PROFESSIONAL MICROSOFT® IIS 8

INTRODUCTION xxvii

▶ **PART I INTRODUCTION AND DEPLOYMENT**

CHAPTER 1   Background on IIS and New Features in IIS 8.0 3

CHAPTER 2   IIS 8.0 Architecture 19

CHAPTER 3   Planning Your Deployment 39

CHAPTER 4   Installing IIS 8.0 63

▶ **PART II ADMINISTRATION**

CHAPTER 5   Administration Tools 97

CHAPTER 6   Website Administration 117

CHAPTER 7   Web Application Administration 153

CHAPTER 8   Web Application Pool Administration 179

CHAPTER 9   Delegating Remote Administration 221

CHAPTER 10 Configuring Other Services 259

▶ **PART III ADVANCED ADMINISTRATION**

CHAPTER 11 Core Server 315

CHAPTER 12 Core Server Extensibility 343

CHAPTER 13 Securing the Server 393

CHAPTER 14 Authentication and Authorization 423

CHAPTER 15 SSL and TLS 471

CHAPTER 16 IIS Scalability I: Building an IIS Web Farm 501

CHAPTER 17 IIS Scalability II: Load Balancing and ARR 545

CHAPTER 18 Programmatic Configuration and Management 597

CHAPTER 19 URL Rewrite 681

CHAPTER 20 Configuring Publishing Options 743

Continued

▶ **PART IV   MANAGING AND OPERATING IIS 8.0**

CHAPTER 21   IIS and Operations Management 779

CHAPTER 22   Monitoring and Performance Tuning 805

CHAPTER 23   Diagnostics and Troubleshooting 851

INDEX 923

PROFESSIONAL

Microsoft® IIS 8

PROFESSIONAL

Microsoft® IIS 8

Ken Schaefer
Jeff Cochran
Scott Forsyth
Dennis Glendenning
Benjamin Perkins

John Wiley & Sons, Inc.

Professional Microsoft® IIS 8

Published by
John Wiley & Sons, Inc.
10475 Crosspoint Boulevard
Indianapolis, IN 46256
www.wiley.com

Copyright © 2013 by John Wiley & Sons, Inc., Indianapolis, Indiana

Published simultaneously in Canada

ISBN: 978-1-118-38804-4
ISBN: 978-1-118-41737-9 (ebk)
ISBN: 978-1-118-43940-1 (ebk)
ISBN: 978-1-118-56642-8 (ebk)

Manufactured in the United States of America

10 9 8 7 6 5 4 3 2 1

For general information on our other products and services please contact our Customer Care Department within the United States at (877) 762-2974, outside the United States at (317) 572-3993 or fax (317) 572-4002.

Wiley publishes in a variety of print and electronic formats and by print-on-demand. Some material included with standard print versions of this book may not be included in e-books or in print-on-demand. If this book refers to media such as a CD or DVD that is not included in the version you purchased, you may download this material at http://booksupport.wiley.com. For more information about Wiley products, visit www.wiley.com.

Library of Congress Control Number: 2012947718

ABOUT THE AUTHORS

KEN SCHAEFER is a senior architect with HP Enterprise Services. For the past three years, he has worked on the Singapore whole-of-government SOE platform transformation program.

Prior to HP, Ken was a lead consultant for global systems integrator Avanade. Avanade is a joint partnership between Microsoft and Accenture and focuses on enterprise projects across the Microsoft product stack.

Ken has worked with IIS for nearly 15 years and was a Microsoft MVP for IIS from 2003 to 2010. He has presented at numerous Microsoft Tech.Ed events across the United States, Australia, and Asia; written articles for Microsoft TechNet; and spent hours talking about IIS at other events, user group meetings, and road shows. He is currently an MCITP, MCTS, MCSE, MCDBA, and holds a Masters in Business and Technology from the University of New South Wales.

Thank you, Julia, Adelaide, Ivy-Jane, Sebastien, and Theo for putting up with the trials, tribulations, and late nights involved in writing a book, again. This would not have been possible without your love and support.

As the lead author, on behalf of all the authors, I'd like to thank Bob Elliott and John Sleeva and the rest of the team at Wiley for their never-ending patience whilst we put this book together. The authors would also like to thank Rob Baugh and Mike Everest for their generous contributions to this work, without which our job would have been that much more arduous.

JEFF COCHRAN is a Senior Network Specialist for the City of Naples, Florida, and has been employed in the computer networking industry for nearly two decades. Beginning with computer bulletin boards on a Commodore 64 in the early 1980s, he has worked with nearly every method of communication via computer. In the early 1990s, he started the first commercial ISP in Southwest Florida, using Windows NT 3.51 systems for mail, web, and FTP servers.

Jeff is married to Zina, a self-employed graphic designer, and spends his free time remodeling a 1950s home in Naples. Although most of his personal hobbies revolve around computers, he enjoys Geocaching and collecting pinball machines, and is still addicted to Age of Empires.

Much of the credit for this book must go to our editor, John Sleeva, for keeping me on track and on point (on deadline is apparently a lost cause), and to our tech editor, Steve Schofield, for fixing my errors in coding and process.

To Zina, without whom there would be no reason to write.

SCOTT FORSYTH is an avid technologist, primarily on the Microsoft web platform for Windows Server, IIS, ASP.NET, Hyper-V, and SQL Server. He worked as Director of Technology for 10 years at Orcsweb, a web host focusing on the Windows platform. This is where he gained the most experience in IIS and building highly available and scalable web farms. Scott is a Microsoft MVP for ASP .NET/IIS, an ASPInsider, and a speaker at code camps, user groups, and technical conferences.

Scott is co-founder and Chief Systems Architect of Vaasnet, a web services company that provides instant, preconfigured virtual machines that can easily be customized for training classes, development environments, or corporate needs. Additionally, he offers consulting services for the web platform on the Microsoft technology stack, and is actively involved in Microsoft community forums and user groups.

Scott lives in Mooresville, North Carolina with his wife and two kids. He can be reached at scott@vaasnet.com. You can follow him on Twitter at http://twitter.com/scottforsyth and find his blog at http://weblogs.asp.net/owscott.

For my wife, Melissa, and my children, Joel and Alisha, who always patiently support me during my long hours of work and writing.

DENNIS GLENDENNING (MA, MBA, MCSA+Msg, MCSE, PMP) is an Enterprise Solutions Architect with Avanade. He has provided technical strategy and design delivery leadership for enterprise clients for more than 14 years. Dennis lives in Cleveland, Ohio with his wife and three children.

To my wife, Melissa, and our amazing children: Bo, T, and Chuck-Do.

BENJAMIN PERKINS (MBA, MCSD.NET in C#, ITIL Management) is currently employed at Microsoft Deutschland GmbH in Munich, Germany as a Senior Support Escalation Engineer on the IIS and ASP.NET team. He has been working professionally in the IT industry for almost 2 decades. Benjamin started computer programming with QBasic at the age of 11 on an Atari 1200XL desktop computer. He takes pleasure in the challenges troubleshooting technical issues have to offer and savors in the rewards of a well-written program. After completing high school, he joined the United States Army and served as a 19 Delta Calvary Scout. After successfully completing his military service, he attended Texas A&M University in College Station, Texas, where he received a bachelor's degree of Business Administration in Management Information Systems.

Benjamin's roles in the IT industry have spanned the entire spectrum from programmer, to system architect, technical support engineer, to team leader and first-level management. While employed at Hewlett-Packard, he received numerous awards, degrees, and certifications. He has a passion for technology and customer service, and looks forward to troubleshooting and creating world-class technical solutions.

"My approach is to write code and design solutions with support in mind, to do it once correctly and completely so we do not have to come back to it again, except to enhance it."

Benjamin is married to Andrea and has two wonderful children, Lea and Noa.

ABOUT THE TECH EDITOR

STEVE SCHOFIELD has been involved in the Microsoft community since 1999, and has been a Microsoft IIS MVP since 2006. Some his community projects include: starting ASPFree.com, being an ASP/ASP.NET MVP, writing a logging utility called IISLogs (`www.iislogs.com`), and sending a monthly IIS Community Newsletter (`www.iisnewsletter.com`). He enjoys helping people in IIS and related Microsoft communities. When not playing with technology, his family keeps him busy. Steve lives in Greenville, Michigan, with his wife, Cindy, and three boys, Marcus, Zach, and Tayler.

CREDITS

EXECUTIVE EDITOR
Robert Elliott

PROJECT EDITOR
John Sleeva

TECHNICAL EDITOR
Steve Schofield

PRODUCTION EDITOR
Christine Mugnolo

COPY EDITOR
Catherine Caffrey

EDITORIAL MANAGER
Mary Beth Wakefield

FREELANCER EDITORIAL MANAGER
Rosemarie Graham

ASSOCIATE DIRECTOR OF MARKETING
David Mayhew

MARKETING MANAGER
Ashley Zurcher

BUSINESS MANAGER
Amy Knies

PRODUCTION MANAGER
Tim Tate

VICE PRESIDENT AND EXECUTIVE GROUP PUBLISHER
Richard Swadley

VICE PRESIDENT AND EXECUTIVE PUBLISHER
Neil Edde

ASSOCIATE PUBLISHER
Jim Minatel

PROJECT COORDINATOR, COVER
Katie Crocker

PROOFREADER
Nancy Carrasco

INDEXER
Johna VanHoose Dinse

COVER DESIGNER
Ryan Sneed

COVER IMAGE
© xiaoke ma / iStockPhoto

CONTENTS

INTRODUCTION   *xxvii*

PART I: INTRODUCTION AND DEPLOYMENT

CHAPTER 1: BACKGROUND ON IIS AND NEW FEATURES IN IIS 8.0   3

IIS Versions 1.0 to 4.0   4
IIS 5.0 and 5.1   4
IIS 6.0   5
  Secure by Default   5
  Request Processing   5
  Additional Features   6
IIS 7.0 and 7.5   7
  ASP.NET Integration   7
  Extensibility   8
  Security   8
  Remote Management   9
  IIS Manager   10
  AppCmd.exe Command-Line Utility   10
  PowerShell Integration   10
  Diagnostics   10
Windows Server 2012 Features   **10**
  Server Versions   11
  The New User Interface   11
  Virtualization and Private Cloud   13
  TLS/SSL   14
IIS 8.0 Features   **15**
  SSL Changes   15
  CPU Throttling   15
  Application Warm-Up   16
  WebSocket   16
  Additional Features   16

CHAPTER 2: IIS 8.0 ARCHITECTURE   19

IIS Architecture Basics   **20**
  Inetinfo.exe   20
  Http.sys   21

ISAPI and CGI   22
IIS Admin Service   22
Application Pools   22
Active Server Pages   23
ASP.NET   23
IIS 7.0 and Later Architecture   **24**
Pipeline Modes   24
Extensibility and Modularity   26
Metabase — Going, Going, Gone!   27
WAS and the Worker Process   29
IIS 8.0 Architecture   **29**
SSL/SNI and Central Certificates   30
Dynamic IP Restrictions   31
Active CPU Throttling   31
Application Initialization   32
PowerShell Improvements   32
Windows Server 2012 Architecture   **33**
Virtualization and Hyper-V   33
Cloud Architecture   35
Resilient File System   36
BitLocker Drive Encryption   36
Network Access Protection   37

CHAPTER 3: PLANNING YOUR DEPLOYMENT   **39**

Windows 2012 Server Deployment Planning   **40**
Windows Server 2012 Requirements   40
Virtualization   41
Which Server Edition?   41
Upgrade or New Installation?   43
Planning Your Hardware   44
Planning Your Network   45
Planning Security   48
Planning Backup and Recovery   51
Windows Server 2012 Cloud Deployment   53
IIS 8.0 Deployment Planning   **53**
IIS 8.0 Requirements   53
Installation Decisions   53
Planning for IIS-Specific Security   54
Planning Development Environments   55
Planning Production Environments   55

Shared Configuration   56
Content Replication   56
Application Deployment Planning   **56**
Automation and Deployment Tools   **57**
Volume Activation   58
Capacity Planning   **58**
Traffic   58
WCAT   59
IIS 8.0 Request Tracing   59
Scalability   60
Application Capacity Planning   60

CHAPTER 4: INSTALLING IIS 8.0   **63**

Windows Server 2012 Server Manager   **64**
The Default IIS 8.0 Installation   **65**
Testing the Installation   66
Installing IIS 8.0 Using Web Platform Installer   73
Installing IIS 8.0's Features   **76**
Installing IIS 8.0 Using PowerShell   **79**
Upgrading from IIS 7.0 to IIS 8.0   **80**
Installing IIS 8.0 on Windows 8   **81**
Installing IIS 8.0 on Windows 7   **84**
Automated Installation and Configuration   **85**
Windows Deployment Services   85
Hosting Service Recommendations   **86**
Directory Structure   87
Web Server Accounts and Application Pools   88
Configuring Shared Hosting with Managed Code   89

PART II: ADMINISTRATION

CHAPTER 5: ADMINISTRATION TOOLS   **97**

Key Characteristics   **98**
IIS Manager   **99**
Appearance   99
Feature Scopes   99
Features View   101
Content View   105
Feature Delegation   105
IIS Manager Extensibility   **106**

Remote Connections	**106**
Configuration Settings	**107**
Configuration File Hierarchy	107
Configuration Levels	108
Location Tags	109
Configuration File Structure	110
Configuration Schema	111
Locking and Unlocking Sections	113
Command-Line Management	**114**
CHAPTER 6: WEBSITE ADMINISTRATION	**117**
Websites, Applications, and Virtual Directories	**118**
Websites	118
Applications	119
Virtual Directories	119
Combining Sites, Applications, and Virtual Directories	120
Creating a New Website	**121**
Creating a Website Using IIS Manager	121
Creating a New Application Pool for Your Site	122
Creating a Website Using AppCmd	124
Creating a New Website Using PowerShell	126
Changes to the applicationHost.config File	126
Configuring Logging	**127**
Enabling Logging	128
Configuring Host Headers	**134**
Administering Applications	**138**
Adding Applications Using IIS Manager	138
Adding Applications Using AppCmd	139
Deleting Applications Using IIS Manager	140
Deleting Applications Using AppCmd	140
Administering Virtual Directories	**140**
Creating Virtual Directories Using IIS Manager	140
Creating Virtual Directories Using AppCmd	142
Adding Virtual Directories Using PowerShell	142
Removing Virtual Directories	142
Authentication	**143**
Configuring Compression	**143**
Configuring Default Document Settings	**146**
Reordering a Document	146
Adding a Default Document	146

Configuring MIME Settings   **146**
Adding MIME Types   147
Editing MIME Types   148
Removing MIME Types   148
Basic Administration Tasks   **149**
Configuring Default Options for IIS   149
Starting and Stopping Services and Websites   150
Isolating Applications   151

CHAPTER 7: WEB APPLICATION ADMINISTRATION   **153**

Application Administration   **154**
ASP Configuration   **154**
ASP.NET Configuration   **155**
IIS 6.0 and Previous Architecture   155
IIS 8.0 Architecture   156
IIS 8.0 and ASP.NET Modules   157
ISAPI Configuration   **172**
CGI Configuration   **173**
FastCGI Configuration   **174**
Installing PHP   174
Installing QDig   175
Installing the FastCGI Module   175
Enabling FastCGI for Use with PHP   175
Windows Process Activation Service   **176**
Application Initialization   **176**

CHAPTER 8: WEB APPLICATION POOL ADMINISTRATION   **179**

A Background of Website Separation   **180**
Defining Applications   **180**
Comparing Virtual Directories to Applications   **183**
Understanding the w3wp.exe Process   **185**
Recycling Application Pools   187
Web Gardens   188
Working with Application Pools   **190**
Creating Application Pools   190
Managing Settings   192
Assigning Applications and Sites to Application Pools   196
Specifying the .NET Framework Version   200
Specifying the Managed Pipeline Mode   202
Managing Active Application Pools   206

Application Pool Security	**212**
Application Pool Configuration Isolation	212
Application Pool SID Injection	213
Site Anonymous User	214
Noteworthy Advanced Settings	**215**
Bitness	215
CPU Limits	215
Processor Affinity	216
Application Pool Users	**216**
Network Service Account	217
Local Service Account	218
Local System Account	218
Windows Application Pool Identity	218
Custom User Account	219
CHAPTER 9: DELEGATING REMOTE ADMINISTRATION	**221**
Introducing the Main Characters	**222**
System Administrator	222
Site Administrator	223
The Two Shall Work as One	223
IIS Manager Remote Access	**223**
Installing the IIS 8.0 Management Service	223
Enabling Remote Connections	224
Authentication Types	229
Authorization at Three Levels	232
.Remote Installation and Usage	234
Extending IIS Manager	235
Delegation Settings	**236**
Delegation of Sections	237
Delegating the Small Details	255
CHAPTER 10: CONFIGURING OTHER SERVICES	**259**
Installing and Configuring an FTP Server	**260**
FTP Basics	260
Planning an FTP Server Installation	261
Creating an FTP Site	265
Creating FTP Sites with PowerShell	271
Testing FTP with Telnet	271
Configuring Existing FTP Sites	**271**
Home Directory	272
Advanced Settings	272

Logging	273
FTP Messages	274
Configuring FTP User Security	**274**
Configuring .NET Accounts for FTP	278
Configuring FTP over SSL	286
Configuring FTP User Isolation	288
Configuring FTP Host Name Support	290
Configuring FTP Request Filtering	291
Configuring FTP IP and Domain Restrictions	292
Configuring FTP Logon Attempt Restrictions	293
Administering FTP with Configuration Files	**294**
Adding FTP over SSL to an Existing Site	294
Configuring Host Name Support	296
The FTP Command-Line Client	**296**
Installing and Configuring an SMTP Server	**298**
How SMTP Works	298
Installing SMTP	298
Configuring the Default SMTP Server	300
SMTP Security and Authentication	302
Configuring Additional Domains	305
SMTP Folders	305
Testing and Troubleshooting SMTP	306
Installing and Using LogParser	**309**
Installing LogParser	309
Using LogParser from the Command Line	309
LogParser Examples	311

PART III: ADVANCED ADMINISTRATION

CHAPTER 11: CORE SERVER	**315**
Background	**315**
Core Server and Modules	**317**
HTTP Modules	319
Server Workload Customization	**326**
Eliminating Overheads	326
A Basic Real-World Example	327
A More Complex Real-World Example	328
Customizing Individual Websites	330
Customization Using IIS Manager	334
ASP.NET and the IIS Pipeline	**336**
Configuring ASP.NET Execution Mode	337
Migrating IIS 7.x ASP.NET Applications to IIS 8	339

Migrating Legacy ASP.NET Applications to IIS 8.0   339
Selecting the ASP.NET Version   340
Legacy ISAPI Support   **340**

CHAPTER 12: CORE SERVER EXTENSIBILITY   343

Extensibility Overview   **344**
IIS Module Concepts   **345**
Events   345
Notifications   347
Return Codes   348
Notification Priority   349
An Example Native Module   **351**
Native Module Design   351
Native Module Creation   352
Native Module Wrap-Up   362
Managed Code Modules   **363**
Managed Event Notifications   364
Further Reading   365
An Example Managed Module   **366**
Managed Module Design   366
Managed Module Creation   366
Managed Module Wrap-Up   371
Event Tracing from Modules   **371**
Adding Tracing Support to a Managed Code Module   372
Extending IIS Configuration   **377**
Adding Configuration Support to Custom Modules   377
Extending the IIS Administration Tool   **381**
Creating an IIS Administration Tool Extension   382

CHAPTER 13: SECURING THE SERVER   393

What Is Security?   **394**
Managing Risk   394
Security Components   395
Types of Attacks   **396**
Denial-of-Service Attacks   396
Privilege Escalation Attacks   396
Passive Attacks   397
Advanced Persistent Threats   398
Securing Your Environment   **398**
Securing Your IIS 8.0 Server   **399**
IP and Domain Restrictions   399
Configuring MIME-Type Extensions   405

Configuring ISAPI Extensions and CGI Restrictions 407
Configuring Request Filtering 413
Application Layer Security 420
Configuring Logging 421

CHAPTER 14: AUTHENTICATION AND AUTHORIZATION 423

Authentication in IIS 8.0 **424**
How IIS 8.0 Authenticates a Client 426
Configuring Anonymous Authentication **428**
Configuring Basic Authentication **430**
Configuring Digest Authentication **433**
Configuring Integrated Windows Authentication **437**
Configuring NTLM Authentication **439**
Configuring Kerberos Authentication 443
Configuring UNC Authentication **448**
Configuring Client Certificate Authentication **449**
Configuring Forms-Based Authentication **453**
Configuring Delegation **456**
Configuring Protocol Transition **461**
Configuring Authorization **462**
URL Authorization 463
Configuring Application Pool Sandboxing 466
Understanding IIS 8.0 User Accounts **468**

CHAPTER 15: SSL AND TLS 471

Securing a Website with TLS **472**
The SSL/TLS Handshake 473
Generating a Certificate Request 476
Submitting the Certificate Request 481
Importing the Certificate into IIS 8.0 483
Configuring Website Bindings 484
Generating a Certificate Using Domain Certificate Request 485
Generating a Self-Signed Certificate 487
Managing an SSL/TLS-Secured Website 487
Enabling Central Certificate Store 492
Managing a Public Key Infrastructure 492
Securing an SMTP Virtual Server with TLS **496**
Securing an FTP Site with TLS **498**

CHAPTER 16: IIS SCALABILITY I: BUILDING AN IIS WEB FARM 501

IIS 8.0 and Web Farms **502**
Shared Configuration 503

Content Configuration   **520**
Local Content   520
Shared Network Content   521
Shared SAN or Storage Spaces Content   523
Content Replication   **524**
Distributed File System   525
Robocopy   528
Offline Folders/Client Side Caching   529
Additional Tools   531
Web Deploy   531
Other Considerations   **532**
Replication   532
.NET Configuration Files and machineKey   535
Session State   536
Security   542

CHAPTER 17: IIS SCALABILITY II: LOAD BALANCING AND ARR   **545**

Load-Balancing Concepts   **546**
Shared Concepts   546
Load-Balancing Solutions   555
Application Request Routing   **558**
ARR Functionality   559
Obtaining ARR   560
Understanding ARR   560
Touch Points   561
Creating a Server Farm   562
Creating Server Farm Rules   565
Health Checks   567
Web Server Bindings   571
Testing URLs Per-Site Per-Server   574
SSL/TLS Offloading   579
Man-in-the-Middle and ARR Helper   580
Server Management   581
Performance Monitoring   584
Caching   584
Miscellaneous Optimizations   588
High Availability for ARR   589
Network Load Balancing   **590**
Frameworks   **594**
Web Farm Framework   594
Windows Azure Services   595

CHAPTER 18: PROGRAMMATIC CONFIGURATION AND MANAGEMENT

CHAPTER 18: PROGRAMMATIC CONFIGURATION AND MANAGEMENT   **597**

Configuration Optimization	**598**
Direct Configuration	**599**
Configuration File Hierarchy	599
Order of Operation	601
Collection Items	602
Section Structure	605
Location Tag	607
Inheritance	610
Locking	611
childConfig/sourceConfig	612
Configuration Path	612
Schema Extensibility	613
Programmatic Configuration	**618**
IIS 8.0 Programming Walk-Through	618
Microsoft.Web.Administration (MWA)	626
Microsoft.Web.Management (MWM)	634
ABO, ADSI, and Legacy API Support	635
IIS WMI Provider	636
AHAdmin	639
Configuration Editor	**641**
Modifying the Custom Extended Schema	642
Modifying the Configuration Item	643
Modifying an Attribute and Viewing the Generated Scripts	644
Command-Line Management	**646**
Using AppCmd.exe	648
Getting Help	648
Using the list Command	650
AppCmd Attributes and Values	653
Managing Objects	653
Determining Which Attributes Are Associated with an Object	654
Backing Up and Restoring	657
Locking and Unlocking the Configuration	664
Piping with XML	664
IIS PowerShell Management	**665**
PowerShell IIS Cmdlets	666
Getting Help	668
Using PowerShell IIS Cmdlets	671
Creating a Website and Viewing the Results	673
Modifying the Attributes of a Website	676

IIS Operational Activities Using PowerShell | 677
Backing Up and Restoring Using IIS PowerShell | 679

CHAPTER 19: URL REWRITE | 681

URL Rewrite Concepts | 682
Conditions | 682
Actions | 683
Obtaining and Installing URL Rewrite | 686
Getting Started Walk-Through | 687
Managing URL Rewrite | 691
Using IIS Manager | 691
Using a Text Editor | 691
Using APIs | 692
Applying URL Rewrite Rules | 692
Global Level — <globalRules> | 692
Global Level — <rules> | 693
Site Level — applicationHost.config | 693
Site Level — web.config | 694
Subfolder Level — web.config | 694
Rule Templates | 695
Inbound Rule Templates | 696
Inbound and Outbound Rules Templates | 697
Outbound Rules Template | 699
Search Engine Optimization Templates | 699
Input Variables | 701
Common URL Parts | 702
Additional Input Variables | 703
Wildcards Pattern Matches | 704
Regular Expressions | 705
10 Things You Need to Know about Regex | 707
Back-References | 712
Rule Back-References versus Condition Back-References | 712
Wildcards Back-References | 713
Capturing Back-References across Conditions | 713
Where to Use Back-References | 714
Setting Server Variables | 715
Request Headers | 715
Allowed Server Variables | 716
Special Considerations | 716
Redirecting to SSL | 716
Checking If a Request Is for a File or a Directory | 718
Considering ScriptResource.axd and WebResources.axd | 719

Caching IIS Output 719
Using String Functions with Rule Actions and Conditions 721
Importing Rules from mod_rewrite 722
Logging Rewritten URLs 722
Rewrite Maps **722**
Common Rules **725**
Redirecting Non-www to www (Canonical Hostnames) 726
Creating a Down for Maintenance Page 726
Preserving Old Urls 728
Preventing Image Hot-Linking 729
Blocking Requests 729
Redirecting a Subdomain to Subfolder 730
Adding HTTP_PROTOCOL 731
Hosting Multiple Domains under One Site 732
Using Query String Logic for Rules 732
Outbound Rules **732**
Outbound Rules versus Inbound Rules 733
Outbound Rule Walk-Throughs 733
Further Outbound Rule Considerations 738
Troubleshooting URL Rewrite **738**
Create a Testing Rule 739
Create a Stopping Rule 739
Reviewing Input Variables 739
Fiddler and Firebug 739
Test Pattern Tool 740
Display Variable Trick 741
Failed Request Tracing 741
Simplify 741

CHAPTER 20: CONFIGURING PUBLISHING OPTIONS **743**

Web Platform Installer **744**
Using Web Platform Installer 744
Web Application Gallery 746
Installing Gallery Applications 746
Web Deployment Tool **751**
Installing Web Deploy with Web PI 751
Installing Web Deploy Directly 751
Deploying Web Applications 753
Migrating and Synchronizing Web Servers 756
FTP Publishing **759**
Configuring FTP Publishing with IIS Manager 760
Configuring FTP Publishing with Configuration Files 762

WebDAV Publishing   **763**
   Installing and Configuring WebDAV   764
Visual Studio Publishing   **768**
   Publishing Websites   769
   Publishing Web Applications   771

PART IV: MANAGING AND OPERATING IIS 8.0

CHAPTER 21: IIS AND OPERATIONS MANAGEMENT   779

Management Approaches   **779**
   ITIL Standards   780
   MOF: Microsoft's ITIL Superset   781
   Applying MOF to IIS Operations Management   784
Operational Tasks   **797**
   Backup and Restore Program   797

CHAPTER 22: MONITORING AND PERFORMANCE TUNING   805

Monitoring Websites   **806**
   How to Monitor IIS 8.0   806
   What to Monitor   824
Performance Tuning   **831**
   Operating System Optimizations   832
   IIS Service Optimizations   835
   Website Optimizations   842

CHAPTER 23: DIAGNOSTICS AND TROUBLESHOOTING   851

Types of Issues   **852**
   Specific Errors   852
   Hang/Time-Out Issues   852
   Resource-Intensive and Slowness Issues   853
Runtime Status and Control API   **854**
   Viewing Worker Processes   855
   Viewing Page Requests   858
   Viewing Application Domains   861
IIS 8.0 Error Pages   **861**
   Customizing Custom Error Pages   863
   Multiple Language Support   866
   HTTP Status Codes   866
   FTP Status Codes   867

Failed Request Tracing	**867**
Setting Up Failed Request Tracing Rules	868
Reading the XML Trace Logs	871
Logging	**873**
ASP.NET Tracing	**874**
Enabling ASP.NET Tracing	876
The ASP.NET Trace Viewer	877
Troubleshooting Tips	**880**
Reproduce	880
Isolate	881
Fix	884
Test	884
Additional Built-In Tools	**885**
Task Manager	885
Event Viewer	885
Reliability and Performance Monitor	888
Logging NTFS Failures to Disk	895
ping, tracert, and pathping	896
telnet	898
Installable Tools	**899**
WFetch	899
Web Capacity Analysis Tool	899
LogParser	900
DelegConfig	901
Process Explorer	902
Process Monitor	904
The Debug Diagnostic Tool	909
ProcDump	914
WinDbg	915
Where to Go Next	921
INDEX	*923*

INTRODUCTION

WINDOWS SERVER 2012 is the latest incarnation of Microsoft's successful server platform. Included is a new version of IIS, now in its eighth incarnation.

IIS 8.0 isn't the revolutionary change in architecture that IIS 7.0 was. However it offers much new functionality, absorbing many of the standalone add-on updates available since IIS 7.0 was released, as well presenting administrators with new security, scalability, and administrative features.

For readers familiar with IIS 7.0, this book has substantial sections devoted to popular add-ons now baked into the product, such as the Application Request Routing (ARR) and URL Rewrite modules, as well as coverage of new features, such as Central Certificate Store and Server Name Indication support.

For readers new to IIS, this book offers complete coverage of IIS fundamentals: the configuration model, delegated administration, extensibility options, and real-time diagnostic and troubleshooting features that have been carried over from IIS 7.0.

Both new and previous users of IIS can benefit from a book covering the whole deployment lifecycle: architecture, installation, configuration, and operations management. Like its predecessor, this book continues to stress both GUI options as well as provide alternative, automated management through comprehensive AppCmd and PowerShell examples.

The authors have focused on capturing the very best of the new features in IIS 8.0 and how you can take advantage of them. The writing styles vary from chapter to chapter because some of the foremost experts on IIS 8.0 have contributed to this book. Drawing on our expertise in deployment, hosting, development, and enterprise operations, we believe that this book captures much of what today's IIS administrators need in their day-to-day work.

WHO THIS BOOK IS FOR

This book is aimed at IIS administrators (or those who need to ramp up quickly in anticipation of having to administer IIS). What differentiates this book is that it doesn't just focus on features and how to configure them using a GUI administrative tool. Instead, we explain how features work (for example, how Kerberos authentication actually works under the covers) so that you can better troubleshoot issues when something goes wrong.

Additionally, since most administrators need to be able to automate common procedures, we have included specific chapters on programmatic administration and command-line tools as well as code snippets (with a focus on using AppCmd.exe and PowerShell) throughout the book.

This book covers features that many other IIS books don't touch (such as high availability and web farm scenarios, or extending IIS) and has a dedicated chapter on troubleshooting and diagnostics.

Real-life IIS administration is about people, processes, and technology. Although a technical book can't teach you much about hiring the right people, this book doesn't focus solely on technology. Operations management and monitoring (key components of good processes) are also addressed.

Overall, we think that this book provides comprehensive coverage of the real-life challenges facing IIS administrators: getting up to speed on the new features of a product, understanding how the product works under the covers, and being able to operate and manage the product effectively over the long term.

HOW THIS BOOK IS STRUCTURED

The book is divided into four major parts:

➤ Part I covers the new features and architecture of IIS 8.0, as well as deployment and installation considerations.

➤ Part II discusses the basics of the administration tools (both GUI and command-line) as well as common administrative tasks for websites, delegated administration, and supporting services (such as FTP, SMTP, and publishing options).

➤ Part III introduces more advanced topics, such as extending IIS 8.0, programmatic administration, web farms and high availability, and security.

➤ Finally, Part IV covers topics that go beyond the initial understanding of the new feature set. We cover topics that administrators will need on an ongoing basis, such as operations management, performance monitoring and tuning, and diagnostics and troubleshooting.

WHAT YOU NEED TO USE THIS BOOK

Although IIS 8.0 ships in both Windows 8 and Windows Server 2012, certain functionality (such as load balancing) is available only in the server edition. Because the full functionality of IIS 8.0 is available in Windows Server 2012, the authors have focused on that product for this book.

For IIS 8.0 extensibility, Microsoft Visual Studio 2012 has been used throughout the book; however, any IDE suitable for .NET development can be used for implementing the code samples presented.

CONVENTIONS

To help you get the most from the text and keep track of what's happening, we've used a number of conventions throughout the book.

PRODUCT TEAM ASIDE

Boxes like this one hold tips, tricks, trivia from the ASP.NET Product Team, or some other information that is directly relevant to the surrounding text.

> **NOTE** *Tips, hints, and tricks to the current discussion are offset and placed in italics like this.*

As for styles in the text:

➤ We *italicize* new terms and important words when we introduce them.

➤ We show keyboard strokes like this: Ctrl+A.

➤ We show file names, URLs, and code within the text like so: `persistence.properties`.

➤ We present code in two different ways:

```
We use a monofont type with no highlighting for most code examples.
```

We use bold to emphasize code that is particularly important in the present context or to show changes from a previous code snippet.

SOURCE CODE

As you work through the examples in this book, you may choose either to type in all the code manually or to use the source code files that accompany the book. All the source code used in this book is available for download at `www.wrox.com`. Once at the site, simply locate the book's title (either by using the Search box or by using one of the title lists), and click the Download Code link on the book's detail page to obtain all the source code for the book.

> **NOTE** *Because many books have similar titles, you may find it easiest to search by ISBN; this book's ISBN is 978-1-118-38804-4.*

Once you download the code, just decompress it with your favorite compression tool. Alternately, you can go to the main Wrox code download page at `www.wrox.com/dynamic/books/download.aspx` to see the code available for this book and all other Wrox books.

ERRATA

We make every effort to ensure that there are no errors in the text or in the code. However, no one is perfect, and mistakes do occur. If you find an error in one of our books, like a spelling mistake or faulty piece of code, we would be very grateful for your feedback. By sending in errata you may save another reader hours of frustration and at the same time you will be helping us provide even higher quality information.

To find the errata page for this book, go to www.wrox.com and locate the title using the Search box or one of the title lists. Then, on the Book Search Results page, click the Errata link. On this page you can view all errata that has been submitted for this book and posted by Wrox editors.

> **NOTE** *A complete book list including links to errata is also available at* www.wrox.com/misc-pages/booklist.shtml.

If you don't spot "your" error on the Errata page, click the Errata Form link and complete the form to send us the error you have found. We'll check the information and, if appropriate, post a message to the book's errata page and fix the problem in subsequent editions of the book.

P2P.WROX.COM

For author and peer discussion, join the P2P forums at p2p.wrox.com. The forums are a web-based system for you to post messages relating to Wrox books and related technologies and interact with other readers and technology users. The forums offer a subscription feature to e-mail you topics of interest of your choosing when new posts are made to the forums. Wrox authors, editors, other industry experts, and your fellow readers are present on these forums.

At http://p2p.wrox.com you will find a number of different forums that will help you, not only as you read this book, but also as you develop your own applications. To join the forums, just follow these steps:

1. Go to p2p.wrox.com and click the Register link.

2. Read the terms of use and click Agree.

3. Complete the required information to join, as well as any optional information you wish to provide, and click Submit.

4. You will receive an e-mail with information describing how to verify your account and complete the joining process.

> **NOTE** *You can read messages in the forums without joining P2P, but in order to post your own messages, you must join.*

Once you join, you can post new messages and respond to messages other users post. You can read messages at any time on the web. If you would like to have new messages from a particular forum e-mailed to you, click the Subscribe to this Forum icon by the forum name in the forum listing.

For more information about how to use the Wrox P2P, be sure to read the P2P FAQs for answers to questions about how the forum software works as well as many common questions specific to P2P and Wrox books. To read the FAQs, click the FAQ link on any P2P page.

PART I
Introduction and Deployment

▶ **CHAPTER 1:** Background on IIS and New Features in IIS 8.0

▶ **CHAPTER 2:** IIS 8.0 Architecture

▶ **CHAPTER 3:** Planning Your Deployment

▶ **CHAPTER 4:** Installing IIS 8.0

1

Background on IIS and New Features in IIS 8.0

WHAT'S IN THIS CHAPTER?

➤ A background of IIS

➤ Windows Server 2012 features

➤ New features in IIS 8.0

Microsoft's Internet Information Services (IIS) has been around for more than 15 years, from its first incarnation in Windows NT 3.51 to the current release of IIS 8.0 on the Windows Server 2012 and Windows 8 platforms. It has evolved from providing basic service as an HTTP server, as well as additional Internet services such as Gopher and WAIS, to a fully configurable application services platform integrated with the operating system.

IIS 8.0 is not as dramatic a change as IIS 7.0 was, but IIS 8.0 benefits from the improvements in the Windows Server 2012 operating system. These benefits make IIS 8.0 far more scalable, more appropriate for cloud and virtual systems, and more integral to Microsoft's application and programming environment.

This chapter provides an overview of the changes in IIS 8.0 as well as a sampling of some of the new technologies. If you are familiar with IIS 7.0, you will want to skim through this chapter for changes before digging into future chapters for specifics. If you are new to IIS, this chapter will provide an introduction to the features in IIS 8.0 and provide you with a basis for understanding future chapters. And if you're the kind of reader who just wants to skip to the part that applies to your immediate needs, this chapter can help you figure out in what area those needs lie.

IIS VERSIONS 1.0 TO 4.0

IIS was released with Service Pack 3 for Windows NT 3.51, as a set of services providing HTTP, Gopher, and WAIS functionality. Although the functions were there, most users chose alternatives from third-party vendors, such as O'Reilly's website or Netscape's server. Although these services had been available for years with the various flavors of UNIX operating systems, native Internet services for Windows were mostly an afterthought, with little integration with the Windows operating system.

With the advent of Windows NT 4.0, IIS also matured in version 2.0. The most notable improvement in IIS version 2.0 was closer integration with the Windows NT operating system, taking advantage of Windows security accounts and providing integrated administration through a management console similar to many other Windows services. IIS 2.0 introduced support for HTTP Host headers, which allowed multiple sites to run on a single IP address, and aligned Microsoft's IIS development with National Computer Security Association (NCSA) standards, providing for NCSA common log formats and NCSA-style map files. IIS 2.0 also introduced a web browser interface for management and content indexing through Microsoft's Index Server.

IIS version 3.0 was introduced with Windows NT Service Pack 3 and introduced the world to ASP (Active Server Pages) and Microsoft's concept of an *application server.* A precursor to the ASP.NET environment, ASP (now referred to as *classic ASP*) is a server-side scripting environment for the creation of dynamic web pages. Using VBScript, JScript, or any other active scripting engine, programmers finally had a viable competitor to Common Gateway Interface (CGI) and scripting technologies available on non-Microsoft platforms, such as Perl.

IIS 4.0, available in the NT Option Pack, introduced ASP 2.0, an object-based version of ASP that included six built-in objects to provide standardized functionality in ASP pages. IIS 4.0 was the last version of IIS that coumld be downloaded and installed outside of the operating system.

IIS 5.0 AND 5.1

With the release of Windows 2000, IIS became integrated with the operating system. Version numbers reflected the operating system, and there were no upgrades to IIS available without upgrading the operating system. IIS 5.0 shipped with Windows 2000 Server versions and Windows 2000 Professional, and IIS version 5.1 shipped with Windows XP Professional, but not Windows XP Home Edition. For all essential functions, IIS 5.0 and IIS 5.1 are identical, differing only slightly as needed by the changes to the operating system.

With Windows 2000 and IIS 5.0, IIS became a service of the operating system, meant to be the base for other applications, especially for ASP applications. The IIS 5.0 architecture served static content, Internet Server Application Programming Interface (ISAPI) functions, or ASP scripts, with ASP script processing handed off to a script engine based on the file extension. Using file extensions to determine the program that handles the file has always been a common part of Windows functionality, and in the case of ASP processing, the speed of serving pages was increased by the automatic handoff of ASP scripts directly to the ASP engine, bypassing the static content handler. This architecture has endured in IIS to the current version.

IIS 6.0

IIS 6.0 shipped with Windows Server 2003 editions and Windows XP Professional 64-Bit Edition, which was built on the Windows Server 2003 Service Pack 1 code base. IIS 6.0 was identical among operating system versions, but there were restrictions or expansions depending on the version of Server 2003 under which IIS was running. For example, Server 2003 Web Edition would only run IIS and a few ancillary services; it could not be used to run Microsoft SQL Server. On the other end of the spectrum, only the Enterprise and Data Center versions of Server 2003 included clustering technology.

Operating system changes also expanded the capabilities of IIS as an application server. Native XML Web Services appeared in Server 2003. Process-independent session states made web farms easier to configure and manage, allowing session states to be stored outside of the application for redundancy and failover. Web farms also became easier with Server 2003's improved Network load-balancing features, such as the NLB Manager, which provided a single management point for NLB functions.

Secure by Default

Windows Server 2003 and IIS 6.0 shipped in a secure state, with IIS no longer installed by default. Even when IIS was installed, the default installation would serve only static HTML pages; all dynamic content was locked down. Managed through web service extensions, applications such as ASP and ASP.NET had to be specifically enabled, minimizing default security holes with unknown services open to the world.

IIS 6.0 also ran user code under a low-privilege account, Network Service, which had few privileges on the server outside of the IIS processes and the website hierarchy. Designed to reduce the damage exposure from rogue code, access to virtual directories and other resources had to be specifically enabled by the administrator for the Network Service account.

IIS 6.0 also allowed delegation for the authentication process; thus, administrators and programmers could further restrict account access. Passport authentication was also included with IIS 6.0, although in real-world use, it never found widespread favor among administrators. Kerberos authentication, on the other hand, allowed secure communication within an Active Directory domain and solved many remote resource permission issues.

IIS 6.0 also would serve only specific file requests, by default not allowing execution of command-line code or even the transfer of executable files. Unless the administrator assigned a specific MIME (Multipurpose Internet Mail Extensions) type to be served, IIS would return a 404 error to the request, reporting the file not found. Earlier versions of IIS included a wildcard mapping and would serve any file type.

Request Processing

IIS 6.0 changed the way IIS processed requests, eliminating what had been a major performance hurdle in scaling prior IIS versions to serve multiple sites. IIS 6.0 used the Http.sys listener to receive requests and then handed them off to worker processes to be addressed. These worker processes were isolated to application pools, and the administrator could assign application pools to specific sites and applications. This meant that many more requests could be handled simultaneously, and it also provided for an isolated architecture in cases of error. If a worker process failed, the effects would not be seen outside of the application pool, providing stability across the server's sites. In addition, worker processes could be assigned a processor affinity, allowing multiprocessor systems to split the workload.

Additional Features

As did its predecessors, IIS 6.0 included additional features and functionality. Some internal features, such as HTTP compression and kernel mode caching, increased performance of the web server and applications served from it. Other features affected configuration, such as the move to an XML metabase, or stability, such as being able to configure individual application pools and isolate potential application failures. Still others added or expanded utility and ancillary functions, such as the improved FTP services or the addition of POP services to the existing SMTP service.

Application Pools

IIS 6.0 changed the way applications behaved in memory, isolating applications into memory pools. Administrators could configure separate memory pools for separate applications, thus preventing a faulty application from crashing other applications outside of its memory pool. This is particularly important in any shared web server environment, especially with ASP.NET applications.

FTP Service

The FTP service grew up in IIS 6.0, providing for greater security and separation of accounts through a new isolation mode using either Active Directory or local Windows accounts. Using Windows accounts or Active Directory accounts, users could be restricted to their own available FTP locations without resorting to naming the home directories the same as the FTP accounts. In addition, users were prevented from traversing above their home directories and seeing what other accounts may exist on the server. Even without NT File System (NTFS) permissions to the content, security in FTP before IIS 6.0 was still compromised because a user could discover other valid user accounts on the system.

SMTP and POP Services

The SMTP service in Windows Server 2003 didn't change much from previous versions, allowing for greater flexibility and security but not altering the core SMTP functions. Most administrators would not use the SMTP service in IIS for anything other than outbound mail, instead relying on third-party servers or Microsoft's Exchange Server for receiving and distributing mail. But the addition of a POP3 service in Server 2003 allowed a rudimentary mail server configuration, useful for testing or small mail domains. Although SMTP can be used to transfer mail, most mail clients such as Microsoft Outlook rely on the POP3 or IMAP protocols to retrieve mail, which was unavailable without additional products until Windows Server 2003 and IIS 6.0.

IIS 7.0 AND 7.5

IIS 7.0 was a complete rewrite of the base code from IIS 6.0 and earlier. Available on Windows Vista and Windows Server 2008, IIS 7.0 adapted to several operating systems, including the new Windows Core Edition and the Windows Web Server edition. IIS 7.5, introduced with Windows 7, consisted of IIS 7.0 plus all the inline updates that had been made to IIS 7.0 since its introduction. Users could essentially update IIS 7.0 to the functionality of IIS 7.5 by installing the appropriate updates and modules.

IIS 7.0 was a ground-up rewrite of IIS 6.0, designed as an integrated web application platform. Integration with the ASP.NET framework combined with fully exposed application programming interfaces (APIs) for complete extensibility of the platform and management interfaces made IIS 7.0 a programmer's dream. Security that included delegation of configuration and a complete diagnostic suite with request tracing and advanced logging satisfied several of the administrator's desires.

Although the most substantial change in IIS 7.0 may have been the integration of ASP.NET into the request pipeline, the extensibility of IIS 7.0, configuration delegation and the use of XML configuration files, request tracing and diagnostics, and the new administration tools were all welcome changes from previous versions of IIS.

Unlike previous versions of IIS, the modular design of IIS 7.0 allowed for easy implementation of custom modules and additional functionality. This increased functionality came from in-house development, third-party sources, or even Microsoft. Because these modules and additional programs could be plugged into IIS at any time, without changing core operating system functions, the Microsoft IIS development team shipped additional supported and unsupported modules outside of Microsoft's standard Service Pack process. IIS 7.5 included most of these inline updates and modules, such as FTP 7.5, that did not originally exist for IIS 7.0. Microsoft's website at www.iis.net is the source for these additional downloads, for the IIS 7.0 and 7.5 versions, as well as for future add-on modules and updates for IIS 8.0.

ASP.NET Integration

One of the most radical changes in IIS 7.0 was its close integration with ASP.NET and the ASP.NET processes. There was a unified event pipeline in IIS 7.0 that merged the previously separate IIS and ASP.NET pipelines from IIS 6.0 and earlier. ASP.NET HTTP modules that previously only listened for events within the ASP.NET pipeline could be used for any request in IIS 7.0. For backward compatibility, IIS 7.0 maintained a Classic pipeline mode, which emulated the separate IIS and ASP.NET pipeline model from IIS 6.0.

IIS 7.0 also changed IIS configuration to match the process used for configuring ASP.NET applications. This greatly improved and simplified the implementation of IIS into the ASP.NET programming environment and allowed for better configurability and easier deployment of both sites and applications. It also made deployment across multiple systems in web farms more straightforward and allowed for extensibility of the configurations. IIS 7.0 introduced the concept of shared configuration, wherein multiple web servers can point to the same physical file for configuration, making deploying configuration changes to web farms nearly instantaneous.

IIS 7.0 introduced the `applicationHost.config` file for storing settings and added configuration options for individual websites or web applications to the `web.config` files, alongside ASP.NET settings, in a new `system.webServer` section.

Extensibility

IIS 7.0 greatly increased the extensibility of IIS as a web application platform. Because of the changes to the request-processing pipeline, the core server itself was now extensible, using both native and managed code. Instead of having to work with ISAPI filters to modify the request process, developers could now inject their own components directly into the processing pipeline. These components could represent the developers' own code, third-party utilities and components, and existing Microsoft core components. This meant that if you didn't like Microsoft's Windows authentication process, you could not only choose to use forms authentication on all files, but also choose to bypass all built-in authentication and roll your own. In addition, if you didn't need to process classic ASP files, you could simply not load that component. Unlike in previous versions, in which components were loaded into memory in a single DLL, IIS 7.0 reduced the memory footprint by not loading unnecessary modules or code.

Security

Componentization also increased the already strong security that existed in IIS 6.0. A perennial complaint against Microsoft had always been that IIS installed by default and that all services were active by default. IIS 6.0 and Server 2003 reversed that course—almost nothing was installed by default, and even when you did install it, the majority of components were disabled by default. To enable ASP.NET, you had to choose to allow ASP.NET as a web service extension. Classic ASP had to be enabled separately, as did third-party CGI application processors such as Perl or PHP.

With the exception of third-party software, however, IIS 6.0 still loaded all the services into memory—it just loaded them as disabled. For example, if you didn't want to use Windows authentication, as would be the case if you were using your own authentication scheme, you could choose not to *enable* it, but the code still resided in memory. Similarly, default IIS 6.0 installations were locked down to processing static HTML files, a good choice from a security standpoint. But what if you were never going to use static HTML files in your application or site? In IIS 7.0, you had the option of never loading the code in the first place.

Minimal Installation

IIS 7.0 continued the tradition of its predecessor with minimal installation the default. IIS was not installed with the default operating system installation, and a basic install only selected those options needed for serving static HTML files. The installation graphical user interface (GUI) for IIS 6.0 allowed a choice of eight different options, including installing FTP, whereas IIS 7.0's setup allowed for more than 40 options. This granularity of setup reduced the memory footprint of IIS 7.0, but more importantly, it reduced the security footprint as well.

Management Delegation

Management of IIS in previous versions meant either granting local administrator privileges to the user or working through Windows Management Instrumentation (WMI) and Active Directory Services Interfaces (ADSI) options to manage the site configurations directly. The only other option was for developers to work through the IIS administrators to change configurations—an option that could often be frustrating for both administrators and programmers. IIS 7.0 changed this through delegation of administration permissions at the server, site, and application levels.

Unified Authentication and Authorization

In IIS 7.0, the authentication and authorization process merged the traditional IIS authentication options with ASP.NET options. This allowed administrators and developers to use ASP.NET authentication across all files, folders, and applications in a site.

In IIS 6.0 and previous versions, controlling access to an Adobe Acrobat (PDF) file was difficult through ASP.NET authentication schemes. You would need to enable Windows authentication or basic authentication on the website, folder, or file and create a Windows account to have access to the file. Then you would need to require the user to provide valid credentials for that Windows account, even if he or she already had logged into your ASP.NET application, to be able to access that PDF file. The alternative was to use impersonation in ASP.NET to access the file using the ASP .NET process account—all to prevent someone from opening the PDF file by pasting the direct URL into their browser. Options involving streaming the content from a protected location were just as cumbersome, and redirecting files to be processed by the ASP.NET DLL was even more problematic.

In IIS 7.0, using ASP.NET authentication no longer required the file to be processed as an ASPX extension; thus, file extensions of all types could be secured with Forms authentication or any other ASP.NET method. This reduced the requirement for Windows Client Access Licenses (CALs) to provide access control, which was prohibitive in an Internet environment.

Remote Management

Although IIS could be remotely managed in previous versions using the IIS Manager over RPC, this wasn't firewall-friendly. An HTML-based management option also existed; however, this didn't allow management of all IIS features. In both cases, users were required to be in the local Administrators group on the machine.

IIS 7.0 introduced a new remote Management Service that permitted the IIS Manager tool to administer remote IIS 7.0 installations over HTTPS. By using the new delegation features in IIS 7.0, remote users could be given access to the entire server, a single website, or even just a single web application. Additionally, features that have not been delegated will not be visible to the end user when connecting remotely.

The Remote Management service also introduced the concept of IIS Users. These user accounts do not exist outside of IIS. An administrator can choose to permit either Windows users or IIS Users access to administer IIS remotely. IIS Users do not consume Windows CALs, nor do they have any permissions outside of IIS itself; thus, they are a cheaper and more secure option for permitting external IIS administration.

IIS Manager

IIS 7.0 introduced a new, unified IIS Manager that combined all management functions for both IIS and ASP.NET in one location. Developers could now manage individual sites and applications without needing local administrator access to the server. The IIS Manager is also extensible through the addition of modules.

AppCmd.exe Command-Line Utility

IIS 7.0 introduced a new command-line utility, AppCmd.exe, which replaced the functionality provided by the various VBScript command-line utilities included with previous versions. AppCmd.exe also expanded command-line control to all IIS configuration functions. For example, to create a virtual directory using AppCmd.exe, you would enter at a command prompt:

```
C:\Windows\System32\inetsrv\appcmd add vdir
/app.name: "Default Web Site/" / /path: /VirtualDiretory1
/physicalPath: C:\InetPub\VirtualDirectory1
```

PowerShell Integration

IIS 7.0 saw the integration of PowerShell commands into IIS management and deployment scenarios with the IIS PowerShell Snap-In. PowerShell has become the scripting tool of choice for Windows administrators, and integration with IIS through cmdlets and specific functions has made enterprise management of IIS servers simpler.

In PowerShell, creating a virtual directory would look something like the following:

```
PS IIS:\> New-Item 'IIS:\Sites\Default Web Site\VirtualDirectory1'
-type VirtualDirectory -physicalPath C:\InetPub\VirtualDirectory1
```

Diagnostics

IIS 7.0 made diagnostic tracing and server state management simple for both administrators and developers. The new Request Tracing module allowed for tracing any request through the pipeline to the point of exit or failure, and provides a logging function for those traces.

Using the Request Tracing module, you could configure logging and tracing of any type of content or result code. Like most IIS settings, request tracing can be configured at the server, site, or application level.

WINDOWS SERVER 2012 FEATURES

Because IIS is integrated into the Windows operating system, many of the changes to IIS 8.0 have to do with changes to the Windows operating system itself. Windows Server 2012 has many new features that affect and enhance IIS 8.0.

Server Versions

Windows Server 2008 came in multiple versions, including Standard, Enterprise, and Datacenter, primarily differentiated by the amount of memory and number of processors accessible. Each was targeted, and licensed, for specific deployment types, and changing the version required a full reinstall.

Windows Server 2008 also had several special editions available. Windows Server 2008 Web Edition was designed to run a web server but could not run applications such as Microsoft Exchange or be used as an Active Directory server. The HPC Edition was designed for high-performance computing, using computing clusters and expandable into a Microsoft Azure data center for cost-effective high-performance tasks. Windows Server 2008 was also available for Itanium processors and also in a Foundation version for the low-cost and low-performance server needs of small companies.

Windows Server 2012 will not support 32-bit or Itanium processors. There is no longer a Web Edition or Foundation version, and the features of the HPC version have been incorporated into the standard operating system. In short, you can buy Windows Server 2012 in only one edition and install it for any system configuration you need, physical or virtual.

Windows Server 2008 and Windows Server 2008 R2 may be directly upgraded to Windows Server 2012, providing that the system meets hardware requirements, but Windows Server 2008 will not be upgradable to future versions of Windows.

The New User Interface

One of the most obvious changes for Windows Server 2012 is the availability of the new graphical user interface. Microsoft designed this interface to unify all forms of Windows, from servers to desktops to tablets to phones, and everything else imaginable. Although seemingly targeted toward the consumers and end user, the new graphical interface (shown in Figure 1-1) also expands the abilities of the server administrator with a new Server Manager interface as well. Live Tiles displays a real-time view of the server and provides a dashboard with live statistics for the administrator.

Windows Server 2012 does not default to the new interface, termed *Server with a GUI*. There are, in fact, three separate interfaces available for Windows Server 2012: the standard Server with a GUI interface used on the desktop; a command-line interface similar to the Server Core installation available in Windows Server 2008; and a new hybrid version, *Minimal Server Interface*, that allows you to run the graphical Server Manager and Microsoft Management Console (MMC) without adding the burden of the browser and interface graphics. Administrators can switch between these versions without having to reinstall Windows, unlike in Windows Server 2008. A simple PowerShell cmdlet allows the change, switching to the Server with a GUI interface from the command-line interface:

```
PS> Install-WindowsFeature Server-Gui-Mgmt-Infra,Server-Gui-Shell -Restart
```

Reversing this and reverting to the Server Core interface is simple:

```
PS> Uninstall-WindowsFeature Server-Gui-Mgmt-Infra,Server-Gui-Shell -Restart
```

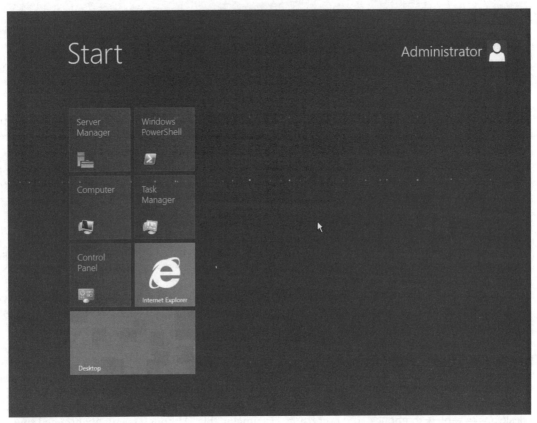

FIGURE 1-1

Most administrators will rarely see the Server with a GUI interface and instead will primarily use the new Minimal Server Interface and the Server Manager (as shown in Figure 1-2) to manage all servers in the enterprise, virtual or physical, whether or not they are based in the cloud.

The new Server Manager allows multiple servers to be administered, even from a Windows 8 workstation. New in Windows Server 2012 is the ability to manage multiple servers with credentials differing from the user's default credentials. These servers can be virtual or physical and may be located in the cloud. Server Manager in Windows Server 2012 will even aggregate server information by server role and other groupings.

> **NOTE** *When you are adding or installing a feature, the requisite source files need to be available. If they are not available as part of the Windows installation, they will be downloaded from the Windows Update website; optionally, the administrator can specify a local Windows Imaging (WIM) file as an installation source. For more information, see* http://technet.microsoft.com/en-us/library/ hh831786.aspx.

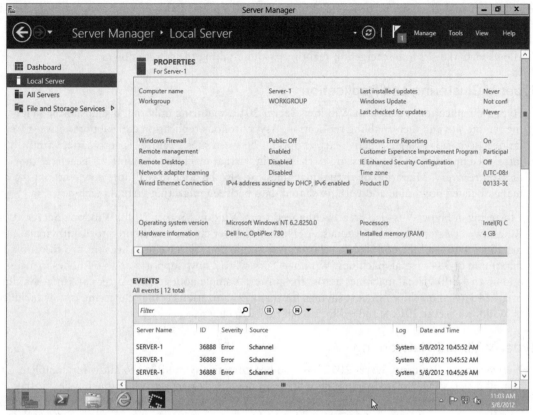

FIGURE 1-2

Virtualization and Private Cloud

Windows Server 2008 supported virtualization and Microsoft's Hyper-V technology, but in Windows Server 2012 virtualization and cloud deployment are the driving force in many of the operating system's architecture changes. Active Directory's changes to accommodate rapid cloud deployment and the virtualization of Active Directory servers make for a seamless management interface. Virtual images and physical servers are treated identically in Windows Server 2012 and can be managed through the same Server Manager interface.

Windows Server 2012 supports both public and private clouds, as well as hybrid clouds, but the private cloud is where the operating system really shines. Management of virtual environments and resources, especially in conjunction with Microsoft System Center 2012, is fully integrated into all levels of the operating system. Hyper-V v.3, Microsoft's latest version of its hypervisor technology, fully integrates PowerShell for local and remote management of all virtual systems. This eases the burden of virtual management by allowing fully scripted and automated solutions.

Windows Server 2012 with Hyper-V also expands the ability to access resources, without the limits on physical versus virtual process imposed in Windows Server 2008. This means that the only limit to virtual machines is the limits of the hardware. Storage management has also become easier in Windows Server 2012 with scalable virtual disks and a new virtual disk format, VHDX. With VHDX, Hyper-V can use virtual fiber channel connections to SMB storage devices. VHDX also allows virtual disks to be merged in real time without taking the system down.

Hyper-V Clustering and Replication

Hyper-V replication is simple in Windows Server 2012, requiring only that a snapshot be sent to the remote site and then enabling replication. Asynchronous replication can support active–passive failover scenarios as well as active–active options between sites. Failover is automatic, with fully integrated updating of IP addressing to the backup virtual machine, allowing for near real-time disaster recovery. Migration of virtual machines can also be done in real time now, without the normal associated downtime and with no shared data between migrating virtual machines.

Clustering in Hyper-V is also greatly enhanced from Windows Server 2008. Windows Server 2008 R2 allowed clusters of up to 16 nodes. A Hyper-V failover cluster was limited to 1,000 virtual machines across all the nodes in the cluster. Any single node in the cluster was limited to running a maximum of 384 virtual machines. Windows Server 2012 now supports up to 64 nodes in a cluster and up to 4,000 virtual machines across the cluster. A single node in the cluster can run a maximum of 1,024 virtual machines. A cost savings for many organizations is that clustering is now included in Windows Server 2012 Standard Edition at no extra charge.

Hyper-V Virtual Networking

Networking in Windows Server 2012 has also been drastically modified to allow for complete virtual networking. Isolated virtual networks can now be created with the same physical infrastructure, a process that could barely be imitated on Windows Server 2008. Windows Server 2012 introduces functions such as DHCP Guard, which prevents a virtual server from exposing services to other virtual networks. This allows for isolating multitenant networks and controlling bandwidth use on the virtual networks, valuable to both hosters and those organizations where a single server farm handles multiple subsidiaries.

Unified Remote Access

Remote access for Windows users has gone from being a convenience to being a necessity, both for mobile clients as well as administrators. Previous Windows Server versions had three separate technologies, virtual private networks (VPNs) and DirectAccess, as well as cross-premises connectivity. In Windows Server 2012, DirectAccess becomes the connection technology, whether the client is using a Windows device or VPN to connect. With wizards to walk the user or administrator through the process, DirectAccess allows for remote client access to systems behind Network Address Translation (NAT) firewalls as well as DMZ use, and simplifies end-user connectivity.

TLS/SSL

The Schannel security support provider (Schannel SSP) provides Transport Layer Security (TLS), Secure Sockets Layer (SSL), and Datagram Transport Layer Security (DTLS) authentication protocols for Windows Server 2012 and adds support for Server Name Indicator (SNI) extensions. Both

SNI and DTLS directly affect the implementation and configuration of IIS 8.0 under Windows Server 2012. SSL and TLS are covered in Chapter 15, "SSL and TSL."

SNI

In Windows Server 2008 and IIS 7.0, a common issue was running multiple virtual web servers on a single server with multiple certificates handled by the one server. During an SSL request, the client requests a certificate from the server to secure the communication and then uses that certificate to encrypt communication to the server. In versions before Windows Server 2012, the client did not inform the server of the target domain during this negotiation, so the server could only issue a single certificate for the request.

Using SNI, the client informs the server of the target domain when it requests the certificate, allowing the server to send a certificate targeted for the specific website so that the secure session is established to the correct virtual web server. In its simplest form, SNI allows an IIS 8.0 server to host multiple SSL sites and certificates on a single IP address, allowing SSL with host headers with individual SSL certificates for each site. In Windows Server 2008 R2, using SSL on sites with host headers allowed for only a single, wild-card certificate across all sites.

DTLS

DTLS comes into play with streaming media, which often uses datagrams for applications such as videoconferencing. DTLS allows secure communications using the Windows Security Support Provider Interface (SSPI). Note that applications must be designed for this functionality, but this now allows secure sessions for gaming applications, video streaming, and other datagram uses.

IIS 8.0 FEATURES

IIS 8.0 has a number of new features and improvements, some of which have been released for IIS 7.5 as out-of-band updates on `www.iis.net`. Many of these new features are due to the updates within the new operating system, though, and cannot be ported back to older versions of IIS. The Application Warm-Up module, for example, was released for IIS 7.5 and is built into IIS 8.0, but a central store for SSL certificates requires Windows Server 2012 and is available only on IIS 8.0.

SSL Changes

Changes to SSL within Windows Server 2012 naturally affect IIS 8.0 as well. In IIS 8.0, certificates are no longer restricted to a site but are managed through a central certificate store, making management of multiple sites in large web farms far less time-consuming. In addition, SSL certificates no longer need to be bound to an IP address, and deployment or configuration of SSL can now be done through simple PowerShell cmdlets. SSL and TLS are covered in Chapter 15.

CPU Throttling

The CPU throttling process in IIS 8.0 has been improved, allowing sites to use more CPU when needed but throttling CPU cycles back to preset limits when there is contention between sites for the CPU. IIS 7.0 on Windows Server 2008 would simply kill a process that required too much CPU, effectively making CPU throttling a dangerous practice on heavily used servers. In IIS 8.0, administrators can set a limit for CPU use that the system will allow a process to exceed if the CPU is available. Otherwise, the process is restricted to the limit and not summarily killed.

Application Warm-Up

The Application Warm-Up module was released for IIS 7.5 and Windows Server 2008 R2, and has been fully implemented in IIS 8.0 on Windows Server 2012. The application is identical; the only real difference is that it ships as part of the server operating system now and there's no need to install it as an add-on module. If you are upgrading from Server 2008, you will need to remove the IIS 7.5 version and upgrade to the shipping version to avoid conflicts.

Application Warm-Up fixes issues with complex applications that take significant time to load caches or generate content for the first HTTP request by allowing administrators to preload or preconfigure those tasks. In addition, the Application Warm-Up module enables administrators to configure a splash page that is displayed to end users while the application is starting. In previous situations, programmers needed to write the routines to handle this; otherwise, users would essentially see a dead browser.

WebSocket

WebSocket is a W3C-standardized API that allows full-duplex bidirectional communications over a single IP address and port. WebSocket requires both client and server support, which is now built into Windows Server 2012 and IIS 8.0, as well as Internet Explorer 10 and above. The web application must also be written to support the WebSocket API.

The big advantage to this API support is for developers, who will now find it much easier to use HTML and connect to data sources asynchronously in cloud deployments. Connections using the WebSocket API are bidirectional and full-duplex, using a single TCP connection but sending streams of messages instead of streams of bytes, thereby greatly increasing the access speed of data connections over standard TCP connections. The WebSocket API uses the standard HTTP port 80, allowing for communication through most firewalls.

Additional Features

As in previous versions, IIS 8.0 includes FTP and SMTP services. SMTP remains unchanged from Windows Server 2008 and IIS 7.5, and FTP is nearly identical to the FTP server available for download from Microsoft's website at www.iis.net. Both FTP and SMTP are covered in detail in Chapter 10, "Configuring Other Services."

FTP

Windows Server 2008 shipped with exactly the same FTP code and functions found in Windows Server 2003 and IIS 6.0, whereas Windows Server 2008 R2 shipped with the updated FTP 7.5, which was released as an inline update through Microsoft's website at www.iis.net. FTP 7.5

included secure FTP using SSL certificates, which had been one of the primary reasons for using third-party FTP servers. In addition, FTP 7.5 integrated with the IIS management functions, including extensibility of the authentication process. This means that FTP can use ASP.NET authentication, including membership and roles features, and does not require Windows CALs.

Windows Server 2012 ships with essentially the same FTP server as in FTP 7.5, with some additional functionality. FTP is covered in detail in Chapter 10.

SMTP

SMTP is again available on Windows Server 2012, as it was on Windows Server 2008, without the need to purchase Microsoft Exchange Server. Unchanged from the Windows Server 2008 implementation, SMTP code is actually developed and owned by the Windows Exchange Server development team. The SMTP service in Windows Server 2012 is not meant to be a full-featured implementation, but rather a simplified service that provides minimum functionality without the need for additional services. Most professional users of IIS will want to install another mail server product, such as Microsoft's Exchange Server.

That doesn't mean that SMTP in Windows Server 2012 is a lightweight product. It is still functional for sending mail from applications on IIS 8.0, and it is a fully compliant implementation of SMTP that functions well in an Internet environment. While not having the configurability of Microsoft's Exchange Server, it will still function with multiple virtual servers and serve multiple SMTP domains while providing for security through relay permissions and IP restrictions as well as Windows login account access.

Chapter 10 goes into more detail on SMTP installation and configuration.

2

IIS 8.0 Architecture

WHAT'S IN THIS CHAPTER?

➤ IIS architecture basics

➤ IIS 7.0 and later architecture

➤ IIS 8.0 architecture

➤ Windows Server 2012 architecture

The origins of IIS as a service to deliver data via HTTP and Gopher requests determined the architecture of IIS for six generations. Over the years, IIS architecture evolved from serving simple requests and providing a Common Gateway Interface (CGI), to including interpreted scripting languages for Active Server Pages (ASP), now referred to as *ASP Classic*. Newer versions added the ability to include the ASP.NET framework for server-processed programs, as well as brand-new technologies such as AJAX and Silverlight.

Understanding the basic architecture of IIS through previous versions will help you understand the changes in IIS 8.0, as well as problems in converting applications and sites from previous versions. IIS has often been compared to the Apache open source server, and often derided as not providing the configurability of Apache. Changes in IIS 7.0 that have been continued through IIS 8.0 have made IIS far more configurable than past versions and allowed many applications that relied on Apache, such as those written with PHP, to not only run on IIS, but also to coexist with applications in many languages, including ASP.NET.

Many organizations chose Apache as their web platform, often because of misinformation, and in some cases have regretted the decision. Although most organizations can work with either web server technology as a base, the choice of web server technology determines many future choices as well, such as the ability to leverage ASP.NET for web applications. In many ways, IIS 8.0 architecture changes void the reasons for choosing Apache as a web platform. IIS 8.0 still supports previous architectures for those who need to reuse applications and sites.

Although IIS 8.0 is not a radical change from IIS 7.0 and shares the same underlying architecture, changes to the architecture of Windows Server 2012 greatly affect some of the functionality of IIS 8.0. These changes include a move to embrace cloud and new storage architectures, as well as expanded acceptance of applications once limited to other platforms. IIS 8.0 functions now integrate well with Microsoft and non-Microsoft technologies, furthering an open web environment.

IIS ARCHITECTURE BASICS

IIS has grown dramatically from its first incarnation in Windows NT and, until IIS 4.0, was pretty much the second or third choice for running web sites and applications. As Windows Server changed, so did IIS. In Windows Server 2000 and IIS 5.0, IIS became an integral part of the operating system. No longer an add-on product, the version of IIS became dependent on the version of the operating system — thus the need to upgrade operating systems to upgrade versions of IIS.

In early versions of IIS, the entire web server was simply an executable, as were other web servers at the time. IIS 4.0 began some changes to the basic architecture, which have been extended over the years, allowing for separation of processes, better security, and faster operations. As IIS grew, it became an essential application platform for Microsoft products such as Microsoft Exchange Server, Microsoft SharePoint Server, and Microsoft SQL Server. The development of programming technologies, such as ASP.NET, has spurred many of the changes to IIS, and now IIS is a fully integrated application environment.

The basic architecture of IIS up to 6.0 is a progression of past principles. Beginning with IIS 7.0 and Windows Server 2003, IIS underwent a full code rewrite and, while the concepts of the architecture remain, major changes to the way the architecture is implemented occurred. These were, in many ways, related to the changing web development environment and have resulted in the IIS you see in version 8.0.

Inetinfo.exe

Throughout the early versions of IIS — indeed, virtually unchanged between IIS 1.0, 2.0, and 3.0 — the IIS Web Server process, `inetinfo.exe`, handled all of the functions of servicing a web request. The client request came in, and whether it needed processing by ISAPI applications or just the web server process, `inetinfo.exe` handled the entire process.

IIS 4.0 changed this architecture by adding *process isolation* to the mix. ISAPI applications could be run in a separate process, meaning that a crash in that application would not bring down the entire WWW service. These out-of-process applications could also be stopped and restarted without affecting other applications, and could be configured to auto-restart the process if it stopped. Applications that still ran in-process would not be affected, but could not be restarted without restarting `inetinfo.exe`, or often the entire server.

IIS 6.0 further extended the architecture of IIS, with the addition of a *worker process isolation mode* and the ability to run multiple application pools. In addition, the HTTP request portion of `inetinfo.exe` was moved into the kernel to further improve performance. IIS 6.0 also introduced recycling of worker processes, an XML metabase, and rapid fail protection.

Http.sys

Http.sys was the new HTTP listener for IIS 6.0. Prior to IIS 6.0, inetinfo.exe listened for HTTP requests as well as routed them to the appropriate handler. Beginning with IIS 6.0, the listener function was broken out of inetinfo.exe, which ran in user mode, and Http.sys became the listener, running in kernel mode.

Kernel Mode versus User Mode

Kernel mode and user mode are the two modes that a process can run in under Windows Server 2003. *Kernel mode* has full access to all hardware and system data, whereas *user mode* processes cannot access hardware directly and have only limited access to system data. In the Intel processor architecture, kernel mode runs in ring 0, whereas user mode runs in ring 3. By running Http.sys in kernel mode, the listener has access to the TCP/IP stack directly and sits outside of the WWW service, unaffected by faulty code or crashes in applications.

By running in kernel mode, Http.sys enjoys a higher priority and can respond to HTTP requests faster than in previous versions of IIS. Http.sys not only improves IIS performance by its priority response, but it also can queue requests while waiting for application responses, even if the application has stopped responding. Each application pool in IIS 6.0 has a kernel mode queue, and Http.sys routes requests to the appropriate queue. This is why performance tuning includes separating intensive applications into individual application pools, allowing other, less intensive applications to benefit by not having to share the same queue. Queue size is configurable for each application pool.

Http.sys also caches requests and will serve requests from this kernel mode cache whenever possible. A cached response will eliminate all processing by IIS, because Http.sys will simply return the response from the cache and bypass any IIS functions for heavily requested material. Because this cache is memory cache and cannot be paged, maximizing RAM in a system is a simple way to increase IIS performance. Maximizing RAM also reduces paging of inetinfo.exe, which, running in user mode, can be paged to disk as needed. Too little RAM for an IIS system will dramatically slow performance.

Other Http.sys Functions

Http.sys also handles TCP/IP connections for HTTP requests and responses, including creating and breaking down the connection itself. Because Http.sys sits directly on top of the TCP/IP stack, it also handles connections and time-outs, as well as the limit for number of connections and bandwidth throttling. Logs are also handled by Http.sys.

Http.sys performs two important functions that improve performance in IIS 6.0. It caches requests in kernel mode, meaning that requests for recently served content, both static and dynamic, can be served from kernel mode without needing to switch to user mode and the inetinfo.exe process.

Http.sys also queues requests until they can be serviced by the appropriate worker process. Each application pool has its own queue, and the size of the queue is configurable to tune performance of specific pools. This queuing also has an advantage for applications that might fail, because requests for a failed application are still queued to the limit of the queue size. These requests can be processed when the application begins responding again and, combined with the ability to auto-restart failed application pools, can keep applications responding with no more indication to the client than a slight delay.

ISAPI and CGI

Early in the development of IIS, Microsoft recognized that the inherent problem with the traditional UNIX-style use of the Common Gateway Interface (CGI) to run applications responding to web requests was that the method did not scale well. Each CGI application request would start a new copy of the CGI application; thus, multiple requests would launch multiple instances, quickly running out of resources and slowing down the web server. Their solution to this was the Internet Service Application Programming Interface (ISAPI). An ISAPI application could respond to multiple requests, conserving resources and scaling far better than a CGI application.

ISAPI and CGI remain important technologies in IIS 8.0. CGI support has grown to allow the running of multiple application types within IIS, such as PHP, which have been a mainstay of Apache and other web servers.

IIS Admin Service

IIS 6.0 broke out everything unrelated to web service and placed it into a separate service, the *IIS Admin service*. This service handles FTP, SMTP, and non-web services other than HTTP. This changed how web applications can run, and no application will now run in process within inetinfo.exe. This further stabilizes the web server and means that all applications run in either a pooled process or an isolated process. The concept of the IIS Admin Service, in a vastly updated form, continues through newer versions of IIS.

Application Pools

IIS 6.0 was the first version of IIS in which you could assign applications to an *application pool*. Multiple applications could be assigned to an application pool, and each application pool could be assigned an ASP.NET process account and identity. The version of ASP.NET framework was also set for each application pool. IIS 6.0 also allowed multiple application pools, something unavailable in IIS 5.0.

By default in IIS 6.0, there was one application pool with one worker process running multiple applications, the equivalent of IIS 5.0's medium application protection. You could also run a single application pool per website, hosting a single worker process and a single application, the equivalent of IIS 5.0's high isolation mode. Both of these are natural extensions of IIS 5.0, and carry the same recommendation of running mission-critical or development applications in their own application pools, and pooling all other applications under one or more multiple application pools. But IIS 6.0 included a third, brand-new worker process configuration for application pools, termed a *web garden*.

Web gardens in IIS 6.0 consisted of multiple worker processes for a single application pool, with one or more applications in the application pool. A web garden thus becomes an application pool that is serviced by multiple worker processes — in effect a "web farm," but all on a single machine. IIS 6.0 also had the ability to support *processor affinity*, meaning that a worker process in a web garden can be assigned to a specific processor in a multiple processor system, potentially improving performance.

Application pools are a great improvement on the IIS architecture because separate websites and web applications can be assigned to combinations of application pools. On a server hosting multiple websites, separating sites into separate application pools can protect one site when the applications in another misbehave.

Active Server Pages

IIS 3.0 introduced *Active Server Pages*, or ASP, often called *ASP Classic* now. ASP was Microsoft's answer to Perl, an interpreted scripting language that was both easy to learn and easy to implement in IIS. Using either *Visual Basic Scripting Language* (VBScript) or *Jscript*, a server-side version of JavaScript, most beginning programmers could master server-side scripting in a much shorter time than it would take to learn C and develop DLLs to run as ISAPI applications.

ASP runs as an ISAPI application itself, lending itself to improved scalability over a Perl script using a CGI executable. Through additional technology, such as ADO and OLEDB access to databases, ASP became the predominant dynamic web-site development technology for IIS servers in a very short time. Today, four IIS generations after ASP was introduced, many organizations still rely on ASP scripting for running web applications. IIS 8.0 includes full native support of ASP, just needing the user to have the ASP Classic module installed.

ASP.NET

ASP.NET and the .NET Framework were released a decade ago as a successor to Microsoft's ASP technology. ASP.NET is built on the principle of a Common Language Runtime (CLR) providing for support for many ASP.NET compatible languages, such as VB.NET, C#.NET, and F#.NET. ASP.NET web pages, called *web forms*, can include various user and custom controls, and the code is compiled and executed on request. Compiled code remains in the system's cache for a period of time (the default is 20 minutes) so that subsequent requests for the same page don't have to be compiled for every request. Code may also be precompiled to a DLL for faster startups, although IIS 8.0 introduces the Application Initialization module to address this speed issue.

In versions of IIS prior to IIS 7.0, ASP.NET ran in a separate pipeline process, similar to ASP code. Once a request was determined to be an ASP.NET page, the code was handed off to a separate ASP.NET ISAPI module for processing. IIS 7.0 changed this with the concept of an integrated pipeline mode; it processes all requests as if they were ASP.NET code, allowing much more extensibility and flexibility for IIS and web applications. These pipelines are discussed later in this chapter.

The 3.5 version of the .NET Framework was the default version for IIS versions prior to IIS 8.0. IIS 8.0 defaults to the 4.5 .NET Framework and can support ASP.NET 2.0 and above. IIS 3.0 and 3.5 are simply extensions of the .NET Framework 2.0 version, adding Windows Presentation Foundation (WPF), ASP.NET AJAX support, and LINQ, among other technologies. IIS 4.0 added Parallel Extensions, supporting multi-core systems, and a number of additional VB.NET and C#.NET features.

ASP.NET 4.5, which is supported only on IIS 7.0 and above, ships standard with Windows Server 2012 and IIS 8.0, with a key feature being support for the new Windows 8.0 interface and modern applications for Windows Phone and Windows 8 devices. Support is also included for HTML 5, as well as WebSockets and asynchronous web modules and HTTP requests. ASP.NET 4.5 also improves network programming as well as WPF functions. Microsoft supports ASP.NET through a website www.asp.net, a sister site to the www.iis.net site for supporting IIS.

IIS 7.0 AND LATER ARCHITECTURE

Although the architecture in IIS 7.0 and later versions is quite different from that of IIS 6.0 and prior versions and the code base has been entirely rewritten, many of the concepts and most of the architecture of the IIS family live on. ISAPI still exists, even though pipeline modules can be written to replace most ISAPI applications. The worker process and application pools are still in place, and inetinfo.exe and Http.sys still perform similar functions. In IIS 7.0 and above, the web server has become the application server, an integral part of the operating system included in all versions of Windows Server 2008 and later. IIS 8.0, which contains the code from IIS 7.0, includes all the functions and processes from IIS 7.0.

Whereas IIS 6.0 was the *supporting platform* for many applications, from ASP and ASP.NET to SharePoint, later versions of IIS have become part of the application itself. In many ways, IIS is now the application framework, supporting the application code and function. The architecture of IIS has been designed around this concept, allowing developers great freedom to alter, tune, and improve not only their applications, but also now the web server itself. The modularity and extensibility of IIS now goes far beyond the capability of ISAPI extensions, which in IIS 6.0 were tacked on as handlers for specific file types. Developers can now modify the server functionality to meet the needs of the application.

Pipeline Modes

A major factor in the growth and development of IIS has been its use as a platform for applications, especially ASP.NET. IIS 7.0 advanced the platform further by integrating ASP.NET directly into IIS, for everything from management to authentication and the request-processing pipeline itself. *Pipeline integration* provides two advantages for IIS: better performance and control for ASP.NET web applications and extensibility through managed code.

ASP.NET performance has been improved because ASP.NET applications no longer need to exit the pipeline and load the ISAPI process to handle ASP.NET code, and then return to the pipeline for response to the client. IIS still supports the classic pipeline mode for application compatibility, but wherever possible you should use the new integrated pipeline mode.

Classic Mode

In IIS 6.0, ASP.NET was enacted as an ISAPI filter, that is, requests exited the pipeline to be processed by aspnet.dll and then returned to the pipeline for further processing of the response to the client. A client's HTTP request in IIS 6.0 would move through the pipeline until a handler was determined, and if the file was an ASP.NET file, it would be shunted to the ASP.NET ISAPI filter, move through the ISAPI process, and return to the pipeline before a HTTP response was eventually sent back to the client. In IIS 7.0 and later, this mode is still available, as the *classic mode*.

Integrated Pipeline Mode

The integrated pipeline mode in IIS 7.0 and above allows developers to integrate their own managed code as a module in the pipeline. In prior versions of IIS, this required development of ISAPI filters or applications, not a trivial task for most developers. In IIS 7.0 and above, modules can be developed with managed code and act as part of the request pipeline. In the integrated pipeline mode in IIS 7.0, ASP.NET files are processed within the pipeline, allowing ASP.NET code at any step in the process. Because ASP.NET is integrated into the pipeline, ASP.NET functions, such as authentication, can be used even for non-ASP.NET content. Every request, regardless of type, is processed by IIS and ASP.NET.

ASP.NET integration also means that ASP.NET authentication can be used across the board for any files, folders, or functions of IIS 7.0. Before IIS 7.0, because ASP.NET exited the pipeline for processing, any files not served by ASP.NET — such as HTML, Perl, or even content such as graphic images — were unaffected by any ASP.NET code and couldn't be secured with ASP.NET authentication schemes. This meant that Windows integrated authentication or a custom authentication scheme had to be used for securing non-ASP.NET content. The integrated pipeline mode greatly simplifies the development of authentication methods.

Moving an Application to the Integrated Pipeline

IIS maintains the classic pipeline mode for compatibility, and you can run ASP.NET applications in the classic pipeline if they have compatibility issues with the integrated pipeline mode. Because the `web.config` configuration file has a different structure in the integrated pipeline mode, if you have `httpModules` or `httpHandlers`, they must be migrated to the new mode. Moving most ASP.NET applications to the new pipeline is relatively straightforward, and IIS commands can be used for the migration.

IIS configures new ASP.NET applications and sites in the integrated pipeline by default. Most applications will run as written, and those that won't will generate configuration errors to tell you what is going on. Using `AppCmd.exe`, IIS provides a command-line method to migrate application configurations to the integrated pipeline, which will correct most errors with incompatible configuration files. From the command line, use the following command:

```
appcmd.exe migrate config {Application Path}
```

Replace {`Application Path`} with the site name and application, similar to `default web site/ application1`. Chapter 8, "Web Application Pool Administration," covers configuration in depth.

Application Pools and the Pipeline

The pipeline mode is set for the application pool in which the application runs. To configure an ASP.NET application to run in the classic pipeline instead of the default integrated pipeline, create an application pool for the classic pipeline, and assign the application to that application pool. You may want to configure an application pool for the classic pipeline and assign applications to it until those applications can be migrated, then simply move the application to an application pool that runs under the integrated pipeline after you have finished your migration.

Extensibility and Modularity

The modular architecture of IIS 7.0 and above differs from the monolithic `inetinfo.exe` in previous IIS versions. More than 40 components are available with IIS 7.0 and above, and custom-written or third-party modules can be added as well. The IIS development team at Microsoft has released several. Creating custom modules to extend the core server is also covered in detail in Chapter 12, "Core Server Extensibility."

The modularity of IIS accomplishes two tasks. The first is that you only need to load those modules required for your application or configuration. This reduces the attack surface of IIS, but it also reduces the amount of useless code loaded into memory. The guiding principle of server management should always be, "If you don't need it, don't load it," and IIS meshes with that principle completely.

The second task accomplished by modularity is the ability to insert custom modules into the pipeline. This extensibility allows developers to add integrated modules as well as for Microsoft to further extend IIS functions after an operating system has shipped.

Modules

IIS 7.0 and above ship with more than 40 modules, handling everything from authentication token caching to the ability to process ISAPI Filters to URL Mapping, all of which can be installed or left out of an installation, according to the website and application requirements. Many of these modules will commonly be installed, such as HTTP Caching and HTTP Logging, which enable kernel mode caching of HTTP requests and standard IIS logging, respectively. Others, such as Digest Authentication or the CGI module, which allow for the use of digest authentication and the ability to use CGI applications, are normally not installed unless you need to support those functions. Some of the types of modules that ship with IIS 7.0 and above include:

➤ **Utility modules** — Utility modules are those that handle internal server operations, not directly acting on any requests. These modules provide caching functions — for files, authentication tokens, and server state — relative to the URI request. Without these modules installed, performance can degrade because caching is reduced.

➤ **Managed Engine: ASP.NET** — This is essentially a single, specialized module, ManagedEngine, that allows for the integration of ASP.NET into the request pipeline. Without this, the IIS request pipeline essentially only runs in classic mode.

➤ **IIS native modules** — Native modules are those written in native code, not dependent on the ASP.NET framework. This includes the majority of the functions from IIS 6.0 that have been moved to modules; code remains in native mode to aid in backward compatibility. These modules also do not require the ASP.NET framework and can thus be run in the core server implementation of IIS 7.0, which does not have an implementation of the ASP.NET framework available. Versions above IIS 7.0 do have ASP.NET available in all installations.

➤ **Managed modules** — Managed modules run in managed code, written using ASP.NET. These modules naturally include those functions that rely on the ASP.NET framework, such as Forms authentication, as well as modules that handle profiles, roles, and the ASP.NET session state.

IIS Manager Extensibility

In IIS 7.0 and above, IIS Manager is a Windows Forms application and is fully extensible, as any other Windows Forms application would be. Extending the administration user interface begins with a module provider, a basic server-side ASP.NET class that contains configuration information for the IIS Manager module. There is a `moduleProviders` section of the `administration.config` file, described below in this chapter, which defines the modules available to IIS Manager. The modules section of the same file lists which modules are actually implemented in the web server.

The corresponding client-side module ("client" as in the IIS Manager, even if it is run on the server) is the Windows Forms application that is used to manage the module in the provider. To aid in programming this form, Microsoft has added the `Microsoft.Web.Management.Client` and `Microsoft.Web.Management.Client.Win32` namespaces that developers can inherit from to ensure consistency and compatibility. More on extending the IIS Manager can be found in Chapter 12.

Metabase — Going, Going, Gone!

IIS 7.0 lost the metabase — well, not completely, because the metabase is still available for IIS 6.0 compatibility. IIS 7.0 removed configurations from the metabase, which was a proprietary and unfriendly format, and stored them in XML configuration files, which are industry standard ASCII text files. Almost all IIS 7.0 and above configurations are in these plaintext XML files that can be edited directly or managed through IIS Manager — "almost all" because some IIS configuration information is still stored in the registry. Because IIS can read configuration files only after IIS is running, those configuration items that must be available as IIS starts must be in the registry.

There are also legacy applications that may require the metabase. FTP and SMTP, for example, have configurations that remain in the metabase as in IIS 6.0, because they are unchanged from IIS 6.0.

FTP is a different story. The FTP server that shipped with Windows Server 2008, along with the SMTP server, was the same that shipped with Windows Server 2003. SMTP has no replacement, but an IIS 7.5 version of FTP is available from www.iis.net, for installation in Windows Server 2008. Windows Server 2008 R2 and Windows Server 2012 ship with the newer version of FTP. Both FTP and SMTP installation and management are covered in Chapter 10, "Configuring Other Services."

applicationHost.config and web.config

The two XML files that control IIS configuration are `applicationHost.config` and `web.config`. The `web.config` file can control configurations at the site and application levels, whereas `applicationHost.config` controls the server itself. Because configurations are inherited, `web.config` settings can override settings at higher levels. With configuration locking and delegation of administration, administrators can allow developers and lower-level administrators to control specific configuration sections while locking others to prevent changes. Chapter 9, "Delegating Remote Administration," covers configuration locking and delegation of administration in greater detail.

The `applicationHost.config` file, located in the `%windir%\system32\inetsrv\config` folder, follows a standard XML format, `<attribute-name>="<default-value>" [<metadata>] [<description>]`. A typical section might look like this:

```
<system.webserver>
    <defaultDocument enabled="true">
```

```
            <files>
                <add value=Default.aspx" />
            </files>
        </defaultDocument>
    </system.webserver>
```

This section is fairly self-explanatory when you read the code. It enables the default document for the server, setting it to `Default.aspx` and only `Default.aspx`. This can be modified at the site level in the `web.config` using the same syntax in the same section, as in the snippet below, which changes the default document from `Default.aspx` to `Home.asx` for the site containing the `web.config` file. Other sites will still inherit from the `applicationHost.config`.

```
    <system.webserver>
        <defaultDocument enabled="true">
            <files>
                <remove value=Default.aspx" />
                <add value=Home.aspx" />
            </files>
        </defaultDocument>
    </system.webserver>
```

In the default installation, IIS does not create a `web.config` file in the root of a site; all settings are contained in `applicationHost.config`. Modifying settings, such as the default document, in IIS Manager for a specific site will create a `web.config` file in the root folder of the site, with configuration information for the site itself. This same `web.config` may also hold ASP.NET application configuration information, but even without ASP.NET, the `web.config` will hold all IIS settings that modify the defaults contained in `applicationHost.config`.

Other XML Configuration Files

There are other XML configuration files that affect websites in IIS 7.0, 7.5, and 8.0. These are also found in the `%windir%\system32\inetsrv\config` folder and include `administration.config`, where configurations for IIS Manager are stored, and `redirection.config`, which holds information for centralized configuration files.

The `redirection.config` file simply holds the information needed to direct the web server to the correct centralized configuration file, along with credentials for accessing that file. It might look something like this:

```
    <configuration>
        <configSections>
            <section name="configurationRedirection" />
        </configSections>
        <configurationRedirection enabled="true"
            path="\\server1\centralconfig$\" userName="domain1.local\config"
            password="Passw0rd1" />
    </configuration>
```

The `administration.config` file holds much more information, such as which modules are available to IIS Manager. A configuration entry similar to the one below will add the default document module to IIS Manager for all sites.

```
    <location path=".">
        <modules>
```

```
        <add name="defaultDocument" />
      </modules>
    </location>
```

The `administration.config` file becomes important when you add custom modules, because they need to be added to the `administration.config` file to be able to use the GUI management interface. Extending IIS core modules with a custom module is covered in more detail in Chapter 12.

Metabase Compatibility

Legacy management interfaces pose a problem for the IIS 7.0 and later management systems with XML configuration files, and some changes made in IIS 7.0 would cause applications and utilities compatible with IIS 6.0 to fail if IIS 7.0 and above could not support these legacy interfaces. *Metabase compatibility* provides this support. Not installed by default in IIS, because it isn't needed, you install metabase compatibility by installing the IIS 6.0 Manager.

Scripts and applications running with metabase compatibility are unable to be delegated in IIS Manager and do not have access to IIS management functions. For this reason, porting these applications to the current model should be a part of any migration.

Metabase compatibility works at the API level with legacy functions, as well as with the ADSI and WMI interfaces to those functions. It remaps calls to the administration functions to the appropriate function in IIS 7.0 and above and also persists these mappings through entries in `applicationHost .config`.

WAS and the Worker Process

IIS 7.0 maintained all the familiar IIS 6.0 components, such as listener processes, worker processes, and application managers, but moved them from the w3svc to the Windows Process Activation Service (WAS). In IIS 6.0 and Windows Server 2003, requests retrieved by `Http.sys` were sent to the HTTP listener process, which handed them off to the appropriate worker process in w3svc, where the application manager would direct them to the specific application. A similar process still exists in current versions of IIS, but WAS will respond to requests other than HTTP, such as TCP, named pipes, and MSMQ. HTTP requests are still retrieved by `Http.sys` and passed to the HTTP manager in w3svc before being passed to WAS, but other requests are directed through the WAS listener adapter interface to the Configuration Manager and Process Manager without passing through w3svc.

Both `Http.sys` and `SMSsvchost.exe`, which host the non-HTTP listeners, now reside outside of IIS. This means that requests received by these listeners can be processed outside of IIS, and Windows communication foundation services can be hosted as services, Windows applications, or other processes outside of IIS. For the adventurous programmer, WAS is extensible, although you will need to write your own listener handler and the accompanying application domain protocol handler.

IIS 8.0 ARCHITECTURE

IIS 8.0 has essentially the same architecture as IIS 7.0 and is fully compatible, with some updates to accommodate the Windows 2012 architecture. IIS 8.0 also has many of the additional updates and modules available for IIS 7.0 integrated into the default IIS 8.0 installation package.

New for the IIS 8.0 architecture are changes to the way SSL and certificates are managed, changes to CPU throttling restrictions, changes to IP restrictions and security options, and the ability to use Non-Uniform Memory Access (NUMA) hardware for web applications. NUMA is basically a hardware-based method of associating processors to their own memory, allowing for faster access and better scaling in large, multiprocessor systems.

Upgraded in IIS 8.0 is the application warm-up package developed for IIS 7.0, now renamed *Application Initialization* and standard in IIS 8.0 as well as retroactive to work in IIS 7.5 on Windows Server 2008 R2. Many of the other IIS 7.0 add-ons now ship with IIS 8.0, such as Application Request Routing (ARR), the URL Rewrite module, and the FastCGI extension. The Web Platform Installer has been integrated into Windows Server 2012 and IIS 8.0, allowing simple installation of applications such as WordPress and DotNetNuke, as well as languages such as PHP.

SSL/SNI and Central Certificates

The network stack in Windows Server 2012 now supports Server Name Indication (SNI) that extends the Transport Layer Security (TLS) and Secure Sockets Layer (SSL) protocols to allow extreme scalability in SSL for multitenant sites and servers. In essence, SNI allows for SSL to handle multiple SSL certificates on a single IP address, often referred to as SSL on host headers.

Host headers, a technology where the requesting client sends an HTTP request to a web server, which then returns a site based on the host requested in the URL, allows for many websites with differing host names to run on a single IP address. Although the DNS record for each host resolves to a single IP, the web process answering on that IP address can read the requested headers and redirect the request to the proper site based on the requested host. This has worked fine for many generations of IIS.

With SSL certificates, which secure a host name and not a specific IP address, host headers do not work because the security handshake takes place before the web server determines the requested host name in the header. Multiple sites secured by SSL certificates could not share the same IP address because the host determination for the handshake would be unable to determine the correct host and certificate name — until Windows Server 2012 and IIS 8.0.

With the support of SNI, which provides a server name indicator within the security handshake process, a web server can now determine the proper host and certificate before the security has been negotiated, allowing the handshake to take place even though multiple sites and certificates are associated to a single IP address. IIS 8.0 has further extended this process with changes to the way certificates are managed and stored in both the server and the browser.

In versions of Internet Explorer and other clients before version 9.0, web certificates to secure specific websites were stored in the browser's personal certificate store. This storage area was never designed to store certificates for many web hosts, otherwise it would likely have been named something like the "Web Hosting" certificate store, which it now is. The personal and web hosting certificate stores behave identically as far as exporting and importing certificates go; the web hosting store has just been beefed up to support many more SSL certificates.

In addition to a new, expanded certificate store, IIS 8.0 and Windows Server 2012 also move the management of certificates to a centralized management system. Not only is it now far easier to configure and manage SSL certificates for your websites, but also the number of supported certificates is far greater. In versions of IIS before IIS 8.0, the web server would load all certificates into memory in case one was requested by a client. Not only is this a cumbersome process when the website is starting, loading 10,000 certificates would result in time-outs for many clients, but searching this list in memory was time-consuming, also resulting in client time-outs. Although there is no defined limit to the number of SSL sites on a single server, in IIS 7.0 and prior versions there became a practical limit because of the access times required.

IIS 8.0 does not load certificates when the server is started; it looks them up from the central manager when required. This dramatically increases the scalability of web servers and the number of supported secure sites. Not only is the startup time greatly reduced, but also the access time to look up needed certificates and negotiate the security process is likewise reduced. The memory profile of the server is reduced, the speed is increased, and there is no longer a requirement to bind a single certificate to an associated IP address and port combination.

SSL and TLS are discussed in detail in Chapter 15.

Dynamic IP Restrictions

IIS 7.5 and earlier versions included IP restrictions as a way of blocking malicious web requests designed to infiltrate your web server. Clunky at best, these restrictions required the administrator to determine the offending IP address or range manually, usually from analyzing log files, and then manually enter those IP addresses into each website from which they wished to block malicious requests. The more entries in the system, the more involved the process became, both to manage and to implement in a web request.

In IIS 8.0, these IP restrictions have been made dynamic. This means that the administrator no longer has to determine the IP addresses to be blocked — the server can now be configured to block any IP address that attempts too many connections to the server or attempts too many requests in a specified period of time.

This blocking of client IP addresses, configurable at both the server level as well as the site level, has been extended to allow the administrator to define the code returned to the client browser. Before this extension, IIS simply returned a standard 403, "access denied," error to the client. Now the server can return a 403, 404 ("page not found"), 401 ("unauthorized"), or simply drop the connection, looking like the web server simply went offline. Similar restrictions are now also available in the FTP server.

Dynamic IP restrictions have been made available for IIS 7.0 as well — the extension can be downloaded from Microsoft's website at www.iis.net. Securing the web server, including using dynamic IP restrictions, is covered in depth in Chapter 14, "Authentication and Authorization." IP restrictions for FTP are covered in Chapter 10, "Configuring Other Services."

Active CPU Throttling

IIS 7.0 introduced throttling to web servers, in a pretty limited manner. An administrator could set the CPU throttling rate for an application pool, but when that limit was hit, the application pool would be recycled and the process killed. Although it prevented runaway applications from taking down multiple application pools, it really didn't help throttle a CPU when there was simply too much traffic. The end-user experience was dismal. The session would simply go away or the browser would time out.

In IIS 8.0 the administrator has additional options. Although CPU throttling is still set for an application pool, the optional outcomes of Throttle and Throttle Under Load have been added. The option to throttle simply restricts the application pool to the percentage of CPU specified. If an application pool is set to throttle at 30,000 (the setting is in the 1/1,000th percent), the pool will never receive more than 30 percent of the CPU time. Instead of killing the process, IIS will simply queue the requests until the CPU is available. This will slow the requests but will not kill the process so they fail and time out.

The Throttle Under Load operation also limits the CPU available, but only when the server is under load. An application pool can use 100 percent of the CPU if nothing else needs it, but when there is a load on the CPU, the application pool will throttle back to allow the CPU to work on the other tasks. In this instance, a setting of 30,000 (30%) will throttle the process back until it reaches 30 percent of the CPU use and then allow it to remain at that level.

Although tuning a website and the application pool has now become a little more involved, the tuning options are much friendlier to the end user and far easier to scale in a multitenant environment. Performance tuning for IIS is further discussed in Chapter 22, "Monitoring and Performance Tuning."

Application Initialization

Application Initialization, previously referred to as the *Application Warm-Up module*, was available as an add-on for IIS 7.5 and is standard in IIS 8.0. There are two basic functions to this module, providing for a quicker startup of applications that require time to initialize connections, query databases, and compile the ASP.NET page code; and to provide an alternate user experience rather than just a spinning hourglass while waiting for the page to load. Although you could precompile code and precache static files in previous IIS versions, Application Initialization provides for more control.

In previous versions of IIS, the first request for an application would result in the worker process spinning up, caching static files, compiling the application, and loading the page. With Application Initialization, the administrator can configure the worker process to spin up and perform these tasks before the request hits the application, allowing for a faster startup without precompiling the application or caching all static files. In an instance where the worker process is recycled, the application will remain available without having to be reloaded.

To improve the end-user experience, Application Initialization gives the administrator the ability to redirect the request to alternate pages while the application is loading. IIS can thus be configured to return a static page while the application is loading, or, by using the URL Rewrite module, the user can temporarily be redirected until the application is ready. The administrator could set the server to play a Silverlight animation until the page is loaded or provide usage tips on a static page.

The Application Initialization module is further discussed in Chapter 22.

PowerShell Improvements

Microsoft has made significant additions to the PowerShell cmdlets shipped with Windows Server 2012, and many provide increased scriptability for IIS 8.0. The most useful addition to IIS 8.0 for PowerShell is not the cmdlets themselves, but rather the ability of the IIS Configuration Editor to generate PowerShell scripts.

The management of IIS changed with the introduction of IIS 7.0 and the use of configuration files instead of the metabase and registry settings of IIS 6.0. Although IIS Manager exposed many of these settings in the GUI, there were several settings where an administrator had to edit the configuration files directly. To alleviate that problem, Microsoft introduced the IIS Configuration Editor for IIS 7.5, and made it available as an extension to IIS 7.0.

The IIS Configuration Editor allowed an administrator to change every configuration feature via this user interface and also introduced the ability to script the configurations out in C# and JavaScript, as well as command-line codes using AppCmd. With IIS 8.0, this editor also allows scripting in PowerShell, which is fast becoming the default scripting language for the Windows administrator. PowerShell for IIS is further covered in Chapter 18, "Programmatic Configuration and Management."

WINDOWS SERVER 2012 ARCHITECTURE

The Windows Server 2012 architecture has not changed dramatically from that of Windows Server 2008. Most of the changes are either refinements or enhancements to the Windows Server 2008 system. Major changes have been made for expanded usability in cloud-based environments, with a new version of Hyper-V, a new Resilient File System that eliminates operating system limits on file or folder sizes (hardware limits obviously still exist) and a new IP address management system that allows for multiple private IP ranges to be dynamically hosted and assigned.

There are some notable changes to Windows Server 2012 in terms of hardware requirements and restrictions. For example, there is no longer a 32-bit option, and Windows Server 2012 will not run on Itanium processors. In today's system availability, these restrictions won't have any effect on new hardware choices, but they will change options for upgrading older systems. Planning installations and upgrades are covered in Chapter 3, "Planning Your Deployment."

Windows Server 2012 increases the maximum memory allowed to 4 TB, from 2 TB in Windows Server 2008; the maximum number of logical processors to 640, from 256 in Windows Server 2008; and failover cluster nodes to 64, from 16 in Windows Server 2008. Windows Server 2012 now requires a minimum of 512 MB of RAM, but nobody will want to install less than 4 GB of RAM for any reasonable use. Likewise, the minimum drive space required is 32 GB, but if you are running more than 16 GB of RAM, the space needed will increase.

Virtualization and Hyper-V

Data-center rack space is at a premium in many organizations, with power consumption and cooling requirements hitting critical levels as well. Efforts at "going green" are also mandating reduced power consumption and hardware requirements. The ability to adapt servers to specific shorter-term needs, especially for development and testing, is also changing data-center requirements. All of these are excellent reasons to look at server virtualization.

Virtual servers have been available for a long time and hark back to the mainframe era when shared systems were the norm. Products such as Microsoft Virtual Server or VMware have been adopted in many organizations. Windows Server 2012 has virtualization baked into the foundation of the operating system, creating a de facto dynamic data center capable of handling many virtualization scenarios.

Virtualization in Windows Server 2012 is hypervisor based, unlike Microsoft Virtual Server, which is a hosted virtualization platform. Hypervisor virtualization does not require a host platform, but virtual machines, such as in Virtual PC and Virtual Server, require a host operating system that supports other operating systems as guests. In hosted virtualization, access to hardware occurs through the hosting operating system. To be totally correct, Microsoft's Virtual PC and Virtual Server do use some hypervisor technology instead of being a pure hosted system, and Microsoft often refers to them as "hybrid" technology.

Windows Server 2012 with Hyper-V provides for a true, fully manageable and fully integrated virtual environment. Using Windows Server 2012, administrators can provision servers with full security and isolation, using virtual networking to link these servers, regardless of physical hardware and location, and migrate these servers into and out of clusters at will. Replication and failover options have improved over Windows Server 2008, and virtual machines and storage options are entirely mobile in Windows Server 2012. Scalability and availability are the keywords to Windows Server 2012's virtualization architecture, whether on systems physically located in a data center or using cloud technology to further expand the capabilities of the organization.

Virtual Networks

Hyper-V in Windows Server 2008 introduced network virtualization, but Windows Server 2012 takes it to a new level with extensible virtual switches that allow switching between virtual machines, the host server, and the external network. Hyper-V can also now use private VLAN technology to isolate virtual systems into networks that are secured from outside systems and other virtual machines on the same host. This greatly expands the capability for multitenant host systems and the ability to merge or separate virtual machines from networks easily.

Virtual networking in Windows Server 2012 allows an administrator to migrate virtual machines between systems and networks easily. It also allows for complete monitoring of the virtual network ports and direct assignment of a virtual network to specific physical network interfaces, and it can be managed programmatically. This isolation allows for policies to be enforced for virtual machines in specific networks and prevents other virtual or physical systems from spoofing virtual machine IP addresses. Naturally, Hyper-V virtual networks are fully supported by PowerShell 3.0.

Clustering, Replication, and Failover

Hyper-V 3.0 is built directly for replication. In past versions, an administrator would often replicate across synchronous high-speed links to identical SAN hardware, resulting in an expensive environment prone to the inevitable corruption being replicated as well as failover issues when the WAN link between sites failed. Hyper-V 3.0, in Windows Server 2012, is hardware independent, meaning that an administrator can replicate between identical hardware SANs, a SAN and a set of servers running simple mirrored drives, or any combination of physical and virtual hardware.

Hyper-V Replica, new to Windows Server 2012, is designed to accommodate failure in WAN links and will not automatically fail over because of network latency. Replication is asynchronous, allowing for lower bandwidth as well as changes in network latency. Hyper-V Replica is also configured on a virtual machine basis, allowing for individual configurations based on the organization's needs for replication and not occurring as a one-size-fits-all solution.

Live Migration

Hyper-V live migration was released with Windows Server 2008 R2 and has been enhanced in Windows Server 2012. One of the main changes is the separation of live migration from clustering, allowing organizations that cannot afford or do not need clustered systems to still use live migration for virtualized systems.

In clustered systems, live migration would move both the server and storage between running virtual machines with no downtime. Essentially, the system just shifted responsibility from one server in the cluster to another. Changes in Hyper-V version 3.0 separate the virtual machine's state, its running processes and memory, from its storage. Although you can still move both *en mass* from one system to another, the ability to shift the virtual machine's state to another, nonclustered, virtual machine makes the administrator's job simple — especially when moving between local systems and a public cloud.

Live storage migration, available with the separation of the migration process, means that an administrator can now move the storage for a virtual machine either together with or separately from the migration of the virtual machine's running state. Although Windows Server 2008 R2 allowed Quick Storage Migration, with live storage migration, there is zero downtime during the move. And an administrator can now move one storage location to another or move storage to various other locations as storage needs and environments become more complex.

Active Directory Changes

The most notable Active Directory change in Windows Server 2012 is that it is entirely installed and managed in a new section of Server Manager. Active Directory is now also aware of changes due to virtualization and updates automatically to accommodate virtualized platform changes. Virtualized domain controllers are fully supported, and domain controllers can be safely cloned in a virtualized or cloud environment.

Cloud Architecture

Windows Server 2012 has been tightly integrated and designed to use Microsoft's Azure cloud hosting service but, owing to this design philosophy, is an outstanding operating system for any public, private, or hybrid cloud deployment. Microsoft even tested the new operating system by converting all the servers in its Bing search service network to Windows Server 2012 while it was still a release candidate, in 16 data centers worldwide and managing 300 PB (petabytes) of data.

The main advantage of cloud technology is the scalability of the system and the agility to respond to changing business needs. Microsoft has moved all of its technologies, from Windows Server 2012 to Microsoft System Center to Microsoft Visual Studio and IIS 8.0, toward cloud integration and management. All Microsoft technologies now seamlessly integrate with public and private cloud deployments, making for easier provisioning of new servers, better use of virtualization technology, and better scalability for seasonal changes in business resource needs.

IP Address Management

One issue with cloud systems, as well as the proliferation of IP-addressable devices in a static and mobile environment, is the management of IP addressing. The advent of IPv6, combined with virtual networks, necessitates the automation of addressing as well as the ability to monitor addressing in real time.

Windows Server 2012 has *IP Address Management* (IPAM) as a feature, which allows for the central management and monitoring of IP addressing, naming, and the IP infrastructure. In Windows Server 2012, IPAM, along with tools such as Microsoft's System Center Virtual Machine Manager, can both manage the Active Directory IP infrastructure systems as well as provide monitoring for compliance and audit policies of the network's IP infrastructure.

Resilient File System

The new filesystem introduced in Windows Server 2012 is an improvement of the NTFS filesystem called the *Resilient File System* (ReFS). ReFS uses B+ Trees for the filesystem on disks, allowing for virtually unlimited file and folder sizes. This is the same technology used by Microsoft's SQL Server for indexes, which is one of the reasons that Microsoft SQL Server has such robust performance. The maximum file size is now 16 EiB (exbibytes), or 1,152,921,504,606,846,976 bytes. With standard 64 KB clusters, that amounts to a yobibyte (YiB), 1,208,925,819,614,629,174,706,176 bytes, as a maximum volume size. Suffice it to say, your only restrictions in data storage are the limits of the hardware you can assemble.

The term *resilient* takes on new meaning with ReFS, in that the filesystem meta data has built-in 64-bit checksums that are independently stored, eliminating the need for utilities such as CHKDSK. In addition, a corrupted file or meta data can be deleted and restored from backup in real time, with no downtime on the filesystem itself. ReFS will also periodically process mirrored data and automatically correct corrupted data from its mirrored copy.

BitLocker Drive Encryption

Windows *BitLocker Drive Encryption* is primarily designed to protect data on laptops that may be lost or stolen, but it is also available on Windows Server 2012. In relation to IIS 8.0, data drive encryption can be used to protect sensitive data stored on servers, adding protection in case the server may be physically accessed in an attempt to bypass authentication within an application or the server operating system itself. This is particularly important on remote servers that may have content covered by data regulations such as the Health Information Portability and Accountability Act (HIPAA) or the Sarbanes-Oxley Act (SBA), among other statutory regulations that may apply in your jurisdiction.

In Windows Server 2012, BitLocker Drive Encryption extends into virtualized and cloud configurations, allowing encryption on virtual machines both in and out of the cloud. Encryption can be used for separate virtual systems on the same physical hardware, further segregating multitenant isolations.

Network Access Protection

Windows *Network Access Protection* (NAP) is designed to prevent clients that do not meet specific health requirements from connecting to the network. *Health*, in NAP terms, is the level of protection that the client has installed, such as required service packs or updates, antivirus protection with current signatures, or other requirements defined by the administrator.

NAP is important to keep in mind for IIS 8.0 for two reasons. First, an IIS 8.0 server should likely not be configured for NAP, because a missed antivirus update could take a server off the network. Although NAP could be used to ensure compliance of IIS 8.0 servers with health requirements, there are better options available, such as Windows updates or Microsoft System Center. The second reason IIS administrators may need to keep NAP in mind is that it can cause network clients to lose access to the web or application server. When you're trying to debug a server issue, always remember that client connectivity may be part, or all, of the problem.

3

Planning Your Deployment

WHAT'S IN THIS CHAPTER?

➤ Windows 2012 Server deployment planning

➤ IIS 8.0 deployment planning

➤ Application deployment planning

➤ Automation and deployment tools

➤ Capacity planning

Deploying Windows Server 2012 and IIS 8.0 is a journey, and, as in all journeys, you need to know three things: your starting point, your ending point, and the path between. The starting and ending points seem to be the most obvious, but the failure to determine them accurately is why the path in many deployments seems to wander astray. There are also many paths in between — all of which lead to the same point, and all of which have different terrain to be negotiated.

In many deployment scenarios, there are two landscapes to be traversed. The first is technical and is often the easiest. Which piece of hardware or which software setting to use for a specific task is often straightforward. But combining that with the second landscape, which is organizational, will determine which technical choices can be made. Many times the best technical choice is not the best organizational choice, and it is often hard for administrators to accept, or even see, the organizational hills and valleys that must be traversed.

In this chapter, you will learn what technical choices are available and some options for applying those choices in the organizational landscape. If your organization has no limits to resources like cash and manpower, you will find your choices unlimited. But, if your organization is like most, resources will dictate your range of choices. You may find that your choices are further limited by management choices, developer needs, and other constraints placed by network access or security concerns. Your choices may even be limited by the skill of in-house staff and, as you read through this chapter, you should honestly assess whether the planning and deployment could be handled by an outside contractor more effectively and efficiently. But even if you will not be responsible for the planning or deployment, this chapter will provide valuable background material that will help you understand why some choices were made.

WINDOWS 2012 SERVER DEPLOYMENT PLANNING

Deploying IIS 8.0 begins with deploying the operating system and platform that IIS 8.0 runs on, and decisions made concerning the operating system will affect IIS 8.0. Most of the decisions for deploying IIS 8.0 are really decisions on deploying the server itself — the operating system, the network topology, backup and recovery, replication, and even whether to upgrade existing systems or install the server from scratch. IIS 8.0 is less often installed to run on its own, serving only static content. It is normally installed to support an application, such as SharePoint or ASP.NET, even if the intent is simply to serve content.

Deploying IIS 8.0 also includes deploying the mechanisms for production of applications and content. The planning stage must encompass the development, testing, and deployment of applications and content, such as whether a development server is used, if a staging server exists for code testing, or if a web farm will be needed for the production system. To a certain extent, planning some deployment features is a guessing game. How many users will you have? How much traffic will be on the network? Where will the bottlenecks be? What if your site or service catches on and you have to expand? These are all scenarios you should plan for, although some may simply be an educated guess. And the scenarios will depend greatly on what your IIS 8.0 deployment is for.

Windows Server 2012 Requirements

Windows Server 2012 requires the following minimum and recommended hardware:

HARDWARE COMPONENT	MINIMUM REQUIREMENT	RECOMMENDED MINIMUM
Processor	x64 — 1.4 GHz Windows Server 2012 supports only 64-bit processors. Itanium processors are no longer supported. Windows Server 2012 supports up to 320 logical processors.	2 GHz or faster
Memory	512 MB	2 GB Maximum supported is 4 TB.
Drive space	32 GB	60 GB

Keep in mind that multiprocessor systems may require more than minimum hardware to install Windows Server 2012. Any system with more than 16 GB of RAM will require more hard drive space for paging and hibernation. Windows Server 2012 also requires a DVD drive to install from the media.

All multiprocessor support for Windows Server 2012 Editions is for physical processors. Multicore processors still count as a single physical processor, no matter how many cores they have. This means that multicore processors are always a good investment, because they provide the advantages of multiple processors without the licensing and operating system requirements.

Virtualization

Windows Server 2012 with Hyper-V has additional considerations for deployment. Windows Server 2012 supports 2,048 logical processors on the host, with up to 64 logical processors per guest operating system. One TB of virtual memory is supported per virtual machine, with up to 1,024 active virtual machines. For virtual clusters, Windows Server 2012 supports up to 64 nodes and up to 4,000 virtual cluster machines.

Single-Root I/O Virtualization (SR-IOV) for Windows Server 2012 supports only 64-bit guest operating systems, so it cannot support a 32-bit Windows 8 guest operating system. SR-IOV also requires hardware and firmware support, so ensure your current or new hardware is compatible.

Which Server Edition?

IIS 8.0, like IIS 4.0, 5.0, 6.0, and 7.0, is tied to the operating system version. You can install IIS 8.0 Express on Windows 7, as a Microsoft Visual Studio development platform, but it is not suitable for production hosting. Developers can use the Express version to develop code and, with the proper configuration, closely duplicate the final deployment environment. The assumption of this book is that you will be using a version of Windows Server 2012 for your IIS 8.0 deployment, although most of the book applies to IIS 8.0 Express installations with few changes.

Windows Server 2012 Editions

Windows Server 2012 is available in four editions, two of which are designed for small businesses. The Enterprise Edition, Web Edition, and Small Business Server Edition are gone, and the Foundation and Essentials Editions are new. The *Foundation Edition* is only available from OEMs, and the *Essentials Edition* is designed to support small businesses. The following table reviews features of each version.

WINDOWS SERVER 2012 EDITIONS

EDITION	FEATURES	LICENSING
Foundation	Simple server with no virtualization rights, no server core installation	15 user accounts only
Essentials	Simplified server with connectivity to cloud services, no virtualization rights, no server core installation	25 user accounts only
Standard	Full server functionality with two virtual instances	Per processor plus client access licensing, two CPUs included
Datacenter	Full server functionality with unlimited virtual instances	Per processor plus client access licensing, two CPUs included

The licensing model aligns to the licensing of Microsoft System Center 2012, which comes in two editions. Standard is licensed for two CPUs in a server and two virtual machines, whereas Datacenter is licensed for two CPUs and unlimited virtual machines. Essentially, Windows Server 2012 Standard is designed to be virtualized and running on a Windows Server 2012 Datacenter host.

Choosing an edition depends on an organization's virtualization strategy. For standalone servers or extremely low virtualization, organizations will choose the Standard Edition. For a highly virtualized or private or hybrid cloud environment, organizations would want the Datacenter Edition. The enhanced functions of the Windows Server 2008 R2 Enterprise Edition, such as failover clustering, are available in the Windows Server 2012 Standard Edition. The only difference between the two is in virtualization abilities and licensing. The functionality of IIS 8.0 is identical on both.

Windows Small Business Server

The Windows Small Business Server Edition no longer exists after the 2011 version. Windows Server 2012 Essentials is designed as a replacement for the small business customer, with connections to cloud services, such as Microsoft Exchange Server and Microsoft SQL Server, instead of having those servers built into the package.

Windows Home Server

Windows Home Server also no longer exists. Windows 8 will have many of the features of Home Server available as an optional download and, as far as IIS 8.0 is concerned, still serve as a home web server. This book will only discuss Windows 8 in passing, although the functionality of IIS 8.0 on Windows Server 2012 is primarily the same as on Windows 8.

Server Core

Windows Server 2012 includes some changes to the Server Core option. This is now the preferred installation option for Windows Server 2012, especially in a virtualized environment — and the ability to run Server Manager, PowerShell, and SQL Server in Server Core makes it possible. Windows Server 2012 Server Core installations have a reduced memory and storage footprint, making them ideal for virtual machines, and the reality is that most organizations are now working with a virtualized or cloud infrastructure.

The other major change to a Server Core installation for Windows Server 2012 is that changing a Server Core installation into a GUI desktop interface no longer requires you to reinstall the operating system. In fact, simple PowerShell commands make the change quick and simple. And it's just as easy to change back.

Server Virtualization

Windows *server virtualization* — running multiple Windows Server 2012 installations on a single physical server using a hypervisor technology — is standard in the Standard and Datacenter Editions of Windows Server 2012. Windows Server 2012 was developed with virtualization as a key feature, and virtualization has become the way of life in many organizations. Reduction of hardware, including the power and cooling needs, as well as reducing physical server space, can yield important savings in many IT departments. Even more important is the security of the virtualized systems from failure due to other resource uses for the hardware. For many organizations, a Domain

Name System (DNS) server, for example, uses very little in the way of CPU, disk space, or memory. Therefore, a single-use system running DNS doesn't make sense. Adding the Dynamic Host Configuration Protocol (DHCP), making the system a domain controller, and having it serve as a virtual private network (VPN) host would allow better use of the available resources, but now each use is at risk if another task has problems and crashes the server. It's also hard to manage peak use of the resources; if all services need the same resource at the same time, it may be unavailable.

Server virtualization solves these issues. It's not a new concept; time sharing on mainframes provided each account with a similar setup, a system that appeared to be only used by that account. Sharing CPU cycles was important from a cost standpoint on those systems, where on PC-based servers the use of CPU cycles is fairly inexpensive. But the concept, extended for today's needs, is still relevant. An example would be a webhosting company selling virtual servers to clients. Instead of needing a physical system for each client, the host can use virtual servers, vastly reducing hardware because dozens of client systems can exist on one physical system.

Hyper-V Version 3

New in Windows Server 2012 is Hyper-V version 3, included in both the Standard and Datacenter Editions of Windows Server 2012.

Upgrade or New Installation?

Choosing to upgrade existing web servers, to migrate to new hardware, or to set up a new server from scratch depends on several factors, not the least of which are the suitability and availability of new hardware resources. If you have existing hardware that meets the minimum requirements for Windows Server 2012 and you are currently running Windows Server 2008, then you have a choice of doing an in-place upgrade. If your hardware is unsuitable for running the new operating system, you can install new hardware and a new operating system and migrate only the applications and content. There are pros and cons to each choice, and the proper choice for one organization may not be the perfect choice for another.

New Installations

A new installation to new hardware, or existing hardware that has had the operating system wiped clean, has the advantage of being a known quantity. You are starting from base, with nothing strange that may get in the way later. It's surprising how many small settings become big problems when an operating system is upgraded. A clean install also ensures that drivers, utilities, and other parts of the operating system are at the most recent level, so that updates begin at a known step as well. If you are deploying multiple servers, a clean install ensures that all are identical, which makes life simpler when managing replication and configuration. If you have existing installations that you upgrade, you don't get the opportunity to rearrange disk partitions as you do with a new install. A new installation is usually the best of all worlds. But you may still have a valid reason to upgrade an existing installation.

Upgrades

Upgrades can be a viable option in several instances — for example, if you have an existing application that you do not want to have to reinstall and reconfigure, or if the time for the upgrade is critically short. An upgrade doesn't take time for reinstalling applications, reconfiguring them, altering security, testing new configurations, and redeploying. In most cases, you can simply upgrade the system and be on your way — with a few caveats.

The first caveat is that you must already be running on hardware sufficient to run the new operating system and applications. Most hardware purchased in the last few years is capable of handling Windows Server 2012, although you may want to upgrade RAM. Drive space requirements also need to be taken into consideration, because during an upgrade you will not have the ability to resize the system partition. If you're short on drive space, a clean install, even on the same hardware, is often the best choice.

Windows Server 2012 can upgrade only from Windows Server 2008 or Windows Server 2008 R2. You cannot upgrade earlier versions of Windows. An in-place upgrade from Windows Server 2003 to Windows Server 2008 R2 to Windows Server 2012 involves many changes to the operating system and settings and is not recommended.

Windows Server 2008 upgrades to Windows Server 2012 are usually quite straightforward, because they share much of the same code and features. After an upgrade, you need to review the system and update drivers, change settings that may have new options, and possibly change some permissions; however, as far as IIS is concerned, sites and applications should work as intended.

A second caveat is that you will carry settings with you to the new operating system and IIS configuration. In the case of the operating system, Windows Server 2012 provides new security and deployment options that may not be configured in an upgrade.

Windows Server 2012 has an upgrade path that may limit your choice for upgrading. Standard, Enterprise, and Datacenter versions of Windows Server 2008 can be upgraded to Windows Server 2012, but previous versions of Windows must be upgraded to Windows Server 2008 first. In other words, if you are running IIS 6.0 on Windows Server 2003, you must upgrade to Windows Server 2008 and IIS 7.0 before you can upgrade to Windows Server 2012 and IIS 8.0, even if your hardware supports Windows Server 2012. In most cases, you will want to perform a fresh installation of Windows Server 2012 to new hardware and then migrate the sites and applications from your Windows 2000 server.

Planning Your Hardware

Hardware planning consists primarily of inventorying existing hardware and determining whether a hardware upgrade is in order, or even hardware replacement. If the hardware will run Windows Server 2012, then it will run IIS, but, depending on applications and configuration, the minimum hardware specifications for Windows Server 2012 may be suboptimal for IIS in a given environment. For example, a system with 1 GB of RAM will run Windows Server 2012, but if you intend to run multiple IIS servers in a virtualized environment, you will be extremely limited in performance as the memory is swapped out. Virtual servers require the same resources as a physical server; thus, memory, drive space, and processor capacity requirements increase in proportion.

Hardware planning for IIS deployments should also take into account the entire development and deployment environment. A development server, staging server, and production server can be on separate physical hardware boxes, virtual installations on a single box, or even clusters of physical boxes for each function. Deployment of large numbers of servers could take place using Windows

Deployment Services, discussed below in this chapter, and require physical systems for that function as well.

Hardware planning also must include communications hardware, including network schemas as well as the physical components of the network. File storage may include planning for a storage area network (SAN) or network-attached storage (NAS), and back-end database hardware adds even more planning.

Planning Your Network

No IIS server is very useful without a network connection, and although there are often limitations imposed on what can be configured, configuring a network to support IIS 8.0 is crucial. Simple choices such as whether to locate a web server inside or outside a firewall can have enormous influence on other deployment choices. For example, a server inside a firewall would require ports opened in the firewall, quite commonly for HTTP, HTTPS, SMTP, FTP, and DNS. Failure to plan for the firewall security required by a choice of server location can result in security holes to other servers inside the network.

Active Directory or Standalone?

In small networks, often with a single server, a workgroup may be used for network connections, but most commonly a domain would be used. You might choose to make your server a part of your domain, separate it into its own domain, or even make it a standalone server outside a domain. In most professional IIS 8.0 installations, the use of an Active Directory domain is generally a given, if the server will be in a domain.

There are several advantages to using a domain for your IIS servers, and a few disadvantages as well. For one, you should not run IIS 8.0 applications on a domain controller, mostly because of security concerns. A domain controller has no local accounts; thus, all process accounts, even the anonymous user account, run as domain accounts with the associated domain access. You must carefully lock down these accounts to prevent them from being used on unintended servers in your network. Additionally, when IIS 8.0 is on a domain controller, compromise of the system through an IIS application can allow full domain access.

The advantages to using a domain primarily come in the administration category. An intranet server, for example, within the same domain as your administrative accounts, can be managed by those same administrative accounts. Domain accounts can be easily delegated access to IIS 8.0 administration tasks without the need for additional accounts within IIS 8.0. If you are managing a web farm, the ability to use domain policies can make server management far easier. Replication and backup become simplified when using domain accounts, and even SQL Server access can be centrally managed in a domain.

A Windows 2012 server should be on a Windows 2012 domain to enable all features within the new operating system. This is especially true if a new server will be installed in a cloud environment, public or private.

A standalone server is a choice made by many organizations, most often when a single IIS server will serve a limited number of sites and applications available to the public. It eliminates the security issues with domains, becoming an island with few connections to other servers or domains for security breaches. A few local accounts, an FTP connection, and the applications in IIS become the only potential targets, and it's far harder to forget to secure an account when there are few to begin with.

The best recommendation for choosing a domain membership option is that if a web server is internal, such as a SharePoint or intranet server, make it a member of the internal domain. If you have one or two dedicated Internet servers with public access, firewalled from your internal domain, consider a standalone server that is not a domain member. If you have multiple public-facing servers, such as a web farm, outside the firewall from your internal network, consider placing them in their own domain with a separate domain controller. Carefully examine the security implications of making this domain a part of your internal domain tree, even with restricted trust relationships. Security changes such as opening domain replication ports in the firewall are risks that you may not be able to balance with the reward of easier management and internal connections.

You will find more on security in Chapters 13, 14, and 15, and you should read those chapters as part of planning your deployment. You will find sample diagrams for typical deployments below in this chapter.

Server Location

Server location isn't a choice of whether to locate the server in the top of the rack or the bottom of the rack, or even whether to locate it in Kansas City or the Cayman Islands. You should already know that rack location will depend on cooling and power availability and that, while having fewer hurricanes, Kansas City isn't as fun a place to make onsite inspections as the Cayman Islands. No, this is a choice of placing your server inside your network, in a DMZ, or outside the firewall, or even co-locating it at an Internet service provider (ISP) or purchasing server space at a hosting company.

Server location depends on two factors: The first factor is the function of the server and who needs access. For example, if your server will be for an intranet, locating it inside firewalls will help with accessibility because you can use network accounts to control access. Security is enhanced because access is restricted to those inside your organization. If a server must be accessed over the Internet, whether as a public server or an extranet server sharing information with partners, you should always place it outside a firewall from your internal network. This maintains the security of your internal network. Placing the firewall in a DMZ — in essence, firewalling it from both the internal local area network (LAN) and the external wide area network (WAN) — is even more secure and should be common practice in most organizations.

When locating servers, you must also address the location of companion servers. For example, if you locate your web servers in a DMZ, you probably want to locate any domain controllers for a web server domain and DNS servers for the web domains in the same DMZ. This simplifies management and restricts any breach of security to the DMZ and not across to the internal network. A little different approach may be more appropriate with database servers. If the server must be accessed by both internal and external accounts, then a location within the internal network may be more feasible. Ports may be opened for SQL communication, although it is wise to run SQL servers on nonstandard ports for further security.

Server Farms

A traditional trend in large-scale IIS implementations is the use of a *server farm* — dozens or even hundreds of systems behaving as a single web server. A primary reason for this is *redundancy*, in which multiple servers are available at any time should one or more fail. A second function is *load balancing*, in which each server receives a portion of the requests, and no server becomes overloaded with requests and slow in response time. Redundancy must be planned for in any server farm because, at any one time, there may be one or more servers offline, either for maintenance or repair.

Working with IIS in a server farm also requires maintaining state in the server farm, so that an application's state is maintained whether or not the next request from the client hits the same server. Load-balancing solutions often involve hardware that will maintain a "sticky IP" and direct a client to the same server for each request. In other cases, a developer may choose to use a SQL server for maintaining state in an ASP.NET application. There are no session state changes between the way IIS 7.0 and IIS 8.0 work; thus, an application that already manages the system state should not need changes to upgrade to IIS 8.0. Working with web farms is covered in more detail in Chapter 16, "IIS Scalability I: Building an IIS Web Farm."

Network Load Balancing

Network load balancing (NLB) is Microsoft's default load-balancing process for all versions of Windows Server 2012, as it was for Windows Server 2008. IIS uses server cookies by default to preserve the session state, and because NLB does not assign requests to servers based on cookies or session state, sessions will often get lost in a standard NLB configuration. If you are planning on using NLB to cluster several IIS 8.0 servers, you should consider the following options for maintaining session state:

➤ **Use client-side cookies** — Read the cookie on each request for session information. The advantage is that the information in a cookie persists even if a connection is dropped, until the cookie is set to expire. A major disadvantage is the limited size of a cookie; that is, you would be unlikely to be able to use cookies for large amounts of session information.

➤ **Use a state server or SQL server to maintain session information** — ASP.NET applications can use a state server to maintain session state across NLB servers, provided that the machine keys in each server's `machine.config` file are identical. You can also write information to a central location such as a SQL server that can be read by all servers.

➤ **Enable client affinity for the NLB cluster** — In the NLB manager, under Port Rules, choose "single affinity" so that a client is always serviced by the same server. The disadvantage to this is that session redundancy is lost because if that server fails, the session is lost.

Clustering

Clustering, as opposed to network load balancing, is a function available in the Standard and Datacenter Editions of Windows Server 2012. *Clustering* is the combination of two or more separate physical servers, or nodes, into a single server cluster, appearing as a single server. In Windows Server 2012, a cluster can consist of up to 64 nodes. Applications on a cluster, as well as other resources, can be designated as running in an active/passive mode, in which one node serves the request and the others act as a failover; or active/active, in which all nodes can service requests for applications or resources.

Clustering in Windows Server 2012 has greatly expanded to handle virtual and cloud environments. There is now a top limit of 4,000 virtual machines in a cluster, with up to 1,024 virtual machines on a single node in the cluster. Failover clustering, previously only available in the Datacenter Edition, is now available in the Standard Edition as well.

Virtualization and Cloud Deployment

Virtualization is a major feature in Windows Server 2012, which is designed for virtualized and cloud environments.

Planning Security

Security is an important part of any network, and this is especially true of a network that provides access to resources from unknown or outside sources, as is the case with a web server exposed to the Internet. Internal IIS applications, such as an intranet, may be easier to define security for, but security should be no less a concern. There are multiple levels where security can be enforced and addressed, from the network level with firewalls and router access lists, to the application level with security for applications themselves. Physical security, hardware security, and operating system security options should also be considered.

Although this section covers security planning, security is covered at various points throughout the book, as well as specifically in Chapters 13, 14, and 15. Chapter 13 covers server security in more detail, but a responsible administrator would be wise to consult multiple sources for all facets of security. Many organizations will have dedicated security administration, and an IIS administrator should consult with them, if available, in planning any deployment.

Network Security

Network security for an IIS server consists of three parts: authorization, access, and auditing. *Authorization* comes from network user accounts; *access* comes from firewall and NTFS security settings; and *auditing* comes from log files. Network security is covered in more depth in Chapter 13, but entire books have been written covering nothing but small portions of network security. The few paragraphs here will give you an idea of what to plan for, but do not consider this to be a treatise on everything you need to do to secure your IIS 8.0 system.

Network User Accounts

Network user accounts are what provide authorization to access resources on the network as well as on the server itself. Windows Server 2012 will try to force you to use strong passwords, although you can bypass this if you want to. A password of eight or more characters with a mix of uppercase letters, lowercase letters, numbers, and non-alphanumeric characters is recommended. A password like *Mix3dP!ckL3$* is far harder to crack than *mixedpickles*, and isn't much harder to remember because the characters look similar. Okay, not that similar, but you get the idea.

The default IIS 8.0 anonymous user account is the IUSR account created during installation. In IIS 8.0, the application pool identity account can be used for anonymous access instead of the default anonymous user account, providing better demarcation between applications and sites on a shared server. This account can be a network user account, making accounts easier to manage and allowing for better access to content on a remote resource. Remote content, such as content located on a network share on a different server, would have access granted for the application pool identity account. More information on access to remote content can be found in Chapter 14, "Authentication and Authorization."

Firewalls and Proxy Servers

Firewalls and proxy servers are important in your network planning because they either allow or block access to your web servers. There are common ports that will normally be open to web servers, such as HTTP on port 80 or HTTPS on port 443, but you will often need other ports opened for access to ancillary services such as DNS and FTP, and even ports for passing Active Directory, Lightweight Directory Access Protocol (LDAP), SQL, and other connections. The Internet Assigned Numbers Authority (IANA) assigns service ports, and a list of current port number assignments is maintained online at the IANA website, www.iana.org/assignments/port-numbers.

Most firewalls can be locked down further than just closing ports — and in most cases, they should be. For example, if all your development servers are in a specific IP address range, it would be prudent to lock FTP access for uploading code and pages to the web server to just that IP range. That way, FTP attempts on your web server are not only stopped by the login and password check, but also, if the attempt is from outside the restricted IP address range, the attempt is blocked before it even hits your web server.

Network Access Protection

Windows Server 2012 includes *Network Access Protection* (NAP), which ensures that systems connecting to the network meet specific minimum health standards in terms of patches, virus protection, and even registry settings. Although NAP doesn't directly affect deploying a web server, you should be aware of any policies in effect in your organization that might cause a test laptop or workstation to be unable to connect to the web server.

IPv6

Windows Server 2012 supports IPv6, and, as with NAP, improper settings can cause network connections to fail. The primary issue with IPv6 as it relates to IIS 8.0 is when troubleshooting, and you should know whether your organization has deployed IPv6 when you choose network options for deploying IIS 8.0. One example is that Windows Deployment Services (WDS), discussed below in this chapter, will not deploy IPv6 networking.

Logging and Auditing

IIS 8.0 has logging functions, which are covered in other chapters in detail, but Windows Server 2012 also has both logging and auditing functions that you need to consider when planning a deployment. Especially critical are *Windows event logs*, which will show many application and system errors related to IIS. Planning a monitoring system for these logs is important, and many organizations already have management software, such as Microsoft's Systems Center Operations Manager, which will monitor event logs and provide auditing functions.

Operations management tools are discussed in Part IV, "Managing and Operating IIS 8.0," but you will need to understand which options are available for planning your deployment. If you do not have a tool already in use, you can use Microsoft's LogParser, discussed briefly in Chapter 10 and available from www.iis.net, to analyze event and other logs. If you need auditing, you can configure Microsoft's auditing functions so that audit information appears in the security event log. One common tactic is to configure successful and unsuccessful login attempts for auditing and use LogParser to track attempts to log in as Administrator or other privileged accounts. If you rename the administrator account and then create a new account named *Administrator* with a complicated password and no access to anything, you can easily report on attacks against the Administrator account, a common target for hackers.

Windows Server Security

Windows server security is covered in Chapter 13, but for planning purposes, you should consider the folder structure and the security assigned to it. In the case of web servers, there are some areas of server security that need more specific planning. The most crucial of these is remote access. Whether by remote desktop, remote administration interfaces, or Windows terminal services, remote access to a server, especially a Windows Server 2012 Server Core installation, is a necessary evil. And with that remote access comes security risks. Remote access to your web servers should always be secured by a VPN or by firewalls limiting access from all but specific IP ranges.

Windows file and folder security is also important to planning your deployment. It is important that the folders your web code and content are in have only the security needed to access them for the needs of your applications. One mistake many administrators make is using a subfolder other than the default Inetpub folder for website home directories. You should use Inetpub or create a new folder off the root to put the home directories of websites in; you should not use a subfolder of the Program Files folder or any other folder. This is because those folders will have permissions for other accounts, and you may run into problems managing security effectively. A bad example of production servers is the default virtual directory configurations used by Microsoft's Visual Studio. The physical folder that the virtual directory points to normally defaults to a folder within a user's profile, making security management a nightmare. In deploying an IIS 8.0 server with ASP.NET applications, a folder structure should be planned that allows for proper security and organization.

Administrators are often concerned about the default administrative shares on Windows servers, with a share name like \\servername\c$. These shares are useful for administrative connections, but you can disable the shares if you are concerned about the security risk they may expose. The risk is simply that they are a known attack point, and if you have secured your server well and the administrative accounts use strong passwords, these administrative shares should not be of undue concern for most administrators. If you are unfamiliar with Windows file and folder permissions, or Windows share-level permissions, you should find a good book or online resource to boost your skills.

Application Security

The security of any Windows server is a function of the security of all the applications on it. An insecure application that allows a server to be compromised is as bad as a server with no password protection. Your planning for Windows server deployments should always include planning for what applications will be running on a server.

In a perfect world, every server would serve a single function — web server, SQL server, Exchange server, and so on. In the real world, however, servers often have to handle multiple applications, and the licensing and hardware costs for additional servers, even virtual servers, don't make financial sense. But some simple planning can provide additional security when servers must share duties. For example, planning to have a web server and SQL server on the same physical hardware is often not the securest of choices. Never mind that SQL is resource-intensive; it also uses different ports for the SQL service, a separate account structure, and separate management tools. This means multiple accounts added to the server, each of which is a potential source of attack; additional ports opened in the firewall; and additional services that may hang and consume resources.

But a DNS server installed on a web server may be a natural fit. The extra ports opened in a firewall present little or no additional attack surface because the DNS service has no known attacks that can be used to gain control of the system. Both DNS and web services are often needed by the same end users, and DNS presents very little in the way of resource use. FTP is another service that is often enabled on web servers for the purpose of transferring content and, in the case of IIS 8.0, does not need to use Windows accounts. FTP on an IIS 8.0 server, covered in Chapter 10, presents very little additional security risk.

ASP.NET and other developed applications can, and usually do, incorporate their own security. This book does not cover this type of application security; programmers should reference other materials for help in this topic. Keep in mind that all security is a trade-off between security and functionality. As long as you understand the risks of applications running on your web server and accept those risks in return for the added functionality, planning to accommodate those risks is a simple task.

Physical Security

Physical security is sometimes overlooked in IIS servers, especially where a web server may be managed by a specific group for intranet or SharePoint use. Sometimes these department servers end up stuck in broom closets, under the manager's desk, or on a table next to a printer, open to public access. This type of location is a poor choice for many reasons, but the most persuasive one is that the server that your department depends on might be turned off by anyone passing by. It could be unplugged to plug in a vacuum cleaner, knocked off a desk, or damaged in a coffee/soda/water incident.

More important in physical security is preventing access to the system by those with more nefarious intent. Any system that can be physically accessed is more easily hacked, especially when other security tenets are not enforced. Leaving a system logged in with a local administrator account and with physical access from unauthorized individuals is like handing out the Administrator password. This is basic security, but for some reason departmental web servers seem to suffer from lapses in security. Always plan to restrict access physically to all deployed systems with at least a lock and key.

Planning Backup and Recovery

Backing up and restoring websites is covered in detail in Chapter 6, but backing up and restoring filesystems and entire services is an important part of administering IIS 8.0 and Windows Server 2012. Many organizations use a third-party product for backing up enterprise systems, but for those systems for which the enterprise backup isn't available or isn't feasible, Microsoft has included a

Windows backup function in all server versions. This function also gets a makeover and improvements in Windows Server 2012.

Volume Shadow Copy Services

In many organizations, Microsoft's Volume Shadow Copy service, introduced in Windows Server 2003, is the first line of defense against lost data. Taking a snapshot of the filesystem and storing changed files on a scheduled basis, Shadow Copies can be restored to provide previous versions of data, including restoring data that has been changed or deleted. Shadow Copies can be restored by end users who have the Volume Shadow Copy client installed, but they are especially handy for administrators who may need to back out changes or restore accidentally deleted files quickly.

One tip for administrators is to install the Volume Shadow Copy client on the server, and then use File Explorer to browse to the administrative share (if you haven't disabled it) to use the client on the same server from which you are trying to restore previous file versions. The client cannot be used locally, but by connecting to the administrative share, you have connected to the server from the server by way of the network, not the filesystem directly.

Volume Shadow Copy files are found in the \System Volume Information folder and consist of two files with a unique globally unique identifier (GUID) and a large file named tracking.log. The amount of space allowed to Shadow Copies can be configured by the administrator, as can the location. The size of these files, as well as the overhead of creating Shadow Copies, should be considered when choosing whether or not to activate Shadow Copies on a server. A good choice is to enable Shadow Copies on development servers, which have a greater chance of accidental file deletions, and not enable them on production servers, because deleted files can be restored by redeploying from a staging or development server. Keep in mind that Shadow Copy services are not a substitute for regular system backups. Owing to the size and performance impact, you should only enable Shadow Copies on data volumes. Planning your server configuration with data stored on a separate volume eases the use of Shadow Copies.

Windows Server 2012 Backup

Windows Server 2012, as with previous Windows versions, includes its own backup utility, Windows Server 2012 Backup. The new version is faster, partly because of its use of the Volume Shadow Copy service, and does block-level backups, allowing more granular restorations than previous versions. You can restore individual items in a backup, or, with applications that support Volume Shadow Copies such as Microsoft SQL Server and SharePoint, you can restore applications. Also, owing to the use of the Volume Shadow Copy service, you can restore an incremental backup from a chosen date without having to restore all incremental backups from the last full backup. Naturally, Windows Server 2012 Backup supports a graphical management interface, but it also supports an extensive command-line backup and remote administration. PowerShell cmdlets are also supported for backup functions and allow for easy scheduling of backups.

Windows Server 2012 Backup supports backing up to remote and cloud-based devices, although it does not support backup to tape. The cloud support makes it easy for an organization to back up servers or data to public cloud networks, solving some disaster recovery issues as well as providing secure backups.

Windows Server 2012 Cloud Deployment

Planning for deploying Windows Server 2012 in a cloud environment, either public or private, is beyond the scope of this book; however, when considering the Windows Server 2012 Essentials Edition, you will want to plan for cloud deployments of any services, such as SQL Server and Exchange Server, both of which require IIS 8.0 to run. Fortunately, IIS 8.0 fits these needs closely and is easily deployed in a cloud environment in support of these applications.

IIS 8.0 DEPLOYMENT PLANNING

Planning your IIS 8.0 deployment becomes easier after you've considered the issues in deploying the Windows Server 2012 operating system, but there are still decisions to be made. You need to ensure that your system and the operating system configuration meet the requirements of your IIS 8.0 deployment. You have some installation decisions to make, such as installing with the operating system, after the operating system is configured, or even installing as part of an upgrade from Windows Server 2008 and IIS 7.0. You will need to plan IIS 8.0 security, such as whether you'll use IIS accounts for managing users and IIS 8.0 installations. You'll need to plan for shared configurations if you're using a web farm and choose to use shared configurations. And you'll need to plan for replication among sites. There are also some IIS-specific planning decisions related to development environments and production environments. The installation of IIS 8.0 is covered in the next chapter, and some of these topics are discussed in more depth throughout the book; therefore, part of your planning should include reading relevant sections of this book for specific information.

IIS 8.0 Requirements

IIS 8.0 requires a Windows 8 operating system or a Windows Server 2012 operating system. Because the version of IIS is tied to the version of the operating system, there is no "IIS 8.0 upgrade" without upgrading the operating system as well. IIS 8.0 is a part of the operating system and, with one exception, cannot be downloaded as an installation. You will need the operating system media at some point for the installation. You can install from the physical media, from a network install point, or use several varieties of automated and unattended installs.

Beyond having the correct operating system, the only other requirement for an IIS 8.0 installation is a network interface with an IP address. It could be a local loopback adapter, with no physical connection to other systems, or any other network interface, but because IIS 8.0 answers requests over TCP/IP, some form of network connection must be available.

Installation Decisions

Naturally, many decisions on how you're going to install IIS 8.0 depend on your installation choices for Windows Server 2012. If you are going to be upgrading your operating system from Windows Server 2008, for example, you have a choice of upgrading IIS 7.0 to IIS 8.0 as part of the process, or of removing IIS 7.0 before the upgrade, then upgrading the operating system and reinstalling IIS 8.0. In most cases, an in-place upgrade will work without any changes in IIS 8.0, although you will need to update for new features, such as SSL with host headers, if you intend to use them.

Planning for IIS-Specific Security

IIS 8.0 has security that is independent, at least to a certain extent, from Windows Server 2012 security. IIS 8.0, as with IIS 7.0, has its own security accounts that can be used for access and delegation; plus, there are security accounts for application pools to run in, shared configuration shares, and FTP or SMTP access. Planning for this security depends greatly on the end function of your IIS 8.0 server.

For example, on an intranet server, maybe running SharePoint, you're likely to use Windows accounts for all access. You may only have a single application pool and a single site, requiring very little in the way of security management beyond the default installation. Or you may run a web host, with hundreds of sites on a server, configured in multiple application pools with separate accounts for each. You may use IIS accounts to delegate management of the sites to the hosting clients, and more IIS accounts for FTP access. A back-end SQL Server may be configured with SQL accounts for these sites, or you may be running SQL Express and using the application pool account for access, with each site in a separate application pool.

Management Accounts and Delegation

IIS 8.0 accounts, as well as Windows accounts, can be used for delegating management of websites, and administrators, developers, or users can be allowed access to IIS Manager to manage specific sections of the server. IIS 8.0 also includes delegation, both for access to the management interface and for locking configuration sections to restrict specific users from making specific changes to the configuration.

Using IIS 8.0 accounts has several advantages, depending on your use of IIS 8.0. For web hosting, or for any use in which managing the server is not going to be done by users who already have Windows accounts with access to the server, IIS 8.0 accounts do not require Windows Client Access Licenses (CALs). IIS 8.0 accounts can also be managed by administrators who have access to the web server but do not have access to accounts in the Active Directory. For intranet use, where Windows accounts already exist, there are few advantages to a separate IIS account system, although administrators may choose to deploy IIS accounts for centralizing web access management.

Delegation, on the other hand, is useful for any organization that needs to restrict IIS management from requiring local administrator access to the system itself, and for allowing developers to make changes to the configurations of their sites and applications while restricting them from any further access. There are actually two parts to delegation: the configuration section locking mode, or overrideMode, and delegation of IIS Manager for managing sections to which the user has access.

Delegating access to configuration sections can be done in IIS Manager or by using the command line with AppCmd.exe. For example, to lock the configuration to prevent custom HTTP errors from being added to a website, you would run the following command, which will lock the configuration of HTTP errors on WebSite1, leaving other sites unlocked:

```
appcmd.exe lock config "WebSite1" -section:httpErrors
```

IIS 8.0 Access Policies

IIS 8.0 has the ability to restrict access to websites, and even folders, by limiting the IP addresses that are allowed access. New to IIS 8.0 is the ability to restrict IP addresses dynamically based on a variety of events, such as too many simultaneous connections. *Request Filtering*, introduced in IIS 7.0, replaces the use of URLScan from previous IIS versions, making it possible to restrict specific requests from being executed. Using these tools, you can lock access to your site from a specific IP address range and serve only a limited set of requests.

One example of restricting IP address access is if you are creating an extranet, allowing access from a specific business partner and denying access from all other sources. If that business partner has a specific IP address range that will access your extranet, you can reject any request coming from other IP addresses. This process shouldn't be used instead of locking down firewall rules, but it does provide an extra layer of security.

Restricting access based on the request can be more flexible. For example, if you do not use MP3 files on your site, you can create a filtering rule that will drop requests for the .MP3 extension. This prevents the server from expending resources to process a request for a file that should not exist on the server and also enforces a policy of not serving MP3 files.

Determining the policy for access and filtering that meets the needs of your organization and your applications should begin with any corporate policy restrictions. Determine what content will be served and to whom, then deny all other requests through IP restrictions or Request Filtering as appropriate. Whenever you implement changes, use the IIS log files to analyze any requests that behaved in an unexpected manner. You may find a developer using a file extension you haven't allowed and need to adjust either the policy or the developer as appropriate.

Implementing access policies using IP address restrictions or Request Filtering is discussed more completely in Chapter 13. You may wish to review the process as you develop your policies to ensure that you understand how to implement your policies.

Planning Development Environments

Most professional IIS 8.0 installations will include a development environment and a production environment, and often a staging server will be used for code testing before deployment. For maximum efficiency, it is important that development environments be configured as close to the production environment as possible. This is simple with IIS 8.0 because both Windows 8 and Windows Server 2012 now share the same web server.

Microsoft has also introduced, with Microsoft Visual Developer 2012, the ability to install an Express version of IIS 8.0 on Windows 7 systems for development use. This allows developers using Windows 7 or Windows 8 to run an identical environment to the deployment environment on IIS 8.0 running on Windows Server 2012. The installation of IIS Express is covered in the next chapter.

Whichever option is used in your organization, planning for differences between development servers and deployment servers is essential. Making the ASP.NET process account a local administrator on the production server is not a valid choice to cure security woes generated by using a less than optimum development environment.

Planning Production Environments

Production environments, while being as close as possible to those used for development, must by nature be more secure and robust. You should plan any production environment to contain the bare minimum of installed IIS 8.0 modules needed to run the deployed applications, and you should minimize any additional programs running on the system. Although development servers may need programs such as Visual Studio installed, production servers would rarely benefit from having such software running on them. In fact, production servers often don't require Internet Explorer or an FTP client, or any other standard client software.

You can enhance security by using a Server Core deployment, which eliminates many GUI-based options. However, with Windows Server 2012, a compromised Server Core installation can reduce security, because a would-be attacker can still run PowerShell commands. Do not count on Server Core as a security fix, especially in public cloud environments.

Production deployments in a cloud environment can benefit from the use of applications that centralize both cloud management and application deployment, such as Microsoft System Center 2012. Microsoft Web Deploy 2.0, introduced as an out-of-band update for IIS 7.0, can help with packaging and deploying applications in an IIS 8.0 cloud setting.

Shared Configuration

IIS 8.0's *Shared Configuration* option allows multiple servers to share the same configuration files, making it easier to keep configurations synced across a web farm, as well as easier to deploy configuration changes. Using shared configurations, deployments to all servers of any configuration changes are almost instantaneous. If you will be using shared configurations, you need to plan a location for the configuration files. This location must be on a Windows share that is accessible to all systems running the shared configuration. Because the shared configuration needs a user account to access this share, you should create a domain user specifically for this shared configuration and assign it read rights to the share, then use this domain user for the shared configuration connection. It is possible to create identical, mirrored, local accounts on each server, but the passwords must be synced for this type of access to work, making this choice more prone to disconnects than using a single domain account.

Content Replication

Although Microsoft's Web Deploy tool can help with content replication, a better option in Windows Server 2012 would be the Distributed File System with Replication (DFS-R). DFS-R works for replication between separate IIS servers and can also provide limited failover capabilities. DFS-R has an advantage in that it uses Remote Differential Compression (RDC) and sends only parts of changed files to the replicated location, increasing the speed of replicating changes. There is still a delay in replication, but most web servers, where the system is simply reading content, won't have any problems.

APPLICATION DEPLOYMENT PLANNING

Rarely is an IIS 8.0 Web Server going to be deployed to serve just static content. Applications will need to be deployed, as well — both the application code and the configuration changes necessary to run the application in IIS 8.0. IIS 8.0 simplifies application deployment, at least as far as the IIS settings go, with a true XCopy deployment scenario. Because all the IIS 8.0 configurations are maintained in XML-formatted configuration files, these can easily be copied to new servers and sites as needed — with the caveat that the new server must have the proper modules installed.

Planning your application deployment should begin with an inventory of what is required by your application in terms of ASP.NET Framework version; IIS 8.0 modules; NTFS file and folder permissions; and ancillary programs and connections, such as Microsoft SQL Server locations and connection strings. These existing requirements must be mapped to the new installation so that code can be deployed, then tested, on the new server. A list of required items for your application might include the following:

➤ ISAPI filters

➤ COM components

➤ ASP.NET assemblies installed in the global assembly cache (GAC)

➤ SSL certificates

➤ Database DSNs (or migrate to a DSN-less connection)

➤ Machine keys (normally copied with ASP.NET configuration files)

➤ Custom registry settings

This list is not comprehensive, but it covers most common application requirements. Each specific application may have its own requirements, and each should be thoroughly tested after migration before deployment for live use.

Packaging and deploying applications is even easier if you use the Microsoft Web Deploy tool. You can write a program, set the configurations, and deploy the application to multiple servers with a single click. Web Deploy can install many of the files and features needed for a new application in ASP.NET as well as other development languages. Web Deploy 2.0 is covered in more detail in Chapter 20.

AUTOMATION AND DEPLOYMENT TOOLS

In the next chapter, you will find instructions for a single-instance installation of IIS 8.0 on Windows Server 2012. However, most professional IIS 8.0 installations won't be manually installing a single instance of IIS on a single server. Automating deployment is important in most organizations, whether it is workstations, applications, servers, or IIS installations. Even when manual installations are feasible in terms of time and location, automated deployments are preferable because exact configurations can easily be achieved.

Over the various versions of Windows and IIS, automated deployment has improved steadily. WMI scripting for configurations, remote installation service (RIS), deployment and unattended installs, and even third-party cloning tools have all been used effectively and made deployment much easier for administrators. While WMI has been deprecated, Windows Server 2012 and IIS 8.0 fully support PowerShell for automation. Web Deploy 2.0 is also available to aid the installation and replication of IIS installations to multiple servers.

Volume Activation

Most professional IIS 8.0 installations are likely using some sort of volume licensing agreement to license Windows Server 2012. Unlike single-server installations, volume licensing options also come with volume activation options. In Windows Server 2012, you have both multiple activation keys, as in Windows Server 2008 licensing, and key management service. With multiple activation keys, each server connects to Microsoft and is authorized, either individually or through a proxy server. Once activated, servers are eligible for Microsoft updates and will function beyond the 30-day activation period.

If you have 10 or more server licenses, or 25 or more Windows 7 or Windows 8 licenses, you are able to run a key management service on your network, activating licenses without connection to Microsoft. Systems activated this way must reconnect to the key management service every 6 months or less to maintain activation. More information on volume activation is available from Microsoft's website.

CAPACITY PLANNING

In many ways, capacity planning for IIS 8.0 is a guessing game. Benchmarking, testing a configuration and saving the results, then making a change and testing again so that the results can be compared, is crucial. However, it's sometimes impossible to test an application on IIS 8.0 if the application is still under development. There are load-testing tools available that can test IIS 8.0 response, and they may or may not make sense in your capacity planning.

IIS 8.0 itself is capable of handling tens of thousands of requests per second. In real-life situations, however, this number is impossible to meet. Bottlenecks can occur at many points in the serving of a request — accessing a back-end database; retrieving data from a mainframe, or an ERP or CRM application; even hardware and network layer delays can reduce the number of serviceable requests.

A common question is, "How many websites can I host on my server?" That question simply cannot be answered with a definitive number. The type of site, the data contained on it, popularity, connection speed, and hardware it runs on are all factors. But a general rule of thumb that works for many hosting companies is that only 15 percent of the sites on a server will be active at a time. That means that you can exceed the estimated capacity of a server by about eight times and be safe. Naturally, for a low-cost web host, maximizing the number of clients on a single server is the way to maximize profits.

Traffic

Traffic is one of the first capacity planning issues you must answer and plan for. How many requests to your servers will come in on average, and what will the peak be? Then you need to test your estimates against your servers to plan for future performance. But estimating traffic before an application or server is deployed is simply an educated guess, and traffic patterns are rarely stable. Just as in street traffic, network traffic comes in bursts, with somewhat predictable peak times. Rush hour on your intranet will be when workers are arriving in the morning, probably after lunch, and right before leaving for home. Nighttime traffic, unless you run night shifts, will likely be minimal.

You can begin to estimate the load on a network connection with some simple math. For each HTTP request, the protocol overhead is about 1,800 bytes. A letter-sized page of text, without graphics, runs about 5K, or 5,120 bytes. A T-1 Internet connection can transfer 1.536 MBps (megabytes per second), or about 26 of those 5K pages, each second. If your average page size is more like 50K, which is small for many of today's graphically rich sites, you'll transmit about 2.6 of those pages per second. Obviously, a good start for increasing capacity would be to reduce the total page size returned on a request. The table below shows estimated bandwidth saturation points for various outbound connection speeds and page content sizes. These numbers should not be relied on in a production environment, however, because many factors can affect the actual bandwidth consumption.

	T-1 LINE (1.536 MBPS)	2 BONDED T-1 LINES (3.72 MBPS)	DS-3 LINE (44.736 MBPS)	OC-3 OPTICAL (155.52 MBPS)
5K file	26 per second	53 per second	760 per second	2,640 per second
50K file	3 per second	6 per second	90 per second	400 per second
500K file	3 seconds each	1.5 seconds each	12 per second	50 per second
5-MB file	5 minutes each	2.5 minutes each	2 seconds each	19 per second
660 MB (CD)	8 hours each	4 hours each	4 minutes each	8 seconds

On the requesting side, your clients may have high-capacity pipelines such as DSL or broadband connections. A typical T-1 line can be saturated by less than a dozen DSL lines with simultaneous requests, which is another reason to ensure that data sent in response to a request is as small as possible. Fortunately, IIS 8.0 includes HTTP compression, which will improve this performance model, as well as rich caching mechanisms to make the end result to the user seem much quicker. Finding the actual response times and overhead on your network and servers will require the use of a tool that can test the web capacity of your specific configuration. Fortunately, Microsoft has such a tool.

WCAT

Microsoft's *Web Capacity Analysis Tool* (WCAT) is designed to simulate a load on your network and web server, allowing you to benchmark your system and apply changes to improve performance. Available as a free download, WCAT comes with preconfigured tests for your site, including HTTP as well as ISAPI and CGI testing. For testing a web server and network, a simple HTML file will work, or you can test application response with WCAT as well. WCAT will also test multiprocessor scalability.

IIS 8.0 Request Tracing

IIS 8.0's *Request Tracing* utility can be used for testing performance as well. Configure a test for a valid response code, 200, and hit your website and application with a browser. The Request Tracing log will show each stage of the request, as well as the time for the stage. You can use this to determine any bottlenecks in your site or application. If the longest time is in authenticating, you might want to look at the SQL Server connection for your authentication database, or possibly optimize indexes on that database. Request Tracing won't tell you what is wrong and how to fix it, but it can provide both a clue to areas that may need work and a valid baseline for testing improvements.

Scalability

Improving *scalability* in websites and servers is a concern for most organizations. IIS 8.0 scales well, having tested with thousands of websites on a single server, and the only limitations are hardware based — the maximum drive space available, maximum RAM in a system, and maximum bandwidth available. But there are still hardware choices and configurations that can help scalability.

Network load balancing, either through Windows NLB or a third-party load balancer, is essential for multisystem configurations. Memory paging in Windows Server 2012 can be improved by locating the paging file on a disk array that does not contain website data or log files, and maximizing RAM can limit the amount of paging the system will do. Choosing a processor with a large L2 cache improves performance for applications like IIS 8.0. Adding or upgrading network adapters, provided you haven't already saturated bandwidth, can improve performance. Setting longer content expiration times for content that rarely changes will mean that proxy servers won't need to refresh content from the server as frequently.

Windows Server 2012 has added networking functionality to support scalability in the network linking IIS 8.0 servers. The Windows TCP/IP stack (`tcpip.sys`) supports IPv6 and expanded IPSec for integrated security. Windows Server 2012 handles intermittent connectivity and recovers quicker from lost packets, making wireless communications faster and providing better transmission across WAN links. Windows Server 2012 can automatically scale the TCP/IP receive window size, and combined, the networking improvements result in up to a 350 percent improvement in throughput.

Windows Server 2012 can also make use of new hardware technologies that offload network processing from the CPU, both removing the CPU as a bottleneck and freeing CPU cycles for processing application requests. Web servers can also benefit from dynamic network connection balancing, which queues network traffic for multiple processors or processor cores, also limiting the need for higher-end servers. More on hardware scalability and networking in Windows Server 2012 can be found on TechNet or through Microsoft's communities.

The greatest increase in scalability in IIS 8.0 comes from the updated Hyper-V 3.0 server in Windows Server 2012. Virtual networks scale easier and more securely than before, and the number of virtual systems on a single host has expanded, too. The ability to scale across virtual systems and cloud servers allows an administrator to add IIS 8.0 sites to a cluster at will, and to remove them when the workload no longer requires them.

Scalability has no single solution for all administrators. Each site's design will contribute to scalability, and the needs for scalability will vary by organization. For more information about performance optimization settings and monitoring IIS 8.0 performance, see Chapter 22, "Monitoring and Performance Tuning."

Application Capacity Planning

Capacity planning for ASP.NET applications is outside this book's scope, but there is a new setting for IIS 8.0 that may help you. ASP.NET 2.0 introduced the `processModel/autoConfig` configuration, which would automate many of the performance configurations such as `MaxIoThreads`, `MaxWorkerThreads`, and so on, setting them at run time for your application. One problem is that this configuration has a 12-request-per-CPU limit, meaning that applications with high latency will not perform as well as they could. IIS 8.0 has a registry key, `MaxConcurrentRequestsPerCpu`, that can overcome this limitation. To use this key, add a `DWORD` key of `MaxConcurrentRequestsPerCpu` to `HKEY_LOCAL_MACHINE\SOFTWARE\Microsoft\ASP.NET\ 2.0.50727.0`, and set it to the number of requests desired. The default if this key does not exist is 12 requests per CPU. The upper limit is still set by the `processModel/requestQueueLimit` configuration, which defaults to 5,000 ASP.NET requests maximum. A setting of 0 will force each request to be immediately processed, and, in cases in which static content is served, this may improve performance. Normally, this is not the setting you want, however. Keep in mind that this process means editing the registry. If you are not comfortable with this, do not perform this modification. Errors in registry settings may cause unforeseen problems, up to and including a non-working server.

Installing IIS 8.0

WHAT'S IN THIS CHAPTER?

➤ Installing IIS 8.0 on Windows Server 2012

➤ Upgrading a Windows Server 2008 IIS 7.0 system to Windows Server 2012 and IIS 8.0

➤ Installing new features in an existing IIS 8.0 installation

➤ Installing IIS 8.0 using PowerShell

➤ Configuring IIS 8.0 for shared hosting recommendations

➤ Installing IIS 8.0 on Windows 8

➤ Hosting service recommendations

WROX.COM CODE DOWNLOADS FOR THIS CHAPTER

The wrox.com code downloads for this chapter are found at www.wrox.com/remtitle .cgi?isbn=1118388046 on the Download Code tab.

There are many ways to install IIS 8.0, from installing it as part of the Windows Server 2012 installation or adding IIS 8.0 to an existing server to upgrading a Windows Server 2008 and IIS 7.0 installation — not to mention automated or unattended installations.

In this chapter, we assume that you've read and understood the deployment planning issues discussed in Chapter 3, "Planning Your Deployment." You might also want to scan several of the upcoming chapters so that you understand which additional features you might want to install. Chapter 5, "Administration Tools," and Chapter 10, "Configuring Other Services," may help you.

Future chapters will cover advanced configuration options for IIS 8.0. Although this chapter covers adding features to an existing IIS 8.0 installation, you may also want to look at Chapter 11, "Core Server," and Chapter 18, "Programmatic Configuration and Management," as companions to this chapter.

WINDOWS SERVER 2012 SERVER MANAGER

Windows Server 2012 has a new look for Server Manager, and some changes to the way it runs. By default, when a user who is a member of the Administrators group logs in, Server Manager starts. To open it from the Start screen, simply click on Server Manager, as shown in Figure 4-1. From the desktop, click Server Manager on the taskbar. If Show Administrative Tools is disabled on a system, Server Manager will not show on the Start screen.

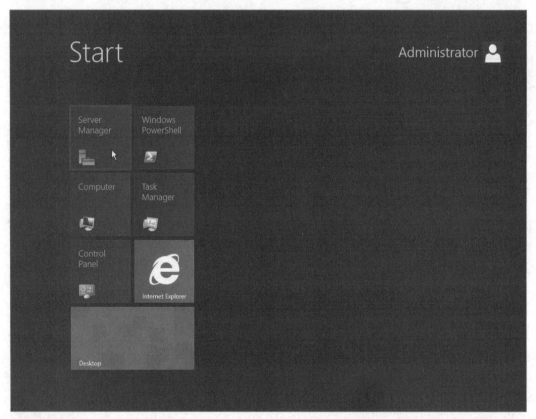

FIGURE 4-1

Naturally, you wouldn't want to install IIS 8.0 if you don't need it, but the number of applications that require IIS and ASP.NET is growing continually. So, even if you're not configuring a "web server," you may very well need IIS 8.0 on the server just for the applications you intend to run. This is especially true if you intend to run many Microsoft products, such as Microsoft Exchange, Microsoft SQL Server, or Microsoft System Center.

IIS 8.0 can be installed on an existing Windows Server 2012 system without the need for additional files or media. In the following examples, the first installation is the bare default with no additional features. Then we'll install popular additional features and roles that are commonly installed but would not be installed in a default IIS 8.0 installation. Adding or removing features can be done during the install or at any time afterward. We'll also install IIS 8.0 using PowerShell commands, as well as install IIS 8.0 on Windows 8.

THE DEFAULT IIS 8.0 INSTALLATION

The default IIS 8.0 installation discussed in this section is the most basic installation of IIS 8.0 possible. At the end of this installation, your server will be able to serve static content. That's enough for some uses, but this is probably the least common installation. It's not uncommon to receive a server from a vendor who has preinstalled the operating system with the default IIS 8.0 installation you'll see here. Adding features during the IIS 8.0 installation is a more common installation, as is adding features to an existing IIS 8.0 installation, but this installation example will familiarize you with what to expect from a basic IIS 8.0 installation.

To perform a default IIS 8.0 installation, perform the following steps:

1. Open Server Manager and select Manage ➪ Add Roles and Features, as shown in Figure 4-2.

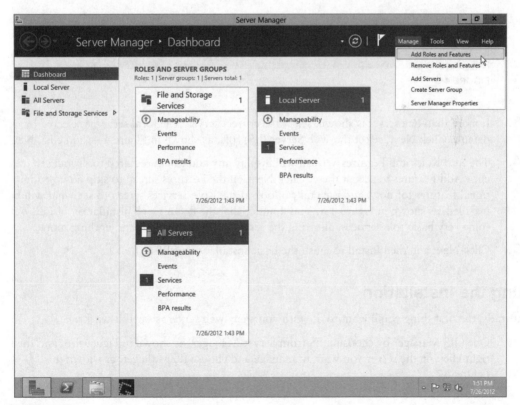

FIGURE 4-2

2. In the Add Roles and Features dialog, click on "Role-based or feature-based installation," as shown in Figure 4-3.

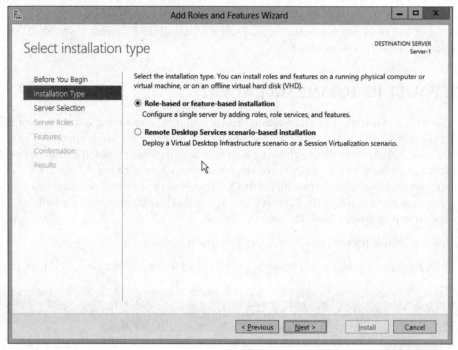

FIGURE 4-3

3. If more than one server is shown, select the correct server. The local server is selected by default. Click Next, select the Web Server (IIS) role, as shown in Figure 4-4, and click Next.

4. The Add Roles and Features Wizard will display any additional required tools and services; click Add Features to accept these. Click Next on the Features screen to skip adding additional features for now, and then take a look at the Role Services screen to see what will be installed, as shown in Figure 4-5. You'll notice that the default web installation installs only some very basic role services, allowing the serving of static content and nothing more.

5. Click Next and then Install to finish the basic installation of IIS 8.0.

Testing the Installation

Naturally, the first thing you'll want to do with your new web server is see if it works:

1. Open IIS Manager by choosing IIS from Server Manager, as shown in Figure 4-6, and then right-click on the server you want to manage and choose IIS Manager, as shown in Figure 4-7.

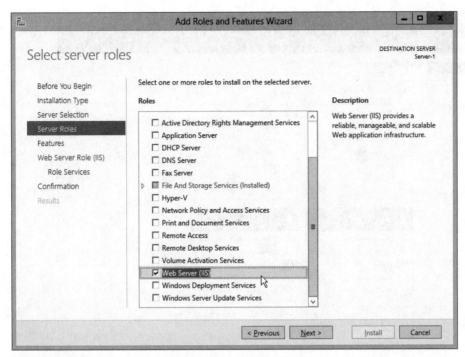

FIGURE 4-4

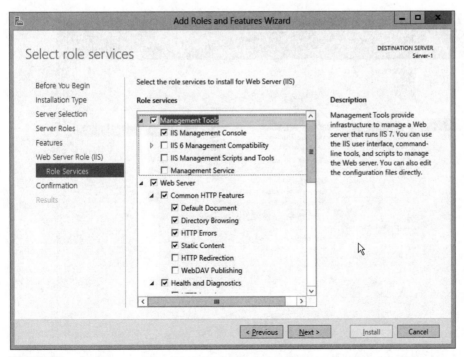

FIGURE 4-5

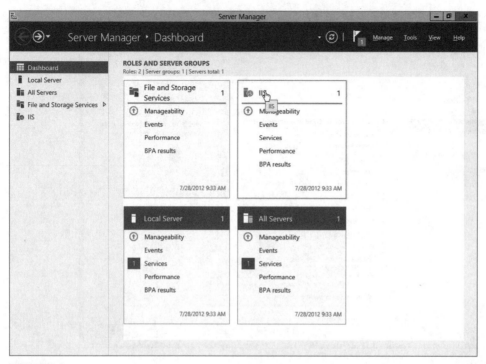

FIGURE 4-6

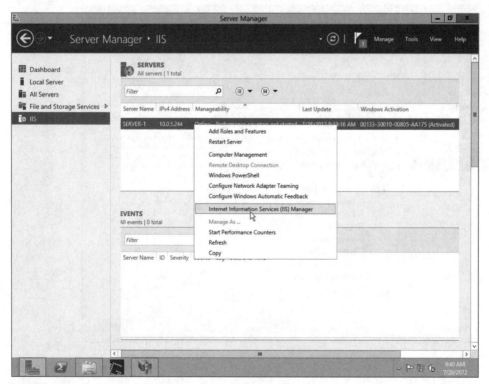

FIGURE 4-7

2. Expand the server to reveal the Default Web Site. You should see the administrative functions, as shown in Figure 4-8.

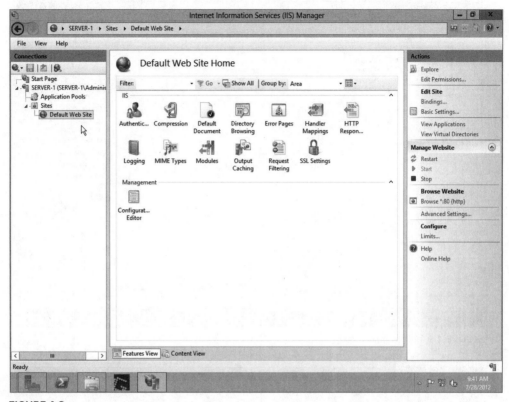

FIGURE 4-8

3. Choose Content View to see the content being served by this website, as shown in Figure 4-9. Notice that several files are already in place by default, including several image files and the HTML file `iisstart.htm`.

4. For a quick look at your new Default Web Site, highlight the file `iisstart.htm` and choose Browse in the Actions pane on the right. Internet Explorer will open your Default Web Site at `http://localhost/iisstart.htm` and you should see the default IIS 8.0 site, as shown in Figure 4-10.

Congratulations. You have now installed a working IIS 8.0 website on your server. At this point, however, it's not very useful, because it only shows the default content. Let's add some of our own.

Return to the Features View in IIS Manager, and then double-click the Default Document feature, as shown in Figure 4-11. You will see the list of documents that IIS 8.0 will serve, as shown in Figure 4-12.

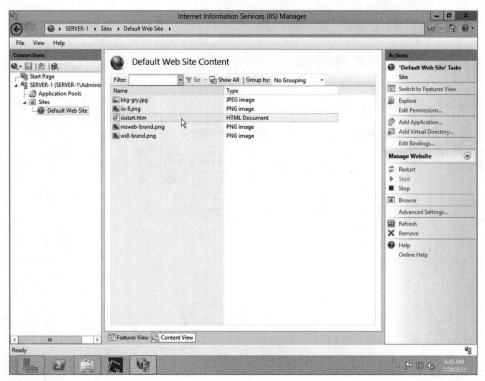

FIGURE 4-9

FIGURE 4-10

FIGURE 4-11

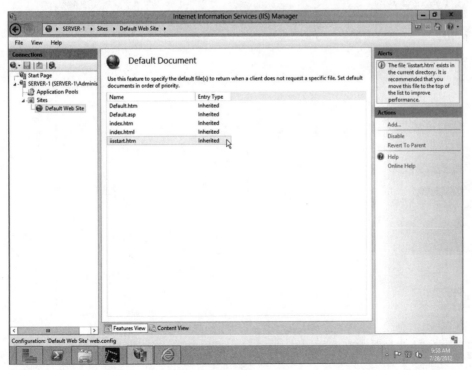

FIGURE 4-12

These documents appear in the order IIS will choose to serve them, if they are available, with iisstart.htm at the bottom. This means that any of the other documents, if they exist in the root of the website, will be served before iisstart.htm.

The conventional means of testing a web server is through the use of a "Hello World!" test page. This is true whether you're testing static content or applications such as ASP and ASP.NET. A basic file, the Hello World! application is designed to be the simplest application you can create that will test the features of your website. For a static HTML file, simply create the following text in a basic text editor such as Notepad, and save it as hello.htm in the website's root folder. The Default Web Site installed with IIS 8.0 has its root at c:\inetpub\WWWRoot\. If you use Notepad, watch out for Notepad adding the .txt extension to your filename.

```
<html>
  <head>
    <title>Hello World!</title>
  </head>
  <body>
    <h1>Hello World!</h1>
    <p>This is a Hello World! HTML file.</p>
  </body>
</html>
```

Once you have saved this file, you can again browse to your web server to view it. Because the file-name hello.htm is not in the Default Document list, you must specify the file on the URL; other-wise, a default document will be served. The URL http:\\{ServerName}\hello.htm, with your server's name replacing {ServerName}, should display in your browser, similar to Figure 4-13.

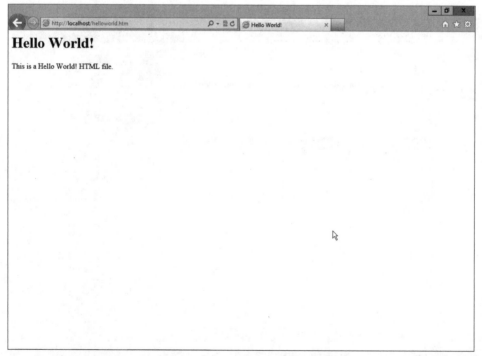

FIGURE 4-13

Note that you can also use the URL `http://localhost/hello.htm` to display the page but, because `localhost` refers to the system that Internet Explorer is installed on, it's not much use outside this kind of simple test. You should always use the Fully Qualified Domain Name (FQDN) of the server to access your websites.

Installing IIS 8.0 Using Web Platform Installer

Microsoft's Web Platform Installer (Web PI), currently at version 4.0, is an easy tool that can be used to install IIS 8.0, roles, and features. Web PI also includes the Microsoft Web Application Gallery, which simplifies installation of many popular web applications running on ASP.NET and PHP.

Web PI is a free utility that can be downloaded from Microsoft from `http://www.microsoft.com/web/downloads/platform.aspx`, where it and the Application Gallery are always up-to-date for the installation or update of the web platform and web applications. To install IIS 8.0 using Web PI, first download and install Web PI from the website, and then simply run the Web PI installer, `wpilauncher.exe`, from the download prompt.

To install IIS 8.0, run Web PI and search for IIS Recommended Configuration, as shown in Figure 4-14.

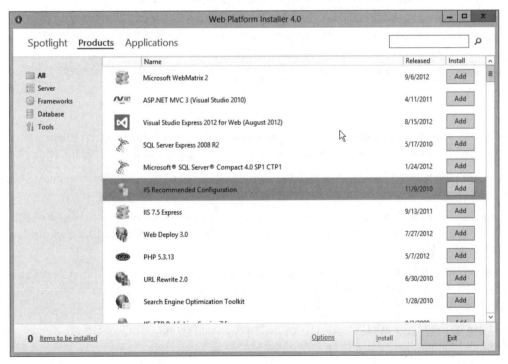

FIGURE 4-14

Click the Add button to add the IIS Recommended Configuration package to the installation, and then click Install to install it. You will see a number of prerequisites, as shown in Figure 4-15. Accept the installation of prerequisites to continue.

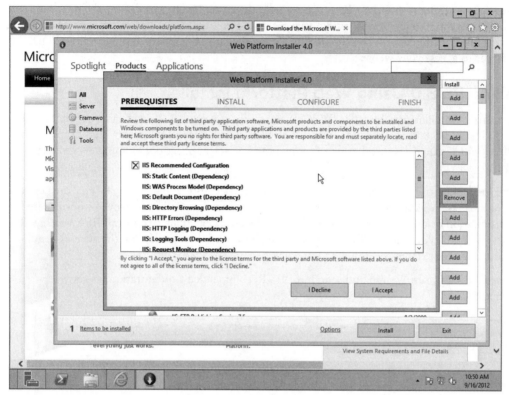

FIGURE 4-15

Web PI will install and configure IIS 8.0 with the recommended base options and configuration. You can also use Web PI to install only selected options by choosing them in the Web PI interface.

If you refresh the Server Manager, you will see IIS in the dashboard pane, as shown in Figure 4-16. Highlight it to see and manage the IIS Server as previously described in this chapter.

You can also use Web PI to configure Windows Server 2012 and IIS 8.0 for web hosting by selecting the Recommended Server Configuration for Web Hosting Providers installation and clicking Add, as shown in Figure 4-17.

Clicking Install will bring up a list of prerequisites, as shown in Figure 4-18, including applications such as ASP.NET MVC, PHP, and the MySQL Connector for MySQL databases. Simply accept the prerequisites to install all the prerequisites.

Web PI can be used to install IIS features, covered in the next section. More details on Web PI can be found in Chapter 20, "Configuring Publishing Options."

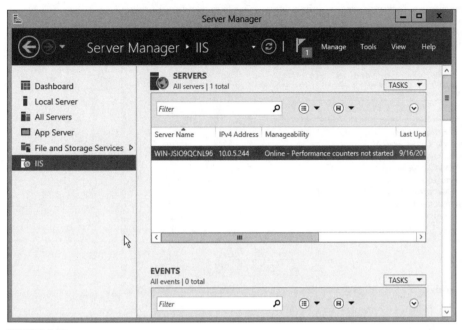

FIGURE 4-16

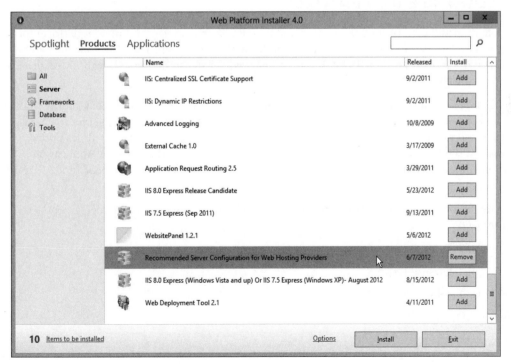

FIGURE 4-17

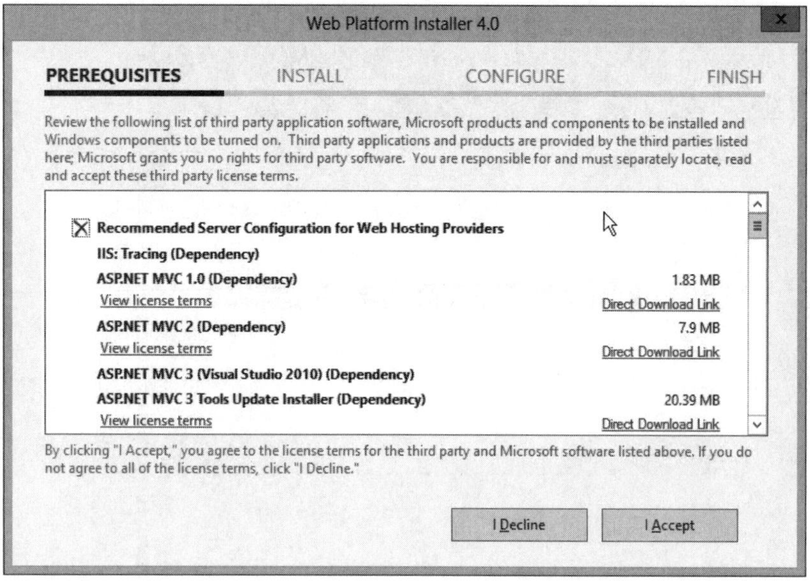

FIGURE 4-18

INSTALLING IIS 8.0'S FEATURES

The default installation of IIS 8.0 serves only static files, so it's not very useful as a platform for web applications. This can be corrected by adding additional features, which can be done during the initial install or any time after IIS 8.0 has been installed. This installation will walk through setting your IIS 8.0 web server up to serve ASP.NET applications.

To add (or remove) features to your IIS 8.0 installation, open Server Manager, click on the Manage link, and choose "Add roles and services" from the dropdown menu. Select the server to change and click Next to get to the Add Roles and Features Wizard. Click on the Server Roles option and expand the Web Server role. Expand Web Server in the list and then expand Application Development, as shown in Figure 4-19. This will allow you to select the roles needed for ASP.NET development.

Select the following options for the most common ASP.NET development and deployment environment:

➤ .NET Extensibility 3.5

➤ .NET Extensibility 4.5

➤ Application Initialization

➤ ASP.NET 3.5

➤ ASP.NET 4.5

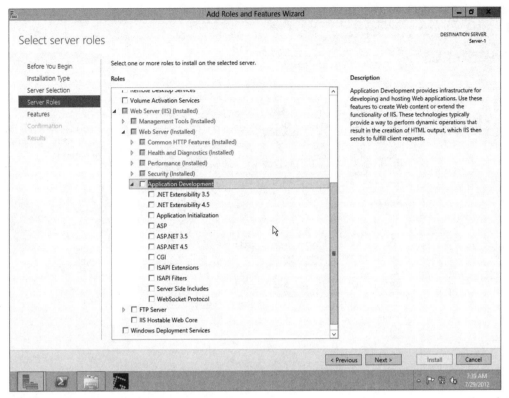

FIGURE 4-19

By default, IIS 8.0 will install ASP.NET 4.5, although upgrades from IIS 7.0 will maintain the ASP .NET 3.5 framework, if it is installed. You can select to install the ASP.NET 3.5 framework (and some applications will ask for it, as shown here), and it will install from the Internet. If you do not have direct Internet access from the server, or are behind a firewall that limits access, you will need to designate a source for missing features. To install the ASP.NET 3.5 framework, refer to the MSDN information at http://msdn.microsoft.com/en-us/library/hh848079%28v=vs.85%29 .aspx.

At each option selected, you may be asked to confirm additional roles and features needed for that installation. You should agree to the additional roles and features as they are requested. Once these are selected, click Next until the Install screen, and then select Install to finish adding the roles and features selected.

Once you have finished the installation and closed the wizard, open IIS Manager, expand the server sites, and select the Default Web Site. In the Features View you will now see a new group for ASP .NET management, as shown in Figure 4-20.

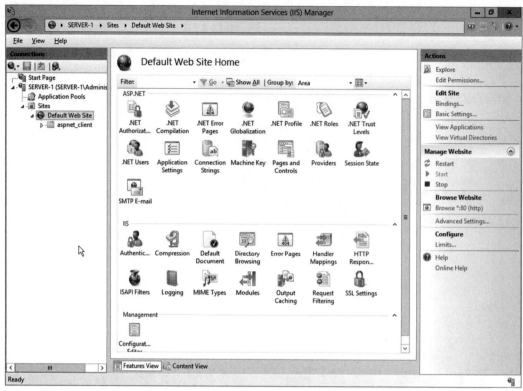

FIGURE 4-20

You can test your ASP.NET installation with a Hello World application, similar to the Hello World HTML page we used in the first installation. For this, we'll use a simple server control to display the traditional line of text on the web page. Create a text document named `hello.aspx` in the root folder of your Default Web Site, just as you created one for the HTML version. Use the following code:

```
<%@ Page Language="VB" %>
<% HelloWorld.Text = "Hello World!" %>
<html>
  <head>
    <title>Hello World! - ASP.NET version</title>
  </head>
  <body>
    <p>
      <asp:label id="HelloWorld" runat="Server" />
    </p>
  </body>
</html>
```

Now open Internet Explorer on your server and browse to the URL `http:\\{ServerName}\hello.aspx`, with your server's name replacing `{ServerName}`. The text "Hello World!" should display in your browser, similar to Figure 4-21.

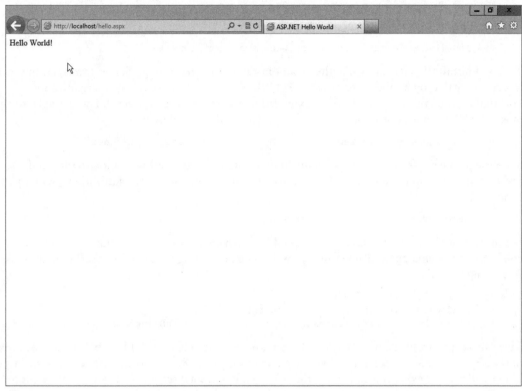

FIGURE 4-21

Okay, that's still not very impressive. But at least ASP.NET has been configured for your website and you can write ASP.NET applications to run on it. This same process can be used to add many additional features to your IIS 8.0 installation. Some of these, such as FTP, are covered in Chapter 10.

INSTALLING IIS 8.0 USING POWERSHELL

IIS 8.0 can be installed via the command line, using PowerShell, which is an easy way to automate installations on remote servers or to install from Windows Server 2012 Server Core. You can also script this installation if you will be installing IIS 8.0 on multiple servers, such as in a web farm recovery situation. Once IIS 8.0 has been installed in this manner, you may also use PowerShell to further configure the system. This installation assumes some familiarity with using PowerShell. If you are unfamiliar with PowerShell, you may want to review Microsoft's Windows PowerShell resources online at `http://technet.microsoft.com/en-us/library/bb978526`.

To use any of the Server Manager features in PowerShell, you must first import the ServerManager module. To do this, open a PowerShell command prompt and enter:

```
PS> import-module ServerManager
```

Installing IIS 8.0 from a PowerShell command is as easy as adding the Web Server feature to Windows. From a PowerShell command, simply run:

```
PS> Add-WindowsFeature Web-Server,web-management-console
```

This will install IIS 8.0 exactly like the default installation done through Server Manager. In other words, you will only be able to serve static HTML files, not much use for most organizations. Fortunately, the same command can be extended to add the features you need. For example, to run most ASP.NET applications, the command would look like the following:

```
PS> Add-WindowsFeature web-server,web-asp-net,web-management-console
```

Simply separate the features in a comma-delimited list. You could throw caution to the wind and install all features, which would be against security policy for most organizations, with the command:

```
PS> Add-WindowsFeature Web-Server -IncludeAllSubFeature
```

Because PowerShell commands can be scripted, you can create a script to deploy a default IIS 8.0 configuration, including needed features as well as default configurations. Your script might look something like this:

```
import-module ServerManager
Add-WindowsFeature web-server,web-asp-net
copy-item -Path c:\DefaultWebFiles\*.* -Destination \c$\inetpub\wwwroot
```

Save this script to a file named `IISInstall.ps1`; place your default web files, such as `Hello.aspx`, in the `DefaultWebFiles` folder; and you're ready to install IIS 8.0 at any time. The paths for installation will need to exist; you can create them using a PowerShell script. Naturally, you'll want to change these paths for deployment to multiple servers and use PowerShell remoting for remote installs. You will also likely wish to set other configurations and features through your script.

By default, PowerShell has scripting disabled. If you receive an error to this effect when running a script, you will need to enable scripting on the system. To do this, open a PowerShell command prompt, using Run As Administrator, and enter the following command:

```
Set-ExecutionPolicy unrestricted
```

This will allow the execution of PowerShell scripts on the system. Note that this may also open security more than some organizations are comfortable with.

You can find help for working with IIS 8.0 and PowerShell at http://www.iis.net/learn/ manage/powershell. PowerShell management of IIS 8.0 is covered in Chapter 18.

UPGRADING FROM IIS 7.0 TO IIS 8.0

Upgrading from IIS 6.0 to IIS 7.0 was a major issue for many organizations. Not only was the operating system being upgraded, but the many changes from IIS 6.0 to IIS 7.0 made programming changes to applications inevitable. With few viable upgrade paths, many organizations chose to upgrade only when a new application version was created. But this is not a problem with IIS 8.0.

There are virtually no changes to IIS 8.0 code from IIS 7.0, only additions. This means that any IIS 7.0 application or website should run directly when deployed into an IIS 8.0 environment, with a few exceptions.

The most notable exception to a clean upgrade is legacy code imported from prior versions of IIS that use various workarounds to run on IIS 7.0. These workarounds will normally work on IIS 8.0 as well, but future upgrades on IIS 8.0 may be in jeopardy. If you have legacy code, a thorough review is in order before upgrading.

The other exception to a direct upgrade path from IIS 7.0 to IIS 8.0 is when the underlying hardware won't support an operating system upgrade. This usually occurs when a 32-bit version for Windows Server 2008 is running on 32-bit hardware. Windows Server 2012 and IIS 8.0 are not compatible with 32-bit hardware. In these cases, a direct operating system upgrade cannot be performed, and a swing, or migration, upgrade is in order.

An in-place upgrade from Windows Server 2008 with IIS 7.0 on compatible hardware is as easy as upgrading the operating system. Insert the DVD with the installation media and choose an upgrade of the existing system. Windows Server 2012 can be installed in an existing Windows Server 2008 network, but you should update any Active Directory servers before any system upgrades.

A swing or migration upgrade from Windows Server 2008 can be performed in several ways, but the easiest would be to use the Microsoft Web Deploy tool, available from `www.iis.net`. Web Deploy is covered in Chapter 20, "Configuring Publishing Options."

You can also migrate sites with PowerShell, using a web configuration backup and restore. You will need to add the PowerShell snap-in to your IIS 7.0 server for this, as well as install PowerShell on your Windows Server 2012 system. First, create a backup of your web configuration with the following PowerShell command:

```
PS> Backup-WebConfiguration -Name IISConfigBackup
```

This will create a subfolder in the `\system32\inetsrv\backup` folder with your configuration files. Copy this folder to the new server, and run the following PowerShell command to restore it on your new web server:

```
PS> Restore-WebConfiguration -Name IISConfigBackup
```

Now just copy the content files and you're ready to go. This example works on most simple installations and even more complex setups such as SharePoint sites, but you may need to further script website configurations for an automated process.

INSTALLING IIS 8.0 ON WINDOWS 8

Although the scope of this book does not include workstation operating systems, IIS 8.0 does have a place on development workstations. Fortunately, IIS 8.0 is functionally identical on workstations and servers, making it easier to develop on and also easier to work within.

To install IIS 8.0 on Windows 8.0, perform the following steps:

1. Open the Programs and Features window by moving the mouse pointer to the lower-left corner of the desktop and right-clicking to open a context menu.

2. Choose Programs and Features from the menu, then click "Turn Windows features on or off" to open the Windows Features dialog. Expand Internet Information Services, as shown in Figure 4-22.

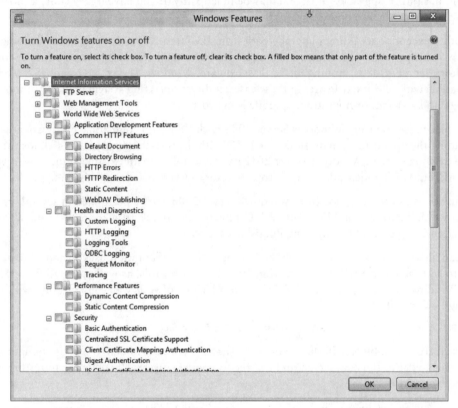

FIGURE 4-22

You'll notice that the selections are the same as when installing IIS 8.0 on Windows Server 2012. For this installation, select the following features:

➤ Web Management Tools

   ➤ IIS Management Console

➤ World Wide Web Services

   ➤ Common HTTP Features

      ➤ Default Document

      ➤ HTTP Errors

> ➤ Static Content

> ➤ Health and Diagnostics

>> ➤ HTTP Logging

> ➤ Performance and Features

>> ➤ Static Content Compression

> ➤ Security

>> ➤ Request Filtering

These selections will install enough to serve basic HTML static pages, and, when you click OK, you should be ready to serve a Hello World HTML file. You may need to restart your system to complete the installation.

3. Open the Computer Management console by moving the mouse pointer to the lower-left corner of the desktop and right-clicking to open a context menu. Choose Computer Management from the menu, expand Services and Applications, and then click Internet Information Services (IIS) Manager. Expand the Server in the Connections pane, and then Sites. Select the Default Site and click OK.

As shown in Figure 4-23, IIS Manager is extremely similar to the Windows Server 2012 version.

FIGURE 4-23

You can follow the same testing process as with the Windows Server 2012 version to test your Windows 8 installation. Adding the additional features to support Visual Studio development can be done using the same process, or you may add features during the Visual Studio installation process.

DEVELOPMENT SYSTEM CONCERNS

When setting up a Windows 8 workstation for developing web applications with IIS 8.0, there are several considerations you should keep in mind. If you create a directory structure identical to your eventual deployment environment and use the same application pool names, deploying your application will be much easier. Using Active Directory accounts for file and folder permissions can simplify the process further. Anything that can be done to match a development station to the deployment environment will make for a smoother deployment.

INSTALLING IIS 8.0 ON WINDOWS 7

Yes, you read that right. For the first time, IIS can be installed on a previous version of Windows for development environment compatibility. This is done by using IIS 8.0 Express, a newer version of IIS 7.5 Express released for IIS 8.0 compatibility. You can download IIS Express from www.iis.net.

IIS Express 8.0 will run on Windows Vista with SP1 and all later versions of Windows. Because IIS 8.0 Express does not run as a service, nearly all functions of IIS 8.0 Express can be handled without elevated privileges, unlike with IIS 7.0. IIS 8.0 Express is also included with the latest version of Microsoft's Web Matrix programming tools.

On Windows Server 2012 and Windows 8, IIS 8.0 Express supports full functionality. Some functions are lost on down-level operating systems, such as the SSL Central, Certificate Store, and Server Name Indication, which require operating system support as well as IIS support.

IIS 8.0 Express uses most of the binaries and configuration settings of the full IIS 8.0 product, to enable simple development of IIS 8.0 applications on Windows 7 workstations. IIS 8.0 Express supports both 32- and 64-bit systems, and also supports installation to a specific home directory, unlike IIS 7.0 on Windows 7. Simply download the appropriate version and use the /userhome parameter when you run iisexpress.exe.

To install IIS Express, you can simply download the .MSI installation file and run it. Agree to the licensing and the installation will run, installing IIS 8.0 Express.

You can manage IIS Express directly within Visual Studio. Simply right-click on your website in Solution Explorer, and choose Use IIS Express from the menu, as shown in Figure 4-24.

You will be asked if you want to configure IIS Express as the web server for this website; answer Yes, and Visual Studio will reload your solution in the new web server. The Properties window for your new server will allow you to manage such things as authentication directly in your solution. To configure all future web projects to use IIS Express, open the Options in Visual Studio, and expand Projects and Solutions, then click on Web Projects. Select the option to always use IIS Express and click OK. Visual Studio 2012 uses IIS 8.0 Express by default.

Because IIS 8.0 Express is intended for development environments, there is no IIS Manager as there would be in IIS 7.0 on Windows 7. You can still manage the IIS environment using the web.config and `applicationHost.config` files as you would any IIS installation. Managing IIS and web applications is covered in Chapters 5, 6, and 7.

FIGURE 4-24

AUTOMATED INSTALLATION AND CONFIGURATION

Many organizations need to install a large number of IIS 8.0 servers in diverse locations — a task not well suited for a single technician with a DVD, or even a herd of technicians. At some point, automated deployment becomes the only feasible method for creating and deploying these servers.

Previous Windows versions used Remote Installation Services, which has been updated to Windows Deployment Services (WDS). WDS is included in Windows Server 2012 as a deployment technology for both server and workstation operating systems. You can also script these deployments through PowerShell, as described earlier.

Windows Deployment Services

Windows Deployment Services (WDS) is designed to deploy Windows Server 20012 and Windows 8 across the enterprise, without the need to physically touch the system and without using the DVD at the new system. Using a network PXE boot, WDS can install a preconfigured Windows Server 20012 operating system with specific IIS 8.0 features and roles.

On the server side, WDS uses a Preboot eXecution Environment (PXE) and Trivial File Transfer Protocol (TFTP) to install an operating system on a client system with no functioning operating system. Boot images are created from an existing client, configured for your needs, and the resulting

WDS installation has identical settings and configurations as the system from which the image was created.

Windows Deployment Services are installed to a system that will act as a WDS server, and that server will store the image files to be supplied to clients. A boot menu is configured for network boots, with client images to be installed, so a user at a new system with no operating system can simply turn the system on and then select the appropriate installation image from the boot menu, which is then installed to the client.

WDS has the capability to image a partition or drive directly and install that to a new system. The limitation is that the system must have been prepared with Sysprep and be offline when the image is captured, normally by booting from a separate CD or DVD.

There are no IIS 8.0–specific settings or changes needed for using WDS to deploy IIS 8.0 servers, but there are settings that must be unique between systems. Sysprep will handle many functions, such as security identifiers, but after installation, an administrator may need to reconfigure IP address settings in IIS 8.0 or connection strings in ASP.NET applications. Naturally these can be scripted as well, using WMI or PowerShell for many changes, to automate complete installations.

Chapter 18 covers PowerShell and other command-based configuration options for IIS 8.0.

HOSTING SERVICE RECOMMENDATIONS

Microsoft has dedicated resources for hosting services using IIS, but these recommendations may apply to any organization running larger numbers of websites on its servers. IIS 8.0 has been tested with thousands of websites per server and scales out well, assuming that adequate hardware resources are available. In general, most hosting companies have a target percentage of sites that will receive requests at any point in time. Microsoft assumes a 90 percent idle factor. This means that only 10 percent of sites will be receiving requests during normal operations. You will probably want to monitor your site activity to balance the ratio for your specific circumstances.

Hosting operations have normally developed a strategy for managing application pools, account access, storage locations, and management environments, but if you are looking for a starting point, Microsoft recommends the following:

➤ Every site gets its own application pool.

➤ Windows domain accounts are used.

➤ No need for multiple accounts: Application pool accounts, anonymous user accounts, and the account connecting to the remote share use the same access account.

➤ Content is stored on a remote (UNC) share on a Storage Area Network (SAN) or other storage device.

This means that you will have at least three pieces of equipment:

➤ **Domain controller** — Active Directory domain accounts are used to ensure security across machines, such as when the content is requested from the remote content server. Using domain accounts also eases management for administrators as the number of sites and servers expands.

➤ **Web server** — Application pools run under domain accounts, and the same account is used for anonymous access. Content and configuration files are stored on a SAN, Network Attached Storage (NAS), or other UNC-accessible device.

➤ **Content hardware** — Web content and configuration files are stored on this equipment, preferably a replicated or clustered system, especially if it is running Microsoft SQL Server. DFS with replication can be used to mirror content between systems.

Directory Structure

Microsoft recommends a specific directory structure and security access to those directories, as shown in the following table. Each site will have a content directory, a log directory, and a directory for Request Tracing logs.

DIRECTORY	SECURITY	NOTES
`<content root>\<sitename>` (e.g., `e:\content\Site1`)	Administrators — full control System — full control `<AppPool ID>` — list folder contents	This is the site root folder. The AppPool ID has to be able to read this folder but does not need write access.
`<content root>\` `<sitename>\wwwroot` (e.g., `e:\content\site1\wwwroot`)	Administrators — full control System — full control `<AppPool ID>` — full control	This is the root of a website belonging to the site owner. The application pool that runs the site needs access to this directory.
`<content root>\` `<sitename>\logs\logfiles` (e.g., `e:\content\site1\logs\logfiles`)	Administrators — full control System — full control `{DomainName}\` `{MachineIdentity}` — full control	This folder is used for web logs. It is parallel to the content directory of the site so that it is not accessible by a visitor browsing the site. Because `Http.sys` is writing log files, you need to give access to the identity that `Http.sys` runs under on the web server. `Http.sys` is running as the machine identity when it writes log files to another machine.

`<content root>\`
`<sitename>\logs\faile-`
`dReqLogFiles` (e.g., `e:\content\site1\logs\failedReqLogFiles`)
	Administrators — full control
	System — full control
	`<AppPool ID>` — full control
		This is the folder used to store Failed Request log files, which allow site owners to diagnose problems with their websites. These logs are written by the AppPool identity, which runs as the Site Owner's identity.

The `icacls.exe` utility, available in several Microsoft resource kits, enables you to create this structure and assign the NTFS permissions using the following batch file (`HostingFolders.bat`):

```
SETLOCAL
REM Save command-line arguments passed as parameters:
SET SITE_ID=%1%
SET CONTENT_ROOT=%2

md %CONTENT_ROOT%\site%SITE_ID%
md %CONTENT_ROOT%\site%SITE_ID%\logs
REM ACL SITE DIRECTORY FOR ADMINS AND the APPPOOL ACCOUNT
icacls %CONTENT_ROOT%\site%SITE_ID% /G {DomainName}\PoolId%1:R /y
icacls %CONTENT_ROOT%\site%SITE_ID% /E /G Administrators:F

REM CREATING FAILED REQUEST LOG DIRECTORY
md %CONTENT_ROOT%\site%SITE_ID%\logs\failedReqLogfiles
icacls %CONTENT_ROOT%\site%SITE_ID%\logs\failedReqLogfiles /G
{DomainName}\PoolId%1:F /y
icacls %CONTENT_ROOT%\site%SITE_ID%\logs\failedReqLogfiles /E /G Administrators:F

REM CREATING WEBLOG DIRECTORY. HTTP.SYS LOGS AS MACHINE IDENTITY
md %CONTENT_ROOT%\site%SITE_ID%\logs\logfiles
icacls %CONTENT_ROOT%\site%SITE_ID%\logs\logfiles /G
{DomainName}\{MachineIdentity}:F /y
icacls %CONTENT_ROOT%\site%SITE_ID%\logs\logfiles /E /G Administrators:F

REM CREATING WEB CONTENT DIRECTORY
md %CONTENT_ROOT%\site%SITE_ID%\wwwroot
icacls %CONTENT_ROOT%\site%SITE_ID%\wwwroot /G {DomainName}\PoolId%1:F /y
icacls %CONTENT_ROOT%\site%SITE_ID%\wwwroot /E /G Administrators:F
```

Replace {DomainName} with your domain's name, and {MachineIdentity} with your server's machine identity under which `Http.sys` will run. Launch this batch file on the content server with the parameters of site ID and content root folder.

Web Server Accounts and Application Pools

On your web server, you will need to set the application pools and the accounts under which they run, as well as the account used for anonymous access. Because you will run all application pools in isolation, you do not need the generic anonymous user account. You can remove the anonymous user account with the following command line:

```
appcmd.exe set config -section:anonymousAuthentication -userName:"" —password
```

You can create the site and matching application pool with the following batch file code (`AppCmdSamples.bat`). Run this file with the parameter of the sitename, which will also be used in creating the application pool. Replace {DomainName} with your domain name, {ServerName} with the name of the web content server, and {ContentShare} with the UNC share name of the content share on the content server.

```
REM Create Application Pool
c:\windows\system32\inetsrv\Appcmd add AppPool -name:Pool_Site%1
    -processModel.username:{DomainName}\PoolId%1
```

```
    -processModel.password:PoolIDPwd%1
    -processModel.identityType:SpecificUser

REM Creating a site with the content, freb and log
REM configuration entries set to the directories we created and
REM secured before.
c:\windows\system32\inetsrv\AppCmd add site
    -name:Site%1
    -bindings:http/*:80:Site%1
    -physicalPath:\\{ServerName}\{ContentShare}\Site%1\wwwroot
    -logfile.directory:\\{ServerName}\{ContentShare}\Site%1\logs\logfiles
    -traceFailedRequestsLogging.directory:\\{ServerName}\
        {--}\Site%1\logs\failedReqLogfiles

REM Now assign the root application of the newly created web-site
REM to its Application Pool
c:\windows\system32\inetsrv\Appcmd set app
    -app.name:"Site%1/"
    -applicationPool:Pool_Site%1
```

Configuring Shared Hosting with Managed Code

If you are a programmer or otherwise familiar with creating and using a console application, you may find management easier using managed code, such as VB.NET or C#.NET. For example, using the Active Directory Service Interface (ADSI), you can configure web server user accounts and application pools for shared hosting through managed code. The following code snippets will manage the same tasks as the batch files above. These code snippets are included in the ManagedCode.txt file.

Creating Users

The following code will create a new Windows domain user account to be used for the application pool identity:

```
using System;
using System.DirectoryServices;
class Program{
   static void Main(string[] args)          {
   DirectoryEntry AD = new DirectoryEntry("WinNT://" +
       Environment.MachineName + ",computer");
   DirectoryEntry NewUser = AD.Children.Add("PoolID1", "user");
   NewUser.Invoke("SetPassword", new object[] { "PoolIDPwd1" });
   NewUser.Invoke("Put", new object[] { "Description",
       "AppPool Account" });
   NewUser.CommitChanges();
   }
}
```

This code creates a new user in Active Directory named PoolID1 with a password of PoolIDPwd1, and a description of the AppPool Account.

Setting Directory Permissions

The following code sets access for the administrator account, assuming that the content is in the e:\ content folder:

```csharp
using System;
using System.IO;
using System.DirectoryServices;
using System.Security.AccessControl;
using System.Security.Principal;

class Program
{
  static void Main(string[] args)
    {
      String dir = @"e:\content";
      DirectorySecurity dirsec = Directory.GetAccessControl(dir);
      dirsec.SetAccessRuleProtection(true, false);

      foreach (AuthorizationRule rule in dirsec.GetAccessRules(true,
      true, typeof(NTAccount)))
        {
          dirsec.RemoveAccessRuleAll
          (
            new FileSystemAccessRule
            (
              rule.IdentityReference,
              FileSystemRights.FullControl,
              AccessControlType.Allow
            )
          );
        }

      dirsec.AddAccessRule
      (
          new FileSystemAccessRule
          (
            @"BUILTIN\Administrators",
            FileSystemRights.FullControl,
            AccessControlType.Allow
          )
      );
      dirsec.AddAccessRule
      (
          new FileSystemAccessRule
          (
            @"BUILTIN\Administrators",
            FileSystemRights.FullControl,
            InheritanceFlags.ObjectInherit,
            PropagationFlags.InheritOnly,
            AccessControlType.Allow
          )
      );

      dirsec.AddAccessRule
      (
          new FileSystemAccessRule
          (
            @"BUILTIN\Administrators",
            FileSystemRights.FullControl,
            InheritanceFlags.ContainerInherit,
```

```
                    PropagationFlags.InheritOnly,
                    AccessControlType.Allow
                )
            );

            Directory.SetAccessControl(dir, dirsec);
        }
    }
```

This code first removes all security from the e:\content folder and then adds specific security settings to allow administrator accounts full control and to allow that access to be inherited by subfolders.

Creating Application Pools

This code will create 100 application pools, consecutively numbered. Depending on your organization, you might want to create generic site and application pools and assign them to users, as needed:

```
// This example is compiled under ASP.NET Framework 4,
// not ASP.NET Framework 4 client
using System;
using System.Collections.Generic;
using System.Text;
using Microsoft.Web.Administration;  //May ned a reference added in project
using System.Diagnostics;

namespace IIS8Demos
{
  class CreateAppPools
  {
    const int NUMBEROFPOOLS     = 100;
    const int APPPOOLBASENUMBER = 1000;
    const string POOLPREFIX     = "Pool_Site";
    const string USERNAMEPREFIX = "PoolId";
    const string PASSWORDPREFIX = "PoolIDPwd";
    const bool ENCRYPTPASSWORD  = true;
    static void Main(string[] args)
    {

      ServerManager mgr = new ServerManager();
      ApplicationPoolCollection pools = mgr.ApplicationPools;
        for (int i = 0; i < NUMBEROFPOOLS; i++)
          {
            CreateAppPool(pools, i + APPPOOLBASENUMBER, POOLPREFIX, USERNAMEPREFIX,
              PASSWORDPREFIX, ENCRYPTPASSWORD);
          }
      mgr.CommitChanges();
    }

    static bool CreateAppPool(ApplicationPoolCollection pools, int i, string
appPoolPrefix, string userNamePrefix, string passwordPrefix,
bool bEncryptPassword)
    {
      try
        {
```

```
                    ApplicationPool newPool = pools.Add(appPoolPrefix + i);
                    newPool.ProcessModel.UserName = userNamePrefix + i;
                    // the SetMetadata call will remove the encryptionprovider in the schema.
                    // This results in clear-text passwords!!!
                    if (!bEncryptPassword)
                      newPool.ProcessModel.Attributes["password"].SetMetadata
                        ("encryptionProvider", "");
                    newPool.ProcessModel.Password = passwordPrefix + i;
                    newPool.ProcessModel.IdentityType =
                      ProcessModelIdentityType.SpecificUser;
        }
            catch (Exception ex)
              {
                Console.WriteLine("Adding AppPool {0} failed. Reason: {1}",
                    appPoolPrefix+i, ex.Message);
    return false;
              }

            return true;
        }
      }
    }
```

This code loops through 100 times, each time creating an application pool, identifying that pool by the APPPOOLBASENUMBER variable incremented by one in each loop. Note that the call to the SetMetadata class removes the encryption provider from the application pool identity, meaning passwords would be in clear text. This is required to set the password in this example.

Creating Sites

This code will create 100 matching sites for the application pools above. It uses the new microsoft .web.administration namespace for IIS 8.0.

```
using System;
using System.Collections.Generic;
using System.Text;
using System.Diagnostics;
using Microsoft.Web.Administration;

namespace IIS8Demos
{
    class CreateSites
    {
        const int NUMBEROFSITES    = 100;
        const int SITEBASENUMBER   = 1000;
        const string POOLPREFIX     = "POOL_";
        const string SITENAMEPREFIX = "SITE";
        const string ROOTDIR        = "e:\\content";

        static void Main(string[] args)
        {
            ServerManager mgr = new ServerManager();
            SiteCollection sites = mgr.Sites;

            for (int i = SITEBASENUMBER; i < NUMBEROFSITES + SITEBASENUMBER; i++)
```

```
            {
                if (!CreateSitesInIIS(sites, SITENAMEPREFIX, i, ROOTDIR))
                {
                    Console.WriteLine("Creating site {0} failed", i);
                }
            }

        mgr.CommitChanges();
    }

    static bool CreateSitesInIIS(SiteCollection sites,
      string sitePrefix, int siteId, string dirRoot)
    {

        string siteName = sitePrefix + siteId;
        // site gets set to Poolname using the following format.
        //Example: 'Site_POOL10'
        string poolName = POOLPREFIX + sitePrefix +  siteId;

        try
        {
            Site site = sites.CreateElement();
            site.Id = siteId;
            site.SetAttributeValue("name", siteName);
            sites.Add(site);

            Application app = site.Applications.CreateElement();
            app.SetAttributeValue("path", "/");
            app.SetAttributeValue("applicationPool", poolName);
            site.Applications.Add(app);

            VirtualDirectory vdir = app.VirtualDirectories.CreateElement();
            vdir.SetAttributeValue("path", "/");
            vdir.SetAttributeValue("physicalPath", dirRoot + @"\" + siteName);

            app.VirtualDirectories.Add(vdir);

            Binding b = site.Bindings.CreateElement();
            b.SetAttributeValue("protocol", "http");
            b.SetAttributeValue("bindingInformation", ":80:" + siteName);
            site.Bindings.Add(b);
        }
        catch (Exception ex)
        {
            Console.WriteLine("Create site {0} failed. Reason: {1}",
                siteName, ex.Message);
            return false;
        }

        return true;
    }
  }
}
```

IIS 8.0 and Windows Server 2012 include a new namespace for ASP.NET, `microsoft.web` `.administration`, that allows control over websites using managed code. This code loops through and creates 100 websites, again incrementing from a base site number for identification. The code sets the site name, site path, and application pool for the site, and creates a virtual directory within that site. The code also configures site binding for HTTP requests, on port 80.

Setting IIS Properties

The following code sets the IIS properties to remove the anonymous user:

```
using System;
using System.Collections.Generic;
using System.Linq;
using System.Text;
using Microsoft.Web.Administration;

namespace ConsoleApplication2
{
  class Program
  {
    static void Main(string[] args)
    {
      SetAnonymousUserToProcessId();
    }

    static void SetAnonymousUserToProcessId()
    {
      ServerManager mgr = new ServerManager();
      try
      {
        Configuration config = mgr.GetApplicationHostConfiguration();
        ConfigurationSection section =
          config.GetSection("system.webServer/security/authentication/
          anonymousAuthentication");
        section.SetAttributeValue("userName", (object)"");
        // if we don't remove the attribute we end up with an encrypted empty string
        section.RawAttributes.Remove("password");
      }
      catch (Exception ex)
      {
        Console.WriteLine("Removing anonymous user entry failed.
          Reason: {0}", ex.Message);
      }

      mgr.CommitChanges();
      return;
    }

  }
}
```

This code also uses the `microsoft.web.administration` namespace and sets IIS properties for the site such that the anonymous user account for the site is the same as the account used for the application pool identity. This makes each site operate under its own user account for anonymous access, segregating site access accounts.

You can find more examples of IIS 8.0 configuration using code in Chapters 6, 7, and 18.

PART II
Administration

▶ **CHAPTER 5:** Administration Tools

▶ **CHAPTER 6:** Website Administration

▶ **CHAPTER 7:** Web Application Administration

▶ **CHAPTER 8:** Web Application Pool Administration

▶ **CHAPTER 9:** Delegating Remote Administration

▶ **CHAPTER 10:** Configuring Other Services

5

Administration Tools

WHAT'S IN THIS CHAPTER?

➤ IIS Manager

➤ Remote connections

➤ Configuration settings

➤ Command-line management

This chapter examines the various tools Microsoft has included to administer IIS 8.0. When building IIS 7.0, Microsoft completely revamped the toolset used to manage IIS. This toolset is largely retained for managing IIS 8.0.

The major changes, beginning with the release of IIS 7.0 and continuing subsequently, are as follows:

➤ The replacement of the IIS 6.0 Manager MMC with a completely new IIS Manager application that provides greater functionality for its expanded role. This new admin tool allows developers and administrators to add their own extensions and tweaks to it through its extensibility features. In addition to these major changes to the administrative tools, they added the ability to set web server configuration through files in the website.

➤ The addition of functionality to the `web.config` file and introduction of the `applicationHost.config` file. Through these files, the developer can completely set up and adjust the website.

➤ The addition of a new, dedicated command line (CLI) tool, `AppCmd.exe`, which allows complete control over every aspect of IIS.

➤ The creation of an IIS PowerShell snap-in, allowing IIS management to join other Microsoft products in being configured and managed through Microsoft's new command line and scripting automation framework.

In this chapter, you will learn about the major tools available to manage IIS 8.0, including IIS Manager, `AppCmd.exe`, and PowerShell.

KEY CHARACTERISTICS

IIS 8.0 was built with the following characteristics in mind:

➤ **Simple to use** — As previously mentioned, IIS 8.0 does not use the same metabase scheme as older versions of IIS, but rather uses a series of plaintext XML files for configuration. With IIS 8.0, the state is in the files, thus a change to the files results in an immediate change to the server, site, or application configuration.

➤ **Securely built** — The default configuration is set to allow only the system administrator to configure the server, sites, and applications. By using Feature Delegation, system administrators can securely make site and application administration available to down-level administrators without giving more permissions on the server than necessary. By default, the system does not store sensitive information like passwords. However, if there is a need to store sensitive information, it is encrypted on the hard disk. In addition to these security features, applications can be isolated to prevent other applications from sharing or reading the settings.

➤ **Extensible** — Just as the IIS Manager is extensible, so is the IIS configuration. This is made easy because the schema of IIS is contained in XML files. To extend the schema, just place an XML file in the schemas folder. You'll see below how the settings are arranged in "sections" within the configuration files.

➤ **Low TCO** — By changing to the XML file-based schema, IIS 8.0 is easier to deploy and manage. The file-based schema allows for web settings to be published in the same files as the website content. With this used in conjunction with Feature Delegation, the system administrator doesn't have to be as involved with every site change made on the server. The `web.config` file can contain both the IIS settings and the ASP.NET settings for a website, permitting centralized control over the site settings. The file-based structure also makes it possible to use standard filesystem-based tools for maintenance (backup and restore) and security.

➤ **Compatible with previous versions** — Applications created for IIS 6.0 will continue to run on IIS 8.0 by calling interfaces such as Admin Base Objects (ABO), the ADSI provider, and the IIS 6.0 WMI provider. Because the .NET Framework has been built into IIS from 7.0 onwards, current .NET applications will continue to work by calling `System.Configuration` and `System.Web.Configuration`. The config files will continue to follow the structure of the `web.config` and `machine.config` files from IIS 6.0, as well as add IIS configuration settings to the files.

➤ **Full automation** — IIS 8.0 can be managed using the GUI; however, as administrators. we are often interested in automation. IIS 8.0 provides this via AppCmd, PowerShell, and also programmatically for .NET developers through the Microsoft Web Administration (MWA) namespace. We touch on AppCmd and PowerShell in this chapter; MWA is covered in Chapter 18, "Programmatic Configuration and Management."

IIS MANAGER

Microsoft had to completely revamp IIS Manager in IIS 7.0 for a few different reasons. ASP.NET has been built into IIS 7.0 from the ground up, and the previous version of the admin tool didn't have the capability to take on the additional features that ASP.NET brought to the table while displaying them in a user-friendly way. With IIS 7.0's move from a metabase configuration to a .NET configuration, administrators can delegate configuration control to the developers through the `web .config` and `applicationHost.config` files. The new interface is able to control what modifications are allowed through the configuration files and show where the configuration is being written. The new interface permits an administrator to create extensions with an easier integration of feature pages, tree view nodes, and menu items. These new extensions are automatically downloaded by remote IIS Manager clients. The new admin tool also makes it possible to administer the server over HTTPS remotely by using the Web Management Service (WMSVC). This new look more closely resembles the Windows Control Panel and presents a more scalable approach to displaying the information needed to control the web server.

Appearance

IIS Manager's look and feel remain the same as with IIS 7.0, with features you would find in a browser, such as the address bar and forward and back buttons. It also has the option to group items by area, category, or "no grouping," which places all the objects together, in manners similar to the Windows Control Panel.

The default page used to manage the server is the homepage. There are two views for IIS Manager: the Features View and the Content View. Both views display a tree view in the left-hand "Connections" column, the feature list in the center column, and a Tasks pane in the right-hand "Actions" column. Figure 5-1 shows the homepage with the three columns and the Features View.

Feature Scopes

IIS 8.0 has five types of nodes in its tree view: server, site, application, virtual directory, and folder. Each node has its own homepage, and each homepage has a feature list.

Although many of the homepages share common features, the server homepage has the following features that are not available in any other homepage. These features appear only at the server level because they perform server-wide configuration or hold server-wide data and information. Note that some of these items may not be present, depending on whether the corresponding IIS feature was added during IIS installation.

- ➤ **Fast CGI settings** — Configures application settings for CGI applications that adhere to the Fast CGI specification.

- ➤ **ISAPI and CGI Restrictions** — Enables or restricts ISAPI or CGI extensions on the web server.

- ➤ **Server Certificates** — (doesn't appear in remote connections) Requests and manages SSL certificates for websites.

- ➤ **Worker Processes** — Views information about currently executing requests inside the worker processes.

➤ **Centralized Certificates** — (doesn't appear in remote connections) Allows for centrally stored SSL/TLS certificates to be used by this web server.

➤ **Feature Delegation** — Configures default delegation state for lower levels.

➤ **IIS Manager Users** — Configures IIS Manager user accounts. These user accounts exist only within IIS and can be used to administer and interact with IIS sites and applications, without a corresponding Windows user account.

➤ **Management Service** — (doesn't appear in remote connections) Configures IIS Manager for delegation and remote access. Remote administration is covered in detail in Chapter 9, "Delegating Remote Administration."

➤ **Shared Configuration** — (doesn't appear in remote connections) Allows multiple IIS web servers to share a centrally stored configuration file. Shared configuration is covered in detail in Chapter 16, "IIS Scalability I: Building an IIS Web Farm."

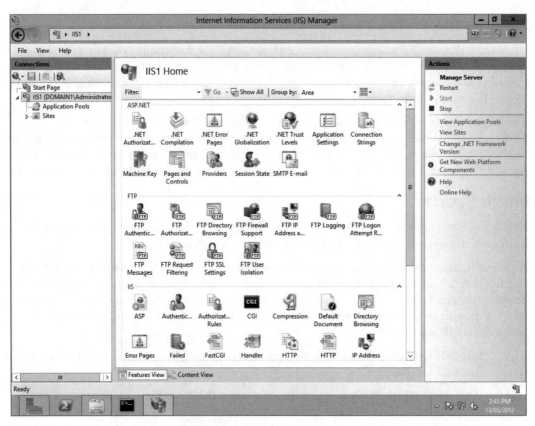

FIGURE 5-1

There are also features that appear elsewhere but do not appear at the server level because they are used specifically by other levels or work better in other locations:

➤ **.NET Profile** — Configures options that track user-selected preferences in ASP.NET applications.

➤ **.NET Roles** — Configures user groups for use with .NET Users and Forms authentication.

➤ **.NET Users** — Manages users who belong to roles and who use Forms authentication.

➤ **SSL Settings** — Specifies requirements for SSL and client certificates.

There are special rules for where the features associated with delegation appear:

➤ Feature Delegation appears only at the root node of a connection.

➤ IIS Manager Permissions appears only on the server, site, and application nodes.

The Tasks pane of the homepage, on the far right side, enables you to access a variety of management tasks, including these tool selections: basic settings, restarting (IIS or Web Site), starting, stopping, advanced settings, and configuring failed request tracing.

If the IIS 8.0 FTP server is also installed, a set of FTP management features also become available. These features are the same at both the server and FTP site levels, except:

➤ **FTP Logon Attempt Retry** — Available at the server level, this allows administrators to block or log remote users who fail to authenticate successfully within the specified parameters. Such failed logons may indicate an attack against the FTP server.

➤ **FTP Current Sessions** — Available at the FTP site level, this feature provides a list of currently logged-on users and statistics about their sessions.

The IIS 8.0 FTP server is covered in detail in Chapter 10, "Configuring Other Services."

Features View

IIS Manager's Features View uses three types of page layouts in addition to the homepages, depending on the type of information being displayed:

➤ List pages

➤ Property grids

➤ Dialog pages

List Pages

List pages show lists of objects. Application pools and sites are two examples of list pages. Within these list pages, you can filter or group the objects. Filtering objects enables you to search for a string in the name column in order to exclude all objects that do not include that string. You also can group objects by categories such as Status or Port, depending on the list page. In Figure 5-2, the grouping options are No Grouping, Status, .NET Framework Version, Managed Pipeline Mode, and Identity.

In the Task pane, you can modify the contents of the list by adding, editing, or removing items. The Task pane also allows you to edit the feature settings that aren't specific to a list item.

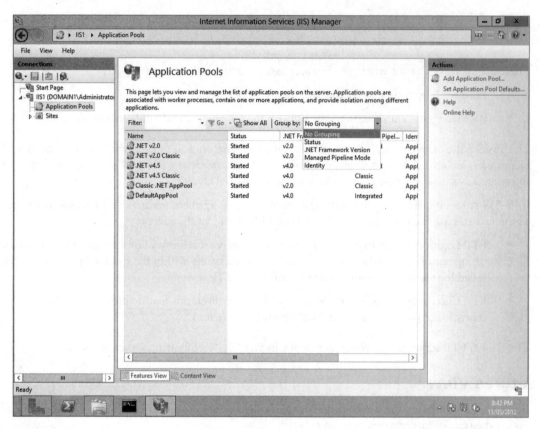

FIGURE 5-2

Property Grid Pages

Property grid pages show grids of properties that relate to one another. By using the Display dropdown list, you can view the properties' Friendly Names, Configuration Names, or Both.

Property grid pages allow you to choose from a selection of variables in a dropdown list or allow you to directly edit the value. In Figure 5-3, the Enable Chunked Encoding property is a dropdown list of True or False, and the Locale ID is a directly editable property.

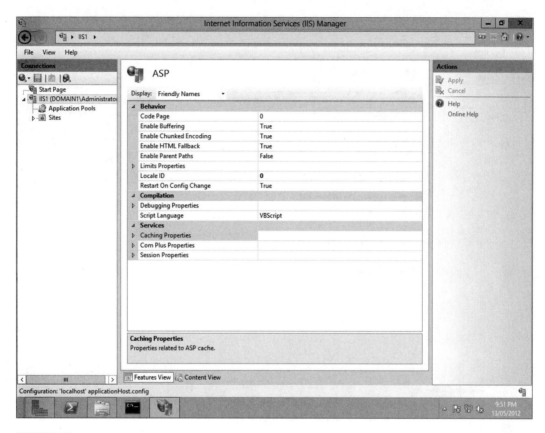

FIGURE 5-3

Dialog Pages

Dialog pages have a similar interface to the old IIS 6.0 Manager, with textboxes, checkboxes, and radio buttons. Apply and Cancel can be selected in the Task pane to save or discard changes, respectively. Figure 5-4 shows the Machine Key dialog page with dropdown menus for encryption and decryption methods, as well as checkboxes for other options.

Website- and Application-Specific Settings

The website- and application-level nodes have basic and advanced settings associated with them. Both the basic and the advanced settings tools can be found in the Actions pane when the site or application has been selected. The basic settings for both types of nodes include Website Name or Alias, Application Pool, Physical Path, and Connect As Selections, as shown in Figure 5-5.

Figure 5-6 shows the advanced settings, which include the basic settings and additional settings such as connection limits and failed request tracing.

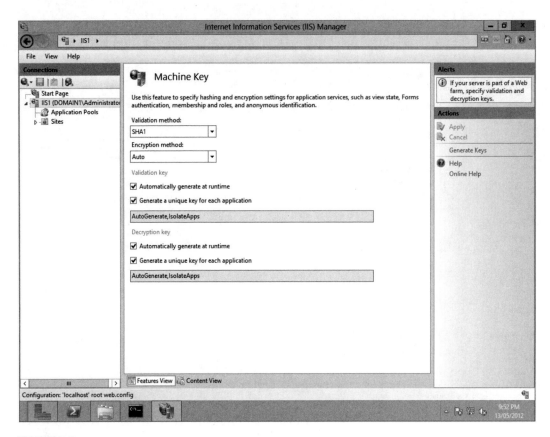

FIGURE 5-4

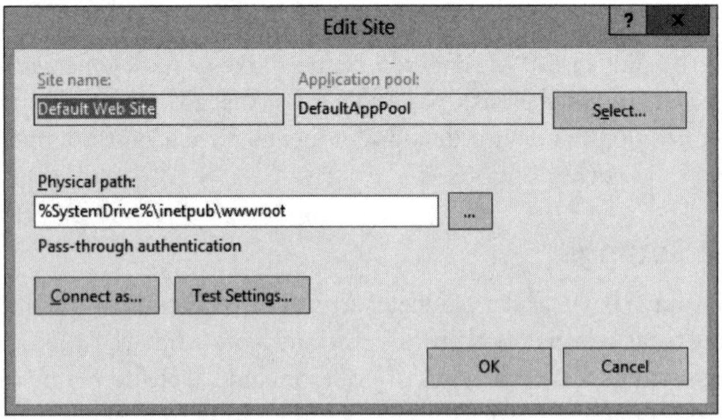

FIGURE 5-5

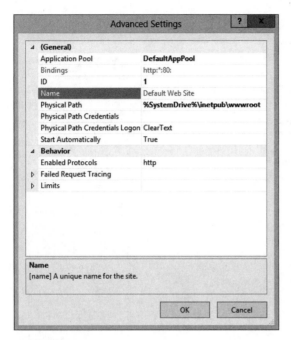

FIGURE 5-6

Content View

Content View is a read-only list page. Actions such as moving, copying, deleting, or creating files or folders are not allowed in this view. You can access Content View by clicking the Content View button at the bottom of the feature (see Figure 5-7), list pane, or by right-clicking a tree view node and choosing Switch to Content View. The Content View is used to set the configuration on a file. To set the configuration, switch to Content View, select the file, and click Switch to Features View. This is the only method that allows a file's configuration to be adjusted in the IIS Manager.

Feature Delegation

Feature Delegation gives the server administrator the ability to delegate control of websites and applications to other administrators or developers. By default, only users in the local Administrators group (including Domain Admins) can manage an IIS 8.0 server. With Feature Delegation, the server administrator can allow non-administrators to manage either websites or applications. These become "site administrators" or "application administrators," respectively. Remember that the hierarchy is server administrators, site administrators, and then application administrators. Chapter 9 goes into greater detail about how to set up and use Feature Delegation.

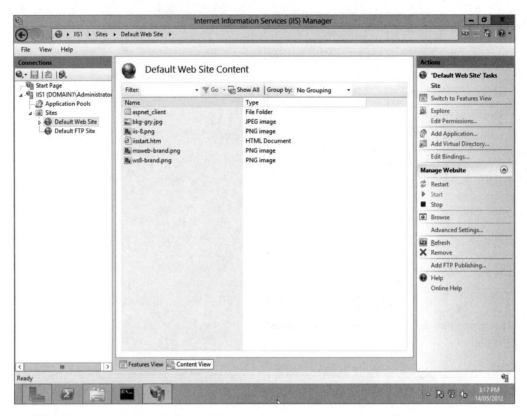

FIGURE 5-7

IIS MANAGER EXTENSIBILITY

Along with the tools that are already built into the IIS Manager, there is also the ability to create your own tools and extend the capabilities of the manager. This feature, known as *IIS Manager extensibility*, allows third-party vendors, developers, or systems administrators to create their own custom tools to work with IIS 8.0.

The `Microsoft.Web.Management.dll` makes extensibility possible by providing access to the entire IIS subsystem. We go into more detail about IIS Manager extensibility and give examples and code in Chapter 12, "Core Server Extensibility."

REMOTE CONNECTIONS

The IIS Manager allows management of both a local IIS 8.0 server and remote IIS 7.0, 7.5, and 8.0 servers. Within the IIS Manager a connection can be created to a remote server, an individual remote website, or even an individual application within a remote website. This granularity allows a server administrator to provide remote management access to only those parts of IIS to which the remote user should have access.

Remote connections use web services over HTTPS, providing a more "firewall-friendly" method of managing IIS remotely compared with RPC used by the IIS Manager in IIS 6.0. Furthermore, permissions can be delegated to both Windows users and IIS Manager users; IIS Manager users only exist within IIS. The latter is a feature that may be of interest to hosting companies, cloud providers, and those in a similar situation, because connections do not require a Windows account (limiting the access that the user account has to the system) and do not require a Windows Client Access License (CAL) for each connection or user.

To open a connection to a remote IIS 7.0, 7.5, or 8.0 server, click the Create New Connection button in the top left of the Connections pane, as shown in Figure 5-8.

Chapter 9 covers delegation and remote access in more detail.

FIGURE 5-8

CONFIGURATION SETTINGS

IIS 6.0 and ASP.NET provided the ability to control certain functions of the website through the web.config file, but all IIS-specific settings were housed in the metabase. Starting with IIS 7.0, Microsoft has changed the configuration storage from the metabase to a series of cleartext XML files. These files provide for a distributed hierarchy in which the configuration is shared among the machine-level configuration files and may optionally be set at the directory level along with the web content. This allows the system administrator to delegate control to the site or application administrators. By default, IIS 8.0 is locked down to allow only the system administrator access to modify the server, site, or application settings. The configuration settings are fully backward-compatible at both the API and XML levels with previous versions of IIS and the .NET Framework.

Configuration File Hierarchy

As with most systems, the configuration files in IIS 8.0 are read and applied in a hierarchical order. The following three files are at the heart of the system:

➤ The applicationHost.config file

➤ The administration.config file

➤ The redirection.config file

➤ The `machine.config` file

➤ The root `web.config` file

The `applicationHost.config`, `administration.config`, and `redirection.config` files are located at `%systemroot%\system32\inetsrv\config`. The `machine.config` and root `web.config` files are both currently located in the `%systemroot%\Microsoft.NET\Framework64\v4.0.30319\` `CONFIG` folder (and in the corresponding 32-bit Framework folder under the `Microsoft.NET` folder for 32-bit applications). When Microsoft releases the next version of the .NET Framework, this path will change.

The `applicationHost.config` file contains the IIS server settings. The `administration.config` file contains modules to be loaded and delegation settings. (Chapter 12 goes into how to extend IIS Manager with new modules.) `Redirection.config` is used by the Shared Config feature (which is covered in Chapter 16).

The `machine.config` and root `web.config` files contain the global default values for the .NET Framework settings. These two separate structures are necessary because IIS and the .NET Framework do not follow the same versioning schedule. IIS uses the Windows Server schedule, whereas the .NET Framework uses the Visual Studio schedule.

Along with the three primary files, additional `web.config` files may be located in the content directories of individual websites or applications to control their behavior and the behavior of the hierarchical levels below them. These `web.config` files can contain settings for IIS, ASP.NET, or any other .NET Framework that can be controlled at that level. The configuration file inheritance hierarchy begins with the `machine.config` file, then the root `web.config`, the `applicationHost.config` file, and then the `web.config` files that may be in the website or application levels.

Configuration Levels

Owing to the hierarchical nature of the configuration, each level of the URL namespace will have a configuration associated with it. The configuration will begin at the server level and then inherit down throughout the child nodes, unless there is an override in place on a child node. These child nodes can include not only folders, but also files. As mentioned above, the best method to set per URL configuration is by using `web.config` files at the root of each individual website.

Occasionally, you will not want to allow `web.config` files to be deployed at levels below the server level. Some of the reasons include:

➤ **Security** — There are times when server administrators need to control the server configuration and cannot allow access by developers through the use of `web.config` files. An example of this could be a production server in an organization that has a policy restricting access only to administrators.

➤ **Administration consolidation** — Consolidating the configuration of all sites on a server to the three main server configuration files presents the administrator with an easy-to-manage, known location for making all the changes needed for the server and sites.

➤ **Remote change notification** — A `web.config` file located on a remote (UNC) share can present problems with usability, scalability, or other issues. A prime example of a potential problem with remote change notification can come when the `web.config` file is located on a non-Windows system that doesn't support the file change notifications in a manner that Windows expects.

➤ **Shared configuration** — If many websites all point to the same central `web.config` for their configuration, by default the `web.config` cannot be isolated in individual `web.config` files at the lower levels.

➤ **File-specific configuration** — When a `web.config` file is applied at a specific level, the file is applied to every file in that folder. If a different configuration for a specific file is needed, a different method has to be used. This is usually accomplished by using location tags.

Location Tags

Location tags present another method to set configuration for lower levels in the configuration hierarchy. The location tags are set at a parent level and then applied to a specific lower level and the hierarchy of configuration below it. These lower levels can be either subfolders or a file in a subfolder. This allows a lower level to have a different configuration from that of the parent level without having to use a separate `web.config` file. Generally, location tags are set at the global level. Location tags use the `path` attribute to set the location for the configuration to be applied. The `path` attribute can be as follows:

➤ `"."` or `" "` — This designates the current level.

➤ `sitename` — This designates the root application of a specific site.

➤ `sitename/application` — This designates a specific application within a specific site.

➤ `sitename/application/vdir` — This designates a specific virtual directory within an application in a site.

➤ `sitename/application/vdir/physicaldir` — This designates a specific physical directory.

➤ `sitename/application/vdir/file.ext` — This designates a specific file. The file can be located anywhere in the folder structure, but the path must specify the location to the file — such as `sitename/application/vdir/folder1/file1.ext`, or, if the file is at the root of the site, `sitename/file1.ext`.

Because location tags generally are located in the `applicationHost.config` file, multiple location tags are allowed in one file. Although the location tags cannot reference the exact same path, they can reference child paths. For example, the global path for `httpLogging` can be set to log only errors by setting the location path to `"."` in the `httpLogging` tag:

```
<location path= ".">
  <system.webServer>
    <httpLogging selectiveLogging= "LogError" />
  </system.webServer>
</location>
```

The logging for the default website can then be set to log every request by setting the location path to the default website in the tag:

```
<location path= "Default Web Site">
  <system.webServer>
```

```
      <httpLogging selectiveLogging= "LogAll" />
    </system.webServer>
  </location>
```

Finally, you can set `file1.htm` to only log errors by setting the location path to point to `file1.htm` in the tag:

```
<location path= "Default Web Site/file1.htm">
  <system.webServer>
    <httpLogging selectiveLogging= "LogError" />
  </system.webServer>
</location>
```

These examples show that by using location tags, different levels of the configuration can have different settings specified without having to use a `web.config` file at lower levels.

Configuration File Structure

Like other XML files, the configuration files are based on sections. *Sections* are groups of related settings that can be deployed as a group and are normally consumed by a single server module. Configuration sections are also the base unit for extensibility. To extend the schema, add a new section with the desired settings.

Sections belong to a section group, to create a logically related group. Sections can be nested inside section groups, but they cannot be nested inside other sections.

Section groups don't have settings in them. Section groups contain one or more sections. They provide a method of organizing the sections into the configuration. Section groups can contain other section groups. This nesting of section groups is used to build the configuration hierarchy within the settings.

Sections have both short and long names. Short names consist of the section itself, whereas long names consist of all the containing section groups and the section name. In this example, `httpLogging` is the short section name, and `system.webServer/httpLogging` is the long section name. The long section name is derived by prepending the short section name, in this case `httpLogging`, with the name of its parent section group(s), `system.webServer`:

```
<system.webServer>
  <httpLogging selectiveLogging= "LogError" />
</system.webServer>
```

This *hierarchical naming structure* provides the method for specifying the correct section to modify when changes are made via any of the IIS 8.0 tools. It also allows multiple sections to be named the same, as long as they are under different section groups. In the example below, `<system .webServer>` and `<httpProtocol>` are both section groups, whereas `<customHeaders>` and `<redirectHeaders>` are both sections within those groups:

```
<system.webServer>

  ...

  <httpProtocol>
    <customHeaders>
```

```
    <clear />
    <add name="X-Powered-By" value="ASP.NET" />
  </customHeaders>
  <redirectHeaders>
    <clear />
  </redirectHeaders>
</httpProtocol>

...

</system.webServer>
```

Configuration Schema

The configuration uses a *declarative schema*, which is housed in multiple files located at %systemroot%\system32\inetsrv\config\schema. You can add new schema files to the configuration by adding them to the schema folder. Once the configuration system has restarted, it will grab the additions to the schema. The new changes will not be used until the configuration system has restarted.

The schema is housed in the following files:

➤ IIS_schema.xml — Provides the schema for the IIS web server settings and the Windows Activation System.

➤ ASPNET_schema.xml — Provides the schema for the ASP.NET settings.

➤ FX_schema.xml — Provides the schema for the other .NET Framework settings.

> **NOTE** *It is highly recommended that these default files not be edited, because that may result in a corrupted schema that will not allow the server to start. If you need to edit a schema file, make a backup copy first. Editing these files can be done only through file access API and XML parsing\editing. The recommended method of adding configuration sections to the schema is to create a new .xml file in the schema folder.*

Schema Organization

As mentioned previously, the configuration consists of a series of sections and section groups. The sections get their layout in the schema. Looking at the IIS_schema.xml file, it is possible to see that the *schema* is a collection of sections. Each of these sections is initiated with sectionSchema. Here the section system.webServer/defaultDocument is detailed in the IIS_schema.xml file. (Notice that the long name is used, showing the section group system.webServer within which the section is contained.) The schema shows an attribute of enabled with a default value of true and an element named files. In addition to those items, it also defines a collection as a subelement of the files element and the collection's properties. (A line break has been added for readability purposes.)

```
<sectionSchema name="system.webServer/defaultDocument">
    <attribute name="enabled" type="bool" defaultValue="true" />
```

```
        <element name="files">
            <collection addElement="add" clearElement="clear"
removeElement="remove" mergeAppend="false">
<attribute name="value" type="string" isUniqueKey="true"/>
            </collection>
        </element>
    </sectionSchema>
```

The schema for `system.webServer/defaultDocument` is then used in the `applicationHost`
`.config` file with this result:

```
<system.webServer>
    <defaultDocument enabled="true">
        <files>
            <add value="Default.htm" />
            <add value="Default.asp" />
            <add value="index.htm" />
            <add value="index.html" />
            <add value="iisstart.htm" />
            <add value="default.aspx" />
        </files>
    </defaultDocument>
</system.webServer>
```

The `enabled` attribute listed in the schema is shown as being set to `true`. The `files` element is
listed with no attributes; however, it is shown to have a collection of elements below it. The collection in the schema becomes a series of elements below `files`. Each of these elements specifies a
filename that the website can use as a default file type. The schema files provide the structure for the
configuration files.

configSections

Although the schema files provide the backbone for the configuration files, there is also a section
in the configuration files named `configSections`. `configSections` is in both `machine.config`
and `applicationHost.config` by default. This part of the configuration may also be added to
any `web.config` for additional structure. The purpose of `configSections` is to register the
sections it lists with the system, including any custom configuration sections. In addition, it
establishes the hierarchy of the section groups. Its purpose is not to define properties of the
sections.

`configSections` uses three pieces of meta data to register a section with the system:

➤   `type` — Used to specify the managed-code section handler for the .NET Framework.

➤   `overrideModeDefault` — Determines whether the section can be overridden at lower levels
    or if it locked down to prevent changes at lower levels. The default is to allow override if it is
    not specified.

➤   `allowDefinition` — Specifies the level in the hierarchy at which the section can be set. The
    options include:

    ➤   `MachineOnly` — Where the section can only be set in the `applicationHost.config`
        or `machine.config` files

➤ `MachineToRootWeb` — Where the section can be set in the `applicationHost.config`, `machine.config`, or the root `web.config` files

➤ `MachineToApplication` — Where the section can be set in the `applicationHost.config`, `machine.config`, the root `web.config`, or the application-level `web.config` files

➤ `AppHostOnly` — Where the section can be set only in the `applicationHost.config` file

➤ `Everywhere` — Where the section can be set in any configuration file

This example of the `applicationHost.config` file shows a small portion of `configSections`:

```
<configSections>
        <sectionGroup name="system.applicationHost">
            <section name="applicationPools" allowDefinition="AppHostOnly"
overrideModeDefault="Deny" />
            <section name="configHistory" allowDefinition="AppHostOnly"
overrideModeDefault="Deny" />
            <section name="customMetadata" allowDefinition="AppHostOnly"
overrideModeDefault="Deny" />
            <section name="listenerAdapters" allowDefinition="AppHostOnly"
overrideModeDefault="Deny" />
            <section name="log" allowDefinition="AppHostOnly"
overrideModeDefault="Deny" />
            <section name="sites" allowDefinition="AppHostOnly"
overrideModeDefault="Deny" />
            <section name="webLimits" allowDefinition="AppHostOnly"
overrideModeDefault="Deny" />
        </sectionGroup>

        <sectionGroup name="system.webServer">
            <section name="asp" overrideModeDefault="Deny" />
            <section name="caching" overrideModeDefault="Allow" />
            <section name="cgi" overrideModeDefault="Deny" />
            <section name="defaultDocument" overrideModeDefault="Allow" />
            <section name="directoryBrowse" overrideModeDefault="Allow" />
            <section name="fastCgi" allowDefinition="AppHostOnly"
overrideModeDefault="Deny" />
```

The first section group is the `system.applicationHost` group and specifies that the sections can only be set in the `applicationHost.config` file. The second section group is the `system.webServer` group. You can see that some of the tags do not use the `allowDefinition` attribute to restrict the file where the configuration can be set. The `allowOverrideModeDefault` is set to `Allow` in some cases, allowing the setting to be overridden (by default) in a lower-level configuration file. The `overrideModeDefault` meta data can also be seen in each of the sections.

Locking and Unlocking Sections

Feature Delegation is one of the new features of IIS 8.0. It enables you to lock or unlock sections, preventing administrators or developers with fewer permissions than a standard system administrator from editing configuration settings. The primary method to lock or unlock a section is by using location tags. The location tags can only be used to unlock a section at the level in which it was locked. Child-level configuration files can never unlock parent-level configuration files. The following section is not locked by default, but can be locked in the `applicationHost.config` file by using the `overrideMode` attribute:

```
<location path="Default Web Site" overrideMode= "Deny">
        <system.webServer>
                <httpLogging selectiveLogging="LogError" />
        </system.webServer>
</location>
```

The previous section set the default website to log only errors in the `applicationHost.config` file, while not allowing `web.config` files at sublevels to change the setting. It is also possible to set the configuration in lower-level files, such as website-level `web.config` files.

In IIS 8.0, locking and unlocking are done with the `overrideMode` attribute, which has the following values:

➤   `Allow` — Unlocks the specified section.

➤   `Deny` — Locks the specified section.

➤   `Inherit` — This is the default value if one isn't specified. The configuration system will determine the lockdown status based on the inheritance hierarchy of the parent files.

IIS 8.0 also supports the legacy attribute `allowOverride`. This is a carryover from the .NET Framework before `overrideMode`. It has the following values:

➤   `true` — Equivalent to `Allow`. Unlocks the specified section.

➤   `false` — Equivalent to `Deny`. Locks the specified section.

➤   [not set] — Equivalent to `Inherit`.

The newer `overrideMode` is the preferred method to establish locking and unlocking of sections. The two locking methods cannot be used in the same location tag. Doing so will cause a failure at run time caused by the illegal configuration.

It is possible when `overrideMode` is used at multiple levels for the same section to have conflicting settings, which can lead to unexpected results or errors. The best policy is to always lock and unlock sections in the `applicationHost.config` file.

You can find additional information about using `AppCmd.exe` to configure locking and unlocking in Chapter 18.

COMMAND-LINE MANAGEMENT

Command-line management in IIS 8.0 is done with the `AppCmd.exe` tool. Microsoft decided to name it `AppCmd.exe` rather than `IISCmd.exe` because, although we primarily use it for administering IIS 8.0, it is also used to manage the Windows Process Activation Service (WAS). This one tool consolidates complete control of the web server, providing a method to control the server with either the command prompt or through scripts. A few examples of what you can do include the following:

➤   Add, delete, and modify websites and application pools.

➤   Stop and start websites and application pools.

➤   View information about worker processes and requests.

➤   List and modify the configurations of IIS and ASP.NET.

For scriptable support, a PowerShell snap-in for IIS 8.0 is available. This provides all the benefits of PowerShell, including support for .NET objects, cmdlets, piping, and remote scripting. PowerShell provides the ability to automate IIS 8.0 in the same way that AppCmd.exe does.

A crash course in AppCmd.exe and PowerShell is beyond the scope of this chapter, and instead is covered in detail in Chapter 18.

> **NOTE** AppCmd.exe *is located in the* %systemroot%\system32\inetsrv *directory, which is available only to members of the administrators group. Additionally, if* applicationhost.config, machine.config, *or* web.config *will be modified, you will need to start the tool with elevated permissions. We recommend placing* AppCmd.exe *in the system path to make it more convenient to use. To place it in the path, open PowerShell using elevated permissions, and use* set-itemproperty *to permanently add the path to the system variables. Type* **Path** *first to determine what folders are currently in the path, and then append* **%systemroot%\system32\inetsrv** *to the current path string. Note that the registry entry is read on system startup, so a reboot would be required to have the change take effect.*

Website Administration

WHAT'S IN THIS CHAPTER?

- ➤ Creating and modifying a website
- ➤ Configuring logging
- ➤ Configuring and managing host headers
- ➤ Administering applications
- ➤ Administering virtual directories
- ➤ Configuring compression
- ➤ Configuring MIME settings
- ➤ Basic tasks to hit the ground running

The daily challenges that you face as a web server administrator are wide and varied — from managing website content or ensuring that the company's website is available for the crucial product release to figuring out why the developer's code that's just been deployed keeps crashing the website. To manage such demands successfully and still be able to sleep at night depends on how well the server is administered and your ability to troubleshoot issues effectively and concisely. To develop these skills, you first need to accustom yourself with the core functionality of IIS and the best practices for managing it.

This chapter discusses the basic administration tasks required to manage an IIS 8.0 web server. In addition to providing an overview of websites, applications, and virtual directories, we will demonstrate the use of the latest tools for managing IIS 8.0, including IIS Manager, AppCmd.exe, and PowerShell.

WEBSITES, APPLICATIONS, AND VIRTUAL DIRECTORIES

In IIS 8.0, websites, applications, and virtual directories form a hierarchy of individual objects in the IIS 8.0 schema. Sites are the root object and contain applications. Applications, in turn, contain virtual directories. Every site has at least one application, called the *root application* and it's signified by (/). Every application also has at least one virtual directory, the *root virtual directory*, also signified by (/), as shown in Figure 6-1. In IIS 8.0, application boundaries apply to both IIS and the technologies that extend IIS, such as ASP.NET.

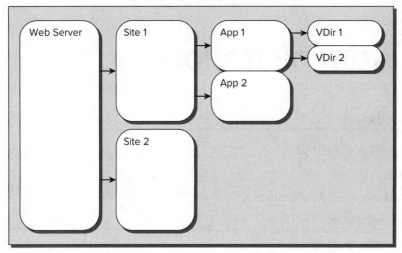

FIGURE 6-1

The relationship among websites, applications, and virtual directories can be one of the more confusing aspects of IIS for new administrators. Having a good understanding of these relationships will significantly ease your IIS administrative headaches.

Websites

A *website* is a collection of pages, images, video, or other digital content that is available via a common host name (e.g., `http://www.mySite.com`) or IP address (e.g., `http://10.10.10.1`). The most common protocols used to access a website are HTTP (Hypertext Transfer Protocol) and HTTPS (HTTP Secure), or its successor, TLS (Transport Layer Security).

Content commonly found within public websites includes HTML, ASPX (ASP.NET), PHP, JSP, Flash, JPG, and PNG formats. These pages can be simple static pages, they can work together to access back-end databases to deliver data through a web browser, or they can be a combination of the two. Websites that serve data from a database are generally called *web applications*. Websites have been around since 1991. The first website was by Tim Berners-Lee, a copy of which is located at `www.w3.org/History/19921103-hypertext/hypertext/WWW/TheProject.html`.

Websites are hosted on *web servers*. IIS 8.0 is Microsoft's latest web server and is a role that is available on Windows Server 2012 and Windows 8. Web servers take requests that are sent from web browsers (or other clients), route them to the responsible website hosted on the server, and then return the website's response back to the client. This chapter explains the process of administering a website on IIS 8.0.

As mentioned previously, sites are *root objects*. They are the containers for applications and virtual directories. Sites provide the unique bindings through which the applications are accessed. The bindings comprise two attributes: the binding protocol and the binding information. The binding protocol determines which protocol the server and the client use to exchange data — for example, HTTP or HTTPS. The binding information determines how the server is accessed by the client. The binding information consists of the IP address, the port number, and the host header (if used). Multiple binding protocols can be used for the same site — for example, if the site uses HTTP to serve standard content but needs HTTPS for the sign-on page.

Applications

An *application* in IIS 8.0 is a collection of files and folders that serves content or provides services over protocols such as HTTP or HTTPS. In IIS 8.0, every site has at least one application, the *root application*, but sites can have many applications, if needed.

Each application can be assigned to a unique *web application pool*. Each web application pool corresponds to at least one Windows w3wp.exe process. Thus, applications are a way of providing Windows resource utilization and security isolation.

Applications in IIS 7.0 support not only HTTP and HTTPS protocols, but other protocols as well. To support a protocol, a listener adapter must be specified in the <listenerAdapters> section in the configuration, and the protocol must be enabled in the <enabledProtocols> section of the configuration. As an example, the FTP protocol can be added to an application to create an FTP binding. For more information on creating an FTP binding, see Chapter 10, "Configuring Other Services."

Applications are discussed in more detail in Chapter 7, "Web Application Administration," and web application pools are discussed in Chapter 8, "Web Application Pool Administration."

Virtual Directories

A *virtual directory* is the directory, or path, that maps a logical directory (e.g., http://www.mysite.com/myPictures) to the physical location of the files on the local or remote server (e.g., c:\myPictures). Virtual directories can use local folders, UNC paths, mapped drives, and Distributed File System (DFS) shares. Like sites, applications always have at least one root virtual directory, although applications can have additional virtual directories as well. Virtual directories are useful for making files available to the application without adding them to the actual on-disk folder structure that houses the application files.

> **NOTE** *We use virtual directories to allow clients to upload images via FTP to their sites without having to give them access to the code base of their websites. The physical folder that they FTP into is isolated in a separate directory structure from their website files, and the virtual directory makes them available to the website. This allows us to maintain an application-level Service Level Agreement (SLA) while allowing the clients to update images on their website whenever they need to.*

Combining Sites, Applications, and Virtual Directories

Consider the sample website shown in Figure 6-2. Under the website root are several regular folders (`Directory1` and `Directory2`), as well an Application (`App1`) and a virtual directory (`vDirectory1`).

Based on the actual configuration of the web server, the sample website is configured as shown in the following table. (It is assumed that the site is accessible via the domain name `mysite.com`.)

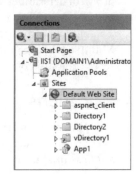

FIGURE 6-2

LOGICAL PATH	ACCESSED AT	PHYSICAL PATH	WEB APP POOL
/	mysite.com	c:\inetpub\wwwroot	Default App Pool
/Directory1	mysite.com/ Directory1	c:\inetpub\wwwroot\ Directory1	Default App Pool
/Directory2	mysite.com/ Directory2	c:\inetpub\wwwroot\ Directory2	Default App Pool
/vDirectory1	mysite.com/ vDirectory1	c:\vDir1	Default App Pool
/App1	mysite.com/App1	c:\App1	App1

Note that the use of a virtual directory (or an application, which must have its own root virtual directory) allows the addition of physical folders to the logical paths of the website. An application additionally allows a different web application pool to be used (separating the website into two separate `w3wp.exe` Windows processes).

The actual configuration of this website, as stored in the `applicationHost.config` file, is as follows:

```
<site name="Default Web Site" id="1">
    <application path="/">
        <virtualDirectory path="/" physicalPath="%SystemDrive%\inetpub\wwwroot" />
        <virtualDirectory path="/vDirectory1" physicalPath="c:\vDir1" />
    </application>
    <application path="/App1" applicationPool="App1">
```

```
            <virtualDirectory path="/" physicalPath="c:\App1" />
        </application>
        <bindings>
            <binding protocol="http" bindingInformation="*:80:mysite.com" />
        </bindings>
    </site>
```

CREATING A NEW WEBSITE

Creating a website is the most fundamental step in hosting your website. You should ensure that you follow good practices for the creation of the site to ensure consistency of the platform. You can create a website using IIS Manager, the command line, or via scripting. The following steps show how to create a basic site to serve contents using all these methods.

Creating a Website Using IIS Manager

IIS Manager presents the administrator with a GUI interface that allows the creation of a website by following these steps:

1. Start IIS Manager: Press WIN+R, enter **inetmgr** in the dialog, and click OK. Alternatively, click Tools on the top right of Server Manager and select Internet Information Server (IIS) Manager.

2. Select the server to administer, click the Sites icon, and then select Add Website from the Actions pane or by right-clicking the Sites icon. This will present the Add Website dialog, as shown in Figure 6-3.

3. Enter a website name that is easily recognized by those who will administer the server (for example, **WebSite1**). A good tip for creating website names when you are doing high-volume hosting is to use a numbering system, or use the domain name without the domain prefix. This can speed up manual administration because it enables you to find the site by typing the name in the website view list.

4. Select the application pool for your site. By default, IIS 8.0 will create a new application pool for your website. Alternatively, you can select one of the existing application pools by clicking the Select button. Normally, when creating a new website, depending on the applications context, choose to have IIS create a new application pool. Application pools are discussed below in this chapter and in more detail in Chapter 8.

5. Set the path to the website files. Note that a local or network UNC path can be accepted in the console — the path must be accessible by IIS Manager or else it will error. The "Connect as..." button allows for a distinct user account to be entered for UNC paths only. This allows content to be published from remote paths, enabling the administrator to specify the user account in the form of servername\username. In the case of high availability or distributed hosting, where the same content is published by several servers, a domain user with rights to read the directories is needed to access the content.

6. Enter the binding details. Note that the type can be set to HTTP or, if a certificate has been assigned to the site, to HTTPS. In this example, choose HTTP. Next, select the IP address to bind the site to. This will be the IP address that the website's domain name will resolve to.

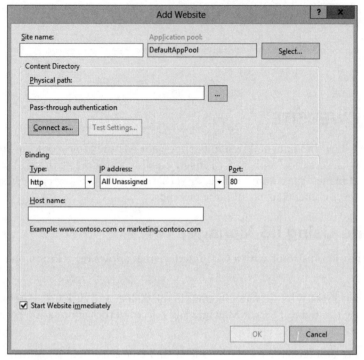

FIGURE 6-3

7. A host header entry is required if there will be multiple websites on the same IP address and a common TCP port (e.g., port 80). When first creating the site, enter your domain to get started, and add additional domains later, as required. There are some requirements when using host headers that are inherent to the HTTP v1.1 specification (which defined host headers). These requirements are discussed below in this chapter.

8. To start the site immediately, leave Start Web Site Immediately checked and click OK.

The site can now be browsed by its domain name, provided the DNS is correctly configured. Figure 6-4 shows WebSite1 in the Sites menu.

To start modifying the site configuration, simply click the site's name under the Sites list; IIS Manager will present the Features View, which gives you access to alter the website's configuration. The Content View shows the website files that are in the root directory of the site.

Creating a New Application Pool for Your Site

It is a good practice to create a new application pool for each site, especially when you are hosting more than one website on the same server. This will ensure that each web application runs inside its own process such that if an application causes a failure, it does not affect any other sites. Further information on application pools is available in Chapter 8. The Add Web Site tool in IIS Manager will automatically create a new application pool and map the site to it. If that option was not chosen when the site was created or if the site was imported through a different method, the web application pool can be created manually.

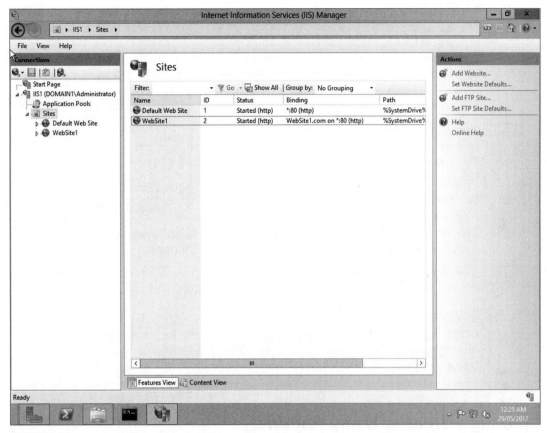

FIGURE 6-4

To create the new application pool, follow these steps:

1. Open IIS Manager, if it is not already open. (Press WIN+R, enter **inetmgr** in the dialog, and click OK.)

2. Select Application Pools under the server name from the Connections pane, and then select Add Application Pool from the Actions pane or right-click the Application Pools icon. This will present the Add Application Pools dialog. Figure 6-5 shows the Add Application Pool tool.

3. Set the name to something that is relevant — in this case, **WebSite1**. (It might seem redundant to add

FIGURE 6-5

AppPool to the end of the name; however, it does help for easing confusion with novice or other administrators.)

4. Select the .NET Framework version for the application pool to default to, and then select the Managed Pipeline Mode. The default pipeline mode is Integrated rather than the IIS 6.0–compatible Classic mode. For more information on the Managed Pipeline, see Chapter 8. By default, the application pool will be created to run with the Application PoolIdentity identity. This identity is a special on-demand Windows identity created by IIS8 when a worker process (w3wp.exe) needs to be started to host the application pool.

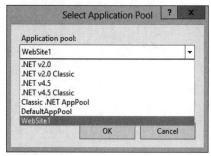

5. Now you can assign the new application pool to your website. To do this, select your website under the Server pane, then right-click or select Advanced Settings from the Actions pane.

6. The Advanced Settings window gives you access to configure other options, such as log locations and so forth. For this instance, select Application Pool and set it to WebSite1 (see Figure 6-6).

FIGURE 6-6

7. As soon as you click OK, the application is moved to the new application pool, which is then recycled. Be wary of this in a production environment, to avoid any unexpected results.

> **NOTE** *Application pools may need to be recycled from time to time to resolve hung applications or to reload a site if new files have been added that IIS is not seeing. For more information, see Chapter 8.*

Creating a Website Using AppCmd

AppCmd.exe is one of the most powerful command-line administration tools shipped with Windows Server 2012. It allows for a great amount of flexibility in the creation and configuration of websites, usually quicker and easier than using the GUI interface. The following example uses AppCmd to create a website with a similar configuration as was created using IIS Manager in the preceding section.

AppCmd.exe is found under %systemroot%\system32\inetsrv\appcmd.exe. Running the tool directly returns the options that are available. More information on this tool can be found in Chapter 18, "Programmatic Configuration and Management." It is important to remember that it must be run with elevated permissions; otherwise, AppCmd.exe will not make changes to the configuration.

To create an application pool using AppCmd.exe, use add with the apppool object. Here, a new application pool for WebSite2 is created:

```
appcmd.exe add apppool /name:WebSite2
```

Running this code returns:

```
APPPOOL object "WebSite2" added
```

Once the application pool is created, you can create the website. Add is used against the site object here to create a new website named www.website2.com. The line of code also details the bindings for the site, port 80, and the physical path to the files for the site, c:\inetpub\wwwroot\website2.

```
appcmd.exe add site /name:"www.website2.com" /bindings:http://www.website2.com:80
/physicalpath:"c:\inetpub\wwwroot\website2"
```

When the site is created, the following lines are returned:

```
SITE object "www.website2.com" added
APP object "www.website2.com/" added
VDIR object "www.website2.com/" added
```

AppCmd.exe is great for creating multiple sites quickly. The following example combines batch scripting with AppCmd.exe to bulk create websites:

```
for /l %1 IN (4,1,50) do mkdir c:\inetpub\wwwroot\website%1 |
c:\windows\system32\inetsrv\appcmd.exe add site /name:www.website%1.com
/id:%1 /bindings:http://www.website%1.com:80
/physicalpath:c:\inetpub\wwwroot\website%1
```

This code uses the for command to create 46 websites. The first site will be www.website4.com. The for command will then increment by 1 to create the next site until it has created www.website50.com, at which point it will stop. During the process, it creates not only the site, but also a folder to house the site's files.

One additional tip when using AppCmd.exe is to issue a /? after the site command to find out which configuration items can be modified on the site.

```
appcmd.exe set site "website1/" /?
```

Running AppCmd.exe with /? shows the following list of items that can be configured for the site. (For readability purposes, FTP site settings were removed from the listing.)

```
ERROR ( message:-name

-id
-serverAutoStart
-bindings.[protocol='string',bindingInformation='string'].protocol
-bindings.[protocol='string',bindingInformation='string'].bindingInformation
-bindings.[protocol='string',bindingInformation='string'].sslFlags
-limits.maxBandwidth
-limits.maxConnections
-limits.connectionTimeout
-limits.maxUrlSegments
-logFile.logExtFileFlags
-logFile.customLogPluginClsid
-logFile.logFormat
-logFile.directory
-logFile.period
-logFile.truncateSize
-logFile.localTimeRollover
-logFile.enabled
-logFile.logSiteId
-traceFailedRequestsLogging.enabled
-traceFailedRequestsLogging.directory
-traceFailedRequestsLogging.maxLogFiles
```

```
-traceFailedRequestsLogging.maxLogFileSizeKB
-traceFailedRequestsLogging.customActionsEnabled
-applicationDefaults.path
-applicationDefaults.applicationPool
-applicationDefaults.enabledProtocols
-applicationDefaults.serviceAutoStartEnabled
-applicationDefaults.serviceAutoStartProvider
-applicationDefaults.preloadEnabled
-virtualDirectoryDefaults.path
-virtualDirectoryDefaults.physicalPath
-virtualDirectoryDefaults.userName
-virtualDirectoryDefaults.password
-virtualDirectoryDefaults.logonMethod
-virtualDirectoryDefaults.allowSubDirConfig
-[path='string'].path
-[path='string'].applicationPool
-[path='string'].enabledProtocols
-[path='string'].serviceAutoStartEnabled
-[path='string'].serviceAutoStartProvider
-[path='string'].preloadEnabled
-[path='string'].virtualDirectoryDefaults.path
-[path='string'].virtualDirectoryDefaults.physicalPath
-[path='string'].virtualDirectoryDefaults.userName
-[path='string'].virtualDirectoryDefaults.password
-[path='string'].virtualDirectoryDefaults.logonMethod
-[path='string'].virtualDirectoryDefaults.allowSubDirConfig
-[path='string'].[path='string'].path
-[path='string'].[path='string'].physicalPath
-[path='string'].[path='string'].userName
-[path='string'].[path='string'].password
-[path='string'].[path='string'].logonMethod
-[path='string'].[path='string'].allowSubDirConfig
```

Creating a New Website Using Powershell

PowerShell is another, powerful, method of managing IIS. To create the same website as the previous examples, first import the webadministration module:

```
PS C:\> import-module webadministration
```

And then run the New-Item cmdlet:

```
PS C:\> New-Item iis:\sites\WebSite1 -bindings
@{protocol="http";bindingInformation=":80:www.website1.com"}
-physicalPath %systemdrive%\inetpub\wwwroot\website1
-applicationPool "DefaultAppPool"
```

For more information on the IIS PowerShell provider, see Chapter 18.

Changes to the applicationHost.config File

If you open the core IIS site configuration file %systemroot%\System32\inetsrv\config\applicationHost.config, you will see that all changes to application pools, websites, and virtual directories create entries in the IIS configuration.

All changes made so far happen under the element `<system.applicationHost>`.

The creation of the application pools is defined under the `<applicationPools>` tag:

```
<applicationPools>
    <add name="DefaultAppPool" />
    <add name="WebSite1" />
    <add name="WebSite2" />
    <applicationPoolDefaults managedRuntimeVersion="v4.0">
        <processModel identityType="ApplicationPoolIdentity" />
    </applicationPoolDefaults>           </applicationPools>
```

The configuration of the site itself is found under the `<sites>` tags:

```
<site name="WebSite1" id="2" serverAutoStart="true">
   <application path="/" applicationPool="WebSite1">
                <virtualDirectory path="/"
                    physicalPath="C:\inetpub\wwwroot\webSite1" />
   </application>
   <bindings>
      <binding protocol="http" bindingInformation="*:80:www.website1.com" />
   </binding>
</site>
<site name="WebSite2" id="3" serverAutoStart="true">
   <application path="/" applicationPool="WebSite2">
                <virtualDirectory path="/"
                    physicalPath="C:\inetpub\wwwroot\webSite2" />
   </application>
   <bindings>
      <binding protocol="http" bindingInformation="*:80:www.website2.com" />
    </bindings>
</site>
```

From these entries, you can see that it is very simple to create your own site by simply editing the `applicationHost.config` file. Note that this is not recommended as a best practice, because there is no configuration check on the direct editing of the file, and errors could result in an invalid IIS configuration, causing the server to fail. It is strongly recommended that if you are going to edit the file directly, make a backup copy or enable Volume Shadow Copies for the `%systemdrive%` volume.

However, it does allow for easy "copy and paste" from a working configuration to a new server.

CONFIGURING LOGGING

Windows Server 2012 ships with several modules that add a great deal of richness to the logging ability of IIS 8.0. The following table describes the default logging modules:

MODULE NAME	MODULE CODE	DESCRIPTION
HttpLoggingModule	`%windir%\System32\inetsrv\loghttp.dll`	Processes request statuses and passes these to `Http.sys`. This module is required for any conventional web server logs to be generated for processing.

continues

(continued)

MODULE NAME	MODULE CODE	DESCRIPTION
FailedRequestsTracingModule	`%windir%\System32\inetsrv\iisfreb.dll`	Logs failed requests as specified in the filter.
RequestMonitorModule	`%windir%\System32\inetsrv\iisreqs.dll`	Watches executing worker processes.
TracingModule	`%windir%\System32\inetsrv\iisetw.dll`	Dumps events for tracing with Event Tracing for Windows.
CustomLoggingModule	`%windir%\System32\inetsrv\logcust.dll`	Loads custom log modules, which can be used to generate custom-formatted logs. Microsoft's ODBC logging option is implemented as a custom log extension.

> **NOTE** *In this chapter, we look at logging from HTTP requests that are passed to the web server core for processing. Logging for diagnostics will only be touched on as to where logs are configured to be stored. Further details on analyzing these logs are in Chapter 23, "Diagnostics and Troubleshooting."*

IIS 7.0 first introduced the options of logging only failed requests, successful requests, or all requests that are processed. On a global configuration level for the server, logging can be configured on a per-site basis or centralized, with two types of centralized logging available: binary and W3C. First, we will discuss the types of standard logging available under IIS 8.0 and the situations in which they are best used.

Enabling Logging

Before you can enable logging, you need to install the Http Logging module in the server roles.

To install the Http Logging module, follow these steps:

1. Open Server Manager, if it is not already open. (Server Manager is pinned to the taskbar by default in Windows Server 2012.)

2. Select Local Server, and then scroll down to the Roles and Features section to verify whether HTTP Logging is installed. If not, choose Add Roles and Features from the Tasks dropdown.

3. Check the HTTP Logging box, click Next, and then click Install.

4. Click Close to finish the dialog, and then close the Server Manager.

Once HTTP Logging is enabled, `<log>` tags are automatically created for the central binary log file and the central W3C log file in the `applicationHost.config` file.

```
<log>
    <centralBinaryLogFile enabled="true"
        directory="%SystemDrive%\inetpub\logs\LogFiles" />
    <centralW3CLogFile enabled="true"
        directory="%SystemDrive%\inetpub\logs\LogFiles" />
</log
```

Here you can see that the `centralBinaryLogFile` and the `centralW3LogFiles` are both set to `enabled="true"`.

Note the `<siteDefaults>` tag, as it shows the log file format and the location of the log files. This tag shows the settings applied in the previous steps.

```
<siteDefaults>
    <logFile logFormat="W3C" directory="%SystemDrive%\inetpub\logs\LogFiles" />
    <traceFailedRequestsLogging
        directory="%SystemDrive%\inetpub\logs\FailedReqLogFiles" />
</siteDefaults>
```

> **NOTE** *It is good practice to place your website log files on a separate drive on your system to prevent the primary disk from being consumed.*

After you have enabled logging for your site, logs will be generated as per the request policy that has been set. The default is to generate per-site logs using the W3C log file standard; this log file type is compatible with most third-party log/web traffic analysis tools. The following is an example of the W3C logs generated for the Default Web Site:

```
#Software: Microsoft Internet Information Services 8.0
#Version: 1.0
#Date: 2012-06-10 10:35:12
#Fields: date time s-ip cs-method cs-uri-stem cs-uri-query s-port cs-username c-ip
    cs(User-Agent) cs(Referer) sc-status sc-substatus sc-win32-status time-taken
2012-06-10 10:35:12 ::1 GET / - 80 - ::1
    Mozilla/5.0+(compatible;+MSIE+10.0;+Windows+NT+6.2;+WOW64;+Trident/6.0)
    - 200 0 0 779
2012-06-10 10:35:12 ::1 GET /iis-8.png - 80 - ::1
    Mozilla/5.0+(compatible;+MSIE+10.0;+Windows+NT+6.2;+WOW64;+Trident/6.0)
    http://localhost/ 200 0 0 38
2012-06-10 10:35:12 ::1 GET /ws8-brand.png - 80 - ::1
    Mozilla/5.0+(compatible;+MSIE+10.0;+Windows+NT+6.2;+WOW64;+Trident/6.0)
    http://localhost/ 200 0 0 38
2012-06-10 10:35:12 ::1 GET /msweb-brand.png - 80 - ::1
    Mozilla/5.0+(compatible;+MSIE+10.0;+Windows+NT+6.2;+WOW64;+Trident/6.0)
    http://localhost/ 200 0 0 38
2012-06-10 10:35:12 ::1 GET /bkg-gry.jpg - 80 - ::1
    Mozilla/5.0+(compatible;+MSIE+10.0;+Windows+NT+6.2;+WOW64;+Trident/6.0)
    http://localhost/ 200 0 0 58
```

Failed Request Tracing Logs

Failed Request Tracing logs are used as a logging tool and a diagnostic utility. In this chapter, you will learn how to enable the trace logs and change the directory to which they are written. Chapter 23 goes into greater detail about the use of the trace logs.

Enabling Failed Request Tracing Logs Using IIS Manager

To enable the Failed Request Tracing logs at the website level using IIS Manager, perform the following steps:

1. Start IIS Manager. (Press WIN+R, enter **inetmgr** in the dialog, and click OK. Alternatively, click Tools on the top right of Server Manager and select Internet Information Server (IIS) Manager.)

2. In the Connections pane, click the website you want to enable Failed Request Tracing on.

3. In the Actions pane, click Failed Request Tracing.

4. In the dialog box, check the Enable box.

5. Select the location where the log files are to be written and the maximum number of trace files.

6. Click OK to close the dialog.

7. Close IIS Manager.

You have now enabled Failed Request Tracing on a website. Refer to Chapter 23 for more information about configuring the logging.

Enabling Failed Request Tracing Logs Using AppCmd

Enabling the Failed Request Tracing logs via the command line is done by using `AppCmd.exe`. There are two properties that need to be set: The `enabled` element needs to be set to `true`, and the `directory` needs to be set to the location you want the logs to be written to.

```
appcmd.exe set site www.WebSite1.com
    /tracefailedrequestslogging.enabled:true
    /tracefailedrequestslogging.directory:c:\logs\failedrequests
```

With the previous command, you have enabled trace logging on `www.website1.com`. There is another command, with its own benefits and shortcomings, that you can use to enable the failed trace logging. It does provide more options for configuring the trace logging; however, it does not provide a method to change the logging directory. The command is

```
appcmd.exe configure trace "www.website1.com" /enablesite
```

This command has more options, which are covered in Chapter 23.

W3C Logging

World Wide Web Consortium (W3C) logging writes log entries using a text-based, customizable ASCII format and is the default log format configured under IIS.

W3C logging is enabled initially on a per-site basis with a default location of `%systemdrive%\inetpub\logs\logfiles\W3SVC1`. The number after `W3SVC` designates the site ID of the website.

Logging can be set to log one file per site or one file for the entire server. This example keeps the log file set to log at the site level.

1. Open IIS Manager and navigate to the server, site, or application you want to configure logging for. Under the Features View, the Logging feature will be available if the module has been installed on the site/server/application.

2. Double-click Logging or select Logging and click Open Feature under the Actions pane, opening the Logging pane. This allows the administrator to enable the logging features.

3. As with previous versions of IIS, you have the option to select the format of your logging or define your own custom log handler. This is only available when configured for logging on a per-site basis, and you have the choice of the following:

   ➤ **IIS**—This is a fixed ASCII text-based format and thus is not customizable for what can be logged.

   ➤ **W3C**—The World Wide Web Consortium log format is discussed in more detail below in this chapter. This is the most widely used log format on web servers today.

   ➤ **NCSA**—NCSA (National Center for Supercomputing Applications) generally is the default log format for Apache and other web servers. This is similar to the IIS format because it is fixed ASCII text that is non-customizable.

4. After determining the log format, select the fields for IIS to record. This example will use the W3C format with the default fields selected. Figure 6-7 shows the W3C Logging Fields dialog box.

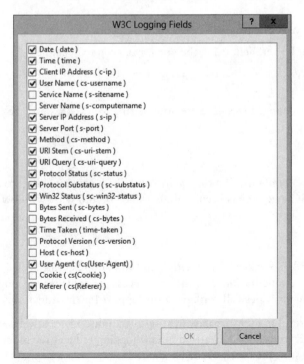

FIGURE 6-7

5. The default location specified for logging is `%systemdrive%\inetpub\logs\LogFiles\w3svc<siteID>`, with the `siteID` value updating to the site ID for each site. Again, for this example, keep the default location for the logs.

6. Encoding can be set to either UTF-8 or ANSI. Use UTF-8 for this example.

7. The log file rollover can be set to create a new log file on a scheduled basis, when the file reaches a set size, or to not create a new log file at all. If the scheduled basis is selected, the time periods are hourly, daily, weekly, or monthly. Additionally, you can set the files to use local time for naming and rollover rather than GMT time. Note that all times logged within the log file use GMT times. Set the log file to roll over on a daily schedule, and use local time for naming and rollover.

8. Click Apply in the Actions pane.

You can enable the HTTP Logging module at the web server, site, or application level. This allows maximum granularity in logging control.

Enabling W3C Logs Using AppCmd

Enabling W3C logging via the command line is done in a similar manner as enabling the failed trace logging. Use `AppCmd.exe` to set the `enabled` property to `true`, and then set the log file location to the desired logging folder. The one additional property is to set the format for the log to use. The available formats are IIS, NCSA, W3C, and custom.

```
appcmd.exe set site WebSite2 /logfile.enabled:true
    /logfile.directory:c:\logs\Website2 /logfile.logformat:W3C
```

Enabling W3C Logs Using PowerShell

Logging can also be managed using PowerShell, using the `Set-ItemProperty` cmdlet:

```
PS C:\> Set-ItemProperty "IIS:\Sites\Website2" -name "logFile.directory" –value
"d:\logfiles\Website2"
```

In this case, the logging directory is changed from the previous setting (`c:\logs\WebSite2`) to a non-system drive (`d:\`).

Centralized Logging

Centralized logging is a global server configuration that writes all HTTP-generated logs to a single log file. Centralized binary and W3C logging has been available since IIS 6.0 with Windows 2003 Service Pack 1.

Centralized Binary Logging

Centralized binary logging was available under IIS 6.0 with Windows 2003 Service Pack 1. However, there was no interface for configuration, and the only access available was through modification of the metabase. IIS 8.0 now provides full configuration support for this function.

This type of logging is extremely useful in high-capacity hosting situations, where a web server may be configured with several thousand websites. Centralized binary logging reduces the requirement on system resources and with no cost to the detail of the log data.

Effectively, when logging takes place in centralized binary logging, raw data are written to the log file for all the websites on the server. Note that the data is in a raw format and thus cannot be read as would W3C logs. A tool is required to interpret these logs. A good tool for analyzing these logs is LogParser (available from Microsoft Downloads); otherwise, a custom tool can be developed.

The following is an example `LogParser` command to query the binary logs for the URI requested order by most requested:

```
LogParser -i:BIN
    "SELECT cs-uri-stem, COUNT(*) AS Total, MAX(time-taken) AS MaxTime,
    AVG(time-taken) AS AvgTime, AVG(sc-bytes) AS AvgBytesSent
    FROM ex*.log GROUP BY cs-uri-stem ORDER BY Total DESC"
```

Enabling Centralized Binary Logging Using IIS Manager

All requests for all sites on a web server are written to a single central log file. This logging format is also available for FTP sites. By default, the log file directory is `%systemdrive%\inetpub\logs\logfiles`. To enable binary centralized logging on the server, follow these steps:

1. Select the server homepage in IIS Manager, and then double-click the Logging icon.

2. On the Logging page, the top dropdown allows a choice between one log file per site (default) and one log file per server. Change this to "per server."

3. In the Log File format dropdown, select Binary.

4. On the directory selection, type the path to a log file directory in the Directory textbox, or click the Browse button to select a directory.

5. For Log File Rollover, select a method that IIS 8.0 uses to create a new log file. If you select MaxSize, type a maximum log file size, in bytes, in the Maximum File Size textbox. Check Use Local Time to use the system's local time zone rather than Greenwich Mean Time (GMT).

6. Click Apply in the Actions pane.

Enabling Centralized Binary Logging Using AppCmd

The following command configures centralized binary logging to be enabled on the server, with daily rotation and writing the log files to `c:\logs\inetpub\logs\LogFiles`:

```
appcmd.exe set config /section:system.applicationHost/log /centrallogfilemode:
CentralBinary /centralbinarylogfile.enabled:true
/centralbinarylogfile.directory:c:\logs\inetpub\logs\logfiles
/centralbinarylogfile.period:Daily
```

Centralized W3C Logging

Enabling centralized logging to use the W3C format has many of the same advantages as centralized logging using the binary format, the primary difference being that the logs are human-readable as they are written. Because the log files are in a readable format, the files are larger than binary files.

Enabling Centralized W3C Logging Using IIS Manager

Setting W3C centralized logging in IIS Manager is done using the same steps as centralized binary logging, except that the log file format should be W3C rather than binary.

1. Select the server homepage in IIS Manager. Double-click the Logging icon.

2. On the Logging page, the top dropdown allows a choice between one log file per site (default) and one log file per server. Change this to "per server."

3. In the Log File format dropdown, select W3C.

4. In the Select Fields list, expand the list categories to select the information to be logged, and click OK. This can be changed at a later date by simply editing the website properties under logging.

5. On the directory selection, type the path to a log file directory in the Directory textbox, or click the Browse button to select a directory.

6. For Log File Rollover, select a method that IIS 8.0 uses to create a new log file. If you select MaxSize, type a maximum log file size, in bytes, in the Maximum File Size textbox. Check Use Local Time to use the system's local time zone rather than Greenwich Mean Time (GMT).

7. Click Apply in the Actions pane.

Enabling Centralized W3C Logging Using AppCmd

The following command is very similar to enabling centralized binary logging. This will enable centralized logging on the server, with daily rotation and writing the log files to `c:\logs\inetpub\logs\logfiles`.

```
appcmd.exe set config /section:system.applicationHost/log /centrallogfilemode:
CentralW3C /centralw3clogfile.enabled:true
/centralw3clogfile.directory:c:\logs\inetpub\logs\logfiles
/centralw3clogfile.period:Daily
```

CONFIGURING HOST HEADERS

Host headers enable you to publish multiple domain names or websites to a single IP address. This allows a web administrator to run several sites on a single IP. It also allows a single website to have multiple names resolve for it, such as `website1.com` and `www.website1.com`.

Host headers are an optional configuration item on site bindings. Bindings are used to configure `Http.sys` to listen on ports and IP addresses. The properties of a binding are the following:

➤ Type — HTTP/HTTPS — HTTPS to enable Secure Sockets Layer (SSL)

➤ IP address

➤ Port

➤ Host header

Each website running on the server must have a unique binding — a unique combination of IP address + TCP port + host header value. By ensuring that each website has a unique binding, incoming requests can be routed to the uniquely identified website, based on the properties of the request.

When a client sends a HTTP request to IIS, it sends an HTTP Host header, indicating the website that it wishes to access. This HTTP Host header, along with the TCP port (by default, port 80 or port 443), plus IP address, is first decoded by the server, allowing the requested location to be extracted from the request and checked against the IIS server's metabase for matching binding entries. In the following example HTTP request, a GET request for the file default.htm was made to a site called www.Website1.com (two CRLFs [carriage return plus line feed] signify the end of the HTTP request):

```
GET /default.htm HTTP/1.1
Host: www.Website1.com
Accept: */*
User-Agent: Mozilla/4.0+(compatible;+MSIE+7.0;+Windows+NT+6.0)
```

If a matching entry is found, the request is forwarded to the website. If there is no host header matching the entry, IIS then looks for a website configured with a matching IP address and port that has a blank host header entry. If there are no matching websites with blank host header entries, the request is then discarded and a HTTP error 400, "Bad Request," is returned to the client. IIS matches requests from the most specific match through to a more general match; bindings that specifically match the IP address + TCP port + host header entry will be matched ahead of bindings that have a blank host header, or specify *All Unassigned* IP addresses.

Consider an IIS 8.0 server configured with two IP addresses, 10.0.0.2 and 10.0.0.3, and websites with the bindings configured as shown in the following table:

SITE ID	IP ADDRESS	TCP PORT	HOST HEADER
1	10.0.0.2	80	Website1.com, www.Website1.com
2	10.0.0.2 10.0.0.3	80	extranet.WebSite1.com
3	10.0.0.2	80	<blank>
4	10.0.0.3	80	intranet.WebSite1.com

Based on these settings, the following behavior would result (assuming that all requests are on port 80):

➤ A request for www.WebSite1.com or Website.com on 10.0.0.2 would be answered by Site 1. Note that this request would be rejected if received on 10.0.0.3.

➤ A request for extranet.WebSite1.com on any of the server's IP addresses (10.0.0.2 or 10.0.0.3) would be answered by Site 2.

➤ A request for any other host (other than www.Website1.com, Website1.com, or extranet.WebSite1.com) on 10.0.0.2 would be answered by Site 3.

➤ A request for intranet.website1.com on 10.0.0.3 would be answered by Site 4. Note that if this request were received on 10.0.0.2, it would be answered by Site 3 instead.

Adding and Removing Host Headers Using IIS Manager

If a website is not given a host header when it is initially set up, you might need to add a host header at a later date. We'll describe the process to add (and remove) a host header via IIS Manager here.

To add a host header, follow these instructions:

1. Open IIS Manager, if it is not already open.

2. Right-click the site, or click the site and from the Actions pane select Bindings under Edit Site. The Site Bindings dialog will appear.

3. Select Add for a new binding, or click an existing binding and click Edit to change the configuration of an existing binding. Figure 6-8 shows the Add Site Binding dialog box.

4. Set the Type to either HTTP or HTTPS, enter the IP address or select it from a list, and then set the port for the website to listen on.

5. Enter the domain name for the host header, and then select OK.

6. Click Close on the Site Bindings dialog box.

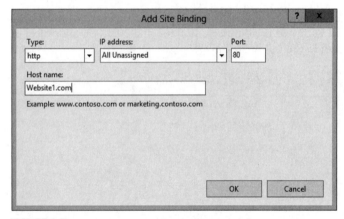

FIGURE 6-8

This will bind the domain to the site. Note that if the host header is already bound to another site, this will be detected and you will be given the option to still assign it to the site. If a binding is duplicated across sites, only one site will be able to start.

Removing a host header follows the same initial steps:

1. Open IIS Manager, if it is not already open.

2. Right-click the site, or click the site and from the Actions pane select Bindings under Edit Site. The Site Bindings dialog will appear.

3. Click the binding that you want to delete, and then click Remove. Click Yes in the verification dialog box.

4. Click Close on the Site Bindings dialog.

Setting Host Headers Using AppCmd

When setting the binding parameter to add the host header, list the bindings in "protocol: domain name: port" format. When adding multiple host headers, use one command and separate the bindings by a comma. Removing bindings with AppCmd.exe is done in a similar fashion. If there are two bindings and you want to remove one, run the add command with only the binding that you want to keep. This will clear all bindings and then re-add the one you want to keep. To remove all bindings, you will need to use the subtraction (–) modifier on the bindings property.

The syntax to add a host header is as follows:

```
appcmd.exe set site < "site name"> /bindings:"<http/https>:<domain name>:<port>"
```

For example, to add the host header for http://website1.com, run the following:

```
appcmd.exe set site "website1" /bindings:"http://website1.com:80"
```

To add multiple host headers, use a comma to separate them in the bindings section:

```
appcmd.exe set site "website1" /bindings:"http://website1.com:80,
http://www.website1.com:80"
```

To remove all the bindings, use the following syntax:

```
appcmd.exe set site "website1" /-bindings
```

To remove only one of the two bindings you set earlier, use

```
appcmd.exe set site "website1" /bindings:http://website1.com:80
```

This results in the website having only the website1.com host header bound to port 80, and the www.website1.com host header has been removed.

If you want to implement Secure Sockets Layer (SSL) on your site, you need to add a binding for the HTTPS protocol and the TCP port (443 being standard). The following command sets the website to listen for all requests to the server over HTTPS.

```
appcmd.exe set site "website1" /bindings:https://website1.com:443
```

Note that a server certificate still needs to be selected for use with the site.

Setting Host Headers Using PowerShell

PowerShell can also be used to set, remove, and edit website binding information, and provides the ability to do this in several ways.

There are dedicated IIS PowerShell cmdlets for manipulating binding information, and these provide the simplest syntax. For example, to add an additional binding to the Website2 that was created earlier in the chapter, first load the WebAdministration module (if not already loaded) and then run:

```
PS C:\> import-module webadministration
PS C:\> New-WebBinding -Name Website2 -IP "*" -Port 80 -Protocol http
-HostHeader "extranet.website2.com"
```

The same can be achieved using the New-ItemProperty cmdlet that was used earlier, but the syntax is somewhat more verbose:

```
PS C:\> New-ItemProperty IIS:\Sites\WebSite2 -name bindings -value
@{protocol="http";bindingInformation="*:80:extranet.website2.com"}
```

To add multiple bindings concurrently, use:

```
PS C:\> New-ItemProperty IIS:\Sites\WebSite2 -name bindings -value
@{protocol="http";bindingInformation="*:80:extranet.website2.com"},
@{protocol="http";bindingInformation="*:80:intranet.website2.com"}
```

To remove a binding, use:

```
PS C:\> Remove-WebBinding -Protocol "http" -Port 80 -IPAddress "*"
-HostHeader "extranet.website2.com"
```

Finally, to clear the bindings completely, run the following command:

```
PS C:\> Clear-ItemProperty 'iis:\sites\WebSite2' -name bindings
```

SSL and Host Headers

Until the updates in Windows 2003 Service Pack 1, it was not possible to use host headers in conjunction with Secure Sockets Layer (SSL) on your website. This was mainly because of complications with the protocol and limitations to the Common Name (CN) properties on certificates applied to a site. Effectively, the CN on the certificate (i.e., www.website1.com) needs to match the name request by the browser client. If these values did not match, an error would be thrown stating that the certificate was not valid for the domain and could not be trusted. Once Service Pack 1 had been applied to an IIS 6.0 server, and also with IIS 7.0, it was possible to use host headers with wildcard SSL certificates. For this to work, a wildcard certificate must be available on the server (i.e., *.website1.com), and the host header must match the wildcard location (e.g., www.website1.com or marketing.website1.com). It was also possible to use certificates that had populated the SAN (Subject Alternate Name) field with additional host names.

With IIS 8.0, SNI (Server Name Indication) is now also supported, in conjunction with browsers that support this functionality. This extension to the SSL/TLS protocols allows a client to indicate which host it is connecting to as part of the SSL/TLS handshake, and for the server to present the correct certificate.

Creating SSL host headers is done using the same method as with standard HTTP Host headers. You can find additional information about configuring SSL in Chapter 15, "SSL and TLS."

ADMINISTERING APPLICATIONS

In this section, we'll discuss adding and removing applications with IIS Manager and via the command line.

Adding Applications Using IIS Manager

To add an application with IIS Manager, follow these steps:

1. Select the website to create the application for and right-click "Add Application," or select "View Applications" from the Actions pane (see Figure 6-9).

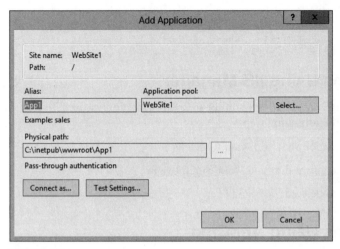

FIGURE 6-9

2. Enter the alias for the application; this will be the path off the website root. Select the application pool for the application to reside in.

3. Note that if the application is not required to be in the same application pool as the parent website, it should be placed into a separate application pool to ensure that any application failures do not affect the site.

4. Enter the physical path of the application, and then select OK.

5. Refresh the Web Sites list, and *alias* will be listed under the site. By selecting the alias, full configuration of the application as a separate application is now possible; thus, everything that can be configured on the parent site can be configured in the application.

6. Select Advanced Settings from the Actions pane. This allows further configuration of the application, with the option to

   ➤ Set path credentials (that is, select a particular user for the application to run under).

   ➤ Set the credential logon type (Interactive/Batch/Network/Clear Text).

   ➤ Change the application pool.

For more information on configuring application pools, see Chapter 8.

Adding Applications Using AppCmd

To create an application under the www.website1.com website with the application name *App1* that maps to App1 to a location outside of the website1 physical path, you need to define the path and location for the application:

```
appcmd.exe add app /site.name:website1 /path:/App1
/physicalPath:c:\wwwroot\App1 /applicationpool:Site1AppPool
```

This returns the following:

```
APP object "www.website1.com/App1" added
VDIR object "www.website1.com/App1/" added
```

Deleting Applications Using IIS Manager

In most cases, deleting an application is very similar to creating an application. To delete an application with IIS Manager, use the following steps:

1. Right-click the application that you want to delete.

2. Select Remove, and confirm that you want to remove it.

The application has now been deleted.

Deleting Applications Using AppCmd

AppCmd.exe can also be used to delete an application. In conjunction with the app object, use the delete command, and specify the application that needs to be removed:

```
appcmd.exe delete app /app.name:<name of app>
```

Replace name of app with the name of the application. In this example, you are deleting the app1/ application:

```
appcmd.exe delete app /app.name:website1/app1
```

ADMINISTERING VIRTUAL DIRECTORIES

Virtual directories are managed using the same tools as sites and applications. IIS Manager, AppCmd.exe, and PowerShell all provide full administration of virtual directories in IIS 8.0.

Creating Virtual Directories Using IIS Manager

To create a virtual directory for a website using IIS Manager, perform the following steps:

1. Open IIS Manager and right-click on the website under which you want to create the virtual directory.

2. Select Add Virtual Directory.

3. In the Add Virtual Directory dialog box, type the alias to be used (see Figure 6-10). This will be the URL from which content is to be accessed.

4. Select the physical location of the directory. The physical path is the location of the content that is to be accessed. This can be a local location or a UNC path to the files. UNC locations can be accessed by specifying remote credentials or by using pass-through authentication of the user accessing the site.

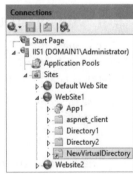

Site name: WebSite1
Path: /

Alias:
NewVirtualDirectory
Example: images

Physical path:
C:\vDir1

Pass-through authentication

Connect as...   Test Settings...

OK   Cancel

FIGURE 6-10

> **NOTE** *When creating a virtual directory to another location on your server or remotely, ensure that the accounts of the site anonymous user (IUSR) and the worker process identity have the required permissions to read and execute as required. This is discussed in greater detail in Chapter 14, "Authentication and Authorization."*

5. Click OK. The virtual directory will be created on the site. By expanding the site under IIS Manager, you can see the virtual directory indicated with a shortcut symbol. Figure 6-11 shows the virtual directory for WebSite1.

Examining the `applicationHost.config` file under the site config, you will see that there is now an additional line for virtual directory `VDir1`:

```
<site name="WebSite1" id="2">
    <application path="/" applicationPool="WebSite1">
        <virtualDirectory path="/"
physicalPath="%SystemDrive%\inetpub\wwwroot" />
        <virtualDirectory path="/NewVirtualDirectory"
physicalPath="C:\vDir1" />
    </application>
    <bindings>
        <binding protocol="http" bindingInformation="*:80:WebSite1.com" />
    </bindings>
</site>
```

Connections

Start Page
IIS1 (DOMAIN1\Administrator)
    Application Pools
    Sites
        Default Web Site
        WebSite1
            App1
            aspnet_client
            Directory1
            Directory2
            NewVirtualDirectory
        Website2

FIGURE 6-11

Creating Virtual Directories Using AppCmd

Again, command-line implementation is made simple with the use of `AppCmd.exe`. To create a virtual directory in the root of the website, use the `vdir` object and the `add` command:

```
appcmd.exe add vdir /app.name:<website name>/
/path:<virtual directory name> /physicalPath:<location of content>
```

The `app.name` parameter in the command corresponds to the website name and the path to which it will refer; thus, leaving just a trailing slash after the website name creates the virtual directory in the root of the site. To create the virtual directory in a place other than the root, the directory name needs to be specified after the root (for example, `/app.name:www.website1.com/vdir1` to create the virtual directory under the `vdir1` folder).

`path` refers to the alias of the site name — in the example, this is `/vdir1` — and `physicalPath` is the location of the contents that is to be served from the filesystem.

To create a virtual directory named *vdir1* under the WebSite1 website, issue the following:

```
appcmd.exe add vdir /app.name:www.website1.com/
/path:/NewVirtualDirectory /physicalPath:c:\vDir1
```

Adding Virtual Directories Using PowerShell

You can easily add virtual directories using PowerShell. To replicate the same `AppCmd.exe` command shown previously, run the following in PowerShell:

```
PS C:\> New-Item 'IIS:\Sites\WebSite1\NewVirtualDirectory' -type VirtualDirectory
-physicalPath c:\vDir1
```

Removing Virtual Directories

Removing virtual directories is almost the same action as adding a virtual directory and can be performed under IIS Manager by right-clicking the virtual directory and clicking Remove, or under the Actions pane by selecting Remove.

To use the command line to delete a virtual directory from the root of the website, run the following command:

```
appcmd.exe delete vdir /vdir.name:www.website1.com/NewVirtualDirectory
```

To delete a virtual directory from an application under the Site1 website, run the following command:

```
appcmd.exe delete vdir /vdir.name:www.website1.com/App1/NewVirtualDirectory
```

Likewise, to remove the same virtual directory using PowerShell, using the `Remove-Item` cmdlet, run the following command:

```
PS C:\> Remove-Item 'IIS:\Sites\Website1\NewVirtualDirectory'
```

AUTHENTICATION

Authentication is the mechanism that allows determining the identity of who is making requests to your web application. Authentication is often combined with *authorization*, which is the process of determining whether access is granted or denied to the authenticated user. Generally, authentication requests require the entering of a username/password combination or other information, such as an access token.

Upon installation, IIS 8.0 allows you to determine which authentication methods will be installed on the server. The authentication options that can be installed are Basic, Windows Integrated, Digest, Client Certificate Mapping, and IIS Client Certificate Mapping. Again, all these options are installed by modules and handlers, allowing you to select which modules are used by the application. If no authentication will be needed on the server, the default Anonymous authentication is always loaded and allows the site to be used without clients having to sign on to the site.

> **NOTE** *Chapter 14 goes into greater detail about authentication methods and setup.*

CONFIGURING COMPRESSION

Prior to IIS 7.0, compression seemed to be more of an afterthought than an integral part of the server. Now compression is easily managed through the main IIS management tools. Compression can provide significant bandwidth savings while delivering content, as well as faster response times for clients (with a possible trade-off of increased memory or CPU usage on the server to compress content), and is thus an important scalability technique.

By default, the Static Compression module is installed when IIS 8.0 is installed. The Dynamic Compression module can be installed during setup or at any point afterward. IIS 8.0 also allows compression to be set at all levels, from server down to virtual directory. The server level allows the most configuration options; all other levels allow only the ability to enable or disable compression.

Enabling both static and dynamic compression is highly recommended. One item to keep in mind is that compression causes the server to work harder and use more processing power. If you choose to enable dynamic compression, you should monitor your server performance to ensure that it is responding within the performance window that your organization has set.

Configuring Compression with IIS Manager

In IIS 6.0, it wasn't possible to configure compression through IIS Manager. With IIS 8.0, however, you can enable compression simply by checking boxes in the Compression section of IIS Manager.

Compression settings can be configured at many levels (Server, Site, Directory). The following example examines server-level compression, because this provides the greatest number of options:

1. Open IIS Manager.

2. Select the server whose settings are to be changed. In the IIS area, double-click the Compression icon. As shown in Figure 6-12, there are two options: to enable dynamic compression and to enable static compression. In addition to the two selections, there are options to configure how static compression is configured.

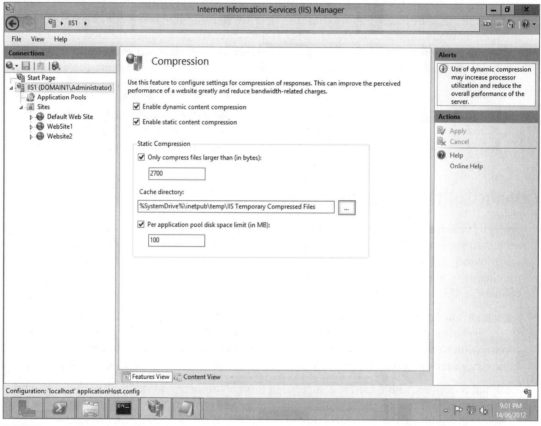

FIGURE 6-12

3. Check the Enable Dynamic Content Compression box. The Enable Static Content Compression box should be checked by default.

4. Optionally, adjust the size of the files that static compression will compress. By unchecking the "Only Compress Files Larger Than (In Bytes)…" checkbox, all files will be compressed. Otherwise, the minimum size of file that IIS will compress can be set; as files get smaller, the benefits in terms of bandwidth saved decrease. As such, compressing very small files may yield marginal benefit. Here you can also set the cache directory and the disk space limit per application pool.

5. Click Apply in the Actions pane to complete the configuration change.

Configuring Compression with AppCmd.exe

To configure compression with `AppCmd.exe`, you will need to work with two separate sections of the configuration: `system.webServer/urlCompression` and `system.webServer/httpCompression`. The `urlCompression` section is where you will enable or disable compression, and the `httpCompression` section gives access to many adjustable properties that are not seen in IIS Manager.

Although static compression is enabled by default, you might need to enable it at some point. Enabling static compression is done with this command:

```
appcmd.exe set config /section:system.webServer/urlCompression -doStaticCompression:true
```

Enabling dynamic compression is done with this command:

```
appcmd.exe set config /section:system.webServer/urlCompression
-doDynamicCompression:true
```

In addition to enabling and disabling compression, `AppCmd.exe` exposes the following additional properties for configuration through `system.webServer/httpCompression`:

```
-sendCacheHeaders
-expiresHeader
-cacheControlHeader
-directory
-doDiskSpaceLimiting
-maxDiskSpaceUsage
-minFileSizeForComp
-noCompressionForHttp10
-noCompressionForProxies
-noCompressionForRange
-staticCompressionDisableCpuUsage
-staticCompressionEnableCpuUsage
-dynamicCompressionDisableCpuUsage
-dynamicCompressionEnableCpuUsage
-staticTypes.[mimeType='string'].mimeType
-staticTypes.[mimeType='string'].enabled
-dynamicTypes.[mimeType='string'].mimeType
-dynamicTypes.[mimeType='string'].enabled
-[name='string'].name
-[name='string'].doStaticCompression
-[name='string'].doDynamicCompression
-[name='string'].dll
-[name='string'].staticCompressionLevel
-[name='string'].dynamicCompressionLevel
```

`system.webServer/httpCompression` is where the cache directory is set. In the following example, the directory is set to the `%systemdrive%\temp\compression` folder (`systemdrive` is usually `c:\`):

```
appcmd.exe set config /section:system.webServer/httpCompression
-directory:%systemdrive%\Temp\Compression
```

CONFIGURING DEFAULT DOCUMENT SETTINGS

IIS uses default documents to determine which file to serve when a site (/) or directory (/folder/) is requested and no explicit filename is specified. The following default documents are set up automatically by IIS 8.0:

➤ `Default.htm`

➤ `Default.asp`

➤ `Index.htm`

➤ `Index.html`

➤ `Iisstart.htm`

➤ `Default.aspx`

IIS serves the files in order from the top down. If both a `default.aspx` and a `default.htm` exist within a directory, the Default Document setting will need to be adjusted to place `default.aspx` higher in the order if that is the file that should be served automatically when the website is accessed.

Reordering a Document

Default Document settings can be adjusted at the server, website, or individual folder level. If the desired document is not at the top of the default list, it can be moved. To do so, open the Default Document setting for the server, site, or folder to be edited, select the desired document, and then click Move Up in the Actions pane until the document is at the top of the list.

Adding a Default Document

There may be times when an additional filename will need to be added that is not in the prepopulated list. To add a new document to the Default Document settings, follow these steps:

1. Open IIS Manager, and select the server, site or directory where the new default document should be added.

2. Double-click the Default Document icon to navigate to the Default Document page.

3. Click Add in the Actions pane. The Add Default Document dialog box will pop up.

4. Type the name of the document you want to add. In this instance, type **testdoc.htm**.

5. Click OK. The `testdoc.htm` page is now at the top of the document order.

6. Close IIS Manager.

CONFIGURING MIME SETTINGS

MIME (Multipurpose Internet Mail Extensions) is an Internet standard that defines the content types delivered by IIS 8.0. Although originating with e-mail, MIME has carried over to be used by other communication protocols, including HTTP. HTTP uses MIME to establish which type of content is being requested by a browser. A browser requests not only content from a web server, but also information that specifies what the content type is. This information is returned from the server as a Content-Type field in the HTTP header. When the browser gets the Content-Type field, it can then determine how to handle the following content: Some content types (e.g., HTML pages or GIF/JPG/PNG images) are handled by the browser natively, whereas other content types, such as DOCX or PDF types, may need to be handed to a helper application. In the event that there is no config-ured helper application, users are usually prompted as to what they want to do with the unknown content.

In IIS 8.0, there is a master list of MIME types that are understood by the server. You can modify this list by adding, editing, or removing MIME types. In the case of IIS, MIME types are differenti-ated by file extension. If a file is requested that doesn't have a corresponding MIME type defined, a 404.3 error is returned to the browser. Additionally, a wildcard (*, application/octet-stream) MIME type can be added that will allow any file to be served, although this results in increasing the attack surface of the server and is not recommended.

Although there is a master list of MIME types in IIS 8.0, additional MIME types can also be set at the server, site, application, virtual directory, and file levels.

Adding MIME Types

Adding MIME types will be your most common activity when managing MIME types. This section covers the methods to add a MIME type in IIS 8.0.

Adding MIME Types Using IIS Manager

Perform the following steps to add MIME types with IIS Manager:

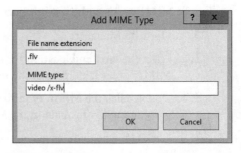

FIGURE 6-13

1. Open IIS Manager.

2. Select the level and location for the MIME type, and then double-click the MIME Types icon.

3. Click Add in the Actions pane. The Add MIME Type dialog box appears, as shown in Figure 6-13.

4. Add the file extension and MIME type, and then click OK. This example adds the `.flv` extension to allow IIS 8.0 to serve Flash videos.

Adding MIME Types Using AppCmd

AppCmd can also be used to add MIME types. AppCmd uses the `config` object with the `set` command to modify the `staticContent` section, adding the file extension and mime type to `applicationHost.config`. The key to adding the MIME type is using the `/+` in the command.

```
appcmd.exe set config /section:staticContent
/+"[fileExtension='<mime extention>',mimeType='<mime type>']"
```

For example, to add the file extension `.flv` and the MIME type `video/x-flv`, run the following command:

```
appcmd.exe set config /section:staticContent
/+"[fileExtension='.flv',mimeType='video/x-flv']"
```

Adding MIME Types Using PowerShell

PowerShell can also be used to add MIME types. To add the `.flv` extension at the server level, run the following command:

```
PS C:\> add-webconfigurationproperty //staticContent -name collection
-value @{fileExtension='.flv';mimeType='video/x-flv'}
```

Alternatively, to add the MIME type at a specific site or folder, add the appropriate path. The following example adds it to the root of the Website1 website:

```
PS C:\> add-webconfigurationproperty //staticContent -Location "IIS:\Sites\WebSite1\"
-name collection -value @
{fileExtension='.flv';mimeType='video/x-flv'}
```

Editing MIME Types

You can edit MIME types using the same tools you used to add MIME types.

Editing MIME Types Using IIS Manager

To edit MIME types with IIS Manager:

1. Open IIS Manager.

2. Select the level and location for which you want to edit the MIME type. Double-click the MIME Types icon to open the feature.

3. Double-click the MIME type you want to edit. The "Edit MIME type" tool will open, and you can modify the data in the MIME type section.

4. Click OK when you have completed making changes.

Removing MIME Types

When it is determined that a MIME type is no longer needed, it is possible to remove it in order to reduce the attack surface of a server.

Removing MIME Types Using IIS Manager

IIS Manager can be used to remove a MIME type with these steps:

1. Open IIS Manager.

2. Select the level and location for which the MIME type should be removed. Double-click the MIME Types icon to open the feature.

3. Right-click on the MIME type to be removed, and click Remove. Select Yes on the verification pop-up.

Removing MIME Types Using AppCmd

To remove a MIME type with `AppCmd.exe`, make sure to specify the extension and the MIME type string — in this case, `video/x-flv`. The key to removing the MIME type is to use `/-` in the command.

```
appcmd.exe set config /section:staticContent
/-"[fileExtension='.flv',mimeType='video/x-flv']"
```

The previous example removed the `.flv` extension and `video/x-flv` MIME type from the server.

BASIC ADMINISTRATION TASKS

This section will provide you with a brief overview of common administration tasks and the quick answers to get your IIS server running with as little pain and time as possible.

Configuring Default Options for IIS

The easiest way to administer an IIS server is to ensure that all your configured sites conform to a standard configuration layout by default and that other requirements are configured as exceptions.

To configure the default options for all websites to inherit, perform the following steps:

1. Open IIS Manager.

2. Click Sites in the Connections pane.

3. Click Set Web Site Defaults in the Actions pane (see Figure 6-14). The Web Site Defaults dialog box will pop up.

4. With this dialog box, you can set a few of the basic behaviors of a website. Under the Behavior section, expand Failed Request Tracing, click Enabled, and then select True from the drop-down menu.

5. Click OK to close the dialog.

Changes to the fields in the Web Sites Default dialog box will apply only to sites created after the change, *not* to sites already created.

Configuring the default website properties with `AppCmd.exe` can be accomplished by using the `config` object and the `set` command. To enable Failed Request Tracing in the default site settings, you need to edit the `siteDefaults.traceFailedRequestslogging.enabled` object to set its value to `true`.

```
appcmd set config /section:sites -siteDefaults.traceFailedRequestsLogging.enabled:true
```

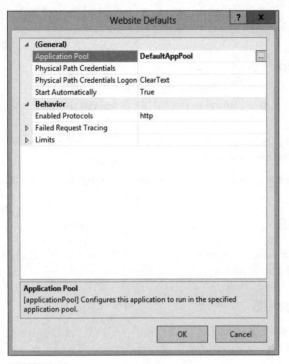

FIGURE 6-14

Starting and Stopping Services and Websites

From time to time, services and sites will need to be manually stopped, started, or restarted to resolve issues on a server.

Stopping and Starting Web Services

Controlling the services that run IIS has not changed from previous versions of IIS. To stop all IIS-related services, issue a `net` command on the IIS Admin Service by its service name:

```
net stop iisadmin /y
```

You can stop the individual services as follows:

➤ **World Wide Web Publishing Service**—`net stop w3svc`

➤ **SMTP Service**—`net stop smtpsvc`

➤ **FTP Publishing Service**—`net stop msftpsvc`

Note that the SMTP Service is no longer part of IIS; it is a separate feature of Windows Server 2012. However, the SMTP Server is often installed along with IIS (to provide e-mail delivery facilities) and has been associated with IIS because it was included with IIS up until IIS 6.0.

Starting the web services follows the same process as stopping them:

```
Net start iisadmin /y
```

You can start the individual services as follows:

➤ **World Wide Web Publishing Service**—net start w3svc

➤ **SMTP Service**—net start smtpsvc

➤ **FTP Publishing Service**—net start msftpsvc

Stopping and Starting Websites

To stop a website with AppCmd, run the following command:

```
appcmd.exe stop site site1/
```

To start a website, run the following command:

```
appcmd.exe start site site1/
```

Isolating Applications

The concept of *application isolation* ensures that applications are separate from other applications and the IIS process, to achieve higher security, to reduce the impact of failure, and to separate management. You can achieve complete application isolation by performing the following steps:

1. Create a new application folder off the folder root.

2. Create a new application pool, or select an appropriate application pool for the user.

3. Create a separate user account for the application, and assign it to the website application.

Once these actions have been completed, the application can be configured as its own entity to prevent any adverse effects of failure of the application.

7

Web Application Administration

WHAT'S IN THIS CHAPTER?

➤ ASP configuration

➤ ASP.NET configuration

➤ ISAPI configuration

➤ CGI and FastCGI configuration

➤ Windows Process Activation Service

➤ Application Initialization

Most websites today are composed of some form of dynamic content. This dynamic content could be an online auction, webmail, forums, blogs, online games, or any type of nonstatic content that is on a website. The content is delivered by a web application. Normally, a *web application* is a three-tiered system, with a web server as the first tier, application servers as the mid-tier, and one or more data sources as the third tier. Increasingly, with the advanced power of Ajax and client-side processing abilities, the browser is also being referred to as a *tier*. For our purposes, the dynamic content technology will be referred to as the *web application*. The web application can be based on a variety of technologies, including ASP, ASP.NET, ISAPI, CGI, and FastCGI. IIS 8.0 natively supports these technologies as well as the Windows Communication Foundation (WCF). These technologies all plug into IIS 8.0 via modules that can be added or removed based on the purpose of the server. This chapter discusses these technologies and their administration as they relate to IIS 8.0.

APPLICATION ADMINISTRATION

The configuration store used by IIS 8.0 is similar to what is used by the .NET Framework, allowing the server or site to have a tighter integration between IIS 8.0 and the .NET Framework technologies such as ASP.NET. As mentioned in Chapter 5, "Administration Tools," the configuration is kept in the applicationHost.config, machine.config, and various web.config files. Owing to tight integration between IIS 8.0 and ASP.NET, the other non-ASP.NET content types now have access to the features of ASP.NET; for example, non-ASP.NET content can use ASP.NET Forms-based authentication (FBA). The "ASP.NET Configuration" section covers some of the shared aspects of ASP.NET. The next section covers ASP as a quick overview to show where ASP.NET came from.

ASP CONFIGURATION

Active Server Pages (ASP) is a server-side scripting engine used to create dynamic, interactive web pages. It debuted with IIS 3.0 in December 1996. ASP is also referred to as *Classic ASP*.

When a server receives a GET request for an ASP page, it runs the server-side code and generates an HTML page, which is then sent to the client's browser. Although rendered ASP pages sent to the browser are standard HTML (and JavaScript, CSS, etc.), the server-side ASP page can contain VBScript/JScript code and COM components for connecting to databases or processing business logic.

To edit the ASP settings with IIS Manager, follow these steps:

1. Start IIS Manager. (Press WIN+R, enter **inetmgr** in the dialog, and then click OK. Alternatively, click Tools on the top-right of Server Manager and select Internet Information Server (IIS) Manager.)

2. Double-click the ASP icon in the IIS section, and the ASP properties page will appear (see Figure 7-1).

3. After making the changes, click Apply in the Actions pane.

Some important properties include:

➤ **Maximum Request Entity Body Limit** — Limits the incoming size of requests from the client. This can have implications for websites where the client is able to upload files (e.g., documents), which are typically sent as part of a request using the HTTP POST method.

➤ **Restart on Config Change** — If set to True, ASP applications are recycled when ASP-related configuration changes are made. Applications that use ASP's built-in session state mechanism will lose all current sessions.

➤ **Script Language** — Sets the default scripting language to use for interpreting server-side ASP code, in which no explicit language declaration is used on the page itself.

➤ **Session Properties: Time-out** — Sets the default time-out for ASP sessions. If no new request is received from the client, that particular session and its state (e.g., any saved session variables) are discarded by the server.

➤ **Send Errors to Browser** — Enables detailed error messages to be sent to the browser, which is useful when debugging code during development. Ensure that this setting is set to False when deploying to a production environment.

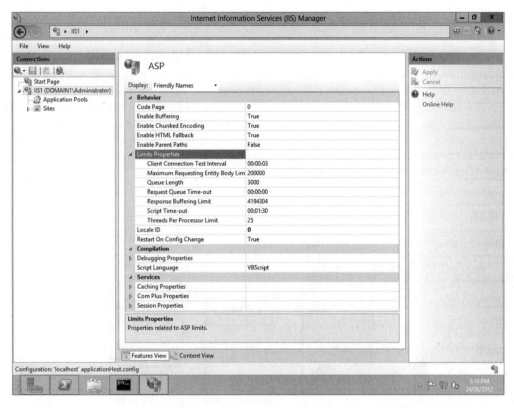

FIGURE 7-1

ASP.NET CONFIGURATION

Since IIS 7.0, ASP.NET is more tightly integrated into IIS than it was in previous versions of IIS. ASP.NET services can now be used to provide functionality to all content types, including PHP, static files, and Classic ASP pages. IIS can be extended using ASP.NET modules, rather than relying on ISAPI filters and extensions. These ASP.NET modules integrate directly into the server pipeline; thus, they can run at any point in the processing pipeline. Additionally, they can be run in any order with native IIS modules. With the integration of ASP.NET and IIS comes the added benefit of a unified server run time. Many features, including configuration, error handling, and tracing, have been unified into the same interfaces for the two systems.

IIS 6.0 and Previous Architecture

Prior to IIS 7.0, ASP.NET was implemented with the `aspnet_isapi.dll`. The route an ASP.NET request would take required IIS first to process the request to determine what needed to be done with the request. If it was determined that it was an ASP.NET request, IIS then passed it off to the `aspnet_isapi.dll` to process the actual request. The `.dll` would then pass the completed request back to IIS to return the results to the client's web browser. This process worked fine for ASP.NET file types; however, other file types couldn't take advantage of the features offered in the ASP.NET architecture, nor could IIS use these features outside of the period before or after the ASP.NET execution path.

Figure 7-2 shows the processing path for an ASP.NET request, under the older processing architecture used in IIS 6.0. This pipeline is available on a per-application pool basis in IIS 8.0 (classic pipeline mode). Here a request comes in to IIS and goes through the Authentication handler and to the Determine handler. At the Determine handler, IIS learns that the request needs to be routed to the `aspnet_isapi.dll`. The request is sent to the ISAPI subsystem and then on to the `aspnet_isapi .dll`. The `aspnet_isapi.dll` then processes the request and sends the result back to the ISAPI subsystem in IIS and then on to the Determine handler. The Determine handler sends the processed results out to the client after logging the request.

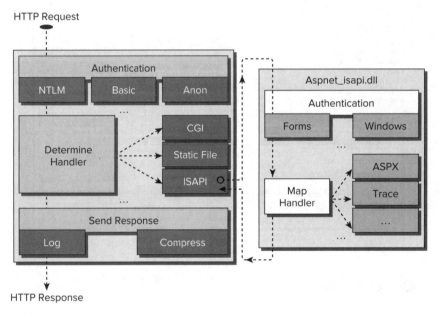

FIGURE 7-2

IIS 8.0 Architecture

The integration between IIS 8.0 and ASP.NET also provides for a much tighter pipeline than the classic pipeline. When using the integrated pipeline, the ASP.NET processing pipeline overlays the IIS pipeline. ASP.NET acts like a wrapper rather than as a plug-in. Figure 7-3 shows the integrated pipeline and how ASP.NET can be called at any point in a request. IIS is able to call ASP.NET from the Authentication phase to use ASP.NET Basic, Forms, Anonymous, or Windows authentication. The ExecuteHandler phase can call ASP.NET to run ASPX files, static files such as htm, ASP.NET traces, or other files such as PHP and ASP. The SendResponse phase can use ASP.NET for compression and logging before sending the response to the client web browser. In addition, ASP.NET modules can be used instead of the built-in IIS modules to replace or add on to IIS functionality, and the ASP.NET APIs can be used to create new modules and handlers.

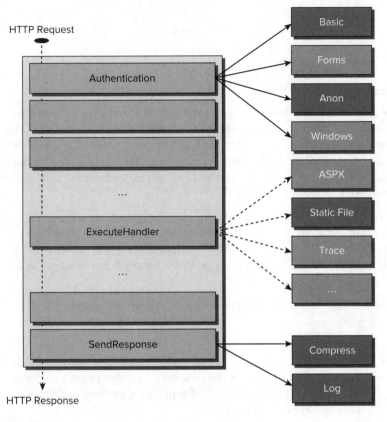

FIGURE 7-3

IIS 8.0 and ASP.NET Modules

The tighter integration between the two technologies enables you to control ASP.NET through IIS Manager. IIS Manager has configuration options for the following ASP.NET modules:

➤ .NET Authorization Rules

➤ .NET Compilation

➤ .NET Error Pages

➤ .NET Globalization

➤ .NET Trust Levels

➤ Application Settings

➤ Connection Strings

➤ Machine Key

➤ Pages and Controls

➤ Providers

➤ Session State

➤ SMTP E-mail

.NET Authorization Rules

.NET Authorization Rules is a .NET feature that allows an application administrator to define access to resources (e.g., files) by specifying Access Control Entries (ACEs) in a `.config` file. This is useful in scenarios in which the application administrator doesn't have access to the actual NTFS permissions on the files. Groups or users can be permitted or denied access (there is no additional granularity to specify write- or delete-type permissions), and these groups and users can be either Windows users or defined in .NET itself.

Note that the .NET Authorization Rules module (by default) only works with managed code resources (i.e., pages or other files handled by ASP.NET) and not static files or files handled by other handlers or CGI (e.g., PHP files). IIS 7.0 introduced a separate module that works with all content — managed or not. As such, the .NET Authorization Rules feature is not as useful as it was under IIS 6.0.

Authorization Rules are discussed in more detail in Chapter 14, "Authentication and Authorization."

.NET Compilation

Before ASP.NET serves a request, it first has to compile the code into the appropriate assembly(ies). These assembly files have the `.dll` extension. With the .NET Compilation module in IIS 8.0, you can control how the ASP.NET code is compiled on the server.

As shown in Figure 7-4, there are three main sections.

➤ **Batch** — The first section, Batch, allows control of the file and batch size as well as the time-out period for batches. Setting batch compilation to `True` tells ASP.NET to compile all of the files in a folder into a single assembly the first time a file in the folder is accessed. This incurs a performance penalty when the first page is accessed but results in faster load times for the other files in the folder. The other settings in the Batch section relate to the maximum size of the files to put in the batch file, the maximum size of the batch, and the time-out period of the Batch file process.

➤ **Behavior** — The second section, Behavior, provides limits to the compiling assemblies. The section sets whether the debug mode is off or on, the number of recompiles before the application is restarted, whether URL line pragmas are set to enabled or not, and whether VB.NET uses explicit compiles and strict compiles or not. *Explicit compiles* are equivalent to specifying "Option Explicit" in VB.NET. Any variable must be explicitly declared in order for it to be used when the code is compiled. The *strict compile option* enables notification when the value of one data type is converted to another data type that has less precision or capacity.

➤ **General** — The final section, General, lists the current assemblies; the default coding language, C# or VB; and the temporary directory to be used during the compiles.

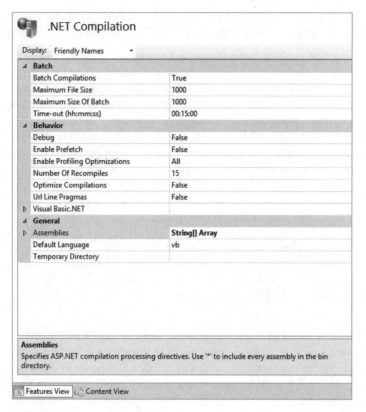

FIGURE 7-4

.NET Error Pages

This feature allows application administrators to configure a custom error page for their ASP.NET application; for example, it may be desirable to present a "friendly" File Not Found (HTTP 404) page to visitors who mistype a link.

Note, however, that error pages configured here only apply to requests for pages handled by the .NET Framework — they do not apply to non-.NET pages. IIS 8.0 has its own *Error Pages* feature located under the IIS section, which allows configuration of custom error pages for any type of request. The main reason for introducing the .NET Error Pages feature was because in IIS 6.0, changing IIS error pages required administrator privileges on the web server: The .NET feature required only editing a web.config file, and thus was useful for customers hosting web applications in which they did not have permissions to the web server itself. Because IIS 8.0 allows configuration of IIS via web.config files, the IIS Error Pages feature is probably of more use to most customers now.

To configure this feature, perform the following steps:

1. Start IIS Manager.

2. At the level (web server, website, application) where the error pages are to be edited, double-click the .NET Error Pages icon in the ASP.NET section.

3. To add a new custom error page for a specific HTTP code, click the Add link in the Tasks page. Enter the HTTP status code (e.g. 404) and the corresponding custom error page to be used.

4. To configure the general settings, click the Edit Feature Settings... link. Choose between having errors On (used both for the browser on the local server and remote users), Off (custom errors note used), or Remote Only (custom errors are sent to remote users, and detailed errors are sent to local browsers). Choose whether the server will redirect to the error page, or rewrite the content of the existing page with the error message (this may affect indexing by search engines). Lastly, supply a Default Page that will be used for all errors where a specific error page matching to an HTTP status was not set in Step 2.

5. Click OK. The settings are now in place.

.NET Globalization

Globalization is a process in which the developer designs the application to work in multiple cultures and locations around the world. Localization then takes the globalized application and customizes the application to the specific culture and location. This process provides for using one code base to deliver application content in any locale. The locale consists of both language and cultural information.

As shown in Figure 7-5, the IIS 8.0 settings for globalization include two sections, Culture and Encoding. The Culture section is used to set the culture-dependent properties, such as time, date, and currency. The UI Culture value determines which resources are loaded for the request. By using the Encoding settings, you can set how a page encodes its response, which enables a browser to determine the encoding without a meta tag.

.NET Trust Levels

The ASP.NET Code Access Security (CAS) policy is set by the trust level of an application. This CAS determines the permissions that are granted to the application on the server. Setting the CAS can be important in multiple scenarios — for example, when one organization (e.g., a hosting company) allows other parties to load arbitrary code onto the server. Another example would be to provide a lock-down to servers, so that in the event of a compromise, the application is limited in what it may be able to reach or alter on the server.

CAS has five levels of trust: Full Trust through to Minimal Trust, with High, Medium, and Low in between. Each level below Full restricts the ability of the .NET application to access certain resources on the server. Server administrators may build their own customized levels, if they wish.

An application with *Full Trust* permissions can access all resources on the server and perform privileged operations. This application is then only restricted by the permissions granted to the Windows User account under which the application is running (or impersonating).

Broadly speaking, *High Trust* is the same as *Full Trust* except that calls to unmanaged code are not permitted. *Medium Trust* no longer permits access to the Registry or Event Log, to the File System outside the application's folder hierarchy, communication to other servers (unless explicitly granted), or the use of OleDb providers to access databases. *Low Trust* blocks the ability to make any out-of-process calls (e.g., to a database) and *Minimal Trust* allows only the most trivial of applications to run.

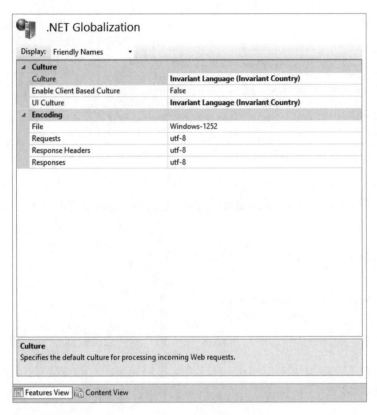

FIGURE 7-5

You can set the trust level for an application in IIS Manager, by using `AppCmd.exe` or PowerShell directly in the configuration, and by using the WMI classes.

In the default settings, there are five different levels of trust: Full, High, Medium, Low, and Minimal. It is also possible to take one of these configurations and use it as a template to create a custom trust level.

The trust configuration files are located in the `%systemdrive\Windows\Microsoft.NET\ <FrameworkPlatform>\\<FrameworkVersion> \CONFIG` folder; for example, the configuration files for the x64 (64-bit) build of v4 of the .NET Framework are located at `%systemdrive%\Windows\ Microsoft.Net\Framework64\v4.0.30319\Config`.

To create a custom trust configuration, copy the configuration level that most closely resembles the settings you need, and then rename it with a defining name. For example, take the `web_minimaltrust.config` file, copy it, and name the copy **web_customtrust.config**. At this point, you would want to modify the new configuration to make the trust changes needed for the site. After making the changes to the configuration file, save and close it. Open the `web.config` file located in the same folder, and find the `<securityPolicy>` section. You will need to add a line to designate the new trust level in the file. Here you see that the last trust level of *Custom* has been added.

```
<location allowOverride="true">
    <system.web>
        <securityPolicy>
            <trustLevel name="Full" policyFile="internal" />
            <trustLevel name="High" policyFile="web_hightrust.config" />
            <trustLevel name="Medium" policyFile="web_mediumtrust.config" />
            <trustLevel name="Low" policyFile="web_lowtrust.config" />
            <trustLevel name="Minimal" policyFile="web_minimaltrust.config" />
            <trustLevel name="Custom" policyFile="web_customtrust.config" />
        </securityPolicy>
        <trust level="Full" originUrl="" />
    </system.web>
</location>
```

When IIS Manager is opened, the Custom Trust level will now be shown in the dropdown selections, as shown in Figure 7-6.

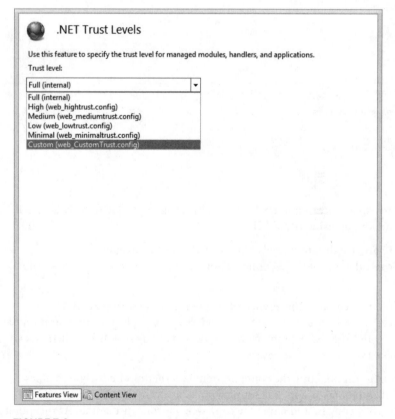

FIGURE 7-6

Application Settings

Application settings allow you to store configuration data in the web.config files in the form of key/value pairs. The settings create application-wide values that can be applied at any point in the web application. Configuration changes are made easily because of the centralized nature of the files. Application settings can be set in IIS Manager by using the following process:

1. Start IIS Manager, if not already open.

2. At the level (web server, website, application) where you want to apply the application settings, double-click the Application Settings icon in the ASP.NET section.

3. Click Add in the Tasks pane. The Add Application Setting dialog box appears, as shown in Figure 7-7.

4. Type in the name of the application setting and the value you want to use.

5. Click OK. The application setting is now in place.

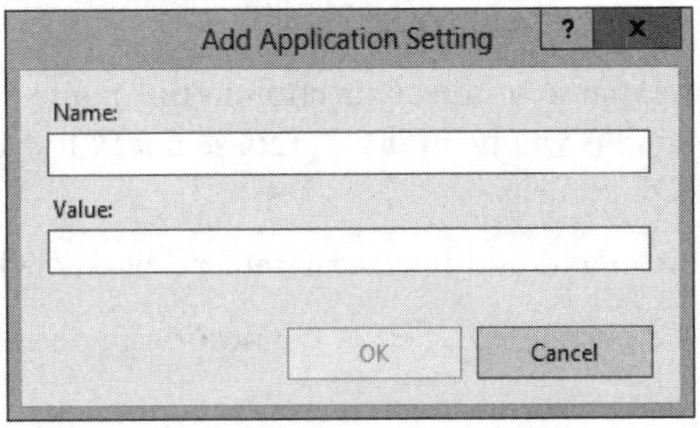

FIGURE 7-7

You can edit or remove application settings through the same section in IIS Manager. In addition to using IIS Manager, you can configure the settings using AppCmd.exe. To add an application setting, use the following syntax:

```
appcmd.exe set config /commit:MACHINE /section:appSettings
    /+"[key='string',value='string']"
```

where key is the attribute you want to set and value is the desired value of the attribute. An example of setting the Buffer attribute to False would look like this:

```
appcmd.exe set config /commit:Machine -section:appSettings
    /+[key='Buffer',value='false']
```

Editing the value follows a similar syntax. Watch where the close bracket moves to and how the value syntax changes:

```
appcmd.exe set config /commit:Machine -section:appSettings
    /[key='Buffer'].value:true
```

Removing the application setting follows the same syntax as adding the settings, except you will need to substitute a – for the +:

```
appcmd.exe set config /commit:Machine -section:appSettings
    /-[key='Buffer',value='false']
```

It is important to remember that any changes to the .NET settings result in an appDomain recycle, which will affect the entire server.

Connection Strings

Connection strings are used to establish communication between an application and a database. The connection string provides the server, database name, user, and password needed for the application to communicate with the database. Within ASP.NET code running on the server, the connection string can then be retrieved from the .config file, rather than having to be hard-coded into each page. In this example, you will add a connection named *DB1* to database DB1 on server SQL1 with user "User1" and password "PW1."

1. Start IIS Manager. (Press WIN+R, enter **inetmgr** in the dialog, and then click OK. Alternatively, click Tools on the top-right of Server Manager and select Internet Information Server (IIS) Manager.)

2. From the IIS Manager homepage, open the Connection Strings module and select Add. The Add Connection String dialog box will appear, as shown in Figure 7-8.

3. If connecting to SQL Server, then enter the name of the connection in the Name box, the server name in the Server line, and the database name in the Database line. Choose whether to use Windows Integrated Security or SQL security.

4. If you use SQL security, select the Set button and add the username and password.

5. If you have a custom connection string (i.e., not a SQL Server connection), you can enter it by selecting the Custom option.

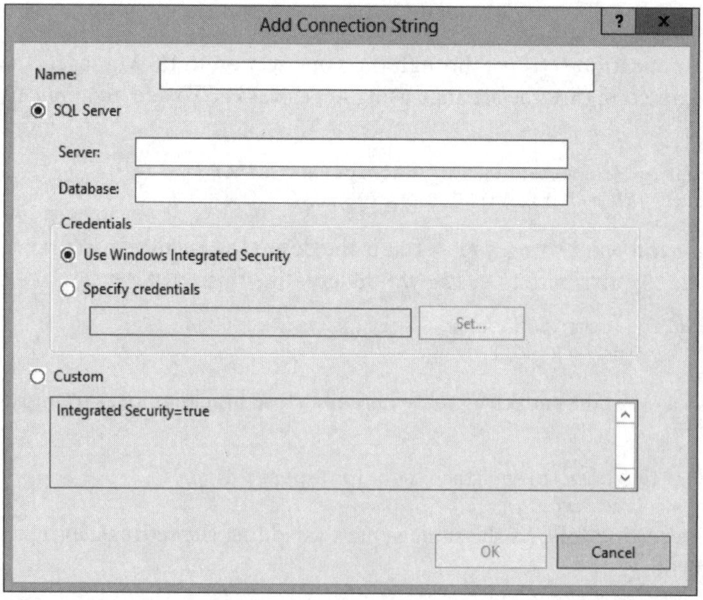

FIGURE 7-8

Machine Keys

ASP.NET uses *machine keys* to protect Forms authentication cookie data and page-view state data. The keys are also used to run sessions out-of-process. Although you can set these machine keys at any level, from server level down to file level, by default they are locked at the server and website levels only. These keys can be shared between servers when a site is run on multiple web servers.

ASP.NET uses two types of machine keys: validation keys and decryption keys.

The *validation key* is used to create a Message Authentication Code (MAC) to verify the integrity of the data. The MAC is then appended to the Forms authentication cookie or the view-state data. If the data is tampered with before being submitted back to the server, the data will no longer generate the submitted MAC. Because the client doesn't have possession of the validation key, the attacker is not able to generate the necessary matching MAC.

The *decryption key* is used to encrypt and decrypt the Forms authentication tickets and view-state data. This prevents a read-only attack against this data.

Setting machine keys in IIS Manager is done by choosing the level at which the key should be used. Figure 7-9 shows the Machine Key page.

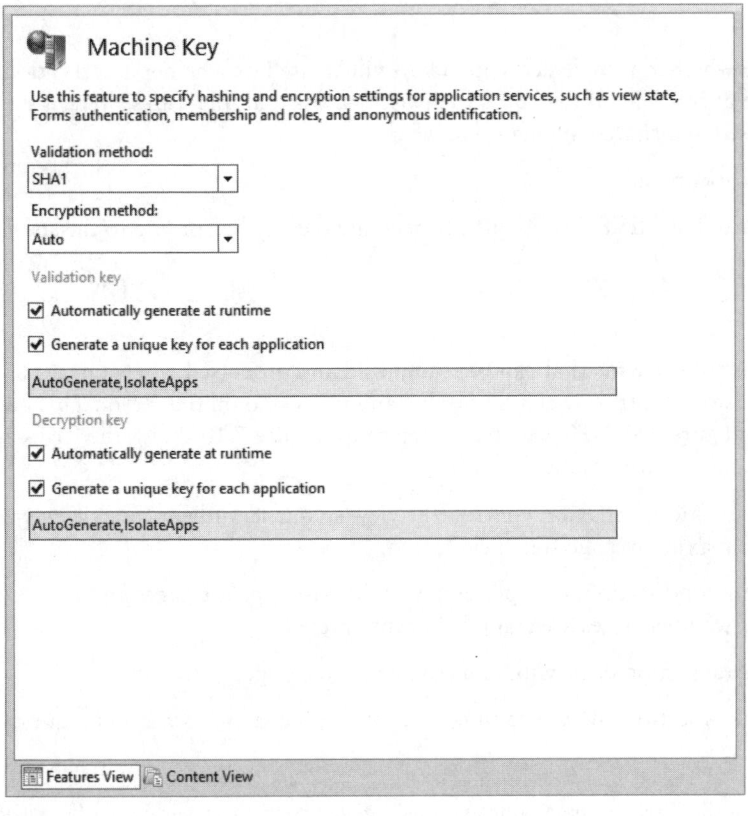

FIGURE 7-9

1. In IIS Manager, select the server, site, or application to which to apply the machine key, then double-click the Machine Key icon in the ASP.NET group on the homepage.

2. Select a validation method.

   The default encryption method is SHA1 (equivalent to HMACSHA1). The other options are AES, MD5, TripleDES, HMACSHA256, HMACSHA384, and HMAC512. As of this writing, MD5 has already seen several collision attacks (attackers are able to produce a matching MD5 hash without knowledge of the validation key) and should be considered insecure. Microsoft's SDL no longer permits the use of MD5 (`http://msdn.microsoft .com/en-us/magazine/ff797918.aspx`). SHA1 is, possibly, also susceptible to techniques that allow collision attacks. Given the rapid advances in the area, you are advised to use, at a minimum, SHA1, but you should regularly review the landscape to determine if there is a need to move to SHA256.

3. Select an encryption/decryption algorithm. The default decryption method is Auto and should be used, because it works with whichever encryption method is used.

4. Determine whether to use a single, fixed, validation key or whether the key will automatically be generated at run time. If the key is to be used across multiple servers, a single validation key must be created and then shared among the servers, using the fixed validation key option.

5. Likewise, determine whether a single decryption key will be used or whether a decryption key should be generated at run time. If the key is to be used across multiple web servers, a single, fixed key must be used and shared among the servers.

6. Click Apply in the Tasks panel.

7. Click Generate Keys to have IIS 8.0 subsequently generate the keys according to the specified parameters.

Pages and Controls

ASP.NET provides for the use of elements that can be recognized and processed when a page is run. It also supports the use of custom controls that are reusable and processed on the server. This allows server code to be used to configure ASP.NET web page properties. Figure 7-10 shows the Pages and Controls module, which includes four sections:

➤ **Behavior** — The first section, Behavior, controls the view state and authenticated view state, as well as setting the maximum page state field length.

➤ **Compilation** — The second section, Compilation, sets the base type for pages and user controls and determines whether pages are compiled or interpreted.

➤ **General** — The General section deals with namespaces for the pages.

➤ **Services** — The Services section allows enabling or disabling the session state and request validation.

The Register Controls link in the Tasks pane enables you to register custom server controls, without having to register them in each individual ASPX page.

FIGURE 7-10

Providers

ASP.NET and applications that are created with the .NET Framework can use databases to store information. To map the applications to the structure of the database, a software module called a *provider* is used. *Providers* are the equivalent of the hardware abstraction layer for applications and databases. IIS 8.0 allows the use of the Provider module for installing custom providers or modifying the standard ASP.NET providers. There are three different provider roles: .NET Roles, .NET Users, and .NET Profile.

The .NET Roles provider has options for creating the authorization store, SQL role, and Windows token provider types. The .NET Users provider can be used to create Active Directory membership or SQL membership provider types. The .NET Profile is used to create SQL profile providers. Figure 7-11 shows the Add Provider dialog box.

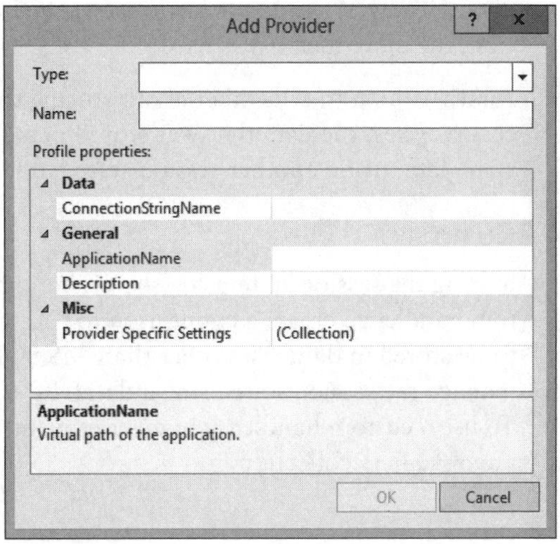

FIGURE 7-11

Adding a provider requires that you select the provider role first and then select .NET Role, .NET User, or .NET Profile. Once the provider role has been selected, you can then click Add to begin the Add Provider dialog. Choose the type of provider you need, name it, and then choose one of the existing connection strings. It is optional to include an application name, description, and provider-specific settings.

Session State

IIS 8.0 uses *session state* to track users browsing a site. This is done by assigning an ID to each user. Additionally, server-side variables and values can be set for each. Because HTTP is a stateless protocol, the server itself keeps no information about the variables the server has already served during previous requests. Instead, IIS 8.0 can use the ASP.NET session state to store and retrieve data for users as they navigate around the website.

Session state can be set in one of the following five modes:

➤ Not Enabled

➤ In Process

➤ Custom

➤ State Server

➤ SQL Server

Not Enabled

Not Enabled, as the name implies, means that the session state is not used on the website.

In Process

In Process keeps the session state stored in the memory bound to the application worker process. This is the default mode in IIS 8.0. This method provides the fastest response to the session state data. However, the downside to using the In Process session state is that the more data in the session, the more memory is used.

Another thing to remember about storing the session state In Process is that when the worker process recycles, the data that was stored in memory is lost. If the application needs to retain the session state data, using another session state mode is recommended.

Custom

Storing the session state using the Custom mode provides for an out-of-process session using a custom handler to create a connection to a database. Using the custom handler allows the session state to be stored in databases other than MS SQL, such as Oracle or Access. It also provides a method to manage the session state using a database schema other than what the .NET Framework provides. To use a custom handler, you must implement a full session state provider in the `<sessionState>`/ `<providers>` collection.

State Server

A second method of storing session state out of process is by using a State Server. The State Server can be either on the same server as the website or on an external server. This State Server mode maintains the data by running a separate worker process from the worker process being run by the ASP.NET application.

If the State Server is being run on the same server as the website, the website can then support running as a web garden. If the website is being run on multiple servers, then one server should be designated as the State Server to share the state among all the web servers.

The State Server mode relies on the `Aspnet_state.exe` service that is installed when ASP.NET is installed. When using a State Server, it is recommended to set the service to start automatically upon server start.

SQL Server

The final mode to keep the session state is to store the state in a SQL Server database. Similar to the State Server mode, the SQL Server can be run on the same server to support a web garden or on a separate server to support a web farm. The advantage of using SQL to store the session state is that the session data is maintained despite worker processes being recycled.

The SQL Server mode also uses the `Aspnet_state.exe` service that needs to be set to start automatically. In addition to the `Aspnet_state.exe` service, the SQL Server mode also needs the `InstallSqlState.sql` script run to configure it for the session state. The script is located at `%systemdrive%\windows\Microsoft.Net\Framework64\v4.0.30319` for 64-bit applications, and in the Framework folder for 32-bit applications.

Cookie Settings

Cookies are text files that contain data used for maintaining information about a user, such as authentication information or site preferences. One method of tracking session state is by using cookies. The cookies are placed on the client's machine and are then referenced by the web server. The cookie is passed back to the web server with every client request in the HTTP header.

Cookies can be set to use one of four modes:

- ➤ Auto Detect
- ➤ Use Cookie
- ➤ Use Device Profile
- ➤ Use URI

Auto Detect

The Auto Detect mode uses cookies if the browser supports cookies. If a mobile device is connecting to the web server and cookies are disabled, no cookies are used. If a desktop or laptop is connecting to the web server and cookies are disabled, the session state is stored in the URL.

When using the Auto Detect mode, session IDs should be set to regenerate. This allows attackers less time to acquire and exploit cookies to penetrate web servers (for example, via a session hijacking attack). The default time limit of 20 minutes should also be reduced to a level you determine as safe.

Use Cookies

When the Use Cookies mode is set, the session cookie associates session information with user information during the duration of the session.

Use Device Profile

The Use Device Profile mode uses cookies for the session state if the client browser supports cookies. If the browser does not support cookies, then no cookies will be used. If the device profile supports cookies, the session state will use cookies despite the user's cookie settings.

Session IDs should be set to regenerate for the same reasons as the Auto Detect mode.

Use URI

By Using the URI (Uniform Resource Identifier) for the session state, the session ID is embedded in the URI as a query string. The URI then is redirected to the original URL. This URI is used for the duration of the session.

Although the Use URI mode removes the disadvantages of cookies, it does have its own issues. Web pages cannot be bookmarked, and absolute URLs cannot be used without losing the session state.

Configuring Session State

You can set the session state using any of the management methods — IIS Manager, AppCmd.exe, editing the configuration files, or using Windows Management Instrumentation (WMI). This section describes how to configure the session state by using AppCmd.exe.

Open a command prompt using administrative permissions, and type the following:

```
appcmd.exe set config /commit:WEBROOT /section:sessionState /mode:InProc
```

This sets the session state to the In Process mode and commits the change to the web-root level of the server.

In addition to setting the session state, you can also set the cookie mode by appending the cookie information to the session state configuration:

```
appcmd.exe set config /commit:WEBROOT /section:sessionState /cookieless:AutoDetect
    /cookieName:website1 /timeout:5 /regenerateExpiredSessionId:True
```

This sets the cookie mode to Auto Detect with the cookie name of website1, a time-out value of 5 minutes, and the regeneration value to True.

SMTP E-mail

Simple Mail Transport Protocol (SMTP) is the protocol used by IIS to send e-mail. ASP.NET has the System.Net.Mail API, which uses SMTP as a means to send mail for web applications. The SMTP E-mail module allows configuration of SMTP for a web application (see Figure 7-12).

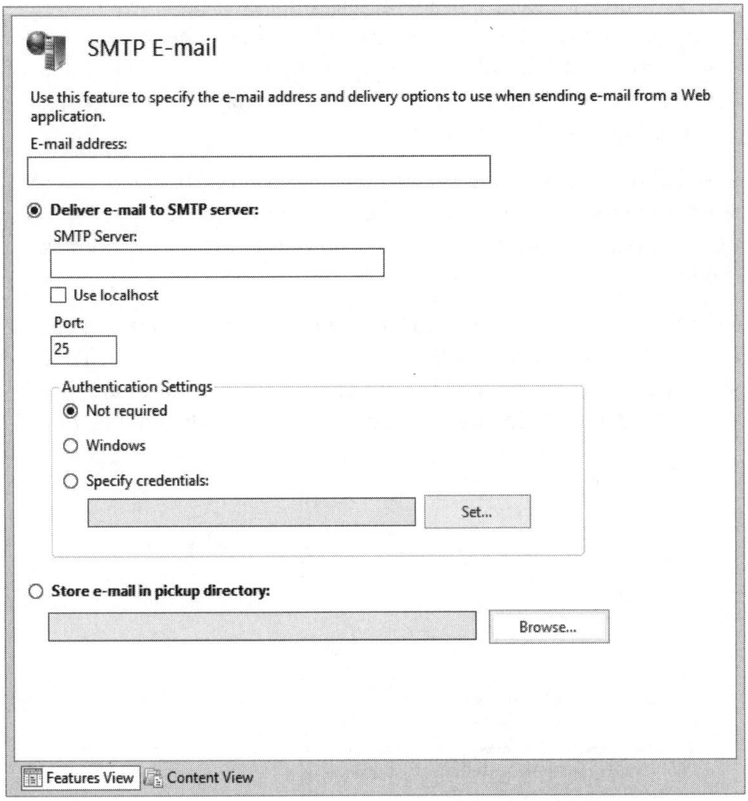

FIGURE 7-12

The SMTP E-mail module can be set to deliver mail to an SMTP server, or it can store the e-mail in a pickup directory for other use. The e-mail address textbox should have the address you wish to be in the "from:" line of the e-mail. If mail will be sent to an SMTP server, determine if the server will be local or a separate server. If separate, give the server name or IP address in the SMTP Server textbox. If SMTP is running locally on the server, then check the "localhost" box. Port 25 is the default port for SMTP and should be kept unless your SMTP server uses a nonstandard port. Indicate the Authentication settings that are needed to connect to the SMTP server. If storing the e-mail in a pickup directory, browse to and select the location for the mail to be saved. For more information on installing and configuring SMTP, see Chapter 10, "Configuring Other Services."

ISAPI CONFIGURATION

Internet Server Application Programming Interface (ISAPI) is a low-level programming interface that is used for running applications, such as ASP.NET, PHP, and Perl. Rather than being a server-side scripting technology, ISAPI is actually a true executable part of IIS. ISAPI applications run as .dlls and can be either extensions or filters. Extensions are applications that have access to the full functionality of IIS. Filters modify or augment the functionality of IIS. Filters check every request until one is found that needs to be processed. This check can be configured to examine either incoming or outgoing traffic. Some examples of ISAPI filters include authenticating and authorizing users, rewriting URLs, and modifying a response back to a client.

In IIS 8.0, ISAPI is being superseded by modules. Because of the integration of IIS 7.0 and ASP .NET, modules can now be written in either C++ or managed code and provide the same speed and security that only ISAPI applications once provided. ISAPI extensions and filters can still be used to provide for backward compatibility.

To run ISAPI applications on the server, two modules need to have the ISAPI information added. The ISAPI and CGI Restrictions module and the ISAPI Filters module both need to have the application information added in order for ISAPI to work. The ISAPI and CGI Restrictions module, shown in Figure 7-13, manages the ISAPI and CGI applications, adding descriptions and enabling or disabling the extensions.

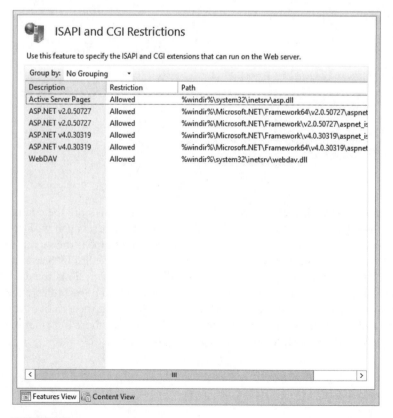

FIGURE 7-13

The ISAPI Filters module, shown in Figure 7-14, provides the filter name and path to the ISAPI filters.

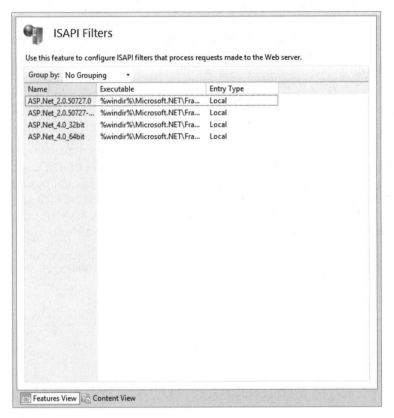

FIGURE 7-14

CGI CONFIGURATION

Common Gateway Interface (CGI) is a standard protocol that provides for communication between an application and a web browser. CGI was invented in 1993, and every version of IIS has supported it. The problem with CGI running on IIS is in the way it handles requests. With each new request for a CGI application, IIS has to create a new process, do the work, and then shut down the process. IIS can handle requests very quickly; however, the overhead of starting and stopping processes can become a bottleneck when running CGI on IIS. This is where FastCGI steps in. The creation of FastCGI resolves part of the bottleneck of using CGI on IIS. The next section provides more details about FastCGI.

FASTCGI CONFIGURATION

FastCGI is a newer version of CGI that adheres to most of the original specifications. However, rather than shutting down a process at the end of a request, the process is allowed to stay running and process other requests. The IIS 8.0 FastCGI implementation, like CGI, is single threaded, but a server can process more requests than with CGI because the processes stay open. On IIS 8.0, FastCGI is implemented as a native module using the built-in APIs.

FastCGI offers significant performance benefits over the original CGI implementation on Windows, due to avoidance of the significant overhead in starting and terminating processes that is incurred when using the original CGI module.

Because FastCGI is a single-threaded application, it has to start multiple processes to handle multiple requests. The processes can be pooled together into groups, and the groups can then be managed together. The properties of a process group can be managed. For example, the number of processes in the group and the number of requests a process can handle before being recycled are each properties that can be managed. In addition to the multiple processes in a process group, FastCGI can have multiple process groups running. Each of these process groups can have its own settings.

Included here is a step-by-step process to install the QDig PHP application on your server using FastCGI. You will need the following prerequisites:

- ➤ IIS 8.0 installed
- ➤ The Default Web Site that was installed by IIS
- ➤ PHP 5.4 (www.php.net/downloads.php#v5)
- ➤ QDig (http://qdig.sourceforge.net/)

The non-thread-safe version can be used, as each FastCGI process can only process a single thread at a time.

Installing PHP

Begin by installing PHP, as follows:

1. Extract the PHP download to c:\PHP.

2. Copy PHP.INI-Production to PHP.INI.

3. Open the PHP.INI file with Notepad.exe.

4. Edit these configuration items:

- ➤ Fastcgi.impersonate should be set to 1.
- ➤ Fastcgi.logging should be set to 0.
- ➤ Cgi.fix_pathInfo should be set to 1.
- ➤ Cgi.force_redirect should be set to 0.
- ➤ Open_baseDir should be set to "c:\inetpub\wwwroot".

5. Save PHP.INI and close it.

Installing QDig

Next, install QDig, as follows:

1. Copy the `index.php` from the QDig download, and place it in `c:\inetpub\wwwroot` (or in a subdirectory of your choosing).

2. Copy some image files (e.g., JPG, GIF, PNG) into the `c:\inetpub\wwwroot` directory (or the subdirectory where the QDig `index.php` file is located).

Installing the FastCGI Module

Now install the FastCGI module in IIS 8.0:

1. Open Server Manager.

2. Click Add Roles and Features.

3. Choose Role Based or Feature Based Installation, and then click Next.

4. Select the local server (or a remote server, if installing to a remote server).

5. On the Server Roles page, check the Web Server (IIS) ⇨ Web Server ⇨ Application Development ⇨ CGI checkbox.

6. Click Next twice to move through the Features dialog and onto the Confirmation page.

7. Click Install.

CGI and FastCGI are now installed on the server, but they are not yet enabled.

Enabling FastCGI for Use with PHP

After installing FastCGI on the server, a handler mapping is required to associate `.PHP` requests to the PHP scripting engine via the FastCGI module. This can be done via any of the IIS 8.0 management interfaces, but this walk-through will use the `AppCmd.exe` tool. Remember to open the command prompt with Administrator privileges.

```
appcmd.exe set config /section:system.webServer/fastCGI
    /+[fullPath='c:\php\php-cgi.exe']
```

This command adds the PHP executable to FastCGI settings and should generate the following response:

```
Applied configuration changes to section "system.webServer/fastCgi" for
    "MACHINE/WEBROOT/APPHOST" at configuration commit path "MACHINE/WEBROOT/APPHOST"
```

Next, you will need to add the PHP handlers to the FastCGI settings:

```
appcmd.exe set config /section:system.webServer/handlers /+[name='PHP-FastCGI',
path='*.php',verb='*',modules='FastCgiModule',
scriptProcessor='c:\php\php-cgi.exe',resourceType='Either']
```

This should generate the response:

```
Applied configuration changes to section "system.webServer/handlers" for
    "MACHINE/WEBROOT/APPHOST" at configuration commit path "MACHINE/WEBROOT/APPHOST"
```

PHP and FastCGI are now set up for use. Open a browser and point to `http://localhost/index` `.php`. QDig should now be available to view the photos in your root directory.

WINDOWS PROCESS ACTIVATION SERVICE

Windows Server 2008 adds a new tool called the *Windows Process Activation Service* (WAS). This service replaces the WWW service in managing application pool configuration and worker processes. The functionality that existed with the WWW service that ran only HTTP sites now allows WAS to run non-HTTP sites in addition to the HTTP sites. WAS is not part of IIS 8.0, but rather an external service that works in conjunction with IIS to manage the application pools and processes.

WAS can be run either with the WWW service or without it if HTTP functionality is not needed. The Windows Communication Foundation (WCF) is an example of a situation in which the HTTP protocol may not be needed. WCF uses a listener adapter to take the requests from WAS and route them to the WCF application, rather than using the HTTP protocol.

WAS is a prerequisite for IIS 8.0 and is automatically installed when you install IIS 8.0 on Windows Server 2012. WAS uses the same `applicationHost.config` file for its configuration that IIS uses. When the server is started, WAS reads the configuration and then shares that information with the listener adapters. The listener adapter then takes the configuration information and creates a communication link between WAS and a protocol listener. At this point, the protocol listeners just sit and listen. When they receive a request, WAS is used to determine if there is a worker process. If there is one, the request is passed to the worker process; if not, a worker process is started to handle the request.

APPLICATION INITIALIZATION

Application Initialization — available as a separate, downloadable module for previous versions of IIS — is now included with Windows Server 2012. As some web applications may require lengthy initialization sequences, the Application Initialization module allows administrators to prime their application prior to receiving HTTP requests from end users.

The Application Initialization module does not have a GUI interface; instead, all modification must be done directly to configuration files.

The Application Initialization module has two main sets of settings:

➤ At the `applicationHost.config` layer, application pools can be configured to start automatically when the IIS World Wide Web publishing service starts.

➤ At the application layer (`web.config`), IIS can request a configured page or pages, so as to "initialize" the application. A temporary holding page can be displayed to end users until the application is ready.

To configure an application pool to be started automatically (rather than the default "on demand" setting), add the `startMode` setting to the application pool's settings in the `applicationHost` `.config` file:

```
<applicationPools>
  <add name="newAppPool" startMode="AlwaysRunning"
      managedRuntimeVersion="v4.0" />
</applicationPools>
```

Each application pool configured this way will have its hosting `w3wp.exe` process started when the IIS World Wide Web publishing service is started (e.g., when the machine starts).

To configure the individual application's initialization page, edit the application's `web.config` file or create the settings in the `applicationHost.config` file using a `<location>` tag:

```
<system.webServer>
  <applicationInitialization remapManagedRequestsTo="Startup.htm"
      skipManagedModules="true" >
        <add initializationPage="/" />
  </applicationInitialization>
</system.webServer>
```

The `initializationPage` setting tells the Application Initialization module which page or pages should be requested during initialization. Use additional `<add />` tags to specify additional pages that should be requested.

The `remapManagedRequestsTo` attribute tells the Application Initialization module which page should be served to end users until the initialization pages have finished running. This would typically be a placeholder page informing users of the temporary unavailability of the application.

Application Initialization enables administrators to provide a better experience for end users by preparing applications for use prior to end users visiting the site. It has additional options (e.g., working with URL Rewrite). For more information on this module, see `www.iis.net/learn/get-started/whats-new-in-iis-8/iis-80-application-initialization`.

8

Web Application Pool Administration

WHAT'S IN THIS CHAPTER?

- ➤ Website separation
- ➤ Virtual directories versus applications
- ➤ The w3wp.exe process
- ➤ Creating application pools
- ➤ Application pool security
- ➤ Application pool user accounts

WROX.COM CODE DOWNLOADS FOR THIS CHAPTER

The wrox.com code downloads for this chapter are found at www.wrox.com/remtitle .cgi?isbn=1118388046 on the Download Code tab.

Websites and applications in IIS 7.0, IIS 7.5, and IIS 8.0 can be separated into processing groups based on your administrative preferences. Called *application pools*, these groups isolate website processes from other website processes on the server, offering strong performance and security benefits.

This chapter covers the various aspects of application pools, from managing worker processes during a recycle event to the dependencies that pools have on the Integrated Pipeline mode. A background and comparison between IIS 5.0 and IIS 6.0 set the stage for understanding why application pools are necessary and the advantages that they bring.

Effective management of application pools requires an understanding of:

- ➤ Virtual directories and applications
- ➤ The w3wp.exe worker process
- ➤ The two pipeline modes
- ➤ Multiple methods of creating application pools

A BACKGROUND OF WEBSITE SEPARATION

Back in the days of IIS 5.0, applications could be placed in one of three isolation modes: low, medium, or high. Low and medium isolation placed all websites in a shared pool that utilized a common user identity and security context. Failures that affected one site often would break other sites that were set to low or medium isolation, requiring a reset of IIS to fix the troubled sites. Those sites in high isolation faired better by partially protecting some sites from one another, but each high-isolation application had an extra memory footprint, and the user identities were shared just as they were in low and medium isolation. This usually meant that a shared Windows identity needed to be granted Read permissions to all sites on the server, creating potential security vulnerabilities.

IIS 6.0 introduced an excellent solution for this by implementing application pools. This allowed the system administrator to create pools of applications bundled together into groups as the administrator saw fit. With this enhancement, it was possible to completely separate sites from one another so that a serious failure in one application wouldn't compromise sites or applications in other pools. In addition, each application pool defined the Windows user identity under which the applications would run, allowing complete separation from a security point of view between application pools.

IIS 7.0, IIS 7.5, and IIS 8.0 build on the strong foundation of application pools first found in IIS 6.0. The core features and concepts implemented in IIS 6.0 remain the same, while additional functions and enhancements were added on that foundation in IIS 7.0 and more again in IIS 7.5. Application pools in IIS 8.0 are the same as you will find in IIS 7.5. In the remainder of this chapter, we discuss features that existed in IIS 6.0, plus enhancements that are new to IIS 7.0 and IIS 7.5.

DEFINING APPLICATIONS

An *application* is a logical grouping of resource files and components. It is a logical boundary that separates data and subsections of a site. This allows IIS to share data within the application threads and to have security and worker process isolation between applications. By default, the root of each website is already an application, and subfolders and virtual directories can also be made into applications.

Classic ASP and ASP.NET are application-aware and use application boundaries to share data and settings. InProcess session state in ASP.NET, for example, executes within the scope of the application boundaries so that all ASP.NET pages within the application have access to the same session state.

Many pre-existing websites expect their site to be installed in an application root. Developers creating a new project in Visual Studio often expect their project to be placed in an application when it is deployed to the production server.

ASP.NET 2.0 has several resources that depend on the application boundaries. There are eight folders, plus a couple of files.

The folders are as follows:

➤ `Bin`

➤ `App_Browsers`

➤ `App_Code`

➤ `App_Data`

➤ `App_LocalResources`

➤ `App_GlobalResources`

➤ `App_Themes`

➤ `App_WebReferences`

The files include the following:

➤ `web.config`

➤ `global.asax`

In addition, there are some common default filenames for various ASP.NET features:

➤ `masterpage.master`

➤ `web.sitemap`

`Bin`, `web.config`, and `global.asax` are the three files and folders that ASP.NET 1.1 is aware of.

Details on these folders are beyond the scope of this book, but it's important to understand their existence and their usage within an application. Each of these files and folders is referenced from the root of the application. Consider the file structure shown in the Connections pane in Figure 8-1.

Notice that the Default Web Site folder has several subfolders. The `Section2` subfolder has a different icon, which shows that it is a separate IIS application. An ASP.NET page in the root or `/admin` folder will use the root `App_*` folders and `bin` folder from the root. But an ASP.NET page in `/Section2` will use the `App_*` folders and `bin` folder within the `Section2` subfolder. The fact that `Section2` is marked as an application sets it as the *application root* for all files and folders under it.

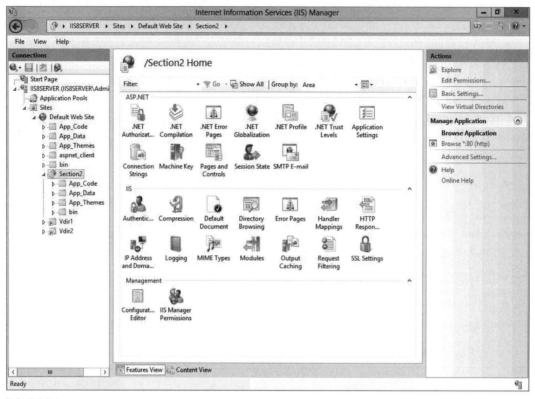

FIGURE 8-1

NOTE web.config *can live outside of application roots, but only a limited number of settings will work without throwing an error. ASP.NET allows you to set the scope of each configuration section. For example, the* processModel *section can only be set in* machine.config, *and when trying to update a* processModel *setting at the website level, it will throw an error. The following four choices are available in the* allowDefinition *attribute of each configuration section:*

➤ Everywhere—Allows the section to be configured in any configuration file, even in a regular physical folder.

➤ MachineToApplication—Allows the section to be configured in any configuration file that is in an application root.

➤ MachineOnly—Allows the section to be configured only in the machine .config file that is in the config folder of the framework version.

➤ MachineToWebRoot—Allows the section to be configured only in the machine.config or root web.config files that are in the config folder of the framework version.

To find out what each section allows, check the machine.config file and notice the allowDefinition attribute of the various sectionGroup elements. If the allowDefinition is not set, the default is Everywhere.

Most commonly, an application coincides with a website, but it can also be a subfolder under a website that is marked as an application. Throughout this chapter, the term "application" will be used frequently. Keep in mind that this is often also a website root, although that is not always the case.

COMPARING VIRTUAL DIRECTORIES TO APPLICATIONS

It is easy to get *virtual directories* and *applications* confused. In IIS 8.0, there is a clear line of separation between them. This chapter is about applications and application pools, not virtual directories, but before moving on, it's important to understand the differences between them.

As stated in the preceding section, an application is a logical boundary that separates data and subsections of a site. A *virtual directory* is the actual pointer to a local or remote physical path. A virtual directory must always exist inside an application, and applications can contain multiple virtual directories.

Consider the following section from `applicationHost.config`:

```
<site name="Default Web Site" id="1">
   <application path="/">
      <virtualDirectory path="/"
        physicalPath="D:\websites\wwwroot" />
   </application>
   <application path="/Section2">
      <virtualDirectory path="/"
        physicalPath="D:\websites\wwwroot\Section2" />
   </application>

   <bindings>
      <binding protocol="http" bindingInformation="*:80:" />
   </bindings>
</site>
```

This section shows applications and virtual directories. One application is the Root Application (/), and the other is /Section2. Each of these contains a virtualDirectory: one points to D:\ websites\wwwroot, which is the site root, and the other points to D:\websites\wwwroot\ Section2, which is a second part of the same site. Because these folders are in two different applications, they will not share the application files and folders.

Notice in Figure 8-2 that the default application pool in IIS, DefaultAppPool, has both applications listed separately.

> **NOTE** *It is not required that these applications be in the same application pool. Because they are two separate applications, they don't share InProc session state or the application files or folders.*

The following example further illustrates the difference between an application and a virtual directory:

```
<site name="Default Web Site" id="1">
```

```
<application path="/">
   <virtualDirectory path="/"
      physicalPath="D:\websites\wwwroot" />
   <virtualDirectory path="/Section2"
      physicalPath="D:\elsewhere\Section2" />
</application>

<bindings>
   <binding protocol="http" bindingInformation="*:80:" />
</bindings>
</site>
```

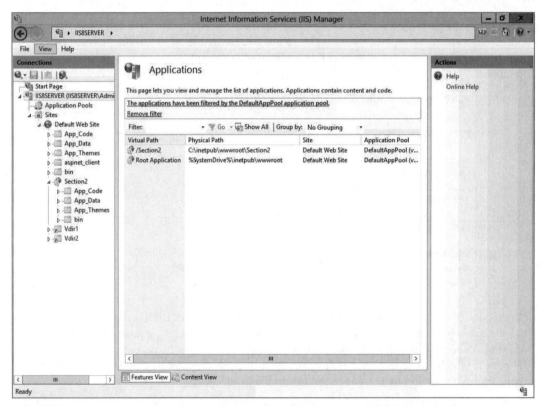

FIGURE 8-2

Here, there is only one application, but two virtual directories. This means that there is no application boundary between the root of the site and /Section2. A page called /Section2/ default.aspx will use the application folders in the root of the site and will ignore the application folders in the /Section2 folder.

There is only one application in the `DefaultAppPool` now. Notice in Figure 8-3 that the icon in the Connections pane on the `Section2` folder is different from the one in Figure 8-1. This is the virtual directory icon and indicates that it is a virtual directory pointing to a separate physical path, though it inherits the application settings from its parent. Even InProc session state and caching will be shared between the two virtual directories given that they are part of the same application.

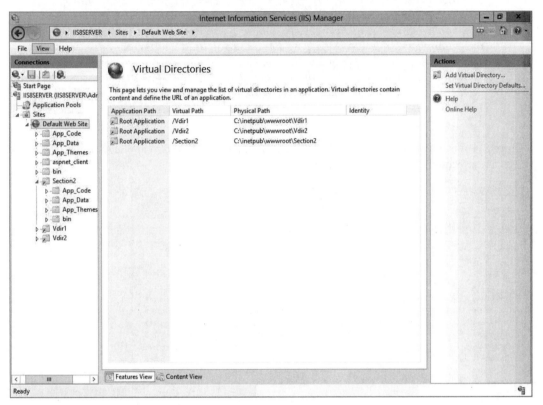

FIGURE 8-3

UNDERSTANDING THE W3WP.EXE PROCESS

Each application pool runs in its own worker process within the operating system so that there is complete separation between application pools. This also allows a specific user identity to be assigned to each worker process for security reasons.

The `w3wp.exe` worker process runs in user-mode and processes requests for content for each application pool.

> **NOTE** *There are no hard limits on the amount of application pools that can run on a single server. IIS can handle hundreds of running application pools and thousands of application pools, assuming that not all of them will be running at once. Each application pool has some memory and potentially CPU overhead that together will eventually tax the server beyond an acceptable level. Mileage will vary depending on hardware and the types of sites on the server. An application pool running a static webpage has about 3 MB of memory overhead, while one running a simple ASP.NET page has a base of 10 MB of memory overhead (give or take a couple of megabytes). You can use these general numbers to determine how much additional overhead is generated by separating sites into their own application pools. RAM is cheap so, when in doubt, separate them out.*

Figure 8-4 shows two `w3wp.exe` worker processes, one for each of two application pools. The web pages are executed within these processes.

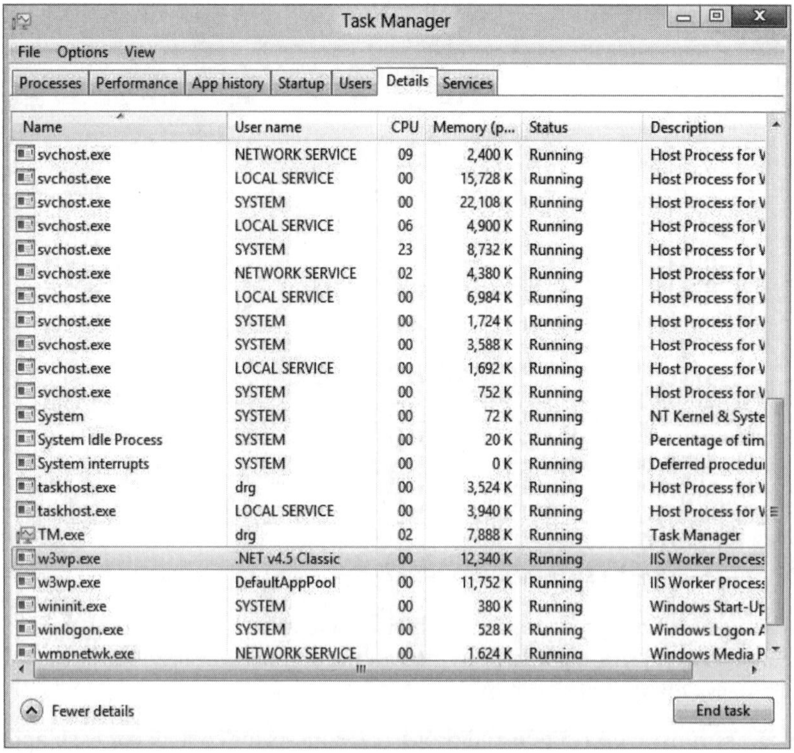
Task Manager
File Options View
Processes Performance App history Startup Users Details Services
Name User name CPU Memory (p... Status Description
svchost.exe NETWORK SERVICE 09 2,400 K Running Host Process for V
svchost.exe LOCAL SERVICE 00 15,728 K Running Host Process for V
svchost.exe SYSTEM 00 22,108 K Running Host Process for V
svchost.exe LOCAL SERVICE 06 4,900 K Running Host Process for V
svchost.exe SYSTEM 23 8,732 K Running Host Process for V
svchost.exe NETWORK SERVICE 02 4,380 K Running Host Process for V
svchost.exe LOCAL SERVICE 00 6,984 K Running Host Process for V
svchost.exe SYSTEM 00 1,724 K Running Host Process for V
svchost.exe SYSTEM 00 3,588 K Running Host Process for V
svchost.exe LOCAL SERVICE 00 1,692 K Running Host Process for V
svchost.exe SYSTEM 00 752 K Running Host Process for V
System SYSTEM 00 72 K Running NT Kernel & Syste
System Idle Process SYSTEM 00 20 K Running Percentage of tim
System interrupts SYSTEM 00 0 K Running Deferred procedu
taskhost.exe drg 00 3,524 K Running Host Process for V
taskhost.exe LOCAL SERVICE 00 3,940 K Running Host Process for V
TM.exe drg 02 7,888 K Running Task Manager
w3wp.exe .NET v4.5 Classic 00 12,340 K Running IIS Worker Process
w3wp.exe DefaultAppPool 00 11,752 K Running IIS Worker Process
wininit.exe SYSTEM 00 380 K Running Windows Start-Up
winlogon.exe SYSTEM 00 528 K Running Windows Logon A
wmpnetwk.exe NETWORK SERVICE 00 1,624 K Running Windows Media P
Fewer details
End task

FIGURE 8-4

A detailed description of the IIS core architecture is outlined in Chapter 2, "IIS 8.0 Architecture." The next section covers how IIS handles recycling application pools.

Recycling Application Pools

Back in the days if IIS 5.0, if there was a failure in a low- or medium-isolation website, one of the only ways to reset the site was to do a complete reset of IIS. This caused an abrupt stop of IIS, and any page requests that came in during the restart failed.

IIS 6.0 introduced a new feature where overlapping processes allow all incoming requests to continue to be served even when an application pool is recycled. This remains true in IIS 8.0. When an application pool is recycled, the existing `w3wp.exe` worker process is not immediately stopped. Instead, a second worker process is started and `Http.sys` will send all new requests to the new worker process once it is ready. After the old worker process has completed all requests in its queue, IIS will shut it down. There is never a page request that is lost during a recycle because `Http.sys` handles and queues the incoming requests before handing them off to the `w3wp.exe` process.

Figure 8-5 illustrates the `DefaultAppPool` during a recycle event. Notice that the old process ID 3920 remains running while the new process ID 3168 is started. It is only when PID 3168 is in the Running state that new requests are sent to it. For those who want to test the theory, it's possible for a brief moment to refresh IIS Manager and see process ID 3168 in a Running state and process ID 3920 in a Stopping state.

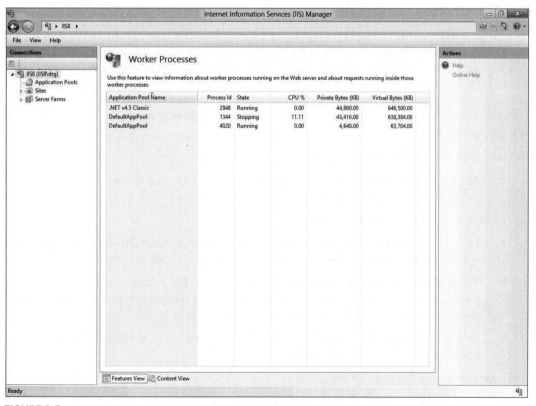

FIGURE 8-5

> **WARNING** *Although no page requests are lost or fail during an application pool recycle, there are some possible adverse effects to a recycle. All data stored in the worker process will be lost. By default, ASP.NET stores session state and caching data In Process (called InProc). This data persists only as long as the worker process is functioning and needs to be re-created anew after a recycle. For this reason, it may be worth considering storing the session state out of process in another system, such as StateServer, SqlServer, or another external session state store. Additionally, there is a first load performance hit when a new worker process is started. Various aspects of IIS and ASP.NET are pre-loaded into the worker process, which takes a noticeable amount of time to load. This often takes several seconds. The first page that runs after an application recycle event will generally take longer to run than those pages rendered after the application pool has already started. This means that an application pool can be recycled with minimal adverse effects, especially if the session state is not important or is stored out of process.*

Web Gardens

A web garden is another concept that was first introduced in IIS 6.0 and is still in effect in IIS 8.0. A *web garden* is an application pool that is serviced by more than one worker process simultaneously. This is enabled by setting the number of worker processes to more than one on the Performance tab of an application pool. When requests for the application begin to queue, IIS automatically creates another worker process for the same application pool and begins to route new requests to the new worker process. When demand is reduced, the worker processes will eventually be spun down and the resources released.

Web gardens are useful in situations where:

➤   There are a high number of concurrent connections, and contention for locks and resources within a single process may limit request throughput.

➤   There is no application session state.

➤   The web application should not be CPU-intensive. Having new CPU-intensive page requests fighting for the CPU with the first page request will cause both to suffer.

➤   The application is subject to synchronous high latency. For example, if the application calls a web service or a remote database and the response is slow, a web garden will allow other requests to be processed while waiting for the long-running applications to complete.

➤   Each process has memory overhead and takes extra time to start. Having too many can quickly use up resources on a server.

Web gardens are problematic where:

➤   Multi-threaded applications access non-multithreaded resources (e.g., flat files).

➤   State information is maintained on the local IIS server.

Figure 8-6 shows three worker processes for `DefaultAppPool` when the Maximum Worker Processes is set to three (3) for this application pool. Recycling the application pool will recycle all three processes.

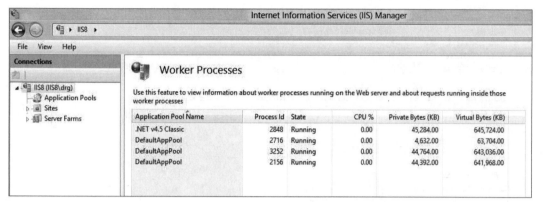

FIGURE 8-6

A web garden can enhance performance and has the following additional benefits:

➤   When one worker process is tied up (for example, if it's processing a number of long-running tasks or if it fails), other worker processes can still handle new requests.

➤   It reduces contention for resources on the web server. During normal operation, each new page request is assigned to the work processes in a round-robin fashion. This helps distribute the workloads of the worker processes.

> **NOTE** *Web gardens and web farms are different concepts, although they share some common characteristics. A* web garden *is composed of multiple processes on a single server handling the same application pool, whereas a* web farm *is composed of multiple servers working together to provide high availability or better scalability.*

One limitation of web gardens is related to session state management. Because a single application is divided across multiple processes, everything that is shared has to be stored out of process. Session state, for example, will not work InProc in a web garden because there will be multiple copies of the session state, with each process reading and writing to a different session state store.

To set the web garden settings, modify the Maximum Worker Processes attribute in the application's Advanced Settings window (see Figure 8-7). Changing the advanced settings of an application pool is covered in depth below in this chapter.

FIGURE 8-7

WORKING WITH APPLICATION POOLS

Effectively creating and managing an application pool generally involves four steps:

1. Create the application pool.

2. Configure any advanced settings that are required.

3. Assign a website or application to the newly created application pool.

4. Manage active application pools.

Creating Application Pools

You can create an application pool in IIS Manager by completing the following steps:

1. Open IIS Manager. (Click WIN + R, enter **inetmgr** in the dialog, and then press OK.)

2. Select the Application Pools section from the Connections pane.

3. Click Add Application Pool... in the Actions pane. Alternately, right-click the Application Pools heading or a blank area in the main pane (see Figure 8-8) and select Add Application Pool.

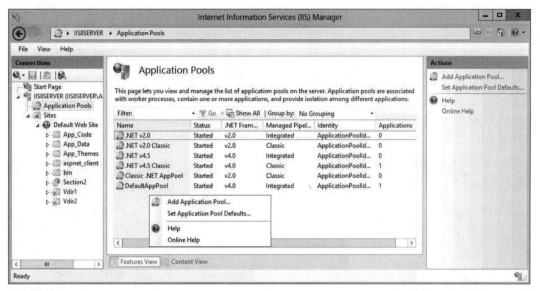

FIGURE 8-8

4. Enter the name of the new application pool into the Name field (see Figure 8-9).

5. Select the .NET Framework version, or select No Managed Code.

6. Set the Managed pipeline mode to Integrated or Classic. The Integrated mode is the default. Further discussion of these two modes is covered in Chapter 2.

7. Click OK.

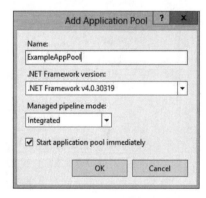

FIGURE 8-9

There are additional advanced settings that may be required, but these are set later and detailed in the following section.

Alternately, you can also create an application pool by using AppCmd.exe—the full use of which is detailed in Chapter 18, "Programmatic Configuration and Management." The following example creates a new application pool, sets the managed runtime version to ASP.NET v4, and sets the pipeline mode to Classic. The last two properties are optional; AppCmd.exe can create a new application pool with just the /name property (this must be run on one line as a single command).

```
appcmd.exe add apppool /name:"ExampleAppPool" -managedRuntimeVersion:v4.0
-managedPipelineMode:Classic
```

Additional code examples are provided in the next section.

Managing Settings

Simply creating an application pool is often the first step. Additional steps, such as changing the application pool user, may be required to properly configure your server. IIS 6.0 had a single dialog box that enabled you to configure all application pool settings. This has changed as of IIS 7.0, where there are three configuration boxes used in IIS Manager to manage additional features: Basic Settings, Recycling, and Advanced Settings. You can access all three tools from either the Links in the Actions section or by right-clicking on the application pool and selecting the appropriate link (see Figure 8-10).

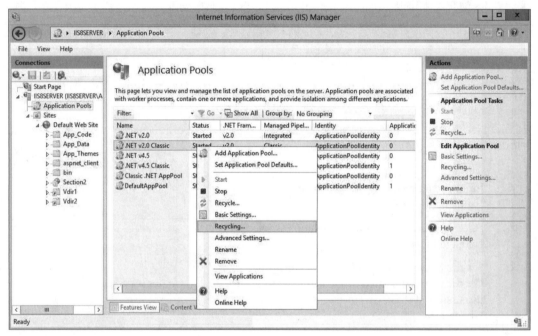

FIGURE 8-10

➤ **Basic Settings**—The Basic Settings configuration box is the same as the one used to create the application pool. This allows editing of the framework version, pipeline mode, and whether or not the application pool should start automatically. Note that the name cannot be edited after it is created; it is in read-only mode here. Both the framework version and the pipeline mode can be edited at any time for any application pool.

➤ **Recycling**—This tool is a two-step wizard (see Figure 8-11). Step one enables you to change settings like the automatic recycling intervals or times. After you have made the appropriate changes to this step, click Next, which brings you to step two of the wizard.

The second step of the wizard enables you to configure Event Viewer logging. Here you have the ability to turn on logging for settings like on-demand recycling or when the application pool notices an unhealthy ISAPI program.

➤ **Advanced Settings**—The third tool to manage the application pool settings is the Advanced Settings tool (see Figure 8-12). Here you can set many of the more advanced properties for the application pool. Everything that can be done in the other two tools can be done here as well. In fact, this tool allows you to set multiple times of the day to recycle the application tool while the Recycle tool itself only allows one.

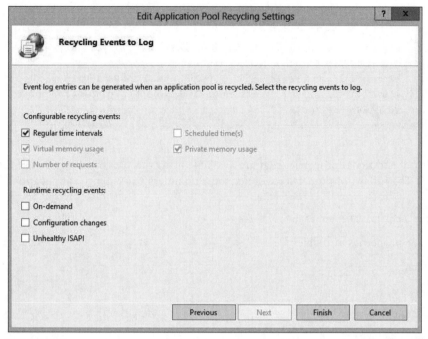

FIGURE 8-11

Be sure to take note of the + and - icons beside each section, as some default to expanded and some default to collapsed.

One handy feature is a brief description of each property in the bottom of the box when a property is selected. This saves you from calling the Help file separately for a summary of each property.

There are a limited number of properties that cannot be set from IIS Manager that can only be set from the command line, but almost everything you need to manage an application pool can be done from here.

Most noteworthy is the Process Model ⇨ Identity settings. Here you can change the identity under which the application pool runs. This is discussed at length below in this chapter. The identity field is not a simple property box like most other options, but an ellipsis button that allows you to set the identity of the application pool.

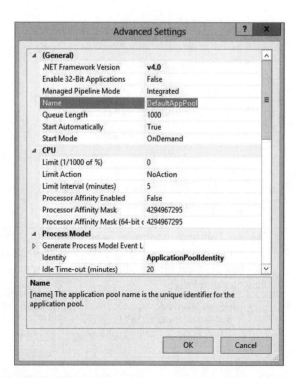

FIGURE 8-12

Like most everything else, changing the application pool settings can be done from the command line or in code. Here it's helpful to be able to see a complete list of properties available in `AppCmd` `.exe`.

> **NOTE** *Everything that is done in the IIS Manager tool uses the same back-end APIs as* `AppCmd.exe` *and* `Microsoft.Web.Administration`. *In addition, the schema files in* `%windir%\system32\inetsrv\config\schema` *are used by all these tools; thus, IntelliSense and the* `/?help` *in* `AppCmd.exe` *are guaranteed to give the complete list of properties.*

To get a complete list of additional properties that are available using the `AppCmd.exe` tool, use the following command. The full list of properties will not show up unless you enter the application pool name.

```
appcmd.exe set AppPool "DefaultAppPool" /?
```

Here is a sample of the properties available:

- ➤ `-queueLength`
- ➤ `-autoStart`
- ➤ `-enable32BitAppOnWin64`
- ➤ `-managedRuntimeVersion`
- ➤ `-managedPipelineMode`
- ➤ `-passAnonymousToken`
- ➤ `-processModel.identityType`
- ➤ `-processModel.userName`
- ➤ `-processModel.password`
- ➤ `-processModel.loadUserProfile`
- ➤ `-processModel.manualGroupMembership`
- ➤ `-processModel.idleTimeout`
- ➤ `-processModel.maxProcesses`

Notice that there are primary application pool properties and that there are properties of elements delimited by a dot (.). You can enter as many properties as you want in a single command. For example, to turn off the IdleTimeout setting and enable logging of manual application pool recycles, run the following:

```
appcmd.exe set apppool "DefaultAppPool"
-processModel.idleTimeout:"00:00:00"
-recycling.logEventOnRecycle:"PrivateMemory, OnDemand, Memory, Time"
```

> **NOTE** *Sometimes it's difficult to know the format of a particular parameter. Neither parameter in this example is straightforward. An easy way to find out the syntax is to make the change using IIS Manager and then open* applicationHost.config *in Notepad (or your favorite text editor) and view the result. This will often give an easy answer to the formatting of the parameter and value.*

Following is sample .NET Visual Basic code you can run in a managed code development studio that demonstrates using Microsoft.Web.Administration to create an application pool and set a couple of its properties:

```
Dim appPool As String = "ExampleAppPool"
Dim sm As ServerManager = New ServerManager
sm.ApplicationPools.Add(appPool)

sm.ApplicationPools(appPool).ManagedRuntimeVersion = "v4.0"
sm.ApplicationPools(appPool).ProcessModel.PingingEnabled = False

sm.CommitChanges()
```

> **NOTE** *For more information on how to implement the preceding .NET sample code, and the other samples that follow, see Chapter 18.*

Using WMI, after you have created an application pool, you can set additional properties, as follows:

```
strAppPool = "ExampleAppPool"

Set oService = GetObject("winmgmts:root\WebAdministration")

'create the app pool
oService.Get("ApplicationPool").Create strAppPool, True

'get the app pool instance
Set oAppPool = oService.Get("ApplicationPool.Name='" & strAppPool & "'")

'set a property
oAppPool.Enable32BitAppOnWin64 = True

'commit them
oAppPool.Put_
```

Creating an application pool in applicationHost.config is quite straightforward. It gets more complex when you need to create virtual directories. Within the applicationPools section, add an element with at least the name attribute set. All other settings are optional.

```
<system.applicationHost>

    <applicationPools>
        ...
        <add name="ExampleAppPool"
            enable32BitAppOnWin64="true">
            <processModel identityType="SpecificUser"
                userName="IISAdminUser" password="..." />
            <recycling disallowOverlappingRotation="true" />
        </add>
        <applicationPoolDefaults>
            <processModel identityType="NetworkService" />
        </applicationPoolDefaults>
    </applicationPools>
        ...
</system.applicationHost>
```

Assigning Applications and Sites to Application Pools

After you have created an application pool, you can assign any number of websites or applications to it. Remember that the application pool sets the .NET Framework version that will be used; therefore, all applications in the same pool must be running the same version of .NET.

Applications are assigned to the application pool at the site or application level. This is done from either the Basic Settings or Advanced Settings tool in IIS Manager. Figure 8-13 shows the application pool setting from the Advanced Settings tool. Because the application pool is central to specifying the framework version and pipeline mode, IIS 8.0 allows the administrator to see these current settings while selecting the application pool.

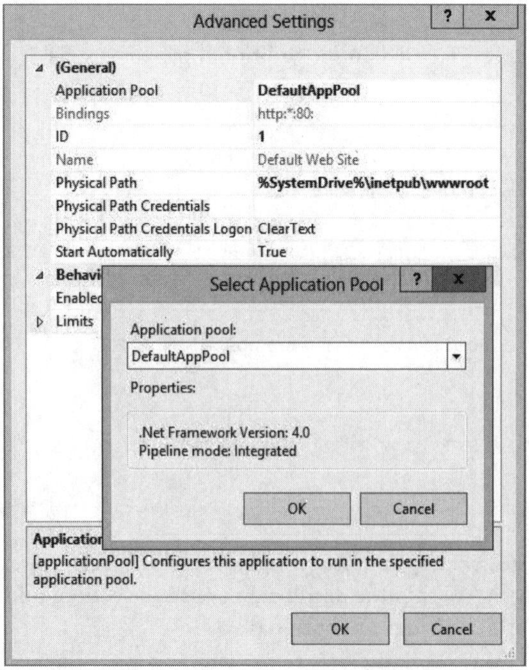

FIGURE 8-13

Three Folder Right-Click Choices

In IIS Manager, if you right-click on a folder, you are given three choices that can be somewhat confusing. Figure 8-14 shows the three choices: Convert to Application, Add Application, and Add Virtual Directory.

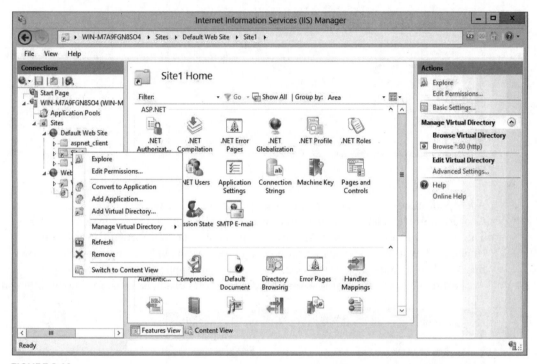

FIGURE 8-14

With these three options, you can mark an existing folder as an application or create a new virtual directory, which is either a simple virtual directory or one that is marked as an application. It's worth reviewing the differences among these three choices.

➤ **Convert to Application**—This option will convert the folder that you right-clicked into an application. It does not allow you to set the alias name or the physical path, as these are derived from the folder you chose. Figure 8-15 shows the dialog box. Within the Add Application dialog box, you can select the "Application pool," set the "Connect as" user credentials, and click the Test Settings button to have IIS Manager run a test against the folder. This process is commonly called "Marking a folder as an application" and creates a new application boundary for your .NET application. It's important to note that the application pool will default to the one set in the `<applicationDefaults />` tag, not the one used by the site. This confuses a lot of people because it doesn't default to what you may assume.

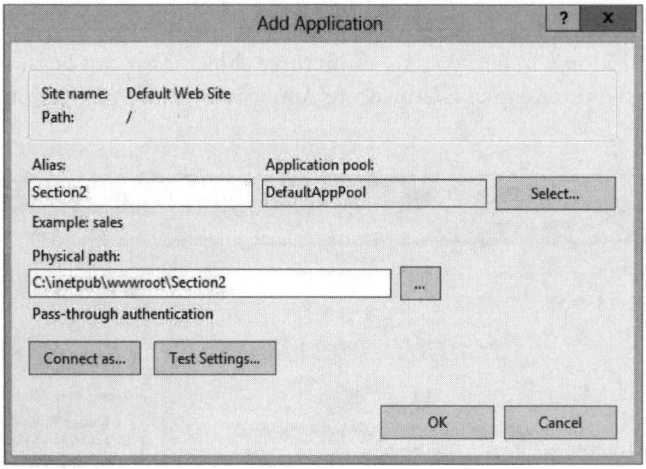

FIGURE 8-15

➤ **Add Application**—The second option allows you to create a new application, but unlike the Convert to Application option, it requires you to complete the alias and physical path fields. This is essentially the Convert to Application option plus the Add Virtual Directory option combined. It will create a virtual directory and mark it as an application. Figure 8-16 shows this Add Application dialog box. Notice that Convert to Application (Figure 8-15) and Add Application (Figure 8-16) share the same Add Application dialog box, but they use it differently.

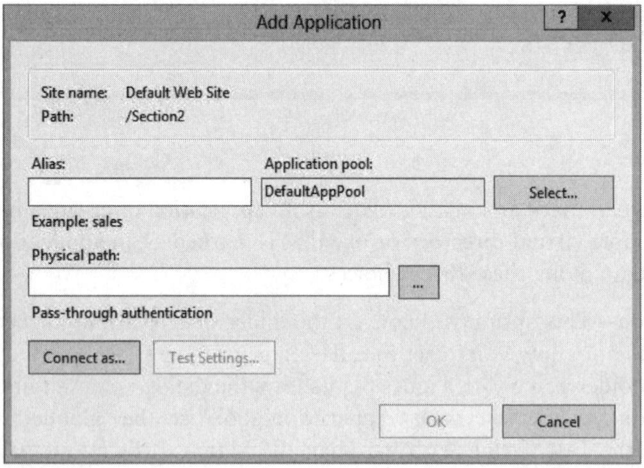

FIGURE 8-16

➤ **Add Virtual Directory**—The third option will create a virtual directory, but it will not set it as an application. Figure 8-17 shows the Add Virtual Directory dialog box. Notice that it does not have the option to select the application pool. This is because the virtual directory will be in the same application and share the same code folders and application boundaries as its parent folder.

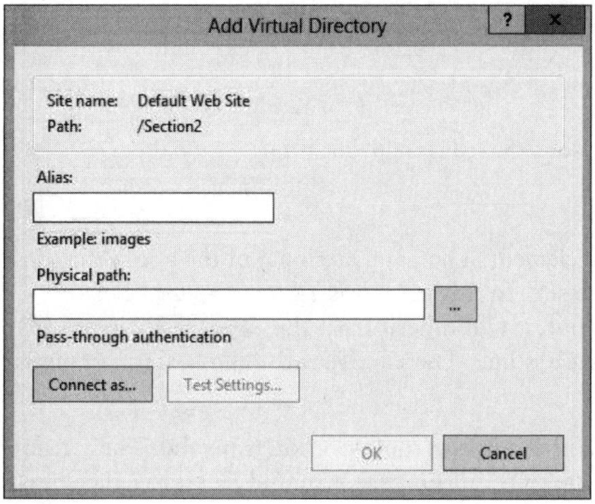

Add Virtual Directory

Site name: Default Web Site
Path: /Section2

Alias:

Example: images

Physical path:

Pass-through authentication

Connect as...   Test Settings...

OK   Cancel

FIGURE 8-17

It's interesting to note that the Convert to Application option will affect the folder that you right-clicked on, but the other two options will create a new virtual directory *under* the folder that you right-clicked on. This is because the latter two options create a new object instead of affecting an existing one.

AppCmd Method

Changing the application pool with AppCmd.exe differs from what you might expect. If the application already exists, it is simply a matter of using the set site command to update the applicationPool property.

```
appcmd.exe set site "Default Web Site"
-[path='/'].applicationPool:"Classic .NET AppPool"
```

It gets more complex when the application doesn't already exist. A website root is already an application, but a subfolder that hasn't been touched yet is not an application or a virtual directory. Before setting the subfolder's application pool, you must first set the subfolder as an application. This is done using the add app command in AppCmd.exe:

```
appcmd.exe add app /site.name:"Default Web Site" /path:/ExampleSubDir
/physicalPath:c:\inetpub\wwwroot\defaultroot\examplesubdir -
applicationPool:DefaultAppPool
```

This will create an application and a virtual directory.

applicationHost.config

Take a look at the XML created in the applicationHost.config file:

```
<sites>
    <site name="Default Web Site" id="1">
        <application path="/ExampleSubDir"
            applicationPool="DefaultAppPool">
```

```
                       <virtualDirectory path="/" physicalPath="c:\inetpub\
                        wwwroot\defaultroot\examplesubdir" />
                 </application>
            </site>
            ...
            <applicationDefaults applicationPool="DefaultAppPool" />
            ...
        </sites>
```

An `application` element is added to the `site` element. The `path` attribute of the `application` element is the relative path from the root of the site. In this case, it is `/ExampleSubDir`. The `applicationPool` attribute is optional; if left out, it will inherit from the `<applicationDefaults />` tag, not from its parent's settings as you may assume. The `<applicationDefaults />` tag is also in the `<sites />` section.

Next, you need to create a virtual directory. Without it, the configuration is invalid. The virtual-Directory path is relative to the application path; thus, in this case it should be set to /. The physical path is also required, which adds some complexity when setting a folder as an application.

The `physicalPath` must be a physical path either on a hard disk drive or a UNC path. A relative path will not work. You can obtain the physical path using `AppCmd.exe` or in code by getting the path to the root of the site and appending the subfolder name to it. In `AppCmd.exe` you can get the physical path to a folder using the following command:

```
appcmd.exe list vdir "Default Web Site/"
```

This will list all the virtual directories for the Site1 site, as shown in the following output:

```
VDIR "Default Web Site/" (physicalPath:%SystemDrive%\inetpub\wwwroot)
```

With this path, you can piece it together to mark the folder as an application. Notice with this example that the site requires the trailing slash (/); otherwise, it will not return a result, not even an error message.

Specifying the .NET Framework Version

If the web server hosts ASP.NET websites, key parts of the .NET run time are loaded into the worker process when the w3wp.exe process is started. They include all the assemblies specific to that particular application, an `HttpRuntime` object, and a cache object (among other things). Only one version can exist in each application pool because these are specific to a particular version of the framework.

This wasn't an issue in IIS 5.0 because ASP.NET lived in a separate process called `aspnet_wp.exe`. This shared process had a different set of disadvantages, but it happened to be easier to maintain.

It was first in IIS 6.0 that the concept of pre-loading the .NET run time into the `w3wp.exe` worker process began. An issue arises if you have multiple websites or applications that have different versions of .NET assigned to them. If these are placed in the same application pool, there would be failures with one or both versions of the framework.

The solution found in IIS 6.0 was to ensure that each application pool had applications that used one, and only one, version of the .NET Framework. IIS 6.0 did not have a good way to manage this or warn the administrator of this issue. Event Viewer would give a helpful recommendation after a failure, but for the average administrator it was easy to miss and difficult to understand what was happening.

FIGURE 8-18

In IIS versions following 6, it is now IIS itself that manages which version of the framework is loaded into the application pool worker process. When you are setting up or editing an application pool, the dialog box shown in Figure 8-18 enables you to select which version of the .NET Framework is set for that application pool. All installed versions of the framework are listed, as well as No Managed Code, which ensures that ASP.NET is not loaded at all.

You can change the .NET Framework version for an application pool using `AppCmd.exe`, as follows:

```
appcmd.exe set apppool "AppPool1"
-managedRuntimeVersion:v4.0
```

This will change the application pool AppPool1 to use ASP.NET version 4.0.

Using `Microsoft.Web.Administration` in Visual Basic .NET, it can be done as:

```
Dim appPool As String = "ExampleAppPool"
Dim runtimeVersion as String = "v4.0"

Dim sm As ServerManager = New ServerManager
sm.ApplicationPools(appPool).ManagedRuntimeVersion = _
    runtimeVersion
sm.CommitChanges()
```

This accomplishes the same as the `AppCmd.exe` example but uses the managed API instead. The example is straightforward, essentially declaring and setting the `appPool` and `runtimeVersion`; setting the runtime version for the application pool; and then committing the changes.

Here is an example of how to accomplish the same using WMI:

```
' set values for the application pool and runtime version
strAppPool = "DefaultAppPool"
strRuntimeVersion = "v4.0"

' Set oIIS and oAppPool
Set oIIS = GetObject("winmgmts:root\WebAdministration")
Set oAppPool = oIIS.Get("ApplicationPool.Name='" _
    & strAppPool & "'")

' Set the ManagedRuntimeVersion and commit the changes
oAppPool.ManagedRuntimeVersion = strRuntimeVersion
oAppPool.Put_
```

The .config XML method can be done by modifying the managedRuntimeVersion attribute in the add element of applicationPools:

```
<applicationPools>
    ...
    <add name="ExampleAppPool" managedRuntimeVersion="v4.0" >
    ...
    </add>
    ...
</applicationPools>
```

Specifying the Managed Pipeline Mode

IIS 8.0 supports two pipeline modes: the Integrated mode, which was introduced in IIS 7.0, and the Classic mode, which models previous versions of IIS. This choice is made at the application pool level, which is great for an IIS administrator because it allows one or both modes to run on the same server. Chapter 2 explains the two modes in more depth.

There are significant web.config differences between the two modes, and many web.config files that work in Classic mode will not work in Integrated mode. AppCmd.exe offers an automated method to migrate configuration files from Classic mode to Integrated mode format. This will be covered below.

First, it is worthwhile to see the structure of each mode and the differences between them.

Classic Mode

The Classic mode models the IIS 6.0 model in which ASP.NET acts as an ISAPI add-on to IIS. This mode is available for backward compatibility and lacks many of the features in the new Integrated mode. In Classic mode, IIS has its own pipeline that can only be extended by creating an ISAPI extension, which has a well-deserved reputation for being difficult to develop. ASP.NET is run as an ISAPI extension that is just one part of the IIS pipeline.

This is best visualized by looking at Figure 8-19. Notice that ASP.NET appears to be an after-thought and doesn't come into play until IIS processes the ISAPI extensions.

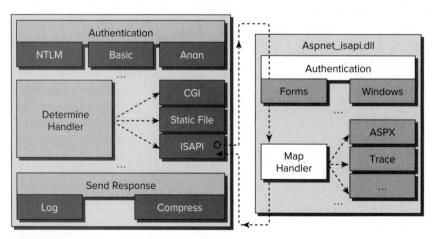

FIGURE 8-19

The file extension determines which ISAPI handler to use. For example, .aspx and .ascx are two of the file extensions mapped to aspnet_isapi.dll. The .asp extension is mapped to asp.dll to handle classic ASP pages, and if installed, the .php extension is mapped to php.dll to handle PHP pages.

Additionally, in IIS 8.0 Classic mode, several features are duplicated. For example, error handling is a duplicate feature where IIS handles non-ASP.NET pages and ASP.NET handles all pages mapped to aspnet_isapi.dll.

> **NOTE** *It's possible to map all file extensions to ASP.NET in IIS 6.0, but there are some limitations. The most noticeable is that default documents are not processed unless they are specifically handled in* global.asax *or an HTTP module. There is a reasonable amount of custom configuration required to have* aspnet_isapi.dll *successfully handle all file types. IIS 7.0 and 8.0 handle this without any additional effort.*

Classic mode will run existing websites without requiring changes to web.config. So, if you have a web farm with mixed versions of IIS, or if you have other reasons why you can't migrate the web .config file to the new syntax, then Classic mode may be a valid option for you.

Integrated Mode

Integrated mode makes ASP.NET an integral part of IIS. Now the IIS server functionality is split into more than 40 modules that split IIS and ASP.NET functionality into subsystems. Modules such as StaticFileModule, BasicAuthenticationModule, FormsAuthentication, Session, Profile, and RoleManager are part of the IIS pipeline. Notice that FormsAuthentication, Session, Profile, and RoleManager were previously part of ASP.NET and didn't have anything to do with IIS.

Figure 8-20 shows the IIS pipeline with modules that were previously part of ASP.NET but are now directly part of the IIS pipeline.

The IIS pipeline has more than twenty events that developers can easily tap into to extend the functionality of the web server. In fact, the modules that are included with IIS 8.0 can be replaced simply by creating custom modules and updating applicationHost.config to use the custom module instead of the ones provided by Microsoft.

Configuration Differences between Modes

IIS 8.0 includes several configuration files that are applicable to the web developer. The <system .webServer> is a section that is recognized in either Classic mode or Integrated mode and can be set in applicationHost.config or in a web.config file. This section controls static pages as well as dynamic pages. Even in Classic mode, this section is honored and enables the web developer to set various IIS configuration settings in the web.config file.

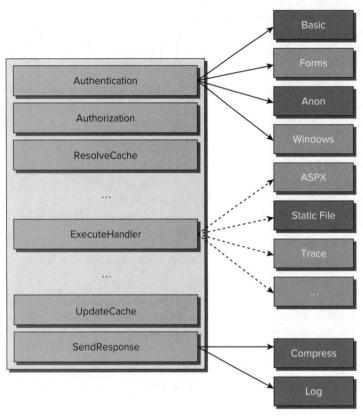

FIGURE 8-20

In Integrated mode, the HTTP modules and HTTP handlers are moved from `<system.web>` to `<system.webServer>`. If you run a `web.config` file that contains HTTP modules or HTTP handlers in Integrated mode, it will fail. Fortunately, Microsoft included a detailed 500.22 error message that includes steps to migrate the `web.config` file (see Figure 8-21).

`AppCmd.exe` is the tool that Microsoft provides to make this migration painless. To migrate the `web.config` file for the Default Web Site, run the following `AppCmd.exe` command:

```
AppCmd.exe migrate config "Default Website/"
```

Here is an example of a `web.config` file that works in Classic mode and in IIS 6.0:

```
<?xml version="1.0" encoding="utf-8" ?>
<configuration>

  <system.web>
    <httpModules>
      <add type="classname, assemblyname"
      name="modulename" />
    </httpModules>
  </system.web>

</configuration>
```

After you run the `AppCmd.exe migrate config` command, the `web.config` file is updated to look like the following:

```xml
<?xml version="1.0" encoding="utf-8" ?>
<configuration>

    <system.web>
       <httpModules>
          <add type="classname,
             assemblyname" name="modulename" />
       </httpModules>
    </system.web>
     <system.webServer>
        <modules>
           <add name="modulename"
              type="classname, assemblyname"
              preCondition="managedHandler" />
        </modules>
        <validation
           validateIntegratedModeConfiguration="false" />
     </system.webServer>

</configuration>
```

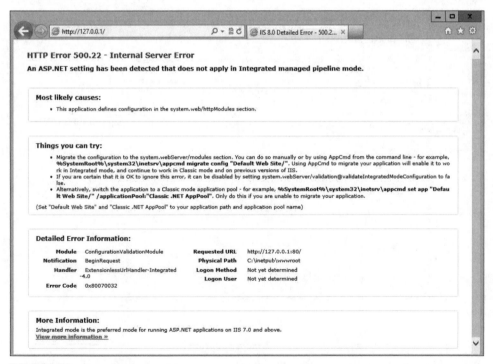

FIGURE 8-21

Notice that the `httpModules` section was left in place for backward compatibility, but it is the `modules` section in `system.webServer` that will take precedence. The `validateIntegratedModeConfiguration` attribute ensures that IIS doesn't complain about the legacy `<httpModules>` section.

Integrated mode is the default mode and has several significant advantages. Just be sure to migrate any existing `web.config` files that have HTTP handlers and HTTP modules so that they run correctly under IIS 8.0.

Managing Active Application Pools

Creating and updating the settings of application pools is only the start. Managing active application pools is essential to effectively managing an IIS server. As mentioned above, each running application pool starts at least one new and separate `w3wp.exe` worker process. If web gardens are enabled, more than one worker process can exist per application pool. IIS and the Windows operating system allow the administrator to view and manage these processes.

More about this is covered in Chapter 22, "Monitoring and Performance Tuning," but common ways to view running worker processes are covered here.

Viewing Running Processes in IIS 8.0

As with IIS 7.0, the running worker processes can be viewed within IIS Manager (see Figure 8-22).

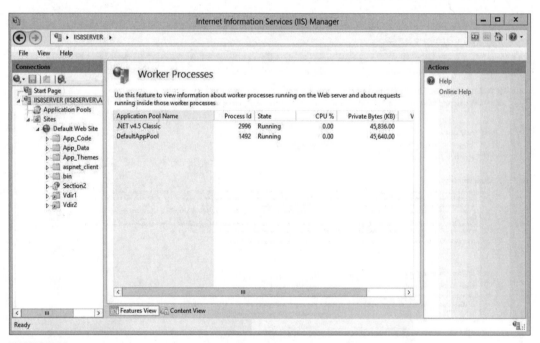

FIGURE 8-22

> **NOTE** *Once an application pool stops during a reboot, restart of the IIS service, or triggered by an idle time out, a new worker process is not started again until the `Http.sys` mechanism receives a first page request for a site served by the application pool. This means that there isn't always a worker process running for every application pool.*

To view the worker processes, in IIS Manager, click the server name and double-click Worker Processes in the IIS section.

The following values are worth noting:

➤ **Process ID**—This is the Process ID (PID) of the worker process on the server. Task Manager will show this same number if the PID column is enabled.

➤ **State**—This shows the current status of the worker process (Stopping, Stopped, Starting, Started, or Unknown).

➤ **CPU %**—This is the CPU % at that instant in time. You can press F5 to refresh the display.

➤ **Private Bytes (KB)**—It's important to understand what this is. This is the allocated physical bytes that the operating system has reserved for that worker process. This is the current size of memory that this process has allocated that cannot be shared with other processes. This corresponds to the "Commit Size" column in Task Manager. Note that the Commit Size column is not shown by default. The application pool can be set to recycle if this value is exceeded.

➤ **Virtual Bytes (KB)**—This is the current size of virtual address space that the process is using. There is no equivalent column in Task Manager in Windows Server 2008, although Performance Monitor will expose this information by selecting the Process object, the appropriate w3wp worker process, and the Virtual Bytes counter. The value in IIS Manager is in kilobytes, whereas the one in Performance Monitor is in bytes, so make sure to multiply or divide by 1024 so that you are comparing apples to apples. The application pool can be set to recycle if this value is exceeded.

Viewing Running Processes in Task Manager

Task Manager is a powerful tool to quickly find key information about a computer. In Windows Server 2012, Microsoft gave Task Manage a welcome facelift. To open it, right-click an open place in the taskbar and click Task Manager from the context menu. Note, the default view in Task Manager shows only those desktop and applications that are currently running. To view more information about systems, click the More Details toggle on the lower-left corner of the Task Manager window.

The Processes tab in this extended Task Manager view shows a list of all running processes that can be accessed by the currently logged-in user (see Figure 8-23). You can find the `w3wp.exe` processes in the Background processes section. The `w3wp.exe` processes found here correspond to application pools defined in IIS Manager that have recently served content.

By default, the PID column is not displayed. It is worth enabling the first time Task Manager is opened on a computer. This change will remain in effect until it is purposely disabled. To do this:

1. Right-click on the top row (where the column name is).

2. Click on PID and the new column will appear.

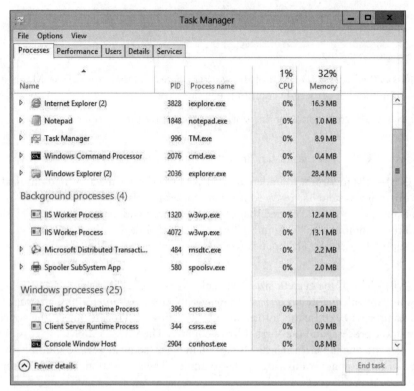

FIGURE 8-23

Now the PID column is visible. Another useful view within the Task Manager is the Details tab. The Details tab in Windows Server 2012 is more like the Processes tab found in Windows Server 2008 and previous operating systems. If each application pool runs under a different user account, the User Name column in the Details tab gives a good clue as to which process belongs to which application pool. To add the PID to the Details tab:

1. Right-click on the top row (where the column name is).

2. Click Select Columns.

3. Check the box next to PID.

4. Click OK on the Select Columns window to close it.

> **NOTE** *In IIS 6.0, there was a tool called* `IISApp.vbs` *that could help match PIDs with application pool names.* `IISApp.vbs` *is no longer available as it has been replaced with* `AppCmd.exe`*.*

Viewing Running Processes Using AppCmd.exe

`AppCmd.exe` will display actively running processes on the computer, along with the PID and application pool name (see Figure 8-24).

```
appcmd.exe list wp
```

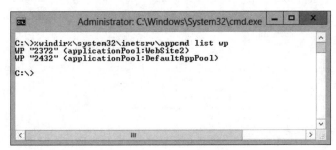

FIGURE 8-24

It is helpful to use either IIS Manager or `AppCmd.exe` along with Task Manager to get a good idea of the running state of the application pool worker processes on a system. Using two or three of the tools together will allow you to match up the PID with the application pool name, then view various performance counters available in each tool.

Performance Monitor is another valuable tool to troubleshoot worker process information and is covered in Chapter 23, "Diagnostics and Troubleshooting."

Viewing Running Page Requests

Not only can you view the active worker processes, something that you could do even in IIS 6.0 using Task Manager, but in IIS 8.0, you can see the currently running page requests using the IIS Manager. This was a welcome new feature in IIS 7.0, something that was very difficult to gain access to in previous versions of IIS. Chapter 23 covers this in more depth, but a short walk-through is given here.

To view the currently running page requests in IIS Manager:

1. Start at the server level, and double-click the Worker Processes icon within the IIS section. This will show all currently running worker processes.

2. Double-click on the worker process for the application pool for which you want to see the currently running page requests. This will bring you to the Requests page, which will show all currently running pages (see Figure 8-25).

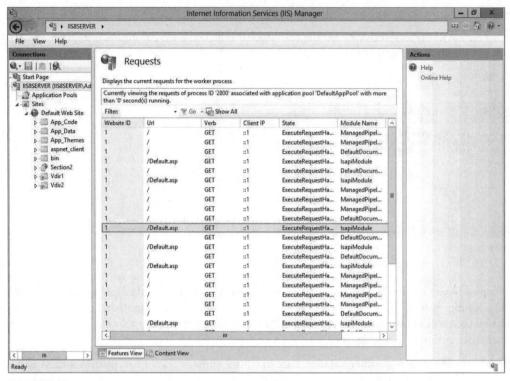

FIGURE 8-25

The Requests page is a list of all currently running processes. If the page completes in subsecond times, it is hard to catch it unless there are many running at a time, but for slow-running pages, this is a great tool to see what is running at any given time.

Starting, Stopping, and Recycling Application Pools

Application pools can be started, stopped, or recycled. There are several reasons that an application pool should be stopped or recycled. Reasons include requiring a fresh start because of a memory leak, a runaway site that is affecting performance on other sites, activating a significant configuration change by restarting an application, or a multitude of other factors.

> **NOTE** *As mentioned above, recycling an application pool doesn't immediately stop an existing process unless all running pages have been completed or the shutdown time limit period has elapsed. In the case of a long running page that is consuming excessive CPU, it may be necessary to kill the* w3wp.exe *worker process directly using Task Manager to have an immediate impact. This is a last resort measure but it will not hurt other worker processes and, depending on the situation, may be necessary for the good of the server. As explained in the above section, you can check the currently running page requests to see what is causing a worker process to stay alive after a recycle.*

Recycling, stopping, or starting an application pool in IIS Manager is a breeze. There are two methods that work equally well. One is to right-click on the application pool and use the dropdown box to take the desired action (see Figure 8-26). The other is to select the application and use the Application Pool Tasks in the Actions pane.

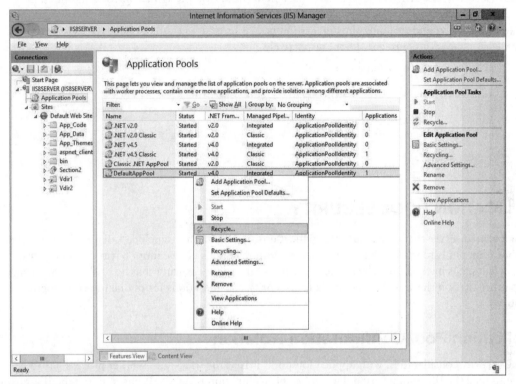

FIGURE 8-26

AppCmd.exe is straightforward as well. The AppPool object is used instead of the WP object in this case.

To recycle an application pool:

```
appcmd.exe recycle apppool "DefaultAppPool"
```

To stop an application pool:

```
appcmd.exe stop apppool "DefaultAppPool"
```

And to start an application pool:

```
appcmd.exe start apppool "DefaultAppPool"
```

The preceding actions can be done from managed code as well, using the Recycle, Stop, and Start, Stop methods of the ApplicationPools object, respectively. The following example shows how to recycle an application pool. Starting or stopping an application pool is just as easy. Simply replace Recycle() with Start() or Stop(), as required.

```
    Dim apppool As String = "DefaultAppPool"

    Dim sm As ServerManager = New ServerManager
    sm.ApplicationPools(apppool).Recycle()
```

Likewise, the `WebAdministration` namespace in WMI allows the same control using the same method names. This example shows how to recycle an application pool. As with the previous example, starting and stopping the application pool is as easy as trading `oAppPool.Recycle` with `oAppPool.Start` or `oAppPool.Stop`, respectively.

```
    strAppPool = "DefaultAppPool"

    Set oService = GetObject("winmgmts:root\WebAdministration")

    'get the app pool instance
    Set oAppPool = oService.Get("ApplicationPool.Name='" & strAppPool & "'")

    oAppPool.Recycle
```

APPLICATION POOL SECURITY

On a shared server that hosts multiple applications, it is essential to include isolation between the application pools to ensure that a site infected with malicious code cannot harm the other sites, or, if one site is hacked, that the hacker's access is limited by ensuring that he or she cannot affect the other sites on the server. There are a few security considerations for managing your application pools.

Application Pool Configuration Isolation

One security consideration with application pools is that the `w3wp.exe` worker process has to be able to read the IIS configuration data to be able to function properly. It has to know the IIS settings specific to all websites that it serves. This means that it has to have Read access to the vast majority of `applicationHost.config` settings. The issue is that if each application pool can read the entire configuration file, it exposes all the information to all the application pools. Therefore, it is essential that each application pool does not have Read or Write permissions to the entire `applicationHost.config` file; otherwise, the wrong person could gain access to sensitive information such as site anonymous user passwords or application pool passwords.

To get around this, the IIS development team came up with a method to allow the `w3wp.exe` worker process to read all the information pertinent to its needs, without having access to the information for any other application data or sensitive global settings. The result is an impressive method to create complete configuration isolation between application pools.

When an application pool is first started, the *Windows Process Activation Service* (WAS) takes only the information pertinent to the application pool and creates a temporary file in `%windir%\inetpub\temp\appPools\`. WAS sets ACLs for the related application pool, and saves the information there. Figure 8-27 shows the folder with the `DefaultAppPool.config` file.

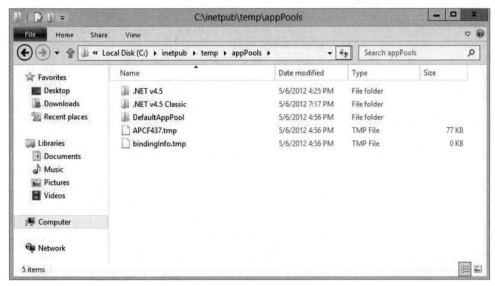

FIGURE 8-27

The `.config` file contains most of the same data that `applicationHost.config` contains, but it does not have any information about the websites in other application pools, and it does not have the application pool settings. It does not need the application pool information, because the `w3wp.exe` worker process is managed by WAS, and the `w3wp.exe` worker process does not need information about itself.

This temporary file is updated only when a change is made that pertains to the data in that file; otherwise, it remains in place until IIS is stopped. Deleting this file will cause IIS to fail for that application pool, and it will only be rebuilt when IIS is restarted. Recycling just the application pool will not properly rebuild the file if you delete it, therefore you should not touch these files except under extreme troubleshooting measures and if you understand their purpose and how they function.

This whole process of creating temporary files was new in IIS 7.0 and automatically ensures that no malicious code in one application pool can read sensitive configuration data from other application pools.

Application Pool SID Injection

What happens when all application pools use the Network Service account? Doesn't this mean that all the `.config` files will have ACLs for the Network Service account and will therefore all have access to the other configuration files?

The answer is no! There is a feature in Windows Server 2012 that allows certain built-in Windows users to have additional unique information injected into both the worker process and Windows security token to isolate resources from each other. IIS uses this feature and injects a unique *security identifier* (SID) for each application pool into the header of the `w3wp.exe` worker process. Each configuration file has the ACLs set to allow access only if both the Network Service account and the application pool SID are a perfect match when reading the configuration file. This ensures that all application pools using the Network Service account are completely isolated from each other automatically.

> **NOTE** *The Application Host Helper Service controls the mappings between IIS and Windows users.*

If you create custom users for your application pool, those custom users will be used to access system resources and the application pool's temporary `.config` file instead of the Network Service account. Note that if you do create your own application pool identity user, be sure to create a custom user for each application pool, because regular Windows users are unable to use the application pool SID injection. Only the Network Service account has this option. In Chapter 14, "Authentication and Authorization," we discuss this SID injection further. This feature is a part of IIS 8.0 and does not need to be manually turned on.

Site Anonymous User

Another security best practice is to change a website's default identity (anonymous user) to the identity created for and used by the application pool. This consolidates security, using just one identity instead of the IUSR or custom anonymous user in addition to the pool identity. This means that all code and service calls, local and across the network, will run under the single context of the application pool's identity.

In IIS 6.0, certain code would run under the anonymous user, and other code would run under the application pool identity. Turning on impersonation would allow you to force most code to use one or the other, but it didn't apply to every situation. In addition, CGI applications, static pages, Classic ASP, and ASP.NET all play by different rules and aren't required to run under one user or the other. This feature in IIS 8.0 allows absolutely everything to run under the application pool identity. If you give each website its own application pool, it is advisable to enable this so that you don't have to manage both anonymous users and application pool users. Managing one user per application pool/website pair makes administration easier.

To enable this, follow these steps in the IIS Manager:

1. From the site level, double-click the Authentication icon.

2. Click Anonymous Authentication, and then click Edit from the Actions pane.

3. From the Edit Anonymous Authentication Credentials dialog box, select "Application pool identity" (see Figure 8-28).

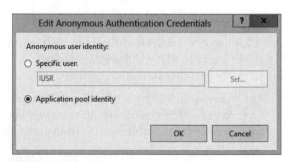

FIGURE 8-28

4. Click OK to save your selection.

To make this the default so that all websites that don't specifically have this set will use the application pool's identity, you can run the following `AppCmd.exe` command:

```
appcmd.exe set config
-section:system.webServer/security/authentication/anonymousAuthentication /userName:""
```

Watch word wrapping, as the preceding is a single command. This command sets the `userName` property to nothing, which will cause it to use the application pool identity.

NOTEWORTHY ADVANCED SETTINGS

It's beyond the scope of this book to detail every available setting because they can be found in the Microsoft Help and in the description section within IIS Manager. But there are some settings that have noteworthy significance.

Bitness

Historically, Windows Server 2003, Service Pack 1 offered support in IIS 6.0 to run 32-bit applications on 64-bit Windows. This way you could have 64-bit Windows and set IIS to run in 32-bit mode to run applications that weren't compatible with 64-bit. There was one major limitation with this option in IIS 6.0. You had to make this setting at the global level for all of IIS. You could not have some sites on the same server run 32-bit while others ran 64-bit.

Starting with IIS 7.0, IIS now supports different bit settings per application pool. You can set some application pools to run 32-bit and others 64-bit. The operating system must be 64-bit to support both bitness modes, and a 32-bit version of Windows can only support 32-bit application pools. This property does not show up in IIS Manager on a 32-bit version of Windows.

If you are running a 64-bit version of Windows, the Advanced Settings for the application pool has a property called Enable 32-Bit Applications which can be set to `true`.

You can change this with `AppCmd.exe` by using the following:

```
appcmd.exe set apppool "AppPool1"
-enable32BitAppOnWin64:true
```

CPU Limits

The CPU limit is one of the easiest settings to misunderstand. At first glance, it would appear that it is possible to set a CPU limit for each application pool so that it will run without using too much CPU. But that is not what the CPU limit does.

The CPU limit sets the maximum CPU that is allowed in the time frame set by "Limit Interval." If the limit is exceeded, IIS will take the action set in "Limit Action." The "Limit Action" choices are (1) No Action and (2) KillW3wp. "No Action" will write an event to the Event Viewer so that there is a record of the excessive CPU, but no further action is carried out. "KillW3wp" will do just that, stop the application pool worker process that exceeded the CPU limit, to prevent the rest of the server from being affected. A new worker process will immediately start up after the first one is stopped. This limit is not a throttle, per se; instead, it is a safety measure to deal with excessive CPU after the fact, but before it goes on too long.

The Limit setting is in 1/1,000th of a percent of the CPU during the Limit Interval time. To calculate the value, multiply the CPU percentage by 1,000. For example, to have a limit of 60 percent over 5 minutes, set the Limit to 60,000 and the Limit Interval to 5. Setting the Limit to 0 will disable the CPU limit.

> **NOTE** *CPU and resource monitoring are covered in detail in Chapter 22.*

Processor Affinity

IIS supports processor affinity, which means that a worker process can be forced to always run on a particular CPU on a multiprocessor server. Enabling a web garden on multiple processors will distribute the processes across the CPUs defined in the affinity mask. The setting in IIS is saved as an unsigned integer (essentially that means that it can only be a positive integer), even though the help mentions that it's a hexadecimal mask. In IIS Manager, in the advanced setting for the application pool, you can enter the value as a hexadecimal number (i.e., 0xF) and it will automatically convert to an integer, or you can enter it directly as an integer.

Be sure to also enable the `Processor Affinity Enabled` property; otherwise, the `Processor Affinity Mask` is ignored. The following table shows some sample affinity options.

HEX MASK (BINARY)	PROC7	PROC6	PROC5	PROC4	PROC3	PROC2	PROC1	PROC0
0x1 (0001)								Yes
0x2 (0010)							Yes	
0x5 (0101)						Yes		Yes
0xF (1111)					Yes	Yes	Yes	Yes
0xF0 (11110000)	Yes	Yes	Yes	Yes				
0xFE (11111110)	Yes	Yes	Yes	Yes	Yes	Yes	Yes	
0xFF (11111111)	Yes	Yes	Yes	Yes	Yes	Yes	Yes	Yes

APPLICATION POOL USERS

Application pools (`w3wp.exe`) run under the user that you specify, which IIS uses to access various system and network resources. For example, they have access to website data on the server's hard disk drive, the ability to perform certain system functions, access to the registry, or access across the network. The default user is the Network Service account, which has limited permissions on the web server and network, but is assigned sufficient permissions to run a standard website. IIS 8.0 allows you to select from three built-in accounts or to create your own custom user (see Figure 8-29).

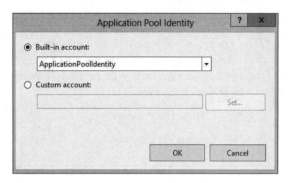

FIGURE 8-29

The built-in accounts are

➤ Network Service

➤ Local Service

➤ Local System

➤ Windows Application Pool Identity

The following sections discuss the four built-in accounts and how to create a custom user account.

Network Service Account

In Windows Server 2008, the default application pool user is the built-in *Network Service* account. Though the *AppPoolIdentity* account (see below) is the default for IIS 8 in Windows Server 2012, the Network Service account remains available. It has minimal permissions on the local computer and network. If you are accessing a resource on another device in the same domain (or in a trusted domain), the Network Service account's network credentials are used to authenticate to the server. This device can be a database, a UNC share, or any other resource that can be accessed across the network. The Network Service account's credentials are in the form of `DomainName\ServerName$`. For example, on the DomainA domain, if a server called WebServer1 was running a site using the Network Service account, and it is doing a database call to SQLServer1, then on SQLServer1, you should grant necessary SQL permissions to the `DomainA\WebServer1$` account.

The following privileges are assigned explicitly to the Network Service account:

➤ Adjust memory quotas for a process.

➤ Bypass traverse checking.

➤ Create global objects.

➤ Generate security audits.

➤ Impersonate a client after authentication.

➤ Replace a process level token.

As a member of the Everyone group, the Network Service account also inherits this privilege:

➤ Access this computer from the network.

Finally, as a member of the IIS_IUSRS group, it inherits this privilege:

➤ Log on as a batch job.

Local Service Account

The *Local Service* built-in user account does not have access to the network like the Network Service account does, but it has similar access to the local system. In Windows Vista and Windows Server 2008 and later, it is given the following additional local privileges that the Network Service account does not have:

➤ Change the system time.

➤ Change the time zone.

You can use the Local Service account if you don't require access to network resources.

Local System Account

The *Local System* built-in user account has full access to the local system. Be sure to use the Local System account with caution, and avoid using it permanently if at all possible. If an unauthorized user exploits a website on the server or gains the ability to upload content and if the application pool is running as the Local System, they could do most anything they please on the web server.

> **NOTE** *Although this user poses a potentially large security risk, it has a practical purpose. When troubleshooting an issue on a website, testing with the application pool identity set as the Local System will confirm whether or not permissions or privileges on the application pool identity are the cause of the issue. Of course, this troubleshooting needs to take into account the possibility of compound issues. Just be sure to set this back to the appropriate user or create a specific user with just the necessary permissions. Also, be sure to test this only on a website for which you know and trust the content and the content developer.*

Windows Application Pool Identity

Windows Server 2008 Service Pack 2 introduced a new built-in feature for running application pools under a unique system credential, referred to as a *virtual account*. Using the Windows Activation Service (WAS), IIS can generate this virtual account for you. There is no need to create either a local or domain account. The WAS will maintain the password for you, and the credential will have the rights of the local server. The virtual account will inherit the name of the application pool.

If you are running IIS 7.5 on Windows Server 2008 R2, you do not have to do anything special to implement a virtual account as an application pool identity. For every pool you create, the WAS will create a virtual account using the name of the application pool and run the pool's worker processes under this account.

If you are running Windows Server 2008 RTM, to take advantage of a virtual account, you have to change the `IdentityType` property of the application pools you create to `AppPoolIdentity`. Here is how to do so in IIS Manager:

1. Open the Application Pools node underneath the server level.

2. Right click the Application Pool and select Advanced Settings....

3. Select the Identity list item and click the ellipsis (the button with the three dots).

4. In the Application Pool Identity selector window, select the Identity Type "ApplicationPoolIdentity" from the combo box.

To do the same using the command line, you can call the AppCmd command-line tool:

```
%windir%\system32\inetsrv\appcmd.exe set AppPool
<your AppPool> -processModel.identityType:ApplicationPoolIdentity
```

Whenever a new application pool is created, the IIS management process creates a security identifier (SID) that represents the name of the pool. Resources can then be secured by using this IIS-managed identity. The identity is not a user-managed user account and will not appear as a user in any Windows User Management Console.

To use the Windows Application Pool Identity to secure file system objects, select a file in Windows Explorer and, for example, add the DefaultAppPool identity to the file's Access Control List (ACL). Here is how you would do this:

1. Open Windows Explorer.

2. Right-click the file and select Properties.

3. Select the Security tab.

4. Click the Edit button and then the Add button.

5. Click the Locations button and make sure you select your machine.

6. Enter **IIS AppPool\DefaultAppPool** in the "Enter the object names to select:" text box.

7. Click the Check Names button and click OK.

Custom User Account

IIS 8.0 allows you to create a custom user. This user can be a local Windows user, or it can be a domain user. Which one you use will depend on your environment and which you prefer for this situation. With a domain user, you can access network resources like UNC shares or a database by giving the application pool identity user access to the network resource. There are a few reasons why you might create a custom user:

➤ **The existing built-in accounts do not adequately meet your needs**—For example, if the Local Service doesn't have enough permission, and the Local System has too much permission, you can create a custom user with the exact permissions needed.

➤ **To separate websites to protect them from each other**—This is particularly important in a shared environment where one web server hosts multiple sites that do not trust each other. A shared web hosting environment is one prime example. Even within the same organization, website isolation is important since, if one website is compromised, websites or applications in other application pools will not be affected if configured correctly.

➤ **To access a network resource with the application pool identity**—If you want to access a network resource, you can create a custom domain user and assign it as the application pool identity. Then anything that runs under the application pool identity that requires access to a network resource will use the custom user that you created.

In IIS 7.0 and later, it is easier than ever to create a specific application pool user. In IIS 6.0, you had to remember to add the user to the IIS_WPG group so that it had adequate permissions to the metabase and operating system and for `Http.sys` to start the application pool. This is handled automatically in IIS through a convenient new feature. When IIS starts a worker process, it will automatically add the specific application pool user to the IIS_IUSRS membership at run time. This eliminates the need to manually add the specific user to the IIS_IUSRS group. This process doesn't permanently place the user in the IIS_IUSRS groups, but instead adds it each time for the lifetime of the worker process.

Like so many other features in IIS, this auto-mapping to the IIS_IUSRS group is configurable if you have a reason to disable it. The `manualGroupMembership` property isn't exposed in IIS Manager, but you can set it through other means, such as through `AppCmd.exe`, a text editor, or programmatically. To set it using `AppCmd.exe`, use the following command:

```
appcmd.exe set apppool "DefaultAppPool"
-processModel.manualGroupMembership:true
```

> **NOTE** *The IIS_IUSRS group is a built-in group with a unique SID that will always be the same on all Windows Server 2008 RTM and later servers. In addition, this user and SID will not change when localized to different languages of the operating system. This allows "xcopy" deployment of websites if the IIIS_IUSRS group is granted permissions on disk.*

Delegating Remote Administration

WHAT'S IN THIS CHAPTER?

➤ Role-based access

➤ Remote access

➤ Delegation settings

WROX.COM CODE DOWNLOADS FOR THIS CHAPTER

The wrox.com code downloads for this chapter are found at www.wrox.com/remtitle .cgi?isbn=1118388046 on the Download Code tab.

Many web environments have a need to distinguish access rights among the system administrators and the website development and management teams. Whether there are two people in these roles or hundreds, it is necessary for the server administration team to specify the access level and settings for the developers or deployment teams.

In the area of delegation, IIS 7.0 broke new ground in two areas. First, IIS administrators could specify and control the website administrators' rights and provide the IIS Manager tool for them to manage their settings through a user-friendly interface. Second, this same access in IIS Manager also enabled site administrators to access web.config files. This may seem strange at first because web.config files used to be for ASP.NET, and it wasn't possible to manage IIS from any type of control file. IIS 8.0 inherits the delegation of configuration from IIS 7.0. You will see that it is powerful, extensible, and distributable. The XML-based format of IIS configuration files allows for easy, granular delegation of the modules and features, ranging from server level settings in the applicationHost.config file to the site or an application level in a web.config file.

The advantages of managing some IIS features from the website's `web.config` file are huge, as you shall see, with the most prominent benefit being that web tool vendors and developers can create websites and then copy them using a simple tool like `Robocopy.exe` or FTP.

Delegation isn't just turning on a switch and allowing developers or administrators to commence work. Done right, it takes planning and understanding of what can and cannot be delegated. This chapter explores the various levels of delegation, how to set them, and what to look out for.

INTRODUCING THE MAIN CHARACTERS

For the sake of this chapter, it is useful to define two different types of personnel by their roles. In the real world, there are many similar situations to the ones we'll use here. For example, in training scenarios, there are teachers and students; in the workplace, there are managers and employees; and in sports, there are coaches and athletes. Likewise, in this world of website delegation, there are the *system administrators*, who have full access to the IIS server; and there are the *site administrators*, who can only do what they have been enabled to do by the system administrators. Sometimes, to the dismay of the developers and often to the delight of the system administrators, the parallels to the examples above are pretty accurate. It is the job of the system administrator to run a tight ship and give access only where it is absolutely necessary. Henceforth, these two roles will be affectionately known as the *system administrator* and the *site administrator*.

> **NOTE** *It is also possible to delegate administration of applications, not just entire websites; however, it gets a bit wordy to say "site and application administrator" over and over again. In this chapter, "site and application" is usually shortened to "site."*

System Administrator

In the IIS world, the *system administrators* are often those who install the operating system and configure IIS exactly to their liking. They may not be in a management position within the company, but they have full rights to the servers that they manage, and anyone else's access is granted only by their say-so.

This role comes with power, but it also comes with great responsibility. It is absolutely essential in almost any workplace to make sure that no security holes are opened and that every setting, change, and access level is completely accounted for. This is the principle of least privilege. The *principle of least privilege* means that every user or program can access only the information or resources that they need for legitimate purposes, without giving them unnecessary access.

Essentially, this means that each person is given the lowest level of access to the system necessary to get the job done. This often is a tricky balance, in which an educated judgment call needs to be made between the level of control someone is given and the security concerns that are introduced with that control.

It is the role of *system administrators* to ensure that every setting is understood and properly configured to the best setting for their environment. Often their jobs and their reputations hinge on things being set exactly right.

Site Administrator

The *site administrators*, on the other hand, should not have full access to the server but should only have access to their immediate area of concern. They do not have access to make security settings at the global level or to manage information for any other sites on the server.

Many people can fit in the role of site administrator. The site administrator can be a developer who is given permission to manage his or her own website; it can be the Quality Assurance (QA) team that needs to test, approve, and sometimes deploy websites; it can be an individual site owner in a shared hosting environment; or, it can even be the system administrator properly locking down his or her own external access to follow the principle of least privilege.

Regardless of the role, this person/group is at the mercy of the system administrator and must make do with the permissions granted or be able to plead his or her case to the system administrator to be granted greater access.

The Two Shall Work as One

Both roles — system administrator and site administrator — are important in most business situations, but even more important, the two administrators should understand each other. A system administrator who doesn't understand how the site administrator thinks is unable to set up a good environment for that person, except perhaps by sheer luck. Likewise, it's worthwhile for the site administrator to understand as much about the server as possible.

IIS MANAGER REMOTE ACCESS

IIS 8.0 offers two methods for enabling site administrators to manage websites remotely: IIS Manager and the `web.config` file. The following sections discuss how to make IIS Manager, with its default settings, available to site administrators. Later, we'll describe using `web.config`. And, finally, we'll wrap up the chapter by interspersing the two methods. First, we need to talk about the components necessary for both delegation options.

Installing the IIS 8.0 Management Service

The first thing to do to allow remote access to the server is to turn on the *Management Service* feature. Unless it is installed and enabled, it is not possible to manage IIS 8.0 remotely through the IIS Manager console. This is the same for IIS 7.0 and 7.5, but differs from IIS 6.0, where remote administration through the console was installed and enabled by default.

When installed, the Management Service runs as the Web Management Service (WMSvc) — a standalone web server and hostable web core (HWC). An HWC is essentially an HTTPS web service inside an out-of-band process, accomplished by making a `LoadLibrary` call to load `hwebcore.dll`.

Naturally, the HWC Web Service enables connections to IIS Manager over an HTTPS connection that does not depend on IIS 8.0.

In case the names seem confusing, *Management Service* is the name that IIS Manager calls the feature, whereas *Web Management Service* (WMSvc) is the name of the Windows service that does the work. The WMSvc Windows service listens for the following four types of requests:

➤ Login requests to `login.axd`

➤ Code download requests to `download.axd`

➤ Management service requests to `service.axd`

➤ Ping requests to `ping.axd`

Although independent of IIS, WMSvc is required for remote management of IIS using IIS Manager. To install the Management Service, perform the following steps:

1. In the Server Manager Dashboard, click "Add roles and features."

2. In the "Before you begin" page of the Add Roles and Features Wizard, click Next.

3. On the Select Installation Type tab, click Next.

4. On the Select Destination Server tab, click on the target server to select it, and then click Next.

5. Confirm that the Web Server (IIS) role is installed; if not, click on the checkbox next to it.

6. Expand the components for the Web Server (IIS) role by clicking on the arrow to the left of the role.

7. Check the box adjacent to the Management Service (see Figure 9-1).

   Confirm any additional features that may be required. If additional features are required, a new wizard will appear listing them. ASP.NET 4.5 is required; if you haven't installed it already, you can expect it to appear in the Add Roles and Features Wizard. If the wizard appears, click Add Features to continue.

8. Click Next on the Server Roles tab to continue.

9. In the Select features tab, click Next.

10. Click Install on the confirmation tab to complete the wizard, and then click Close to finish.

Enabling Remote Connections

After installing the Management Service, you need to enable remote connections, which are disabled by default. Although it means that no remote access is possible unless you specifically configure it, installing a service as disabled by default makes it that much harder for malicious parties to take control of your server.

NOTE *When using IIS Manager, only administrators on the local server can manage the Management Service. It is not possible to manage it remotely, even after you have configured the system for remote management.*

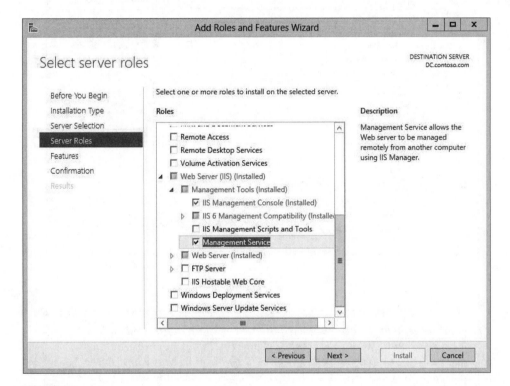

FIGURE 9-1

To enable remote connections, in IIS Manager:

1. At the server level, double-click the Management Service icon in the Management section.

2. Check "Enable remote connections" (see Figure 9-2).

3. Optionally, check "Windows credentials or IIS Manager credentials" if you will be using the IIS Manager credentials. This will be covered shortly.

4. The other settings can be left at the default setting or adjusted depending on your requirements.

5. Click Apply on the Actions pane.

FIGURE 9-2

> **NOTE** *"Management Service" is grayed out when WMSvc is started and cannot be edited until WMSvc is stopped. You can do that from the Actions pane. Obviously, any existing connections will be terminated if you stop the service to make any changes. A warning is presented explaining this, but even the best of administrators can miss the warning and panic when the screen is grayed out.*

After configuring WMSvc, be sure to start it. You can do so from the Actions pane by clicking Start or from the command line by using `net start WMSvc`.

> **NOTE** *By default, WMSvc has a start-up type of Automatic [Delayed Start]. This means that after your first server reboot, WMSvc will be started. To set the start-up type to Manual or Disabled, you can use the Services MMC snap-in from Administrative Tools (or by typing* **services.msc** *at the command line). Another option is to do it from the command line, as follows (note the spacing):*
>
> ```
> sc config WMSvc start= demand
> ```

After starting WMSvc, you can confirm that your server is listening by using `netstat`, as shown in the following example:

```
C:\>netstat -a | findstr 8172
   TCP    0.0.0.0:8172          IIS8Server:0      LISTENING
   TCP    [::]:8172             IIS8Server:0      LISTENING
```

The Connections and IP Address Restrictions sections enable you to customize how IIS Manager is accessed remotely. The individual settings are as follows:

➤ **Identity Credentials** — This takes a longer description, which will be covered shortly.

➤ **IP Address** — This can be left as All Unassigned or set to a particular IP Address. Multiple bindings are not possible in WMSvc because they are with sites in IIS.

➤ **Port** — This is the TCP port used. Make sure that all firewalls between the client computer and the server allow access to this port. Windows Firewall on the web server will, by default, allow IIS Manager access through port 8172, which is convenient. Yet, if you change the port, Windows Firewall will not automatically update the port; therefore, make sure to remember to update Windows Firewall whenever you make any port changes to Management Service.

➤ **SSL Certificate** — Windows Server 2012 creates a self-signed certificate when Management Service is installed. This works great as far as encryption is concerned, but it doesn't prove who you are. For that reason, IIS Manager will give a warning if you try to connect using the default certificate. You can change the default certificate. The recommended certificate should match the exact URL that you provide to the site administrator (or you can use a certificate type known as a *wildcard*). Chapter 15 describes installing certificates in more detail.

➤ **Log requests to** — This is straightforward. By default, logging is enabled and points to `%SystemDrive%\Inetpub\logs\WMSvc`. You can disable logging and/or change the path using this section. Note that this is for traffic coming in, not for errors. Errors with Management Service are logged to Event Viewer, so be sure also to check Event Viewer when troubleshooting configuration errors with Management Service.

➤ **The IP address restrictions** — Lets you allow or disallow access by IP address or range of IP addresses. Without the IP domain restrictions, all that is needed to gain access to the server is the username and password. The IP address, port, sitename, and application name come into play too, but they are often easy to guess. With properly configured IP restrictions, it is much more difficult to gain uninvited access to the server. The settings are fairly easy to understand but are slightly different from IP restrictions in previous versions of IIS.

The "Access for unspecified clients" dropdown list allows you to specify the default permission for anyone not set in this list. When set to Allow, any Allow IP entries will be ignored, and when set to Deny, any Deny IP entries will be ignored. Then why have them? The advantage of this method is that if you have a long list of IPs, you don't lose them if you temporarily switch between Allow and Deny, as you did in prior versions of IIS.

➤ **Restart/Start/Stop** — Be sure to start the service when changes have been completed; otherwise, any promises that you made to the site administrators that they can manage their sites remotely will be untrue until you remember to do this.

> **NOTE** *The settings for Management Service are not set in* `applicationHost` `.config` *like most other settings in IIS. Instead, they are saved in the registry under* `HKEY_LOCAL_MACHINE\SOFTWARE\Microsoft\WebManagement\Server`.

This configuration is stored in the registry and can be manipulated directly in the registry. The following is a sample VBScript using the WSH class that will enable remote management, set remote management to support Windows and IIS Manager Credentials, and set the service mode to start automatically and start the service. (User Access Control can interfere with this script because it is making changes to the registry.)

```
Const HKLM = &H80000002

strComputer = "."
strService = "WMSvc"

'Connect to the root namespace in WMI
Set objRegistry = GetObject("winmgmts:\\" & strComputer & _
   "\root\default:StdRegProv")

strKeyPath = "Software\Microsoft\WebManagement\Server"

'Turn on Remote Management
strValueName = "EnableRemoteManagement"
strValue = 1
call objRegistry.SetDWORDValue(HKLM, _
   strKeyPath, _
   strValueName, _
   strValue)

'Enable IIS Manager with Windows and IIS Manager Credentials
strValueName = "RequiresWindowsCredentials"
strValue = 0
objRegistry.SetDWORDValue HKLM, _
   strKeyPath, _
   strValueName, _
   strValue

'Connect to the cimv2 namespace in WMI
Set objWMIService = GetObject("winmgmts:" _
   & "{impersonationLevel=impersonate}!\\" & strComputer _
   & "\root\cimv2")

'Get all services called WMSvc (there will only be 1)
Set colServiceList = objWMIService.ExecQuery _
   ("Select * from Win32_Service where Name='" & _
      strService & "'")

For Each objService in colServiceList
   'Change the service account to start automatically
   errChangeMode = objService.Change( , , , , "Automatic")
   'Start the service
   errStartService = objService.StartService()
Next
```

To run this, create a file called `EnableRemoteManagement.vbs`, and paste this code into it. You can run it from the command line by typing **cscript EnableRemoteManagement.vbs** or by double-clicking on it.

Authentication Types

In versions 5 and 6 of IIS, Windows authentication was the only method of authentication available for IIS-related access. This held true in disk-level permissions for the site, application pools, and in IIS FTP. A local user needed to be created in Windows Users and Groups or in a domain before access could be granted to an IIS resource.

Starting with IIS 7.0, there is a method specific to IIS for remote management: *IIS Manager authentication.*

IIS Manager Authentication

IIS Manager authentication is managed at the server level, and users are assigned authorization at either the site or application level. Because IIS Manager users are not local Windows or domain users, you do not require a server Client Access License (CAL), and creating an IIS Manager user does not grant any rights to the server except what IIS allows. This makes IIS Manager Users users ideal for a shared web hosting or for a company that needs to manage several users with minimal rights. Within IIS Manager, you can manage the IIS Manager Users at the server level by clicking on the server in the left-hand pane and within the Management section in the middle pane, and double-clicking IIS Manager Users, as shown in Figure 9-3.

FIGURE 9-3

From the IIS Manager Users dialog box, you can create any number of new users or edit existing users by resetting the password, disabling or deleting them. Setting up authorization for these users comes later and is done from a different area. Figure 9-4 shows the IIS Manager Users tool in IIS Manager.

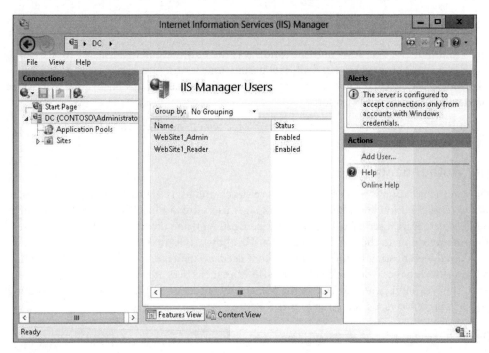

FIGURE 9-4

These users are stored in the `administration.config` file in the `%SystemDrive%\System32\inetsrv\config` folder by default, or they can be saved to a shared configuration location. The password is never stored; instead, the SHA256 hash is saved to disk. This enables you to move the hash between servers and ensures that others cannot read the password.

When IIS Manager creates users, they are placed in the `system.webServer` section of the `administration.config` file, as shown in the following snippet:

```
<system.webServer>
  <management>
    <authentication defaultProvider="ConfigurationAuthenticationProvider">
      <providers>
        <add name="ConfigurationAuthenticationProvider" type=... />
      </providers>
      <credentials>
        <add name="User1" password="12A303C224C250D07C81691DE6E0FD..." />
        <add name="User2" password="6025D18FE48ABD45168528F18A82E2..." />
        <add name="User3" password="5860FAF02B6BC6222BA5ACA523560F..." />
      </credentials>
    </authentication>
  . . .
  </management>
</system.webServer>
```

Creating IIS Manager users programmatically is described in Chapter 18, "Programmatic Configuration and Management."

> **NOTE** *Don't forget that the default option for Management Service is "Windows credentials only"; therefore, be sure to select "Windows credentials or IIS Manager credentials" from the Management Service section. Figure 9-4 shows the alert in the top-right corner that you will receive if you do not select "Windows credentials or IIS Manager credentials."*

Windows Authentication

Windows users and groups are another option for authentication. IIS can authenticate users stored in either the IIS server's local security directory or in an Active Directory domain.

There are many situations in which creating a domain account is preferred. For example, if you already have a user account for the site or application administrator, you can easily authorize it to manage a site using his or her existing user account. Additionally, if you plan to give this same user access to other resources or tools, it is worthwhile to use Windows user accounts so that you need only maintain one set of users and passwords. Another key difference between Windows authentication and IIS Manager user authentication is how the WMSvc service accesses the configuration files on disk.

When using Windows authentication, it is the Windows user token that makes all calls to the configuration files on disk. This means that you must grant the Windows user write permissions to the configuration files.

When using IIS Manager user authentication, it is the process identity of the WMSvc NT service that is used to read from and write to the configuration files. By default, this is the *Local Service* account. If using a shared configuration over a UNC path, make sure to update the service account to one that has rights to the configuration files. If you are using IIS Manager user authentication on a shared server where you need to ensure isolation between sites, be sure to assign a custom Windows user for the WMSvc service to run as, and give that user read/write rights to the web .config files for all sites that will be using IIS Manager delegation.

If you want to aggregate users to give whole groups access to a site or application, you must use Windows authentication or build your own custom provider, because IIS Manager Users does not support groups. With Windows authentication, it is possible to create users, assign them to a Windows group, and give that group permission to manage a site or application.

Windows users and groups are managed outside of IIS, either through the Local Security Authority Subsystem Service (LSASS) or through Active Directory. To add a Windows user to the local IIS server:

1. Press WIN+R, type **lusrmgr.msc** in the open field, and then press Enter.

2. Expand Local Users and Groups to create or manage a user or group from there. Figure 9-5 shows the Local Users and Groups tool.

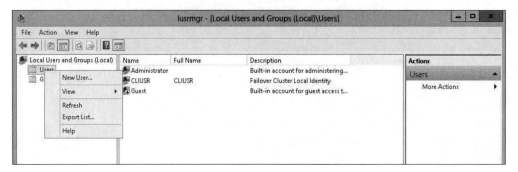

FIGURE 9-5

The same concept can be accomplished from Active Directory Users and Computers (ADUC) if you are using Active Directory users and groups.

Build Your Own

In addition to IIS Manager user authentication and Windows authentication, a third option for user authentication in IIS is to build your own provider. Authentication and authorization are extensible mechanisms implemented on top of a provider model. This means that you can easily (depending on your programming expertise) write your own authentication provider that authenticates against whatever back-end user store that you set.

For example, you can create a SQL back-end user store so that all your users are maintained in one place, or you can build something on top of the .NET membership provider. This allows you to share the same users with any other tools that you have developed. This is just one example; the sky is the limit as to what you can create.

Authorization at Three Levels

Now that we have covered authentication, it's time to determine the sites or applications to which users will have access. Authorization exists at three levels: the web server, the website, and the web application.

Web Server-Level Authorization

At the server level, users in the Administrators group are automatically given permission to manage the server remotely as long as Management Service is started. IIS 8.0 does not allow you to give an IIS Manager user access to the server level.

Website- and Web Application-Level Authorization

You can, however, grant permission to a Windows or IIS Manager user to manage a website or application. Unlike creating IIS Manager users, which are managed at the IIS application or service level, authorization is managed directly within the site or application.

> **NOTE** *You can see all permissions for the entire server from the server level. Select the server, and then double-click the IIS Manager Permissions icon. This allows read-only access to view the site or applications and users that are granted remote management permissions on this server.*

To authorize a user to access a website or application in the IIS Manager console:

1. Navigate to the site or application to which you want to grant management rights.

2. Double-click the IIS Manager Permissions icon, found in the Management section in the central pane (see Figure 9-6).

If you don't see the icon, look to see if the Management Service had been installed and the WMSvc service is running.

FIGURE 9-6

3. Click Allow User from the Actions pane.

4. Select either Windows or IIS Manager from the radio options. Both options have a Select button to allow you to choose from available users, as shown in Figure 9-7, or you can type in the user directly.

5. When selecting a Windows user, you can select a group instead of a user. It's important to note that the default object type is User, so if you use the Select wizard to assign a group, be sure to click the "Object types" button and check the Groups checkbox, as shown in Figure 9-8.

6. After entering a valid Windows user or group, or an IIS Manager User user, click OK.

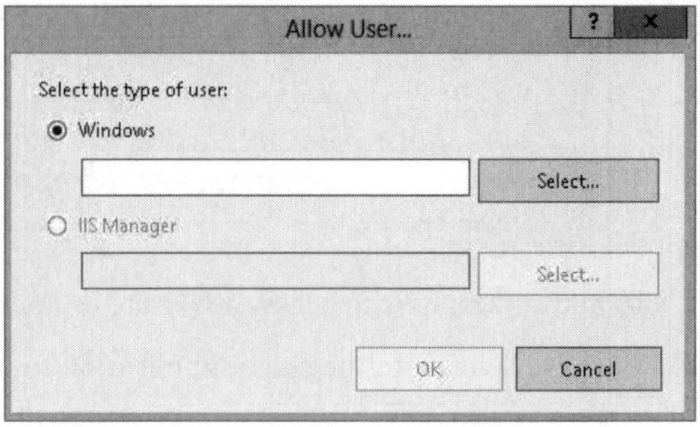

FIGURE 9-7

FIGURE 9-8

That user will now have access to the site or application.

Remote Installation and Usage

After configuring the server to allow remote management, the next steps are to make IIS Manager available to the site administrator and to provide the information he or she needs to connect to the IIS 8.0 server.

Both Windows Server 2008 and Windows clients since Vista SP1 include the IIS Manager client tool (aka Remote Manager) to connect to an IIS 8.0 Web Server, although it is not installed by default.

IIS Manager is compatible with and available for Windows XP and Windows Server 2003 through a separate download, available at www.iis.net/go/1524.

Connecting to the Server/Site/Application

After installing IIS Manager, it's time to connect to IIS 8.0 for remote management. The information necessary to connect to the server varies, depending on which level of access you require. Following is a list of the information that you need to provide, or be provided with, to connect to IIS 8.0 remotely:

➤ Required for all levels of access:

　➤ Server name, IP, or domain name

　➤ Server Port (if it's different from the default port 8172)

　➤ Username (don't forget the server name or Active Directory name if required)

　➤ Password

➤ Additional information for site or application access:

　➤ Website name (this needs to be spelled exactly right, but it's not case-sensitive). Spaces are allowed because IIS supports spaces in website names.

　➤ Application name

Connecting to IIS 8.0 Remotely

There are multiple ways to connect to a server, site, or application via a remote instance of IIS Manager:

➤ From the Start page, click any of the "Connect to a" links — for example, "Connect to a site."

➤ Click the upper-left icon in the Connections pane, and select one of the three choices (see Figure 9-9).

➤ Right-click Start Page, and select one of the three choices.

Once selected, it's as easy as following the wizard by plugging in the details. The wizard will guide you through the questions and provide some simple examples of the field syntax. You will also be presented with a field asking you for the connection name. This is just a friendly name for your own reference; it doesn't need to correspond with anything on the server.

It is possible to establish a connection to multiple servers, sites, or applications at once and use a single management tool to manage all of them, but you cannot connect remotely to the same site twice from the same server, even if using different methods of authentication. Be sure to save IIS Manager so that your connection is available next time you need to use it to manage a site.

Extending IIS Manager

One of the powerful features of IIS 8.0 is the capability to extend almost every area of the platform. IIS Manager is fully extensible and allows the IIS administrator or developer to extend onto the existing infrastructure. For example, if a new tool or feature is added to IIS, it can be made available remotely through IIS Manager. More impressive yet, all communication is still performed through the same port and then run locally on the web server, ensuring that even complex features do not need additional ports opened on any firewall.

The www.iis.net website has several custom applications that can extend IIS Manager. They can be accessed remotely just like the native IIS features. Chapter 12, "Core Server Extensibility," takes this further and walks you through extending IIS Manager yourself.

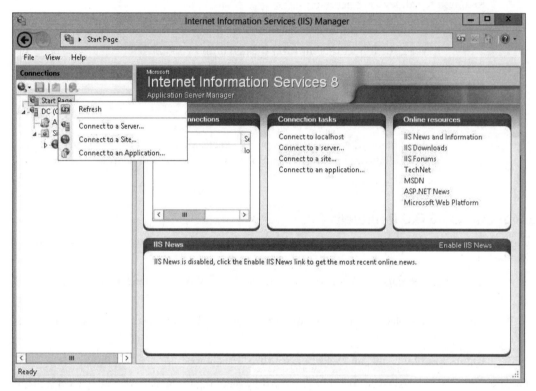

FIGURE 9-9

DELEGATION SETTINGS

So far, we've discussed remote management of IIS 8.0 using IIS Manager. Now it's time to look at the granular control available to you for remote administrator access.

> **NOTE** *IIS 8.0 does not have the capability to control access per user, per site. Each site can be adjusted to suit your needs, but all users that have permission to manage that site will have the same level of access.*

IIS 8.0 enables you to control two types of remote access:

➤ **IIS manager features** — Available rights are No Visibility, Read Only, and Read/Write.

➤ **Web.config access** — Available rights are Read Only and Read/Write.

Remote access through IIS Manager and `web.config` can be micromanaged to the finest detail by allowing every setting to be set on a per-site or per-application basis. Management access can be granted for whole sections, elements, collections, attributes, and even individual items within a collection. Additionally, access can be set so that "everything is granted except" or "only grant specific settings." If planned correctly, even the most complex lockdown requirement can be accommodated in IIS 8.0.

> **NOTE** *It's important to note in this section that only a small part of managing delegation is available from IIS Manager. Most of the fine-tuning adjustments must be made directly in* `applicationHost.config` *and* `administration.config` *files, or with one of the command-line or development methods.*

Delegation of Sections

Delegation at this level can get confusing because IIS Manager has two parts to cover in this discussion. Part one concerns the system administrator who uses IIS Manager to establish access settings for the site administrator. The other part is the site administrator doing what he or she has been granted permission to do.

Moving on from there, we see what the system administrator is able to set in IIS Manager for the site or application administrator. After looking at what can be achieved in IIS Manager, we look at the more granular configuration control that can be done directly from the configuration files.

The first thing to do is to open up the Feature Delegation section within IIS Manager, as shown in Figure 9-10, by double-clicking on the icon.

The Feature Delegation tool allows you to lock or unlock entire sections. Section examples include Error Handling, Compression, Authentication, and many others. IIS Manager does not allow you to lock or unlock more granular settings like attributes or elements, but that can be done manually, which will be covered later in this chapter. Figure 9-11 shows the Feature Delegation section.

FIGURE 9-10

Within the Feature Delegation tool, you can change the Delegation setting, depending on the item, to one of the following rights:

➤ Read/Write

➤ Read Only

➤ Not Delegated

➤ Reset to Inherited

➤ Configuration Read/Write

➤ Configuration Read Only

This can be done by selecting the item in the main window and clicking on the appropriate action in the Action pane, or by right-clicking on the item itself in the main window and selecting the appropriate action from the choices in the dropdown control.

These three options are covered in more detail later, but to really understand what they are doing, it's important to understand what is happening behind the scenes. The following sections dig in deeper to some of the more subtle settings.

FIGURE 9-11

Default Delegation versus Custom Website Delegation

The first thing to note is that when you open the Feature Delegation section, you will always start in the Default Delegation mode, labeled "Feature Delegation" at the top. This means that any change you make is global and will apply to all sites (unless the site has its own setting that overrides the default). To customize a delegation set that is specific to a site, click Custom Site Delegation in the Actions pane.

It's easy to get confused here because the differences between the two modes aren't very obvious. Apart from the subtle wording in the Actions pane, the two differences are the title and the existence of the Sites dropdown box only in the Custom Web Site Delegation mode. Figure 9-12 shows the Custom Site Delegation mode, and Figure 9-13 shows the Default Delegation mode.

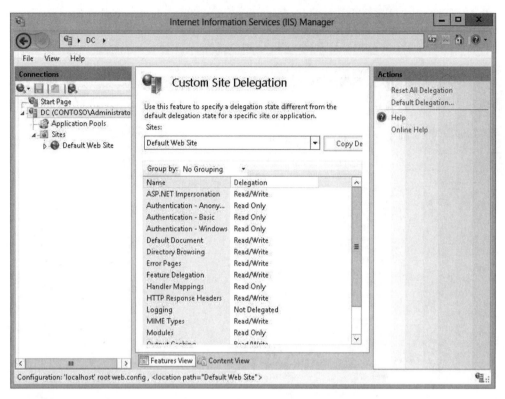

FIGURE 9-12

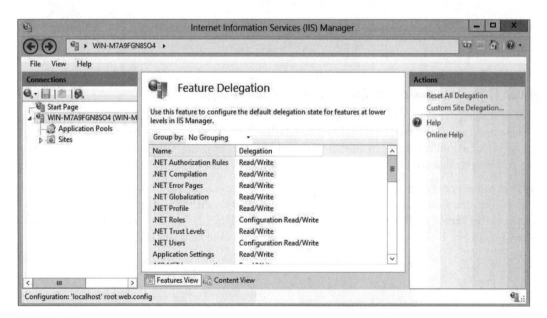

FIGURE 9-13

It's important to understand these two modes, because changes will be applied differently in each of the modes. In the background, every change is placed in a `<location />` tag in the `applicationHost.config` or `administration.config` file, which we cover in the next section (or in `machine.config` or the root `web.config` files for .NET settings). One or more of three location tags may be created, if they aren't already there. One location tag is set with `overrideMode="Allow"`, another with `overrideMode="Deny"`, and sometimes a third with `overrideMode="Inherit"`. When a setting change is made within IIS Manager, that section — for example, `windowsAuthentication` — is placed within one of the location tags.

When you are in Default Delegation mode, all changes are set in a `<location />` tag, where the path is set to `path="."` or `path=""` (both `path=""` and `path="."` function the same), as in the following example. This means that it applies to all sites, unless it is also set at the site or application level.

```
<location path="" overrideMode="Allow">
    <system.webServer>
        <security>
            <authentication>
                <windowsAuthentication enabled="true">
                    <providers>
                        <add value="Negotiate" />
                        <add value="NTLM" />
                    </providers>
                </windowsAuthentication>
            </authentication>
            <ipSecurity allowUnlisted="true" />
        </security>
    </system.webServer>
</location>
```

In the preceding example, the location path is `""` with an `overrideMode` of `Allow`, which means that it overrides the default `overrideMode` values. It then specifically grants read/write permissions to the `windowsAuthentication` section.

When you are in Custom Site Delegation mode, all your changes are placed into `<location />` tags, where the path is set to the website or application name, as shown in the next example (which is specific for the Default Web Site):

```
<location path="Default Web Site" overrideMode="Deny">
    <system.webServer>
        <security>
            <authentication>
                <windowsAuthentication>
                    <providers />
                </windowsAuthentication>
            </authentication>
        </security>
    </system.webServer>
</location>
```

In this example, the path is `Default Web Site` with an `overrideMode` of `Deny`. This means that Windows authentication cannot be set for the Default Web Site by a site administrator. Because the first location tag allows Windows authentication for all sites but the second location tag denies it for the Default Web Site, all site administrators except for the Default Web Site administrators can manage Windows authentication. The site administrators for the Default Web Site can view the settings, but they cannot update Windows authentication settings on their sites.

In a situation like this, it is always the setting furthest down the configuration hierarchy that takes effect. In this example, the first location section is applied first because it's a generic global section. Then the second location section is applied. This isn't because of the order listed (although they may be listed in that order) but because the second location is more specific and further down the configuration hierarchy path.

Another thing to notice in the first example above is the `ipSecurity` setting, which the second example does not have. This means that IPSec is allowed for all sites on the server, and because it isn't specifically denied for the Default Web Site, it is allowed there, too.

> **NOTE** *You may be wondering why only a few elements are set in the location tag when there are so many other sections. This is because there are defaults set earlier in the* `applicationHost.config` *file (or* `machine.config` *file for .NET-related settings), so if you have not changed a section, it will not show up in the location tag. This is covered in more depth in the next section.*

In IIS Manager, when you switch between the two modes, it does not change any settings in the background. In fact, next time you come back into that section in IIS Manager, it will revert back to the Default Delegation mode. Therefore, don't be afraid to switch between the two modes in IIS Manager and then make adjustments at whatever level you deem necessary.

<section> Settings

At the top of the `applicationHost.config` and `machine.config` files are the `<configSections>` sections. Within them are many `<configGroup>` tags, and under them are `<section>` tags. The `configGroups` are containers that don't do anything except hold `<section>` tags.

The `<section>` tags, on the other hand, define the rules for the section — where they can be configured, what their default `overrideMode` should be, and whether they can be defined in location tags. The following table lists the three properties you can set to control how a section can be managed:

PROPERTY	DEFAULT	VALUES	DESCRIPTION
allowDefinition	Everywhere	MachineOnly MachineToApplication AppHostOnly Everywhere	Defines where the section can be set. If not set, or set to Everywhere, then this section can be defined in applicationHost.config or any web.config file or location tag within the site hierarchy. It can even be set in folders not marked as applications. MachineOnly applies to .NET and means that this section can only be set in machine.config. MachineToApplication means that this section can be run in applicationHost.config, the website root, or any application folder. It cannot, however, run in a regular folder that isn't an application. AppHostOnly means that it can only run in applicationHost.config and cannot run anywhere under a website.
overrideMod-eDefault	Allow	Allow Deny	This sets the default overrideMode for this section. When set to Allow, changes in location tags or web.config files lower down in the site hierarchy can override the settings higher up. Essentially, it means that the value is read/write. Deny means that no sections below this can modify this value. Or, to put it another way, this value is read only.

continues

(continued)

PROPERTY	DEFAULT	VALUES	DESCRIPTION
allowLocation	True	true false	This can be set to false to disallow settings within a location tag. You can still set them in web.config files, but because they cannot be set in location tags, the web.config file needs to reside in the actual folder to which you want the setting to apply.

The combination of these three properties determines what is and is not allowed for the section to run at different levels. All three conditions need to be satisfied for a setting to be allowed outside of the main sections of applicationHost.config, machine.config, or the root web.config files. The default on all three is to allow as much access as possible, but many sections in applicationHost.config have an overrideModeDefault value of Deny.

> **NOTE** *Although you can change the* overrideModeDefault *directly, this may not be the best option. Instead, consider using a* <location> *tag in the bottom area of* applicationHost.config *(or in* machine.config *or the root* web.config *files for .NET settings) with* overrideMode *set to* Allow *or* Deny*. This way, you can leave the IIS defaults untouched while still setting the* overrideMode *at the server, site, or application level.*

The Role of the Configuration Files

The previous section covered changing sections to Read Only or Read/Write permissions. Those changes are applied to the applicationHost.config, machine.config, or root web.config files and apply to both IIS Manager and web.config. We have yet to describe the overall role of web.config files and that of the IIS Manager, so we will pause to cover those now.

As you are probably well aware, IIS 8.0 enables website developers and administrators to control some IIS settings from the web.config file. Settings such as defaultDocuments no longer require the IIS system administrator or a custom control panel to change them. Consider the following web.config file, which sets defaultDefault to default.aspx. When you or your site administrator places this file in your website or application root, IIS will pick up the setting and change the default document.

```
<?xml version="1.0" encoding="UTF-8"?>
<configuration>
  <system.webServer>
    <defaultDocument>
      <files>
        <clear />
```

```
        <add value="default.aspx" />
      </files>
    </defaultDocument>
  </system.webServer>
</configuration>
```

It's important to note that changes by a site administrator made through IIS Manager will always flow into the website `web.config` file; thus, IIS Manager and `web.config` go hand-in-hand. IIS Manager is simply a user-friendly tool to help you do what you could have done in `web.config` manually.

Changes made by a site administrator in IIS Manager do not flow into the `applicationHost.config` file. If you happen to have jumped into this section without reading the first couple of pages of this chapter, it's important to note that "site administrator" is referring to someone who is connecting to IIS Manager using specific site or application credentials. A system administrator, on the other hand, can make changes in IIS Manager that are written to `applicationHost.config`.

This `web.config` control allows application developers to create complete website projects that include everything from the web pages to the IIS configuration, ready for straightforward deployment. For this to work effectively, it is important that the website developers and site administrators not be given more permission than they should be trusted with, yet they need enough access to do their jobs properly. It is up to the system administrator to implement the necessary settings.

The default configuration allows only a limited amount of control from the site `web.config` file. The IIS team has locked it down to only the most obviously safe settings. It is up to the system administrator to turn on sections that he or she deems safe. Examples of sections that are allowed changes are as follows:

➤   `defaultDocument`

➤   `directoryBrowse`

➤   `httpRedirect`

➤   `urlCompression`

Some sections that are not allowed by default are as follows:

➤   `httpCompression`

➤   `windowsAuthentication`

➤   `httpTracing`

➤   `isapiFilters`

What happens when a developer uploads a `web.config` file that violates the rights granted to him or her? Because the website `web.config` file is not allowed to set `windowsAuthentication`, as in the following example, when the website is viewed, a 500.19 error is thrown.

```
<system.webServer>
  <security>
    <authentication>
      <windowsAuthentication enabled="false">
        <providers>
```

```
            <remove value="Negotiate" />
            <remove value="NTLM" />
            <add value="NTLM" />
         </providers>
      </windowsAuthentication>
   </authentication>
   </security>
</system.webServer>
```

Fortunately, because the error messages in IIS 8.0 are much more informative than those in the past, it is easy to tell what is wrong. Figure 9-14 shows the error message that is displayed when you view it from the web server (or if you have `<httpErrors errorMode="Detailed" />` set in web `.config` and are viewing it remotely).

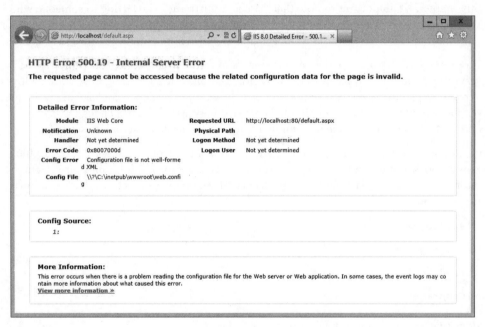

FIGURE 9-14

Note the Config Error and Config Source sections, which are especially useful, allowing you to discern exactly what is wrong.

It is also worth noting that the `windowsAuthentication` settings in the site `web.config` are exactly the same as they are in `applicationHost.config`. An error will be thrown if there is any attempt to set anything in the `windowsAuthentication` section, even if the net result doesn't change.

Customizing Application Folders Using Location Tags

You can also configure customized settings for folders set as applications. This is done simply by creating a `<location>` tag in `applicationHost.config` with a `path` attribute pointing to the application. The following example disallows setting the default document within the `/app` subfolder:

```
<location path="Default Web Site/app" overrideMode="Deny" >
  <system.webServer>
```

```
        <defaultDocument enabled="true">
          <files>
            <clear />
            <add value="Default.aspx" />
            <add value="Default.htm" />
            <add value="Default.asp" />
          </files>
        </defaultDocument>
      </system.webServer>
    </location>
```

If the web.config file in the app subfolder tries to set the defaultDocument, a 500.19 error is thrown because it is explicitly denied the ability to set default documents within the app subfolder. If the following web.config file in the app folder is set, a 500.19 error will be thrown because it violates the policy set in applicationHost.config:

```
<system.webServer>
  <defaultDocument>
    <files>
      <clear />
      <add value="default.aspx" />
    </files>
  </defaultDocument>
</system.webServer>
```

The question that arises, then, is how do you set the defaultDocument when you don't have permission to set it in the app subfolder? You can still set it in the website's web.config file, assuming that it's not also denied there, too. This is done using the <location /> tag in the website's web.config file, which is in the root of the site's path, as follows:

```
<location path="app">
  <system.webServer>
    <defaultDocument>
      <files>
        <clear />
        <add value="default.aspx" />
      </files>
    </defaultDocument>
  </system.webServer>
</location>
```

Notice that the location tag's path property is set to app, which means that even though it lives in the root of the website, it sets the default document for the app folder. The ability to control different sites and applications from location tags is powerful and allows you some flexibility to specify IIS settings from locations that make more sense for a system administrator — for example, from applicationHost.config, which the system administrator has access to but the site administrator does not.

Where Settings Are Applied

An interesting concept with IIS 8.0's delegated configuration structure is that *locking settings defines where IIS Manager applies changes.* IIS Manager will always enforce changes made at the lowest level possible along the configuration path.

If a section is unlocked and you make a change in IIS Manager to an application, IIS Manager will update the `web.config` file located in the application path. If the application does not have permission to apply the setting, it will write the setting in a location tag in the site `web.config` file. If the website is not granted permission to apply the setting, then the `applicationHost.config` file is updated instead. Of course, as mentioned above, if a setting needs to be applied to the `applicationHost.config` file, only a system administrator is able to make the change. It is read only for all site and application administrators.

IIS Manager does not allow you to specify the location where it makes changes, but it does show you precisely where it applies the setting. This is shown in the status bar at the bottom, as shown in Figures 9-15 and 9-16.

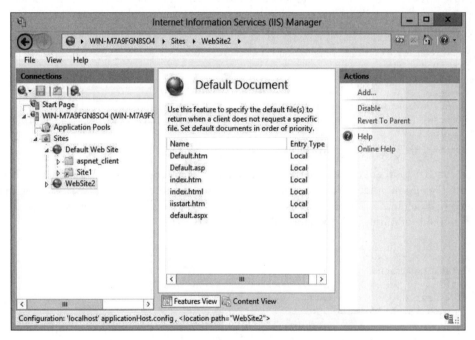

FIGURE 9-15

> **NOTE** *If you turn off delegation for a particular feature in IIS Manager, it does not automatically move settings around to protect websites from breaking. It is up to the website administrators to update that setting in their* `web.config` *files; otherwise, their websites may fail until they fix it.*

IIS Manager

We've covered IIS Manager from an administrator's perspective; now it's time to look at Read Only and Read/Write settings for delegation to site administrators. Let's look at the different IIS Manager delegation options in more depth to see what they really do.

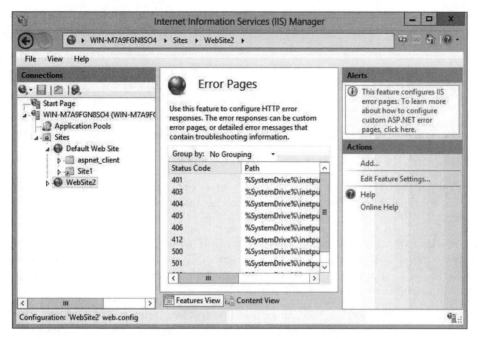

FIGURE 9-16

Read Only

Read Only access means that for that section, the site administrator cannot make changes to the `web.config` file. In IIS Manager the situation is the same. The site administrator can see the settings but is unable to modify them. When the site or application administrator clicks the Edit Feature Setting link, the settings will appear, but they will be grayed out and cannot be changed. A message will inform you in the Alerts window that the setting is Read Only.

Read/Write

With *Read/Write permissions*, a site or application administrator can edit settings in that section, either through `web.config` or from IIS Manager, as covered above.

Not Delegated

What if you want to completely hide the icons in IIS Manager so that they don't show at all (for example, if you do not want a site administrator even to see the ISAPI Filters icon)?

The `applicationHost.config` file allows you to set `<location />` tags with `overrideMode="Allow"`, `overrideMode="Deny"`, or `overrideMode="Inherit"`. That takes care of Read Only and Read/Write permissions, but it doesn't do anything about the actual icons in IIS Manager.

This is where the `administration.config` file comes into play. The `administration.config` file is specifically for the IIS Manager Users interface and various settings that it relies on — for example, management of IIS Manager users. In `administration.config`, you can remove modules, which, in turn, hides the icons in IIS Manager. Using this method, you are able to have each site or application show a different set of icons/tools.

The following excerpt in `administration.config` can be used to remove the ISAPI Filters icon for just the Default Web Site:

```
<location path="Default Web Site">
  <modules>
    <remove name="IsapiFilters" />
  </modules>
</location>
```

This is specific to just the Default Web Site, and it will remove the IsapiFilters module, which essentially means that the ISAPI Filters icon will not even show up for any site administrator for this website.

Within the `administration.config` file, concepts for `<clear />`, `<add />`, and `<remove />` apply the same to this as to `applicationHost.config` and even .NET itself. If an object already exists, you must first `<remove />` it or do a `<clear />` to remove all objects in a collection. If you do not do this first, you will run into errors because of duplicate objects.

In Feature Delegation in IIS Manager, you can set a section to "Not Delegated" for a particular site or application. When you do this, two changes are made to the configuration files in the background. A `<remove />` tag is added for that section in `administration.config`. Also, in `applicationHost.config`, that section is moved to a `<location />` tag with `overrideMode="Deny"`, and the `path` attribute is set to the name of the site or application. This causes it to become read only.

If you set a section to "Not Delegated" in Default Delegation mode (for all sites), it will actually remove the tag in `administration.config` rather than using a `<remove />` tag. It will also set it to read only in `administration.config`.

To look at it another way, when you select Not Delegated, you are hiding the icon in IIS Manager, and you are setting that setting to read only for `web.config` administration.

> **NOTE** *By editing the configuration files directly, you can hide the icons but still leave the settings as read/write for* `web.config` *management. Be careful that this doesn't fool you or future administrators into thinking that the section is locked down, just because it doesn't show up in IIS Manager.*

You can switch back to either read only or read/write, which will add the module back to `administration.config`, and, if you selected read/write, it will also update `applicationHost.config` to accommodate your request.

Configuration Read/Write and Configuration Read Only

There are two other types of section delegation settings: *Configuration Read/Write* and *Configuration Read Only*. There are two sections in which these settings apply: .NET Roles and .NET Users. These two sections are specific to ASP.NET users and roles that are stored in a database. Changing them will only affect the configuration settings and not the data itself. The reason they are called *Configuration Read/Write* and *Configuration Read Only* is to serve as a warning to let you know that you aren't locking users out of the data itself, but only the configuration. It's the database part that makes it unique.

The Not Delegated setting for a .NET User or Role is the same as for any other section. It will hide the icon and set the section to read only.

Reset to Inherited

The *Reset to Inherited* option sets the particular section to inherit from its parent. The way it does this differs depending on whether you're in the Default Delegation or the Custom Site Delegation mode.

When in Default Delegation mode, if you click "Reset to Inherited" and the section is within a location tag, it will add the tag back to administration.config and move the tag back up to the main section in applicationHost.config (or the machine.config or the root web.config files for .NET settings). Your custom settings will remain, however. If the section is not within a location tag, meaning that it already has the default setting, it will not change anything.

When in Custom Site Delegation mode, it will handle this differently. When you select the Reset to Inherited option, it will ensure that the tag is added back to administration.config; and in applicationHost.config, it will move the section to a location tag that has overrideMode set to Inherit. Even if the section isn't in a location tag already, it will move it down to the Inherit location tag.

Here is what applicationHost.config looks like when a section is set to Inherited:

```
<location path="Default Web Site" overrideMode="Inherit">
  <system.webServer>
    <isapiFilters />
  </system.webServer>
</location>
```

The other way to set a section to Inherited is to delete it from the location tags using a test editor like Notepad.

Reset All Delegation

The final option in the Actions pane of IIS Manager for delegation is the *Reset All Delegation* link. This also functions differently depending on the situation. Essentially, the rules are the same as for Reset to Inherited, covered in the previous section.

If you are in Default Delegation mode and click on "Reset All Delegation," it will move all sections from location tags and place them back in the main section of applicationHost.config, machine.config, or the root web.config. If you've placed any specific settings there, it will make sure to preserve them for you.

If you are in Custom Site Delegation mode, it will copy all of the sections into location tags with overrideMode="Allow" or overrideMode="Deny", except that it will leave the overrideMode="Allow" untouched. This results in whole new sections being created at the bottom of the configuration files, which you may or may not prefer.

If you would like to ensure that a particular website always inherits from the master default, you will need to update `applicationHost.config` manually and either delete the location tags if there aren't any specific settings in them, or change the `overrideMode` to Inherit.

Copy Delegation

When in Custom Site Delegation mode, there is a button called *Copy Delegation*. From here, it is possible to copy the delegation settings from one website to another.

To do so, select the website that you want to copy *from* in the dropdown box, and then click the Copy Delegation button (see Figure 9-17). This will open a dialog box with an option to select any number of the other websites on the server.

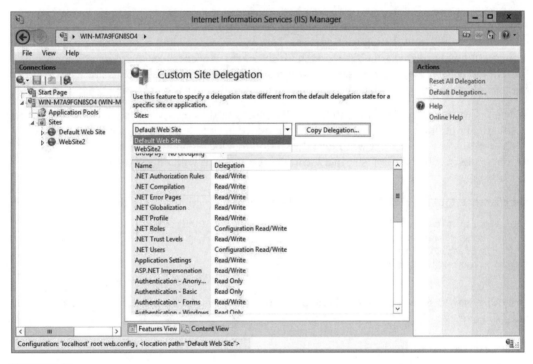

FIGURE 9-17

Select the sites that you want to copy *to* and click OK. This will create a duplicate copy of the location tags and section assignments in both the `applicationHost.config` and `administration.config` files. It is also careful to preserve any specific settings on each site.

It's interesting to note, however, that the Copy Delegation tool will create a copy of the entire resultant settings. The following example illustrates this point.

Here is a snippet of some example settings in `applicationHost.config` before copying. Notice that `customHeaders` has been set to read only for the Default Web Site, and a custom ISAPI filter is configured for WebSite2.

```
<location path="Default Web Site" overrideMode="Deny">
    <system.webServer>
```

```
                <httpProtocol>
                    <customHeaders />
                </httpProtocol>
            </system.webServer>
        </location>

        <location path="WebSite2" overrideMode="Deny">
            <system.webServer>
                <isapiFilters>
                    <filter name="Example" path="c:\windows\system32\file.dll" />
                </isapiFilters>
            </system.webServer>
        </location>
```

After copying the delegation from the Default Web Site to Site 2, the settings look like this:

```
        <location path="Default Web Site" overrideMode="Deny">
            <system.webServer>
                <httpProtocol>
                    <customHeaders />
                </httpProtocol>
            </system.webServer>
        </location>

        <location path="WebSite2" overrideMode="Deny">
            <system.webServer>
                <httpErrors />
                <modules />
                <handlers />
                <httpProtocol>
                    <customHeaders />
                    <redirectHeaders />
                </httpProtocol>
                <isapiFilters>
                    <filter name="Example" path="c:\windows\system32\file.dll" />
                </isapiFilters>
                <!--section removed to shorten the example -->
            </system.webServer>
        </location>
        <location path="WebSite2" overrideMode="Allow">
            <system.webServer>
                <urlCompression />
                <directoryBrowse />
                <security>
                    <authorization />
                </security>
                <!-section removed to shorten the example -->
            </system.webServer>
        </location>
```

There are three important things to notice here. First, the Copy Delegation tool preserves the custom ISAPI filter — for which we can all be thankful. Second, the Copy Delegation tool actually fills out the section of the site(s) to which it was copied. Third, the Copy Delegation tool will not copy specific settings to other sites. It will only apply delegation-related settings by placing elements in their appropriate location tag. In the example above, the isapiFilter called Example would not be copied to the Default Web Site if you used the Copy Delegation tool to copy from Site2 to the Default Web Site.

You may or may not prefer how IIS Manager does this. If you do not like how it does the copy, you are free to do it manually in `applicationHost.config` using a text editor like Notepad. There's nothing wrong with this, except that any changes to the delegation settings further up the hierarchy will not be automatically inherited after a copy is carried out.

AppCmd.exe and Delegation

You can use `AppCmd.exe` to lock and unlock sections and reset them to their inherited settings. It does not handle the advanced attribute, element, and item locking (which are covered in the above sections), but it does allow most of the delegation controls that IIS Manager supports.

> **NOTE** *Chapter 18, "Programmatic Configuration and Management," covers the* `AppCmd.exe` *tool.*

The `appcmd.exe config` command is used for a lot more than just configuring delegation settings, but the settings that apply to delegation are `lock`, `unlock`, `clear`, and `reset`.

The `lock` and `unlock` commands work the same as in IIS Manager, as covered above. Remember that locking makes a section read only, and unlocking makes a section read/write.

The syntax to lock a section is straightforward. You can leave out the site or application path so that it applies at the server level, or you can include it to make the section change more specific. Here is an example of how to lock the `directoryBrowse` section at the global level:

```
appcmd.exe lock config -section:directoryBrowse
```

This will place the `directoryBrowse` section in a location tag with `overrideMode` set to `Deny`.

To unlock a section, simply change `lock` to `unlock`. The rest of the syntax is the same. For example, to unlock the `customErrors` section for just the Default Web Site, run the following command:

```
appcmd.exe unlock config "Default Web Site" -section:customErrors
```

This will do exactly what the Read/Write link does in IIS Manager. It will place the `customErrors` section in a location tag, with `overrideMode` set to `Allow`.

There are also `clear config` and `reset config` functions, about which you can find more details by running `AppCmd.exe clear config /?` or `AppCmd.exe reset config /?`, respectively. These are not fully featured, but they do allow the most common changes. For example, `reset config` works only at the global level and does not support resetting inheritance at the site level.

With `AppCmd.exe`, it is possible to lock and unlock sections, reset global level settings, and clear out existing settings to do some housekeeping. In this section, we have looked at section locking and unlocking from IIS Manager, `AppCmd.exe`, and Notepad. Now it's time to look at attribute, element, and item locking.

Delegating the Small Details

So far, we have covered delegation of full sections. But what if you want to lock down more granular elements, collections, attributes, or even individual items? This is possible in IIS 8.0; in fact, the IIS team has you covered. By learning about a half-dozen properties, you can configure customized delegation, not only for sections, but for about anything else you can imagine.

Elements/Collections/Attributes

Before explaining how to lock or unlock elements, collections, and attributes, it's important to understand what they are. An *element* is a basic building block of XML, composed of a start tag, the contents, and an end tag. *Collections* contain multiple elements that can be added or removed individually. An *attribute* is a parameter used to attach information to the element. The best way to visualize this is to see an example:

```
<anonymousAuthentication enabled="true" userName="IUSR" />
<windowsAuthentication enabled="true">
  <providers>
    </clear>
    <add value="Negotiate" />
    <add value="NTLM" />
  </providers>
</windowsAuthentication>
```

➤ **Element** — In the above example, "`anonymousAuthentication`" and "`windowsAuthentication`" are elements. Elements can contain attributes, collections, or other elements within them.

➤ **Collection** — The `providers` collection allows multiple objects to be grouped together. In this case, they are a `<clear>` tag and two `<add>` tags.

➤ **Attribute** — `enabled` and `username` are attributes. They can only have one value (although the value can be a comma-delimited list of multiple values).

The scheme file `IIS_schema.xml` contains the real definition, where you can specifically see the elements, collections, and attributes. This is shown in the following example:

```
<sectionSchema name="...windowsAuthentication">
  <attribute name="enabled" type="bool" defaultValue="false" />
  <element name="providers">
    <collection addElement="add" clearElement="clear" removeElement="remove">
      <attribute name="value" type="string" isUniqueKey="true" />
    </collection>
  </element>
  <attribute name="authPersistSingleRequest" type="bool" defaultValue="false"
    />
  <attribute name="authPersistNonNTLM" type="bool" defaultValue="false" />
  <attribute name="useKernelMode" type="bool" defaultValue="false" />
</sectionSchema>
```

Now that we have looked at elements, collections, and attributes, it's time to look at how to lock or unlock them as needed.

Locking Attributes

The first attribute to consider is `lockAttributes`. This is a comma-delimited list of attributes that you want to lock. When this attribute is set, all child websites and applications can read the value, but they cannot update it. It can accept an asterisk (*) also, which means that all attributes are locked.

The following example shows how you can use `lockAttributes` to prevent any child sites or applications from changing the `enabled` attribute in `directoryBrowse`:

```
<location path="." overrideMode="Allow">
  <system.webServer>
    <directoryBrowse lockAttributes="enabled" />  </system.webServer>
</location>
```

This allows anything to be changed except for enabling or disabling `directoryBrowse`. As another example, to also lock `showFlags`, you can set `lockAttributes` to `lockAttributes="enabled, showFlags"`.

If an attempt is made to change the `enabled` attribute in a `web.config` file, a 500.19 locking violation error will be thrown when the website is viewed.

When you attempt to change an attribute in IIS Manager, a warning dialog will pop up, letting you know which line number on which file caused the error.

> **NOTE** *Here's an interesting one. If the section is set to Read/Write mode, setting changes made in IIS Manager will be applied to the website or application* `web.config` *file. If the setting that you want to make is not allowed because of the* `lockAttribute` *setting, you will get the error listed above. However, if the delegation mode is set to Read Only, then IIS Manager will apply the settings to the* `applicationHost.config`, `machine.config`, *or root* `web.config` *files, which aren't blocked by the* `lockAttribute` *setting. Basically, this means that if a section is set to Read Only, then the* `lockAttributes` *setting will be ignored by IIS Manager, but for a Read/Write section, the* `lockAttributes` *will prevent the setting from being changed, even by IIS Manager when running as a system administrator.*

Locking Elements

The next attribute that we'll look at is `lockElements`. This allows entire elements to be locked. You must place the `lockElements` attribute in the parent tag, as in the following example:

```
<httpProtocol lockElements="customHeaders">
  <customHeaders>
    <clear />
      <add name="X-Powered-By" value="ASP.NET" />
  </customHeaders>
  <redirectHeaders>
    <clear />
```

```
        </redirectHeaders>
      </httpProtocol>
```

By setting this in the `applicationHost.config` file, you can specify that child sites and applications cannot change the `customHeaders`, but they can still change the `redirectHeaders`, because you didn't specifically lock it.

Like `lockAttributes`, the `lockElements` attribute can use an asterisk (*) to signify all elements, and you can specify multiple elements by separating them with a comma.

Locking Collections

You can also use the `lockElements` attribute to lock collections. Collections typically have three directives: add, remove, and clear. You can prevent site and application administrators from using any combination of directives. For example, you may want to allow them to add new items to the collection but not to remove or clear out the existing items.

This is done the same way as with locking elements. The following example illustrates this:

```
<requestFiltering>
  <fileExtensions allowUnlisted="true" lockElements="clear,remove">
    <add fileExtension=".asa" allowed="false" />
  </fileExtensions>
</requestFiltering>
```

This will allow elements to be added but not removed. As expected, a 500.19 locking violation will be thrown if an attempt is made to `<clear />` or `<remove>` any items in the collection.

Locking Individual Items

A third attribute that can be used for delegation locking is the `lockItem` attribute. The two values of `lockItem` are `true` and `false`. This allows you to lock a particular item so that it cannot be changed. This is useful in a collection in which you require that a particular item always be set. Here is an example of this:

```
<httpProtocol>
  <customHeaders>
    <clear />
    <add name="X-Powered-By" value="ASP.NET" />
    <add name="X-Copywrite" value="Wrox" lockItem="true" />
  </customHeaders>
</httpProtocol>
```

This will allow site or application administrators to change or remove `X-Powered-By` and to add new items, but it will prevent them from changing or removing `X-Copywrite`.

Locking All Attributes and Elements Except Those You Specify

The final two attributes, `lockAllAttributesExcept` and `lockAllElementsExcept`, are counterparts to the attributes just discussed. They enable you to lock all attributes or elements, respectively, except for those you specify. Each attribute takes comma-delimited values, just like their counterparts, but they do not allow the asterisk (*) wildcard because that would be a double negative, which would be confusing and counterproductive. As an example of `lockAllAttributesExcept`, the following line allows the enabling or disabling of the directory browsing but ensures that nothing else can be changed:

```
<directoryBrowse lockAllAttributesExcept="enabled" enabled="false" />
```

The `lockAllElementsExcept` attribute is essentially the same, as shown in the following example:

```
<httpProtocol lockAllElementsExcept="customHeaders">
    <customHeaders>
        <clear />
        <add name="X-Powered-By" value="ASP.NET" />
    </customHeaders>
    <redirectHeaders>
        <clear />
    </redirectHeaders>
</httpProtocol>
```

Notice that the `lockAllElementsExcept` attribute is set with a value of `customHeaders`. This means that if you set a custom header, it will be allowed, but if you try to set the `redirectHeaders`, you will get a 500.19 lock violation error.

The `lock` attributes are useful to mitigate unknown changes when patching or loading future versions of IIS or ASP.NET and you want to ensure that no matter what, only the specific attributes or elements that you specify can be changed.

10

Configuring Other Services

WHAT'S IN THIS CHAPTER?

- ➤ Planning an FTP Server installation

- ➤ Installing and configuring an FTP Server

- ➤ Managing an FTP Server both through the GUI interface and programmatically

- ➤ Installing and configuring an SMTP Server

- ➤ Managing an SMTP Server both through the GUI interface and programmatically

- ➤ Installing LogParser and performing basic log-file analysis

WROX.COM CODE DOWNLOADS FOR THIS CHAPTER

The wrox.com code downloads for this chapter are found at www.wrox.com/remtitle .cgi?isbn=1118388046 on the Download Code tab.

In previous chapters you learned to plan, install, configure, and manage the basic IIS 8.0 Web Server functions. IIS 8.0 and Windows Server 2012 come with ancillary services that an administrator may want to use, such as an FTP Server and an SMTP Server. There are additional services and third-party tools that may also be helpful to IIS administrators, such as Microsoft's LogParser. Although the capabilities of Microsoft's additional services might be more limited than those of other commercial products, such as comparing the SMTP Server to Microsoft's Exchange Server, for many functions the included utilities and services provide all the functionality needed and with no additional costs.

Not all IIS servers will benefit from these additions, and an administrator should install only the services required. The security exposure of unneeded services should deter administrators from installing them, but these services can bring additional performance overhead, reducing the performance available for the needed functions of the server. Fortunately, all these services can be installed or uninstalled without affecting the IIS 8.0 functions, either during the IIS installation or at any time after IIS has been installed.

If you are familiar with these services in Windows Server 2008 and IIS 7.0, you should find no significant changes in the versions that ship with Windows Server 2012. The SMTP service has seen no changes in Windows Server 2012, but the FTP service has been extended to handle many requested functions, such as FTP logon attempt restrictions and added extensibility options.

There are planning decisions that you need to make before installing and configuring these services; however, the configurations are less than intuitive, especially when configuring FTP. Obviously, each installation environment will dictate how these are configured. For example, intranet use of these services differs from an Internet webhosting service. Plan your installation carefully, and you'll find these services, even with limitations, quite capable and robust.

INSTALLING AND CONFIGURING AN FTP SERVER

Microsoft's FTP service has been around since the Windows NT days, and the core code has always been a solid implementation of the RFCs describing the FTP service. This makes the FTP service extremely compatible with compliant FTP clients on all platforms. It has also historically caused some limitations in the service, including large file transfers and the lack of secure FTP services, which are in high demand today.

Windows Server 2012 has increased the security of FTP and supports FTP over SSL (FTPS) as well as account-lockout policies, IP restrictions, and request filtering. FTP also still supports user isolation, as it did in previous versions; traditionally, Microsoft's FTP service used a single FTP root folder and relied on Windows permissions for securing these folders. User isolation also seems to have caused the most problems for IIS administrators in configuring FTP services. In Windows Server 2012, the FTP service has the option of configuring user isolation based on IIS user accounts or Windows user accounts.

The transfer of larger files is supported, assuming that the hardware meets the requirements, and Windows Server 2012 supports larger file partitions. Time-out control of FTP sites makes it easy to support both longer file transfer sessions and less reliable connections. Administrators will find that Microsoft's FTP service provides the features that all but the most demanding organizations will need.

FTP Basics

At its root, File Transfer Protocol (FTP) is a simple protocol for transferring files between systems. It operates on standard ports — one for control and one for data flow — and the basic functionality has changed little since the early days of networking. The original description for FTP in RFC 114 was written in 1971, and the Internet Engineering Task Force standardized it in RFC 959 in 1985. The PASV command, allowing Passive FTP and also called *Firewall Friendly FTP*, was standardized in 1994.

FTP operates at the application level and uses the Transmission Control Protocol (TCP) as the transport protocol. Unlike many common protocols today, FTP uses two ports, one for the data stream and one for control, with TCP ports 20 and 21, respectively, the standard for Active FTP. Passive

FTP uses a negotiated port above 1024 for the data, which is initiated by the client and thus normally passes through firewalls with less trouble. By virtue of using a control port and a data port, large transfers can cause problems with FTP when the control port times out with no activity while the data port is transferring the file.

Security has been a concern with FTP since the beginning. By default, logons and passwords are passed in clear text, allowing network sniffers to retrieve the packets and reveal the logons and passwords. Two separate methods for addressing this issue exist, often referred to as *Secure FTP*. The first, which is true Secure FTP (SFTP), is FTP over SSH, wherein an FTP session is tunneled over an SSH connection. This is a tough act, because FTP uses separate control and data ports, whereas SSH protects a single port. However, FTP over SSH is available in various products and implementations. The second method, FTP combined with SSL/TLS, is normally referred to as *FTPS*. The term *SFTP*, often used to describe either of these methods, actually refers to SSH File Transfer Protocol, which isn't FTP but, rather, a new protocol designed to address FTP deficits. FTP Server on Windows Server 2012 includes FTP over SSL.

FTP on Windows servers can also be a major resource concern. Because each session is persistent in FTP, meaning that it remains open until closed, resources are tied up longer than they would be with an HTTP connection, which is not persistent. The default settings for FTP allow 100,000 connections with a time-out of 120 seconds, and many administrators will extend the time-outs to allow for larger file transfers through firewalls. For that reason, a busy FTP Server should always be a dedicated server and serve no HTTP or other traffic if possible. Installing FTP to allow content and code deployment to a website is a common function on web servers; if this is your purpose, Microsoft's FTP service is ideal for you.

Planning an FTP Server Installation

Installing and managing an FTP Server in IIS 8.0 requires some planning, especially in the case of folder structure for user isolation. If FTP is being installed merely to allow updating a website, no specific folder structure is needed, beyond that for the website. Users, often .NET user accounts, can publish websites and applications directly to the IIS 8.0 site structure, using FTP. Using FTP for publishing sites and applications is covered in Chapter 20, "Configuring Publishing Options."

To use FTP as a file transfer process in a traditional FTP Server setup, you need to understand and choose an isolation method and create the directory structure for it. Planning this structure is not difficult, but you need to decide on a proper structure, for security and privacy, for your organization.

User Isolation

Microsoft's implementation of FTP had a security concern prior to IIS 6.0 and Windows Server 2003: the inability to separate users into their own folder structure. Although a work-around existed before Windows Server 2003 and IIS 6.0, the concept of user isolation introduced in IIS 6.0 eliminated this security concern for administrators. In Windows versions since then, FTP users can be "Anonymous or Non-Isolated," "Isolated without Active Directory," or "Isolated with Active Directory." Depending on your specific needs, all three have a place on IIS 8.0 servers, and, in fact, all three can be run on the same server in different sites. When creating a new FTP site, you have three choices for user isolation.

Do Not Isolate Users

Under the "Do Not Isolate Users" setting, the FTP Server behaves as it did prior to Windows Server 2003 and IIS 6.0. Users may or may not have a home directory under the FTP root, and NTFS permissions determine whether separate users can access each other's files and folders. This setting is primarily used for anonymous access or where multiple users having access to the same files and folders is not an issue.

Isolate Users

The "Isolate Users" setting isolates users, based on their Windows logon, into separate home directories. NTFS permissions still affect the users, but they have no direct access to the home directory structure of other users. This setting allows for both local and domain user accounts to be used.

Isolate Users Using Active Directory

The "Isolate Users Using Active Directory" setting authenticates and isolates users through Active Directory and maps their home and root directories based on FTPDir and FTPRoot settings in Active Directory for each user. Naturally, this setting cannot be used outside of an Active Directory domain.

Directory Structure

One of the most confusing and least intuitive settings in configuring a Microsoft FTP site is the directory structure required for each user isolation method. If this directory structure is not used, then user isolation will not function, and clients will receive an error when logging in, indicating that the user's home directory is inaccessible. This is one of those configurations that made sense to a developer somewhere and became a required configuration regardless of usability. It is also one of the distinguishing factors between choosing to use the Microsoft FTP Server and a third-party product.

> **NOTE** *The directory structure for your FTP site must already exist when you create the site.*

Do Not Isolate Users

If you choose not to isolate users, the FTP site's root directory becomes the default home directory, unless there is a directory underneath the FTP root that exactly matches the user account logon. Whenever there is a matching directory, the user will be dropped into that directory on logon, but the only separation between users relies on Windows NTFS permissions on the files and folders.

The directory structure for this setting is the least exclusive of all FTP directory structures. You need an FTP root directory, which is specified in the configuration and can be anything, and that's it. If you want users to be dropped into folders based on their logons, you will also need a subfolder off the FTP root with the exact spelling of the logon name. For example, if user John Smith has a logon (SAM account name, not UPN) of *user1*, then the folder must be `user1` as well. Figure 10-1 shows examples of FTP folders created for the user account names User1, User2, and User3.

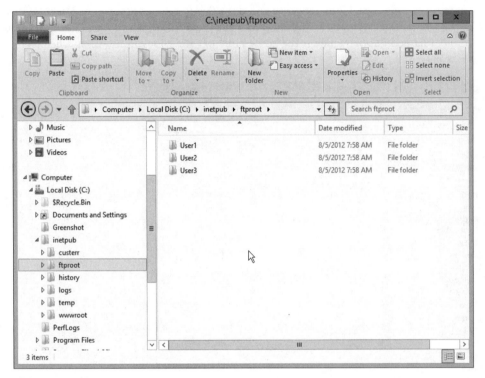

FIGURE 10-1

One common use of the non-isolated setup is for anonymous user downloads and uploads. When we go through security settings later in the chapter, we'll configure an anonymous upload folder that is invisible and doesn't allow downloads, often called a *blind FTP*. If you will use an anonymous access FTP for uploads or downloads, your best option is to configure a specific site for this and use a specific FTP root that is separate from any other. This setup is most prone to abuse, and instead of isolating the users, you can protect yourself better by isolating the entire site. An even better option is not to allow anonymous access but, rather, use a shared published account — perhaps *Upload* as a user for anonymous uploads and *Download* for anonymous downloads. You can then require a logon and password and rotate this on a schedule to reduce the opportunity for abuse of the FTP site.

Isolate Users without Active Directory

Standard user isolation requires a slightly more specific folder structure. In addition to the FTP root for the site, you need a subfolder off it named *LocalUser* for local accounts and/or the domain name for domain accounts. Off this folder, the subfolders must be named for each user account that will have FTP access. Each user is dropped into his or her folder upon logon as their root folder and is prevented from navigating up the folder structure to see the other folders. In user isolation, the user's home directory is the root of his or her FTP site.

Figure 10-2 shows examples of FTP folders configured for the domain user accounts User4, User5, and User6 in the Domain1.local domain and local user accounts User1, User2, and User3. You must also create a folder named *Public*, which is the home directory for anonymous access when using standard user isolation.

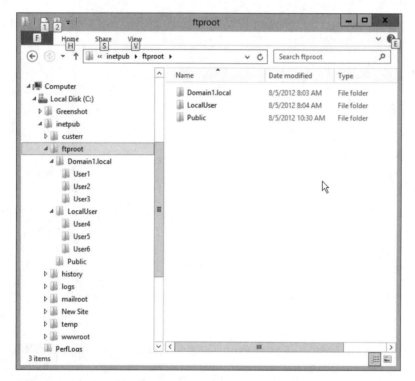

FIGURE 10-2

Isolate Users Using Active Directory

Active Directory isolation has no required folder structure because the user's home directory maps according to the home directory setting in his or her Active Directory account. Only valid Active Directory accounts can access the user's home directory and this FTP site.

Unless you installed FTP as part of the installation of IIS, you need to install it using Server Manager. Open Server Manager, click the Manage menu, and choose the Add Roles and Services option. Choose "Role-based or feature-based installation," select the appropriate server, expand the Web Server (IIS) role, and then choose the entire FTP Publishing Service tree, as shown in Figure 10-3, which includes FTP Server and FTP Extensibility. There's no configuration to be done while installing the service; you will set configuration options when you create FTP sites. If you will not use ASP.NET or IIS user accounts to deploy applications to websites, you do not need to install the FTP Extensibility role.

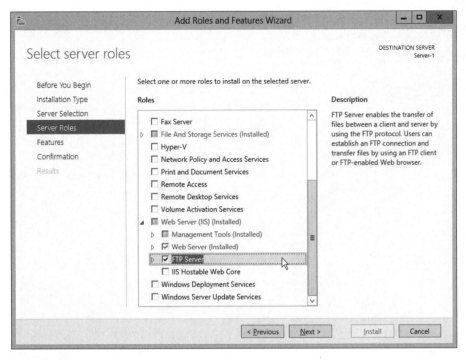

FIGURE 10-3

Installing the FTP service creates a directory under \Inetpub on the %SystemDrive% called Ftproot, which is the home directory of the default FTP site. This directory can be changed in the properties of the site, and additional sites on the system will need additional directories created, too. These directories can be on UNC network locations, but valid credentials to the share must be supplied. In other words, if you choose to use a network location and a UNC path, the target server must have that UNC share with proper permissions for the FTP account accessing it. If you choose to do this, the most effective method is with Active Directory accounts and Active Directory isolation.

Creating an FTP Site

To create a new FTP site, perform the following steps:

1. Open Internet Information Services (IIS) Manager and select the appropriate server. You will notice a new section in the Features View named FTP, as shown in Figure 10-4.

2. Expand the server in the Connections pane and right-click on the Sites folder. Choose Add FTP Site, as shown in Figure 10-5, to open the Add FTP Site wizard.

3. Enter an FTP site name and choose a physical path to the FTP file location. In this case, create a public FTP site and use the folder location c:\inetpub\ftproot\Public for the file location, as shown in Figure 10-6. Click Next.

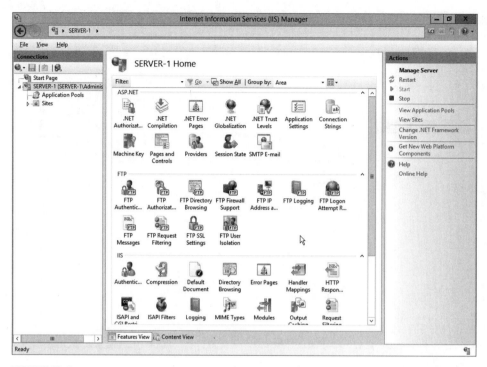

FIGURE 10-4

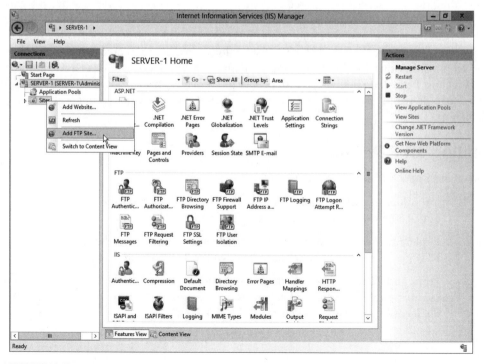

FIGURE 10-5

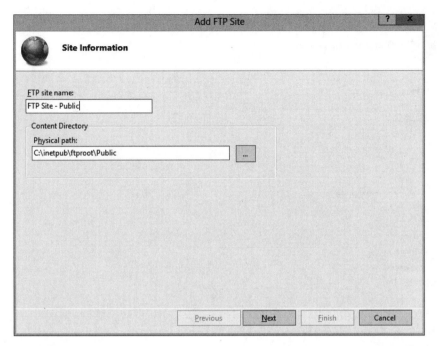

FIGURE 10-6

4. In the Bindings and SSL Settings dialog, choose the IP address for the FTP service to answer on.

Do not leave this set to All Unassigned, because this opens the FTP service on any IP address on the server that does not currently have an FTP site assigned. This is a security hole that an administrator will not want. Just as with websites, you can bind a specific FTP site to a specific IP address, separating multiple FTP sites on your server.

Unless you have a specific need, you should also leave the FTP port at the default of 21. As with web servers, FTP Servers answer on a specific IP address and port combination, and the default for the protocol is port 21. If you change this port, the end user must specify the port in the connection, as in `ftp://ftp.domain1.com:2121/`, if you set this for port 2121. This is useful for secure FTP sites but can be confusing for end users, because clients will assume the default FTP port of 21 when a user does not specify one. You must also remember to open the port in your firewall for access.

In IIS 8.0, you can now enable a virtual host name, similar to host headers for a website. Configuring FTP headers and SSL is covered later in this chapter. For now, do not choose a virtual host name. Choose No SSL, as shown in Figure 10-7, and click Next.

5. In the Authentication and Authorization Information dialog, choose Anonymous authentication. This will allow any user to authenticate to this FTP site. Also allow Authorization for all users and apply both read and write permissions, as shown in Figure 10-8, and then click Finish.

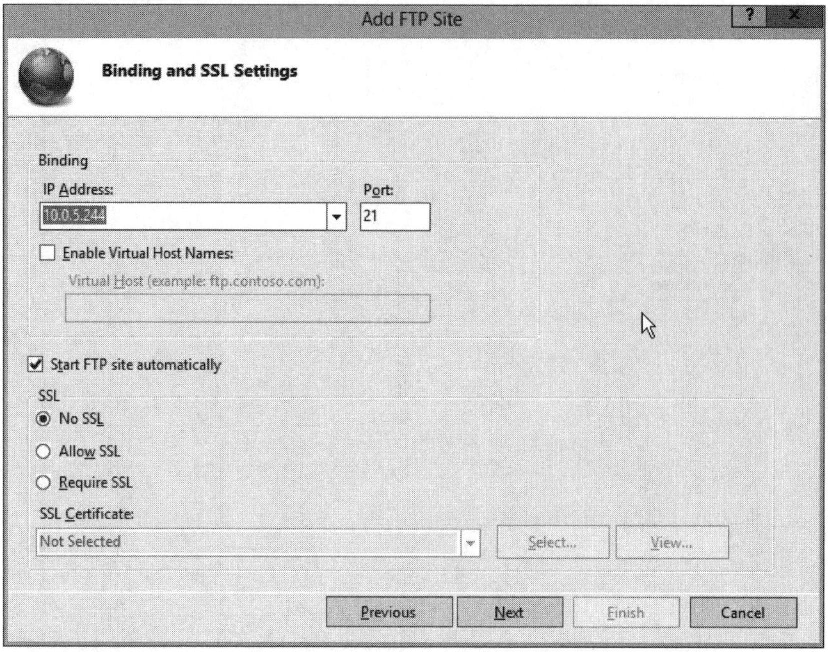

FIGURE 10-7

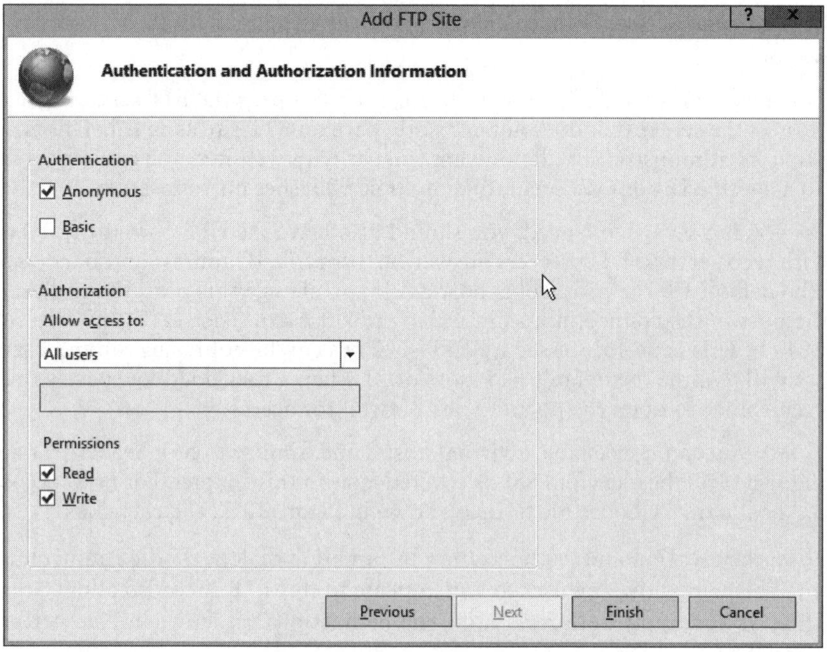

FIGURE 10-8

Never choose Anonymous authentication on a production system! Doing so creates an anonymous FTP Server available for any user on the Internet to upload and download files.

After adding the FTP site, when you open IIS Manager, you should find a new FTP site in the IIS Manager Sites folder, with the name *FTP Site — Public*. If you highlight the site, you should see the FTP features displayed, as shown in Figure 10-9.

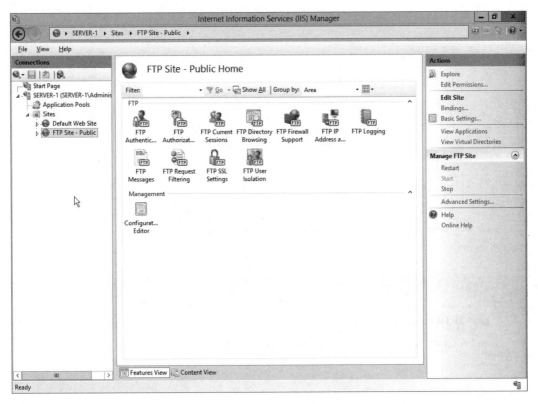

FIGURE 10-9

To test your new FTP site, simply open Internet Explorer and browse to the IP address of your FTP site using the FTP protocol. The URL should look similar to `ftp://{IP_Address}/`, substituting your site's IP address. You should see the default screen, as shown in Figure 10-10.

If you add some files to your FTP site root folder and reload your browser window, you will see those files listed, as in Figure 10-11. In this case, we created three dummy text files: `File1.txt`, `File2.txt`, and `File3.txt` in the `c:\inetpub\ftproot\Public` folder.

The Windows command-line FTP client is covered later in this chapter. This client is an easy way to test the functionality of an FTP site without potential issues caused by using another client, such as Internet Explorer, in testing.

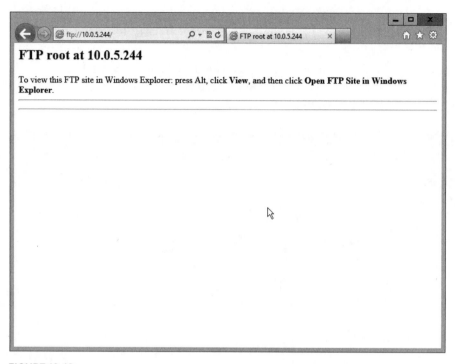

FIGURE 10-10

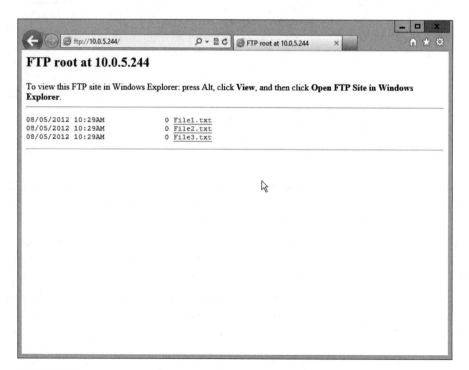

FIGURE 10-11

Creating FTP Sites with PowerShell

Windows Server 2012 and IIS 8.0 ship with PowerShell 3.0, which has many new cmdlets for managing both the server and IIS. Using PowerShell, you can script the creation of websites, described in Chapter 4, as well as create and manage FTP sites. This book is not a PowerShell manual, however; if you are unfamiliar with PowerShell, you may want to review Microsoft's Windows PowerShell resources, at `http://technet.microsoft.com/en-us/library/bb978526`.

Creating an FTP site using PowerShell is quite easy, using the `New-FtpSite` PowerShell cmdlet. The only required parameter is the site name, so the following command, in a PowerShell prompt, will create a site:

```
PS>New-WebFtpSite -Name NewFtpSite -Port 21
```

This creates a site, named *NewFtpSite*, that answers on all IP unassigned addresses and the default port of 21. The root of this site is in the FTP root folder under `c:\inetpub`. Often, these parameters are not what an administrator desires. Therefore, to create a website where you control the root path, the IP address, and a host name, use the following command:

```
PS>New-WebFtpSite -Name NewFtpSite -PhysicalPath c:\inetpub\ftproot\NewFtpSite
    -HostHeader NewFtpSite -IPAddress 127.0.0.1 -Port 21
```

Naturally, you should replace the IP address with your server's IP address. The local host designation of `127.0.0.1` won't work from any system other than the server itself.

Testing FTP with Telnet

One of the easiest tests for determining if the FTP Server is available on port 21 is to try using Telnet to reach the port. From a system outside your network, open a command prompt and type the following:

```
Telnet {ServerName} 21
```

where `{ServerName}` is the fully qualified domain name (FQDN) or IP address of your FTP Server. You should see a response something like this:

```
220 Microsoft FTP Service
```

If you see this response, your FTP Server is available and answering connection requests. This means that network connectivity exists between the test system and your FTP Server, including firewalls allowing traffic to pass on port 21.

CONFIGURING EXISTING FTP SITES

Newly created FTP sites will usually need some further configuration to meet the needs of an organization. Setting security, logging properties, and User Isolation all takes place in IIS Manager for the specific FTP site.

All of the basic permissions, binding information, and site information are available through menu options in the Actions pane for the FTP site. Bindings and basic settings were configured when the site was created but can be changed at any time. For example, changing the home folder location or the port the site answers on are just simple changes in these menus. But there are some advanced settings an administrator may want to change.

Home Directory

The home directory for an FTP site is set in the Basic settings for the site, found under the Actions pane. FTP Servers can be pointed to network shares as well as local directories. The key to this is providing access to the share for the authenticated FTP account or using "Connect as" to specify the user account with access to the share. If you use a share, the share permissions also come into play when determining the FTP user account's access to the FTP content.

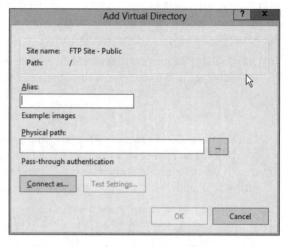

FIGURE 10-12

FTP sites can use virtual directories in the same manner that websites can. Virtual directories provide two valuable functions for FTP sites: redirection from the forced directory structure of standard isolated user sites, and redirection to common folders for isolated users. You can also use virtual directories to redirect non-isolated sites to alternate drives or folder structures. Virtual directories are below the FTP site home directory, so you must specify them in the FTP path for access. Many FTP clients allow you to set the default directory on the FTP Server that you will be placed in.

The process for creating a virtual directory in an FTP site is similar to the process for creating a virtual directory in a website. First, create the physical folder. Then open IIS Manager and browse to the FTP Server where the virtual directory will be. Select Virtual Directories from the Actions pane, and then select Add Virtual Directory... from the Actions pane. The Add Virtual Directory wizard will open, as shown in Figure 10-12, and ask for an alias (the name of the virtual directory). You can then browse to the physical directory, choose it, and, if needed, assign specific connection credentials by clicking on Connect as....

Advanced Settings

If you open the Advanced Settings dialog by clicking on Advanced Settings in the Actions pane, you will see General and Behavior settings that can be configured, as in Figure 10-13. In most cases, the general settings will have been configured while setting up the site, but the behavior settings assume some defaults that an organization may need to change. If you are having no issues with your FTP site, leave these at the default settings.

The time-out settings for a site work well in most situations, but you may want to increase or decrease these for specific sites. For example, a heavily used site may benefit from a shorter control time-out, which will close an inactive FTP session. A site with slow connections, on the other hand, might require setting the data channel time-out to a higher number to allow for inconsistent transmissions. Any changes made here should be noted and monitored for performance changes, and reset to the defaults if needed.

Max Connections is one setting that should never be set too low — 100,000 connections should be an absolute minimum. Otherwise, your server may suffer a denial-of-service attack from a system making too many connections at a time. Once the maximum number of connections is reached, legitimate connections will be blocked until a previous connection is dropped. Likewise, "Reset on Max Connections" should be set to `False` to keep your system from resetting all FTP connections during such an attack. Most modern firewalls will also block these types of attacks.

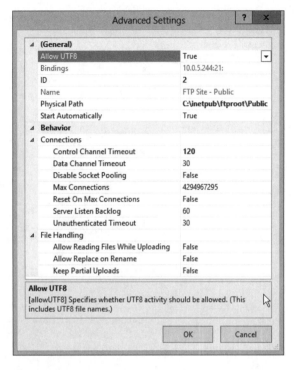

FIGURE 10-13

Logging

FTP logging is configured through the Logging feature for the FTP site. Unlike previous versions of FTP, logging is now enabled by default. If you open the Logging dialog by clicking on Logging in the FTP Features View, as shown in Figure 10-14, you can change the default settings for the logs. Logging uses the W3C extended log file format, and you can choose the location of the log files. Many hosting services will point these logs to a folder accessible through the FTP Server account assigned to the customer with that FTP site so that the customers can manage their own logs.

You can configure the W3C log fields captured by clicking on the Select W3C fields... button. Useful log options include Client IP Address, Method, URI Stem, Bytes Sent, and Bytes Received. For most organizations, the default settings will be appropriate. Current W3C log file format and fields can be found online, at `www.w3.org/TR/WD-logfile.html`.

Log file rollover settings are also usually adequate for most sites. If your site receives a lot of traffic, you may want to limit log file sizes. You can also configure the naming and timing for daily file rollover to be in local time. Log files in the W3C format are timed by Greenwich Mean Time (GMT), and changing the rollover and naming to local time will not change the actual logs. Conversion with a time offset from GMT must be done in your analysis software.

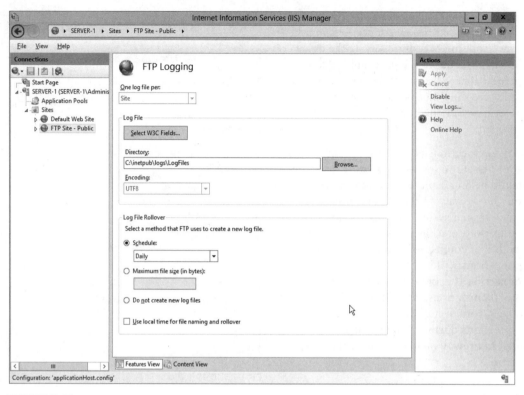

FIGURE 10-14

FTP Messages

Messages displayed by the FTP site can be configured using the FTP Messages feature for the site, as shown in Figure 10-15. Many organizations will not configure FTP messages because they are rarely seen by modern FTP clients, such as Internet Explorer; however, for some organizations, these messages should be configured. In particular, if your site requires specific permissions or is a restricted site, you may want to announce that in your Banner or Welcome message. These messages are configured and displayed according to standard FTP protocols. The Banner displays when a connection is made, and the Welcome text is displayed when a user is authenticated and allowed access. Some organizations suppress all messages, even the default ones, to provide anonymity. This was a popular security technique in the early days of FTP, but it no longer has any real effect on security.

CONFIGURING FTP USER SECURITY

Creating a new site for anonymous access isn't much use for many FTP needs, which require Write access for only specific users. You can configure a range of security options in FTP, including authorization and authentication security to provide restricted access for specific users. For example, let's remove Write access for anonymous users and add Read and Write access for the administrator account on our FTP site. Start by selecting the FTP site in the sites tree of the Connections pane.

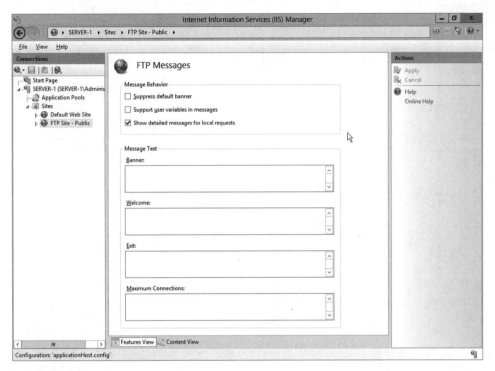

FIGURE 10-15

Because we configured this site for both Read and Write access for Anonymous, or unauthenticated, users, Authentication and Authorization must be configured for the Administrator account, and it must be granted both Read and Write access. We will also remove Write access for the Anonymous users. Start by adding Basic authentication in addition to the existing Anonymous authentication so that there is a method for authenticating a user account that logs in. To do this, open the FTP Authentication feature, and you'll see that, as shown in Figure 10-16, although Anonymous authentication was enabled when the site was created, Basic authentication is disabled. Highlight Basic Authentication and enable it by choosing Enable in the Actions pane. Now you have a method for authenticating a user account.

After enabling the authentication method, you need to authorize the Administrator account for the FTP site. Open the FTP Authorization feature, as shown in Figure 10-17.

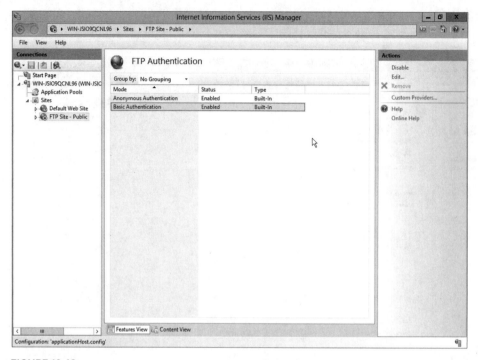

FIGURE 10-16

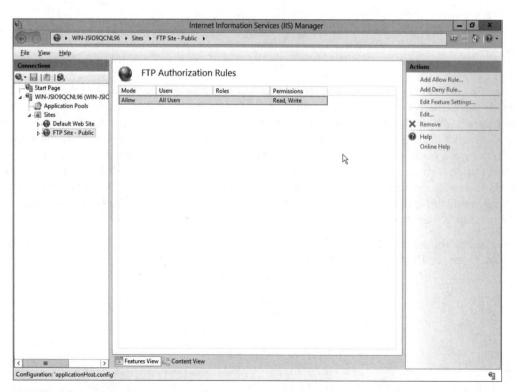

FIGURE 10-17

You'll see that all users are allowed, with Read and Write permissions. Select this authorization rule and click on Edit in the Actions pane, which brings up the Edit Allow Authorization Rule dialog. Change the access section to "All Anonymous Users," remove Write permission, as shown in Figure 10-18, and then click OK. Now Anonymous users will no longer be able to write files to the FTP site.

To add the Administrator account with Read and Write permissions, click on Add Allow Rule in the Actions pane. As shown in Figure 10-19, you can allow access to all users, all anonymous users, specified roles or user groups, or specified users.

The All Users and All Anonymous Users choices are self-explanatory, and naturally should be used carefully because they can allow unintended access to a site. The "Specified roles or user groups" option enables you to assign access to a group, and then user accounts can be allowed or denied access simply by adding or removing them from the group, without ever changing authorization roles for the FTP site. *Roles* are groups of IIS user accounts, whereas *user groups* are standard Windows groups using Windows accounts.

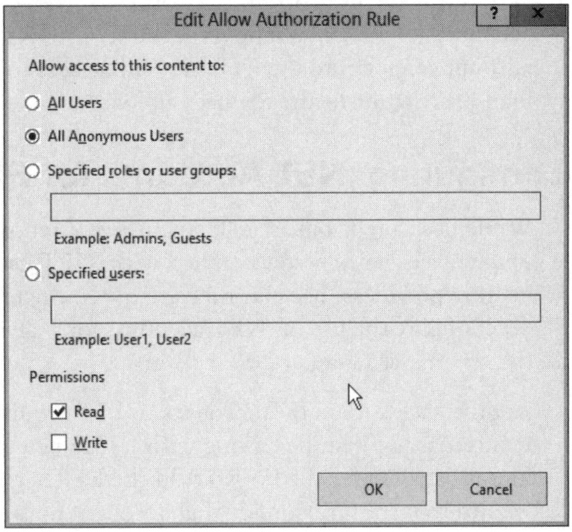

FIGURE 10-18

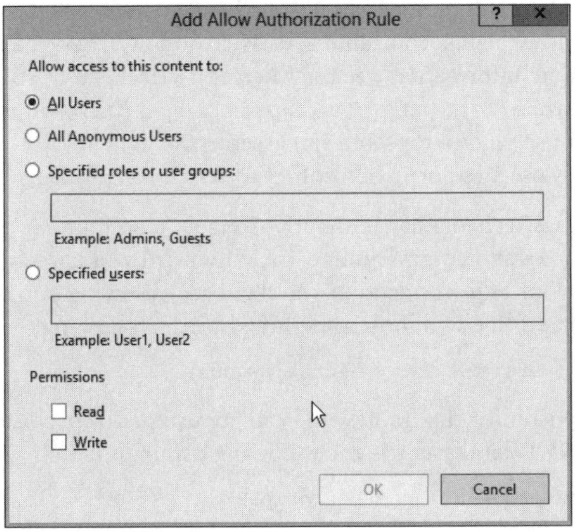

FIGURE 10-19

Windows accounts will require a Client Access License (CAL) and are most useful for intranet situations. IIS user accounts and ASP.NET user accounts do not require Windows CALs and are useful in hosting situations in which accounts only need access to manage IIS or use FTP. For our needs, we are going to add the Administrator account with Read and Write access allowed.

> **NOTE** *For more on licensing, you should review the agreement with your operating system or check with Microsoft Licensing, at* www.microsoft.com/licensing/.

Simply add the user Administrator, using the syntax {Domain}\{UserName} if this is a domain account, not a local Windows account, with Read and Write permissions. Now the Administrator account can log into the FTP site with access to upload files, but anonymous users can only download files that have already been uploaded.

Configuring .NET Accounts for FTP

While licensing is one issue facing using Windows accounts for FTP access, simply using FTP to update websites is better handled with .NET user accounts. These are natural accounts to use for hosting providers, because they are likely already configured for access to the website to begin with. To configure the use of .NET accounts for FTP on IIS 8.0 websites, you must add FTP publishing to the server. See Chapter 20 for details.

Adding access for .NET accounts to FTP requires that the FTP Extensibility Role be installed. If this was not installed along with FTP, open the Add Roles and Features wizard, and you will find it listed under the IIS Role, in the FTP Server category. Check the box and click through the wizard to install it. Configuring accounts for a website, as opposed to an FTP site, will also require FTP Publishing.

Configuring .NET Membership

In order to use .NET accounts, you must have Microsoft SQL Server installed and accessible and configured for the ASP.NET membership database schema. You can install Microsoft SQL Server 2012 Express using the Web Platform Installer. For more information, see the Microsoft website at http://www.microsoft.com/sqlserver/en/us/editions/2012-editions/express.aspx. Microsoft SQL Server Express is a free SQL server designed for use on desktops and single servers in light applications, such as an ASP.NET website. You can also use a remote Microsoft SQL Server instance.

You can configure the .NET membership database schema using aspnet_regsql.exe, found in the framework folder. If you run aspnet_regsql.exe at a command line, a GUI wizard will launch to walk you through the process of setting up your SQL connection and database, allowing you to choose which features to configure. The command line will look something like the following:

```
C:\%windir%\Microsoft.NET\Framework\<versionNumber>\aspnet_regsql.exe
```

Replace <versionNumber> with the specific version for the framework you are using. To specifically add the membership database to an existing .NET database, use the following command:

```
aspnet_regsql.exe -E -S DatabaseInstance -A mr -d MembershipDB
```

The E parameter assumes you are using Windows authentication on your SQL server and that your current account has access. The S parameter specifies the database instance. The A parameter is a directive to add, and the `mr` modifier is for membership and roles. Lastly, the `d` parameter specifies the name for the membership database.

> **NOTE** *For more information on* `aspnet_regsql.exe,` *visit* `http://msdn` `.microsoft.com/en-us/library/ms229862%28v=vs.80%29.aspx.`

You must create a SQL Server user account for the .NET membership database. Your SQL server will need to be set for Windows and SQL Authentication, and you will need to add a SQL Server Login and User for database access. Normally, this will be the IIS Application Pool Identity; by default, the user account is `IIS AppPool\DefaultAppPool`. Replace `DefaultAppPool` with the name of the application pool if you use a different application pool.

> **NOTE** *For more details on working with SQL Server logins, check SQL Books Online or the Microsoft article at* `http://msdn.microsoft.com/en-us/library/` `aa337562.aspx.`

You must also have Microsoft ASP.NET Framework 4.0 installed in order to use .NET accounts; it is installed by default in Windows Server 2012. You can also add .NET 4.5 and the associated roles and services using the Add Roles and Features option in Server Manager. You will also need to implement ASP.NET 4.0 Forms authentication in order to use ASP .NET accounts for FTP. You can find the instructions for this at `http://msdn.microsoft` `.com/en-us/library/xdt4thhy%28v=vs.100%29.aspx.` A full example of configuring .NET accounts is in Chapter 20.

Configuring .NET membership for FTP access requires editing the root `web.config` file, normally found at `%SystemRoot%\Microsoft.NET\Framework64\v4.0.30319\config\web.config`. Open the file in a text editor, such as Notepad or Microsoft Visual Studio, and scroll to the bottom of the file. Just before the closing `</configuration>` tag, add the following code (`ASP.NET FTP Membership.txt`):

```
<location path="FTP Site - Public/ftpsvc">
 <connectionStrings>
   <add connectionString="Server=localhost;
     Database=aspnetdb;Integrated Security=true"
     name="FtpLocalSQLServer" />
 </connectionStrings>
   <system.web>
     <membership defaultProvider="FtpSqlMembershipProvider">
       <providers>
         <add name="FtpSqlMembershipProvider"
           type="System.Web.Security.SqlMembershipProvider,
```

```
            System.Web,Version=2.0.0.0,Culture=neutral,
            PublicKeyToken=b03f5f7f11d50a3a"
              connectionStringName="FtpLocalSQLServer"
              enablePasswordRetrieval="false"
              enablePasswordReset="false"
              requiresQuestionAndAnswer="false"
              applicationName="/"
              requiresUniqueEmail="false"
              passwordFormat="Clear" />
          </providers>
        </membership>
        <roleManager defaultProvider="FtpSqlRoleProvider" enabled="true">
          <providers>
            <add name="FtpSqlRoleProvider"
              type="System.Web.Security.SqlRoleProvider,
              System.Web,Version=2.0.0.0,Culture=neutral,
              PublicKeyToken=b03f5f7f11d50a3a"
                connectionStringName="FtpLocalSQLServer"
                applicationName="/" />
          </providers>
        </roleManager>
      </system.web>
    </location>
```

Save and close the root `web.config` file, and you have enabled ASP.NET Forms authentication for the "FTP Site – Public" we created in earlier examples.

Configuring the ASP.NET Membership Provider

To use ASP.NET Forms authentication for FTP, you must configure the provider, including adding a connection string, role provider, and membership provider, before adding an account for FTP access. Begin by adding a connection string.

Adding a Connection String

Open IIS Manager and select the website to be configured, and then double-click the Connection Strings feature. This will bring up the Connection Strings list, as shown in Figure 10-20.

Click on Add in the Actions pane to bring up the Add Connection String dialog, and then enter the following details:

➤ **Name** — FtpLocalSQLServer

➤ **Server** — localhost

➤ **Database** — aspnetdb

This assumes you are using a local installation of SQL Express and configured the root `web.config` according to the code sample above. If your configuration is different, such as using a remote SQL Server, you will need to change these settings accordingly.

Leave the security at Windows Integrated Security, though you may need to add the ASP.NET Application Pool Identity as a user in the SQL Database, depending on your setup. The dialog should look something like Figure 10-21.

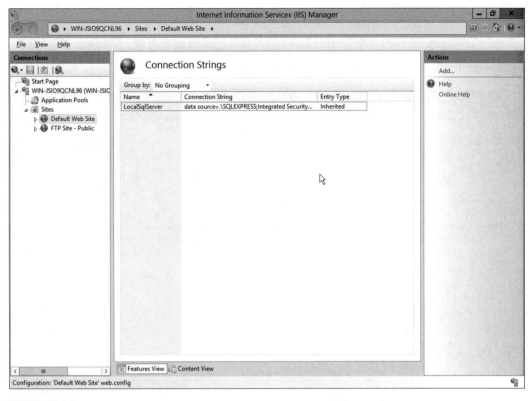

FIGURE 10-20

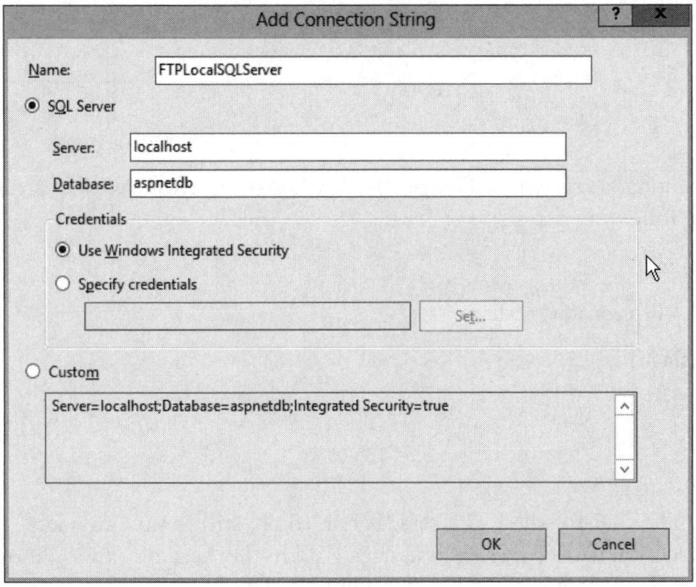

FIGURE 10-21

Adding a Role Provider

Next, you must add a role provider for the .NET accounts. In IIS Manager, highlight the website and double-click the Providers feature. In the Providers feature, as shown in Figure 10-22, select .NET Roles in the dropdown and click Add in the Actions pane.

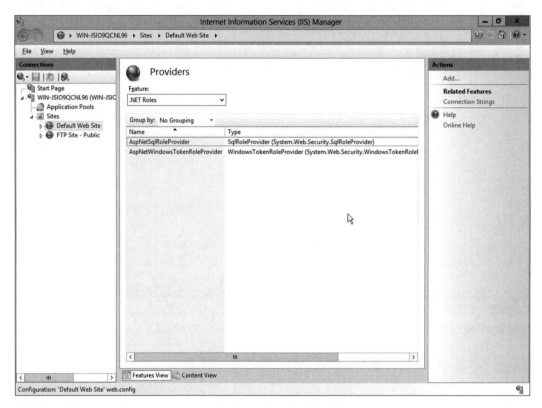

FIGURE 10-22

This will open the Add Provider dialog, as shown in Figure 10-23. Choose SQLRoleProvider from the Type dropdown and enter the following details:

➤ **Name** — FtpSqlRoleProvider

➤ **Connection string name** — FtpLocalSQLServer

➤ **Application name** — / (a slash)

Click OK to add the provider.

Adding a Membership Provider

You must also add a membership provider for the FTP users. While you're still in the Providers feature, change the drop-down selection to .NET Users and click Add in the Actions pane. Choose SQLMembershipProvider from the drop-down and enter the following details:

➤ **Name** — FtpSqlMembershipProvider

➤ **Connection string name** — FtpLocalSQLServer

➤ **Application name** — / (slash)

Leave the Behaviors at the defaults of False and click OK to add the provider.

Adding a Membership Role

Now that you have providers in place for supporting ASP.NET users for FTP sites, you need to add a .NET role for these accounts. In IIS Manager, select the website and open the .NET Roles Feature by double-clicking on it. Enter a name for the role, such as **FTPRole**, and click OK. There is no configuration for the role.

FIGURE 10-23

Adding a User Account

To add a user account for FTP, highlight the website and double-click the .NET Users feature to open it, as shown in Figure 10-24.

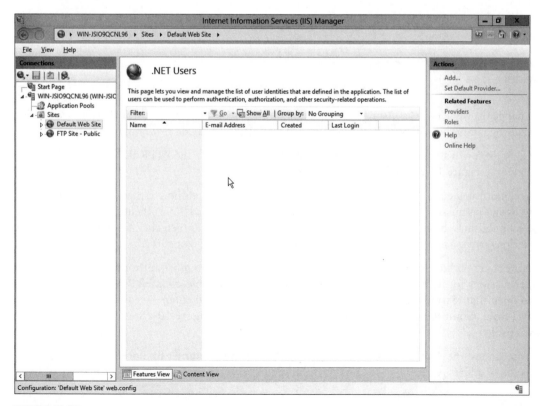

FIGURE 10-24

Click Add in the Actions pane to open the Add .NET User dialog, and enter a username and password, as shown in Figure 10-25. Choose a security question and enter an answer. You can eliminate the security question and answer by editing the line in the root or site `web.config` that reads:

```
requiresQuestionAndAnswer="true"
```

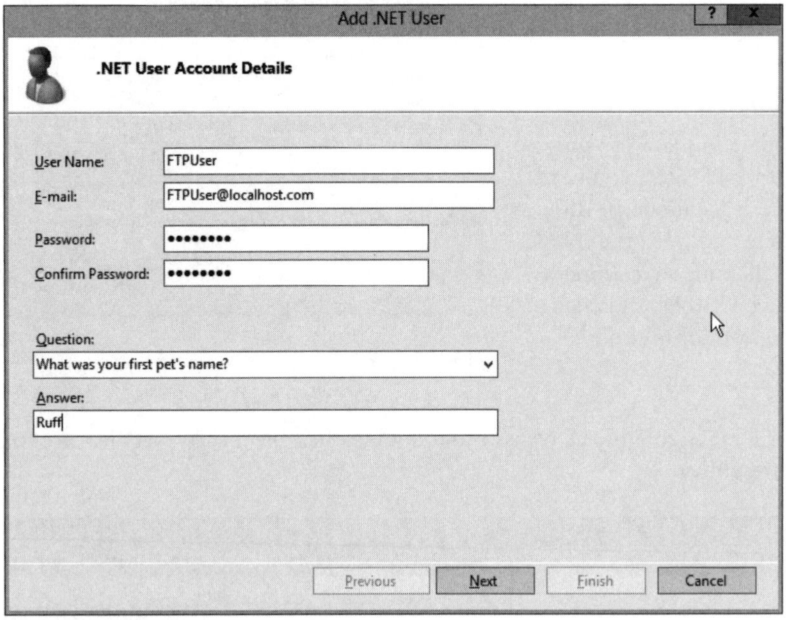

FIGURE 10-25

Change the value to `false`, and you will not require this security step. This will also remove the security challenge from the ASP.NET Retrieve Password module, if it is used on your application server.

Click Next to advance to the .NET User Role dialog and assign the FTPRole created earlier, as shown in Figure 10-26, and then click Finish.

You must now enable Membership Authentication in FTP and authorize the FTPRole created earlier to assign permissions to that role. In IIS Manager, double-click FTP Authentication (requires that FTP publishing be enabled for a website — see Chapter 20), and then click Custom Providers in the Actions pane. Choose the AspNetAuth provider, as shown in Figure 10-27, and click OK.

Now that you have a .NET account role with a user in it, you must authorize that role and grant permissions for it. In the Features View for the website, double-click FTP Authorization Rules to open that feature. Select Specified roles or user groups and enter the role created earlier, FTPRole. Grant Read and Write permissions, as shown in Figure 10-28, and click OK to enable that role.

You can test the ASP.NET user account for FTP by opening Internet Explorer and browsing to the IP address or name of the server. Because this server was configured to answer on all IP addresses, the local host address, `127.0.0.1`, will work fine. In Internet Explorer, enter the URL `ftp://127.0.0.1/` and press Enter. You should be directed to a logon prompt for the site, since we do not have Anonymous FTP access granted for the website. Enter the user name and password created above, as shown in Figure 10-29, and click "Log on." You should see a list of files in the root directory of the server.

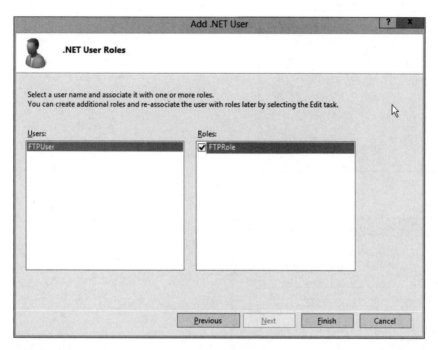

FIGURE 10-26

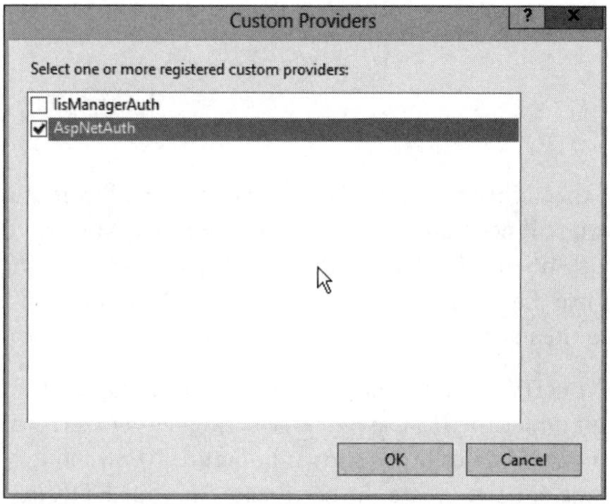

FIGURE 10-27

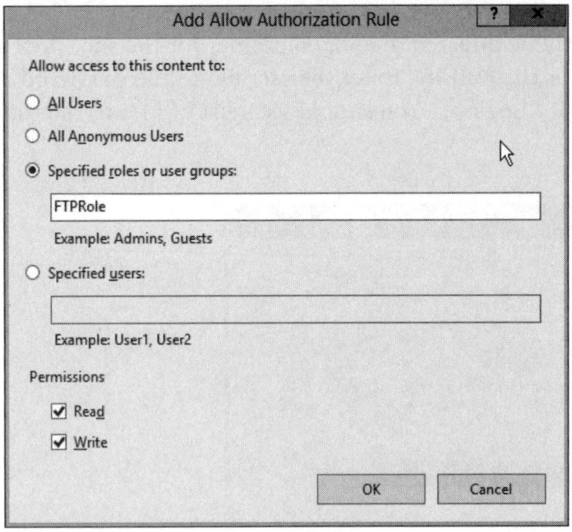

FIGURE 10-28

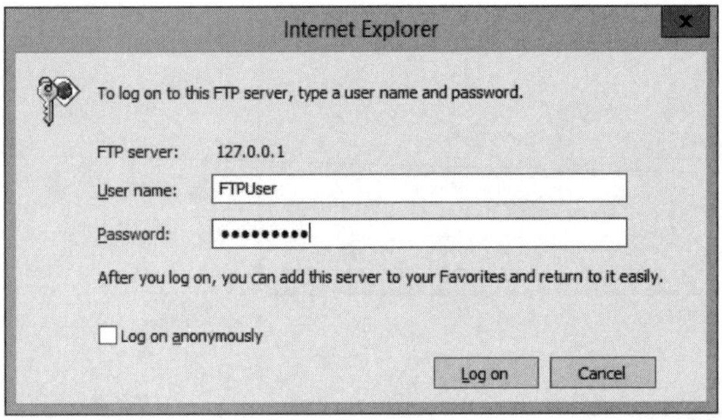

FIGURE 10-29

Configuring FTP over SSL

One of the most significant changes in IIS 8.0 is the ability to use a secure channel for FTP communications using FTP over SSL (FTPS). Although you still need an SSL certificate to do this, Microsoft has provided simplified self-signed certificates for both IIS and FTP use. Naturally, if you have a certificate from a recognized certificate authority, you can use that, but for simply creating a SSL connection for FTP, a self-signed certificate is both secure and quite usable.

The first step in configuring FTPS is to create the certificate. You can do this in IIS Manager by selecting the server in the Connections pane, and under the IIS Category, selecting Server Certificates. When this feature opens, you will see the current certificates or, as shown in Figure 10-30, none. Select Create Self-Signed Certificate in the Actions pane to create the certificate for your FTP site.

You need to enter a friendly name for the certificate, as shown in Figure 10-31. Choose the Web Hosting store and click OK to create the certificate. Self-signed certificates are good for one year and may not be acceptable for public websites because they can generate a security message that may deter users.

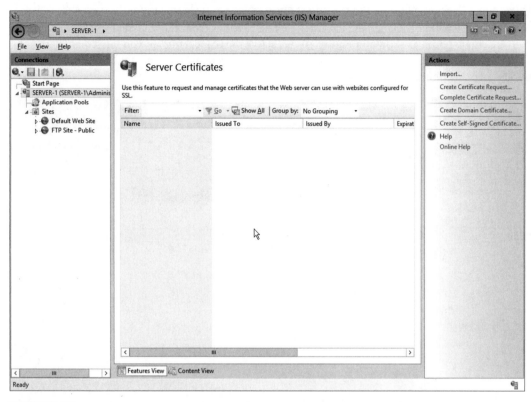

FIGURE 10-30

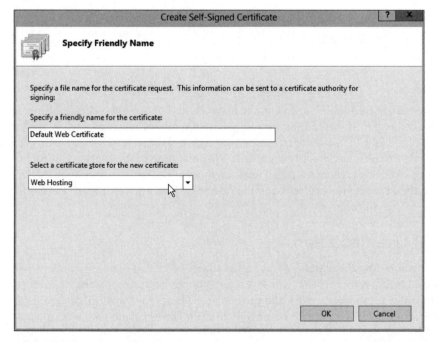

FIGURE 10-31

The steps to add the SSL certificate to the FTP site are quite simple. Highlight the site in the sites tree of the Connections pane, and choose FTP SSL Settings from the FTP features. In the FTP SSL Settings dialog box, as shown in Figure 10-32, select the SSL certificate you just created, and check Allow SSL connections. This allows the Administrator account to connect with SSL and the anonymous users to connect without using SSL.

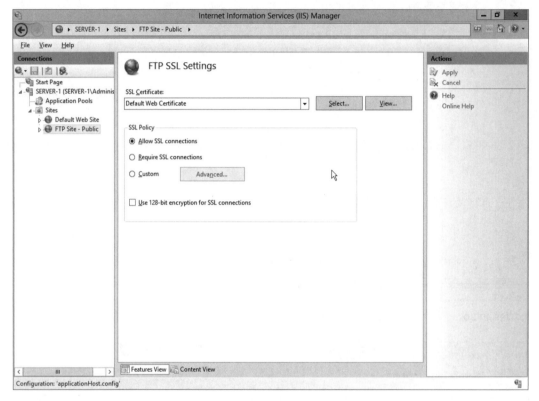

FIGURE 10-32

Connections that don't use SSL could be sniffed on the network for connection credentials, but revealing anonymous credentials is virtually no risk. If you do not allow anonymous users, such as in a webhosting service that uses FTP for clients to upload content to their websites, then requiring SSL connections will lock down the access to only using SSL. This will protect the connection from network sniffers and from exposing credentials on an unsecured network. You can specify that clients need to use SSL for only the credentials by selecting the Advanced button. See Chapter 15 for more information on using SSL certificates.

Configuring FTP User Isolation

Although the user isolation introduced in IIS 6.0 is still available in FTP, it is less useful because FTP sites can be bound to a specific website, which was a major reason for user isolation in the past. However, you might still want to isolate users and provide an FTP site for transferring data from client systems. Isolating users in FTP is much easier than in prior versions, and you have options for isolation as well.

To isolate users, browse to the FTP site in the sites tree of the Connection pane, and then select the FTP User Isolation feature. The FTP User Isolation configuration, as shown in Figure 10-33, offers two options for where to start users: the root directory or their username directory. Normally, you would want to start them in their username directories; however, if you're using isolation, you probably want to leave the FTP root directory for Anonymous users to access. You can also select to isolate users by username or Active Directory settings, and you can choose whether to allow global virtual directories.

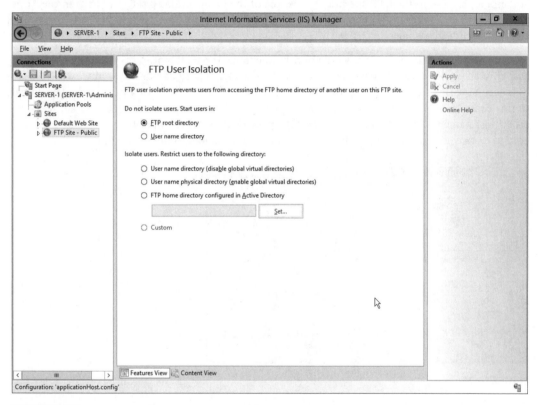

FIGURE 10-33

User isolation requires the proper folder structure and that the folders exist, prior to configuring the website. Configuration of the IIS FTP Server is covered earlier in this chapter. The following table shows the required directories for each type of access:

USER ACCOUNT TYPES	PHYSICAL HOME DIRECTORY SYNTAX
Anonymous users	`%FtpRoot%\LocalUser\Public`
Local Windows user accounts (requires Basic authentication)	`%FtpRoot%\LocalUser\%UserName%`
Windows domain accounts (requires Basic authentication)	`%FtpRoot%\%UserDomain%\%UserName%`
IIS Manager or ASP.NET custom authentication user accounts	`%FtpRoot%\LocalUser\%UserName%`

Configuring FTP Host Name Support

Host name support for FTP is similar to using host headers for a website. Normally, an FTP site will answer on an IP address and port pair, so you can have only a single FTP site using a standard port on a single IP address. Host name support changes this for FTP. To add a host name to your FTP site so that you can create a separate site on the same IP address and standard port, using a different host name, browse to the FTP site in the sites tree of the Connections pane, and then in the Actions pane, select Bindings. This will show the current bindings for the site. Highlight the FTP binding, and choose Edit to change it.

As shown in Figure 10-34, you have the option to change the FTP bindings, including the host name that this site will answer to. We're going to use `ftp.domain1.com` as our host name, which means that accessing this site from now on will be done by specifying this host name, not the IP address. In this case, `ftp://ftp.domain1.com/` will open the FTP site, whereas using the IP address or any other host name will not. You must ensure that your DNS has the proper host entry for the FTP host in `domain1.com` pointing to the IP address this site is configured to answer on.

FIGURE 10-34

When using the virtual host option in FTP, the logon process changes for the client. Because the FTP protocol has no concept of a virtual host name, it will not pass the host name to the server as part of the user logon. The client must log in using a {domain}/{username} syntax, specifying the logon domain that the FTP protocol won't pass. There is a proposal for a change to the FTP protocol to allow a HOST feature, which is supported by Microsoft FTP, but FTP clients must support this HOST feature as well. Many current clients do.

Configuring FTP Request Filtering

FTP Request Filtering is new with IIS 8.0 and allows many of the same filtering options that are available for websites. You can now filter FTP requests by file extensions, URL sequences, and specific FTP commands, either specifically allowing or denying each one.

> **WARNING** *Adding filters can result in denying access to the FTP site, so be sure to test them before you put them into production.*

To add a filter to restrict executable files on your FTP Server, for example, open the Request Filtering feature for the site, and choose the File Name Extensions tab. Click Deny File Name Extension in the Actions pane, and enter the file extension you wish to block. As shown in Figure 10-35, we blocked both `.exe` and `.msi` extensions. Files with those extensions cannot be uploaded to or downloaded from this site.

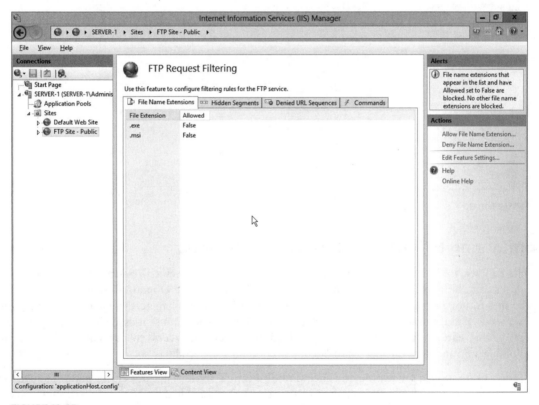

FIGURE 10-35

If you open the Edit FTP Request Filtering Settings dialog by clicking Edit Feature Settings in the Action pane, you will see, as shown in Figure 10-36, that you can block all unlisted file extensions by unchecking "Allow unlisted file name extensions" and then use the extension filters to specifically allow individual file extensions.

Opening the Hidden Segments tab will show that the request segment _vti_bin is already filtered by default. This will block any directory changes to the /_vti_bin folder and keep it from being displayed in any file listings, as a security precaution. You don't need people downloading your code or uploading new code that will cause damage to your site or its visitors.

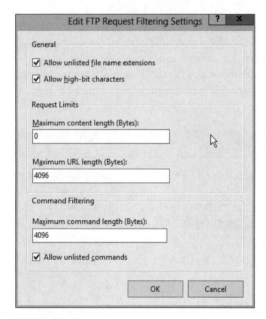

FIGURE 10-36

Configuring FTP IP and Domain Restrictions

The FTP service in IIS 8.0 allows you to configure access from specific IP addresses, ranges of address, or domains. This is done through the FTP IP Address and Domain Restrictions feature for the site. Although this is not designed to block rogue FTP clients from accessing your system, if you know the IP range or domain from which they are coming, you can use it as such. A more practical use for this feature is to allow only a single IP address or domain access to a specific FTP site, as in allowing a business partner access to documentation on your products.

To do this, first open the feature and click on Edit Feature Settings in the Actions pane. Change the "Access for unspecified clients" setting to Deny, check the "Enable domain name restrictions" box, as shown in Figure 10-37, and then click OK.

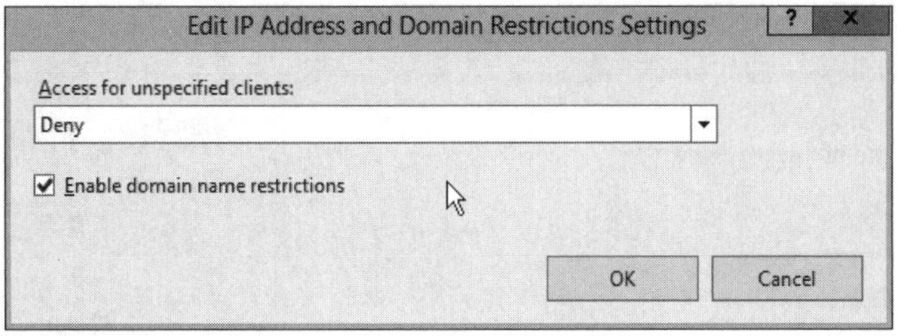

FIGURE 10-37

Ignore the warning about reverse IP lookups. For this example, accept the additional network load so that you can allow only a specific partner domain. Add the domain name, as shown in Figure 10-38, and click OK to accept that you will only allow access from any IP address that points back to that domain.

Beware that by restricting access to a single domain, you have blocked every other domain, including yours. If you need access, be sure to add your domain or IP address as allowed.

Configuring FTP Logon Attempt Restrictions

Also new to FTP with IIS 8.0 is the ability to restrict logon attempts for FTP sites. Using this feature, you can stop brute force or dictionary attacks on your server. Although best handled in a separate firewall device to reduce the load on the server, this has been a requested feature for FTP for many years.

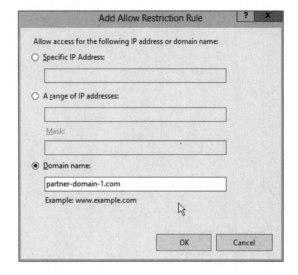

FIGURE 10-38

FTP logon attempt restrictions is a feature at the server level and is not configurable for individual sites. Highlight the server in the Connections pane and select "FTP logon attempt restrictions," then simply enable the FTP logon attempt restrictions through the checkbox, as shown in Figure 10-39. By default, this feature will block those IP addresses from where the attempt was made, although you can choose simply to log the attempts while testing. These addresses are blocked for the time period selected; by default, therefore, an IP address that fails a logon attempt four times in 30 seconds is blocked for the remainder of that 30 seconds. You may wish to increase this timeframe, but setting it too high may lock out legitimate users who have simply forgotten their password.

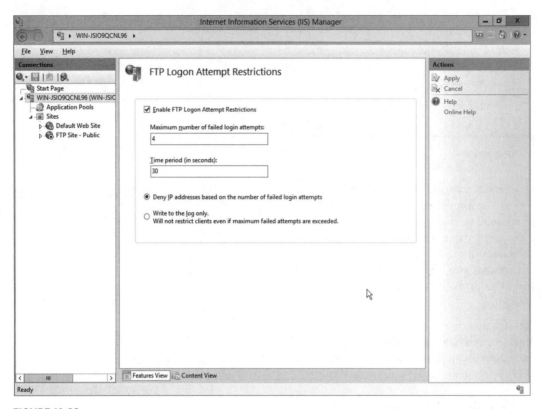

FIGURE 10-39

ADMINISTERING FTP WITH CONFIGURATION FILES

Because FTP uses the same XML-based configuration files as IIS 8.0, you can configure the settings for FTP sites by editing the applicationHost.config file, and you can create sites from scratch in the same manner. Although we don't explore every available option, we discuss some of the basic FTP configurations here. All the code in this section uses the FTPConfiguration.txt code file.

> **NOTE** *Remember that because the configurations are in* applicationHost
> .config, *you can use IIS 8.0's shared configuration option to configure servers
> automatically across a web farm as soon as the* applicationHost.config *file is
> updated.*

Adding FTP over SSL to an Existing Site

To add FTP over SSL to an existing website, you need to retrieve the SSL hash to include in the applicationHost.config file. Browse to the web server in the Connections pane, select the Server Certificates feature, and then find the FTP certificate. Double-click on the certificate to open the properties dialog, choose the Details tab, and scroll until you find Thumbprint. Because this thumbprint is needed in the `applicationHost.config` file, keep this dialog open while you edit the `applicationHost.config` file or copy the thumbprint to a Notepad file for use later. Next, open the `applicationHost.config` file in Visual Studio or any text editor, and find the section for your website with FTP. It should look something like this:

```
<site name="Web Site 1" id="99">
    <application path="/">
        <virtualDirectory path="/" physicalPath="%SystemDrive%\inetpub\website1" />
    </application>
    <bindings>
        <binding protocol="http" bindingInformation="*:80:" />
        <binding protocol="ftp" bindingInformation="*:21:" />
    </bindings>
    <ftpServer>
        <security>
            <authentication>
                <anonymousAuthentication enabled="false" />
                <basicAuthentication enabled="true" />
            </authentication>
        </security>
    </ftpServer>
</site>
```

You need to add the SSL certificate to the site, which is done through an SSL setting below the FTP Server Authentication section. SSL is set for the FTP site level. To require SSL for both the control and data channels of the FTP protocol, add the following line:

```
<ssl serverCertHash="{Certificate Hash}"
    controlChannelPolicy="SslRequire" dataChannelPolicy="SslRequire" />
```

where {`Certificate Hash`} is the value of the thumbprint without spaces. It will look something like this when finished:

```
<site name="Web Site 1" id="99">
    <application path="/">
        <virtualDirectory path="/" physicalPath="%SystemDrive%\inetpub\website1" />
    </application>
    <bindings>
        <binding protocol="http" bindingInformation="*:80:" />
        <binding protocol="ftp" bindingInformation="*:21:" />
    </bindings>
    <ftpServer>
        <security>
            <authentication>
                <anonymousAuthentication enabled="false" />
                <basicAuthentication enabled="true" />
            </authentication>
            <ssl serverCertHash="28d132014f72050177444aa34bba952912f47ff6"
                controlChannelPolicy="SslRequire"
                dataChannelPolicy="SslRequire" />
        </security>
    </ftpServer>
</site>
```

Configuring Host Name Support

Adding host name support to our site can easily be done in the `applicationHost.config` file as well. Let's start by looking at the FTP site configuration in the `applicationHost.config` file:

```
<site name="FtpSite1" id="42">
    <application path="/">
      <virtualDirectory path="/" physicalPath=
          "%SystemDrive%\inetpub\FTPRoot\ftpsite1" />
    </application>
    <bindings>
        <binding protocol="ftp" bindingInformation="192.168.1.10:21:" />
    </bindings>
    <ftpServer>
       <security>
          <authentication>
              <anonymousAuthentication enabled="false" />
              <basicAuthentication enabled="true" />
          </authentication>
       </security>
    </ftpServer>
</site>
```

You just need to add the binding for the host name, and thus the edited version will look like this (changes are in bold):

```
<site name="FtpSite1" id="42">
  <application path="/">
    <virtualDirectory path="/"
        physicalPath="%SystemDrive%\inetpub\FTPRoot\ftpsite1" />
  </application>
  <bindings>
    <binding protocol="ftp" bindingInformation="192.168.1.10:21:ftp.domain1.com" />
  </bindings>
  <ftpServer>
    <security>
      <authentication>
        <anonymousAuthentication enabled="false" />
        <basicAuthentication enabled="true" />
      </authentication>
    </security>
  </ftpServer>
</site>
```

THE FTP COMMAND-LINE CLIENT

Windows Server 2012, as in previous versions of Windows, includes a command-line FTP client that can be effectively used to diagnose issues with the FTP service. Because the command-line client echoes each command and response, diagnosing the response codes is easier than with other FTP clients, including Internet Explorer, which may not show accurate return codes. Return codes are discussed in the next section.

The default syntax for beginning an FTP session with the command-line client is simply:

```
ftp {ServerName}
```

You can designate the server by name or IP address, and, if needed for a nonstandard port, append the port address with a colon. The default launching of the FTP client, when followed by a server designation, assumes an open command for that server. If you merely launch the FTP client by typing **ftp** and pressing Enter, you will find yourself at the FTP command prompt without an open connection.

The most commonly used FTP commands are open, close, dir, cd, get, put, and quit. The open and close commands will open or close a connection to the FTP Server specified as a parameter for the command, respectively. The dir command simply displays a directory at the level you are at within the FTP folder hierarchy, and the client also supports the UNIX-style ls command to list directories and files. The cd command enables you to change directories, the same as on the local system at a command prompt. The get and put commands are used to get a file from the FTP Server or put a file on the FTP Server, respectively, essentially downloading or uploading files.

A full FTP session that logs into a site, changes to the upload directory, uploads the file MyFile.txt, and then exits would look something like the following. (User-typed commands are in bold.)

```
c:\>ftp ftp.domain1.com
connected to ftp.domain1.com
220 Microsoft FTP Service
User <ftp.domain1.com:<none>>: jsmith
331 Password required for jsmith
Password: Passw0rd
ftp> cd upload
250 CWD command successful
ftp> put MyFile.txt
220 Port command successful
150 Opening ASCII mode data connection for MyFile.txt
226 Transfer complete
ftp: 10 bytes sent in .01 Seconds 756.00 Kbytes/sec.
ftp> close
221
ftp> quit
c:\>
```

The response codes returned by the server — 220, 331, 250, 150, 226, and 221 — provide a concise path through the transaction. Errors or unexpected response codes are visible in the command-line client so that you can see the exact command that fails along with the response from the server at the point of failure.

For example, if you had entered

```
ftp> cd uplode
```

and the actual physical directory name was spelled correctly, as in our first example, you should have seen a response code of 550, because the directory does not exist. Knowing that the 550 response occurred on that command helps you to diagnose that the directory does not exist or cannot be seen by the client logon ID, probably because of permissions.

INSTALLING AND CONFIGURING AN SMTP SERVER

Microsoft's SMTP Server has been deprecated on Windows Server 2012 and the management scripts have been removed. Although SMTP still works as it did in Windows 2008 R2, the management scripts are no longer available. Administrators and programmers should begin using `System.Net .Smtp` for sending mail, using an external SMTP Server such as a Microsoft Exchange Server.

> **NOTE** *Information on* `System.Net.Smtp` *can be found online at* `http://msdn .microsoft.com/en-us/library/ms164240.aspx`.

The SMTP Server in IIS 8.0 provides mail transport functions between servers. It is designed for sending mail from the IIS 8.0 server to another SMTP Server and can act as a relay server as well. Although SMTP does send and receive mail messages, it is not designed as a "user" technology to provide a mailbox for messages. That functionality is provided by an e-mail server that implements a mailbox protocol such as POP3 or IMAP.

How SMTP Works

In Windows Server 2012, SMTP is an in-process service and runs in the `Inetinfo.exe` process. It monitors the SMTP port (25, by default) for incoming messages and the `Pickup` folder for outgoing messages. When a message appears in the `Pickup` folder, SMTP will determine the destination domain from the header. If the domain is local, the message is moved to the `Drop` folder. If not, the destination SMTP Server is determined through a DNS lookup for the mail exchanger (MX) record for the destination domain. Once the destination SMTP Server is resolved, a connection attempt is made on port 25. If the destination server accepts the connection, the message is transferred to the destination server for delivery to the recipient's mailbox.

If the destination server rejects the message, the SMTP Server will try to deliver a non-delivery report to the original sender. This report will include the original message and the reason that delivery could not be made, such as the destination address not existing. If the message cannot be returned to the original sender, it is moved to the `Badmail` folder.

Installing SMTP

SMTP is not installed by default on Windows Server 2012. It also is not listed as a role service, as other IIS 8.0 components are, but, rather, as a server feature. Open Server Manager, click the Manage menu, and choose the Add Roles and Features option. Choose "Role-based or feature-based installation," select the appropriate server, and then select the SMTP Server feature from the Features option. You will be prompted to confirm, adding other required features, as shown in Figure 10-40, such as the IIS 6.0 Manager, if not already installed. The SMTP Server has not changed since IIS 6.0 and is still managed through the IIS 6.0 Manager. If you launch this manager from the Start screen, you should see the IIS 6.0 Manager and your new SMTP Server, as shown in Figure 10-41.

Installing the SMTP Server feature will configure a default SMTP Server answering on port 25 on all unassigned IP addresses. You will want to configure this server further before you use it. The installation also creates the following on your system:

FIGURE 10-40

➤ First, a service (Simple Mail Transfer Protocol service) is created. This service runs within the existing `inetinfo.exe` process but can be started and stopped separately from IIS.

➤ Second, an SMTP virtual server is created. This SMTP virtual server is configured to accept mail destined for the fully qualified domain name of the local server but is not started by default. Additional SMTP virtual servers can be created if desired.

➤ Finally, a set of folders is created, by default, within the `%systemdrive%\inetinfo\mailroot` folder, named `badmail`, `drop`, `pickup`, and `queue`. Their purpose is described in detail later in the chapter.

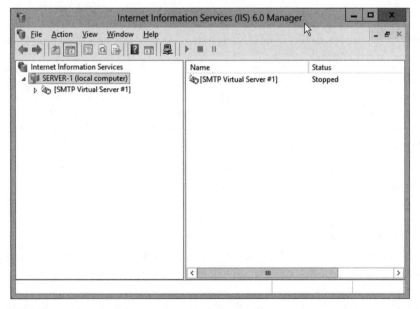

FIGURE 10-41

A common technique for developers sending mail was to drop messages into the SMTP pickup folder. This is no longer possible using `System.Net.Smtp`.

Configuring the Default SMTP Server

If you open the IIS 6.0 Server Manager and expand the local computer, you will see the SMTP Servers configured on this physical system. Expanding the SMTP Server will show the SMTP domains and current sessions on that SMTP Server. Right-clicking on the SMTP Server and choosing Properties will allow you to configure the server, as shown in Figure 10-42.

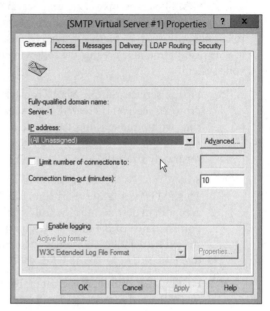

General Settings

On the General tab of the SMTP Server Properties dialog, there are several important configuration changes that can be made. To begin with, here is where you assign a specific IP address, and the port if you have a reason to change it. You should always assign a specific IP address to your SMTP Server to ensure that you don't accidentally respond to SMTP requests on an unintended address. If you have more than one virtual SMTP Server, you will need to assign separate IP addresses or separate ports, and

FIGURE 10-42

many programs will assume the default SMTP port of 25. Assigning specific IP addresses to each server addresses this need. SMTP does not support host header style technology. You may also wish to assign multiple identities to this server, to provide SMTP services from two separate domains, for example. You can do this through the Advanced button.

You may also restrict the number of connections and set the connection time-out in this dialog. Limiting the number of connections can reduce load on the server, but in most cases, it will also cause delays in mail deliveries as connections are unavailable when the mail is sent. Ten minutes is a sufficient time-out for even the slowest mail servers, but you may want to lower this so that dropped connections recycle quicker, especially if you limit the number of connections.

Log files are disabled on the SMTP Server by default, but most administrators will want to enable them. Configuring and interpreting SMTP log files are covered more completely below in this chapter.

Messaging Limit Configurations

The Messages tab of the SMTP Properties dialog, shown in Figure 10-43, allows configuring several message limits to match your needs for this specific SMTP Server. The maximum message size and the maximum session size are both measured in
kilobytes (KB). Using these, you can restrict the amount of data that can be sent in a single message or a single session. The defaults are normally adequate for sending messages from ASP.NET applications but restrict the sending, and receiving, of large files or bulk mail. By increasing the message size limit, you increase the data in a single message, but if you leave the session size limit at the default, you will still throttle performance for sending bulk mail.

Similarly, you can limit the number of messages sent in a single connection, which will force the SMTP Server to renegotiate a new connection after the maximum has been reached. This can increase performance of the server because it will make multiple connections to the destination server, but the destination must also allow multiple connections. You may also limit the number of recipients in a single message. The default is 100, the minimum required by RFC 2821 for an SMTP Server to use this feature.

It is suggested that for most SMTP Server needs, you leave the defaults as is. Increasing the message and session size limits, as well as the number of recipients in a single message, or unchecking the selections so there are no limits, can increase the server's delivery rate for bulk mail, such as found in many newsletter applications or applications that e-mail website updates to clients. Increasing these settings and sending one message to many recipients will increase the load on the server and can cause the server to be blacklisted by other SMTP Servers as a spam source.

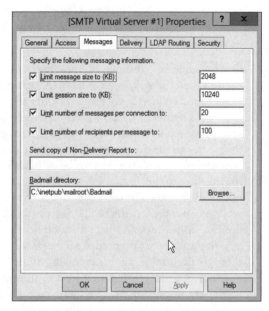

FIGURE 10-43

What happens when these limits are exceeded really depends on the remote SMTP Server. For any server supporting EHLO, and most do, the servers will pass their limits to each other for review. This prevents attempts at sending messages outside the limits, and a non-delivery report (NDR) will be generated before a transfer is attempted. If a message exceeding the maximum number of recipients is received by the SMTP Server, it will be split into multiple messages, and no NDR will be generated.

Non-delivery reports are sent to the message sender, but you can have copies sent to another e-mail address as well. This can be useful for notifying an administrator of delivery problems, but in most cases, you will only enable this when tracking a problem. There are many legitimate reasons for an NDR to be generated, such as a typo in the recipient's e-mail address, that are not delivery problems that normally need to be addressed by an administrator.

Delivery Configurations

The Delivery tab allows two important configu-rations to be changed. The first are the retry intervals and options for outgoing messages that cannot be delivered on the first attempt. The defaults, as shown in Figure 10-44, are adequate for almost all situations and should only be adjusted in situations in which network connections might be slow, spotty, or otherwise play havoc with SMTP connectivity. It is important to be aware of the defaults in order to understand SMTP delivery delays. The retry intervals are listed for the first, second, and third attempts at redelivering a message that could not be delivered, and each subsequent delivery attempt. Normally, a server will also send an NDR to the message sender indicating that there was a delivery delay, as defined by the delay notification time. After a default 2 days of attempts, the server will give up and return the message as undeliverable, with a matching NDR. Consistent SMTP message delivery delays could indicate a problem with connectivity between SMTP Servers or a problem with the destination server, such as an overload of messages.

On this same tab, you can set outgoing connection limits as well as the port used, with the "Outbound connections" button. Under the Advanced options, you can specify the use of a smart host for e-mail delivery, relaying through that server to the destination server. The smart host server takes on the responsibility of delivering the message to the destination SMTP Server. You might want to use a smart host outside the firewall to better protect the SMTP Servers inside the firewall from attack. A smart host would also be appropriate where you needed all messages to pass through a central server for archiving and compliance needs, or to add required footer information to all outgoing messages. The smart host entry expects the fully qualified domain name of the smart host SMTP Server, such as `smtp.domain1.com`. You may also use an IP address by enclosing it in square brackets, as in `[192.168.1.10]`.

FIGURE 10-44

The Masquerade Domain and Fully Qualified Domain name configurations may be used to change how the SMTP message is addressed and delivered. The Masquerade Domain will replace the local domain listed in the "Mail From" lines of the SMTP header. Because this can trigger some anti-spam filters, you should test the use of this option carefully. By setting the Fully Qualified Domain name, you override the default domain being used for DNS lookups. This can help speed name resolution by using both the domain's MX record and the host name for resolution.

LDAP Routing

Lightweight Directory Access Protocol (LDAP) routing can be used to force the SMTP Server to consult an LDAP server, such as an Active Directory server for resolving both senders and recipients. This is really only useful if mail is destined locally within the realm of your LDAP domain, and in almost all cases, the use of a mail server such as Microsoft's Exchange Server is a much better option.

SMTP Security and Authentication

SMTP Servers provide a risk to organizations for being compromised and used to relay spam and virus attacks. Misconfigured or insecure servers can be used for phishing attacks, denial-of-service attacks, and transportation of pornography and pirated software. All of these mischievous-to-criminal acts are traceable right back to the SMTP Server, putting an organization at risk for lawsuits or criminal charges. In many ways, the worst effect on an organization can be the black-listing of the SMTP Server, preventing e-mail from being transferred to or from the organization and its clients.

SMTP security is set on the Access tab, as shown in Figure 10-45, not the Security tab as expected from the name. The Security tab is used for determining which users or groups can administer this SMTP virtual server.

Authentication

Clicking the Authentication button on the SMTP Server Properties dialog's Access tab brings up the authentication options, shown in Figure 10-46.

FIGURE 10-45

FIGURE 10-46

You can force incoming connections, whether from an SMTP client such as Windows Mail, another server relaying through this one, or just a message being delivered by a remote server, to authenticate using similar mechanisms to those in IIS 8.0. You can have "Anonymous access," "Basic authentication," or "Integrated Windows Authentication." Each of these behaves as it does in IIS 8.0, with Anonymous Access allowing anyone to connect without providing credentials, and Basic authentication and Integrated Windows authentication requiring a valid Windows username and password. The Microsoft SMTP Server does not support ASP.NET authentication or the use of non-Windows user accounts. Basic authentication has the advantage that most clients support it, and it can be secured using TLS encryption. Integrated Windows authentication uses NTLM v2 to pass credentials to the SMTP Server; thus, enabling this option requires clients that support NTLM v2, such as Microsoft Outlook Express or Windows Mail. In these programs, the use of NTLM is called *Secure Password Authentication*. Enable this option in those clients if you are using IWA on your SMTP Server.

> **NOTE** *These authentication requirements apply only to inbound SMTP connections. Formatted mail messages dropped directly into the SMTP virtual server's* Drop *directory are not affected by these settings. The* Drop *directory is discussed in detail below in this chapter.*

TLS Encryption

TLS encryption is a function of SSL and requires an SSL certificate. You may use the self-signed certificates you can create in IIS Manager, although the SMTP service will only use a single certificate for the server. You must create the certificate or apply for one from a certificate authority and install the certificate before you can use TLS to encrypt transmissions. More information on SSL certificates can be found in Chapter 13.

Connection Control

The Connection button in the Access tab allows restricting access to the SMTP Server according to the IP address range or domain, as shown in Figure 10-47. You may set the list as systems to exclude from connections ("All except the list below") or as the only systems to include in allowing connections ("Only the list below"). In most cases, you will want to allow all systems to connect so as to be able to accept messages from other networks, but you may want to restrict this if you are only accepting mail from internal clients or if you will be using this server only for outbound messages.

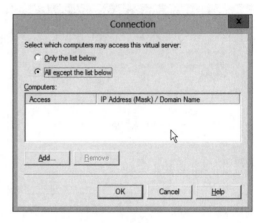

FIGURE 10-47

Relay Restrictions

More important than connection restrictions are *relay restrictions*, those systems that are allowed to send mail through this SMTP Server. *Relaying* is the process of sending mail through the SMTP Server that is not destined for final delivery to a remote SMTP Server. Typically, only your legitimate users should be able to relay mail to remote systems. If the system is misconfigured to allow anyone to relay mail, then it is possible for spammers or other malicious users to use your mail server to deliver spam (or worse) to any e-mail address.

> **NOTE** *The default settings, shown in Figure 10-48, allow only those clients that authenticate to your server, by providing a valid username and password, to relay mail through your server. SMTP clients, such as Outlook, as well as an ASP.NET script using* system.net.mail, *can be configured to provide authentication required by your server. Outside systems will not be able to relay unless they also know the authentication credentials. In more recent times, it has become increasingly common for attackers to attempt to guess passwords for well-known or commonly used user accounts (e.g., the built-in Administrator account). If attackers are able to guess a username and corresponding password, they may be able to authenticate to your SMTP Server and relay mail through it. For this reason, unless you have a requirement to allow relay by external roaming users, you should disable the "Allow all computers which successfully authenticate to relay..." checkbox.*

 If you have systems that will send mail through this server that for some reason cannot authenticate, you can add them into the allowed list. Typically, this would include only the IP addresses of your internal clients. This allows those clients to relay through your SMTP Server, while denying relay privileges to external machines.

Configuring Additional Domains

By default, the SMTP virtual server that is created when you install the SMTP service accepts mail only for the fully qualified domain name of the local server (i.e., mail destined for *@server1.example.com). If you want the SMTP Server to accept mail for your entire organization or a sub domain of your organization (e.g., *@example.com), you will need to configure the SMTP virtual server to accept mail for that domain or sub domain.

FIGURE 10-48

To do so, perform the following steps:

1. Open the Internet Information Services (IIS) 6.0 Manager from the Administrative tools folder. Expand the SMTP Virtual Server node that you wish to configure, and locate the Domains node. Right-click and choose New ➪ Domain.

2. You will be asked to specify whether the new domain you are adding is a local domain or a remote domain. For the SMTP Virtual Server to accept mail for a domain, choose the Alias domain. Adding a Remote domain allows you to specify how mail should be delivered to that remote domain, overriding the global settings for the virtual server. You may wish to configure a specific Remote domain entry if mail should be delivered to a specific mail server rather than relying on public DNS MX records.

3. Enter the domain name from which you wish the SMTP Virtual Server to accept mail (e.g., example.com). Click Finish to close the wizard and commit the changes.

SMTP Folders

When SMTP is installed, it creates a folder structure under %systemdrive%\Inetpub\Mailroot. This structure becomes the SMTP message store and includes several important folders. Based on where a message file appears in these folders, you can diagnose many mail delivery problems.

Badmail

The Badmail folder contains messages that could not be delivered after all delivery attempts have been tried and that cannot be returned to the sender with a non-delivery report. Additionally, all messages from your internal clients that do not have a resolvable From: domain are placed into the Badmail directory. Administrators can examine the messages in this folder, because all files can be opened with any text editor, to see why they may not have been deliverable. Undeliverable messages will have a .bad extension. The Badmail folder can be configured on the Messages tab of the SMTP Server's properties.

Drop

Incoming SMTP messages are placed in the Drop folder. Because Windows Server 2012 does not have a POP application that would place messages in individual mailboxes, without an additional application, such as Microsoft Exchange Server, users cannot retrieve these messages using POP or IMAP clients like Microsoft Outlook. Because these are text files, they can be read in any text editor, or you could write an ASP.NET application to read these messages. The Drop folder for each domain can be configured in the properties for the domain under the SMTP Server in the IIS 6.0 Manager.

Pickup

Outgoing SMTP messages will be placed in the Pickup folder. Normally, a message will only stay in this folder long enough for the connection to the destination SMTP Server to be made and the message transferred. If the connection cannot be made for some reason, the SMTP Server will hold the message in the Queue folder until the next retry period and attempt delivery again. If the number of retries is exceeded, the message will be moved to Badmail, along with an explanation of why the message could not be delivered. Messages destined for the domains served by the local SMTP Server are immediately moved to the Drop folder.

Queue

Messages that cannot be delivered on the first delivery attempt will be moved to the Queue folder. By default, the server will wait 15 minutes on the first retry, 30 minutes on the second, 60 minutes on the third, and then 240 minutes for each subsequent retry. The default maximum is 2 days for retrying a connection before moving the message to the Badmail folder. Therefore, if a destination server is down for the weekend, your message may end up in Badmail even if the destination server is eventually available. If you find this is the case, simply rename the file with the .bad extension to have no extension, and move it to the Pickup folder. As long as the destination server is now available, the message will be delivered.

Testing and Troubleshooting SMTP

Once SMTP is configured and working, the service itself is pretty bulletproof. SMTP is a simple and time-tested process, and there really aren't many things that can go wrong. When things do go wrong, troubleshooting the problem is usually quite simple with a combination of SMTP logs and non-delivery reports (NDRs) as well as messages left in the \Badmail folder. Many of the problems with SMTP delivery are actually outside the service itself, such as a firewall block or network problems between the SMTP Server and the destination.

Testing with SMTPDiag

Microsoft's SMTPDiag tool, deprecated with Microsoft Exchange 2010, works fine to test SMTP installed on an IIS 8.0 server. Download the tool from http://www.microsoft.com/en-us/download/details.aspx?id=11393 and install it according to the instructions. It has a simple command line, consisting of:

```
smtpdiag {senderaddress} {destinationaddress} /v
```

Replace {senderaddress} and {destinationaddress} with valid e-mail addresses to test communications. Running SMTPDiag with the /v argument will result in a verbose listing of the entire connection and testing process, complete with response codes. You will be shown the results as the connection progresses, including DNS responses, through the conclusion of the connection, whether successful or not. Use these results to trace errors in the SMTP connection process.

Testing with Telnet

One of the easiest tests for determining if the SMTP Server is available on port 25 is to try using Telnet to reach the port. From a system outside your network, open a command prompt and type:

```
Telnet {ServerName} 25
```

where {ServerName} is the FQDN or IP address of your SMTP Server. You should see a response something like this:

```
220 {ServerName} ESMTP Server (Server Type and Version)
```

where the server type and version shown are the same as your SMTP Server. If you see this response, your SMTP Server is available and answering connection requests. This means that network connectivity exists between the test system and your SMTP Server, including firewalls allowing traffic to pass on port 25. To further test the SMTP function, you can follow the process in Microsoft's Knowledge Base article number 323350, at http://support.microsoft.com/kb/323350.

SMTP Log Files

Analyzing log files is an important step to troubleshooting many problems, and SMTP is no exception. By default, the log files for SMTP are not enabled, but any administrator will want log files available for diagnosing problems in connection and delivery of messages. Once the logs are enabled, deciphering the logs can be an adventure in itself. With some simple analysis using nothing more than a text editor, you can diagnose many SMTP connection and delivery problems.

Configuring SMTP Logging

To configure logging of SMTP connections, you need to enable the log files. Log files can be in a text format or logged to an Open Database Connectivity (ODBC) database. Because ODBC logging will consume resources normally needed for IIS and SMTP, administrators will want to choose text log files. If the logs need to be maintained in a database for future analysis, then importing the text logs into a database like Microsoft SQL Server is the recommended solution.

In text format, you have a choice of W3C Extended log file format, NCSA Common log file format, or Microsoft IIS log file format. As with IIS, the most information available will be found in the W3C Extended log file format. This format is widely used by many applications, so it can be analyzed using most common third-party analysis tools. The other log file formats mainly exist for backward compatibility reasons. Unless you need to use another format to match an analysis program you already use, the W3C Extended log file format is recommended.

To configure SMTP logging, enable logging on the General tab of the SMTP Server Properties and select a log format — the default W3C Extended log file format is usually appropriate. The logs are always saved with a filename that includes the date of the log file, but you can specify a directory if you wish. A hosting company, for example, might wish to designate a log directory within the site so that clients can download and process the logs.

You set this directory on the General tab of the Logging Properties dialog, as shown in Figure 10-49. Here you would also set the schedule for starting a new log file, referred to as the *rollover*, as well as whether to use the local time for naming and rolling over the file.

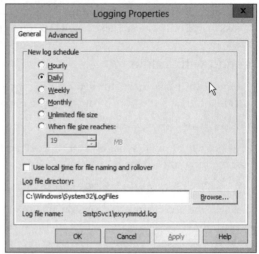

The W3 Extended specification requires times to be logged in Greenwich Mean Time (GMT). This avoids potential issues arising from changes to local times (e.g., when entering or leaving Daylight Savings Time). You will need to use an offset from GMT when you analyze them. Most log analyzer programs allow you to specify an offset when analyzing log files.

The Advanced tab of the Logging Properties dialog allows you to choose the items logged. Most often, you will want to select the Date, Time, Method, Protocol Status, Bytes Sent, and Bytes Received.

FIGURE 10-49

These are the more useful fields for log analysis in SMTP Server, but you might find that you want to use others as well. The included IIS 8.0 logging utilities do not all work directly with SMTP, but many analysis programs will work fine because the W3C Extended log file format is a universal standard. You can also use Microsoft's LogParser utility, described below, to analyze these logs.

Interpreting SMTP Logs

SMTP logs might seem daunting at first, but like IIS logs, they are fairly easy to understand once you know what you are looking at. Using the W3C Extended log file format, you will have a header for each log file with four lines, each preceded by a pound sign. These are, in order, the Software, Version, Date, and Fields. The version is which log file version you chose — 1.0 is the W3C Extended log file format. The date is year/month/day and hours/minutes/seconds in 24-hour time. Because this time will be GMT, when you analyze the logs, you will need to use the appropriate offset for your time zone. The configuration for using local time in naming and rollover does not change the GMT setting for the log itself, only for the date used in the filename and the time the log rolls to a new one and archives the old one.

The fields will be those that you chose while configuring the SMTP logs. Although fields like Date and Time have obvious data in them, some of the important fields that are not self-explanatory include the following:

➤ cs-method — The cs-method is the SMTP command and will be HELO, MAIL, RCPT, DATA, or QUIT. HELO is the initialization of a connection, and QUIT is the termination of the connection. MAIL is the Mail From or reverse path information, and RCPT is the RCPT TO or forward path information for the message — basically, where it's coming from and where it's going to. DATA is the actual data included in the message. Microsoft's SMTP Server supports most HELO extensions, as well.

➤ sc-status — The sc-status method is the protocol status or the codes returned by the SMTP Server. You can use these to determine the connection status and sometimes what caused a connection to drop, such as a time-out being reached.

➤ sc-bytes, cs-bytes — The sc-bytes and cs-bytes methods are the bytes sent and bytes received, respectively. You can use these to determine the amount of data sent to or received from a particular client or remote SMTP Server. Analyzing this can give you an idea of the total volume of SMTP traffic, and a large jump in traffic may mean that your server is being used to send bulk e-mail.

INSTALLING AND USING LOGPARSER

Originally included as an unsupported utility in the IIS 6 Resource Kit, LogParser is a simple command-line program that can parse almost any log file and generate output in a wide array of formats. The current version of LogParser can be downloaded from www.iis.net or the Downloads section of Microsoft's website.

Installing LogParser

LogParser is probably the easiest add-on to your web server that you will ever install. The LogParser download is a Microsoft installation file. Simply double-click the LogParser.msi file, and follow the installation prompts to install the entire package. The default installation is to a LogParser folder in \Program Files (x86).

LogParser consists of an executable file and a DLL, and you may want to copy those to a folder in the environment path, such as %WinDir%\System32\. This will allow you to execute LogParser from any folder; otherwise, you will need to specify file paths when using LogParser.

The LogParser installation also includes a compiled HTML help file, LogParser.chm, which includes full instructions and samples for running LogParser. Of particular interest is the reference section of the help file, which includes the query syntax as well as input and output formats.

Using LogParser from the Command Line

LogParser is a command-line tool and uses a query language similar to a SQL Server query to parse many types of log files, including IIS, FTP, and SMTP logs. The command line for LogParser is simply:

```
LogParser {Command}
```

If the command requires a user-supplied parameter, that parameter follows the command with a colon, as in:

```
LogParser {Command}:{Parameter}
```

If the user-supplied parameter has spaces in it, you need to enclose the parameter in quotes, as in:

```
LogParser {Command}:"{Parameter with spaces}"
```

LogParser has several modes: query mode, conversion mode, defaults override mode, and help mode. Help mode is simply prefixing the command with -h, which then displays help on that particular command or command sequence. For example, to get help on using the IISW3C format log file as input, use the LogParser command:

```
LogParser -h -i:IISW3C
```

The defaults override mode allows the LogParser default parameter values of input and output formats, as well as global switches, to be changed by the user. The syntax uses `-saveDefaults` and `-restoreDefaults` to save custom parameters or restore the factory default settings.

The conversion mode of LogParser provides for conversion from one format to another, for BIN, IIS, and W3C log formats. The mode syntax requires input and output formats, as well as input file and output file information. To convert from IIS to W3C format, the command might look like this:

```
LogParser -i:IIS -o:IISW3C iisfile.log w3cfile.log
```

Most useful to IIS administrators is the query mode. Using queries, an administrator can analyze log files for performance issues, error codes, or page hits, or just about any other query a user can dream up. LogParser is faster than traditional log analyzers designed to provide site statistics and can dig deeper into logs based on very specific queries. A simple query to find the top 10 requested URIs in a log file would look like this:

```
LogParser -i:IISW3C "SELECT TOP 10 cs-uri-stem, COUNT(*) AS Hits FROM u_ex*.log
    GROUP BY cs-uri-stem ORDER BY Hits DESC"
```

This query, entered all as one line, uses the IISW3C format as an input format. The default input format is text line, so the format is specified on the command line. The query selects and counts the `cs-uri-stem` field entries as hits from the `ex*.log` files in the folder in which this command is run. The `ex*.log` format will pick up all IIS log files in the folder, which are normally named by the date of the log preceded by "ex" with a `.log` file extension. The query groups the output by `cs-uri-stem`, which is the file and path beginning from the website's root, and adds the hits for each, displaying the top 10. Reading 200,000 lines of log files and outputting the top 10 takes about a half second, far faster than log analyzers designed to provide site statistics.

LogParser queries can be contained in a query file, called on the command line using the `file` command. For example, the top 10 hits query above can be saved as a text file. The SQL extension is a convention used in LogParser query files, but any extension can be used. Save the following as Top10Hits.sql:

```
SELECT
TOP 10
cs-uri-stem,
COUNT(*) AS Hits
FROM u_ex*.log
GROUP BY cs-uri-stem
ORDER BY Hits DESC
```

Run this file with the following command line:

```
LogParser -i:IISW3C file:Top10Hits.sql
```

Saving queries to a file makes repeating the command easier. Note that the input file format is not part of the query and must be entered on the command line.

LogParser Examples

There are any number of queries an IIS administrator might run using LogParser, and there are some examples included with the LogParser installation. More samples can be found in the LogParser forums at `www.iis.net`. The examples here are presented in the query file format. You may run them according to the information in the previous section.

Files Not Found

Requests for files that don't exist can indicate a problem with links in the website. This simple script displays the top 10 requested files that generated a 404 response:

```
SELECT
        TOP 10
        Count(*) AS Total,
        cs-uri-stem
FROM u_ex*.log
WHERE
        (sc-status = 404)
GROUP BY cs-uri-stem
ORDER BY Total DESC
```

This script can be modified for any response code. For example, whereas 404 errors are files that weren't found, the 404 subcode of 404.3 indicates that the request can't be served because of a MIME map policy. Changing the WHERE clause to (sc-status = 404.3) would limit the list to only those requests with faulty MIME maps.

Daily Bandwidth Use

The amount of bandwidth used by a site is a common statistic requested from IIS administrators, and LogParser can provide this quickly and simply. The following script adds the total cs-bytes and sc-bytes, the amount of data coming and going from a website, then divides those totals by 1,048,567 to change from bytes to megabytes. The results are grouped by day, with the megabytes, both incoming and outgoing, transferred.

```
SELECT
        TO_STRING(TO_TIMESTAMP(date, time), 'MM-dd') AS Day,
        DIV(To_Real(Sum(cs-bytes)), 1048567) As Incoming(Mb),
        DIV(To_Real(Sum(sc-bytes)), 1048567) As Outgoing(Mb)
FROM u_ex*.log
GROUP BY Day
```

Maximum Time Taken

Requests that take longer to generate a response may indicate a problem with that URI, from a larger than desired file to a problematic script or a poorly formed database query. This script will quickly display the 10 URLs with the longest response times. These files may warrant further investigation.

```
SELECT
        TOP 10
        cs-uri-stem,
```

```
      MAX(time-taken) AS MaxTime
FROM u_ex*.log
GROUP BY cs-uri-stem
ORDER BY MaxTime DESC
```

File Leeching

File leeching — the linking to files on your website from an outside source, especially links to copyrighted material or images, which can pose legal problems as well as representing unauthorized bandwidth use — is a sore point for many administrators. LogParser can help identify these external systems that link to a website's resources, through a modification in the top 10 hits query in the previous section. The only change is the addition of a WHERE clause to the query, to limit the results to those from outside referrers. For this example, any file with a JPG or GIF extension will be counted, unless it is requested from the fully qualified domain name of the website itself. The query changes all filenames to lowercase so that both "JPG" and "jpg" will be counted, because each will result in serving the same file.

The query also uses the EXTRACT_FILENAME function and the EXTRACT_TOKEN function, to retrieve the filename from the path in cs-uri-stem and to split the cs-referrer string to just the referrer URL. More information on these functions can be found in the LogParser help file. This script will look for referrers who are outside the www.domain1.com domain. Replace that with whatever domain you'll be using.

```
SELECT
      TOP 10
      TO_LOWERCASE (cs-uri-stem) as ImageFile,
      COUNT(*) AS Hits,
      TO_LOWERCASE (EXTRACT_TOKEN(cs(Referer),0,'?')) as OutsideReferer
FROM u_ex*.log
WHERE
      (EXTRACT_TOKEN(cs(Referer),2,'/') <> 'www.domain1.com')
      AND
      (cs(Referer) IS NOT NULL)
      AND
      EXTRACT_EXTENSION(TO_LOWERCASE(cs-uri-stem)) IN ('gif'; 'jpg')
      AND
      (sc-status IN (200; 304))
GROUP BY ImageFile, OutsideReferer
ORDER BY Hits DESC
```

This script evaluates logged requests that have a status of either 200, which is a successful request; or 304, which indicates that the requested file has not been modified and should be served from the browser's cache. In-depth explanations of the query syntax can be found in the LogParser help file.

ADDITIONAL EXAMPLES

The LogParser help file includes examples for most commands, and with a little work they can solve most LogParser query questions. The LogParser forums at www.iis.net are an excellent resource for additional tips and scripts, or for help in adapting a script of your own.

PART III
Advanced Administration

▶ **CHAPTER 11:** Core Server

▶ **CHAPTER 12:** Core Server Extensibility

▶ **CHAPTER 13:** Securing the Server

▶ **CHAPTER 14:** Authentication and Authorization

▶ **CHAPTER 15:** SSL and TLS

▶ **CHAPTER 16:** IIS Scalability I: Building an IIS Web Farm

▶ **CHAPTER 17:** IIS Scalability II: Load Balancing and ARR

▶ **CHAPTER 18:** Programmatic Configuration and Management

▶ **CHAPTER 19:** URL Rewrite

▶ **CHAPTER 20:** Configuring Publishing Options

11

Core Server

WHAT'S IN THIS CHAPTER?

➤ Native and managed modules

➤ Removing unused modules

➤ An overview of the IIS request pipeline

As you learned in Chapter 2, "IIS 8.0 Architecture," IIS 7.0 introduced a brand new architecture to the IIS family. In previous versions, the boundaries between what is part of the web server and what is a plug-in or extension were intuitively apparent. IIS 8.0 continues the usage of this module structure introduced in IIS 7.0, which results in these boundaries being less obvious.

In this chapter, we take a closer look at how the underlying IIS web server works, and how it is now possible to define for yourself exactly what functionality is provided by the core server, to maximize performance for your specific applications, and to minimize resource overheads.

BACKGROUND

In the early days of the web, a *web server* was nothing more than a single executable. It listened on port 80 for incoming requests, translated the request URI to a local file, and then delivered that file to the client. Figure 11-1 shows this simple web server form.

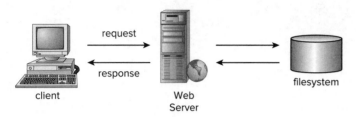

FIGURE 11-1

The *Common Gateway Interface* (CGI) is an extension of this simple web server form that allows the web server to pass URI parameters (for example, form field data, query strings, and so on) to external programs, and thus deliver dynamic content produced by the external program or script. Figure 11-2 represents how the CGI interfaces between the simple web server and applications running on the web server host.

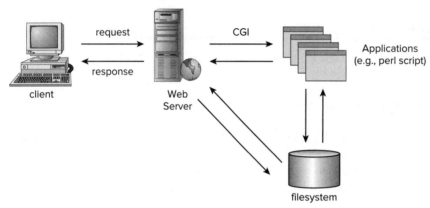

FIGURE 11-2

Over time, although the web server implementation has become significantly more complex, dealing with performance, scalability, and extensibility factors, the basic functionality remains the same: listener, interpreter, and applications.

Like most other web server platforms, IIS has grown in complexity and sophistication with each major version release. The core server has been enhanced and extended, continually improving the performance characteristics and functionality. Over the years, new IIS releases have boasted new logging options, new authentication capabilities, new methods of caching content, new scripting technologies, and more.

Each version release caused some web server administrators to jump for joy, while leaving others wanting more.

As more features were added, the system resource overhead grew. For those web applications that do not require or use those advanced features, they become nothing more than a waste of valuable resources and unnecessary or cumbersome overhead. IIS 8.0 puts an end to the wild, resource-hungry web server platform, and delivers performance, functionality, and flexibility.

This chapter takes a closer inspection of IIS 8.0 core server components and highlights why the structure of the new web server can be used to manage that performance and functionality depending on the application requirements.

CORE SERVER AND MODULES

IIS 8.0 provides a sleek core server system cut down to the bare bones of a high-performance and robust processing engine. The basic functionality is broken into four basic components that act as the foundation of arguably the most innovative and flexible web server system ever released:

➤ **Http.sys** — The HTTP listener does nothing more than listen on port 80 for inbound web requests and then pass those requests to the IIS 8.0 core.

➤ **WAS** — The Windows Process Activation Service manages the worker process and application pool configurations. WAS allows you to run a website that uses a protocol other than HTTP — for example, using the TCP protocol for hosting a web service through a WCF listener.

➤ **WWW Service** — The World Wide Web Publishing Service is a listener adapter for the HTTP listener (i.e., Http.sys). The WWW Service is responsible for updating Http.sys, the configuration of Http.sys and alerts WAS when a request enters the request queue.

➤ **w3wp.exe** — One or more worker processes that handle all the remaining request processing.

At first glance, the IIS 8.0 core server appears similar to previous versions. IIS 6.0 introduced the concept of *independent worker processes* to isolate independent applications running on the same physical server and thereby prevent a failure in one application from affecting any other. Figure 11-3 depicts the IIS 8.0 structure, highlighting the basic components identified above.

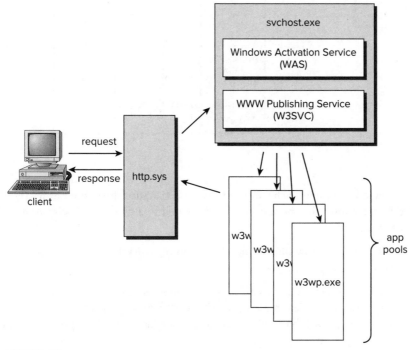

FIGURE 11-3

There is no significant difference between how IIS 7.5 and IIS 8 manage HTTP requests. The request is managed by the HTTP listener, the Web Activation Service, the Web Publishing Service, and the worker process. IIS 8.0 executes each request inside independent application pools in an extremely optimized manner.

To understand how the worker process execution in IIS 8.0 is such a major departure from pre IIS 7.0 versions, refer to Chapter 2, which introduces the request-processing pipeline that handles requests in a more linear fashion than previous versions of IIS. Figure 11-4 presents a close-up of the IIS 8.0 application pool processing pipeline.

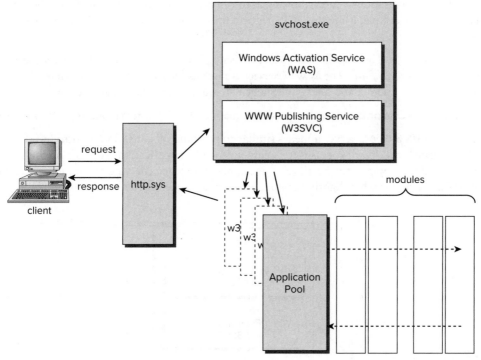

FIGURE 11-4

Figure 11-4 highlights the modular design of the application pool structure. Just about every piece of functionality handled by the application pool process is delegated to a module, which can be enabled and/or disabled as required.

The application pool process itself can now be considered as a simple workflow or processing pipeline, as shown in Figure 11-5.

Each stage in the request life cycle is referred to as an *event*, and modules provide the relevant functionality for the event processing. For example, when the worker process reaches the `authenticateRequest` event stage, it will hand off processing to any active module providing that function.

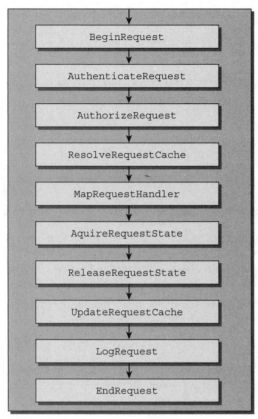

FIGURE 11-5

> **NOTE** *Chapter 12, "Core Server Extensibility," provides a more detailed treatment of the request-processing pipeline and request events.*

HTTP Modules

Out-of-the-box, IIS 8.0 ships with more than 40 individual modules. The default installation activates many of these, which, as you will discover later in this chapter, are not all required. In fact, you can obtain a perfectly functional web server using only a handful of the default modules.

To understand how the core server works, it is useful to take a closer look at each of modules that ship with IIS 8.0. There are two basic categories:

➤ **Native Code Modules** — Generally, a binary `.dll` file, developed using languages such as VB and C++.

➤ **Managed Code Modules** — Developed using scripted and runtime interpreted languages, including C# and ASP.NET.

The next few pages offer a brief description of the discrete functionality of the modules that ship with IIS 8.0.

Native Modules

The following tables list the native modules that ship with IIS 8.0, grouped into categories by general functionality.

HTTP Modules

The following modules provide HTTP-specific tasks related to client–server interaction:

MODULE	DESCRIPTION
HttpRedirectionModule	Supports configurable redirection for HTTP requests to a local resource.
ProtocolSupportModule	Performs protocol-related actions (such as setting response headers and redirecting headers), implements the Trace and Options HTTP verbs, and manages keep-alive support via configuration controls.

Security Modules

The following table lists the modules that perform security-related functions. A separate module exists for each authentication mechanism, allowing you to select which authentication mechanisms are supported on your server and to remove those that you don't need.

Note that you must install at least one authentication module. Without at least one authentication module, IIS cannot determine whether the request is authorized to access the relevant system resources. IIS checks for a valid user object after the authentication phase and returns a 401.2 error if it doesn't find one.

MODULE	DESCRIPTION
AnonymousAuthenticationModule	Performs Anonymous authentication when no other authentication method succeeds, or if no other authentication module is present. Typically, this module would be removed for an intranet or secured membership application. It is installed enabled by default and therefore needs to be disabled or removed if unwanted.
BasicAuthenticationModule	Performs Basic authentication as described in RFC 2617.

MODULE	DESCRIPTION
DigestAuthenticationModule	Performs Digest authentication as described in RFC 2617. The IIS host must be part of an Active Directory domain.
IISCertificateMappingAuthenticationModule	Maps SSL client certificates to a Windows account. SSL must be enabled with the requirement to receive client certificates for this module to work.
CertificateMappingAuthenticationModule	Similar to the previous module, but performs Certificate Mapping authentication using Active Directory.SSL must be configured for this module to work, and the IIS host must be a member of an Active Directory domain. *Caution:* Requests may be allowed if Active Directory Certificate Mapping is configured to protect a directory but the module is removed!
RequestFilteringModule	Performs UrlScan tasks such as configuring allowed verbs and file extensions, setting limits, and scanning for bad character sequences. (See Chapter 13, "Securing the Server," for further details about this feature.) This module is the successor of the ISAPI filter `UrlScan.dll` and was available for download separately from IIS.
UrlAuthorizationModule	Performs URL authorization based on configuration rules.
WindowsAuthenticationModule	Performs Windows authentication (NTLM or Kerberos).
IpRestrictionModule	Restricts access to IPv4 clients based on a list of addresses in the IIS configuration. (See Chapter 13 for some further details about this feature.)
DynamicipRestrictionModule	Dynamically restricts access to IPv4 and IPv6 clients based on the number of concurrent requests or the number of requests over a period of time.

Content Modules

The following modules provide functionality related to static web-site content, such as images and plain HTML:

MODULE	DESCRIPTION
DefaultDocumentModule	Displays a default document from a list of default files in the configuration when no explicit document has been identified in the request. If a matching default document is not found, a 404 result will be returned.
DirectoryListingModule	Lists the contents of a directory if no file is explicitly requested — for example, when the request is something like `http://www.Site1.com/path/` or just `http://www.Site1.com`. Note that if the DefaultDocumentModule is installed, a default document match will be attempted first. If this module is not installed, and either the default document module is not installed or there is no matching default document found, a 404 (not found) error will result.
ServerSideIncludeModule	Implements server-side includes for those requests ending in `.stm`, `.shtm`, or `.shtml`.
StaticFileModule	Delivers static file content such as plain HTML and images. The list of file extensions supported is determined by the `staticContent/mimeMap` configuration collection.If this module is not present, requests for static content return an HTTP 200 (OK) response, but the entity body (page) will be blank.

Compression and Performance Modules

The following two compression modules perform gzip compression in the request-processing pipeline. Most modern web browsers and search engine indexers support this compression technique. The Application Initialization module can return static content, whereas the web application initializes after a recycle.

MODULE	DESCRIPTION
DynamicCompressionModule	Applies gzip compression to outbound responses produced by applications.
StaticCompressionModule	Performs gzip compression of static content in memory as well as persistent in the file system.
ApplicationInitializationModule	Performs initialization activities prior to serving the first request after a recycle.

Caching Modules

The following modules manage caching of responses to requests. Note that for user mode caching, the cache resources are defined under the user account mapped to the request, whereas the kernel mode cache is handled by the Http.sys identity.

MODULE	DESCRIPTION
FileCacheModule	Provides user mode caching for files and handles on files opened by the server engine and modules, reducing file access overheads and improving request delivery times.
HTTPCacheModule	Provides kernel mode and user mode caching in Http.sys and manages the output cache, including cache size and cache profiles as defined via configuration controls.
TokenCacheModule	Caches Windows security tokens for password-based authentication schemes (Anonymous, Basic, IIS client certificate). For example, a password-protected HTML page that references 50 images that are also protected would normally result in 51 logon calls to the local account database, or, even worse, to an off-box domain controller. Using the TokenCacheModule, only one logon event is called and the result is cached, with the remaining reference requests authorized through that cached authentication token.
UriCacheModule	Provides user mode caching of URL information, such as configuration settings. With this module, the server will read configuration data only for the first request for a particular URL, and reuse it on subsequent requests until it changes.

Logging and Diagnostics Modules

The following modules provide support for functions related to web-site and web-application diagnostics and logging. Logging includes ordinary web request logs, as well as application execution logging during run time or failure.

MODULE	DESCRIPTION
CustomLoggingModule	Provided for legacy support of custom logging modules, such as ODBC support. This module also supports the ILogPlugin COM interface, but you should use the new Http Module API for any new development.
FailedRequestsTracingModule	Implements tracing of failed requests, taking definition and rules for failed requests via configuration.
HttpLoggingModule	Implements the standard web-site logging functions by Http.sys.

continues

(continued)

MODULE	DESCRIPTION
RequestMonitorModule	Implements the IIS 8.0 Runtime State and Control Interface (RSCA). RSCA allows its consumers to query for runtime information like currently executing request, start/stop state of a website, or currently executing application domains.
TracingModule	Reports events to Microsoft Event Tracing for Windows (ETW).
CustomErrorModule	Sends rich HTML content to the client on server error, and allows you to customize that default content. Without this module, IIS will send blank pages with minimal information on any server error, including 404.
ConfigurationValidationModule	Validates configuration issues, such as when an application is running in Integrated mode but has handlers or modules declared in the `system.web` section, and displays relevant error information if a problem is detected.

Extensibility Support Modules

The following modules support extending the web server platform to produce dynamic content and special functionality:

MODULE	DESCRIPTION
IsapiModule	Implements functionality for ISAPI Extensions mapped in the `<handlers>` section (`modules="IsapiModule"`) or called by a specific URL request to the dll.
IsapiFilterModule	Implements ISAPI filter functionality, such as legacy mode ASP.NET or SharePoint.
ManagedEngine	Provides integration of managed code modules in the IIS request-processing pipeline. If this module is not installed, managed code modules will not work, even if they are installed.
CgiModule	Implements the Common Gateway Interface (CGI) to allow the execution of external programs like Perl, PHP, and console programs to build response output.
FastCgiModule	Supports FastCGI, which provides a high-performance alternative to CGI.
WebSocketModule	Supports server applications that communicate using the WebSocket protocol.

Managed Modules

In addition to native modules, IIS 8.0 ships with several modules developed using managed code. Some of the managed modules, such as UrlAuthorization, have a native module counterpart that provides a native alternative to the managed module. Although modules developed using native code are generally faster and more efficient with memory and other system resources, native code modules can often be a less time-consuming and flexible alternative to develop. Note that managed modules require that the ManagedEngine module be installed.

The following table lists the managed modules that ship with IIS 8.0:

MODULE	DESCRIPTION
AnonymousIdentification	Manages anonymous identifiers, which are used by features that support anonymous identification such as ASP.NET profile.
DefaultAuthentication	Provides an authentication object to the context when no other authentication method succeeds.
FileAuthorization	Verifies that a user has permission to access the requested file.
FormsAuthentication	Supports authentication by using Forms authentication.
OutputCache	A managed code alternative to the native HttpCacheModule.
Profile	Manages user profiles by using ASP.NET profile, which stores and retrieves user settings in a data source such as a database.
RoleManager	Manages a RolePrincipal instance for the current user.
Session	Supports maintaining the session state, which enables storage of data specific to a single client within an application on the server. Note that without this module, the session state will be unavailable in your applications.
UrlAuthorization	Determines whether the current user is permitted access to the requested URL, based on the username or the list of roles that a user is a member of.
UrlMappingsModule	Supports configurable mapping of a real URL to a more user-friendly URL (that is, URL Rewrite).
WindowsAuthentication	Sets the identity of the user for an ASP.NET application when Windows authentication is enabled.

Almost all of the feature set of IIS that was implemented as part of the core web server system in previous versions is now delivered as a set of modular plug-in components.

Components can be installed or removed as needed, thus streamlining the server workload and customizing to the specific application. Since this modular structure is based on the worker process object, this customization can be applied to any level, from discrete applications to the global web server environment.

SERVER WORKLOAD CUSTOMIZATION

This new modular architecture provides server administrators and developers with the capacity to tune IIS to optimal performance and security by selecting which modules to include and which to "weed out" from the server workload.

For example, if you want to deliver a public website with only static HTML, including user authentication and CGI handling is not just a waste of system resources, but it may also open your web server to potential threats from attacks against yet-unknown vulnerabilities in those modules.

> **NOTE** *Many of the examples encountered below assume that several optional components not included in a default IIS installation have been already installed. Please review Chapter 4, "Installing IIS 8.0," for further information on installing optional IIS components prior to activating those components using the methods demonstrated below.*

Eliminating Overheads

Now it is possible to load only those modules required. Try this exercise as a demonstration. Note that you will need administrator privileges.

> **WARNING** *Performing this exercise on a production system will cause disruption to website delivery! You should use a development or test system for this process.*

1. On your IIS 8 server, open the default IIS home page (`http://localhost`), and then open Task Manager. (Click WIN+R, enter **taskmgr** in the dialog, and then click OK.)

2. Look for the worker process task (`w3wp.exe`) in the processes list, and observe the memory resource usage (around 3 or 4 MB for a default full install). This represents the amount of system memory resource consumed by each worker process task. This may be relatively insignificant for a small web facility, but as the load grows, with potentially hundreds of worker processes, the resource utilization builds and can become quite significant.

   Now you will remove *all* modules from the running system.

3. Create a backup of the system in case you need to restore it back to the original state, using the AppCmd utility from a command shell:

   ```
   %windir%\system32\inetsrv\appcmd add backup original
   ```

   Alternatively, you can use the PowerShell IIS snap-in and execute the following command:

   ```
   PS IIS:\>Backup-WebConfiguration -NAME original
   ```

Now you can restore your configuration to this state at any time by executing the following command:

```
%windir%\system32\inetsrv\appcmd restore backup original
```

Alternatively, you can use the PowerShell IIS snap-in and execute the following command:

```
PS IIS:\>Restore-WebConfiguration -NAME original
```

4. Click WIN+R, enter **notepad.exe %systemroot%\system32\inetsrv\config\applicationhost .config** in the dialog, and then press Enter.

5. Search for the configuration section for HTTP modules `<modules>`.

6. Cut everything between `<modules>` and `</modules>`, and then save the file. (Do *not* close the file just yet so that you can restore with a simple Undo!)

7. Restart the IIS service. (Click WIN+R ⇨ **net stop w3svc** ⇨ OK, and then WIN+R ⇨ **net start w3svc** ⇨ OK.)

8. Refresh the `http://localhost` view.

Like magic, there is nothing but a blank response!

Now take another look at the worker process image in Task Manager. The worker process task now has a significantly smaller memory footprint, thanks to a complete lack of included modules.

Congratulations! You have created arguably the world's fastest and most secure web server! It is fast because it doesn't really *do* anything, and therefore it is secure because it does not expose any system resources.

To restore your IIS install to its former glory, simply Edit ⇨ Undo the changes to the config file and Save. Refresh your browser window, and confirm that the home page is back.

The creation of such a secure and speedy system, of course, is purely academic, but this demonstration provides some indication of the value of fine-tuning the installed modules.

A Basic Real-World Example

For a real-world example of how IIS 8.0 can be tuned to suit a specific purpose, consider a plain old static HTML website, such as might be made available to schoolchildren to publish their simple web pages. The functionality is essentially the most basic of web server implementations, similar to that pictured in Figure 11-1.

For this application, there is no need for any application processing, no need for individual user authentication or authorization, and no requirement for directory listing or compression. Even logging is effectively optional for this simple application.

For a static HTML website, only the following modules are required:

➤ **StaticFileModule** — Provides access to the file system.

➤ **AnonymousAuthenticationModule** — Defines the user credentials with which to access the file system.

The following module is optional:

> ➤ **DefaultDocumentModule** — Appends a default document (for example, iisstart.htm) to the request URI when a document name is not explicitly requested.

The following exercise demonstrates how to achieve this configuration task.

> **NOTE** *You will need Administrator privileges to perform the following tasks.*

1. Start by creating a backup of the system in case you need to restore it back to the original state, using the AppCmd utility from a command shell:

   ```
   %windir%\system32\inetsrv\appcmd add backup original
   ```

   Now you can restore your configuration to this state at any time by executing the following command:

   ```
   %windir%\system32\inetsrv\appcmd restore backup original
   ```

2. Click WIN+R, enter **notepad.exe %systemroot%\system32\inetsrv\config\applicationhost .config** in the dialog, and then press Enter.

3. Search for the configuration section for HTTP modules <modules>, and replace the contents with

   ```
   <modules>
       <add name="DefaultDocumentModule" />
       <add name="StaticFileModule" />
       <add name="AnonymousAuthenticationModule" />
   </modules>
   ```

4. Save the file. (Do *not* close the file just yet so that you can restore with a simple Undo!)

5. Restart the IIS service. (Click WIN+R ⇨ **net stop w3svc** ⇨ OK, and then WIN+R ⇨ **net start w3svc** ⇨ OK.)

This configuration provides just the very bare essential functions to deliver plain, static data from the server file system. With this configuration, you will be able to access the default content by opening a web browser on the server console and browsing to `http://localhost`.

As an exercise, try removing the `DefaultDocumentModule`. Now, when you try `http://localhost`, you will receive a "File Not Found" response. Browse to `http://localhost/iisstart.htm` to view the default page.

For some specific web server applications (for example, an image gallery server), this even tighter configuration might be appropriate.

A More Complex Real-World Example

A more complex example of a real-world web application might take the form of an extranet Perl application using client authentication to the Windows user base.

To support this kind of application, you will want to include the following:

> ➤ **WindowsAuthenticationModule** — To authenticate the web-site visitor using a Windows-integrated (NTLM) mechanism.

➤ **DefaultDocumentModule** — To display a default document if not provided in the request.

➤ **StaticFileModule** — To display static content, such as images and so forth.

➤ **RequestFilteringModule** — To block suspicious requests. (It is always sensible to block suspicious web requests, even on a secure, firewalled intranet, and especially when clients are accessing from beyond the secure environment.)

➤ **DynamicCompressionModule** — To reduce bandwidth on the network from ASP pages.

➤ **StaticCompressionModule** — To reduce bandwidth from images and static content.

➤ **FileCacheModule** — To cache file system access.

➤ **TokenCacheModule** — To cache authentication and session tokens.

➤ **UriCacheModule** — To cache URL mapping to local resources.

➤ **HttpLoggingModule** — To log requests in standard file format.

➤ **IsapiFilterModule** — To implement Perl as an ISAPI filter.

The following exercise demonstrates how to use the `applicationHost.config` file to achieve this configuration result.

> **NOTE** *You will need Administrator privileges to perform the following tasks.*

1. Start by creating a backup of the system in case you need to restore it back to the original state, using the AppCmd utility from a command shell:

```
%windir%\system32\inetsrv\appcmd add backup original
```

Alternatively, you can use the PowerShell IIS snap-in and execute the following command:

```
PS IIS:\>Backup-Configuration -NAME original
```

Now you can restore your configuration to this state at any time by executing the following command:

```
%windir%\system32\inetsrv\appcmd restore backup original
```

Alternatively, you can use the PowerShell IIS snap-in and execute the following command:

```
PS IIS:\>Restore-Configuration -NAME original
```

2. Click WIN+R, enter **notepad.exe %systemroot%\system32\inetsrv\config\applicationhost .config** in the dialog, and then press Enter.

3. Search the configuration section for HTTP modules <modules>, and replace the contents with:

```
<modules>
<add name="UriCacheModule" type="" preCondition="" />
<add name="FileCacheModule" type="" preCondition="" />
<add name="TokenCacheModule" type="" preCondition="" />
<add name="HttpCacheModule" type="" preCondition="" />
<add name="DynamicCompressionModule" type="" preCondition="" />
<add name="StaticCompressionModule" type="" preCondition="" />
```

```
            <add name="DefaultDocumentModule" type="" preCondition="" />
            <add name="StaticFileModule" type="" preCondition="" />
            <add name="WindowsAuthenticationModule" type="" preCondition="" />
            <add name="DigestAuthenticationModule" type="" preCondition="" />
            <add name="RequestFilteringModule" type="" preCondition="" />
            <add name="CustomErrorModule" type="" preCondition="" />
            <add name="HttpLoggingModule" type="" preCondition="" />
            <add name="IsapiFilterModule" type="" preCondition="" />
        </modules>
```

4. Save the file. (Do *not* close the file just yet so that you can restore with a simple Undo!)

5. Restart the IIS service. (Click WIN+R ➪ **net stop w3svc** ➪ **OK**, and then WIN+R ➪ **net start w3svc** ➪ **OK**.)

Now all worker processes for all websites active on your web server will be loaded with the required modules included.

Customizing Individual Websites

So far, all the workflow customization demonstrated has been applied to the entire web server, and it thus affects all websites on that system.

It is rare, however, that all websites on a given server have identical feature and functionality requirements; therefore, you will often want to customize `<module>` configuration for each website, rather than (as above) across the entire web server.

The following example assumes that there are two websites on the server: Site1 and Site2. Site1 delivers a simple web server platform as described in the first example above, "A Basic Real-World Example." Site2 delivers the extranet application described in the second example above, "A More Complex Real-World Example."

It is hardly unlikely that two websites with such different requirements are running on the same web server. The following process demonstrates how to achieve customization of each.

Refer to Figure 11-4, and notice that the modules are loaded inside the actual worker processes. It is important to understand that in order to customize a specific *website* different from others on the same server, then that website must use an independent *application pool*. Fortunately, when using IIS Manager, websites are created with a unique application pool by default.

The following exercise demonstrates how to first create the two websites and then customize each application pool, as described previously.

> **NOTE** *This exercise assumes a default install with IIS content at* `C:\InetPub`. *Also, note that you will need Administrator privileges to perform the following tasks.*

1. Open IIS Manager. (Click WIN+R, enter **inetmgr** in the dialog, and then click OK.)

2. Expand the tree to the Sites node.

3. Right-click the Sites node, choose Add Website, and then complete the dialog as shown in Figure 11-6. Note how the application pool name changes when you enter the site name.

4. Repeat Step 3, replacing all occurrences of *Site1* with *Site2*.

Now you need to review the list of modules available on this server, by opening the `applicationHost.config` file and confirming the list of available modules.

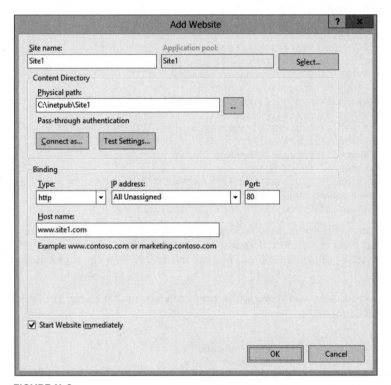

FIGURE 11-6

5. Click WIN+R, enter **notepad.exe %systemroot%\system32\inetsrv\config\applicationhost .config** in the dialog, and then press Enter.

6. Make sure that the modules to be enabled for the specific websites are available to IIS. To make these available to IIS, they must be defined in the `<globalModules>` configuration section of the `applicationHost.config` file.

7. Search for the `<globalModules>` configuration block, and observe the list of available modules. Ensure that all the modules required for the two sample websites are present in this location:

```
<add name="DefaultDocumentModule"
   image="%windir%\System32\inetsrv\defdoc.dll" />
<add name="StaticFileModule"
   image="%windir%\System32\inetsrv\static.dll" />
<add name="AnonymousAuthenticationModule"
   image="%windir%\System32\inetsrv\authanon.dll" />
<add name="UriCacheModule"
   image="%windir%\System32\inetsrv\cachuri.dll" />
<add name="FileCacheModule"
   image="%windir%\System32\inetsrv\cachfile.dll" />
```

```
<add name="TokenCacheModule"
  image="%windir%\System32\inetsrv\cachtokn.dll" />
<add name="HttpCacheModule"
  image="%windir%\System32\inetsrv\cachhttp.dll" />
<add name="DynamicCompressionModule"
  image="%windir%\System32\inetsrv\compdyn.dll" />
<add name="StaticCompressionModule"
  image="%windir%\System32\inetsrv\compstat.dll" />
<add name="WindowsAuthenticationModule"
  image="%windir%\System32\inetsrv\authsspi.dll" />
<add name="DigestAuthenticationModule"
  image="%windir%\System32\inetsrv\authmd5.dll" />
<add name="RequestFilteringModule"
  image="%windir%\System32\inetsrv\modrqflt.dll" />
<add name="IsapiFilterModule"
  image="%windir%\System32\inetsrv\filter.dll" />
<add name="CustomErrorModule"
  image="%windir%\System32\inetsrv\custerr.dll" />
<add name="HttpLoggingModule"
  image="%windir%\System32\inetsrv\loghttp.dll" />
```

You will recognize this list as those modules selected in the two previous examples. It is okay, of course, if there are more than just these modules listed, but any module that is *not* listed under `<globalModules>` will not be available to any web-site application pool to load.

8. Search for the `<modules>` configuration section and confirm that all the available modules are loaded by default:

```
<modules>
        <add name="DefaultDocumentModule" />
        <add name="StaticFileModule" />
        <add name="AnonymousAuthenticationModule" />
        <add name="UriCacheModule" type="" preCondition="" />
        <add name="FileCacheModule" type="" preCondition="" />
        <add name="TokenCacheModule" type="" preCondition="" />
        <add name="HttpCacheModule" type="" preCondition="" />
        <add name="DynamicCompressionModule" type="" preCondition="" />
        <add name="StaticCompressionModule" type="" preCondition="" />
        <add name="WindowsAuthenticationModule" type="" preCondition="" />
        <add name="DigestAuthenticationModule" type="" preCondition="" />
        <add name="RequestFilteringModule" type="" preCondition="" />
        <add name="CustomErrorModule" type="" preCondition="" />
        <add name="HttpLoggingModule" type="" preCondition="" />
        <add name="IsapiFilterModule" type="" preCondition="" />
    </modules>
```

9. Close the `applicationHost.config` file.

It is important at this stage to clarify the difference between the two configuration sections visited so far:

➤ `<globalModules>` — Determines which modules are available for the application pools to load.

➤ `<modules>` — Determines which modules are actually loaded into the application pools.

Furthermore, the `applicationHost.config` file determined the default configuration for all websites on that web server. As with the previous examples, at this stage in this exercise, all websites will load with the same set of modules.

The next step is to define the modules to be loaded for each of the two websites, beginning with Site1. Because this configuration task is for a specific website, the local `web.config` file is used.

10. Enter the following configuration elements into a blank text file:

```xml
<?xml version="1.0" encoding="UTF-8"?>
<configuration>
    <system.webServer>
        <modules>
          <clear/>
          <add name="DefaultDocumentModule" />
          <add name="StaticFileModule" />
          <add name="AnonymousAuthenticationModule" />
        </modules>
    </system.webServer>
</configuration>
```

11. Save this file to the website root (File ⇨ Save As, enter **C:\inetpub\Site1\web.config** for the file name, and then click Save).

Note the use of the `<clear/>` element in this file. By default, the worker processes for this website will inherit the list of modules from the `<modules>` section of the `applicationHost.config` file. Starting the `<modules>` configuration block with the `<clear/>` element blocks inheritance of the default `<modules>` configuration defined in `applicationHost.config`. After that, it is a simple matter of just adding the modules required in exactly the same format as in the first example above.

12. Next, create the configuration file for Site2. Create a new, blank text file, and enter the following configuration elements:

```xml
<?xml version="1.0" encoding="UTF-8"?>
<configuration>
    <system.webServer>
        <modules>
            <remove name="AnonymousAuthenticationModule" />
        </modules>
    </system.webServer>
</configuration>
```

13. Save this file to the website root (File ⇨ Save As, enter **C:\inetpub\Site2\web.config** for the file name, and then click Save).

You will notice that this time, instead of using the `<clear/>` tag to remove all inherited modules, one single `<remove name="modulename" />` was used to achieve the same result as `<clear/>` followed by all required module definitions.

After these configuration steps are completed, all worker processes loaded into the Site1 application pool will load up with only those modules required for the simple static website described in the first example above, yet worker process images loaded into the application pool for Site2 contain all those additional modules required for the example extranet application.

Using these basic principles of `<globalModules>` configuration sections in `applicationHost`
`.config` and `<modules>` sections of each `web.config` file, you are able to fully customize and fine-
tune your application pools independently for each website on your IIS 8.0 web server.

Customization Using IIS Manager

IIS Manger provides a graphical interface that allows quick and easy results when making ad hoc
changes to workflow customization.

The following exercise demonstrates how to add and remove modules that you want to be made
available to worker processes, define the default set of modules to be loaded, and customize the
server workflow for individual application pools.

> **NOTE** *You will need Administrator privileges to perform the following tasks.*

1. Open IIS Manager. (Click WIN+R, enter **inetmgr** in the dialog, and then click OK.)

2. To view and manage the list of modules to be loaded by default into all worker processes
across all websites and applications, in the IIS Administration Tool, click the main Server
Node [for example, SERVER1 (SERVER1 \Administrator)], and then double-click the
Modules icon in the Features View.

You will see the default set of modules displayed over the Features View pane, similar to
that shown in Figure 11-7.

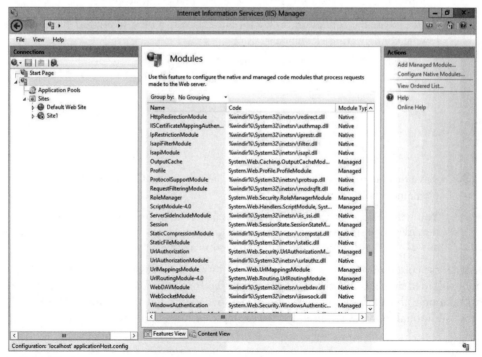

FIGURE 11-7

3. To remove a module from the default list, simply right-click on the module to be removed, and choose Remove from the Context menu.

4. To add the module back into the list, click Configure Native Modules in the Actions pane to add a Native module, select the module to add, and click OK. To add a managed module back into the list, select Add Managed Module in the Actions pane.

Note that removing a module from the list in this way does not remove the availability of that module to application pools, but it does prevent that module from loading *by default* with all applications. If a specific website or application web.config has that module explicitly included using the `<add name="modulename" />` described above, then the module will still be loaded for those worker processes.

Likewise, adding a module to this list does not guarantee that it will be loaded into every worker process for every website and application root. If the respective web.config file uses the `<clear/>` directive to remove all inherited module configuration, or if the `<modules>` configuration section includes a matching `<remove name="modulename"/>`, then that module will not be loaded in those respective worker process tasks.

5. To achieve the same outcome as editing the `<globalModules>` configuration section in applicationHost.config, in the module list described above, first right-click on the selected module, and choose Remove from the Context menu.

6. Click Configure Native Modules in the Actions pane, and again select the module to be removed. Click the Remove button to prevent this module from loading in *any* worker process of any application pool.

Note that if the removed module is explicitly defined in any individual application pool web.config, IIS will display an error when any visitor attempts to access that website.

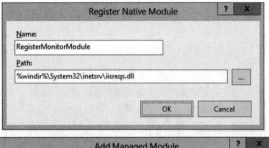

7. To add a module into the global list, simply click Configure Native Modules in the Actions pane for a Native module, and then click the Register button. Enter the module details, as per the example shown in Figure 11-8, and then click OK. To add a Managed module, select Add Managed Module from the Actions pane.

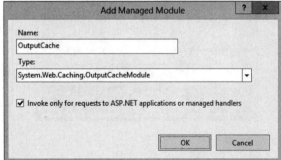

FIGURE 11-8

8. To customize the modules loaded into a specific website or application, simply browse to the relevant node in the object tree of IIS Manager, and click on the node to be configured.

9. Double-click on the respective Modules icon to display the module list specific to that application. Any changes to the list of modules under a given website or application affect only that node and any child node inheriting those settings.

ASP.NET AND THE IIS PIPELINE

Prior to IIS 7.0, ASP.NET support was provided as an ISAPI filter only. As Figure 11-9 demonstrates, this implementation double-handled many stages of the request processing. Furthermore, some tasks were simply impossible to achieve within the ASP.NET framework. For example, it was not possible to use ASP.NET Forms authentication to manage static content like images without writing complex file-handling routines within the ASP.NET application or mapping images to the ASP.NET ISAPI extension.

Also, basic request processing like mapping the request URL to a local system resource had already been completed before even the ASP.NET framework was loaded, and therefore it was not previously possible to use ASP.NET code to execute tasks like modifying the raw request parameters (for example, rewrite URLs).

With the integrated request-processing mechanism, however, IIS 8.0 integrates ASP.NET natively, and thus the ASP.NET framework is more powerful and pervasive than ever before. With ASP.NET running natively, you can use Forms authentication to secure all content delivered by IIS 8.0, rewrite request URLs before they are mapped to local resources, and do much more that was never before possible using managed code.

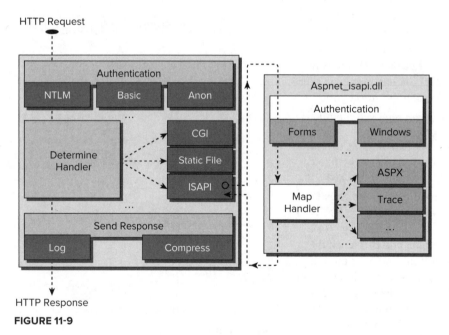

FIGURE 11-9

Figure 11-10 shows how the integrated request-processing pipeline exposes more processing events to the .NET framework than ever before.

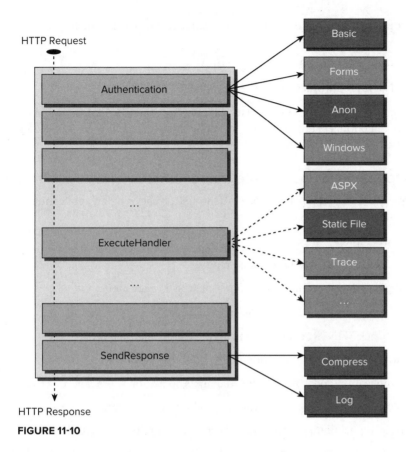

FIGURE 11-10

Configuring ASP.NET Execution Mode

Although IIS 8.0 provides great flexibility and tight integration, there may be situations that require you to run an application in the same environment as IIS 6.0. For example, when installing a legacy application under IIS 8.0, you may experience unexpected errors or application misbehavior. A quick solution might be to simply run the application under the old IIS 6.0 execution model. Since the difference between integrated and classic modes is entirely related to the execution of the worker process tasks, it is not unexpected to find this configuration control under the application pool properties.

Selecting the Execution Mode

When creating your own application pools, you can control the execution mode using the application pool properties configuration:

1. Open IIS 8.0 Manager. (Click WIN+R, enter **inetmgr** in the dialog, and then press Enter.)

2. Expand the navigation tree and click the Application Pools node.

3. Double-click on your application pool, and select the required execution state for the Managed Pipeline Mode:

> **Integrated** — The IIS 8.0/7.0 mode.

> **Classic** — The IIS 6.0 worker process legacy mode.

Note that legacy applications written for the IIS 5.0 platform and requiring IIS 5.0 Isolation mode under the IIS 6.0 platform are no longer supported. Those applications must either be recoded or remain deployed to IIS 5.0 and IIS 6.0 platforms.

Setting an Application to Run in Legacy or Integrated Mode

Selecting the required request-processing pipeline mode is as simple as choosing an application pool running in the required mode.

By default, IIS 8.0 installs two application pools:

> **DefaultAppPool** — Executes in IIS 8.0 Integrated mode.

> **Classic .NET AppPool** — Executes in IIS 6.0 worker process Legacy mode.

If you do not need to create your own application pool, simply choose one of the existing pools:

1. Open IIS Manager. (Click WIN+R, enter **inetmgr** in the dialog, and then press Enter.)

2. Expand the navigation tree to your application node under the relevant website.

3. Right-click on the application node, and choose Manage Application ⇨ Advanced Settings.

4. Click Application Pool, and then click on the ellipsis (...) button to the right of the value field.

5. Select the appropriate application pool from the list provided, and then click OK to all.

If a unique application pool for your application is required or preferred, you can create a new application pool as follows:

1. Open IIS Manager. (Click WIN+R, enter **inetmgr** in the dialog, and then press Enter.)

2. Expand the main Server node to expose the Application Pools node.

3. Click the Application Pools node, and then click Add Application Pool in the Actions pane.

4. Complete the dialog as shown in Figure 11-11, choosing the required execution mode.

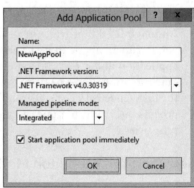

After creating the application pool, you can now follow the preceding steps to assign that new application pool to your application.

FIGURE 11-11

Migrating IIS 7.x ASP.NET Applications to IIS 8

An ASP.NET application that was specifically written for IIS 7.x (7.0 or 7.5) and that operates in the integrated managed pipeline mode can be migrated to IIS 8 without significant effort. In a majority of cases, after setting up and configuring the website, simply moving the forms, content, and components from the IIS 7.x instance to the IIS 8 instance should be all that is required.

> **NOTE** *If your ASP.NET application uses any third-party components, you need to make sure those components can run on IIS 8 and the newest version of Windows Server.*

Migrating Legacy ASP.NET Applications to IIS 8.0

Although the integrated pipeline model of IIS 8.0 is designed to support existing applications seamlessly, there are some configurations that may cause problems under this framework.

Generally, most scenarios that would cause an application designed to run under IIS 6.0 are related to configuration file layout. IIS 8.0 provides built-in assistance for migrating your application configurations by displaying helpful error text when a legacy application fails.

You can easily resolve configuration issues by using the AppCmd utility that ships with IIS 8.0. To use the AppCmd utility to check and migrate legacy .NET applications to take advantage of the new Integrated Mode request-processing pipeline, use the following command syntax:

```
%windir%\system32\inetsrv\appcmd.exe migrate config <Application Path>
```

For example, for an application called *app1* under the IIS *Default Web Site*, you would enter the following:

```
C:\windows\system32\inetsrv\appcmd.exe migrate config Default Web Site/app1
```

It is quite safe to simply install a legacy application to the IIS platform in exactly the same manner as you have always done with IIS 6.0. If there is any issue with the application configuration, IIS will display an informative error.

Usually, the error message displayed by IIS for a failed application will include the command (similar to the above example) to be executed. Executing the AppCmd instruction will check and correct any configuration issues, and migrate your application to the new platform. Once the migration process is completed, the application will still run properly in Classic Mode.

There may be some cases in which an application will not function correctly in IIS 8.0 Integrated Mode. For example, client impersonation is not available in some early request-processing stages. If your application requires `web.config` to define `<identity impersonate="true" />`, which is common with intranet applications, then IIS will generate a warning error message. In most cases, you can simply disable the error as shown below to ignore this error, and your application will run with no adverse repercussions. If, however, problems in application function are experienced or errors are encountered, you will need to configure the application to run using the Classic ASP.NET mode as previously demonstrated.

You can disable the configuration migration error messages by adding the following configuration item to the application's `web.config` file:

```
<system.webServer>

    <validation validateIntegratedModeConfiguration="false" />

</system.webServer>
```

Selecting the ASP.NET Version

There may also be conditions that require use of previous ASP.NET framework versions to support some legacy code, sometimes even multiple different versions running side-by-side on the same server or even under the same website.

Previously, this flexibility was supported by configuring alternative script maps under the application virtual folder. Because of the limitation that only one ASP.NET version can be loaded into a single worker process, if two applications mapped to different ASP.NET versions were configured to load into the same worker process, only the first application to load would operate under the correct version.

With IIS 8.0, although the same limitation is true, application pool configuration specifies the ASP.NET version to prevent the common misconfiguration issue from causing difficulty. Therefore, for each application running a different version of the .NET framework, you will also need to create a separate application pool and set the .NET runtime version in the application pool Advanced Properties.

The request-processing engine of IIS 8.0 provides seamless integration of ASP.NET applications. Although applications designed for previous versions are generally supported, in some cases legacy applications may fail under the new Integrated Mode processing.

It is important to note that the IIS5 Isolation Mode is no longer supported. Legacy applications depending on this mode will no longer run under IIS 8.0 without an appropriate rewrite of the affected code.

LEGACY ISAPI SUPPORT

When introduced with IIS 4.0, the Internet Server API (ISAPI) opened doors to a whole new world of server programming. ISAPI provided developers with a means to build on the stable and powerful IIS platform to create web applications with virtually limitless functionality.

With IIS 8.0 and the HttpModule API, ISAPI may well be considered redundant. Although the IIS team has been careful to state that support for ISAPI will not be removed any time soon, there are no strong arguments to compel developers to create new applications using this, now legacy, API.

There are many reasons why the new HttpModule API is superior to ISAPI, including:

➤ **New object-oriented design** — The C++ class-based HttpModule API provides a more familiar programming environment with more intuitive objects and structures.

➤ **Improved resource management** — New support functions make management of memory and resources more robust and accessible.

➤ **Improved request-state management** — With ISAPI, passing state information between various event notifications requires construction of custom objects and complex data structures. The CHttpModule class supports global property definitions, offering a more intuitive mechanism.

➤ **Choice of language** — System-level server programming was previously the exclusive domain of native code developers. Now, with support for managed code HTTP modules, this level of control is open to the widest possible developer audience.

With the vast array of third-party and proprietary components available based on ISAPI, it is safe to expect that ISAPI support will continue to be available for some time. However, developers will most certainly opt for the new HttpModule API from here on. The following chapter takes a detailed look at the new API and how you can take advantage of these new features.

12

Core Server Extensibility

WHAT'S IN THIS CHAPTER?

➤ An overview of module extensibility

➤ Basic module concepts

➤ An example native code module

➤ An example managed code module

➤ Event tracing from modules

➤ IIS configuration extensibility

➤ Extending the IIS Administration Tool

WROX.COM CODE DOWNLOADS FOR THIS CHAPTER

The wrox.com code downloads for this chapter are found at www.wrox.com/remtitle .cgi?isbn=1118388046 on the Download Code tab. The code is in the chapter 12 download.

You may be getting the idea by now that the modular structure of IIS 8.0 is one of the most important features in the IIS product. The previous chapter demonstrated how it is possible to customize the server workload by simply plugging in and unplugging the relevant modules, thereby customizing functionality, reducing resource overheads, and improving performance.

This chapter concentrates on the underlying module system and how independent components can be seamlessly integrated into the core system to enhance or modify the functionality of the basic core system.

EXTENSIBILITY OVERVIEW

The application programming interface (API) provided for developers to extend IIS is quite certainly the most powerful yet delivered by the IIS developer team. This API, in fact, is exactly the same API used by the IIS team itself to create the default modules supplied with IIS out-of-the-box.

This means that the creators and maintainers of IIS are no longer required to wait for a major OS release or service pack, update, or patch to deliver enhanced or new functionality. Cosmetic adjustments, flaws, or security vulnerabilities alike can be addressed by simply replacing the relevant module without affecting the remaining system in general.

As developers, the exciting implication is that we can now not only add our own functionality by creating a custom pluggable module, but we can also completely replace any default module shipped with IIS.

Indeed, if you are so inclined, you could take the basic core server, strip out all default modules, and write your own modules from scratch. (Why anyone would want to do that, though, is questionable!)

Those of you already familiar with the old IIS 6.0 ISAPI model will find the existing API strikingly familiar. The HTTP Module API provides all the notifications available to ISAPI and more, including access to user objects; global notifications, such as application startup or shutdown; and change notifications, including changes to configuration and content.

For this reason, although the IIS Developer Team has been careful to state that ISAPI will remain a part of IIS in the future, it is almost certain that developer focus will very quickly move away from ISAPI in favor of the HTTP module API.

To extend core server functionality, two basic module types are available:

➤ **Request Modules** — For extensions that are relevant to request processing (for example, authentication, URL mapping and rewriting, or logging functionality).

➤ **Global Modules** — For extensions that provide additional functionality to the core server that are not necessarily related to request processing (for example, application pool control, configuration, and content change management).

One of the most exciting features in IIS 8.0 is the wide choice of development languages for building server extensions. In legacy versions, to extend the core server in ways like new authentication mechanisms, URL rewriting, and so forth, we had little choice other than to use a native development language like C++ or VB. Now, with the core server, language choices include ASP.NET managed code like C# or VB.NET.

Native code like C++ still provides enhanced control and performance over managed code modules because of the execution mode, and managed code cannot be used to develop global-level modules, but with support for managed code extensibility, you can create core server extensions with the ease and rapid development cycle attainable from the managed code development environment.

Although there are some important differences between the API for native and managed code, the basic principles are similar, and thus for ease of presentation, this chapter concentrates first on native code and then discusses managed code modules.

IIS MODULE CONCEPTS

Before you begin developing your own custom IIS modules, it is useful to first review the concepts of events, notifications, priorities, and return codes.

Although the following section describes these concepts in the context of the native code API, it is recommended that those readers more familiar with a managed code development environment continue reading in order to cover some important basic concepts of IIS module design. Once encountering the native code sample, managed code developers may want then to skip to the "Managed Code Modules" section to understand how these concepts relate specifically to a managed code environment.

Events

In earlier chapters, we presented the IIS 8.0 request pipeline and discussed the various stages of request processing. In the context of IIS extensibility, each of these steps can be considered an event.

PIPELINE REQUEST-PROCESSING EVENT	DESCRIPTION
BeginRequest	IIS has received the request and is ready to begin processing.
AuthenticateRequest	IIS is ready to check the supplied credentials.
PostAuthenticateRequest	IIS has established the identity of the user.
AuthorizeRequest	The credentials have been checked, and now IIS is ready to determine whether the user is allowed access to the requested resource.
PostAuthorizeRequest	The user has been authorized.
ResolveRequestCache	IIS is ready to check the cache for an existing match to this request.
PostResolveRequestCache	IIS has checked the cache for an existing match to this request.
MapRequestHandler	IIS is ready to determine which handler should be used (static file, ASP, CGI, other) to service the request. MapRequestHandler is triggered only when the worker process is running in Integrated Mode and .NET 3.0 or greater.
PostMapRequestHandler	IIS has determined which handler to use.
AcquireRequestState	IIS is ready to load state information, such as session data and application variables.

continues

(continued)

PIPELINE REQUEST-PROCESSING EVENT	DESCRIPTION
PreRequestHandlerExecute	IIS is ready to pass the request to the relevant handler, determined by the MapRequestHandler event.
PostRequestHandlerExecute	The event handler has completed execution of the request.
ReleaseRequestState	IIS is ready to store and release state information such as session data and application variables.
PostReleaseRequestState	IIS has stored state information
UpdateRequestCache	IIS is ready to determine whether or not to cache the request.
PostUpdateRequestCache	IIS has completed updating the cache modules that can be used to serve future requests.
LogRequest	IIS is ready to pass data to the IIS logging system. Is triggered only when running in Integrated Mode and .NET 3.0 or greater.
PostLogRequest	IIS has completed processing all LogRequest event handlers. PostLogRequest is triggered only when the worker process is running in Integrated Mode and .NET 3.0 or greater.
EndRequest	IIS is finished processing the request.

Additionally, the following events are nonsequential and might occur at any place in the pipeline:

NONSEQUENTIAL EVENT	DESCRIPTION
AsyncCompletion	An asynchronous processing event has been completed (for example, data written to a response buffer has been sent).
CustomRequestNotification	A custom notification set by a module has been encountered.
MapPath	A URL path has been mapped to a physical path on the system (may occur several times during processing of a single request).
ReadEntity	Data are read from the HTTP request structure.
SendResponse	Data are sent to the HTTP client.

Several global events are also defined that do not necessarily relate to any HTTP request processed within the pipeline:

GLOBAL EVENT	DESCRIPTION
GlobalApplicationResolveModules	When IIS resolves the registered modules.
GlobalApplicationStart	When IIS starts an application.
GlobalApplicationStop	When IIS exits an application.
GlobalCacheCleanup	When IIS clears the cache.
GlobalCacheOperation	When IIS performs a cache-related operation.
GlobalConfigurationChange	When a change is made to a configuration file.
GlobalCustomNotification	When a module raises a user-defined notification.
GlobalFileChange	When a file within a website is changed.
GlobalHealthCheck	When a health-related operation is executed.
GlobalPreBeginRequest	Before a request enters the integrated request-processing pipeline.
GlobalRSCAQuery	When a Runtime Status and Control query is executed.
GlobalStopListening	When IIS stops accepting new requests.
GlobalThreadCleanup	When IIS returns a thread to the thread pool.
GlobalTraceEvent	When a trace event is raised.

Notifications

When creating your own IIS 8.0 module, you will want to instruct IIS 8.0 to call your own specified code when one or more of the previously covered events are encountered during processing of the request pipeline. Each HTTP module installed into IIS registers to the core server a request for notification of certain events.

For example, suppose you want to create a custom authentication module to check credentials against a local text file or SQL database. For such a module, you would want to register your module to receive notifications of the AuthenticateRequest event.

In the IIS Module code samples provided later in this chapter, you will see how the APIs provide special functions to allow your modules to instruct IIS to pass control to your custom processing upon encountering specified events. IIS will pass control to your module by calling a function provided by your custom module according to the API. For many events, IIS provides two separate notifications: one at the beginning of the event, and one when the event has completed. The functions are implemented in your custom module as methods within your module class.

The following table lists the methods executed at each event notification. Your custom module implementation might register for one or more notifications. For each notification your module registers for, you must implement at least one of the notification methods:

EVENT NOTIFICATION	EVENT NOTIFICATION METHOD	POST-EVENT NOTIFICATION METHOD
BeginRequest	OnBeginRequest	OnPostBeginRequest
AuthenticateRequest	OnAuthenticateRequest	OnPostAuthenticateRequest
AuthorizeRequest	OnAuthorizeRequest	OnPostAuthorizeRequest
ResolveRequestCache	OnResolveRequestCache	OnPostResolveRequestCache
MapRequestHandler	OnMapRequestHandler	OnPostMapRequestHandler
AcquireRequestState	OnAcquireRequestState	OnPostAcquireRequestState
PreExecuteRequest-Handler	OnPreExecuteRequestHandler	OnPostPreExecuteRequest-Handler
ExecuteRequestHandler	OnExecuteRequestHandler	OnPostExecuteRequestHandler
ReleaseRequestState	OnReleaseRequestState	OnPostReleaseRequestState
UpdateRequestCache	OnUpdateRequestCache	OnPostUpdateRequestCache
LogRequest	OnLogRequest	OnPostLogRequest
EndRequest	OnEndRequest	OnPostEndRequest
AsyncCompletion	OnAsyncCompletion	None
CustomRequest-Notification	OnCustomRequestNotification	None
MapPath	OnMapPath	OnPostMapPath
ReadEntity	OnReadEntity	OnPostReadEntity
SendResponse	OnSendResponse	OnPostSendResponse

Return Codes

After your custom module has completed processing, control will be returned to the IIS pipeline to continue dealing with the request. Depending on the outcome of your custom processing, you may want to allow control to flow back to IIS and other default or custom modules, or to stop processing any further modules for the given event.

This control is achieved by returning one of the following three return codes:

➤ RQ_NOTIFICATION_CONTINUE — Indicates that IIS should continue processing additional request-level notifications.

➤ RQ_NOTIFICATION_PENDING — Indicates that an asynchronous notification is pending (for example, data are added to an output buffer and awaiting delivery to the client) and returns request-level processing to IIS.

➤ RQ_NOTIFICATION_FINISH_REQUEST — Indicates that IIS has finished processing request-level notifications and should not process any additional request-level notifications.

For example, if a custom authentication module determines that the user credentials supplied with the request are invalid, then you will want to instruct IIS to finish the request without any further processing by returning the RQ_NOTIFICATION_FINISH_REQUEST result. If the credentials are considered valid, however, you will want IIS to continue processing the request as usual by returning RQ_NOTIFICATION_CONTINUE.

Notification Priority

It is possible, of course, to install multiple modules that all register for the same event notification. For example, the log inhibitor module described above could be installed together with the default logging module shipped with IIS.

If both modules are installed at the same time and both modules are registered for the LogRequest notifications, then how does IIS determine which one to call first? The answer is priority. The module API provides a SetPriorityForRequestNotification function to set the priority of your module to one of the following values:

PRIORITY VALUE	DESCRIPTION
PRIORITY_ALIAS_FIRST	Indicates that the module should be processed before all other modules.
PRIORITY_ALIAS_HIGH	Indicates that the module should be processed with high priority.
PRIORITY_ALIAS_MEDIUM	Indicates that the module should be processed with medium priority.
PRIORITY_ALIAS_LOW	Indicates that the module should be processed with low priority.
PRIORITY_ALIAS_LAST	Indicates that the module should be processed after all other modules.

Modules that do not call SetPriorityForRequestNotification are treated as PRIORITY_ALIAS_MEDIUM by default.

Again referring to the example used previously in this chapter, you would probably want to check the IP address of the client before any other request logging actions are taken, and therefore you would set your module priority to PRIORITY_ALIAS_FIRST. When more than one module of the same priority value is registered to the same event notification, the module that appears first in the <globalModules> configuration section of the applicationHost.config file will take precedence. (Refer to Chapter 5, "Administration Tools," for more details about the contents of the applicationHost.config file.)

An alternative method of ordering priority of modules with the same event notification priority is provided in the IIS administration application. Open the IIS manager, and double-click the *modules* icon. In the Actions pane, click View Ordered List. Now the display orders the modules in default priority from first to last. IIS will pass processing control to those modules first by order of priority set using SetPriorityForRequestNotification, and *then* in the order shown in this List View, where multiple modules have the same internal priority.

When listing modules in this way, you will also notice that the Actions pane now provides tools to modify the module order with *move up* and *move down* functions.

After completing the Native Module Tutorial in the following section, you will see that an individual SetPriorityForRequestNotification call is made for each event registration. Therefore, it is possible to register for different event notifications with differing priorities. For example, you may want to create a module that is first to process OnAuthentication events but last to process OnLog events.

Figure 12-1 represents how modules interact with the IIS pipeline.

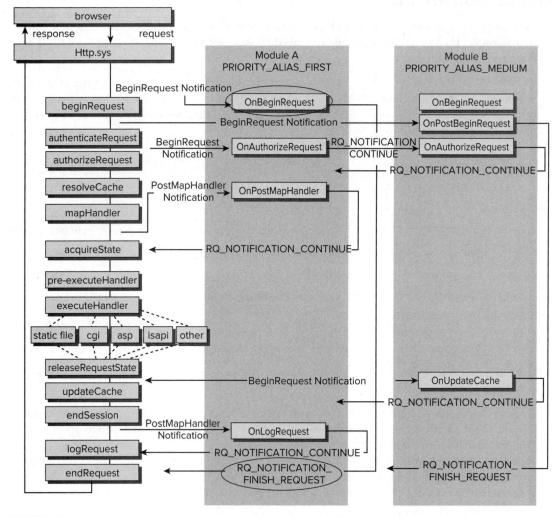

FIGURE 12-1

Note how Module A returns RQ_NOTIFICATION_FINISH_REQUEST after processing OnBeginRequest and thus prevents Module B or any other module (even default, out-of-the-box modules) from processing its own implementations. The same is true when Module B returns the `RQ_NOTIFICATION_FINISH_REQUEST` result, bypassing all further modules (except for the `LogRequest` and `EndRequest` notifications).

Now that we've covered the basics, you are ready to proceed to the next section to create custom HTTP modules. The following section explains the steps required to create an HTTP module using C++ native code.

AN EXAMPLE NATIVE MODULE

For this tutorial, consider a requirement to prevent cross-linking of content on your website from some other website. A typical situation in which this might be useful is where your website contains some graphical content that some other website includes in its own web pages. Every time someone views the other web page, it causes a hit on your own web server, wasting valuable bandwidth and system resources.

> **NOTE** *As usual, MSDN is your best friend when it comes to an authoritative and up-to-date reference. For a complete reference to the Native Code Module development API, refer to* `http://msdn2.microsoft.com/en-us/library/ms692081.aspx` *or* `http://learn.iis.net/page.aspx/112/iis-70-on-server-core/`. *At the time of this writing, there are no specific IIS 8 references.*

Native Module Design

Note that it is assumed that you are familiar with CGI variables and how to use them to examine certain properties of a web request. In this tutorial, you will use the following CGI variables:

➤ `HTTP_REFERER` — Contains the URI of the website where the request was initiated. A blank value may indicate that the request was initiated from a bookmark or manual entry, or possibly a search engine robot, and the like. A request that was initiated as a result of following a link on a web page (whether a internal reference such as an image link or actual user click on an href link) will contain the fully qualified URI of the originating web page (if any) — for example, `http://www.Site1.com/path/file.html`.

➤ `SERVER_NAME` — Contains the hostname of the server to which the request is directed — for example, `www.Site1.com`.

Registering a module to receive `OnBeginRequest` notifications will enable you to intercept the request before IIS processes it any further. By examining and comparing the contents of the CGI variables (also known as *server variables*) `HTTP_REFERER` and `SERVER_NAME`, it is possible to determine whether the request was initiated from the same website or from a remote website. If the value contained in `SERVER_NAME` is found in `HTTP_REFERER`, then it is safe to assume that the request has been initiated from a web page on the local website. If it is not found, or the `HTTP_REFERER` value is blank, then the request may be treated as if initiated from an external link. If the request is found to be a cross-site link, this module will terminate the request immediately and return a 403 error (http-access-denied) to the client.

The following walkthrough is based on Visual Studio 2012. Although the source code should work under other IDE versions and titles, some of the basic menu and interface options may differ.

Native Module Creation

Before starting, you need to download and install the Windows Software Development Kit (SDK) for Windows 8, which can be found at `http://msdn.microsoft.com/en-us/windows/hardware /hh852363`.

After downloading and installing the Windows SDK, complete the following steps to create your HTTP module for IIS. The following sections describe these steps in detail.

1. Include SDK files.
2. Create the new project files.
3. Define the `HttpModule` class.
4. Export the `RegisterModule` method.
5. Register the module for event notifications.
6. Implement the notification method(s).
7. Set the notification priority (optional).
8. Build the module.
9. Install the module.
10. Test the module.

Including SDK Files

If this is the first time that you have used Visual Studio 2012 with Windows Platform SDK, you will need to make sure that the IDE is aware of the location of the relevant Include files.

1. Open Visual Studio 2012.
2. Click Tools ➪ Options.
3. Expand the Projects and Solutions node in the tree view, and then click VC++ Directories.
4. In the Show directories for the drop-down box, select Include files.
5. Verify that the path where you installed the SDK Include files is listed. If the path is not listed, click the New Line icon, and then add the path where you installed the SDK Include files.
6. Click OK.

> **NOTE** *In Visual Studio 2010 and newer, you are not required to perform the previous steps. The VC++ Directory settings are now set by default.*

Creating a New Project

The next step creates the new project files. Although you are free to name the project something different from the suggested *BlockCrossLinks*, it is recommended that you follow the sample verbatim at least one time.

1. Choose File ⇨ New ⇨ Project.

2. In the Project Types pane, expand the Installed ⇨ Templates ⇨ Visual C++ node, and then click Win32.

3. In the Templates pane, select Win32 Project.

4. In the Name box, type **BlockCrossLinks**.

5. In the Location box, type the path for the sample or accept the default, then click OK.

6. When the Win32 Application Wizard opens, click Application Settings.

7. Under Application type, click DLL.

8. Under Additional options, click "Empty project," and then click Finish.

> **NOTE** *If you have configured the Visual Studio environment for another programming language, you can change the environment settings to C++ by selecting Tools ⇨ Import and Export Settings... ⇨ Reset all Settings...⇨ Yes/No, and then selecting your preferred collection settings.*

Defining the HttpModule Class

In this step, you will create only the basic source code structure, including only the `HttpModule` class definition as well as construction and export functions.

There are three basic components to the module source code:

➤ The `HttpModule` class — The base class for this module. In this class, you will implement the request notification methods that are called by IIS at the relevant request-processing events.

➤ The `HttpModule` factory — Manages the creation and removal of the module for each request to be processed.

➤ The `RegisterModule` function — The exported function to allow IIS to load the module.

Create the basic structure by following these steps:

1. In Solution Explorer, right-click Source Files, point to Add, and then click New Item. The Add New Item dialog box opens.

2. Expand the Installed ⇨ Visual C++ node in the Categories pane, and then click Code.

3. In the Templates pane, select the C++ File (.cpp) template.

4. In the Name box, type **BlockCrossLinks,** and leave the default path for the file in the Location box.

5. Click Add.

6. Insert the following code:

```
#define _WINSOCKAPI_
#include <windows.h>
#include <sal.h>
#include <httpserv.h>
// Create the module class.
class CBlockCrossLinks : public CHttpModule
{
    //TODO
    // Implement Notification Method/s
};
// Create the module's class factory.
class CBlockCrossLinksFactory : public IHttpModuleFactory
{
public:
    HRESULT
    GetHttpModule(
        OUT CHttpModule ** ppModule,
        IN IModuleAllocator * pAllocator
    )
    {
        UNREFERENCED_PARAMETER( pAllocator );
        // Create a new instance.
        CBlockCrossLinks * pModule = new CBlockCrossLinks;
        // Test for an error.
        if (!pModule)
        {
            // Return an error if the factory cannot create the
            // instance.
            return HRESULT_FROM_WIN32( ERROR_NOT_ENOUGH_MEMORY );
        }
        else
        {
            // Return a pointer to the module.
            *ppModule = pModule;
            pModule = NULL;
            // Return a success status.
            return S_OK;
        }
    }
    void
    Terminate()
    {
        // Remove the class from memory.
        delete this;
    }
};
// Create the module's exported registration function.
HRESULT
__stdcall
RegisterModule(
```

```
            DWORD dwServerVersion,
            IHttpModuleRegistrationInfo * pModuleInfo,
            IHttpServer * pGlobalInfo
    )
    {
    HRESULT hr = S_OK;
    UNREFERENCED_PARAMETER( dwServerVersion );
        UNREFERENCED_PARAMETER( pGlobalInfo );
    // TODO
    // Register for notifications
    // Set notification priority
    return hr;
    }
```

This code lays out the basic framework for the new module. First, the module is defined as an `HttpModule` class with `CBlockCrossLinks : public CHttpModule`. Within this construct, you will implement the runtime functionality, as indicated by the TODO comment placeholder.

Next, the `class CBlockCrossLinksFactory : public IHttpModuleFactory` block defines the factory class called by IIS to construct instances of your module and to later unload them from memory. Any special global initialization can be processed in the `GetHttpModule()` method and then cleaned up in the `Terminate()` method.

Lastly, in this code segment, the `RegisterModule()` function must be provided for use by IIS to obtain runtime information about the module, including which events are required and which functions internal to the module class should be called for each notification. As indicated by the TODO comment placeholders, this is where you will define the notifications and notification priorities for your module.

Exporting the RegisterModule Method

Now that the basic code has been laid out, the following steps are required to export the `RegisterModule` function and thus define the entry point for IIS to access the module:

1. On the Project menu, right-click BlockCrossLinks ⇨ Properties.

2. Expand the Configuration Properties node in the tree view, expand the Linker node, and then click Command Line.

3. In the Configuration dropdown box, select All Configurations.

4. In the Additional Options box, type **/EXPORT:RegisterModule**, and then click OK.

At this stage, you can attempt to build the project to confirm correct implementation thus far.

Select Build Solution from the Build menu (or just press F7). You should see the following text in the output window:

```
- Build started: Project: BlockCrossLinks, Configuration: Debug Win32 -
Build started 4/11/2012 7:27:39 AM.
InitializeBuildStatus:
  Creating "Debug\BlockCrossLinks.unsuccessfulbuild" because "AlwaysCreate"
  was specified.
ClCompile:
  BlockCrossLinks.cpp
ManifestResourceCompile:
```

```
   All outputs are up-to-date.
Manifest:
   All outputs are up-to-date.
LinkEmbedManifest:
   All outputs are up-to-date.
   BlockCrossLinks.vcxproj -> C:\Users\Administrator\documents\visual studio
   12\Projects\BlockCrossLinks\Debug\BlockCrossLinks.dll
FinalizeBuildStatus:
   Deleting file "Debug\BlockCrossLinks.unsuccessfulbuild".
   Touching "Debug\BlockCrossLinks.lastbuildstate".

Build succeeded.

Time Elapsed 00:00:01.84
========== Build: 1 succeeded, 0 failed, 0 up-to-date, 0 skipped ==========
```

If any errors appear in the output, you will need to resolve those before proceeding.

Registering for Event Notifications

Now it is time to register the module for the required request events. You will recall from the preceding "Native Module Design" section that the BeginRequest notification will be used to deliver the required outcomes.

Notification registration is done in the RegisterModule function by calling SetRequestNotifications. Returning to VS2012, locate the RegisterModule function in your source code file (near the end of the file), and add the following code:

```
HRESULT hr = S_OK;
UNREFERENCED_PARAMETER( dwServerVersion );
UNREFERENCED_PARAMETER( pGlobalInfo );
// TODO
// Register for notifications
// Set notification priority
// Set the request notifications
hr = pModuleInfo->SetRequestNotifications(
        new CBlockCrossLinksFactory,
        RQ_BEGIN_REQUEST, // Register for BeginRequest notifications
        0
);
return hr;
```

This code instructs IIS to call your module whenever a BeginRequest event is encountered. See the table under the "Notifications" section previously discussed in this chapter for the full list of notification events available. When this module is installed, whenever a BeginRequest event is encountered, IIS will attempt to call the OnRequestBegin() method of your module class, which must be implemented next.

Implementing the Notification Method(s)

Now that you have registered your module to receive request notifications, IIS will attempt to execute the relevant notification method of your module. Because this module registers for RQ_BEGIN_REQUEST notifications, you must implement one of either OnBeginRequest or OnPostBeginRequest methods.

Refer to the table of available notification events in the "Notifications" section above for a full list of the relevant methods required to register for those notifications.

Again, because this module needs to check the request properties and reject processing depending on the source of the request, the `OnBeginRequest` method is selected in this case.

Back to VS2012, look for the `BlockCrossLinks` class implementation, and add the following `OnBeginRequest` notification:

```
// Create the module class.
class CBlockCrossLinks : public CHttpModule
{
        //TODO
        // Implement Notification Method/s
        REQUEST_NOTIFICATION_STATUS
        OnBeginRequest( IN IHttpContext * pHttpContext,
                        IN IHttpEventProvider * pProvider
                        )
        {
            // TODO:
            // Implement Method
        }
};
```

Now it is time to add the code that does the real work! The following code replaces the `TODO: Implement Method` comment above.

First, assign some buffers and static variables:

```
            // We won't be using this, so confirm that to avoid compiler warnings
            UNREFERENCED_PARAMETER( pProvider );
            // The images folder to be protected
            // Change this value to reflect the images
            // path for your own website
            PCSTR pszProtectedPath = "/images/";
            // controls whether to permit loading of images from
            // bookmarks or type the url into the browser location
            BOOL permitBookmarks = false;
            // Create an HRESULT to receive return values from methods.
            HRESULT hr;
            // Buffer size for returned variable values.
            DWORD cbValue = 512;
```

Using the `AllocateRequestMemory` function provided by the API, all memory allocated will be handled by IIS.

```
            // Allocating buffers for relevant
            // CGI environment variable values
            PCSTR pszServerName =
                (PCSTR) pHttpContext->AllocateRequestMemory( cbValue );
            PCSTR pszReferer =
                (PCSTR) pHttpContext->AllocateRequestMemory( cbValue );
            PCSTR pszPathInfo =
                (PCSTR) pHttpContext->AllocateRequestMemory( cbValue );
            if(pszPathInfo == NULL ||
               pszServerName == NULL ||
```

```
        pszReferer == NULL
        )
{
    // looks like a memory allocation problem
    // bail out and let IIS take care of it.
    return RQ_NOTIFICATION_CONTINUE;
}
```

The GetResponse function provides a handle to the HTTP request data. The data structure returned provides access to various request variables, as well the GetServerVariable() method used to retrieve CGI variable values. This function is first used to determine whether the request is seeking a file within the protcted path defined at the beginning of this function. If it is not, then the return code RQ_NOTIFICATION_CONTINUE is used to send control back to IIS to continue as usual.

It is worth noting at this stage that although this sample tests the PATH_INFO for the existence of the string defined in pszProtectedPath above, you could just as easily test the string value for some other property, such as a file extension matching a known image format, such as .jpg, .gif, or .png.

```
// Retrieve a pointer to the response.
IHttpResponse * pHttpResponse = pHttpContext->GetResponse();
// start by inspecting the path
hr = pHttpContext->GetServerVariable("PATH_INFO",
                                        &pszPathInfo,
                                        &cbValue);
if( hr != S_OK )
{
    // Can't determine whether this is an image folder request,
    // so give it back to IIS to finish it off.
    return RQ_NOTIFICATION_CONTINUE;
}
// is it the folder of interest?
if( strstr( pszPathInfo, pszProtectedPath ) == NULL )
{
    // not a path of interest - let it go through unchallenged
    return RQ_NOTIFICATION_CONTINUE;
}
```

At this stage, the request is identified as a request for a file within the protected path. The following code retrieves the CGI variables SERVER_NAME and HTTP_REFERER. Note that in the case of any error, control is simply passed back to IIS to continue processing as usual.

```
// Look for the "SERVER_NAME" variable.
hr = pHttpContext->GetServerVariable("SERVER_NAME",\
                                        &pszServerName,
                                        &cbValue);
if( hr != S_OK )
{
    // No point continuing if we have no SERVER_NAME
    // give it back to IIS to finish it off.
    return RQ_NOTIFICATION_CONTINUE;
}
// now retrieve the HTTP_REFERER value
hr = pHttpContext->GetServerVariable("HTTP_REFERER",
                                        &pszReferer,&cbValue);
```

If SERVER_NAME appears within the HTTP_REFERER value, then this request was generated by a link from the same website. In that case, control is passed back to IIS as before. If not, however, RQ_NOTIFICATION_FINISH_REQUEST is used to terminate the request immediately — no further notifications for any other modules (including those shipped with IIS) will be processed.

```
// check for a valid result
if( hr == S_OK )
{
   // if the referrer is the same website, then pszServerName
   // will appear in pszReferer
   if( strstr(pszReferer, pszServerName) != 0 )
   {
      // it is there, so this is a valid link
      return RQ_NOTIFICATION_CONTINUE;
   }
   else
   {
      // the referer does not match server_name
      return RQ_NOTIFICATION_FINISH_REQUEST;
   }
}
```

If HTTP_REFERER is not found in the list of CGI variables, then the request has not been generated by a website link. Possible causes include access from a browser bookmark, directly typing the URI into the browser location, or a request made by a search index robot. The value of the permit_bookmarks variable defined at the beginning of this function determines how to handle this kind of request.

```
if( hr = ERROR_INVALID_INDEX )
{
   // the referer value is missing from the header
   if( permitBookmarks )
      return RQ_NOTIFICATION_CONTINUE;
   else
      return RQ_NOTIFICATION_FINISH_REQUEST;
}
// we only arrive here if there was an error
// allow IIS to deal with the rest.
// Return processing to the pipeline.
return RQ_NOTIFICATION_CONTINUE;
```

You can change the value of the local variable permit_bookmarks to change the default behavior. If you want to allow delivery for requests with missing HTTP_REFERER values, set permitBookmarks = true.

Setting Notification Priority

When several modules (including those shipped with IIS) are loaded, IIS uses a notification priority scheme to determine the order in which to pass request processing. Setting the notification priority for your module is optional. If you do not explicitly set the notification priority here, your module will be treated as the default PRIORITY_ALIAS_MEDIUM priority.

Returning to the RegisterModule() function, add the following additional code:

```
HRESULT hr = S_OK;
```

```
UNREFERENCED_PARAMETER( dwServerVersion );
UNREFERENCED_PARAMETER( pGlobalInfo );
// TODO
// Register for notifications
// Set notification priority
// Set the request notifications
hr = pModuleInfo->SetRequestNotifications(
        new CBlockCrossLinksFactory,
        RQ_BEGIN_REQUEST, // Register for BeginRequest notifications
        0
);
if( hr == S_OK ) // Do this only if there was no error
{
        hr = pModuleInfo->SetPriorityForRequestNotification(
                        RQ_BEGIN_REQUEST,     // which notification
                        PRIORITY_ALIAS_FIRST  // what priority
                        );
}
        return hr;
```

Because this module needs to check the request properties and reject processing if the request is determined to be related to a cross-linked request, it makes sense to set the priority to the maximum available so that it will be the first module called by IIS when a request is received.

However, if you want to pre-qualify the request via some other custom module before determining whether to allow or reject a request, you may want to set a lower priority, such as PRIORITY_ ALIAS_MEDIUM or PRIORITY_ALIAS_LAST.

Building the Module

Now build the module by choosing Build Module from the Build menu (or simply press F7). Confirm that there are no errors by observing the results displayed in the output window:

```
- Build started: Project: BlockCrossLinks, Configuration: Debug Win32 -
Build started 4/11/2012 7:29:21 AM.
InitializeBuildStatus:
  Creating "Debug\BlockCrossLinks.unsuccessfulbuild"
            because "AlwaysCreate" was specified.
ClCompile:
  BlockCrossLinks.cpp
ManifestResourceCompile:
  All outputs are up-to-date.
Manifest:
  All outputs are up-to-date.
LinkEmbedManifest:
  All outputs are up-to-date.
  BlockCrossLinks.vcxproj -> C:\Users\Administrator\documents
                                \visual studio
                                \12\Projects\BlockCrossLinks
                                \Debug\BlockCrossLinks.dll
FinalizeBuildStatus:
  Deleting file "Debug\BlockCrossLinks.unsuccessfulbuild".
  Touching "Debug\BlockCrossLinks.lastbuildstate".

Build succeeded.
```

```
Time Elapsed 00:00:02.31
========== Build: 1 succeeded, 0 failed, 0 up-to-date, 0 skipped ==========
```

Installing the Module

Now it is time to install the custom module into IIS. The following steps use IIS Manager for this task. You can also complete this task by editing the `applicationHost.config` file, as described in Chapter 18, "Programmatic Configuration and Management."

Note that the following method will install the module to *all* websites on this server. Refer also to Chapter 11, "Core Server," for more detail on independently managing modules for individual websites.

1. If IIS 8.0 is running on a different server than your copy of Visual Studio, copy the file `BlockCrossLinks.dll` generated by the VS2012 build process to some location on the IIS system.

2. To open IIS Manager, press WIN+R, enter **inetmgr** in the dialog, and then press OK.

3. Click the base container (SERVER1/Administrator).

4. Double-click the Modules icon in the Features View.

5. Click Configure Native Modules in the Actions pane.

6. Click Register.

7. Enter **BlockCrossLinks** as the name, and the full path to the `BlockCrossLinks.dll` file.

8. Click OK.

9. Confirm that `BlockCrossLinks` now appears in the list of available modules and that the checkbox is checked.

10. Click OK.

Congratulations! Your first native code HTTP module is installed and ready to test.

> **WARNING** *A native module generally compiles as a 32-bit module, by default. When it is registered in IIS, there is a pre-condition set for running it in 32-bit mode. For this to load, the worker process you are running under must have Enable 32-Bit Applications set to True.*

Testing the Module

Although there are a variety of ways to test this module, the following process assumes a standard default installation of IIS 8.0. The standard default install will establish the *Default Web Site* referred to in the following demonstration, as well as the default homepage graphic iis-8.png. If your own installation is nonstandard, simply modify the following steps accordingly:

1. Open the IIS default website root in Windows Explorer by pressing WIN+R, entering **C:\inetpub\wwwroot**, and then clicking OK.

2. Create a new folder called `images`.

3. Copy (or move) the file `iis-8.png` into the new `images` folder.

4. Open the `iisstart.htm` file in a text editor. (Right-click on the file, and choose Open With ⇨ Notepad.)

5. Find the following text:

```
<img src="iis-8.png"
    alt="Microsoft Internet Information Services 8.0"
    class="hero">
```

and replace it with the following:

```
<a href="http://127.0.0.1">
   <img src="http://127.0.0.1/images/iis-8.png" />
</a>
```

6. Save the file and exit.

Now open Internet Explorer on the server console (or by a terminal server session), type **http://localhost** in the IE location field and hit Enter.

You will see that the homepage now displays only a broken image icon instead of the IIS Welcome graphic. Now click the broken link icon, and observe the default homepage in all its glory!

Native Module Wrap-Up

When accessing the default homepage that you modified previously in Steps 4 and 5 using the URL `http://localhost`, the image link is requested using the IP address (`127.0.0.1`) instead of the hostname (`localhost`). Thus, when the custom module processes the request for the image file, the value of `SERVER_NAME` evaluates to `127.0.0.1`, and the value of `HTTP_REFERER` is `http://localhost/iisstart.htm`.

Since the `SERVER_NAME` value does not exist in the `HTTP_REFERER`, the request is detected as cross-linked and rejected.

When you click on the link to open the homepage now as `http://127.0.0.1`, the value of the `SERVER_NAME` is `127.0.0.1` and the `HTTP_REFERER` is `http://127.0.0.1/iisstart.htm`, and thus the request is allowed to complete.

As a further exercise, you might want to conduct further processing in the `OnBeginRequest` method of your custom module to add further functionality:

➤ Replace the requested image with an alternative image, perhaps containing some copyrighted text alerting the viewers to the fact that the website they are visiting is (perhaps unintentionally) referring to content delivered to another website without permission.

➤ Modify the IIS response code to return a more descriptive result, say, 403 (Request Denied), instead of the default 200 (OK).

MANAGED CODE MODULES

Although there are several important differences, the Managed Code API shares some basic concepts with the Native Code API, and therefore the earlier section, "IIS Module Concepts" is recommended reading prior to beginning this section. You may also consider reviewing the sections covering the IIS 8.0 pipeline in Chapter 2 and ASP.NET integrated mode in Chapter 11 prior to proceeding with this section.

For those of you already familiar with `HttpApplication` events in previous versions of ASP.NET, the IIS 8.0 API will be a familiar and empowering extension.

IIS 8.0 ships with the special ManagedEngine utility module, which acts as a native code module wrapper for managed code modules. Figure 12-2 represents how the ManagedEngine module exposes IIS request-processing pipeline events to the managed code environment.

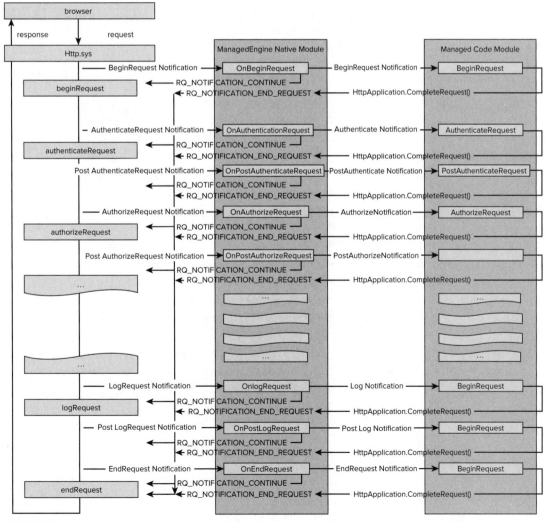

FIGURE 12-2

Notice that one major difference between the managed and native code functionality is that managed code modules do not set a return code back to IIS; instead, the modules use the CompleteRequest method of the HttpApplication class to interrupt the request-processing pipeline and go directly to the EndRequest event.

Another important difference is that not all the native notification events are available. For example, there is no equivalent of PostBeginRequest for managed code modules.

Nonetheless, the ability for managed code to now execute in the same stages as IIS modules makes many tasks previously only accessible to native ISAPI filters and extensions now possible in managed code, using the familiar ASP.NET APIs and full functionality of the .NET platform. For example, it is now possible to use managed code to achieve the following:

➤ Custom authentication modes that replace built-in methods.

➤ Modification of the incoming request contents, such as request headers or rewrite URLs.

➤ Filtering of outgoing responses for all content types, including images and multimedia files.

Managed Event Notifications

The complete pipeline contains the following stages, exposed as HttpApplication events in ASP.NET:

REQUEST EVENT	DESCRIPTION	POST-EVENT
BeginRequest	The request processing is starting.	<none>
AuthenticateRequest	The request is being authenticated. IIS and ASP.NET authentication modules subscribe to this stage to perform authentication.	PostAuthenticateRequest
AuthorizeRequest	The request is being authorized. IIS and ASP.NET authorization modules check whether the authenticated user has access to the resource being requested.	PostAuthorizeRequest
ResolveRequestCache	Cache modules can check whether the response to this request exists in the cache and return it instead of proceeding with the rest of the execution path. Both ASP.NET Output Cache and the new IIS Output Cache features execute here.	PostResolveRequestCache

REQUEST EVENT	DESCRIPTION	POST-EVENT
MapRequestHandler	This stage is internal in ASP .NET and is used to determine the request handler. This Request Event will fire only if running in Integrated Mode and .NET 3.0 or greater.	PostMapRequestHandler
AcquireRequestState	The state necessary for the request execution is being fetched. ASP.NET Session State and Profile modules obtain their data here.	PostAcquireRequestState
PreRequestHandlerExecute	Any tasks before the execution of the handler can be performed here.	PostRequestHandlerExecute
ReleaseRequestState	ASP.NET has completed the execution of all request event handlers.	PostReleaseRequestState
UpdateRequestCache	The response is stored in the caching modules.	PostUpdateRequestCache
LogRequest	Any task before logging of the request can be performed here. Event and Postevent will fire only in Integrate Mode and .NET 3.0 or greater.	PostLogRequest
EndRequest	The request has been processed. Any task before the response is sent can be performed here.	<none>

Further Reading

Managed module functionality is provided within the System.Web namespace. As before, you should allow MSDN to become your best friend when it comes to a concise reference for IIS development. You will find the relevant APIs documented at http://msdn2.microsoft.com/en-us/library/system.web.aspx.

This MSDN reference provides details on all the objects and structures available for extending IIS. Probably the best way to learn how to use them is to jump right in and create a sample module.

AN EXAMPLE MANAGED MODULE

If you have already completed the previous tutorial in this chapter and completed the development of a custom module using native code, then you will be familiar with the example functionality of the Cross Link Blocker. Otherwise, you should review the information on Module Design previously covered in this chapter.

Managed Module Design

As with the native module design, the BeginRequest event will be the notification used to implement this module. Also, the request information used will be the values of the SERVER_NAME and HTTP_REFERER variables provided by the CGI framework.

The example native code module used the RQ_NOTIFICATION_FINISH_REQUEST return code to interrupt the request processing when a cross-linked request was discovered. Although this might be a good way to reduce the performance and bandwidth hit that cross-link requests would otherwise create, it does not necessarily provide the most eloquent solution.

The following example delivers an alternative pre-defined image in place of the requested file. The replacement image may be very small, or blank, to minimize bandwidth overheads, or may carry some copyright or "access denied" text. This tutorial demonstrates use of a small text-carrying image, but you can use any file you like — even a nasty surprise for the cross-linker!

Managed Module Creation

Although the IDE used in this sample is Visual Studio 2012, you can use other IDE versions and products. You can even use a plaintext editor like Notepad to complete this sample. Simply replace the IDE steps provided with equivalent steps for your selected IDE.

This example can be completed in five basic steps:

1. Define the IHttpModule interface.
2. Register for notifications.
3. Implement the notifications.
4. Install the module.
5. Test the module.

Defining the IHttpModule Interface

The first task is to define the module framework. IHttpModule is a System.Web namespace interface that provides the initialization and disposal methods for IIS modules.

1. Open Visual Studio 2012.
2. Click File ➪ New ➪ File.
3. Select Text File from the General node, and then click Open.

4. Click File ⇨ Save TextFile1.txt As….

5. Use the File Save As dialog to browse to the location of your website root (for example, `c:\inetpub\wwwroot`), and create a new folder called **App_Code**.

6. Save the file as **BlockLinks.cs** into the `App_Code` folder.

7. Insert the following code:

```
using System;
using System.Web;
namespace CustomModules
{
    public class BlockLinks : IHttpModule
    {
        public BlockLinks()
        {
            // Class constructor.
        }
        // Classes that inherit IHttpModule
        // must implement the Init and Dispose methods.
        public void Init(HttpApplication app)
        {
            // TODO:
            // Add initialization code
            // Including notifications
        }
        public void Dispose()
        {
            // TODO:
            // Add code to clean up the
            // instance variables of a module.
        }
        // TODO:
        // add event notification methods
    }
}
```

This code simply lays out the basic module framework. All implementations of `IHttpModule` must provide the basic constructor (`public BlockLinks()`), initialization (`public void Init(HttpApplication app)`), and disposal (`public void Dispose()`) methods.

Next, you will proceed to add the custom functionality of the module.

Registering for Notifications

In this step, you need to determine which event notification will be handled by this module. As outlined in the design discussion, only the `BeginRequest` notification is required for this module.

Find the module's `Init` method and add the following code:

```
// Classes that inherit IHttpModule
// must implement the Init and Dispose methods.
public void Init(HttpApplication app)
{
    // TODO:
```

```
// Add initialization code
// Including notifications
app.BeginRequest += new EventHandler(app_BeginRequest);

}
```

This line registers the module's event handler method `app_BeginRequest` to the IIS request pipeline.

Implementing the Notifications

Now that you have registered the `app_BeginRequest` method, you need to implement it. Add the following code to your class:

```
// TODO:
// add event notification methods
// Define a custom BeginRequest event handler.
public void app_BeginRequest(object o, EventArgs ea)
{
    HttpApplication httpApp = (HttpApplication)o;
    HttpContext ctx = HttpContext.Current;
    NameValueCollection coll;  // to handle the CGI variables
    String ServerName = String.Empty; // variable to store the SERVER_NAME
    String Referer = String.Empty;    // and HTTP_REFERER CGI variables.
```

This code simply sets out a few variables and objects to simplify later manipulation. The `HttpContext` class provides access to the HTTP request details as well as to HTTP response structures if needed.

Notice the use of the `NameValueCollection` class for the `coll` object. This utility class is included to simplify processing of the CGI variables, but you will need to include the namespace in the C# headers to be able to use this:

```
using System;
using System.Web;
using System.Collections.Specialized;
```

Now let's return to the notification method implementation. The next step in this implementation is to inspect the URL requested by the remote client and determine whether it is an image file.

```
String ServerName = String.Empty;
String Referer = String.Empty;
// retrieve the URL requested
String RequestUrl = ctx.Request.RawUrl;
if (RequestUrl.EndsWith(".jpg", StringComparison.OrdinalIgnoreCase) ||
    RequestUrl.EndsWith(".gif", StringComparison.OrdinalIgnoreCase) ||
    RequestUrl.EndsWith(".png", StringComparison.OrdinalIgnoreCase))
{
        // Is an image file
}
}
```

The next bit of code simply extracts the data of interest from the request structure and then tests whether the request is the result of a link from the local website:

```
// Is an image file
// Load ServerVariable collection into NameValueCollection object.
```

```
coll = ctx.Request.ServerVariables;
// Get names of all keys into a string array.
ServerName = coll["SERVER_NAME"];
Referer   = coll["HTTP_REFERER"];
if (!Referer.Contains(ServerName))
{
    // NOT initiated by a link from a local web page!
}
```

You might already recognize that when `Referer.Contains(ServerName)` is `false` (that is, `!Referer.Contains(ServerName)` is true), there are two possible causes:

➤ The `HTTP_REFERER` is a remote website — for example, the `SERVER_NAME` is `www.Site1.com` and the `HTTP_REFERER` is `www.Site2.com/path/page.html`.

➤ The `HTTP_REFERER` is blank. In this case, the request was initiated by a bookmark or direct entry to the browser location, or by a non-browser entity (a search engine robot, for example).

If you want to permit access in case of the second cause, you will need to add a further test for a specifically blank string (that is, `Referer == ""`). Otherwise, continue with the following code to deny all requests that are not the result of a local web page request.

The following code uses the `RewritePath` method of the `HttpContext` class to change the requested file to a different file of your own choosing:

```
if (!Referer.Contains(ServerName))
{
    // NOT initiated by a link from a local web page!
    ctx.RewritePath(
        "/images/",  // replacement file
        "denied.bmp",    // replacement path
        ""               // replacement query string
        );
}
```

And that completes the coding for this module.

Installing the Module

Now it is time to install the custom module into IIS. The following steps use IIS Manager for this task. This task can also be completed by editing the `applicationHost.config` file. Refer to Chapter 18 for details of that method.

Note that the following method will install the module to *all* websites on this server. Refer also to Chapter 11 for more detail on independently managing modules for multiple websites.

1. To open IIS Manager, press WIN+R, enter **inetmgr**, and then click OK.

2. Expand the node tree, and click on the Sites container (for example, Default Web Site).

3. Double-click the Modules icon in the Features View.

4. Click on Add Managed Module in the Actions pane.

5. Enter **BlockLinks** in the Name field, and select .CustomModules.BlockLinks from the list.

6. Click OK.

Congratulations! Your first managed code HTTP Module is installed and ready to test.

> **ALTERNATIVE INSTALL**
>
> An alternative to installing the managed module as source code in the `App_Code` path under the website root is to compile the code as a DLL, copy it to the `bin` folder (for example, `C:\inetpub\wwwroot\bin`) of the website, and then follow the preceding steps.
>
> Running the module from `App_Code` means that during development, you will be able to make quick modifications to your modules while viewing the results in your web browser, without needing to run the compiler or restart services. Installing the module as a binary DLL, however, provides some savings on resource overheads, making your modules significantly more efficient when running on production systems, as well as providing some protection of your intellectual property if you are distributing your code on a commercial basis.

Testing the Module

Although there are a variety of ways to test this module, the following process assumes a standard default installation of IIS 8.0. The standard default install will establish the Default Web Site referred to in the following demonstration, as well as the default homepage graphic `iis-8.png`. If your own installation is nonstandard, simply modify the following steps accordingly:

1. To open the IIS default website root in Windows Explorer, press WIN+R, enter **C:\inetpub\wwwroot**, and click OK.

2. Create a new folder called `images`.

3. Copy (or move) the file `iis-8.png` into the new `images` folder.

4. Open the file `iisstart.htm` in a text editor (right-click on the file, and choose Open With ⇨ Notepad).

5. Find the following text:

```
<img src="iis-8.png" alt="IIS8" width="571" height="411" />
```

and replace it with the following:

```
<a href=http://127.0.0.1>
    <img src="http://127.0.0.1/images/iis-8.png" />
</a>
```

6. Save the file, and exit.

7. Right-click inside the `images` folder, choose New ⇨ Bitmap Image, and enter the filename **denied.bmp**.

8. Right-click on the new file, and choose Open With ⇨ Paint.

9. Use the text tool to add some text (for example, **Access Denied**), and save the changes.

Now open Internet Explorer on the server console (or by a terminal server session), enter **http://localhost** in the location field, then press Enter.

You will see that the homepage now displays the replacement image instead of the IIS Welcome graphic. Click on the broken link icon and observe the default homepage in all its glory!

Managed Module Wrap-Up

When accessing the default home page that you previously modified in Steps 4 and 5 using the URL http://localhost, the image link is requested using the IP address (127.0.0.1) instead of the hostname (localhost). Thus, when the custom module processes the request for the image file, the value of SERVER_NAME evaluates to 127.0.0.1, and the value of HTTP_REFERER is http://localhost/iisstart.htm.

Since the SERVER_NAME value does not exist in the HTTP_REFERER, the request is detected as cross-linked and rejected.

When you click the link to open the homepage now as http://127.0.0.1, the value of SERVER_NAME is 127.0.0.1, and the HTTP_REFERER is http://127.0.0.1/iisstart.htm — thus, IIS is permitted to deliver the requested image file.

As a further exercise, you might want to further process the custom module to incorporate further functionality, such as adding notification text to the web server log file using the AppendToLog method of the Response object.

EVENT TRACING FROM MODULES

Although the sample modules in the preceding examples are relatively simple, they demonstrate how it is now possible to add virtually limitless enhanced functionality to the core web server system as well as web applications.

As you no doubt know, however, the more complex applications become, the more difficult it is to diagnose when something goes wrong. In the past, the diagnosis of misbehaving web applications and extensions was arguably the single-most difficult and time-consuming task in running and managing web applications.

The designers of IIS 8.0 recognized this fact and provided debugging and diagnostic tools. Chapter 23, "Diagnostics and Troubleshooting," provides an in-depth treatment of the tracing tools and how to capture and manage tracing information.

For the module programmer, though, the capacity to hook into the built-in tracing subsystem provides some major time-saving capabilities. The advantage of using the tracing system in favor of alternative methods, such as writing debug output to a text file or Event Viewer logging, is that the code has no effect unless a trace listener is attached. Therefore, any diagnostic resource overheads are limited until it is required, and then the diagnostics can be activated by the user when and as required.

Adding Tracing Support to a Managed Code Module

This tutorial expands on the managed code module example, adding some tracing output. You will perform the following steps, as detailed in the following sections:

1. Include a namespace reference.

2. Declare a global TraceSource variable.

3. Initialize the TraceSource object.

4. Add trace events.

5. Compile and deploy the module.

6. Add a trace listener to IIS.

7. Enable tracing and route trace events to IIS.

8. View the trace results.

> **NOTE** *This tutorial requires that the event tracing module is installed and active. For further details on adding and removing optional IIS components, refer to Chapter 4, "Installing IIS 8.0."*

Including a Namespace Reference

The first step to adding event tracing to your IIS module is to include a reference to the relevant namespace. IIS event tracing is supported by System.Diagnostics, which you will find fully documented in MSDN at http://msdn2.microsoft.com/en-us/library/system.diagnostics.aspx.

In this example, the TraceSource class from the System.Diagnostics namespace will be used to produce output that can be routed to IIS for display.

To begin, open the C# source created in the previous tutorial (BlockLinks.cs), and include System.Diagnostics below the existing using declarations:

```
using System;
using System.Web;
using System.Collections.Specialized;
using System.Diagnostics;
```

Declaring a Global TraceSource Variable

To produce trace output from any location within your module, you need to create a global variable to store the TraceSource object.

Add a Tracesource object declaration at the beginning of the Blocklinks class:

```
public class BlockLinks : IHttpModule
{
    TraceSource ts;
```

Initializing the TraceSource Object

The best place to create the `TraceSource` object is in the `Init()` method of the custom module code. This function is called when the module object is created for each request, and any system resources allocated here will be cleaned up upon request completion.

Initialize the `Tracesource` object with the following code:

```
public void Init(HttpApplication app)
{
    // TODO:
    // Add initialization code
    // Including notifications
    app.BeginRequest += new EventHandler(app_BeginRequest);
    ts = new TraceSource("BlockLinks");
}
```

Note that the text string `BlockLinks` is defined in order to clearly identify output generated by this module.

Adding Trace Events

Now you are free to add trace events at any stage of your module. It is a recommended best practice to always add `Start` and `Stop` events to each of your module notification methods, so that trace output will always confirm module entry to and exit from your custom module.

Precisely where and in how much detail tracing events are added is entirely up to you. For example, the following code includes the recommended `Start` and `Stop` events, plus one `Information` event and one `Warning` event:

Add four trace events with the following additional code:

```
public void app_BeginRequest(object o, EventArgs ea)
{
    ts.TraceEvent(TraceEventType.Start, 0,
            "[BlockLinks] START BeginRequest");
    HttpContext ctx = HttpContext.Current;
    NameValueCollection coll;
    String ServerName = "";
    String Referer = "";
    int loop1;
    // retrieve the URL requested
    String RequestUrl = ctx.Request.RawUrl;
    if (RequestUrl.EndsWith(".jpg", StringComparison.OrdinalIgnoreCase) ||
        RequestUrl.EndsWith(".gif", StringComparison.OrdinalIgnoreCase) ||
        RequestUrl.EndsWith(".png", StringComparison.OrdinalIgnoreCase))
    {
        // Is an image file
        ts.TraceEvent(TraceEventType.Information, 0,
                "[BlockLinks] Detected request for image");
        // Load ServerVariable collection into NameValueCollection object.
        coll = ctx.Request.ServerVariables;
        // Get names of all keys into a string array.
        ServerName = coll["SERVER_NAME"];
        Referer   = coll["HTTP_REFERER"];
```

```
        if (!Referer.Contains(ServerName))
        {
            // NOT initiated by a link from a local web page!
            ts.TraceEvent(TraceEventType.Warning, 0,
                    "[BlockLinks] Cross-Linked request detected from" + Referer);
            ctx.RewritePath(
                        "/images/",  // replacement file
                        "denied.bmp",   // replacement path
                        ""               // replacement query string
                        );
        }
    }
    ts.TraceEvent(TraceEventType.Stop, 0,
            "[BlockLinks] END BeginRequest");
}
```

Note the use of the `TraceEvent()` method of the `TraceSource` object to generate the trace information. In this sample, the `TraceEvent` method is supplied three arguments:

➤ Trace event type

➤ A numeric identifier

➤ A text string message

The event message is displayed by the connected Event Listener (demonstrated below) and can be any text string. The Identifier is an integer between 0 and 65,535 (inclusive) and used for display purpose only. The Trace Event Type can be one of the following:

TRACE EVENT	DESCRIPTION
TraceEventType.Critical	Fatal error or application crash
TraceEventType.Error	Recoverable error
TraceEventType.Information	Informational message
TraceEventType.Resume	Resumption of a logical operation
TraceEventType.Start	Starting of a logical operation
TraceEventType.Stop	Stopping of a logical operation
TraceEventType.Suspend	Suspension of a logical operation
TraceEventType.Transfer	Changing of correlation identity
TraceEventType.Verbose	Debugging trace
TraceEventType.Warning	Noncritical problem

Compiling and Deploying the Module

In order to produce tracing events, you must compile the module with the /d:TRACE option. This option is not available in the runtime compiler; thus, you will need to compile and install the module as a binary DLL. One way to achieve this task is to use an Administrator command shell.

An alternative method to build and install your C# code using Visual Studio 2012 is demonstrated later in this chapter with the example in the section, "Extending the IIS Administration Tool."

1. Create a bin directory in the website root:

```
C:
cd \inetpub\wwwroot
mkdir bin
cd bin
```

2. Move the source code to the bin folder:

```
move ..\App_Code\BlockLinks.cs
```

3. Compile the module into a binary DLL:

```
%SystemRoot%\Microsoft.NET\Framework64\v4.0.30319\csc.exe
        /target:library
        /out:BlockLinks.dll
        /debug
        /d:TRACE
        /R:System.Web.dll
        /R:%windir%\system32\inetsrv\Microsoft.Web.Administration.dll
        BlockLinks.cs
```

4. Press WIN+R, enter **inetmgr**, and then click OK to open IIS Manager.

5. Expand the node tree, and click on the Sites container (for example, Default Web Site).

6. Double-click the Modules icon in the Features View.

7. If the BlockLinks module appears in the list, remove it.

8. Click on Add Managed Module in the Actions pane.

9. Enter **BlockLinks** in the Name field, and select .CustomModules.BlockLinks from the Type list.

10. Click OK to all dialogs.

Adding a Trace Listener to IIS

To make the trace events provided by your module available to IIS, you need to connect an IIS listener to the TraceSource that you defined in the module Init() method.

Open the web.config file in your website root (for example, C:\inetpub\wwwroot\web.config), and add the following configuration elements:

```
<configuration>
  <system.diagnostics>
    <sharedListeners>
```

```
          <add name="IisTraceListener"
              type="System.Web.IisTraceListener, System.Web, Version=2.0.0.0,
                  Culture=neutral , PublicKeyToken=b03f5f7f11d50a3a" />
      </sharedListeners>
      <switches>
        <add name="DefaultSwitch" value="All" />
      </switches>
      <sources>
        <source name="BlockLinks" switchName="DefaultSwitch">
          <listeners>
            <add name="IisTraceListener"
                type="System.Web.IisTraceListener,
                    System.Web, Version=2.0.0.0, Culture=neutral,
                    PublicKeyToken=b03f5f7f11d50a3a" />
          </listeners>
        </source>
      </sources>
    </system.diagnostics>
      <system.webServer>
```

Note the use of `name="BlockLinks"`, which corresponds to the use of
`ts = new TraceSource("BlockLinks")` in the module's `Init()` method.

Enabling Tracing and Routing Trace Events to IIS

Now that your module is ready to produce trace output to any connected listener, you will need to
set up IIS 8.0 to capture that information.

Chapter 23 includes some additional detail on administration of IIS using Failed Request Tracing
features. The following steps demonstrate one way to achieve this task:

1. Open IIS Manager (press WIN+R, enter **inetmgr**, and click OK), and then navigate to the
Sites node (for example, Default Web Site).

2. Double-click the Failed request Tracing Rules in the Features View.

> **NOTE** *If the Tracing Rules icon is not displayed, then you will need to install
> this feature. Refer to Chapter 4 for additional information on installing and
> managing optional features.*

3. Click Add in the Actions pane.

4. Click Next.

5. Enter **100-999** in the Status Codes field to enable tracing for all requests.

6. Select All Sources, and click Finish.

7. Click Edit Site Tracing in the Actions pane, check the box labeled Enable, and then click OK.

Viewing Trace Results

To see the event tracing in action, perform the following steps:

1. Open a web browser on the IIS Server console, and view `http://localhost`.

2. In IIS Manager, click the website node, double-click the Failed Request Tracing Rules in the Features View, and then click View Trace Logs in the Actions pane.

3. Open the `logs` folder to view the list of request trace files. You should see two files for each page request: one for the `iisstart.htm` request and one for the image request.

4. Open the last trace file in the list to see the trace event output.

EXTENDING IIS CONFIGURATION

If you have followed through with the examples, you will recall that some of the static variables hard-coded into the module source may vary from application to application.

For example, the native code module example used the variable `pszProtectedPath` to determine which path to protect from cross-link requests. Another website may store images in a different path, and to use the same module on that other website, you would need to edit the source code and then recompile a special DLL just for that application.

Obviously, it would be a far better solution to permit configuration of the custom module without requiring access to the source.

The following section demonstrates how you can use IIS 8.0's extensible configuration to manage and control custom modules, to provide seamless integration of your custom module configuration parameters.

Adding Configuration Support to Custom Modules

This section uses the example managed code module discussed above to demonstrate extending the configuration system.

If you have followed the tutorial above, you will already be familiar with the module design and functionality. You may recall that the BlockLinks module will supply an alternative image if the request for an image file contains a blank `HTTP_REFERER` value. This means that if the request is generated by a non-link source, such as a bookmark or search index robot, the requested image will not be delivered.

It might be useful to allow the Server Administrator to determine whether to allow or deny this type of request, and thus the following walkthrough demonstrates how to extend the IIS configuration to allow the server administrator to control the behavior when a blank `HTTP_REFERER` is encountered, without resorting to changes to the module source code.

This example is accomplished by the following general stages:

1. Extend the configuration schema.

2. Register the configuration extension.

3. Create the configuration entry.

4. Access the configuration information.

5. Include the namespace reference.

6. Define a global configuration variable.

7. Extract the configuration data.

8. Add the processing logic.

9. Install and test the module.

Extending the Schema

First, you need to extend the IIS 8.0 configuration schema. This is achieved by creating a file named `CUSTOM_Schema.xml` in the IIS configuration schema folder at `%systemroot%/system32/inetsrv/config/schema`.

1. Press WIN+R, enter **notepad.exe %systemroot%\system32\inetsrv\config\schema\ CUSTOM_Schema.xml** in the dialog, and then click OK.

2. Add the following code:

```
<configSchema>
  <sectionSchema name="BlockLinksSection">
    <attribute name="permitBookmarks" type="bool" defaultValue="false" />
  </sectionSchema>
</configSchema>
```

3. Save the file.

Now the IIS configuration schema has been extended to recognize the new item, to expect one attribute named `permitBookmarks`, of Boolean type (`true|false`) and with the default value of `false` if not explicitly set otherwise.

Registering the Extension with IIS Config

Now you need to add this configuration extension into the IIS configuration. This is done using the master configuration file `applicationHost.config` in the configuration path at `%systemroot%/system32/inetsvr/config`.

1. Press WIN+R, enter **notepad.exe %systemroot%\system32\inetsrv\config\applicationHost .config** in the dialog, and then click OK.

2. Locate the `<configuration>` section.

3. Add the following code:

```
<configSections>
    <section name="BlockLinksSection" />
    <sectionGroup name="system.applicationHost">
```

This step adds the new custom entry to the live IIS configuration. Now you can add configuration information for your module.

Creating the Configuration Entry

Because the custom schema defined above includes a default value (`false`) for the `permitBookmarks` configuration attribute, this step is optional if you want to deny requests that have a blank `HTTP_REFERER` value. In this case, however, the attribute will be explicitly set to `true`, indicating that requests with blank `HTTP_REFERER` values are permitted access.

Again using `applicationHost.config`, add the following line as the last item before the end of the `<configuration>` section:

```
    <BlockLinksSection permitBookmarks="true" />
</configuration>
```

If you want to deny bookmark links and web robots, of course, you should set the attribute value to `false` or omit this entry to use the default attribute value (also `false`).

Accessing Configuration Information

Now it is possible to read the configuration information defined above from inside the sample custom module. This is achieved using the `Microsoft.Web.Administration`, provided by the DLL in the IIS system folder at `%systemroot\system32\inetsvr`.

In the next steps, you will add code to the BlockLinks custom module created earlier in this chapter to access the custom configuration entities created in the previous steps.

Including the Namespace Reference

Open the `BlockLinks.cs` source code created in the last (Event Tracing) sample, and add the namespace declaration to the top of the file:

```
using System;
using System.Web;
using System.Collections.Specialized;
using System.Diagnostics;
using Microsoft.Web.Administration;
```

Defining a Global Configuration Variable

Next, create a global variable in the module class to store the value of the configuration item.

```
public class BlockLinks : IHttpModule
{
    TraceSource ts;
    String permitBookmarks = "false";
```

Note the default value again set to `false`. This default value will be used in case of any problems reading the detail from the configuration system. You can change this default to `true` if you prefer, without affecting the basic functionality of this example code.

Extracting the Configuration Attribute

You have a few choices for where to add code to extract the configuration data, but you will want to be careful that the value of the global variable is consistent throughout your module execution. Here, the Init() method is used so that the configuration information is retrieved every time the module is initialized as each request is received into the IIS pipeline.

```
public void Init(HttpApplication app)
{
    // TODO:
    // Add initialization code
    // Including notifications
    app.BeginRequest += new EventHandler(app_BeginRequest);

    ts = new TraceSource("BlockLinks");
    // create the server management object
    ServerManager sm = new ServerManager();
    // Open the applicationHost.config data
    Configuration conf = sm.GetApplicationHostConfiguration();
    // Open the configuration section
    ConfigurationSection sect = conf.GetSection("BlockLinksSection");
    // Read the attribute value
    permitBookmarks = sect.GetAttributeValue("permitBookmarks").ToString();
}
```

Here, you will see that the configuration info is retrieved in three steps:

1. Open the IIS configuration using GetApplicationHostConfiguration().

2. Open the custom configuration section with GetSection("BlockLinksSection").

3. Read the attribute value with GetAttributeValue("permitBookmarks").

Adding Processing Logic

Now that the module has initialized with the relevant configuration attribute received into the global variable, all that is required is to add the processing logic.

In the original code sample, if the HTTP_REFERER value was blank, the request was treated the same as any cross-linked request. With the new configuration attribute, it is now possible to test for a blank HTTP_REFERER and act accordingly.

Therefore, the next step is to modify the original code to include a test for a blank HTTP_REFERER and perform the relevant action depending on the value of the permitBookmarks attribute global variable.

```
if (!Referer.Contains(ServerName))
{
    // NOT initiated by a link from a local web page!
    if (Referer == "")
    {
        if (permitBookmarks == "false")
        {
            ts.TraceEvent(TraceEventType.Warning, 0,
                    "[BlockLinks] Bookmark request detected");
            ctx.RewritePath(
```

```
                                        "/images/",  // replacement file
                                        "denied.bmp",     // replacement path
                                        ""                // replacement query string
                                        );
                }
        }
        else
        {
                ts.TraceEvent(TraceEventType.Warning, 0,
                        "[BlockLinks] Cross-Linked request detected");
                ctx.RewritePath(
                                "/images/",  // replacement file
                                "denied.bmp",     // replacement path
                                ""                // replacement query string
                                );
        }
}
```

Installing and Testing the Module

When this new code is compiled in the same way as the previous sample, you will be able to observe the new functionality. Note that if the BlockLinks module is already installed, you may need to first remove the module from the list of installed modules, and then read as per the method described in the earlier section, "Installing the Module."

Open a fresh web browser (close any open browser windows first) and enter the URL to the IIS 8.0 image. If you have followed all the previous examples, the URL will be `http://127.0.0.1` `/images/iis-8.png`.

Because this request will carry no `HTTP_REFERER` information, it will be detected as a cross-link.

With the configuration item in `applicationHost.config` set to `true`, you will see the image displayed:

```
<BlockLinksSection permitBookmarks="true" />
```

Setting the configuration option to `false` will cause the denied image to be displayed instead:

```
<BlockLinksSection permitBookmarks="false" />
```

You will recall that a blank `HTTP_REFERER` variable in a request indicates that the request has been initiated by access to a client bookmark, manual entry to the browser location field, or by a non-browser client such as a search engine or web crawler/robot. To permit delivery of the resource to all these types of requests, set the `permitBookmarks` attribute to `true`. To deny all requests of this nature, set the attribute to `false`.

As a further exercise, you might like to try extending the IIS configuration to also support configuration of the `pszProtectedPath` global variable via the IIS Configuration System.

EXTENDING THE IIS ADMINISTRATION TOOL

The ability to extend the IIS configuration to support custom modules provides the IIS developer with a unique capacity to develop custom web service plug-ins with a seamless interface to the core system.

In the previous section, the custom configuration support provided for the sample "BlockLinks" module requires that the end-user edit the IIS configuration files directly in order to control the module behavior.

IIS 8.0 also provides extensibility to the Administration Tool GUI to support simple and intuitive configuration support for your custom modules.

This section provides an example of how to implement GUI control of the permitBookmarks configuration item created in the previous section.

Creating an IIS Administration Tool Extension

As previously mentioned, this walkthrough is based on Microsoft Visual Studio 2012. It is quite possible to use other IDE titles and versions by simply translating the various steps to the equivalent for your selected IDE.

During this example, you will note that the relevant custom GUI component is also called a *module* despite the fact that these objects are very different from the HttpModule encountered in previous sections.

This example is accomplished by the following general stages:

1. Create a new project.

2. Add namespace references.

3. Create a configuration dialog.

4. Add the control to the IIS Administration Tool.

5. Build and install.

Creating a New Project

Start by creating a new project:

1. Click File ➪ New ➪ Project.

2. Under the Visual C# templates, choose the Class Library template, as shown in Figure 12-3.

3. Enter the name **BlockLinksConf** as the project name, and then click OK.

Adding Namespace References

Since a couple of namespaces required for this example are not included in the default template, add these as follows:

1. Right-click the References node in the VS2012 project view, and then click Add Reference....

2. Select System.Windows.Forms, and then click OK.

3. Right-click References again, and choose Add Reference....

4. Select the Browse tab, enter **%systemroot%\system32\inetsrv** in the name field, and then press Enter.

5. While holding down the Ctrl key, click Microsoft.Web.Administration.dll and then on Microsoft.Web.Management.dll, and then click OK twice.

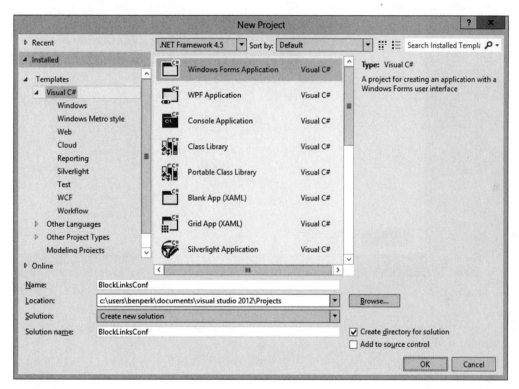

FIGURE 12-3

Creating the Configuration Control

The next step is to create the configuration control that will be used to enter the configuration settings. Because there is only a single attribute used in this example (permitBookmarks value), the control will be very simple, containing just a single checkbox to enable or disable delivery of "bookmark" requests, and a Save button to write the value to the active configuration.

1. In the VS2012 Project View, right-click the BlockLinksConf item, and choose Add ➪ User Control.

2. Name it **BlockLinksConfForm.cs,** and click Add.

3. Add two elements to the form: a checkbox labeled **permitBookmarks** and a button labeled **Save,** as shown in Figure 12-4.

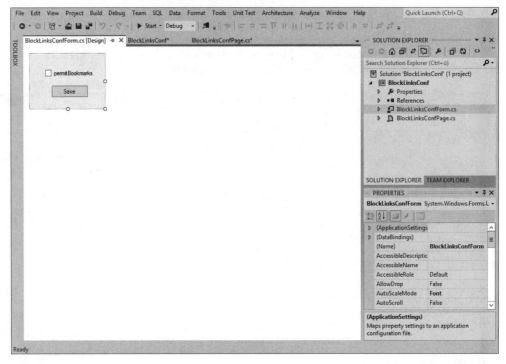

FIGURE 12-4

4. Open the configuration dialog's code view by right-clicking the `BlockCrossLinksConf.cs` object and choosing View Code.

5. Add the namespace reference:

```
using System;
using System.Collections.Generic;
using System.ComponentModel;
using System.Drawing;
using System.Data;
using System.Linq;
using System.Text;
using System.Windows.Forms;
using Microsoft.Web.Administration;
```

6. Declare the following variables:

```
namespace BlockLinksConf
{
    public partial class BlockLinksConfForm : UserControl
    {
        private ServerManager mgr;
        private Boolean permitBookmarks;
```

7. Modify the constructor method to take one argument, and set the private member accordingly:

```
public BlockLinksConfForm(ServerManager mgr)
{
```

```
        this.mgr = mgr;
        InitializeComponent();
}
```

Important: Note the addition of `ServerManager` `mgr` in the argument list of the constructor definition.

8. Create a method to read the configuration data:

```
public BlockLinksConfForm(ServerManager mgr)
{
    this.mgr = mgr;
    InitializeComponent();
}
private void ReadSettings()
{
    Configuration config =
        mgr.GetApplicationHostConfiguration();
    ConfigurationSection sect =
        config.GetSection("BlockLinksSection");
    permitBookmarks =
        (Boolean) sect.
            GetAttributeValue("permitBookmarks");
}
```

You may recognize the functions `GetWebConfiguration()` and `GetSection()`, which are essentially identical to the mechanism used to retrieve configuration item attribute values in the example for the previous section, "Extending IIS Configuration."

9. Create a public initialization function to allow the current value of the `permitBookmarks` setting to be loaded into the dialog when opened:

```
public BlockLinksConfForm(ServerManager mgr)
{
    this.mgr = mgr;
    InitializeComponent();
}
private void ReadSettings()
{
    Configuration config =
        mgr.GetApplicationHostConfiguration();
    ConfigurationSection sect =
        config.GetSection("BlockLinksSection");
    permitBookmarks =
        (Boolean) sect.
            GetAttributeValue("permitBookmarks");
}
public void Initialize()
{
    ReadSettings();
    checkBox1.Checked = permitBookmarks;
}
```

10. Finally, for this stage, implement the action when clicking the Save button:

```
private void button1_Click(object sender, EventArgs e)
{
    ServerManager mgr = new ServerManager();
```

```
                  Configuration conf =
        mgr.GetApplicationHostConfiguration();
                  ConfigurationSection sect =
        conf.GetSection("BlockLinksSection");
                  sect.SetAttributeValue("permitBookmarks",
        checkBox1.Checked);
                  mgr.CommitChanges();
            }
```

Again, a `ServerManager` object is used to obtain a reference to the `applicationHost.config` configuration entry, but this time `SetAttributeValue()` is used to write the attribute value to active configuration, and then `CommitChanges()` to save those changes.

Creating an IIS Administration Tool Module Container

Now everything is in place to add the control created in the previous steps into the IIS Administration GUI. This is achieved by creating a Module page, which is the middle pane of the IIS Manager console when a module icon is clicked. The Module page is a Windows Forms control onto which the BlockLinksConfForm created above will be added.

The Module page acts as a container (or wrapper) for the custom configuration control.

1. Right-click the BlockLinksConf node in the Visual Studio 2012 project view, and click Add ⇨ Class.

2. Name the class **BlockLinksConfPage.cs**, and then click Add.

3. Add the following namespace reference:

```
using System;
using System.Collections.Generic;
using System.Linq;
using System.Text;
using System.Threading.Tasks;
using Microsoft.Web.Management.Client;
using Microsoft.Web.Management.Client.Win32;
using Microsoft.Web.Management.Server;
using Microsoft.Web.Administration;
```

4. Modify the BlockLinksConfPage class definition as follows, and implement the constructor:

```
public class BlockLinksConfPage : ModulePage
{
    private ServerManager mgr;
    private BlockLinksConfForm cf;

    public BlockLinksConfPage()
    {
        mgr = new ServerManager();
        cf = new BlockLinksConfForm(mgr);
        Controls.Add(cf);
    }
}
```

(Note the addition of `ModulePage` as the class derived from.)

IIS Manager calls the OnActivated() method of the Modulepage class when opened. You need to override the default OnActivated() method to include a call to the initialization function implemented above. This will make sure that the configuration control dialog will load with the active configration value displayed.

5. Override the default OnActivated() method by adding the following code:

```
public BlockLinksConfPage()
{
    mgr = new ServerManager();
    cf = new BlockLinksConfForm (mgr);
    Controls.Add(cf);
}
protected override void OnActivated(bool initialActivation)
{
    base.OnActivated(initialActivation);
    if (initialActivation) cf.Initialize();
}
}
```

6. Add the Module wrapper method:

```
public class BlockLinksConfModule : Module
{
    protected override void Initialize
            (
            IServiceProvider serviceProvider,
            Microsoft.Web.Management.Server.ModuleInfo moduleInfo
            )
    {
    base.Initialize(serviceProvider, moduleInfo);
    IControlPanel controlPanel =
        (IControlPanel)GetService(typeof(IControlPanel));
    controlPanel.RegisterPage
            (
            new ModulePageInfo
                (
                this,
                typeof(BlockLinksConfPage),
                "BlockLinks",
                "Configuration for the BlockLinks Custom Module."
                )
            );
    }

    protected override bool IsPageEnabled(ModulePageInfo pageInfo)
    {
        Connection conn = (Connection)GetService(typeof(Connection));
        ConfigurationPathType pt = conn.ConfigurationPath.PathType;
        return pt == ConfigurationPathType.Server;
    }
    }
}
```

Note that the overridden IsPageEnabled() method determines when the configuration control is available. In this case, since the permitBookmarks variable is defined globally across all websites, the ConfigurationPathType.Server is defined. Alternative values to make the configuration control available to discrete server items include:

➤ ConfigurationPathType.Site — Shows the configuration icon on individual websites.

➤ ConfigurationPathType.File — For individual files.

➤ ConfigurationPathType.Folder — Physical or virtual paths.

➤ ConfigurationPathType.Application — For web application configuration.

7. Finally, the top level of this hierarchy is the ModuleProvider. Add the following method:

```
public class BlockLinksConfModuleProvider: ModuleProvider
{
    public override Type ServiceType
    {
        get { return null; }
    }
        public override bool SupportsScope(ManagementScope scope)
    {
        return true;
    }
        public override ModuleDefinition GetModuleDefinition
            (IManagementContext context)
    {
        return new ModuleDefinition
            (Name, typeof(BlockLinksConfModule).AssemblyQualifiedName);
    }
}
```

Build and Install

The final stage of this example is to build and install the IIS Administration Tool add-in.

Loading the configuration module into the IIS Administration Tool requires strong naming by code signing, thus the first step is to add a signing key to the DLL.

1. Double-click the Properties node in the VS2012 Project view.

2. Choose the Signing tab, check the box labeled "Sign the Assembly," and then choose New, as shown in Figure 12-5.

3. Enter **BlockLinksConf.key** as the Key File Name, uncheck the password box, and click OK.

4. Now compile the project by right-clicking the BlockLinksConf item in the VS2012 Project view and choosing Build. Unless you have made any changes to the compiler settings, the BlockLinksConf.dll will be saved in the project folder bin/Debug path.

5. Open a Visual Studio command prompt and change to the dll folder — for example:

```
cd \Users\Administrator
cd Documents\Visual Studio 12\Projects
cd BlockLinksConf\BlockLinksConf\Bin\Debug
```

6. Install the dll to IIS using the gacutil.exe utility:

```
gacutil -i BlockLinksConf.dll
```

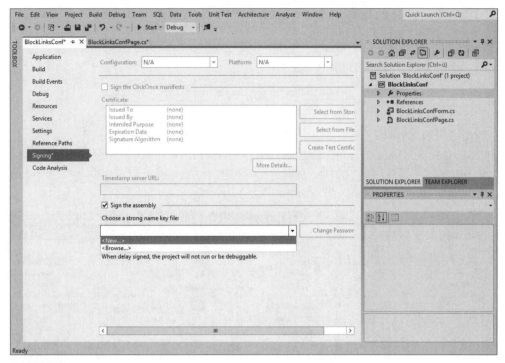

FIGURE 12-5

7. Use the `gacutil.exe` utility again to determine the public key token created by the strong name signing. For example:

```
>gacutil -l BlockLinksConf
Microsoft (R) .NET Global Assembly Cache Utility. Version 4.0.30319.17379
Copyright (c) Microsoft Corporation. All rights reserved.
The Global Assembly Cache contains the following assemblies:
  BlockLinksConf, Version=1.0.0.0, Culture=neutral,
  PublicKeyToken=0e92b0551681fe73, processorArchitecture=MSIL
```

The value of the `PublicKeyToken` displayed in this command is needed to install the module to the IIS Administration Tool. Note that this value will be different for every installation!

8. Open the IIS Administration configuration file. Press WIN+R, enter **notepad .exe %systemroot%\System32\inetsrv\config\administration.config**, and then click OK.

9. Locate the `<moduleProviders>` configuration section, and add the following, all on one line, directly below the `<moduleProviders>` start tag:

```
<moduleProviders>
    <add name="BlockLinksConf"
type="BlockLinksConf.BlockLinksConfModuleProvider,
    BlockLinksConf, Version=1.0.0.0, Culture=neutral,
    PublicKeyToken=0e92b0551681fe73" />
```

Note that the `PublicKeyToken` value reflects the value determined from Step 7.

10. In the same file, locate the `<location>` section, add the following item, and then save the file and close:

```
<!- For all Sites ->
<location path=".">
    <modules>
        <add name="BlockLinksConf" />
```

Viewing the Result

Open the IIS Administration tool and click the Server node (for example, SERVER1/Administrator) to display the Features View, and observe the new configuration item displayed, as shown in Figure 12-6.

FIGURE 12-6

Click on the BlockLinks config icon to open the configuration dialog, as shown in Figure 12-7. Now you can enable and disable the `permitBookmarks` configuration item created in the previous example ("Extending the IIS Configuration") using this simple and intuitive GUI control.

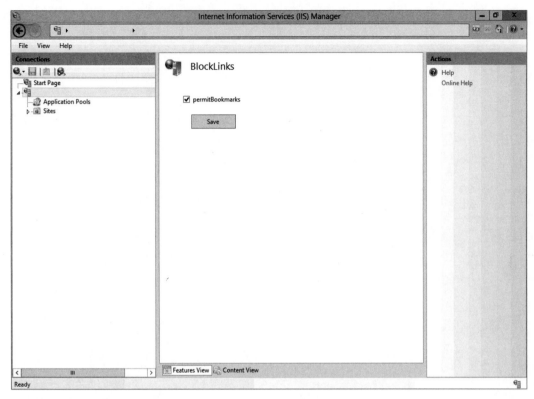

FIGURE 12-7

You can confirm operation of the GUI module by observing the behavior of the website, as per the "Installing and Testing the Module" section; however, it may be more instructive to observe the effect of modifying the permitBookmarks checkbox control on the relevant configuration item in the applicationHost.config file.

Checking the custom configuration control checkbox results in applicationHost.config to include the following line:

```
<BlockLinksSection permitBookmarks="true" />
```

Clear the checkbox to set permitBookmarks to false:

```
<BlockLinksSection permitBookmarks="false" />
```

13

Securing the Server

WHAT'S IN THIS CHAPTER?

➤ Overview of security

➤ Types of attacks

➤ Securing your IIS 8.0 server

➤ Application layer security

➤ Configuring logging

"We have just installed Application X onto IIS. What steps do we need to take to make IIS secure?" This is one of the most common questions faced in the security arena, and this hasn't changed from when IIS ran on NT to the present day. The question, however, presupposes that there is some set of discrete steps that can be undertaken to secure IIS and that there is some finite endpoint that can be described as "secure."

Certainly there are a lot of products and organizations that claim to make your server secure or that secure your application or secure your organization. As a security implementer (or even just someone with a dilettante interest), to what extent should you place credence in such claims?

This introductory chapter on security covers the following topics:

➤ The basic principles of network and computer security

➤ Configuring IIS 8.0 to enhance the security of your web server

➤ Additional items (such as application layer security) that you will need to consider when evaluating overall environmental security

Beyond this chapter, the next two chapters delve into more specific security areas. Chapter 14, "Authentication and Authorization," deals with authentication and authorization, and Chapter 15, "SSL and TLS," with SSL and TLS. These chapters should be read together to get a good understanding of the security technologies and infrastructure that are most important when managing an IIS 8.0 installation.

WHAT IS SECURITY?

Security can be defined as a state of freedom from attack or danger. Current security orthodoxy teaches us that the only totally secure computer is one that is switched off, encased in concrete, and dumped at the bottom of the ocean. And this should tally with any system administrator's experience. There are very few, if any, nontrivial software products that have shipped to date that haven't contained some kind of security vulnerability. Even if the software itself is completely bug-free, it may be compromised because of the way in which it interacts with other systems, or because of poor operational practices (for example, the use of easily guessable passwords).

Even the type of totally secure system mentioned above (encased in concrete at the bottom of the ocean) might not be classified as a secure system. A *secure system* will deny access to those who are unauthorized, yet allow access to those who are authorized. In other words, it's usable by those permitted to use it and no one else. The machine at the bottom of the ocean fails this usability test. In fact, this need to distinguish between legitimate users and those who should be denied access is one of the things that makes security difficult. It's easy to write a system that gives access to everyone, or conversely denies access to everyone, but much more difficult to write a system that allows the good guys in but keeps the bad guys out.

What security researchers and books try to focus on is educating readers on security principles and practices that they can apply to their environments that allow them to have "secure enough" computers. This section presents a condensed summary of security principles. With these principles in mind, you can then look over the rest of this chapter, as well as the subsequent two security-related chapters, to determine which policies are best suited to your specific environment.

Managing Risk

When you see a product that claims to be secure or a security guide to secure your system, it's worth asking the following two questions: "secure from *whom*?" and "secure against *what*?" Does your new communications system secure you against a casual eavesdropper? A dedicated attacker? Or a national intelligence agency? Is your new application secure against a shoulder surfer (someone who looks over your shoulder to steal a password)? Someone who physically steals your server? Collusion between malicious systems administrators? In some cases, the answer is no — not because the products are necessarily insecure, but because the developers of the product make certain assumptions (conscious or otherwise) about how they will be used. Most server applications assume that the application will be hosted on a machine that is physically secured against attackers. Even well-known security technologies like SSL/TLS assume that the implementer will take the necessary steps to secure the endpoints.

In the computing world, there are almost a limitless number of possible attacks against your systems, ranging from common viruses and worms, through to malicious internal staff. Facing limitless possible attacks without any single way of combating all of them (unless you count the "computer at the bottom of the ocean" idea) requires some kind of framework that security professionals can use to determine whether the security measures being put in place are appropriate for the situation.

To help deal with this challenge, security specialists borrow concepts from risk-management disciplines (among other areas).

The same threat may have differing consequences across differing organizations. For example, a common self-propagating worm may be somewhat more than an annoyance in the average organization if it causes some machines to become unusable; however, it may be fatal in a hospital if it disables a critical machine. Likewise, differing threats can have different consequences within the same organization, and even the same threat can have differing consequences for different parts of the same organization. For example, a compromised public web server at a bank might allow an attacker access to the web application's code, and possibly intercept transactions between the bank and customers — definitely a serious problem, but probably not as serious as if the bank's central customer, accounts, or credit databases were compromised.

To determine which threats to address, at the most rudimentary level, we can look at the concept of risk-weighted costs. We take the expected cost that would result from a threat eventuating and multiply it by the likelihood of that threat eventuating:

(Cost if Risk Eventuates) * (Likelihood of Risk) = Risk Weighted Cost of Compromise

Knowing the risk-weighted cost of compromise helps guide us in prioritizing the threats we face, from the most serious to the trivial. We can then deploy our resources, time, and effort to mitigating the more serious threats.

> **NOTE** *By no means should you rely on this one simplistic calculation when determining your security design and policies! Especially in more complex environments, you are encouraged to enlist the aid of security and risk specialists in developing and maintaining their security policies.*

Security Components

Developing a secure system relies on having, at a minimum, the following components:

➤ **Authentication** — This is the process of remote users identifying themselves and then proving their identity (typically through a shared secret such as a password).

➤ **Authorization** — After a user has been authenticated, the user's requested action is checked against an access control list (ACL) maintained on the server to determine if the user is permitted to perform the action (e.g., access/read the web page).

➤ **Auditing** — The user's actions must be recorded and not be subject to dispute (what is known as "non-repudiation"), so as to definitively determine which users performed which actions.

When determining your security strategy, it is important to verify that your solution encompasses these three components. Although an individual product may perform all three things perfectly, it is important to factor in two other areas where vulnerabilities can creep in — through human error or through one product interacting with another.

TYPES OF ATTACKS

A complete taxonomy of possible attacks against your IIS server is beyond the scope of this book. Attacks come in all shapes and sizes, and thus it is difficult, if not impossible, to be comprehensive.

Denial-of-Service Attacks

A *denial-of-service* (DoS) attack typically involves an attacker making spurious requests to a server in order to consume resources and deny legitimate users access to the service (hence, "denial of service").

The attack could be as simple as overwhelming the server with a sufficiently large number of requests, or it could involve making requests that consume large amounts of resources (for example, invoking long-running database queries). In the former case, a single attacking machine may not have the necessary CPU or bandwidth to overwhelm a well-provisioned server; thus, the attacker may enlist the use of a large number of individual machines to attack the server simultaneously — an attack known as a *distributed denial-of-service* (DDoS) attack.

Privilege Escalation Attacks

A *privilege escalation attack* involves an attacker gaining access to, and performing actions on, resources to which they would not otherwise be permitted. Privilege escalation can involve both gaining additional permissions on a single system (for example, a regular user gaining Administrative privileges) as well as gaining access to other systems in the network to which the user wouldn't otherwise have access at all (for example, getting access to a domain controller or other back-end server).

Typically, a privilege escalation attack is merely a precursor to some other form of attack (for example, data theft, data destruction, and so on). By escalating their privileges, attackers are now able to perform a malicious action they wouldn't otherwise have been able to. They may alter files (for example, defacing your website), they may steal sensitive information, or they may even create additional "backdoor" accounts that can be used to return to the system even after you have closed off the initial attack vector.

There are several ways that a malicious attacker can attempt to gain privileges that they would not otherwise be entitled to. Some of the most common are the following:

➤ **Social engineering attacks** — An attacker attempts to convince another user of the system that they should be given access (for example, by pretending to be a Helpdesk technician or by sending an e-mail purporting to be from a legitimate source). The user then provides credentials or otherwise gives the attacker access because he or she has been fooled into thinking that the attacker is a legitimate user.

➤ **Vulnerability exploitation** — An attacker exploits a vulnerability in an application or operating system. High-profile worms and viruses that exploited vulnerabilities include Conflicker, Sasser, and Stuxnet. Typically, applications themselves also have vulnerabilities due to poor coding practices. Typical vulnerabilities in web-based applications include: SQL Injection attacks, cross-side scripting attacks, and session replay attacks.

The Open Web Application Security Project (OWASP) is an excellent platform-neutral resource for a system administrator looking to understand application-level vulnerabilities. In particular, the OWASP publishes a Top 10, available at `www.owasp.org/index.php/ Category:OWASP_Top_Ten_Project`.

➤ **Poorly secured systems** — Many systems are poorly secured, and this presents an attacker with an easy way in with minimal effort. For example, the use of blank or easily guessable passwords, or the re-use of passwords across multiple systems, can allow an attacker to gain access without any need to exploit any vulnerabilities or to interact with any legitimate staff. Unfortunately, access gained this way can be very difficult to detect because the attacker (once he or she has access) looks just like a legitimate user.

Preventing, detecting, and combating these types of attacks can be difficult. In an environment that doesn't follow good management practices, it becomes almost impossible to do anything about these attacks. It's not a matter of *if* such an attack will succeed, but *when*.

In this chapter (and the succeeding chapters on security), we discuss some of the technologies and resources you can use to secure your environment. However, good security relies on good operational procedures:

➤ **Documented baseline** — A documented baseline for your environment is necessary. This includes knowing which privileged accounts should exist and what they are for, which services exist on your network, and what they should be doing.

➤ **Security patches** — Ensuring that security patches, best-practice configuration, and appropriate password/access control policies are in place is a prerequisite for ensuring that the environment can be kept secure.

➤ **Detection tools** — Detection tools (for example, an intrusion detection system) and operations management tools (such as Microsoft System Center Operations Manager 2012) that enable detection of unusual activity that deviates from your accepted baseline are necessary. This could include detection of services not working, unusual account logons/password guessing, known malicious traffic on the network, and many other symptoms of an attack in progress. More recently, Security Incident and Event Management (SIEM) systems, which correlate log data from many disparate systems, have become commonplace.

In Chapters 21 and 22, we discuss these concepts in more detail.

Passive Attacks

Passive attacks are much harder to detect than active attacks. Here, attackers are not trying to change anything on your network (although they may have had to perform a previous attack to gain access in the first place). Instead, *passive attackers* are merely observing existing activity. This could be "sniffing" the network for sensitive information or logging keystrokes on a computer to capture usernames and passwords.

Technologies such as SSL/TLS or Internet Protocol Security (IPsec) can be used to secure traffic in transit and help prevent such passive attacks, and anti-malware or Host Intrusion Protection System (HIPS) applications may assist in preventing passive attacks from running on host systems. Additionally, organizations deploy HoneyPot systems (systems designed to present an inviting attack surface in the hope that they do get attacked) or network probe devices in order to analyze and detect the traffic passing across their networks.

Advanced Persistent Threats

Advanced persistent threats (APTs) have become a common buzzword. APTs do not have a particular technical implementation; instead, they are a category of threat that may include any number of technical or social vectors. They are called "advanced" because they typically incorporate a number of vectors and are executed by bodies (e.g., national governments or criminal organizations) with substantial resources and expertise.

A typical APT attack does not involve opportunistic or short-term compromise. Instead, attackers have specific strategic or commercial objectives and will deploy substantial resources over time to gradually work their way to the objective. Recent examples of successful APT-based attacks include Stuxnet (conjectured to be deployed by intelligence agencies to attack Iranian nuclear facilities) and attacks against RSA (the initial vector was an attack against Adobe Acrobat Reader via targeted e-mail) and Symantec. In both of these latter cases, substantial costs were incurred by the corporations in managing the resulting publicity and migrating customers away from any potentially compromised platform.

For systems administrators, APTs mean that even the least important servers may be a target — not because they are intrinsically valuable, but because they may be a staging point toward a more valuable target.

> **NOTE** *The remainder of this chapter (and the next two chapters) focuses on technologies in IIS 8.0 that can be used to secure your web servers, your applications, and the data they use. Specifically, this chapter outlines some basic IIS 8.0 functionality that can be configured to either disable functionality or restrict access, or alternatively may need to be reconfigured from defaults to permit functionality.*
>
> *In Chapter 14, "Authentication and Authorization," we look at the various client authentication technologies that IIS 8.0 supports and how these are configured. We also look at the various user accounts and identities that IIS 8.0 uses for processing requests and how to configure these to support your application.*
>
> *In Chapter 15, "SSL and TLS," we look at certificates and PKI management, server authentication, and traffic data encryption for websites, FTP sites, and SMTP servers.*

SECURING YOUR ENVIRONMENT

Before securing IIS 8.0, it is important that your overall network environment itself is secure. Securing a Windows environment, let alone a heterogeneous environment, is a book (or several) in itself. There are numerous technologies, white papers, best practices, and tools available that will assist in initially configuring the environment, ensuring that the configuration remains and monitoring the environment for any changes.

The TechNet Security portal (`http://technet.microsoft.com/security/`) is the first stop for administrators seeking guidance on securing a Windows network, including the latest prescriptive advice, security and patch bulletins, analysis tools that can warn of possible misconfiguration, and step-by-step implementation guides.

SECURING YOUR IIS 8.0 SERVER

After securing the environment, you can now look to secure your IIS 8.0 server itself. There are several configuration options in IIS 8.0 that can be used to restrict access or deny certain types of requests without any knowledge of who the end user is. These configuration options are the focus of this security chapter.

Chapter 14, "Authentication and Authorization," examines how to provide protected access to resources based on who the end user is. This covers authentication technologies (such as Basic, Digest, and Kerberos authentication) as well as authorization configuration (how to configure access to resources to permit only certain users access), and also information on the various identities that are used by IIS 8.0 internally to provide access to functionality.

> **NOTE** *A security best practice is to install only those components that are required for the functionality you need to provide end users. Beginning with Windows Server 2003, IIS 6.0 has shipped in a locked-down state with only a minimal set of functionalities available in a default configuration. By not installing unnecessary functionality, your server cannot be compromised by possible vulnerabilities in components that you aren't using (or didn't even know were installed). This lock-down mentality should extend to administrator configuration as well. Only install those components that are required to deliver the services that end users need. This reduces the surface area that attackers can attempt to exploit and also reduces the administration overhead of the server by reducing configuration options and reducing the number of patches required to be installed.*
>
> *Windows Server provides an option for a "Core" installation, which removes many consumer features, GUI components, and the Explorer shell from the server. (`cmd.exe` is used as the shell instead.) This option reduces the potential attack surface of a server.*

IP and Domain Restrictions

Configuring IP address and domain name restrictions allows you to selectively permit or deny access to the web server, websites, folders, or files. Rules can be configured for remote IP addresses or based on a reverse DNS lookup of the remote IP address, based on static or flexible criteria.

> **NOTE** *The IP and Domain Restrictions module (`iprestr.dll`) is not installed in a default IIS installation. You will need to install this module specifically if you want to use its functionality. Website administrators and web-application administrators can configure IP and domain restrictions for websites and applications that they are permitted to manage, provided that the configuration elements are not locked at a higher level. See Chapter 9, "Delegating Remote Administration," for more information.*

Default Policy and Domain Name Restrictions

When configuring IP and domain name restrictions, there is always a default policy. The default policy applies to clients where a specific rule is not defined. It either permits all access except for those clients specifically rejected or rejects all clients except for those specifically permitted. When IIS 8.0 is first installed, all clients are permitted unless specifically rejected.

The same dialog that is used to set the default policy is also used to enable or disable the ability to allow or reject clients based on a reverse DNS lookup, as well as set the response to be sent to clients.

To configure the default rule, perform the following steps:

1. Open the IIS Manager MMC console.

2. At the web server, website, application, folder, or file node at which you want to configure this setting, select IP and Domain Name Restrictions.

3. Click Edit Feature Settings. The Edit IP and Domain Restrictions Settings dialog box appears, as shown in Figure 13-1.

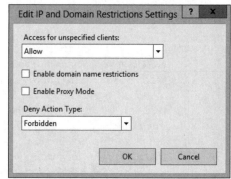

FIGURE 13-1

4. Select Allow to allow all clients by default, or select Deny to deny all clients by default.

5. Optionally, to configure rules based on the client's DNS name, check the Enable Domain Name Restrictions checkbox. A warning will be presented that performing DNS lookups is a potentially expensive operation. Click Yes to enable DNS lookup restrictions.

6. Choose the Default Deny Mode response that IIS should send back to clients: It can send back 401 (Unauthorized), 403 (Forbidden), 404 (Not Found), or terminate the request. Note that sending back a 401 response may result in an authentication dialog appearing at the remote end if a browser-based client is being used. This may result in spurious authentication attempts to IIS.

7. Choose whether IIS should parse the incoming request for an X-Forwarded-For HTTP header. This may indicate that the request has been proxied by a reverse proxy server, load balancer, or similar, and that this header should be examined for the ultimate remote client. Note that this header can be forged, so it may be best to rely on dedicated edge devices (e.g.,

firewalls) to determine whether this header has been sent by a reliable, known, proxy server or not.

8. Click OK to exit the dialog.

> **NOTE** *Performing reverse DNS lookups is a potentially expensive operation that can severely degrade the performance of your IIS server. DNS lookups may be adversely affected because of slow response times from remote DNS servers or because the remote client does not have an entry in the* inAddr.arpa *reverse lookup domain. On the other hand, in an intranet scenario in which your organization has full control over internal DNS servers and client DNS registration and there are fast links between your IIS servers and internal DNS servers, this can be a useful tool for restricting access to certain client machines within your environment.*

You can alter the default rule settings using AppCmd. For example, to change the default settings (that is, disallow all unspecified clients and also enable Domain Name restrictions), run the following command:

```
appcmd.exe Set config -section:system.webServer/security/
    ipSecurity /allowUnlisted:false /enableReverseDns:true
```

This command configures this setting for the entire server. Setting the config parameter permits configuration at an individual website or web-application level.

Configuring Rules

You can create rules for specific remote hosts, remote subnets, or remote DNS hosts or domains (if the reverse DNS lookup option is enabled). To create rules that allow or deny access:

1. Start IIS Manager. (Click WIN+R, enter **inetmgr** in the dialog, and click OK. Alternatively, click Tools on the top-right of Server Manager and select Internet Information Server (IIS) Manager.)

2. At the web server, website, application, folder, or file node at which you want to configure this setting, select IP and Domain Name Restrictions.

3. Click the Create Allow Entry or Create Deny Entry links in the Actions pane. Figure 13-2 shows the interface for creating an Allow Entry.

    a. To create a rule for a specific remote host, select Specific IP Address and enter the remote IP address. This is equivalent to selecting "A range of IP addresses" and entering a specific IP address and a subnet mask of **255.255.255.255**.

    b. To create a rule for a remote subnet, select "A range of IP addresses," and enter the subnet and subnet mask. For example, to permit or deny access to all IP addresses in the 127.0.0.0/8 subnet, enter **127.0.0.0** as the subnet and **255.0.0.0** as the subnet mask.

    c. If you have enabled Domain Name Restrictions in the previous step, then you will have the ability to set restrictions based on DNS names. This option will not be available if

Domain Name Restrictions has not been enabled. To create a rule for a remote domain name or domain, select "Domain name." Enter the remote reverse DNS name. If you want to permit or deny access to a whole domain, use the * wildcard (for example, ***.example.com** would permit or deny access to all hosts in the example.com domain).

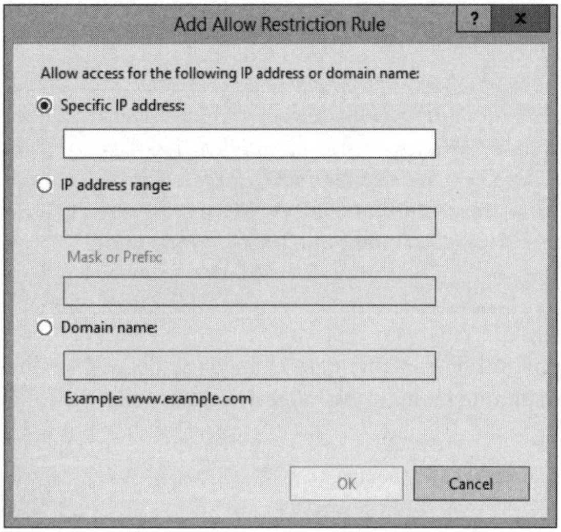

FIGURE 13-2

> **NOTE** *When using DNS names, you must use DNS names that have corresponding PTR records in the inAddr.arpa reverse lookup domain. You cannot use any arbitrary DNS name that resolves to the remote IP address. When a client connects to IIS, IIS is only aware of the client's remote IP address. IIS must do a reverse DNS lookup to determine what DNS name the client has. If you want to determine what reverse DNS name an IP address has, you can use the command* ping -a xxx.xxx.xxx.xxx *(where* xxx.xxx.xxx.xxx *is the remote IP address). The* -a *switch performs a reverse DNS lookup.*

You can also use AppCmd or PowerShell to create Allow and Deny rules. The following code samples explain how to configure global Allow and Deny rules for an individual IP address and for a particular subnet. The first rule permits access from 192.168.0.1, and the second rule denies access to all addresses in the 192.168.2.0/24 subnet.

```
appcmd.exe set config -section:system.webserver/security/ipSecurity
    /+"[ipAddress='192.168.0.1',allowed='true']"

appcmd.exe set config -section:system.webserver/security/ipSecurity
    /+"[ipAddress='192.168.2.0',subnetMask='255.255.255.0',allowed='false']"

PS C:\> add-webconfiguration /system.webServer/security/ipSecurity
```

```
        -location "IIS:\Sites\Default Web Site" -value
        @{ipAddress="192.168.0.1";allowed="true"} -pspath IIS:\

PS C:\> add-webconfiguration /system.webServer/security/ipSecurity
        -location "IIS:\Sites\Default Web Site"
        -value @{ipAddress="192.168.0.1";subnetMask="255.255.255.0";allowed="true"}
        -pspath IIS:\
```

Rule Priority

A *priority system* is used to evaluate potentially conflicting rules. Rules are evaluated in order of priority until a rule that matches the remote client is reached. Depending on whether that rule permits or denies access, the resource or an error message is sent back to the client.

It is important to note that Deny rules do not override Permit rules (unlike some systems, such as NTFS Access Control Entries) and that more specific entries do not override more general entries (unlike some systems, such as Active Directory subnet definitions). The only consideration is rule ordering. As soon as a rule that matches the remote client's IP (or reverse DNS name if applicable) is reached, that rule is evaluated and no further rule evaluation occurs.

To illustrate this, consider the following scenarios. In each case, the remote client is 127.0.0.1.

RULE PRIORITY	RULE	EXPLANATION
1	Allow 127.0.0.0 / 255.0.0.0.	Allow all hosts in the 127.0.0.0 subnet (127.0.0.1–127.255.255.254).
2	Deny 127.0.0.1/255.255.255.255.	Deny host 127.0.0.1.

Result: In this scenario, the remote client 127.0.0.1 is allowed access, despite the fact that Rule 2 is more specific. Rule 1 matches the remote client and permits access. No further rule processing is done.

RULE PRIORITY	RULE	EXPLANATION
1	Allow 127.0.0.1/255.255.255.255.	Allow host 127.0.0.1.
2	Deny 127.0.0.0/255.0.0.0.	Deny all hosts in the 127.0.0.0 subnet (127.0.0.1–127.255.255.254).

Result: In this scenario, the remote client 127.0.0.1 is permitted access, despite the fact that Rule 2 is an explicit Deny rule. Rule 1 again matches the remote client and permits access. No further rule processing is done.

Perform the following steps to view and change rule priority:

1. Open the IIS Manager MMC console.

2. At the web server, website, application, folder, or file node at which you want to configure this setting, select IP and Domain Name Restrictions.

3.   Click the View Ordered List option in the Actions pane. The Move Up and Move Down options enable you to reorder the rule priorities. Rules located higher up in the list have higher priority. The Move Up and Move Down options are not visible if no rules are defined that apply to that server, website, folder, or file. If rules have been defined at a higher node, the options are available and allow you to override the settings at a lower-level node. To return to the screen that allows you to add and remove rules, click View Unordered List.

Enabling Dynamic Restrictions

IIS 8.0 introduces a new dynamic IP address restriction feature. This allows IIS 8.0 to dynamically determine whether to block certain remote clients, based on criteria preset within IIS. To set this feature:

1.   Start IIS Manager. (Click WIN+R, enter **inetmgr** in the dialog, and click OK. Alternatively, click Tools on the top-right of Server Manager and select Internet Information Server (IIS) Manager.)

2.   At the web server, website, application, folder, or file node at which you want to configure this setting, select IP and Domain Name Restrictions.

3.   Click Edit Dynamic Restriction Settings. The Dynamic IP Restriction Settings dialog opens, as shown in Figure 13-3.

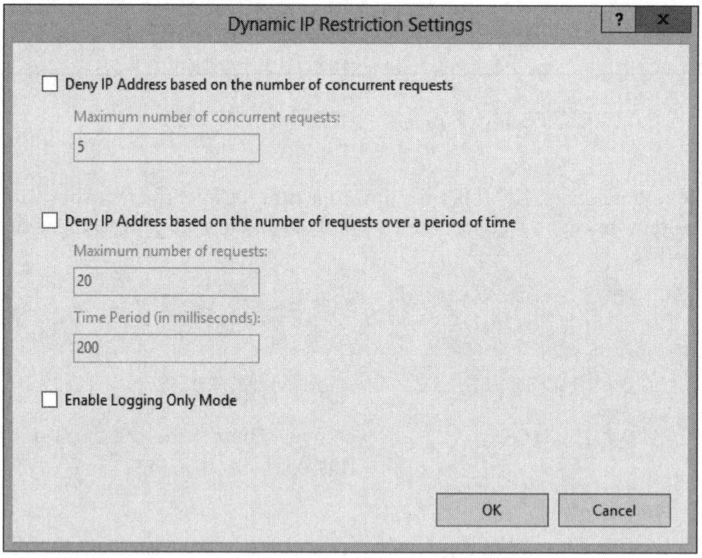

FIGURE 13-3

4.   Choose whether you want to enable restrictions based on:

➤   The number of concurrent HTTP connection requests from clients. Most well-behaved clients open a maximum of two concurrent HTTP connections and use HTTP Keep-Alives to reuse those connections.

> ➤ The number of requests received over a period of time. A client requesting many resources over a period of milliseconds may be attempting a denial-of-service attack.

5. Enable the Logging Only checkbox if you want IIS merely to log requests that would be rejected, without actually rejecting the requests from the client. This may be useful to model any potential changes before an actual implementation.

Comparing IP and Domain Name Restrictions

While IP and domain name restrictions enable an IIS administrator to determine which remote machines can connect to IIS, other mechanisms that provide the same functionality may be more appropriate, depending on the scenario.

Generally, it is advisable to configure connection restrictions at the lowest level in the ISO OSI model as possible. This prevents a misconfiguration or vulnerability in a lower-level component from allowing an attacker to bypass higher-level restrictions. For example, if a vulnerability in Windows or IIS is discovered, it may be possible for an attacker to compromise the server before any IIS IP and domain name restriction rules are evaluated. To mitigate this scenario, restrictions could be configured on any firewalls in the environment. At the next highest level, routers typically can be configured with routing rules or access control lists (ACLs) that do not permit traffic from hosts. At a host level, IPsec or the Windows Firewall provides a lower-level connection control.

IIS IP and domain name restrictions may be more appropriate in the following situations:

> ➤ As a server, website, or web application administrator, you do not have access to any lower-level options for configuring connection control. For example, you might be hosting your application with a third-party hosting company.

> ➤ You need to configure differing restrictions for different websites, folders, or files. Most lower-level access restrictions apply filters based on IP address. They are unable to differentiate between different requested URLs all located at the same host. Some firewalls, such as Microsoft's Forefront Threat Management Gateway (TMG) 2010, are able to do further "application-layer" inspections of packets and are thus aware of HTTP namespaces and able to apply URL-based restrictions.

IIS IP and domain name restrictions are generally more secure than attempting to configure these restrictions within your application. A vulnerability or misconfiguration of ASP or ASP.NET would allow an attacker to potentially bypass any restrictions coded into your application before your code has a chance to run. Prior to IIS 7.0, Administrator Privileges were required on the server to be able to configure IIS IP and domain name restrictions. With IIS's support for delegated administration, the option now exists for individuals to configure these restrictions within IIS rather than relying on application-level code.

Configuring MIME-Type Extensions

Multipurpose Internet Mail Extensions (MIME)–type restrictions were first introduced in IIS 6.0. These restrictions prevent undefined file types from being served by IIS. This can help protect your server by preventing malicious attackers from downloading sensitive files (such as configuration files, data files, or system binaries).

Although these files would not typically be stored within your website's root folders, either a system misconfiguration or URL canonicalization vulnerability (for example, that exploited by the NIMDA worm) may allow an attacker to gain access to sensitive files.

When a client attempts to download a file that does not have a defined MIME type, a 404.3 HTTP status is logged in the IIS log files.

> **NOTE** *The MIME Type Extensions security setting only applies to files that are handled by the IIS Static File HTTP handler. If the file extension is handled by a different handler (for example, by an ISAPI Extension such as ASP or ASP.NET), then a MIME type does not have to be defined. See the section, "Configuring ISAPI Extensions and CGI Restrictions," for more information on HTTP handlers.*

IIS 8.0 ships with approximately 350 defined MIME types that cover files such as text (`.txt`, `.css`, `.js`), HTML (`.html`, `.htm`), images (`.jpg`, `.gif`, `.png`), and common audio and video formats. These are enabled if you install the Static File option when installing IIS 8.0.

Adding a New MIME Type

If you have a custom file extension that needs to be downloadable by clients, you will need to add a new MIME type. MIME types can be added at the server, website, web-application, or folder level.

To add a new MIME type:

1. Open the IIS Manager MMC Console.

2. At the web server, website, application, or folder node where you want to configure this setting, select MIME Types.

3. Click Add to add a new MIME type. The Add MIME Type dialog appears, as shown in Figure 13-4.

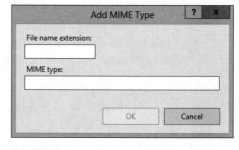

FIGURE 13-4

4. Enter the file extension and an appropriate MIME type. MIME types are defined in IETF RFCs 2045, 2046, 2047, 2048, and 2077.

5. Click OK to add the new MIME type and exit the dialog box.

Removing an Existing MIME Type

If you are certain that your IIS server should not serve a particular file type, you can remove the associated MIME type to prevent accidental download of that file. To remove a MIME type:

1. Open the IIS Manager MMC Console.

2. At the web server, website, application, or folder node where you want to configure this setting, select MIME Types.

3. Select the MIME type that you no longer want to serve, and then click the Remove link from the Actions pane.

Configuring MIME Types Using AppCmd

You can configure MIME types programmatically by using AppCmd or PowerShell. To add a new MIME type for a file extension "ext" with a type of "text/plain" across all websites on the server, run the following code:

```
appcmd.exe set config -section:system.webServer/staticContent
    /+"[fileExtension='.ext',mimeType='text/plain']"

PS C:\> add-webconfiguration /system.webServer/staticContent
    -value @{fileExtension=".ext";mimeType='text/plain'} -pspath IIS:\
```

Configuring ISAPI Extensions and CGI Restrictions

IIS provides a mechanism for extending the functionality of the server via an API known as ISAPI. Developers can write *ISAPI extensions*, which allow for additional functionality when particular types of files are requested. Common ISAPI extensions include ASP.NET and its predecessor ASP (Active Server Pages). A PHP ISAPI extension implementation also exists.

ISAPI extensions work on the basis of file extensions, which can be "mapped" to an ISAPI extension (for example, .aspx files are mapped, by default, to the ASP.NET ISAPI extension). When a file with that extension is requested, processing is handed over to the ISAPI extension, which determines what additional work should be done. In the case of ASP and ASP.NET, these extensions scan the file for custom code that should be run server-side.

Common Gateway Interface (CGI) is a platform-independent way of extending web servers. Typically, CGI applications are implemented as .exe files when run on Windows, and read the browser's request from standard input, process the request, and return a valid HTTP response to standard output. CGI is not as popular on IIS as ISAPI extensions because each request spawns a new process, and process creation/destruction is relatively expensive in Windows, leading to poor scalability for most CGI applications.

A new CGI implementation (FastCGI) is available in IIS 8.0. FastCGI provides the ability to service multiple requests within a single process, either in a single-threaded environment (servicing one request after another) or a multithreaded environment (if the actual CGI executable supports this).

> **NOTE** *For more information about CGI, see Chapter 7, "Web Application Administration."*

IIS 8.0 provides the ability for a server administrator to configure what ISAPI extensions and what CGI applications are permitted to run on the server. This setting can only be configured at a server level by default. For administrators familiar with IIS 6.0, this configuration item corresponds to the Web Service Extensions node in the IIS 6.0 MMC Administrative Tool.

> **NOTE** *The "ISAPI and CGI Restrictions" option will not appear unless you have installed either the ISAPI extensions or CGI support modules. Neither of these two modules is included in a default installation of IIS 8.0. If you choose to install a built-in ISAPI extension like ASP or ASP.NET, then ISAPI extension support is installed as well.*

To configure ISAPI and CGI restrictions, open IIS Manager and navigate to the server node. If you have previously installed any CGIs or ISAPI extensions, they will be listed, as shown in Figure 13-5.

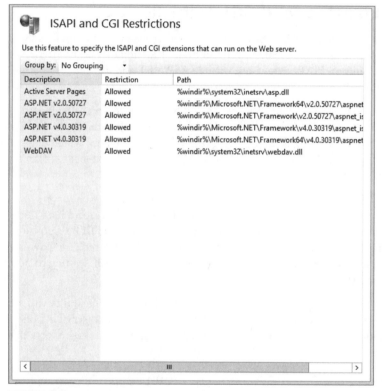

FIGURE 13-5

IIS 8.0 allows each CGI or ISAPI extension to be set to an Allowed or Disallowed state. For those CGIs or ISAPI extensions that are set to Disallowed, a 404.2 HTTP status will be logged in the IIS log file if a client attempts to request a resource that invokes the ISAPI extension or CGI application.

Adding a New ISAPI Extension or CGI Restriction

To add a new ISAPI extension or CGI restriction:

1. Open IIS Manager and navigate to the server node.

2. Double-click the ISAPI and CGI Restrictions icon to open the feature.

3. Click the Add link in the Actions pane. The Add ISAPI or CGI Restriction dialog box appears, as shown in Figure 13-6.

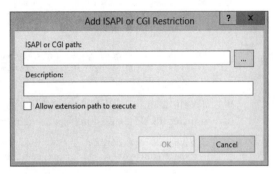

4. Enter the path to your ISAPI extension (typically, a `.dll` file) or CGI application (typically, an `.exe` file). Optionally, add a description.

5. To allow the ISAPI extension or CGI restriction, check the "Allow extension path to execute" checkbox. If this is not selected, the Restriction setting will be set to Not Allowed.

FIGURE 13-6

6. Click the OK button to commit your changes.

Changing Default Settings

By default, only specifically permitted ISAPI extensions and CGI applications are permitted to run; all other ISAPI extensions and CGI applications will be denied. To change these defaults so that all ISAPI extensions or CGI applications are permitted to run except those specifically denied, perform the following steps:

1. Open IIS Manager and navigate to the server node.

2. Double-click the ISAPI and CGI Restrictions icon to open the feature.

3. Click Edit Feature Settings. The Edit ISAPI and CGI Restrictions Settings dialog box appears, as shown in Figure 13-7.

FIGURE 13-7

4. Select the "Allow unspecified CGI modules" checkbox to allow all CGI modules except those specifically denied.

5. Select the "Allow unspecified ISAPI modules" checkbox to allow all ISAPI extensions except those specifically denied.

> **NOTE** *Allowing all unspecified CGI applications or ISAPI Extensions is a security risk. If an attacker is able to load a CGI application onto your server (for example, via upload functionality), he or she will be able to execute it remotely.*

Configuring ISAPI and CGI Restrictions with AppCmd

AppCmd and PowerShell can also be used to configure the ISAPI and CGI Restrictions Policy.

➤ To add an additional entry to the ISAPI and CGI restrictions configuration, run either of the following commands:

```
appcmd.exe set config  -section:system.webServer/security/isapiCgiRestriction
    /"[path='c:\program files\myCustomCGI.exe'].description:"My Custom  CGI""
    /commit:apphost
```

```
PS C:\> Add-Webconfiguration /system.webServer/security/isapiCgiRestriction
    -value @{path="c:\program files\myCustomCGI.exe";allowed="true";description="My
    Custom CGI"}
```

➤ To allow unlisted ISAPI extensions, run the following command (be aware that allowing unlisted ISAPI extensions is a security risk):

```
appcmd.exe set config
   -section:system.webServer/security/isapiCgiRestriction /notListedIsapisAllowed:True
```

```
PS C:\> Set-Webconfigurationproperty /system.webServer/security/isapiCgiRestriction
-name notListedIsapisAllowed -value True
```

➤ To allow unlisted CGI executables, run the following command (be aware that allowing unlisted CGI executables is a security risk):

```
appcmd.exe set config -section:system.webServer/security/isapiCgiRestriction
    /notListedCGIsAllowed:True
```

```
PS C:\> Set-Webconfigurationproperty /system.webServer/security/
isapiCgiRestriction
    -name notListedCgisAllowed -value True
```

➤ To disable unlisted ISAPI extensions or CGI executables, run the listed commands, but replace the `True` property with `False`.

Additional Configuration for ISAPI Extensions and CGI Applications

In order for an ISAPI extension or CGI application to process requests, a script mapping must also be configured. This associates files with a certain extension with the ISAPI extension (for example, .asp files with the Active Server Pages ISAPI extension) or CGI application.

If you are familiar with IIS 5.0 or 6.0, this script mapping corresponds with the Mappings tab option in the IIS 6.0 and IIS 5.0 MMC Administrative Tools.

> **NOTE** *If you configure a script map before configuring the ISAPI and CGI Restriction Policy setting, IIS Manager will ask you if you want to have an entry placed automatically into the ISAPI and CGI Restriction Policy and have the status set to Allowed. This can save one additional configuration step.*

You can configure script maps at a server, website, or web-application level. This allows the flexibility of executing certain ISAPI extensions only within a restricted area. Perform the following steps to configure a script map:

1. Open IIS Manager and navigate to the server, website, or web application where the script mapping should be added.

2. Select the Handler Mappings option.

3. Select Add a Script Map. The Add Script Map dialog box appears, as shown in Figure 13-8.

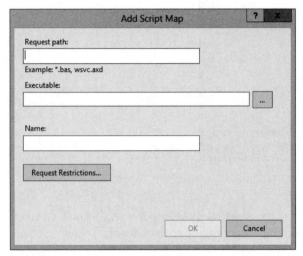

FIGURE 13-8

4. Enter the path to the ISAPI extension or CGI executable and the file extension or specific file that the ISAPI should handle. To add multiple file extensions, you will need to repeat this process from Step 3 for each additional extension that you want to have processed by the ISAPI extension or CGI application.

5. Optionally, add a name for your ISAPI extension or CGI application.

6. The Request Restrictions option allows for further restrictions on the operation of the ISAPI extension. Click the Request Restrictions button to access these options. On the Mapping tab, decide whether to allow the ISAPI extension to respond only for requests to files or to also allow requests to URLs that have no file (for example, http://servername/folder/). The Verbs tab enables you to limit requests to specific permitted HTTP verbs (e.g., GET only), and lastly, the Access tab allows interpretation (read a file from disk, run interpreted script contained within a file, execute a file, write to a file) to be set. Enter the optional restrictions, as shown in Figure 13-9.

7. Click OK to exit the dialogs.

IIS automatically configures script mapping to invoke the necessary supporting modules based on the file extension of the executable supplied in Step 4. If the file extension is a DLL, then the ISAPIModule is configured. If the file extension is .exe, then the CGIModule is configured. You can override this by editing the applicationHost.Config file.

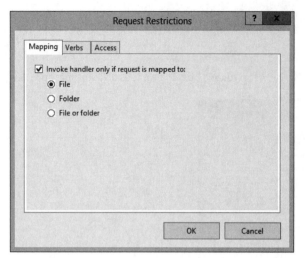

FIGURE 13-9

The following XML configuration snippet shows the ISAPIModule (ASP) and CGIModule (PHP) configuration for two popular application programming environments:

```
<handlers accessPolicy="Read, Script">
   <add name="PHP-CGI"
      path="*.php"
      verb="GET,HEAD,POST"
      modules="CgiModule"
      scriptProcessor="c:\setup\php\php-cgi.exe"
      resourceType="File" />
   <add name="ASPClassic"
      path="*.asp"
      verb="GET,HEAD,POST"
      modules="IsapiModule"
      scriptProcessor="%windir%\system32\inetsrv\asp.dll"
      resourceType="File" />
</handlers>
```

> **NOTE** *For more information on ISAPI extensions and CGI applications, see Chapter 7.*

ISAPI extensions and CGI executables provide a powerful way to extend the functionality of IIS 8.0. Out-of-the-box, Windows Server 2012 does not install or enable either ISAPI or CGI support; however, both ASP.NET and ASP are supplied as part of the operating system and can be added from the Server Manager MMC Console.

As with adding any additional functionality to your server, configuring additional ISAPI extensions or CGI executables requires that you take additional steps to ensure the ongoing security of your server. Monitor the vendor's website for patches that may be released to fix security or configuration vulnerabilities in the product. Additionally, if you install any custom applications (for example, a third-party ASP.NET application), ensure that you monitor that vendor's website to ensure that there are no vulnerabilities in the application itself (see the section, "Application Layer Security," below in this chapter).

Lastly, functionality exists with IIS to allow unlisted ISAPI extensions or CGI executables to be run, effectively disabling the restriction policy. There may be circumstances in which this setting may be useful — for example, when developers are uploading new versions of a CGI application that may vary in name. It is a security risk in production environments, because an attacker may be able copy an unauthorized executable or ISAPI extension to your server and then have that run.

Configuring Request Filtering

Request Filtering provides a configurable set of rules that enables you to determine which types of requests should be allowed or rejected for the server, website, or web application.

Administrators of previous versions of IIS may be familiar with the URLScan tool, which delivers similar functionality. In IIS 8.0, Request Filtering is improved over URLScan for the following reasons:

➤ Request Filtering is implemented as a module rather than an ISAPI filter.

➤ Request Filtering rules can be implemented for specific websites or web applications, rather than a single set of rules that applies to an entire server.

➤ Request Filtering logging is integrated with IIS logging functionality (rejected requests will be logged to the regular IIS log file), whereas URLScan maintains its own separate log file, making troubleshooting potential issues more time-consuming.

➤ Request Filtering has a GUI interface, allowing administrators to verify settings quickly in a one-off situation.

The Microsoft IIS website (`http://learn.iis.net/page.aspx/938/urlscan-3-reference/`) provides information on the latest version of URLScan, with more detailed configuration information available in Microsoft KB Article 326444 (`http://support.microsoft.com/?id=326444`). If you are migrating an existing URLScan-protected server to IIS 8.0, these two documents can help with a migration strategy.

Request Filtering is implemented in `%systemroot%\system32\inetsrv\Modrqflt.dll`.

Request Filtering offers the following options for allowing or denying specific requests. Each type of filter can be applied at the web-server, website, or web-application level. There are many filters that can be configured, all of which are accessible from the Request Filtering option within IIS Manager:

1. Start IIS Manager. (Click WIN+R, enter **inetmgr** in the dialog, and click OK. Alternatively, click Tools on the top-right of Server Manager and select Internet Information Server (IIS) Manager.)

2. At the web server, website, application, folder, or file node where you want to configure this setting, select Request Filtering.

The tabs across the feature, as shown in Figure 13-10, show the various types of filters that can be configured. Each option is discussed below.

FIGURE 13-10

Filtering by Filename Extensions

The File Name Extensions tab allows filtering by file extension. File extensions that are not matched by a specific rule can be set to Allowed or Disallowed (that is, a default rule can be configured). This functionally corresponds to the [AllowExtensions] and [DenyExtensions] functionality in URLScan.

Adding Allow or Deny entries for file extensions via the GUI is as simple as clicking the Allow File Name Extension... or Deny File Name Extension... links in the Action Pane, respectively. To configure fileExtensions filtering using a configuration file, you can use the following XML tags within a <system.Web> section:

```
<security>
        <requestFiltering>
                <fileExtensions allowUnlisted="false" >
                        <add fileExtension=".asp" allowed="true"/>
```

```
            </fileExtensions>
        </requestFiltering>
    </security>
```

The <fileExtensions> parent node enables you to define a default rule. In the preceding example, all file extensions not specifically listed are denied. You can then use the <add>, <remove>, and <clear> tags to manipulate the file extensions that are permitted to be requested. In the preceding example, files with the .asp file extension are permitted to be requested.

If a request is rejected because of a fileExtensions request filter, a 404.7 HTTP status is logged in the IIS log file.

The fileExtensions section does provide for an applyToWebDAV attribute to be set. This allows requests that are tagged as WebDAV authoring requests to bypass this filter. To configure this attribute, set:

```
    <fileExtensions allowUnlisted="false" applyToWebDAV="false">
```

In order for the WebDAV exception to apply, the WebDAV module must be installed. If the WebDAV module detects a WebDAV HTTP request, it sets a server variable. If any applyToWebDAV exceptions have been configured, the RequestFiltering module verifies whether this server variable has been set. If it has, then RequestFiltering rules that have the applyToWebDav attribute set do not apply to the marked requests.

Filtering by HTTP Verb

The HTTP Verbs tab permits or denies requests that use specified HTTP verbs (such as GET and POST). Like fileExtensions above, verbs that are not matched by a specific rule can be set to Allowed or Disallowed. This functionality corresponds to the [allowVerbs] and [denyVerbs] functionality in URLScan.

To configure verbs filtering using a configuration file, you can use the following XML tags within a <system.Web> section:

```
    <security>
        <requestFiltering>
            <verbs allowUnlisted="false" >
                <add verb="GET" allowed="true" />
                <add verb="POST" allowed="true" />
            </verbs>
        </requestFiltering>
    </security>
```

In this example, all requests that do not use the GET or POST HTTP verbs are denied by IIS. GET and POST requests are permitted.

If a request is rejected because of a verbs request filter, a 404.6 HTTP status is logged in the IIS log file.

Similar to the fileExtensions section, the verbs section allows for WebDAV verbs to be exempted from filtering. To configure this attribute, set the following:

```
    <verbs allowUnlisted="false" applyToWebDAV="true">
```

Filtering by URL Sequence

The URL tab enables you to reject requests that contain certain substrings within the requested URL. A commonly rejected sequence is "..", which may indicate a possible directory traversal attack. In this attack, an attacker attempts to move up or down the directory tree until she can reach a resource she wouldn't otherwise be allowed to reach. The infamous Code Red virus used this technique when attacking vulnerable IIS 5.0 servers.

There is no capability to configure a default rule in this section. You can explicitly configure sequences to be rejected (and all other requests will be accepted). You cannot configure Request Filtering to reject all requests except the specific URLs that you want to allow.

This functionality corresponds to the [DenySequences] functionality in URLScan. When a request is rejected because of a denySequences request filter, a 404.5 HTTP status is logged in the IIS log file.

```
<security>
    <requestFiltering>
        <denyUrlSequences>
            <add sequence=".."/>
        </denyUrlSequences>
    </requestFiltering>
</security>
```

In this example, any request that contains ".." will be rejected.

> **NOTE** *Outlook Web Access (OWA) functionality in Microsoft Exchange Server 2000, 2003, and 2007 creates URLs for messages based on the subject line for each e-mail message. If the subject line contains "..", then the end user will be unable to view the message via OWA if the above example is implemented on an Exchange front-end server (also known as a Client Access Server in Exchange 2007).*

Filtering by Hidden Segment

The Hidden Segments tab enables you to reject requests that contain a URL segment. This varies from the previous denyURLSequences in that URL segments (for example, a folder name is a segment) are evaluated rather than raw strings. The Hidden Segments tab corresponds to the hiddenSegments section in a .config file.

Consider the URLs www.example.com/products/water and www.example.com/products/waterbeds. If you want to allow requests to the second URL (waterbeds) but not the first (water), then using denyURLSequences would not help, because adding the sequence *water* would result in requests to both folders being denied.

The hiddenSegments Request Filtering section permits us to deny the first URL but allow the second. To configure hiddenSegments filtering using a configuration file, the following XML tags may be used within a <system.Web> section:

```
<security>
      <requestFiltering>
            <hiddenSegments>
                  <add segment="water" />
            </hiddenSegments>
      </requestFiltering>
</security>
```

Similar to the `fileExtensions` section, the `hiddenSegments` section allows for WebDAV verbs to be exempted from filtering. To configure this attribute, set the following:

```
<hiddenSegments applyToWebDAV="true">
```

When a request is rejected because of a `denySequences` request filter, a 404.8 HTTP status is logged in the IIS log file.

Filtering by Header Size

The Headers tab allows you to set a limit on the size of any particular HTTP header. See the "Configuring Request Limits" section below for how these settings are stored in the IIS configuration file.

Configuring Request Limits

The `requestLimits` option enables you to restrict the size of requests made by clients. This can help prevent malicious requests (for example, requests that send too much data or use too long a URL for your application) from having an adverse impact on your server or application.

Access the Request Limits option by clicking the Edit Feature... link in the Action Pane. There are three specific limits that you can configure from this link:

➤   `maxAllowedContentLength` — This is the maximum size of the HTTP request that can be sent from the client to the server. It is measured in bytes. If a request is rejected because it exceeds a `maxAllowedContentLength` request filter, then a 404.13 HTTP status is logged to the IIS log file.

➤   `maxURL` — This is the maximum size of the URL that can be requested, including the domain name, path, and port, but excluding the query string (the part after a ? in a URL). If a request is rejected because it exceeds a `maxURL` request filter, then a 404.14 HTTP status is logged to the IIS log file.

➤   `maxQueryString` — This is the maximum size of a query string that can be sent by the client to the server. If a request is rejected because it exceeds a `maxQueryString` request filter, then a 404.15 HTTP status is logged to the IIS log file.

In the following example, the maximum allowed content length is 1,000,000 bytes, the maximum URL length is 260 characters, and the maximum query string length is 25 characters:

```
<security>
      <requestFiltering>
            <requestLimits
                  maxAllowedContentLength="1000000"
                  maxUrl="260"
```

```
                        maxQueryString="25" />
            </requestFiltering>
        </security>
```

Note that the HTTP header request size limits are also contained within this section of a `.config` file. The following example limits the `Accept` header to 1,024 bytes:

```
<requestLimits>
    <headerLimits>
        <add header="Accept" sizeLimit="1024" />
    </headerLimits>
</requestLimits>
```

Request Filtering by Rule

The last remaining option available in the Request Filtering feature allows you to configure a combination of the above restrictions: Certain strings can be detected within the URL, QueryString, or one or more HTTP headers, and optionally when files of a certain type are requested. For example, you may want to deny access to image files (`.jpg`, `.gif`, `.png`), to certain types of bots, or to other user agents. This is possible using the Rules tab.

To configure a rule:

1. Select the Rules tab within the Request Filtering feature, and click the Add Rule link in the Actions pane.

2. Enter a name for your new rule.

3. Decide whether to filter the URL and/or QueryString and select the relevant checkboxes (see Figure 13-11).

4. To have the rule scan HTTP headers for specific text, enter the HTTP header names in the Header section.

5. Add the file extensions to which this rule should apply (e.g., `.gif`).

6. Lastly, enter the string(s) that will trigger the Deny rule.

Request Filtering Logging

The new Request Filtering options in IIS 8.0 provide a powerful mechanism for administrators to define known good or known bad requests, and to configure IIS to handle those requests appropriately. Because Request Filtering logging is now integrated with IIS logging, you can use regular log file analysis tools to evaluate the effectiveness of configured Request Filtering policies.

The following table summarizes the HTTP status codes for requests rejected because of a configured Request Filtering policy:

REQUEST FILTERING REASON	HTTP STATUS CODE
Request Filtering: URL sequence denied	404.5
Request Filtering: Verb denied	404.6

REQUEST FILTERING REASON	HTTP STATUS CODE
Request Filtering: File extension denied	404.7
Request Filtering: Denied by hidden segment	404.8
Request Filtering: Denied because request header is too long	404.10
Request Filtering: Denied because URL doubled escaping	404.11
Request Filtering: Denied because of high bit characters	404.12
Request Filtering: Denied because content length too large	404.13
Request Filtering: Denied because URL too long	404.14
Request Filtering: Denied because query string too long	404.15
Request Filtering: Denied by Rule	404.19

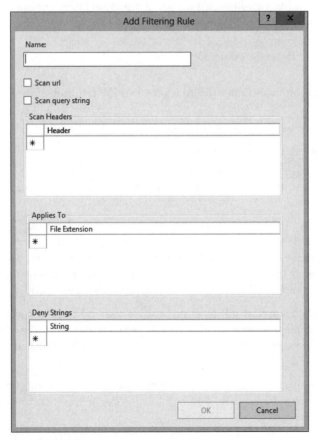

FIGURE 13-11

Application Layer Security

Even after securing your environment and IIS 8.0 itself, it is important not to neglect application security. Both off-the-shelf (OTS) and custom-developed code may suffer from a range of vulnerabilities. In recent years, more attention has been devoted to breaking applications rather than server software itself because of the larger number of vulnerabilities available. For example (at time of writing), Secunia (an independent vulnerability tracking site) reports just six vulnerabilities in IIS 7.0 in the four years since release: `http://secunia.com/advisories/product/17543/?task=advisories`. Note that vulnerabilities in non-IIS components (such as Schannel, but that might be exposed by IIS) are not counted by Secunia as IIS vulnerabilities per se. On the other hand, SecurityFocus's BugTraq list announced more than 30 vulnerabilities in various third-party web-based software applications in just a two-week period at the time of writing (`www.securityfocus.com`).

A wide array of vulnerabilities can affect application layer software. Some of the most common are the following:

➤ **SQL injection attacks** — Poor input validation allows an attacker to submit carefully crafted input to your application that is then executed inside a database supporting your application. The most trivial would exploit some code such as the following:

```
strSQL = "SELECT * FROM users WHERE username = '" &
Request.Form("username") & "'  AND userPassword = '" &
Request.Form("Password") & "'"
```

By submitting `';TRUNCATE TABLE Users` as input, the attacker turns the resulting SQL statement into

```
SELECT * FROM Users WHERE Username = '';TRUNCASE TABLE Users – '
```

which would cause the entire Users table to be deleted.

Alternatively, the attacker could enter SQL code that would create a new user (via an `INSERT INTO` statement) or bypass your authentication mechanism by setting "1=1" as a search criterion.

➤ **Cross-site scripting (XSS) attacks** — An attacker injects some script into your database, which is then displayed to other users visiting your website. This is a common attack vector against forum/bulletin board software but could also be used against any software that displays user input to other users (for example, even to administrators). The script runs on the victim's machine and could steal cookies and other data and send them to the attacker.

➤ **Session replay attacks** — Application software produces predictable session key values, and an attacker is able to easily determine previously good session keys and replay a prior user's session, potentially bypassing the need to authenticate and/or accessing sensitive information to which the prior user had access.

It is important for administrators to subscribe to both vendor update bulletins as well as third-party disclosure forums like BugTraq (`www.securityfocus.com`) and Full Disclosure (`http://lists.grok.org.uk/mailman/listinfo/full-disclosure`).

For custom development, Microsoft maintains a security developer section at http://msdn .microsoft.com/security. In particular, the Patterns and Practices section is worth visiting: http://msdn.microsoft.com/en-US/practices/bb190386.aspx.

The Open Web Application Security Project (OWASP) produces an excellent, platform-independent guide to application security threats and mitigations. You can find it at www.owasp.org.

Configuring Logging

An effective auditing and logging strategy allows administrators to detect possible malicious activity and possibly prevent compromise. In the event of a successful attack, comprehensive and untainted log files can still help, by identifying the method by which the attacker gained access (and allowing that hole to be closed), and also potentially providing proof of who the attacker was.

IIS 8.0 logging configuration and options are covered in Chapter 6, "Website Administration." Windows also provides the Windows Event Logs, where several other important pieces of information are logged (for example, account logon events that might indicate a password guessing attack, or application crash events that might indicate an attempt to exploit an application).

Suffice it to say that administrators should consider the following when developing a logging strategy:

➤ Move IIS log files from the Windows system partition (typically, the c: drive). An attack that floods a server with requests could result in the log files growing very large and filling the disk, resulting in a denial of service.

➤ Enable auditing (via the local security policy or domain-based group policy) for account logon events (both successes and failures). A large number of failed logon events can indicate an attempt to brute-force the password for an account. Most operation-monitoring tools (such as Microsoft System Center Operations Manager 2012) can be configured to alert when a certain number of failed logon attempts are detected within a specified period. Successful logons should also be audited, because several failed logons followed by a successful logon may indicate that an attacker has managed to get a password.

➤ In higher-security environments, archive your Windows Event Logs rather than allowing older events to be overwritten as needed, or use a log archival product (e.g., a Syslog client) to send your logs to a dedicated log management system. (Syslog is a commonly used product in many environments.) An attacker may generate several spurious events to fill the Event Logs to cover possible incriminating events generated earlier. Windows Server 2012 sets the default log size for the Security and System logs to 20 MB; however, old events are overwritten as needed. An automated tool can generate a large number of spurious events in a very short period of time, potentially overwriting events that you may need to reconstruct an attack.

14

Authentication and Authorization

WHAT'S IN THIS CHAPTER?

➤ Configuring Anonymous authentication

➤ Configuring Basic authentication

➤ Configuring Digest authentication

➤ Configuring Integrated Windows authentication

➤ Configuring NTLM authentication

➤ Configuring UNC authentication

➤ Configuring Client Certificate authentication

➤ Configuring Forms-based authentication

➤ Configuring delegation

➤ Configuring protocol transition

➤ Configuring authorization

➤ Understanding IIS user accounts

Configuring authentication and authorization for IIS and applications running on top of IIS is one of the more complex IIS security operations. This is in part because of the number of different authentication options available, in part because IIS has offered multiple request processing pipelines, and in part because authentication and authorization are often conflated, even though they are distinct concepts.

Authentication is the process of identifying and proving that identity to a remote service (in this case IIS). Typically, a client or user will provide an identifier (for example, a Windows username) and then will be required to prove that identity. Typically, proof of identity takes the form of something you know (a password), something you have (security token), or something you are (some kind of biometric identification). Two-factor or multifactor authentication systems combine these concepts, requiring multiple pieces of authentication information to prove the end user's identity.

Authorization occurs after authentication, and is the process by which a user requests permission to perform an operation (for example, view a file), and the system verifies that operation against an access control list (ACL) maintained for the file or resource. The ACL consists of a set of access control entries (ACEs) that define which users can or cannot perform certain operations. By "operations," we mean being able to read a file, or modify its contents, or update its properties, or impersonate a user, or perform a backup, or shut down a system, or any other possible thing that can be done. Most operating systems allow the definition of both Allow ACEs and Deny ACEs, and, by default, if a user is not explicitly listed on an Allow ACE, then he or she is denied access even without a specific Deny ACE being present. In IIS, a Deny ACE will explicitly deny a user permission to perform an operation, even if there is a corresponding Allow entry defined as well.

The processes of authentication and authorization are often confused because typically they occur at the same time as far as an end user is concerned. Credentials are supplied, and an immediate answer is provided by the server.

This chapter covers these distinct concepts, enabling you to develop a security strategy for your applications, configure the appropriate settings, and troubleshoot potential issues that arise. In particular, this chapter discusses:

➤ Authentication options available with IIS 8.0

➤ How to configure permissions correctly on resources to allow permitted users to access resources, while denying unauthorized users

➤ The built-in Windows accounts that IIS 8.0 uses

AUTHENTICATION IN IIS 8.0

IIS 8.0 provides six authentication options, plus the ability to configure a fixed user identity for connecting to network resources (making seven in total). These are briefly described below. For each authentication mechanism, more detailed information including configuration options, minimum requirements, and potential weaknesses is described subsequently in the chapter. The following authentication mechanisms are supported by IIS 8.0:

➤ **Anonymous authentication** — Here the end user does not supply credentials, effectively making an anonymous request. IIS 8.0 impersonates a fixed user account when attempting to process the request (for example, to read the file off the hard disk). This authentication mechanism would be used for public-facing websites where visitors are not required to supply credentials.

➤ **Basic authentication** — The end user is prompted to supply credentials, which are then transmitted unencrypted across the network. Basic authentication was originally defined in RFC 1945 (the HTTP 1.0 specification) and is thus supported in all current browsers. Although the user's password is BASE64-encoded, it is not encrypted, requiring a separate technology to secure the password (e.g., TLS or IPSec).

➤ **Digest authentication** — The end user is prompted to supply credentials, but unlike in Basic authentication, the user's password is not passed in cleartext across the network. Digest authentication was originally defined in RFC 2069 and updated in RFC 2619. Digest authentication involves hashing the user's password using MD5. Windows is unable to store MD5 hashes of passwords for local accounts, thus Digest authentication is only available for Active Directory accounts.

➤ **Integrated Windows authentication** — Technically, this incorporates two separate authentication mechanisms: NTLM v2 (also known as NT Challenge/Response from previous versions of IIS) and Kerberos. Enabling Integrated Windows authentication (IWA) via IIS Manager typically enables support for both of these two mechanisms. Neither mechanism sends the user's password in cleartext across the network. NTLM works in a similar way to Digest authentication (with a hashed version of the user's password). Kerberos relies on shared secrets between the client, Active Directory domain controller, and the IIS server to authenticate the user. Kerberos is only available for Active Directory accounts, whereas NTLM can be used for local accounts as well. IIS 8.0 does not present Kerberos as a discrete authentication option to the client, instead sending a "Negotiate" option, though non-Kerberos responses can be blocked. NTLM can be presented as a discrete authentication option to the client.

➤ **Client Certificate authentication** — When using Client Certificate authentication, the client presents a certificate to the server. The server is configured to map certificates to one or more Windows user accounts (that is, it is possible to map multiple certificates to a single user account or to map each certificate to an individual user account). IIS logs on the mapped user account. Client Certificate authentication requires that SSL/TLS be enabled for the resource being secured. More information on SSL/TLS, and in particular the handshake that sets up a secured session, can be found in Chapter 15, "SSL and TLS."

➤ **Forms-based authentication** — Unlike the previous authentication mechanisms, which rely on the transport of credentials as part of the HTTP headers (technically, client certificate mapping occurs at the TCP level below HTTP), Forms-based authentication (FBA) relies on the user authenticating via an HTML form. In this way, the request for the login form is an anonymous request. After authenticating via the HTML form, an authentication cookie is set by the server. The client must return this cookie with each subsequent request in order for the request to be authenticated. No other HTTP authorization data is carried in the HTTP headers. Although this authentication can be configured in part using IIS Manager, it is effectively ASP.NET's FBA. Forms-based authentication can be combined with either ASP.NET's authorization features (available with previous versions of ASP.NET) or IIS 8.0's built-in URL Authorization feature to protect access to resources.

➤ **UNC authentication** — When IIS 8.0 needs to retrieve files from a remote network resource (for example, a remote file server), a virtual directory in IIS 8.0 can be mapped to a UNC (Universal Naming Convention) path. When configuring this virtual directory, it is possible to specify a fixed user account that will be used to connect to that remote share, regardless of the identity of the end user, or to have the user's credentials passed through to the remote file server for authorization.

> **WHAT HAPPENED TO PASSPORT AUTHENTICATION?**
>
> Microsoft's attempt at a federated identity management system, Hailstorm (and then later known as Microsoft Passport in IIS 6.0, and now known as Microsoft Live ID) has been overtaken by subsequent developments in identity federation technologies. Microsoft now offers Active Directory Federation Services (ADFS) as an identity federation product that is not tied to Microsoft's own identity servers. The relatively low uptake of the Passport service by the wider community has seen Passport authentication removed from IIS.

These authentication mechanisms (with the exception of UNC authentication, which is per virtual directory that is connected to a remote server) can be configured at a website, folder, or individual file level. This provides flexibility in securing a website. For example, a website could be largely public but have a secure section where users are required to authenticate in order to gain access.

How IIS 8.0 Authenticates a Client

Regardless of what authentication mechanism or mechanisms are configured on a resource (website, folder, or file), the browser begins by making an anonymous request. The exception to this is Client Certificate authentication. This is because Client Certificate authentication occurs during the SSL/TLS handshake, and that handshake occurs before the client browser makes its first HTTP request. Client Certificate authentication is discussed in more detail below in this chapter, and in Chapter 15, we discuss SSL/TLS in detail.

> **NOTE** *It is possible for users to install third-party utilities that may remember passwords on behalf of the user and automatically submit those to a website. In that case, the first request may include credentials rather than be an anonymous request.*

If Anonymous authentication is configured for the resource being requested, then IIS 8.0 will attempt to log on the configured anonymous user account. If Anonymous authentication is not configured but one of the other mechanisms is configured, then the server will present a list of available authentication options to the client.

> **NOTE** *If no authentication mechanism is configured at all for a resource, then IIS 8.0 will respond with a 401.2 ("Unauthorized: Logon failure due to server configuration") HTTP error.*

This is done through the use of WWW-Authenticate HTTP headers, one for each possible enabled mechanism. IIS 8.0 will order these from the most preferable to the least preferable (IWA, Digest,

Basic). Within IWA, it is now possible to present a desired order of mechanisms to the client (e.g., Negotiate or NTLM can be presented first). This is an improvement in IIS 8.0 over IIS 7.0. The client will pick the most preferable authentication mechanism that it supports from the list.

> **NOTE** *Browsers typically do not support a "fallback" mechanism that allows them to attempt to use a weaker authentication mechanism if using a stronger authentication mechanism fails. Instead, the browser will continue attempting to use the strongest selected authentication mechanism unless or until either the server or browser configuration is changed.*

For each subsequent request to the server, the browser will continue sending the same credentials. This means that if the previous request was anonymous, then the next request will also be anonymous. If the previous request involved sending credentials, then the next request will contain the same credentials using the same authentication mechanism. This will continue until either:

➤ The client browser process is terminated. It may not be sufficient to simply close the browser if there are still additional spawned windows that exist in the same Windows process. If using a browser that supports tabbed browsing, closing a tab is generally not sufficient either. When the user next visits the resource, he or she will be prompted to supply credentials again.

➤ The server responds with a 401 Unauthorized HTTP status. This causes the browser to prompt the user to supply alternate credentials.

This has important implications for authentication mechanisms, such as Basic authentication, that do not encrypt the user's credentials. After accessing a resource that requires Basic authentication, the browser will continue sending credentials for all subsequent requests even if the subsequent file does not require authentication.

> **NOTE** *There are a few exceptions to this rule. FBA is cookie-based, and as such not reliant on authorization HTTP headers sent from the client. It is possible to create persistent FBA cookies that survive browser restarts, allowing users to authenticate without having to re-enter their credentials. Another exception occurs when using NTLM authentication and a HTTP POST request is made, which is discussed in the "Configuring NTLM Authentication" section.*

Now we discuss each authentication mechanism in detail, including a discussion of the way the mechanism works, minimum requirements on the client and server sides, and configuration options for each. The discussion assumes that the default authentication modules supplied with Windows Server 2012 are used, rather than custom authentication modules. For more information on developing custom modules or replacing supplied modules, see Chapter 12, "Core Server Extensibility."

CONFIGURING ANONYMOUS AUTHENTICATION

When *Anonymous access* is permitted, a remote user is not required to supply credentials to access a file. Instead, IIS 8.0 attempts to use a pre-configured account to access the resource (for example, to read a file off the hard disk). If that account has appropriate rights, then the action (typically to read the file) is performed. If the pre-configured account does not have permission to access the resource, but some other authentication mechanism is enabled that both server and client support, then the user has an opportunity to supply credentials that can access the resource. If no alternate authentication mechanism is enabled or there is no alternate authentication mechanism that both client and server support enabled, then a 401.3 ("Unauthorized due to ACL on resource") HTTP status is generated.

By default, the configured anonymous access account is the IUSR account created when IIS 8.0 is installed. This account replaces the IUSR_<machinename> account used in previous versions of IIS.

> **NOTE** *The AnonymousAuthenticationModule (`authanon.dll`) must be installed and enabled to allow Anonymous authentication. This module is installed by default using an interactive install. Requests for .NET resources (such as ASP .NET ASPX pages or ASMX web services) are not made using the IUSR account. Instead, requests for those resources use the Web Application Pool's identity (by default, NT Authority\Network Service) if ASP.NET impersonation is not enabled. For more information on impersonation, see the "Configuring Authorization" section below in this chapter.*

Anonymous authentication can be configured at a server, website, folder (including virtual directories), or file level. You must be an Administrator on the server, or have delegated permissions, to be able to enable Anonymous authentication for the node in question.

To configure Anonymous authentication:

1. Start IIS Manager. (Press WIN + R, enter **inetmgr** in the dialog, and click OK. Alternatively, click Tools on the top-right of Server Manager and select Internet Information Server [IIS] Manager.)

2. Locate the server, website, folder, or file that you want to configure Anonymous authentication for. Select the Authentication Feature option.

3. Select the Anonymous Authentication option, and click Enable in the Actions pane to enable Anonymous authentication. Click Disable in the Actions pane to disable Anonymous authentication (if currently enabled), as shown in Figure 14-1.

4. Click Edit in the Actions pane to edit Anonymous authentication options, as shown in Figure 14-2. By default, the IUSR account is used for anonymously authenticated access for static files and Classic ASP files (ASP.NET file access occurs under the Web Application Pool's identity).

5. Click the Set button to change the Anonymous authentication identity, supplying the username and password to be used. Alternatively, to return the network identity to IUSR, enter

IUSR as the username, leaving the password blank. To use any other in-built identity (such as LocalSystem, Local Service, or Network Service), supply the username, leaving the password field blank.

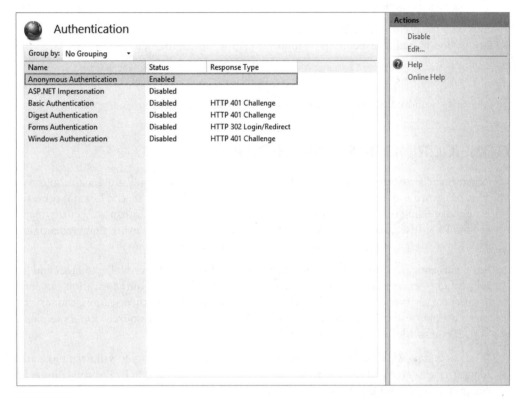

FIGURE 14-1

6. To disable the use of a distinct Anonymous user account and rely entirely on the application pool's identity for all requests, select the "Application pool identity" radio option. The implications for disabling a separate Anonymous authentication user account are discussed below in this chapter.

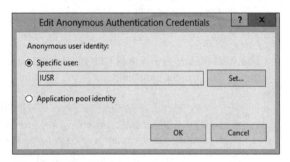

FIGURE 14-2

7. Click OK to confirm your changes.

Enabling and disabling Anonymous authentication can also be performed programmatically using AppCmd or PowerShell. To set a default of enabling Anonymous authentication using AppCmd, execute the following line of code:

```
appcmd.exe set config -section:system.webServer/security/authentication/
anonymousAuthentication /enabled:true
```

To enable Anonymous authentication for a specific website (or other location) using PowerShell, run the following command, setting the -location parameter appropriately:

```
Set-WebConfigurationProperty -filter/system.WebServer/security/authentication/
anonymousAuthentication -name enabled -value true -location "Default Web Site"
```

Enabling the use of a specific pool identity for requests, rather than relying on the default identity, can be configured by executing the following AppCmd command:

```
appcmd.exe set config -section:system.webServer/security/authentication/
anonymousAuthentication /userName:Username /password:Password
```

Identities used by IIS, and their user rights, are discussed later in this chapter.

CONFIGURING BASIC AUTHENTICATION

When *Basic authentication* is enabled, users are prompted to supply a username and password. This password is encoded using Base64 encoding and sent to the server. It is important to note that Base64 encoding is not encryption, and the use of an underlying transport security technology such as SSL/TLS, IPsec, or some VPN technology is recommended to ensure that credentials are not exposed to attackers or devices that are monitoring network traffic.

Basic authentication was introduced as part of the HTTP v1.0 protocol standard, and as such is supported by every major browser. Owing to its simplicity, Basic authentication can safely be used across proxy servers and through firewalls. When using Basic authentication, the server has the user's username and password and can directly access network resources (for example, a remote SQL Server or file server) on behalf of the user.

When accessing a file secured using Basic authentication, the browser will first make an anonymous request. The server will reply with an HTTP 401 (Unauthorized) HTTP status. (Some HTTP headers are not shown for brevity.)

```
HTTP/1.1 401 Unauthorized
Server: Microsoft-IIS/8.0
WWW-Authenticate: Basic
Date: Wed, 25 Jul 2012 09:02:51 GMT
```

The WWW-Authenticate HTTP header indicates that the server supports Basic authentication for clients who want to authenticate.

> **NOTE** *If multiple authentication mechanisms are supported, multiple WWW-Authenticate headers will be returned — for example:*
>
> ```
> HTTP/1.1 401 Unauthorized
> WWW-Authenticate: Negotiate
> WWW-Authenticate: Basic
> ```

To authenticate, the client will take the user's username, append the user's password (separating them with a colon), and Base64-encode the result. For example, for a user User1 and password

Password1, the client would append these two, resulting in User1:Password1, which would then be Base64-encoded to give the result: VXNlcjE6RG9tYWluQQ==.

The client then makes a second request, passing these credentials in an Authorization HTTP header. The request would look similar to the following. (Again, some HTTP headers are omitted for brevity.)

```
GET /default.htm HTTP/1.1
Host: server1
Authorization: Basic VXNlcjE6RG9tYWluQQ==
```

The server will validate the user's credentials and attempt to access the resource. If the user's credentials are invalid or the user is otherwise unable to access the resource, the server will return another 401 HTTP status response. If the user is able to access the resource and perform the requested action (for example, read the file or write data), the server will return a 200 (OK) HTTP response.

The server will continue to respond to invalid credentials with a 401 HTTP status each time a request is made; however, by default, most browsers will allow a user three incorrect attempts before displaying an Unauthorized message in the browser window. The user would need to make another request for the resource (for example, by refreshing their browser window) in order to attempt to authenticate again.

Basic authentication can be configured at a server, website, folder (including virtual directories), or file level. You must be an Administrator on the server or have delegated permissions to be able to enable Basic authentication for the node in question.

> **NOTE** *The use of Basic authentication requires that Anonymous authentication be disabled. When a browser requests a resource, it does not initially send credentials (the request is anonymous). If Anonymous authentication is also enabled, IIS 8.0 will process the request as is and will not challenge the user for credentials (unless the configured anonymous user does not have access to the resource). To force the user to be prompted, Anonymous authentication should be disabled.*
>
> *The Basic Authentication module (`authbas.dll`) must be installed and enabled to allow Basic authentication. This module is not installed by default using an interactive install.*

To configure Basic authentication:

1. Start IIS Manager. (Press WIN + R, enter **inetmgr** in the dialog, and click OK. Alternatively, click Tools on the top-right of Server Manager and select Internet Information Server [IIS] Manager.)

2. Locate the server, website, folder, or file that you wish to configure Basic authentication for. Select the Authentication Feature option.

3. Select the Basic authentication option, and click Enable in the Actions pane to enable Basic authentication. Click Disable in the Actions pane to disable Basic authentication (if currently enabled).

4. Click Edit in the Actions pane to edit Basic authentication settings (Figure 14-3).

5. You may optionally choose to configure a default domain. In the event that a user does not supply a domain (or machine) as part of his or her username, the configured default domain will be inserted by IIS prior to the username. For example, if the user supplies *User1* only as the username and the default domain is configured as *Domain1*, then IIS will attempt to log on the user as Domain1\User1. If no default domain is specified, then the local IIS 8.0 machine's security accounts database (SAM database) will be assumed.

6. You may optionally choose to configure a realm. This information is displayed to the user in the browser's credentials prompt (as shown in Figure 14-4). By making this value the same as the default domain value, users will be aware of which domain IIS 8.0 will be attempting to log on to in the event that a domain is not specified by the user.

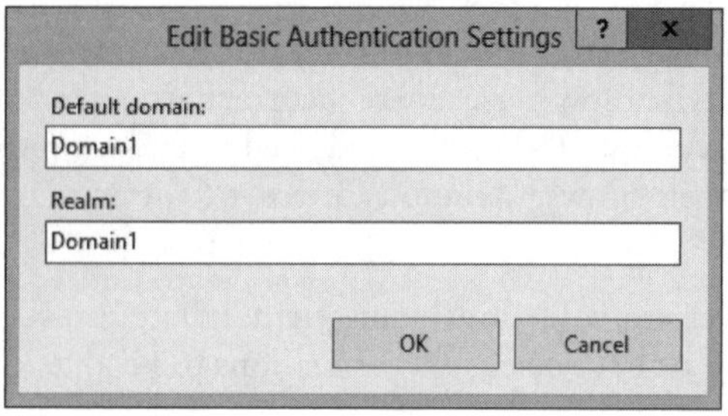

FIGURE 14-3

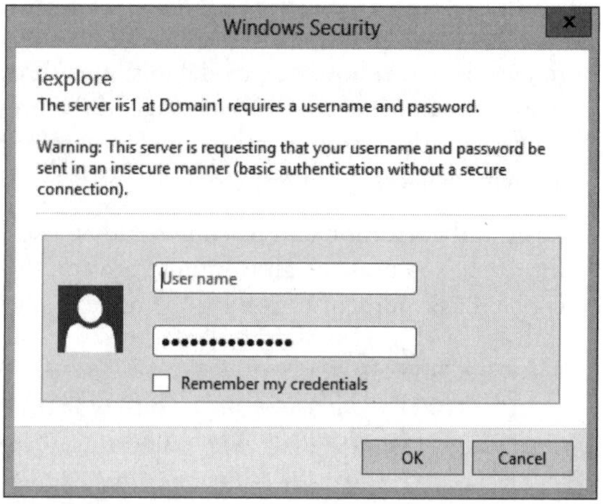

FIGURE 14-4

7. Click OK to commit changes and exit the dialog box.

Enabling and disabling basic authentication can also be performed programmatically. To enable Basic authentication using AppCmd, execute the following line of code:

```
appcmd.exe set config -section:system.webServer/security/authentication/
basicAuthentication /enabled:true
```

To configure the default domain and realm, execute the following command:

```
appcmd.exe set config -section:system.webServer/security/authentication/
basicAuthentication /defaultLogonDomain:DomainName /realm:realmName
```

To enable Basic Configuration for a particular website (in this case, the Default Web Site) using PowerShell, run the following command:

```
Set-WebConfigurationProperty -filter /system.WebServer/security/authentication
/basicAuthentication -name enabled -value true -location "Default Web Site"
```

CONFIGURING DIGEST AUTHENTICATION

When *Digest authentication* is enabled, users are prompted to supply a username and password, similar to Basic authentication. Although the user's username is returned in cleartext to the server, the user's password is not, making Digest authentication significantly more secure than Basic authentication.

Digest authentication was defined in RFC 2069 and updated in RFC 2619. Digest authentication is supported by all major browsers. Like Basic authentication, Digest authentication works through proxy servers and firewalls and can thus be used in most Internet-facing scenarios.

Digest authentication uses hashing algorithms (MD5 in all the cases seen by the authors) to secure the user's password. A hashing algorithm is a mathematical process that is easy to compute, but, given the hash of a value, difficult (or impossible) to determine the original value. For example, when using the mathematical functions Sine and Cosine, a value is easy to compute, but deducing the original value is impossible because, for every given value of $Sin(x)$, there are an infinite number of starting possible values when attempting to perform the inverse function.

In order to validate the user's identity, the server must also have an MD5 hash of the user's password. The local Security Accounts Manager (SAM) database has no facility for storing the MD5 hash of a user's password; thus, Digest authentication cannot be used for local accounts. In a Windows 2000 (or Mixed Mode) domain, passwords must be stored using the "Reversible Encryption" option for the user's Active Directory account. After enabling this option, the user's password must be changed to allow a domain controller to store a copy that can be decrypted. When authenticating a client using Digest authentication, the domain controller can decrypt this copy and perform an MD5 hash on it.

For a Windows Server 2003 (or higher) functional level domain, various hashes of user passwords are calculated automatically when a user's password is set, and stored in the `AltSecID` attribute of the user's account in the directory. For these functional level domains, no additional configuration is required to use Digest authentication. However, it is important to note that the MD5 hashing algorithm is case sensitive; the realm value must be set to the case-sensitive value of the Domain name or, alternatively, the realm field can be left blank when users are in the same domain as the IIS server. This is shown later in this section.

> **NOTE** *The previous section looked at Basic authentication, where the server has the user's username and password in cleartext. In that scenario, if IIS 8.0 needs to pass the user's credentials to another back-end server (for example, to a back-end database server like Microsoft SQL Server), it can do so directly. When you use a protocol such as Digest authentication, IIS 8.0 does not have the user's password. In order to access a back-end service using the user's credentials, you need to enable both delegation and protocol transition. These are discussed below in this chapter.*

When accessing a file secured using Digest authentication, the browser will first make an anonymous request. The server will reply with an HTTP 401 (Unauthorized) HTTP status. (Some HTTP headers are not shown for brevity.)

```
HTTP/1.1 401 UnauthorizedServer: Microsoft-IIS/8.0
WWW-Authenticate: Digest qop="auth",
algorithm=MD5sess,
nonce="+Upgraded+v1cd489ce150a8bac955cb7dd6dfca6ab709ccc0287170cd01330d4c9d4455e
05bf894cd3dece97a47998dc0060be74c4122a220b77089f2a7",charset=utf-8,
realm="Digest"
Date: Wed, 25 Jul 2012 05:39:18 GMT
```

The WWW-Authenticate HTTP header is presented as a single line by the server. Line breaks were added for readability purposes only.

RFC 2619 defined two options for the QOP (Quality of Protection) field: *auth* and *auth-int* (authentication with integrity). The second option is not currently implemented by IIS 8.0. The algorithm field specifies the hashing algorithm to be used by the client. The Nonce value is randomly determined by the server and is to be used by the client as part of the authentication protocol. The realm value is also used by the client as part of the authentication process. If the server does not define a realm value, the value "Digest" is used.

To authenticate, the client performs several operations, resulting in a final authentication code that is returned to the server. (Some HTTP headers are omitted for brevity.) Additionally, the Authorization header, when sent from the browser, does not contain line breaks — they have been inserted for readability purposes only.

```
GET / HTTP/1.1
Authorization: Digest
  username="User1",
  realm="Digest",
nonce="+Upgraded+v1cd489ce150a8bac955cb7dd6dfca6ab709ccc0287170cd01330d4c9d4455e05bf894
cd3dece97a47998dc0060be74c4122a220b77089f2a7",uri="/iisstart.htm",
cnonce="+Upgraded+v1d25a8f7ab4b201f03ea7b337b15cc2296653d76e690a5e91ca3ee768061d320f",
  nc=00000001,
  algorithm=MD5-sess,
  response="3d92886ae6777254d37b125fcc08ccc4",
  qop="auth",
  charset=utf-8,
Host: iis1
```

The Response field above contains the authentication information generated by the client. It is calculated as follows:

1. The user's username, realm (in this case, Windows domain), and password are concatenated (each item is separated by a colon) and then hashed to generate a temporary value (Value1).

2. The HTTP method (in this case, GET) and the requested URI (in this case, the root folder /) are concatenated (again separated by a colon) and hashed to generate a second temporary value (Value2).

3. The following items are then concatenated (again with a colon separating each item) and a hash generated: Value1, server-supplied nonce (nonce above), request counter (nc), client

nonce (cnonce), quality of protection field (qop), and Value2. This final value is the Response field provided by the client to the server.

Because the server has access to the same information (with the exception that a domain controller stores Value1 as a pre-calculated value when the user's account is created in a Windows Server 2003 or higher functional level domain), it is able to perform the same calculations and derive a Response value. If the client-provided Response value matches the one calculated by the server, then the user is deemed authenticated.

Digest authentication protects users and applications against a variety of malicious attacks by incorporating pieces of information about the request as inputs to the hashing algorithm. For example, by incorporating the URI and HTTP method, the response code varies as a user requests different files, preventing an attacker from reusing a captured response code to request other files. Additionally, the client must always supply higher values for the request counter when using the same server nonce (for example, by incrementing the value for each request), resulting in an altered response code, even for subsequent requests for the same file. The server remembers the last received nc (request counter) value for each nonce that it currently has issued, and rejects requests that supply nc values that are the same or lower than the last used value. This prevents replay attacks, where an attacker captures packets on the network and then retransmits them to the server later, effectively impersonating the original user.

Digest authentication can be configured at a server, website, folder (including virtual directories), or file level. You must be an Administrator on the server or have delegated permissions to be able to enable Digest authentication for the node in question.

The use of Digest authentication requires that Anonymous authentication be disabled. When a browser requests a resource, it does not initially send credentials (the request is anonymous). If Anonymous authentication is also enabled, IIS 8.0 will process the request as is and will not challenge the user for credentials (unless the configured anonymous user does not have access to the resource). To force the user to be prompted, Anonymous authentication should be disabled.

> **NOTE** *The Digest Authentication module (*authmd5.dll*) must be installed and enabled to allow Digest authentication. This module is not installed by default using an interactive install.*

To configure Digest authentication:

1. Start IIS Manager. (Press WIN + R, enter **inetmgr** in the dialog, and click OK. Alternatively, click Tools on the top-right of Server Manager and select Internet Information Server [IIS] Manager.)

2. Locate the server, website, folder, or file that you want to configure Digest authentication for. Select the Authentication Feature option.

3. Select the Digest Authentication option and click Enable in the Actions pane to enable Digest authentication. Click Disable in the Actions pane to disable Digest authentication (if currently enabled).

4. Click Edit in the Actions pane to edit the Digest authentication settings (Figure 14-5).

Optionally, you can choose to configure a realm. This information is displayed to the user in the browser's credentials prompt (as shown in Figure 14-6).

5. Click OK to commit changes and exit the dialog.

Edit Digest Authentication Settings	?	X

Realm:

[   ]

[OK] [Cancel]

FIGURE 14-5

Windows Security [X]

iexplore
The server iis1 at Domain1 requires a username and password.

[User name]

[●●●●●●●●●●●●●]

[ ] Remember my credentials

[OK] [Cancel]

FIGURE 14-6

> **NOTE** *If using Windows 2000, functional-level user passwords must be stored using Reversible Encryption. This can be configured in two ways: on the account properties page of the user account in Active Directory, or by using a Group Policy Object (GPO). If configuring a GPO, the setting is found under Computer Policy ⇨ Windows Settings ⇨ Security Settings ⇨ Account Policies ⇨ Password Policies ⇨ Store Passwords using Reversible Encryption. Be aware that storing passwords using Reversible Encryption is a security risk*

> **NOTE** *The MD5 hashing algorithm is case-sensitive. This means that the hash of the value "User1" is different from the hash of the value "USER1" and is different again from the hash of the value "user1." Because a Windows Server 2003 functional level domain does not store passwords using reversible encryption by default, it is not possible for a domain controller to examine the case of the username supplied by the browser and then calculate the appropriate MD5 hash on-the-fly (as the domain controller does not have the password). Therefore, several pre-computed hashes are stored: one hash generated using the exact case of the user's sAMAccountName as well as additional variations (e.g., username entirely in lowercase and entirely in uppercase). The user must supply his or her username in one of these cases; otherwise, authentication will fail.*

> *Additionally, if a realm value is configured, it must be entered using the case-sensitive value of the domain name. Alternatively, if users and the IIS server exist in the same domain, the realm field can be left blank, and IIS will automatically assume that the user is in the same domain.*

Enabling and disabling digest authentication can also be performed programmatically using AppCmd or Powershell. To set Digest Authentication to enabled as a default for all sites using AppCmd, execute the following command:

```
appcmd.exe set config -section:system.webServer/security/authentication/
digestAuthentication /enabled:true
```

To enable Digest Authentication for a specific site using PowerShell, run the following command:

```
Set-WebConfigurationProperty -filter /system.WebServer/security/authentication/
digestAuthentication -name enabled -value true -location "Default Web Site"
```

To configure the realm using AppCmd, execute the following command:

```
appcmd.exe set config -section:system.webServer/security/authentication/
digestAuthentication /realm:realmName
```

CONFIGURING INTEGRATED WINDOWS AUTHENTICATION

IWA encompasses two separate authentication protocols: NTLM and Kerberos. By default, both of these two options are made available when enabling IWA.

In this first section, we will cover the common IWA features, and how to adjust between NTLM and Kerberos. In the subsequent two sections we will cover NTLM and Kerberos, respectively, in depth, including prerequisites, usage scenarios, and relative strengths and weaknesses.

To configure IWA:

1. Start IIS Manager. (Press WIN + R, enter **inetmgr** in the dialog, and click OK. Alternatively, click Tools on the top-right of Server Manager and select Internet Information Server [IIS] Manager.)

2. Locate the server, website, folder, or file that you want to configure IWA for. Select the Authentication Feature option.

3. Select the Windows Authentication option and click Enable in the Actions pane to enable IWA. Click Disable in the Actions pane to disable IWA (if currently enabled).

4. Click Advanced Settings in the Actions pane to edit the IWA authentication settings (Figure 14-7):

    a. Choose whether to offer or require Extended Protection (see note below). By default Extended Protection is off.

    b. Choose whether to use kernel-mode authentication. Kernel-mode authentication provides improved performance during authentication, and can also simplify Service

Principal Name (SPN) management in some scenarios. SPNs are discussed later in this chapter. Kernel-mode authentication is enabled by default.

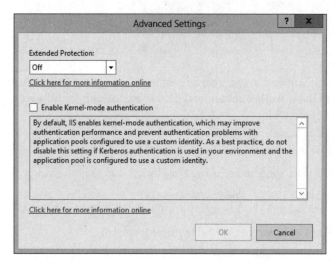

FIGURE 14-7

5. Click OK to commit changes and exit the dialog.

6. Click the Providers link in the Action pane to change the IWA options that IIS will present to end users (Figure 14-8):

   a. By default Negotiate and NTLM providers are enabled (in that order). Negotiate allows the client and server to negotiate between Kerberos and NTLM.

   b. To have IIS present authentication options in a different order, select either Negotiate or NTLM and click the Move Up or Move Down buttons.

   c. To add an additional provider, select an available provider from the drop-down list and click Add. Negotiate:Kerberos is the most likely to be used here;

FIGURE 14-8

   it presents Negotiate as an authentication option to clients but blocks non-Kerberos responses. Negotiate:PKU2U is typically used in Windows 7 Home Group situations and other peer-to-peer scenarios that Microsoft may devise in the future.

7. Clikc OK to commit changes and exit the dialog.

> **NOTE** *Extended Protection is a security feature added to IIS to help address the security issues identified in KB 974926* (http://technet.microsoft.com/ en-us/security/advisory/974926). *It is designed to protect against "man in the middle" replay attacks, where an attacker can obtain a client's authenticator (e.g., by tricking the user into visiting a malicious website) and then re-use that authenticator to connect to another server pretending to be the end user. Extended protection does this by adding some additional information to the authentication process that includes identifiers of the service being connected to by the original end user. When the authenticator is subsequently re-used for another service, the information no longer matches. Detailed information on Extended Protection can be found at* http://blogs.technet.com/b/srd/ archive/2009/12/08/extended-protection-for-authentication.aspx.
>
> *Using Extended Protection requires support from both the client and server. Microsoft has released updates for all operating systems from Windows XP onward, and for IE5.01 SP4 onwards to support Extended Protection. Extended Protection is most likely to be useful in controlled environments where both clients and servers can be updated to support this functionality.*

CONFIGURING NTLM AUTHENTICATION

NTLM is a proprietary Microsoft protocol suite that can be used both for HTTP-based authentication and non-HTTP-based authentication. It provides similar capabilities as Digest authentication, but predated the development of Digest authentication. Recognizing the need for a more robust authentication mechanism than Basic authentication and with the necessary security infrastructure already existing in Windows, Microsoft adapted both Internet Explorer and IIS to support NTLM-based authentication (also known as *NT Challenge/Response Authentication* in IIS 4.0).

Despite being a proprietary Microsoft protocol, most modern browsers in addition to Internet Explorer v3 and higher (such as Chrome, Mozilla/Firefox, and Opera) support NTLM-based authentication. When used to authenticate clients over HTTP, NTLM authentication is a connection-oriented mechanism. This requires that the HTTP connection be maintained through the use of HTTP keep-alive functionality. If the server or browser is configured not to use keep-alives, then NTLM authentication will fail. For this reason, it is sometimes said that NTLM authentication does not work through forward proxy servers, because forward proxy servers typically do not permit an end-to-end persistent HTTP connection that can be reused by the end-client for subsequent HTTP requests. In the event that clients are behind a forward proxy server, it must be NTLM-aware in order for NTLM authentication to work.

NTLM authentication can be used for both domain and local accounts, unlike Digest authentication (or Kerberos authentication), which can only be used for domain accounts. This makes NTLM ideal for use in workgroup scenarios or between domains where no trust relationship exists.

Two versions of NTLM exist (v1 and v2). IIS 8.0 only supports NTLM v2; NTLM v1 has been shown to be cryptographically compromised and is not recommended for use. When configuring a Windows computer's local security policy (or configuring its settings via domain-based Group Policy), NTLM v2 support must remain enabled for NTLM authentication over HTTP to work. For brevity, the rest of the chapter will not explicitly mention the NTLM version number — v2 is assumed.

After enabling IWA in IIS 8.0, two WWW-Authenticate headers are sent to clients by default. The following table outlines under which circumstances NTLM will be used:

HEADER SENT	AUTHENTICATION ATTEMPTED
WWW-Authenticate: Negotiate	Kerberos, if requirements for it are met; otherwise, NTLM v2. See the "Configuring Kerberos Authentication" section later in this chapter for Kerberos requirements. The Negotiate header uses the Microsoft implementation of SPNEGO and GSSAPI to allow a client to negotiate an acceptable authentication mechanism.
WWW-Authenticate: NTLM	NTLM v2. The NTLM header uses the Microsoft NTLM SSP (Security Support Provider) to authenticate the client using NTLM v2.

Steps to customize which HTTP headers are sent to the client are discussed in the previous section.

Internet Explorer, by default, will attempt to automatically log in the current user when a website is using NTLM or Negotiate security, and the website is in the browser's intranet security zone. This can allow an organization to obviate the need for users to authenticate to their workstations, and then authenticate again to internal websites, effectively implementing a rudimentary form of Single Sign On (SSO). What Internet Explorer determines to be the intranet security zone automatically is listed in the Microsoft KB article 258063 (http:// support.microsoft.com/?id=258063).

Internet Explorer's behavior can be altered by editing the settings at Tools ⇨ Internet Options ⇨ Security ⇨ Intranet zone ⇨ Custom Level ⇨ "Automatic logon only in Intranet zone" (Figure 14-9). This setting can also be set centrally via a Group Policy Object if a large number of machines need to be configured.

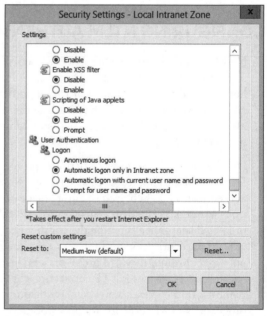

FIGURE 14-9

When accessing a file secured using NTLM authentication, the browser will first make an anonymous request. The server will reply with an HTTP 401 (Unauthorized) HTTP status. As NTLM is a three-step challenge/response process, the client needs to send two requests in addition to the initial anonymous request to authenticate successfully. The server's response to the initial anonymous request will be as follows (Some HTTP headers are not shown for brevity.)

```
HTTP/1.1 401 Unauthorized
Server: Microsoft-IIS/8.0
WWW-Authenticate: NTLM
Date: Wed, 15 Aug 2012 05:56:21 GMT
Proxy-Support: Session-Based-Authentication
```

The client now replies with an NTLM Type 1 request. This request contains several individual pieces of information: the version of NTLM used, what levels of encryption are supported, and whether message signing is supported.

This information is Base64-encoded and sent to the server, as shown below. (Some HTTP headers are omitted for brevity.)

```
GET http://localhost/iisstart.htm HTTP/1.1
Accept: */*
Accept-Encoding: gzip, deflate
Connection: Keep-Alive
Authorization: NTLM
TlRMTVNTUAABAAAAB7IIogcABwAsAAAABAAEACgAAAAGAjogAAAAD0lJUzFET01BSU4x
Host: localhost
```

The server now responds with an HTTP 401 (Unauthorized) HTTP status and a Type 2 NTLM message. This message includes information about the security features supported by the client (e.g., message signing), as well as those that are required by the server. Additionally the "challenge" (similar to the nonce in Digest authentication) is sent as part of this message. The next request from the client will be the "response" (hence Challenge/Response authentication).

The data above is Base64-encoded and sent to the client. (Some HTTP headers are omitted for brevity.)

```
HTTP/1.1 401 Unauthorized
Server: Microsoft-IIS/8.0
WWW-Authenticate: NTLM
TlRMTVNTUAACAAAADgAOADgAAAAFwomi7BcvirGGndJQUKTsFgAAAJIAkgBGAAAABgI6IAAAAA9
EAE8ATQBBAEkATgAxAAIADgBEAE8ATQBBAEkATgAxAAEACABJAEkAUwAxAAQAGgBEAG8AbQBhAG
kAbgAxAC4AbABvAGMAYQBsAAMAJABJAEkAUwAxAC4ARABvAG0AYQBpAG4AMQAuAGwAbwBjAGEAb
AAFABoARABvAG0AYQBpAG4AMQAuAGwAbwBjAGEAbAAHAAgAgAM7bsIa16zQEAAAAA
Date: Wed, 15 Aug 2012 06:13:48 GMT
Proxy-Support: Session-Based-Authentication
```

In the final part of an NTLM authentication handshake, the client now replies with a Type 3 NTLM message. This contains the client's authentication information derived from the user's password and the challenge sent by the server in the Type 2 message.

The NTLM response data is derived as follows:

1. The MD4 algorithm is applied to the Unicode user password, resulting in Value1.

2. The uppercase username is concatenated with the uppercase target realm (domain or server name), and the HMAC-MD5 algorithm is applied to this value using Value1 as a key. This results in Value2.

3. A random 8-byte client nonce is created.

4. The server challenge is concatenated with the random client nonce, and the HMAC-MD5 is calculated using Value2 as a key. This results in a 16-byte value (Value3).

The data above is Base64-encoded and sent to the client. (Some HTTP headers are omitted for brevity.)

```
GET http://localhost/iisstart.htm HTTP/1.1
Accept: */*
Accept-Encoding: gzip, deflate
Connection: Keep-Alive
Host: localhost
Authorization: NTLM
TlRMTVNTUAADAAAAAAAAAFgAAAAAAAAWAAAAAAAABYAAAAAAAAAFgAAAAAA
AAWAAAAAAAAABYAAAABcKIogYCOiAAAAAPBL6murVga0NdTxvOVAeKbg==
```

As the server (or domain controller, for domain accounts) has access to the same information, it is able to perform the same calculations and derive a Response value. If the client-provided Response value matches the one calculated by the server, then the user is deemed authenticated.

> **NOTE** *Owing to the multistep authentication process, IIS log files will record two 401 HTTP status requests while a client is authenticating, followed by a 200 OK request. This is expected behavior.*

NTLM authentication varies from other authentication mechanisms in that the underlying HTTP connection is authenticated. As such, for subsequent requests, no credentials are sent by the client to the server. Instead, the underlying HTTP connection must be kept open via HTTP *keep-alive* functionality (this allows a HTTP connection to be kept open for subsequent HTTP requests). If the connection is closed, the authentication process must begin again.

> **NOTE** *An exception is when a client needs to send data using the HTTP POST method. Because it is possible that the server may reject the client's credentials (resulting in multiple additional requests, all reposting the same information, consuming bandwidth and delaying the final response), the client does not attempt an authenticated POST request. Instead, it preemptively sends a Type 1 message (but without the POST data). This initiates another NTLM handshake so that the client can verify that the existing credentials are acceptable to the server. Only with the Type 3 message does the client post the form data to the server.*

NTLM authentication can be configured at a server, website, folder (including virtual directories), or file level. You must be an Administrator on the server or have delegated permissions to be able to enable NTLM authentication for the node in question.

The use of NTLM authentication requires that Anonymous authentication be disabled. When a browser requests a resource, it does not initially send credentials (the request is anonymous). If Anonymous authentication is also enabled, IIS 8.0 will process the request as is and will not challenge the user for credentials (unless the configured anonymous user does not have access to the resource). To force the user to be prompted, Anonymous authentication should be disabled.

> **NOTE** *The Windows Authentication module (*`authsspi.dll`*) must be installed and enabled to allow NTLM authentication. This module is not installed by default using an interactive install.*

Configuring Kerberos Authentication

Kerberos v5 authentication is an open, industry-standard, ticket-based authentication method first developed at MIT. It uses a variety of techniques to avoid eavesdropping/passive sniffing attacks and replay attacks. It supports mutual authentication of the client and server to each other.

Kerberos authentication relies on a trusted third party. In a Windows domain, this is a domain controller. For this reason, Kerberos authentication can only be used for Active Directory domain accounts. A client needs to contact a domain controller to obtain the necessary Kerberos tickets. For this reason, Kerberos authentication is commonly said to fail across firewalls. This is not because firewalls cannot pass Kerberos traffic, but because firewalls are typically deployed at the edge of a network (that is, bordering an internal network and the wider Internet), and most firewalls deny traffic from the Internet to internal domain controllers.

Kerberos authentication was first introduced with Windows Server 2000 and can be used for HTTP and non-HTTP authentication. Internet Explorer 5.0 was the first version of IE to support Kerberos authentication. Kerberos authentication can only be used for Active Directory domain accounts and thus is not available in workgroup scenarios or for local accounts. Internet Explorer will attempt Kerberos authentication in the following circumstances:

➤ IWA (requires a restart) is enabled under Internet Explorer ➪ Tools ➪ Internet Options ➪ Advanced. This is enabled by default, except under certain circumstances on Windows 2000. For more information, see `http://support.microsoft.com/Default.aspx?id=299838`.

➤ The client operating system must be Windows 2000, Windows XP, Windows Vista, Windows 7, Windows 8, or Windows Server 2000 (and newer). Windows NT and Windows 9x do not support Kerberos authentication by default.

➤ The website must be in Internet Explorer's Intranet security zone or the Trusted Sites security zone. If the website is in the Internet security zone, then IE will not attempt Kerberos authentication, as typically the browser cannot contact a domain controller in an Internet scenario. For more information on how IE determines whether a site is in the Intranet zone, see `http://support.microsoft.com/?id=258063`. For the Trusted Sites zone, the website must be added manually or via Group Policy Objects (GPO). To add a site via GPO to the Intranet or Trusted Sites zones, open Group Policy Editor and navigate to Computer/User Configuration ➪ Administrative Templates ➪ Internet Explorer ➪ Internet Explorer Control Panel ➪ Security Page ➪ Site to Zone Assignment.

➤ The client must be able to contact a Kerberos KDC (Key Distribution Center). In an Active Directory domain, this is hosted on domain controllers. The KDC must have a corresponding registered SPN or be able to refer the client to another KDC that does have the SPN registered.

➤ An appropriate SPN must be registered. When installing IIS 8.0, SPNs are automatically registered for `http://servername` and `http://servername.ADDomain` in Active Directory. If you are using a custom name (either NetBIOS or fully qualified domain name) to access the server, you may need to register an appropriate SPN. SPNs are explained in more detail below in this section.

How Kerberos Authentication Works

As Kerberos authentication is a far more complex mechanism than previously described protocols, a brief section here will explain the process by which a client authenticates using Kerberos.

Kerberos authentication involves three parties: the client, the remote service that the client wants to access, and a trusted third party. The third party is known as the Kerberos Key Distribution Center (KDC) and is hosted on each domain controller in a Windows Active Directory domain.

To authenticate to the remote service, the client initially contacts the KDC to get a Ticket Granting Ticket (TGT). The TGT enables the client to subsequently contact the KDC for additional authentication tickets. It obviates the need for the client machine to continually ask for the user's password or to cache the user's password in memory. The TGT has a validity of 8 hours by default on a Windows Active Directory domain.

To get a TGT, the client contacts the KDC (specifically, a service called the Authorization Service, or AS), indicating its name. In an Active Directory domain, a process called *pre-authentication* is performed to authenticate the client, but that is beyond the scope of this book. The KDC verifies that the client (user or machine) exists in Active Directory, and if so generates two pieces of information. The first is a session key (Session Key 1) that will be used to secure communications between the KDC and the client. The second is the TGT.

The first piece of information is encrypted using a key derived from the user's password. Since both the KDC and the user know what this is, the user will be able to decrypt the session key. The TGT is encrypted using a secret known only to the KDC. If you have ever wondered what the disabled *krbtgt* user account is for in a Windows Active Directory domain — its password is used to derive the key to encrypt the TGT.

The KDC returns both pieces of information to the client. The client decrypts the session key using its knowledge of the user's password. The client is now able to authenticate to the KDC to obtain service tickets for remote services.

To authenticate to a remote HTTP website, the client contacts the KDC for a service ticket. As before, the client contacts the TGS. The client supplies its details encrypted with Session Key 1, as well as the previously provided TGT. Since only the client could decrypt the package containing Session Key 1, the KDC knows that the client is legitimate.

The TGS of the KDC now prepares two pieces of information to give back to the client. The first is a new session key (let's call this Session Key 2) that the client will use when talking to the remote HTTP service. This data is encrypted using Session Key 1. The second piece of data contains identifying pieces of information about the client (for example, the username) as well as a second copy of Session Key 2. This data is encrypted using a key derived from data that only the KDC and the HTTP service know (namely, the machine or user account password that the HTTP service is running under). This is known as the "service ticket."

The client receives these two pieces of information. It can only decrypt the first piece, and it extracts the session key that it should use to communicate with the HTTP service.

In the final step of the authentication process, the client now sends two pieces of information to the HTTP service. The first is the service ticket received from the KDC. The second is the current time on the client, and this is encrypted using Session Key 2 (the key used to secure transmission between the client and HTTP service). This is known as the "authenticator."

The HTTP service receives the two pieces of information. It decrypts the first part using its own password. This contains a copy of Session Key 2, as well as the client's identity. The HTTP service uses Session Key 2 to decrypt the authenticator and extract the time stamp. It compares the time to its own current system time. If a significant discrepancy exists (more than 5 minutes, after accounting for time zone differences, in a default Active Directory configuration), then a replay attack is assumed to be occurring. Otherwise, the client is considered authenticated.

Figure 14-10 illustrates the process. The following information is exchanged:

1. Initial client request

2. Session Key 1 (encrypted with user password) and TGT

3. Request for service ticket (encrypted with Session Key 1) and TGT

4. Session Key 2 (encrypted with Session Key 1) and Service Ticket (encrypted with HTTP service's password)

5. Time Stamp/Authenticator (encrypted with Session Key 2) and Service Ticket (encrypted with HTTP service's password)

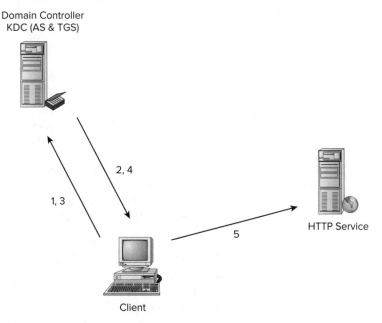

FIGURE 14-10

Service Principal Names

Kerberos authentication relies on the trusted third party (KDC) to vouch for the authenticity of the client to the server. To do this, the KDC encrypts information about the client using a secret known only to itself and the service.

In order for the KDC to know which secret to use, the client must tell the KDC what service it wishes to access, and the KDC needs some way of determining the appropriate secret for that service. This occurs through the use of Service Principal Names (SPNs).

Service Principal Names (SPNs) are attributes of user or computer objects in Active Directory. When a client wishes to access a particular service, it tells the KDC the SPN of the service it wishes to access, and the KDC searches Active Directory for that SPN. If there is a match, the KDC uses the password of the machine or user that the SPN is registered under as the basis of the secret.

For this reason, it is important not to have duplicate SPNs within Active Directory. If an SPN is accidentally registered under two different objects, then the KDC will not know which password should be used to encrypt the service ticket, and Kerberos authentication will fail.

You can add and remove SPNs by using the `SetSPN.exe` command-line tool, included with Windows Server 2012. `SetSPN.exe` does not need to be run on a domain controller, but rather any domain-joined machine that is Windows 2000 or later. For operating systems that do not have SetSPN included, it can be downloaded from Microsoft's website, at `http://support.microsoft.com/kb/970536`.

Registering an SPN requires the following information: a protocol prefix, the machine name (for example, the NetBIOS name or the fully qualified domain name) used by the client to access the service, an optional port number, and the user or machine account that the SPN should be registered under. For example, to access a website at `www.domainA.local` that is running on machine server1, you would use the following code:

```
setspn.exe -A HTTP/www.domainA.local domainA\server1
```

To remove an existing SPN, use the `-D` option, as follows:

```
setspn.exe -D HTTP/www.domainA.local
```

To list all SPNs registered under a particular user or computer account, use the `-L` option:

```
setspn.exe -L domainA\server1
```

When adding a machine to a domain, default SPNs are added for HOST/machinename and HOST/machinename.domainname. This provides Kerberos authentication to websites accessed using either `http://machinename` or `http://machinename.domainname` (HTTPS access also works). If accessing a website by any other name(s) (for example, a custom FQDN), then an SPN must be registered for that FQDN.

In prior versions of Windows (for example, Windows Server 2003), the SPN was registered under the server's machine account if the web application pool (`w3wp.exe` process) was running under an intrinsic security principal (LocalSystem, Network Service, or Local Service). If the web application pool was being run under a custom domain user account, then SPN was registered under that domain user account. If the web application pool was being run under a custom local user account, Kerberos authentication could not be used.

As mentioned in the earlier section on configuring IWA, Windows Server 2012 offers an option to use *kernel-mode authentication*. In this case, the SPN is registered under the machine account no matter which security principal is used to host the worker process. This simplifies SPN management and also improves performance by moving authentication to kernel mode.

If you elect *not* to use kernel-mode authentication, then the same rules that applied to previous versions of Windows apply. If the web application pool is being hosted under a custom domain account, the SPN must be registered under that user account, rather than the machine account. Additionally, since an SPN is based on a machine name, all web applications hosted at that machine name (for example, www.domainA.local) must run in the same web application pool or separate web application pools running under the same account. That account must be the account that the SPN is registered under.

In a *web farm scenario* (where there are multiple load-balanced web servers, using either Windows Network Load Balancing or an external hardware load balancer), the following rules apply:

➤ The KDC does not know ahead of time which physical machine will receive the request. In order to encrypt the service ticket, it must be encrypted using credentials that can be decrypted on any of the machines in the web farm.

➤ To facilitate this, the web application pools participating in the farm must be run under a custom domain user account, and the SPN for the virtual host name must be registered under this domain user account. The KDC can use the password of this account as the basis for encrypting the service ticket.

➤ Kernel-mode authentication must be disabled on each website participating in the web farm. As a result, the custom user account being used as the identity of the web application pool can decrypt the service ticket from the client.

Enabling Kerberos Authentication

You can configure Kerberos authentication at a server, website, folder (including virtual directories), or file level. You must be an Administrator on the server or have delegated permissions to be able to enable Kerberos authentication for the node in question. The steps for enabling and configuring Kerberos authentication are shown under the "Configuring Integrated Windows Authentication" section earlier in this chapter.

> **NOTE** *The use of Kerberos authentication requires that Anonymous authentication be disabled. When a browser requests a resource, it does not initially send credentials (the request is anonymous). If Anonymous authentication is also enabled, IIS 8.0 will process the request as is and will not challenge the user for credentials (unless the configured anonymous user does not have access to the resource). To force the user to be prompted, Anonymous authentication should be disabled.*

CONFIGURING UNC AUTHENTICATION

UNC authentication allows you to configure IIS to use a specified user account when accessing resources on a remote share. When creating a virtual directory (or web application) that points to a UNC (Universal Naming Convention) share, credentials can be provided for accessing that share. If no credentials are provided, then IIS 8.0 will attempt to use the currently impersonated user. The currently impersonated user may be:

➤ The application pool's user identity (if Anonymous authentication is being permitted). If the application pool's identity is Network Service, then the machine account (machinename$) is used.

➤ The authenticated end user's account is used, if Basic authentication is used.

➤ The web application pool's user account if Digest or NTLM authentication is used. For these two authentication mechanisms, IIS 8.0 does not have the user's password and therefore is unable to authenticate as the user to the remote resource unless protocol transition is configured and enabled (see the section, "Configuring Protocol Transition," below in this chapter).

➤ The authenticated end user if Kerberos authentication is used and delegation is configured (see the "Configuring Delegation" section later in this chapter). Otherwise, if delegation is not configured or fails, the access will be by the user account hosting the web application pool.

To configure UNC authentication:

1. Open IIS Manager. (Press WIN + R, enter **inetmgr** in the dialog, and click OK. Alternatively, click Tools on the top-right of Server Manager and select Internet Information Server [IIS] Manager.)

2. Locate the server, website, or folder at which you wish to add a new virtual directory or web application. Right-click and choose Add Virtual Directory.

3. Enter the alias that the directory should be accessed under and the UNC path (`\\servername\sharename`) to the remote resource. Do not use the drive letters used, as drive-letter mappings are valid for the logged-on user only (see Figure 14-11).

4. Click the "Connect as" button to alter the credentials used to connect to the remote share. Choose the Specific User option to set a user account to be used regardless of the end user. Enter the username and password when prompted. Alternatively, select the Application User ("Pass-through authentication")

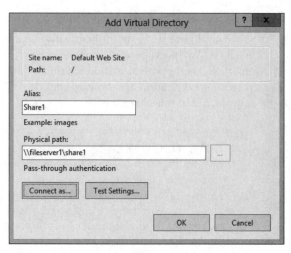

FIGURE 14-11

option if the end user's credentials (or the web application pool's credentials in the absence of an end user's credentials) should be used (see Figure 14-12).

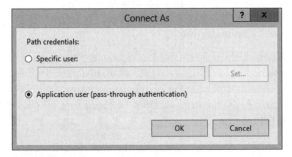

FIGURE 14-12

5. Click OK to exit the dialog.

> **NOTE** *The web application pool's account must also have access to the remote share. This has been a requirement since IIS 7.0 and is a result of that account needing to be able to read any* web.config *files that may be located on the remote share. In previous versions of IIS, all configuration was stored in the central metabase and therefore no access rights were required for the web application pool identity. If the web application pool identity is Network Service, then granting the machinename$ account access to the remote share is sufficient. This is only possible in an Active Directory domain scenario.*

CONFIGURING CLIENT CERTIFICATE AUTHENTICATION

Client Certificate authentication works by having a client present a user authentication certificate issued by a trusted root Certificate Authority, which is then mapped to a Windows security principal (user account).

> **NOTE** *The Client Certificate is presented by the client to the server as part of an SSL or TLS handshake. As such, use of Client Certificates for authentication requires enabling SSL/TLS on a website. For more information on SSL/TLS, see Chapter 15.*

IIS 8.0 supports three Client Certificate authentication mechanisms:

➤ **One-to-One Client Mapping** — When this is enabled, each individual trusted user certificate is mapped, one by one, to a Windows user account. Some certificates may be mapped to a shared user account, or each certificate may be mapped to an individual user account. When the certificate is presented to IIS 8.0, it logs on the corresponding user.

➤ **Many-to-One Client Mapping** — When this is enabled, multiple trusted user certificates are mapped to a single Windows user account. This is similar to the One-to-One mapping but doesn't provide the fine-grained options of restricting certain users to certain parts of the website. Instead, all certificates that are trusted will be permitted the same access. This option provides less flexibility but reduces administration.

➤ **Active Directory Mapping** — When enabled, certificates are passed to Active Directory. If the certificate has been explicitly assigned by a domain Administrator to a user within the directory, then that user is logged on. Alternatively, if the certificate contains a UPN (Universal Principal Name: user@domainA.local) that matches a UPN assigned to a user account in Active Directory, then that user is logged on.

One-to-One and *Many-to-One client mappings* are most useful when users accessing the site are external to your organization, or your organization does not have an internal PKI (Public Key Infrastructure). In this case, you must manually associate issued certificates with valid Windows users within your internal Active Directory domain or with valid local Windows users on the IIS 8.0 server.

Active Directory mapping is most suitable when your users are internal, and most useful when you have Active Directory Certificate Services (formerly Microsoft Certificate Services) deployed as an Enterprise (AD Integrated) Certificate Authority. Using Group Policy Objects (GPOs), users can automatically be enrolled for certificates, which are then also automatically associated with their Active Directory accounts. These certificates can then be automatically presented to IIS 8.0 and then user-authenticated.

Active Directory mapping cannot be used with either One-to-One or Many-to-One certificate mapping.

> **NOTE** *The Certificate Mapping Authentication module* (`authcert.dll`) *must be installed and enabled to use Active Directory certificate mapping authentication. This module is not installed by default using an interactive install. At the time of this writing, IIS 8.0 supports enabling Active Directory certificate mapping only at the server level.*

1. Start IIS Manager. (Press WIN + R, enter **inetmgr** in the dialog, and click OK. Alternatively, click Tools on the top-right of Server Manager and select Internet Information Server [IIS] Manager.)

2. Locate the server that you wish to configure Active Directory Certificate Mapping authentication for. Select the Authentication Feature option.

3. Select the Active Directory Client Certificate Authentication option, and click Enable in the Actions pane to enable Active Directory Client Certificate authentication. Click Disable in the Actions pane to disable Active Directory Client Certificate Authentication (if currently enabled).

Like Active Directory Certificate mapping, enabling One-to-One or Many-to-One certificate mapping requires that the website in question be SSL/TLS-enabled. Steps for requesting and installing a server authentication certificate for SSL/TLS are covered in Chapter 15.

There is no dedicated UI option for enabling and configuring one-to-one or many-to-one certificate mapping. Administrators may use the IIS Manager's Configuration Editor option, manually edit configuration files, or use programmatic means to set up the mappings.

> **NOTE** *The IIS Certificate Mapping Authentication module* (authmap.dll) *must be installed and enabled to use Active Directory certificate mapping authentication. This module is not installed by default using an interactive install.*

One-to-one mapping maps a certificate's thumbprint to a specified user account. Many-to-one mapping maps properties of certificates (e.g., OU values) to a user account.

To configure either option:

1. Start IIS Manager. (Press WIN + R, enter **inetmgr** in the dialog, and click OK. Alternatively, click Tools on the top-right of Server Manager and select Internet Information Server [IIS] Manager.)

2. Locate the server or website that you wish to configure Certificate Mapping authentication for. Select the Configuration Editor option.

3. In the section drop-down, select system.webServer ➪ Security ➪ Authentication ➪ IISClientCertificateAuthenticationMapping. The IISClientCertificateAuthenticationMapping settings will be displayed (see Figure 14-13).

FIGURE 14-13

4. Set the Enabled property to True to enable mapping, or back to False to disable this feature.

5. To enable a one-to-one mapping:

    a. Click the ellipses on the end of the oneToOneMappings field.

    b. Click the Add button.

    c. Paste the binary value extracted from an x509 certificates .cer file (remove the "----Begin Certificate----" and "----End Certificate----" text).

    d. Enter the username and password that this certificate should be mapped to.

    e. Repeat steps (b) through (d) for each certificate. Close the dialog once all users have been mapped.

    f. Install the certificates on end user's machines, as required.

6. To enable a many-to-one mapping:

    a. Click the ellipses on the end of the manyToOneMappings field.

    b. Click the Add button to add a new mapping.

    c. Enter the username and password that the certificate should be mapped to, as well as a description (optional) for the rule and a name for the rule.

    d. Click the ellipses at the end of the Rules field to specify the mapping rules.

    e. In the Rules dialog specify the certificate fields that should be searched and the values that would constitute a match. Multiple rules can be created.

    f. Install the certificates on end user's machines as required.

7. Click OK to exit all dialogs.

AppCmd provides a relatively simple way to configure oneToOne and manyToOne certificate mapping. To enable the mapping functionality, run the following command:

```
appcmd.exe set config "Default Web Site" -
section:system.webServer/security/authentication/iisClientCertificateMappingAuthenti
cation /enabled:"True" /manyToOneCertificateMappingsEnabled:"True" -commit:apphost
```

Subsequently, to configure a manyToOne rule for mapping, run the following command:

```
appcmd.exe set config "Default Web Site" -
section:system.webServer/security/authentication/
iisClientCertificateMappingAuthentication/
+"manyToOneMappings.[name='Mapping1',description='Mapping1',userName=User1',password
='Password'].rules.[certificateField='Subject',certificateSubField='CN',matchCriteri
a='User1']"
```

To configure a oneToOne mapping, run the following command:

```
appcmd.exe set config "Default Web Site" -
section:system.webServer/security/authentication/
iisClientCertificateMappingAuthentication /
+"oneToOneMappings.[userName='User1',password='Password',certificate=BLOB']"
```

Replace BLOB with the binary certificate data extracted from the x509 certificate .cer file.

CONFIGURING FORMS-BASED AUTHENTICATION

Forms-based authentication (FBA) is a non-HTTP-based mechanism for authenticating users. Instead of using HTTP headers, users are redirected to a normal HTML page that contains form elements (such as textboxes) where they can enter credentials. Upon submitting the form, back-end .NET code will process the credentials against a pre-configured user store (for example, Active Directory, an XML file or database). If the user is authenticated, a cookie is set that permits access to further pages.

Although IIS Manager offers an option to configure FBA, this feature is still truly an ASP.NET feature, which has been available with the .NET Framework since v1 was released in 2002. All settings are stored in the `<system.web>` configuration section rather than IIS 8.0's `<system.webServer>` section. Traditionally, ASP.NET's FBA feature has been used in conjunction with ASP.NET's URL Authorization feature. However, IIS 8.0 contains a native (non-managed) URL Authorization module as well. The native URL Authorization module can be used for requests for all resources (both ASP.NET and other files), whereas the managed .NET URL Authorization module can only be used, by default, when a request is for a .NET resource (similar to how this functionality worked in IIS 5.0 and IIS 6.0)

Although IIS Manager exposes options to configure FBA settings, if you wish to configure ASP .NET authorization rules, you must still edit ASP.NET configuration files. The following table summarizes the main configuration items required to enable FBA:

CONFIGURATION ITEM	EXPOSED IN IIS MANAGER	DESCRIPTION
Enabling/Disabling FBA	Yes	Enables or disables FBA.
Configuring the Login URL and authentication cookie setting	Yes	The page to which users should be redirected can be configured in IIS Manager, as can various security settings for the authentication cookie.
Users	No	Users must be defined so that access rules (to permit or deny access) can be configured. This must be done manually.
Roles	No	Users can be grouped into roles (similar to groups), and access can be permitted or denied based on role membership. This must be configured manually.
Provider details	No	Configuration information must be provided that tells the FBA module where to look (for example, XML file, SQL database) for user and role information. This must be configured manually.
Access rules	No	Access rules must be configured that permit or deny access to specified users or roles. This must be configured manually.

FBA is most useful in situations in which a website creator does not have the ability to set NTFS permissions or create/delete Windows users accounts, such as in a hosting scenario. FBA provides developers with the ability to configure authentication and authorization rules based simply on ASP .NET configuration files and, optionally, a database to store user and role details.

You are encouraged to examine the IIS 8.0 URL Authorization feature as an alternative to ASP .NET's URL Authorization features. The two URL Authorization options are discussed later in this chapter.

You can configure FBA at a server, website, folder (including virtual directories), or file level. You must be an Administrator on the server or have delegated permissions to enable FBA for the node in question.

> **NOTE** *The use of FBA requires that Anonymous authentication be enabled. As login credentials need to be entered on an HTML form, forcing HTTP-based authentication will prevent the user from ever being able to load the form unless the user also has a set of Windows credentials. The Forms Authentication module (*System.Web.Security.FormsAuthenticationModule*) must be installed and enabled to allow FBA. This module is not installed by default using an interactive install.*

To configure FBA:

1. Start IIS Manager. (Press WIN + R, enter **inetmgr** in the dialog, and click OK. Alternatively, click Tools on the top-right of Server Manager and select Internet Information Server [IIS] Manager.)

2. Locate the server, website, folder, or file that you wish to configure FBA for. Select the Authentication Feature option.

3. Select the Forms-Based Authentication option, and click Enable in the Actions pane to enable FBA. Click Disable in the Actions pane to disable FBA (if currently enabled).

4. Click the Edit link to edit configuration information for FBA. You can specify the following items in the options dialog box (see Figure 14-14):

   a. Login URL — This is the page to which users will be redirected to enter their credentials.

   b. Cookie time-out — After the set period of inactivity (no requests from the browser), the user will need to reauthenticate.

   c. Cookie mode — Allows the Administrator to choose whether to use cookies, store authentication information in the URL, allow .NET to detect whether the device supports cookies via JavaScript, or assume cookie support based on the browser's user-agent string (this is the default setting).

   d. Cookie name.

e. Whether the cookie is protected from tampering through the use of encryption and validation.

f. Require SSL for requests.

g. Whether to use a sliding cookie renewal — When using sliding renewal, each request resets the cookie time-out setting. If sliding renewal is disabled, the user will have to reauthenticate regardless of whether they are active or inactive when the cookie times out.

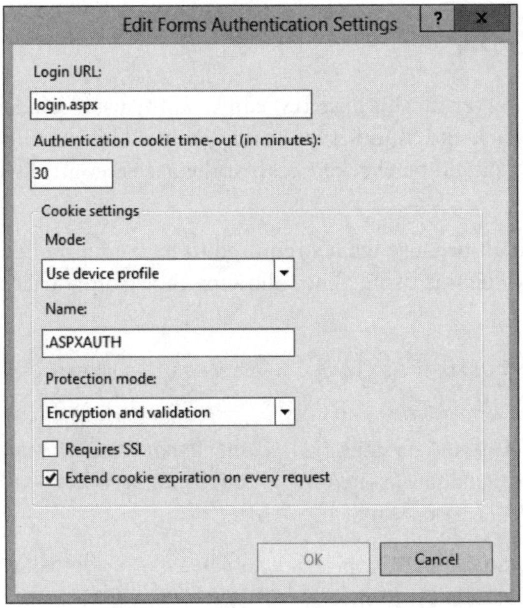

Edit Forms Authentication Settings

Login URL:

login.aspx

Authentication cookie time-out (in minutes):

30

Cookie settings

Mode:

Use device profile

Name:

.ASPXAUTH

Protection mode:

Encryption and validation

☐ Requires SSL

☑ Extend cookie expiration on every request

OK   Cancel

FIGURE 14-14

5. Click OK to commit your changes and exit the dialog.

> **NOTE** *FBA settings are stored in the ASP.NET configuration section. This can either be the machine-wide root* `web.config` *file or in the* `<system.web>` *section of a website's or web application's* `web.config` *file. FBA settings are not stored in IIS configuration files or sections.*

By default, Forms-based authentication applies only to requests for files managed by .NET (e.g., ASPX pages), and not to other types of files (e.g., static files). To alter this configuration, so that Forms-based authentication is used for all file types:

1. Open IIS Manager.

2. Locate the server node, and open the Modules feature.

3. Double click the FormsAuthentication module, and deselect the "Invoke only for requests to ASP.NET applications or managed handlers" option.

4. Click OK to commit your changes, and exit the dialog boxes.

This option can be altered in the `applicationHost.config` file by removing the `managedHandler` precondition for the FormsAuthentication module:

```
<add name="FormsAuthentication" type="System.Web.Security.FormsAuthentication
Module" preCondition="managedHandler" />
```

CONFIGURING DELEGATION

Delegation is a process by which a server (in this case IIS) can send the user's credentials to another back-end server (for example, to a back-end SQL Server or file server). This may be useful in situations in which the user's credentials should be checked against the access control list (ACL) maintained by the back-end server.

Configuring delegation can be difficult because what's required to be configured depends on what authentication mechanism the client is using. The following table summarizes the major implications:

AUTHENTICATION MECHANISM	USER ACCOUNT USED BY IIS	DELEGATION CONFIGURATION
Anonymous	IUSR for non-ASP.NET content. Application pool identity (Network Service) for ASP.NET content.	machinename$ account used to access back-end services.
Basic	End user for non-ASP.NET content. Application pool identity (Network Service) for ASP.NET content.	IIS has user's username and password in cleartext. Can log on directly as the end user for remote content. Enable Impersonation for ASP.NET to have .NET access back-end resources as the end user.
Digest, NTLM	End user for non-ASP.NET content. Application pool identity (Network Service) for ASP.NET content.	IIS does not have user's password. Cannot access back-end resources (except as machinename$) unless protocol transition is configured.
Kerberos	End user for non-ASP.NET content. Application pool identity (Network Service) for ASP.NET content.	Can access back-end content as end user if Kerberos delegation is configured. Enable Impersonation for ASP.NET to have .NET access back-end resources as end user.
FBA	IUSR for non-ASP.NET content. Application pool identity (Network Service) for ASP.NET content.	In ASP.NET code, impersonate a Windows principal in order to access back-end resources as that user.

This section concentrates on configuring delegation to enable Kerberos-authenticated clients to delegate to back-end services. For NTLM- and Digest-authenticated users, protocol transition enables the IIS server to obtain a Kerberos ticket for a back-end service even though the initial authentication mechanism (from client to IIS) was not Kerberos. The next section focuses on enabling protocol transition.

> **NOTE** *ASP.NET separates out authentication and impersonation. Although you can configure Windows authentication as an authentication option in ASP.NET, all code still runs as the application pool's identity (Network Service, by default) unless you also enable impersonation. Once you enable impersonation, the end user's credentials can be delegated to back-end services. For ASP or static files, impersonation occurs automatically.*

In a Kerberos delegation scenario, the following takes place (Figure 14-15):

1. The client browser supplies a Kerberos service ticket to the web server. The process that happens in obtaining a service ticket was described above and shown in Figure 14-10.

2. The HTTP service, seeing the need to open a connection to SQL Server using the end user's credentials, obtains the necessary ticket from the KDC.

3. The KDC returns a ticket if the HTTP service is permitted to delegate.

4. The server opens the connection, sending the ticket obtained from the KDC.

5. The SQL Server permits the connection to be opened or returns an error indicating that the user is not permitted to log in to the SQL Server.

6. The web server returns the web page to the end user.

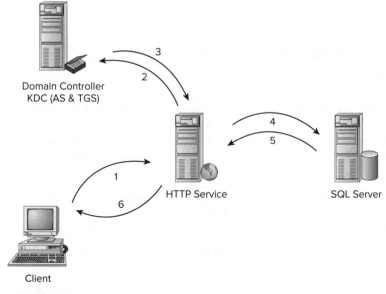

FIGURE 14-15

To configure delegation requires some configuration within Active Directory. Specifically, the HTTP service must be permitted to delegate, and the end user's account must not be configured to be non-delegatable.

To configure an IIS server to be permitted to delegate:

1. Open the Active Directory Users and Computers MMC tool.

2. Locate the computer account corresponding to the IIS server (or user account if you are running the worker process hosting the website under a custom user account).

3. Right-click and choose Properties. Open the Delegation tab (see Figure 14-16).

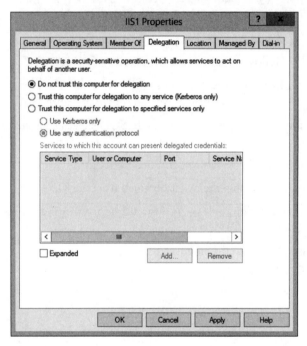

FIGURE 14-16

4. The "Trust this computer for delegation to any service (Kerberos only)" option corresponds to what was known as *unconstrained delegation.* If the domain functional level is Windows 2000 or Mixed Mode, then this is the only option. The IIS server will be able to delegate to any back-end server; however, protocol transition will not be available. Protocol transition is discussed in the next section.

5. The "Trust this computer for delegation to specified services only" option is a more secure option (because it limits what back-end services this server may attempt to gain access to). The sub-option ("Use any authentication protocol") is what allows protocol transition.

6. Select this option, and click Add to add back-end services that the IIS server should be permitted to delegate to.

7. Enter the machine account name (if the back-end service is running under a built-in principal such as LocalSystem or Network Service) or user account name (if the back-end service is running under a custom account), and click OK to retrieve a list of registered SPNs. For a back-end Microsoft SQL Server, this will be MSSQLSvr. Click OK to add the service (see Figure 14-17).

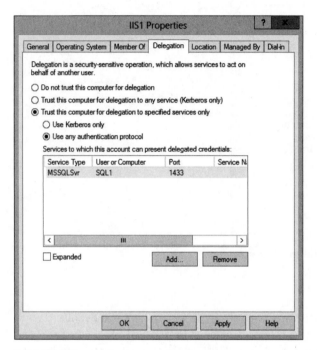

FIGURE 14-17

8. Lastly, verify that any users that should be able to authenticate are not marked as non-delegatable. To do this, locate the user accounts in Active Directory, right-click and choose Properties. On the Account tab, ensure that the "Account is sensitive and cannot be delegated" option is *not* checked (by default, it is not checked), as shown in Figure 14-18. If this checkbox is checked, delegation for that user account is not possible.

There is an additional configuration step required if:

➤ You are accessing an ASP.NET resource (for example, an .aspx page);

and

➤ The resource is hosting in a web application pool running in integrated pipeline mode.

In this situation, it is required that you configure <identity impersonation="true" /> for your ASP.NET application. This permits your ASP.NET application to impersonate the end user and, furthermore, to use those credentials to access the back-end resource.

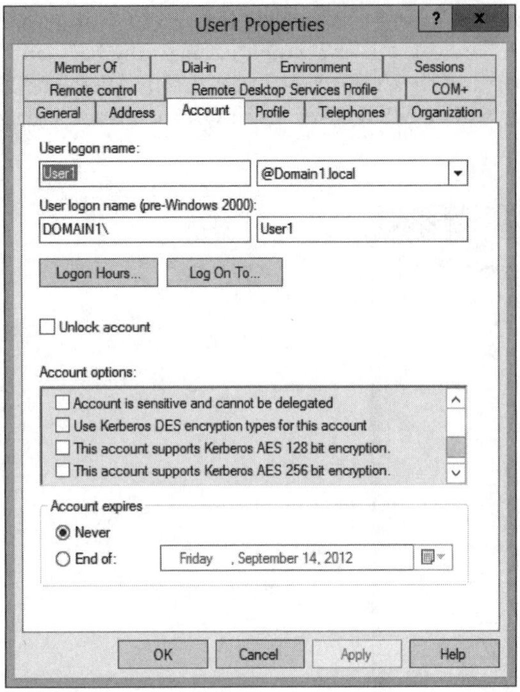

FIGURE 14-18

However, in order for this to work when using the new integrated pipeline mode, the `validateIntegratedModeConfiguration` setting must be disabled. If this setting is enabled, then a 500.24 HTTP status will be sent to the client. This error is thrown because authentication occurs after the `BeginRequest` and `AuthenticateRequest` events, and identity impersonation cannot occur during those two events.

You can use AppCmd to disable the `validateIntegratedModeConfiguration` setting. This setting can be configured for the server, a website, or an individual web application. For example, to disable this setting for a web application called *Webapp1* located on a website called *Website1*, run the following command:

```
appcmd.exe set config "Website1/Webapp1" /section:validation /
validateIntegratedModeConfiguration:false
```

As mentioned in the earlier section on configuring Kerberos authentication, service principal names (SPNs) must be correctly registered for the accessed web application. Additionally, when using delegation, correct SPNs must also be registered for the back-end services so that IIS 8.0 can obtain the necessary service tickets. For a product such as Microsoft SQL Server, default SPNs are registered when installing the product. For third-party applications, you might need to register an SPN manually.

CONFIGURING PROTOCOL TRANSITION

First implemented in Windows Server 2003, *protocol transition* is a feature that allows a client to authenticate to IIS 8.0 using a protocol other than Kerberos (for example, NTLM or Digest). By utilizing Services for User to Self (S4U2S) and Services for User to Proxy (S4U2P), IIS 8.0 is able to get a Kerberos ticket to the back-end service. For more information on S4U2P and S4U2S, see http://adopenstatic.com/cs/blogs/ken/archive/2007/07/19/8460.aspx.

In a protocol transition scenario:

1. The client authenticates to IIS 8.0 using an HTTP authentication protocol other than Kerberos (for example, NTLM or Digest authentication).

2. IIS 8.0 obtains a Kerberos ticket on behalf of the user. The process for obtaining Kerberos tickets is discussed above.

3. The IIS 8.0 server authenticates to the back-end server application using Kerberos. The back-end service must support Kerberos authentication.

In a default IIS 8.0 configuration, nothing additional needs to be configured in IIS 8.0 to support protocol transition. The only configuration that is required is on your domain controllers. To support protocol transition, the domain functional level must be Windows Server 2003 or higher. Additionally, protocol transition relies on constrained delegation. This requires that the IIS 8.0 server and back-end server be in the same domain. The client can be in any trusted domain or forest.

To configure Active Directory for protocol transition, ensure that required SPNs are registered, as discussed previously. Then, to configure IIS 8.0 to support protocol transition:

1. Open the Active Directory Users and Computers MMC tool.

2. Locate the computer account corresponding to the IIS server (or user account, if you are running the worker process hosting the website under a custom user account, and not using kernel-mode authentication).

3. Right-click and choose Properties. Open the Delegation tab.

4. Select the "Trust this computer for delegation to specified services only" option, and ensure that the "Use Any Protocol" sub-option is also selected.

5. Click Add to add back-end services that the IIS server should be permitted to delegate to.

6. Enter the machine account name (if the back-end service is running under a built-in principal such as LocalSystem or Network Service) or user account name (if the back-end service is running under a custom account), and click OK to retrieve a list of registered SPNs. For a back-end Microsoft SQL Server, this will be MSSQLSvr. Click OK to add the service (refer to Figure 14-17).

After you have configured these options, users will be able to authenticate to IIS 8.0 using any HTTP authentication protocol, and have IIS 8.0 pass their credentials to the supported back-end services.

CONFIGURING AUTHORIZATION

As mentioned above, authentication and authorization are discrete steps in determining the final response to be sent to the end user. The authorization process occurs after the user has been authenticated and involves determining if the user has access to the resource or not. Typically, the resources accessed are files on a hard disk (or possibly a database), and NTFS permissions are used to control access. Once the end user has been determined, NTFS permissions then determine if the user is able to access the resource in the requested way.

Depending on how the user authenticated, how IIS 8.0 is configured, and what type of resource the user is attempting to access, the actual user account being used is different!

The following table summarizes the common accounts used:

AUTHENTICATION MECHANISM	USER ACCOUNT BEING USED BY IIS
Anonymous	IUSR for non-ASP.NET content. Application pool identity (Network Service) for ASP.NET content.
HTTP (Basic, Digest, NTLM, Kerberos)	End user for non-ASP.NET content. Application pool identity (Network Service) for ASP.NET content.
URL authorization	IUSR for non-ASP.NET content. Application pool identity (Network Service) for ASP.NET content.

The IUSR account is used for non-ASP.NET content unless the Application Pool Identity option is configured. See "Configuring Anonymous Authentication" above in this chapter for more information on this setting.

Configuring NTFS permissions to permit (or deny) access can be done using various tools. The Explorer shell provides a useful mechanism for one-off changes. Alternatively, for many changes or on Windows Server 2008 Core edition, you can use the `icacls.exe` command-line tool.

To be able to load web pages, images, or similar resources, NTFS Read permissions are required. For CGI applications, Execute permissions are required. If your application permits users to upload files (or you are using an authoring technology like WebDAV), then Write permissions are required.

> **NOTE** *If you are using FBA/ASP.NET URL Authorization or native IIS 8.0 URL authorization, authorization rules are stored in ASP.NET configuration files and IIS configuration files, respectively. For more information on adding, editing, or removing those configuration file entries, see "URL Authorization" later in this chapter.*

To alter NTFS permissions using Explorer:

1. Open an Explorer window, navigate to the file or folder that you want to set permissions on, right-click, and choose Properties. Select the Security tab (see Figure 14-19).

2. Click the Edit button to alter permissions. To alter permissions for an existing user or group, select the user or group in the top panel, and check or uncheck permissions checkboxes in the lower panel.

3. To add a new user or group, click the Add button and enter the user or group to add.

4. Click the Advanced button to configure advanced properties, such as propagating changes to all subfolders, enabling auditing, or changing the ownership of the file or folder.

5. Click OK to confirm the changes and exit the dialog.

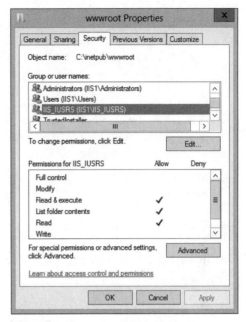

The `icacls.exe` command-line tool can be used to configure NTFS permissions. It can be used to export permissions for an existing file/folder or configure permissions on an existing file/folder. For example, to grant Read/Execute permissions to User1 to File1.txt, the following command would be used:

FIGURE 14-19

```
icacls.exe file1.txt /grant Domain1\User1:(RX)
```

For more information on using `icacls.exe`, type **icacls.exe /?** at a command prompt.

URL Authorization

URL authorization is a feature in IIS 8.0 that can be used to permit or deny access to resources, by storing access rules in a data store (such as an XML file or database), rather than relying on traditional NTFS permissions.

IIS 8.0 ships with two URL authorization modules. The first is a managed module, which provides the same functionality as ASP.NET has provided when installed with previous versions of IIS. By default, this module is added in `applicationHost.Config` (in the default `<modules>` section), and by default, it applies only to requests for .NET managed file extensions:

```
<add name="UrlAuthorization" type="System.Web.Security.UrlAuthorizationModule"
preCondition="managedHandler" />
```

IIS 8.0 also ships with a new, native code module, which also implements URL-based authorization. This module is also added in the `applicationHost.Config` file but in the `<globalModules>` section:

```
<add name="UrlAuthorizationModule" image="%windir%\System32\inetsrv\urlauthz.dll" />
```

The native URL Authorization module applies to all requests, whether they be for .NET managed files or other types of files (e.g., static files or ASP files). Additionally, the IIS Manager MMC console provides a graphical interface for configuring this native URL Authorization module.

> **NOTE** *If you are using the Authorization Manager (AzMan) features in IIS 6.0, URL authorization provides enhanced functionality over the AzMan implementation in IIS 6.0.*

Both URL Authorization mechanisms can be used to secure access to resources through the alteration of configuration stores (e.g., XML files or a database). This makes URL Authorization a viable way of securing access to resources when the site administrator is unable to directly set NTFS permissions (e.g., in a hosting scenario).

Additionally, URL Authorization mechanisms can be used by any of the various authentication mechanisms. This means that Forms Based Authentication or some form of HTTP-based authentication, or even Client Certificate Authentication can be combined with a URL Authorization module to permit or deny access to users.

Configuring the Managed (ASP.NET) URL Authorization Module

To configure ASP.NET authorization module rules:

1. Start IIS Manager. (Press WIN + R, enter **inetmgr** in the dialog, and click OK. Alternatively, click Tools on the top-right of Server Manager and select Internet Information Server [IIS] Manager.)

2. Locate the server, website, folder, or file that you wish to configure Authorization for. Select the .NET Authorization Feature option.

3. By default, an Allow rule already exists for all users. Additional rules can be added by clicking the Add Allow Rule or Add Deny Rule links in the Actions pane.

4. To add a new Allow Rule, click the Add Allow Rule link. Select whether this rule should apply to All Users, All Anonymous Users (i.e. all users who have not authenticated), specific users or groups (see Figure 14-20). Additionally, the rule can be limited to a subset of HTTP verbs.

5. Click OK to commit the new rule.

A typical configuration will have a Deny rule for All Anonymous Users, with an Allow rule for All Users, or specific groups of users. ASP.NET Authorization rules are evaluated in the order that they are stored in, until a match is found, so ensure that any Deny rules are higher in the list order than Allow rules. Additionally, rules are evaluated from the lowest web.config file through to the root web.config file. This means that it may be possible to override higher level settings at a lower level in the website folder hierarchy.

> **NOTE** *ASP.NET URL Authorization settings are stored in the ASP.NET configuration section. This can either be the machine-wide root* web.config *file or in the* <system.web> *section of a website's or web application's* web.config *file. These settings are not stored in IIS configuration files or sections.*

FIGURE 14-20

Configuring the Native (IIS 8.0) URL Authorization Module

Fully configuring the native URL Authorization feature is beyond the scope of this book, as URL Authorization can leverage the ASP.NET membership providers to access user and role information in multiple different data stores (e.g., a database, Active Directory, or other authentication store). The steps below involve functionality native to IIS 8.0 — rules are stored in IIS 8.0 configuration files. For the more advanced option of using ASP.NET's membership provider model, information on configuring membership providers can be found on the ASP.NET website: http://www.asp.net.

URL Authorization can be configured at a server, website, folder (including virtual directories), or file level. You must be an Administrator on the server or have delegated permissions to enable URL authorization for the node in question.

> **NOTE** *The URL Authentication module (*urlauthz.dll*) must be installed and enabled to allow URL authorization. This module is not installed by default using an interactive install.*

To configure URL authorization:

1. Start IIS Manager. (Press WIN + R, enter **inetmgr** in the dialog, and click OK. Alternatively, click Tools on the top-right of Server Manager and select Internet Information Server [IIS] Manager.)

2. Locate the server, website, folder, or file that you want to configure Authorization for. Select the Authorization Rules feature.

3. Select the Add Allow Rule from the Actions pane to configure a new permitted access rule. Access can be permitted to any request (including users who have not authenticated), only authenticated users, authenticated users within specific roles, or only specific users (see Figure 14-21).

FIGURE 14-21

4. Optionally, restrict the HTTP verbs that this rule applies to. Click OK to add the rule.

5. To configure a Deny rule, select the Add Deny Rule from the Actions pane.

6. Select the Users or Roles links to configure users or roles. To add a Windows Domain user account, specify Domainname\Username. To specify a local Windows account, use Servername\Username. For other, non-Windows accounts, simply use the defined username.

7. Click OK to exit the dialog.

IIS Authorization Rules are evaluated from `applicationHost.config` down to the lowest `web.config` file. By utilizing the lock settings feature, it is possible to prevent lower level administrators from overriding rules set at a higher level. Unlike ASP.NET Authorization rules, Deny rules take precedence over Allow rules.

Configuring Application Pool Sandboxing

In previous versions of IIS, it has sometimes been difficult to isolate web application pools from each other. If multiple web application pools are configured to run as the same identity (for example, Network Service), then code running inside one web application pool would be able to use File System objects to access configuration files, web pages, and similar resources belonging to another web application pool. This was because it was impossible to allow one process running as Network Service access to a file, but prevent another process also running as Network Service access to the same file.

In IIS 8.0, it is possible, with some work, to prevent this from occurring. As part of IIS 8.0's built-in functionality, each web application pool has an application pool configuration file generated on-the-fly when that application pool is started. These are stored, by default, in the `%systemdriver\` `inetpub\temp\appPools` folder. Each web application pool has an additional SID (Security Identifier) generated for it, and this is injected into the relevant `w3wp.exe` process. The application pool's configuration file is ACLed to allow only that SID access. Since each `w3wp.exe` process has its own SID, each application pool's configuration file is ACLed to a different SID. Figure 14-22 illustrates the process.

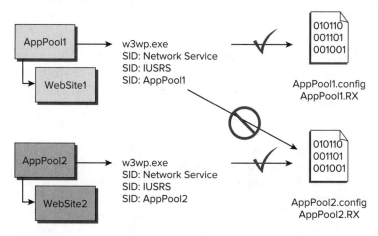

FIGURE 14-22

You can use the `icacls.exe` tool, as follows, to determine the SID applied to any given application pool's configuration file:

```
icacls.exe %systemdrive%\inetpub\temp\appPools\appPool.config /save output.txt
```

The retrieved SID can now be used to secure website content in the same way. To do this:

1. Configure each website (or web application) to run in its own web application pool.

2. Configure Anonymous authentication to use the application pool identity rather than the IUSR account. See the "Configuring Anonymous Authentication" section earlier in this chapter for more information.

3. Remove NTFS permissions for the IUSRS group and the IUSR account from the website's files and folders.

4. Use the `icacls.exe` tool to permit the retrieved SID Read (and optionally, Execute and Write) access to the website's files and folders. Either the SID can be used, or the user "IIS APPPool\ApplicationPoolName" can be used.

After configuring these NTFS permissions, only the SID that has been injected into a particular `w3wp.exe` process will be able to read the contents of the website in question. All code running in other `w3wp.exe` processes, even though the process identity may also be "Network Service," will be unable to read this particular website's content. For more information, see `http://adopenstatic.com/cs/blogs/ken/archive/2008/01/29/15759.aspx`.

This technique may be most useful to web hosters or similar administrators that need to accept content from various external or distrusted parties.

UNDERSTANDING IIS 8.0 USER ACCOUNTS

User accounts are greatly simplified in IIS 8.0. The Anonymous User account (previously IUSR_<machinename> in IIS 6.0 and earlier) is now a well-known SID called *IUSR*. This means that this account has the same name and the same SID on all IIS 8.0 machines. Additionally, accounts such as IWAM_<machinename> and aspnet_wp.exe that you might be familiar with from previous versions of IIS are no longer used.

Lastly, the IIS_WPG group introduced with IIS 6.0 has been replaced with the IIS_IUSRS group from IIS 7.0 onwards. In IIS 6.0, accounts that would be used as web application pool identities needed to be placed into the IIS_WPG group by an administrator. In IIS 8.0, by default, any account configured as a web application pool identity is automatically and dynamically added to the IIS_IUSRS group, if required.

> **NOTE** *You can disable this behavior and stop an application identity from being automatically added to the IIS_IUSRS group by editing the configuration for that application pool, as follows:*
>
> ```
> <applicationPools>
>     <add name="DefaultAppPool">
>         <processModel manualGroupMembership="true" />
>     </add>
> </applicationPools >
> ```
>
> *This configuration prevents the identity of the DefaultAppPool application pool from automatically being added to the IIS_IUSRS group.*

The following table summarizes the user and logon rights granted to the accounts natively used by IIS 8.0. The IUSR account is not specifically listed, as it has no rights specifically assigned to it. Instead, it inherits rights from the default Users group.

RIGHT	LOCALSYSTEM	NETWORK SERVICE	LOCAL SERVICE	IIS_IUSRS
Act as part of the operating system (seTCBPrivilege)	x			
Adjust memory quotas for a process (seIncreaseQuotaPrivilege)		x	x	
Bypass traverse checking (seChangeNotifyPrivilege)		x	x	
Change the system time (seSystemTimePrivilege)			x	

Change the time zone (seTimeZonePrivilege)			x	
Create global objects (seCreateGlobalPrivilege)		x	x	
Generate security audits (seAuditPrivilege)		x	x	
Impersonate a client after authentication (seImpersonatePrivilege)		x	x	x
Log on as a batch job				x
Replace a process-level token (seAssignPrimaryTo-kenPrivilege)		x	x	

The LocalSystem account is used to run IIS 8.0 services, and is also an option for application pool identities. The LocalSystem account has "Act as part of the operating system" privileges (which allows it unfettered access to Windows). It also has many other privileges by default (which are not listed individually below). Suffice it to say that a process running as LocalSystem has almost full control over your server. Running application pools as *LocalSystem* is a security risk and needs to be carefully investigated prior to implementation.

Network Service is a low-privilege account and the default web application pool identity. Network Service is able to access network resources using the computer's machine account (machinename$). Local Service is similar to Network Service, but cannot access other resources on the network (except those that permit anonymous access).

15

SSL and TLS

WHAT'S IN THIS CHAPTER?

➤ Securing a website with SSL/TLS

➤ Securing an SMTP virtual server with TLS

➤ Securing an FTP site with TLS

When looking at a strategy to secure your application server infrastructure, it is important to examine several discrete elements:

➤ Secure the actual server that the application is running on.

➤ Ensure that only permitted users of the application are able to access the allowed functionality (and that all other users, including malicious attackers, are denied access).

➤ Ensure that your users know that they are connecting to the correct server, and, if required, secure traffic between the client and server.

Chapters 13 and 14 discuss many of the security options available with IIS 8.0. This chapter addresses security between the client and the server. Secure Sockets Layer (SSL) and Transport Layer Security (TLS) are industry standard technologies for authenticating machines (or users) and for encrypting traffic between two devices.

IIS 8.0 introduces three new features to help administrators manage and scale TLS-protected websites:

➤ A central certificate store that can be used by multiple IIS 8.0 servers

➤ Support for Server Name Indication (SNI), which provides functionality that allows multiple, disparate websites to be supported on a single IP address

➤ A new certificate store (Web Hosting) where IIS loads certificates "on demand," allowing a greater density of TLS-enabled hosts on a single server

> **NOTE** *SSL is a technology originally developed by Netscape, with v2.0 being the first publicly available release. TLS is an IETF standard that is the successor to SSL, and the latest draft version is TLS v1.2. Currently, the terms SSL and TLS are used interchangeably in the popular press when discussing secured HTTP traffic. "TLS" is almost always used when discussing securing other protocols (such as FTP or SMTP).*

TLS should be considered whenever there is a need to secure the transmission of data from eavesdropping attacks (including credentials) or to ensure message integrity (that data aren't altered in transit). Additionally, to ensure that the two parties in a conversation (the client and server) are able to trust each other's server (and optionally client), authentication is built into the TLS handshake process.

> **NOTE** *TLS is a Layer 4 protocol implementation. This typically means that the use of TLS requires the use of an alternative port. For example, when securing HTTP traffic, TLS-secured traffic operates on port 443, rather than port on 80, which is used for unsecured traffic. For internal applications, IPec should also be considered. Because this operates at Layer 3, the security provided by IPsec is transparent to applications, and no modification is required. Instead, routing devices and firewalls need to allow access for additional IP protocols. This is generally not an issue in internal networks.*

SECURING A WEBSITE WITH TLS

TLS uses X.509 certificates and asymmetric (public/private) key cryptography to establish the identity of the server (or client) and, subsequently, symmetric encryption to traffic securely between the client and server. A handshake between the server and client is used to set up a secure session between the two machines. If at any point during the handshake a failure occurs, then either the session is not established or, in the case of recoverable errors, the user is warned of a potential issue and must manually choose to continue with the establishment of the session.

> **NOTE** *Since Windows Server 2003 SP1, administrators have been able to use kernel mode SSL, using functionality provided by* `ksecdd.sys`. *This significantly cuts the processing overhead involved in negotiating an SSL/TLS connection and in maintaining it during the session. When using kernel mode SSL/TLS, the overhead is approximately 10 percent of capacity to service requests. Because the SSL/TLS handshake process is far more computationally intensive than the communication afterward, the greater the number of shorter sessions, the greater is the impact on a server's performance.*

The SSL/TLS Handshake

The process by which a client and a server establish a secure connection is known as the *SSL/TLS handshake*. The handshake involves the verification of the server's identity (authentication) by the client, as well as a mutual agreement between the client and server as to what encryption technologies (ciphers) should be used to secure the connection.

When a user requests a resource using the secured HTTPS URI, and assuming that the server is configured to support SSL/TLS, the client makes the request, indicating the various ciphers that it supports for securing the connection. The server, assuming that it also supports one of the ciphers indicated by the client, returns its certificate as the second step in the handshake.

The client typically performs several checks on this certificate before proceeding. Most browsers will perform all the following checks unless the default configuration is altered by the user. For non-browser clients (e.g., automated tools), all, some, or none of these checks may be performed:

➤ The client compares the validity dates embedded in the certificate with the current system time. Each certificate is valid from a starting date to an ending date (typically a period of between 1 and 5 years). If the current client system date and time are outside of the certificate's validity period, the user will be presented with a warning.

➤ The client compares the fully qualified domain name (FQDN) of the website being accessed with the Common Name (CN) and Subject Alternate Name (SAN) properties of the certificate presented by the server. This helps mitigate Domain Name System (DNS) poisoning or DNS hijacking attacks, in which an attacker may have redirected the DNS entry of a legitimate website to a server that he or she controls. In such circumstances, the attacker is unlikely to also have a legitimately issued certificate that matches the DNS name.

➤ The client verifies that the certificate has been issued by a trusted certificate authority (CA) and that the certificate has not been tampered with. Each Windows machine stores a list of trusted root and subordinate (or intermediate) CAs. Because the certificate presented by the remote server contains the name of the CA that issued the certificate, Windows first verifies that the name of the issuing CA matches one that the machine already trusts. The certificate also contains a verification hash that was generated by the issuing CA and embedded into the certificate. The client can use the public key embedded in the copy of the issuing CA's certificate that is stored on the machine to verify that the details in the certificate have not been altered. Because the hash is created using the private key of the issuing CA's signing certificate, which is a secret known only to the CA, it is currently computationally infeasible for someone to create both a fake certificate and matching fake verification code.

Each version of Windows ships with a built-in list of commercial third-party trusted CAs. Deploying Windows Server 2012 Active Directory Certificate Services (ADCS, formerly known as "Windows Certificate Services") in Enterprise mode results in domain-joined clients automatically trusting that CA. Administrators can also manually add trusted CAs (e.g., for partner organizations).

To view a list of installed trusted CAs:

1. At the Windows Start screen, type **mmc.exe**, and then press Enter.

2. Choose File ⇨ Add/Remove Snapin.

3. Select Certificates and click Add.

A prompt will appear offering a selection of the current user's account, a nominated service account, or the machine's account. Each account has its own store of certificates. In a default configuration, the list of trusted root CAs is the same between all options. Select Computer Account.

4. Select Local Computer to display certificates installed on the local machine (or enter a remote machine name as appropriate), and click Next.

5. Click Finish and OK to exit the Add/Remove Snapin dialog, and then expand the Trusted Root Certification Authorities node to view a list of installed trusted root CAs, as shown in Figure 15-1.

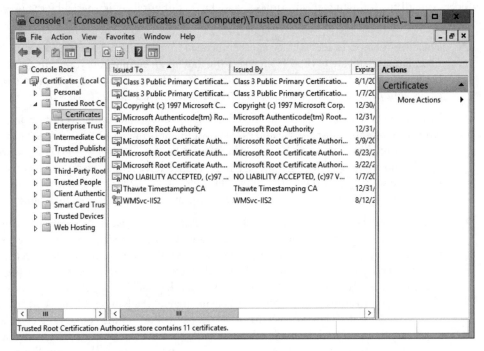

FIGURE 15-1

Depending on the client operating system, the user may be presented with a variety of error messages if one of these checks fails. Clients such as Windows XP and Windows Server 2003 running the default Internet Explorer 6 browser display the error message shown in Figure 15-2 when connecting to a website with a nonmatching Common Name in the certificate.

Figure 15-3 shows the error message when the certificate is issued by an untrusted CA.

For users of Internet Explorer 7 or newer (Windows Vista, 7 or 8, Windows Server 2008 or 2012), the error message is indicated in the first line of gray text, when encountering a website with a certificate error, as shown in Figure 15-4.

FIGURE 15-2

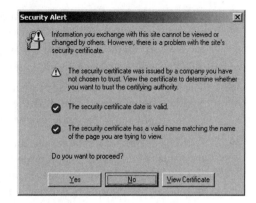

FIGURE 15-3

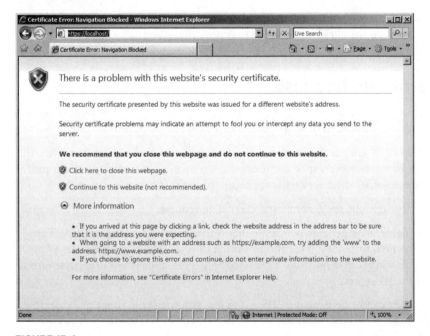

FIGURE 15-4

Assuming that the certificate passes the three standard checks or that the user decides to continue to the site despite the warning, the next steps in the TLS handshake are as follows:

1. The client may optionally contact the CA to determine if the server's certificate has been revoked. A CA can choose to publish a certificate revocation list (CRL), which is used to list certificates that are no longer valid (e.g., if they were incorrectly issued in the first place or a server hosting a certificate has been compromised). Internet Explorer 10 (which ships with Windows 8/Windows Server 2012) will check published CRLs in a default configuration.

2. If the server's certificate has not been revoked or the client chooses not to verify the certificate against a published CRL, the client will then generate a random numeric value to be used as the basis for cryptographic work involved in this particular session. Specifically, what is generated depends on the cipher to be used to secure the session.

3. The client extracts the server's *public key* from the server's certificate and encrypts the generated random numeric value. Because certificates use asymmetric key (private/public key pairs) cryptography, only the server can decrypt this value, using its secret *private key*.

4. Both the client and the server use the generated random numeric values as a shared secret that is used to derive the encryption keys needed for the session. (What keys specifically need to be generated depends on the cryptographic ciphers that both client and server support.) In general, symmetric keys are generated and used by both client and server. Symmetric keys are used because the overhead incurred when encrypting and decrypting data is far less than when using asymmetric (public/private) key pairs.

Once this exchange has been completed, the SSL/TLS handshake is completed for this session. Information exchange between the client and the server is now encrypted and considered secure against both interception (eavesdropping) and man-in-the-middle attacks.

Generating a Certificate Request

The first step in making content available over HTTPS is to generate a *certificate request*. This request can be submitted to a CA, which will, in turn, generate a certificate that can be installed on the server.

Alternatively, in the absence of a separate CA, a self-signed certificate can be generated. Here the server signs its own certificate; however, such certificates are generally only used for development or testing purposes because no other machines trust the signer of the certificate by default.

IIS Manager provides three options for generating a certificate request:

➤ A certificate request can be generated as a file that is manually submitted to a CA. This method would be used to request a certificate from a third-party CA or if there is a CA within the organization that is not Active Directory–integrated, or is not otherwise directly contactable by the IIS server.

➤ A certificate request can be generated by IIS 8.0 that is automatically submitted directly to an Active Directory–integrated installation of Active Directory Certificate Services (known as *Microsoft Certificate Services* in Windows Server 2003 and earlier). The Request Domain Certificate option in IIS Manager provides this functionality.

➤ IIS 8.0 can automatically generate a self-signed certificate. Previously, an IIS 6.0 Resource Kit tool (SelfSSL.exe) could be used to create a self-signed certificate. In IIS 8.0, this facility is built into the user interface.

Each of these possible mechanisms for generating a certificate request is discussed in turn below. Full steps for generating a certificate request to send manually to a CA are detailed. For the other, alternative mechanisms for requesting a certificate, only the steps that are different are detailed.

Certificates and certificate requests can only be configured at a server level. Once a certificate has been installed, it can then be configured for use at a website level. You must be an Administrator on the IIS server (or delegated permissions to manage the whole IIS server) to be able to generate a certificate request.

To create a certificate request to send to a CA, perform the following steps:

1. Start IIS Manager. (Press WIN+R, enter **inetmgr** in the dialog, and click OK. Alternatively, click Tools on the top-right of Server Manager and select Internet Information Server (IIS) Manager.)

2. At the server-level node, select the Server Certificates option. A list of existing installed server authentication certificates is presented. If the IIS 8.0 Remote Management service is installed, a self-signed certificate issued to `WMSvc-<servername>` will be listed, because this certificate is used to secure connections to the Remote Management service.

3. Select Create Certificate Request to begin the certificate request generation process.

4. Enter the details for the certificate that you want to generate, as shown in Figure 15-5. The Common name property should be filled in with the server name (either a NetBIOS name or FQDN) upon which the website will be answering requests. If the server's name in the URL being requested by a client does not match the common name in the certificate presented by the server, the client will show an error to the user (refer to Figure 15-4).

   The remaining fields should be filled in according to the legal status of your organization. Depending on the CA you submit this request to and the type of certificate you are requesting, the CA may verify these details before issuing you a certificate.

   Click Next to continue.

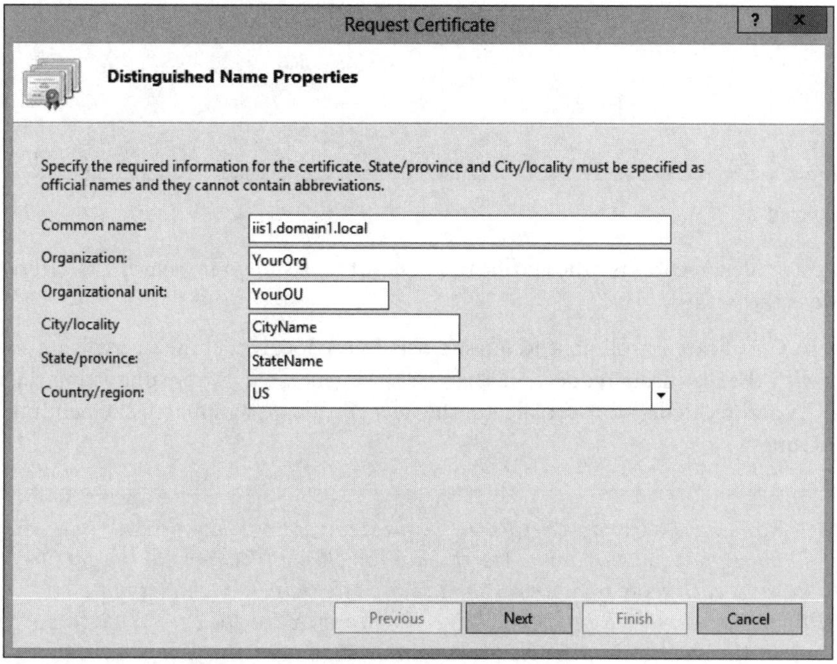

FIGURE 15-5

5. Select the cryptographic provider and bit length that you want to use for this certificate, as shown in Figure 15-6. RSA is the mostly widely used on the public Internet.

At the time of writing, 2,048-bit key lengths are considered secure for the foreseeable future. (NIST estimates that 2,048-bit RSA keys can be considered secure until 2030.) Longer key lengths can be chosen to provide additional security; however, selecting a longer key length puts additional load on both the client and server when performing the SSL/TLS handshake. For busy sites, dedicated hardware devices (either add-in cards or separate network devices) to offload the processing of SSL/TLS should be examined.

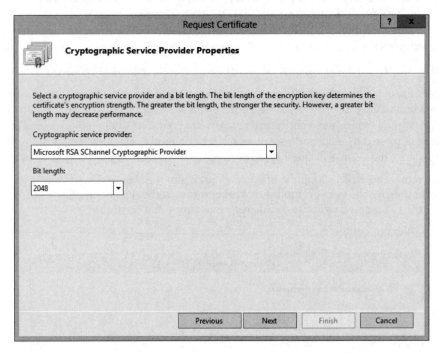

FIGURE 15-6

6. Choose a filename to save the certificate request to, as shown in Figure 15-7, and click Finish to close the wizard.

At this point, a Certificate Enrollment Request exists in the local machine's certificate store that corresponds with the certificate request file that was just generated. After submitting the certificate request to a CA and receiving your certificate, the new certificate will match the pending Certificate Enrollment Request.

> **NOTE** *Running the Create Certificate Request wizard again will result in a new certificate request file and a new Certificate Enrollment Request in the certificate store. A certificate resulting from a certificate request file must match a Certificate Enrollment Request in the certificate store for the certificate to be imported. If you delete a pending Certificate Enrollment Request or otherwise overwrite it by rerunning the wizard, then discard the earlier certificate request file and only use the newly created one.*

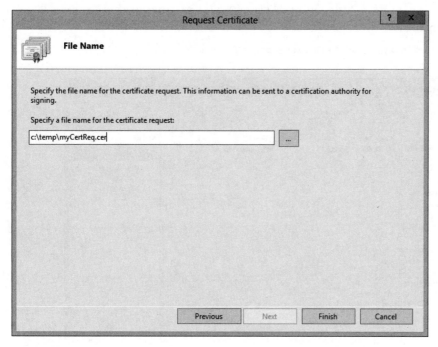

FIGURE 15-7

To view the Certificate Enrollment Request:

1. At the Windows Start screen, type **mmc.exe**, and press Enter.

2. Select File ⇨ Add/Remove Snapin.

3. Select the Certificates snap-in and click Add. Click OK to exit all the dialogs.

4. Expand the Certificate Enrollment Requests node to see all pending requests, as shown in Figure 15-8.

The generated certificate request file is now submitted to a CA, which generates a signed certificate. Most commercial third-party CAs have a range of certificates that vary in price. The higher-assurance certificates (that tend to cost more money) involve additional due diligence by the CA to ensure that the certificate request comes from a legitimate business or individual that is entitled to use the requested certificate Common Name. In practice, it is debatable whether end users are sufficiently aware of the different assurance levels offered by various types of certificates. In an attempt to combat this, Microsoft, in conjunction with partners, has launched *Extended Validation (EV) certificates*. Sites secured using EV certificates have the URL bar displayed in green, rather than the traditional white. You can find examples and further explanation at http://windows.microsoft.com/en-US/windows-vista/Will-the-real-website-owner-please-stand-up-How-EV-certificates-reveal-who-is-really-behind-a-website.

A certificate request can also be generated from the command line using the certreq.exe tool. When using the certreq.exe tool to generate a certificate request, the -new option must be specified, and a settings file must be specified that contains information about the request. The full syntax of the command is:

```
certreq.exe [-binary] [-user|machine] policyfile.inf certRequestFileName
```

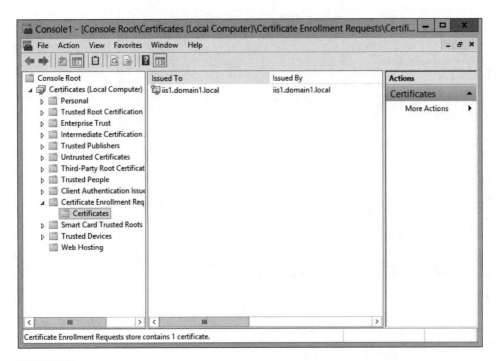

FIGURE 15-8

The `policyfile.inf` file contains information used to generate the certificate request file. The `certRequestFileName` is the name of the file that you wish to have `certreq.exe` save the resulting certificate request as. The optional -binary switch forces `certreq.exe` to save the resulting certificate request in binary format rather than the Base64-encoded format. The optional -user or -machine determines whether the pending request is stored in the user's certificate store or the machine's certificate store. When creating a request for a server authentication certificate suitable for use with IIS 8.0, the -machine option should be used.

The INF policy file follows standard INF conventions, with section headers delimited by square brackets ([ ]), name value pairs for settings, and comments beginning with the semicolon (;) character.

The INF for use with `certreq.exe` requires only a single section header:

```
[NewRequest]
```

However, to ensure that the certificate can be used for server authentication, the *Object Identifier* (OID) for server authentication should be explicitly specified. This is specified in the [ExtendedUsage] section.

For name value pairs, only the `subject` value is required — other fields are optional. However, you will most likely want to specify certain fields (e.g., key length) to ensure that you are generating a sufficiently secure certificate for the correct purpose. A typical INF would look like this:

```
[NewRequest]
Subject = "cn=server1, o=organization, l=city, s=state, c=country"
KeySpec = 1
KeyLength = 2048
Exportable = true
MachineKeySet = true
PrivateKeyArchive = false
ProviderName = "Microsoft RSA SChannel Cryptographic Provider"
ProviderType = 12
RequestType = PKCS10
KeyUsage = 0xa0

[EnhancedKeyUsageExtension]
; server authentication
OID=1.3.6.1.5.5.7.3.1
```

Running `certreq.exe` using the INF file will result in a PKCS10 certificate request similar to the CER file generated earlier using the wizard in IIS Manager. You can then submit this request file, as detailed in the next section.

Submitting the Certificate Request

The procedure for submitting the generated certificate request and retrieving the resulting certificate varies from CA to CA. For lower-assurance certificates, the contents of the certificate request file are typically sent to the CA, and after some verification of the ownership of the domain, a certificate is generated that can be downloaded and installed into IIS. For higher-assurance certificates, additional physical evidence (such as business-registration papers) may need to be supplied to the CA.

In this chapter, the certificate request will be submitted to a CA running Microsoft Active Directory Certificate Services, which provides an approximation of the process involved.

Certificate requests can be submitted to Active Directory Certificate Services in three main ways:

➤ **By using the Certification Authorities MMC tool** — This MMC console is installed on any server running Active Directory Certificate Services. It can optionally be installed on other Windows Server 2008 machines by using the Server Manager tool.

➤ **By using the optional web interface** — Using the web interface requires that IIS be installed on the same machine running Active Directory Certificate Services. A `/certsrv` virtual directory is created underneath the Default Web Site to allow users to request and retrieve certificates.

➤ **By using the command-line certreq.exe tool** — The command-line `certreq.exe` tool can be used with the `-submit` option. You need to specify your certificate request file and the name of the CA to submit the request to.

This chapter covers the detailed steps for using the web interface, because this procedure is the most similar to requesting a certificate from a commercial CA.

> **NOTE** *By default, only users in the Domain Admins and Enterprise Admins security groups are able to issue server authentication certificates. For information on changing this configuration, see the section "Managing a Public Key Infrastructure" later in this chapter.*

To request a certificate using the optional web interface:

1. Open a browser window and navigate to `http://CAServerName/certsrv/`, where `CAServerName` is the name of the server that has Active Directory Certificate Services installed.

2. Click the Request a Certificate link.

3. Click the Submit an Advanced Certificate Request link.

4. Click the "Submit a certificate request by using a base-64-encoded CMC or PKCS #10 file ..." link, as shown in Figure 15-9.

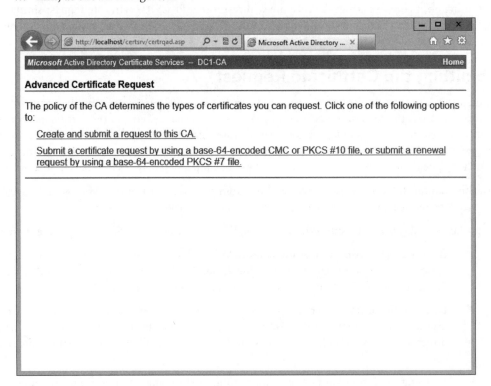

FIGURE 15-9

5. Using Notepad (or similar text editor), open the certificate request file that was generated previously, and copy the contents of that file into the Base-64-encoded certificate request textbox, including the " -----BEGIN NEW CERTIFICATE REQUEST-----" and "-----END NEW CERTIFICATE REQUEST-----" text.

6. Select "Web Server" as the certificate template that should be used to generate the new certificate (see Figure 15-10). Click the Submit button to submit the request.

FIGURE 15-10

Active Directory Certificate Services will process the certificate request and generate a signed certificate that can be downloaded using your browser. Click the DER Encoded link to download the newly issued certificate. The DER Encoded certificate can be imported into IIS 8.0. In some cross-platform situations, it may be necessary to use the "Base-64-encoded" option instead. Depending on the platform, you may need to decode the Base-64-encoded file before importing it. Click the "Download Certificate" link to download the certificate to the local server.

Importing the Certificate into IIS 8.0

The certificate issued, whether from a commercial CA or from Active Directory Certificate Services, can now be installed on the local machine. This can be done using the Certificate MMC or by using IIS Manager, as follows:

1. Start IIS Manager. (Press WIN + R, enter **inetmgr** in the dialog, and click OK. Alternatively, click Tools on the top-right of Server Manager and select Internet Information Server (IIS) Manager.)

2. At the server-level node, select the Server Certificates option.

3. Select the Complete Certificate Request option.

4. Enter the path to the certificate file that was issued by the CA. Additionally, enter a Friendly Name to describe this certificate. This Friendly Name will be displayed in IIS Manager. The name should help you identify what the certificate is being used for (e.g., the name of the website that will be using the certificate, as shown in Figure 15-11). Change the Certificate Store dropdown to Web Hosting to take advantage of the new, scalable certificate store, or leave it set to Personal Store for backward compatibility.

5. Click OK to install the certificate.

FIGURE 15-11

Configuring Website Bindings

To use the newly installed certificate, you must update the website bindings. This allows a website to listen on an additional port for SSL/TLS connections — typically, port 443.

> **NOTE** *Although binding configuration is updated at an individual website level, the binding configuration information is stored in the server's* applicationHost .config *file, not in individual* web.config *files under each website. Allowing individual website owners to change the bindings for their websites is a security risk.*

To update the binding for a website to allow it to accept SSL/TLS connections, perform the following steps:

1. Open IIS Manager with a user that has permissions to update the `applicationHost.config` file (by default, users in the local Administrators group).

2. Locate the website to which you want to allow SSL/TLS connections, and click the Bindings link in the Actions pane.

3. Click the Add button to add an additional binding.

4. Set the binding type to `https`, and, optionally, select the IP address(es) that the website should listen on for SSL/TLS connections. Alternatively, the All Unassigned option can be used to have the website listen for SSL/TLS connections on any IP address not already assigned to another website.

5. Select the installed certificate that should be used for this website, as shown in Figure 15-12. Setting the host header and SNI is covered later in this chapter.

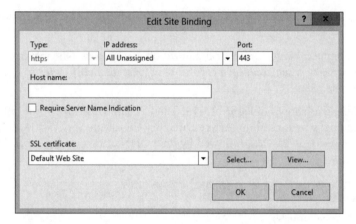

FIGURE 15-12

6. Click OK twice to exit the dialogs and update the website's bindings.

You can also update a website's bindings by using the `AppCmd` command-line tool. To add an HTTPS binding to an existing site called Site1, run the following command:

```
appcmd.exe set site /site.name:"Site1"
/+bindings.[protocol='https',bindingInformation='*:443:']
```

Editing bindings and other website configuration details are covered in detail in Chapter 6, "Website Administration."

Generating a Certificate Using Domain Certificate Request

If Active Directory Certificate Services (ADCS) is installed in the organization in Enterprise (Active Directory Integrated) rather than Standalone mode, then the IIS 8.0 Domain Certificate Request feature can be used to automatically submit a certificate request to the CA and have the resulting certificate issued installed on the IIS 8.0 machine.

Because the process uses RPC, this process is not suitable where there are firewalls or similar equipment interposed between the IIS 8.0 server and the ADCS CA. Additionally, by default, only users in the Domain Admins and Enterprise Admins groups have permissions to enroll server authentication certificates automatically. The Domain Certificate Request wizard must be run by a user in a group that has permission to enroll certificates based on the Web Server certificate template.

> **NOTE** *For information on altering the default configuration to allow other users or groups to enroll server authentication certificates, see the section "Managing a Public Key Infrastructure" later in this chapter.*

To request and install a certificate using the Domain Certificate Request wizard, perform the following steps:

1. Open IIS Manager. At the server-level node, select the Server Certificates option.

2. Select the Create Domain Certificate option to begin the certificate request generation process.

3. Enter the server's Common Name and your organization's properties. The information entered here is the same as when creating a certificate request manually (refer to Figure 15-5). Click Next to continue.

4. Enter your CA address, as shown in Figure 15-13. The CA name takes the form of the Common Name entered when installing Active Directory Certificate Services (by default, `<domain-name>`-`<servername>`-CA), followed by the FQDN of the machine that ADCS is running on.

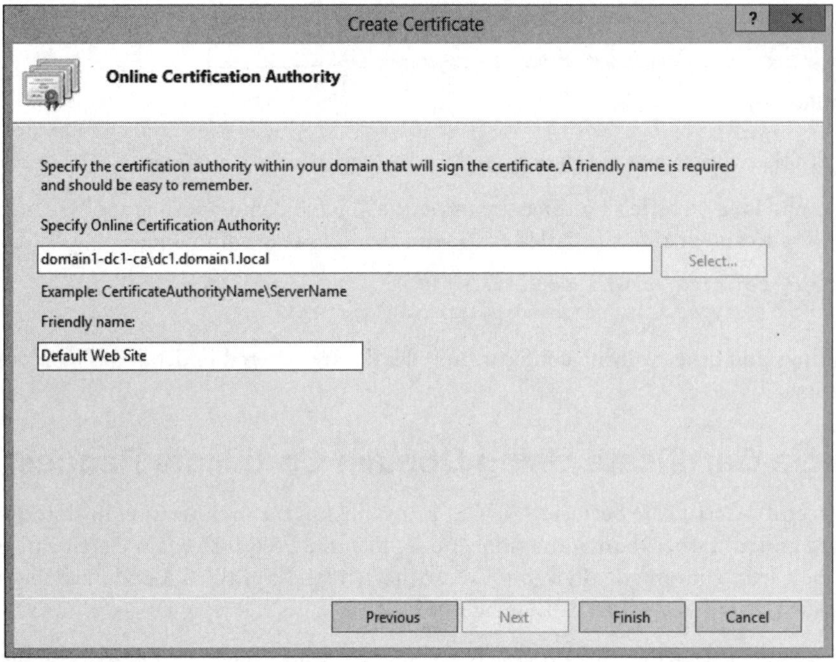

FIGURE 15-13

5. Enter a Friendly Name to describe this certificate. This Friendly Name will be displayed in IIS Manager. The name should help you identify what the certificate is being used for (e.g., the name of the website that will be using the certificate).

6. Click Finish to complete the wizard and submit the request to the designated CA. The certificate will automatically be issued by the CA and installed into the local machine certificate store on the IIS 8.0 server.

To configure a website to use this newly issued certificate, follow the steps under "Configuring Website Bindings" earlier in this chapter.

Generating a Self-Signed Certificate

When a CA is not available, a self-signed certificate may be all that is required. This is particularly true in development environments where a developer may simply wish to test that his or her application works over SSL/TLS. A self-signed certificate is one where the server signs its own certificate. Because no machine other than the server trusts it as a CA, any remote machine accessing the site will result in a warning being displayed to the user (for an example, refer to Figure 15-3).

To generate and install a self-signed certificate:

1. Open IIS Manager. At the server-level node, select the Server Certificates option.

2. Select the Create Self-Signed Certificate option to begin the certificate request generation process.

3. Enter a Friendly Name for your certificate, as shown in Figure 15-14. This Friendly Name will be displayed in IIS Manager. The name should help you identify what the certificate is being used for (e.g., the name of the website that will be using the certificate). Change the Certificate Store dropdown to Web Hosting to take advantage of the new, scalable certificate store, or leave it set to Personal Store for backward compatibility.

4. Click OK to generate and install the certificate automatically into the local machine's certificate store. To configure a website to use this newly issued certificate, follow the steps under "Configuring Website Bindings" above in this chapter.

Unlike other certificate request mechanisms, there is no need to supply a Common Name or any organizational details when generating a self-signed certificate. With a self-signed certificate, the Common Name is automatically set to the FQDN of the local IIS 8.0 server, and the Organizational Unit and Organization details are left blank.

Managing an SSL/TLS-Secured Website

After configuring a website to SSL/TLS connections, additional management or configuration may be required from time to time.

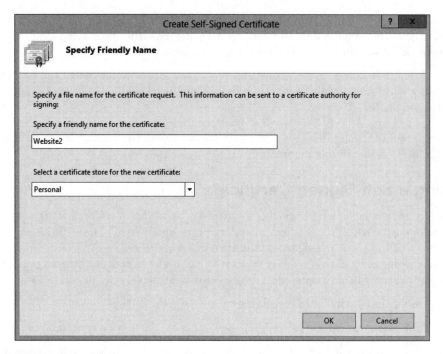

FIGURE 15-14

Configuring Additional SSL/TLS Options

An SSL/TLS-secured website has the following additional configuration options:

➤ **Require an SSL connection** — If this is selected, the website will no longer listen for HTTP requests, but only access HTTPS-secured requests.

➤ **Require 128-bit key encryption** — Key lengths less than 128 bits are not considered secure, and forcing this option requires the end client to negotiate a more secure connection. In some countries, U.S. export restrictions prevent technology supporting 128-bit key lengths from being exported from the United States.

➤ **Client certificates** — The website can be configured to accept, require, or ignore client certificates. Client certificates can be used in mutual authentication scenarios where the server uses a client certificate to authenticate the end user. For more information on configuring client certificates, see Chapter 14, "Authentication and Authorization."

To configure any of these additional options:

1. Open IIS Manager and navigate to the website node where you wish to configure these settings.

2. Open the SSL Settings feature.

3. Select the options required, and click Apply in the Actions pane to save the changes.

Exporting and Importing Certificates

In certain circumstances, you might need to export an existing certificate (e.g., to move it to a new server or to import into a dedicated hardware device such as an SSL offload device). The following steps can be used to export an existing server authentication certificate and import it into a different IIS 8.0 server.

To export an existing certificate:

1. At the Windows Start screen, type **mmc.exe**, and press Enter.

2. Choose File ⇨ Add/Remove Snapin.

3. Select Certificates and click Add. A prompt will appear offering a selection of the current user's account, a nominated service account, or the machine's account. Select Computer Account and click Next. Accept the default Local Computer and click Finish.

4. Expand the Personal or Web Hosting node where the certificates are stored, and then the Certificates node underneath.

5. Select the certificate you want to export from the middle pane, as shown in Figure 15-15.

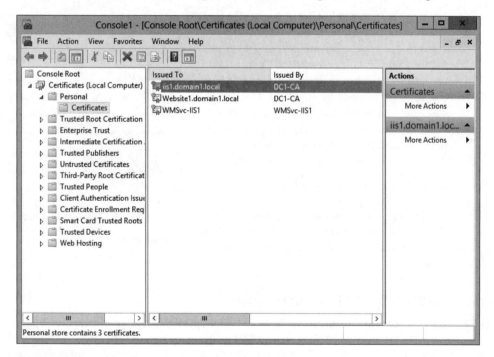

FIGURE 15-15

6. Right-click on the certificate, and choose All Tasks, Export.

7. Click Next on the introductory screen of the wizard. On the second page, choose Yes, export the private key, and click Next.

8. Accept the default Personal Information Exchange PKCS #12 format. If your certificate was issued by a subordinate or intermediate CA and you wish to export the entire certificate chain for import onto the new server, check the "Include all certificates in the certification path." Typically, this is required if you need to install intermediate CA certificates into the local machine store when installing the server authentication certificate. Click Next to continue.

9. Enter a password to secure the private key. You will need this password when importing the certificate on the new device. Click Next to continue.

10. Enter a filename to save the exported certificate as, and then click Next.

11. Review the confirmation screen — click Finish to close the wizard, or click Back if you want to change any of your selections.

To import a certificate on a new IIS 8.0 server, perform the following steps:

1. Open IIS Manager. At the server-level node, select the Server Certificates option.

2. Click the Import link in the Actions pane.

3. Enter the path to the PKCS#12 (.pfx) file that was previously exported, and enter the password to decrypt the private key, as shown in Figure 15-16. If you ever wish to export this certificate in the future, ensure that the "Allow this certificate to be exported" checkbox is checked. Change the Certificate Store dropdown to Web Hosting to take advantage of the new, scalable certificate store, or leave it set to Personal Store for backward compatibility.

4. Click OK to import the certificate.

FIGURE 15-16

The certificate can now be configured for use with a website. Follow the instructions on configuring website binding above in this chapter to configure a website for SSL/TLS connections.

Configuring SSL and HTTP Host Headers

HTTP Host: headers are a feature of the HTTP v1.1 specification that allows a web server to host multiple websites on a single IP address and TCP port, while simultaneously allowing HTTP v1.1 clients to specify the website to which they wish to connect. The process requires that the client send a Host: HTTP header as part of the HTTP request specifying a website it wishes to access, and the web server having a website configured with a corresponding HTTP Host: header value. For more information on configuring Host: headers for use with websites, see Chapter 6.

When using SSL/TLS, the entire HTTP request is encrypted, including the HTTP Host: header. This means that the web server needs some separate mechanism for determining which website the request should be routed to. Traditionally, this has required each SSL/TLS-secured website to be run on a unique combination of IP address and TCP port.

Since Windows Server 2003 SP1, IIS has had support for newer types of certificates that allow responses to more than a single domain name. This has allowed a site (or combination of sites) to respond to requests for multiple websites. There are two particular types of certificates:

➤ **Wildcard certificates** — Wildcard certificates contain `*.domain.tld` (e.g., `*.example.com`) in the CN (Common Name) field and can be used for a request for any host name within that domain.

➤ **Certificates with the Subject Alternate Name (SAN) field populated** — Sometimes called *Unified Communications* (UC) *certificates*, these certificates have a host name specified in the CN field (just like regular certs), plus a list of additional host names in the SAN field. The host names in the SAN field do not have to belong to the same domain: These certificates can be used to answer a request for any of the specific host names listed in the CN or SAN fields.

To be able to use HTTP `Host:` headers with SSL/TLS-secured websites, where those websites run on the same IP address and TCP port, there must be no ambiguity about which certificate to present to the client. For example, if there is a certificate with a CN of *website1.example.com* and a SAN field of `website2.example.com`, then it would be possible to:

➤ Create a single website with the SSL host headers of both `website1.example.com` and `website2.example.com`. Configure this website to use the available certificate.

➤ Create two websites using the SSL host headers of `website1.example.com` and `website2 .example.com`, respectively. Use the available certificate for both websites.

In both cases, there is no ambiguity as to which certificate should be provided to the client: The TLS handshake can be completed, and the underlying HTTP request sent to IIS. `http.sys` will be able to parse the HTTP request and, based on the decrypted `Host:` header, route the request to the correct website.

Server Name Indication

The preceding configuration can help in environments where one website needs to listen for multiple host names, or in a corporate environment where the same certificate can be shared across multiple websites. In a hosting environment, however, this is probably not suitable. Here, each customer has his or her own certificate, and the hosting provider may wish to host these all on a single IP address.

Server Name Indication (SNI) gets around the limitation of relying entirely on wildcard or UC certificates. It is an extension to the underlying TLS specification (defined in RFC 6066) that allows a client to specify the website host name being requested during the TLS handshake. This allows the server to present a corresponding certificate to the client. Thus, SNI requires support from both the client and server, unlike wildcard or UC certificates, which request server support only. As of this writing, most major browsers support SNI, including IE 7 (and newer) on Windows Vista (or newer); there is no support on Windows XP, Firefox v2 (and newer), and Chrome 6 (or newer).

SNI is enabled on IIS by checking the Require SNI checkbox (refer to Figure 15-12). There is no specific configuration required on the client side.

Enabling Central Certificate Store

Central Certificate Store is a new IIS 8.0 feature designed to simplify certificate management in cases in which multiple web servers (e.g., in a load-balanced web farm) all need access to the same TLS certificates. Before IIS 8.0, these certificates needed to be installed and renewed on each IIS server individually. Using the new Central Certificate Store, these certificates can be stored on a common file share and accessed by all configured IIS servers. Thus, ongoing management (e.g., renewal of certificates) can be performed at one single location.

There are some requirements for using Central Certificate Store. These are as follows:

➤ All certificates (stored as `.pfx` files) must have a common password protecting the private key. This may present some challenges in a hosting environment in which certificates are issued by third-party CAs and provided by customers to the hosting company.

➤ All certificate `.pfx` files must follow a specific naming convention so that IIS can match the certificate to the site. The file should be named `<domainname>.pfx` (e.g., `www.example.com .pfx`). For wildcard certificates, the host-name portion should be replaced with an underscore (e.g., `_.example.com.pfx` for a certificate that has a Common Name of `*.example.com`).

To enable Central Certificate Store on an IIS 8.0 server:

1. Open IIS Manager. At the server-level node, select the Centralized Certificates option.

2. Click the Edit Feature Settings link in the Action pane to configure the Central Certificate Store.

3. Check Enable Centralized Certificates to enable this feature. In the dialog, enter a UNC path to the file share containing the certificates, as well as the username and password that IIS should use to connect to the file share. Additionally, enter the password used to protect the private keys of the certificates (see Figure 15-17).

4. Click OK to save the settings and enable the feature.

Managing a Public Key Infrastructure

Implementing and managing a Public Key Infrastructure (PKI) is a book in itself; this section merely touches on some considerations. Readers are advised to consider Microsoft TechNet resources or *Microsoft Windows Server 2008 PKI and Certificate Security* (Microsoft Press, 2008) for more information on managing a Microsoft PKI.

If you are looking to protect a public-facing website (e.g., an e-commerce site), obtaining a certificate from a major third-party CA is the best route forward. However, if you need to protect internal websites, then deploying an internal PKI may be more economical, especially if you also need to deploy certificates for other purposes — for example, to permit users to encrypt files via the Encryptable File System (EFS) or to deploy 802.11x network access authentication.

Deploying Microsoft Active Directory Certificate Services in Enterprise mode (i.e., integrated with Active Directory) has several benefits. The CA is automatically added to the trusted root certification authorities store on domain-joined client machines. Additionally, clients can take advantage of auto-enrollment features, to automatically enroll for certificates without intervention by users.

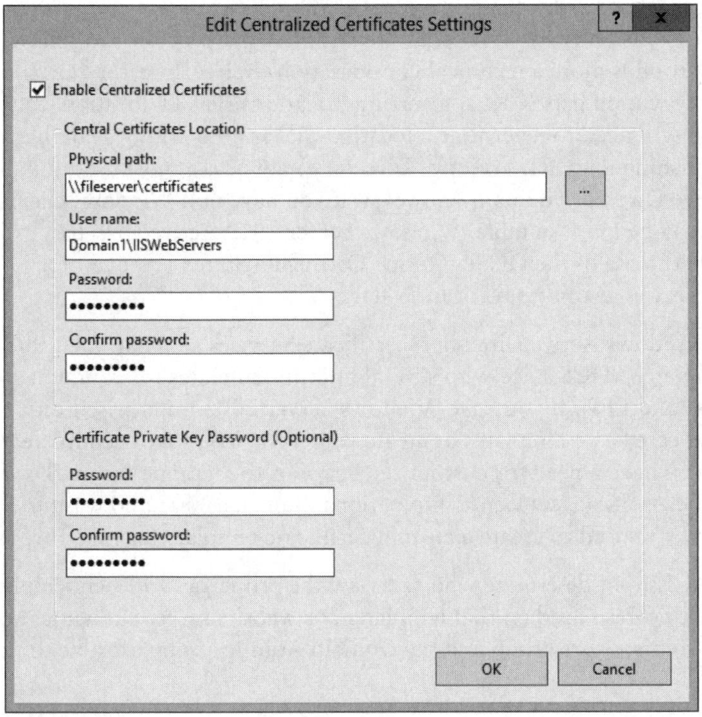

FIGURE 15-17

When deploying a PKI, it is essential to know that the CA's certificate is the "key to the kingdom." If an attacker is able to compromise a CA and obtain the CA's certificate, then no certificates issued by that CA can be trusted, nor can the identity of any machine presenting a certificate be guaranteed.

To mitigate this risk, many organizations deploy a two-tier CA infrastructure. A root CA (top-level CA) is initially configured (typically as a standalone CA, not joined to a domain). This CA then signs a certificate for a second CA. This second CA (known as a *subordinate CA*) issues certificates to end users or computers and is typically domain-joined (if using Microsoft Active Directory Certificate Services). There may be one, or more, subordinate-issuing CA.

In the event that the subordinate-issuing CA is ever compromised, the subordinate CA's certificate can be revoked by the root CA (thus invalidating any certificates signed by the subordinate CA) and a new certificate issued to the subordinate CA.

To mitigate the risk of compromise of the root CA, the root CA is typically maintained in an offline state (powered off or disconnected from the network). Additionally, tamper-resistant hardware devices (known as *hardware security modules*, or HSMs) can be used to store the root CA's certificate.

As part of the deployment process, you need to determine your certificate revocation policy. This determines under what circumstances a certificate will be revoked (rendered invalid) and how clients will be advised of that revocation. The first is a decision regarding what processes to follow within your organization. The second is more a technical consideration. Active Directory Certificate Services can publish certificate revocation lists (CRLs) to various locations (HTTP location, Active Directory, and so forth), and you will need to determine a location that is both highly available and accessible by all clients. Publishing the CRL to Active Directory may be the most useful if all clients are members of your Active Directory domain. However, if you have non-Windows clients, an HTTP location or file share may be more suitable. Windows Server 2012 Active Directory Certificate Services also supports the use of the OCSP (Online Certificate Status Protocol) for responding to client requests on server certificate revocation status.

When issuing certificates from Windows Active Directory Certificate Services (ADCS), each certificate is based on a certificate template. ADCS ships with several built-in templates for common scenarios (e.g., server authentication and EFS). If you have Windows Server 2003 Enterprise Edition (or higher), you can edit the supplied certificate templates or create your own. You may need to create additional security templates if you have a need for customized usage or to facilitate new OIDs. For example, if you are deploying Microsoft System Center Operations Manager 2007 and want to use the Gateway Server functionality, you need to create a custom certificate template for that purpose.

Certificate templates also have ACLs that determine who can view the properties for each template and who is permitted to issue certificates based on that template. For website server authentication certificates, users in the local Administrators group and the Domain Admins group are able to issue certificates.

Certificate template management can be performed (on your ADCS server) by doing the following:

1. At the Windows Start screen, type **mmc.exe**, and then press Enter.

2. Choose File ⇨ Add/Remove Snapin, and select the Certificate Templates snap-in. Click OK to add the snap-in and exit the dialog.

   Existing certificate templates are now displayed (see Figure 15-18).

3. To duplicate an existing template for editing, right-click on an existing template and choose Duplicate Template.

4. To edit an existing template, including issuing permissions, double-click on a template. Enrollment permissions are defined on the Security tab (see Figure 15-19). To permit an additional user or group to issue this particular certificate, add the user or group and grant them the Enroll permission.

Managing a PKI involves good processes. To ensure the ongoing security of your PKI and all the applications that depend on it, it is essential to define clear processes for certificate issuance, new template creation, certificate revocation, CA backup and recovery, and associated tasks. Additionally, a clear delineation of responsibility among IT staff for these tasks is essential. Readers considering deploying their own PKI are encouraged to read the Certificate Services deployment information available on the Microsoft TechNet website.

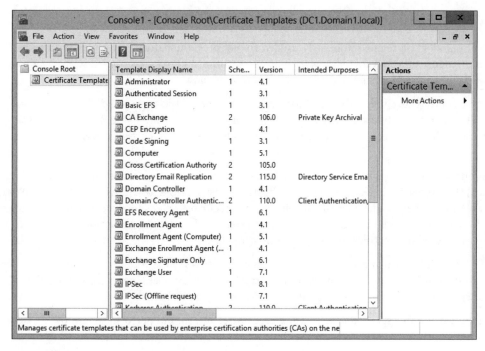

FIGURE 15-18

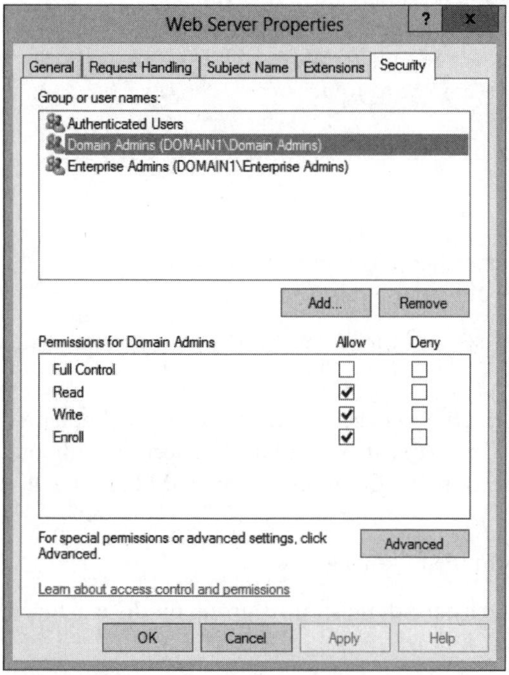

FIGURE 15-19

SECURING AN SMTP VIRTUAL SERVER WITH TLS

Although SSL and TLS are most popularly used with websites, the nature of TLS allows it to be used to secure many other protocols as well. The Microsoft SMTP server supplied with Windows Server operating systems has supported TLS for many years now.

TLS can be used to secure both inbound traffic and outbound traffic separately. The encryption offered by TLS can be useful especially if requiring users to authenticate using Basic authentication, because without TLS, the user's credentials would be passed in cleartext across the network or Internet.

Securing connections using TLS requires a suitable server authentication certificate to be installed on the local IIS 8.0 machine. Generating a certificate request suitable for securing an SMTP virtual server is the same as generating a certificate suitable for securing a website, except that a self-signed certificate should not be used because e-mail clients typically do not have an option to present a prompt to the user about certificates issued by untrusted CAs.

Unlike HTTP/HTTPS, which provides a separate port (port 443) for SSL/TLS secured communications, the Microsoft SMTP server requires only port 25 to be available. Clients should use the START TLS command to initiate a TLS-secured session over port 25.

After installing a suitable server authentication certificate, you should perform the following steps to secure transmissions:

> **NOTE** *Managing SMTP virtual servers requires using the IIS 6.0 Manager, rather than the native IIS Manager. The IIS 6.0 Manager is installed as a dependency when you install the SMTP server via Server Manager. The IIS 6.0 Manager is located in the* Administrative Tools *folder beside the IIS 7.0 Manager.*

To secure inbound connections:

1. In Server Manager, select Tools ⇨ IIS Manager (6.0). You must be in the local Administrators group on the machine to be able to use this tool.

2. Locate the SMTP virtual server that is to be secured for inbound connections, right-click, and choose Properties.

3. On the Access tab, check the Require TLS Encryption checkbox. The dialog will update with information indicating whether a suitable TLS certificate is available for securing inbound connections, as shown in Figure 15-20. Additionally, Event 550 (Source SMTPSvc) will be logged in the Windows Event Log.

To secure outbound connections using TLS, perform the following steps:

1. Open IIS Manager (6.0). You must be in the local Administrators group on the machine to be able to use this tool.

2. Locate the SMTP virtual server that is to be secured for outbound connections, right-click, and choose Properties.

3. On the Delivery tab, click the Outbound Security button, and then check the "TLS encryption" checkbox, as shown in Figure 15-21.

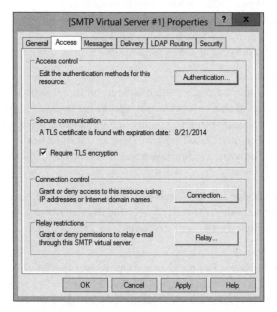

FIGURE 15-20

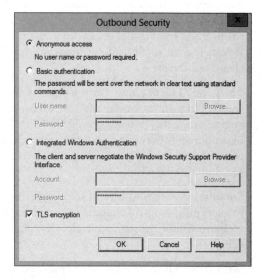

FIGURE 15-21

4. Unlike the dialog box for securing inbound connections above, no information is presented as to whether there is a suitable certificate available. However, if a suitable certificate can be configured for outbound TLS encryption, Event 2000 will be logged in the Windows System Event Log, as shown in Figure 15-22.

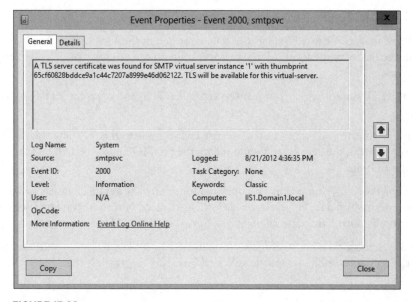

FIGURE 15-22

SECURING AN FTP SITE WITH TLS

FTP supports an anonymous access mode, which typically is used for public read-only FTP sites. For private sites (read-only, or read/write–enabled), enabling a password requirement results in the user's username and password being transmitted in cleartext between the FTP client and FTP server. The use of TLS allows the administrator to encrypt the transmission of information between client and server.

The use of TLS to secure transmission of data *does* incur a processing overhead on both client and server. For a server with many concurrent connections, this can become a significant overhead. To help alleviate this potential problem, FTP 7 supports encrypting the control channel (used for sending commands between client and server), the data channel (used for transferring data), or both channels. Additionally, an option exists to encrypt only the credentials sent across the control channel, and nothing else.

For administrators who want to protect the usernames and passwords of their end users, the option to encrypt the control channel only will be attractive. Files transferred over the data channel in this scenario will be transferred in cleartext; however, they won't incur any overhead in encryption and decryption.

With IIS's FTP server, it is possible to add an FTP binding to an existing, defined website. With this option, you can easily enable content to be published to a website using FTP and have that secured using TLS. Alternatively, you can explicitly define FTP sites (which need not be related to existing websites at all) and then configure TLS for those FTP sites.

Securing an FTP site using TLS requires a suitable server authentication certificate to be installed on the local IIS 8.0 machine. The process for generating a certificate request for a certificate is the same for FTP sites as that for websites discussed above in this chapter. Before configuring TLS for an FTP site, follow the steps documented above to request, generate, and install a suitable server authentication certificate.

To configure TLS for an existing FTP site:

1. Open IIS Manager. Because bindings can only be stored in the `applicationHost.config` file, you will need to be in the local Administrators group on the machine, or delegated appropriate permissions.

2. Locate the FTP site for which you want to configure TLS, and open the FTP SSL Settings feature.

3. Choose a certificate you want to use to secure connections to this FTP site. Ideally, the Common Name in the certificate should match the NetBIOS name or FQDN that is used to access the FTP site.

4. Choose whether TLS connections are optional for control and data channels or are required for both control and data channels, or click the Advanced button to configure individual settings for both control and data channels, as shown in Figure 15-23.

5. Optionally, choose whether to enforce a minimum 128-bit key length by selecting the "Use 128-bit encryption for SSL connections" checkbox. Key lengths less than 128 bits are no

longer considered secure, although in some countries, U.S. export restrictions on cryptography may mean that clients do not support 128-bit SSL keys.

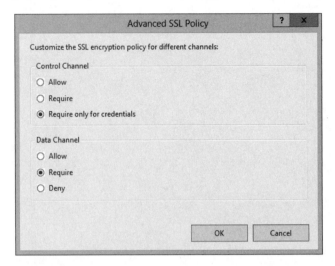

FIGURE 15-23

6. Click Apply in the Actions pane to apply the configuration.

> **NOTE** *IIS FTP supports FTPS (FTP over SSL/TLS). There is a separate protocol, SFTP, that involves tunneling FTP over SSH (Secure Shell). When evaluating client applications to use with the IIS FTP server, ensure that the clients support FTPS rather than SFTP.*

To configure a secure FTP binding for an existing website, perform the following steps:

1. Open IIS Manager. Because bindings can only be stored in the `applicationHost.config` file, you will need to be in the local Administrators group on the machine or delegated appropriate permissions.

2. Locate the website to which you wish to add a secure FTP binding, and click the Add FTP Publishing link in the Actions pane. The wizard will guide you through the process of adding a new FTP site and configuring TLS.

3. Choose the IP address, TCP port, and virtual host name upon which the FTP site should listen. For more information on configuring FTP 7, see Chapter 10, "Configuring Other Services."

4. Choose the SSL/TLS certificate that should be used for secured connections to this FTP site, and optionally select the Require SSL checkbox to force TLS connections, as shown in Figure 15-24.

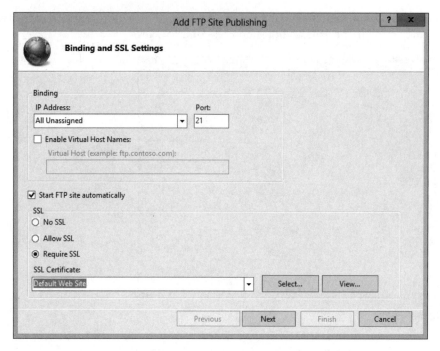

FIGURE 15-24

5. Click Next to continue, and configure access and authorization restrictions. Click Finish to add the new binding.

6. To configure advanced TLS properties for this secure FTP site, refresh the view in IIS Manager. The FTP SSL Setting feature will now become available, and configuration options described in the previous section can now be configured.

After updating your FTP site's bindings, clients can connect to your TLS-secured site by sending an AUTH TLS command when connecting to your FTP site. Detailed information on managing the IIS FTP server can be found in Chapter 10.

16

IIS Scalability I: Building an IIS Web Farm

WHAT'S IN THIS CHAPTER?

➤ IIS Shared Configuration

➤ Creating a machine-neutral IIS configuration

➤ Staggered installations and upgrades

➤ Shared web content options

➤ Session state and other shared technologies

WROX.COM CODE DOWNLOADS FOR THIS CHAPTER

The wrox.com code downloads for this chapter are found at www.wrox.com/remtitle .cgi?isbn=1118388046 on the Download Code tab.

For years IIS has been the web platform of choice for Fortune 1000 sites, and for good reason. Even back at version 6.0, IIS scaled to hundreds of servers to handle any load thrown at it. However, when IIS 7.0 was released, IIS took a large step forward. Now web farm support is a core part of IIS and, whether you're scaling to 2 or 200 servers in your web farm, you will find that it's straightforward, powerful, and flexible.

IIS 8.0 builds on the previous version by focusing on large scale configurations. Although versions 7.0 and 7.5 supported large shared configuration files, IIS 8.0 can handle very large files with ease, substantially enhancing the performance of even the largest configurations. This allows web hosts and other companies with similar needs to grow the configuration without worrying about performance. For example, you can add tens of thousands of sites to a web farm with thousands of servers, even if many of the sites are rarely used.

IIS 8.0 made significant changes to Secure Sockets Layer (SSL) performance, too. Previously a web farm with large numbers of certificates took a long time to spin up after a reboot. Now the performance hit for large SSL situations is negligible. Additionally, IIS 8.0 introduced the Central Certificate Store (CCS), which allows sharing SSL certificates between web servers. This was discussed in Chapter 15, "SSL and TLS."

Over the next two chapters, we're going to take a look at what you need to know to build out a highly scalable web farm. This chapter covers the Shared Configuration infrastructure, which provides centralized IIS configuration files for all servers in a web farm. It also looks at what you need to consider to ensure that there isn't any single point of failure and that your web farm is able to withstand almost any type of hardware or software failure, while still maintaining a fully operational website. We will also look at content replication, load-balancing options, and several other considerations to manage a web farm of any size effectively.

The next chapter discusses the topic of load balancers so that you can distribute traffic to your web farm using your algorithm of choice. We'll look at different load balancing solutions, the various configuration options, and Application Request Routing (ARR), Microsoft's best solution for load balancing web farms.

IIS 8.0 AND WEB FARMS

For IIS to scale out to multiple servers and remain manageable, it needs to ensure that the least amount of effort possible is required for each individual server. Ideally, you should be able to manage a large server farm with no more effort than you would take to manage a single server.

One of the key enhancements that was introduced in IIS 7.0 is Shared Configuration. It allows the configuration to be generalized so that everything unique to each server is removed. Then, that one configuration file can be shared by all the servers. With that in place, whenever a change is made to IIS, that change is essentially applied to all the servers at the same time. There is no longer any manual work to make changes to multiple servers or to manually run scripts to keep the servers in sync.

Surrounding Shared Configuration are many other smaller enhancements — for example, the ability to make the configuration file completely machine neutral, support for system environment variables in the configuration files, and a configuration infrastructure that allows multiple servers to read and write to the same configuration file without any locking or sharing violations.

Sharing the IIS configuration is by no means the only consideration needed for managing a highly available web farm, so we will also look at the other aspects of setting up and managing your web farm.

NOTE *Microsoft provides an entire framework for managing web farms — the Web Farm Framework (WFF). This framework will handle much of the work discussed in this chapter for you. It can take servers out of rotation for patching or upgrades, roll out new servers to handle scale, sync the configuration and content, and much more. If you have a medium-to-large web farm, you should give WFF serious consideration. There is a bit of a learning curve to make sure that it's set up correctly and works for your environment, but if you have multiple web farms or multiple servers in your web farm, then take a look at WFF. You can read about it and download it at* www.iis.net/download/webfarmframework.

Shared Configuration

As mentioned, Shared Configuration enables you to store IIS configuration files in a location of your choosing: in a local folder or across the network. It also ensures that sensitive information like the IIS user passwords are encrypted.

NOTE *Since version 7.0, IIS has been based on a distributed configuration. This means that the configuration is partially stored in the global configuration files* (applicationHost.config *and* administration.config), *but much of the configuration also lives within the site's* web.config *files, too. Therefore, when you set up a web farm, not only do you need to ensure that the shared configuration files are kept in sync, but you must sync the site content too. In most cases, you would anyway, but it's important to be aware of this requirement.*

Additionally, the runtime information, called the Runtime Status and Control API (RSCA), *is per server and isn't saved in any configuration file. This includes information like the application pool or website state, if they changed state automatically during an unexpected failure, and some statistics — for example, in ARR (discussed in the next chapter). This also means that recycling application pools or resetting IIS is only performed on the server upon which you run them. The live runtime state is not included with Shared Configuration.*

A standalone server stores the configuration in %windir%\System32\inetsrv\config. With Shared Configuration you can choose pretty much any other location for the configuration. When Shared Configuration is enabled, the redirection.config file in the old location is used to point to the new configuration location, but the applicationHost.config and administration.config files in the old location are ignored.

One of the first decisions that you need to make is whether to store the configuration locally or at a central location across a Universal Naming Convention (UNC) path, such as `\\server1\site1`. The potential concern with a central location is that the network or the central location may temporarily or permanently fail while the web farm is in operation. IIS does help us with that. If you point to a network share and the network share becomes unavailable, IIS will continue to run from a cached version of the configuration until the network location is available again. However, one issue with an unavailable network location is that IIS cannot start correctly if the web server reboots or IIS restarts and the configuration isn't available. Additionally, a non-redundant UNC path introduces a single point of failure if you cannot bring it back online before the web servers need to restart. A web farm, by nature, usually needs more redundancy, not less. Don't worry, there is a solution for that with the Offline Files feature, discussed later in the chapter.

Later in this chapter we'll look at both local and network options for the Shared Configuration location. We'll look at Distributed File System Replication (DFS-R) and offline folders, both of which offer good options for either local or network configuration locations. First, though, let's jump right in and take a look at how to set up Shared Configuration.

Enabling Shared Configuration is a two-step process:

1. Export the configuration files to the destination location.

2. Set IIS to point to that location.

Note that it is necessary to ensure that the exported configuration does not contain elements that are specific to any of the servers. The items that you need to be aware of are discussed later in this chapter.

Exporting the Configuration Files

IIS Manager allows you to export the configuration files and save them to a location of your choosing. After exporting the files, you can copy them wherever you want, or leave them there. The goal in IIS 8.0 is to make sure that the configuration files are generic text files that can be edited in a simple file editor like Notepad or copied between locations using simple tools like XCopy. IIS 8.0 has met this goal, making the entire architecture simple and scalable.

When exporting the configuration files, the following three files are saved to the new file destination:

➤   `applicationHost.config`

➤   `administration.config`

➤   `configEncKey.key`

From IIS Manager, this is done at the server level. Double-click the Shared Configuration icon to open that tool (see Figure 16-1).

The Shared Configuration tool has two parts: the main section, used for pointing to the configuration files, and the right-hand Actions pane, used for exporting the configuration.

To export the configuration files, click Export Configuration in the Actions pane. This opens the Export Configuration dialog window, as shown in Figure 16-2.

FIGURE 16-1

FIGURE 16-2

The Export Configuration dialog box has three required fields and the optional Connect As section:

➤ **Physical path** — The physical path can be a local path or a UNC path. The ellipsis (...) opens the Browse For Folder dialog box, allowing you to navigate to the folder instead of typing it in. You can enter a hidden network path, too, if you so desire.

➤ **Connect As button** — The Connect As button opens the Set Credentials dialog box. This is an optional setting and often isn't needed. This is only used this once, to connect to the folder and network share that you will export the configuration files to. If you don't set anything in the Set Credentials dialog box, the user that you are currently logged on as will be used instead. You would set credentials here if the user that you are logged into IIS Manager with doesn't have Write permissions to the destination folder or share.

➤ **Encryption Keys** — An encryption key is used to encrypt the `configEncKey.key` file that will be exported through this tool. (This will be explained in more depth shortly.) The password needs to be a complex password that includes uppercase and lowercase letters, numbers, and symbols, and is at least eight characters. Be sure to remember this password since it is required to configure the other servers in the web farm.

When you click the OK button, the current configuration is exported to the destination that you specified. If you are re-exporting the configuration, it will overwrite the existing files.

It's helpful to understand what the `configEncKey.key` file is. This file contains the RSA keys that will be installed on each of the servers when they are first configured for Shared Configuration. This ensures that all the servers in the web farm have the same RSA keys so that they can properly encrypt and decrypt sensitive information like the IIS Manager Users and application pool passwords. Think of it this way — the password entered in the export tool is used to encrypt the `configEncKey.key` file, which, in turn, contains keys that are used to encrypt and decrypt sensitive information in the configuration files.

Completing this dialog box is all that is required for the first step. This exports all the configuration files that are necessary for this server to share its configuration with other servers. Those files are ready to be shared and used by the other servers.

Relocating the Configuration Files

Now that you have the file exported, you must tell this server and all the other servers in the web farm where and how to point to those files. Until this point, you are still running off your original configuration files in the `%windir%/System32/inetsrv/config` folder.

Enabling the Shared Configuration and pointing to the Shared Configuration files is done from the same Shared Configuration tool, from the main section. Before walking through this, it's important to understand the two different password prompts.

The first password prompt is the username that is entered into this main window, shown in Figure 16-3. This is the user that is used to authenticate to the Shared Configuration path during normal operation. Since the Windows Process Activation Service (WAS) Windows service user is Local System by default, it's important to be able to specify a custom user to access network resources. Setting a domain user allows you to access a network share using the permissions that you specify. The domain user must have access to the shared folder; both the Windows share and the NTFS permissions. No additional Windows user rights need to be specifically granted to this user besides the share and file access.

FIGURE 16-3

> **NOTE** *Interestingly, the user entered here in the Shared Configuration is only used for read access by IIS Manager, WAS, and the programming APIs. But, any time that you write to the configuration files from IIS Manager or the programming APIs, it will not run under this user. Instead, for IIS Manager, it will run under the user that you are authenticated as, or it will run under the WMSvc service account user if you are using delegated administration and IIS Manager Users authentication. When making changes to the configuration using one of the programming APIs, the user account that the code runs under will be used to connect to the Shared Configuration store for write access. Therefore, it's important that you keep track of the permissions used for reading from and writing to the configuration since you may need to grant additional access to the Shared Configuration files.*

After clicking Apply, a second password prompt will appear, asking you to enter the Encryption Keys Password. This is used to decrypt the `configEncKey.key` file. The password is the same one that you entered in the export configuration tool in the previous section.

Following are the steps necessary to enable Shared Configuration for a server after you have already performed the export from the first server.

1. At the server lever, double-click the Shared Configuration icon to open the Shared Configuration tool.

2. Check the "Enable Shared Configuration" checkbox.

3. Enter the path in the "Physical path" textbox. This can be a local path or a UNC path. This will often be the same path that was set when using the Export Configuration tool, although it doesn't have to be, since you have a lot of flexibility in how you configure this.

4. If you are using a local path, leave the User name and Password fields blank; otherwise, enter the username used for authentication to the configuration folder. Usually this will be a domain user who has been granted access to the Windows share and NTFS permissions — for example, Domain01.local\User1 (or just User1, if it's a local user).

5. Click Apply.

6. You will be asked to enter another password, as shown in Figure 16-4. This is the Encryption Key password that was entered in the Export Configuration tool. This password is used to decrypt the configEncKey.key file, which, in turn, installs the RSA keys on the server. Enter the password that you entered previously and click OK.

FIGURE 16-4

7. You will be asked to acknowledge two prompts. The first prompt tells you that the current encryption keys have been backed up in the current configuration directory on your local computer. The second prompt mentions that both IIS Manager and the Management Service need to be restarted for the change to take effect.

8. Repeat these steps for all servers in your web farm, or see the section below for automation if you have several servers.

That's it. At this point, IIS will be running off the directory that you specified. After all servers are pointed to the same configuration any IIS change made to any of the servers will immediately be picked up by all servers.

UNC Polling for Shared Configuration

IIS 7.5 introduced the ability to poll the UNC path for configuration changes rather than relying on File Change Notification (FCN). This is useful if the UNC path doesn't support FCN, as may be the case for some non-Windows file servers.

You can manage this manually by adding attributes to configurationRedirection in the redirection file at %windir%\System32\inetsrv\config\redirection.config. The two new attributes work together and only come into play if the path is a UNC path; otherwise, for a local path, FCN will continue to be used. The attributes are as follows:

➤ enableUncPolling — When true, polling will be used rather than FCN. The default is false.

➤ pollingPeriod — Specifies the time interval between checks for changes to the configuration files. This is only used when enableUncPolling is set to true. The default is 00:03:00 (3 minutes).

The following example shows a polling period of 1 minute:

```
<configurationRedirection
 enabled="true"
 path="\\nas01\IISSharedConfig$"
 userName="domain01\IISSharedConfigUser"
 password="..."
 enableUncPolling="true"
 pollingPeriod="00:01:00"
/>
```

Automating RSA Key Sync

For your sanity it's important to automate the Shared Configuration steps if you have more than a few servers to manage; maintenance can become tedious if you need to do everything manually. While the IIS Shared Configuration isn't extra easy to automate, it is possible. There are three main steps that are necessary to automate Shared Configuration on a server:

➤   Sync the RSA machine key.

➤   Copy the two configuration files.

➤   Update `redirection.config`.

Syncing the RSA Machine Key

The Windows RSA machine keys — not to be mistaken with the ASP.NET machineKey — are used for the encryption and decryption of encrypted information in the IIS configuration. When those keys exist on all the servers of the web farm, they can all work correctly with the encrypted information in the configuration files.

It is possible to script the export and import of the RSA keys using `aspnet_regiis.exe` from the ASP.NET framework folder. To do so, first navigate to any of the framework folders that have the `aspnet_regiis.exe` file (e.g., `%windir%\Microsoft.NET\Framework\<version>\`). Then run the following two commands:

```
aspnet_regiis.exe -px iisWasKey "iisWasKey.xml" -pri
aspnet_regiis.exe -px iisConfigurationKey "iisConfigKey.xml" -pri
```

The `-px` says to export the keys, and the `-pri` says to include the private keys with it. Running this will generate two files in the current folder. Copy those to the destination server, and run the same two commands again from that server, but this time change the `-px` (for export) with `-pi` (for import), drop the `-pri`, and give the key a unique name. It should look like this:

```
aspnet_regiis.exe -pi iisWasKeyNew "iisWasKey.xml"
aspnet_regiis.exe -pi iisConfigurationKeyNew "iisConfKey.xml"
```

This should get you started to create your own scripts to import the RSA keys on a new server. Obviously, you can use your own paths and take care of copying the files across the network.

> **NOTE** *The RSA keys are saved in the All Users Profile in the path* `%ALLUSERSPROFILE%\Microsoft\Crypto\RSA\MachineKeys\`. *Because they are system files, if you want to see them from the command prompt, you must type* **dir /as** *to show the system files.*

After you have completed this step once on a server you don't need to do it again on the same server. You can perform just the following two steps if you need to perform maintenance on a server and remove or re-add the server into Shared Configuration.

Copying the Configuration Files

The next step is to copy the two configuration files to the new server. The files that are needed are `applicationHost.config` and `administration.config`. You can take these from whichever authoritative location you are currently using for the server farm. If you're setting up a new web farm then you can copy them directly from `%windir%\System32\inetsrv\config` from your golden server; otherwise, copy them from the location that your existing server farm is using. If you're using a central location or replicating the configuration path automatically, this step is already taken care of.

Updating redirection.config

The final step is to update `%windir%\System32\inetsrv\config\redirection.config` so that the Shared Configuration is enabled and pointing to the new location. There are two ways to achieve this. One is to edit the XML of the file, and the other is to copy a master/example `redirection.config` file over the existing file. This second method is easy because you can create it on one server, save to a master location, and then script it with a simple file copy.

To create the master file you can use IIS Manager to set up Shared Configuration one time and then save that `redirection.config` file. This will create the encrypted password for you, and since you would have completed the RSA file sync mentioned above, the encrypted password will work on all servers. Following is an example of what the `redirection.config` file looks like when set up to use a UNC path with a username and password.

```
<configuration>

  <configSections>
    <section name="configurationRedirection" />
  </configSections>

  <configProtectedData>
    <providers>
      <add name="IISRsaProvider" type="" description="Uses
        RsaCryptoServiceProvider to encrypt and decrypt"
        keyContainerName="iisConfigurationKey" cspProviderName=""
        useMachineContainer="true" useOAEP="false" />
    </providers>
  </configProtectedData>

  <configurationRedirection enabled="true"
    path="\\domain01.local\WebfarmConfig\site1"
    userName="domain01.local\User1"
password="[enc:IISRsaProvider:jAAAAAECAAADZgAAAKIUpmPJCNUjMGpYbz0PEdto7bbO5+lYUI5P+
X5YyR5hZogAU82H6LD2qNqWzBWKnb6VFfhHLwkPcFbQh5w43wFFMHkQuosJjFfORJ6US4SKKt3vbSVOyXh1E
qhzaRkc4K0U+aMeY1NjEASwMaBZmDjDyGTjiaFXJi:enc]" />

</configuration>
```

You should perform an `iisreset` after completing this step since some settings in `administration.config` will not be picked up unless IIS is restarted.

Now that you have these steps completed, your server will be set up for Shared Configuration. In a similar way, you can automate adding and removing the servers from Shared Configuration for upgrades and staggered installs. Simply move the two configuration files around as needed and update or replace `redirection.config` so that it's either enabled or disabled.

Reconnecting to Shared Configuration

It's not uncommon to need to reconnect to Shared Configuration. This is common after a staggered software install (mentioned later in this chapter) or other maintenance. If you follow the common practice of trying to connect to the same location again using IIS Manager you will be prompted for a password. If you happen to have the password handy, then it's not too big of a deal; but if you want to save the effort of digging up the password each time, there are a couple of little-known tricks to reconnect without needing to know the password.

> **NOTE** *It doesn't hurt to re-export again if you have lost the password and you need to join a fresh server to the web farm. It will overwrite the existing key — but it won't hurt anything — and then you can join the new server. If you are reconnecting an existing server to Shared Configuration, however, keep reading.*

The `configEncKey.key` file, which is created when you perform a Shared Configuration export, is only needed once per server so that the machine key can be imported for that server. After that is performed once, you no longer need the `configEncKey.key`. With that in mind, there are two ways to reconnect to Shared Configuration without reentering the password.

The first option is to manually edit `redirection.config` located at `%windir%\System32\inetsrv\config\redirection.config`. When you update this file using your favorite text editor, the change will be picked up immediately. The `configurationRedirection` element is the one that should be changed. When enabled, it should look like this:

```
<configurationRedirection
  enabled="true"
  path="c:\inetpub\IISSharedConfig" />
```

You can also disable it by setting enabled to `false`. It's fine to leave the path attribute set even if it's disabled.

Using this method of editing `redirection.config`, you can automate the install of your web farm, or you can do this manually.

The second trick to reconnecting to an existing Shared Configuration location is to rename the `configEncKey.key` to something like `configEncKey.key.backup`. When you do this and join a server to that location, you will receive the prompt shown in Figure 16-5.

FIGURE 16-5

Simply click Yes, and your server will be added to Shared Configuration without you needing to specify the password.

Again, to be clear, you cannot do this the first time you join a server to a Shared Configuration location, but you can do this every time afterward.

Creating Machine-Neutral Configuration Files

Having a single set of configuration files for multiple servers requires that the configuration files be generic enough to work on all servers, regardless of the unique settings on each server. This takes some forethought and planning. This section explains how to do this and the necessary considerations to accommodate your specific environment.

Access Control Lists

If you are intimately familiar with IIS 6.0, you know that the IIS 6.0 metabase had its own set of *Access Control Lists* (ACLs) for each section of the metabase, just as the NTFS file system has ACLs on files and folders. This allowed the administrator to lock down particular settings so that only certain users could read, write, list, or control specified sections.

In concept, this was powerful and allowed a lot of control, but in reality, it was difficult to maintain and to configure properly. For this reason, IIS 7.0 (and including 8.0) completely removed ACLs within the configuration and instead depends on ACLs at the file level plus some other configuration improvements.

This was necessary for web farm and Shared Configuration support. In the past, the ACLs would get in the way when trying to keep multiple servers in sync, and often a tool called `metaacls.vbs` was needed to repair permissions that got out of sync between servers. In IIS 8.0, this is a non-issue, since the configuration file doesn't contain any ACL information.

No action is required on your part, but it is helpful to be aware of how this improved since IIS 6.0.

System Environment Variables

System environment variables are an integral part of the Windows operating system and allow unique settings on each server to be defined in a variable that can be called from many different applications. These are commonly used in batch files, .NET applications, Windows programs, and most anywhere else you can imagine.

IIS 8.0 supports them as well. Starting with IIS 7.0, you can set environment variables in the configuration files instead of hard-coding the values. Common system environment variables that you may already be familiar with are `%windir%` and `%SystemDrive%`. The `%windir%` variable is a system environment variable that points to your Windows directory (which is usually `C:\Windows`), and `%SystemDrive%` is usually `C:\`. There are other environment variables, of course, and you can define your own, as discussed below.

By default, `applicationHost.config` already uses several system environment variables. In fact, by default, you won't see c:\ or d:\ hard-coded anywhere in the configuration files. Instead, all paths are relative to the environment variables. For example, the default site's `physicalPath` is set to `%SystemDrive%\inetpub\wwwroot`. Although it's rare to change a system path like the C drive, it's still cleaner to use environment variables every opportunity that you have.

Using system environment variables allows you to have unique paths on each server while still sharing the same configuration file. In an ideal situation, all the servers in a web farm will be identical and have the same paths and settings between them. That isn't always possible, however, especially for companies or individuals on a tight budget or who are trying to reuse servers for multiple purposes.

Because of this support for environment variables, it's a good idea to use environment variables when possible for paths. For example, if you use `d:\websites` as the root folder for your websites, create an environment variable called `WebsitePath` and set it to `d:\websites`. This way, if you ever change the path, or if you build a new machine that doesn't use the same path, you can simply update the server's system environment variable — no other change is required in the configuration files.

Now, that said, in all practicality creating system environment variables for your site paths may be more effort than it's worth since it involves creating them on each server and setting all paths in IIS to use them. Just be aware of this recommendation so that you can make your own judgment call on whether or not to use system environment variables for static site paths.

> **NOTE** *IIS 8.0 doesn't support environment variables on all attributes — just on the path-related attributes like* `physicalPath` *or* `Path`. *This is controlled in the schema files (most likely* `IIS_schema.xml`) *by setting the corresponding attribute to* `expanded="true"`. *To find out for sure which attributes support environment variables, open* `%windir%\System32\inetsrv\config\schema\IIS_schema` `.xml`, *search for* `expanded="true"`, *and take note of the attributes where it's set.*

If you create your own custom attributes, you can set `expanded="true"` so that you can use environment variables. Here is an example of one line from `IIS_schema.xml`:

```
<attribute name="physicalPath" type="string" expanded="true" />
```

To use an environment variable, simply set it surrounded by `% %`, as shown in the following example:

```
<site name="Site01" id="2">
  <application path="/">
    <virtualDirectory path="/"
      physicalPath="%WebsiteRootPath%\Site01" />
```

```
      </application>
      <bindings>
        <binding protocol="http" bindingInformation="*:80:" />
      </bindings>
    </site>
```

Notice the `WebsiteRootPath` environment variable in `physicalPath` instead of a hard-coded `d:\` websites value.

This is supported in IIS Manager, as well. When entering the path, simply type the environment variable name surrounded by the `% %`. Figure 16-6 shows a site's properties with the physical path set to an environment variable. Note that if you use the path selector in IIS, it will not use an environment variable for you. You must set it manually.

FIGURE 16-6

PowerShell is probably the best tool to manage system environment variables. Be sure to run in an elevated administrator window. To get a list of all environment variables type:

```
    Get-ChildItem env:
```

This includes both *user* environment variables and *system* environment variables. IIS will only pick up the system environment variables or the environment variables for the user that the IIS app pool runs under. Setting system environment variables is more convenient than messing with IIS user environment variables.

To set a new system environment variable in PowerShell 3.0, you can run the following command, replacing `WebsiteRootPath` with the variable name and `c:\inetpub` with the variable value.

```
    [Environment]::SetEnvironmentVariable("WebsiteRootPath", "d:\websites", "Machine")
```

After you set this new value, it will not show up immediately in your PowerShell windows and it will not work within IIS. You must restart IIS Manager and the IIS services for IIS to pick up the new environment variable. You can restart IIS by typing **IISReset** from the command line. For PowerShell to pick up the new variable, simply close and start a new PowerShell window.

With a little bit of environment variable management, you can neutralize the configuration files so that they will work in your web farm, even if the paths are different between different servers in the web farm.

Handling Per-Server Bindings

A common question with web farm configuration is how to handle the different IP addresses or bindings across a web farm. Your web farm load-balancing method (covered in the next chapter) may require a unique IP address per server, and you may have multiple testing URLs that are also unique for each server.

It's surprisingly easy to manage this as long as you understand a simple principle: *Unused site bindings are ignored; they will not throw an error.*

Even IP addresses that don't exist on the server will be ignored. When using IIS Manager and setting up a new site binding, you will be offered a dropdown list of all the IP addresses on the server. Don't let this fool you. That is a handy method of quickly selecting a valid IP that is already on the server, but you can type in another IP address free-form instead of using the options in the dropdown box.

This means that the unique site bindings on each server can be added to all servers and will be ignored on the servers where they don't apply. With this in mind, to properly manage a web farm of servers using Shared Configuration with different site bindings on each server, simply add all the bindings one time and they will be available to the servers as needed.

Now that you know that unused site bindings are ignored, you can set up almost any environment to have neutral configuration files so that all servers can share the same set of configuration files.

Distributed web.config Files

With the distributed `web.config` file structure in IIS 8.0, it's possible to use the `web.config` files to separate unique settings from each server in the web farm so that each server can have a unique configuration specific to its differences.

With the ability to pull settings out of `applicationHost.config` and set them in the website `web.config` file instead, it is possible to have different `web.config` files for each server on the web farm. See Chapter 9, "Delegating Remote Administration," for more information on applying settings in the `web.config` file instead of `applicationHost.config`.

Since most web farms will have shared or replicated content, it's not common to have a unique `web.config` file per server. This makes diversified `web.config` files a non-solution in many web farms, but it's good to be aware of the options.

configSource

If you must have unique settings per site per server, consider the `configSource` configuration attribute. The `configSource` attribute can be applied to configuration sections or individual items of the `web.config` file to pull out sections and store them in their own configuration files. This is particularly useful if you want to protect certain sections from being overwritten, or if you want to set NTFS ACLs on sections so that only certain people can manage them.

> **NOTE** For `configSource` to be used in a shared web farm to provide uniqueness to the configuration, you need to ensure that your configuration files are not replicated with the rest of the site. However, the `configSource` path must be a relative path in the same folder as the `web.config` file. This limitation is on purpose, for security reasons.

The following example shows how to create a separate configuration file for the defaultDocument section of a site.

Create or update your website's `web.config` file so that it looks like the following:

```
<?xml version="1.0" encoding="UTF-8"?>
<configuration>
    <system.webServer>
        <defaultDocument configSource="defaultDoc.config">
        </defaultDocument>
    </system.webServer>
</configuration>
```

Next, create a new document called `defaultDoc.config` and place it in the same folder as your `web.config` file:

```
<defaultDocument>
    <files>
        <clear />
        <add value="default.aspx" />
    </files>
</defaultDocument>
```

Notice that this allows the `<defaultDocument>` section to be placed in its own file rather than being managed from the `web.config` file. The list of default documents will now be controlled from `defaultDoc.config` instead of `web.config`.

The biggest issue on a web farm is that `configSource` is not supported within `applicationHost.config`. Without this being supported at the `applicationHost.config` level, it's not a common solution for web farms. This will only work for settings that are delegated to `web.config`.

Additionally, `configSource` will only work with *relative* paths; therefore, even in the `web.config` files, it's not possible to point to an *absolute* physical path on the server.

It's good to be aware of this, though. If you do have a unique requirement, you can use this as part of your solution.

childSource

The `childSource` attribute, on the other hand, does have more potential for a web farm. It only works for the `<site>` section in `applicationHost.config`, but that just may be the section that you want to save out to a different file. The concept is the same as the `configSource` attribute mentioned in the above section.

The `childSource` attribute's path is relative to the temporary application pool's folder (`%systemdrive%\inetpub\temp\apppools`), so it's best to use an absolute path — since absolute paths are supported with `childSource`. This means that you can point to a configuration file on your local server, which achieves the purpose of having unique site settings on each server while still sharing the same general configuration files.

The `childSource` attribute differs from `configSource` in that it doesn't manage any of the attributes for the parent. It only manages the child elements. Here is what `applicationHost.config` should look like:

```
<site name="Site1" id="1" childSource="c:\SiteConfig\site1.config" >
</site>
```

Notice the absolute path to the file on disk, and notice that the name and ID are still set in `applicationHost.config`. The `site1.config` file looks like this:

```
<site>
  <application path="/">
    <virtualDirectory path="/" physicalPath="%SystemDrive%\inetpub\wwwroot" />
  </application>
  <bindings>
    <binding protocol="http" bindingInformation="*:80:" />
  </bindings>
</site>
```

Notice that the `<site>` element is completely empty in `site1.config`. That is a requirement of the `childSource` because the attributes are defined in `applicationHost.config`. Changes you make to this file will be immediately picked up by IIS Manager, but they will not be picked up by WAS until IIS is restarted or `applicationHost.config` is "touched" in some way. One way to deal with this if you are making changes to the child configuration file directly is to add an irrelevant space to `applicationHost.config` to cause the change to take effect. When making changes from IIS Manager, they take effect immediately. Therefore, another option is to add a dummy binding to the site and then remove it again. That will also cause changes in the child configuration file to be picked up.

Unfortunately, `childSource` is not supported within the `location` or `system.webServer` elements so many of the non-delegated site settings cannot be configured in this manner. As you've seen, both `configSource` and `childSource` have their limits; however, they also have potential uses, so being aware of them does give you more options if you have a unique situation where you need to get creative.

Staggered Installations

Installing additional IIS features and third-party IIS-related applications can potentially make registry key changes, install components locally, and make changes to the IIS configuration files. This adds complexity to a web farm environment using the Shared Configuration because whatever is set on one server needs to be set on all the others, and if they are set out of order, errors can occur.

For example, consider a case in which an install is done on the first server in a web farm where the installer places files in the GAC or file system, makes a registry change, and then updates the configuration files. Because the configuration files are shared by all servers in the web farm, this will result in only one server having the necessary GAC components, files, and registry changes, while all other servers use the updated configuration. This can cause serious problems until the installer is run on the other servers. To make matters worse, when you attempt the install on the other servers, it may check the IIS configuration files first, determine that it is already installed, and not complete the install. Or, it may complete the install but add redundant entries to the configuration file, causing new errors.

A final potential concern with using third-party installers is that not all installers are intelligent enough to reference the `redirection.config` file to find the actual location of the Shared Configuration files. They may cut corners and update `%windir%\system32\inetsrv\applicationHost.config` directly. This will mean that, although it might appear that the installer has completed the install, nothing takes effect.

Fortunately, IIS will often give a warning and will not allow an install when Shared Configuration is installed, but you can't always depend on that to remind you to take care when dealing with an install with Shared Configuration enabled.

There are a few ways to address these install issues. One is to work with the vendor and get a manual install. With that manual install, you can create a script that can be applied to all the servers. If the vendor doesn't have a manual install, you may need to dig into the application or the vendor's documentation to learn what the installer does. Then you can script your own manual way to push the installs out across the web farm.

The obvious other solution is to use the installer on all the web farm servers. Be careful with something like this because you're at the mercy of the application vendor. You're particularly vulnerable running the installation as an administrator because the installation program can do pretty much anything the vendor dreams up, malicious or otherwise. It is generally good practice to get a manual install for each third-party package to ensure that you are in control of everything added to the server.

Regardless of the method, when performing an install on a web farm, you will need to perform what is called a staggered install. This means that each server will be upgraded at different times, and when it is not receiving live traffic.

> **NOTE** *As mentioned previously, Web Farm Framework is a solution that can take care of this entire process for you. If you have more than a few servers, you should consider it to help with these types of tasks (and more).*

Here are some tips and suggestions to keep in mind when performing a staggered installation.

1. The first step is to notify all other administrators who are working at that time that you have moved this web farm to a lockdown state and that they must not make any changes to IIS until you have finished. If they do make changes while you have only partially completed the install, the configuration can be out of sync, and their changes will be lost.

2. Take one of the servers out of the web farm so that it is not handling new traffic. Wait until all current page requests have finished and the load balancer is not sending any further traffic to that server.

3. Turn off Shared Configuration. This is done in reverse to how it was described in the "Shared Configuration" section at the beginning of this chapter. From the server level, double-click the Shared Configuration icon. Uncheck the Enable Shared Configuration checkbox and click Apply. You will be prompted with three choices, as shown in Figure 16-7. You are asked if you want to import the current Shared Configuration into your local server or if you want to use the old one that is already on your local server. Unless you have some reason to use the old configuration from before you enabled Shared Configuration, you should click Yes. The Shared Configuration files will be copied to your `%windir%\system32\inetsrv\config` folder. This means that your server will function with the same settings as it did while using Shared Configuration even though it is reading them from the local configuration. As long as no one makes any changes to the configuration on any of the servers, it is OK if the servers are reading from local configuration files for this period of time. Perform an `iisreset`.

FIGURE 16-7

4. Now it is time to run the installer or add the IIS feature. This will install everything locally and update the local configuration files without touching the other servers in the web farm.

5. At this point, you can add this server back to the load balancer so that your server farm has enough servers to handle the load while the other servers are updated. Just don't export the configuration to the shared location yet or it will break the other servers that haven't had the install performed.

6. Repeat this process for all the servers in the web farm. Since only you know your web farm well enough to plan the specifics, you can do half of your servers while transferring your load over to the other half, or you can take them out and replace them one by one, or you can point your traffic to a "Down for maintenance" website during this maintenance. Whichever method you decide, make sure to plan it well so that you don't cause failures during the install.

7. When you have completed the install on all the servers in the web farm, take one of the servers and export the configuration to the Shared Configuration location. Perform an `iisreset` after adding the server back to the web farm. This is needed if there are significant changes, and it is worth doing to be safe.

8. Add the remaining servers back to Shared Configuration as you did with the first server.

9. After finishing the previous steps, complete your final cleanup. Enable all servers on the load balancer, notify all other administrators and customers that the maintenance is complete, and complete any documentation and post-project housekeeping.

As with everything else, be sure to test the whole process thoroughly in a staging environment first before installing it in production. Don't allow a lack of processes or planning to be the weak link in your web farm environment.

So far, this chapter has covered the Shared Configuration mechanism in IIS 8.0 and how to make the configuration files machine-neutral so that they will work successfully on all servers of the web farm.

Additionally, the bulk of the IIS functionality for web farms has been covered. It really is that straight forward. Keep reading, though, because there are some specific considerations to keep in mind, and there will be some discussion about content replication and protecting the IIS configuration files from any network hiccup.

It's time to switch gears and move away from IIS specific settings and take a look at content replication, which can be applied to various aspects of the web farm to keep the servers in sync. The rest of this chapter is mostly non-IIS-specific and covers the tools necessary to build and maintain a web farm environment.

CONTENT CONFIGURATION

Before diving into the technologies that support a web farm, it's important to understand some high-level concepts for configuring the content for a web farm and to know which method you will use.

There are essentially three web farm file content configurations:

➤ Local content

➤ Shared network content

➤ Shared SAN content

The solution that you choose will often be based on the project requirements, budget, your previous experience, and/or available hardware. Each solution has its own set of advantages and limitations.

Local Content

Figure 16-8 shows a web farm configuration using *local content*. Each of the web servers keeps the content locally, and therefore it's up to the system administrator to set up either an automatic method of replication or a way to push content to all nodes after it has gone through the quality assurance team and is ready for deployment. In the case of the website writing files or changes to disk, it's important that the content be immediately replicated to the other servers so that they remain in sync.

There are several advantages and disadvantages of a web farm file content configuration using local content. Following are some advantages:

➤ There is complete isolation between servers. If something goes wrong, usually only one of the servers is affected, and if the load balancer properly takes it out of rotation, end users won't be affected.

➤ It has the ability to distribute load evenly. Each server handles its own load, removing disk I/O pressure from a central location.

➤ Because there are fewer moving parts, local content configuration is straightforward.

➤ It can be less expensive since another content server isn't required.

➤ Testing and troubleshooting can sometimes be easier because taking a server out of the web farm allows modifying the content without affecting any of the other servers.

This method also has some disadvantages or limitations:

➤ A solution for replication between servers is required. The more servers there are, the more complex this can become.

➤ If the website writes to disk (e.g., with a wiki), the other servers won't have that content available until the replication software copies it to the other servers. Depending on the replication solution and/or file locking, this may take a while.

➤ There are more copies of the data, which costs more if the website content is very large; that is, for a very large website (in terms of disk space usage), there will be as many copies of the data as there are servers (plus backups).

The advantages and limitations need to be considered within your particular environment to see if this is best for you. Many high-traffic websites on the Internet today use local content.

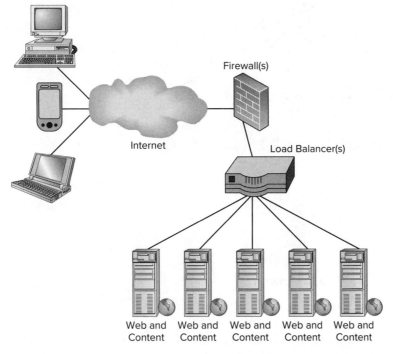

FIGURE 16-8

Shared Network Content

Shared network content utilizes a central location to manage the content, often using a Network Attached Storage (NAS) server, and all the web servers point to that location. Often they are mirrored to another server with some method of failover, but the web servers primarily point to a single location.

In contrast to local content, Figure 16-9 shows shared content using a NAS device. All the servers on the web farm point to the network storage over a UNC path. This is fully supported in IIS 8.0 (as it was in previous versions). Network shares are easy to configure on Windows or non-Windows servers, so using a network device for sharing content is easy to do for most any size web farm.

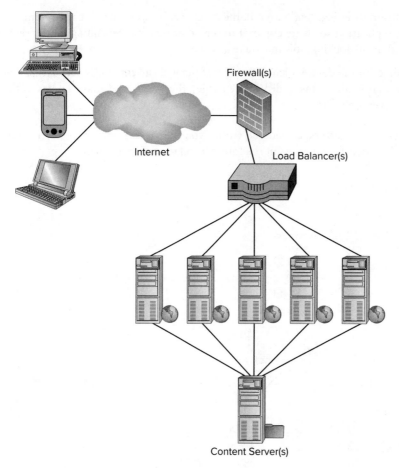

Firewall(s)

Internet

Load Balancer(s)

Content Server(s)

FIGURE 16-9

Shared network content has its own set of advantages and limitations. The advantages of a single shared network content storage location are as follows:

➤ Anything written to disk is immediately available on all the servers. In addition to website content, FTP, Web Deploy, and other means of transferring the website data, you only need to write to the one place for it to become immediately available to all the web servers.

➤ Adding the content on additional servers is as easy as pointing to a UNC path.

➤ Only a few copies of the website need to be kept. For websites that use a large amount of space, this can be beneficial. The hard drives on the web servers need to contain only the operating system; it's up to the content servers to maintain all the content. For a large web farm, this may mean two copies of the data (plus backups) instead of having copies for each of the web servers.

The disadvantages and limitations of this method are as follows:

➤ There is a single point of failure. This can be minimized with a good solution like DFS or a file cluster.

➤ More pressure is placed on the content location. As the site gets busier, if it overtaxes the content server, it's often difficult to scale out quickly to address the load. Disk I/O can become a bottleneck.

➤ Network bandwidth can become a concern on a busy web farm because, in addition to the bandwidth generated from the website visitors (common to all methods), there is additional traffic between the web servers and the shared network devices, which can be quite substantial.

➤ Cost can be a consideration since a set of content servers is required.

➤ The network device must support Server Message Block (SMB) File Change Notifications, which are not supported by all operating systems. Most Windows versions from Windows 2000 Server and on support at least SMB v1. Windows Server 2012 has enhanced support with SMB v3 and should be considered for the network server, if possible.

➤ There are more moving parts — for example, additional NAS devices or servers, network components, network shares, and NTFS permissions.

➤ The feature introduced in IIS 7.0 that injects the application pool SID into the NETWORK SERVICE token does not work across the network, so you should use custom application pool identity users instead.

➤ There can be potential locking issues because multiple servers use the same files. Be sure that your website considers this.

Don't let the list of disadvantages scare you. There are many environments where shared content over a network share is the best solution. Weigh the pros and cons of each method to decide which is best for you.

Shared SAN or Storage Spaces Content

A third option is to use a *Storage Area Network* (SAN) or the new Storage Spaces feature in Windows Server 2012. This will allow the storage space to be attached as a local volume so that it can be mounted as a drive letter or a folder on the system. The new drive or folder should be attached the same way to all servers in the web farm and be provided with the same drive letter or path.

The challenge with SAN or Storage Spaces is to ensure that all servers in the web farm can have read/write access at the same time. In previous versions of Windows this was only possible if you use a different file system besides NTFS — one that supports multiple access.

Windows Server 2012 introduced support within Cluster Shared Volumes (CSV) for general application data. This allows web servers to read/write data using a SAN or Storage Spaces, giving similar functionality as a UNC path does, except without some of the network path issues.

SANs and Storage Spaces generally offer more robust hardware with flexibility in the drive configuration to carve off only the space that you need. Some SAN solutions offer advanced replication settings, snapshots, de-duplication, thin provisioning, powerful RAID options, and preemptive responding to failures. Generally you can connect to the same using Fiber Channel, iSCSI, or FCoE.

Storage Spaces allows you to use a JBOD (Just a Bunch of Disks) disk array with commodity hard drives. This offers quite powerful functionality at very affordable rates. It does not have all the features that the enterprise SANs offer, but it is a good cost effective solution if you don't need the extra features found with other SAN products. You can mix and match disk types to create a combination of SSD and hard drives to give a tiered solution.

SANs and Storage Spaces share many of the advantages and disadvantages of local content and network storage. The advantages that SANs offer above local content and network storage are the following:

➤ Usually higher-end hardware with a high level of redundancy and flexibility to scale up and out.

➤ Easier to manage and adjust for growth using the built-in tools and features.

There are a few disadvantages:

➤ **Up-front cost** — Some will argue that a SAN is less expensive in the long run, but a small web farm may not reach that point. However, both Storage Spaces and SANs have aggressive pricing nowadays, often making them as affordable as a home-grown NAS solution.

➤ **File system requirements** — You cannot simply use NTFS as the file system. You must use another file system or setup a Windows cluster and CSV.

A good SAN solution can be costly up-front, but it has its advantages too.

CONTENT REPLICATION

A key part of virtually any web farm is keeping the various nodes of the web farm in sync. This applies to each of the three types of web farm configurations described above.

➤ For local content, you need one or many-way replication between the content nodes to keep them all up-to-date.

➤ For a NAS or SAN device you may just rely on backups if you believe that you have enough redundancy in place, but often you may want to consider a replicated copy of your storage solution as a fallback option.

In addition to the web content, there are various components that make up a web farm's website. They include, but aren't limited to, the IIS configuration, SSL certificates, content, session state, database, components in the Global Assembly Cache (GAC), and COM+ components. Often it is necessary to automatically keep this content in sync between the server nodes.

Various tools and programs exist to support this. Microsoft provides a few options, and there are many third-party vendors that have created extensive applications to take care of content replication. This section covers some of Microsoft's solutions and briefly discusses additional tools.

The two most obvious aspects of a web farm that would use replication are website content and IIS Shared Configuration files. Both are stored at the disk level, so a disk replication tool is necessary to keep them in sync.

You might be asking why replication is necessary when the IIS configuration can point to a UNC share. Without redundancy of the configuration files, the web farm hinges on a single point of failure, and therefore the content store needs to have a good replication and failover solution. This is covered below.

Distributed File System

Distributed File System (DFS), which is available as part of the Windows operating system, offers an impressive solution for keeping servers in sync. DFS is made up of DFS Namespaces (DFS-N or DSFN) and DFS Replication (DFS-R or DFSR). The two work together, using the same management interface. Together they offer a powerful solution for high availability and redundancy.

With DFS-N, if one entire server fails, the other will immediately take over without any configuration changes required on your part. DFS-N uses Active Directory (itself a fully redundant system if configured as such) and provides a fully redundant UNC path. This UNC path can be used from IIS, or elsewhere, and will continue to work even if the primary content server fails. It's worth noting that DFS also supports stand-alone DFS roots, which can also be used in a web farm, but they do not use Active Directory, and they do not offer the redundant DFS Namespaces described here.

It is also possible to use the two independent of each other. For example, it's possible, and fairly common, to just use DFS-R without using DFS-N. It is also possible, although less common, to use DFS-N without DFS-R. Examples of the former will be covered shortly.

Figure 16-10 shows an image of the DFS Management tool that is configured with a pair of replicated folder targets. The UNC path \\Domain01.local\WebfarmConfig\Site1 is a redundant path that can handle a failure on either server with almost instant failover capability.

DFS is part of Windows Server 2012 and doesn't require a separate download. To install it, perform the following steps:

1. Select Server Manager ⇨ Manage ⇨ Add Roles and Features. Follow the wizard until the Server Roles step.

2. Expand File and Storage Services ⇨ File and iSCSI Services, and select the DFS choices that you want.

3. Select Next and follow the wizard to completion.

Much more can be said about DFS than is covered in this chapter — be sure to research it well and test it well before depending on it in a web farm environment — but this information and the next few sections will get you pointed in the right direction.

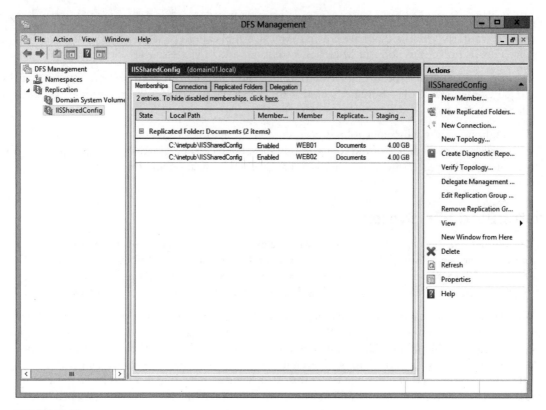

FIGURE 16-10

DFS Replication

DFS-R offers the ability to replicate data over either a LAN or a WAN with support for remote differential compression (RDC), a client-server protocol to efficiently replicate data over a limited-bandwidth connection by detecting insertions and changes so that only the changes to the files are replicated across the network.

This makes DFS-R extremely efficient over long distances, or on a local network. Once set up, DFS-R "just works." Little maintenance is required after it is properly configured. There are a few options for handling the replication method. You can have two-way replication or use a full mesh, or you can use a combination of these to create your own style of replication between all the servers.

Changes made to one server are immediately replicated to the other servers as long as there aren't any locks on the file. DFS-R also supports file creation, renames, deletions, or changes to the file itself.

DFS-R isn't for every situation, however. You should not use it if you have multiple servers writing to the data at the same time, or if there are often locks on the file. Microsoft Exchange and SQL Server will not work with DFS-R for that reason. Web applications tend to be prime candidates for DFS-R, and IIS 8.0 Shared Configuration is another technology that works well on DFS-R; it is discussed in more depth below.

DFS Namespaces

DFS Namespaces offer failover support for when a server becomes unavailable by immediately switching over to use the next server in the priority order. There are two modes for DFS Namespaces. The more robust is using domain-based namespaces, and the second is stand-alone namespaces.

Domain-based namespaces benefit from the redundancy of Active Directory and store the namespace information both in Active Directory and in a memory cache on each of the namespace servers. If configured currently, there is redundancy in Active Directory, multiple namespace servers, and multiple target folders, thus allowing redundancy at every part of the system.

Priorities can be placed on each folder so that a particular folder is always used first, as long as it's available. Additionally, DFS Namespaces can be configured so that the highest-priority server becomes the primary server again when it has recovered.

DFS Namespaces enable you to point to a UNC path (e.g., \\Domain01.local\WebfarmConfig\ Site1), which will always be available, even if any single server on the network fails.

DFS-R and the IIS Configuration Files

DFS-R is an excellent solution for the IIS Shared Configuration. It can be used in one of two ways:

➤ Use DFS-N and DFS-R together to provide a single UNC path to which all servers point. This path is fully redundant and can handle a failure on any server on the network (or more if configured for additional redundancy) and still provide uninterrupted service.

➤ Use DFS-R, but don't use DFS-N. DFS must be installed on each web server and will keep the configuration files in sync locally on each server. Set IIS Shared Configuration to point to a physical path on each server instead of using a UNC path.

Both options are fully acceptable, and really there aren't too many advantages or disadvantages for each one. The one that you choose is more a matter of preference.

The first option depends on the stability of the network, since IIS reads the configuration across the network when it first starts, and it watches for any changes to the configuration. It's convenient in that there is a central place that all new servers can be pointed to, and it doesn't require DFS to be installed on all the web servers.

The second option is potentially more stable because a network failure won't affect the IIS configuration, as long as general Internet traffic can still get through. If there is a network failure, the configuration may get out of sync until the network connection is available again, but IIS will continue to run normally since the configuration is local on the same server.

When using the second method, it is advisable to pick one server that you consider the configuration master server, and you should only make changes from that server. This ensures that changes aren't made to two servers at the same time when they are disconnected from each other, causing conflicts that DFS may not be able to resolve.

In either situation, be sure to use the IIS Export Configuration tool in IIS Manager to ensure that the encryption keys are exported and will work on all the servers. The first part of this chapter covered that in depth.

Whichever option you choose, be sure to test it well before releasing it into production, so that you are well aware of how it will respond in every situation.

DFS-R and Content Replication

Keeping the web content (files, folders, images, etc.) in sync between nodes is also key to any web farm environment. DFS can be used for any of the three web farm configurations. Just like in the previous section on the IIS configuration files, it can be used for replication between servers without using DFS-N, or it can be used to mirror a server to provide redundancy in case of a failure.

If used for replication of local content, DFS-R needs to be installed on all the web servers. Once configured, a new server can be added to the mix at any time. Just be extra careful when adding a new server that you don't make it the master server by mistake, causing it to replicate a blank or invalid folder, which, in turn, will blow away all the files on the rest of the web farm. It's important to test this in advance to be sure you can join this correctly to the domain 100 percent of the time.

Robocopy

Another tool that Microsoft has had for many years is *Robocopy* (Robust File Copy for Windows), which is available by default in Windows Server 2012. Robocopy is a command-line tool that will replicate content between servers, either one-way or two-way. It is not nearly as robust as DFS, but it's been around for years and has proven itself worthwhile.

Unlike DFS-N, Robocopy doesn't offer a method to redirect to the backup server if the primary server fails. Where it really shines is in easy-to-configure replication between folders. It can be set up in a batch file, scheduled using Windows Task Scheduler, and left alone. No installation is needed on the servers, and it will work with previous versions of Windows.

There are dozens of command parameters and ways to use Robocopy, including the ability to copy or move folders; choose how many subfolders to traverse; copy NTFS permissions; add or remove file attributes; determine which files, folders, or types to include or exclude; and much more. It is very powerful and flexible, but it has its limitations, as well.

One of the shortcomings of Robocopy is that it runs when you tell it to run, often from Windows Task Scheduler if you configure it as such. Therefore, it does not have a file handle on the files to know when they are created, updated, or deleted. This means that if a file is created on a server but that file is not on the other server, it does not know if it was just created on Server1 or just deleted on Server2. There is a /MON parameter that enables Robocopy to remain running and monitor for changes, but it does not run as well as something like DFS-R. This means that two-way mirroring is not completely trustworthy. One way to handle this is to consider one of the servers as the primary and the other as just a copy of the primary server. You can create a true copy with the /PURGE or /MIR (mirror) properties. With these properties set, Robocopy will delete files on the destination server if they are not on the source server. In the event that you need to failover to the secondary server, you should immediately disable /PURGE or/MIR so that new files that are created are not deleted again on Robocopy's next run. Another way to deal with this is to not use /PURGE or /MIR so that new files on either server will not be deleted by mistake. This will result in a need to do housekeeping over time because deleted files will not truly be deleted unless you delete them from both servers.

Here is an example of a batch file that does two-way replication between two servers. Create a file called `robocopyexample.bat`, and add the following to it:

```
robocopy.exe "D:\Domains" "\\10.0.0.10\domains$" /E /W:10 /R:3 /SEC /XO

robocopy.exe "\\10.0.0.10\domains$" "D:\Domains" /E /W:10 /R:3 /SEC /XO
```

This is just a small sample of the commands possible. The usage is as follows:

```
ROBOCOPY source destination [file [file]...] [options]
```

Let's take a look at this example and try to understand it. If you have spaces in your path, make sure to surround the path in quotes, as shown in this example. The `/E property` says to copy all sub-folders even if they are empty. The `/W:10` says to wait 10 seconds between retries (the default is 30 seconds), and the `/R:3` says to retry three times before giving up (the default is 1 million). The `/SEC` copies all the NTFS security settings. Finally, the `/XO` says to exclude files with older timestamps, which will result in the files with the newest timestamp taking precedence. Notice that there are two commands, one for each direction.

To see a complete list of commands, run `robocopy.exe /???` from the command line. With other tools like DFS-R, Robocopy has less of a place in a web farm than it did in times past, but there are times when Robocopy might be the tool for you, whether because of corporate policy, the inability to install DFS-R on your production content servers, your desire to have more flexibility on the files or folders that are replicated, or whatever other factors drive your decision.

Robocopy is also a great tool for an initial replication between servers for a migration. And you can also use Robocopy for IIS Shared Configuration. You can have configuration files that are pushed to all other servers on the web farm using Robocopy.

Offline Folders/Client Side Caching

Another option for the IIS Shared Configuration or web content is to use offline folders (aka *client-side caching*, or CSC), which offers faster performance when the network is slow, and offline files when the network is completely down. This allows the configuration files to always be available, even if there is a problem with the network. During a network failure, or a failure with the remote server, it will use the cached version until the network connection is restored. Windows takes care of this seamlessly once it is properly set up. This is the recommended configuration if you are accessing a UNC path for the IIS Shared Configuration.

To set up an offline folder for the IIS Shared Configuration, there are a few steps to configure the first time. Offline folders aren't enabled by default, so the first step is to enable and reboot. Here are the steps necessary for offline folders:

1. First, install the Desktop Experience, which is required for Offline Files to work. To do so, open Server Manager and choose Manage ⇨ Add Roles and Features. Step through the wizard until the Features step. Expand User Interfaces and Infrastructure and click Desktop Experience, as shown in Figure 16-11. Complete the wizard and reboot.

2. Enable Offline Files. Open the start screen and type **offline**. Click Settings ⇨ Manage offline files. If the "Manage offline files" link doesn't appear, give it a few seconds since it can take a minute to index the new link. Reboot.

3. After the reboot, open Windows Explorer so that you can see the UNC path to the IIS configuration files.

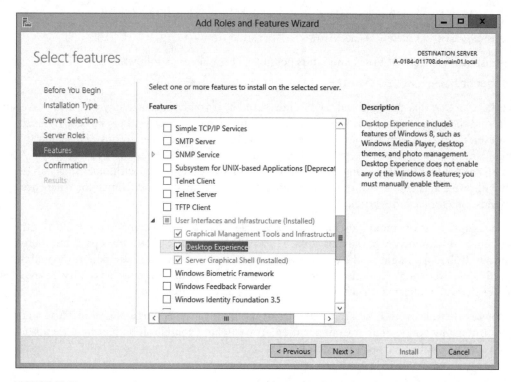

FIGURE 16-11

4. Right-click on the configuration folder (e.g., IISSharedConfig) and select "Always available offline," as shown in Figure 16-12.

5. Click OK.

After the wizard completes, your folder will have a sync icon beside it (see Figure 16-13).

Configuring and using offline folders will protect the configuration files against any network hiccup and ensure that IIS can read or write to the configuration even when disconnected from the main UNC share.

> **NOTE** *Offline folders can be used along with DFS Namespaces and Replication to give even greater resiliency to network blips. Generally, if you are pointing to a UNC share for IIS Shared Configuration, enable offline files for that folder.*

Keep in mind that if you have a failure to the UNC path so that you are in Offline mode, try to avoid making changes to IIS until the server is back online again so that you don't have mismatched versions. Otherwise, only one set of changes will take effect, while the other will be overwritten. If you specify one of the web servers as the primary configuration server, it will help avoid this issue and ensure that all servers have the same configuration at all times.

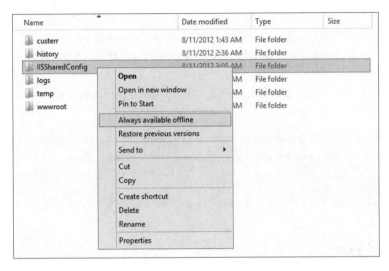

FIGURE 16-12

FIGURE 16-13

Additional Tools

The tools mentioned so far for redundancy and failover are by no means the only options available. There are many mature third-party solutions on the market that will help with not only the file-level content, but also many other aspects of deploying your applications from your testing environment to your production environment. Another option is Windows Web Farm Framework, which was mentioned briefly above. If these solutions mentioned so far don't meet your needs, with a bit of research, you can find many other good options available to you.

Web Deploy

Web Deploy (MSDeploy.exe) is a powerful command-line tool with many uses. At a high level, it's a deployment tool that can be used to migrate the IIS configuration, content, and many other

Windows components. It is also the foundation for publishing tools and Microsoft Web Platform. This is a powerful tool for web farms because it allows you to sync some of those more difficult components, such as the registry, the GAC, custom IIS configuration, and web content.

Web Deploy can work in Remote mode or Offline mode.

In Remote mode, one of the servers is set up as the server and listens for incoming requests (by default over port 80), while the other functions as the client, so that you can do a migration or sync between the servers in one step.

In Offline mode, no installation is necessary and you can export to a saved path, manually copy to the other server, and import on the other end.

> **NOTE** *See Chapter 20, "Configuring Publishing Options," for instructions on how to get started with Web Deploy. It is a powerful and versatile tool for the IIS and web farm administrator.*

OTHER CONSIDERATIONS

Just setting up load balancing and IIS Shared Configuration isn't all that is required to configure and manage a web farm effectively. The following few sections discuss other applicable technologies and how to configure them for your web farm.

Replication

Not everything will copy between servers as easily as the IIS Shared Configuration files or the web content. This section touches on a few things to keep in mind that DFS-R, Robocopy, and offline folders don't address.

SSL Certificates

If you use *Secure Socket Layer (SSL) certificates* on your web servers, they need to be installed on all the servers in a web farm. There are a couple of rules of thumb to note.

First, as long as the same certificate is installed on each server, then the shared IIS configuration will correctly use the right certificate, regardless of the server. As long as you ensure that this is true, you should be set, but there are some common misunderstandings about SSL certifications that are addressed here.

After you create a *Certificate Signing Request (CSR)* and send it to a CA, the certificate that the CA generates will work only on the server where the CSR was generated. You cannot apply the certificate from the vendor on any of the servers on the web farm except for the one that generated the CSR.

The solution is to go through the entire SSL issuing process on one of the servers on the web farm. After you have successfully installed the certificate on the one server, you can export it and use it all you want on the other servers. In other words, the CSR can be used only on one server, but an exported certificate can be used on multiple servers. Be sure to guard the certificate carefully and password-protect it so that no one else is able to gain access to it. Note that some certificate authorities will skip the CSR step and will provide you with the entire certificate.

Make sure that the certificate authority you use allows you to use the certificate on multiple servers. Some have requirements to use it on a limited number of servers, unless you pay extra.

> **NOTE** *See Chapter 15, "SSL and TLS," for a detailed discussion of CCS and how to create and manage certificates.*

Be sure that you don't install a new unique certificate for each server on the web farm since the certificates will not work correctly with IIS Shared Configuration. The only way for SSL certificates to work with the IIS Shared Configuration is to create the certificate on one server and then export that to all the other servers.

If your web farm is more than a couple of servers, you will most likely want a way to automatically keep the SSL certificates in sync so that you don't need to manage them manually on each server. IIS 8.0 introduced a whole new certificate store that makes this much easier than in times past. This is called the Central Certificate Store (CCS). This allows you to replicate certificates using a simple file store.

Registry Settings

Windows *registry settings* may need to be updated for one reason or another. Obviously, registry settings aren't replicated between servers by default. This is probably a good thing because it gives a chance to pull back the changes if something goes wrong with the first server that is updated. However, this also means that changes need to be applied to all servers somehow.

Registry keys generally aren't changed very often, so even a manual system can be acceptable for a small web farm, but if you make regular changes that need to be applied to all servers in a web farm then you will need some sort of automation.

Web Deploy is built for this and offers a good solution for registry key replication. PowerShell also makes it easy to script synchronization between servers. For the registry there usually aren't many settings that you would want to replicate. Usually you would just replicate license keys or some application specific section if you find that it changes often.

GAC

Files installed in the .NET *Global Assembly Cache* (GAC) also need to be kept in sync between the nodes of the web farm. Many assemblies would be placed in the bin folder of the application and don't live in the GAC, so syncing the GAC isn't necessary except for specific assemblies which are installed there.

You can sync the GAC manually or automatically. To manage the GAC manually, you can use the Fusion Cache Viewer by navigating to `%windir%\Assembly\` or by using `gacutil.exe` (which is available after installing Visual Studio or one of the Visual Studio Express editions).

Automation options for the GAC include `gacutil.exe`, Web Deploy, and Web Farm Framework.

Often an assembly is part of a larger install; therefore, be sure to understand the full installation process so that you can either install it manually on all nodes or run the vendor's (or your development team's) installer.

> **WARNING** *When viewing the GAC through the* `%windir%\assembly` *folder, you will see a unique interface that masks the disk-level folder structure. This is called the Fusion Cache Viewer. Interestingly enough, when viewing this over a UNC path, for example,* `\\machinename\windows\assembly\`, *it will show you the local GAC and not the remote one. Be careful that this doesn't cause you to update the wrong GAC.*

COM+

With the advent of .NET and managed code, *COM+* is quickly fading from existence, but there are still some legacy applications and code around that require COM+ support, or, if you have developers who are set in their COM+ ways, it's possible that new development may still use COM+.

There are a few ways to keep the COM+ catalog and files in sync between servers.

On a smaller web farm, you can manually register the rare COM+ component that needs to be registered or updated. This is done using whichever steps you currently use for individual servers.

Microsoft provides the `comrepl.exe` tool, located in `%windir%\System32\com`, to help keep the COM+ catalog completely in sync between servers without needing to register the components on all servers manually. It will also copy files between the servers, although it doesn't give you flexibility to set the path for the components on disk; instead, it will handle this automatically, as shown in the following example. Running it is as simple as navigating to that path and entering the following:

```
comrepl.exe <source server> <list of servers separated by spaces>
```

The two optional parameters are potentially helpful. The `/n` parameter disables any confirmation prompts. Ensure that you use this in any batch files, but be careful because the prompts are there for a reason. The `/v` parameter gives verbose log information in the command line rather than forcing you to dig it out of the log file.

The following is an example of using `comrepl.exe` from the command line with the `/v` parameter:

```
C:\WINDOWS\system32\Com>comrepl localhost 10.0.0.10 /v

WARNING: The entire catalog on 10.0.0.10 will be
replaced with the catalog from localhost
Replication is an irreversable action.

Please enter YES (upper case) to continue:YES

Replication started - logging to C:\Program Files\
ComPlus Applications\Replication\comrepl.log
```

```
COM REPLICATION LOG  - [DATE:10,13,2007 TIME: 03:54 pm]

STATUS [localhost]: Preparing to replicate from source computer.
STATUS [localhost]: Exporting application 'ASPEasyPDF' to 'C:\Program Files\ComPlus
Applications\Replication\ReplicaSource\Def\{41E90F3E-56C1-4633-81C3-6E8BAC8BDD70}\{
E6223F6B-A7B3-4386-9EEE-E71B5D3C15F6}\comrepl.msi'
STATUS [10.0.0.10]: Preparing to replicate to target computer.
STATUS [10.0.0.10]: Copying all exported application files from the source computer
to 'C:\Program Files\ComPlus Applications\Replication\ReplicaNew' on the target.
STATUS [10.0.0.10]: Removing old replica files in 'C:\Program
Files\ComPlusApplications\Replication\ReplicaOld'.
STATUS [10.0.0.10]: Renaming 'C:\Program Files\ComPlus Applications\Replication\
ReplicaCurrent' to '\ReplicaOld'.
STATUS [10.0.0.10]: Renaming 'C:\Program Files\ComPlus Applications\Replication\
ReplicaNew' to '\ReplicaCurrent'.
STATUS [10.0.0.10]: Installing application from 'C:\Program Files\ComPlus
Applications\Replication\ReplicaCurrent\Def\{41E90F3E-56C1-4633-81C3-6E8BAC8BDD70}\
{E6223F6B-A7B3-4386-9EEE-E71B5D3C15F6}\comrepl.msi'.
STATUS [10.0.0.10]: Setting identity for app 'ASPEasyPDF'.
STATUS [10.0.0.10] : Replicating Partition Users.
STATUS [10.0.0.10]: Removing the computer list.
STATUS [10.0.0.10]: Copying computer list from 'localhost'.
STATUS [10.0.0.10]: Copying local computer properties from 'localhost'.
Replication succeeded.
```

This example shows all the steps that comrepl.exe takes to copy over the components, user permissions, and catalog. This should be run only on systems that are configured virtually the same, as the change is made to all COM+ packages and does not allow you to pick and choose.

To create an automated solution, create a batch file to do this for you. You can then run it manually after each install on the primary or staging machine, or schedule it to run at regular intervals. Be careful, however, as this will copy the entire catalog over to the target servers.

You can also consider scripting the creation and syncing of COM+ using PowerShell or your favorite scripting language.

.NET Configuration Files and machineKey

The .NET and ASP.NET configuration files live in the .NET Framework config folder. Be sure that all changes made to these files are applied on all other servers. Also, don't forget that there are configuration files for each version of the framework. If you will support multiple versions of the framework, be sure that all configuration files for all versions of the framework are applied to all servers.

Another important configuration item is the .NET machineKey. For all the servers to work together as one, ASP.NET requires that the machineKey be the same on all servers. This ensures that if something like "viewstate" is encoded on one server and the user's second page request is handled by a different server, the different server is able to successfully decode "viewstate." The same applies to everything else that depends on the machineKey.

The machineKey tag has two keys:

➤ validationKey — Used to validate encrypted data like "viewstate" to ensure that it hasn't been tampered with.

➤ decryptionKey — Used to encrypt and decrypt forms authentication data and viewstate data when validation is set to TripleDES.

The default setting for each key is AutoGenerate, IsolateApps. AutoGenerate is as it sounds; it means that a key will be automatically generated rather than you specifying one. In a web farm, you don't want this because you want each server to have the same keys. IsolateApps generates a unique encrypted key for each application by using the application's ID. IsolateApps is okay in a web farm.

You can apply this at the server level so that it will apply to all sites, but just for the default framework version. Therefore, this tool isn't very consistent if you want to update the machine key for all framework versions. It's best to update the global configuration files manually if you will update this at the server level.

However, you can also set this at the site or application level. In that case, the tool in IIS Manager is helpful to save you having to look up the syntax and doing it manually. Note that if you make a change with IIS Manager at the site or application level, you need to update your source control version of web.config with the updated version so that it's not overwritten on the next deployment.

To configure this using the IIS Manager GUI, perform the following steps:

1. At the server, website, or application level, double-click the Machine Key icon (but at the server level it isn't recommended, since it only accounts for one framework install).

2. Uncheck the two checkboxes for "Automatically generate at runtime," as shown in Figure 16-14.

3. Click Generate Keys from the Actions pane.

4. The "Generate a unique key for each application" box is optional. The default is often good unless you have a site that needs to use Forms authentication across application boundaries.

5. Click Apply.

This will apply the change to a web.config file at the server, site, or application level. Any time web.config is touched, all sites and applications affected by that file will have their AppDomains reset. In other words, don't do this when handling production load unless you're aware of the brief AppDomain recycle (InProc session state will be lost) and slow first load.

Session State

Many websites require a way to maintain state between pages so that variables, like user settings, can be passed around the website throughout a person's visit. A common situation that often uses session variables is a shopping cart that needs to know the user and what he or she has added to their cart. Session variables are common, and the websites that you support may have a requirement for session state.

Session variables are maintained by the web server, and a small cookie is saved to the client. In this way, when a new page request is made, the cookie will let the server know who this is, and the server will retrieve the session information from wherever it stores it.

The issue on a web farm is that if one page request is handled by one web server but the next page request is handled by another web server, the two web servers each need to have that same data available.

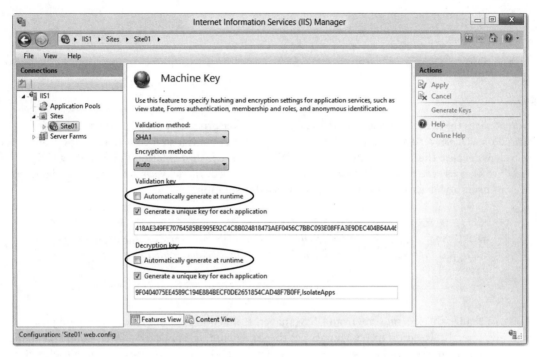

FIGURE 16-14

There are three solutions for this:

➤ Have your load balancer implement sticky sessions so that the same user gets the same server each time. In this way, the session information can be stored locally on each server and is only lost if a server fails. It only affects the users on that server when it does fail. This may be required for Classic ASP, which doesn't have any built-in session state solution that works with a web farm.

➤ Don't support session state. This isn't always feasible, but technically it's a solution. In fact, many website developers do decide to build their websites without a dependency on session state because of the web farm requirements.

➤ The third option is to ensure that your session state provider saves the session state off the server, or that it replicates the session data so that each server has all the data. It's this third option for ASP.NET that will be discussed now.

Since the most commonly used development platform on IIS web servers is ASP.NET and since it is Microsoft's solution for dynamic data-driven websites, it will get preference in this discussion. Many other development platforms or languages support a session state solution for web farms; thus, be sure to check with their documentation for the best solution.

ASP.NET has five options for session state:

➤ InProc

➤ StateServer

➤ SQLServer

➤ Custom

➤ Off

InProc

InProc saves the state In-Process, in the `w3wp.exe` worker process. This means that the data is stored on each server and is not available on the other servers. It also means that an application pool recycle will cause the session state to be lost. While it's the fastest solution (not counting Off), it won't work on a web farm unless sticky sessions are applied. If sticky sessions are applied and you are not using a web garden, then InProc is a workable solution.

> **NOTE** *See Chapter 8, "Web Application Pool Administration," for more information on web gardens, which can be confusing because they differ from web farms.*

You can change the session state from IIS Manager, from code, or from editing the configuration files directly. To edit it in IIS Manager at the server, site, or application level, double-click the Session State icon to open the Session State tool. Figure 16-15 shows the Session State tool with the default setting of InProc.

To set the session state to InProc from your `web.config` or other configuration file, add a `sessionState` tag to the `<system.web>` section of your configuration file, as follows:

```
<configuration>
   <system.web>
      <sessionState mode="InProc" />
   </system.web>
</configuration>
```

StateServer

StateServer is another solution provided by Microsoft, but it doesn't have any failover option. When ASP.NET is installed on a server, there is a service called *ASP.NET State Service* that is installed in Windows Services. This is disabled by default but can be easily enabled. Be sure to set the startup mode to Automatic so that it starts after every reboot.

By default, the ASP.NET SessionState can't be accessed remotely. To enable it to run remotely, set `HKEY_LOCAL_MACHINE\SYSTEM\CurrentControlSet\Services\aspnet_state\Parameters\AllowRemoteConnection` to 1 in the registry.

To enable StateServer from IIS Manager, follow the steps described in the "InProc" section above, but select StateServer instead. If you prefer to change this from a text editor, the setting will look like the following:

```
<sessionState mode="StateServer" />
```

If you are not using the default state server on the local server, you can set the parameters to what you need, as seen here:

```
<sessionState mode="StateServer" stateConnectionString="tcpip=10.0.0.10:42424" />
```

This configuration tag must be in the `<system.web>` section of your configuration file.

While StateServer is easy to configure and can manage session state in a web farm because all servers can share it, it doesn't have any sort of redundancy. You should use it only if you can accept that risk and have a way to switch to another state server if the first one fails.

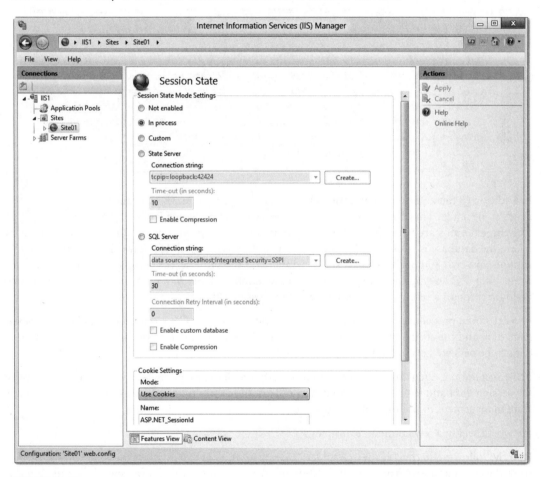

FIGURE 16-15

SQLServer

The third solution provided by Microsoft is *SQLServer session state*. If you have a SQLServer cluster in place, this is a good solution. SQLServer session state has the most performance overhead of any of the built-in options, but the added redundancy is often worth the slight performance penalty. Be sure to test it in your environment to ensure that it performs and scales well.

To use SQLServer session state, you must prepare your database to have the SQL Server state schema. This can be done from `aspnet_regsql.exe`, which is in the `framework` folder. This can only be done from the command prompt. The `aspnet_regsql.exe` GUI (opened by double-clicking the icon from Windows Explorer) is for other database features of ASP.NET and is not for SQLServer session state.

You can run `aspnet_regsql.exe` by using Windows credentials (the credentials that your command prompt is running as) or by using SQL authentication with a username and password that you provide. A third option is to generate a SQL script file, which you can run manually on the server.

> **NOTE** *Unfortunately, you cannot run this with just dbo permissions on the database because* `aspnet_regsql.exe` *uses msdb system-stored procedures and makes changes to the msdb database. None of the SQL Server roles are sufficient except for sysadmin. People have successfully used the* -sqlexportonly *parameter of* `aspnet_regsql.exe` *to generate the SQL script file and manually modified it to work in an environment where the database user only had dbo permissions. It requires several changes and is not supported by Microsoft. A detailed walkthrough of this hack is outside the scope of this book except to say that it is possible should you have that requirement.*

In addition to the authentication options for `aspnet_regsql.exe`, there is another decision that needs to be made. This decision is for the `-sstype` parameter, which is the SQLServer session type. The three options are t (temporary), p (persistent), and c (custom). The difference between them is where the database is stored. Both t and p create a database called *ASPState*. This means that you cannot have two SQLServer session state instances on the same server because the database name is not unique. The t option saves the session state data in the *tempdb* database and does not persist the data through a reset. The session state data is lost if SQL Server is restarted.

Several stored procedures are created in the ASPState database. The p option causes both the session state data and the stored procedures to be saved in the ASPState database and allows the session data to be persisted even if SQL Server is restarted.

The third option, c (custom), enables you to specify the database name that is used for both storing the session data and for the stored procedures. This allows multiple instances of SQLServer session state management to use the same SQL server.

It's worth seeing a few common examples.

Run the following in the `framework` folder (`%windir%\Microsoft.NET\Framework\<version>\`) from the command line. You can run it from any server with the .NET Framework installed; it does not need to be run from the SQL Server. Be sure that port 1433 is opened on the firewall.

```
aspnet_regsql.exe -ssadd -sstype c -S sql.domain01.local -d SQLState -U
User1 -P Pa$$word1
```

The `-ssadd` parameter says to add SQLServer session state (note: the `-ssremove` parameter is the opposite and will remove it again). The `-sstype c` parameter is the option that was just described to specify the type. You specify the server with the `-S sql.domain01.local` option. The `-d` is for the database, `-U` for the user, and `–P` for the password.

> **NOTE** *The parameters are case-sensitive, so be sure to match the case correctly.*

The following example does the same, except that the -E causes it to use Windows authentication instead of SQL authentication:

```
aspnet_regsql.exe -ssadd -sstype c -S sql.domain01.local -d SQLState -E
```

The following example is the same as the previous example, except that the sstype is p, which means that it will create a database called *ASPState* instead of one that you specify. Notice that the -d parameter is not used in this case.

```
aspnet_regsql.exe -ssadd -sstype p -S sql.domain01.local -E
```

Once the database has been prepared, you must change your configuration file to point to SQLServer session state management. You can do this as described in the "InProc" section from IIS Manager or by editing the configuration file directly.

When using IIS Manager, you must select SQL Server and set a valid connection string. The Create button will open a dialog box that will help you create the connection string.

The configuration file section should look like this:

```
<sessionState
  mode="SQLServer"
  sqlConnectionString=
    "Server=sql.domain01.local;Database=sqlstate;User ID=User1;Password=Pa$$word1"
/>
```

Once this has been completed, your website will be using SQLServer session state management, and if SQL Server is properly configured in a cluster, it will provide a fully redundant session state solution for your web farm.

> **NOTE** *As with most command-line tools,* aspnet_regsql.exe *allows you to view the detailed help with* aspnet_regsql.exe /?.

Custom

ASP.NET supports implementing your own session state provider, so if you want to implement something other than Microsoft's solution, you can do so. As with the others, once you've developed it and installed it on the server, either your site web.config or root web.config file can be updated to point to your custom provider.

Off

Session state can be turned off completely, and this is worth doing if you don't use session state, since there is a slight performance penalty to using session state, even if you don't use it. To turn it off, follow the instructions in the "InProc" section above, except turn it Off instead of setting it to In Process. IIS Manager calls this *Not enabled*. In your configuration file, it should look like this:

```
<configuration>
    <system.web>
        <sessionState mode="Off" />
    </system.web>
</configuration>
```

THIRD-PARTY SESSION STATE

Microsoft's AppFabric Caching Services (http://msdn.microsoft.com/ windowsserver/ee695849.aspx), ScaleOut Software (www.scaleoutsoftware .com), and Alachisoft (www.alachisoft.com) are reputable third-party options who have developed session state solutions for web farms. Their products are built for highly available, highly scalable web farms and either maintain session data in-process and replicate all changes immediately, or store the session data out-of-process through a custom worker process that resides on each server. Memcached (www.memcached.org) is an open source option.

Security

By default, the IIS application pools run as the ApplicationPoolIdentity user. This means that if you are accessing remote content over a UNC path, the computer machine account must have permission to access the remote resource.

It may not be desirable to use ApplicationPoolIdentity as the application pool identity because if you give access to the machine account, everything on that server now has access to it. It's an all-or-nothing permission setting. While it may be acceptable in some situations, it's more advisable to create a custom user for each application pool and assign that user to the remote resources instead.

Using Active Directory accounts makes this easier to manage because you only need to maintain the passwords in Active Directory and IIS. If you create a new server to add to the web farm, you can point to the same IIS Shared Configuration, and it will work immediately.

Using local users and groups is also acceptable; it just means that the same username and password need to be assigned to each server. As long as the password is the same, it will use pass-through authentication, which allows the different servers to function together even though they don't share a central username/password configuration store.

Code Access Security

In the past there was one other consideration when planning or growing a web farm that used ASP .NET and UNC paths: to create a *Code Access Security* (CAS) policy. ASP.NET implements CAS to ensure that website content resides on the local server or an approved UNC path. You had to tell ASP.NET that the UNC path that you are using was approved; otherwise, your site would not run correctly.

As of ASP.NET 3.5 SP1, this is no longer a concern. By now you are most likely using ASP.NET 3.5 SP1 or higher, so you don't need to be concerned about the CAS configuration for a UNC path. However, if you are using an older version of the .NET Framework, the `CasPol.exe` tool adds the UNC path to CAS's approved list. It is located in the .NET `Framework` folder (`%windir%\Microsoft.NET\Framework\<version>\`). To approve a UNC path, run the following command:

```
CasPol.exe -m -ag 1 -url "file://\\{NAS1.Domain01.local}\*" FullTrust -exclusive on
```

Running this will modify the `security.config` file in the framework's `config` folder. If `security.config` does not already exist, it will create the file. Once run, your website will allow a UNC path to the website content. In the example above, the `\\NAS1.Domain01.local\` path will be approved for access over the network.

There are a few things to note:

➤ Replace `NAS1.Domain01.local` with your server name. You don't need the whole path; that's what `\*` is for. You just need to enter the UNC path to the server.

➤ Enter the command exactly as written. If you put a domain name here but an IP address in the IIS path, it won't work.

➤ Run the command for both 32-bit and 64-bit of the framework that you support. However, you do not need to run it for ASP.NET 4.0 or higher.

➤ Run the command for all servers that you trust and that will be used by this server. If you have backup or alternate servers, be sure to add them as well.

➤ Don't run the command twice, or ASP.NET will fail because of a duplicate entry. `CasPol.exe` isn't smart enough to check if you already made that entry. The command will update a file called `security.config` in the `config` subfolder off the framework folder.

17

IIS Scalability II: Load Balancing and ARR

WHAT'S IN THIS CHAPTER?

➤ Load-balancing concepts and methods

➤ Hardware, software, and other load-balancing solutions

➤ Setting up testing URLs

➤ Application Request Routing

➤ Microsoft Network Load Balancing

➤ Web Farm Framework

➤ Windows Azure Services

The previous chapter discussed concepts relating to keeping servers in sync with each other and ensuring that your site can be served up from multiple servers. Taking this further, the next step is load balancing the traffic between multiple servers to support scalability and high availability.

This chapter looks at various load-balancing options to direct traffic throughout the web farm and ensure that even the load balancer is highly available and can survive a critical failure without impacting your web farm.

First, we will discuss some general load-balancing concepts to understand it at a high level. Then we'll look in depth at a Microsoft solution for load balancing: Application Request Routing (ARR). We'll take a look at Network Load Balancing (NLB), Microsoft's previous load-balancing solution, which still has a role complementing ARR to make it highly available.

Finally, we will look at two newer frameworks from Microsoft meant to pull together all the previously discussed technologies to function as a cohesive unit: Web Farm Framework (WFF) and Windows Azure Services.

LOAD-BALANCING CONCEPTS

A web farm is only as strong as its weakest link. If any part of the architecture fails and is not prepared to handle that failure, the entire architecture fails. A fully resilient web farm needs to be planned all the way through.

Each item has a different failure rate and also a different cost to make it fully redundant; therefore, the cost/risk decision needs to be determined by you and the decision makers around you. You may find that it's worth the risk to leave some parts without redundancy for less critical web farms, or you may have double or triple contingencies at each part of the process.

When planning your web farm, be sure to ask the following question: Do you have redundancy or failover options at network feeds from upstream providers, power, all network equipment, firewalls, domain controllers, DNS servers, web servers, content servers, database servers, session state, documentation, processes, and staffing?

You may have a requirement for geographical redundancy so that if an entire city were to be taken out by a natural (or unnatural) disaster, your websites would remain online. This often requires a complete copy of your primary location with equipment that sits idle, waiting for the once-in-a-lifetime failure to occur.

The point in all this is to make sure to sit back, put your feet up, and think through every part of your architecture. Simply having a web farm with multiple web servers doesn't make a fail-proof system. Your network team, firewall team, web team, database team, Active Directory team, and your management team need to have a well-thought-through plan for each and every type of situation. The old saying to plan for the worst and pray for the best is very true here. Don't be caught with unexpected downtime because one part of the system failed and you didn't have a contingency plan in place.

One more thing: Test, test, test! Make sure to schedule regular testing windows where you can "pull the plug" (virtually or literally) on different devices in your web farm and watch it continue to hum away just as though nothing happened.

This chapter looks at the load-balancing aspect, to ensure that the part of the system that distributes the load between the web servers meets your needs and is itself redundant and not a single point of failure.

Shared Concepts

Many concepts relating to load balancing are the same, regardless of which type of load balancer you use. This section looks at some of these shared concepts to lay the foundation for the specifics later in the chapter.

The OSI Model

It's helpful to understand some basic concepts. The *Open Systems Interconnection* (OSI) model defines logical layers of the network and application stack. This is useful in understanding load balancing because it gives us some common terminology to use when comparing various load-balancing solutions.

There are seven layers in the OSI model:

➤ **Layer 1** — Physical layer

➤ **Layer 2** — Data Link layer

➤ **Layer 3** — Network layer

➤ **Layer 4** — Transport layer

➤ **Layer 5** — Session layer

➤ **Layer 6** — Presentation layer

➤ **Layer 7** — Application layer

It's outside the scope of this book to look at the OSI model is depth, so let's just look at a simple reference list as it pertains to web traffic:

➤ **Layer 1** — Think actual cabling and physical devices.

➤ **Layer 2** — Think MAC addresses.

➤ **Layer 3** — Think IP addresses.

➤ **Layer 4** — Think TCP/UDP and ports.

➤ **Layer 5/6** — Supports layer 7.

➤ **Layer 7** — Think host header, URL, and other site data.

For our discussion about load balancing, there are two layers that interest us the most: 4 and 7. Most modern load balancers can direct traffic based on data from all seven layers, but some are more limited — for example, they may support up to layer 4, which includes the port (e.g., 80/443) and Transport layer protocols (e.g., TCP, UDP), but they do not support layer 7, which is load balancing based on the domain name, URL, or other server variables.

When choosing which load balancer to use, make sure that it meets your needs. If you are deciding on a new solution, there should be little reason to obtain a solution that doesn't support all seven layers. For example, being unable to load balance based only on the domain name, URL structure, or web cookies is very limiting in today's world.

Traffic Distribution

Various load balancers have different methods of distributing traffic, but for the most part they share similar concepts. Following is a list of common traffic distribution options:

➤ **Round-robin** — Each request is assigned to the next server in the list in a round-robin fashion, one server after the other, and then back to the beginning again.

➤ **Weight-based** — Each server is given a weight, and requests are assigned to the servers according to their weight. This allows some servers to handle more traffic than others.

➤ **Random** — Each request is randomly assigned to a server.

➤ **Sticky sessions (affinity)** — The load balancer keeps track of the sessions and ensures that return visits within the session or time-out period always return to the same server.

➤ **Least current request** — Since the load balancer usually has a handle on how many outstanding requests there are, it can route traffic based on the server that currently has the least current requests. The assumption is that the server with the least requests is also the most ready to take new requests.

➤ **Response time** — Similar to the least current request algorithm, the load balancer usually knows the response time of each server and can send new requests to the server with the fastest response time.

➤ **User or URL information** — Some load balancers offer the ability to distribute traffic based on the URL or the user information. Users from one geographic region may be sent to one server or sets of servers, while users in another region can be routed differently. The same can apply to the URL, query string, cookies, or other information.

Load-Balancing Methods

Load balancers need some method of forwarding requests to the web server while ensuring that the general communication between the client and web server appears relatively seamless. There are a few creative ways to achieve this.

Reverse Proxy

A reverse proxy takes an incoming request and then makes another request on behalf of the user. This makes it a middle-man between the client and the server, which means that the load balancer maintains two separate TCP connections: one with the user and one with the web server (see Figure 17-1).

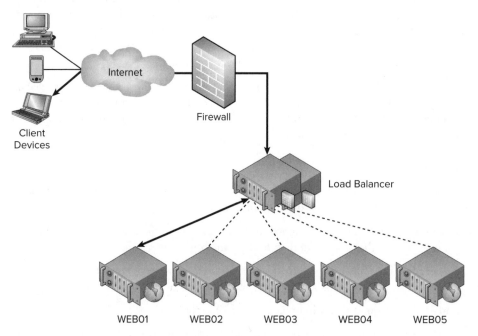

FIGURE 17-1

There are several advantages to this layer 7 method, and a couple of considerations. This configuration requires minimal changes to your network architecture. The web servers don't need to change their default gateway and the IP addresses of the load balancer, and web servers can be on the same network or different networks.

In this configuration, the load balancer has full access to all the traffic on the way through. This allows the load balancer to add treatments and potentially check for any attacks, and it can manipulate any of the URL or header information on the way through.

However, there are some potential issues. One is that the reverse proxy server maintains the connection with the client, so if there is a really long session — for example, a large download — the proxy server needs to determine if it's still an active session or a timed-out session. Setting the time-out value too high can open the server up for denial of service (DoS) attacks, but setting it too low can cause timeouts for legitimate traffic.

Another issue is that the load balancer, being the middle-man, is seen by the web servers as the client. This means that logging or any logic in code using headers like REMOTE_ADDR or REMOTE_HOST will all see the IP address of the proxy server rather than the original client who made the request. However, there are relatively easy ways around this by adding software to the web servers to rewrite the server variables to fool the web server into thinking that the web server had a direct line of communication with the client.

Transparent Reverse Proxy

This transparent reverse proxy mode is similar to the reverse proxy mode except that the TCP connection between the load balancer and the web server is set with the client IP as the source IP. This layer 7 method avoids the man-in-the-middle issue since the web server thinks that the request came from the original client. However, it requires that the web servers use the load balancer as their default gateway. This does require more network changes than a non-transparent reverse proxy, but that's not necessarily a bad thing, depending on your situation. While a non-transparent reverse proxy and a transparent reverse proxy are different, Figure 17-1 is a good representation of both. The difference between the two is how the load balancer passes the traffic on to the web servers.

As in a non-transparent reverse proxy, there are two separate TCP connections: one between the client and one between the web server. This gives the load balancer full control of the packets to add any treatments or enhanced functionality that it wants.

Direct Server Return

A long time tried and true method is called Direct Server Return (DSR). Some load balancers give it a different name: *nPath routing, 1 arm LB, Direct Routing* (DR), or *SwitchBack*. This method forwards the incoming request to the web server by setting the web server's MAC address. As a result, the web server responds directly back to the client. This gives a direct path back to the client from the server — thus, the name. See Figure 17-2 for a visual perspective. There is a single TCP connection established directly between the client and the web server.

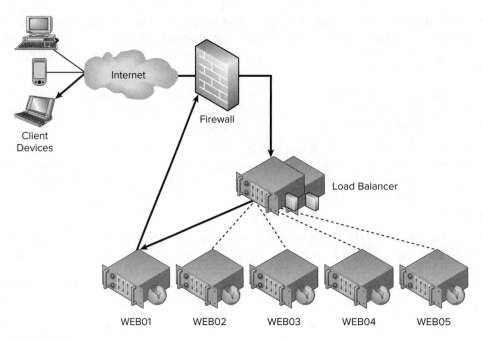

FIGURE 17-2

To achieve this, the web server needs to be fooled into thinking that it owns the IP address of the load-balanced IP, but it can't actually announce that IP address on the network. This can be achieved through a loopback adapter. (In Windows, that's the Microsoft Loopback Adapter.)

This was more popular in past years, when computing speed was more limited; it's less common now that computing power is easier to come by. DSR is extremely fast because it simply updates the MAC address of the packet.

This layer 4 method of load balancing has some advantages and disadvantages. The main advantage is performance. The HTTP request is often tiny — basically just asking for a particular URL to be served up. However, the HTTP response is the large part of the HTTP communication since it has the body of the webpage and all dependencies. If the server responds directly to the client, the load balancer doesn't need capacity to handle all the request and response communication. This allows even smaller load balancers to handle large amounts of traffic at near line speed.

DSR doesn't have the man-in-the-middle issue since the connection is established directly between the client and the web server.

However, DSR usually requires more effort to set up since a loopback IP needs to be created on the web servers. The biggest disadvantage is that since the traffic doesn't pass back through the load balancer, it cannot support many of the enhanced features that many of the other load-balancing methods support. For example, it cannot support SSL offloading, compression, or SEO treatments.

WEAKHOST REQUIRED FOR THE LOOPBACK ADAPTER

If your load-balancing configuration uses the Microsoft Loopback Adapter, there is a change that needs to be applied to Windows Server 2012. By default, `stronghost` is enabled, which prevents cross-interface forwarding. This means that a request coming in through a network adapter cannot be handled by the loopback adapter since it's a different network adapter from the one that the original traffic came on. To switch from `stronghost` to `weakhost`, run the following from the command line (run as a single-line command):

```
netsh int ipv4 set int "Local Area Connection"
weakhostreceive=enabled weakhostsend=enabled
```

Be sure to change the name of the network adapter from "Local Area Connection" to the name of your network adapter that receives the Internet traffic for that website.

NAT Load Balancing

Yet another option is Network Address Translation (NAT) based load balancing. This layer 4 method of load balancing is achieved by changing the destination IP address of the packets. When the load balancer sits inline between the client (generally over the Internet) and the web servers, it can perform NAT, which forwards packets from one network to another. This method uses one TCP connection directly between the client and the web server. To achieve this, the web server must set its default gateway to that of the load balancer. Figure 17-3 shows NAT load balancing.

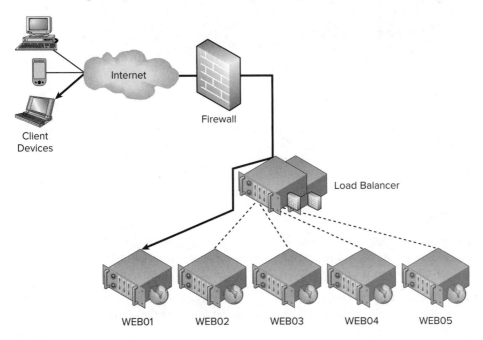

FIGURE 17-3

This may be a good option if your firewall or gateway device is also your load balancer, because it might already be the default gateway for your web servers. This option doesn't have the man-in-the-middle issue since to the web server it appears like a direct connection with the client.

Microsoft NLB

Microsoft Network Load Balancing (NLB) gets a category all to itself. It performs layer 2 load balancing by manipulating the MAC address of the network adapters so that incoming traffic arrives to all the servers in the web farm. Then the servers talk among themselves to decide who will respond to the request. Figure 17-4 shows how this works.

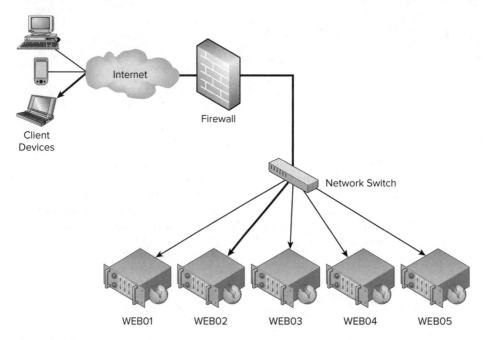

FIGURE 17-4

With NLB, the TCP connection is established directly between the client and the web server, which also means that there isn't a man-in-the-middle issue.

Not all switches support the MAC address changes, so it can require extra configuration on the network switch to allow NLB to work.

Load Balancer Features

Load balancers often serve additional purposes. They are already handling traffic for high traffic sites, so it makes sense to address other common needs on the way through. It's these features that really differentiate the various products.

Note that when using DSR, many of these options are not possible since the traffic doesn't come back through the server, so it's the other load-balancing methods that make many of these features possible.

Some examples of additional functionality include:

➤ **Sorry server or minimum servers** — When the count of healthy servers drops below a certain level, additional logic kicks in to handle this situation. For example, if all web servers are marked as "unhealthy" or "down for maintenance," you can point to another "down for maintenance" site on a different server.

➤ **SSL offloading** — Many load balancers provide the option to offload SSL. This means that SSL traffic is decrypted on the load balancer, and then communication between the load balancer and the web servers is over HTTP, not encrypted. This offloads the SSL performance overhead from the web servers so that they can focus on the job that they do best.

➤ **Intrusion prevention systems (IPS)** — The load balancer may offer DDoS, IDS, IPS, and other checks on the traffic on the way through to watch for attacks of various types. It can then report on it or, in many cases, block or minimize the attack.

➤ **Traffic treatment** — Some load balancers will treat the traffic on the way through to optimize it for performance or search engines. Some examples include HTTP compression, page consolidation, whitespace removal, server identification removal, and search engine treatment.

➤ **Caching** — Many load balancers can cache static content, or sometimes dynamic content, for rapid response and to offload some work from the web servers.

➤ **TCP offloading and buffering** — The load balancer may offer features to consolidate multiple HTTP sessions into less sessions so that the web servers don't need to keep the same level of sessions open. They can also buffer the requests so that long-lasting sessions don't have a negative impact on the web servers.

➤ **Content filtering** — Some load balancers can change the traffic on the way through to rewrite the page content, URL, or HTTP headers.

➤ **QoS and prioritization** — Some load balancers offer the ability to give some traffic higher precedence (Quality of Service, or QoS) than other traffic so that if bandwidth or resources are limited, the more important traffic gets priority. The other reason for QoS is to ensure that heavy traffic is throttled if necessary to even out the traffic to save on bandwidth costs.

➤ **Client authentication** — This offers the ability to authenticate clients at the firewall (e.g., from the domain) before the request is allowed through. This can offload authentication from the content servers.

➤ **Firewall** — Although load balancers can function as firewalls, it's not uncommon for firewalls to function as load balancers. Sometimes the roles will tend to blend. Regardless of what the device is called, they can often perform firewall tasks to block or allow traffic based on various rules.

➤ **API support** — You may want to add automation to your load balancers to manage web farms from other tools, or to further extend the functionality. Many load balancers have a method to do this programmatically rather than just through the load balancer's custom tools.

➤ **Health checking** — This is a fundamental feature of most load balancers and will be discussed in more depth later in the chapter. Most load balancers have the ability to check the status of the servers in the web farm and to mark them as unhealthy and respond differently if they don't respond to the health checks correctly.

Client Affinity

The previous chapter discussed session state and other variables that may require you to have users "stick" to a particular server. Some applications or websites have dependencies on a single server. If that applies to you, you may need some type of persistence for the traffic. This is often called *client affinity*, *sticky sessions*, or *maintaining client state*.

The primary advantage of client affinity is that applications that have dependencies on a single server can work in a web farm without a code rewrite or needing to implement other technologies to remove the single server dependencies.

There also are some disadvantages of client affinity. First, if the server to which a client is bound fails, the client will need to be re-routed to another server anyway; thus, you can't guarantee a highly available solution with client affinity. Another issue is that the traffic may become unbalanced if a number of heavy users happen to be bound to one server while another server gets a lighter load. Likewise, if one node has a performance issue that comes up, such as a runaway CPU thread, then all users bound for that node will be impacted even though there may be plenty of available resources elsewhere on the web farm. And yet another consideration is being able to recognize the same user on subsequent visits.

Different load balancers implement client affinity in different ways. One way is to use the client's IP address. This had the advantage of being straightforward and very fast, as the IP address is readily available in the TCP packet header. However, there are issues with some proxy servers and large networks. Some ISPs and large corporate environments share the same IP for multiple users. What the load balancer sees is the exact same IP address for multiple users — or in the case of proxy servers like AOL, the opposite occurs. The load balancer can see multiple IP addresses for one user since they can be assigned a different IP at any time. AOL does have a semi-solution to this now by including the X-FORWARDED-FOR header with the client's own IP address; however, many load balancers are not aware of this. One solution is to obtain the full list of IP addresses that AOL uses and consider them one potential user. As you can imagine, however, that creates an imbalance to one server in the web farm, which has to handle all AOL users.

Another solution for client affinity is to use cookies. Since most web browsers and web applications support cookies and have them enabled, this works quite consistently. However, it's not without issues, too. It is possible for users to block cookies and for some web applications to not support them. When that occurs, the cookie-based client affinity fails. Cookie-based affinity may use an active or passive cookie, which means a cookie just for a single browser session, or a longer-term cookie that outlasts the browser session.

It's also possible to use a unique URL for client affinity, but this isn't very common. The SSL session ID is yet another option.

As you can tell, client affinity works pretty well and is pretty solid, but it's not 100 percent accurate. If you can avoid stickiness/client affinity, you'll be better off. However, if you have no other choices, you can use one of the options mentioned in this section, provided that your load balancer supports it.

Failure Handling

In a perfect world, servers and sites would never fail, would never need maintenance, and would always work as expected. However, we all know that that is an unrealistic goal.

One of the critical roles of a load balancer is to handle failure situations, whether they are planned or unplanned. With whatever load-balancing solution you choose, make sure that the health checking and error handling meet your needs.

An essential feature that you should expect to find is the ability to check the status of a page (or set of pages) for each server, for each load-balanced site. When a failure occurs on a server, it should take that server out of rotation. This health checking may mark a server as unhealthy after the first failure, or it may keep track of the number of failures and only mark the server as unhealthy when a certain number of failures occur.

After the failure occurs, it should continue to retry until it receives a good response again, after which it should bring the server back into rotation.

The status of the page should be based on a time limit, a HTTP status code, and a page content match.

Another consideration for your health tests is to make sure that when you have scheduled maintenance planned, your health test doesn't mark the entire web farm as unhealthy when you didn't expect it to. This is a common oversight by deployment teams until they get the process down pat. It's easy to perform a change on the site that causes even the health testing page to respond incorrectly, essentially taking down the entire web farm.

Another feature included with many load balancers is the ability of the web farm to fail over to an entirely different server when all other servers fail. This is sometimes called a *sorry server* or a *backup server*. The purpose of a sorry server is to take over if the primary servers all fail due to maintenance or a common dependency. Often the sorry server will be a safe "down for maintenance" type of page that does not share any dependencies with the primary web farm.

Testing URLs Per-Site Per-Server

Planning testing URLs per-site-per-server is an important part of any load-balancing strategy. We'll look at this topic in a fair bit of depth later in the chapter, using ARR for a creative solution.

Load-Balancing Solutions

There are many load-balancing solutions, ranging from hardware to software and combinations thereof.

Hardware

Hardware solutions have been the most widely used solutions over the few years that the Internet and web farms have existed. They are usually backed by their manufacturers with a full support package and regular updates, giving you someone to lean on when you run into problems. Hardware solutions often have product tiers so that you can order a device that is guaranteed to handle your traffic requirements.

Third-party companies have created very powerful and robust solutions for load balancing, with ever-increasing features that extend beyond load balancing.

Most third-party hardware devices sit in front of the web farm with dedicated hardware that forwards the incoming requests to the server that is ready to handle those requests. The load balancers themselves can usually be ordered in pairs that are fully redundant, so that if either load balancer fails, the other one can pick up without missing a beat.

These balancers often support up to OSI layer 7, both for monitoring and for distribution of traffic, and almost all hardware load balancers support DSR (although, as mentioned previously, DSR does not support many of the advanced features).

Some other considerations when deciding on the best solution include scalability (can it handle your peak load both now and in the future?), features (can it handle all your requirements?), API and programming support, staff expertise (is someone on your staff already familiar with a particular brand and model?), the vendor's reputation for support, brand name (yes, sometimes the brand is used in the decision-making), and price.

Choosing a hardware load balancer is a big decision with a lot of options from which to choose. With careful planning and research, you can find the product that will fit your environment well.

Software

Another type of load balancer is a software load balancer, in which you can provide your own hardware while using the vendor-supported software for load balancing. The main advantage of a software solution is that you can provide your own hardware to meet your needs — often with more power and at a lower price than hardware-based solutions. You may also have the ability to extend it to give more flexibility to automate the usage.

A good part of this chapter is devoted to Microsoft's software solution, Application Request Routing (ARR), which serves as a powerful reverse proxy and is a serious contender to consider for load-balancing solutions.

There are fewer software load-balancer solutions available than hardware solutions, but they do exist. HAProxy (http://haproxy.1wt.eu) is one of the most widely used software load balancers, although it doesn't run on Windows. An example of a commercial Windows solution is KEMP LoadMaster, from KEMP Technologies (http://www.kemptechnologies.com/us/load-balancer.html).

A software load balancer usually sits in front of the web farm on dedicated or virtual servers. It may also be possible to install them on the web servers themselves to save hardware in smaller environments. It is also up to the product to ensure that you have a highly available solution so that if one of the servers fails, then the other one takes over.

NLB and round-robin DNS are technically types of software solutions, but they deserve categories of their own since they function in significantly different ways from most software load balancers.

Network Load Balancing

NLB has a unique way of balancing the traffic by changing the MAC addresses on the servers to cause all incoming traffic to arrive at all the web servers; and then for each server, NLB knows whether it should respond to the traffic or ignore it. This allows it to work in a highly available manner without needing new hardware to sit in front of the web farm.

NLB is quite limited in functionality, but it has its place, including complementing ARR to make it highly available, as we'll discuss later in this chapter. There's a whole section devoted to NLB later in this chapter where we'll look at this in more depth, including a full walk-through.

Round-Robin DNS

Another method for load balancing is called *round-robin DNS* load balancing (also known as a *poor man's load balancer*). To be true, it's not really load balancing because it doesn't "balance" based on the load of the server. Instead, it sends each new request to the next server in the list, regardless of the state of the server. In fact, it will continue to send traffic to servers even if they are partially or fully unavailable.

Additionally, it's not possible to have any type of stickiness when using DNS load balancing because DNS doesn't have any intelligence for maintaining information about the traffic.

There are two common ways to configure DNS load balancing. One way is for each name server (e.g., primary and secondary) to have two or more Host (A) records. Most DNS servers can reply in a round-robin fashion so that traffic is roughly balanced between the servers (or clusters of servers, depending on your setup).

The other useful configuration is to offer geo-redundancy to provide load balancing across data centers. This can be set up so that the primary and secondary name servers aren't automatically kept in sync, and so that each name server has a single Host (A) record that points to an IP address at its data center. Then, if a data center goes offline, it cannot send any traffic to the server(s) at its location. DNS is resilient already, so end users' DNS clients will try the next name server in the list — thus getting the data center that is available.

This solution requires that you have an active-active solution, in which both data centers can handle the traffic simultaneously. If you have read/write data in your database, this can cause problems.

So, when is DNS load balancing worth considering? For a small web farm in a Windows environment, DNS load balancing is rarely worth considering. With ARR and other third-party solutions readily available, DNS load balancing doesn't bring much to the table.

Where it is worth considering is for larger solutions that can support active/active traffic and if you scale larger than a single cluster can handle. If you outgrow your server farm in terms of scalability, you can consider having multiple clusters and use DNS load balancing to balance the clusters. DNS should have a Host (A) record for each cluster's virtual IP addresses, and it will send the traffic evenly to each cluster.

When configuring DNS load balancing, make sure that the time to live (TTL) is set low so that new requests continue to distribute around the servers or clusters, and so that if you make a change, it will take effect as soon as possible.

DNS load balancing isn't the most common method, but it does have its place, especially if you need to create multiple clusters.

Global Server Load Balancing

Another form of DNS load balancing is Global Server Load Balancing (GSLB), which is meant for load balancing across physical locations. There are different blends of GSLB configurations, including authoritative and non-authoritative configurations, and proxy and server methods. The concept is similar to what was discussed in the "Round-Robin DNS" section above, except that dedicated GSLB devices tend to have much more powerful functionality, including health checking and also the ability to change the DNS records to respond to health checking rather than always assuming an active/active configuration.

Frameworks

In addition to load balancers, there are frameworks that pull the load balancers and other functionality together into a cohesive set of functionality. Later in this chapter we'll discuss the Web Farm Framework (WFF) and Microsoft Azure Services — frameworks that provide additional functionality on top of the load balancing.

APPLICATION REQUEST ROUTING

In 2009, Microsoft released the first version of the Application Request Routing (ARR) module, which plugs into IIS 7.0 or greater and functions as a reverse proxy load balancer. This is an elegant solution because of its quick and clean installation and rich functionality. When looking for a load-balancing solution, ARR is worth serious consideration.

ARR leverages URL Rewrite for the routing, giving it powerful functionality for routing decisions. And because it sits on top of IIS, all the site bindings, security, error handling, and other rich functionality are readily available.

You may have heard ARR described as a reverse proxy, which technically is true; however, that description alone downplays its significance. ARR functions as a full-blown load balancer as long as your requirements fit within ARR's feature set.

Following are the main advantages of ARR:

> ➤ Cost — As long as you provide the hardware, the software costs only a Windows license. Windows Server 2012 Web Edition is the only requirement, and it's an affordable one.

> ➤ Staff expertise — Since ARR plugs into IIS, if you know IIS, the ARR learning curve is minimal.

➤ **Performance** — The first resource limit that ARR usually runs into is network. Because most networks support 1 Gbps or more, that says a lot. ARR can handle very large sites with ease.

➤ **Flexibility** — ARR offers full layer 7 load balancing, giving you flexibility to direct traffic based on any server variable, any part of the URL, cookie, or more.

Does ARR have any disadvantages? It's not without some considerations. It is not as feature rich as many of the commercial productions on the market that can offer SEO treatments, enhanced firewalls, IPS, DDoS handling, and more — although even some of those can be addressed with IIS add-ons such as Dynamic IP Restrictions, Request Filtering, and Caching. For the price, ARR is hard to beat, which is why we're spending a good part of this chapter introducing you to it and digging into the details.

ARR Functionality

ARR includes many, but not all, of the features mentioned previously in this chapter. Following is a generalized list of the functionality provided by ARR:

➤ Works as a reverse proxy

➤ Support for all common load-balancing algorithms

➤ Health checking

➤ Configurable caching

➤ Media and streaming media caching

➤ Request consolidation for media streaming

➤ Can work as a content delivery network (CDN)

➤ SSL offloading

➤ HTTP compression

➤ Powerful layer 4 and 7 routing decisions with URL Rewrite

➤ Usage reporting

➤ Cookie-based client affinity

➤ A unique server affinity feature for web hosts

➤ Firewall functionality using Windows Firewall

➤ Dynamic IP restrictions

➤ Rich programming and automation support

Note that ARR load balances only HTTP/HTTPS traffic. It cannot load balance any other protocols, such as RDP, NNTP, FTP, or other non-HTTP traffic.

Obtaining ARR

You can obtain and install ARR using the Web Platform Installer (Web PI) or by going to `www.iis .net` and searching for ARR and installing it from the website. One of the top search options (currently the top option) is the ARR main page, which includes the installer. The installer uses Web PI so that it can properly install the dependencies. One of the dependencies is URL Rewrite, which is covered in depth in Chapter 19.

Once ARR is installed, start or restart IIS Manager. There will be a new section in the left-hand side called *Server Farms* (see Figure 17-5).

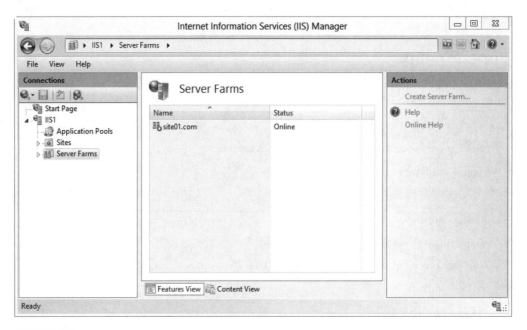

FIGURE 17-5

Understanding ARR

ARR is an add-on module to IIS, so it installs like any Windows application and is referenced in `applicationHost.config` and `administration.config`. Management is commonly performed using IIS Manager, and since ARR is schema backed like the rest of IIS, you can script it using any of the IIS scripting methods and manage it and generate sample scripts with Configuration Editor.

ARR works by using URL Rewrite to watch for your web farm traffic and to send that traffic to ARR. Then ARR processes the site by distributing the traffic to the appropriate server.

Next, we'll look at how IIS, ARR, and URL Rewrite play together.

Touch Points

To understand ARR properly, it's helpful to understand the three touch points for ARR traffic flow. Because ARR leverages IIS and URL Rewrite, it may not be immediately obvious how the traffic flows and how it's handed off on the way through the server.

An easy way to understand it is to visualize it as three touch points. These are three places where the incoming request touches down on the way through the ARR server. The three touch points, in order, are as follows:

1. The IIS site binding

2. The URL Rewrite rule

3. The ARR server farm

Figure 17-6 shows the three touch points visually represented in IIS Manager. Notice that they aren't in order from top to bottom.

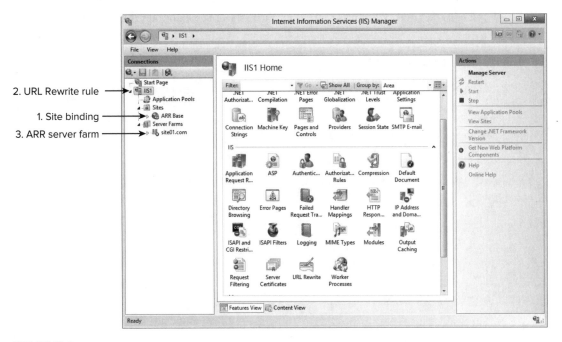

FIGURE 17-6

When an incoming request arrives at the ARR server, first it is caught by the IIS binding. Therefore, a standard binding needs to exist on a website. You can choose to create a generic website. The same website can be shared by multiple load balanced IPs, too. For example, you can create a site called "ARR Base" to be used for the HTTP and HTTPS bindings for the load-balanced IP addresses. It's here that SSL bindings occur and HTTPS requests are decrypted.

After the request is caught by the website, it will be caught by URL Rewrite, as long as an appropriate rule exists. URL Rewrite at the server level is run at the `PreBeginRequest` step in the IIS pipeline, which means that it is handled before other site functionality is performed. The URL Rewrite rule should have an action to redirect the request to one of the server farms. URL Rewrite rules can also edit server variables on the way through.

Finally, when the server farm gets the request from URL Rewrite, it processes it as instructed. It determines which server to reverse proxy the request to, based on the load balancing algorithm and client affinity settings.

Creating a Server Farm

There is a lot more to learn about ARR, but first let's take a look at creating a basic server farm so that we can visualize it better before digging deeper. In this walk-through, you will set up a web farm of two servers and an ARR server that functions as a load balancer to balance your traffic between the two web servers.

The following names and IP addresses are used throughout the examples in this chapter:

- ➤ Web Server 1 — `WebServer01`
  - ➤ IP — `10.1.5.31`
- ➤ Web Server 2 — `WebServer02`
  - ➤ IP — `10.1.5.41`
- ➤ Web Server 3 — `WebServer03`
  - ➤ IP — `10.1.5.51`
- ➤ ARR Server 1 — `ARR01`
  - ➤ IP — `192.168.1.50`
- ➤ ARR Server 2 — `ARR02`
  - ➤ IP — `192.168.1.60`
- ➤ Site 1 — `Site01.com`
- ➤ Site 2 — `Site02.com`
- ➤ Site 3 — `Site03.com`
- ➤ Testing Virtual IP Address on ARR server — `192.168.1.50`
- ➤ NLB load balanced IP — `192.168.1.70`

These IP addresses and names will be used throughout the ARR section of this chapter so that you can build a full testing environment as you move through this chapter. The examples are based on two (sometimes three) web servers and two ARR servers, but that is by no means the limit of IIS or ARR. You can scale to hundreds or even thousands of servers in your server farms by following the principles discussed here.

The example subnets used are `192.168.1.0/24` for the ARR server and `10.1.5.0/24` for the web servers. If you do not have a network setup for both of these subnets, you can use your own IP address scheme. The ARR server and web servers can be in the same subnet or in different subnets, whichever you choose. As you move through the walk-through, just convert the IP addresses to ones that work in your environment.

To get started, first you must set up three servers that will be included in this server farm. To set up the web servers, perform the following steps:

1. Install Windows 8 or Windows Server 2012 on a fresh server or virtual machine, and install IIS. Call the server **WebServer01** and ensure that it is assigned a unique IP address (e.g., **10.1.5.31**).

    This will be the first web server. A default installation of IIS will suffice as long as you also include ASP.NET. However, you should review the features that you install to make sure that they reflect your needs. The first time you open IIS Manager, you will be asked about the Microsoft Web Platform Installer. You do not need to use it for this part of the walk-through.

2. Delete the existing site called *Default Web Site*. Alternatively, you can update the bindings for Default Web Site to something other than the default wildcard setting since we'll use the same bindings in step 3.

3. Create a new website, called **site01.com,** and leave the Host name field blank, the IP set to (All Unassigned), and leave the port value at 80. This binding is more general than you would normally use in production, but it is kept this way to allow the walk-through to remain straightforward.

4. Create a simple "Hello World" page for that website called "default.aspx" with the following content:

    ```
    This server is <%= System.Environment.MachineName %>
    ```

5. Repeat steps 1-4 to set up a second web server, called **WebServer02**. If you want, at this point, you can create any number of additional web servers to be added to the server farm. You can also set up Shared Configuration, as described in Chapter 16, "IIS Scalability I: Building an IIS Web Farm". This walk-through assumes that you will have two web servers and does not require that you use Shared Configuration.

Now that you have created the web servers, you are ready to set up the server farm in ARR. First, you must build the server, create a site, and set the site bindings for the incoming requests.

1. Build another server, called **ARR01,** using Windows 8 or Windows Server 2012. Assign it a static IP address (e.g., **192.168.1.50**). Install IIS like you did in the first part of this walk-through.

2. Start IIS Manager. If it's the first time that you started IIS Manager on this server, you should receive a pop-up message asking if you want to use Microsoft Web Platform Installer. You can also open Microsoft Web Platform Installer by searching for it under the Windows start screen. Use the Web Platform Installer to install Application Request Routing (ARR) and allow it to install all the dependencies for ARR that it recommends.

3. On the new ARR01 server, delete the existing site called *Default Web Site*. Alternatively, you can update the bindings for Default Web Site to something other than the default wildcard setting since we'll use the same bindings in step 4.

4. Create a new site called **ARR Base** pointing to a blank folder located at `C:\Domains\ArrBase` on disk.

5. Create a site binding on ARR Base with the IP set to (All Unassigned), leave the Host name field blank, and leave the port value at 80.

Note that the default site that is created when IIS is installed is called *Default Web Site* and can be used instead of *ARR Base*, but it's helpful to create a specific website for ARR for clarity and so that you understand where the site bindings come into play.

Next, perform the following steps to create the Server Farm and the URL Rewrite rule:

1. Open IIS Manager and right-click Server Farms in the Connections pane and choose Create Server Farm.

2. Name the server farm **site01.com** and click Next.

3. Enter the address of your first web server, `WebServer01`, and click Add. You can enter the server by valid IP address, DNS name, or server name.

4. Repeat step 3 for `WebServer02`.

5. Click Finish after you have added your web servers.

6. You will see a message box asking if you would like to have a URL Rewrite rule created automatically. This rule is very basic and will catch all traffic without any filtering per domain name, so usually it's best to say "No" to this question. However, for this walk-through, allow the wizard to create the rule for you. Click Yes.

7. Let's make one more change to make it easier to test. In the Connections pane, click on the server farm you just created, and then double-click Load Balance. Change the load balancing algorithm to "Weighted round robin," leave the load distribution at the default of "Even Distribution," and click Apply.

Now on the ARR server you will have a site, URL Rewrite rule, and server farm created for you. Before testing your new server farm, you will need `site01.com` and `www.site01.com` to resolve to the IP address assigned to ARR01. You can do this by creating a `hosts` entry on the workstation computer that you are testing from:

1. Open an elevated command prompt window.

2. Run the following three commands, swapping `192.168.1.50` for your IP address for ARR01:

```
cd %windir%\System32\Drivers\etc
echo 192.168.1.50 site01.com >> hosts
echo 192.168.1.50 www.site01.com >> hosts
```

Now you're ready to test the load-balanced website. Open your web browser and browse to `http://site01.com`. You should see the test page that you set up on your first web server. Each time you refresh your web browser it should alternate through your web servers.

If it doesn't alternate between servers, it may be because of `favicon.ico`, which can add another request for each refresh that you do. If you have two servers in your web farm and two requests per request, then it will appear that ARR isn't performing a proper round-robin. One quick way around this for testing is to add one or more images to your test page so that there is one more page request than servers in your web farm. This will give the impression that it's rotating through the web servers. You can also get a pulse on the success of the new setup from the server farm's Monitoring and Management page.

You have just successfully set up your first ARR-based web farm.

Creating Server Farm Rules

Remember that you have full layer 7 control over the incoming request to route it however you like. For example, you can route based on the IP address, host header, query string, URL, client IP, or any other layer 7 information. This is handled with URL Rewrite rules at the server level.

You can create as many server farms and URL Rewrite rules as you want. Additionally, as discussed later, there are tricks to edit the domain name on the way through to give you more flexibility on the web server bindings.

Let's take a look at the URL Rewrite rules and manually create our own to get a feel for how this all works together.

In IIS Manager, navigate to the server level (the top level, above *Application Pools* and *Sites*) and double-click on URL Rewrite. If you just completed the walk-through, you should see a rule called "ARR_site01.com_loadbalance." This rule, which was created automatically, is too generalized — it will catch traffic for all domain names and IP addresses. If you have more than one load-balanced site, this needs to be more specific.

The first thing to do is to delete this rule. There are a couple of reasons why this is recommended. While at first it seems easier to allow ARR to handle the rules, ARR isn't smart enough to maintain your custom changes. If you make any changes to the rule and then make a change to the rule from the ARR server farm (e.g., turning off SSL offloading), it will remove all your hard work. This can be frustrating and will cause downtime to the site while you fix it. The safest way to avoid that is to maintain your rules yourself.

Continuing where the last walk-through left off, let's create our own rule now that has two conditions: the IP address of ARR01 (`192.168.1.50`) and a domain name of `site01.com`. The following steps assume that you performed the preceding walk-through. If you have not, you can use your own information in place of the example information below.

1. Open IIS Manager and double-click on the URL Rewrite icon at the server level.

2. From the list of existing URL Rewrite rules, delete the automatically generated rule that is there from the previous walk-through.

3. Click Add Rule from the Actions pane.

4. Double-click "Blank rule."

5. Name the rule **VIP – site01.com**.

6.   Change the Using option to Wildcards.

7.   Set the Pattern value to an asterisk (*).

8.   Expand the Conditions section and click Add.

9.   For the Condition input, enter {**HTTP_HOST**}. This refers to the domain name.

10.   Enter ***site01.com** for the Pattern. This will work for either `site01.com` or `www.site01`
`.com`. See Chapter 19 for a full discussion on more powerful conditions using regular
expressions.

11.   Add another condition with an input of {**SERVER_ADDR**} and pattern set to 192.168.1.50,
the IP address of `ARR01`. Neither of these conditions is required for a simple test, but they
show the flexibility that you have in creating your rules to ensure that they are specific
enough.

12.   In the Actions section, select Route to Server Farm for the Action Type.

13.   Select your server farm `site01.com` from the Server farm dropdown menu.

14.   Click Apply from the Actions pane.

15.   Test your website by visiting `http://site01.com` in your web browser to confirm that the
new rule works as promised.

If you are curious or need to double-check, the generated rule that is saved in `applicationHost`
`.config` should look like the following:

```
<rule name="VIP - site01.com" patternSyntax="Wildcard">
  <match url="*" />
  <conditions>
    <add input="{HTTP_HOST}" pattern="*site01.com" />
    <add input="{SERVER_ADDR}" pattern="192.168.1.50" />
  </conditions>
  <action type="Rewrite" url="http://site01.com/{R:0}" />
</rule>
```

As a further point of reference, here is an equivalent rule using regular expressions. This will make
sense if you know URL Rewrite (or after you've read Chapter 19).

```
<rule name="VIP - site01.com">
  <match url=".*" />
  <conditions>
    <add input="{HTTP_HOST}" pattern="^(www\.)?site01\.com$" />
    <add input="{SERVER_ADDR}" pattern="^192\.168\.1\.50$" />
  </conditions>
  <action type="Rewrite" url="http://site01.com/{R:0}" />
</rule>
```

These are examples of rules that are scoped to the domain name and IP address, and route to the
server farm of your choosing.

You have tremendous flexibility in your rules. As you can see, you can catch the incoming request using a wide variety of conditions and then redirect to a server farm of your choosing. For example, you could route images to one server farm and dynamic content to another server farm, or, if you are receiving an unexpected amount of traffic due to a marketing campaign, you can route overtaxed pages to a server responding with a simple static page.

See Chapter 19 for detailed examples and instructions on other URL Rewrite rules. The sky is the limit once you start realizing the flexibility you have.

Health Checks

A server farm would be pretty limiting if it couldn't automatically detect when a web server is unhealthy. ARR addresses this with two types of health checks.

➤ Live traffic testing

➤ Explicit URL testing

Live Traffic Testing

The live traffic test watches for errors with the live traffic. If it sees what you define as a failure, it marks that server as unhealthy.

Note that by default live traffic testing isn't enabled because the failover period is set to 0.

The advantage of this method of health checking is that it is able to watch for errors with any type of page request, not just a single testing URL. So, if one part of the site starts to fail on one server, this test will notice and take the server out of rotation.

However, there are some disadvantages to this method. If you have a problem page due to a bad release from the developers (preposterous!) and someone notices that problem page and presses F5 in his or her web browser a bunch of times, it's possible that it will take a server out of rotation. In fact, since that problem page is seen by all the servers in the web farm, it's possible for that one user to create a DoS attack and take all servers out of rotation, essentially breaking the whole site because of a problem on a single page.

The other consideration with live traffic testing is that when a server node is taken out of rotation because of a failure, it cannot be brought back into rotation again until you have the explicit URL testing configured, or until you manually mark the problem server as healthy. Therefore, it's essential that you never set up live traffic testing without also setting up the explicit URL testing. You need to decide if the disadvantages for live traffic testing outweigh the advantages and whether live testing is useful for you.

To configure live traffic testing, select your server farm and double-click on the Health Test icon. Figure 17-7 shows the Health Test tool expanded so that you can see all available options.

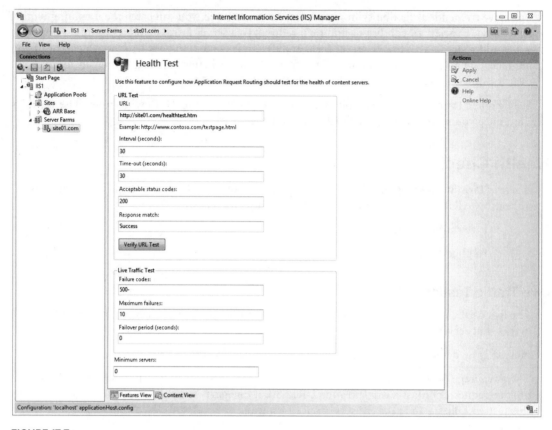

FIGURE 17-7

Live traffic testing is in the second section, entitled, conveniently enough, Live Traffic Test. You can configure the following three fields:

➤ **Failure codes** — You can define a comma-delimited set of HTTP status codes that you consider a failure. You can also set a range of values with a hyphen (-). The default value of 500- will catch anything with a 500 or higher status code. You could also be specific, with something like 500,510-599. Sub-status codes are not supported.

➤ **Maximum failures** — This is the number of failures that must occur during the failover period before a server is marked unhealthy.

➤ **Failover period (seconds)** — The value in this field is used along with the maximum failures to determine if there are too many failures during the failover period. If there are, the server is marked as unhealthy. When the value is set to 0, the live traffic test is disabled.

Explicit URL Testing

The second type of test is explicit URL testing. This checks a specific test page on each server in the server farm at a regular interval to see if it responds within the allocated time with the correct status and content match. If it doesn't, it marks the server as unhealthy.

Explicit URL testing is important to add to all production server farms to ensure that they dynamically handle failures on individual servers. Unlike live traffic testing, this cannot cause a DoS attack and is an essential part of any server farm.

Setting up the URL test is straightforward. First, select your server farm in IIS Manager and double-click the Health Test icon.

Explicit URL testing is not enabled by default because the URL is blank. The top section, URL Test, pertains to this discussion about Explicit URL testing.

> **URL** — This is the URL used for the health testing. You must include the protocol (e.g., `http://site01.com/healthtest.htm`). What's interesting about the health test is that for the test to be performed on every server in the server farm, the server's IP is used when communicating with the web server, rather than the address in the URL field. However, the domain name from the URL is still passed through and will be used for the site binding on the web server. Thus, the server's IP plus the host header will be used to locate the web server and binding. This means that you can use a host header for the health testing URL even if the IP address resolves to something else. In fact, you can use a made-up binding if you prefer, such as `http://site01/healthtest.htm`. Simply ensure that the binding exists on the website on the web servers.

> **Interval (seconds)** — This is the time, in seconds, between tests. This is also the value used to determine the interval for testing during a failure. When there is a failure, the health test will continue to test at this same frequency.

> **Time-out (seconds)** — This is the time, in seconds, before the health test gives up on a page that takes too long. When a page doesn't complete in this much time, it will mark the server as unhealthy.

> **Acceptable status codes** — This functions the same as the failure codes in the live traffic testing. You can enter a comma-delimited list of HTTP status codes and use a hyphen (-) to specify a range. A valid example is 200,301-307. If the status code from the test doesn't match this, the server with the invalid status code will be marked as unhealthy. Sub-status codes are not supported.

> **Response match** — You can also perform a content match to ensure that a certain word or phrase can be found on the page. Simply enter the phase, and the test will be successful only if that phrase is found on the page.

Click the Verify URL Test button to see the results of a test for every server in the server farm. This is helpful to confirm that your health test is set up correctly and to see the status of each server.

For the most part, there aren't any disadvantages of using explicit URL testing, as long as you have a consistent page to test. However, there are some considerations to keep in mind.

The health test doesn't have a specific Windows worker process to run under, so it runs within every `w3wp.exe` worker process already started. This is not a problem if you have a single worker process, but it is a problem if you have multiple worker processes on the ARR server, as every worker process will test every server in every server farm at each interval. And this is doubled if you have two ARR servers in a highly available configuration. This can potentially overload the web servers, or at the very least clutter the logs when you're troubleshooting. The solution is to try to consolidate application pools whenever possible on the ARR server. If the ARR server is dedicated to ARR tasks, it's pretty easy to keep your application pool count to just one or two.

Another slight weakness with an ARR health test implementation is that it will mark a server as unhealthy after a single failure. Some load balancers will allow multiple failures before the health test takes a server out of rotation. It's not uncommon to have a single failure on a website even if the server is healthy. With this in mind, it's beneficial with ARR's health testing to keep the interval value reasonably low so that if a server is marked as unhealthy, it will retry and notice that it's healthy again pretty quickly.

Minimum Servers

Another setting related to health testing is available at the bottom of the Health Test screen: Minimum servers.

The idea with this setting is that if you need a certain number of servers to handle the load, the health test shouldn't allow the server farm to drop below that level. Let's say, for example, that you have a 10-server web farm and it takes six servers to handle the traffic during an average day. If you had failures on five of the servers, you would have only five servers handling traffic. Since you need six servers to properly handle the traffic, the performance for all users would suffer. The thinking is that if this situation arises, it's better to make all servers available so that five out of 10 users receive a good experience, rather than all users being impacted. Of course, there's no guarantee what will happen, especially if you don't have client affinity enabled. Users may receive intermittent failures, depending on which server serves up their requests. It's a trade-off between the server farm being completely useless due to overloading or partially useless due to unhealthy servers being marked as healthy again.

The way that the "Minimum servers" value works is that if there are fewer healthy servers than the minimum servers, health testing is ignored and all servers are brought back into rotation.

The "Minimum servers" setting will depend on your environment, but you may find that setting it to at least 1 will ensure that you won't have a situation in which all servers are taken out of rotation. In addition, if you have a large server farm, you may want to set this to a level such that if the minimum count is reached, your server farm would be pretty much unusable. On the other hand, if you feel that a failed server exposes any sensitive information, leaving this value at a default of 0 is the best course of action.

Recommendations

There are a couple of recommendations that are helpful when planning health testing.

As mentioned previously, live traffic testing must be combined with explicit URL testing so that after a failure it can recover automatically when the server recovers. Understand that the live traffic test and URL test can fight with each other and cause some flapping.

Additionally, the live traffic test can open a door for DoS attacks, so use it carefully and be sure to understand the risks.

The URLs for your health test shouldn't test your database or application layer, unless you have a specific reason to do so. The reason is that if the database is to fail, all servers will be taken out of rotation, causing all parts of your site to fail, including your friendly error pages. Unless you have a specific reason to take all servers out of rotation in this situation, your health test shouldn't test the database or any other external shared dependency.

Furthermore, you may find that even testing ASP.NET is not beneficial since it's more likely to have a failure on all nodes (e.g., during a site deployment as files are being changed) than for ASP.NET itself to fail.

With this in mind, a good test is often a simple test of a static HTML page for the website. This will ensure that the server is online and that the application pool is running. All other failures are most likely shared across all servers.

You may want to consider a page that tests for the performance of the application pool — for example, testing part of your site so that if it doesn't complete in time, it will be taken out of rotation. Just keep in mind that it's also very possible that you'll get false positives with the occasional slow page load that happens under healthy circumstances. You will need to weigh this for your specific situation.

The rule of thumb should be that your health test needs to test only what is specific to each server and nothing more.

Of course, you should still monitor your database, ASP.NET applications, and all other dependencies, but they should be handled with your monitoring tools and not with a load balancer's health test.

Another thing to keep in mind is how your health test is handled during maintenance. You should make sure that your "down for maintenance" method doesn't cause your health test to fail; otherwise, any attempt to present a friendly "down for maintenance" page will be thwarted by the health test taking all servers out of rotation.

Web Server Bindings

Setting up an ARR web farm requires getting the bindings correct on both the ARR server(s) and the web servers. The bindings on the ARR server are pretty straightforward and have already been discussed. Let's now take a look at the considerations for the bindings on the web servers.

Web server bindings are made up of four parts:

➤ Domain name (host header)

➤ IP address

➤ Port

➤ Protocol (HTTP/HTTPS)

After an incoming request arrives at the ARR server, ARR uses the load balancing algorithm to choose which server to forward that request to. When the request is made to the web server, the binding information may change. Understanding what happens with the bindings allows you to be creative in how your web server site bindings work.

Domain Name (Host Header)

As the request passes from the ARR server to the web server, the domain name remains untouched. If the domain name started off as `www.site01.com`, it will still be `www.site01.com` when the request arrives at the web server.

This means that you can use the domain name for the bindings on the web servers. Additionally, if you know that all your visitors will use a limited number of domain names, you can create bindings for the domain name with the IP address set to (All Unassigned). In this way, it will work on every server in the web farm from a single binding. See Figure 17-8 for an example. Note that this example doesn't account for testing URLs, which will be discussed later.

FIGURE 17-8

With URL Rewrite, you can get fancy and edit the domain name using the `HTTP_HOST` server variable. You can change the domain name on the ARR server to whatever you want, even if it's not an FQDN. Then on the web servers you can use another rule to change it back again. This will allow it to bind to specific sites as needed, but since you change it back again, all the functionality in code will continue to work. This can be useful if you set up a shared-site situation in which each site owner gets his or her own dedicated IP address.

You can have a URL Rewrite rule on the ARR server that sets `HTTP_HOST` to a unique name for that site (e.g., `site01` without the `.com`). It should also set a variable like `HTTP_X_ORIGINAL_HOST` to `HTTP_HOST`. Then, on the web server, you can have a binding for that domain name (e.g., `site01`) so that the correct site handles the request. Then, with URL Rewrite, you can set `HTTP_HOST` to `HTTP_X_ORIGINAL_HOST`. This is just one example of creative things that you can do with URL Rewrite and `HTTP_HOST`.

It's important to note that if you don't use SSL offloading, host headers aren't nearly as straightforward, so you need to handle them as you would any other HTTPS site binding.

If you know that the site handles only a small number of domain names, then using the domain name for the bindings on the web servers is usually easiest. However, if you provide the site owner with a dedicated IP address or if you have a large number of domain names, you may need to explore one of the other options.

IP Address

The IP address (as seen by the web server) will become the IP address of the server — namely, the IP address specified in ARR. For example, if the load balancing algorithm chooses a server that has an IP address of 10.1.5.31, the IP address that can be used for the bindings on the web server is 10.1.5.31. The original IP address obtained from a DNS resolution of the domain name will not be used on the path from the ARR server to the web server.

At this point, you can get creative by adding multiple internal IP addresses to the web servers to give unique bindings on a per-site per-server basis. This can get messy if you have either a lot of sites or a lot of servers. So, if possible you should consider using the domain name for the web server binding. However, if you can't use the domain name for the bindings, unique IP addresses for the bindings can work well.

Figure 17-9 shows the bindings for a site with a unique IP address binding per web server node. To edit the binding for a site, select the site in IIS Manager and then select Binding from the Actions pane. Note that this example doesn't account for testing URLs, which will be discussed later.

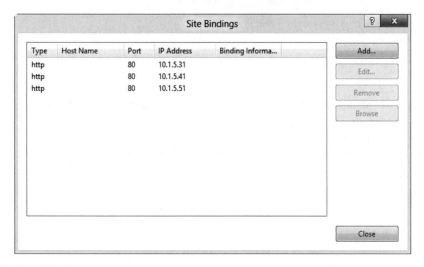

FIGURE 17-9

Port

The port is set when you set up the server farm. You may have missed the port setting, as the advanced fields are collapsed behind the Advanced Settings link when adding a new server to a server farm. When adding a new server to a server farm, you can specify the HTTP port and HTTPS port, which are port 80 and port 443, respectively, by default. The ports set here are used for the binding on the web server.

You can also get creative here by using several unique ports. For example, give Site1 port 81, Site2 port 82, and so forth. This doesn't use up IP addresses for the bindings to the web servers. It also has the advantage of only requiring one unique port per site, allowing the bindings per site to remain low.

However, using unique ports can easily throw off web applications, especially third-party web applications. It's not uncommon for developers to use the port number for determining whether a page is secure or for other logic in code. Custom ports are a tool available to you for the site bindings, but use them as an option of last resort.

Figure 17-10 shows the bindings for a site with a unique port binding. Notice that only one binding is necessary for all servers on the web farm. This example doesn't account for testing URLs, which will be discussed later.

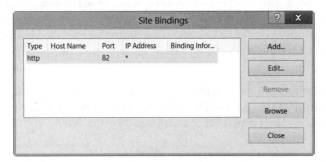

FIGURE 17-10

Protocol

The protocol (HTTP or HTTPS), also called *Scheme* in IIS Manager, is defined in the URL Rewrite rule. When using SSL offloading, it will always be HTTP; otherwise, two rules are needed, one for HTTP and one for HTTPS. The protocol seen by the web server will be whatever is defined in the URL Rewrite rule — either HTTP or HTTPS. Figure 17-11 shows where it's set in a URL Rewrite rule.

FIGURE 17-11

Testing URLs Per-Site Per-Server

When testing a web farm, it's important to be able to test each site on each server to ensure that they all respond correctly and to be able to troubleshoot, as needed.

There are a few ways to create these testing URLs for all your sites. At a high level, there are two solutions:

➤ Unique binding on each site on each server. Testing is performed directly against the web servers.

➤ Use ARR so that all testing goes through ARR while still allowing per-site per-server testing.

The advantage of unique binding directly on the web servers is that there is one less moving part; it's pretty straightforward to understand. However, as your number of sites or servers grows, this can become increasingly cumbersome.

The advantages of going through ARR are that you can share a single IP address per server, and you can share a single certificate on the ARR server. You have a single location to manage all the URLs.

Let's take a look at these two options. Either option is acceptable — just pick the one that works best for you, and be sure to plan and maintain it well.

Unique Bindings on Web Servers

To create unique bindings on the web servers, you can use the IP address, domain name, or port to give a unique binding. Your needs will likely sway you one way or the other. For example, some testers require that the public domain name be used for testing, and they update the hosts file (`%windir%\System32\Drivers\etc\hosts`) on their computers to change which server is being tested.

If you use private IP addresses or custom ports, you may need to be on the local network or use a virtual private network (VPN) for testing since the IP address or port may not be publicly available. You may prefer this anyway, but in any case it's an important consideration.

Let's take a look at three ways to create unique bindings. Here are examples of different sets of URLs for three servers and three sites. The following table is an example of host header-based bindings:

SERVER	SITE	URL	IP	PORT
Server01	Site01	site01.server01.domain.com	10.1.5.31	80/443
Server01	Site02	site02.server01.domain.com	10.1.5.31	80/443
Server01	Site03	site03.server01.domain.com	10.1.5.31	80/443
Server02	Site01	site01.server02.domain.com	10.1.5.41	80/443
Server02	Site02	site02.server02.domain.com	10.1.5.41	80/443
Server02	Site03	site03.server02.domain.com	10.1.5.41	80/443
Server03	Site01	site01.server03.domain.com	10.1.5.51	80/443
Server03	Site02	site02.server03.domain.com	10.1.5.51	80/443
Server03	Site03	site03.server03.domain.com	10.1.5.51	80/443

With this method, you will need to use an existing domain name or purchase one for this purpose. You can then set up a wildcard certificate for each server (e.g., `*.server01.domain.com`) that points to the primary IP of the server. However, the limitation with this is for SSL testing. You will need to set up a wildcard certificate and binding on each server to handle multiple URLs over a single IP address. See Chapter 15, "SSL and TLS," for a discussion on SSL bindings.

IP Address-Based Bindings

You can also use unique IP addresses, as shown in the following table:

SERVER	SITE	URL	IP	PORT
Server01	Site01	Flexible	10.1.5.31	80/443
Server01	Site02	Flexible	10.1.5.32	80/443
Server01	Site03	Flexible	10.1.5.33	80/443
Server02	Site01	Flexible	10.1.5.41	80/443
Server02	Site02	Flexible	10.1.5.42	80/443
Server02	Site03	Flexible	10.1.5.43	80/443
Server03	Site01	Flexible	10.1.5.51	80/443
Server03	Site02	Flexible	10.1.5.52	80/443
Server03	Site03	Flexible	10.1.5.53	80/443

This offers flexibility for both certificates and domain names, but it can quickly become unruly as your environment grows.

Port-Based Bindings

A third option is to use unique ports per site, as shown in the following table:

SERVER	SITE	URL	IP	PORT
Server01	Site01	Flexible	10.1.5.31	81/444
Server01	Site02	Flexible	10.1.5.31	82/445
Server01	Site03	Flexible	10.1.5.31	83/446
Server02	Site01	Flexible	10.1.5.41	81/444
Server02	Site02	Flexible	10.1.5.41	82/445
Server02	Site03	Flexible	10.1.5.41	83/446
Server03	Site01	Flexible	10.1.5.51	81/444
Server03	Site02	Flexible	10.1.5.51	82/445
Server03	Site03	Flexible	10.1.5.51	83/446

This allows you to share the IP address while giving full flexibility for the domain name. This may work well to start; however, as you add more ports, it can become difficult to manage, and some applications get confused with a custom port. As a general rule, if you can avoid port-based testing URLs, you'll probably be better off.

ARR for Testing URLs

Another option for your testing URLs is to leverage ARR to front all the URLs. While both options are good, going through ARR gives you more flexibility and control than creating unique bindings on the web servers. You can share a single certificate for all testing URLs and even rewrite the domain name so that it appears to the web server as though you are testing with the production domain name. All this is possible through a single simple rule and a few simple DNS settings.

Note that it's not really the full ARR that you'll be using, but the reverse proxy functionality, which is available when both URL Rewrite and ARR are installed.

If your testing URLs are planned well, you will not need to make any changes to ARR when you add new servers or new sites, so long as the sites' domain names follow a consistent pattern.

There are many ways to implement the rules for your testing URLs. The option we'll explore below is a generic and powerful solution, although it may not work for every situation. Hopefully, this implementation will give you good ideas that will work in your environment.

The concept is similar to the previous discussion about testing URLs per server, except that every URL will go through the ARR server. Here's an example of what the URLs and IPs will look like, with the IP address 192.168.1.50 being the IP address of the ARR server. That can be a private or public IP address.

SERVER	SITE	URL	IP	PORT
Server01	Site01	site01.server01.domain.com	192.168.1.50	80/443
Server01	Site02	site02.server01.domain.com	192.168.1.50	80/443
Server01	Site03	site03.server01.domain.com	192.168.1.50	80/443
Server02	Site01	site01.server02.domain.com	192.168.1.50	80/443
Server02	Site02	site02.server02.domain.com	192.168.1.50	80/443
Server02	Site03	site03.server02.domain.com	192.168.1.50	80/443
Server03	Site01	site01.server03.domain.com	192.168.1.50	80/443
Server03	Site02	site02.server03.domain.com	192.168.1.50	80/443
Server03	Site03	site03.server03.domain.com	192.168.1.50	80/443

Following are the steps to set up this URL testing scheme through the ARR server:

1. Set up DNS to point to the appropriate servers. The following table shows the records that need to be created for a three-server web farm:

A RECORD	IP
`*.server01.domain.com`	IP of ARR server
`*.server02.domain.com`	IP of ARR server
`*.server03.domain.com`	IP of ARR server
`server01.domain.com`	IP of `Server01`
`server02.domain.com`	IP of `Server02`
`server03.domain.com`	IP of `Server03`

Your DNS server needs to support wildcard records, which most DNS servers do.

2. Add the following rule to the ARR server at the server or site level:

```
<rule name="Testing URLs" enabled="true" stopProcessing="true">
    <match url="(.*)" />
    <action type="Rewrite" url="http://{C:2}.domain.com/{R:0}" />
    <serverVariables>
        <set name="HTTP_HOST" value="{C:1}.com" />
    </serverVariables>
    <conditions>
        <add input="{HTTP_HOST}" pattern="^(.+)\.(server\d\d)\.domain\.com$" />
    </conditions>
</rule>
```

3. Edit the rule so that `domain.com` and `domain\.com` reflect the domain name that you use for the testing URLs. You can use whichever domain name you prefer, whether it's your primary domain name or a domain name purchased for this purpose.

4. Ensure that the proxy functionality is enabled in ARR. At the server level in IIS Manager, select Application Request Routing Cache, and then choose Server Proxy Settings from the Actions pane. Ensure that Enable Proxy is selected and click Apply.

5. Add wildcard or static site bindings to the ARR server, including your SSL bindings. You can use your "ARR Base" site with a blank host header, if it doesn't clash with anything else on that server.

Let's take a look at what this rule does. (Note that Chapter 19 covers URL Rewrite in much more depth.)

➤ The condition is met if the testing URL has a pattern of `something` `.server{digit}{digit}.domain.com`

➤ If the condition is met, it replaces the domain name (HTTP_HOST) with `something.com`, where `something` is taken from the condition. Note that this assumes that all your domain names are `.com` domain names. You can tweak this to follow a pattern that works for you, including using a longer testing URL to include the top-level domain (TLD). By setting the domain name to this value, you can fool your site into thinking that the request was for that domain name; so, if you have any logic in code that watches for the domain name, it will work correctly.

➤ Rewrites (via reverse proxy) to `server{digit}{digit}.domain.com`. Since you have wild-card DNS records for your web servers, this will proxy the request to the appropriate web server.

The assumption is that you can bind by domain name on the web server because of site bindings that you've already set up. However, if you cannot, there are other creative ways to make this work since you have full control of the `HTTP_HOST` value. You can set the `HTTP_HOST` to any arbitrary value — for example `{C:1}`, which is the `site01` part of the URL — and then add that as a binding to the site on the web servers. You can create a global URL Rewrite rule on the web servers that writes `site01` to `site01.com`. This allows you to use a binding URL like `site01`, which can be anything you set, but also fools the code on the site into thinking that the request came in as `site01.com`.

There are many ways to approach testing URLs, but they are outside the scope of this chapter. Hopefully, this lets you see the potential that you have with your testing URLs.

SSL/TLS Offloading

ARR supports SSL/TLS offloading, which takes the pressure off the web servers to handle the computationally expensive decrypting/encrypting. Additionally, it removes the requirement to install certificates on every web server.

Note that Transport Layer Security (TLS) is essentially an update to Secure Sockets Layer (SSL); so, for the sake of simplicity, we'll call this *SSL offloading*, but it is really SSL or TLS offloading.

To be true, the SSL performance overhead often isn't a big deal with today's hardware, but there are situations in which the overhead is noticeable and offloading is helpful.

The way that ARR works is that it will always decrypt the traffic when it arrives to the ARR server, regardless of the configuration. The real question is whether you want to re-encrypt it again for the path between the ARR server and web servers. ARR does not support packet pass through, in which the SSL packets are untouched, so every request is decrypted on the ARR server.

ARR decides whether to perform SSL offloading based on how the URL Rewrite rules are created. If you have a rule that routes to one server farm using HTTP, SSL offloading is enabled. If you have two rules that route to the corresponding protocol, SSL offloading is not enabled. The following rule is for a site with SSL offloading enabled:

```
<rule name="VIP - site01.com" patternSyntax="Wildcard">
   <match url="*" />
   <conditions logicalGrouping="MatchAll" trackAllCaptures="false">
      <add input="{HTTP_HOST}" pattern="site01.com" />
   </conditions>
   <action type="Rewrite" url="http://site01.com/{R:0}" />
</rule>
```

The following pair of rules is for a site that does not have SSL offloading enabled. Notice the condition to check whether HTTPS is on or off.

```
<rule name="VIP - site01.com" patternSyntax="Wildcard">
   <match url="*" />
   <conditions logicalGrouping="MatchAll" trackAllCaptures="false">
      <add input="{HTTP_HOST}" pattern="site01.com" />
```

```
            <add input="{HTTPS}" pattern="off" />
        </conditions>
        <action type="Rewrite" url="http://site01.com/{R:0}" />
    </rule>
    <rule name="VIP - site01.com_SSL" patternSyntax="Wildcard">
        <match url="*" />
        <conditions logicalGrouping="MatchAll" trackAllCaptures="false">
            <add input="{HTTP_HOST}" pattern="site01.com" />
            <add input="{HTTPS}" pattern="on" />
        </conditions>
        <action type="Rewrite" url="https://site01.com/{R:0}" />
    </rule>
```

Note that there's another way to use a single rule rather than a pair of rules — by using the CACHE_URL input variable, as discussed in Chapter 19.

In the case of no SSL offloading, the incoming request to the ARR server is decrypted, and then encrypted again before it leaves for the web server. This does require more processing overhead than solutions that just forward the request on, but it gives you full control over the incoming request since URL Rewrite has access to the unencrypted header data. In both cases, you must install the SSL certificate on the ARR server. Only when you do not enable SSL offloading do you need to also install the certificate on the web servers.

Note that you may still want to install certificates on the web servers for direct per-site-per-server HTTPS testing; however, if you don't mind a certificate warning, you can use a self-signed certificate, or you can use an internal domain certificate.

As you can see, SSL offloading simplifies things in more ways than one, but the real decision needs to be security in your environment. You should use SSL offloading only if you have a trusted switched network between your ARR server and web servers.

Next, let's take a look at how the web servers respond to SSL offloading and how you can fool them into not knowing the difference.

Man-in-the-Middle and ARR Helper

A reverse proxy, which ARR is, has the issue of being a middleman between the client and the web servers. This means that the web servers will see incoming requests as coming from ARR rather than directly from the client.

SSL offloading has a similar issue. Because ARR offloads SSL, the incoming request to the web servers is seen as over HTTP, even if the original request uses SSL. This can cause the following issues:

➤ REMOTE_ADDR and REMOTE_HOST server variables will be the ARR server rather than the client. This can break functionality in code if those variables are used.

➤ The IIS logs also reflect the ARR server instead of the client.

➤ The HTTPS and SERVER_PORT variables always appear to be HTTP related, even for SSL traffic.

➤ The certificate server variables are empty, even for SSL traffic.

For some situations this isn't a deal breaker, but for others, it can be inconvenient or critical to the operation of a site. Fortunately, there are good solutions for this.

Many load balancers, ARR included, save the original client information in a different server variable so that it's available on the web server. The server variables that ARR conveniently sets are as follows:

➤ HTTP_X_FORWARDED_FOR — This is the IP and port of the original client request. For example, it may be something like 69.132.57.48:51402.

➤ HTTP_X_ARR_LOG_ID — This is a globally unique identifier (GUID) that can be used to line up the logs between ARR and the web server.

➤ HTTP_X_ARR_SSL — If the request arrives as an SSL request, this server variable is set with the certificate information. This will include the certificate issuer, subject, common name, and other certificate information.

➤ HTTP_X_ORIGINAL_URL — It's URL Rewrite that sets this for us in this situation. It's the value of URL before the rule was applied, so if you changed the URL at some point, you can still tell what the original URL was.

Now that the important information is available on the web servers, there are a couple of ways to use this information. One way is to update all code references to use these variables. However, there is a better way.

Microsoft's Anil Ruia provided a simple little utility, ARR Helper, that takes the information that was tucked away in the server variables and writes it back to the original locations. This essentially fools the web server into thinking that the request came directly from the client and that SSL requests were actually SSL requests. As far as your code is concerned, on the web server it would never be aware that ARR was in the mix or that SSL offloading was performed.

You can obtain ARR Helper by going to www.iis.net and searching for "ARR Helper." There is a 32-bit and a 64-bit installation.

Note that you should install ARR Helper on the web servers, not on the ARR server. ARR already takes care of the server variables for you; ARR Helper takes care of putting the original server variables back again on the web servers.

The installation process is a simple Next/Next/Finish installation; however, keep in mind that if you're using shared configuration, you need to take the servers out of shared configuration before you can perform the installation. It does require IIS 7.0 or greater for the web server. If you have a non-Microsoft or an IIS 6 solution, you need to find another way to resolve this issue.

Once ARR Helper is installed, it will just work for all sites. No configuration is necessary (or possible). ARR Helper has negligible performance overhead and doesn't hurt for direct non-ARR sites, so it's safe and should be installed on all IIS 7+ web servers that will be added to your web farm.

Server Management

As you would assume, you can readily add or remove servers from a server farm at any time. Additionally, you can temporarily take a server out of rotation without deleting it.

Adding Servers

Servers can be added when you first create the server farm or after the fact. In either case, there is an Advanced Settings link that allows you to set a custom HTTP and HTTPS port and define a weight for each server to be used for custom distribution load balancing.

To add a server to an existing server farm, simply expand the server farm from the Connections pane and click on the Servers node. Click Add Server from the Actions pane, and then follow the wizard, optionally entering advanced settings.

To add a server from the command line, perform the following, entering in your own server farm name and server address (run as a single-line command):

```
appcmd.exe set config -section:webFarms
 /+"[name='site01.com'].[address='10.1.5.31']" /commit:apphost
```

Editing Server Settings

Surprisingly, you cannot edit the HTTP or HTTPS port, or the weight of a server from IIS Manager after it's been created. If you want to edit these settings, you can use the command line tool, or you can delete the server and re-create it on the ARR web farm in IIS Manager.

Following is the AppCmd syntax to edit the HTTP and HTTPS ports, and the weight of an existing server (run as a long single-line command):

```
appcmd.exe set config  -section:webFarms
 /[name='site01.com'].[address='10.1.5.31'].applicationRequestRouting.weight:"70"
 /[name='site01.com'].[address='10.1.5.31'].applicationRequestRouting.httpPort:"81"
 /[name='site01.com'].[address='10.1.5.31'].applicationRequestRouting.httpsPort:"44
4"
 /commit:apphost
```

Removing Servers

You can remove a server from a server farm just as easily. From IIS Manager, simply select your server from the Connections pane, and then click Remove Server from the Actions pane.

To remove a server using the command line, run the following, replacing the variables as needed (run as a single-line command):

```
appcmd.exe set config -section:webFarms
 /-"[name='site01.com'].[address='10.1.5.31']" /commit:apphost
```

Disabling or Enabling Servers

Here's where it's easy to get confused. IIS and ARR have the concepts of runtime state and permanent state. In a server farm, the *runtime state* just applies to one server; any changes you make are not replicated to other servers in the server farm. However, the *permanent state* is replicated. Figure 17-12 shows the ARR runtime state that appears in the Monitoring and Management section of the server farm. You can make changes to any of the servers, although all changes made in the Monitoring and Management section are temporary and apply only to this ARR server. After a reboot or restart of IIS, the setting will revert back to the permanent state.

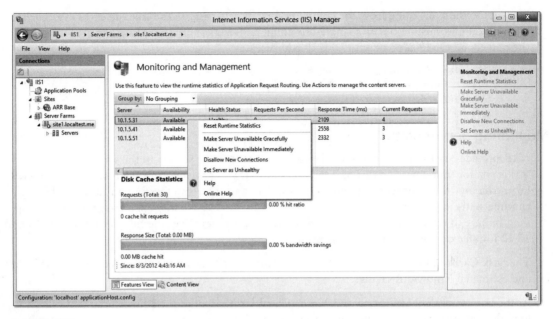

FIGURE 17-12

You can also make permanent changes to a server in a server farm, including taking it offline and bringing it back online again. This is performed from the Servers area, as shown in Figure 17-13.

FIGURE 17-13

You can do the same thing from the command line by setting `enabled` to `true` or `false`. The following example must be run as a single-line command. Make sure to replace `site01.com` with your site name, and the IP address with your IP address.

```
appcmd.exe set config -section:webFarms
 /[name='site01.com'].[address='10.1.5.31'].enabled:"False"
 /commit:apphost
```

Monitoring Server Status

ARR provides useful information for the runtime status of the servers in the server farm. Note that this is just for traffic passing through each server, so if you have multiple ARR servers in an ARR farm, you may find it beneficial to configure them in an active/standby configuration so that all runtime statistics are collected on one active node. If you do have them in an active/active configuration, be sure to review the runtime statistics on all the servers to get the full picture. Refer to Figure 17-12 for an example of some of the runtime statistics.

The Disk Cache Statistics section of the Monitoring and Management screen shows you the hit ratio and estimated bandwidth savings.

At the bottom of the Monitoring and Management screen is a date and timestamp that reflects how long the statistics have been collecting. You can reset that from the Actions pane to start fresh.

Performance Monitoring

ARR version 2.0 introduced the following performance monitor counters, giving you additional options for monitoring your ARR server:

➤ Application Request Routing Server

➤ Application Request Routing Cache

Together, these counters provide 22 performance objects for ARR caching and for ARR in general. Each of the counters has details per server farm. You can find a list of the counters at `http://tinyurl.com/9e71f8f`.

Caching

For a site to perform optimally and to offload processing and bandwidth from the web server, you should leverage caching to whatever degree makes sense in your environment. Caching allows often-used content to be saved at a location that is quicker to access, whether that is in memory, on faster disks, or on a different server created for this purpose. It also allows slow-running pages to be saved for quicker access while saving on bandwidth between the ARR and web servers.

ARR has several options for caching, plus the ability to function as a content deliver network (CDN) to front entire web farms and to cache as much read-only content as possible. For a video walk-through about setting up a CDN using ARR, visit `http://tinyurl.com/8voudsj`.

Enabling ARR Caching

Caching is not enabled until you set the cache location on disk, so the default settings are to not use caching at all. Therefore, it's important to understand caching so that you can at least turn on the safe settings so that you can dig deeper and get the most out of caching.

Following are the steps to enable caching.

1. In IIS Manager, from the server level, double-click Application Request Routing Cache.

2. Click Add Drive from the Actions pane.

3. Set the drive location to a path on disk for the cache to live, and, optionally, set the maximum size limit for the cache drive.

4. Click OK.

Now files will immediately start caching. A good way to test is to create a `test.css` page with something simple in it. View the `test.css` page directly in your web browser using the FQDN that uses ARR. Refresh it a couple of times in your browser. Now update the page to have something else for the content. If you refresh it within 60 seconds, it should remain the same; however, after 60 seconds, it should update. Understanding caching will help you support your development team, too, since changes that they make may not be updated immediately after caching is enabled.

You can add additional drives the same way you created your first drive, and you can also add a secondary drive. The secondary drive is meant to be a shared location between multiple ARR servers, primarily for CDN situations. This allows multiple ARR servers to save content to a shared resource for faster access.

What Is Cached

ARR caching is based on the "cache-ability" of the request, as defined in RFC 2616 (`www.ietf.org/rfc/rfc2616.txt`). After ARR caching is enabled, by default, static content is cached. This means that static files like images, CSS, and JavaScript files are cached at the ARR layer.

You can choose in ARR what to do with differences in the query string. For example, if there is a static HTML page with a unique query string, do you want to cache that uniquely, not cache it at all, or lump it together with the other requests for that page, regardless of the query string?

FIGURE 17-14

You have the ability to override the caching within ARR, if you so choose. This is done at the server level by changing the cache control rules. The cache control rules support wildcards, with an asterisk (*) for the host name and URL, allowing you flexibility on what is cached and what isn't. Figure 17-14 shows the configuration dialog.

When cache control rules are set, they will override all cache control directives in the response header of the file, so basically this control rule wins out.

You can manage this from IIS Manager by navigating to Application Request Routing Cache at the server level and clicking on Cache Control Rules from the Actions pane. The filtering per site is handled by host name within each rule rather than applying settings at the site level.

Setting the Cache Duration

The cache duration is determined in a few ways. At the server farm level, the ARR cache duration is set as shown in Figure 17-15.

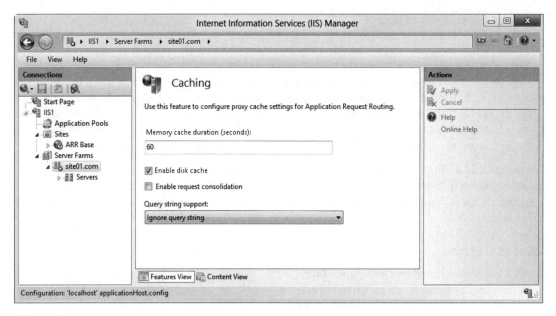

FIGURE 17-15

The "Memory cache duration (seconds)" setting specifies how long ARR will cache requests before it calls back to the web server to see if there have been any updated instructions. The default for ARR 1.0 was 5 seconds, but it was updated to 60 seconds in ARR 2.0. This setting shouldn't be too high; otherwise, ARR will be too aggressive and won't make updates when there are changes on the web servers. If it's too low, however, you won't benefit from the caching.

Additionally, as mentioned above, the cache control rules override both the memory cache duration and the types of files that are cached.

When a file is changed on the web server, the If-Modified-Since header in the page response will be updated to the new timestamp. When ARR's memory cache duration has been reached (the one with a default of 60 seconds), ARR will notice the change and will update its local cache — and henceforth serve up the latest file.

These various levels work together to determine what is cached and for how long.

Managing Cached Content

ARR also supports the ability to manage the cached content. A few useful options are available in IIS Manager, at the server level, within the Application Request Routing Cache tool:

➤ **Browse Cache Content** — This allows you to navigate the site and folder hierarchy to see all cached files. You can also see the size, modified date, and on which drive the cached files are located. You can delete individual files from here, as well.

➤ **Reset Cache Statistics** — This resets the caching runtime statistics data.

➤ **Delete Specific Cached Objects** — This allows you to enter a specific URL, and it will remove that cached item from cache. This works well when you know the full URL and want to quickly ensure that it's removed from cache.

➤ **Delete All Cached Objects** — This is useful during testing or as a quick option while troubleshooting when you want to clear out the entire cache.

Additionally, you can view the HTTP response cache with the following command, run from the command line:

```
netsh http show cache
```

Pre-Caching Objects

Another useful feature in ARR is the ability to pre-cache objects so that they are ready when needed, often in anticipation of high demand, and regardless of how frequently they are used. This is a one-time event, so the Pre-cache Objects tool needs to be rerun if the cache is emptied or pages have dropped from cache.

To use the Pre-cache Objects tool, you must create a text file with FQDNs, one per line. These FQDNs must match the caching requirements that you have, so unique tests per query string may need to be accounted for if your caching rules depend on a unique query string. Then from the ARR at the server level, click "Pre-cache Objects" and enter the path to the text file and a path to an output log file.

However, instead of this functionality, you may want to consider the new Application Initialization functionality. The Application Initialization module is included with IIS and just needs to be enabled as an IIS feature. It provides a lot of additional functionality that surpasses the original, built-in pre-cache objects' functionality in ARR.

Security

Security is a critical consideration with caching in ARR, because cached content always has the possibility of being read by the wrong user. There are some important things to note.

Authorization cannot be delegated to ARR, so if you have sensitive content that requires authorization and is cacheable, you should disable caching for that server farm.

Furthermore, cookies aren't taken into consideration with caching, so if you have content that is cached and needs to be unique depending on the user's cookie, caching should be disabled for that server farm.

You can browse the cache to confirm that none of the sensitive information is cached. Another good test before you enable caching in ARR in production is to start with the cache emptied and then log in with a user with sensitive information. Then log in with another user and access the same pages. Make sure that they get fresh content specific to the correct user. But this is an over-simplification of the testing process, so be sure to test it well with your application so that you can feel confident that no sensitive information is exposed.

Miscellaneous Optimizations

There are some performance optimizations that should be performed on your ARR servers. The following three recommendations are not an exhaustive list, but simply suggestions that are not mentioned elsewhere in this chapter.

First, turn off the Idle Time-out setting for your ARR application pools. Frankly, unless you do bulk hosting, you should turn this off anyway. This keeps your site actively running while maintaining the health checking, even during quiet times.

You can change this by navigating to your application pool from IIS Manager and clicking Advanced Settings. Locate "Idle Time-out (minutes)," set it to 0, and click OK, as shown in Figure 17-16.

To perform the same thing from the command line, run the following command, entering your own application pool's name:

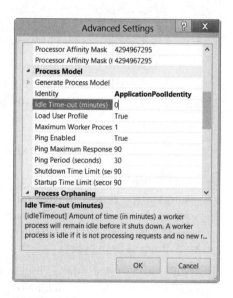

FIGURE 17-16

```
appcmd.exe set apppool "ARR Base" -processModel.idleTimeout:"00:00:00" /commit:apphost.
```

Another performance optimization that benefits caching is to disable the creation of 8.3 file names and directories (DOS-style file names). The creation of the 8.3 name creation can negatively impact performance of the directory enumeration. From the command prompt, run the following on all your web servers:

```
fsutil.exe behavior set disable8dot3 1
```

A third consideration applies if you stream media. Request consolidation is helpful because it will consolidate all the streaming requests in-flight to greatly reduce the number of requests. This also works with tiered cache nodes. This is set at the server or server farm level under the Caching feature. Figure 17-17 shows the setting at the server farm level.

FIGURE 17-17

DIGGING DEEPER

This chapter is not an exhaustive list of all caching features in ARR. You can discover more functionality through IIS Manager Help, by exploring the options in the Actions pane, or by perusing the schema file at %windir%\System32\inetsrv\ config\schema\arr_schema.xml.

High Availability for ARR

ARR doesn't have any high availability features built in. If the server fails or is down for maintenance, the entire web farm will be unavailable. Of course, this defeats the purpose of a web farm, which you want to ensure doesn't have any single points of failure.

To achieve high availability for ARR, you must use a complementary technology to make ARR itself highly available. There are two good options for this:

➤ Use your existing (or new) hardware load balancer. Of course, if you already have a load balancer, you may not need ARR unless it provides additional functionality or ease of use that your hardware load balancer doesn't have.

➤ Use Microsoft Network Load Balancing (NLB), which works well with ARR to provide a high availability solution.

The first option will depend on your expertise and knowledge of your hardware solution.

The second option is a commonly recommended solution for making ARR highly available in an affordable way. NLB is rather limited as a load balancer, but it and ARR make a great pair. This configuration requires that you have NLB installed and configured on the ARR servers. The ARR server should have shared configuration enabled, as discussed in Chapter 16. The following section describes using NLB as a load balancer, as well as using NLB with ARR.

NETWORK LOAD BALANCING

NLB has already been mentioned in this chapter, but let's take a look at it in more depth now. NLB, sometimes referred to as *Network Load Balancing Services* (NLBS), was previously Microsoft's solution for load balancing web farms. While it's still supported by Microsoft, it is less often used directly for load balancing and is starting to take on roles like complimenting ARR, as discussed here.

NLB is a type of load balancer that uses its own unique method to balance the load across all the servers. Incoming traffic is routed to all the servers, but only one of them will actually respond to the traffic while the others ignore that traffic. Therefore, it doesn't have any load balancing device in front of the web servers. All the servers work together as peers for a shared cause.

ARR has functionality that far surpasses NLB. That makes ARR a better load-balancing solution, except for one problem. ARR doesn't have its own built-in solution for high availability, so it can't handle failures to the server hosting ARR. As a result, it becomes a single point of failure, completely defeating the purpose of a web farm.

That's where NLB comes in. NLB is a cost-effective, Microsoft-supported solution for high availability, and ARR is a powerful reverse proxy load balancer. Together, they make a strong team.

Let's take a look at what it takes to set up an NLB cluster. One common configuration change that may be needed at the network level is to set static ARP records on Cisco switches. For a good article from Cisco, see `www.cisco.com/en/US/products/hw/switches/ps708/products_configuration_example09186a0080a07203.shtml`.

Note that it's beyond the scope of this book to explain NLB in depth. The following walk-through is a high-level overview only.

Before starting this walk-through, create another server configured the same as `ARR01`. Call it **ARR02** and give it an IP address of **192.168.1.60**. For this to function correctly so that you rarely need to touch `ARR02`, you should set up Shared Configuration, as discussed in Chapter 16.

Next, install NLB services on `ARR01`.

1. Open Server Manager and select Manage ➪ Add Roles and Features.

2. Step through the wizard until you reach the "Select features" screen.

3. Check Network Load Balancing, as shown in Figure 17-18.

4. Select Add on the dialog box that appears.

5. Click Next and then Install.

6. Repeat for ARR02.

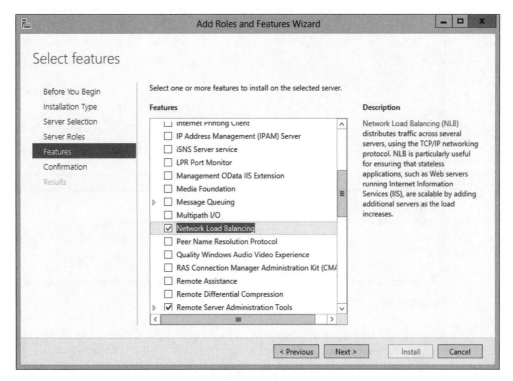

FIGURE 17-18

To create an NLB cluster, perform the following steps:

1. Open Server Manager and select Tools ⇨ Network Load Balancing Manager.

2. Click Cluster ⇨ New, as shown in Figure 17-19.

3. Enter the host name (IP, DNS, or NetBIOS name) of the first server in the cluster, and then select Connect.

4. Select the network adapter that you will use as the cluster interface from the choices at the bottom, and then click Next.

5. In the New Cluster : Host Parameters dialog box, you can select the priority. Even though the servers generally function as peers to each other, they need to be assigned a unique host identifier, which also serves as the priority. Normally, the default here is good.

6. The Dedicated IP address is the IP address for that particular server. The default is usually good. You will enter the Cluster IP address on the following screen. Ensure that the IP address and subnet are correct. Click Next.

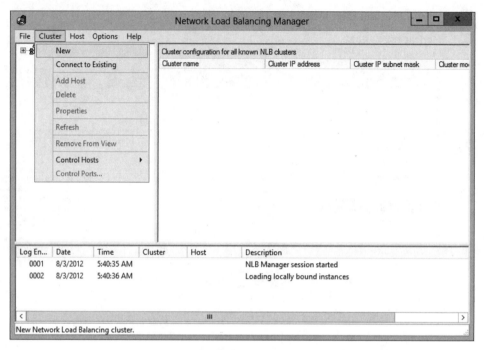

FIGURE 17-19

7. Enter **192.168.1.70** for the cluster IP address of the New Cluster : Cluster IP Addresses dialog box. This is the virtual IP address that is shared by all servers in the cluster. Click Next.

8. In the New Cluster : Cluster Parameters dialog box, ensure that the settings are correct. You can leave the "Full Internet name" blank, or you can set it to the domain name that points to the cluster IP address specified in that section.

9. Now you are presented with one of the more difficult questions in this wizard. The "Cluster operation mode" has three choices: "Unicast," "Multicast," and "IGMP multicast."

If your network supports it, usually "Multicast" or "IGMP multicast" is the best solution. NLB does its magic by messing with the MAC address of the network adapters on the servers. Unicast and Multicast work differently at both the switch layer and the network adapter on the server. The biggest issue with Unicast mode is that it will not allow the same network adapter that is used for the cluster IP address to also be used to manage the server using the server's original IP address. Essentially, that means that the NLB virtual IP will take over the network adapter and render the other IP address useless. Therefore, unless you're guaranteed to never want to manage a cluster node directly (highly unlikely), you must configure a second network adapter on the server to be used for directly managing the server. Multicast doesn't have this limitation and is preferred, unless your network doesn't support it. (Most networks support multicast.) You may need to discuss this with your networking team to see what's supported. If possible, however, this is the one time in the wizard when it's usually best to break away from the NLB default, as long as your network supports it.

Make your selection and click Next.

10. The New Cluster : Port Rules dialog box is where most of the rules are configured. If you click Next too quickly, you will accept the defaults and miss a lot of the customization that NLB offers. Instead, click Edit on the default port rule. You can limit the rule to a particular cluster IP address, port range, and protocol, as shown in Figure 17-20.

11. You can change the filtering mode to "Multiple host," "Single host," or "Disable this port range." If you select "Multiple host," you have three sub-options for the level of affinity. Here is where you can choose if you want users to come back to the same server on their repeat visits and whether "users" means everyone with the same IP address or everyone in the same network (class C), or if you don't want any affinity at all. The default of "Single" (host) means that the same IP address comes back to the same server on each subsequent

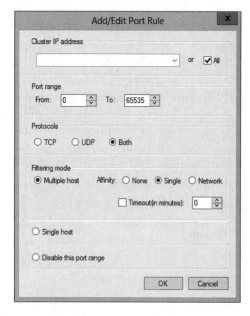

FIGURE 17-20

visit. Selecting "Single host" is a good choice if you want to have one ARR server normally handle all traffic so that statistics are consolidated. After your first server is added, the Port Rules section will also have an option for the load weight. This enables you to give some servers a higher weight (and thus more traffic) than the others.

12. Click OK and then Finish to complete the wizard.

Since the preceding steps set up only one of the cluster servers, you must add additional servers to NLB now.

1. From Network Load Balancing Manager, select the cluster node and ⇨ click Cluster ⇨ Add Host.

2. Complete the wizard using the same principles as for the original setup but for ARR02 this time.

That's it. Now you should have a virtual IP address (192.168.1.70) that is highly available between ARR01 and ARR02. If either server fails, the other server will take over.

At this point, you should edit your DNS bindings and URL Rewrite rules to use 192.168.1.70 for all your website traffic instead of the primary IP of ARR01. This ensures that neither ARR01 nor ARR02 is a single point of failure.

Using Network Load Balancing Manager, you can manage the nodes in the cluster by starting, stopping, performing a drainstop (basically a graceful stop), or by temporarily suspending them.

NLB handles server failures automatically using a heartbeat pulse between the servers; when one server fails, the others immediately take over. Because the HTTP and HTTPS protocols are so forgiving, when there is a failure, the web application (usually a web browser) will retry for a period of time before giving up. Because NLB recovers from a failure more quickly than the standard time-out in most browsers, the end user just sees a bit of a delay while waiting for the page to load. This essentially means that there will be no downtime when a server fails.

There are other types of failures that aren't as graceful, though. If there is an ASP.NET or IIS failure, NLB will not be aware of it, and it will continue to handle traffic on that unhealthy server. The only way to get extensive monitoring is to develop your own testing and, through code, disable a server if it fails any of the tests that you specify. System Center Operations Manager (SCOM) also offers support for NLB to enhance its intelligence and functionality.

For the most part, NLB is no longer the best standalone product now that other tools have superseded its functionality. However, NLB's new claim to fame is being a supported Microsoft solution to make ARR highly available. The ARR and NLB partnership makes a powerful load balancing solution.

FRAMEWORKS

In addition to hardware and software load balancers, framework tools are available that pull together additional functionality so that you have a central toolset for managing your web farm. Microsoft has two framework solutions: Web Farm Framework and Windows Azure Services.

Web Farm Framework

The Microsoft Web Farm Framework (WFF) is a module add-on to IIS that adds considerable new functionality to your web farm, making it much easier to manage servers, application installs, load balancers, and more. Some features of interest include:

➤ **Server provisioning** — WFF keeps track of all product installations on the server so that at any time you can provision entire servers with almost no effort, often called *elastic scale*. The provisioning process takes an available server with just the operating system installed and brings it up to the same status as the existing web servers.

➤ **Application provisioning** — WFF seamlessly rolls out application installations across a web farm by taking servers out of rotation one by one, installing the application, and then adding the servers back to the web farm again. There is support for provisioning using Web PI applications or using Web Deploy to provision other applications.

➤ **Content provisioning** — WFF also manages the process of provisioning your application content and managing updates.

➤ **Load-balancing support** — WFF has built-in support for ARR and third-party load balancers so that it can manage server and sites for you. This is important for many of the other features, because servers and sites need to be taken out of rotation and added back in again.

> ➤ **Log consolidation and statistics** — WFF offers up-to-date status and trace logs from all servers in the web farm, giving you useful insight into the web farm as a whole.

> ➤ **Extensible** — WFF is highly configurable, allowing you to integrate your own applications and processes into WFF.

If you have a large server farm or multiple server farms, WFF is well worth considering. In fact, when you use WFF, many of the details included in the ARR section of this chapter (and the "Shared Configuration" and deployment sections mentioned in Chapter 16) don't need to be managed manually; WFF takes care of the heavy lifting for you. You can find the WFF home page at www.iis.net/downloads/microsoft/web-farm-framework.

There are some caveats. The current version of WFF, version 2.2, has a dependency on a single controller node; therefore, if the controller node fails, WFF will be unable to monitor or manage the server farm until it is back online again.

WFF is a solution that introduces a number of new components, which means it can also introduce points of instability if you don't understand it well enough. Before using WFF, make sure that you have researched it and understand it thoroughly, including perusing the forums to apply recommended settings. You can find the forums at http://forums.iis.net/1167.aspx. WFF has a lot of potential and can make your life in the web farm world a lot better, but be sure that you know it well.

Windows Azure Services

When people who know at least something about Windows Azure hear the term *Windows Azure*, they often think of Microsoft's hosted cloud solution. What many don't realize is that Microsoft has now provided similar functionality for hosting service providers so that they can build their own environment on-premises and offer product offerings with the same functionality as Windows Azure — namely, websites, databases, and virtual machine hosted solutions. This framework, called *Windows Azure Services*, has powerful functionality built in to allow large-scale, shared hosting solutions, scaling to tens of thousands of sites, databases, and virtual servers. This is compatible with Windows Azure's cloud solution to offer a consistent platform for site administrators and developers, whether they host all their sites with Microsoft or with another company. Additionally, the service management portal allows self-service functionality, which may benefit corporate environments with staff that needs to set up sites for their own projects.

For smaller environments, Windows Azure Services may be overkill; however, if you are a hosting provider or if you have large deployments and want elastic scale, you may want to consider utilizing it for your environment.

Windows Azure Services is a complete package for hosting providers that includes the technologies and guidance to set up the various roles for large-scale hosting so that they work as a cohesive unit. It includes support for websites, hosted virtual servers, and MySQL and SQL Server databases. The server roles include the web servers, content servers, database servers, management servers, provisioning servers, and System Center servers. There is strong API support for programmatic management of the environment and to build tools for your users or customers.

While the architecture is based on IIS, it is a distributed version that has major architectural modifications. For example, there is no longer an `applicationHost.config` file. The entire configuration lives in a database. Sites can be provisioned on any of the web servers, so they don't need to stay running all the time and they are usually bound to a limited number of the web servers at a time, based on the number of worker roles set for the site. Troubleshooting and management is usually handled through the service management portal or System Center reports, rather than local tools on the web servers.

Windows Azure Services isn't the solution for a standard website, but it's a useful framework to be aware of for larger solutions. It's a technology to keep your eye on over time because Microsoft will most likely invest into this area of large-scale hosted solutions. Further information can be found at `www.microsoft.com/hosting/en/us/services.aspx`.

18

Programmatic Configuration and Management

WHAT'S IN THIS CHAPTER?

- ➤ Configuration optimization
- ➤ Direct configuration
- ➤ Programmatic configuration
- ➤ Configuration Editor
- ➤ Command-line management
- ➤ PowerShell management

WROX.COM CODE DOWNLOADS FOR THIS CHAPTER

The wrox.com code downloads for this chapter are found at www.wrox.com/remtitle
.cgi?isbn=1118388046 on the Download Code tab.

There are many management and programmatic configuration options in IIS 8.0. The latest release of IIS maintains the large steps taken in the area of management and upholds the foundation for extensive customization.

The configuration has been optimized in IIS 8.0; nonetheless, the schema continues to be fully extendable. This schema expansion allows all the programming methods to use the custom extensions immediately. The schema is not hard-coded into IIS and can therefore be significantly expanded.

Moreover, mimicking the ASP.NET structure by use of the XML Configuration construct, IIS 8.0 fully supports many of the configuration methods familiar to .NET developers.

If you have invested in custom programs in previous versions of IIS, you will be happy to know that the IIS development team has taken great care to ensure that IIS 8.0 is backward compatible with existing scripts, allowing you to continue to use your existing code.

This chapter is broken into three main sections: direct configuration, programmatic configuration, and command-line management. *Direct configuration* refers to understanding the configuration model and many of the underlying principles that can be managed using a simple text editor. After a detailed explanation of the configuration model, we discuss programmatic configuration and methods such as the managed AHAdmin that lies at the programming API core, the .NET-managed code wrapper, and IIS 8.0 Windows Management Instrumentation (WMI). Additionally, ABO, IIS 6.0 WMI, ADSI, and legacy code support are covered. Lastly, in the command-line management section, the AppCmd and the IIS PowerShell 3.0 module are discussed. Details covering the creation, management, and monitoring of a website from the command line using these tools are provided.

We also discuss the configuration file hierarchy, location tags, and how to reference configuration files or location tags specifically. Some areas of IIS tend to mask this complexity, but there are times when it's important to modify a particular location tag within a particular configuration file. This chapter covers how this is done from a manual configuration perspective and how to do this programmatically.

The goal of this chapter isn't to give multitudes of code examples, but rather to give you the tools that you need to understand the configuration files and the programmatic APIs so that you can do far more than what is shown in the examples here.

CONFIGURATION OPTIMIZATION

The schematized XML configuration system in IIS 8.0 remains the same as it was in IIS 7.x. This means that all IIS and website configurations remain within the .xml and .config files. Having this single location where all IIS and website configurations are stored can result in performance bottlenecks. As the number of hosted applications on a single Windows server increases, the suboptimal performance becomes more obvious. Not only that, but as the number of unique website and IIS configurations increases, the physical memory required to store those configurations also increases.

The configuration optimization actions taken in IIS 8.0 fall into the following two categories:

➤ IIS and website configuration memory utilization

➤ Performance of change provisioning

Because there is a lot of server consolidation happening in the IT industry, the number of cohosted websites will likely increase. As websites migrate to these single instances of Windows Server, administrators and companies expect the same performance and administration requirements as if they were hosted on a single server. This means that there should be no change of behavior of the website simply because it is cohosted with another website.

The number of cohosted websites that we are discussing here is in the thousands. Administrators of IIS instances that provide webhosting or administrators within large enterprise organizations will realize the greatest benefit. For example, using IIS 7.x on a single web server with more than 2,500 cohosted websites could use more than 500 MB of memory. However, on Windows Server 8, using IIS 8.0, the amount of memory used can be up to 50 percent less. This means that developers can use this additional memory to create more feature-rich applications or the administrators can run additional processes to make their systems more responsive or available.

The memory utilization optimization is based on how the creation and loading of the configurations are stored into the object model and then written into memory. Refer to the section, "Configuration File Hierarchy," later in this chapter for more on how the configuration hierarchy is structured.

> **NOTE** *Each time there is a modification to a website's configuration, the temporary application pool configuration file will be re-created and rewritten to the* `%SystemDrive%\inetpub\temp\appPools` *directory, and an AppDomain restart will be triggered.*

The second configuration optimization introduced into IIS 8.0 is related to the provisioning of global configuration modifications across all active websites on the Windows Server. For example, if the IIS administrator wants to disable Basic authentication for all hosted websites, this modification must be provisioned to each of the websites' configuration settings.

In IIS 7.x the provisioning of these changes across approximately 500 websites would take several minutes. The time requirement, that is, the performance hit, increases as the number of websites that are updated increases. Ultimately, it could take 5 to 6 minutes for a global modification to be propagated completely. In IIS 8.0, the algorithm for finding the configuration files needing an update has been optimized so that it recognizes the difference between a file and a folder. If the algorithm determines that the namespace is a file, it will stop and move to the next namespace. This code optimization resulted in the reduction of time required to propagate global configuration changes to seconds, even for the largest of cohosted website instances.

DIRECT CONFIGURATION

IIS can be managed in many different ways. You are probably very familiar with using IIS Manager to configure and administer IIS, and you may have edited the configuration files directly or developed some applications that manage IIS. With so many features in IIS 8.0, it's well worth your time to understand the entire configuration structure and many of the features that are available so that you can tackle even the most complex situation with relative ease.

IIS 8.0 has taken great strides to ensure that the entire schema can be extended and configured and that all programming APIs have full access to the extended configuration.

This section lays a foundation that is necessary for both the administrator and the IIS programmer to be able to understand the configuration files, why they are configured as they are, the benefits that they have over previous versions, and how to manage them well.

Configuration File Hierarchy

Since the introduction of the Integrated Pipeline, ASP.NET is not a second-class citizen. This means that ASP.NET continues to play a significant role within the IIS 8.0 platform. It also means that IIS and ASP.NET need to work together in a cohesive way.

The decision that led up to the current IIS configuration structure could be considered a battle of configuration dominance between IIS and ASP.NET. The IIS development team had to decide which configuration structure should become the standard. The configuration structure that has been ASP .NET's since day one is the one that IIS uses today. Older metabase configuration types are done away with, and sole preference is now given to the XML-based method.

This is welcomed for those who are familiar with ASP.NET because there is little additional learning necessary. The schema structure and rules that have guided ASP.NET continue to guide IIS, and by the time the configuration files have been read and a website is displayed, the two are merged into one joint system. This means that the `web.config` files of the websites and applications control both ASP.NET and IIS configuration.

There are three root configuration files and some other administration files that live at the global level. The hierarchy of configuration files contains the following:

FILE	PATH	DESCRIPTION
`machine.config`	`%windir%\Microsoft.NET\ Framework\<version>\config\`	Contains most of the .NET Framework sections and settings. This isn't new to IIS 8.0 but shows how IIS and the .NET Framework function as one.
`web.config` (root)	`%windir%\Microsoft.NET\ Framework\<version>\config\`	Contains more of the ASP. NET-specific sections and settings. Like `machine.config`, this is not new to IIS 8.0.
`applicationHost .config`	`%windir%\System32\inetsrv\config` (by default)	Contains the IIS global web server, configuration sections, and site settings using `location` tags.
`administration .config`	`%windir%\System32\inetsrv\config` (by default)	Contains the configuration for IIS Manager and the IIS Manager users.
`redirection .config`	`%windir%\System32\inetsrv\config`	This is used for shared configuration, which allows `applicationHost.config` and `administration.config` to be relocated.
`web.config` (site)	Website root path	Contains ASP.NET or IIS settings for the site. Or, if a `location` tag is used, it can manage the setting for subfolders or files. This file is not new to IIS 8.0.

web.config (application)	Website application path	The same as the site web .config file, except that it can be specific to an individual application.
Web.config (folder)	Website folder path	Although it's not commonly placed in a regular folder, some sections in web.config can run at the folder level.

Figure 18-1 shows how IIS and .NET work together and the order in which they are loaded. The .NET Framework configuration files are processed parallel to the IIS configuration files. After all global configuration files are loaded, the site's web.config file is processed.

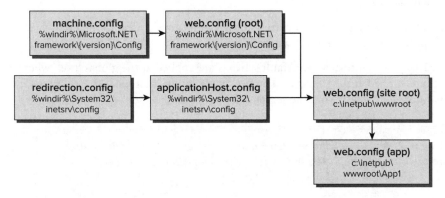

FIGURE 18-1

Order of Operation

As the configuration files are loaded, it's possible to have the same setting exist in multiple places at the same time. For example, you can set directory browsing settings in applicationHost.config, in site web.config files, and in location sections within those files. When settings exist in more than one place at a time, it's the last one loaded that actually takes effect.

Additionally, there are location sections within each configuration file that can also exist. Location sections are processed with the file that they live in, but after any generic section within that file.

Consider the following example:

APPLICATIONHOST.CONFIG

```
<system.webServer>
    ...
    <directoryBrowse enabled="false" />
    ...
</system.webServer>
```

APPLICATIONHOST.CONFIG LOCATION TAG

```
<location path="Default Web Site">
   <system.webServer>
      <directoryBrowse enabled="true" />
   </system.webServer>
</location>
```

SITE WEB.CONFIG

```
<system.webServer>
   <directoryBrowse enabled="false" />
</system.webServer>
```

In this example, the `directoryBrowse` element will first be processed by the general section of `applicationHost.config`, causing the value to be set to `"false"`. Then the `location` tag (still in `applicationHost.config`) will be processed, causing the value to become `"true"`. Finally, the site's `web.config` will be processed, setting the actual value back to `"false"`. The final result of `directoryBrowse` will be `"false"`.

This is not unlike Active Directory or NTFS permissions. The settings closest to the final object are the ones that are applied last, and ultimately win the fight.

To look at it another way, the more generic default settings are applied at the global level, whereas the specific settings are applied at the site level. The site owner knows best what the site needs, but the server administrator knows best what the server defaults should be.

> **NOTE** *Even though the site administrator makes the decision on settings, the server administrator needs to be able to deny the ability to override certain settings. This is covered in the "Locking" section.*

Collection Items

The earlier `directoryBrowsing` example is a simple attribute. That is an easy example because an attribute can be set in multiple configuration locations at once without any conflict. Although an attribute is as simple as it gets, collection items are a different matter. You cannot add the same collection item multiple times without throwing an error.

A *collection item* is part of a group of items that can be added, removed, or cleared. For example, the `defaultDocument` element contains a `files` section, which often contains multiple collection items, as illustrated by this example:

```
<defaultDocument enabled="true">
   <files>
      <add value="default.aspx" />
      <add value="default.htm" />
      <add value="default.asp" />
      <add value="index.htm" />
      <add value="index.html" />
```

```
        </files>
    </defaultDocument>
```

In this example, the `<add />` element adds to the collection, resulting in five default documents specified by this configuration section.

The issue arises when the same items are added again, either right there in the same tag or in another configuration file or location section down the structure hierarchy.

> **NOTE** *Some common collections are* modules, handlers, defaultDocuments, httpErrors, customHeaders, filesExtensions, *and* windowsAuthentication *providers.*

The solution is easy enough, but you must understand it to master the IIS and ASP.NET configuration model. If a collection item already exists and you want to replace it with your own item, you must first "remove" the individual item or "clear" the set of items and add back what you want.

This is best understood with an example. Consider setting a `customHeader`. By default, there is already one with a name of `X-Powered-By` and a value of `ASP.NET` set in `applicationHost.config`. If you want to change the value of `X-Powered-By` in your website's `web.config` file and add a second collection item called `X-Managed-By`, you might erroneously try the following:

```
<httpProtocol>
    <customHeaders>
        <add name="X-Powered-By" value="ASP.NET v4.5" />
        <add name="X-Managed-By" value="The Best Admin" />
    </customHeaders>
</httpProtocol>
```

Because the `X-Powered-By` collection item already exists, you would run into the error shown in Figure 18-2.

To configure your `web.config` file properly, you would need to *remove* the `X-Powered-By` collection item first or *clear* the whole section and add back what you need. Both of the following examples are valid:

VALID OPTION 1

```
<httpProtocol>
    <customHeaders>
        <remove name="X-Powered-By" />
        <add name="X-Powered-By" value="ASP.NET v4.5" />
        <add name="X-Managed-By" value="The Best Admin" />
    </customHeaders>
</httpProtocol>
```

VALID OPTION 2

```
<httpProtocol>
    <customHeaders>
```

```
            <clear />
            <add name="X-Powered-By" value="ASP.NET v4.5" />
            <add name="X-Managed-By" value="The Best Admin" />
        </customHeaders>
    </httpProtocol>
```

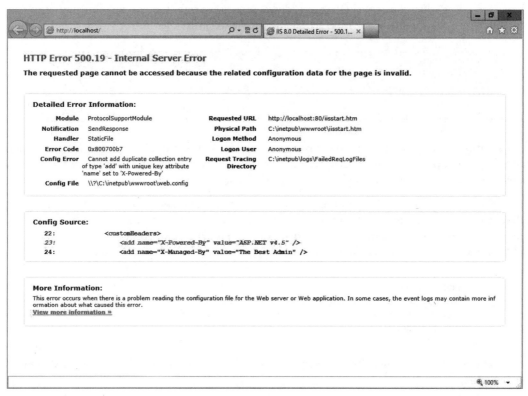

FIGURE 18-2

In the first example above, you may have noticed in the Remove tag that the value property isn't set like it is in the Add tags. This is because the value is not required to specify an item uniquely and to remove it from the collection. In fact, an error will be thrown if you have the value in the Remove tag. Only enough information to identity the item uniquely is necessary.

In these examples, when IIS processes all the configuration files, it will first add the X-Powered-By collection item at the global level when applicationHost.config is processed. Then, in the first example, it will remove the item again, causing it not to exist anymore. Then it will add it back and also add X-Managed-By. In the second example, when web.config is processed, it will clear *all* the previous collection items (in this case, there is only one) and then will add both items in the example. In neither situation is there a time when a duplicate entry exists.

> **NOTE** *It is possible to have duplicate collection items with the same key if it is specifically allowed in the schema. This is possible when a collection element has the* `allowDuplicates` *attribute set to* `"true"`. *This doesn't occur often, and* `applicationHost.config` *doesn't have any duplicate collection items allowed.*

There is one more thing worth noting about collection items. There are three commands that can be applied to a collection item. They can be added, removed, or cleared, although IIS doesn't always call them `add`, `remove`, and `clear`. In fact, the schema file allows those command names to be changed, as shown in the following excerpt from `IIS_schema.xml`:

```
<sectionSchema name="system.webServer/httpErrors">
    . . .
    <collection addElement="error" clearElement="clear" removeElement="remove">
    . . .
</collection>
```

The `httpErrors` section uses `error` for the Add command instead of `add`. As you can see from that excerpt, it's possible to create a custom command name for Clear and Remove too, although it's never changed by default in any of the configuration files.

Section Structure

The IIS and .NET configuration files are made up of section groups, sections, elements, attributes, and collections. It's helpful to understand the structure of each of the global configuration files, both for IIS and .NET. The following subsections describe the core configuration files.

applicationHost.config

At the core of IIS is the `applicationHost.config` configuration file, which contains settings that pertain to the activation service like application pools, sites, logging settings, listeners, and the like. By default, it is located in `%windir%\System32\inetsrv\config`, but it can be redirected to a different location, as explained in Chapter 17. Figure 18-3 shows an example structure of the `applicationHost.config` file.

administration.config

The `administration.config` file is for the IIS Manager user interface (UI) and settings that pertain to that, such as the IIS Manager users. Like `applicationHost.config`, this file is located in `%windir%\System32\inetsrv\config` but can be redirected to a local or network folder. Figure 18-4 shows the configuration structure for `administration.config`.

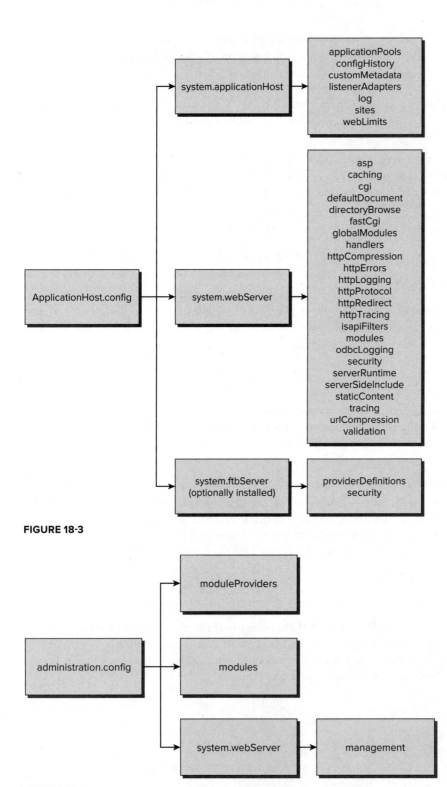

FIGURE 18-3

FIGURE 18-4

redirection.config

The `redirection.config` file is used to configure the location of `applicationHost.config` and `administration.config` to allow the shared configuration mechanism to function. Located in the `%windir%\System32\inetsrv\config` folder, `redirection.config`'s structure is very simple because of its narrow focus, as shown in Figure 18-5.

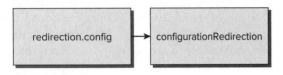

FIGURE 18-5

machine.config

The `machine.config` file is specific to .NET and isn't new to IIS 8.0, but because of the tight integration between .NET and IIS, it is a key player in IIS 8.0. It is located in the `%windir%\Microsoft.NET\Framework\<version>\config\` folder and contains most of the .NET Framework sections and settings. Because this file exists for each version of the framework, there is often more than one on each server.

web.config (Root)

The root `web.config` file is similar to `machine.config` except that it has ASP.NET-related sections and settings. It is also located at `%windir%\Microsoft.NET\Framework\<version>\config\`. Like `machine.config`, there will be one root `web.config` file for each version of the framework.

Location Tag

An essential part of configuring ASP.NET, and now IIS, is the `location` tag. This has been covered already in previous chapters, but it's worth covering again now because of its central role in the IIS configuration.

Within any of the configuration files, the settings within the top-level `<configuration>` tag are applied to the directory in which the configuration file resides, and all the child paths beneath it. In the case of global configuration files, the settings in the `applicationHost.config` and the other root configuration files are the default settings for all sites.

The `location` tag enables you to specify unique settings to specific child paths without needing a `web.config` file actually to exist at that level. This is done by setting the `path` property to the site, application, folder, or file that you want to configure, as seen in the following `applicationHost.config` section example:

```
<location path="Default Web Site">
    <system.webServer>
        <defaultDocument enabled="true">
            <files>
                <clear />
                <add value="default.aspx" />
            </files>
        </defaultDocument>
```

```
        </system.webServer>
    </location>
```

The `path` in this example is set to "Default Web Site," which means that everything in that tag will be applied to the site located at `c:\inetpub\wwwroot`, even though the configuration is set in `%windir%\System32\inetsrv\config`.

When set in the global configuration files, the `path` property must start with a reference to the site and then optionally include the path to folders or files under the site. If the `.config` file is for a site instead of being a global configuration file, it cannot include the website name but instead it must start with a relative path under the `web.config` file. Absolute paths are not supported; everything must be relative to the `.config` file where the `location` tag exists.

The following table explains the possible values for the path attribute:

VALUE	GLOBAL CONFIGURATION EXAMPLE	SITE OR APPLICATION EXAMPLE	DESCRIPTION
"." (or "")	path="."	path="."	The current level. In the global configuration files, this refers to the defaults. In a site or application's `web.config` file, this refers to the location where the `web.config` file resides. Because this is the default value, leaving the `path` attribute off will do the same.
"sitename"	path="Default Web Site"	N/A	The *site name* specifies a site and is valid from any of the global configuration files. You cannot set the path to a site name from a site's `web.config` file.
"application"	path="Site1/App1"	path="App1"	At the site or application level, the application name must be a relative path.
"vdir"	path="Site1/Vdir1"	path="Vdir1"	At the global level, the site name must be included; but at the site level, the site name cannot be included.

"physicaldir"	path="Site1/ PhysicalDir1"	path="PhysicalDir1"	A simple folder doesn't need to be an application or virtual directory to have IIS or ASP .NET settings applied, but understand that most settings are locked so that they cannot be set outside of an application root.
"file.ext"	path="Site1/ default.aspx"	path="login.aspx"	Files can also be configured. In fact, using a location tag is the only way to configure settings for a file.

Multiple location tags can exist in the same configuration file, and it's even possible to have multiple location tags with the same path as long as they don't reference the same sections or if they have a different overrideMode as described in Chapter 9, "Delegating Remote Administration."

The order in which the location tags are listed isn't important to the configuration system, but you may want to consider keeping it organized for your own sake.

You cannot nest a location tag in the top-level sections or under other location tags. When creating a location tag, the entire path to the section must be included. For example, if you want to set the default document for Site1 in the applicationHost.config file, you would create a location tag that looks like this:

```
<location path="Default Web Site">
    <system.webServer>
        <security>
            <authentication>
                <basicAuthentication enabled="true" />
            </authentication>
        </security>
    </system.webServer>
</location>
```

Notice that even the <system.webServer></system.webServer> must be included within the location tag.

You can use the location tag for various reasons:

➤ To control the settings for a site or application that is different from where the configuration file is located

➤ To centralize all settings into a single file for neater housekeeping

➤   To apply settings to a file (instead of a folder)

➤   To lock certain sections, as will be explained shortly

➤   To disable inheritance, as will also be explained shortly

➤   To apply default settings in the global configuration files while still leaving the default installation settings untouched

Inheritance

By default, all settings that are applied at any level will inherit down to all child sites, applications, folders, and files, wherever the setting is relevant. What's interesting when working with ASP.NET applications is that the application folders and files do not inherit across application boundaries. This means that files in \bin and \app_code and other system folders will only be processed within the bounds of that application.

This can cause some issues when there are references in web.config that are inherited by its child applications, but when the files and classes that are referenced don't exist at that level. Consider a situation in which a module exists in the root of the site in \bin and is referenced in web.config in the <module> section, but a subfolder called App1 is marked as an application. The reference in web.config to the module would still be there in the App1 application because of the web.config inheritance, but the module binary itself wouldn't be loaded as long as it only exists in the root \bin folder. This would cause an error in the App1 application, preventing anything from working.

To look at it another way, consider the following:

➤   \web.config — Contains a reference to an HTTP module

➤   \bin\module.dll — The module itself

➤   \App1\ — Marked as an application

In the App1 application, the web.config settings will still be the same as in the root application, because the web.config files inherit across application boundaries. But the \bin\module.dll will not be loaded in the \App1\ application because ASP.NET files and folders do not inherit across application boundaries. Because the web.config reference is looking for the class within the module.dll file but cannot find it, an error will be thrown.

There are a few ways to work around this (purposely) inconsistent inheritance where web.config is inherited, but not the other ASP.NET system files and folders:

➤   Under the App1 folder, place a copy of the \bin folder and other necessary system folders. This will keep ASP.NET happy even if it doesn't use the module. Of course, make sure to understand your application to know if the module would be helpful or if it would hurt having it load in the App1 folder.

➤   "Remove" the module, as described in the preceding "Collection Items" section. As of ASP.NET v2.0, if you remove a module, it will not load the module at any time. Note that before v2.0, this didn't work because the module would be loaded into memory when the site's web.config file was processed before the application's web.config file had a chance to remove it. Either `<remove />` or `<clear />` will work, but when using `<clear />` be sure to add back any modules that you need for the site to operate properly.

➤ ASP.NET v2.0 introduced a new attribute called `inheritInChildApplications`. This is extremely useful in these situations in which you don't want something to inherit to the child applications. It is explained further now.

The `inheritInChildApplications` attribute allows you to wrap a section within a `location` tag, mark it so that it doesn't inherit, and then put in whatever settings you want to live only at that level. The path attribute can be "." or something more specific, whatever your needs are. Consider the following example from the `web.config` file in the root of the site:

```
<location path="" inheritInChildApplications="false">
  <system.webServer>
    <modules>
      <add name="CustomModule" type="…"
        preCondition="managedHandler" />
    </modules>
  </system.webServer>
</location>
```

This will only be applied to the root of the website and not to any child applications because of the `inheritInChildApplications` setting.

One caveat is that a section cannot be in two places at once. This means that you *cannot* have the top-level section contain some modules and a `location` tag with `inheritInChildApplications="false"` contain the rest of the modules. It's all or nothing for each unique section within the path.

Locking

Often the Server Administrator has full access to the server, whereas the site owners need to be isolated to their own area and are given only as much access as they need to manage their sites properly. One of the main ways to ensure that this happens is through section, attribute, and element locking. This is explained in depth in Chapter 9, "Delegating Remote Administration," but is briefly reviewed here.

Using the `location` tag, you can set configuration items so that they cannot be overwritten. The attribute name that controls this is `overrideMode`. The three options for `overrideMode` are *Allow*, *Deny*, and *Inherit*. The following example shows how to set the `windowsAuthentication` section so that it cannot be overwritten further down the path hierarchy:

```
<location path="Default Web Site" overrideMode="Deny">
    <system.webServer>
        <security>
            <authentication>
                <windowsAuthentication>
                    <providers />
                </windowsAuthentication>
            </authentication>
        </security>
    </system.webServer>
</location>
```

Usually this is set in the global configuration files so that website and application operators cannot change those settings. Many sections are locked down by default but can be changed to lock or unlock sections of the configuration files.

childConfig/sourceConfig

The configuration system can be further configured by using the `childConfig` and `sourceConfig` attributes to break out parts of the configuration into other `config` files. There are several reasons why you may do this:

➤ **Security** — Sections of the configuration can be delegated to different administrators and have NTFS ACLs applied so that only the necessary users or roles have access to make changes.

➤ **Manageability** — Separating the configuration into sections can allow different people to manage different parts of the configuration without stepping on each other's toes.

➤ **Section isolation** — Breaking the configuration into parts can protect parts of the configuration from being overwritten when unrelated changes are uploaded to the server. This is especially useful for the `web.config` files in a website because it is common to use FTP or some other remote deployment method to upload an old copy to the `web.config` file. This upload can potentially overwrite changes that were made through IIS Manager on the server.

> **NOTE** *Updating the* `childConfig` *or* `sourceConfig` *files will not cause an AppDomain recycle as changing the other* `.config` *files will. This means that the changes will not take effect until the next time the configuration files are reloaded, or until you purposefully "touch" the main configuration files. To touch a configuration file, add a space to an insignificant place and save the file. This will cause an AppDomain recycle, causing the configuration change to take effect.*

By default, the three main global configuration files — `applicationHost.config`, `machine.config`, and root `web.config` — don't use either `childConfig` or `sourceConfig`. It's important to note that `sourceConfig` does not work in `applicationHost.config`, and `childConfig` does not support the section's attribute values.

Both `configSource` and `childSource` are described further in Chapter 17.

Configuration Path

Understanding the configuration paths in IIS 8.0 is important, both from tools like `AppCmd.exe`, PowerShell, and for programming with the programming APIs.

In IIS 6.0 and prior versions, the configuration path was in the form of LM/W3SVC/1/ROOT, where 1 is the site ID. Because there was just the one metabase file for the entire configuration, there wasn't a need to reference the configuration file from any tool or programming API.

In IIS 8.0, with ASP.NET working as such an integral part, there are multiple configuration files. Plus, it is possible to have settings at multiple levels, so it's necessary to have a method to specify where a particular setting should be applied. This is done by offering a method to target specific locations of a given setting.

In the new system, the configuration path has the following syntax:

```
MACHINE/WEBROOT/APPHOST/{Sitename}/{Vdir or App}
```

MACHINE corresponds to `machine.config`, WEBROOT to the root `web.config` file, and APPHOST to `applicationHost.config`; when referencing the site, the MACHINE/WEBROOT/APPHOST is optional. What is interesting about this configuration path structure is that it never references a setting directly. It only references the configuration file and `location` tag. This is different from IIS 6.0, which often required the whole path direct to the property — for example, LM/W3SVC/1/ROOT/ `ServerComment`. The IIS 8.0 configuration settings are set as a separate step.

You can use just part of the path to access specific configuration files. For example, `machine .config`'s path is simply MACHINE. Additionally, the `redirection.config` file's path is MACHINE/ REDIRECTION.

A good way to illustrate how this works is by using `AppCmd.exe`, which makes use of the configuration path. The directory browsing setting makes for a good example because by default it is allowed to be set in the site's `web.config`. This means that changing the setting in IIS Manager will result in the site's `web.config` file being changed rather than setting it in a `location` tag in `applicationHost.config`. This may not be your preference, so using the configuration path, you can have the setting apply to a `location` tag within `applicationHost.config` instead. This can be done with the following command:

```
AppCmd.exe Set Config "Default Web Site/" /section:directoryBrowse
/enabled:true /COMMIT:MACHINE/WEBROOT/APPHOST
```

Notice the /COMMIT property, which allows you to force `AppCmd.exe` to apply the setting to the place of your choosing. This is optional and often isn't needed, but in this situation it is used to ensure that the setting is applied directly to `applicationHost.config` instead of the site's `web .config` file.

For additional information about `AppCmd.exe`, see the "Command-Line Management" section later in this chapter. It is also possible to modify the `applicationHost.config` file and administer IIS using PowerShell; see the "IIS PowerShell Management" section later in this chapter for examples.

Understanding this configuration hierarchy is important when using `AppCmd.exe` and for programming, which is covered in following section.

Schema Extensibility

In legacy IIS versions, there wasn't a consistent schema or configuration structure to the metabase. Much of this was hard-coded into IIS and wasn't available to be modified or extended. There was an `MBSchema.xml` file, which enforced some data integrity, but there was room for improvement. IIS 8.0 builds substantially on this and has a schema folder that includes schema files for IIS and the .NET Framework. These can be extended by Microsoft, third-party companies, or by you directly.

The four core schema files are as follows:

➤ `IIS_schema.xml` — This covers the Windows Process Activation Service (WAS) and settings for the IIS Web Server.

➤ `FX_schema.xml` — This covers the .NET Framework configuration sections.

➤ `ASPNET_schema.xml` — This covers the ASP.NET settings.

➤ `rscaext.xml` — This is the schema for the Runtime Status and Control (RSCA) API extension configuration. This works along with `IIS_Schema.xml` but adds the runtime state schema.

> **WARNING** *It is strongly recommended that you don't change any of the native schema files. Instead, you should use your own schema file to extend it. This ensures that you don't make any changes that will keep IIS from starting and also ensures that hot fixes and upgrades will not override the changes that you make.*

These schema files, along with the configuration sections in the config files, define rules and guidelines that IIS and .NET must abide by. What makes this even more powerful is that it can easily be extended to include anything that you need, such as website contact names or phone numbers.

In addition to the built-in schema and the extensible schema, there are dynamic properties that allow properties and their values to be generated dynamically, as needed. Together this makes a powerful, extensible infrastructure. Although there is no high-level programmatic method to get and set schema files except using traditional XML APIs, it is easy to do this from a text editor and easy to deploy by using XCopy and other common tools.

The best way to understand this is to see it in action. Suppose you want to add owner information to the website so that your custom tools can tell who the owner is and have information about him. In this example, it's desirable to add an element section called *OwnerInfo*. This section will include two attributes: name and e-mail, both of type string. Finally, it will have a role attribute of type enum that has three possible options: Admin, Tech, and Billing.

To extend the schema, you can place a file with any name into the schema folder as long as it has an extension of `.xml`. To create this and write code to update the site with the new owner information, follow these steps:

1. Create an empty text file in the schema folder (`%windir%\System32\inetsrv\config\schema`) called **OwnerInfo.xml**. You can do this from the command prompt or from Windows Explorer.

2. Add the following text to the file:

```
<configSchema>
  <sectionSchema name="system.applicationHost/sites">
    <collection addElement="site">
     <element name="OwnerInfo" >
        <attribute name="name" type="string"/>
```

```
            <attribute name="email" type="string"/>
            <attribute name="role" type="string">
                <enum name="Admin" value="0" />
                <enum name="Tech" value="1" />
                <enum name="Billing" value="3" />
            </attribute>
        </element>
    </collection>
  </sectionSchema>
</configSchema>
```

Your schema has been extended and is ready to use. This will extend onto the existing `system .applicationHost/sites` schema. A good way to find out the correct syntax is to use the `rscaext.xml` file as an example. It already extends onto many existing sections and has examples for the sectionSchema, collections, elements, attributes, and enums.

> **NOTE** *If you ever have a hard time getting IIS to start after you make a bad change and doing an* iisreset *doesn't show you the real error, there is still hope. The best way to find out what is wrong with a schema file or any of the configuration files is to use IIS Manager. Even if IIS can't be started, IIS Manager will continue to work, and if there are any errors, it will do a good job of telling you what is wrong.*

This schema addition will add to the existing `Site` collection and create a new element called `OwnerInfo` with the three attributes.

> **NOTE** *When you save the file in the schema folder, it will be immediately noticed by IIS — no reset of IIS is necessary. Be careful because an error here could cause IIS to fail. At the risk of stating the obvious, be sure to test this extensively in a testing environment before releasing it to production.*

Because the `sites` section is already in `applicationHost.config`, no changes need to be made there at this time. The next example in this section covers how to add a new section that doesn't already exist in any of the configuration files.

The next step is to create a tool to write the owner information to the site. You can use any of the programming methods described later in this chapter or edit the configuration file directly from a text editor. The following example will work with the Managed Code API, which is described later in this chapter. If IIS programming is new to you, you should jump to the "Programmatic Configuration" section of this chapter and come back to this later. In addition, as covered in more depth later in the chapter, be sure to reference `Microsoft.Web.Administration.dll` from `%windir%\System32\inetsrv` and import the `Microsoft.Web.Administration` namespace. Using whichever programming tool you choose, add the following code:

```
Dim SM As New ServerManager
Dim config As Configuration = SM.GetApplicationHostConfiguration
Dim section As ConfigurationSection = _
```

```
    config.GetSection("system.applicationHost/sites")

Dim mySite As Site = SM.Sites("Default Web Site")

Dim ownerInfo As ConfigurationElement = mySite.GetChildElement("OwnerInfo")

ownerInfo.GetAttribute("name").Value = "Abraham Lincoln"
ownerInfo.GetAttribute("email").Value = "16@whitehouse.gov"
ownerInfo.GetAttribute("role").Value = "Admin"

SM.CommitChanges()
ServerManager SM = new ServerManager();
Configuration config = SM.GetApplicationHostConfiguration();
ConfigurationSection section =
        config.GetSection("system.applicationHost/sites");

Site mysite = SM.Sites["Default Web Site"];

ConfigurationElement ownerInfo =
        mysite.GetChildElement("OwnerInfo");

ownerInfo.GetAttribute("name").Value = "Abraham Lincoln";
ownerInfo.GetAttribute("email").Value = "16@whitehouse.gov";
ownerInfo.GetAttribute("role").Value = "Admin";

SM.CommitChanges();
```

Finally, run your program. That's all there is to it. You will notice in the Microsoft.Web
.Administration section that the code to manage your custom schema is exactly the same as the
code used to manage built-in IIS settings.

You can see the new settings by opening applicationHost.config and looking in the sites
section. It should look something like this:

```
<site name="Default Web Site" id="1">
  <application path="/">
    <virtualDirectory path="/" physicalPath="%SystemDrive%\inetpub\wwwroot" />
  </application>
  <bindings>
  <binding protocol="http" bindingInformation="*:80:" />
  </bindings>
  <OwnerInfo name="Abraham Lincoln" email="16@whitehouse.gov" role="Admin" />
</site>
```

Notice the OwnerInfo element with the values filled in. This is amazingly easy and powerful!

The previous example showed how to extend onto the existing sites section in applicationHost
.config. The next example shows you how to create a *new* section. First, add a file into the schema
folder called **MyCustomSection.xml**, and add the following to it:

```
<configSchema>
  <sectionSchema name="myCustomSection">
    <attribute name="name" type="string" />
    <attribute name="Length" type="int" defaultValue="100" />
    <attribute name="IsActive" type="bool" defaultValue="true" />
    <attribute name="Color" type="enum" defaultValue="Red" >
        <enum name="Red" value="0" />
        <enum name="Yellow" value="1" />
```

```
            <enum name="Green" value="3" />
            <enum name="Blue" value="4" />
        </attribute>
    </sectionSchema>
</configSchema>
```

Because this is a new section, you must also add it to the `configSections` section of the configuration file. This example will add this to `administration.config` to show that it's not just `applicationHost.config` that can be extended. Because this is a main section, it must be placed directly under `<configSections>`, as follows:

```
<configuration>
    <configSections>
        <section name="myCustomSection" />
        <section name="moduleProviders" ... />
    ...
    </configSections>
    ...
</configuration>
```

The code to work with your new custom section is essentially the same as before. Here is a code sample to set these four attributes:

```
Dim SM As New ServerManager
Dim config As Configuration = SM.GetAdministrationConfiguration
Dim section As ConfigurationSection = _
config.GetSection("myCustomSection")

section.GetAttribute("name").Value = "TheName"
section.GetAttribute("Length").Value = 200
section.GetAttribute("IsActive").Value = True
section.GetAttribute("Color").Value = "Blue"

SM.CommitChanges()
ServerManager SM = new ServerManager();
Configuration config = SM.GetAdministrationConfiguration();
ConfigurationSection section = config.GetSection("myCustomSection");

section.GetAttribute("name").Value = "TheName";
section.GetAttribute("Length").Value = 200;
section.GetAttribute("IsActive").Value = true;
section.GetAttribute("Color").Value = "Blue";

SM.CommitChanges();
```

After running this, it will add a new section to the administration configuration file:

```
<myCustomSection name="TheName" Length="200" IsActive="true" Color="Blue" />
```

> **NOTE** *It is possible to create a strongly typed class that will provide IntelliSense support for your custom schema. To do so, you would create a class that corresponds to the custom schema that you just created. Then use one of the* `GetSection` *overrides that allow you to set the* `System.Type` *of the section. This will provide full IntelliSense support as if you were using Microsoft's Managed Code APIs directly.*

As you can see, the schema is a foundational part of IIS, is used for many of the tools and programming within IIS, and can be extended to fit your needs. The sky is the limit on what you can do with IIS to make it more customized for your environment.

This completes the direct configuration section, which covered many of the key concepts of the configuration files. Now it's time to move on to programmatic configuration, where you will learn the various programming API choices, which you would want to use, and how you would do so.

PROGRAMMATIC CONFIGURATION

When dealing with a small number of web servers and infrequent changes, IIS Manager and manual methods of administrating IIS work well, but it doesn't take long to outgrow this manual administration and look for a better way to manage the server.

Programmatic configuration is nothing new in IIS, but it's been greatly improved while keeping full support for legacy code. There is no need to throw out your old code, yet you can use the latest and greatest methods of programming to manage your IIS servers from now on.

Virtually everything that can be done through IIS Manager and through editing the configuration files directly can be done programmatically. You can program to automate monotonous tasks like the creation of new sites, managing many servers at once, or to develop tools so that non-administrators can make changes — for example, to shut down a site because of non-payment. Whatever the reason, pretty much anything that you dream up can be built.

Since there are code samples scattered throughout the book, this section focuses more on the key concepts so that, coupled with the code snipped throughout the book, you will have the tools necessary to program whatever you need. It's hard to cover everything that you need for programming without writing at least a full book, but the key foundational concepts for various programming methods are covered.

You may be a seasoned developer who just needs reference material, or you may be a programmer who needs to know how to program against IIS 8.0, or you may be a system administrator who has never programmed before but who is looking to create some tools to simplify your work.

The next few pages are targeted at the person who is not yet a programmer but would like to know how to take advantage of many of the coding examples that have been scattered throughout the book. You will be taken on a walk-through to create a tool that will use a web page to create an application pool and website. This will be done using free tools that you can easily download online.

For the more seasoned programmer, stick around, because there is a lot to cover that will benefit you too. But feel free to skim parts that you already know well.

IIS 8.0 Programming Walk-Through

This walk-through takes you on a brief journey to get your feet wet in the world of IIS administration programming. It is by no means a detailed walk-through — full books have been written for that — but it does lay a foundation upon which you can build.

System Requirements

This walk-through uses only three tools: Visual Web Developer 2010, IIS 8.0, and any commonly used web browser. Additionally, it is much easier to develop when the development machine has IIS installed, rather than doing development remotely. The assumption is that you are doing your development on a Windows Server 2008 R2 or Windows Server 8 that has IIS installed. It is possible to set up remote debugging, but explaining how to do so is outside of the scope of this book.

> **NOTE** *The full Visual Studio 2012 is even better than Visual Web Developer because of the extra tools and features that it comes with. Because this walk-through uses features that both products have, you can use whichever one to which you have access. Because the steps are pretty much the same, you should have no problem using either tool and still following this walk-through. For this walk-through, Visual Web Developer is used.*

To obtain Visual Web Developer, a good place to start is `www.asp.net` or with a Bing search. Searching for Visual Web Developer should get you a good download page within the top few links. Be sure that you're downloading it directly from `www.asp.net` or `www.microsoft.com` and not some third-party download.

Installing Visual Web Developer is straightforward. SQL Server Express is not required for this walk-through, so selecting that during the Visual Web Developer installation is optional.

Getting Started with Visual Web Developer

Before starting Visual Web Developer, you need to decide on the disk location where you will develop the website. Visual Web Developer has its own web engine, called *ASP.NET Development Server* (aka Cassini), so IIS does not need to be used for development. However, once you have it developed, you will probably want to run it under IIS on either the same server or a different server.

Be sure to prepare a folder that makes the most sense for both development and operational use. This demo uses `C:\inetpub\WebSite1`.

> **NOTE** *When running Cassini, your currently logged-in user will need access to the disk and to make changes to IIS. With User Access Control (UAC) in Windows Server 2008 R2 and Windows Server 2012, you may run into an issue where you need to elevate to Administrator rights, even if you are logged in as a user who is an administrator. To get around this, there are three potential solutions:*
>
> ➤ Make sure that the folder where your website exists has specific permissions for your currently logged-in user. Just having the Administrators group will not be enough. This is usually the preferred method because it doesn't require bypassing UAC.
>
> ➤ Right-click the Visual Web Developer icon before you start it and click "Run as administrator." This will ensure that everything within Visual Web Developer, including Cassini, will run as the Administrator.
>
> ➤ In theory, you could disable UAC so that it doesn't get in the way, but that's not the recommended work-around.

Once Visual Web Developer or Visual Studio is installed, fire it up — it's time to begin. Note that you can develop in Visual Basic or C#. Both will accomplish the same thing — it's just a matter of syntax. This walk-through provides examples in both Visual Basic and C#.

1. Click File ➪ New Web Site.

2. Ensure that ASP.NET Web Site is selected.

3. Ensure that File System is selected in the Location dropdown box.

4. In the Location textbox, enter **C:\inetpub\WebSite1**.

5. Select your preferred language. Figure 18-6 shows the completed New Web Site dialog box.

6. Click OK.

FIGURE 18-6

This will create a new website with a couple of default documents. `Default.aspx` and `Default.aspx.vb` (`.cs`) are the starting files in the new website template. For simplicity in the walk-through, they will be used instead of creating new files. Note that `Default.aspx` `.vb` (`.cs`) may be collapsed under `Default.aspx`. If it is, click the plus (+) beside `Default` `.aspx` to expand it. `App_Data` will not be used, so you can ignore or delete that folder.

7. `Microsoft.Web.Administration.dll` needs to be added as a reference to the project. To add the reference, click the Website menu item and then Add Reference.

8. Go to the Browse tab and navigate to `%windir%\System32\inetsrv` (`%windir%` is usually `C:\Windows`).

9. Select `Microsoft.Web.Administration.dll` and click OK, as shown in Figure 18-7. To save time navigating through the folders and files, you can directly type **%windir%\ System32\inetsrv\Microsoft.Web.Administration.dll.**

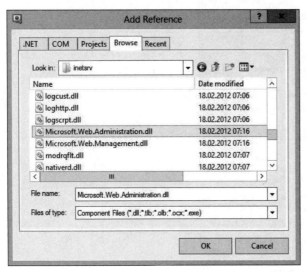

FIGURE 18-7

Designing the Web Form

Now that Visual Web Developer is started and the reference to `Microsoft.Web.Administration` `.dll` is in place, it's time to design the web form that takes the information about the website.

1. Open `Default.aspx` from Solution Explorer on the right. If Solution Explorer is not shown, you can open it from the top menu by clicking View ⇨ Solution Explorer.

2. Click the Design tab at the bottom of the main window. This will switch to Design View, which is a graphical representation of the web page.

3. Right-click in a fresh place on the design surface and click Properties. This will place you in the Properties menu, which is usually on the right side.

4. Change the Title property to `Create Web Site`.

5. On the design surface, type **Create Web Site** inside the `div` tag (the dotted square box), and press Enter twice.

6. From the toolbox on the left, drag a Label control to the empty space below the words you just typed (still inside the `div` tag). If the toolbox isn't displayed, you can show it by clicking View from the top menu and clicking Toolbox.

7. Position your cursor after the Label and press Enter twice.

8. Next, create a table to make the page look better. To create the table, from the top menu click Table ⇨ Insert Table.

9. In the dialog box that appears, enter **6** for the rows and **2** for the columns, as shown in Figure 18-8. The defaults are good unless you feel the urge to clean it up further.

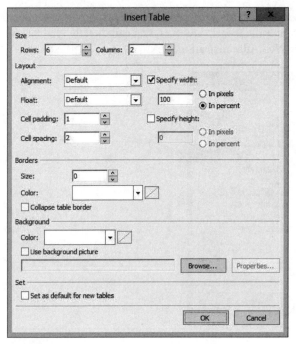

FIGURE 18-8

10. Click OK to accept the settings.

11. In the top five left-hand column cells, enter the following text: **Site Name, Site IP, Site Port, Site Host Header,** and **Site Path,** respectively.

12. Drag a TextBox control from the toolbox to each of the top five right-hand column cells.

13. Drag a Button control from the toolbox to the bottom left-hand column cell.

14. Now it's time to name the controls properly. Right-click the Label control and select Properties.

15. In the Properties windows delete everything in the Text property.

16. Still in the Properties window, change the ID to StatusLabel.

17. The third change to make to the Label is to enter **Red** for the ForeColor property.

18. Each of the TextBoxes needs to be renamed. Just as you changed the ID property for the Label, do the same for the TextBoxes. They should be named **NameTextBox, IPTextBox, PortTextBox, HostHeaderTextbox,** and **PathTextBox.** Be certain to name these exactly right, because they need to match the code later in this walk-through.

19. Edit the properties for the Site Port TextBox, and set the Text value to 80. This is the standard default port for HTTP.

20. Change the Button Text property to **Create Site,** and the Button ID to **CreateSiteButton.**

21. On the right-hand side of the TextBox beside Site IP, type **Leave blank for (all unassigned).**

22. On the right-hand side of the TextBox beside Site Host Header, type **Leave blank for all host headers**.

23. Feel free to adjust the column widths to improve the aesthetics.

This completes the design area of the web page.

24. Finally, double-click the Create Site button to be positioned in the code section of `Default .asp.vb` (`.cs`), and prepare to write some code.

Writing the Code

Now that the web page UI has been completed, it's time to write some code. This is surprisingly easy with Visual Web Developer and IntelliSense, which will autocomplete the namespaces, classes, and objects for you.

Copy or type the following code into the code window, or type it manually so that you get a chance to understand it better. A further explanation is coming shortly. Note that there is already some code in the code window. That should all be replaced with this:

```
Imports Microsoft.Web.Administration

Partial Class _Default
    Inherits System.Web.UI.Page

    Protected Sub CreateSiteButton_Click(ByVal sender As Object, _
                                         ByVal e As System.EventArgs) _
                                         Handles CreateSiteButton.Click
        'Declare and instigate ServerManager
        Dim SM As New ServerManager
        Dim bindingInfo As String
        Dim mySite As Microsoft.Web.Administration.Site

        'Create the bindingInfo variable which will be in the
        'form for "IP:Port:HostHeader".  Example ":80:" is
        'everything on port 80.
        bindingInfo = IPTextBox.Text & ":" & _
          PortTextBox.Text & ":" & _
          HostHeaderTextBox.Text

        'Create an App Pool for this site
        SM.ApplicationPools.Add(NameTextBox.Text)

        'Create the Site
        mySite = SM.Sites.Add(NameTextBox.Text, _
                 "HTTP", _
                 bindingInfo, _
                 PathTextBox.Text)

        'Add site to app pool.  Application(0) is the first and only
        'application in the site so far.
        mySite.Applications(0).ApplicationPoolName _
            = NameTextBox.Text

        'Changes will not take effect until CommitChanges is called.
```

```
          SM.CommitChanges()

          StatusLabel.Text = "Website " & NameTextBox.Text & " was created."

      End Sub
  End Class
  public partial class _Default : System.Web.UI.Page
  {...
    protected void CreateSiteButton_Click(object sender, EventArgs e)  {
        ServerManager SM = new ServerManager();
        String bindingInfo;
        Site mySite;

        bindingInfo = IPTextBox.Text + ":" + PortTextBox.Text + ":" +
                      HostHeaderTextBox.Text;
        SM.ApplicationPools.Add(NameTextBox.Text);

        mySite = SM.Sites.Add(NameTextBox.Text, "HTTP",
                         bindingInfo, PathTextBox.Text);
        mySite.Applications[0].ApplicationPoolName = NameTextBox.Text;

        SM.CommitChanges();

        StatusLabel.Text = "Website " + NameTextBox.Text + " was created.";
    }
  }
```

It's worth stopping here for a minute to explain the code.

The `Imports` (`using`) command at the top will import the `Microsoft.Web.Administration` namespace, so you don't need to type it each time you need to reference any of its classes. For example, notice the following line:

```
Dim SM As New ServerManager(ServerManager SM = new ServerManager).
```

You could instead enter **Dim SM As New Microsoft.Web.Administration.ServerManager (Microsoft.Web.Administration.ServerManager SM = new Microsoft.Web.Administration .ServerManager)**, which is the full name of the class. Because it can be pretty monotonous to type **Microsoft.Web.Administration** every time, especially if it's used more than once, importing the namespace is a good practice.

The `Protected Sub CreateSiteButton_Click` (`protected void CreateSiteButton_Click`) is an Event subroutine that is called when the Create Site button is clicked. This will not run when the page is first loaded. It will only run when someone specifically clicks the Create Site button.

Next, three variables are declared: the `ServerManager` object, which is the main entry point for managing the server; the `bindingInfo` string variable; and the `mySite` site variable.

Next, the `bindingInfo` variable is populated in the format that IIS needs. The format is `IP:Port:Host Header`. For example, to create a site binding for IP address 10.0.0.10 on port 80 and using a host header of `Site1.DomainA.local`, the site binding would be `10.0.0.10:80:Site1 .DomainA.local`. The IP and host header are optional, but the port is required; therefore, `":80:"` is also valid.

The `add` method allows you to set only one binding. If you need to add multiple bindings, you must add them after the site has been created. This simple example supports only a single host header and binding when initially creating the website.

Be sure to add **SM.CommitChanges()**, as it is the method required to actually apply the changes to the server.

Finally, the StatusLabel is updated with a message to state that the website was created.

Running the Create Web Site Website

No, that title isn't a typo. Now that you've created a website that creates an IIS site, it's time to try it out. To run this using the ASP.NET Development Server (aka Cassini) that is part of Visual Web Developer:

1. Choose Debug ➪ Start Debugging, and then acknowledge the prompt asking you if you want to enable debugging in `web.config`.

   This will start the ASP.NET Developer Server and start your web browser running your new application.

2. Enter in the values that you want for your new website.

   Note that this example doesn't do any error checking, so be sure to enter only valid values. The site name can contain spaces, but most other special characters are not supported. The site IP should be an IP address on the web server. Leaving it blank is supported. The default port of 80 is often good, but feel free to change that. The site host header can be set or left blank, which essentially gives a wildcard host header. Finally, the site path needs to be a valid path on disk to your website, for example, `c:\inetpub\Site2`. Figure 18-9 shows a picture of what your Create Web Site website should look like with some possible values filled in.

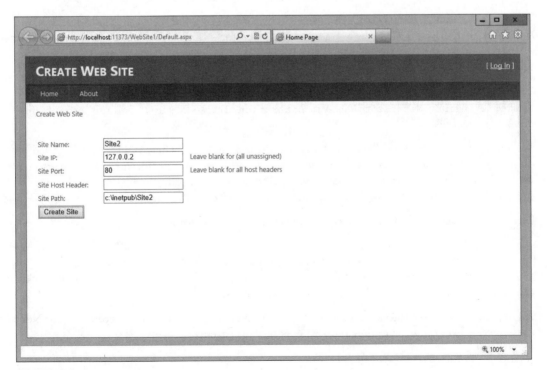

FIGURE 18-9

3. Once everything is filled in, click the Create Site button, and the site will be created in IIS!

> **NOTE** *This is a bare-bones example showing the essentials to installing Visual Web Developer and creating a simple website that will create a site in IIS. To keep the code example clean and easy to understand, this does not include error checking, and it does not attempt to use all programming best practices. Use this as a stepping-stone to get you started in IIS 8.0 administrative programming.*

That's it! That was easy, wasn't it? Whether you're a seasoned programmer or this is your first program, I'm sure you can see the powerful simplicity that is available at your fingertips. Now, use this along with the other references in this chapter to start dreaming up and developing your own tools to help yourself and those around you be even better IIS administrators.

Microsoft.Web.Administration (MWA)

The `Microsoft.Web.Administration` API offers a strongly typed set of .NET classes for IIS administrative programming. It is a wrapper over the Application Host Administration API (AHAdmin) native code interface library, which is discussed in its own section below. These sets of classes make programmatic management of IIS extremely easy. With tools like Visual Studio or Visual Web Developer, it's easy to create anything from a few simple scripts to a full-blown corporate program to manage IIS. Because the classes are strongly typed, IntelliSense and design-time error checking make programming so much easier than in past versions.

The walk-through previously covered in this chapter used `Microsoft.Web.Administration` and will most likely be the preferred programmatic method for .NET developers. Unless you have a specific need for using any of the other APIs or WMI, `Microsoft.Web.Administration` is well worth considering as your primary programming method.

This API needs to be referenced in your project or `web.config` file. It's located at `%windir%\System32\inetsrv\Microsoft.Web.Administration.dll`, so be sure to add this after you first create a project.

It's important to understand the class structure in this namespace. There is a set of predefined classes that make management of the most common IIS objects straightforward, but you also have the ability to change individual elements and attributes directly. Additionally, from code, you can specify the configuration file and the `location` tag that you want to manage.

The root-level class is `ServerManager`, which is the foundation for the other classes (see Figure 18-10).

The class structure is easy to visualize. Picture five main objects: `Site`, `Application`, `VirtualDirectory`, `ApplicationPool`, and `WorkerProcess`. There are also some matching classes that enable you to set the default settings for these objects.

An `Application` belongs to a `Site`, and a `VirtualDirectory` belongs to an `Application`. None of these objects lives on its own; they must be part of their parents.

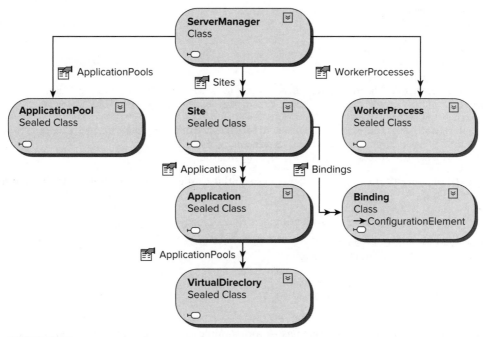

FIGURE 18-10

The WorkerProcess class allows you to view real-time configuration data about the server! You can gain access into the currently running worker processes and even the running requests.

Additionally, the ServerManager class has a set of methods to manage the configuration files directly. Don't worry if you aren't a seasoned programmer and this seems overwhelming. At first you may imagine a complex XML-based configuration method, but it's really quite simple. If you are a seasoned developer, you'll be equally impressed with the power that you have.

The next three sections cover programming the configuration setting, dynamic runtime data, and how to edit attributes and elements directly.

Configuration Classes

The core configuration classes include ApplicationPool, Site, Application, and VirtualDirectory, and a matching set of classes to set the default values for each object. Creating these various objects in IIS couldn't be easier.

The following example shows how to create a site in IIS. (Don't forget to import the Microsoft .Web.Administration namespace, because ServerManager is really Microsoft.Web .Administration.ServerManager.)

```
Dim SM As New ServerManager
SM.Sites.Add("Site1", "http", ":80:", "c:\websites\Site1")
SM.CommitChanges()
ServerManager SM = new ServerManager();
SM.Sites.Add("Site1", "http", ":80:", "c:\\websites\\Site1");
```

```
SM.CommitChanges();
Unhandled Exception: System.ArgumentException: The specified HTTPS binding is in
valid.
   at Microsoft.Web.Administration.BindingCollection.Add(Binding binding)
   at Microsoft.Web.Administration.BindingCollection.Add(String bindingInformati
on, String bindingProtocol)
   at Microsoft.Web.Administration.SiteCollection.Add(String name, String bindin
gProtocol, String bindingInformation, String physicalPath, Byte[] certificateHas
h, String certificateStore, SslFlags sslFlags)
   at Microsoft.Web.Administration.SiteCollection.Add(String name, String bindin
gProtocol, String bindingInformation, String physicalPath)
   at ConsoleApplication2.Program.Main(String[] args)
```

This creates an instance of the ServerManager class and uses the Sites collection's Add method to create the "Site1" site.

To create an application pool, use the following:

```
Dim SM As New ServerManager
SM.ApplicationPools.Add("Site1AppPool")
SM.CommitChanges()
ServerManager SM = new ServerManager();
SM.ApplicationPools.Add("Site1AppPool");
SM.CommitChanges();
```

Once created, you can change various settings — for example, to set the application pool's framework version back to version 1.1, you could add the following code. Note that SM is not defined again because this is meant to be a continuation of the previous code example.

```
Dim apppool As ApplicationPool
apppool = SM.ApplicationPools("Site1AppPool")
apppool.ManagedRuntimeVersion = "v4.5"
SM.CommitChanges()
ApplicationPool appPool = SM.ApplicationPools["Site1AppPool"];
appPool.ManagedRuntimeVersion = "v4.5";
SM.CommitChanges();
```

Another way to accomplish the previous two code examples would be to set the new application pool as a variable of type ApplicationPool. This will give you a handle to the application pool so that you can immediately make changes to it.

```
Dim SM As New ServerManager
Dim apppool As ApplicationPool

apppool = SM.ApplicationPools.Add("Site2AppPool")
apppool.ManagedRuntimeVersion = "v4.5"
SM.CommitChanges()
ServerManager SM = new ServerManager();
ApplicationPool appPool = SM.ApplicationPools.Add("Site2AppPool");
appPool.ManagedRuntimeVersion = "v4.5";
SM.CommitChanges();
```

To create a new application (not an application pool), all that is needed is the following:

```
Dim SM As New ServerManager
Dim site As Site

site = SM.Sites("Site1")
```

```
site.Applications.Add("/app1", "C:\websites\Site1\App1")
SM.CommitChanges()
ServerManager SM = new ServerManager();
Site site = SM.Sites["Site1"];
site.Applications.Add("/app1", "C:\\websites\\Site1\\App1");
SM.CommitChanges();
```

As you can see, development with the `Microsoft.Web.Administration` Managed Code API is straightforward. This is just the beginning of what you can do. Using this as a springboard, the sky is the limit on the possibilities available.

Dynamic Runtime Classes

In addition to the classes that configure sites and application pools (static data), you can start and stop sites, recycle application pools, and even see the currently running worker processes, application domains, and page requests.

Here's an example of how to view all the running processes on the server. Remember that this data is dynamic and changes based on what is running at any given time. Applications that exist in IIS don't always have a worker process running at all times.

```
Dim SM As New ServerManager

For Each wp As WorkerProcess In SM.WorkerProcesses
  Console.Writeline(wp.AppPoolName & " " & wp.ProcessId)
Next
ServerManager SM = new ServerManager();
foreach (WorkerProcess wp in SM.WorkerProcesses)
{
    Console.WriteLine(wp.AppPoolName + " " + wp.ProcessId);
}
```

In this example, the method used for writing the information to the screen is `Console.Writeline`, which makes sense for a console application. If you are developing this for the web, you can write the information to a Label control, or, if it's for testing, the quick and easy way is to use `Response.Write` instead of `Console.Writeline`.

> **NOTE** *User Access Control (UAC) can fight with you here. If you don't get any results, be sure to elevate your permissions to an Administrator so that UAC doesn't prevent you from gaining access to the process information.*

The following code shows all running page requests. Notice `GetRequests(0)`. The 0 is the time that the page has been running in milliseconds. Setting it to 0 means that it will get all page requests, but you can set it to a higher number, for example, `10000` for 10 seconds, to see all pages that have been running for longer than that period of time.

```
Dim SM As New ServerManager

'loop through each running worker process
For Each wp As WorkerProcess In SM.WorkerProcesses
  Console.Writeline("App Pool Name: " & wp.AppPoolName)
```

```
        Console.Writeline("Worker Process PID: " & wp.ProcessId)

        'loop through each running page request
        For Each request As Request In wp.GetRequests(0)
            Console.Writeline("   Request:" & request.Url)
        Next
    Next
ServerManager SM = new ServerManager();
foreach (WorkerProcess wp in SM.WorkerProcesses)
{
    Console.WriteLine("App Pool Name: " + wp.AppPoolName);
    Console.WriteLine("Worker Process PID: " + wp.ProcessId);
    foreach (Request request in wp.GetRequests(0))
    {
        Console.WriteLine("      Request: " + request.Url);
    }
}
```

Additionally, you can start and stop sites, and start, stop, and recycle application pools. To recycle the application pool called AppPool1, you can do the following:

```
Dim SM As New ServerManager
SM.ApplicationPools("Site1").Recycle()
ServerManager SM = new ServerManager();
SM.ApplicationPools["Site1"].Recycle();
```

You get the point. It doesn't take much to figure out each of these from scratch, plus there are code examples scattered throughout this book.

Accessing a Remote Server

Connecting to a remote IIS server is as simple as calling `ServerManager.OpenRemote`. The following example shows how to define a variable of type `ServerManager` and connect to a remote host:

```
Dim SM As ServerManager = ServerManager.OpenRemote("10.0.0.10")
ServerManager SM = ServerManager.OpenRemote("10.0.0.10");
```

In the previous code examples in this chapter, you will notice that SM is defined as `Dim SM As New ServerManager`. Just replace that line with the line in this code example, and you will be able to connect to a remote server instead of the local IIS server. You can use an IP address, host name, or domain name for `OpenRemote`'s `serverName`. This is a good place to add a `Try...Catch` block to handle any failures connecting to the remote server.

Editing Attributes and Elements

In addition to the classes for the most common configuration objects, you can view, create, update, or delete any attribute or element within the configuration files using the base class `ServerManager`. You can edit any of the IIS configuration files, which include `applicationHost.config`, `administration.config`, `redirection.config`, and all site and application configuration files.

To do so, as you are used to by now, you must declare and instantiate a variable of type `ServerManager`, as follows:

```
Dim SM As New ServerManager
ServerManager SM = new ServerManager();
```

Then you have a few choices for the various configuration files:

➤ `ServerManager.GetApplicationHostConfiguration`

➤ `ServerManager.GetAdministrationConfiguration`

➤ `ServerManager.GetRedirectionConfiguration`

➤ `ServerManager.GetWebConfiguration`

The `GetWebConfiguration` method enables you to specify a specific site's configuration file. The other three don't take any parameters and point directly to the corresponding configuration file that is obvious from the method name.

To get the `applicationHost.config` file, for example, you would do something like this:

```
Dim config As Configuration = SM.GetApplicationHostConfiguration
Configuration config = SM.GetApplicationHostConfiguration();
```

To get a specific site's `web.config` file, you would use this:

```
Dim config As Configuration = SM.GetWebConfiguration("Site1")
Configuration config = SM.GetWebConfiguration("Site1");
```

And to get an application's `web.config` file, you would use this:

```
Dim config As Configuration = SM.GetWebConfiguration("Site1", "/App1")
Configuration config = SM.GetWebConfiguration("Site1", "/App1");
```

Now that you've created the configuration object for the configuration file that you want, it's time to call the section. Picking a particular `location` tag is covered in the next section. For now, only the default section will be covered. Using the section structure covered above in this chapter, you can pick the section that you want to change. For example, to pick the `defaultDocument` section from the `system.webServer` section group, you would do the following:

```
Dim section As ConfigurationSection = _
            config.GetSection("system.webServer/defaultDocument")
ConfigurationSection section =
            config.GetSection("system.webServer/defaultDocument");
```

As you can probably tell already, the `system.webServer` in this code example corresponds to the `<system.webServer>` section group in the configuration file. The `defaultDocument` corresponds to the `<defaultDocument>` section.

Once you have chosen the group, then it's time to pull out an attribute or element. The following example pulls this all together into a complete example and reads the enabled attribute value from Site1's `web.config` file:

```
Dim SM As New ServerManager
Dim config As Configuration = SM.GetWebConfiguration("Site1")
Dim section As ConfigurationSection = _
    config.GetSection("system.webServer/defaultDocument")

Dim enabled As ConfigurationAttribute = section.Attributes("enabled")

Console.Writeline(enabled.Value)
ServerManager SM = new ServerManager();
```

```
Configuration config = SM.GetWebConfiguration("Site1");
ConfigurationSection section =
    config.GetSection("system.webServer/defaultDocument");

ConfigurationAttribute enabled = section.Attributes["enabled"];

Console.WriteLine(enabled.Value);
```

You can also read, update, and delete elements and collections. The following example gets the default documents for a site:

```
Dim SM As New ServerManager
Dim config As Configuration = SM.GetWebConfiguration("Site1")
Dim section As ConfigurationSection = _
    config.GetSection("system.webServer/defaultDocument")

Dim filescollection As ConfigurationElementCollection

filescollection = section.GetCollection("files")

For Each item As ConfigurationElement In filescollection
    Console.Writeline(item.Attributes("value").Value)
Next
ServerManager SM = new ServerManager();
Configuration config = SM.GetWebConfiguration("Site1");
ConfigurationSection section =
    config.GetSection("system.webServer/defaultDocument");
ConfigurationElementCollection filesCollection =
    section.GetCollection("files");
foreach (ConfigurationElement item in filesCollection)
{
    Console.WriteLine(item.Attributes["value"].Value);
}
```

Don't forget to change `Console.Writeline` to `Response.Write` if you are creating a web page instead of a console application. Notice the `filescollection` variable, which gets all the collection elements. Then the `For Each` (`foreach`) loop writes out the value (name) of each of the default documents.

Dealing with location Tags

Many times you will need to make a change to a specific `location` tag instead of the default section. This is fully supported and fairly straightforward once you know how to do it.

The thing to keep in mind is that it's when you choose the section in the configuration file that you also choose the location. In the previous code example, it's the line that starts with `Dim Section` (`Section`) that can be tweaked to specify the `location` tag. The `GetSection` method has an override to allow you to specify the `locationPath`. The `locationPath` is in the form of *Site1* or *Site1/App1*.

To set the `defaultDocument-enabled` attribute to `false` in the `location` tag for "Site1" in `applicationHost.config`, you can use the following example (notice that this example is also managing a remote server at IP address 10.0.0.10):

```
Dim SM As ServerManager = ServerManager.OpenRemote("10.0.0.10")
Dim config As Configuration = SM.GetApplicationHostConfiguration
Dim section As ConfigurationSection = _
    config.GetSection("system.webServer/defaultDocument", "Site1")
ServerManager SM = ServerManager.OpenRemote("10.0.0.10");
Configuration config = SM.GetApplicationHostConfiguration();
ConfigurationSection section =
    config.GetSection("system.WebServer/defaultDocument", "Site1");
```

Notice that the GetSection method has the site name as the second parameter. For the GetSection method, the following:

```
GetSection("system.webServer/defaultDocument")
```

is identical to

```
GetSection("system.webServer/defaultDocument", "")
```

A question comes to mind. What happens if there are multiple location tags for the same path, but with different overrideMode values? Suppose, for example, that you have the following three sections in applicationHost.config:

GENERAL SECTION

```
<system.webServer>
    . . . {various sections} . . .
</system.webServer>
```

LOCKING LOCATION TAG

```
<location path="" allowOverride="false">
    <system.webServer>
        . . . {various sections} . . .
    </system.webServer>
</location>
```

ALLOWING LOCATION TAG

```
<location path="" allowOverride="true">
    <system.webServer>
        . . . {various sections} . . .
    </system.webServer>
</location>
```

That's a trick question actually. Configuration elements can only appear once per unique path, so it's not possible to have a section in all three locations at the same time. When updating a section, you only need to specify the configuration file and the site or application. If you do need to indicate a specific location tag with a specific overrideMode setting, you can do that by using the overrideMode property of ConfigurationSection, as follows:

```
. . .
Dim section As ConfigurationSection = _
    config.GetSection("system.webServer/defaultDocument", "Site1")

section.OverrideMode = OverrideMode.Deny

. . .

ConfigurationSection section =
```

```
config.GetSection("system.WebServer/defaultDocument", "Site1");

section.OverrideMode = OverrideMode.Deny;
```

As you can see, you have granular control over the location tag paths and even the overrideMode specific tags within any of the configuration files.

Microsoft.Web.Administration offers a powerful programming solution for IIS 8.0 administration. The IIS team has done a tremendous job of making it very powerful and flexible, yet easy to work with.

Microsoft.Web.Management (MWM)

The second Managed Code API that IIS offers is Microsoft.Web.Management. This provides the framework to create user interface (UI) features in IIS Manager and create and manage IIS Users and permissions. Because many of the built-in features and icons in IIS Manager use this same namespace in the background, you can use it to create features that look and feel identical to the built-in IIS features.

There is both a server side and a client side to this API, including rich features for lists, properties, grids, group panels, and wizards, and access into the action and other panes within IIS Manager. IIS User management allows you to create users, update users and passwords, and assign either IIS Manager users or Windows users to sites and applications for remote delegation.

You must reference %windir%\System32\inetsrv\Microsoft.Web.Management.dll within your project or web.config file to use Microsoft.Web.Management. There are four subnamespaces within the Microsoft.Web.Management namespace: Client, Features, Host, and Server.

Extensive development in Microsoft.Web.Management is not covered here, but one example will be provided. This example creates an IIS Manager user and grants it permissions to a specific Site1. Additionally, a Windows user will also be granted permissions to the same site.

First, be sure to import Microsoft.Web.Management.Server, which is the namespace for ManagementAuthentication and ManagementAuthorization, as follows:

```
Imports Microsoft.Web.Management.Server
using Microsoft.Web.Management.Server;
```

The code to create the IIS Manager user and grant the two users permissions to the site is straightforward:

```
Dim user As ManagementUserInfo
'create IIS Manager user
user = ManagementAuthentication.CreateUser("IISUser1", "password")

'grant the freshly created user permissions to the site
ManagementAuthorization.Grant(user.Name, "Site1", False)

'additionally, grant the Windows user permission to the site
ManagementAuthorization.Grant("DomainA.local/User2", "Site1", False)
ManagementUserInfo user =
    ManagementAuthentication.CreateUser("IISUser1", "password");
```

```
ManagementAuthorization.Grant(user.Name, "Site1", false);
ManagementAuthorization.Grant("DomainA.local/User2",
                             "Site1", false);
```

> **NOTE** *Chapter 12, "Core Server Extensibility," discusses this further and gives a walk-through using* `Microsoft.Web.Management` *to extend IIS Manager.*

ABO, ADSI, and Legacy API Support

Anyone who has existing scripts for their IIS 6.0 web servers will be pleased to know that IIS 8.0 maintains support for existing APIs. Although the IIS 8.0 underlying structure is substantially different, an emulation layer exists that maps Admin Base Objects (ABOs) and manages calls to the configuration system using a component called *ABOMapper.* This means that your existing code can function as it always did without needing to completely rewrite your code before migrating to IIS 8.0.

The ABOMapper works as an intermediary layer between legacy code and the new IIS configuration system. It does this by interpreting all the code, discovering the differences between the old and the new, and making the appropriate Read or Write operations directly against the configuration files. It does not work against the in-memory configuration.

Active Directory Service Interface (ADSI) and IIS 6.0 WMI depend on ABO and are supported in IIS 8.0. The whole set of ABO APIs and dependency APIs are included in this discussion. This applies to the .NET `System.DirectoryServices` namespace, too, which works on top of ADSI.

> **NOTE** *IIS 6.0 WMI support and IIS 7/8.0 WMI support are two different things. Make sure to note which version of WMI is being referred to whenever "WMI" is mentioned. There is legacy support for existing WMI code, which is called "IIS 6.0 WMI."*

To be able to support ABO, the metabase compatibility components need to be installed, as they are not installed by default. This is done in the Add Roles and Features section of Server Manager. The relevant options are shown in the following table.

ROLE	DESCRIPTION
IIS 6 Management Compatibility	Provides forward compatibility for scripts and applications that use the Admin Base Object (ABO) and the Active Directory Service Interface (ADSI) API. Existing IIS 6 scripts can be used to manage the IIS 7 web server.
IIS 6 Metabase Compatibility	Provides the capabilities to configure and query the metabase. These capabilities let you migrate scripts and applications that use the ABO or ADSI API.

continues

(continued)

ROLE	DESCRIPTION
IIS 6 WMI Compatibility	Provides interfaces to programatically manage and automate tasks in IIS 8 Web server.
IIS 6 Scripting Tools	Provides the ability to use IIS 6 scripting tools, built to manage IIS 6 in IIS 7/8.

The IIS 6.0 Metabase Compatibility option is a requirement for the other two, and IIS 6.0 WMI Compatibility is a requirement for IIS 6.0 Scripting Tools.

There are some things to keep in mind with the IIS 6.0 scripting options. They do not support the features of IIS 8.0, only features that already existed in IIS 6.0. This also means that the new distributed configuration is not supported. You cannot specify which `location` tag or which configuration file is being used. You must leave that decision to the ABOMapper.

Additionally, the ServerComment field in IIS 6.0 wasn't a required field, and it wasn't required to be unique, but the site name is a required field in IIS 8.0; therefore, the ABOMapper takes care of that new requirement by adding numbers to the name to ensure uniqueness. This means that the site name will end up being different from what was entered in the script. Also, calls that ABO makes to back up, restore, import, and export will be ignored because the configure files work much differently in IIS 8.0. For these reasons, it's advisable to migrate to the new API options when possible.

Some features — namely, the FTP version that is shipped with the product, NNTP, and SMTP — will still use the regular call to `metabase.xml`. Everything else will go through the ABOMapper.

When you are developing or troubleshooting using any of the IIS 6.0 scripting APIs, the error logs will not be recorded to the Event Log; instead, they will be saved to `%windir%\System32\Abomapper.log`, so be sure to watch that log file for any clues to issues that you may run into.

IIS WMI Provider

Windows Management Instrumentation (WMI) is used for managing various aspects of the Windows operating system. You were able to manage IIS with WMI in previous versions of IIS, and support is still partially maintained for existing IIS 6.0 scripts.

Although there have been no modifications to WMI since IIS 7.x, the WMI capabilities in IIS 8.0 provide some nice syntax for the WMI provider, ensuring consistency across the whole provider and making scripting with WMI easy but powerful. The IIS 6.0 WMI API is maintained for backward compatibility, but it has its limitations and shouldn't be used for new development unless you have a compelling reason to do so. The WMI provider in IIS 8.0 is the newest, and through the rest of this chapter, any time that "WMI" is mentioned without specifying the version, it will always refer to the WMI provider on IIS 8.0.

One of the most common uses for WMI is within Windows Scripting Host (WSH), which gives you the ability to create a script that can be run right from the computer, almost like an executable program except that you can edit it directly from Notepad.

Before you try to use the WMI provider, make sure that you have the required components installed to support WMI. They are installed from Server Manager by Adding a Role. The IIS WMI provider feature is under Management Tools ⇨ IIS Management Scripts and Tools.

Once you have the role installed, you are ready to start creating your own WMI scripts. The following section will give a walk-through of how to create an application pool and a site and then add the site to the application pool.

WMI Walk-Through

WMI can be used in many different ways, but a common programming method is to use WSH. In this section you will write a WMI example script to create an application pool and a website and add the website to the application pool.

To start, open Notepad or your favorite text editor. Enter the following code sections, in order:

```
Option Explicit

Dim oIIS, oBinding, oApp
Dim siteName, physicalPath, bindings
siteName = "Site1"
physicalPath = "c:\inetpub\wwwroot"
bindings = ":80:Site1.DomainA.local"
```

First, `Option Explicit` is set, ensuring that all variables are declared. If they aren't, an error is thrown early. This is generally a good practice and makes it easier to catch typos early.

Once the variables are defined, they are populated with the desired values:

```
' Set oIIS to the WebAdministration class
Set oIIS = GetObject("winmgmts:root\WebAdministration")
```

The `oIIS` object is set to the `WebAdministration` class. This will be used many times throughout this script.

```
' Create application pool
oIIS.Get("ApplicationPool").Create(siteName)
```

That's all there is to creating the application pool! Running the script will be covered shortly. Now it's on to creating the site bindings:

```
'Create the binding for the site
Set oBinding = oIIS.Get("BindingElement").SpawnInstance_
oBinding.BindingInformation = bindings       .
oBinding.Protocol = "http"
```

The bindings are set in the `BindingElement` class to be used shortly in the next step. Notice the variable called `bindings`, which was set at the beginning of the script.

```
' Create the site
oIIS.Get("Site").Create siteName, array(oBinding), physicalPath
```

Creating the site is also easy. The `Create` method takes the site name, the `BindingElement` object as an array, and the physical path.

```
' Get the application that was created
```

```
Set oApp = oIIS.Get("Application.SiteName='" & siteName & "',Path='/'")

' Assign the new app pool to the application
oApp.ApplicationPool = siteName

' Commit the changes
oApp.Put_
```

To add the new site to the application pool, you must first get the application of the site that was created and then update the application's application pool. To ensure that the change is applied, you must run oApp.Put_, which commits the changes.

```
' Write out a message
WScript.Echo "Site " & siteName & " has been created."
```

Finally, it's helpful to output something so that you have feedback on the status of the script.

> **NOTE** *This code example doesn't have any error handling so that it is a concise example, but if you try to create this and the application pool or site already exists, it will fail. To properly create this for a production environment, it's wise to check first if the application pool and site already exist and handle any other errors that may occur.*

Now, take all the preceding code and piece it together into the text document. Then save the text document to your computer with an extension of .vbs.

WSH runs in one of two modes, WScript or CScript. If it is set to run in WScript on your computer, then everything will run the same, but the final message saying that the site has been created will display in a Windows message box. If there are any error messages, a Windows message box will be used for them also. If you are using CScript and you ran the program by double-clicking on it, then you will probably see the message flash on the screen briefly and then disappear. That is because it displays it in a command prompt instead of a pop-up window. Essentially, the differences between CScript and WScript are just in the output method. CScript is command-line-based, whereas WScript is more Windows-based. The actual code execution is the same.

To control which script host you are using, you can either change the default or you can start the script from the command prompt using the script host that you choose. In this example, start by opening the command prompt. If you forget the syntax, you can always get it by typing **cscript /?**. To change the default script host:

➤ For CScript, type **cscript //H:CScript**.

➤ For WScript, type **cscript //H:WScript**.

The way to run it without permanently changing the default script host is to start it from the command prompt and prefix the filename with the script host under which you want it to run. For example:

➤ ```cscript CreateSite.vbs```

➤ ```wscript CreateSite.vbs```

> **NOTE** *Although WScript can be more friendly in some ways because of the Windows message boxes, be careful about running a script that outputs a lot of information in individual pieces, for example, if you are testing something within a* `while` *loop and doing a* `wscript.echo` *often. If you aren't careful, you'll need to click the OK button a lot of times. If you use CScript, it will output the data in the command prompt without waiting for you to acknowledge anything. That makes CScript better when you have a lot to output.*

This has given a brief overview of how to create a script using WSH and some differences between WScript and CScript and how to use each script host.

Connecting to a remote server is also fully supported in WMI. For the line in the preceding code sample that has set `oIIS = GetObject("winmgmts:root\WebAdministration")`, you can use the following instead, and replace the `serverName` with your server name or IP:

```
set oIIS = GetObject("winmgmts://ServerName/root/WebAdministration")
```

Much more could be said about WMI programming, but this is enough to get your feet wet and give you the tools that you need to start creating scripts in your enterprise to manage IIS 8.0.

AHAdmin

The Application Host Administration API (AHAdmin) interface is the foundational native code COM-friendly interface, which you can use directly from native code applications and module development, or indirectly using the IIS WMI provider or the managed code wrappers. AHAdmin replaces the role of ABO, although ABO is still supported, as discussed above.

AHAdmin is straightforward to develop with and builds on the configuration path and `location` tag principles already discussed in this chapter. With it you can target a specific `location` tag and use the distributed configuration system introduced in IIS 7.0.

When developing using AHAdmin, you start by getting an instance of `IAppHostAdminManager` for read-only access to the config. To have read/write access, you use `IappHostWritableAdminManager`, which derives from `IAppHostAdminManager` but has additional methods: `CommitChange` to commit the changes to disk and `CommitPath` to specify where the configuration settings are written.

For example, in VBScript in WSH, you can write the following:

```
Set ahRead = CreateObject("Microsoft.ApplicationHost.AdminManager")
Set ahWrite = _
    CreateObject("Microsoft.ApplicationHost.WritableAdminManager")
```

The `ahRead` object can read the configuration, whereas the `ahWrite` object can read and write to the configuration.

Here's an example of how to disable the anonymous user using AHAdmin from a WSH file using VBScript. Create a file called **DisableAnonymousAuth.vbs** and save the following to it:

```
configFile = "MACHINE/WEBROOT/APPHOST/"
siteName = "Default Web Site"
```

```
configPath = configFile & siteName
configSectionName = _
   "system.webServer/security/authentication/anonymousAuthentication"

'create the ahManager object
Set ahManager = CreateObject("Microsoft.ApplicationHost.WritableAdminManager")

'get the anonymous authentication section
set anonymousAuth = _
   ahManager.GetAdminSection(configSectionName, configPath)

'set the enabled attribute to false
anonymousAuth.Properties.Item("enabled").Value = False

'commit the changes
ahManager.CommitChanges()
```

Notice that you can specify the configuration file and `location` tag to which the configuration is written. See the "Configuration Path" section above in this chapter for more discussion on setting that. See the "WMI Walk-Through" section in this chapter to get an overview of writing and running WSH scripts.

The AHAdmin `WritableAdminManager` object is created, and the enabled property is set. Finally, the changes are committed.

WSH can also use JScript instead of VBScript simply by naming the file with a `.js` extension instead of a `.vbs` extension and, of course, using JScript for your development instead of VBScript. Following is an example of how to enable shared configuration and set the path, username, and password. Save the file with the filename `SetSharedConfiguration.js`.

```
try{

var configPath = "c:\\SharedConfig";
var username = "User1";
var password = "User1";

var config =
WScript.CreateObject(
   "Microsoft.ApplicationHost.WritableAdminManager" );

config.CommitPath = "MACHINE/REDIRECTION";

var section = config.GetAdminSection(
   "configurationRedirection",
   config.CommitPath);

section.Properties.Item( "enabled" ).Value = true;
section.Properties.Item( "path" ).Value = configPath;
section.Properties.Item( "userName" ).Value = username;
section.Properties.Item( "password" ).Value = password;

//comment the changes
config.CommitChanges();
}
//catch and output any error
catch(e)
```

```
{
WScript.Echo(e.number);
WScript.Echo(e.description);
}
```

This example uses MACHINE/REDIRECTION for the commit path, which means that the changes are made to the %windir%\System32\inetsrv\config\redirection.config file.

IIS Manager, IIS WMI, Microsoft.Web.Administration, and Microsoft.Web.Management use AHAdmin under the covers. As you can guess, AHAdmin can do almost anything you dream up and is recommended by Microsoft for native code applications and module development. If you aren't using .NET and the Managed Code APIs, or WMI, then AHAdmin is the API that you should consider for your development needs.

CONFIGURATION EDITOR

The Configuration Editor is a relatively new feature in IIS that provides an administrator access to all the elements contained within the applicationHost.config. You may have experienced in the past that there are some configurations that cannot be performed from within the IIS Management console or that the place to make the modification was not easily found. Alternatively, you used AppCmd; PowerShell; or the dangerous way, using a generic text editor. For example, it may not be easy to find where to set batchTimeout, uiCulture, attributes of custom modules, or perhaps an attribute of a custom extended schema. Figure 18-11 shows the Configuration Editor feature.

FIGURE 18-11

Refer to the previous "Schema Extensibility" section in this chapter and recall the creation of the custom `OwnerInfo` schema. If the attributes of this schema need to change, you may be tempted to open the `applicationHost.config` using Notepad and make the change directly. However, now that you know you can make those modifications using the Configuration Editor, that temptation can be wiped out.

> **WARNING** *If you happen to make a typo when modifying any of the configuration files using Notepad that results in a malformed XML file, it can result in a significant amount of time to find where the problem is. Try to use a tool to make changes to the configuration instead of a text editor.*

In this section you will:

➤ Modify the e-mail address, name, and role of the custom extended `OwnerInfo` schema.

➤ Modify the `BlockLinksSection`, `permitBookmarks` value created in Chapter 12.

➤ Modify the `batchTimeout` attribute and view the generated C#, JavaScript, AppCmd, and PowerShell scripts.

Modifying the Custom Extended Schema

Earlier in this chapter when the `OwnerInfo` schema was created, modified, and extended, Notepad was used to perform those actions. Using Notepad is no longer required now that the custom schema has been implemented. Changes to it can be made using the Configuration Editor. As shown in Figure 18-12, you can find the `OwnerInfo` schema and attributes in the `system.applicationHost/sites/` path.

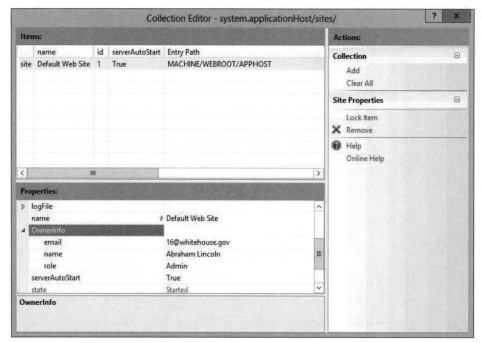

FIGURE 18-12

Modify one of the attributes, close the window, and click the Apply link found on the Actions pane to commit the changes. If you return to the entry and view the elements value, you will find that the new value exists. You can also check within the `applicationHost.config` file directly to confirm the changes.

Modifying the Configuration Item

Recall from Chapter 12, "Core Server Extensibility," where the BlockLinks custom module and section were created. In that example, you created a configuration control that provided a GUI-like page within IIS for changing the `permitBoomarks` attribute. It is also possible to change this value from the Configuration Editor.

The first action to take is to open the IIS Manager console and navigate to the Configuration Editor. To quickly find the BlockLinksSection, select the Search Configuration... link located in the Actions pane. Doing this opens a window as shown in Figure 18-13.

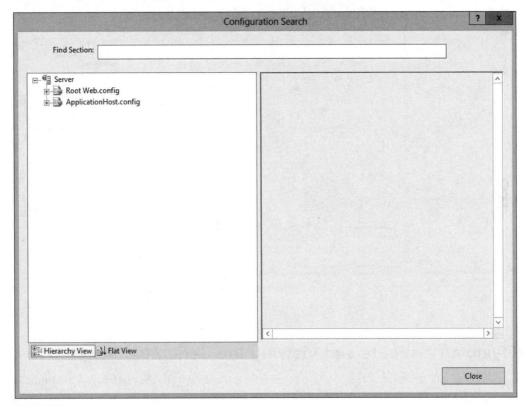

FIGURE 18-13

Enter **BlockLinksSection** into the Find Section text field, and you will see the section. Take a note of where it is in the hierarchy so that you can navigate to it from within the Configuration Editor drop-down. Click the section to see the current value.

> **NOTE** *The attribute is findable only if you completed the example referred to in Chapter 12.*

Close down the window and navigate to the root section, click BlockLinksSection, and an interface to modify the value is provided, as shown in Figure 18-14. Make the required change, and select the Apply link in the Actions pane to commit them to the configuration.

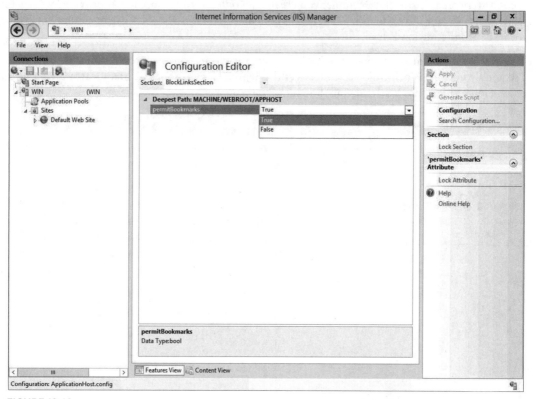

FIGURE 18-14

Modifying an Attribute and Viewing the Generated Scripts

It is possible to change most of the configuration settings from within the configuration editor. For example, if you needed to change the `maxBatchSize` value found in the `system.web/compilation` path, simply navigate to that location and modify its value.

Notice that when the modification is made, the Generate Script link found on the Actions pane becomes enabled. Click the link, and a window shown in Figure 18-15 is displayed.

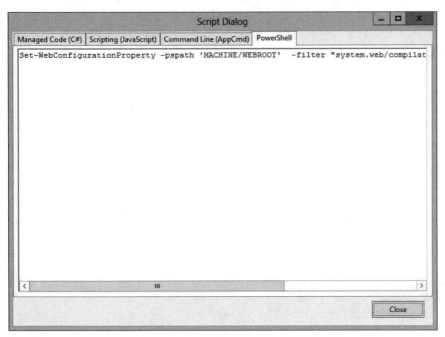

FIGURE 18-15

This is a really nice feature that generates Managed Code (C#), Scripting (JavaScript), AppCmd, and PowerShell syntax examples. If you ever get stuck and cannot get the syntax of a script correct, you can use this tool for some help. The AppCmd- and PowerShell-generated scripts are shown in the following snippets:

```
Appcmd set config -section:system.web/compilation
                  /maxBatchSize:"2000"
                  /commit:webroot /clr:4.0

Set-WebConfigurationProperty
      -pspath 'MACHINE/WEBROOT'
      -filter "system.web/compilation"
      -name "maxBatchSize"
      -value 2000
```

> **NOTE** *The PowerShell script generator is new to IIS 8.0.*

To apply the changes, select the Apply link on the Actions pane. You can then navigate to the IIS Console GUI configuration control and see that the modification was, indeed, applied. Figure 18-16 displays the interface that can also be used to modify or check the value of the IIS, or in this case, ASP.NET, configuration.

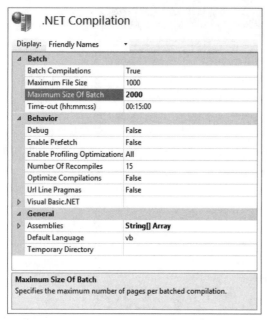

FIGURE 18-16

Now you should have a good understanding of what the Configuration Editor can do and the benefits it provides to an administrator. The following two sections dive deeper into the capabilities of AppCmd and PowerShell.

COMMAND-LINE MANAGEMENT

One of the tools for command-line management in IIS 8.0 is AppCmd.exe. This one tool contains functions that give the administrator complete control of the web server. A few examples of what you can do include the following:

➤ Add, delete, and modify websites and application pools.

➤ Stop and start websites and application pools.

➤ View information about worker processes and requests.

➤ List and modify the configurations of IIS and ASP.NET.

AppCmd.exe provides a consistent set of supported commands for performing queries and tasks against a set of supported object types. You can run these commands individually or in combination with other commands to perform complex tasks or queries.

OBJECT NAME	DESCRIPTION
site	To administer virtual sites
app	To administer applications

`vdir`	To administer virtual directories
`apppool`	To administer application pools
`config`	To administer general configuration sections
`wp`	To administer worker processes
`request`	To administer HTTP requests
`module`	To administer server modules
`backup`	To administer server configuration backups
`trace`	To administer failed request trace logs

Supported commands include the following:

➤ `add`

➤ `clear`

➤ `configure`

➤ `delete`

➤ `inspect`

➤ `install`

➤ `list`

➤ `lock`

➤ `migrate`

➤ `recycle`

➤ `reset`

➤ `restore`

➤ `search`

➤ `set`

➤ `start`

➤ `stop`

➤ `uninstall`

➤ `unlock`

`AppCmd.exe` is located in the `%systemroot%\system32\inetsrv` directory, which is available only to members of the Administrators group. Additionally, if `applicationhost.config`, `machine .config`, or `web.config` will be modified, you will need to start the tool with elevated permissions. We recommend placing `AppCmd.exe` in the system path to make it more convenient to use. To place it in the path, open PowerShell using elevated permissions, and use `set-itemproperty` to add the path to the system variables permanently. Run `Path` first to determine what folders are currently in the path and then append "`%systemroot%\system32\inetsrv`" to the current path string.

```
set-itemproperty -path "HKLM:\SYSTEM\CurrentControlSet\Control\Session Manager\
Environment" -name path -value "%systemroot%;%systemroot%\system32;%systemroot%\
system32\WindowsPowerShell\v1.0\;%systemroot%\system32\inetsrv"
```

Using AppCmd.exe

`AppCmd.exe` interacts with server management objects to expose methods in order to perform a variety of actions on those objects as well as exposing attributes that can be inspected and manipulated. For example, the `app` object provides methods to list, set, add, and delete applications. These objects contain attributes that can be searched for, inspected, and set.

Getting Help

To determine the objects supported for use with `AppCmd.exe`, use the following command:

```
appcmd.exe /?
```

This returns the following:

```
General purpose IIS command line administration tool.

APPCMD (command) (object-type) <identifier> </parameter1:value1 ...>

Supported object types:

    SITE        Administration of virtual sites
    APP         Administration of applications
    VDIR        Administration of virtual directories
    APPPOOL     Administration of application pools
    CONFIG      Administration of general configuration sections
    WP          Administration of worker processes
    REQUEST     Administration of HTTP requests
    MODULE      Administration of server modules
    BACKUP      Administration of server configuration backups
    TRACE       Working with failed request trace logs

(To list commands supported by each object use /?, e.g. 'appcmd.exe site /?')

General parameters:

/?              Display context-sensitive help message.

/text<:value>   Generate output in text format (default).
                /text:* shows all object properties in detail view.
                /text:<attr> shows the value of the specified
                attribute for each object.
/xml            Generate output in XML format.
                Use this to produce output that can be sent to another
                command running in /in mode.
/in or -        Read and operate on XML input from standard input.
                Use this to operate on input produced by another
                command running in /xml mode.
```

```
/config<:*>     Show configuration for displayed objects.
                /config:* also includes inherited configuration.
/metadata       Show configuration metadata when displaying configuration.

/commit         Set config path where configuration changes are saved.
                Can specify either a specific configuration path, "site",
                "app", or "url" to save to the appropriate portion of the
                path being edited by the command, or "apphost", "webroot",
                or "machine" for the corresponding configuration level.
/debug          Show debugging information for command execution.

Use "!" to escape parameters that have same names as the general parameters,
like "/!debug:value" to set a config property named "debug".
```

To determine the supported commands for a specific object, type **AppCmd.exe** followed by the object you want more information about and **/?** — in this case, **app** (application):

```
appcmd.exe app /?
```

This returns the following:

```
Administration of applications

APPCMD (command) APP <identifier> <-parameter1:value1 ...>

Supported commands:

  list      List applications
  set       Configure application
  add       Add new application
  delete    Delete application

(To get help for each command use /?, e.g. 'appcmd.exe add site /?'.)
```

Once you know the command to use against the object, you can learn the attributes that you can configure with the command. Here the object is app, and the command is list:

```
appcmd.exe list app /?
```

This returns:

```
Administration of applications

APPCMD (command) APP <identifier> <-parameter1:value1 ...>

Supported commands:

  list      List applications
  set       Configure application
  add       Add new application
  delete    Delete application

(To get help for each command use /?, e.g. 'appcmd.exe add site /?'.)

c:\Windows\System32\inetsrv>appcmd list app /?
List applications

APPCMD list APP <identifier> <-parameter1:value1 ...>
```

```
List the applications on the machine.  This command can be used to find a
specific application by using its identifier or url, find all applications
belonging to a specified site or application pool, or match zero or more
applications based on the specified application attributes.

Supported parameters:

 identifier

    Application path or url of the application to find

 /app.name

    Application path or url of the application to find (same as identifier)

 /?

    Display the dynamic properties that can be used to find one or more
    application objects


Examples:

 appcmd list apps

    List all applications on the machine.

 appcmd list app "Default Web Site/"

    Find the application "Default Web Site/" (root application of the site
    "Default Web Site").

 appcmd list app http://localhost/app1

    Find the application associated with the specified url.

 appcmd list apps /site.name:"Default Web Site".

    Find all applications belonging to the site "Default Web Site".

 appcmd list apps /apppool.name:"DefaultAppPool".

    Find all applications belonging to the application pool "DefaultAppPool".

 appcmd list apps /path:/app1

    Find all applications that have the "path" configuration property set to
    "/app1".
```

Using the list Command

The list command can be used with every object to find the instances or attributes of the object. You can modify the results of the query by changing the criteria being searched for. The results can then be inspected, exported, or used with another command to perform actions.

Listing All Object Instances

To list all the instances of an object, use AppCmd.exe with list and the object:

```
appcmd.exe list app
```

This returns a list of all web applications running on the server. A server with only the default setup would return this result:

```
APP "Default Web Site/" (applicationPool:DefaultAppPool)
```

Listing Unique Object Instances

If you are searching for a specific instance of an object, you can fine-tune list by adding an attribute of the object. For example, to list an application named *Default Web Site/*, use the following:

```
appcmd.exe list app "Default Web Site/"
```

This will list the Default Web Site application as well as attributes associated with it:

```
APP "Default Web Site/" (applicationPool:DefaultAppPool)
```

Listing Object Instances by Criteria

You can also use the list command with object attributes to return all the object instances that meet specified criteria:

```
appcmd.exe list app /apppool.name:"defaultapppool"
```

This returns a list of all applications that use the application pool DefaultAppPool:

```
app "Default Web Site/" (applicationPool:DefaultAppPool)
```

Remember that the command is placed before the object, and the attributes to be used are placed after the object. This creates a structure similar to a sentence or statement telling the object to do something — in this case, the app object should list all the applications that belong to the application pool DefaultAppPool.

AppCmd.exe Output

When you list objects, AppCmd.exe provides a method to return varied amounts of detail based on the parameters given. If you use only the default list command against an object, the data returned is short, usually consisting of one line of text that provides basic information about the object. Here we are using the app object Default Web Site:

```
appcmd.exe list app "Default Web Site/"
```

This returns the application name and the application pool that the Default Web Site uses.

```
APP "Default Web Site/" (applicationPool:DefaultAppPool)
```

Listing Detailed Information

To return much more data from the list command, append /text:* to it, as follows:

```
appcmd.exe list app "default web site/" /text:*
```

This returns the path, application name, and site name, as well as application information, default virtual directory settings, and current virtual directory information:

```
APP
  path:"/"
  APP.NAME:"Default Web Site/"
  APPPOOL.NAME:"DefaultAppPool"
  SITE.NAME:"Default Web Site"
  [application]
    path:"/"
    applicationPool:"DefaultAppPool"
    enabledProtocols:"http"
    [virtualDirectoryDefaults]
      path:""
      physicalPath:""
      userName:""
      password:""
      logonMethod:"ClearText"
      allowSubDirConfig:"true"
    [virtualDirectory]
      path:"/"
      physicalPath:"%SystemDrive%\inetpub\wwwroot"
      userName:""
      password:""
      logonMethod:"ClearText"
      allowSubDirConfig:"true"
```

Listing by Property

AppCmd.exe also enables you to return only data that meets a specific property. To do this, add /text:<property> to the command. For example, to list all applications that use the default application pool as their application pool, use:

```
appcmd.exe list app /text: /apppool.name:DefaultAppPool
```

The query returns:

```
APP "Default Web Site/" (applicationPool:DefaultAppPool)
```

This shows that the Default Web Site is the only site using the default application pool.

You may also want to use the data that is output by AppCmd.exe with other command-line tools or shell commands. You can take the AppCmd.exe string and insert it into another command. The following command lists the files in the logfile directory used by the Default Web Site:

```
FOR /F %f IN ('AppCmd.exe list site "default web site"
    /text:logfile.directory')
DO DIR %f
```

Listing Configuration Objects

AppCmd.exe uses a series of objects to manipulate IIS 7.0. Each of these objects maps to a section in a configuration file — for example, the Default Web Site. You can query the configuration for the Default Web Site using this command:

```
appcmd.exe list site "default web site" /config
```

This returns:

```
<site name="Default Web Site" id="1">
  <bindings>
    <binding protocol="http" bindingInformation="*:80:" />
```

```
        </bindings>
        <limits />
        <logFile />
        <traceFailedRequestsLogging />
        <applicationDefaults />
        <virtualDirectoryDefaults />
        <application path="/">
          <virtualDirectoryDefaults />
          <virtualDirectory path="/" physicalPath="C:\inetpub\wwwroot" />
        </application>
    </site>
```

The returned data is a list of the sections that can be configured for the object being queried.

AppCmd Attributes and Values

The attributes of an object provide a method to limit the results of a list or modify the values of the object. The previous example showed how the attribute apppool.name could limit the results of a query of the applications on the server. In this case, the limit was to return only objects that had the attribute value of DefaultAppPool. It is possible then to take the object that was returned by the query and modify it by changing the value of the attribute. In this instance, assume that you have an app object named WebSite1 that uses the DefaultAppPool and an application pool named WebAppPool1.

```
appcmd.exe set app "WebSite1/" /applicationpool:"WebAppPool1"
```

This then changes the application pool of WebSite1 from DefaultAppPool to WebAppPool1.

How did we know to use the applicationpool attribute? We'll show you that one shortly.

Managing Objects

We've already shown you about list and used set in one example, but you can also create and delete instances of objects by using add and delete.

Adding New Objects

The add command enables you to create new instances of an object:

```
appcmd.exe add apppool /name:"WebAppPool2"
```

This command created a new application pool object named WebAppPool2. The only attribute needed by this command was name; however, other objects may need additional attributes when creating a new object. This command would have been used to create the application pool that was used in the previous example.

Deleting Objects

Deleting an object is exactly what it appears to be, removing it completely from the server:

```
appcmd.exe delete apppool /apppool.name:"WebAppPool2"
```

When deleting objects, object-specific identifiers are required. Here the identifier was the app pool name WebAppPool2.

Modifying Objects

The `set` command has two modes of use. The first mode combines `set` with the help syntax to determine what attributes an object has that can be modified:

```
appcmd.exe set site "WebSite1" /?
```

The second mode modifies the attributes of the object. As seen above with: `AppCmd .exe set app "WebSite1/" /applicationpool:"WebAppPool1"`, WebSite1 was set to use WebAppPool1. Similar to the `Delete` command, object-specific identifiers are required with the `Set` command.

UPDATING LIVE WEBSITES

When updating live websites, it's recommended that you make a copy of the existing web folder, apply the updates to the new folder, and then point the website to the web folder. Following is a script that uses user-defined variables for the `src` (source) and `dest` (destination) folders. `Xcopy.exe` then copies the data in the `src` folder into the `dest` folder, and `AppCmd.exe` points the web virtual directory to the new folder.

```
echo off

Set /P Src=[old folder date]
Set /P Dest=[new folder date]

xcopy c:\inetpub\wwwroot\WebSite1\%src%
        c:\inetpub\wwwroot\WebSite1\%dest% /c /e /i /o /y

AppCmd.exe set vdir WebSite1/
            -physicalpath:"c:\inetpub\wwwroot\WebSite1\%dest%"
```

Determining Which Attributes Are Associated with an Object

`AppCmd.exe` makes it possible to control every aspect of IIS through the command line, including managing sites, applications, virtual directories, and application pools. We've already shown a few examples in which sites, applications, and application pools have either been modified or listed. To make some of the changes to the objects, you have to know which attribute needs to be modified to achieve the desired result.

Above we changed the application pool for WebSite1 from the DefaultAppPool to the WebAppPool1 application pool and used an attribute named applicationpool. How did we know about the attribute named applicationpool? Using the `list` command with `/text:*` on the object WebSite1/ allows us to see every attribute associated with the WebSite1 application:

```
appcmd list app "WebSite1/" /text:*
```

The command returns the following:

```
APP
  path:"/"
  APP.NAME:"WebSite1/"
```

```
APPPOOL.NAME:"WebAppPool1"
SITE.NAME:"WebSite1"
[application]
  path:"/"
  applicationPool:"WebAppPool1"
  enabledProtocols:"http"
  [virtualDirectoryDefaults]
    path:""
    physicalPath:""
    userName:""
    password:""
    logonMethod:"ClearText"
    allowSubDirConfig:"true"
  [virtualDirectory]
    path:"/"
    physicalPath:"C:\inetpub\wwwroot"
    userName:""
    password:""
    logonMethod:"ClearText"
    allowSubDirConfig:"true"
```

In this case, `applicationPool` is one of a few attributes available to be modified. Some object types will have only a few attributes, and some objects will have many. In this example, the `applicationPool` attribute is directly under the application element. However, some attributes fall under subelements. If you want to modify the virtual directory default path, you would need to use element path notation. Here `virtualdirectorydefault` is the subelement, and `path` is the attribute we are changing.

```
appcmd.exe set app "WebSite1/" /virtualdirectorydefaults.path:"/"
```

This command makes the virtual directory default path `"/"`.

Controlling Object State

In addition to the tasks already shown, you can also use `AppCmd.exe` to gather state information for sites, application pools, worker processes, and currently executing requests. For some objects, the state can also be changed. Examples include starting/stopping a site and starting/stopping/recycling an application pool.

> **NOTE** *To gather the state information,* `AppCmd.exe` *uses the RSCA (Runtime Status and Control API). The IIS Manager and WMI also use the RSCA to gather information. You can find additional information on using functionality in IIS 8.0 to analyze running processes and problems in Chapter 23, "Diagnostics and Troubleshooting."*

Determining Site and Application Pool State

It is possible to determine the state of a site or application pool and then, based on the current state of the object, start, stop, or recycle it. Here we will use the `list` command on the `apppool` object:

```
appcmd.exe list apppool
```

The result of the query on a default system is

```
APPPOOL "DefaultAppPool" (MgdVersion:v2.0,MgdMode:Integrated,state:Started)
APPPOOL "Classic .NET AppPool" (MgdVersion:v2.0,MgdMode:Classic,state:Started)
```

At the end of the string state is the list for both application pools as "Started." You can also use a query to return all the objects that meet specific criteria. This example returns all the application pools whose state is set to started:

```
appcmd.exe list apppools /state:started
```

As before, the result of this query on a default system is

```
APPPOOL "DefaultAppPool" (MgdVersion:v2.0,MgdMode:Integrated,state:Started)
APPPOOL "Classic .NET AppPool" (MgdVersion:v2.0,MgdMode:Classic,state:Started)
```

Once you know the state of the object, you can change it to meet your needs. In this case, we will stop the `DefaultAppPool`:

```
appcmd.exe stop apppool /apppool.name:"DefaultAppPool"
```

This returns

```
"DefaultAppPool" successfully stopped
```

Determining Worker Process State

By finding the worker process state, the Process ID (PID) number is given and can be used along with Task Manager to determine the health of an application pool process. As with other objects, the worker process object can be queried either with a list query with no attributes to narrow the search or with a specific query that returns only objects that match the attributes listed in the query. The nonspecific query uses the `list` command against the `wp` object. Before running this example, restart the `DefaultAppPool` and navigate to `http://localhost/` on your server.

```
appcmd.exe list wp
```

If your `DefaultAppPool` were started and you navigated to `http://localhost/`, the query should return a result similar to the following:

```
WP "1044" (applicationPool:DefaultAppPool)
```

In this example "1044" is the PID number for the `DefaultAppPool` application pool. If you know either the PID number or the name of the application pool that you want to query, it is possible to fine-tune the query to return only the result needed, rather than all active worker processes:

```
appcmd.exe list wp /apppool.name:"DefaultAppPool"
```

or

```
appcmd.exe list wp /wp.name:"1044"
```

Both of these queries will return only the `DefaultAppPool` worker process status.

Monitoring Currently Executing Requests

Requests that are currently being executed can be determined by using the `request` object:

```
appcmd.exe list request
```

Like other objects used with `AppCmd.exe`, the `request` object can use attributes to focus the information it returns. The attributes can be used to return information on a specific site, application pool, worker process, URL, or requests that have been executing for longer than a specified time (in milliseconds). Examples of attributes used with `request` include the following:

➤ Requesting based on site ID:

```
appcmd.exe list request /site.id:1
```

➤ Requesting based on application pool:

```
appcmd.exe list request /apppool.exe:DefaultAppPool
```

➤ Requesting based on worker process:

```
appcmd.exe list request /wp.name:"1044"
```

➤ Requesting based on site name:

```
appcmd.exe list request /site.name:"Default Web Site"
```

➤ Requesting based on the time for which the process has been running:

```
appcmd.exe list request /elapsed:"1000"
```

Here is an example of the information returned by a request:

```
REQUEST "3d0000018000a2f1" (url:GET /default.aspx, time:324 msec, client:192.168.0.132)
```

The information returned includes the request ID, URL, time the request has taken, and the client IP address. This provides a useful tool to look at requests that are taking longer to execute than desired.

Backing Up and Restoring

`AppCmd.exe` is also used to back up, list, and restore the global server configuration. We recommend making a backup before installing any component or making any modification that changes the global server configuration. When the backup is made, it contains the `applicationhost.config`, `administration.config`, `redirection.config`, `metabase.xml`, and `mbschema.xml`. (The last two contain metabase data that is still used by SMTP and FTP.)

To create a backup, use:

```
appcmd.exe add backup
```

Once the backup has been created, the command prompt will return. The backups consist of folders named automatically based on the date and time of the backup and placed in the `%systemroot%\system32\inetsrv\backup` directory. It is also possible to name the backups by appending the backup name at the end of the string.

```
appcmd.exe add backup test1
```

To list a backup, use:

```
appcmd.exe list backup
```

The result is a list of all backups stored in the backup folder:

```
BACKUP "20070709T221615"
BACKUP "20070709T223557"
BACKUP "20070709T223601"
BACKUP "test1"
```

To restore a backup, use:

```
appcmd.exe restore backup /backup.name:"20070709T221615"
```

When restoring a backup, IIS stops and performs an overwrite of the server's state. Once the configuration files have been overwritten, IIS restarts. If you prefer not to have IIS stop and restart, you can also use /stop:false. This allows you to stop and restart the services manually at a time that you desire.

```
appcmd.exe restore backup /backup.name:"20070709T221615" /stop:false
```

To remove a backup, use:

```
appcmd.exe delete backup test1
```

Remember that 30 seconds spent backing up can save hours spent rebuilding your server.

Setting the Configuration

The configuration of IIS 8.0, as mentioned previously in this chapter, is set in a series of XML files. The specifics of these files are covered below, but for now, know that AppCmd.exe can also be used to manage the configuration. Tasks included in managing the configuration consist of listing, editing, and clearing the configuration; locking and unlocking sections; and searching through the configuration.

Listing the Configuration

AppCmd.exe views the configuration as a series of sections and subsections. Starting at the top with no modifiers, it is possible to list the configuration of the server. You can narrow the focus of the list by adding site or application names or URLs. Beyond that, by using specific section identifiers in relation to a site or URL, you can gather the exact information that you need. Each level is seen as a section or subsection and inherits the settings from the level above it, unless explicitly overwritten.

To list the entire configuration for a server, use:

```
appcmd.exe list config
```

Listing the configuration for the Default Web Site is just as simple:

```
appcmd.exe list config "Default Web Site/"
```

To narrow the focus down to a specific section in the Default Web Site, use:

```
appcmd.exe list config "Default Web Site/" /section:system.net/settings
```

This would return the following result:

```
<system.net>
  <settings>
    <httpWebRequest />
    <ipv6 />
    <performanceCounters />
    <servicePointManager />
    <socket />
    <webProxyScript />
  </settings>
</system.net>
```

AppCmd.exe will show only sections of the configuration that are explicitly set. To display inherited or default values, append /config:* to the string:

```
appcmd.exe list config "Default Web Site/" /section:system.net/settings /config:*
```

By adding the /config:* to the string, the results that are returned contain all the information, even if it wasn't specifically set at that section level.

```
<system.net>
  <settings>
    <httpWebRequest maximumErrorResponseLength="64"
maximumResponseHeadersLength="64" maximumUnauthorizedUploadLength="-1"
 useUnsafeHeaderParsing="false" />
    <ipv6 enabled="false" />
    <performanceCounters enabled="false" />
    <servicePointManager checkCertificateName="true"
checkCertificateRevocationList="false" dnsRefreshTimeout="120000"
enableDnsRoundRobin="false" expect100Continue="true" useNagleAlgorithm="true" />
    <socket alwaysUseCompletionPortsForAccept="false"
           alwaysUseCompletionPortsForConnect="false" />
    <webProxyScript downloadTimeout="00:02:00" />
  </settings>
</system.net>
```

How do you discover what the available sections are? Use this command:

```
appcmd.exe list config -section:?
```

Here is a portion of what the previous command returns:

```
system.net/authenticationModules
system.web/deployment
system.web/httpModules
system.webServer/directoryBrowse
system.webServer/cgi
configPaths
system.web/compilation
system.webServer/security/access
system.web/deviceFilters
system.transactions/defaultSettings
system.webServer/management/authorization
system.applicationHost/customMetadata
system.web/authorization
system.web/globalization
system.webServer/handlers
configurationRedirection
configProtectedData
system.web/browserCaps
system.net/mailSettings/smtp
system.web/xhtmlConformance
system.xml.serialization/dateTimeSerialization
system.webServer/urlCompression
system.web/pages
system.web/trace
appSettings
system.web/profile
```

```
system.webServer/isapiFilters
system.web/customErrors
system.net/webRequestModules
system.web/caching/outputCacheSettings
```

Editing Configuration Properties

When `AppCmd.exe` is used to edit the configuration, the section being edited consists of an object or series of objects and the attributes associated with the object. In the previous example, the section was `system.net/settings`, the object being "`settings`" with a series of properties listed below it that can be edited. To differentiate whether the change you are setting will be at a global level or site-specific, you must add the URL if the change is to be at site level. You can take the previous example and use the information gathered by using `list` with `/config:*` to determine what property we need to adjust. The `set` command is then used to make a global configuration change to enable IPv6 and then a site-specific change to disable IPv6 that will override the global configuration only for the one site.

```
appcmd.exe set config /section:system.net/settings -ipv6.enabled:"true"
```

The global configuration has been set to enable IPv6, and now it will be disabled on the Default Web Site.

```
appcmd.exe set config "http://localhost"
                      /section:system.net/settings
                      -ipv6.enabled:"false"
```

In this case, `http://localhost` had to be used as the site name for the Default Web Site because it had no other site name.

Editing Configuration Collections

Sections can contain elements known as *collections*. Collections can, in turn, contain more elements. `httpErrors` is an example of a section that contains a collection. It contains both standard elements and a collection:

```
appcmd.exe list config /section:httpErrors
```

Following is the result:

```
<system.webServer>
  <httpErrors>
    <error statusCode="401"
           prefixLanguageFilePath="%SystemDrive%\inetpub\custerr"
           path="401.htm" />

    <error statusCode="403"
           prefixLanguageFilePath="%SystemDrive%\inetpub\custerr"
           path="403.htm" />

    <error statusCode="404"
           prefixLanguageFilePath="%SystemDrive%\inetpub\custerr"
           path="404.htm" />

    <error statusCode="405"
           prefixLanguageFilePath="%SystemDrive%\inetpub\custerr"
```

```
                    path="405.htm" />

        <error statusCode="406"
                prefixLanguageFilePath="%SystemDrive%\inetpub\custerr"
                path="406.htm" />

        <error statusCode="412"
                prefixLanguageFilePath="%SystemDrive%\inetpub\custerr"
                path="412.htm" />

        <error statusCode="500"
                prefixLanguageFilePath="%SystemDrive%\inetpub\custerr"
                path="500.htm" />

        <error statusCode="501"
                prefixLanguageFilePath="%SystemDrive%\inetpub\custerr"
                path="501.htm" />

        <error statusCode="502"
                prefixLanguageFilePath="%SystemDrive%\inetpub\custerr"
                path="502.htm" />

    </httpErrors>
  </system.webServer>
```

In this example, each error status code is an element in the `error` collection. Refer to `IIS_schema` at `%systemroot%\system32\inetsrv\config\schema` to see the schema for `httpErrors`:

```
<sectionSchema name="system.webServer/httpErrors">
    <attribute name="errorMode" type="enum" defaultValue="DetailedLocalOnly">
      <enum name="DetailedLocalOnly" value="0" />
      <enum name="Custom" value="1" />
      <enum name="Detailed" value="2" />
    </attribute>
    <attribute name="existingResponse" type="enum" defaultValue="Auto">
      <enum name="Auto" value="0" />
      <enum name="Replace" value="1" />
      <enum name="PassThrough" value="2" />
    </attribute>
    <attribute name="defaultPath" type="string" expanded="true" />
    <attribute name="defaultResponseMode" type="enum" defaultValue="File">
      <enum name="File" value="0" />
      <enum name="ExecuteURL" value="1" />
      <enum name="Redirect" value="2" />
    </attribute>
    <attribute name="detailedMoreInformationLink"
                type="string"
                defaultValue="http://go.microsoft.com/fwlink/?LinkID=62293"
                required="false" />
    <collection addElement="error" clearElement="clear" removeElement="remove">
      <attribute name="statusCode" type="uint" required="true"
                isCombinedKey="true"
                validationType="integerRange"
                validationParameter="400,999" />
      <attribute name="subStatusCode" type="int" defaultValue="-1"
```

```
                    isCombinedKey="true"
                    validationType="integerRange"
                    validationParameter="-1,999" />
        <attribute name="prefixLanguageFilePath" type="string" expanded="true"
                    defaultValue="" required="false" />
        <attribute name="path" type="string" expanded="true"
                    required="true" validationType="nonEmptyString" />
        <attribute name="responseMode" type="enum" defaultValue="File">
          <enum name="File" value="0" />
          <enum name="ExecuteURL" value="1" />
          <enum name="Redirect" value="2" />
        </attribute>
      </collection>
    </sectionSchema>
```

Notice that there is a series of attributes and that, toward the bottom, is the collection `error`. You can add, edit, or delete any of these elements in the collection by using the `set` command against the `config` object. Here we will be changing the 401 error page from "`401.htm`" to "`defaulterror.htm`." `/[statusCode='401']` determines which element will be edited, and `.path:defaulterror.htm` states that the new path should be to the `defaulterror.htm` file.

```
appcmd.exe set config /section:httpErrors /[statusCode='401'].path:defaulterror.htm
```

The new result for the 401 status code is:

```
<error statusCode="401"
       prefixLanguageFilePath="%SystemDrive%\inetpub\custerr"
       path="defaulterror.htm" />
```

You can also add or remove elements from a collection by using a plus sign (+) or a minus sign (−). For example, the following adds a status code of 503 and points to the file `503.htm` in the `SystemDrive%\inetpub\custerr` folder:

```
appcmd.exe set config /section:httpErrors              /+[statusCode='503',
          prefixLanguageFilePath='%SystemDrive%\inetpub\custerr',
          path='503.htm']
```

The following removes the 503 status code:

```
appcmd.exe set config /section:httpErrors /-[statusCode='503']
```

When adding an element to a collection, you must specify every attribute. When deleting an element, however, you only need to specify the name of the element.

Configuration Location

Because the configuration of IIS 8.0 is a hierarchical system of layered levels, starting at the server level and working down to the application, you can set the configuration at any of these levels and it will be inherited by the levels below it. However, you can also set a configuration property at a higher level and have it apply only to a specific lower level. This is done by using the `commit` parameter. For example, with the `commit` parameter, it is possible to have HTTP logging log only errors by default at the server level, but force a specified URL to have HTTP logging log everything.

You can set the `commit` parameter at the following levels:

➤ (omitted) — The default; writes configuration at the level for which it is set.

➤ `url` — Same as default; writes configuration at the level for which it is set.

➤ `site` — Writes configuration in `web.config` at the site root of the URL for which it is set.

➤ `app` — Writes configuration in `web.config` at the application root of the URL for which it is set.

➤ `apphost` — Writes configuration at the server level, in the `applicationHost.config` file.

➤ `<PATH>` — Writes configurations at the specified configuration path.

To set logging to log everything for the Default Web Site, you would use the following:

```
appcmd.exe set config "http://localhost"
            /section:system.webServer/httpLogging
            -selectiveLogging:LogAll
            -commit:apphost
```

In this example, the `commit` was executed against the `apphost` level; thus, the configuration change will be made to the `applicationHost.config` file rather than the `web.config` file of the Default Web Site.

Locating Configuration Settings

Because of the layered hierarchical structure of the configuration, a system is needed to determine the location(s) where a setting is being applied. Above in this chapter, `list` was used to find the configuration objects that needed to be edited. Here, this is reversed, and `search` is used to find every location where a setting has been applied. This is needed because a setting for the same object might be applied in multiple places.

> **NOTE** *The following examples return a result only if a match is found. If you do not have a website called "Default Web Site," searching for it will result in a blank line. When running these search commands, use search criteria that exist in your environment.*

To return all locations where configuration is set on a server, use `search` with no arguments:

```
appcmd.exe search config
```

This returns the following results on the server:

```
CONFIGSEARCH "MACHINE/WEBROOT/APPHOST"
CONFIGSEARCH "MACHINE/WEBROOT/APPHOST/Default Web Site"
CONFIGSEARCH "MACHINE/WEBROOT/APPHOST/WebSite1"
```

You can determine where the configuration for a specific site is set by including the site name in the command:

```
appcmd.exe search config "default web site"
```

The results show that the Default Web Site has configuration set at both the `apphost` level and in the Default Web Site's `web.config` file:

```
CONFIGSEARCH "MACHINE/WEBROOT/APPHOST"
CONFIGSEARCH "MACHINE/WEBROOT/APPHOST/Default Web Site"
```

To determine all the locations where a specific configuration is being set, add the section to the search:

```
appcmd.exe search config /section:system.webServer/httploggin
```

This search shows that only the `apphost` level is being used to configure the `httpLogging` section.

```
CONFIGSEARCH "MACHINE/WEBROOT/APPHOST"
```

To determine all the locations where a specific property is being set, add the section and the property to the search:

```
appcmd.exe search config /section:system.webServer/httpLogging /selectiveLogging
```

This can be further refined to return only the locations where the property is set to a specific value. To determine all the locations where a specific property is being set, add the section and the property value to the search:

```
appcmd.exe search config /section:system.webServer/httpLogging
                        /selectiveLogging:LogError
```

Locking and Unlocking the Configuration

As discussed above in the "Locking" section of this chapter, sections of the configuration can be locked to prevent them from being set at lower levels, or unlocked to allow delegation of authority to other users. Most IIS settings are locked by default. To allow delegation of authority, you need to unlock these sections. This is done with the `unlock` and `lock` commands. The command is given, followed by the section that needs to be locked or unlocked. The following command unlocks the `authentication` section in the Default Web Site:

```
appcmd.exe unlock config "default web site" /section:system.web/authentication
```

To lock the section, use:

```
appcmd.exe lock config "default web site" /section:system.web/authentication
```

Piping with XML

You can use the `/xml` modifier with the `appcmd list` command to create complex tasks or perform large batch functions. The `/xml` modifier enables you to export the results of a query into a standard XML format that can be used by other command-line tools or shell commands. For example, to list all the application pools that are started and export the information to an XML format, issue the following command:

```
appcmd.exe list apppool /state:Started /xml
```

which results in:

```
<?xml version="1.0" encoding="UTF-8"?>
<appcmd>
    <APPPOOL APPPOOL.NAME="DefaultAppPool"
```

```
              PipelineMode="Integrated"
              RuntimeVersion="v2.0" state="Started" />
    <APPPOOL APPPOOL.NAME="Classic .NET AppPool"
              PipelineMode="Classic"
              RuntimeVersion="v2.0" state="Started" />
    <APPPOOL APPPOOL.NAME="WebSite1"
              PipelineMode="Integrated"
              RuntimeVersion="v4.0" state="Started" />
</appcmd>
```

The results returned show that there are three application pools started, their names, the mode of each application pool, and the runtime version of each pool.

We can also take this XML data and pipe it directly into another `AppCmd.exe` command to cause an action to happen to the objects that were returned in the first query. Here we will recycle all the application pools that were returned in the first query:

```
appcmd.exe list apppool /state:Started /xml | appcmd.exe recycle apppool /in
```

This piping function gives great flexibility in creating scripts to administer sites and servers.

In this section, how to create, manage, and monitor a website using the AppCmd has been discussed in detail. Information covering getting help with the commands and finding the syntax for those commands was also provided. The following section covers the similar topics using the IIS PowerShell module.

IIS POWERSHELL MANAGEMENT

PowerShell is a very powerful command-line and scripting language that can be used to administer applications running on the Windows platform. It is tightly integrated with the .NET Framework and provides full access to existing COM, WMI, and .NET capabilities. PowerShell tasks are executed using cmdlets, which are small pieces of code that perform a specific function. PowerShell can also be used to administer a system remotely, and it can be used to monitor the health or change the configuration of the Windows operating system itself.

This section discusses PowerShell capabilities specific to IIS. Examples of what you can do with IIS from PowerShell include the following:

➤ Add, modify, and delete websites and application pools.

➤ Stop, start, recycle, and monitor the health of application pools.

➤ Enable and disable global modules.

➤ Back up and restore a web configuration.

> **NOTE** *Execute* `get-command` *for a list of all the available commands.*

This section discusses the following topics:

➤ The available IIS PowerShell cmdlets

➤ Using the help methods to better understand what the cmdlet does

➤ Examples of numerous cmdlets to add, modify, and delete configurations

➤ Monitoring and controlling the state of objects

➤ Backing up and restoring the IIS configuration

PowerShell IIS Cmdlets

PowerShell works together with the server management objects and allows an administrator to perform a large number of IIS actions. Those objects also expose attributes, such as web requests and object status, that are used to monitor the current health of the web server. To view the IIS-specific cmdlets, perform the following steps:

1. Open the PowerShell console.

2. Enter **import-module WebAdministration**.

3. Enter **cd IIS:**.

4. Enter **get-command-module WebAdministration**.

After entering the command in Step 4, the following cmdlets are rendered:

Add-WebConfiguration	Add-WebConfigurationLock
Add-WebConfigurationProperty	Backup-WebConfiguration
Clear-WebCentralCertProvider	Clear-WebConfiguration
Clear-WebRequestTracingSetting	Clear-WebRequestTracingSettings
ConvertTo-WebApplication	Disable-WebCentralCertProvider
Disable-WebGlobalModule	Disable-WebRequestTracing
Enable-WebGlobalModule	Enable-WebRequestTracing
Get-WebAppDomain	Get-WebApplication
Get-WebAppPoolState	Get-WebBinding
Get-WebCentralCertProvider	Get-WebConfigFile
Get-WebConfiguration	Get-WebConfigurationBackup
Get-WebConfigurationLocation	Get-WebConfigurationLock
Get-WebConfigurationProperty	Get-WebFilePath
Get-WebGlobalModule	Get-WebHandler
Get-WebItemState	Get-WebManagedModule

Get-WebRequest	Get-Website
Get-WebsiteState	Get-WebURL
Get-WebVirtualDirectory	New-WebApplication
New-WebAppPool	New-WebBinding
New-WebFtpSite	New-WebGlobalModule
New-WebHandler	New-WebManagedModule
New-Website	New-WebVirtualDirectory
Remove-WebApplication	Remove-WebAppPool
Remove-WebBinding	Remove-WebConfigurationBackup
Remove-WebConfigurationLocation	Remove-WebConfigurationLock
Remove-WebConfigurationProperty	Remove-WebGlobalModule
Remove-WebHandler	Remove-WebManagedModule
Remove-Website	Remove-WebVirtualDirectory
Rename-WebConfigurationLocation	Restart-WebAppPool
Restart-WebItem	Restore-WebConfiguration
Select-WebConfiguration	Set-WebBinding
Set-WebCentralCertProvider	Set-WebCentralCertProviderCredential
Set-WebConfiguration	Set-WebConfigurationProperty
Set-WebGlobalModule	Set-WebHandler
Set-WebManagedModule	Start-WebAppPool
Start-WebCommitDelay	Start-WebItem
Start-Website	Stop-WebAppPool
Stop-WebCommitDelay	Stop-WebItem
Stop-Website	

The names of the cmdlets are very intuitive. For example, no further explanation should be necessary for New-Website, Backup-WebConfiguration, and Get-WebAppPoolState cmdlets. However, *how* to use them, *when* to use them, and *which* parameters are required/optional are important topics, and are discussed in the following sections.

Getting Help

PowerShell includes only a small amount of help documentation. It is expected that you access and read help topics online. The entry point for getting PowerShell help within the console is by executing the following command:

```
PS IIS:\>get-help
```

The `get-help` command results in the following output:

```
TOPIC
    Windows PowerShell Help System

SHORT DESCRIPTION
    Displays help about Windows PowerShell cmdlets and concepts.

LONG DESCRIPTION
    Windows PowerShell Help describes Windows PowerShell cmdlets,
    functions, scripts, and modules, and explains concepts, including
    the elements of the Windows PowerShell language.

    Windows PowerShell does not include help files, but you can read the
    help topics online, or use the Update-Help cmdlet to download help files
    to your computer and then use the Get-Help cmdlet to display the help
    topics at the command line.

You can also use the Update-Help cmdlet to download updated help files
    as they are released so that your local help content is never obsolete.

    Without help files, Get-Help displays autogenerated help for cmdlets,
    functions, and scripts, which includes the syntax, aliases, and remarks.

  ONLINE HELP
    You can find help for Windows PowerShell online in the TechNet Library
    beginning at http://go.microsoft.com/fwlink/?LinkID=108518.

    To open online help for any cmdlet or function, type:

        Get-Help <cmdlet-name> -Online

  UPDATE-HELP
    To download and install help files on your computer:

1. Start Windows PowerShell with the "Run as administrator" option.
        2. Type:   Update-Help

    After the Help files are installed, you can use the Get-Help cmdlet to
    display the help topics. You can also use the Update-Help cmdlet to
    download updated help files so that your local help files are always
    up-to-date.

    For more information about the Update-Help cmdlet, type:

        Get-Help Update-Help -Online  or go to:
```

```
        http://go.microsoft.com/fwlink/?LinkID=210614

GET-HELP
    The Get-Help cmdlet displays help at the command line from content in
    help files on your computer. Without help files, Get-Help displays
    autogenerated help for cmdlets, functions, and scripts. You can also
    use Get-Help to display online help.

    To get help for a cmdlet, type:  Get-Help <cmdlet-name>

    To get online help, type:  Get-Help <cmdlet-name> -Online

    The titles of conceptual topics begin with "About_".
    To get help for a concept or language element, type:

        Get-Help About_<topic-name>

    To search for a word or phrase in all help files, type:

        Get-Help <search-term>

    For more information about the Get-Help cmdlet, type:

        Get-Help Get-Help -Online   or go to:
        http://go.microsoft.com/fwlink/?LinkID=113316

    EXAMPLES:
        Save-Help             : Downloads help files from the Internet and saves
                                them on a file share.
        Update-Help           : Downloads and installs help files from the
                                Internet or a file share.
        Get-Help Get-Process  : Displays help about the Get-Process cmdlet.
        Get-Help Get-Process -Online  : Opens online help for the Get-Process cmdlet.

        Help Get-Process      : Displays help about Get-Process one page at a time.
        Get-Process -?        : Displays help about the Get-Process cmdlet.
        Get-Help About_Modules : Displays help about Windows PowerShell modules.
        Get-Help remoting     : Searches the help topics for the word "remoting."

    SEE ALSO:
        about_Updatable_Help
        Get-Help
        Save-Help
        Update-Help
```

One important point found in the previous get-help output is the description of the
`'get-help <cmdlet-name>'` command and parameter. This command provides quick access
to the syntax for executing a specific cmdlet.

There are a large number of cmdlets available for IIS administration, each having a different set
of parameters; therefore, you may not always remember or know the syntax. To get the syntax
required to execute a specific cmdlet, enter the following command and view the result in the
command window. An example is shown in Figure 18-17.

```
Get-Help Disable-WebGlobalModule
```

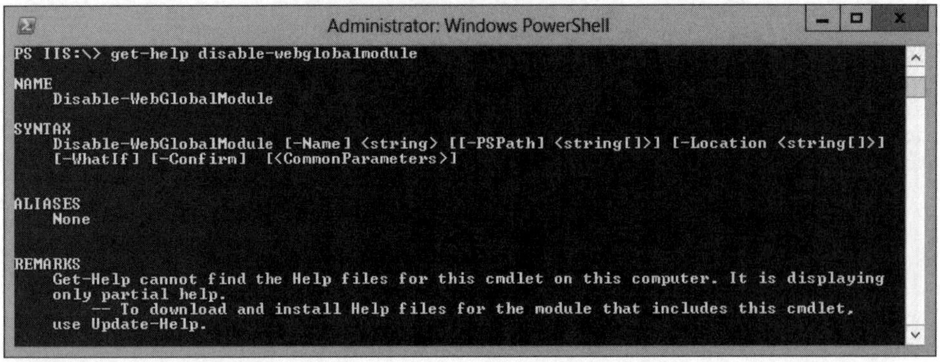

FIGURE 18-17

Notice that the following parameters are supported by the `Disable-WebGlobalModule` cmdlet:

PARAMETER	TYPE	REQUIRED	DESCRIPTION
Name	String	Yes	The module name to disable
PSPath	String[]	No	The configuration path
Location	String[]	No	The module's location
WhatIf	...	No	Shows the results of execution without executing them
Confirm	...	No	Prompts for confirmation before execution

The `get-help` command provides some additional parameters that provide even more information about a cmdlet. For example, in the previous table there is a column called "Required"; however, in the output from the `Get-Help Disable-WebGlobalModule`, this information is not visible. Use the following parameters to extend the information provided by the `get-help` command:

PARAMETER	DESCRIPTION
-Full	Lists cmdlet parameters and their specific attributes (e.g., Required)
-Detailed	Lists the specific parameters and their descriptions
-Examples	Shows an example of how to execute the cmdlet

> **NOTE** *Many of the methods do not contain locally installed examples and descriptions. These are stored online and can be referenced there.*

A partial example of using the `Full` `get-help` parameter is rendered by executing the following command:

```
Get-Help Disable-WebGlobalModule -full
```

The result is shown in Figure 18-18.

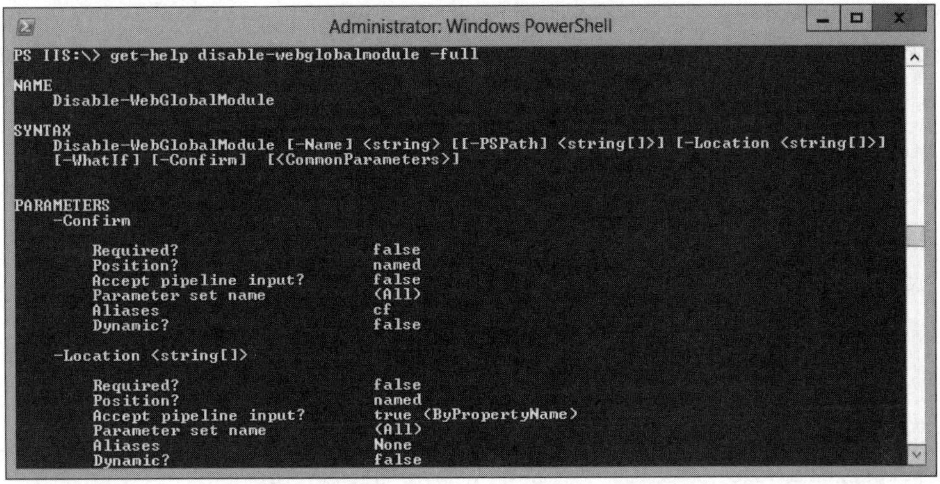

```
Administrator: Windows PowerShell

PS IIS:\> get-help disable-webglobalmodule -full

NAME
    Disable-WebGlobalModule

SYNTAX
    Disable-WebGlobalModule [-Name] <string> [[-PSPath] <string[]>] [-Location <string[]>]
    [-WhatIf] [-Confirm]  [<CommonParameters>]


PARAMETERS
    -Confirm

        Required?                      false
        Position?                      named
        Accept pipeline input?         false
        Parameter set name             (All)
        Aliases                        cf
        Dynamic?                       false

    -Location <string[]>

        Required?                      false
        Position?                      named
        Accept pipeline input?         true (ByPropertyName)
        Parameter set name             (All)
        Aliases                        None
        Dynamic?                       false
```

FIGURE 18-18

Now you know how to install the module, see which cmdlets exist, and how to find the parameter. In the following section, you learn how to use them.

Using PowerShell IIS Cmdlets

A sound approach when beginning to use the IIS PowerShell cmdlets is first to understand their capabilities and then group them together into different administrative activities. For example, the IIS cmdlets can be grouped into the following three activities:

➤ Creating new websites

➤ Modifying existing websites

➤ Managing the operations of existing websites

Review the available PowerShell IIS cmdlets on the previous pages, and notice that they all begin with the action that is taken, followed by what object that action is executed upon. For example, executing the Remove-WebBinding cmdlet removes the specified binding from a website and is associated with the "Modifying existing website" group.

CREATING NEW WEBSITES	
New-WebApplication	New-WebAppPool
New-WebBinding	New-WebFtpSite
New-WebGlobalModule	New-WebHandler
New-WebManagedModule	New-Website
New-WebVirtualDirectory	

MODIFYING EXISTING WEBSITES	
Add-WebConfiguration	Add-WebConfigurationLock
Add-WebConfigurationProperty	Clear-WebCentralCertProvider
Clear-WebConfiguration	Clear-WebRequestTracingSetting
Clear-WebRequestTracingSettings	ConvertTo-WebApplication
Disable-WebCentralCertProvider	Disable-WebGlobalModule
Disable-WebRequestTracing	Enable-WebGlobalModule
Enable-WebRequestTracing	Remove-WebApplication
Remove-WebAppPool	Remove-WebBinding
Remove-WebConfigurationBackup	Remove-WebConfigurationLocation
Remove-WebConfigurationLock	Remove-WebConfigurationProperty
Remove-WebGlobalModule	Remove-WebHandler
Remove-WebManagedModule	Remove-Website
Remove-WebVirtualDirectory	Rename-WebConfigurationLocation
Set-WebBinding	Set-WebCentralCertProvider
Set-WebCentralCertProviderCredential	Set-WebConfiguration
Set-WebConfigurationProperty	Set-WebGlobalModule
Set-WebHandler	Set-WebManagedModule

MANAGING THE OPERATIONS OF EXISTING WEBSITES	
Backup-WebConfiguration	Get-WebAppDomain
Get-WebApplication	Get-WebAppPoolState
Get-WebBinding	Get-WebCentralCertProvider
Get-WebConfigFile	Get-WebConfiguration
Get-WebConfigurationBackup	Get-WebConfigurationLocation
Get-WebConfigurationLock	Get-WebConfigurationProperty
Get-WebFilePath	Get-WebGlobalModule
Get-WebHandler	Get-WebItemState
Get-WebManagedModule	Get-WebRequest
Get-Website	Get-WebsiteState
Get-WebURL	Get-WebVirtualDirectory

Restart-WebAppPool	Restart-WebItem
Restore-WebConfiguration	Select-WebConfiguration
Start-WebAppPool	Start-WebCommitDelay
Start-WebItem	Start-Website
Stop-WebAppPool	Stop-WebCommitDelay
Stop-WebItem	Stop-Website

It should be clear now what features exist within the IIS PowerShell module, how to get help, and how to find the syntax to use them. Let's now move on and perform some actions. In the next sections, the following activities are discussed:

➤ Creating a website and viewing the results in IIS Manager and within PowerShell

➤ Modifying the website attributes

➤ Performing operational activities

Creating a Website and Viewing the Results

When you create a new website from within IIS Manager, the required elements are the following:

➤ Site name

➤ Application pool

➤ Physical path

➤ Binding Type, IP Address, and Port (contain default settings)

When using PowerShell to create your website, you need to take additional precautions. Although the following command creates a new website with the corresponding output shown in Figure 18-19, it does not create an application pool:

```
New-Website -Name Site1 -Port 81 -PhysicalPath "C:\inetpub\Site1"
```

FIGURE 18-19

Next, enter a standard DOS-like command **cd sites** followed by **dir**. This will display a list of all the websites on the server, including the Name, ID, State, Physical Path, and Bindings. The output is shown in Figure 18-20.

FIGURE 18-20

Finally, change the directory to the specific site — for example cd Site1 and enter the **dir** command to list the contents of the website, as shown in Figure 18-21.

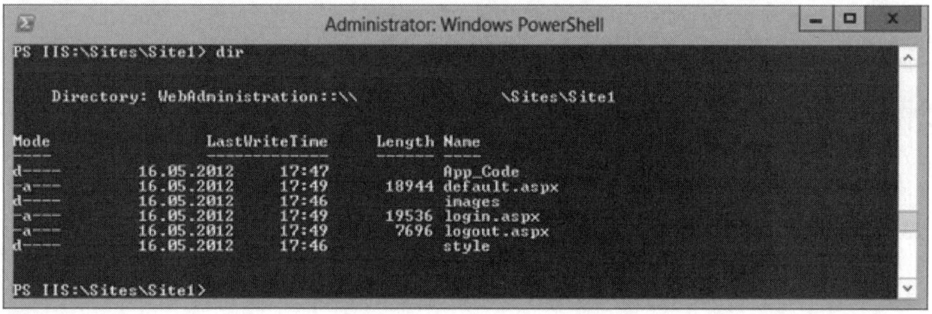

FIGURE 18-21

Another useful directory to check into is IIS:\AppPools. Navigate to the directory by executing cd IIS:\AppPools and then enter **dir** to list all the currently existing application pools, their state, and the applications that are using them. Notice in Figure 18-22 that the website just created uses the DefaultAppPool application pool. That means that if you do not include the -ApplicationPool attribute, the DefaultAppPool is used by default.

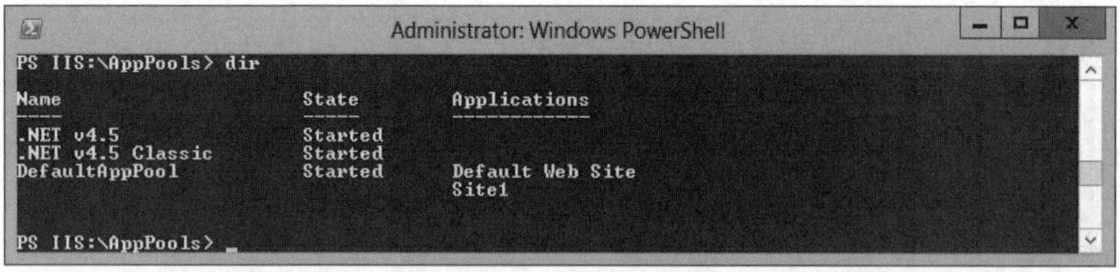

FIGURE 18-22

The application pool must already exist when used with the -ApplicationPool attribute. Unlike when you create a new website within IIS Manager, where a new application pool is created along with the website, this is not currently the case with the New-Website cmdlet. Therefore, you must create a specific application pool for the website, if you want the website to have its unique application pool.

> **NOTE** *You should link each website to a unique application pool.*

Execute the following command to create an application pool called Site1. Then modify the Site1 website configuration so that it uses it. Once complete, execute another directory list, the results of which are shown in Figure 18-23.

```
New-WebAppPool -Name Site1

Set-WebConfigurationProperty
        -PSPath 'MACHINE/WEBROOT/APPHOST'
        -Filter
"system.applicationHost/sites/site[@name='Site1']/application[@path='/']"
        -Name "applicationPool"
        -Value "Site1"
```

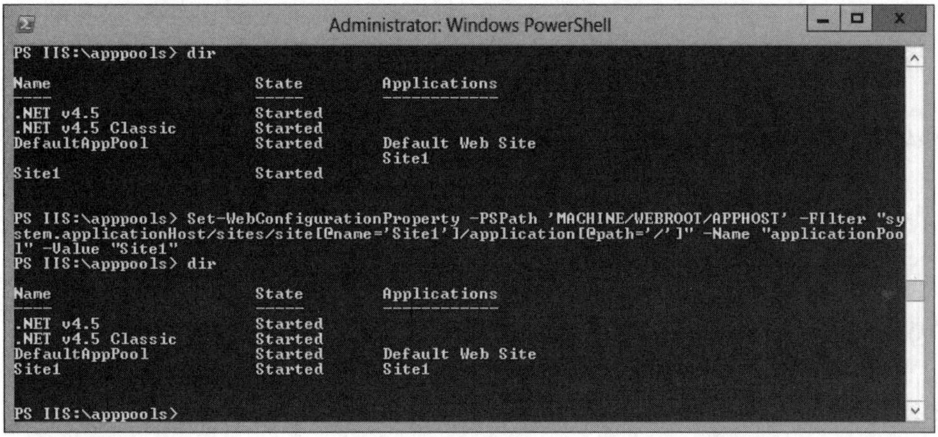

FIGURE 18-23

Notice that prior to the Set-WebConfigurationProperty command, the Site1 application was associated to the DefaultAppPool application pool; afterward, it is associated to the Site1 application pool. That is what is expected.

The syntax for the Set-WebConfigurationProperty can be found by using the get-help command. However, if you have no idea about how to build this statement, an even better tip is that you can use the Configuration Editor, which was discussed above in this chapter. Make the change to the system.applicationHost/sites/site/applicationPool attribute, close down the windows, and then click on the Generate Script link located in the Actions pane. This tool is useful when you begin using the IIS PowerShell cmdlets, but over time the syntax will become more and more intuitive.

You may be wondering about which .NET Framework Version, Identity, and Managed Pipeline mode has been associated to the new Site1 application pool by default. You can either look at the application pools "Advanced Settings..." in IIS Manager, as shown in Figure 18-24, or you can use `Get-WebConfigurationProperty` to select its attributes.

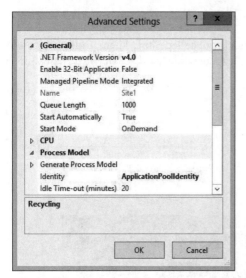

FIGURE 18-24

Up to now you have created a website and an application pool and linked the two together. Now it is time to perform some modifications to the website just created.

Modifying the Attributes of a Website

Recall Chapter 11, "Core Server," where you learned that removing or disabling unused modules resulted in less memory consumption of the worker process. In the following, you will remove the Windows authentication and Forms authentication from the Site1 website. In the real world, to minimize the memory utilization of the website, you would remove all the modules that your website doesn't need. For sake of brevity, in the example, only two are removed.

Execute the following IIS PowerShell cmdlet to remove the WindowsAuthentication module from the Site1 website:

```
Remove-WebConfigurationProperty
-PSPath 'MACHINE/WEBROOT/APPHOST/Site1'
      -Filter "system.webServer/modules"
      -Name "."
      -AtElement @{name='WindowsAuthentication'}
```

This cmdlet results in the following being written to the `web.config` file located in the physical directory of the Site1 website:

```
<configuration>
  <system.webServer>
```

```
            <modules>
              <remove name="WindowsAuthentication" />
            </modules>
          </system.webServer>
      </configuration>
```

Perform that same `Remove-WebConfigurationPorperty` command and replace `WindowsAuthentication` with `FormsAuthentication`; it too will not be loaded into memory when the website is accessed. If you wanted to remove the module from the whole server, you could use the `Remove-WebGlobalModule` cmdlet.

> **NOTE** *If you receive a "Lock violation" error, navigate to the Modules feature at the server level, click on the module you want to disable, and select Unlock from the Actions pane.*

To remove any lock violations using IIS PowerShell, use the `Remove-WebConfigurationLock` cmdlet:

```
Remove-WebConfigurationLock
        -PSPath 'MACHINE/WEBROOT/APPHOST'
        -Filter "system.webServer/modules/add[@name='FormsAuthentication']"
```

> **NOTE** *Remember that you can use the Generate Script feature within the Configuration Editor tool to help build your PowerShell syntax. The PowerShell syntax generator is new to IIS 8.0.*

At this point, you should have a good overview of creating, updating, selecting, and deleting website and IIS configuration information. Let's now move to the IIS PowerShell capabilities that provide a real-time operational view of a website and ways to change its state.

IIS Operational Activities Using PowerShell

There are many tools that are capable of monitoring the health and status of a website. IIS PowerShell provides several cmdlets that can quickly check the status of a website and application pool and then take action if required.

The first few actions an administrator takes when there are reports of a website being unavailable are to check the status of the web service and the status of the application pool. To check the status of a specific website, execute either of the following cmdlets, which render the result shown in Figure 18-25:

```
Get-WebsiteState -Name Site1
Get-WebUrl IIS:\Sites\Site1
```

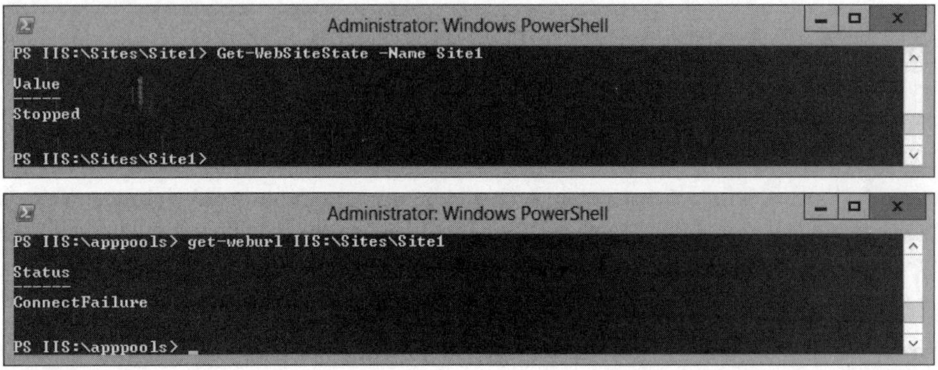

FIGURE 18-25

Notice that the value of the website state is `Stopped` and the Status of the web URL is `ConnectionFailure`. This is not good; it means that requests to the website are not being responded to. Users are likely receiving a `'cannot display the webpage'` error. To start the web service again, execute the following command, and the value returned from the `Get-WebSiteState` should be `Started`.

```
Start-WebSite -Name Site1
```

If the `Get-WebSiteState` returns `Started` to begin with, you may want next to check the state of the associated application pool. To check the state of the application pool for the given website, use `Get-WebAppPoolState`. Note that this cmdlet requires the application pool name as a parameter, so you need to find that value before running the command if you do not already know it. Do you remember how to do this? To do this, change your location to `IIS:\AppPools`, and list the contents of the directory as shown in Figure 18-23 previously. You can then see which application pools belong to which websites. Execute the following cmdlet to see the current state of the application pool:

```
Get-WebAppPoolState -Name Site1
```

If the Value is anything other than `Started`, you should execute the `Start-WebAppPool` cmdlet passing the name of the application pool in the command window. Then reexecute the `Get-WebAppPoolState` for the given application pool and confirm that it has been started.

Lastly, if the website and application pool both have a valid status, try running `Get-WebRequest`, which may get you closer to the root cause of any issue with the website. Figure 18-26 displays the results of the following command:

```
Get-WebRequest -AppPool Site1
```

The result of `Get-WebRequest` contains information about the request that the web server is currently processing. You can see the filename and the amount of time taken to perform the request. If either seems out of the ordinary, then that would be a place to dig deeper into the issues' cause.

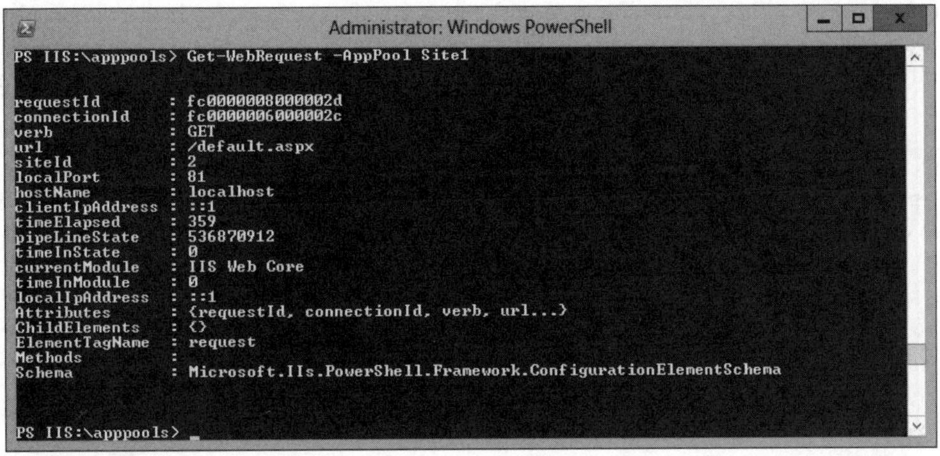

FIGURE 18-26

Backing Up and Restoring Using IIS PowerShell

Backing up before making changes can save you hours of work trying to find and/or roll back a change that caused a feature not to function as expected. Performing a backup is relatively simple and can be done quickly. Take backups before making any configuration change, no matter how small it may seem.

The IIS PowerShell module provides two cmdlets to support the backing up and restoring of a website's configuration:

➤ `Backup-WebConfiguration`

➤ `Restore-WebConfiguration`

Figure 18-27 shows the execution and result of the `Backup-WebConfiguration`.

```
Backup-WebConfiguration -Name Backup-05-31-2012
```

FIGURE 18-27

The value provided for the `-Name` attribute will be the name of the directory in which the backup is stored. You will find the new directory created within `%windir%\System32\inetsrv\backup`.

After performing the backup, you can proceed with the planned modifications. If there are problems or unexpected results and the manual rollback doesn't seem to get the website back to its original state, you can quickly use the `Restore-WebConfiguration` cmdlet. Execute the following command:

```
Restore-WebConfiguration -Name Backup-05-31-2012
```

If no error message is rendered, then the web configuration has been restored successfully and the state of the website is as it was before any modification.

19

URL Rewrite

WHAT'S IN THIS CHAPTER?

- ➤ URL Rewrite concepts
- ➤ Obtaining and installing URL Rewrite
- ➤ Getting started walk-through
- ➤ Managing URL Rewrite
- ➤ Applying URL Rewrite rules
- ➤ Rule templates
- ➤ Input variables
- ➤ Wildcards pattern matches
- ➤ Regular Expressions
- ➤ Back-references
- ➤ Setting server variables
- ➤ Special considerations
- ➤ Rewrite maps
- ➤ Common rules
- ➤ Outbound rules
- ➤ Troubleshooting URL Rewrite

WROX.COM CODE DOWNLOADS FOR THIS CHAPTER

The wrox.com code downloads for this chapter are found at www.wrox.com/remtitle
.cgi?isbn=1118388046 on the Download Code tab.

Imagine if you could take all incoming requests to your web server and manipulate them at will. Imagine changing the HTTP headers on the fly or redirecting the user to another URL, only under certain circumstances that you specify. Or, envision yourself providing a friendly URL for the sake of the search engines while using query strings in the background. URL Rewrite offers extensive power and flexibility for all this, and more.

This chapter introduces URL Rewrite and the various concepts necessary to effectively use it. URL Rewrite isn't tied directly to IIS, so updates may occur between major versions of IIS. The current version at the time of this writing is URL Rewrite 2.0.

URL REWRITE CONCEPTS

It's easy to get overwhelmed when you first start working with URL Rewrite; new rules can be difficult to create, especially when you use the Regular Expression (regex) syntax for them. However, once you understand some basic concepts, you will find that URL Rewrite is quite reasonable to learn, and soon you will be writing powerful rules with ease.

Before going further, we need to define the term "rule" as it pertains to URL Rewrite. For URL Rewrite, a rule is the main entity. For example, you can create a URL Rewrite rule to redirect your domain name from `domain.com` to `www.domain.com`. The whole set of conditions and actions is called a *URL Rewrite rule*. Here's an example of a fairly straightforward rule:

```
<rules>
  <rule name="Redirect domain.com to www" patternSyntax="Wildcard">
    <match url="*" />
    <conditions>
      <add input="{HTTP_HOST}" pattern="domain.com" />
    </conditions>
    <action type="Redirect" url="http://www.domain.com/{R:0}" />
  </rule>
</rules>
```

At a high level, URL Rewrite enables you to filter requests based on a *condition* and then take the appropriate *action*. Simply boiling URL Rewrite down to conditions and actions removes most barriers that many people have in understanding URL Rewrite.

However, that ten-thousand-foot overview misses a couple of other parts, but we'll cover them later and it will make more sense when the time comes. The other aspects of URL Rewrite rules include outbound rules, the ability to change the server headers on the way through, the rules' names, and the Match URL pattern.

Conditions

A *condition* is a way to tell if an incoming request applies to your rule, and a fundamental building block of URL Rewrite rules. Consider, for example a redirect from HTTP to HTTPS for your login page. You can create three conditions checking if the user: 1) is on the login page, 2) is on your particular site (you don't want to apply this rule for an unrelated site on the same server), and 3) is using HTTP instead of HTTPS. When all three conditions are met, you can redirect users to the HTTPS version of the same URL.

You can have any number of conditions, and you can even use the results of conditions within other conditions. These are called *back-references* and are discussed later in this chapter.

When you have multiple conditions, you can choose whether to MatchAll or MatchAny, with MatchAll being the default. As one would assume, MatchAll ensures that all conditions are met before the rule is applied. MatchAny applies the rule if any of the conditions are met.

With conditions, you can also choose whether it's a positive match (default, or negate="false") or a negative match (negate="true"). A positive match will check if something is true, such as if the domain name is a particular domain name. Using the same example, with negate set to true, it will do the opposite and it will pass if the domain name does not match a particular domain name. Both states are common in URL Rewrite rules.

Because conditions are a fundamental part of URL Rewrite rules, and offer a lot of power and flexibility, they will be a key topic throughout the remainder of this chapter.

Actions

An *action* is simply what you want to do with the page request if the conditions are met. URL Rewrite provides the following five actions:

➤ Redirect

➤ Rewrite

➤ None

➤ Custom Response

➤ Abort Request

The most common actions are *Rewrite* and *Redirect*, but all actions have their place. Additionally, Application Request Routing (ARR) introduces a sixth action, Route to Server Farm, which is a type of the rewrite action.

Redirect

A *Redirect* action is a client-side redirect that is handled by sending a response to the web browser (or search engine or other user agent), which will cause the browser to redirect to another location. Causing a redirect from one location to another is a standard part of the HTTP protocol.

It's easier to understand redirects with some examples:

➤ Redirect from a non-www site to a www site — for example, from domain.com to www.domain.com

➤ Redirect from an HTTP site to an HTTPS site — for example, from http://domain.com/logon/ to https://domain.com/logon/

➤ Redirect from an old site location to a new site location — for example, from www.domain.com/files/oldarticle.aspx to www.domain.com/articles/interesting-article/

Because the Redirect action immediately redirects the user to another URL, no further rules are processed for this request.

> **NOTE** *If your redirect happens to come back to the same server, the rules are processed again, starting from the top — but that's a fresh request and not part of the original request.*

URL Rewrite supports four types of redirects:

➤ Permanent (301)

➤ Found (302)

➤ See Other (303)

➤ Temporary (307)

The differences among these are subtle but helpful to understand.

Permanent (301)

A Permanent (301) status code is supported by HTTP 1.0 and greater and is still fully supported today. This signifies to a web browser, search engine, or other user agent that the URL has been permanently moved to a new location. The web browser or agent will usually keep track of the original and new URLs, and when it sees a request for the original URL it will go directly to the new URL. As a result, it won't stop by the server to see if there are any updated instructions. It will go directly to the new location.

A 301 status code is useful when you perform site updates and need to leave instructions for search engines and browsers that the old URL now has a new permanent home.

> **WARNING** *Testing a 301 status code — the default redirect in URL Rewrite — can become a challenge during testing, because your browser will remember the redirect and won't go back to the server for updated instructions. As a result, your changes on the server won't be noticed. During testing, you should use one of the other status codes instead.*

Found (302)

A Found (302) status code, also called Moved Temporarily, is supported by HTTP 1.0 and greater but is mostly replaced by a 307 status code now. Due to some arbitrary wording in the original HTTP specification, there is some confusion on how the 302 is to be implemented, and it doesn't always follow a consistent behavior in how it handles redirects in which the original URL uses a POST (or other non-GET) verb. A 302 status code is generally a safe choice if your original and new URLs are both GET requests; otherwise, you should use a 303 or 307 status code.

See Other (303)

This status code, introduced in HTTP 1.1, essentially makes sure that the redirect is made using a GET verb. This is normally used in situations where you POST to a page, such as a form submission, which completes the POST and redirects to another page, such as a thank you page. In this case, a 303 status code should be used for the redirect from the submission to the thank you page.

Temporary (307)

The Temporary (307) status code, also called a Temporary Redirect, was introduced in HTTP 1.1 and is mostly a replacement for a 302 status code. This redirects to the same verb (POST, GET, etc.) as the original request. So, if the original request is a POST, it will redirect using a POST again. Likewise, if the original is a GET, it will redirect using a GET request.

Rewrite

The second common action in URL Rewrite is a Rewrite. A *Rewrite* is a server-side method of rewriting server variables on the way through, often times rewriting the path before it fully arrives at the site.

It's easy to get redirects and rewrites confused. The big difference is that a redirect is a client-side change that sends an instruction to the web browser (or other web agent) to go one step further to find the correct page. A rewrite, on the other hand, is a server-side change that takes the URL from the web browser (or other web agent) and, on the server, it will change the URL before the server sees the request.

Consider an example in which a website, which has been around for years and isn't easy to change, has a URL such as www.site.com/article.aspx?id=143&type=productinfo. Search engines prefer URLs that look like actual files or folders on disk, not to mention marketing folks, who like something friendlier to add to printed material. Since it may not be easy to update the entire site to use friendly URLs, you can use URL Rewrite to front those URLs with more friendly ones. An example of a friendly URL is www.site.com/articles/productinfo/143/. Notice how this looks like a subfolder folder on disk rather than a URL with a long query string. We'll talk further in the chapter about rewrite maps, which can take this one step further and map friendly names to IDs.

A Rewrite action can take any request that arrives at the server and rewrite it to any other path. Examples include the following:

➤ Fronting a non-friendly URL with a friendly URL for search engine optimization (SEO).

➤ Having a single IIS website handle multiple sites, each with its own domain name, and all sites appearing to be dedicated sites.

➤ Rewriting server variables such as HTTP_HOST, which is the domain name.

None

Yes, you guessed correctly — the *None* action is really an action telling URL Rewrite to do nothing. Of course, the original request, which isn't related to URL Rewrite, will continue to run normally. This action does have practical uses. There are multiple common situations in which you might want to take no action.

During troubleshooting and even when a rule is running in production, you may want to watch for a certain URL pattern and say that no further action will be taken, and to stop processing more rules. Consider, for example, a health-test page used on a server farm. It's important that no other rules ever break the health-test page; otherwise, the server may be taken out of rotation prematurely. To protect the health test page, you can create a rule that watches for the URL pattern for the health-test page, has an action of None, and is set to "Stop processing of subsequent rules." This will prevent all other rules from running for that one page.

A similar situation is for troubleshooting. You can create a stopping rule above a set of rules so that the rest of the rules are ignored, enabling you to rule them out, as needed.

Another reason to use the None action is when you want to change the server variables. You can create a rule that changes the server variable but doesn't take any other actions.

Custom Response

The *Custom Response* action enables you to set any HTTP response type that you would like. For example, you can offer a 403 Forbidden response, a 405 Method Not Allowed, or a 500.101 Made Up Error. Those are just three examples; it's up to you which response you want to provide.

This action enables you to set a status code, sub-status code, reason, and error description. It's useful for providing a custom response that's not handled with any of the other actions, and it is also useful for quick testing response messages when troubleshooting.

Abort Request

The *Abort Request* action causes URL Rewrite to return a 504 - Receive Failure response and drop the connection. No useful information about the server is returned. You can use this to block specific URL patterns before they are run.

OBTAINING AND INSTALLING URL REWRITE

URL Rewrite is an add-on module and isn't natively a part of IIS. Fortunately, it's easy to obtain and install.

Microsoft's preferred method of obtaining URL Rewrite is using the Web Platform (WebPI) installer. To install URL Rewrite, open WebPI, filter for URL Rewrite, and download.

Because WebPI isn't installed by default, you may not have it on your system yet. It's still easy to obtain URL Rewrite. Visit www.iis.net in your web browser and search for URL Rewrite. It should be a top choice. At the time of this writing, URL Rewrite Module 2.0 is the latest version. You should be presented with two options: Install with Microsoft Web Platform Installer or download for x86 / x64. You can take your pick. URL Rewrite doesn't have any dependencies, so either will work. When using Microsoft Web Platform Installer, it will be able to detect your "bitness" for you. If you are installing manually, use x86 if your operating system is 32-bit, and use x64 if your operating system is 64-bit. Since Windows Server 2012 is available only in 64-bit, it's an easy discussion when installing on Windows Server.

After downloading URL Rewrite, simply follow the wizard to complete the installation. If IIS Manager was already open on your desktop before the install, close and re-open it.

GETTING STARTED WALK-THROUGH

Enough talking! Let's perform a simple walk-through so that you can see URL Rewrite in action and get a feel for how the rules really work. The following walk-through creates a Canonical Domain Name rule to redirect from `localtest.me` to `www.localtest.me`. There is also a template for this particular situation, which we'll cover later.

> **NOTE** *The domain* `localtest.me` *and all subdomains point to the loopback IP address* `127.0.0.1`. *As long as you have Internet access, you can use it for testing on your local machine, without any special DNS configuration. You can set the appropriate bindings on your IIS sites and immediately start testing. We'll use that for a number of examples in this chapter. If you don't have Internet access on your test machine, add all test URLs to your hosts file first.*

For this example, you will create the rule at the site level so that it doesn't impact anything else on the server, and use the *Wildcards* match syntax since it's straightforward for the first walk-through. You'll use IIS Manager as the tool to create the rules since it gives the best visual way to understand the rule structure.

First, let's get started by setting up a test site for this and further examples in this chapter. To set up the test site, perform the following steps:

1. To ensure that User Account Control (UAC) doesn't fight with you, you can grant your user specific Full Control permissions to the `c:\inetpub` folder. UAC ignores your membership in the Administrators group with the default NTFS permissions. This will be helpful later.

   If you are prompted by some folders because the permissions cannot be set, simply acknowledge the prompt and continue. Those folders are not applicable to URL Rewrite.

2. Create a new folder, called **localtest.me**, under the `c:\inetpub\` folder.

3. In the `localtest.me` subfolder, create a file called **default.htm** that has simply "Hello World" for the content.

4. Start IIS Manager.

5. Create a new site called **localtest.me**. (See Chapter 6, "Website Administration," for details, as necessary.)

6. Leave the IP Address as All Unassigned.

7. Set the Host name to `localtest.me`.

8. Click OK. See Figure 19-1.

9. Still in IIS Manager, select the newly created site from the Sites window (or the left-hand pane), and click Bindings.

10. Add another binding for `www.localtest.me`, with the IP address set to All Unassigned.

11. Right-click the `localtest.me` site from the left-hand pane and click Edit Permissions. From the Security tab, add the application pool identity (see Chapter 8, "Web Application Pool

Administration"), or, for quick non-production testing, ensure that the Users group has at least Read permissions.

12. Click OK to save and close the dialog.

Your test site is setup and ready for use. It will listen for `www.localtest.me` and `localtest.me`.

FIGURE 19-1

Now that you have a good working site, you can create the URL Rewrite rule, as follows:

1. Start IIS Manager.

2. Select the website that you just created.

3. Double-click the URL Rewrite icon.

4. Click Add Rule(s)....

5. In the Inbound rules section, select Blank rule and click OK.

6. Give the rule a name — for example, **Redirect localtest.me to www**.

7. For the Using property, select Wildcards from the dropdown box.

8. For the Pattern field, enter an asterisk (*), without the parentheses (see Figure 19-2).

9. Further down in the main window, expand the Conditions section and click Add....

10. In the Condition input field, enter {HTTP_HOST}.

11. In the Pattern field, enter **localtest.me,** and then click OK. You should see the new condition appear, as shown in Figure 19-3.

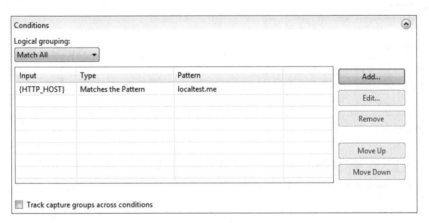

FIGURE 19-2

FIGURE 19-3

12. Back in the main pane, scroll down to the Actions section and select Redirect for the Action type.

13. For the Redirect URL field, enter **http://www.localtest.me/{R:0}.** The {R:0} is called a *back-reference* and will be discussed later in this chapter.

14. When testing, it's recommended to set the Redirect type to Temporary (307) so that your tests aren't cached in the browser, which can make testing difficult. Set the redirect type to Temporary (307). Figure 19-4 shows what the completed Action section should look like.

15. Click Apply in the Actions pane.

Now that the rule is created, it's easy to test. The first test is to open your favorite web browser, visit `http://localtest.me`, and ensure that it redirects to `http://www.localtest.com`.

The configuration that is generated, which we'll discuss later, should look like this:

```
<rule name="Redirect localtest.me to www" patternSyntax="Wildcard"
stopProcessing="true">
  <match url="*" />
  <conditions>
    <add input="{HTTP_HOST}" pattern="localtest.me" />
  </conditions>
  <action type="Redirect" url="http://www.localtest.me/{R:0}"
redirectType="Temporary" />
</rule>
```

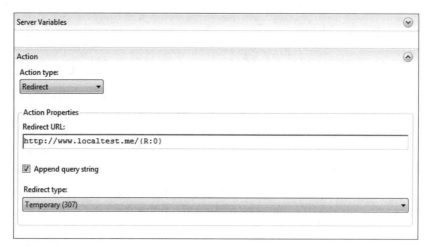

FIGURE 19-4

The equivalent rule using the Regular Expressions syntax will look like this:

```
<rule name="Redirect localtest.me to www-regex" stopProcessing="true">
  <match url=".*" />
  <conditions>
    <add input="{HTTP_HOST}" pattern="^localtest\.me$" />
  </conditions>
  <action type="Redirect" url="http://www.localtest.me/{R:0}"
redirectType="Temporary" />
</rule>
```

It is also helpful to confirm that the full path and query string come through the redirect. The `{R:0}` in the action and the Append query string checkbox in the rule take care of that. We'll cover the `{R:0}` in the "Back-References" section later in this chapter. To test that the full URL works, visit the following in a web browser: `http://localtest.me/default.htm?id=123`. This should redirect to `http://www.localtest.me/default.htm?id=123`, exactly like the original URL but with the www prefix added.

> **GETTING AROUND CACHING**
>
> One trick that you may find useful is to use the InPrivate (Internet Explorer) or
> Incognito (Chrome) feature of your web browser so that you can be sure that noth-
> ing is cached. It's common for redirect rules and your browser cache to fight with
> you, but when you start an InPrivate session, caching is (usually) forgotten.
>
> Another trick is to add a unique query string to the end of the URL, such as
> `?id=somethingnew123`.

MANAGING URL REWRITE

As this book has covered in other chapters, there is more than one way to manage IIS, and URL
Rewrite is no exception.

It's important to understand the different methods so that you can follow along in this chapter and
so that you have flexibility in your day-to-day management of URL Rewrite rules. URL Rewrite
can be managed through all of the regular methods, including IIS Manager, Configuration Editor,
AppCmd, PowerShell, a text editor, and all the Application Programming Interface (API) methods.
Let's take a look at the three most common.

Using IIS Manager

IIS Manager fully supports URL Rewrite rules, and unless you work with URL Rewrite on a daily
basis so that you can memorize the full syntax, you may find that it's easiest to do everything
through IIS Manager.

However, if you want to communicate a rule to someone else — whether you're asking for help or helping someone else — it's often useful to show the XML configuration, as discussed in the next section. So,
you may find that you will use a combination of IIS Manager plus a text editor to manage the rules.

You will likely find that it's easy to read XML-based rules and re-create them in IIS Manager.
Throughout this chapter there will be XML examples that don't explain all the IIS Manager steps,
but you will probably find that you can create them in IIS Manager quite easily.

Using a Text Editor

If you like to work directly with the configuration through a text editor, or if you want to share
your rules with someone else, you may prefer to use a text editor. The advantage is that you have
direct insight into the changes and can easily duplicate them, back them up, or copy rules between
machines. Be careful, however, because mistakes in the XML syntax can break your site.

Many examples in this chapter will show the XML configuration method since it's the most concise
syntax. The "Applying URL Rewrite Rules" section discusses the XML configuration structure and
the file locations on disk where the configuration is stored.

Using APIs

You can manage URL Rewrite by using any of the APIs. Since IIS 8 is schema-backed, everything that you want to do is fully supported from all APIs. This chapter will not show examples, as doing so could fill a whole book on its own. However, a good starting place is to use Configuration Editor to create a new rule, and to use the Generate Script command to get a starting point for generating sample code to be used from a .NET program by referring to `Microsoft.Web.Administration`, or from a script using JavaScript, AppCmd, or PowerShell. Additionally, Chapter 18 covers programmatic configuration and management.

APPLYING URL REWRITE RULES

URL Rewrite rules can be applied at different levels. Understanding these levels will help you know where to create the rules.

Rules are processed starting with the server level on down to the site and subfolders. URL Rewrite itself is processed very early in the IIS pipeline, before most IIS-related functionality. However, it runs after the site binding, so all page requests must be bound to a website, even if you use URL Rewrite. If the rule redirects back to the same server, you will need a binding for both URLs.

For global rules (`<globalRules />`), URL Rewrite runs during the `PreBeginRequest` event in the IIS pipeline, whereas for other rules (`<rules />`), URL Rewrite runs in the `BeginRequest` event in the IIS pipeline. The following shows the flow of the request as it pertains to URL Rewrite:

> Incoming request ⇨ Site binding ⇨ If the request arrives using SSL, the packet is decrypted ⇨ URL Rewrite runs ⇨ Site is processed

Next, let's take a look at the different levels where rules can be applied.

Global Level — <globalRules>

Global rules apply to all traffic, regardless of the site, although you can apply conditions to rules so that they are filtered to just certain traffic.

Global rules are set in `%windir%\System32\inetsrv\config\applicationHost.config` in the following section:

```
<configuration>
 <system.webServer>
  <rewrite>
   <globalRules>
    <rule />
   </globalRules>
   <outboundRules>
    <rule />
   </outboundRules>
  </rewrite>
 </system.webServer>
</configuration>
```

In IIS Manager, you can set global rules at the server level by selecting the server on the left-hand side and double-clicking on the URL Rewrite icon.

Rules set at this level are not displayed in IIS Manager at the site level and are therefore not able to be edited at the site level. They are available only at the server level.

Global Level — <rules>

A mostly undocumented location exists that also supports inbound URL Rewrite rules. Global rules and site rules have different purposes. It's possible to create site-level rules but save them at the top level so that they apply to all sites.

Top-level site rules can be overwritten at the site level by site administrators. These rules are useful if you want to create a default rule but allow site administrators to disable or edit it.

IIS Manager does not support creating or editing these rules. You must manage them with one of the other configuration editing options. This applies only to inbound rules. Outbound rules can only be set in one place at the global level and are supported from IIS Manager.

These rules are also set in `%windir%\System32\inetsrv\config\applicationHost.config` in the following section:

```
<configuration>
  <system.webServer>
    <rewrite>
      <rules>
        <rule />
      </rules>
    </rewrite>
  </system.webServer>
</configuration>
```

Site Level — applicationHost.config

Rules can be applied to specific sites but set in `%windir%\System32\inetsrv\config\applicationHost.config`. Setting rules at this level prevents AppDomain recycles as you're editing them, and they aren't saved to the site's `web.config` file, so they won't be overwritten mistakenly. They are good for permanent or rarely edited rules at the site level.

These rules apply only to the site for which they are defined, so you do not need to create a condition to filter to a particular site, as you may do for global rules. However, all other conditions still apply, especially if you have multiple domain names and don't want the rule to apply to all the domain names for that site.

Like top-level site rules, IIS Manager does not support creating or editing these rules. You must manage them with one of the other configuration editing options.

These rules are set within a `location` tag in `applicationHost.config` in the following section:

```
<configuration>
 <location path="{site or app name}">
  <system.webServer>
   <rewrite>
    <rules>
     <rule />
    </rules>
```

```
        <outboundRules>
          <rule />
        </outboundRules>
      </rewrite>
    </system.webServer>
  </location>
</configuration>
```

Site Level — web.config

Site-level URL Rewrite rules are applied to the site's `web.config` file and only impact the site. They are similar to site-level `applicationHost.config` rules, except that they are saved in the `web.config` file at the root of the website.

IIS Manager will save site-level rules to this location. Remember that changes made to `web.config`, even through IIS Manager, will "touch" the `web.config` file, causing an AppDomain recycle. This may have an impact on your production website.

The rules are set in your site's `web.config` file in the following section:

```
<configuration>
 <system.webServer>
  <rewrite>
   <rules>
    <rule />
   </rules>
   <outboundRules>
     <rule />
   </outboundRules>
  </rewrite>
 </system.webServer>
</configuration>
```

You can create and manage these rules from IIS Manager by navigating to the website and starting the URL Rewrite tool from the URL Rewrite icon.

Subfolder Level — web.config

It is possible to apply rules at the subfolder level, too. This can be accomplished either through a `location` tag in the site's `web.config` file or in a `web.config` file in the subfolder. The subfolder does not need to be marked as an application to process URL Rewrite rules.

As one would assume, rules applied at the subfolder level apply only to traffic that arrives to that subfolder.

The configuration structure is the same as the site-level `web.config` or the site-level `applicationHost.config` that uses a `location` tag.

RULE TEMPLATES

URL Rewrite comes with a number of templates for common rules. These templates can be used to generate somewhat customized rules for you. Don't worry if some of the patterns or settings in the generated rules seem difficult to understand. The rules will make more sense as we progress through the chapter.

All templates share some common functionality, so rather than repeating them for each rule below, let's look at a mini-walk-through on how to start using a template:

1. In IIS Manager, navigate to the URL Rewrite tool at the site, server, or folder level by double-clicking on the URL Rewrite icon.

2. Click Add Rules(s)... from the Actions pane.

3. Select the appropriate template (see Figure 19-5) and click OK.

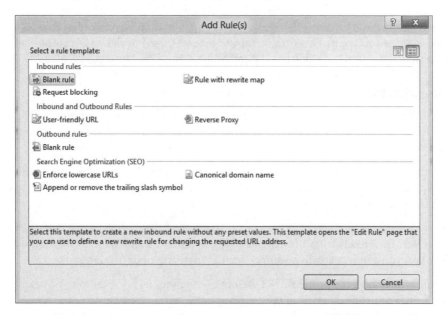

FIGURE 19-5

> **NOTE** *The current version of URL Rewrite has three rules that don't exist at the server level. So, if you don't see the rule, it may be because you're looking at the server level instead of the site level. All URL Rewrite templates are available at the site or subfolder level.*

It's from this point that we will pick up the rules below. The templates are broken into four categories:

➤ Inbound rules

➤ Inbound and Outbound rules

➤ Outbound rules

➤ Search Engine Optimization (SEO)

Inbound Rule Templates

These three templates will process incoming traffic on the way through. All three templates exist at the server, site, and subfolder level.

Blank Rule

As one would assume, the "Blank rule" template sets up a fresh, blank rule that enables you to create the rule however you want. This is the template that was used in the walk-through above, and the template that you will most likely use if none of the other templates work for you.

Rule with Rewrite Map

The "Rule with rewrite map" template is great for handling a large number of unique URLs that don't follow a fixed pattern. It enables you to create a rewrite map — a list of key/value pairs — and ties it to a rewrite or a redirect rule.

Before creating a rule using this template, you must create a rewrite map. You can do that from the URL Rewrite main screen in the Actions pane by selecting View Rewrite Maps. We'll look at that in more depth later in this chapter.

After creating a rewrite map, you can create a rule from the "Rule with rewrite map" template. This enables you to create a redirect or a rewrite rule. If you haven't decided on all the values for the rewrite map yet, you can just create an empty rewrite map and update it later.

A rewrite rule will change the original URL before the site sees it. For example, you can have an original URL that someone enters into the browser (e.g., `/article/how-to-use-urlrewrite/`) and URL Rewrite will rewrite it on the fly (e.g., `/article.aspx?id=123`). However, a rewrite cannot rewrite between different application pools. The original request and the page that handles the rewritten request must be in the same application pool.

A redirect rule is similar, except that it causes a client-side redirect. The rewrite map's original value should be a relative URL, such as `/productinfo/`. The new value can be a relative URL, such as `/article.aspx?id=123`, which will redirect to the same domain, or an absolute URL, such as `http://www.domain01.com/article.aspx?id=123`.

The "Rule with rewrite map" template is particularly useful when you do a site redesign and change the paths to your files. This is a great way to map old URLs to new URLs. It's also useful for mapping search engine-friendly URLs to less search engine-friendly URLs, like in the example above.

Request Blocking

The "Request blocking" template gives a number of options for blocking visitors based on different criteria.

First, you must choose the input variable on which to filter. The choices are: URL Path, User-agent Header (for search engine spiders or certain types of browsers or devices), IP Address, Query String, Referrer (spelled HTTP_REFERER in this context), and Host Header.

> **NOTE** *It's interesting that the word "Referer" in HTTP headers is a misspelling that is formally part of the HTTP/1.0 RFC 1945. In 1996, when the RFC was submitted, the word "referrer" was not commonly used, and neither the correct nor incorrect spelling was in the Unix spell checker that was used to check the RFC document. The misspelling has remained part of HTTP ever since.*

You can choose Wildcards or Regular Expressions for the using syntax type and whether to match on a positive match (Matches the Pattern) or a negative match (Does Not Match the Pattern).

Finally, you can choose which HTTP status code to return. The choices are: 401 (Unauthorized), 403 (Forbidden), 404 (Not Found), or Abort Request (504 - Receive Failure).

As with any of the templates, you can further customize the generated rule after it has been created.

Inbound and Outbound Rules Templates

There are two templates that enable you to create both inbound and outbound rules: User-friendly URL and Reverse Proxy. These templates work well together to offer a complete set of functionality.

User-Friendly URL

The User-friendly URL template is a fairly common template that enables you to create new friendly URLs to front less friendly URLs. The following table shows some examples:

OLD URL	NEW URL
/article.aspx?id=55	/article/55/
/store.aspx?n=5&i=5323	/shop/item/5323/5/
/about_us.aspx	/about_us/

The User-friendly URL template is also helpful if you need a kick-start in creating other rules. You can start with this template to see the rule that is generated for you, and then tweak the rule, as needed.

For this template, you must first enter a pattern for your existing URL. The protocol and host part (http://domain.com) is optional. It will intelligently make some recommendations for you. One thing to be careful of is that you don't have a friendly URL that is so vague that it catches other, unrelated URLs. For example, a URL pattern of `^([^/]+)/?$` will catch any URL with a pattern like `/{something}/`. This means that it can catch a URL like `/aboutus/` or `/members/`, which may or may not be your intention.

The main inbound rule that is generated from this template handles the friendly URL only if someone visits it directly, but it doesn't fix any of the original URLs within the HTML of the page. That's where the check box options come into play.

There are three ways to handle all the old URLs in your site. One way is to update your entire site's links and code so that it uses the new, friendly pattern. That requires access to your code base, which may not always be possible for older legacy sites or third-party sites. The second method is to change the URLs within the HTML of the page each and every time the page is rendered. This is handled with an outbound rule. The third way is to watch for any rules that were missed by the previous two options and perform a client-side redirect back to the friendly URL. Usually it takes time to update all the URLs, so a combination of all three options is the best approach.

Whether you update your code is up to you, of course; URL Rewrite can't help with that. However, the two check box options in this template wizard can help with the other ways to handle new URLs. The two options are:

➤ **"Create corresponding redirect rule"** — Selecting this check box will cause an inbound rule to be created that will catch everything that you didn't handle otherwise and cause a client-side redirect to the friendly URL. Basically, it's for all the leftovers and/or before you handle the other URLs through other methods.

➤ **"Create corresponding outbound rewrite rule"** — Selecting this check box will cause an outbound rule to be created that will parse your webpage just before it's displayed to your site visitors and watch for the old pattern in any `a`, `form`, or `img` tags; if it finds the old URL pattern, it will update to the new pattern. As you can guess, this has some performance overhead because it needs to parse the entire page each time, but for many situations the performance overhead is negligible.

The User-friendly URL template is a powerful tool to clean up your URL and to put you in the good books for your marketing team and search engines.

Reverse Proxy

The Reverse Proxy template is available after URL Rewrite is installed, but it will not work unless Application Request Routing (ARR) is also installed. See Chapter 17, "IIS Scalability II: Load Balancing and ARR," for details about ARR.

The Reverse Proxy template is a powerful feature that functions as a proxy between the original request and a remote site. For example, you can have a request come into one server but actually serve up a page from another server. This is commonly useful when you have a server in your DMZ that is available on the Internet and you want to serve up a page or site from an internal server. Your web server can proxy between the user on the Internet and your internal server.

If you use the full ARR functionality, you will have a fully featured reverse proxy with load balancing, health monitoring, caching, and other powerful features. However, if you want just the simple proxy feature in URL Rewrite, you can perform reverse proxy requests to remote resources without needing to set up server farms and the like. That's where this template comes in.

The Reverse Proxy template enables you to specify the IP or domain name of the remote server. It can be an internal IP on your network, a public URL, or any resource that your web server has access to, even if the web visitor doesn't have direct access to it.

You can also choose whether to used SSL offloading. When checked (the default), SSL requests will be decrypted on the server and the proxied request to the remote server will always be over HTTP, regardless of the original protocol. Be careful, however, because if the request is not on a trusted network, it's critical for your users and for your trustworthiness to keep the request encrypted all the way to the final resource, unless you have a trusted network between your proxy and the final site. If you uncheck this feature, the request will be decrypted on the server, enabling you to make URL Rewrite decisions with the unencrypted request, and then it will be decrypted again and use SSL for the request to the remote server.

When you use the Reverse Proxy template and select "Rewrite the domain names of the links in HTTP responses," an outbound rule will be created for you that will rewrite all URLs in the a, form, or img tags in the page HTML. This generally would be used to replace the domain name of the remote resource with your domain name.

Note that outbound rules will clash with page compression because URL Rewrite can't look through compressed page to be able to make any changes; therefore, if the remote resource uses compression, URL Rewrite will throw an error. One possible trick is to update the HTTP_ACCEPT_ENCODING server variable in your inbound rule to have a value of "none." This should cause the remote resource to not compress the request, enabling you to use outbound rules.

The XML configuration works by using a subtle difference in how the action URL is used. The generated rule will look something like this:

```
<rule name="ReverseProxyInboundRule1" stopProcessing="true">
    <match url="(.*)" />
    <action type="Rewrite" url="http://server05/{R:1}" />
</rule>
```

URL Rewrite can tell what is a Reverse Proxy rule because it is a "rewrite" that starts with the protocol (http or https).

Outbound Rules Template

There is only one outbound template: a "Blank rule" template that enables you to create any type of outbound rule. This is covered in depth later in the chapter.

Search Engine Optimization Templates

The URL Rewrite development team was thoughtful enough to include some SEO tools for us. The SEO templates are unique in that the generated rules are automatically placed at the top of the list of rules, while all other generated rules are placed at the bottom.

Enforce Lowercase URLs

The Enforce Lowercase URLs template is available at the server and site level. When the rule is generated, it will cause a client-side redirect if there is an uppercase letter in the path. The purpose of the rule is primarily so that search engines see a single URL regardless of the casing. If the search engines consider different casing as different instances, the page rank can be split among multiple pages.

Note that the domain name part of the URL (e.g., `www.localtest.me`) is already handled by the HTTP protocol and the web browser, and it is assumed that it will already be lowercase. Try it out in your web browser now. Visit `http://www.BiNg.com`. It will appear to be a client-side redirect, but it's a browser function and not a function of IIS. All major browsers take care of that for you.

The query string part (e.g., `?id=5`) is also not handled by this rule.

What the generated rule does take care of is the path (e.g., `/articles/articlepage.aspx`). If there is an uppercase letter anywhere in the path, URL Rewrite will perform a redirect back to the same URL, while changing the URL to become all lowercase.

The Enforce Lowercase URLs template is easy to use since there aren't any options. Simply select the template and click Yes when the template wizard asks for your confirmation. A new rule with a standard default name will be created for you.

Canonical Domain Name

A rule generated from this template will redirect all traffic from one domain name to the primary domain name, usually used for SEO reasons to add or remove the www on a domain name so that traffic isn't split between multiple domain names.

This template is available only at the site or subfolder level; it is not available at the global level.

Creating a Canonical Domain Name rule from the template is similar to what we covered in the walk-through previously in this chapter. The template wizard simply asks what your primary domain name will be by providing you with a list of domain names in the site's binding list, or by enabling you to enter your own.

After you complete the short template wizard, the generated rule will be placed in your site and cause all traffic that doesn't match your primary domain name to redirect to that domain name.

Append or Remove the Trailing Slash Symbol

The third SEO template will generate a rule that either appends or removes trailing slashes on URLs that aren't specifically mapped to the file or directory structure. This is helpful with your page rankings because some search engines will see two different pages even if they only differ by a slash at the end. Ensuring that both with and without a slash funnel into a single URL pattern can prevent you from splitting your rankings in the search engines.

The template wizard is straightforward. Simply choose whether you want to add or remove the trailing slash, and a rule will be created that will create a Permanent (301) redirect when the slash is the opposite of what you prefer.

INPUT VARIABLES

When URL Rewrite processes an incoming request, a lot of information is available in the form of input variables, made up of request headers and server variables. They include information such as the domain name, URL, and client's IP address. This information is used for the rule conditions to determine which requests your rule applies to, and it can also be used in the rule action paths.

Some examples of the more common input variables include:

➤ {HTTP_HOST}

➤ {SERVER_ADDR}

➤ {REMOTE_ADDR}

➤ {URL}

➤ {QUERY_STRING}

➤ {HTTPS}

➤ {REQUEST_URI}

A useful trick is to create a simple page that generates all the server variables with their values. Simply create a page within your website called servervariables.aspx (or whatever you want to call it) and place the following in it:

```
<%
For Each serverVar As String in Request.ServerVariables
    Response.Write(serverVar & " " & Request(serverVar) & "<br />")
Next
%>
```

If you prefer C#, you can use the following instead:

```
<% @ Page Language="C#" %>
<%
foreach (string serverVar in Request.ServerVariables)
{
    Response.Write(serverVar + " " + Request[serverVar] + "<br>");
}
%>
```

Now when you call the page in your web browser, it will display a list of most of the server variables and their values. One important distinction between this script and URL Rewrite is that URL Rewrite runs before the default document, whereas this script runs after it. Therefore, if you call a default document implicitly, these variables may not match. Some other variables, such as APP_POOL_ID, are not available in URL Rewrite.

To see a nearly complete reference of the standard variables available to URL Rewrite, create a blank rule and add a condition. For the Condition input field, start with the { character. You'll get a dropdown list of all system input variables available to you. Even this list misses some variables, such as{CACHE_URL}, which is mentioned later, and the application warm-up variables, which are not discussed in this chapter.

The most commonly used input variables pertain to the URL, so let's take a look at the URL parts. Then we'll examine some of the other common input variables.

Common URL Parts

Consider the following URL example:

```
https://localtest.me:80/events/article.aspx?id=123
```

This complete URL is made up of five parts that correspond to different input variables, as shown in Figure 19-6 and discussed below.

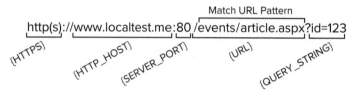

FIGURE 19-6

Protocol

First, the `https://` or `http://` protocol can be determined with the {HTTPS} input variable, which has a value of on or off. You can see if an incoming request is a secure request by checking for {HTTPS} = on or {HTTPS} = off.

Domain Name

The domain name part (localtest.me) is reflected in the {HTTP_HOST} input variable. This is the exact domain name without the protocol or other parts of the URL.

Port

The port isn't always present in the URL. When it's not present, it defaults to 80 for HTTP and 443 for HTTPS. Regardless of whether it's set explicitly or implicitly in the URL, it is available as {SERVER_PORT}. In the example above, it will have a value of 80.

URL and Match URL Pattern

The next part of the URL goes by multiple names and has multiple ways to call it. The {URL} input variable is useful because it will retain the URL exactly, except that the beginning slash is always included. In the preceding example, it will be /events/article.aspx.

An alternative to {URL} is the Pattern in the Match Rule section of IIS Manager, or the `<match url="" />` element when seen in a text configuration. This is an important, dedicated part of the URL Rewrite rules, and it always has the beginning slash removed. It can also be called in back-references, which are discussed later in the chapter. Throughout this chapter, it's called the *Match URL pattern*. In the preceding example, it will be events/article.aspx.

Query String

The {QUERY_STRING} input variable is everything after the question mark (?). In the example above, it is id=123.

Full URL and Query String

In addition to the five parts just mentioned, you can use the {REQUEST_URI} variable, which includes the entire URL path, including the query string. In the example above, it is /events/article .aspx?id=123.

Additional Input Variables

In addition to the URL parts, there are plenty of other input variables, ranging from the client IP, server IP, additional options for the URL parts, and more. You also can set your own custom server variables.

The following table is not exhaustive, but it gives a good idea of common input variables that you can use. A useful list from Microsoft is available at http://msdn.microsoft.com/en-us/ library/ms524602.aspx. Although it's an article from IIS 6, it is still applicable today.

For the following table, refer to the following example URL. For the variables that aren't URL-related, we'll make up some sample data.

    http://localtest.me/sub/vars.aspx/postpath/321?id=123

Note the /postpath/ part of the URL. That's used most commonly for CGI paths, but otherwise is not used frequently. However, including it in the example shows how some of the different URL-related input variables handle it differently.

INPUT VARIABLE	SAMPLE DATA
{HTTPS}	off
{HTTP_HOST}	localtest.me
{SERVER_PORT}	80
{URL}	/sub/vars.aspx
"Match URL Pattern"	sub/vars.aspx/postpath/321
{QUERY_STRING}	id=123
{REQUEST_URI}	/sub/vars.aspx/postpath/321?id=123
{SERVER_PORT_ SECURE}	0
{REQUEST_METHOD}	GET
{SERVER_ADDR}	192.168.1.20 (public website's IP)

continues

(continued)

INPUT VARIABLE	SAMPLE DATA
{REMOTE_ADDR}	`10.0.0.20` (client's IP)
{HTTP_REFERER}	Referrer URL, such as `www.bing.com`
{REQUEST_FILENAME}	`c:\inetpub\localtest.me`
{SERVER_ADDR}	`127.0.0.1`
{UNENCODED_URL}	Usually the same as `REQUEST_URI` but can differ for different character encoding or some unique paths. It's the URL before IIS treatments. One way to see the difference is to use a tool such as Fiddler and visit `http://localtest.me/sub/../sub/`. The `UNENCODED_URL` variable contains the `../sub`, whereas `REQUEST_URI` has the cleaned-up version. Since most browsers also clean it up, you can't easily test this in a web browser. The usage is limited for URL Rewrite but more common for ISAPI extensions or some PHP applications.
{CACHE_URL}	`http://localtest.me:80/sub/vars.aspx/postpath/321?id=123`
{PATH_INFO}	`/sub/vars.aspx/postpath/321`
{CERT_*}	Many certificate-related fields for SSL
{HTTP_ACCEPT_LANGUAGE}	`en-US,en;q=0.8`
{HTTP_COOKIE}	Cookies from the browser
{REMOTE_USER}	`Server01\User01`
{AUTH_TYPE}	Negotiate (blank for Anonymous)
{HTTP_USER_AGENT}	Mozilla/5.0 ...

Again, this is by no means an exhaustive list. See the discussion above for ways to see other options. This is a good reference for the frequently used server variables and the format of the data.

WILDCARDS PATTERN MATCHES

The default pattern match is ECMAScript, which is a Perl-compatible syntax for regex. Most examples in this chapter are based on Regular Expressions rather than Wildcards because of the high level of flexibility. However, two other pattern syntaxes, Wildcards and Exact Match, are also good options.

Exact Match is straightforward and doesn't need any further explanation. It means just what its name implies.

Wildcards, on the other hand, do require further mention. There are two reasons why you might consider Wildcards pattern matches. First, they are easy to learn and figure out. Second, they perform faster than Regular Expressions. So, for very high-performance situations you can use the Wildcards pattern match rather than Regular Expressions to get a bit of extra performance out of the server. See the Note in the next section for further information about performance.

There is just one special character to keep track of for Wildcards pattern matches. The * (asterisk) character is a wildcard match of zero or more characters of any type. It is also used for back-references, as discussed later in this chapter.

> **WARNING** *Although the* ? *is documented in the URL Rewrite documentation, it is not a supported special character. The documentation about the* ? *character is incorrect. See the following forum thread in which one of the IIS product team members provides the story on the* ? *character:* `http://forums.iis .net/t/1167455.aspx`.

The other difference between Wildcards and Regular Expressions is that the pattern for the Wildcards syntax assumes the entire string. A pattern match of {`HTTP_HOST`} = "`domain.com`" will not match `www.domain.com` since there is no * at the beginning of the pattern. This is different from Regular Expressions, which have their own method of specifying the beginning and ending of a string, as discussed below.

One useful trick if you want to get all third-level domains (e.g., `cityname.domain.com`) but not include just a second-level domain (e.g., `domain.com`) is make sure to include the dot (.) in the pattern match. For example, *.`domain.com` will not match for a domain name of `domain.com` because of the dot difference.

REGULAR EXPRESSIONS

Even though the walk-through earlier in this chapter used Wildcards in the example, the Regular Expressions (regex) offers the greatest degree of power and flexibility. Wildcards pattern syntax quickly becomes limiting when you start creating useful rules. This is where regex takes over. Regex is the default syntax, or it can be specified explicitly in the rule with a pattern syntax of ECMAScript.

> **NOTE** *Throughout this chapter, the term* Regular Expressions *is used when referring to the URL Rewrite syntax choice. However, the actual syntax is lovingly referred to as* regex *by most heavy users of regular expressions. When discussing regular expressions in general, we'll use the term* regex*, although both can be used interchangeably.*

Regex offers a powerful way to match strings with certain patterns to see if they match — and if they do, to highlight useful information into what is called a *back-reference* to be used later.

However, when IT people hear the term "regular expressions" (or "regex"), it's not uncommon for their face to pale and their knees to buckle. Regex is one of the most concise, cryptic, and difficult to understand syntaxes that an IT pro has to work with. Unless you've worked with it enough to get a good feel for it, it can be overwhelming. There is nothing intuitive about regex.

> **NOTE** *Regular Expressions take more computing power than Wildcards or static values, so if you are really driving for high end performance, you may want to use Wildcards for the simpler rules and use Regular Expressions for the rest. Even though Regular Expressions do take more computing power, you can have hundreds of rules on a busy server with ease. In the vast majority of cases, the performance penalty is negligible. Don't be scared to use Regular Expressions as the default and then review them only if you have an extreme situation that demands performance optimizations.*

It doesn't have to be that way. Let's see if we bring regex down to earth and make it straightforward and easy to understand the key things needed to work with URL Rewrite.

To start, let's use two examples to get a general feel of things. Consider this pattern:

```
<conditions>
    <add input="{HTTP_HOST}" pattern="^domain.*(com|net)$" />
</conditions>
```

This will check the value of `HTTP_HOST` (the domain name) and see if it matches the pattern of `^domain\.(com|net)$`. Later we'll look at what the different parts of the pattern mean, but basically this rule will see if the domain name is exactly `domain.com` or `domain.net`.

```
<conditions>
    <add input="{QUERY_STRING}" pattern="id=(\d+)" />
</conditions>
```

This condition will check the query string for `id=` at least one, but possibly more, number digits (0-9).

As you can see, regex is about creating pattern strings that need to match an input value to see if it matches. It is much more concise than using `if/else`-type statements in different programming languages like C#. Instead, a single pattern can match complex queries within a single URL Rewrite condition.

You may have found that it almost starts to make sense just from looking at those examples, but continue reading. The next section discusses 10 things you need to know about regex to be able to create useful and powerful URL Rewrite rules.

10 Things You Need to Know about Regex

Regex is made up of many special characters. You might not remember all these patterns the first time, but if you come back and reference them, you'll soon become proficient with them.

^ to Start and $ to End

If you don't specify the beginning and ending of a string, it can consider a match successful even if you didn't expect it. To ensure that your match is an exact match, you must start it with a ^ (caret) character, which signifies the beginning of the pattern, and you must end with a $ (dollar sign) character, which signifies the end of the pattern. Note that ^ has a different meaning if it's in the middle of the pattern.

Consider this example:

```
<conditions>
    <add input="{HTTP_HOST}" pattern="localtest.me" />
</conditions>
```

As a regex pattern, it does not say that the pattern needs to start with `localtest.me`; it just says that it has to exist somewhere in the matching string. So, if the domain name is `www.localtest.me` or `charlotte.localtest.me` or just `localtest.me`, it will match the pattern. The back-reference will be different, but we'll cover that a little later.

To ensure that you get exactly `localtest.me` (well, almost exactly — more on that in the next section), you can instead use a pattern of `^localtest.me$`.

By learning what ^ and $ mean, you can now create patterns of "starts with," "ends with," "contains," and "is exactly."

To check for something that starts with www, you can match with a pattern of `^www`. Notice that the ^ at the beginning specifies that the beginning of the string must have www, but after the www it doesn't matter what comes next.

"Ends with" can be specified in the example "com$". That will get anything that ends with "com."

"Contains" wouldn't have either special character, and "is exactly" would have both.

\ to Escape Special Characters

Because regex is made up of many specific characters, there needs to be a way to say when you want to use the real value of a specific character. Consider, for example, the $ character. If you want to check for $ in a query string, you could check for `id=\$5`, which would match `id=$5`. If you forgot to use the \ in the pattern, it would prematurely specify the end of the pattern and wouldn't work correctly. By using `\$`, it means to actually use $.

The special characters that need to be escaped are as follows:

```
[ \ ^ $ . | ? * + ( )
```

The most common special character for URL Rewrite rules is the . (dot). It's most commonly used because it's a special character, but also because it's used in all FQDNs. Thus, you should use a \. instead of just the . character by itself.

With the two rules you've learned so far, you can precisely match the domain name `localtest.me` with the following pattern:

```
<conditions>
    <add input="{HTTP_HOST}" pattern="^localtest\.me$" />
</conditions>
```

. for Any Single Character (but not \r or \n)

The next special character to consider is the . (dot), which signifies a single wildcard character.

Interestingly, if you don't escape the dot, it could still match your pattern, but you won't be able to trust it for sure.

Consider a pattern of `^localtest.me$` for `{HTTP_HOST}`. If your domain name is `localtest.me`, it will pass because what it is really checking for is `localtest{any character}me`. So, `localtest4me` will also work. Because `localtest4me` isn't a valid domain name, you're safe in this situation.

However, it's recommended to get in the habit of always escaping your dot so that you don't overlook a situation where you need a literal dot. Consider the situation where you are checking the IP address with `{SERVER_ADDR}` = `"10.1.1.1"`. If you are sloppy and do not enter the ^ or $, or escape the dots, this could match more than just `10.1.1.1`. That same pattern will also match IPs such as `110.1.1.1`, `210.1.1.1`, `10.111.12.34`, and `110.111.111.111` — the options are nearly endless. So, the moral of the story is to escape the dot by using \. whenever you expect a literal dot.

The dot applies to everything except for the \r or \n special instructions, which are used for a carriage return (CR) and a line feed (LF), respectively. You don't tend to see those with web requests anyway.

* to Repeat 0 to infinity; + to repeat 1 to infinity

The * (asterisk) after another character or section means that you want the possibility to exist any number of times, including zero times.

The + (plus sign) has a slight but important difference. When it is used after another character or section, it means that you want the possibility to exist any number of times, but at least once.

Let's look at an example to understand these characters well. Two inputs commonly used for the Match URL pattern are the .* and .+ combinations. Remember that the dot means any single character. Therefore, the .* means that you would want zero or any number of characters. Or, to put it another way, you don't care what the URL is, even if it's blank.

The .+ combination, on the other hand, means that you want at least one character, but you don't care what it is. To put it another way, you want at least something.

To summarize:

> ➤ .* equals anything, even if empty

> ➤ .+ equals something, but we don't care what

The repeat characters are used frequently for URL Rewrite rules. They can also be used in other situations — for example, after sections (which we'll cover shortly) or shorthand character classes. Consider a pattern of `^[0-9]*$`. This will match an empty string or digits, but nothing else. On the other hand, `^[0-9]+$` specifies that there must be at least one digit.

| for "or"

The | (pipe) character is an easy one — it means "or." A common place to use it for URL Rewrite is for the top-level domain (TLD) choices, such as in the following situation:

```
<conditions>
    <add input="{HTTP_HOST}" pattern="^www\.domain\.(com|net|org)$" />
</conditions>
```

The com, net, and org are grouped together by the parentheses and flagged with the "or" so that if the domain name TLD matches any of them, it's considered a successful match.

? for Optional

The ? (question mark) character marks the preceding item as optional. Another way to look at it is that it will match if the proceeding item exists zero or one times. A common usage for this in URL Rewrite is for the optional www. in the domain name.

```
<conditions>
    <add input="{HTTP_HOST}" pattern="^(www\.)?domain\.com$" />
</conditions>
```

This will match whether the domain name is www.domain.com or just domain.com. Just don't forget to keep the slash dot (\.) inside the parentheses since it is also optional.

Shorthand Mini-Expressions

There are some shorthand mini-expressions that represent common patterns. The most common examples include the following:

- ➤ \d — Digits
- ➤ \w — Word characters (letters, digits, underscores)
- ➤ \s — Whitespace (spaces, tabs, and line breaks)
- ➤ \D — Not digits
- ➤ \W — Not word characters
- ➤ \S — Not whitespace

Here is an example that checks the query string for id=(number):

```
<conditions>
    <add input="{QUERY_STRING}" pattern="id=(\d+)(&|$)" />
</conditions>
```

This example condition will be considered a successful match only if the query string has a parameter called id with a value that is a number. The (&|$) ensures that either the id parameter is the last parameter in the query string or that the next value after the number is an &, which is for another parameter. This ensures that the id parameter cannot have a value that starts with a number but isn't a true number (e.g., 123abc).

( ) to Create Groups for Back-References or Decisions

You've probably started to notice by now that you can create groups for more advanced logic. Groups, specified within parentheses ( ), are used for back-references (discussed below) and can also be used for sub-dividing your patterns into smaller parts. This has a number of practical purposes in regex, as shown in many of the examples in this chapter. You are free to create groups wherever you want. They won't hurt as long as you update your back-references, as needed. The following condition is legitimate, although not helpful:

```
<conditions>
    <add input="{HTTP_HOST}" pattern="^(d)(o)(m)(a)(i)(n)(\.com)$" />
</conditions>
```

This example of a condition checks to see if the domain name is "domain.com". Although you probably would not have a reason to write such a condition, it shows that groups can be created at will, as you see fit.

Following is an example with two conditions that shows how groups can be used:

```
<conditions>
    <add input="{HTTP_HOST}" pattern="^(domain1|domain2)\.com$" />
</conditions>

<conditions>
    <add input="{HTTP_HOST}" pattern="^www\.(.+)$" />
</conditions>
```

In this example, the first condition shows that you can check whether the domain name is one of two possible choices. The parentheses will group together the second-level domains (domain1 and domain2) with an "or" between them. A back-reference called {C:1} is also created that will result in one of the following three possibilities:

➤ {C:1} = domain1 if the domain name is domain1.com.

➤ {C:1} = domain2 if the domain name is domain2.com.

➤ The condition will not pass if the domain name is neither domain1.com nor domain2.com, and the rule will not complete.

The second example checks to see whether the domain name starts with www. If it does, a back-reference called{C:1} is created that contains the part of the domain after www.

Back-References in Regex

Regex back-references enable you to pull out the important part of the matched string, which you can use later in the rule. Consider the following example:

```
<conditions>
    <add input="{QUERY_STRING}" pattern="id=(\d+)" />
</conditions>
```

This checks for a pattern of `id={at least one digit}` in the query string. With the added parentheses, a back-reference is created for the digits that are captured. This enables you to use the `id` value later in the rule, as in the following example:

```
<rule name="Handle friendly URL">
    <match url="^article/(\d+)/(\d+)$" />
    <action type="Rewrite"
      url="article.aspx?id={R:1}&amp;memberid={R:2}"
      appendQueryString="false" />
</rule>
```

This example starts to get elaborate because it includes a couple of the patterns that you just learned about. Note that `\d` means any digit, so this will match a pattern of articles/{digits}/{digits}. Because the digits are in parentheses, they become back-references: {R:1} and {R:2}.

The {R:0} refers to everything captured and isn't used in this particular rule, but is commonly used in other rules. The first section defined with parentheses is {R:1}, the second section is {R:2}, and so on.

The {R:0} is important to keep track of because it can be confusing. A pattern match for {HTTP_HOST} = "localtest.me$" will match multiple domains, including www.localtest .me and localtest.me. It matches both of these because the ^ (beginning character) isn't specified at the beginning. However, the {R:0} back-reference will only include localtest.me since that's the part of the string that matches the pattern. So, {R:0} isn't always the same as the input variable; rather, it's whatever is matched in the pattern.

You can use the URL Rewrite Test Pattern tool in IIS Manager when creating rules to see what your back-references will be. See the "Test Pattern Tool" section later in the chapter for more on this. See also the upcoming "Back-References" section for more about how back-references are used.

[ ] for Character Class

Where regex gets extra interesting is that characters have different meaning depending on how they are used. Character classes are the main place where this occurs. Many of the things that you learned previously do not apply to character classes.

A character class is marked by square brackets (`[ ]`) and used to match a single character against a set of specified values. The specified values can be individual characters or ranges of characters. Common examples include:

➤ `[a-zA-Z0-9]` for all letters and numbers. The `0-9` means all characters from 0 to 9. Likewise, the `a-z` and `A-Z` specify the full range of letters from a to z (lowercase) and A to Z (uppercase). Because URL Rewrite rules default to case insensitivity, you can leave off the A-Z and it will still work.

➤ `[-_a-z0-9 ]` includes all letters, numbers, -, _, and a space.

➤ `[0-1][0-9]` for all numbers from 00 to 19. This enables you to put multiple character classes beside each other. This will not match 0, however, since the pattern requires two digits.

You can use the previously discussed options such as *, +, or ? after the character class to allow repeating or to make it conditional. For example, a pattern of `[0-1]?[0-9]` will make the first character optional, which will allow a value of 05 or 5 to match.

There are some special rules for character classes. The following rules are worth noting:

➤ If the - (hyphen) is the first character, it signifies a literal hyphen; otherwise, it's used for a range of values, such as `a-z`.

➤ A \ (backslash) has the same meaning as outside of the character class.

➤ A ^ (caret) as the first character negates the character class. So, to get something that doesn't contain a slash, you could use `[^/]+`.

➤ The shorthand mini-expressions (e.g., `\d`, `\w`) work within character classes, too.

With character classes, you can get creative on different patterns. For example, a Canadian postal code has a pattern of "letter number letter space number letter number" — for example, "B0P 2H0." You can find that with a pattern of `[a-z][\d][a-z] ?[\d][a-z][\d]`. Notice that the space character in the middle is made optional, too. This rule will accept uppercase and lowercase, with and without the middle space, but only in the correct Canadian postal code format.

Remember that URL Rewrite defaults to case insensitivity, so you don't need to include `A-Z` along with `a-z` in pattern matches.

> **NOTE** *This discussion doesn't include the entire regex syntax, but it gives the most common examples used for URL Rewrite. There are other interesting concepts, such as lazy or greedy loading, repetition ranges, and more. A handy cheat sheet is available at* `www.regular-expressions.info/reference.html/`.

BACK-REFERENCES

URL Rewrite rules often make use of back-references. These are references to information obtained from earlier in the rule. If you're jumping right to this section in the chapter, you might want to review the previous sections, which discuss the regex syntax for back-references.

Rule Back-References versus Condition Back-References

URL Rewrite has two types of back-references: rule back-references and condition back-references. A rule back-reference is taken from the Match URL pattern part of the rule, whereas a condition back-reference is taken from the conditions. A rule back-reference is identified by {R:N}, where N is from 0 to 9, and a condition back-reference is identified in a similar way by {C:N}.

To use back-references, you must first capture the data, and then you can use the data. Before explaining further, let's look at an example.

```
<rule name="Subdomain redirect" enabled="true" stopProcessing="true">
    <match url=".*" />
    <conditions>
```

```
        <add input="{HTTP_HOST}" pattern="^www\.localtest\.me$" negate="true" />
        <add input="{HTTP_HOST}" pattern="^([^\.]+)\.localtest\.me$" />
    </conditions>
    <action type="Redirect" url="http://localtest.me/{C:1}/{R:0}" />
</rule>
```

This rule watches for a URL like `sub.localtest.me/article.aspx` and redirects to `localtest.me/sub/article.aspx`. This is a good example of back-references because it makes use of both types.

The rule back-reference is identified by `{R:0}`. In the preceding example, the `<match url=".*" />` is the rule, and the `{R:0}` value is the URL (e.g., `article.aspx`).

The condition back-reference gets its reference from the last condition, if there are more than one, and is identified by the `{C:1}`. In the preceding example, the last condition is `<add input="{HTTP_HOST}" pattern="^([^\.]+)\.localtest\.me$" />`. The back-reference in this example is to the `sub` part of `sub.localtest.me`.

Note that there is an exception to how condition back-references are obtained, which is for the `trackAllCaptures` option, which we'll look at shortly.

Now that we have the general idea and an example, let's dig in deeper.

Wildcards Back-References

Back-references are captured in one of two ways, depending on the pattern syntax used for the rule.

When ECMAScript (the default: regex) is set, it uses the regex back-reference. Refer to the earlier "Back-References in Regex" section for further information on regex back-references.

When the Wildcards pattern syntax is used, the back-reference is used when the `*` (asterisk) is set. For example, consider a Match URL pattern value of `*.localtest.*`. For the Wildcards pattern syntax and an example value of `www.localtest.me`, the back-references will be as follows:

- ➤ `{R:0}` www.localtest.me
- ➤ `{R:1}` www
- ➤ `{R:2}` me

The `{R:0}` back-reference gets the entire matched string. The `{R:1}` is a back-reference for the first asterisk (`*`), and the `{R:2}` is a back-reference for the second asterisk (`*`).

Capturing Back-References across Conditions

URL Rewrite 2.0 introduced the ability to capture back-references from all conditions, not just the last condition. While the default setting tracks only the back-references from the last condition, you can change this behavior by setting the `trackAllCaptures` property to `true` on the conditions section, as shown in the following example. When `trackAllCaptures` is set to `true`, all conditions are tracked, starting with the first one and moving down the list of conditions. The `{C:0}` back-reference is the full string match from the first condition. `{C:1}` through to `{C:N}` include each specific captured regex back-reference group.

When using IIS Manager to create the rules, you can turn on tracking across all conditions by checking the "Track capture groups across conditions" check box in the Conditions section. A good example of where tracking across all conditions can be used is when working with query strings. Consider this example:

```
<rule name="Redirect based on querystring" stopProcessing="true">
    <match url="^info\.aspx$" />
    <conditions trackAllCaptures="true">
        <add input="{QUERY_STRING}" pattern="name=(\w+)-(\w+)" />
        <add input="{QUERY_STRING}" pattern="age=(\d)" />
    </conditions>
    <action type="Rewrite"
      url="/lookup.aspx?firstname={C:1}&amp;lastname={C:2}&amp;age={C:3}"
      appendQueryString="false" />
</rule>
```

Note that the & character — a common URL character — needs to be written as & in the XML configuration since it's a specific character in XML. So, this example is a bit more cluttered than some others.

In this example, if someone visits `http://localtest.me/info.aspx?name=John-Doe&age=99`, the URL will be rewritten to `http://localtest.me/lookup.aspx?firstname=John&lastname=Doe&age=99`. Using the back-references, you're able to pull out the data that you want from the query strings.

You can also use `{C:0}`, which has the value of the entire first condition's capture, which is `"name=John-Doe"`.

As a review, if you don't set `trackAllCaptures`, or if you set it to `false`, then `{C:0}` will be `"age=99"` and `{C:1}` will be `99`. Yet, with `trackAllCaptures` set to true, you can obtain data from all the conditions. If you don't add a reference area with ( ) (parentheses) to a condition, it won't contribute to the list of back-references.

For Wildcards back-references, the concept is the same, except that all asterisks are used for back-references rather than the parentheses sections.

Where to Use Back-References

Back-references can be used in the following locations:

➤ In the `condition` input string

➤ In the rule `action`:

    ➤ The `url` attribute of Rewrite and Redirect action

    ➤ The `value` attribute of Rewrite action in outbound rules

    ➤ The `statusLine` and `responseLine` of a `CustomResponse` action

➤ In the `key` attribute within a rewrite map

SETTING SERVER VARIABLES

URL Rewrite 2.0 introduced the ability to create or set your own server variables. This enables you to set custom information that will be available to other rules and to the website itself. You can set variables like `HTTP_X_ORIGINAL_HOST`, or pretty much any other server variable, pre-existing or made up.

The value of the server variable can be a literal string, or you can use other server variables or back-references. This gives you full flexibility in setting server variables.

Figured 19-7 shows two example server variables: one set with a server variable and one set with a literal string.

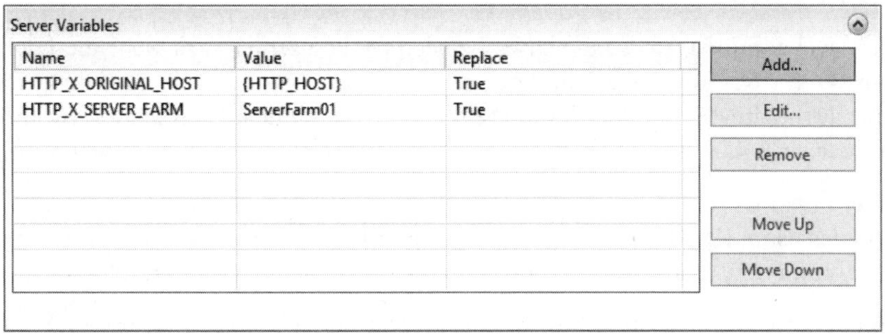

FIGURE 19-7

Following is an example of a rule that has the two server variables set. Notice that this is a good place to use the None action, if you don't want to perform an action on the rule.

```
<rule name="Set Server Variables">
    <match url=".*" />
    <serverVariables>
        <set name="HTTP_X_ORIGINAL_HOST" value="{HTTP_HOST}" />
        <set name="HTTP_X_SERVER_FARM" value="ServerFarm01" />
    </serverVariables>
    <action type="None" />
</rule>
```

When running this rule, you may receive a 500.50–URL Rewrite Module Error. This will occur if you created the rule at the site level, rather than the server level, and the two variables haven't been granted permission to run at the site level. The upcoming "Allowed Server Variables" section explains how to approve server variables to be changed at the site level.

Request Headers

Request headers work slightly different from server variables. Initially, they are set the same way as server variables, except for a couple of considerations. Most importantly, they must start with the `HTTP_` prefix. This defines them as a request header. Consider, for example, the request header called "host." This is written as HTTP_HOST when used for URL Rewrite. Additionally, the following rules apply when converting from the URL Rewrite variable to a request header:

➤   All underscore (_) symbols in the name are converted to dash symbols (-).

➤   All letters are converted to lowercase.

➤   The HTTP_ prefix is removed.

You can set or define your own request headers by starting your server variable with HTTP_. A custom request header, discussed in Chapter 17, is HTTP_X_ORIGINAL_HOST. Using the preceding rules, you can see that it will become a request header called "x-original-host."

Allowed Server Variables

Site-level and subfolder-level administrators may have the need to set a server variable using URL Rewrite. This is supported in URL Rewrite 2.0 and greater. However, before an IIS administrator can set a server variable at the site or subfolder level, the server variable must be approved by an IIS administrator at the server level. If it is not approved, a runtime error will be displayed when the site is loaded.

To approve server variables using IIS Manager, select URL Rewrite from the server level, and then select View Server Variables. From there, you can add, rename, or remove server variables.

From the configuration perspective, you can set allowed server variables in applicationHost .config in the rewrite section as follows:

```
<configuration>
  <system.webServer>
    <rewrite>
      <allowedServerVariables>
        <add name="HTTP_X_ORIGINAL_HOST" />
      </allowedServerVariables>
    </rewrite>
  </system.webServer>
</configuration>
```

SPECIAL CONSIDERATIONS

There are a few additional considerations to keep in mind when using URL Rewrite. Understanding the following considerations will make working with URL Rewrite much more productive.

Redirecting to SSL

IIS has the built-in ability to enforce SSL for sites, folders, or files. However, this isn't very friendly because it doesn't provide a redirect to the new location. Instead, it simply displays an error message if users visit the page over HTTP.

URL Rewrite offers a nice solution for this since it can seamlessly redirect a page from HTTP to HTTPS, or vice versa. You can use it for situations like ensuring that the login page, order page, or credit card page always use SSL, whereas the rest of the site redirects back to HTTP.

There are some important considerations for SSL to note.

The order of operations is important. When a request arrives at the server, it must first bind to the website and then URL Rewrite rules, and then site-level functions are performed. The order is as follows:

> Incoming request ⇨ Site binding ⇨ SSL Packet decrypted ⇨ URL Rewrite runs ⇨ Site is processed

This is important for a couple of reasons. First, this shows that URL Rewrite has access to the decrypted information, which is very useful. Whether a request is SSL or not, URL Rewrite handles it the same.

Second, URL Rewrite doesn't have any control over which certificate is used in an incoming request. If the domain name doesn't match the certificate common name (for example, if the request is for `domain.com` but the certificate is for `www.domain.com`), a warning may be presented to the end user. URL Rewrite can't help with this for the incoming request, because it has access to the request too late.

However, URL Rewrite may have been able to help at an earlier stage. If a different URL Rewrite rule redirected to the HTTPS page, make sure that that rule uses the correct domain name. One way to avoid the SSL warning is to be explicit in your action paths — that is, rather than using `https://{HTTP_HOST}`, you should use `https://www.domain.com`. Furthermore, if you have a Canonical Domain Name rule to enforce a certain domain name, you can just ensure that it's run prior to your SSL rules.

Another consideration for SSL traffic is to make sure that if you create a rule to redirect HTTPS back to HTTP, you exclude your page dependencies, such as JavaScript, CSS, and images; otherwise, some page dependencies will incorrectly redirect to HTTP and your HTTPS pages will block those dependencies.

Alternatively, rather than excluding your dependencies, you can be more explicit in your HTTPS to HTTP rule and only include files with certain extensions, such as `.aspx`, `.htm`, and `.html`. Using file extensions won't work for friendly URLs based on Microsoft ASP.NET MVC or similar frameworks, since the file extensions are hidden, so make sure to account for that, too.

In addition to URL Rewrite rules, it's helpful to find a way in your site links and code to redirect back to HTTP from your HTTPS pages, and to always link to the HTTPS version of your secure pages. This prevents an extra redirect. Then you can consider URL Rewrite just a safety net.

Following is an example of a two-rule combination that will enforce SSL for your secure pages while redirecting back to HTTP for your other pages. Understand that it will not catch all situations; otherwise, the rule can be overly complex. It's an example only, so be sure to test it well in your environment.

```
<rule name="http to https" stopProcessing="true">
    <match url="^(login|signup|payment|login.aspx)/?$" />
    <conditions>
        <add input="{HTTPS}" pattern="off" />
    </conditions>
    <action type="Redirect" url="https://localtest.me{URL}" />
</rule>
```

```
<rule name="https to http" stopProcessing="true">
    <match url="^(login|signup|payment|login.aspx)/?$" negate="true" />
    <conditions>
        <add input="{HTTPS}" pattern="on" />
        <add input="{URL}" pattern="^(.*\.(aspx|htm|html|php)|[^\.]*)$" />
        <add input="{URL}" pattern="/css|/js$" negate="true" />
    </conditions>
    <action type="Redirect" url="http://localtest.me{URL}" />
</rule>
```

Let's make sure that we understand the parts of this. The Match URL pattern in both rules is exactly the same, except that the second rule has `negate="true"`. This example accounts for all pages that end with `login`, `signup`, `payment`, or `login.aspx` with an optional `/` at the end.

The first rule redirects to HTTPS if the page is not secure but should be, and the second rule redirects to HTTP if the page is not already set that way but should be. Notice in the actions that one redirects to HTTP and the other to HTTPS.

The final trick to make the HTTPS-to-HTTP redirect work correctly is by using the `{URL}` pattern match in the second rule. It's a bit of a busy rule, but it's pretty powerful. It causes this rule to run only if there are extensions with `.aspx`, `.htm`, `.html`, or `.php`, or if there is no dot (`.`) in the path, in which case we can pretty safely assume that it's not a `.css` or `.js` type file. One final condition makes sure that the rule isn't applied if the URL path ends with `/css` or `/js`, which are used by ASP.NET 4.5's bundling and minification functionality.

To test this rule, first ensure that you have both HTTP and HTPS bindings on your site and then visit `http://localtest.me/login` and ensure that you are redirected to `https://localtest.me/login`. Likewise, if you visit `https://localtest.me/something-else`, it should redirect back to `http://localtest.me/something-else`.

Checking If a Request Is for a File or a Directory

You have the option within a rule to check if the request is for a file or directory. Many times you may need to perform some URL modifications for all virtual requests but not for actual files and directories, or vice versa. This can be achieved by using the `matchType` of `IsFile` or `IsDirectory`. In IIS Manager, the Add Condition dialog box enables you to check for a file or directory, as shown in Figure 19-8.

The following rule is an example of this. This rule will cause all paths that don't really exist on disk to be handled by a page called `dynamic.aspx`.

```
<rule name="Rewrite Dynamic" stopProcessing="true">
    <match url="(.*)" />
    <conditions>
        <add input="{REQUEST_FILENAME}" matchType="IsFile" negate="true" />
        <add input="{REQUEST_FILENAME}" matchType="IsDirectory" negate="true" />
    </conditions>
    <action type="Rewrite" url="\dynamic.aspx" />
</rule>
```

This will check for the existence or non-existence of files and folders, and respond accordingly. A good test is to add this example rule to your site and visit `http://localtest.me/non-existent-page`. The request should be processed by `dynamic.aspx`. Or, if you haven't created `dynamic.aspx` for this test, the error page should show that a call to `dynamic.aspx` is being attempted. Likewise, after ensuring that you have a page called `dynamic.aspx` in your site, visit `http://localtest.me/default.aspx`; you should see that your `default.aspx` page is called, not `dynamic.aspx`.

There is an important consideration — the `.axd` file types, which we'll look at next.

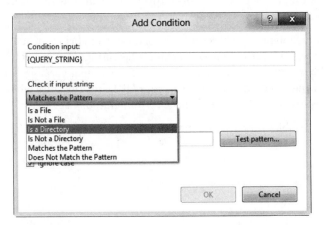

FIGURE 19-8

Considering ScriptResource.axd and WebResources.axd

ASP.NET has two types of special virtual files that serve up content dynamically for purposes such as dynamic JavaScript, which is needed for certain ASP.NET functionality. If you create a rule that checks for the existence of files or folders, you should also take into account `ScriptResource.axd` and `WebResource.axd`, which aren't really files or directories, but, for the sake of your rule, may need to be categorized as such. To account for these types of virtual files in a rule, you can simply add a condition that checks `{URL}` for `\.axd$`. The following example is the same as in the previous section but with this added consideration:

```
<rule name="Rewrite Dynamic" stopProcessing="true">
    <match url="(.*)" />
    <conditions>
        <add input="{REQUEST_FILENAME}" matchType="IsFile" negate="true" />
        <add input="{REQUEST_FILENAME}" matchType="IsDirectory" negate="true" />
        <add input="{URL}" negate="true" pattern="\.axd$" />
    </conditions>
    <action type="Rewrite" url="\dynamic.aspx" />
</rule>
```

Caching IIS Output

IIS has a feature, called *Output Caching* that will cache certain page requests for performance reasons. These can be cached in kernel mode or user mode. Because the cached pages will be presented to the end user before URL Rewrite even sees them, there is the possibility that URL Rewrite will not work as expected with page caching.

URL Rewrite controls Output Caching by altering certain caching properties or by disabling caching when certain input variables are used. The result of the URL Rewrite changes to caching will either optimize kernel mode and user mode Output Caching for better performance or prevent caching of responses when certain input variables are used that may conflict with the caching logic. URL Rewrite will not enable Output Caching if it is already disabled.

Generally, you don't need to make any setting changes as a result of this functionality within URL Rewrite. This all happens behind the scenes.

However, you do need to be mindful of which input variables prevent responses from being cached. There is a whitelist of input variables that will not affect Output Caching when using them in URL Rewrite rules. Input variables in the whitelist can be safely used, whereas all other input variables will prevent caching of responses. Using non-whitelisted input variables in your URL Rewrite rules will not impact the functionality of your site, except that it will no longer benefit from Output Caching.

Following is the list of whitelisted input variables that are safe to use without affecting Output Caching:

- CACHE_URL
- DOCUMENT_ROOT
- HTTP_URL
- HTTP_HOST
- PATH_INFO
- PATH_TRANSLATED
- QUERY_STRING
- REQUEST_FILENAME
- REQUEST_URI
- SCRIPT_FILENAME
- SCRIPT_NAME
- SCRIPT_TRANSLATED
- UNENCODED_URL
- URL
- URL_PATH_INFO
- APP_POOL_ID
- APPL_MD_PATH
- APPL_PHYSICAL_PATH
- GATEWAY_INTERFACE
- SERVER_SOFTWARE
- SSI_EXEC_DISABLED

> **WARNING** *Be careful with all input variables not on the whitelist, as they can have a greater impact on performance than you expect.*

Using String Functions with Rule Actions and Conditions

URL Rewrite offers three string functions that can be used with the rule actions and conditions:

➤ `ToLower` — Returns the string as lowercase.

➤ `UrlEncode` — Returns the string as a URL-encoded format.

➤ `UrlDecode` — Returns the string as a decoded string.

The syntax to use a string function is `{function_name:string}`. The string can be a literal string or it can be a variable. The following single-line examples show the different variable types using either a literal string or variable:

```
<add input="{UrlDecode:{QUERY_STRING}}" pattern="Raúl" />
<action type="Rewrite" url="default.aspx?name={UrlEncode:Desirée}" />
<action type="Redirect" url="http://domain.com{ToLower:{URL}}" />
```

Like back-references, you can use the string functions in the following locations:

➤ In the `condition` input string

➤ In the rule `action`:

   ➤ The `url` attribute of Rewrite and Redirect action

   ➤ The `value` attribute of Rewrite action in outbound rules

   ➤ The `statusLine` and `responseLine` of a `CustomResponse` action

➤ In the `key` attribute within a rewrite map

Following is an example that shows how to use UrlDecode in a rule. This rule checks if there is a value in the query string of id=Raúl. Because Raúl contains a special character, it will not work correctly unless you use UrlDecode, as in this example:

```
<rule name="Decode an encoded querystring" stopProcessing="true">
  <match url=".*" />
  <conditions>
    <add input="{UrlDecode:{QUERY_STRING}}" pattern="id=Raúl" />
  </conditions>
  <action
    type="Redirect"
    url="http://localtest.me/person.aspx?id=111"
    appendQueryString="false" />
</rule>
```

To test, visit `http://localtest.me/?id=Raúl`. You should be redirected to `http://localtest.me/person.aspx?id=111`. If you replace the input with just `"{QUERY_STRING}"`, it should not redirect.

Importing Rules from mod_rewrite

IIS URL Rewrite has a tool available to import rules from Apache's `mod_rewrite` module. This tool, called *Import mod_rewrite Rules* is available within IIS Manager by going to URL Rewrite from the site level or subfolder level and clicking on Import Rules. The tool is not available at the server level.

The import tool takes a best-effort approach to import rules from `mod_rewrite`. It will get most rule types, although it may not be able to import every situation due to the wide range of creative rules that people can write.

The "Import mod_rewrite Rules" tool enables you to import rules by either pointing to a `.htaccess` file from Apache or copying and pasting the rule(s) into the tool's main window. Doing so will convert the rule for you and enable you to set your own rule names.

If you are moving over from Apache (good for you!), or if you happen to see some good `mod_rewrite` examples that you want to learn from, this tool can be a tremendous help.

For further information, visit `www.iis.net/learn/extensions/url-rewrite-module/importing-apache-modrewrite-rules`.

Logging Rewritten URLs

Since URL Rewrite can manipulate the URL using the Rewrite action, you can choose whether to log the original URL or the rewritten URL. The default is to log the original URL. This applies only to the Rewrite action. You can log the rewritten rule from IIS Manager as shown in Figure 19-9, or as shown in the following `action` element.

```
<action type="Rewrite" url="{C:1}" appendQueryString="false" logRewrittenUrl="true" />
```

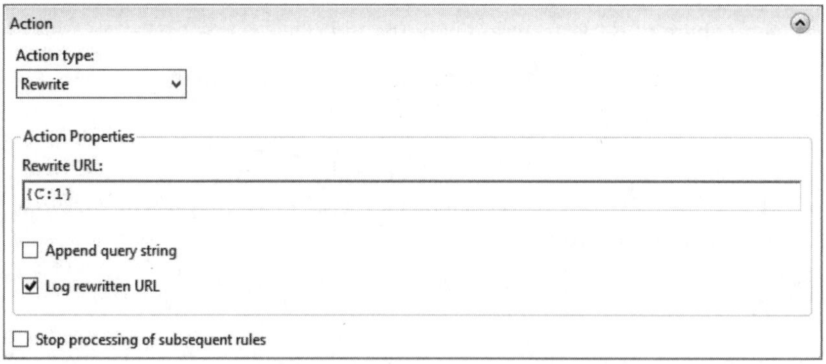

FIGURE 19-9

REWRITE MAPS

Standard URL Rewrite rules are very powerful when it comes to pattern matches, but what if you want to maintain a list of before/after URL mappings, or if you want a list of values to use in your logic where a pattern doesn't work? That's where rewrite maps come in. A rewrite map is a list of key/value pairs that can be used for substitution in redirects, rewrites, or most any other URL Rewrite rule situation.

Figure 19-10 shows a sample rewrite map, using IIS Manager to manage them.

FIGURE 19-10

Rewrite maps are also useful for a list of keys, even if the value isn't used. (You will see some examples of this shortly.) In that case, you can set the value to some arbitrary value, such as 1, as in the following example (displayed as the XML configuration):

```
<rewriteMap name="ApprovedDomains">
    <add key="www.localtest.me" value="1" />
    <add key="localtest.me" value="1" />
    <add key="staging.localtest.me" value="1" />
    <add key="admin.localtest.me" value="1" />
</rewriteMap>
```

Creating the actual rewrite map is pretty straightforward. You can create a rewrite map in IIS Manager at the server, site, or subfolder level. You can use IIS Manager to manage rewrite maps by opening IIS Manager, navigating to the place where you want to create the rewrite map, double-clicking on the URL Rewrite icon, and selecting View Rewrite Maps from the Actions pane. This will show you a list of all the rewrite maps. You can add a rewrite map from the Actions pane if you need to create a new one, or you can double-click on an existing rewrite map to edit it.

Additionally, you can set the default value for a rewrite map, which can come in handy for certain types of rules that assume that there is always a match with a unique value. By default, an empty string is used as the default value.

The syntax for using a rewrite map is {RewriteMapName:String}. The string can be any string value, whether it's a literal string, an input variable, or a back-reference. When the string matches any key in the rewrite map, the resultant value is the value of the matching key.

Consider the following example:

```
<rewrite>
 <rewriteMaps>
  <rewriteMap name="OldNewRewrites" defaultValue="">
    <add key="/about_us.htm" value="/about/" />
    <add key="/company_info.htm" value="/company/" />
```

```
      </rewriteMap>
    </rewriteMaps>
  </rewrite>
```

With this rewrite map you can do any number of comparisons. Probably the most common is to check if the {URI} matches any name in a rewrite map, and if it does, then replace it, as in the following condition:

```
<add input="{OldNewRewrites:{URI}" pattern="(.+)" />
```

This example of a condition achieves two important goals. First, it sees if the condition is valid. The condition will be true only if one of the "Original Values" in the OldNewRewrites rewrite map matches the URI. Second, the pattern (.+) creates a back-reference that can be used later in the rule. That's where the "New Value" in the rewrite map comes into play.

Let's piece it all together and take a look at a complete example with rewrite map and rule:

```
<rewrite>
  <rules>
    <rule name="Redirect rule">
      <match url=".*" />
      <conditions>
        <add input="{StaticRedirects:{URL}}" pattern="(.+)" />
      </conditions>
      <action type="Redirect" url="http://localtest.me{C:1}" />
    </rule>
  </rules>
  <rewriteMaps>
    <rewriteMap name="StaticRedirects" defaultValue="">
      <add key="/about_us.htm" value="/about/" />
      <add key="/company_info.htm" value="/company/" />
    </rewriteMap>
  </rewriteMaps>
</rewrite>
```

Note that if you use {URL}, it will ignore the query string, whereas {REQUEST_URI} will include it. You can use whatever makes the most sense for you.

Let's look at this one more way. Consider the following condition:

```
<add input="{OldNewRewrites:{URL}" pattern="(.+)" />
```

For the example above of a URL Rewrite condition using a rewrite map, the following table shows the possible {URL} values, the resultant input value, and the {C:0} back-reference value:

{URL}	INPUT VALUE	{C:0} VALUE
/about_us.htm	/about_us.htm	/about/
/company_info.htm	/company_info.htm	/company/
/home.htm	{blank}	N/A

Now let's look at a more powerful example. Suppose that you want to create a list of approved domain names, but you want to accept them regardless of whether they start with www without needing to create a www entry for each domain name in the rewrite map. This can be achieved with a combination of back-references and a rewrite map, as in the following site-level example:

```
<rewrite>
 <rules>
  <rule name="Block non-whitelist domains" stopProcessing="true">
   <match url=".*" />
   <conditions>
    <add input="{HTTP_HOST}" pattern="(www\.)?(.*)" />
    <add input="{WhiteList:{C:2}}" pattern="(.+)" negate="true" />
   </conditions>
   <action type="AbortRequest" />
  </rule>
 </rules>
 <rewriteMaps>
  <rewriteMap name="WhiteList">
   <add key="admin.localtest.me" value="1" />
   <add key="localtest.me" value="1" />
  </rewriteMap>
 </rewriteMaps>
</rewrite>
```

This has a simple rewrite map with the domain name as the key. There doesn't need to be an entry for www. The value of 1 means that we don't really care what it is as long as it's not blank.

The fun comes with the two patterns. Using the skills you've learned so far in this chapter, you can check for an optional www. and create a back-reference of {C:2} for just the part after the www. Then, using {C:2}, you can check to see if it's not in the whitelist and abort the request if it's not an approved domain name. Using this rule pattern, there are four possible domain names that will work: admin.localtest.me, www.admin.localtest.me, localtest.me, and www.localtest.me.

Rewrite maps can be used in the following locations:

➤ In the condition input string

➤ In the rule action:

  ➤ The url attribute of Rewrite and Redirect action

  ➤ The statusLine and responseLine of a CustomResponse action

Rewrite maps are useful when you have a list of values that can't be determined from a pattern. You can use just the key for a list, as in the domain name list above, or you can use a key/value pair to replace one value with another.

COMMON RULES

URL Rewrite is extremely flexible and has diverse usages, but certain questions tend to come up more frequently than others. Following are some examples of common rules that you can use as a base when creating your own rules.

Redirecting Non-www to www (Canonical Hostnames)

Forcing your page to redirect from domain.com to www.domain.com is a common practice for SEO. As mentioned previously, you can use the Canonical Domain Name template to create a rule that will redirect all traffic for a website to a single URL. The following example can be placed at the server or site level. It will cause a redirect to www.localtest.me if the domain name is localtest.me:

```
<rule name="Redirect localtest.me to www">
    <match url=".*" />
    <conditions>
        <add input="{HTTP_HOST}" pattern="^localtest\.me$" />
    </conditions>
    <action type="Redirect" url="http://www.localtest.me/{R:0}" />
</rule>
```

The other common option is to reverse the direction if you prefer to drop the www from the URL:

```
<rule name="Redirect localtest.me from www">
    <match url=".*" />
    <conditions>
        <add input="{HTTP_HOST}" pattern="^www\.localtest\.me$" />
    </conditions>
    <action type="Redirect" url="http://localtest.me/{R:0}" />
</rule>
```

You can test by applying the first rule and visiting http://localtest.me. Your page should redirect to http://www.localtest.me. The second rule is the opposite; it will redirect from http://www.localtest.me back to http://localtest.me.

> **NOTE** *See the upcoming "Adding HTTP_PROTOCOL" section to see how you can extend this rule to maintain the HTTP or HTTPS (protocol) when redirecting.*

Creating a Down for Maintenance Page

If you want to perform maintenance on your site, it's important that you don't show error pages to the search engines; otherwise, your rankings may drop. Choosing the incorrect status code to serve up a maintenance page can also hurt.

The HTTP 503 status code is meant for this purpose because it implies that the status is temporary. If your search engine tries to index your site when there is a 503 status code, it will hopefully ignore your site or page until the next time.

Using the lessons learned previously in this chapter, it's straightforward to create a down for maintenance URL Rewrite rule. You will need a condition specific to the part of your site that is down for maintenance, and then you can use the Custom Response action. The following example will mark your /tools/ folder down for maintenance. Using the pattern of ^tools($|/) will get anything that is exactly tools or that starts with tools/.

```
<rule name="Down for maintenance" stopProcessing="true">
    <match url="^tools($|/)" />
    <action type="CustomResponse" statusCode="503"
        statusReason="Down for maintenance"
        statusDescription="This site is currently down for maintenance" />
</rule>
```

It is also possible to create a custom friendly page. Just make sure that within the code for your page you return a 503 status code. Following is an example that will do something similar to the previous rule, except that it will load a custom page rather than return a dynamically generated response. This example does not account for any of the dependencies on the page, so you may need to add a condition to exclude the images, style sheet, and JavaScript from the rule.

```
<rule name="Down for maintenance page">
    <match url="^tools($|/)" />
    <action type="Rewrite" url="/downformaintenance.aspx" />
</rule>
```

Similarly, you can create a "down for maintenance" page that applies to the whole site by making your match url="" less specific, as in the following example. Note that the following example also demonstrates how to exclude your images and style folders from the maintenance so that your maintenance page itself can reference dependencies from that folder without them failing:

```
<rule name="Down for maintenance page">
  <match url=".*" />
  <conditions>
    <add input="{URL}" pattern="^/images" negate="true" />
    <add input="{URL}" pattern="^/style" negate="true" />
  </conditions>
  <action type="Rewrite" url="/downformaintenance.aspx" />
</rule>
```

For all three examples, make sure that as you perform your maintenance, you don't overwrite the web.config file if it's a site-level rule. And if you use a .aspx page for being down for maintenance, you need to ensure that you don't make any changes that will break ASP.NET. Basically, you need to ensure that your maintenance itself doesn't break your "down for maintenance" page.

Following is an example of a "down for maintenance" page that returns a 503 HTTP status along with your own custom wording. As you can assume, you can edit it so that it matches your site's look and feel, and so that it looks much better than this example. Save the file to the root of the site as **downformaintenance.aspx.**

```
<%
Response.StatusCode = 503
Response.TrySkipIisCustomErrors = True
%>

<html>
<head><title>Down for Maintenance</title></head>
```

```
<body>
<h1>Down for Maintenance</h1>
<div>We are currently upgrading our website to the latest and greatest.
Please come back in a few minutes to see our newly upgraded site.</div>
</body>
</html>
```

To test the last rule, apply it to your site and create the `downformaintenance.aspx` page into the root of the site. When you visit your site, you should receive the "down for maintenance" page rather than your normal site. When your maintenance is complete, you can simply disable the rule so that it's ready for next time.

Preserving Old Urls

After a major site change, it's common to have old URLs that have different paths on the new sites. The issue with this situation is that they rarely follow a consistent pattern, so you need to map the original and destination one by one, which is where rewrite maps come in. The following example handles this with a 301 client-side redirect. The advantage of a 301 redirect is that the search engines should update and use the redirected URL, not the original URL.

```
<rewrite>
    <rules>
        <rule name="Redirect Old to New" stopProcessing="true">
            <match url=".*" />
            <conditions>
                <add input="{Old to New:{REQUEST_URI}}" pattern="(.+)" />
            </conditions>
            <action type="Redirect" url="{C:1}" appendQueryString="false" />
        </rule>
    </rules>
    <rewriteMaps>
        <rewriteMap name="Old to New">
            <add key="/about.aspx" value="/about/" />
        </rewriteMap>
    </rewriteMaps>
</rewrite>
```

The new value can be a FQDN URL, too (e.g., `http://domain.com/about/`).

You can also preserve old URLs without the redirect by silently handling the page in the background with a rewrite. You must have the original and updated path in the same site, though. Here's what the rule would look like:

```
<rewrite>
    <rules>
        <rule name="Rewrite Old to New">
            <match url=".*" />
            <conditions>
                <add input="{Old to New:{REQUEST_URI}}" pattern="(.+)" />
            </conditions>
            <action type="Rewrite" url="{C:1}" appendQueryString="false" />
        </rule>
    </rules>
```

```
    <rewriteMaps>
        <rewriteMap name="Old to New">
            <add key="/about.aspx" value="/about/" />
        </rewriteMap>
    </rewriteMaps>
</rewrite>
```

To test the first example, apply it to your site and add an entry to your rewrite map with a key of
/oldpage.aspx and a value of /. When you visit http://localtest.me/oldpage.aspx, you
should be redirected to http://localtest.me/.

The second example will perform nearly the same, except that the URL in the browser's address bar
shouldn't change. It will display your site's homepage even though the URL should still be http://
localtest.me/oldpage.aspx.

Preventing Image Hot-Linking

URL Rewrite can also be used to prevent other sites from serving up your images from their
site — called *hot-linking*. Hot-linking can cause undue traffic to your site without you receiving the credit, or it may cause copyright issues. You can prevent hot-linking by watching for the
HTTP_REFERER — the referring website. If it's not your own site, you can assume that it's a hot-link
attempt. You must ensure that the domain name matches exactly, so it's wise to precede the hot-
linking rule with the Canonical Domain Name rule, which is explained earlier in this chapter. If you
change your domain name, all your images will start failing until you update this rule.

The following example will replace the attempted image with your own image, called
nohotlinking.png. This rule is not unbeatable since malicious users can hide the referrer, but it
will greatly minimize hot-linking to your images.

```
    <rule name="Prevent image hot-linking">
        <match url=".*\.(jpg|gif|png)$" />
        <conditions>
            <add input="{HTTP_REFERER}" pattern="^$" negate="true" />
            <add input="{HTTP_REFERER}" pattern="^http://localtest.me.*" negate="true" />
        </conditions>
        <action type="Rewrite" url="/images/nohotlinking.png" />
    </rule>
```

To test this rule, first apply it to your site. Copy an example PNG image to /images/
nohotlinking.png or create your own image. From another site, create a test HTML page that
references the image. For example, from a second site, create a page that has a reference to <img
src="http://localtest.me/image.gif" />. When you view the page in your second site, it
should show the nohotlinking.png image instead of image.gif.

Blocking Requests

You may want to block certain requests or only allow requests to come from pages by IP or some
other criteria. There are many ways to do this, all of which we can't include, but following are some
common options. Also, don't forget to look at the Dynamic IP Restrictions module or the built-in IP
Address and Domain Restrictions feature in IIS for blocking by IP address, or using the built-in IIS
functionality to remove Read permissions to the folder or file to block access.

To block all requests except from one IP address:

```
<rule name="Block for all but one IP" stopProcessing="true">
    <match url=".*" />
    <conditions>
        <add input="{REMOTE_ADDR}" pattern="^127\.0\.0\.1$" negate="true" />
    </conditions>
    <action type="AbortRequest" />
</rule>
```

To block access if the domain name doesn't exactly match the domain name, you can use this example:

```
<rule name="Block if wrong domain name" stopProcessing="true">
    <match url=".*" />
    <conditions>
        <add input="{HTTP_HOST}" pattern="^(www\.)?localtest.me$" negate="true" />
    </conditions>
    <action type="AbortRequest" />
</rule>
```

To test the last example, first apply it to the test site, ensuring that you have a binding on the site for `test.localtest.me`, and then visit `http://test.localtest.me`. You should receive a failure rather than the normal homepage. If you visit `http://www.localtest.me`, it should display your normal homepage.

Redirecting a Subdomain to Subfolder

A common question is something like the following: Is it possible to rewrite `http://sub.domain .com/resources/default.htm` to `http://domain.com/sub/resources/default.htm`?

This can be achieved with a redirect or a rewrite, depending on how you want it handled. Here's an example of a redirect:

```
<rule name="Subdomain redirect" stopProcessing="true">
    <match url=".*" />
    <conditions>
        <add input="{HTTP_HOST}" pattern="^www\.localtest\.me$" negate="true" />
        <add input="{HTTP_HOST}" pattern="^([^\.]+)\.localtest\.me$" />
    </conditions>
    <action type="Redirect" url="http://localtest.me/{C:1}{URL}" />
</rule>
```

This example will change the URL in the browser's address bar. Alternatively, you can use a rewrite. This won't change the domain name, but it will call `/sub/…` in the background and preserve the original URL without updating the browser's address bar. That rule would look like this:

```
<rule name="Subdomain rewrite" stopProcessing="true">
    <match url=".*" />
    <conditions>
        <add input="{HTTP_HOST}" pattern="^www\.localtest\.me$" negate="true" />
        <add input="{HTTP_HOST}" pattern="^([^\.]+)\.localtest\.me$" />
    </conditions>
```

```
    <action type="Rewrite" url="/{C:1}{URL}" />
</rule>
```

To test the first rule, which causes a redirect and is easy to test, first apply the rule to your site, and then visit `http://dallas.localtest.me`. Your browser's address bar should change to `http://localtest.me/dallas`. Even if you get a "page not found" error, you can see that the redirect works.

You can test the second rule in a similar way, except that you should make sure that the `/dallas` folder already exists and has a default document, or when the rewrite occurs, take note of the error message to see what the rewritten path is.

Adding HTTP_PROTOCOL

The `{HTTPS}` or `{SERVER_PORT_SECURE}` variables enable you to check whether the incoming request is over SSL, but they don't give you the actual HTTP or HTTPS as a variable to use in your rule actions. There may be times when you need to perform a redirect or a proxy rewrite where the protocol is needed. Here is a trick that can be used to create a server variable called `HTTP_PROTOCOL` that contains either HTTP or HTTPS, and can be used for other rules on the server.

```
<rule name="Create HTTP_PROTOCOL">
    <match url=".*" />
    <conditions>
        <add input="{CACHE_URL}" pattern="^(.+)://" />
    </conditions>
    <serverVariables>
        <set name="HTTP_PROTOCOL" value="{C:1}" />
    </serverVariables>
    <action type="None" />
</rule>
```

After this rule is created, you can use `HTTP_PROTOCOL` from other rules in URL Rewrite.

Alternately, rather than using a two-rule pattern, you can apply this within a single rule. The following example extends the "Redirect localtest.me to www" rule that was covered previously in this chapter. This example will maintain the original HTTP or HTTPS as it applies the redirect.

```
<rule name="Redirect localtest.me to www" stopProcessing="true">
  <match url=".*" />
  <conditions>
    <add input="{HTTP_HOST}" pattern="^localtest\.me$" />
    <add input="{CACHE_URL}" pattern="^(.+)://" />
  </conditions>
  <action
    type="Redirect" url="{C:1}://www.localtest.me/{R:0}" />
</rule>
```

To test this rule, make sure that you have both an HTTP and an HTTPS binding on your site, and then apply the example to your site and visit `http://localtest.me`. It should redirect to `http://www.localtest.me`. Now test again, but this time, visit `https://localtest.me`. You should be redirected to `https://www.localtest.me`.

Hosting Multiple Domains under One Site

With URL Rewrite, it's possible to host multiple domain names under one site. You can do this by rewriting to different subfolders, depending on the domain name.

Note that there are additional configuration inheritance considerations for running a site under a subfolder, especially if another complex site exists in the site root.

The following example will run the domain `localtest.me` from the `\localtest\` subfolder of the site. It will exclude anything that already starts with `/localtest/` in the path since those are usually legacy paths that shouldn't be caught by the rule.

```
<rule name="Subfolder site-localtest.me">
    <match url="^localtest($|/)" negate="true" />
    <conditions>
        <add input="{HTTP_HOST}" pattern="^(www\.)?localtest\.me$" />
    </conditions>
    <action type="Rewrite" url="/localtest{URL}" />
</rule>
```

Much more can be discussed about this situation. You can find a detailed walk-through of hosting multiple domains under one site at `http://bit.ly/LVoiFs`.

Using Query String Logic for Rules

A question that occasionally comes up is how to capture the query string values regardless of the order in which they appear. With URL Rewrite 1.0, you had to use a creative way to achieve this. With URL Rewrite 2.0, however, it's much easier because of the feature to capture back-references across conditions. See the earlier section "Capturing Back-References across Conditions" for a further explanation and example.

OUTBOUND RULES

Version 2.0 of URL Rewrite introduced support for outbound rules. These rules can change not only the headers but also the entire page body as it leaves the server before it reaches the end user.

This is useful when you can't easily make code changes, or if you are using a third-party application that you can't control. Using outbound rules, you can make edits such as changing URLs or other strings within the body of the webpage, or updating the URL in a client-side redirect.

Outbound rules can rewrite either the body of the response or a server variable.

For response rewrites, URL Rewrite will parse the body of the page and make changes as needed. Content filters can narrow the focus to just certain tags — for example, a `form`, `a`, or `img` tag for URL edits.

The other type of outbound rule will change server variables (for example, `X-PoweredBy`), or server variables can be replaced with a setting of your choice.

Outbound Rules versus Inbound Rules

Fundamentally, outbound rules are the same as inbound rules, but the structure of the rules is surprisingly different, so there are some new concepts to note.

The first thing to be mindful of is that outbound rewrite rules will parse the entire body of the page, which, as you can guess, can be CPU-intensive. There are filters to make this more efficient, but it's still important that you perform the full parsing only when you have to. This is where preconditions come in.

Preconditions are specific to outbound rules and enable you to check for certain conditions before the rest of the rules are applied. Unlike inbound rules, which process the condition after the Match URL pattern is processed, the preconditions in outbound rules are processed first. A common precondition is to check whether the content type is text/HTML so that you don't parse images and other non-text content. Preconditions can be shared between outbound rules.

The next concept to be aware of with outbound rules is the filter. A filter will ensure that only certain elements within the page are checked for a match. This makes the parsing engine much faster, and it also makes the comparison more specific.

The third concept worth noting is that outbound rules can update only one server variable at a time. Unlike inbound rules, which have a simple key/value replacement concept for multiple rules, an outbound rule has a lot more logic necessary for each server variable, so essentially the entire rule is focused on a single server variable.

Fourth, response headers have a prefix of RESPONSE_, which is in contrast to request headers for inbound rules, which have a prefix of HTTP_. So, a response header of "Server" would use a URL Rewrite outbound pattern of RESPONSE_SERVER. Like request headers. the underscore (_) is replaced with a dash (-), and the RESPONSE_ prefix is removed when it is stored as a response header.

If you understand inbound rules and these four concepts, you should find it reasonably easy to create outbound rules.

Outbound Rule Walk-Throughs

To understand how to create outbound rules and what the various settings do, let's perform a walk-through of three different types of outbound rules.

Updating the Server Response Header

For the first walk-through, let's update the server response header so that rather than showing "Microsoft-IIS/8.0," we can mask this and show something else instead. While we should be proud that we're using IIS 8.0, some security specifications require that we don't reveal which server type we are using to host your website.

Fiddler is a good tool for viewing the response headers, although you can use your favorite tool, such as Firebug, Firebugger, Internet Explorer's built-in developer tools, or whichever you prefer.

Before starting on the rule, let's take a look at what the response headers look like. Figure 19-11 shows a page request in Fiddler with the Server response header circled. Notice that the value is Microsoft-IIS/8.0.

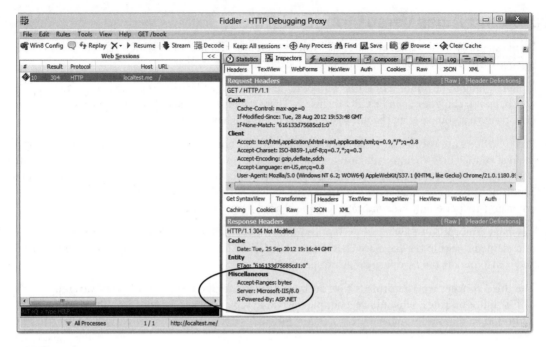

FIGURE 19-11

To create a rule to mask this value, perform the following steps:

1. Open IIS Manager, navigate to your site, and open URL Rewrite.

2. Click Add Rules and double-click on the outbound blank rule.

3. Give your new rule a name of **Mask server response header.**

    Since we want this to occur for all page responses, we don't need to select a precondition.

4. In the Matching scope dropdown, select Server Variable.

5. For the variable name, enter **RESPONSE_SERVER.** Remember that RESPONSE_ will be removed before the header is saved, so the actual response variable will become "Server."

6. For the pattern, enter .*, which will always be true, regardless of the original server value. This is where you could filter to only replace the header under certain circumstances. But, we don't want to for this example.

    Likewise, you can ignore the conditions for now, although for other rules you can create whatever conditions you want.

7. In the Action Properties Value textbox enter **Custom Web Server 1.0.**

8. Click Apply.

Now in Fiddler you should see that the server header is Custom Web Server 1.0, as shown in Figure 19-12.

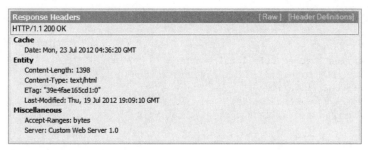

FIGURE 19-12

The configuration should look like this:

```
<rewrite>
 <outboundRules>
  <rule name="Mask server response header">
   <match serverVariable="RESPONSE_SERVER" pattern=".*" />
   <action type="Rewrite" value="Custom Web Server 1.0" />
  </rule>
 </outboundRules>
</rewrite>
```

This walk-through showed how you can update response headers and manipulate them to a value of your choosing.

Catching and Updating Redirects

Another situation in which you might need to update response headers is when you want to catch redirects before they occur and swap them with your own value. This may occur if you have a third-party site or even ASP.NET Forms authentication where there is a server-side redirect generated. This will send a client-side request, which is really a `location` response header with a target URL path.

You can watch for a `location` response header to occur and update it before the end user sees it. This will enable you to use an updated URL instead of the one generated by the server.

For the following example, let's do a straight rewrite from `newyork.localtest.me` to `seattle.localtest.me`. To achieve this, you can perform the same steps as in the previous walk-through, except for the following four differences:

➤ Give the rule a different name, like **Update redirects to seattle.localtest.me.**

➤ Set the match Server Variable to **RESPONSE_LOCATION.**

➤ Set the match Pattern to **(.*)newyork\.localtest\.me(.*).**

➤ Set the action Value to **{R:1}seattle.localtest.me{R:2}.**

This will check for `{anything}newyork.localtest.me{anything}` and replace it with `{anything}seattle.localtest.me{anything}`. Be careful, however, as this checks if the old domain (`newyork.localtest.me`) is contained anywhere in the "location" string, so it may not account for subdomains. You may need to update this to be more specific to your situation.

The configuration, which is in a different section in `web.config`, should look like this:

```
<rewrite>
  <outboundRules>
    <rule name="Update redirects to seattle.localtest.me">
      <match
        serverVariable="RESPONSE_LOCATION"
        pattern="(.*)newyork\.localtest\.me(.*)" />
      <action type="Rewrite" value="{R:1}seattle.localtest.me{R:2}" />
    </rule>
  </outboundRules>
</rewrite>
```

To test, you can create a simple page called `redirect.aspx` with the following in it:

```
<% response.redirect("http://newyork.localtest.me") %>
```

Then visit your `redirect.aspx` page (e.g., `http://localtest.me/redirect.aspx`). While the redirect would normally go to `newyork.localtest.me`, the outbound rule will change that, and you will instead go to `seattle.localtest.me`.

Updating the Response Body Text

As mentioned above, outbound rules enable you to change the body text. This third walk-through will show how to update `newyork.localtest.me` to `seattle.localtest.me` for all a, form, and img tags in the response body text. This walk-through will show how to use preconditions and, like the previous walk-through, will show back-references.

Because of the filter for just a, form, and img tags, this will run reasonably fast, but understand that extremely large pages or extra busy sites may be impacted by the extra CPU overhead with parsing the entire content page.

Let's get started:

1. Open IIS Manager, navigate to your site, and open URL Rewrite.

2. You need to create the precondition. Click View Preconditions from the Actions pane.

3. Click Add. Ensure that you don't already have an HTML precondition. If you do, you can skip to step 7.

4. Name the precondition **IsHtml**.

5. Click Add and create a condition with a Condition input of {**RESPONSE_CONTENT_ TYPE**} and a value of **^text/html** (see Figure 19-13). Click OK and OK again.

6. Click Back to Rules from the Actions pane.

7. Click Add Rules and select a new outbound blank rule.

8. Name it **Update links to seattle.localtest.me.**

9. Select the IsHtml precondition from the dropdown.

10. In the "Match the content within:" dropdown, select A, Form, and Img.

11. For the pattern, enter **(.*)newyork\.localtest\.me(.*)**.

12. Click Apply.

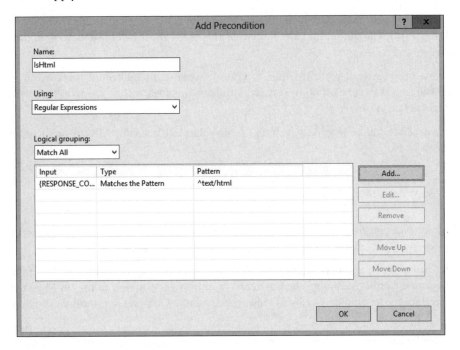

The configuration should look like this:

```
<rewrite>
 <outboundRules>
  <rule name="Update links to seattle.localtest.me" preCondition="IsHtml">
   <match filterByTags="A, Form, Img" pattern="(.*)newyork\.localtest\.me(.*)" />
    <action type="Rewrite" value="{R:1}seattle.localtest.me{R:2}" />
  </rule>
  <preConditions>
   <preCondition name="IsHtml">
    <add input="{RESPONSE_CONTENT_TYPE}" pattern="^text/html" />
   </preCondition>
  </preConditions>
 </outboundRules>
</rewrite>
```

To test, first create a site with a site binding for newyork.localtest.me, apply the preceding rule, and then create a page that simply has the following:

```
<a href="http://newyork.localtest.me">Link to your city</a>
<a href="http://newyork.localtest.me/default.aspx?abc=def">Other link</a>
```

Now if you view that page in your web browser and then view the HTML source, you will notice that the links have been updated to seattle.localtest.me. This is just one example, but as you can see, you can change any string pattern with another by using outbound rules.

Further Outbound Rule Considerations

You can parse the entire page rather than just some elements. To do so, simply don't set any of the filters when creating the outbound rule. Note that this is the most CPU-intensive type of rule, especially for large pages.

If the page is compressed, it will throw an exception, because the outbound rule cannot parse the page. One solution is to turn off compression, although this means that you won't receive the benefits that compression offers.

If you have access to make server-level changes, the solution offered by Microsoft's Ruslan Yakushev is as follows:

1. Set the `LogRewrittenUrlEnabled` registry key:

   ```
   reg add HKEY_LOCAL_MACHINE\SOFTWARE\Microsoft\InetStp\
   Rewrite /v LogRewrittenUrlEnabled /t REG_DWORD /d 0
   ```

2. Make sure that the `dynamicCompressionBeforeCache` property is set to `false` for the `/system.webServer/urlCompression` configuration element.

3. Re-order the IIS modules to have the URL Rewrite module (RewriteModule) run before the Dynamic Compression module (DynamicCompressionModule). In the IIS Manager user interface in the module's ordered view, the Dynamic Compression module should be above the URL Rewrite module.

This may not be the easiest solution, but it offers a workaround to the compression issue in outbound rules.

URL Rewrite enables you to create your own custom filter tags. This can be done in IIS Manager or directly in the configuration.

Two performance options are not set by default. These are not available in IIS Manager, so you must set them directly in the configuration.

The first tweak is to set `rewriteBeforeCache`, which will allow the rewritten page to be cached. Note that you should not use this if chunked transfer encoding is used for responses. You can set this on the `outboundRules` element, as follows:

```
<outboundRules rewriteBeforeCache="true">
```

The second tweak for outbound rules is to limit the amount of occurrences, if you are able to. For example, if you know that a certain pattern will occur a maximum of one time in the page, you can set the occurrences to 1, and it will not parse the rest of the page after the first match. This is not available in IIS Manager, either. You can set it in the configuration within each rule, as follows:

```
<match pattern="newyork" occurrences="1" />
```

TROUBLESHOOTING URL REWRITE

When URL Rewrite works, it works great. And when a rule is created successfully, there is rarely a situation where it starts failing. However, what can cause you to pull your hair out is when creating the rules in the first place. Some things just don't just respond as you would expect, and it can be difficult to track down what's wrong. Following are some quick tips to help troubleshoot URL Rewrite.

Create a Testing Rule

One of the easiest and most flexible ways to troubleshoot URL Rewrite is to create a testing rule to confirm that a bare-bones rule will work. There are a few ways to do this.

If your site is still in development, the most elementary option is to create a rule at the server level with a "Match URL Pattern" of .* and an Abort Request action. To test, simply ensure that you can view your site before the rule is created, and then confirm that the request is aborted after the rule is created. After you've confirmed that URL Rewrite does indeed work, you can start adding back parts of your good rule until you track down the issue.

While unlikely, it is possible that URL Rewrite was installed incorrectly. (It has happened, although rarely.) Confirming that a basic rule works is a good way to confirm that URL Rewrite was installed correctly.

If you're running in production, your testing rules will need to have a condition filtered to just traffic used for testing. For example, you could add a condition for {REMOTE_ADDR} equaling your own IP address.

You don't need to have the rule abort the request, either. A less intrusive test is to add a server variable that you can display on your page through code.

If you created a site-level rule, creating a testing rule can help confirm that the correct site is handling the request. It's not uncommon for a rule to be created correctly but that a different site binding is catching this request.

Create a Stopping Rule

Along the lines of the previous tip, you can create a *stopping rule*, which is a rule meant to catch the request and stop all further rules from being run. This is useful if you have a large number of rules and are not sure which one is handling the request. You can create a stopping rule that essentially watches for your incoming test request — based on your IP address or whatever conditions you need to filter to just your test traffic — and stops processing further rules. You can then move that rule up the list until it stops your other rules from running. This helps narrow down which rule came into play.

Reviewing Input Variables

See the "Input Variables" section earlier in this chapter, which gave a script to see the variables available to URL Rewrite. It's possible that the variables you think URL Rewrite sees aren't what URL really does see.

Fiddler and Firebug

Tools such as Fiddler and Firebug are invaluable for the web administrator, and troubleshooting URL Rewrite is no exception. When you can see the request in-flight, it can sometimes become obvious where the issue is. These tools enable you to see the page output, whether the server responded, what that status request type was, and more.

Test Pattern Tool

IIS Manager has a Test Pattern tool that can be used to validate your rules or conditions. This is especially helpful when building regex patterns, as well as to find out what the back-references will be.

The following walk-through shows how to navigate to the tool for building or testing your own patterns, using Regular Expressions. You can also use the same steps when creating or editing a real rule, although this walk-through will take you right to the tool in the fewest number of steps.

1. Open IIS Manager.

2. Click on the server level (or site or subfolder level) from the left-hand pane.

3. Double-click the URL Rewrite icon.

4. Click Add Rule(s) from the Actions pane.

5. Double-click Blank Rule.

6. Click the "Test pattern" button in the top part of the middle pane.

7. Enter your regex pattern in the Pattern field.

8. Enter your test data in the "Input data to test" field. The value that you enter into this field should simulate what your data will be. For example, if your rule will have a condition that uses HTTP_HOST, then enter a valid domain name in the "Input data to test" field. For the best testing, try to think of each unique pattern of data that you may receive.

9. Click the Test button. This will tell you that "the input data to test does not match the pattern," or it will display the captured groups to be used in back-references, as shown in Figure 19-14.

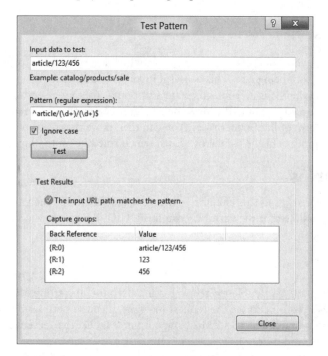

FIGURE 19-14

10. Adjust your input data or pattern and repeat until you feel comfortable with your pattern. When you click Close, you will be given an option to save the updated Pattern. You can accept or reject that prompt.

You would perform nearly the same steps to test a Wildcards pattern. The only difference is that after Step 5, change the "Using" from Regular Expressions (the default) to Wildcards. After you do that, the Test Pattern tool will use the Wildcards syntax rather than the Regular Expressions syntax.

The same tool is also available in the Add Condition dialog when you add conditions to a rule. It functions exactly the same, except that the back-references will be for conditions (e.g., {C:1}) rather than for rules (e.g, {R:1}).

Display Variable Trick

Here's a trick that will enable you to see the value of a particular variable. Feel free to replace bing .com with your own test page. We give no promises that Bing will continue to support arbitrary query string values. At the time of this writing, Bing's homepage doesn't prevent this type of request, and we can assume that they don't mind using their site for this.

Create the following rule at the site or server level and replace {REQUEST_URI} with whatever input variable you want to test. When you visit your site, it will redirect to bing.com with var={value} in the URL. It's a simple but effective trick.

```
<rule name="Test Variables">
 <match url=".*" />
 <action
  type="Redirect"
  url="http://www.bing.com/?var={REQUEST_URI}"
  appendQueryString="false" redirectType="Temporary" />
 <conditions>
   <!-- add appropriate conditions here so that production traffic isn't impacted -->
 </conditions>
</rule>
```

Failed Request Tracing

URL Rewrite is fully integrated into Failed Request Tracing (FRT). See Chapter 23, "Diagnostics and Troubleshooting," for more details on how to use it. When FRT is enabled and you perform a test run on your site, the FRT log will show the URL Rewrite logic, what matched, the values in the conditions, and which rules were applied.

Simplify

As with most anything, if you can simply it, you can kill two birds with one stone. Not only does rewriting a complex rule to a simpler one offer a greater chance of it being resolved, but it's easier to maintain over time. When you run into a wall while troubleshooting URL Rewrite rules, maybe it's time to find an easier way to write your rule.

20

Configuring Publishing Options

WHAT'S IN THIS CHAPTER?

➤   Web Platform Installer

➤   Web Deployment Tool

➤   FTP publishing

➤   WebDAV publishing

➤   Visual Studio publishing

WROX.COM CODE DOWNLOADS FOR THIS CHAPTER

The wrox.com code downloads for this chapter are found at www.wrox.com/remtitle
.cgi?isbn=1118388046 on the Download Code tab.

Microsoft provides several options for publishing web pages and applications to IIS 8.0. Some
of these options, such as the Web Platform Installer (Web PI) and the Web Deployment Tool
(Web Deploy), are designed to install full application sets and configurations, whereas others,
such as FTP publishing, are designed to simply publish files, folders, and content to your sites.

In this chapter, you will find information on configuring and using FTP for publishing.
Chapter 10, "Configuring Other Services," covers the installation of the FTP service for use as
a traditional FTP server, to transfer files to and from the server, and this chapter extends that
to allow publishing websites and applications using FTP.

Microsoft also supports WebDAV for publishing and deploying of sites and applications,
although interest in WebDAV has been waning over the years. Microsoft's FrontPage Server
Extensions has been deprecated and has not been supported since IIS version 7.5. WebDAV
or FTP publishing are the only options for those using old versions of Microsoft's FrontPage
or SharePoint Designer development tools. Microsoft's current replacements for both the

FrontPage and SharePoint Designer products are Microsoft Expression Web and the current versions of Microsoft Office, which allow editing websites and pages. WebDAV also allows files and folders to be transferred using HTTP protocols, making it very compatible with current web browsers for file transfers. This chapter covers installing and configuring WebDAV for file transfers as well as publishing sites and applications.

Of particular interest to administrators of larger networks of IIS 8.0 systems will be Microsoft's Web Deploy. It was developed for IIS 7.0 and released as a tool on Microsoft's website, and it has been updated several times over the past few years. The current version, 3.0, works with IIS 8.0 to not only deploy applications, but also to handle site migration and replication across multiple servers. Web Deploy is covered in this chapter for both application deployment as well as site migration and replication.

The Web Platform Installer (Web PI), while not just a publishing option, is also covered here. Many administrators will use Web PI for configuring and deploying commercial applications, such as WordPress, Umbraco, and DotNetNuke, but developers can also use Web PI and the Microsoft Application Gallery to publish their works for easy installation by others.

WEB PLATFORM INSTALLER

Microsoft's Web Platform Installer (Web PI) is a free tool that can be used to install IIS 8.0, SQL Express, the .NET Framework, and many applications from the Web Application Gallery. You can find detailed information for the current version online at `http://www.microsoft.com/web/downloads/platform.aspx`, and currently available applications in the Web Application Gallery at `http://www.microsoft.com/web/gallery/`.

Using Web Platform Installer

Microsoft's Web PI is small and quick to install from the link above. The download saves the file `wpilauncher.exe` to your system. Simply double-click it to run it and install Web PI. (In Internet Explorer 10 you can run the download directly or save the file and run it without needing to double-click.) Web PI will display a list of products and applications, as shown in Figure 20-1, with spotlighted applications on the main list.

To install a product or application, simply find it in the list and click the Add button to add that item to your installation package. You can select as many or as few items as you want, although you should try to select only those products you know you will be using. For example, although you can install PHP quite easily, if you will not be running PHP websites, you should not install PHP.

If you highlight the Products list, you will see that many of the products, such as IIS components, may already be installed. Web PI does not let you uninstall or modify products or applications, so any installed products will be grayed out and unelectable. As a demonstration, try selecting a product you do not have installed, such as the Search Engine Optimization Toolkit (SEO Toolkit). You can either scroll through the Products list to find it, as highlighted in Figure 20-2, or type a part of the term, such as **Search Engine**, into the Search field at the top right of the Web PI wizard to find it quicker.

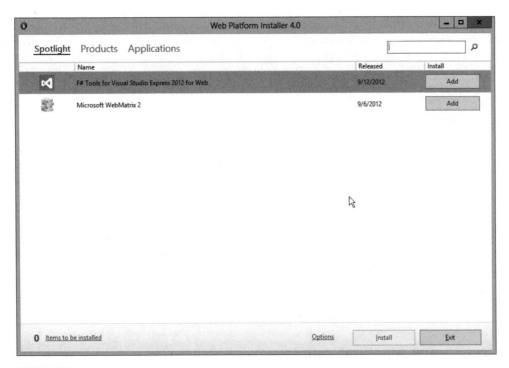

FIGURE 20-1

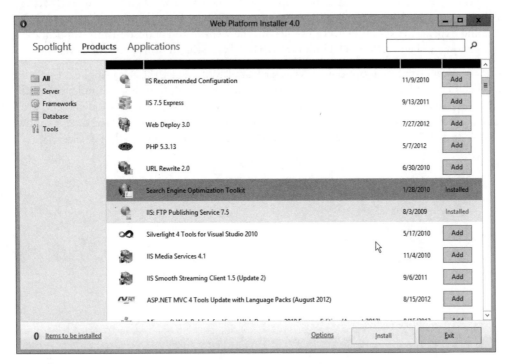

FIGURE 20-2

Click the Add button to add the SEO Toolkit to your installation, and then click Install to install your selection. Accept the licensing terms for the SEO Toolkit, and Web PI will complete the installation for you. If you had selected products or applications that needed to be configured, Web PI would launch those configuration wizards. The SEO Toolkit has no further configuration needed before use, so the installation will simply complete.

Web Application Gallery

The Microsoft Web Application Gallery (http://www.microsoft.com/web/gallery/) is a repository of applications developed for Microsoft's IIS web platform and installable using Web PI. Many are widely popular applications, such as WordPress, DotNetNuke, and Joomla!, configured for easy installation by novice administrators who may only have a need to run the application and do not want or need to understand the underlying mechanics.

Developers can have their own applications listed in the Web Application Gallery, which currently supports ASP.NET and PHP applications. Applications must meet some basic criteria, listed at the Web Application Gallery site, but, once listed, will be available for many end users through both the Web Application Gallery and the control panels at many popular web hosters. Applications submitted for listing must be available to the public for free, but many application developers provide free community versions of products to bring in commercial clients.

Installing Gallery Applications

Applications may be installed from the Web Application Gallery, from Web PI, or directly from within IIS Manager for IIS 8.0. To install an application directly from IIS Manager, open IIS Manager and expand the sites folder. Right-click on the website and choose Install Application from Gallery, as shown in Figure 20-3. The link is also available in the Actions pane for a website.

All the application installation options — whether from IIS Manager, the Web Application Gallery, or using Web PI — will launch Web PI to perform the actual installation. For example, to install DotNetNuke Community Edition on your IIS 8.0 server from the Web Application Gallery, browse to the gallery at http://www.microsoft.com/web/gallery/. Search for DotNetNuke, as shown in Figure 20-4, and click Install to install the DotNetNuke application to your IIS 8.0 server.

FIGURE 20-3

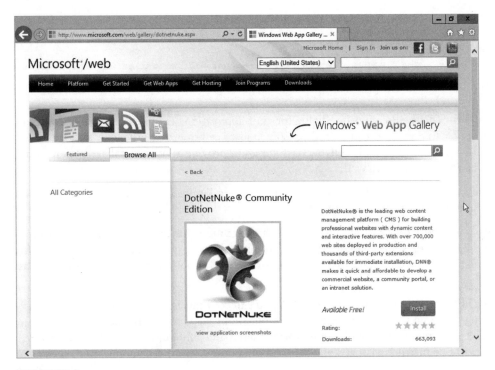

FIGURE 20-4

Application installation starts with a page that shows the licensing and system requirements for installing the application. Click on Install Now to launch Web PI, and then choose Run from the options presented by Internet Explorer. Web PI will display the application to be installed, as shown in Figure 20-5. Click on Install to continue the installation.

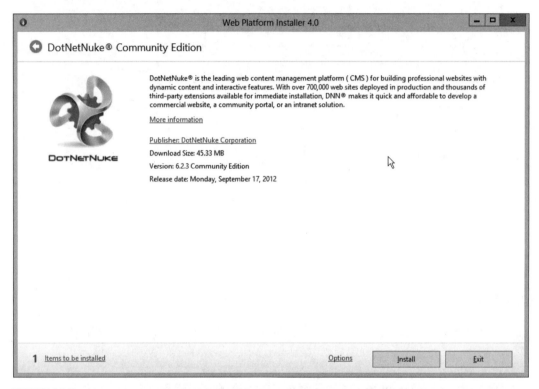

FIGURE 20-5

Web PI will bring up the Prerequisites dialog for your application, as shown in Figure 20-6. In this case, SQL Server Express is already installed, so you just need to provide the login details and click Continue. If you needed to install SQL Server Express or provide another database option, you would see options for those, as well.

Web PI will ask you to accept the installations, as shown in Figure 20-7. Click I Accept to agree to the licensing terms and begin the installation.

Web PI will next move to the Configure dialog, which is unique for each application. In the case of DotNetNuke, there are some configurations regarding which website to use, the name of the site, and an application directory, if desired. For this sample, click Continue to accept the defaults, as shown in Figure 20-8.

When Web PI finishes, as shown in Figure 20-9, you can continue by launching the application and finishing the setup for DotNetNuke. Some applications may have no further setup, but many in the Web Application Gallery will require further setup and configuration for the application itself. You will find instructions for doing this at the support sites for each application, such as `http://www.dotnetnuke.com/` for DotNetNuke. The support sites are listed in the application description on the Web PI website.

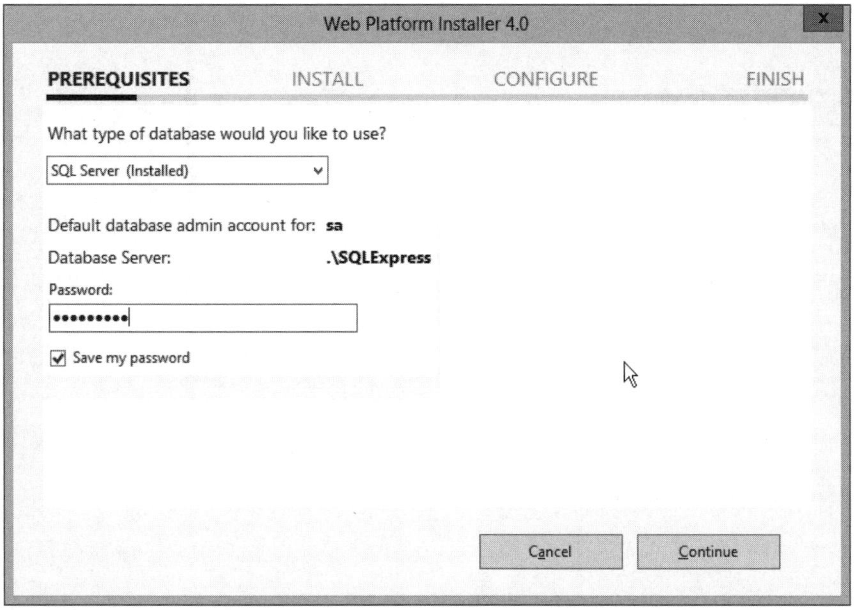

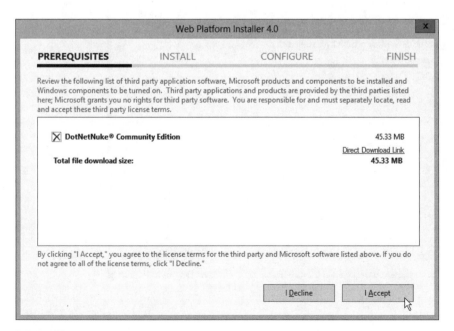

FIGURE 20-6

FIGURE 20-7

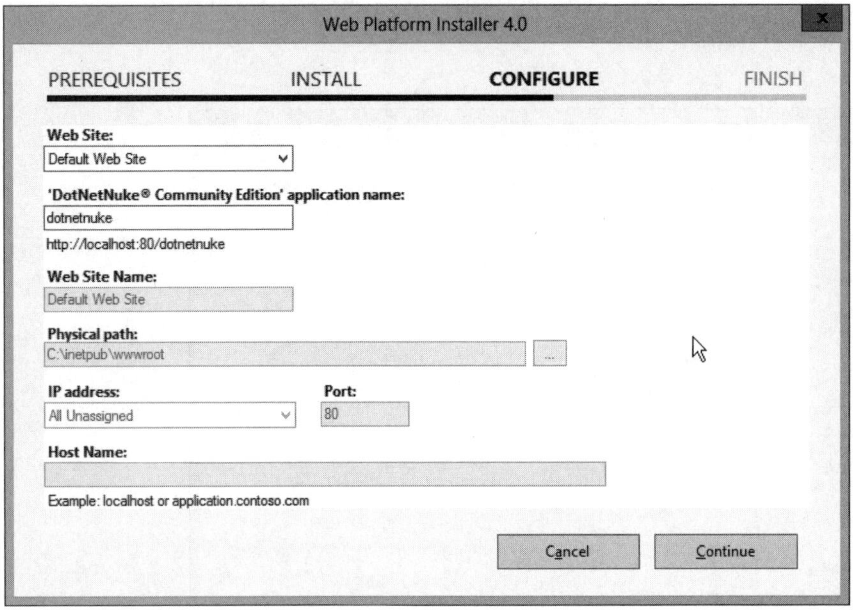

FIGURE 20-8

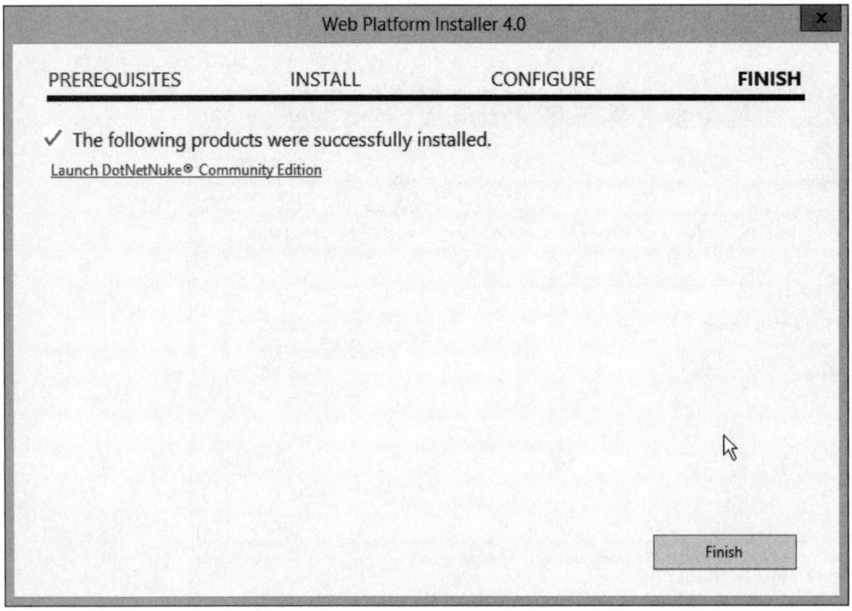

FIGURE 20-9

WEB DEPLOYMENT TOOL

The Microsoft Web Deployment Tool (Web Deploy, previously called *MS Deploy*) is fully integrated into IIS 8.0, Visual Studio 10, Web Matrix, and the Web PI. The latest version, 3.0, is available online at http://www.iis.net/download/webdeploy and can be installed by loading the module directly or by using the Web PI. Installation requires that Windows Server 2012 be already installed, but the web server and module can be installed together using Web PI.

Web Deploy is faster than other methods, such as FTP, for publishing or syncing files, because it transfers only changes between the source and destination systems. Web Deploy also supports Microsoft SQL Server directly, scripting databases for deployment to the new location. A major advantage of Web Deploy over other deployment methods is its capability to handle transformations during deployment, such as changing a database connection string from a development system to a production system as well as settings within IIS 8.0.

When you finish this section, you should be able to install Web Deploy and use it to back up IIS 8.0 configurations, migrate sites between servers, and deploy application packages from products such as Visual Studio. Other deployment options exist and will be covered later in the chapter.

Installing Web Deploy with Web PI

To install Web Deploy, first download the Web Platform Interface (Web PI) and install it as previously described. Open Web PI and search for **Web Deploy**, and then add it to your installation. If you have not installed the Recommend Server Configuration for Web Hosting Providers, search for it and also add it to your Web Deploy installation. This will configure the web server with the most common deployment for web hosting providers and guarantee that IIS 8.0 prerequisites for Web Deploy are installed. Click Install to continue the installation.

Several dependencies, such as SQL Server Shared Management Objects and SQL Server, are selected for you, as shown in Figure 20-10. These are installed as part of the Web PI prerequisites, as well as the Web Service Management Handler, which are not installed automatically if you install Web Deploy directly. For that reason, most administrators should use the Web PI installation. Accept the license agreement, and Web PI will install Web Deploy 3.0 for you.

Installing Web Deploy Directly

Installing the Web Deploy module directly, without using Web PI, is simple and straightforward. First, download the Web Deploy module from www.iis.net/download/webdeploy. Make sure you download the x64 version for Windows Server 2012. You can also directly install the application using Web PI from the IIS website. Once you have downloaded Web Deploy, launch the installer, click Next to pass the Welcome screen, and accept the license agreement.

Three setup types are available: Typical, Custom and, Complete (see Figure 20-11).

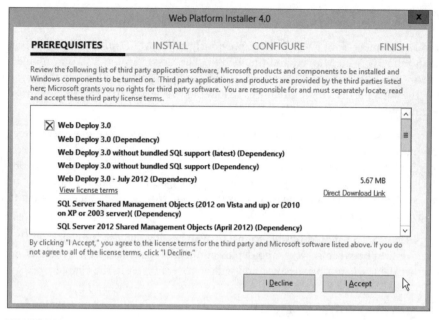

FIGURE 20-10

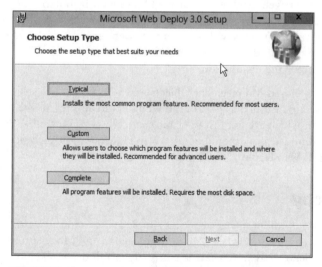

FIGURE 20-11

The only difference between the three choices is whether you'll install the Remote Agent Service. This service simply listens for Web Deploy requests, and you likely will want it installed for many functions. Simply choose Complete, and it will install the Web Deploy module with the Remote Agent Service, as if you had chosen Custom and selected the service for installation. Click through the wizard and Web Deploy will install.

Installing Web Deploy directly does not install the SQL Shared Management Objects (SMO), which is required for SQL Server database deployments, or the Web Management Service handler, which is required for non-administrator deployments; neither does it configure the Web Management Service for non-administrator deployments, unless PowerShell v2 is installed. Therefore, using Web PI to install Web Deploy is recommended for most administrators and configurations.

Deploying Web Applications

With Web Deploy installed, a developer or administrator can easily package and deploy applications. An application is simply exported from an original location and imported into the new location, using tools within IIS Manager. There are a few requirements for using Web Deploy to deploy your own web applications or to synchronize websites, which may or may not be installed or configured as part of your web development system:

➤ You must install the .NET 3.5 Framework in IIS 8.0, which is not installed by default when you choose the Application Server role. If you did not install this previously, use the Add Roles and Features process to add the .NET 3.5 Framework, including HTTP Activation. You will also need the Advanced Logging Module for IIS, which can be installed in the same way.

➤ When using Web Deploy, you must have access to the systems involved. The examples assume two servers in the same Active Directory domain and do not include FQDNs or paths — just system names. In cross-domain instances, you will need to provide authentication for the destination domains, as well as name resolution. This is also true when using Web Deploy from local systems to commercially hosted systems. The commands must be able to find the destination systems by name and be authenticated to allow access for Web Deploy.

➤ When Web Deploy is installed on a Windows Sever 2012 system, both 32-bit and 64-bit versions will be installed. You must use the version that matches the other server involved so that if you are creating a deployment package on a Windows Server 2012 system, which is 64-bit, to deploy on a 32-bit Windows Server 2008 system, you must use the 32-bit version of Web Deploy on both systems.

Exporting Applications

To export an application using Web Deploy, perform the following steps:

1. Open IIS Manager and expand the site with the application to be exported.

2. Right-click on the application and choose Deploy ➪ Export Application, as shown in Figure 20-12.

3. In the Export Application Package wizard, select the appropriate package contents, if they are not already selected, and click Next.

In the Parameters window, you can add parameters to your package, such as a new SQL connection string to match the deployment environment.

In the Add Parameter window, add the Name, Default Value, and other information about the parameters you will request during deployment, such as tags that determine how the parameter will be displayed and input validation in the form of Boolean values or regular expressions.

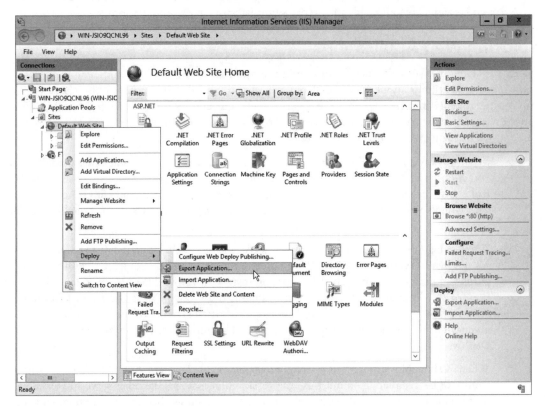

FIGURE 20-12

4. Click Next and enter a physical location for the package to be saved. It will be saved as a compressed ZIP file by default.

5. Click Ok. The wizard will complete the package export and leave you with an application package that can be imported into another site.

Once you have exported a package and saved the resulting package file to a location that can be reached by the new server, the process is reversed to install the application. Open IIS Manager on the new server, expand the sites folder, and right-click on the site to receive the new application import. Select Deploy ➪ Import Application, as shown in Figure 20-13, to launch the Import Application Package wizard.

You will be asked for the path of the application package and then presented with the contents of the package. You should see, as shown in Figure 20-14, that the package contents are the same as those you exported when creating the package.

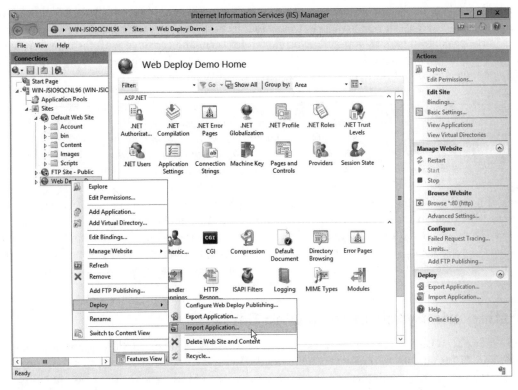

FIGURE 20-13

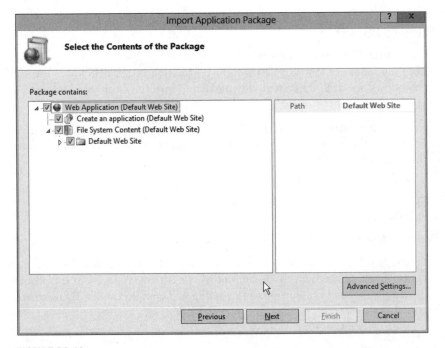

FIGURE 20-14

You will be asked for the application root where the application should be installed and allowed to accept the same root as the application was exported from. If you have added any additional parameters in the package at export, you will be prompted for them and provided with the default values you entered during the application export. Finishing the wizard will complete the installation of the package. You should find the application installed and active on the new site.

> **NOTE** *The Web Deploy application import process requires the site to be running version 2.0 of the ASP.NET framework. After the package is installed, you can reset the framework to that appropriate for the new application.*

Exporting and importing applications can be used to provide snapshots of applications before upgrade, but they do not produce a reliable backup for running applications. If you decide to use the export/import process for backups, remember that data and settings in a dynamic application environment can change quickly and that any export is of an application at a specific time. Also remember that any application designed for deployment to other systems or clients should be sanitized before export to remove unnecessary data and settings.

Migrating and Synchronizing Web Servers

You can use Web Deploy to migrate and synchronize websites between IIS 8.0 versions and from IIS 6.0 or IIS 7.0 versions to IIS 8.0 servers. Using Web Deploy, you need to review the dependencies on the source site, install them on the destination site, and then sync the site from the source to the destination. This is easily accomplished with the command line and can be scripted for mass migrations.

Migrating IIS 6.0 Sites to IIS 8.0

To use MS Deploy to migrate an IIS 6.0 site running on Windows Server 2003, you must have MS Deploy installed on both the source system (IIS 6.0) and the destination system (IIS 8.0). To install Web Deploy on your Windows Server 2003 system, download and install it from `www.iis.net/downloads/microsoft/web-deploy`.

MS Deploy also requires administrator access to the system. This means the user must be logged in as an administrator or the commands must be run as an administrator, on both the source system (IIS 6.0) and the destination system (IIS 8.0).

Begin by reviewing the IIS 6.0 source site's dependencies using the following command: (`MSDeploy.exe` is installed in the `C:\Program Files(x86)\IIS\Microsoft Web Deploy V3` folder by default. You can add it to the path, if needed.)

```
msdeploy -verb:getDependencies -source:metakey=lm/w3svc/1
```

The `metakey` for `lm/w3svc/1` is for site number 1 on the server, usually the default website. An easy way to find the site number in IIS 6.0 is to go to the site's properties dialog and look at the properties for the log file. The log file name in the bottom of the dialog will contain the site ID number you will use in the command line `metakey`.

Once you have the dependencies information, install those dependencies on the destination server. This may include applications, services, and other settings, and there is no simple shortcut for exporting these and importing them to the new site. Scripting the installation of dependencies using PowerShell is recommended for large numbers of sites, such as client sites for hosting companies. Common dependencies would be things like the ASP.NET framework, ASP.NET Authentication, and so on, but exporting some sites may involve many dependencies.

Once the proper dependencies are installed on the destination server, there are two ways to migrate a site using Web Deploy. One method is to create a site package, similar to exporting and importing an application package, and the second method is to use the Web Deployment Agent Service to migrate directly between servers.

For the package method, run the following command:

```
msdeploy -verb:sync  -source:metakey=lm/w3svc/1
    -dest:package=c:\Site1.zip > WebDeployPackage.log
```

Again, the `metakey` is the site ID number. This time, we'll pipe the process to a log file, in case we need to review it. After creating the compressed package file, copy it to a location that can be reached by the destination IIS 8.0 server, and, on the IIS 8.0 server, run the command, again paying attention to the site ID in the `metakey`, which can be changed to match the new site location:

```
msdeploy -verb:sync -source:package=c:\Site1.zip
    -dest:metakey=lm/w3svc/1 > WebDeploySync.log
```

This command will sync the site to the new server, and you should be ready simply to start the site to complete the migration.

The Web Deploy command also has a parameter to run the sync operation in a "what if" situation, and display the results of what would happen if the command were run for real. To do this, simply add the `-WhatIf` switch to the command line, as follows:

```
msdeploy -verb:sync -source:package=c:\Site1.zip -dest:metakey=lm/w3svc/1
    -whatif > WebDeploySync.log
```

To use the Web Deployment Agent Service to move to or from a remote server, install Web Deploy on the remote system and start the agent service, as follows:

```
net start msdepsvc
```

Once the service is running, you can push your site synchronization from a local system to the remote system with the following command line, again paying attention to the site ID and adding the computer name:

```
msdeploy -verb:sync -source:metakey=lm/w3svc/1 -dest:metakey=lm/w3svc/1,
    computername=Server1 -whatif > msdeploysync.log
```

A pull from a remote IIS 6.0 server to the local IIS 8.0 server is simply:

```
msdeploy -verb:sync -source:metakey=lm/w3svc/1,computername=Server1
    -dest:metakey=lm/w3svc/1 -whatif > msdeploysync.log
```

Web Deploy is often the best way to automate migration from older IIS 6.0 sites to new servers. It is also quite useful for syncing IIS 7.0 and 8.0 sites, in a manner very similar to working with IIS 6.0 sites.

Migrating or Syncing IIS 7.0 and IIS 8.0

Migrating or synchronizing sites between IIS 7.0 and IIS 8.0 is similar to migrating IIS 6.0 sites, with slightly different command lines. Begin by reviewing the source (IIS 7.0) site's dependencies using the following command: (MSDeploy.exe is installed in the C:\Program Files(x86)\IIS\ Microsoft Web Deploy V3 folder by default.)

```
msdeploy -verb:getDependencies -source:apphostconfig="Default Web Site"
```

The name used in the apphost.config is for the default website. Change this to the name of the site you intend to migrate. An easy way to determine the site name is to look at Advanced Settings for the site, as shown in Figure 20-15.

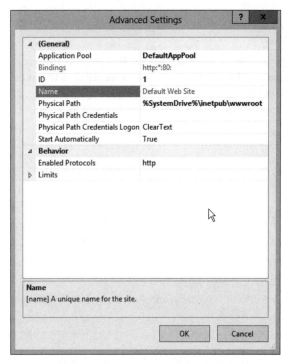

FIGURE 20-15

Once you have the dependencies information, install those dependencies on the destination server. Scripting the installation of dependencies using PowerShell is recommended for large numbers of sites, such as client sites for hosting companies. Common dependencies would be things like the ASP.NET framework, ASP.NET Authentication, and so on, but exporting some sites may involve many dependencies.

Once you have the proper dependencies installed on the destination server, there are two ways to migrate a site using Web Deploy. One method is to create a site package, similar to exporting and importing an application package, and the second method is to use the Web Deployment Agent Service to migrate directly between servers.

For the package method, run the following command:

```
msdeploy -verb:sync  -source:apphostconfig="Default Web Site"
    -dest:package=c:\site1.zip
```

Again, pay attention to the site name. After creating the compressed package file, copy it to a location that can be reached by the destination server, and, on that server, run the command, setting the site name, which can be changed to match the new site location:

```
msdeploy -verb:sync -source:package=c:\site1.zip
    -dest:apphostconfig="Default Web Site" > msdeploysync.log
```

This command will synch the site to the new server and you should be ready simply to start the site to complete the migration.

The Web Deploy command also has a parameter to run the sync operation in a "what if" situation and display the results of what would happen if the command were run for real. To do this, simply add the -WhatIf switch to the command line, as follows:

```
msdeploy -verb:sync -source:package=c:\site1.zip
    -dest:apphostconfig="Default Web Site" -whatif > msdeploysync.log
```

To use the Web Deployment Agent Service to move to or from a remote server, install Web Deploy on the remote system and start the agent service, as follows:

```
net start msdepsvc
```

Once the service is running, you can push your site from a local IIS 7.0 system to the remote IIS 8.0 system with the following command line, again paying attention to the site name, but this time adding the appropriate computer name as well:

```
msdeploy -verb:sync -source:apphostconfig="Default Web Site"
    -dest:apphostconfig="Default Web Site",computername=Server1 > msdeploysync.log
```

A pull from a remote IIS 7.0 server to the local IIS 8.0 system is simply:

```
msdeploy -verb:sync -source:apphostconfig="Default Web Site",computername=Server1
    -dest:apphostconfig="Default Web Site" > msdeploysync.log
```

The Web Deployment Agent Service also supports the -WhatIf parameter on the command line, as in working with IIS 6.0 sites.

FTP PUBLISHING

Configuring a website for FTP publishing is often the simplest method to allow developers to publish applications to a web server. It is secure and allows administrators to restrict access to sites through FTP settings. FTP publishing is integrated into Visual Studio 2012 and is a simple way to publish applications with nothing more than an FTP account linked to the website. FTP publishing requires that the Microsoft FTP service be installed, as discussed in Chapter 10.

Configuring FTP Publishing with IIS Manager

FTP publishing for IIS 8 is easy to configure to allow IIS site administrators to manage the content on their sites, using IIS security accounts. FTP must be installed first. (See Chapter 10 for installation instructions.) You also need to have a website created in order to configure FTP publishing for that site.

Open IIS Manager, highlight the website you want to configure in the Connections pane, right-click on it and choose Add FTP Publishing, as shown in Figure 20-16. You will find yourself in the Add FTP Site Publishing wizard, as shown in Figure 20-17.

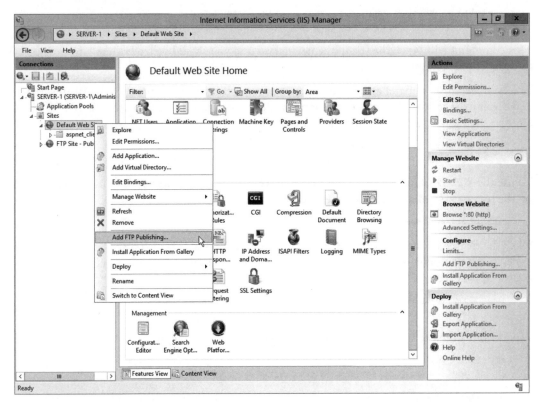

FIGURE 20-16

Select the IP address to use for FTP (the same IP address that the site is bound to is the best choice) or check the Enable Virtual Host Names box to allow multiple FTP sites on one IP address. Virtual host names are similar to host headers for websites and allow FTP clients to reach multiple FTP sites on the same IP address based on the host name requested. For most organizations, a separate IP address is more desirable.

For most uses, you should leave the port address at the default of 21. As with websites and HTTP ports, any non-standard port binding requires the port to be specified on the URL, as in `ftp://server1:2121/`, if the IP port of 2121 were specified. For more secure, automated uploads, a non-standard port may be useful, but clients will try to connect to the default port of 21 if no alternate port is specified on the URL.

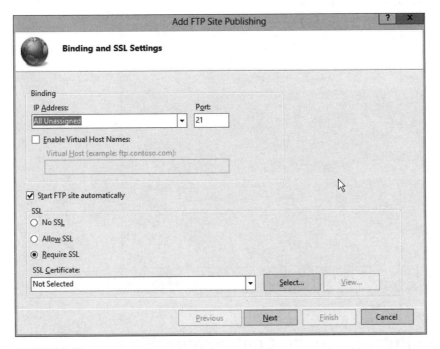

FIGURE 20-17

FTP over SSL, often referred to as *FTPS*, is possible for IIS 8.0 by simply checking the appropriate SSL choice. You must supply a certificate for SSL, either self-generated or assigned by a known SSL root certificate store. Self-generated SSL certificates will produce a warning in the client, so if you are serving the general public, a certificate issued by a root authority is the better choice. SSL options are covered in Chapter 15, "SSL and TLS."

When you have finished with the binding choices, click Next to select the authentication and authorization for FTP access, as shown in Figure 20-18. These are the same options described in Chapter 10, with a choice of Anonymous or Basic authentication. Authentication and authorization are also covered in Chapter 14. Anonymous authentication allows any account access without logging in and is unwise for FTP publishing since anyone with a FTP client could change the programming and content on a site. Basic authentication is sent in clear text, so for the most secure access, you should use SSL for your FTP publishing. SSL is covered in Chapter 15, "SSL and TLS."

Authorization allows you to choose the user account or group that is allowed access to the FTP site. Hosting companies would likely choose to allow access to those accounts used for managing the website, while some organizations may find it easier to grant access to a user group and control the membership through that group. Click Finish to finalize configuring FTP publishing for the website. You will now be able to use FTP publishing from Visual Studio and other development environments.

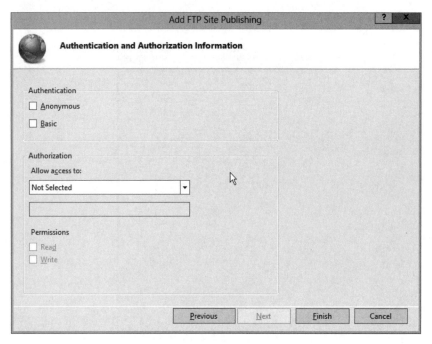

FIGURE 20-18

Configuring FTP Publishing with Configuration Files

Once the FTP role has been installed on an IIS 8.0 server, it may be easier for administrators or developers used to working configuration files to enable and configure FTP publishing by editing the files directly. Adding FTP publishing to a website is a simple edit of the applicationHost.config file using Visual Studio or any text editor. For example, let's add FTP publishing to Website 1 and set it for access by the Administrator account for Read and Write access. Code examples for this section are in the FTPPublishing.txt code file. In our applicationHost.config file, we already have the website information, which looks like this:

```
<site name="Web Site 1" id="99">
    <application path="/">
        <virtualDirectory path="/" physicalPath="%SystemDrive%\inetpub\website1" />
    </application>
    <bindings>
        <binding protocol="http" bindingInformation="*:80:" />
    </bindings>
</site>
```

Our site name is Web Site 1 with an ID of 99, located in the \Inetpub\website1 folder. HTTP is bound to the default port number, 80. First, we add a binding element for FTP on port 21, so that the site information will look like this, with the added line in bold setting the binding:

```
<site name="Web Site 1" id="99">
    <application path="/">
        <virtualDirectory path="/" physicalPath="%SystemDrive%\inetpub\website1" />
```

```
    </application>
    <bindings>
        <binding protocol="http" bindingInformation="*:80:" />
        <binding protocol="ftp" bindingInformation="*:21:" />
    </bindings>
</site>
```

We now need to add an FTP Server section to the site with the authentication configured for no anonymous access and Basic authentication for the FTP site. FTP authentication is configured for the site, whereas website authentication can be configured for an individual URL. When this section is added, shown in bold in the following code, the `<site>` section will be as follows:

```
<site name="Web Site 1" id="99">
    <application path="/">
        <virtualDirectory path="/" physicalPath="%SystemDrive%\inetpub\website1" />
    </application>
    <bindings>
        <binding protocol="http" bindingInformation="*:80:" />
        <binding protocol="ftp" bindingInformation="*:21:" />
    </bindings>
    <ftpServer>
        <security>
            <authentication>
                <anonymousAuthentication enabled="false" />
                <basicAuthentication enabled="true" />
            </authentication>
        </security>
    </ftpServer>
</site>
```

The last thing to do is to add a `<location>` section for the website with the FTP authorization for the Administrator account with Read and Write access to the FTP site. This `<location>` section looks like the following:

```
<location path="Web Site 1">
  <system.ftpServer>
    <security>
      <authorization>
        <add accessType="Allow" users="Administrator" permissions="Read, Write" />
      </authorization>
    </security>
  </system.ftpServer>
</location>
```

After the `applicationHost.config` is saved, the server will reread it and your site will now have FTP publishing, with Read and Write access for the Administrator account.

WEBDAV PUBLISHING

Web Distributed Authoring and Versioning (WebDAV) is an HTTP extension designed to allow editing and versioning of web-based files. As an extension, WebDAV adds protocols to HTTP that allow you to create and delete folders, transfer files, lock files, and determine ownership and update properties. This is, essentially, the original goal that the web designers had in mind — the ability to collaborate and share information.

WebDAV is still a usable protocol, although it has fallen out of favor as technologies such as Web Deploy have taken its place. An alternative to FTP, WebDAV, like Web Deploy, uses HTTP transports and will normally operate through firewalls that will pass web traffic. Microsoft used a previous concept of Web Folders — Windows folders accessible across a HTTP connection — that had limitations in both extensibility and compatibility with non-Windows clients. WebDAV is now fully compliant with RTFC 4918, which defines WebDAV. WebDAV is also fully supported by many current client operating systems, including Windows, Linux, and Apple systems.

For the purposes of IIS 8.0, WebDAV is primarily relevant as a publishing alternative to FTP. In IIS 8.0, WebDAV is integrated to IIS Manager and supports locking mechanisms to prevent accidental updates and overwrites of application files. WebDAV is supported over SSL connections and supports authoring rules based on specific URLs.

Installing and Configuring WebDAV

Open Server Manager and use the Add Roles and Features option in the Management tools to add WebDAV publishing to your web server. You'll find it under the Server Roles ➪ Web Server (IIS) role ➪ Common HTTP Features. Simply check WebDAV Publishing, as shown in Figure 20-19.

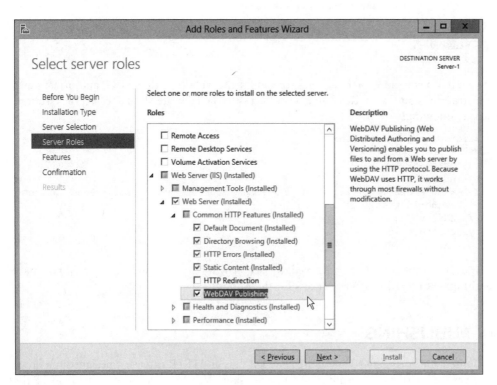

FIGURE 20-19

There are no features to install with WebDAV, so click Next to continue to the confirmation dialog. There is an option here to restart the destination server automatically if required, although WebDAV normally will not need a server restart. Click Install, as shown in Figure 20-20, to complete the installation.

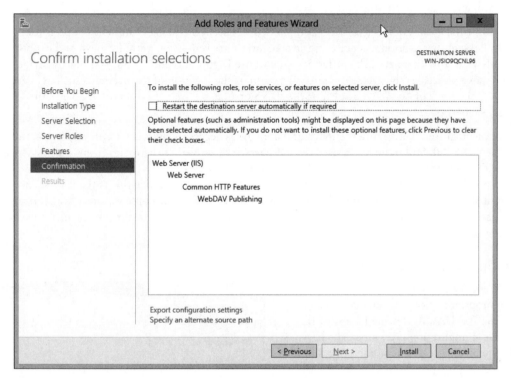

FIGURE 20-20

The WebDAV feature will install to your server.

Accounts for Using WebDAV

When configuring WebDAV, you should never allow access for All Users, just as you would never grant Everyone administrator access to the server. You have several options for WebDAV accounts, including local Windows user accounts and groups, Active Directory domain Windows accounts and groups, and .NET user accounts and groups. The choice of account type will depend on many factors, such as whether this is an intranet situation, whether an Active Directory domain is present, and whether licensing allows for an adequate number of Windows accounts.

Different account types may also require enabling different authentication options in IIS 8.0, including, in order from most secure to least secure, Windows Integrated authorization (IWA), Digest Authentication, and Basic Authentication. If multiple authentication methods are enabled, IIS 8.0 will attempt connections in the order from most secure to least secure, until a connection is established.

IWA uses Kerberos version 5, if available, and NTLM authentication. This requires a Windows account, either local or Active Directory, and will not work over an HTTP proxy connection. This is an ideal authentication method for an intranet, where user accounts are in a Windows Active Directory domain. In these cases, where the authentication is trusted between systems, the user will not be prompted for a username and password.

Digest authentication requires a user ID and password. Essentially, Digest authentication is the same as Basic authentication, except that the credentials are sent using an MD5 hash and cannot be openly viewed with a network sniffer. If you will use Digest authentication, you must provide a realm name as well as the account name. The realm is the location of the account, such as the domain in the form of `Domain\UserID`, or the DNS or Active Directory domain in an e-mail address, such as `UserID@Domain.TLD`.

Basic authentication, while more secure than Anonymous access, is the least secure authentication available in IIS 8.0. Still requiring a user ID and password, as well as the realm being specified, the authentication credentials are sent across the network in clear text. This means that packet sniffers and protocol analyzers can easily read the user ID and password. Since this is the least secure option, it should be used where there is little security concern over the content. Basic authentication is compatible with almost any web client, so it may be required in some instances in which the client software cannot be dictated.

Configuring Authoring Rules

Once WebDAV is installed and you have created appropriate accounts, you need to configure the WebDAV Authoring Rules for the site. This configuration is on a per-site basis so that publishing can be confined to a single site by setting the proper access rules for the proper user accounts. Open IIS Manager and expand the Sites tree, and then select the site to configure and double-click the WebDAV Authoring Rules feature to open it. Click on Add Authoring Rule in the Actions pane. You'll see the Add Authoring Rule dialog, as shown in Figure 20-21.

You can choose to allow WebDAV publishing access to all content or only to specific files or folders. For publishing from Visual Studio, unless you have a specific reason to restrict this, leave it at the default, "All content." IIS 8.0 Request Filtering rules can also affect WebDAV publishing, so you might need to configure request filters to allow specific file types to be published. Request Filtering is discussed in Chapter 13, "Securing the Server."

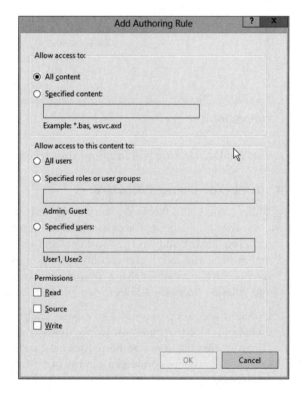

FIGURE 20-21

Next, choose the user accounts to allow access to. These can be .NET or Windows user accounts or groups. Using a group for accounts with access can make it easier for an administrator to manage the accounts that have WebDAV access. Simply add or remove an account from a group to change access. You must also grant the permissions allowed for the user account. Read and Write permissions are required for most publishing, and Source permission supports publishing from Visual Studio and other development environments. Creating and using .NET accounts are covered in Chapters 10 and 14. For Windows accounts, you must enable IWA on the website. After clicking OK, you will have allowed WebDAV access to the specified content and accounts.

Configuring WebDAV with Configuration Files

Once you have installed WebDAV, you can configure WebDAV on a website by editing the configuration files for that site — a process that lends itself to automation by administrators. This process requires that you have Administrator permission since you will be editing the `applicationHost .config` file; Windows User Account Control will not allow this unless you are an administrator. The code from this section can be found in the `WebDAVPublishing.txt` file.

Using Visual Studio, or any text editor, open the `applicationHost.config` file, normally located in the `%SystemRoot%\System32\inetsrv\config` folder. At the bottom of the file, find the `<location>` section, or create one if it doesn't exist, and edit it to include the following:

```
<location path="Default Web Site">
  <system.webServer>
    <security>
      <authentication>
        <anonymousAuthentication enabled="true" />
        <basicAuthentication enabled="false" />
        <digestAuthentication enabled="false" />
        <windowsAuthentication enabled="true" />
      </authentication>
    </security>
  </system.webServer>
</location>
```

Within this `<location>` section, you will need a `<webdav>` section. You will also need to make sure you have enabled the appropriate authentication methods. Your `<location>` section will look something like this:

```
<location path="Default Web Site">
  <system.webServer>
   <security>
   <webdav>
     <authoring enabled="true" />
     <authoringRules>
      <add users="administrator" path="*"
        access="Read, Write, Source" />
     </authoringRules>
   </webdav>

     <authentication>
      <anonymousAuthentication enabled="true" />
```

```
            <basicAuthentication enabled="false" />
            <digestAuthentication enabled="false" />
            <windowsAuthentication enabled="true" />
          </authentication>
      </security>
    </system.webServer>
  </location>
```

This will add the Administrator account to WebDAV publishing with Read and Write access, but allow no other accounts access. It will also enable WIA for the Windows account administrator. Naturally, you will want to modify this code to fit your own organization's needs and account types. For a .NET account group, it might look something like the following:

```
<location path="Default Web Site">
  <system.webServer>
   <security>
   <webdav>
     <authoring enabled="true" />
     <authoringRules>
      <add roles="WebDAVUsers" path="*"
        access="Read, Write, Source" />
     </authoringRules>
   </webdav>

     <authentication>
      <anonymousAuthentication enabled="true" />
      <basicAuthentication enabled="false" />
      <digestAuthentication enabled="false" />
      <windowsAuthentication enabled="true" />
     </authentication>
    </security>
  </system.webServer>
 </location>
```

Naturally, the WebDAVUsers role listed here would need to exist as a .NET user role and have .NET user accounts in it to be usable. .NET accounts and roles make sense in many situations, such as web hosting or development environments, where .NET accounts are already in use for other tasks.

VISUAL STUDIO PUBLISHING

A major reason for the publishing functions in IIS 8.0 is for publishing from Microsoft's development tools, such as Visual Studio. Beginning in IIS 7.0 and extended in Visual Studio 2010 and 2012, publishing websites and applications directly from Visual Studio has become very convenient for developers, either for production or development systems. Publishing from Visual Studio, both 2010 and 2012, is similar in this regard; it involves using FTP or Web Deploy, both of which were described earlier in the chapter. Once they are installed, publishing websites and applications from Visual Studio is easy to configure.

Publishing Websites

Publishing a website created in Visual Studio 2012 using FTP is accomplished by opening Visual Studio 2012 and opening the website solution. Right-click on the root of the website in Solution Explorer and choose Publish Web Site, as shown in Figure 20-22.

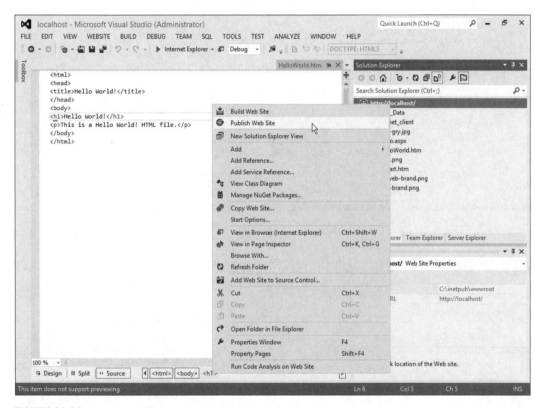

FIGURE 20-22

This will open the Publish Web Site dialog, as shown in Figure 20-23, where you select the target location. Enter the path to the target as an FTP URL, similar to `ftp://localhost/`, using the FQDN of your FTP-enabled website, the host name, or the IP address the FTP service is bound to.

Click OK to continue. You will be asked for the login credentials for the FTP site. Enter the username and password allowed during configuration of the FTP site. This will open a warning message that passwords are sent in clear text — one of the drawbacks of FTP publishing. Click OK, and you will see the publishing process in the Output pane of Visual Studio 2012, as shown in Figure 20-24.

Publishing a website from Visual Studio 2012 using Web Deploy is almost the same as using FTP. Follow the same process to publish the website in Visual Studio 2012, except in the Publish Web Site dialog, use the `HTTP://` protocol instead of `FTP://`, as shown in Figure 20-25.

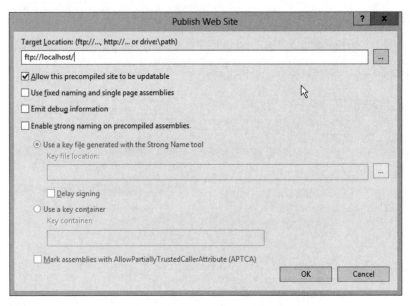

FIGURE 20-23

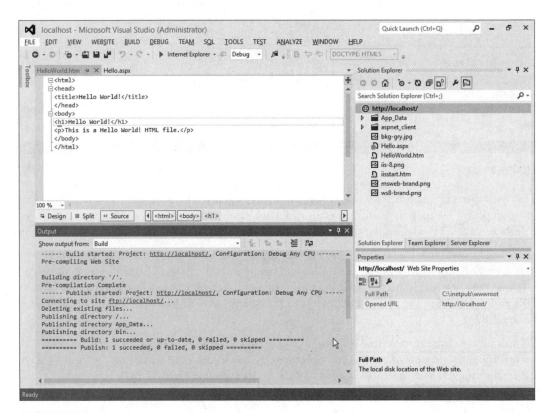

FIGURE 20-24

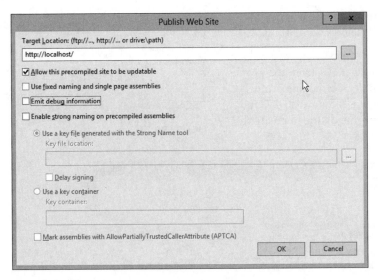

FIGURE 20-25

Publishing Web Applications

Publishing a web application using FTP or Web Deploy is somewhat more involved. Create or open a web application project in Visual Studio. For the demo, we simply created a new project in Visual Studio 2012, selecting Web Forms Application as the template. Once the application is created or opened in Visual Studio 2012, right-click on the application root in Solution Explorer and choose Publish, as shown in Figure 20-26. This will open the Publish Web Application wizard.

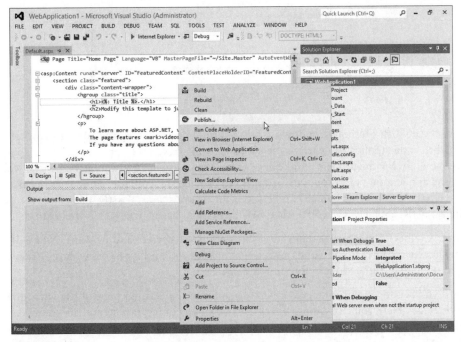

FIGURE 20-26

Provide credentials as requested, and you will again see the results in the Output Pane of Visual Studio 2012.

The first step of the wizard is to open or create a publishing profile. For the demo, choose <new> from the profile dropdown to create a new profile. Name this profile **FTP Publishing Profile**, as shown in Figure 20-27, and you will be prompted with a profile dialog to create the profile, as shown in Figure 20-28.

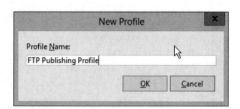

FIGURE 20-27

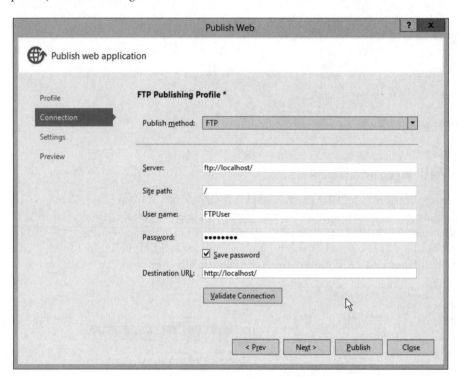

FIGURE 20-28

Select FTP from the Publish Method dropdown, and then provide the server and site path, as prompted. The path is the application path to the site, so if you created the application in the root, a single slash, as shown in the diagram, will take care of it. If your application root is below the website root, enter the application path. You will also need to provide the FTP username with access to this server, as well as the password, which can be saved for future access. Lastly, you'll want to provide the destination URL, which is the URL that web clients will use to access this application.

Click on Validate Connection to ensure that the profile details are correct and working. You will receive a green checkmark next to the Validate Connection button or a link to see what failed in the connection. Fix any failed connections before moving on.

Once you have a valid connection profile, click Next to move to the Settings page of the wizard, as shown in Figure 20-29. Here you can choose a Release or Debug configuration, and choose whether to delete all existing files during the publication.

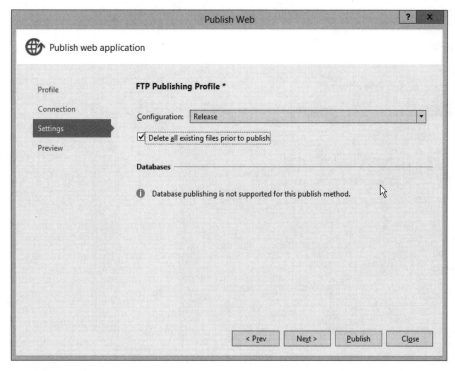

FIGURE 20-29

You'll also notice that databases cannot be published with FTP — a good reason to use Web Deploy for application publishing. If you have no databases, or if you will be publishing the database separately, this is not an issue.

Clicking Next will bring you to the preview page of the wizard, and your last chance to return to previous pages and change selections. Assuming that everything is correct on this page, click Publish to finish publishing the application to the site using FTP.

Visual Studio 2012 will show the publication process in the Output pane and will launch the application in the default web browser.

Using Web Deploy to publish an application is similar, although Web Deploy has more flexibility and functionality for publishing. Begin by again right-clicking the application root in Solution Explorer in Visual Studio 2012 and selecting Publish. Ensure that Profile is selected as the first step in the wizard, and again select <new> from the dropdown to create a new publishing profile, this time for Web Deploy. Name your profile and click OK to continue to the connection dialog of the wizard.

As shown in Figure 20-30, Web Deploy is looking for a service URL, the location used by the Web Deploy connection, in the form of an HTTP or HTTPS URL. This is almost always the site URL, but it may not be if you publish to a URL internal to your network and deploy to an external URL for web client access. More confusing is the prompt for Site/Application, which is the IIS site name and the application name.

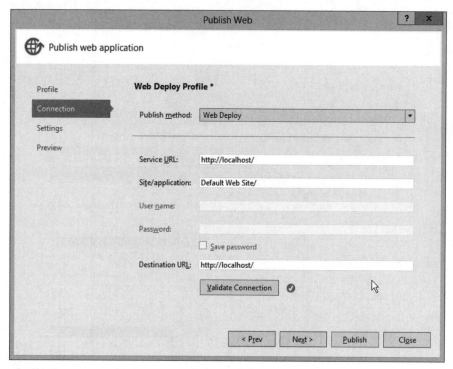

FIGURE 20-30

If the service URL is not on the local network, you will need to enter the username and password required for access to the site. If the service URL is local, Windows and the Web Deploy publishing process will pass the credentials of the logged in user, which must have authentication for WebDAV and ASP.NET to access the site.

Once the connection validates, click Next to continue to the Settings dialog of the Publish Web Application wizard, as shown in Figure 20-31. You have the same configuration choices as for FTP publishing, but you also have the ability to publish the database and set connection strings. This is especially useful if your development environment uses a connection string different from that of the deployment environment. Through this setting, you can change to the deployment connection string at the time of publication.

In this dialog, you can also configure the deployment of updates to the database for your application. You can add new database schemas and SQL scripts that will change the existing database configuration for your updated application. When you click Next to continue to the preview, you will see the options you have selected, as well as an option to preview the actual deployment. Click on Start Preview, as shown in Figure 20-32.

The preview will show you all the changes that will be made on the site, as shown in Figure 20-33. You can unselect any changes you do not want to make or go back to previous screens to change publishing options. If you click Publish, the web application will be published as confirmed in the preview.

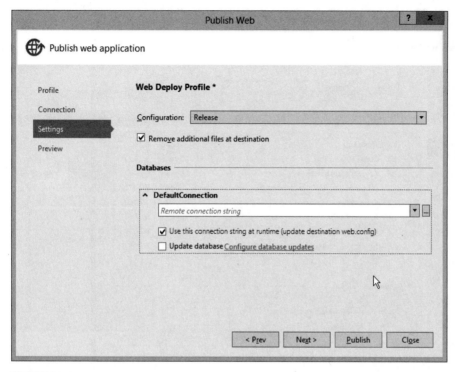

FIGURE 20-31

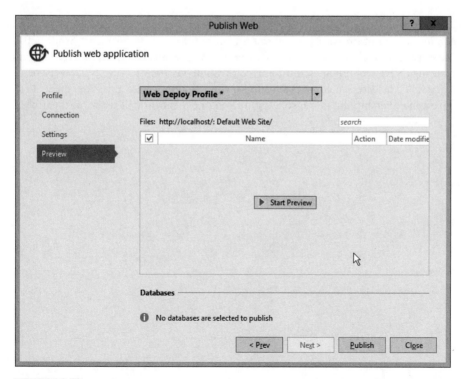

FIGURE 20-32

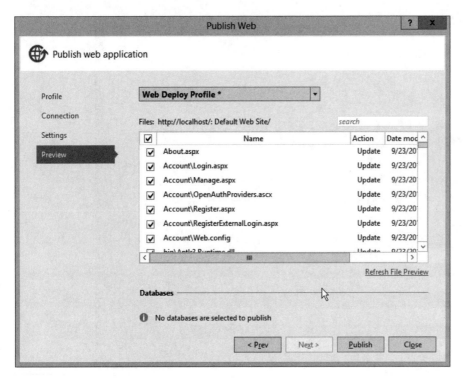

FIGURE 20-33

You will again see the publication process in the Output pane of Visual Studio 2012, and the application will launch in the default browser for you to test. More information on Visual Studio 2012 and its publishing options is available from www.microsoft.com/visualstudio/. Development of web applications using .NET technologies is supported through Microsoft's ASP.NET website, at http://www.asp.net/. This site is a companion site for the IIS support site at http://www.iis .net/. They share a membership database, so a login from one location will work on the other.

PART IV
Managing and Operating IIS 8.0

▶ **CHAPTER 21:** IIS and Operations Management

▶ **CHAPTER 22:** Monitoring and Performance Tuning

▶ **CHAPTER 23:** Diagnostics and Troubleshooting

21

IIS and Operations Management

WHAT'S IN THIS CHAPTER?

➤ IT Infrastructure Library standards

➤ The Microsoft Operations Framework

➤ Change management

➤ Backup and restore

After a website has been deployed into a production environment, what then? How do you ensure uptime for your website in an environment that is subject to ongoing changes, is exposed to the hailstorm of the Internet, and may be subject to more traffic than any other server? After deploying a web server, in some ways, the work has just begun.

Maintaining a web server involves a range of knowledge, skills, and abilities. There are a few different approaches to managing the operations of IIS servers, and all of them have some merit. You will, undoubtedly, want control and predictability from your server on an ongoing basis. For this purpose, most technicians value a steady flow of information and metrics.

This chapter introduces some important topics related to managing production IIS servers. To keep your servers up and the hosted applications functioning properly, you need a way to organize your team differently from the application development team. You need a system and organization suited to respond to the daily troubles that plague today's web server, and to be proactive about ensuring the viability of your investment in the hosted application. You first need to review some of the best sources for putting together a world-class structure for ensuring uptime. This chapter begins by looking more at organizational processes and then returns to a more technical focus.

MANAGEMENT APPROACHES

Professional websites almost always require some level of predictable uptime and some sort of minimum performance goals. Few would be happy with a website that responded inconsistently or sporadically every day. Of course, the margin of error, or window of acceptable downtime, will vary greatly depending on the nature of the website and the role it plays in fulfilling the mission of a business. A professional website is a valued tool, whether it's used occasionally for simple text updates or used extensively by customers to conduct e-commerce transactions.

In many cases, a particular website is just one site among many and might be hosted on a server that depends on a network infrastructure with complex (and often fragile) ties to other systems in your organization. The point here is that not only may a website break on its own, but it can also fail for reasons beyond the web server administrator's control. In this kind of environment, ensuring uptime and performance is a matter of operational management.

Managing operations for IIS applications and servers is about meeting expectations for the website every day. Control, predictability, and information flow are all key elements of IT operations management. If you have web servers in operation, yet lack operational systems, then where can you turn to get started?

Two excellent sources for great tools are the widely recognized authorities on technical management: the IT Infrastructure Library (ITIL) and the closely related Microsoft Operations Framework (MOF).

ITIL Standards

The *IT Infrastructure Library*, or ITIL (www.itil-officialsite.com), is a leading authority for technical management principles and practices. Based in the United Kingdom and deployed across the globe, the ITIL offers a body of knowledge, training practicum, and certification that is known as the standard for technical management assets and templates.

Chartered in the 1980s by the British government, and originally written as 31 volumes, the foundation publications were retitled later in the 1990s to be seen as guidance and not as a formal method. This made the ITIL assets extensible and applicable to broad audiences outside the original design. Since then, ITIL adoption gained worldwide momentum. This wider adoption and awareness led to several other standards, including ISO/IEC 20000, which is now the conceptual framework within which the latest version of ITIL operates.

A version of ITIL v3 first became available in May 2007, although it fully matured into its current form in June 2011. The new version recasts the ITIL assets against the modern business and technical landscape and organizes the body of knowledge into five core texts, including:

➤ Service Strategy

➤ Service Design

➤ Service Transition

➤ Service Operation

➤ Continual Service Improvement

With v3, ITIL extends its relevance to cover the technical priorities of modern business, including IT service management.

An essential part of the framework is the all-important toolkit. The *ITIL Toolkit* is a collection of resources brought together to inculcate the principles of ITIL and help you implement ITIL systems in your daily operations. The materials included in the toolkit are intended to assist in both understanding and implementation and are targeted at both existing ITIL users and beginners alike. The toolkit includes:

➤ A detailed guide to ITIL and service management

➤ The ITIL Factsheets — 12 two-page documents, serving as a concise summary of each of the ITIL disciplines

➤ A management presentation for ITIL (which doubles as a proposal for service management)

➤ A service management audit/review questionnaire and report in Microsoft Excel workbook form

➤ Materials to assist in the reporting of the above results (i.e., templates)

When developing applications on the platform, ITIL can bring you two levels of benefits. First, you can take the ITIL templates and use them to identify the common requirements, risks, and techniques used across the globe for building, deploying, and maintaining web applications. The templates are comprehensive aides to planning. Second, you can base your designs and directions on the strategic guidance found in the ITIL white papers, leveraging industry-proven principles.

ITIL is a terrific source for many things, but it's not the only recognized source for guidance. Other widely used frameworks include the Information Services Procurement Library (ISPL), the Application Services Library (ASL), the Dynamic Systems Development Method (DSDM), the Capability Maturity Model (CMM/CMMI), the Control Objectives for Information and Related Technology (COBIT), the Project Management Institute's Project Management Body of Knowledge (PMBOK), and, of special note, the Microsoft Operations Framework (MOF). MOF is a Microsoft-centric superset of ITIL, and it makes perfect sense to use MOF when talking about managing IIS operations.

MOF: Microsoft's ITIL Superset

Before we apply the MOF processes to a couple of sample IIS operations, let's take a moment to introduce it properly. The *Microsoft Operations Framework* (MOF) is a set of publications providing both descriptive and prescriptive guidance on IT service management. It's an actionable version of ITIL specifically for IT services based on Microsoft servers. Whereas ITIL is a consortium of expertise, MOF is constrained to Microsoft's perspective on managing IT using Microsoft's software. This limited focus is also the benefit of MOF, because the framework has the advantage of Microsoft's insider knowledge of its own products. You can get everything you need from MOF by visiting www.microsoft.com/mof.

Microsoft published the first elements of MOF in 2000 to help their customers achieve reliability, availability, and manageability goals for mission-critical systems that operate on the Microsoft platform. MOF is definitely one of the best sources for guidance covering operational systems for IIS servers. MOF v4 is the current release, which began to emerge in 2007 and finally superseded all previous content in 2011. Built from the precursor standards found in the ITIL, MOF provides in-depth technical guidance covering the spectrum of technology. MOF addresses the people, process, and technology issues that define today's complex and heterogeneous environments.

The top-level structure of MOF is composed of the following:

➤ **Lifecycle Phases** — The formal chapters of service delivery

➤ **Management Reviews** — The tasks involved in starting and ending Lifecycle Phases

➤ **Service Management Function (SMF)** — Sections or stages within the three Phases where activities are defined

Figure 21-1 depicts the elements and relationships between these top-level structures.

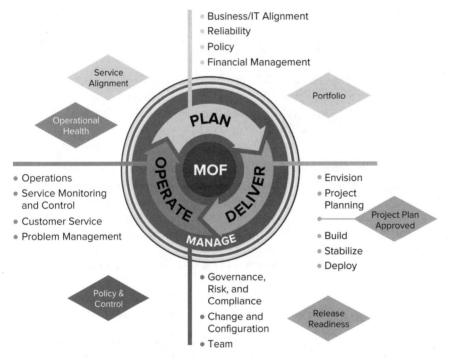

FIGURE 21-1

In fact, much of MOF is a bunch of IT activities that Microsoft identified and then grouped into an SMF. The SMFs combine to comprise a "Phase." The three Phases together describe the life cycle of an IT service, from imagineering to retirement:

➤ **Plan Phase** — This is where you decide on an approach and define your strategy for bringing your service to life and maintaining it over time.

➤ **Deliver Phase** — This is where you do the work that brings your service to life and ready it for your operations team.

➤ **Operate Phase** — This is the run time for your service, during which your service is consumed by live users.

The Phases are surrounded, in a manner of speaking, by a *Manage Layer*. In each Phase, the Manage Layer asks you to consider GRC (governance, risk, and compliance) challenges, including change and configuration management.

The following table outlines the different SMFs found in each MOF area:

MOF AREA	MOF FUNCTION	BENEFIT TO IIS OPERATIONS
Plan Phase	Business/IT Alignment	Cohesive backing for your IIS services throughout your organization; recoup budgets for aspects that are no longer valued.
	Reliability	Clear expectations and support for high availability and disaster recovery requirements.
	Policy	Certain IT policies need to reflect the business and legal principles that protect your organization, such as privacy and partner contracts.
	Financial Management	Accurate accounting and program management keep organizations responsive to new opportunities.
Deliver Phase	Envision	Start with a solid concept and approach, and begin working to address risks that can affect you later if unattended.
	Project Planning	If you don't have a plan, you have a plan for failure. Translate the requirements and concepts into an action plan, line up your team, and make room in your schedule to get the work done.
	Build	Use the tools to build components predictably and apply testing techniques that validate your work.
	Stabilize	Ensure a quality release by putting your website or application through comprehensive testing.
	Deploy	Promote your application to production and transfer runtime responsibilities to your operations team.
Operate Phase	Operations	Uptime! Plus, keep your team proactive instead of reactive.
	Service Monitoring and Control	Know when services go down before end users, and know more about why.
	Customer Service	Finally, incorporate end users' feedback to make their experience the best it can be.
	Problem Management	Accelerate root cause analysis and use a model to prepare for future issues.
Manage Layer	Governance, Risk, and Compliance	Be assured that only trusted people work on defined areas, and keep the lawyers at bay by keeping in line with regulations.
	Change and Configuration	Minimize human error and miscommunications.
	Team	Avoid unattended tasks, get people with the right skills, avoid miscommunications — and come to work happy!

MOF service functions have detailed documents that offer rich process definitions, templates, and other collateral that can flesh out how you shape your IIS operations. If you are interested in a more thorough and expert inculcation of MOF, there are several professional training options made available through Microsoft and a network of training partners. Use your favorite search engine to search for "MOF training."

Now that we have given you a general introduction to MOF, here are some more specific ways you can leverage it for IIS operations.

Applying MOF to IIS Operations Management

The following sections describe just a few ways in which you can use the MOF library to structure your operations to meet your requirements for uptime and performance (for example, SLA obligations). The two sections we picked are especially relevant to IIS. We first cover role-based administration to show how operations teams can be layered to provide full coverage of your IIS operations challenges. Afterward, we cover change management to illustrate how operations teams can reduce the risks of downtime when deploying changes to their web servers. Figure 21-2 shows how these major elements interoperate in the MOF model. Note how Service Management Functions — like Change Management — act as Solution Accelerators within a Service Improvement Project.

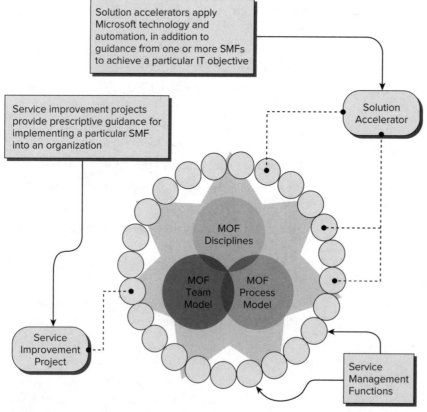

FIGURE 21-2

Role-Based Administration

IIS operations usually involve a team-based approach. Many players can be involved in managing web applications, including developers, system engineers, service desk personnel, and managers of all types. To keep your environment secure and performing well, each person involved in the operations program should have only the rights and privileges necessary to do the job at hand. The widely accepted network administration concept of *Least-Privileged User Account* (LUA) provides a great justification for limiting access, both from a security point of view as well as managing your SLA obligations. The following table describes the roles that your web application team might consider for managing the operations of all their web servers. The roles listed in the following table map to the "role clusters" from the MOF Team Model, as described at `http://technet.microsoft.com/en-us/library/cc539245.aspx`.

MOF ROLE CLUSTER	ROLE NAME	ROLE RESPONSIBILITIES
Operations	IIS Admin	Routine maintenance, audit, lockdown, enable extensions, and aid in the deployment of new web applications as per the organization's policies. Ensure that the web server is maintained in a state so that it can satisfy all SLA requirements. Participate in monitoring and audit processes.
Security	IIS Security Admin	Implement Active Directory policies. Lead security audit. Ensure IIS security by implementing best practices.
Operations	IIS Application Admin	Administer applications and websites (does not have rights to all of IIS, only to particular websites). Configure resources for websites. Participate in monitoring and audit processes and take care of all security concerns raised by the application.
Infrastructure	IIS Deployment Admin	Deploy the web servers. Ensure that service packs and patches are current and that configuration settings conform with organization rules. Ensure that the web servers have antivirus protection.
Support	IIS Incident Admin	Implement incident response for incidents. Provide web server incident management policy. Isolate and resolve problems and issues from incidents and propagate requests for changes. Interface with partners if there are issues regarding hardware or technology they have provided, and maintain a support loop with them.

Additional roles can be added to support application-specific needs, such as publishing files or making changes to the config files.

In addition to the Team Model Role Cluster, MOF includes a Team SMF to help you identify the right roles for your organization. You can read more about the Team SMF at `http://technet` `.microsoft.com/en-us/library/cc543311`.

Once you have your Team Model, IIS 8.0 makes it easy to delegate tasks to application owners and infrastructure engineers alike. Application roles usually require fewer privileges and should not interfere with any of the organization's roles. They also need to be restricted to the application or applications in scope for the personnel and have boundaries to block access to areas outside of their charge. For this purpose, IIS 8.0 provides granular access to resources through adaptation of Group Policy Objects (GPO), inheritance of permissions on folders, and integration with the Windows Server security mechanisms. Delegating rights for the IIS server, websites, and application pools is covered in detail in Chapter 9, "Delegating Remote Administration."

One context in which roles are important is when a change to an IIS platform has to be deployed. Some changes, such as new versions of IIS applications, can present high levels of risk for downtime should the change have unknown and undesired consequences upon deployment. The next topic we look at is the Change and Configuration Management SMF.

Change Management

Like many of the SMFs, many large tomes have been written on the subject of change management — both by Microsoft and by other venerable institutions. If you don't have a mature change management process, then you should develop a system to support both your website development processes and the ongoing operations that keep your production site going. If you have a change management process already and it hasn't been crafted specifically for web solutions, review it for appropriateness for website applications and servers.

A good change management system provides a disciplined process for introducing changes into the web-server environment and maintains minimal disruption to ongoing operations when the change is introduced. Keeping your servers up while they undergo software or hardware upgrades, for example, can best be done when you have a realistic plan. To achieve this goal, a change management process includes the following objectives:

➤ Formalize the process of initiating change through the submission of a request for change (RFC) and a change approval board (CAB).

➤ Assign a priority and a category to the change, and appraise urgency and impact on tertiary services, the infrastructure, and end users.

➤ Plan the deployment of the change. Be careful to include "go/no-go" checkpoints where the change deployment progress can be verified or delayed depending on the new levels of risk that you may uncover as the change plan matures.

➤ Work with the Change and Configuration SMF, which manages the release and deployment of changes into the production environment. For more information about the Release Management SMF, see `http://technet.microsoft.com/en-us/library/cc543211`.

➤ Conduct a post-implementation review of whether the change has achieved the goals that were established for it and determine whether to keep the change or roll it back.

The Change and Configuration Management SMF extends these objectives into specific tasks, and it's worthwhile to view those and incorporate the relevant tasks into your IIS operations program.

An important principle of how the SMF sets up and relates change managements tasks is that you don't take anything for granted. Be sure that you have all the relevant people reviewing the change and the deployment plan, and be sure that everyone involved understands and agrees on what to expect after the change is implemented.

To that end, the following table lays out how you may wish to involve team members in change management decisions. The first column calls out the different teams that can be involved in IIS operations as defined by the MOF Team Model. The remaining columns indicate whether the team should be involved based on the severity (that is, scope, risk, impact) of the change.

MOF ROLE CLUSTER	CHANGE TYPE			
	MINOR CHANGE	STANDARD CHANGE	SIGNIFICANT AND MAJOR CHANGE	EMERGENCY CHANGE
Infrastructure	Not involved	Preauthorized	CAB member	CAB member
Operations	Not involved	Preauthorized	CAB member	CAB member
Partner	Not involved	Preauthorized	CAB member	CAB member
Release	Authorizer	Authorizer	CAB member	CAB member
Security	Not involved	Preauthorized	CAB member	CAB member
Support	Not involved	Preauthorized	CAB member	CAB member
Service	Not involved	Preauthorized	CAB member	CAB member

To make both the Team Model SMF and Change and Configuration Management SMF more palpable, let's go through two examples of how these MOF principles can help you manage your IIS operations. First, we look at how to scope, plan, and manage an emergency change. Then we look at a typical change management task: applying server hotfixes.

MOF Example: Change Management for Emergency Updates

Emergency updates to an IIS environment are those that need to be applied to restore performance or to avoid an imminent loss of performance. This is the kind of change that usually accompanies pressure to skip the normal considerations you would take before introducing change. The process outlined in the example below, taken from the MOF Change and Configuration Management SMF, will help you deploy changes to an IIS environment without losing confidence in your results.

For this example, let's assume that you received alerts from your IIS server that indicate an unexpected spike in CPU and I/O utilization. Let's assume that an application team has recently deployed a website onto the same shared IIS 8.0 server cluster from which you received the alerts. Furthermore, let's assume that the cluster includes three web servers in a load-balanced configuration. The cluster provides key services for financial and marketing personnel who report to executives in your company and who are suddenly dissatisfied with the responsiveness. Upon approaching the application team who recently added the website, you have been informed that they have a fix they would like to apply immediately. You communicate to the application team that this fix must first be applied through your team's change management process, which is based on MOF and illustrated in Figure 21-3.

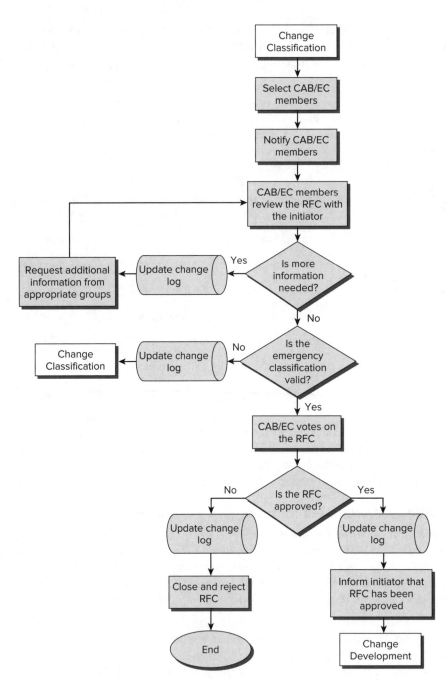

FIGURE 21-3

The first thing to talk about is the *change manager* (CM). The CM, as we may think of the role, is the pivot point for the entire process. The CM pushes and redistributes all communications between the CAB members and stakeholders and ensures that the CAB establishes a plan and governs execution of the change deployment according to the terms set by the CAB. The CM is usually a technical manager but can be a project manager or a team leader from either the infrastructure or application group who is familiar with the environment. The CM is involved with the change from start (request) to finish (debrief), and although the CM is not responsible for the decisions made by the CAB, the CM is responsible for the time it takes for the CAB to act.

Taking our example, the upcoming sections describe the following steps for progressing through the deployment of your application fix:

1. Appoint CAB members.

2. Notify CAB members.

3. CAB members review the request for change.

4. CAB members vote on the RFC.

Appoint CAB Members

The CAB includes several standing members, including subject matter experts from your systems engineering team, the application group that manages websites on your servers, security representatives, networking specialists, and hardware representatives. Depending on the nature of the emergency, you can add or remove members from this core list. For our change, we will want the following represented in our CAB:

➤ Network administrator responsible for the IIS cluster

➤ Networking engineer or architect who is responsible for the IIS cluster

➤ Application engineers from all teams that host applications on the applicable cluster

We will exclude the security and hardware representatives. The more people who are asked to join an emergency CAB meeting, the more difficult it becomes to schedule a meeting that all members can attend, especially when given short notice and if such a meeting is not part of the normal work day. An example of when you would extend the circle of the CAB to include others would be when a change affects areas that lie outside of the knowledge and authority of the standing members. The change initiator for a particular change request is an exception. This person needs to be a member of the CAB to provide quick answers to their questions. Ideally, the standing members alone should possess sufficient knowledge and authority to make a decision.

The CAB has a short timeframe in which to meet and act. An emergency change can be requested at any time, for any number of business and technical circumstances, and because the emergency change must be deployed quickly, the CAB must be large enough to have enough authority to act without impediment and be small enough to decide how to act very quickly. Because voting requires a quorum (when adhering strictly to MOF), the standing members or appointed deputies of the CAB must always be able to attend the meetings for emergency changes given short notice. This demand for instant availability can be ensured by using second and third parties who can back up the primary when he or she is not available. Depending on the nature of an emergency change, the CAB members may be called into duty anytime, at any time of day or night — either in person, over the phone, or by using other technology solutions.

For an emergency change, the recommended voting is that the change requires unanimous approval. Given this recommendation, this is another good reason to keep the CAB members to a minimum.

Notify CAB Members

The CM is responsible for contacting each CAB member personally to inform him or her of the emergency change request, and arrange for when it will be reviewed, and what form the meeting will take. The CM has to be aggressive about communicating and organizing. Normal communications methods may not be sufficient to get the CAB aligned in the timeframe necessary for an emergency change. If e-mail meeting requests are used, invitees should be given a short time period to acknowledge the meeting to the CM; otherwise, more direct methods of contacting CAB members must be used.

In all cases, the CM would contact enough of the members from the standing CAB membership roster to cover the required teams.

CAB Members Review the Request for Change

In our example, an initial review meeting has to happen within 4 hours to ensure that follow-up tasks can be accomplished following the initial meeting. In the initial review of the RFC, the CAB applies the same common-sense approach and criteria used for all changes. A key difference between the emergency change and most other changes is that the testing effort will not be as exhaustive, if it is done at all. The risk assessment, as factored by the likelihood and impact estimates, may be more important for an emergency change because the risks are typically higher given the available — or unavailable — room for testing.

Having all the right resources at the review will facilitate the decision-making process. The presence of the change initiator at the review allows questions about the change and its impact to be put directly to the initiator and to be answered quickly. There may be a need to collect additional information and re-present the RFC to the CAB before a decision can be made. In this case, the RFC is placed in a pending state until the CAB can reconvene, likely within a very short time (an hour, for example).

The outcome of the initial review can range from canceling the change to accepting the change as a fast-track candidate. The CAB may decide that the change is not an emergency change and should be handled by the normal change process. In this case, the CM reclassifies the change and updates the change log with the reason for reclassification. If the change initiator wants the RFC to be considered again as an emergency change, this person must provide additional supporting evidence to justify the need and resubmit the RFC to the CM. The CM can then bring the RFC, containing the new information, back to the CAB.

The decisions and actions of the CAB for an emergency change happen as quickly as possible. In our example, the CAB meets at the behest of the CM who received your change request, which you initiated based on the alerts you received concerning the resource constraints. The change request that the CAB has been called to review includes your personal testimony about the resource metrics (alerts) and complaints proffered by the finance and marketing departments. In addition, you include log files that describe the activities of the web services since the application team applied their website to the cluster, which show that the services used by the financial and marketing personnel are interrupted whenever the new application that shares the IIS server is in use. The final data point that the CAB considers as part of the request for change is the change description. In our case, your change request is to roll back the new application off the server cluster until it can be system-tested in a lab environment and proven compatible with the services used by the finance and marketing teams.

Along with the recommended change, you include both a risk assessment and a risk mitigation plan. The risk assessment includes the likelihood and impact of several undesired outcomes that are unlikely but possible. In our case, you would indicate that rolling back an application can cause damage to other systems if too many files or configurations are removed, or other elements of the application are removed on which the remaining applications rely. Your mitigation plan includes running Process Monitor (formerly RegMon and FileMon) on a lab server during a test installation of the problem application to identify the relevant files and registry keys. You also will back up the server and ensure that you can completely restore it should you need to roll back the change.

You will want to present your recommendation and supporting points in an organized brief. Figure 21-4 shows a sample form that you can use to present your case.

REQUEST FOR CHANGE SUMMARY					
Division			Date		
Current State					
Desired State					
Change Recommendation					
Type	Priority	Services Affected		Impact	
Risks		Likelihood × Impact (1–5)		Mitigation	
				1. 2.	
				1. 2.	
Change Owner:			Technical Lead:		
Project Manger:			Business Liaison:		

FIGURE 21-4

Some of the fields in this template are more intuitive than others, and one cannot overlook the need for training across your entire team on this and other aspects of your change processes. Here are some descriptions of the fields that you would use in this form:

➤ **Division** — Include the business or technical division name where the change will take effect.

➤ **Current State** — A short narrative that describes the deficiency in the affected system that needs to be changed.

➤ **Desired State** — A short narrative that characterizes the intended functionality.

➤ **Change Recommendation** — The steps needed to change from the current state to the desired state.

➤ **Type** — The MOF change types include:

  ➤ **Major** — A change where the impact on the group could be massive — for example, a department- or corporate-wide change, or a network-wide or service-wide change

  ➤ **Significant** — A change where the effect is widespread, but not massive — for example, a change affecting a group within a department or a specific group of CIs

  ➤ **Minor** — A change affecting small numbers of individuals or CIs — for example, a change to a printer used by a department consisting of just a few members

  ➤ **Standard** — A change that has been performed before and is part of the operational practice of the business — for example, an update to a user profile

As with the change priority, the change category will also vary with the makeup of the business. A change affecting a particular department may be deemed significant in some organizations but may only be considered a standard category in another organization in which that department is regarded as less critical to the business.

A set of standard changes and standard procedures for implementing them is normally predefined by the CAB. This set of standard changes can be automatically approved without needing to be voted on by the CAB or the CM, thereby taking a shorter route through the change approval process.

➤ **Priority** — The suggested priorities include:

  ➤ **Emergency** — A change that, if not implemented immediately, will leave the organization open to huge risk — for example, applying a security patch

  ➤ **High** — A change that is important for the organization and must be implemented soon — for example, an upgrade in response to new government legislation

  ➤ **Medium** — A change that should be implemented to gain functional benefits from the upgrade — for example, adding a customer feedback service

  ➤ **Low** — A change that is not pressing but would be advantageous — for example, a "nice to have" addition to a user profile

These definitions will mean different things to different organizations. Depending on organizational size, structure, and the underlying Service Level Agreements (SLAs) between IT and the business it serves, organizations might need to modify their own priority definitions. There is also the matter of perception and political influence. It's a well-known practice to escalate changes that come from certain managers for reasons other than business optimization.

It is important to note, however, that an emergency priority change differs from the other change priorities in that it takes a different path through the review process in order to implement the change as quickly as possible. This priority is reserved for only those changes that, if not implemented quickly, might seriously affect service levels or result in a large cost to the business.

➤ **Services affected** — Outline the technical systems or services that will or may be affected. Be sure to include all the services that depend on the servers you plan to change, not just the services that are tied directly to the server. By identifying tertiary services, you empower the CAB to fully evaluate the scope and therefore the impact and risk of the change.

➤ **Impact** — Share the goal of the change and how the business services will be positively or negatively affected.

➤ **Risks** — Think through the unintended consequences that may occur as a result of the intended change. List the possible outcomes that would affect the uptime and performance of the target server and of the systems that depend on it.

➤ **Likelihood × impact** — These are numerical values that can be multiplied to provide a weighted measure of severity.

The *likelihood* is a measure of the probability of the risk turning into an issue. A rating of 1 represents the lowest probability, whereas a rating of 5 represents the highest level of certainty.

The *impact* is a measure of the risk's scope, or breadth and depth of the effect. Again, a rating of 1 is the low end, which means you can tolerate this risk if it materializes. A rating of 5 would indicate that the end users of the system would not tolerate the risk if it happened.

Note that if a risk has a high likelihood of occurring but has a low impact — an undesired but negligible consequence — then the value for this field is $5 \times 1 = 5$. In another case, if a risk has a moderate likelihood but a fairly problematic consequence if it does happen, then you could expect a value approximating $3 \times 4 = 12$. The point here is that just because a risk is likely to occur doesn't necessarily mean that you need to expend resources to mitigate the risk, if the impact is low.

➤ **Mitigation** — These either are the steps that you will take to reduce the likelihood of the risk actually coming to pass, or the steps that you will take to lessen the impact in the case that the risk materializes.

➤ **Change Owner** — This is the person who is accountable to the rest of the organization for the success of the change. This person will usually be the direct supervisor of the Technical Lead identified below.

➤ **Project Manager** — The Project Manager (PM) is the person responsible for managing scope, staffing, and communication for the team that is planning and deploying the change.

➤ **Technical Lead** — Having responsibility for the technical design, deployment, and transfer to operations, the Technical Lead is the person responsible for the quality of the technical solution.

➤ **Business Liaison** — This person or persons represents the class of end users who will be most affected by the change. The Business Liaison ensures that their constituents are informed about the change deployment and represented in the change planning process. Liaisons can tell you what the work schedules are, what the workers' priorities are, and many more details about the constraints you'll have to work around to keep from interrupting operations during the deployment of the change.

Now look at the following form in Figure 21-5, which is filled out for our particular situation in the running example of processing an emergency change. The form shows how you might present your argument in a formal request to the CAB for an emergency update.

REQUEST FOR CHANGE SUMMARY			
Division	eComm	Date	Sep 19, 2012
Current State			
IIS 8.0 Server Cluster X is intermittently unresponsive. The downtime is linked to resources required by a recently installed application.			
Desired State			
IIS 8.0 Server Cluster X must comply with the SLA expectations for the finance and marketing systems.			
Change Recommendation			
Restore the IIS Server Cluster X to the pre-application state, where resources were sufficient to accommodate the financial and marketing systems.			

Type	Priority	Services Affected	Impact
Emergency	High	IIS 8.0 Sever Cluster X: +Finance App XYZ +Marketing App XYZ +New App XYZ	Restore SLA compliance w/ finance + mkt systems. Tmp end service for the problem application and launch compatibility testing project.

Risks	Likelihood × Impact (1–5)	Mitigation
Finance + mkt systems will be disabled during roll back of the new application.	2 × 5 = 10	1. Validate new app footprint using RegMon and FileMon. 2. Back up server for possible restore.
Removing the new application does not resolve the issue.	1 × 5 = 5	1. Plan to restore the server to a point prior to the detection of the service failure. 2. Activate application engineers standby for possible triage duty.

Change Owner:	Ken Schaefer, x3845	Technical Lead:	Dennis Glendenning, x3123
Project Manger:	Ken Schaefer, x3845	Business Liaison:	Mike Everest, x4572

FIGURE 21-5

Note that this form can provide only an overview or summary; it's a good way to get the CAB review started and to keep it structured. But it's not all that you would want to present, or have ready to present. Be sure to include supplemental evidence, including log files, best-practice articles, and testimony from business leaders in the form of e-mails or your own personal notes. This supplemental data will round out your argument and provide substance to position against the inevitable questioning that a good CAB review will provoke.

CAB Members Vote on the RFC

Once the CAB members agree that all the necessary information has been collected and reviewed, a vote on whether to continue fast tracking the change can take place. For an emergency change to be approved, a unanimous vote should be required. In this case, a majority is not sufficient, considering the risks involved in making an emergency change.

When a change is approved, it moves on to the change deployment stage, which follows an expedited path to implement the change as soon as possible. Whichever decision is made, the change initiator and all other interested parties are informed of the decision, and the change log is updated.

For our example, the CAB approves your change request to roll back the problem application, provided you follow through with your risk mitigation plan. Upon this decision, the CM communicates the decision throughout the organization and documents the disposition (for or against) of the CAB pertaining to the emergency change request.

In following this MOF Change Management SMF, your team has accomplished the following:

➤ Involved leaders with sufficient authority to approve change

➤ Included subject matter experts with sufficient knowledge to evaluate the change request

➤ Consulted with the stakeholders (i.e., the application teams)

➤ Communicated the final disposition to all team members and end users

The above example illustrates how emergency changes to an IIS application can be enacted with predictable results. By enabling a team of informed representatives to communicate and to track progress, the MOF Change Management SMF reduces the risk of a problem with deployment affecting uptime.

MOF Example: Change Management for Applying Hotfixes

Applying hotfixes to IIS servers is considered by many as the single most important security task involved in maintaining a web server. As the type of server with the most exposure to external attacks in many organizations and the kind of server that often handles more network traffic, IIS servers require every possible defense.

Although the task of installing a hotfix is usually simple, the effect of not applying the hotfix can be disastrous. The possible impact aside, installing a hotfix is a minor change. In an overwhelming majority of cases, applying a hotfix to a server poses only a minimal risk to the server.

Any minor change to a server, by definition, has both low impact and low risk. A change of this nature differs from a standard change in that the change may not have been performed before and therefore has to be approved. What actually constitutes a minor change depends on the criteria set by your organization. Because the impact and risk of a minor change are low, as is the need for deployment resources to implement the change, a minor change does not normally need to go before the CAB for review. Instead, the area leader or CM has the authority to approve or reject the change.

Figure 21-6 shows the process that the CM uses to authorize minor changes.

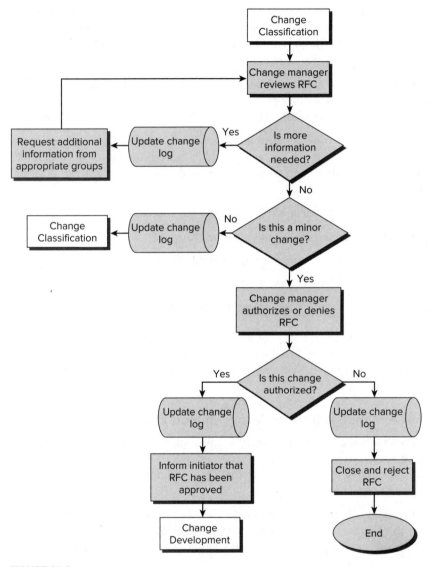

FIGURE 21-6

Comparing the process for approving and deploying a minor change to that for an emergency change, you can see that there are fewer steps and less concern and that the process for a minor change is more streamlined. The complexity and scale of the change approval process should reflect both the complexity and scale of the change under review. Although there is a definite need for some process regardless of the scope of change, the simple change does not justify the effort required of most other types of changes.

The priorities of the change review board remain the same, however, when considering major or minor changes. The board must, in both cases, be concerned that the change has been correctly classified, that the unintended outcomes have been identified and mitigated, and that — above all else — communication and organizational processes will be enacted correctly.

OPERATIONAL TASKS

The first half of this chapter covered the management approaches you can use to build an operations program that yields a higher rate of success in meeting the uptime and performance demands of your website. In the remaining sections of this chapter, we cover some specific tasks to which every IIS administrator must attend: backing up and restoring web servers.

Backup and Restore Program

One operation that stands at the top of priorities for any administrator of any server is ensuring an adequate backup/restore program. Should an administrator fail in this task, the server and the applications that it hosts are in serious jeopardy of failing miserably should anything unfavorable occur to the server. Although IIS 8.0 is the most secure and stable web platform that Microsoft has released to date, given their position in the perimeter network and their high traffic profiles, IIS servers are more susceptible to attack and failure than any other infrastructure server. In this light, maintaining operational fallbacks (backup) and defense (antivirus) are relatively inexpensive insurance policies against the likely faults to which any IIS server is susceptible.

In this section, we outline a disaster recovery program sufficient for enterprise-class SLAs. The program we present below is just a sample, however, and you should take this as a starting point only. Our discussion includes a stepwise review of some basic backup tasks and an approach to backups as an operational program with checks and balances.

Backup Scope

When designing a backup/restore program, the first element to consider in your design is what exactly needs to be backed up. The answer, in general terms, comes in two parts:

1. Back up all data and configurations that are important to the mission of the server.

2. Back up everything that would restore more efficiently (and with lower risk of loss) from backup media than from the original installation media.

Your two top priorities for selecting backup points are then *coverage* and *efficiency*. Those are the general terms. More specifically, when backing up an IIS server, you need to consider these main categories of data:

➤ **Website data** — Files that contain code and configurations necessary to present the user with interfaces, manage data, and apply the computational logic of the hosted application. Examples include HTML, ASP.NET, and .DLL files.

➤ **Transaction data** — Data collected in the course of using the website, such as logs, session data, product data, and sales records. Transactional data can be stored on the local server in the form of log files, on a dedicated session state server, or on a special database server (for example, Microsoft SQL, Sybase ASE 15, Oracle 1Xg).

➤ **IIS 8.0 configurations** — Settings that customize the service for the hosted applications, including settings that define the website object, application pools, and core IIS service. Example configurations include authentication schemes, file directories, and modular switches that are found in the `.config` files. These files are introduced in Chapter 2 and reviewed in detail in Chapter 5.

➤ **OS and dependent service configurations** — Any configurations and supporting files that help provide the working engines for your hosted applications. Examples include resource kit tools, monitoring agents, and local/group policies.

Be sure that you review all the above categories and include the appropriate files in your backup set. Use the preceding list as a basic checklist to reduce the chances that you will leave anything out that is mission critical to your IIS server.

Backup Methods and Media

Now that you have an introduction to what data to back up, the next item to consider is the backup method and media. The following list covers the main options for backup media in a business setting.

➤ **No backup** — In rare cases, all files come straight from installation media and you have only to reinstall from a CD-ROM disk. An example of this scenario is an e-mail relay server that uses a simple SMTP and IIS service and is not mission critical. It's hard to beat the convenience of reinstalling from CD-ROM, but be sure that you have an infallible system for storing and retrieving your CD-ROM media.

➤ **Tape or cartridge** — Tape drives have been staples for backing up servers for decades. Tape media have the benefits of providing high storage capacities and the portability of moving backups off site. Tapes come in a range of technologies and are affordable enough to allow you to leverage a library of tapes to accommodate normal, differential, and incremental backups.

➤ **Local disk** — Backing up data on a separate disk is affordable and fast. Restoring data from a separate disk is as easy as it gets. Adding a secondary hard disk drive is easy for most administrators and offers a low-maintenance solution. Certain disk arrays can also provide a form of backup if data is written to more than one disk.

➤ **External disk array** — An array of disks is more expensive than using local storage but comes with the added benefits of better management options and a much higher level of fault tolerance. Most disk arrays can withstand one or more drive failures while maintaining operations. Robust and highly engineered arrays, such as a storage area network (SAN) or network-attached storage (NAS), can endure several failures without data loss and provide the most scalable and tolerant solutions.

➤ **Array of servers** — This option includes posting data to two separate servers that are clustered together to appear as the same server. Use the integrated Microsoft Clustering Service to evoke network load balancing (NLB) for IIS servers or a dedicated clustering appliance such as those offered by Cisco, F5, and Citrix. If you can spare the budget, a hardware option for load balancing is always preferred. Using more than one server to provide a service can also increase performance.

The following table compares the backup options presented above:

OPTION	PROS	CONS	SPEED	COST
No backup	Economical, convenient	Risk of data loss is virtually guaranteed in a failure event.	Restores can be very slow, depending on the installation times and complexity.	None
Tape	High-capacity media; removable for off-site storage	Drives and a full media library can be expensive, and backups are slow; media fail periodically without notice.	1–10 MBps (megabytes per second)	$0.25–$0.50 per gigabyte
Local disk	Fast; highest capacity for unattended, automated backup	Not portable; server remains as a single point of failure.	100–320 MBps	$1 per gigabyte or less
External disk array	Fast; highest capacity for workgroup backups; fault tolerant	Fitting disks for fault tolerance (RAID 1, 5, or 10) can be expensive.	100–320 MBps	$4–$10 per gigabyte
Server array	Highest level of fault tolerance; smallest response time for restorations	Expensive; highest maintenance and operations burden.	Ethernet 100 MBps to Gigabit Ethernet 1,000 MBps	Varies

Approaches

Your approach to backups has to reflect the expectations (or, in some cases, demands) that your end users have for restoration times. For example, if you have an agreement with a customer or another workgroup in your company that specifies your availability and performance boundaries, such as a Service Level Agreement (SLA), that promises 99.999 percent uptime, then you can afford no more than 5 minutes per year of downtime.

Your backup and restoration program needs to be part of an overall program for high availability. If your end users accept up to 4 hours or more of downtime a few times a year, then your backup approach can be very different from the one in which you have to guarantee 99.999 percent uptime. Both scenarios are covered below. To round out the scenarios, let's start with the situation in which there are few or no expectations.

Low Service Expectations

If your service can be down for extended periods of time, then the hardware used is typically not redundant. Often, the IIS platform with low service expectations is a single server with one or more hard disk drives. For this scenario, backups should be thorough, although your users can tolerate a flexible window for restoring the service. The following table shows the backup priorities for IIS systems with low service expectations:

SCOPE	PRIORITY	PERIOD	METHOD/MEDIA
Website data	High	Monthly–yearly	Tape or install files
Transaction data	Low	Never	None
IIS 8.0 configurations	Low	Never (just document them)	None (checklist)
OS and dependent services	Low	Never (just document them)	None (checklist)

When you have plenty of time to restore a server, you can simply rebuild it from scratch using the Windows media, a checklist, and any backup media that has the website content.

Moderate Expectations

If your end users need your faulty IIS server back within a fixed window of time, then you should focus on being able to recover the website data and IIS service configurations quickly. The following table shows the backup priorities for IIS systems with moderate service expectations:

SCOPE	PRIORITY	RATE	METHOD/MEDIA
Website data	High	Daily–hourly	Tape–disk
Transaction data	High	Daily–hourly	Tape–disk
IIS 8.0 configuration	Moderate	Monthly	Tape
OS and dependent services	Moderate	Monthly–yearly	OS image

When you have a fixed amount of time to restore a server, you can rebuild the server from scratch or from an image file that you create using something like the Microsoft Deployment Toolkit or another similar imaging technology.

High Availability

For the IIS servers that are critical to business continuity, those that must continue to provide service regardless of whatever technical difficulties may arise, a backup program may focus less on recovering from a hardware fault and more on maintaining the history and continuity of service in the event of faults. The following table shows the backup priorities for IIS systems with high service expectations:

SCOPE	PRIORITY	RATE	METHOD/MEDIA
Website data	High	Hourly–constant (Mirror)	Array of servers, geographically distributed
Transaction data	High	Hourly–constant (Mirror)	Array of servers, geographically distributed

| IIS service configuration | High | Never | Array of servers |
| OS and dependent services | High | Never | Array of servers |

Conducting Backups

In many cases, your organization will use an industrial-strength backup solution. Several vendors have backup solutions for IIS service. For IIS operations, you can pick from many excellent options for backup software. Windows Server 2012 is new as of this writing, and only a few backup solutions are compatible. However, the leading providers will undoubtedly keep pace and release compatible solutions. The following table lists some of the best options to consider:

VENDOR	SOFTWARE	WEBSITE
Symantec	Backup Exec 2012	`www.symantec.com/backup-exec`
CA	ARCserve	`www.arcserve.com`
EMC	Avamar, Data Domain, Data Protection Advisor, NetWorker	`www.emc.com/backup-and-recovery/` `backup-for-microsoft.htm`
IBM	Tivoli Storage Manager	`www.ibm.com`
APTARE	StorageConsole	`www.aptare.com`
CommVault	Simpana Software	`www.commvault.com`
Hewlett-Packard	HP Data Protector	`www8.hp.com/us/en/software-solutions/software` `.html?compURI=1175640#.UDr2TEJC8UU`
Microsoft	Web Deploy 3.0	`www.iis.net/download/WebDeploy`
IIS.NET Community	iBackupIIS7	`www.iis.net/community/default` `.aspx?tabid=34&g=6&i=1892`

For the purposes of this chapter, we follow up with Microsoft's native Windows Server Backup toolset. Although it is almost never used in production enterprise scenarios, it's somewhat common in non-production and smaller environments. However, the version proffered by Microsoft in Windows Server 2012 is substantially more robust than the minimalist version found in the Windows Server 2008 RTM version.

The new Windows Server Backup supports a wide range of backup targets, including the previously supported volume-level backups and system states. You can also restore folder- and file-level data, which is functionality deprecated by Microsoft in Windows Server 2008. Additionally, at the time of this writing, a remote backup service is in beta for both Windows 8 and Windows Server 2012 as part of Windows Live.

Windows Server Backup now supports internal and external drives, optical media, removable drives, and Hyper-V virtual machines. Altogether, Microsoft's native backup tool for LAN uses comes in three forms:

➤ **Wbadmin Management Console** — Officially called the "Windows Server Backup Microsoft Management Console," this is a graphical interface for backup and restore that exposes the functionality of the `Wbadmin.exe` command-line tool in a user interface. The Console isn't available in Server Core installs, so you'll have to rely on the command-line or PowerShell tools if you want to manage backups remotely.

➤ **Wbadmin.exe** — Command-line backup and restore management tool that replaced `ntbackup.exe`.

➤ **PowerShell cmdlets** — Microsoft provides a number of management cmdlets for use with IIS, including backup and restore functions.

Perform the following steps using Server Manager to install the Windows Server Backup feature, along with the command-line support tool `Wbadmin.exe` and the PowerShell cmdlets:

> **NOTE** *To install the Windows Server Backup feature, you must be a member of the Backup Operators or Administrators group or have been delegated the right.*

1. In the Server Manager Dashboard, click "Add roles and features."

2. In the "Before you begin" page of the Add Roles and Features Wizard, click Next.

3. On the "Select installation type" tab, click Next.

4. On the "Select destination server" tab, click on the target server to select it, and then click Next.

5. On the Server Roles tab, click Next.

6. In the "Select features" pane in the Features tab, click on the checkbox next to Windows Server Backup, and then click Next (see Figure 21-7).

7. On the Confirmation page, review the choices you made and choose Install and then Close after the wizard completes.

8. After the features are installed, click the "refresh" icon (two arrows in a circle between the navigation URL and the alert Flag) on the Server Manager Dashboard.

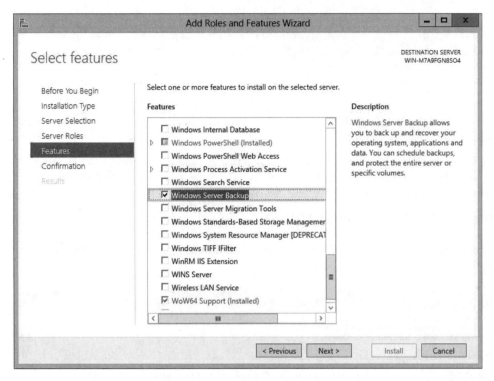

FIGURE 21-7

9. Launch the Windows Server Backup Management Console by clicking on the Tools menus from the top menu bar and choosing Windows Server Backup (see Figure 21-8).

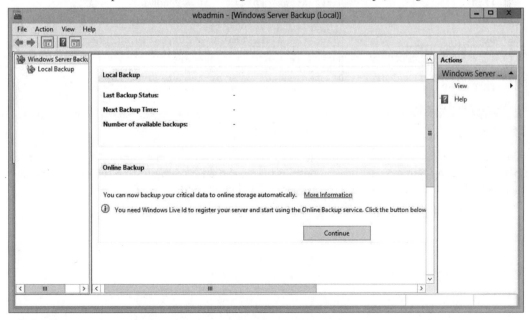

FIGURE 21-8

> **NOTE** *At the time of this writing, you only have the option to install Windows Server Backup. Unlike Windows Server 2008 R2, you cannot elect the components individually.*

You can also install the Windows Server Backup feature and execute all the backup/restore functions of the feature using PowerShell.

Note that Windows Server Backup is based on the Volume Shadow Copy Service (VSS). Using VSS, Windows Server Backup will take snapshots of an entire volume and allow you to restore either the entire volume or individual files.

Alternatively, you can use the command-line tool to set up and manage your backup and restore tasks. To use the command-line WBadmin tool, click the Start button, type **cmd** in the search field, and then hit Return. In the new command shell, type **WBadmin /?** and hit Return. The results are illustrated in Figure 21-9.

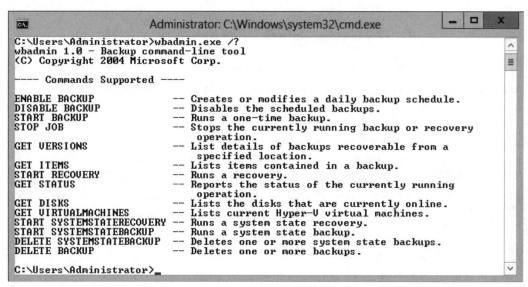

FIGURE 21-9

Like the Windows Server Backup Console, you can use the WBadmin command-line tool to back up and restore the system state, which contains many of the IIS configuration settings. To make a backup of the system state, execute the following DOS command:

```
Wbadmin start SystemStateBackup -backupTarget:[volume name]
```

22

Monitoring and Performance Tuning

WHAT'S IN THIS CHAPTER?

➤ Server Manager

➤ Task Manager

➤ Resource Monitor

➤ Performance Monitor

➤ What to monitor

➤ Operating system optimizations

➤ IIS service optimizations

➤ Website optimizations

After covering operations frameworks and processes in the previous chapter, it's time to talk about the changes you can make to improve performance and ensure the uptime of your web service. We can't cover it here, but the major performance factors are managed at an architectural level, where decisions are made about which roles each server will fill and how they may or may not be load balanced. Chapter 16, "IIS Scalability I: Building an IIS Web Farm," and Chapter 17, "IIS Scalability II: Load Balancing and ARR," touch on these decisions. Additionally, *IT Service Management* (ITSM) is a popular body of knowledge that emphasizes end users when prescribing approaches to ensuring that IT systems behave as designed. Monitoring and tuning are both core to that philosophy. For a user-centric approach and toolset, use your favorite search engine to learn more about ITSM.

It doesn't take much research to see that, from an ITSM perspective, monitoring is about more than just troubleshooting problems with data. Effective monitoring can get you ahead of a problem, detecting an impending outage or performance issue *before* it impacts your end users. Having it in place obviously doesn't preclude problems, but when problems occur, your mean time to resolution will be monumentally lower if you have monitoring in place. Of course, the right solution includes monitoring and alerting across both the application and infrastructure systems involved, such as the base OS services, Domain Name System (DNS), and networking systems.

This chapter focuses on monitoring and tuning for IIS. As you will see, *monitoring* is about both collecting data and making sense of it, and *tuning* is about using that data to build the configuration designed for your user's best experience.

MONITORING WEBSITES

With *performance data*, you can establish patterns that define peak periods of activity, audit capacity, build detailed upgrade plans, and learn how all the parts of your system really interact. Unfortunately, administrators are often unable to act on the data they collect — sometimes because they don't have a roadmap. The goal of this chapter is to help you not only collect the right data, but also to beat the odds and intelligently tune your system in the process of maximizing performance across the entire web service.

To help you with your task, the following major performance and optimization areas are discussed in this chapter:

➤   Http.sys (kernel mode request processing)

➤   Memory usage

➤   Processor utilization

➤   Disk I/O

➤   Network bandwidth

➤   Bandwidth throttling

➤   Web connections

➤   HTTP compression

➤   Site configuration

We'll dig deeper into each of these areas and provide what you need to know for a comprehensive monitoring program. Before going into the details of what to monitor, it makes sense first to talk about *how* you monitor an IIS server. After all, the tools you use will dictate the options you have for monitoring. The following section introduces some of the tools that you can use on a Windows Server 2012 server running IIS 8.0.

How to Monitor IIS 8.0

For complex web applications that span two or more servers, with business demands for consistent performance, you may find it necessary to invest in a commercial monitoring solution, if you don't already have one in place. The leading options offer a great menu of features, including customizable reports covering both the Windows platform and web services data, alerting and autocorrection scripts, and other management functions — all of which will provide you with a consolidated, comprehensive toolset for monitoring your application. Like many other computing subsystems, website monitoring can be offloaded to a third-party provider. For example, HP offers two options: Application Performance Management as a Service and Service Management as a Service.

Of course, as with all the options, your "mileage will vary." If you are hosting your website in a third-party facility, your provider may provide monitoring services. You should treat their solution with the same critical approach that you would if you were purchasing the solution for your onsite service. Some of the main points to consider in selecting a monitoring solution include the following:

➤ **The business value of the application** — Critical to casual. You should align your budget with the relative value of your website to your business.

➤ **The sophistication of your application** — Match it to the feature set of the monitoring solution.

➤ **Monitoring impact** — Monitors can have an impact on performance, depending on how you implement them. Launching the Microsoft toolset on the web server itself, for example, can affect hard disk drive performance.

➤ **Consolidation of logs** — Aggregating event data from all the servers in your service set is of great benefit when tracking the performance of distributed applications.

➤ **Granular metrics** — These are of use only if your tuning options are equally granular. Collecting data that you cannot act on is a waste of resources.

Some of the major providers for computing-system monitoring are named in the following table. Each application offers terrific options for monitoring web applications of all types. Many include a per-server fee, an investment that will return dividends many times over if your application has scale. The list is not meant to be comprehensive, but it should get you started with a list of best-of-class options.

SOFTWARE	VENDOR	DESCRIPTION
System Center Operations Manager 2012	Microsoft	Operations Manager is an extensible monitoring and alerting platform. It includes rich instrumentation written by the Microsoft product teams, including Active Directory, DNS, and IIS. The instrumentation for IIS, embedded in what is called a "management pack," includes detailed models that cover both the system design and health aspects of an IIS application. Microsoft's health models are based on the Systems Definition Model (SDM), which enables Operations Manager to analyze the performance, availability, configuration, and security of IIS applications.

continues

(continued)

SOFTWARE	VENDOR	DESCRIPTION
SiteScope	Hewlett-Packard Development Company	SiteScope is a monitoring and alerting solution based on an agentless architecture. It monitors more than 65 different targets for critical health and performance characteristics, such as utilization, response time, usage, and resource availability. It sets thresholds to receive proactive alerts before end users experience problems. SiteScope is a specialized solution for website monitoring and management, including unique features such as URL content monitoring, URL sequence monitoring, and link checks.
Performance Center	Hewlett-Packard Development Company	Performance Center is aimed at integrating development, testing, infrastructure, and operations teams. This option channels production data back into its scripting engine to help with root-cause analysis as well as providing a production-like space in which to develop.
LoadRunner	Hewlett-Packard Development Company	Build synthetic transactions using a script editor and see how your application performs under load to validate readiness for a production environment.
ProactiveNet	BMC Software	ProactiveNet is a suite of tools built around protecting the end-user experience, including performance, capacity, and experience instrumentation.
Tivoli Monitoring for Web Infrastructure	IBM	Tivoli is another popular solution that equips you with the resources for identifying issues and alerting appropriate personnel. It includes automated problem correction using a bank of IBM's best practices.
WebTrends Analytics	WebTrends, Inc.	WebTrends Analytics measures and tests the online experience, capturing metrics from both the visitor's point of view and the system metrics. It does more with session context, providing details surrounding the source and nature of web sessions. WebTrends ties analysis into other reporting and business solutions via industry-standard open access technologies.

The options listed in the preceding table are all terrific, proven performance management solutions for distributed IIS applications. They can make the difference between success and failure when keeping a complex system available. Again, the list isn't meant to be comprehensive but, rather, an illustration of what is available today.

Alternatively, Windows Server 2012 offers a set of native performance management tools. Even if you install a commercial-grade solution, you may find that from time to time you need to use one of the native tools to supplement your real-time data needs. The following table lists the native tools that you can use to manage performance:

SOFTWARE	DESCRIPTION
Server Manager	Presents a centralized dashboard for role administration, including the IIS role. Context menus provide quick insight into performance and Best Practice Analyzer (BPA) data.
Windows Task Manager	Provides real-time data on locally running processes and services and metrics on CPU and memory.
Windows Performance Monitor	Measures the effect that programs have on your computer's performance, in real time and via log data.
Resource Monitor	Enables you to view and manage resource utilization, including CPU, RAM, hard disk drive, and networking.
Resource and Performance Monitor	Enables you to view performance data, both in real time and from log files; keeps you informed on the impact of running processes on your system.

Having reviewed a few commercial options, it's time to focus on the many native tools that accompany Windows Server 2012. We start off with Server Manager, which has been updated from the ground up for the new operating system.

Server Manager

Server Manager is the new dashboard for centralized administration introduced with Windows Server 2012. It's a Microsoft Management Console (MMC) but in a style different from previous platforms. With Server Manager, you can define your management scope, aggregate servers into management pools, and dive into a number of links to get real-time data on the performance and health of your farm. Microsoft recommends that you use Server Manager to provision and administer up to 100 servers remotely; if your fleet is greater than 100, turn to a systems-management application like HP Server Automation or System Center Configuration Manager.

Some of the uses of Server Manager include:

➤ **Service management** — Start and stop services, configure accounts, and scan servers for compliance with best practices.

➤ **Performance monitoring** — View real-time performance of key server components, including processor, memory, network throughput, hard disk drive I/O, and more.

Once started, Server Manager begins with a Welcome tile with quick links for the new user. Scrolling down, you see the thumbnails that give you a quick view of the status for a role on either a server or a group of servers (see Figure 22-1).

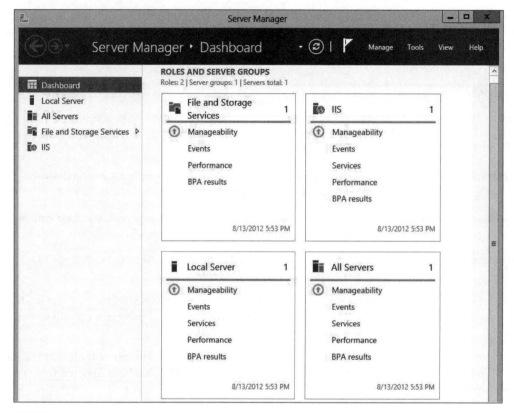

FIGURE 22-1

The thumbnails can be configured to your liking. Each row in the thumbnail is explained below:

➤ **Manageability** — Typically reports up/down status, reporting link status, remote management link status, and other access indicators.

➤ **Event** — Configure as necessary using options for severity levels, sources, event IDs, and other parameters.

➤ **Services** — Report against expected service states — for example, startup type.

➤ **Performance** — Alerts for your configured thresholds for resource performance will be raised here.

➤ **BPA results** — When BPA scans return data that is incongruous with your configured thresholds, alerts will be raised in this row.

You can export the Server Manager configuration and import it across all your management servers.

If an alert has been raised, the top of the thumbnail will burn red (when otherwise green), and alert summaries will appear in the thumbnail margins. Figure 22-2 reflects several stopped services and a critical event. Figure 22-3 is an example of the details you find when clicking on the Services summary.

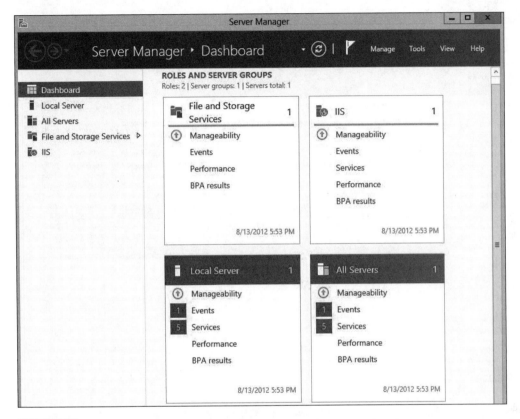

FIGURE 22-2

Of special note, you can pull up a dashboard for the IIS role server (or server group) by clicking on the IIS node on the left navigation pane. The role-specific dashboard includes the following embedded controls:

➤ **Servers control** — Shows the status details of each server in the group.

➤ **Events control** — Summarizes those events raised within the default (or custom) filter.

➤ **Services control** — Summarizes the state of each service aligned with the role.

➤ **Best Practices Analyzer control** — Reports the result of the latest scan.

➤ **Performance control** — Renders a snippet of the performance log data for CPU and RAM.

➤ **Roles and Features control** — Lists the installed roles.

Figure 22-4 shows a few of the controls, including the Performance control.

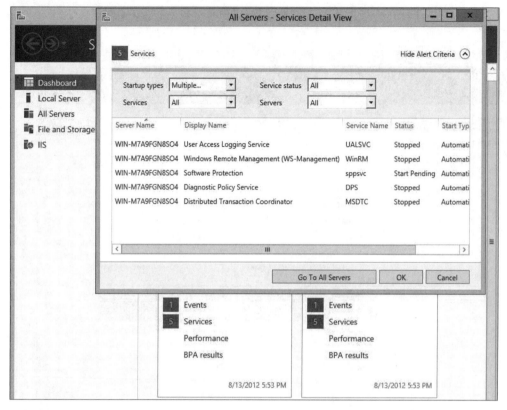

FIGURE 22-3

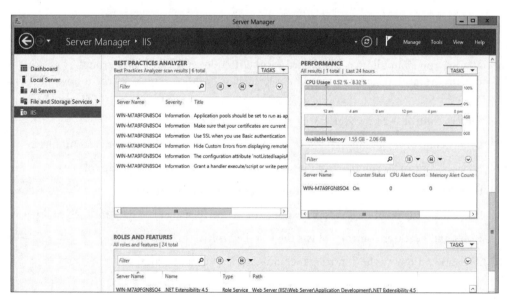

FIGURE 22-4

For each control, you have the following common configuration options:

➤ **Tasks** — Configure various options, such as add/remove alerts, refresh the control data, and execute a BPA scan.

➤ **Filter** — Enter a keyword in the textbox, and click the search icon to filter the data displayed in the control.

➤ **Column headers** — Right-click on the column headers to add or remove columns.

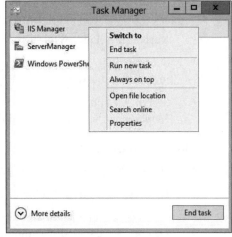

Windows Task Manager

Task Manager was first introduced in Windows 95. The version that comes with Windows Server 2012 looks truly futuristic compared with the veritable original. It's been extended into a dynamic tool that unfolds nested data through a new, colorful user interface (UI). Figure 22-5 shows the default view of Task Manager.

FIGURE 22-5

Task Manager is a simple display of the running applications. To open it, click the "More details" arrow. You will see the Processes, Performance, Users, Details, and Services tabs. Figure 22-6 shows Performance tab.

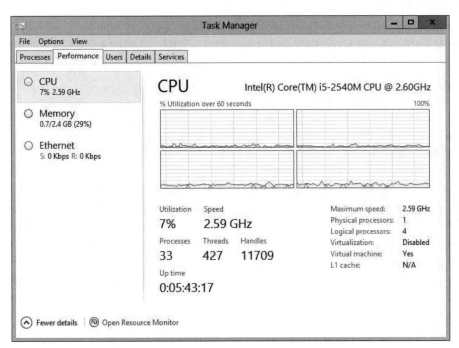

FIGURE 22-6

You can open Task Manager in several ways:

➤ **Mouse** — Right-click on the taskbar and select Task Manager from the context menu.

➤ **Shortcuts** — Press Ctrl+Alt+Delete, and then click Task Manager from the options on the system screen. Or, simply press Ctrl+Shift+Esc.

➤ **Keyboard** — Press WIN+R to launch the Run window, enter **TM.exe**, and then press Enter.

➤ **Start screen** — Launch the Start screen and click on the Task Manager icon, which is included in the System section by default.

➤ **Search** — Launch the desktop Search application from the Quick Launch bar, and type **Task Manager** in the Apps box, and then click the search icon.

Managing Processes

The *Process tab* includes the following features:

➤ Resource utilization is color-coded in shades of yellow, with darker colors for heavier use.

➤ Processes are mapped to application names and status and listed with usage metrics for CPU, memory, hard disk drive, and network resources.

➤ You can suspend an application from Task Manager.

➤ The Details tab provides the legacy Task Manager.

Managing Performance

The *Performance tab* provides real-time performance data in graph and table formats. CPU and RAM usage is monitored in an easy-to-view graph that depicts details of utilization metrics. This tab also is used as a shortcut to the Resource Monitor MMC console by clicking the Open Resource Monitor button.

Some of the more germane features of this tab include the following:

➤ There are sections for CPU, memory, disk, Ethernet, and wireless network resources.

➤ Real-time metrics are presented in graphs, scoped over the last 60 seconds, that can be clicked to show details.

➤ The CPU section can be toggled to show aggregate usage or usage per logical core.

➤ When configured to show usage per logical core, mousing over the logical core shows the NUMA node index.

➤ The CPU section shows utilization on heat-mapping tiles in blue, with darker colors for heavier utilization.

Figure 22-7 shows the new CPU toggling options.

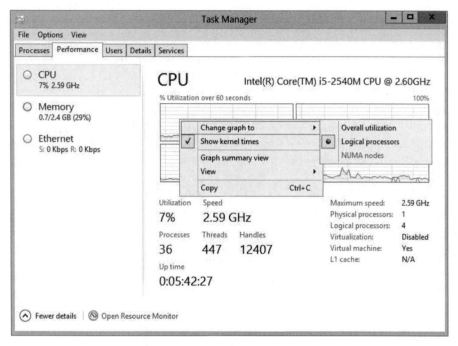

FIGURE 22-7

Managing Services

You can use the Services tab to start and stop services and to view several important aspects of the services, both running and available, on your server. You can see the Process ID (PID), description, status, and group associated with each service (see Figure 22-8). You can also use this pane to jump to the underlying process in the Details tab by right-clicking on the process and clicking on the "Go to details" option.

To start or stop a service, right-click on its name on the Services tab, and then click either "Start Service" or "Stop Service." Using the Services tab, you can map a running service to its PID, which is useful in running scripts to automate the management of services.

Resource Monitor

Resource Monitor provides a way to get to the details of how software affects your server. It has lost the reporting functions found in previous versions and is now most useful in real-time diagnostics. To access Resource Monitor, press WIN+R to launch the Run window, enter **Perfmon.exe /res** (or **resmon.exe**), and then press Enter. Figure 22-9 shows the new Windows Server 2012 Resource Monitor.

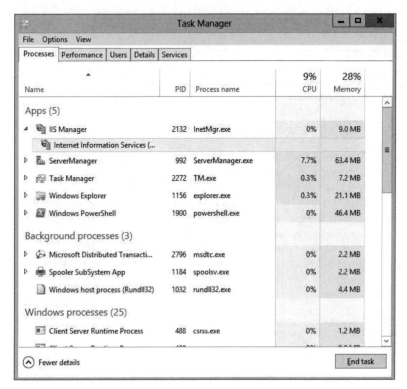

FIGURE 22-8

Performance Monitor

Performance Monitor, as its name suggests, identifies how programs affect a computer's performance. You can look at real-time data through the graphic interface of Performance Monitor or analyze performance over time using log data. Like System Monitor in Windows Server 2003 and Reliability and Performance Monitor in Windows Server 2008, the new version of Performance Monitor relies on performance counters, event trace data, and system configuration information.

Access Performance Monitor by following these steps:

1. Press WIN+R to launch the Run window, type **Perfmon.exe**, and then press Enter.

2. To connect to a remote computer, right-click on the top Performance node and select "Connect to another computer."

3. Click on the Performance Monitor node under the Monitoring Tools node.

The Performance Log Users group is a built-in group in Windows Server 2012 that enables users who are not local administrators to perform many of the functions related to performance monitoring and logging. For members of the Performance Log Users group to initiate data logging or modify Data Collector Sets, the group must first be assigned the user right to log on as a batch job. To assign this user right, use the Local Security Policy MMC snap-in.

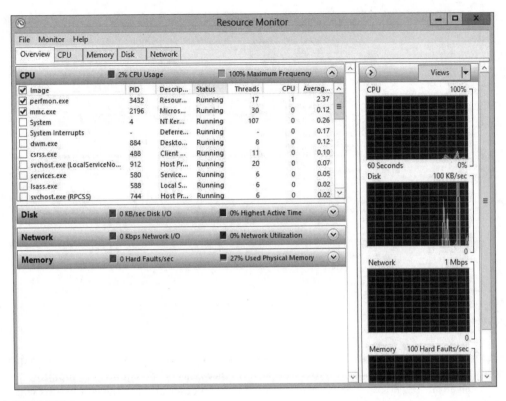

FIGURE 22-9

Membership in the local Administrators group, or equivalent, is the minimum required to complete this procedure. To assign the "Log on as a batch job" user right to the Performance Log Users group, follow these steps:

1. Press WIN+R to launch the Run window, type **secpol.msc,** and then press Enter. The Local Security Policy snap-in will open in Microsoft Management Console.

2. In the navigation pane, expand Local Policies and click User Rights Assignment.

3. In the console pane, right-click "Log on as a batch job," and click Properties.

4. In the Properties page, click Add User or Group.

5. In the Select Users or Groups dialog box, click Object Types. Select Groups in the Object Types dialog box, and click OK.

6. Type **Performance Log Users** in the Select Users or Groups dialog box, and then click OK.

7. In the Properties page, click OK.

In Performance Monitor, you can render the data in graphs, histograms, or tabular reports. Figure 22-10 shows the Windows Server 2012 Performance Monitor.

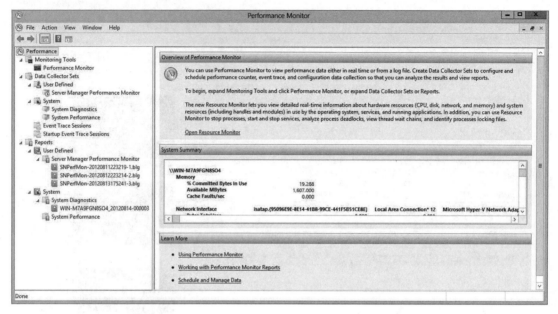

FIGURE 22-10

To configure Performance Monitor, add counters by clicking the green plus sign (+) on the top menu bar and using the Add Counters screen to select performance objects and counters to monitor. Be sure to check the box next to "Show description" to view a description of the counters as you browse through them.

The following table describes how to perform common tasks in the Add Counters dialog box:

TASK	PROCEDURE
Choose the source computer for counters.	Select a computer from the dropdown list, or click Browse to find other computers. You can add counters from the local computer or another computer on a network to which you have access.
Display a description of the selected counter group.	Select "Show description" in the lower-left corner of the page. The description will update as you select other groups.
Add a group of counters.	Highlight the group name and click Add.
Add individual counters.	Expand the group by clicking on the down arrow, highlighting the counter, and clicking Add.

Search for instances of a counter.	Highlight the counter group or expand the group and highlight the counter you want to add, type the process name in the dropdown below the "Instances of selected object" box, and click Search. The process name that you type will be available in the dropdown list to repeat the search with other counters. If no results are returned and you want to clear your search, you must highlight another group. If there are not multiple instances of a counter group or counter, the Search function will not be available.
Add only certain instances of a counter.	Highlight a counter group or counter in the list, select the process you want from the list that appears in the "Instances of selected object" box, and click Add. Multiple processes can create the same counter, but choosing an instance will collect only those counters produced by the selected process.

Once you have added counters to the Performance Monitor display, you can adjust the view from the tool menu bar to help identify information that you are looking for.

Figure 22-11 shows the Add Counters window for Performance Monitor.

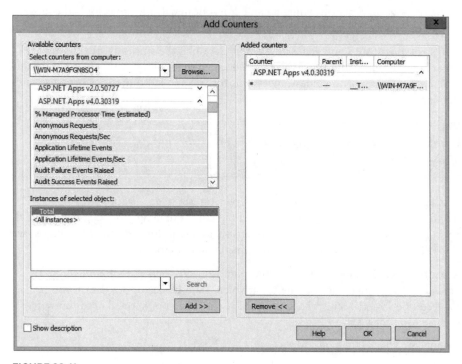

FIGURE 22-11

Data Collector Sets

Windows Server 2012's Resource and Performance Monitor includes a configuration concept known as *Data Collector Sets*. A Data Collector Set organizes multiple data collection points into a single component that you can use to review or log performance. A Data Collector Set can be created and recorded, grouped with other sets, incorporated into logs, viewed in Performance Monitor, configured to generate alerts, and used by non-Microsoft applications.

There are two ways to create a Data Collector Set:

➤ **From a template** — This is the simplest way to create a new Data Collector Set. There are several templates from which to choose. Templates are XML files and can be exported and imported. To build a collector set from a template, open Resource and Performance Monitor, locate the Data Collector Set node in the navigation pane, and double-click it to expand it. Right-click the User Defined node and choose New, then Data Collector Set to start the wizard. After providing a name for your new Data Collector Set, choose Create From A Template, click Next, and then complete the wizard.

➤ **Manually** — Open Performance Monitor and double-click the Data Collector Sets node to expand it. Then right-click the User Defined node and point to New and click Data Collector Set to start the wizard. After providing a name for your new Data Collector Set, choose Create Manually, click Next, and then complete the wizard.

You can obtain system diagnostics and generate a report detailing the status of local hardware resources, system response times, and processes on the local system, along with system information and configuration data. This report includes suggestions for ways to maximize performance and streamline system operation.

> **NOTE** *You must be a member of the local Administrators group to run the default Data Collector Set.*

Here are the missing details on how to create a Data Collector Set from within Performance Monitor. Before you begin, however, add some counters to collect data against. Begin with the display of counters in Performance Monitor. If you are unsure about adding additional counters, see the "What to Monitor" section below for advice on which counters to use.

1. Right-click the User Defined node within the Data Collector Sets parent node, point to New, and click Data Collector Set. The Create New Data Collector Set wizard starts. The Data Collector Set created will contain all of the data collectors selected in the current Performance Monitor view.

2. Type a name for your Data Collector Set and click Next.

3. The Root Directory setting will contain data collected by the Data Collector Set. Change this setting if you want to store your Data Collector Set data in a different location from the default. Browse to and select the directory, or type the directory name.

> **NOTE** *If you enter the directory name manually, you must not enter a backslash at the end of the directory name.*

4. Click Next to define a user account for the Data Collector Set to run as, or click Finish to save the current settings and exit.

5. After clicking Next, you can later update the Data Collector Set to run as a specific user. Click the Change button to enter the username and password for a different user from the default listed.

> **NOTE** *If you are a member of the Performance Log Users group, you can configure Data Collector Sets that you create to run under your own credentials.*

6. Click Finish to complete the wizard and to return to Windows Resource and Performance Monitor.

To view the properties of the Data Collector Set or to make additional changes, select Open Properties for this Data Collector Set. You can get more information about the properties of Data Collector Sets by clicking the Help button in the Properties page.

➤ To save and start the Data Collector Set immediately (and begin saving data to the location specified in Step 4), click "Start this data collector set now."

➤ To save the Data Collector Set without starting collection, click Save and close.

Reports

Performance Monitor includes two default system reports for assessing system health and diagnosing system-performance issues. It also includes one default User Defined report, Server Manager Performance Monitor. It may also include a third report for network issues. The default reports correlate to the default system collector sets and are described below:

➤ **System Diagnostics** — Details on the status of hardware drivers, system services, security systems, and disk drives

➤ **System Performance** — Detailed metrics covering the resource utilization of hardware devices and the impact of running applications

In the scenario we use below to show you how to collect data and view reports, you will collect data to view the System Performance Report.

Keep in mind the prerequisites for viewing a report. To view system reports, ensure that you meet the following requirements:

➤ You are logged on as a member of the local Administrators group, or you have started Resource and Performance Monitor with elevated privileges.

➤ Resource and Performance Monitor is running.

> **NOTE** *The System Performance Report uses the Windows Kernel Trace provider, which can only be accessed by members of the local Administrators group.*

After launching Performance Monitor and ensuring that you have data to report by enabling the Data Collector Set, perform the following steps to view a diagnosis report:

1. In the navigation tree, expand Data Collector Sets and then System.

2. Right-click System Performance and click Start. Data collection will begin (see Figure 22-12).

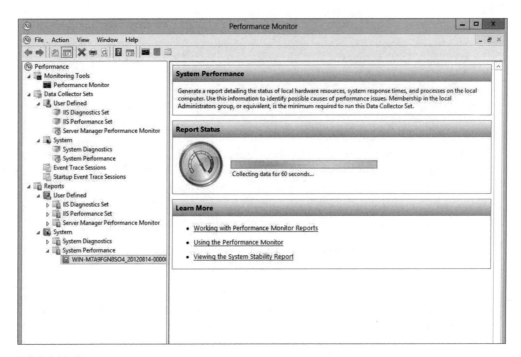

FIGURE 22-12

3. In the navigation tree, expand Reports, then System, then System Performance, and click the report stamped with the current date and time.

4. When data collection and report generation are complete, the System Performance Report will appear in the console pane (see Figure 22-13).

Each report presents data in categories and subcategories. Here are a few tips on navigating through a System Report from the Performance Monitor:

➤ Use the arrow icons on the right side of a category bar to expand and collapse the category.

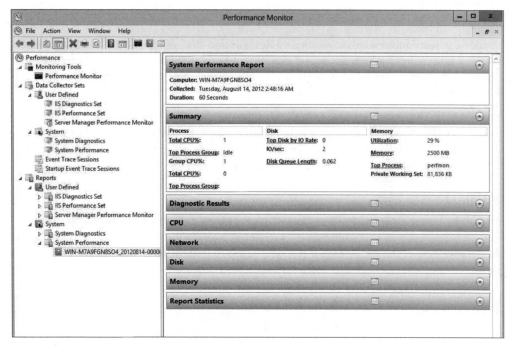

FIGURE 22-13

➤ Use the data icons on the center of a category to pull up a summary menu of all the data points in the report and navigate using the quick links therein.

➤ Toggle between Report view and Performance Monitor view by clicking on the desired icon on the top menu bar. Click the black icon with the red line to view the data in graph form. Click the green icon with the white box to see the data in report form (see Figure 22-14).

FIGURE 22-14

Note an important caveat about logging: Using Performance Monitor on the local server will add to the load that the server must handle. Usually, you can assume that logging increases most of the captured data by 5 percent, but that can vary greatly, and the best thing you can do to ensure that your performance data is accurate is to monitor from another server. Open Performance Monitor on a Windows Server 2012 server that does not host your web application and point the monitoring counters toward the remote web-host server. The data you collect, then, will not be tainted by the demands of the monitoring and logging process. Creating and viewing reports on collected data can also spike the demand for resources on a server; thus, doing that on a server other than those that are hosting your web application will further protect your web server's resource load.

What to Monitor

When picking objects and counters to monitor, you will find that you have tens of objects and hundreds of counters from which to choose. Picking counters that have meaning to you can be a daunting task. The following sections are based on Microsoft's best practices and will help you pick meaningful counters that will become the basis for useful reports on your system.

We cover the main components of the server as well as the core services that make an IIS server tick. In each case, we offer a description of the counters that you will find in Windows Server 2012. As we mentioned in the Monitoring sections above, these counters are performance objects that are written into the operating system by Microsoft and enable you capture the metrics over time.

Memory Usage

Memory can be a source of performance degradation. Memory issues should be reviewed before investigating other web server components (for example, processor utilization). The following table provides an overview of the counters that can be tracked to find memory, caching, and virtual memory (paging) bottlenecks:

AREA	COUNTERS	DESCRIPTION
Physical and virtual memory usage	Memory\Available Kbytes Memory\Committed Bytes	Memory\Available Kbytes is the amount of physical memory available to processes running on the server. Memory\Committed Bytes is the amount of committed virtual memory. If the server has little available memory, you may need to add memory to the system. In general, you want the available memory to be no less than 5% of the total physical memory on the server. Generally, the committed bytes value should be no more than 75% of the total physical memory. Capture data during peak periods.
Memory caching	Memory\Cache Bytes Internet Information Services Global\Current File Cache Memory Usage Internet Information Services Global\File Cache Hits %	Memory\Cache Bytes represents the total size of the filesystem cache. Internet Information Services Global\Current File Cache Memory Usage represents the current memory used by the IIS file cache. Internet Information Services Global\File Cache Hits % represents the ratio of cache hits to total cache requests and reflects how well the settings for the IIS file cache are working. A site with mostly static files should have a very high cache hit percentage (70%–85%).

Memory page faults	Memory\Page Faults/sec Memory\Pages Input/sec Memory\Page Reads/sec	A *page fault* occurs when a process requests a page in memory and the system cannot find it at the requested location. If the requested page is elsewhere in memory, the fault is called a *soft page fault*. If the requested page must be retrieved from disk, the fault is called a *hard page fault*. Most processors can handle large numbers of soft faults. Hard faults, however, can cause significant delays.
		Page Faults/sec is the overall rate at which the processor handles all types of page faults.
		Pages Input/sec is the total number of pages read from disk to resolve hard page faults.
		Page Reads/sec is the total disk reads needed to resolve hard page faults.
		Pages Input/sec will be greater than or equal to Page Reads/sec and can give you a good idea of your hard page fault rate. If there are a high number of hard page faults, you might need to increase the amount of memory or reduce the cache size on the server.

Processor Utilization

Before you review processor utilization, first ensure that any memory issues have been resolved. *Processor utilization* on an IIS server is a factor of processing HTTP requests, code execution, and I/O writes. Note that each processor installed in a server will have its own counter objects. The following table lists the most valuable counters to include in your data set:

AREA	COUNTERS	DESCRIPTION
Thread queuing	System\Processor Queue Length	System\Processor Queue Length displays the number of threads waiting to be executed. These threads are queued in an area shared by all processors on the system. If this counter has a sustained value of 10 or more threads, you'll need to upgrade or add processors.
CPU usage	Processor\% Processor Time	Processor\% Processor Time displays the percentage of time the selected CPU is executing a non-idle thread. Track this counter separately for each processor instance. If the values are high (>75%) while the network interface and disk I/O throughput rates remain low, you'll need to upgrade or add processors.

Disk I/O

Disk throughput is not a common cause of performance degradation because of the high performance of today's storage systems. If a server has heavy disk read and write duties, the server's overall performance can be degraded first by memory constraints, because memory reads and writes are much faster than disk I/O. To reduce the disk I/O, manage the server's memory to ensure that the page.sys file is used only when necessary. The following table includes the counters you should monitor to measure disk I/O performance:

AREA	COUNTERS	DESCRIPTION
Overall drive performance	PhysicalDisk\% Disk Time	PhysicalDisk\% Disk Time is the percentage of elapsed time that the selected disk drive was busy servicing read or write requests. If the % Disk Time value is high and the processor and network connection remain nominal, the system's hard disk drives may be contributing to performance degradation. For example, if the system's processor utilization was at or below 50%, network utilization was at 20%, and % Disk Time was at 90%, this would indicate a problem.
Disk I/O	PhysicalDisk\Disk Writes/sec PhysicalDisk\Disk Reads/sec PhysicalDisk\Avg. Disk Write Queue Length PhysicalDisk\Avg. Disk Read Queue Length Physical Disk\Current Disk Queue Length	PhysicalDisk\Disk Writes/sec and PhysicalDisk\Disk Reads/sec are the number of writes and reads per second and measure disk I/O activity. PhysicalDisk\Avg. Disk Write Queue Length and PhysicalDisk\Avg. Disk Read Queue Length — In combination, these counters tell you how many write and read requests are waiting to be processed. In general, you want there to be very few waiting requests. Keep in mind that the request delays are proportional to the length of the queues minus the number of drives in a redundant array of independent disks (RAID). In most cases, the average disk queue lengths should be less than 4.

Network Bandwidth

To determine the throughput and current activity on a web server's NIC, monitor the performance counters in the following table:

AREA	COUNTERS	DESCRIPTION
Network traffic	Network Interface\Bytes Total/sec	Network Interface\Bytes Total/sec is the rate at which bytes are sent and received over each network adapter, including framing characters. If the total bytes-per-second value is more than 50% of the total bandwidth under a typical load, you might have problems under peak times.

Web Service Counters

The following counters describe the main ways in which a website posts activity. From these counters, you can get a great sense of the demands that your website visitors are placing on your website components, and the utilization of your website service. The following table lists the most valuable counters to include in your data set:

AREA	SETTING	DESCRIPTION
Web service demand	Web Service\Current Connections Web Service\Connection Attempts/sec	Web Service\Current Connections is the current number of connections established with the web service. Web Service\Connection Attempts/sec is the rate, in seconds, at which connections to the WWW service have been attempted since the service started.
Web service utilization	Web Service\Bytes Total/sec Web Service\Total Method Requests/sec	Web Service\Bytes Total/sec is the total rate at which bytes are transferred by the web service. Web Service\Total Method Requests/sec is the rate at which all HTTP requests are made.
Web service utilization	Web Service\ISAPI Extension Requests/sec Web Service\CGI Requests/sec	Web Service\ISAPI Extension Requests/sec is the rate at which ISAPI extension requests are received by the web service. Web Service\CGI Requests/sec is the rate at which CGI requests are received by the web service. If these values decrease because of increasing loads, you might need to redesign the applications.
Web service utilization	Web Service\Get Requests/sec Web Service\Post Requests/sec	Web Service\Get Requests/sec is the rate at which HTTP requests using the GET method are made. GET requests are the most common HTTP request. Web Service\Post Requests/sec is the rate at which HTTP requests using the POST method are made. POST requests are generally used for forms and are sent to ISAPIs (including ASP) or CGIs. GET requests make up almost all other requests from browsers and include requests for static files, ASPs and other ISAPIs, and CGI requests.
Web server storage capacity	Web Service Cache\File Cache Hits %	Web Service Cache\File Cache Hits % is the total number of successful lookups in the user-mode file cache (since service startup). If the cache is performing its function well, this counter will be high for static content. This value might be low if the counter known as the "Kernel URI Cache Hits % Age" is high.

continues

(continued)

AREA	SETTING	DESCRIPTION
Web server processor capacity	Web Service Cache\ Kernel:URI Cache Flushes Web Service Cache\ Kernel:URI Cache Misses Web Service Cache\ Kernel:URI Cache Hits %	Web Service Cache\Kernel:URI Cache Flushes should be as low as possible, relative to the number of requests. Note that this number increases every time a file is flushed from the `Http.sys` response cache, which means that the content has not been accessed in the past 2–4 minutes. The only way to decrease this number is to flush the cache less often, although frequent flushing can cause `Http.sys` to use more memory for content that is not being accessed. Web Service Cache\Kernel:URI Cache Misses is the total number of unsuccessful lookups in the Kernel URI cache (since service startup). The lower the number of misses the better. (Each request for dynamic content increases the value of the counter by one.) Web Service Cache\Kernel:URI Cache Hits % is the ratio of Kernel URI cache hits to total cache requests (since service startup). The higher the ratio the better — up to 100. (This counter applies to static unauthenticated content and dynamic content that is marked as cacheable.)

ASP.NET Counters

You can audit your capacity, stability, and throughput metrics for your ASP.NET code using the counters in the following table:

AREA	SETTING	DESCRIPTION
ASP.NET stability	ASP.NET Apps vX\ Errors Total ASP.NET vX\Application Restarts ASP.NET vX\Worker Process Restarts	ASP.NET Apps vX\Errors Total, where X is the .NET version number, is the total number of errors that have occurred in ASP.NET applications. ASP.NET vX\Application Restarts is the number of times the application has been restarted during the web server's lifetime. ASP.NET vX\Worker Process Restarts is the number of times a worker process has restarted on the machine.

ASP.NET throughput	ASP.NET Apps vX\ Requests/Sec ASP.NET vX\Requests Queued	ASP.NET Apps vX\Requests/Sec, where X is the .NET version number, is the number of requests executed per second for ASP.NET applications. ASP.NET vX\Requests Queued is the number of ASP .NET requests waiting to be processed.
ASP.NET capacity	ASP.NET vX\Requests Rejected ASP.NET vX\Worker Process Running	ASP.NET vX\Requests Rejected, where X is the .NET version number, is the total number of requests that were not executed because of insufficient server resources. This counter represents the number of requests that return a 503 HTTP status code. ASP.NET vX\Worker Process Running is the number of worker processes running on the machine.

Centralized Binary Logging

When an IIS server hosts many websites, the process of creating hundreds or thousands of formatted log files can consume valuable CPU and memory resources from the server. When using a production web server as your basis for monitoring and logging, you can actually create performance and scalability problems.

Centralized binary logging is an option that minimizes the amount of system resources that is used for logging. With this format, IIS creates one log file for all sites on the web server. Every site writes request hit information as unformatted binary data. The binary output file, which is a far more efficient filesystem than other logging formats, takes up to 50 percent less space than an ANSI text file.

Centralized binary logging is a server property, not a site property. When you enable centralized binary logging, you cannot record data from individual websites in a different format. The centralized binary logging log file has an Internet binary log (.ibl) filename extension.

Settings for binary logging can be found in the following XML configuration file:

```
%SystemRoot%\system32\inetsrv\config\applicationHost.config
```

Enable central binary logging by setting the centralLogFileMode attribute to CentralBinary and the enabled attribute to True. The log file is created in the W3SVC folder, which by default is located at systemroot\System32\LogFiles\. If possible, move the central log file to a dedicated logging partition. You can also configure logging using IIS Manager, as shown in Figure 22-15.

1. Select the server node in the left pane.

2. Double-click the Logging icon in the IIS section.

3. In the Logging settings, select Server as the setting for the "One Log file per" option. Binary logging will then be the default option for log format.

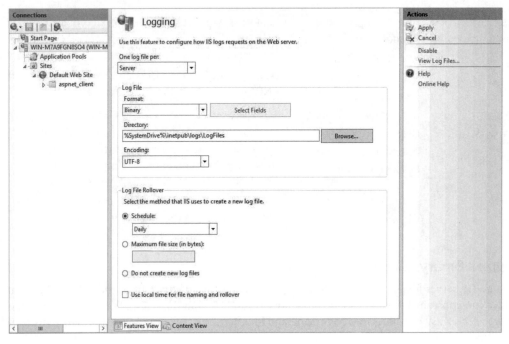

FIGURE 22-15

When you are ready to extract data from a raw log file, you can do one of the following:

➤ Create a custom application (for example, VB, VB.NET) that locates and extracts the data that you want from the raw file, and convert the data into formatted text. You can view header file and log file format descriptions in the IIS 8.0 SDK.

➤ Use the Log Parser tool to extract data from the raw file. The Log Parser tool and its accompanying user documentation are included as a separate download from `www.microsoft.com/downloads`.

Centralized binary logging records the following information, which is similar but not identical to the W3C Extended log file format:

➤ Date

➤ Time

➤ Client IP address

➤ Username

➤ Site ID

➤ Server name

➤ Server IP address

➤ Server port

➤ Method

➤ URI stem

➤ URI query

➤ Protocol status

➤ Windows status

➤ Bytes sent

➤ Bytes received

➤ Time taken

➤ Protocol version

➤ Protocol substatus

Note that the following fields are reported in W3C Extended log files, but they are not recorded in centralized binary logging log files:

➤ **Host** — The host header.

➤ **User Agent** — The browser type of the client. This string is too large to be practical for the binary format.

➤ **Cookie** — The content of the cookie that was sent.

➤ **Referrer** — The site that the user last visited.

At this point in the chapter, we change topics from *collecting* data to *using* data. Using the data collected from your monitoring solution, you can make incremental changes to your website configuration, hardware platform, or operating system services with confidence that your changes will actually amount to improved performance.

PERFORMANCE TUNING

The mandates for tuning websites range from emergency fixes to creating more headroom for growth in an existing environment. One of the most compelling reasons for tuning performance is that your visitor base goes up, but your budget for hardware does not. By fine-tuning your application, you can get more life from your existing platform as demands go up.

The Windows platform has several tuning points — knobs or levers that you can adjust to match your resource alignment with expected traffic. This hasn't changed much with Windows Server 2012 and IIS 8. Microsoft has added the following tuning features in IIS 8:

➤ **Application initialization** — Start certain applications upon boot, ensuring a snappy response when the first request arrives.

➤ **NUMA support** — Native support Non-Uniform Memory Access (NUMA) hardware with up to 128 processor cores, significantly moving up the bar for high-performance servers.

➤ **CPU throttling options** — New options to the IIS 7.x set for managing CPU and memory resources per application pool.

Ideally, you would conduct your first round of performance tuning before the website is released into production. That way, you can be sure that when your application goes into production, it will perform well, and you will know what that application's limitations will be before they are reached. In any event, the main configuration points that you can consider when making incremental changes are listed first in brief below, then in detail in the sections that follow. For each category of configuration change, we included a few examples of what can be done for illustration purposes. It's not a comprehensive list, but it should give you a good idea of what to consider.

Tuning your web server and website involves these areas:

➤ **Processor** — Change the processor type or add processors to the server.

➤ **Memory** — Change the memory type or add memory to the server.

➤ **Operating system** — Stop unnecessary services from using resources, and adjust settings to prioritize IIS traffic processing.

➤ **Load balancing** — Add system capacity and fault tolerance by pairing servers and clustering servers to handle extra demands.

➤ **Application partitions** — Add system capacity by partitioning your web application into tiers and hosting those tiers on separate, dedicated servers.

➤ **IIS and website** — Configure IIS and your websites to maximize performance and stability.

In the next sections, we cover the details of the areas introduced above, starting with some of the more important operating system configurations, and go into detail subsequently on how to tune IIS and websites.

Operating System Optimizations

We mention just a couple of areas related to optimizing the operating system here, but you should give thought to how you can do more. Pick up a book on Windows Server 2012 or do an online search. You can uncover an entire universe of settings that are beyond the scope of this book. Again, the IT Service Management (ITSM) framework mentioned at the beginning of this chapter can provide insight for configuration and change management. The areas of the operation system configurations that are covered here include the operating system architecture, service hardening, data throughput, application performance, TCP stack tuning options, and storage settings.

If you don't use a configuration management tool and your computer domain doesn't deliver group policies to servers, you can use the Security Configuration Wizard (SCW) to export the settings once you have hardened your system.

Disable Unnecessary Services

Because Windows Server 2012 has a modular architecture, there will be few unnecessary services after you install the IIS role. You may have installed features or roles that you don't need, however, and by removing those you make more resources available to IIS and present a smaller attack surface for malicious code. Going a step further, your server should ideally be dedicated to the IIS role and should be provisioned on a fresh build.

Use the Services console (press WIN+R, type **services.msc** into the Run box, and then hit Enter) to disable services by right-clicking on the service and updating the Startup Type to Manual or Disabled. The following table lists the services that you normally will not need on an IIS server:

SERVICE NAME	DESCRIPTION
Application Experience	Processes application-compatibility cache requests for applications as they are launched.
Distributed Link Tracking Client	Maintains links between NT File System (NTFS) files within a computer or across computers in a network. Disable this service only if your IIS content is local to the web server.
IP Helper	Provides automatic IPv6 connectivity over an IPv4 network. If this service is stopped, the machine will only have IPv6 connectivity if it is connected to a native IPv6 network.
Network List Service	Identifies the networks to which the computer has connected, collects and stores properties for these networks, and notifies applications when these properties change. Note that the Notification Service depends on the Network List Service and may be required for activating your operating system.
Print Spooler	Loads files to memory for later printing. Most IIS servers do not have printer access, so you can safely disable this service.
Remote Registry	Enables remote users to modify Registry settings on this computer. If this service is stopped, the Registry can be modified only by users on this computer.
Secondary Logon	Enables starting processes under alternative credentials. If this service is stopped, this type of logon access will be unavailable. If this service is disabled, any services that explicitly depend on it will fail to start. Usually, administrators who log on to IIS servers have the necessary rights required to administer the server and do not require the Run As service.

Disable the preceding services only after giving careful thought to whether the web server requires them.

Application Performance

The configuration options on the *Application Performance* area of the System Properties console (`sysdm.cpl`) determine the responsiveness of foreground and background applications. To adjust the configuration options for application performance, follow these steps:

1. Press WIN+R, type **sysdm.cpl** into the Run box, and hit Enter.

2. In the System Properties dialog box, select the Advanced tab, and then click Settings in the Performance section.

3. On the Visual Effects tab, select "Adjust for best performance." This will reduce the load on the system when displaying windows and menus.

4. On the Advanced tab, ensure that Background Services is selected. This setting is used because the IIS processes should be run as background services. By default, Background Services is selected.

5. Also on the Advanced tab, click the Change button in the Virtual Memory section, and configure the paging file according to the following principles:

   ➤ Ideally, place the paging file on a different disk or disk array from the one that holds the system and boot partitions. In high-performing systems, you should use the RAID-0 (Stripe Set) array to store the paging file.

   ➤ Avoid placing a paging file on a fault-tolerant drive, such as a RAID-1 or a RAID-5 volume. Paging files do not need fault tolerance, and some fault-tolerant systems suffer from slow data writes because they write data to multiple locations.

   ➤ Do not place multiple paging files on different partitions on the same physical disk drive.

   ➤ Set the initial paging file size to be at least 1.5 times larger than the amount of physical RAM.

   ➤ Set the maximum paging file size to be equal to the initial size, which stops the paging file from changing sizes and fragmenting the hard disk drive.

TCP Stack Tuning Options

Microsoft has improved the network stack considerably in Windows Server 2012. Network performance is more stable and flexible, and faster. Here is an abridged list of benefits over previous operating systems:

➤ Automated TCP/IP performance tuning, using improved algorithms to assess the best way to communicate with networks.

➤ An ability to offload TCP/IP processing away from the CPU onto a compatible NIC adapter, saving CPU cycles for other services.

➤ Receive-side scaling (RSS) allows faster network performance by spreading the packet-reception processing load across multiple processors.

➤ Dual layer implementations of IPv4 and IPv6 network stacks.

In addition to the improvements in the network stack, you can configure settings to fine-tune the server. You should thoroughly test any and all changes you make to the Registry, and rarely will you want to introduce such a change into a production environment without first proving the value (and stability) of the change in a controlled laboratory environment.

The following table shows some of the ways you can optimize the TCP network services stack for your IIS server:

REGISTRY VALUE	DESCRIPTION
`TCPWindowSize`	The maximum data (in bytes) in a TCP transmission burst. The range is 1–65,535 bytes using the following Registry value: `HKEY_LOCAL_MACHINE\System\CurrentControlSet\Services\Tcpip\Parameters\TcpWindowSize.` The default values for common interfaces are: Gigabit (1,000 M bps) — 65,535 Ethernet (100 Mbps) — 16,384 Others — 8,192. This value should be set to: `End-to-end network bandwidth (bytes/s) x Bandwidth-Delay product (the round-trip delay in seconds)`
`MaxHashTableSize`	The TCP hash table tracks open TCP connection states. Set during installation, the default size is figured by multiplying the number of processors times 128. `HKEY_LOCAL_MACHINE\System\CurrentControlSet\Services\Tcpip\Parameters\MaxHashTableSize` The maximum is 0x10000 or 65,536 bytes for this Registry value. For high-performance servers, use the maximum value regardless of the number of processors.
`MaxUserPort`	Windows makes 5,000 port connections available for each IP address. Your site may require more concurrent port connections and can raise the following Registry value up to 65,534: `HKEY_LOCAL_MACHINE\System\CurrentControlSet\Services\Tcpip\Parameters\MaxUserPort`

IIS Service Optimizations

Having optimized other aspects of the operating system, the next area to think about before we cover website configuration is the IIS 8.0 service. As you read through these options, keep in mind that most of the tuning options covered here are set at the *server* level and will apply uniformly to all the websites hosted on the server. If your web server hosts more than one site, be careful to consider the requirements for all the sites on the server before making any changes to the IIS service.

Http.sys Optimizations

`Http.sys`, the front end of IIS, is defined in Chapter 2, "IIS 8.0 Architecture." Because of the separation of the HTTP protocol stack in *kernel mode* from the worker processes in *user mode*,

`Http.sys` uses its own error-logging scheme that is controlled by the kernel mode conventions. The following are some examples of events that use kernel mode error logging:

➤ Connection time-outs.

➤ Worker process in user mode unexpectedly terminates or closes its application pool; outstanding requests are logged.

➤ When IIS does not immediately destroy connections that the client terminates before a response for the last request on these connections is complete ("Zombie sessions").

The kernel mode request processing handled by the `Http.sys` stack has a separate log file from those files that log website activity. The default location for the `Http.sys` error log is at:

```
%SystemRoot%\System32\LogFiles\HTTPERR
```

To change the configuration of `Http.sys`, you have to edit the Registry. `Http.sys` reads the configuration only once during startup. The `Http.sys` configuration is global and will affect all web traffic. The parameters are located under the following Registry key:

```
HKEY_LOCAL_MACHINE\System\CurrentControlSet\Services\HTTP\Parameters
```

You can make adjustments to values within the HTTP\Parameters key to further tune how the `Http.sys` service receives and responds to raw requests. To optimize the `Http.sys` I/O processing, review the options in the following table:

REGISTRY VALUE	DESCRIPTION
UriEnableCache	This Registry value enables the kernel mode response and fragment cache. For most workloads, the cache should remain enabled. Consider disabling the cache if you expect very low response and fragment cache utilization. To disable the fragment cache, change the data for this value to 0.
UriMaxCacheMegabyteCount	Specifies the maximum memory available to the kernel cache. When set to 0, the operating system adjusts the amount of memory available to the cache. Note that specifying the size only sets the maximum, and the system may not allow the cache to grow to the specified size.
UriMaxUriBytes	This is the maximum size of an entry in the kernel cache, which offers a faster response to requests by keeping them in memory and off the hard drives. Responses or fragments larger than the data set in this Registry value will not be cached. The default value is 262,144 bytes (256 KB). You should increase this limit to take advantage of installed memory greater than 2 GB. If memory is limited and large entries are crowding out smaller ones, it may help to lower this limit.

`UriScavengerPeriod`	The `Http.sys` cache is flushed by a scavenging process, which fires according to the time period set in this Registry value. Setting the scavenger period to a high value reduces the number of scavenger scans. However, the cache memory usage may grow as older, less frequently accessed entries are allowed to stay in the cache. Setting this period to too low a value causes more frequent scavenger scans and may result in excessive flushes and cache churn. The default value is 120 seconds. Consider increasing that amount by as much as 100% if your data is static.

This last set of `Http.sys` Registry values is centered on connection options. You can tune the connection parameters to make the most of the installed resources on the local server. The Registry-based tuning options for connections are listed in the following table:

REGISTRY VALUE	DESCRIPTION

`IdleConnectionsHighMark`
`IdleConnectionsLowMark`
`IdleListTrimmerPeriod`
	Manage the structures that handle `Http.sys` connections, ensuring a minimum and maximum capacity as well as the polling period where capacity is audited.

`InternalRequestLookasideDepth` `RequestBufferLookasideDepth`	Change buffer management parameters for tuning for load fluctuations.
`MaxConnections`	Number of concurrent connections that the `Http.sys` will allow. Each connection uses non-paged-pool memory. On a dedicated web server, the value can be set higher than the default, which is set conservatively, to enable the server to handle more simultaneous requests.

Application Pool Optimizations

IIS 8.0 builds on the options first introduced in IIS 6.0 for optimizing application pool and worker process performance. Chapter 8, "Web Application Pool Administration," explains how pooling applications into a common worker process benefits websites and how to manage the pooling feature using code, configuration files, and IIS Manager.

You can tune application pools using the same tools, including WMI scripting, `web.config` files, `appcmd.exe`, and IIS Manager.

To view the options for setting application pool settings using AppCmd, type the following line into a command window (replace `DefaultAppPool` with the name of any application pool on your server):

```
appcmd.exe set AppPool "DefaultAppPool" /?
```

To use IIS Manager, perform the following steps to access the tuning window:

1. Open IIS Manager.

2. In the Connections pane, double-click on the server that you want to manage.

3. Click the Application Pools node under the target server.

4. In the center pane, right-click on the application pool that you want to tune, and select Advanced Settings to view the tuning options (see Figure 22-16).

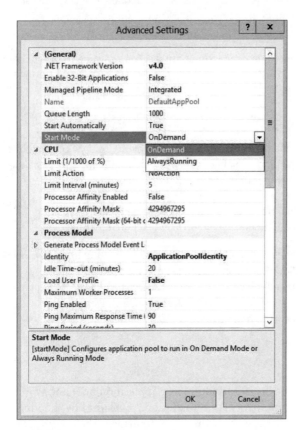

FIGURE 22-16

The following three tables list some of the key settings to consider when tuning IIS application pools. Use the values suggested as a baseline, and further fine-tune these settings based on the performance data collected.

This following table describes the general attributes:

PARAMETER	DESCRIPTION
.NET Framework Version	Configure IIS to load the .NET Framework version specified here, or choose "No Managed Code."
Enable 32-Bit Applications	Set to `True` to instantiate worker processes in a WOW64 session to support 32-bit applications on a 64-bit server.
Managed Pipeline Mode	Configure ASP.NET to run in either classic mode (as an ISAPI extension) or in integrated mode. See Chapter 2 for more details.
Queue Length	Set the maximum number of requests allowed in the queue for this pool. The default is 1,000. Visitors will receive an IIS error 503 "Service Unavailable" when the queue is full.
Start Automatically	When `True`, the application pool will start when IIS starts.
Start Mode	On Demand mode is the default setting, which sets the pool to spawn a worker process when the first request arrives. The other option, "Always Running mode," causes the pool to spawn a process immediately.

The following table covers the application pool CPU tuning options:

PARAMETER	DESCRIPTION
Limit (1/1000 of %)	Maximum percent of CPU time (in 1/1,000-ths of a percent) that the worker processes in an application pool are allowed to use within the interval specified below. 0 disables this limit and is the default setting. Use this setting if code in the website is unstable and consumes CPU resources over time.
Limit Action	This determines how IIS reacts when the pool reaches the limit set in the Limit setting. NoAction is the default. KillW3WP forces the pool to shut down while the pool is reset. Throttle limits the CPU access to the limit provided above. ThrottleUnderLoad limits CPU access only if there is conflicting demand for it.
Limit Interval (minutes)	Interval for monitoring the limit of CPU time that the application pool is allowed to use, as specified above. At the end of this interval, the counter is reset. 0 disables CPU monitoring; 5 minutes is the default setting.
Processor Affinity Enabled	This forces the worker processes for this application pool to spawn as a thread on a particular processor. Use this setting on multiprocessor systems that host websites that are not written using .NET managed code (which is multithreading-aware).
Processor Affinity Mask	Hexadecimal value, or CPU ID, that represents the target CPU to which the application pool will assign new worker processes.

The next table includes options for application pool process model tuning. These settings affect the worker process behavior and can have a big impact on the user's experience.

PARAMETER	DESCRIPTION
Idle Time-out (minutes)	Shuts down a worker process after being idle for more than a specified amount of time. This can save some resources on limited-memory systems, but it is not recommended in situations that will require frequent spawning of new worker processes under heavy CPU load, because of the overhead associated with process creation.
Load User Profile	When `True`, IIS will load the user profile of the account specified in the Identity field. This is new to IIS 8.0 and allows you to further configure security and logging based on the application pool identity account profile.
Maximum Worker Processes	You can control the total number of worker processes in a Web Garden mode of operation. In Web Garden mode, several worker processes handle the request load under a single application pool. There is no preassignment of worker processes to websites via different application pools. In some cases, one worker process is not enough to handle the load (indicated by poor CPU usage and long response times), and increasing the number of worker processes may improve throughput and CPU usage. One case in which the Web Garden mode may be considered is with hosting multiple sites. Multiple worker processes can also offer more reliability in case of an incidental crash of one of them, with little chance of total service disruption. Web Garden mode is easier to set up and control than multiple preassigned application pools. The default is one worker process to handle all requests.
Ping Enabled	Enables health monitoring of the application pool using a periodic request for acknowledgement that is sent to the pool (according to the two settings below). If the pool is unresponsive, it is recycled. `True` by default, this is an excellent option for most pools.
Ping Maximum Response Time (seconds)	Maximum time that a worker process is given to respond to a health-monitoring ping. The process is terminated by IIS if it does not respond. This is set to 90 seconds by default.
Ping Period (seconds)	Interval between health-monitoring pings.
Shutdown Time Limit (seconds)	Period of time a worker process is given to finish processing requests and shut down. If the process exceeds the limit, it will be forced to terminate by IIS. This is set to 90 seconds by default.
Startup Time Limit (seconds)	Period of time a worker process is given to start. If the process exceeds the limit before it becomes responsive, it will be restarted by IIS. This is set to 90 seconds by default.

The following table covers the application pool process orphaning options:

PARAMETER	DESCRIPTION
Enabled	Set to `True` to abandon an unresponsive worker process. This can help debug errant applications.
Executable	Launches a program when a pool is unresponsive and abandoned. Microsoft gives an example, "`C:\dbgtools\ntsd.exe`," which can be used for debugging.
Executable Parameters	These parameters will be used when executing the program above.

The following table includes application pool rapid-fail protection:

PARAMETER	DESCRIPTION
Service Unavailable Response Type	This is part of a load-balancing support structure. When the pool is stopped, setting this to HttpLevel causes an HTTP 503 error. If set to TcpLevel, the connection will reset.
Enabled	If set to `True`, the pool is shut down if the worker process crashes more than the tolerated number set below.
Failure Interval (minutes)	The time in minutes during which worker process crashes must stack up to trigger a rapid-fail protection event, which will shut down the pool.
Maximum Failures	Total number of worker process crashes tolerated before the pool is killed by a rapid-fail protection event.
Shutdown Executable	Launches a program when a pool is shut down. This can reconfigure your load balancer and trigger another application or event.
Shutdown Executable Parameters	These parameters will be used when executing the program above.

The final table in this section covers the application pool recycling tuning options. Like the settings in the preceding table, the options in the table below can affect the user's experience significantly and deserve careful consideration:

PARAMETER	DESCRIPTION
Disable Overlapped Recycle	When `True`, the existing worker process will be shut down first before another is started. Use this setting when your application does not support multiple instances.
Disable Recycling for Configuration Changes	This stops the recycling act that would accompany a configuration change to the application pool.

continues

(continued)

PARAMETER	DESCRIPTION
Private Memory Limit (KB, kilobytes)	Maximum amount of private memory a worker process can consume before causing the application pool to recycle. A value of 0 means that there is no limit.
Regular Time Interval (minutes)	Periodic recycling based on time. The default value is 1,740. Use this value if your application is unstable and becomes inoperable over time. Otherwise, set this to 0 to stop the application pool from automatically recycling based on this time interval.
Request Limit	Periodic recycling based on the (cumulative) number of requests. 0 means that there is no limit. Use this value to cap the number of requests as a means to reset your application pool in case that the server ceases to be responsive.
Specific Times	Recycling at given time settings. You can provide them several times during the day, or in one entry. Use to recycle the application pool during a maintenance window.
Virtual Memory Limit (KB, kilobytes)	Memory-based recycling (disabled by default) allows recycling of a worker process if it has reached the limit defined here. 0 indicates no recycling based on virtual memory usage.

Website Optimizations

Having covered the tuning options for the operating systems and for the IIS service, it's now time to work directly with the website configurations. Tuning a website is not as complex as writing optimized website code, but it's every bit as important. Each of the tuning options covered below applies to the website where you make the change; other websites that you may host on the server will not be affected.

HTTP Page Headers

Every web page that IIS sends includes *HTTP page headers*, extra data that is prefixed to the page stream before it is sent. The extra data in the page headers tells the visitor's browser how to handle the web page. There are two types of HTTP page headers that you can use to help optimize your website performance: Content Expiration and HTTP keep-alives.

HTTP Keep-Alives

A browser typically makes multiple requests in order to download an entire web page. To enhance server performance, most web browsers request that the server keep the connection open across these multiple requests, which is a feature known as *HTTP keep-alives*.

Without HTTP keep-alives, a browser that makes numerous requests for a page containing multiple elements, such as graphics, might require a separate connection for each element. The additional connections also make a browser much slower and less responsive, especially across a slow connection.

HTTP keep-alives are required for integrated security or connection-based authentication services, such as Integrated Windows Authentication (IWA). If you disable HTTP keep-alives for websites that use IWA, requests to the website fail.

Content Expiration

Consider setting file expiration dates where possible. *Content expiration* is how IIS determines whether or not to return a new version of the requested web page if the request is made after the web page content has expired. IIS will mark each web page before it's sent using the settings you provide for content expiration. The end user's browser will translate the expiration mark. The options for expiring content are as follows:

➤ **Immediately** — Expires content immediately after it is delivered.

➤ **After** — Sets the number of days after which the content will expire.

➤ **On** — Sets an exact date when the content will expire.

By setting content expiration other than immediately, you can reduce second-access load times by 50 to 70 percent. This setting will not affect dynamically generated content.

Enabling HTTP Header Tuning

To enable content expiration or HTML keep-alives, follow these steps:

1. Open IIS Manager.

2. Double-click on the target server that you want to administer. To set the options to apply to all servers, continue to Step 3. To apply these settings to a single website, double-click on the Sites node under the target server, and then select the website you want to administer.

3. Ensure that your center panel shows the Features View tab (located at the bottom left of the center pane).

4. In the HTTP Response Headers pane, right-click on an empty space, and select the Set Common HTTP Response Headers option from the context menu.

   Figure 22-17 shows the "Enable HTTP keep-alive" and "Expire Web content" options.

5. Select the configuration options most suitable for the website and click OK.

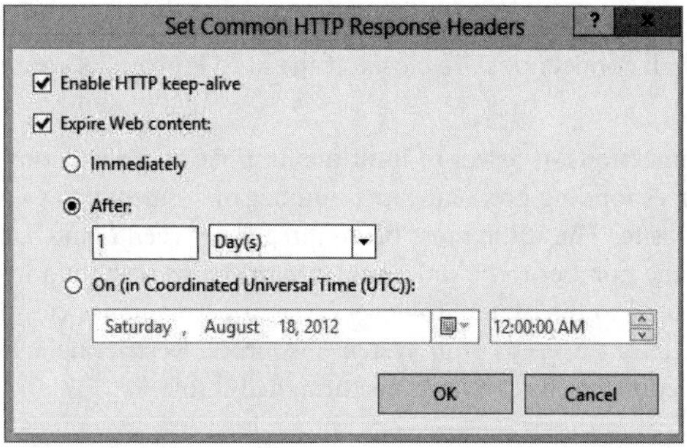

FIGURE 22-17

Bandwidth Throttling

Bandwidth throttling can be set at the Global Websites node and at each individual website. At the global websites level, you can limit the total network bandwidth available for all websites on the server. Bandwidth throttling can also be set at the website level, allowing you to limit the amount of bandwidth consumed by each site. The default for bandwidth throttling at any level is Disabled and is the recommended setting.

If a minimum amount of bandwidth for a particular site is required or a site uses too much bandwidth that affects other sites, then bandwidth throttling is an optional solution. Also, adding server NICs or offloading the website/application to another server would alleviate bandwidth bottlenecks.

1. Open IIS Manager.

2. Double-click on the target server that you want to administer.

3. Double-click on the Sites node under the target server.

4. Select the website you want to administer.

5. Ensure that your center panel shows the Features View tab (located at the bottom left of the center pane).

6. In the Actions pane, in the Manage Web Site\Configure group, click the Limits link. The following options are available for controlling bandwidth usage for the site (see Figure 22-18):

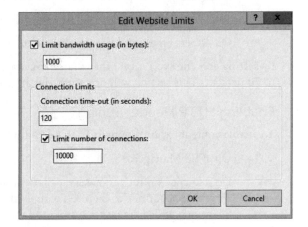

FIGURE 22-18

➤ **Limit bandwidth usage (in bytes)** — Select to limit the amount of traffic allowed to a website based on bandwidth usage. In the corresponding box, enter a value, in bytes, at which you want to limit the website traffic. The value must be an integer between 1,024 and 2,147,483,647.

➤ **Connection timeout (in seconds)** — Type a number in the box to set the length of time, in seconds, before the web server disconnects an inactive user. This setting guarantees that all connections are closed if the HTTP protocol cannot close a connection.

➤ **Limit number of connections** — Select to limit the number of connections allowed to a website. In the corresponding box, enter the number of connections to which you want to limit the website. The value must be an integer between 0 and 4,294,967,295 (unlimited). Setting the number to be unlimited circumvents constant administration if your connections tend to fluctuate. However, system performance can be affected if the number of connections exceeds your system resources. Restricting a website to a specified number of connections can keep performance stable.

Output Caching

You can configure *output caching* to improve performance. As you know, when a user requests a web page, IIS processes the request and returns a page to the client browser. With output caching enabled, a copy of that processed web page is stored in memory on the web server and returned to client browsers in subsequent requests for that same resource, eliminating the need to reprocess the page each time it is requested. This is helpful when your content relies on an external program for processing, such as with a Common Gateway Interface (CGI) program, or when the site includes data from an external source, such as from a remote share or a database.

With the output caching management in IIS 8.0, cached items are retained in memory, but they are dumped if resources run low on the server. The page will then be recached the next time a user requests that resource if the server determines that the page is sufficiently popular to be cached.

To access the tuning options for output caching, follow these steps:

1. Open IIS Manager.

2. Double-click on the target server that you want to administer.

3. Double-click on the Sites node under the target server.

4. Select the website you want to administer.

5. Ensure that your center panel shows the Features View tab (located at the bottom left of the center pane).

6. In the center pane, double-click the Output Caching Rules icon in the IIS grouping.

7. In the Actions pane, click the Edit Feature Settings link. Figure 22-19 shows the resulting Edit Output Cache Settings dialog box.

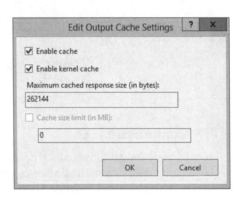

FIGURE 22-19

The options for caching are as follows:

➤ **Enable cache** — Enables the IIS output cache, which stores cached responses in user mode. The IIS output cache is similar to the ASP.NET output cache. However, the IIS output cache is a native output cache that offers increased performance over the managed output cache in ASP.NET.

➤ **Enable kernel cache** — Enables the kernel cache, which stores cached responses in kernel mode. Performance is improved when responses are returned from the kernel cache without transitioning to user mode.

➤ **Maximum cached response size (in bytes)** — Specifies the maximum size of a cached response for both the user-mode and kernel-mode caches. The default value is 262,144 bytes.

➤ **Cache size limit (in MB)** — Configures the size limit of both the user-mode and kernel-mode caches.

8. Make any changes and after establishing the feature settings, you can add caching rules. To create a new caching rule, click Add in the Actions pane and complete the configuration window. The options are listed and explained in the following table:

ELEMENT NAME	DESCRIPTION
File name extension	Displays the filename extension for which the caching rule applies (e.g., `.aspx`).
User-mode caching	File Cache Monitoring options include: ➤ Using file change notifications ➤ Time intervals ➤ Prevent all caching Click the Advanced button to set caching based on the URL and/or HTTP headers.
Kernel-mode behavior	File Cache Monitoring options include: ➤ Using file change notifications ➤ Time intervals ➤ Prevent all caching
Entry Type	Shows the scope of the output caching rule. The value is either Local or Inherited. This setting is read only.

HTTP Compression

If network bandwidth is a concern, consider using the IIS compression service. *HTTP compression* will shrink data before the IIS server sends it; the client's browser decompresses the data before rendering it for the website visitor. Using HTTP compression gives you these benefits:

➤ Reduces the amount of data sent (improves bandwidth utilization)

➤ Increases the page display speed (increases transfer times)

➤ Allows for consolidation of web applications into a smaller web farm (reduces server sprawl)

HTTP compression requires support of HTTP 1.1 by the client's browser. Most current browsers support HTTP 1.1 and have the feature enabled by default; older browsers may not support HTTP 1.1. Older browsers will still be able to retrieve files from your site; they will not take advantage of HTTP compression. Before enabling HTTP compression on production servers, it is imperative that all the applications on the web server are tested fully.

Using IIS Manager, you can apply compression settings at the global website level. IIS Manager allows you to configure global compression for the following:

➤ Static files only

➤ Dynamic application responses only

Here are the steps to install the IIS compression services, which are essential if you want to use HTTP compression:

1. Open Server Manager.

2. Click the Manage menu in the top-right corner and choose Add Roles and Features.

3. On the Installation page, click Next to add a Role-based or feature-based installation.

4. Click Next on the Server Selection page.

5. On the Server Roles page, scroll down and expand the Web Server (IIS) role in the Roles box.

6. Expand the Performance node and select Static Content Compression and/or Dynamic Content Compression (see Figure 22-20).

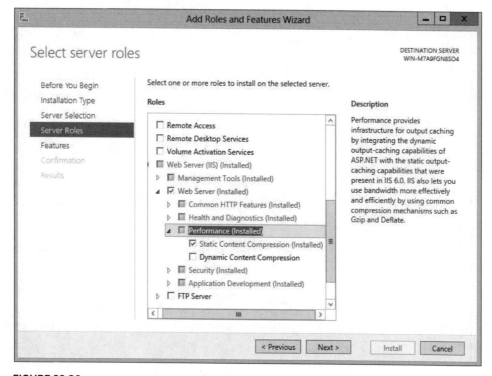

FIGURE 22-20

7. Click Next, click Next again, and then Install. Click Close after the role services are installed.

Now that the services are installed, you can configure compression for a website. Here are the steps for enabling HTTP compression in IIS:

1. Open IIS Manager.

2. Double-click on the target server that you want to administer. If you want to set the options to apply to all servers, continue to Step 3. To apply these settings to a single website,

double-click on the Sites node under the target server, and then select the website you want to administer.

3. Ensure that your center panel shows the Features View tab (located at the bottom left of the center pane).

4. In the center pane, double-click the Compression icon in the IIS grouping.

5. In the center pane, click the checkboxes of the kind of compression you want to employ.

When setting compression settings at the server level, you have more options to consider. Figure 22-21 shows the options for server-level compression settings.

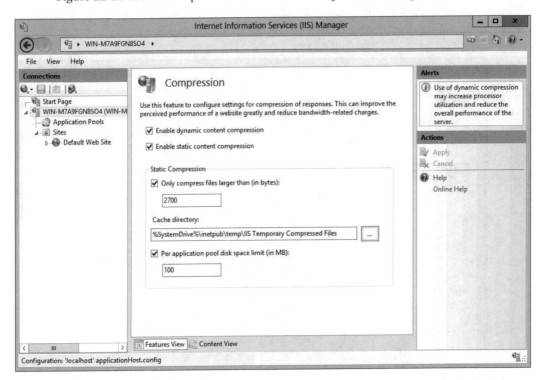

FIGURE 22-21

You can set the following compression settings at the server level:

➤ **Enable dynamic content compression** — Configures IIS to compress dynamic content. Compression of dynamic application responses can affect CPU resources because IIS does not cache compressed versions of dynamic output. If compression is enabled for dynamic responses and IIS receives a request for a resource that contains dynamic content, the response that IIS sends is newly compressed every time it is requested. Because dynamic compression consumes significant CPU time and memory resources, use it only on servers that have clients with slow network connections but that have CPU time to spare.

➤ **Enable static content compression** — Configures IIS to compress static content. Unlike dynamic responses, compressed static responses can be cached on disk across multiple requests without degrading CPU resources. On the next request, a compressed file can be retrieved from disk, which improves performance because the CPU does not have to compress the file again.

➤ **Only compress files larger than (in bytes)** — Defines the minimum file size that you want IIS to compress. The default size is 256 bytes.

➤ **Cache directory** — Defines the path of a local directory where a static file is cached after it is compressed, either until it expires or until the content changes. For security reasons, this temporary directory must be on a local drive on an NTFS-formatted partition. The directory cannot be compressed and should not be shared.

➤ **Per application pool disk space limit (in MB)** — Sets the maximum amount of space, in megabytes, that you want IIS to use when compressing static content. When the "Limit disk space usage" setting is defined, IIS automatically cleans up the temporary directory when the set limit is reached. The default limit is 100 MB per application pool.

When tuning at the website level, you only have the option to turn compression on or off by selecting the checkbox next to either "Enable dynamic content compression" or "Enable static content compression."

6. In the Actions pane, click Apply.

Note that dynamic content cannot be compressed and then later cached. An important caveat about compressing dynamic content is that it must be generated and compressed on every hit to the web page. When hosting dynamic content, you should evaluate the cost/benefit ratio of compressing dynamic content. You benefit from better bandwidth management, but it comes at the cost of CPU processing. If your site uses dynamic content extensively and processor utilization (% Processor Time) is already high, you may have to first upgrade the server's processors before enabling HTTP compression.

Website Connections

Using the website Performance tab, IIS provides a means for an unlimited number of concurrent connections and an option to limit the number of connections at both the *web server* (global) level and for a particular *website*. For internal IIS servers, setting the value to an unlimited number avoids additional benchmarking and administration if your connection loads burst beyond anticipated levels.

For externally facing sites, IIS performance will plummet if the number of connections exceeds your system resources — affecting all sessions. All IIS systems have a performance ceiling. For Internet-facing servers, provide a maximum connection figure to protect against denial-of-service scenarios. To arrive at a realistic figure, establish a benchmark for concurrent connections during peak performance, and then add 10 percent to 20 percent as a margin of error.

To access the website tuning options, follow these steps:

1. Open IIS Manager.

2. Double-click on the target server that you want to administer.

3. Double-click on the Sites node under the target server.

4. Select the website you want to administer.

5. In the Actions pane, under the Manage Web Site group, click Advanced Settings. The Advanced Settings window is shown in Figure 22-22.

6. In the Behavior group, make any necessary adjustments to the Connection Limits field as appropriate to the nature of your website.

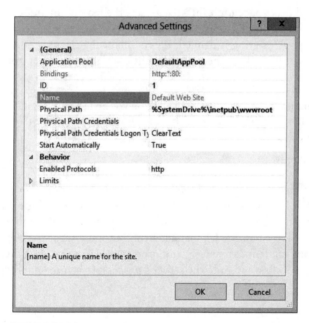

FIGURE 22-22

Ideally, your web application will be tested to identify performance expectations at given connection/activity levels. For example, if an Internet-facing application realizes 200 concurrent connections and performance indicators point to 100 percent utilization of the server farm, then capping the connection rate to 95 percent — or 190 concurrent connections — will ensure that servers will remain responsive during a burst in requests.

23

Diagnostics and Troubleshooting

WHAT'S IN THIS CHAPTER?

➤ Types of Issues

➤ Runtime Status and Control API

➤ IIS 8.0 error pages

➤ Failed Request Tracing

➤ Logging

➤ ASP.NET Tracing

➤ Built-in troubleshooting tools

➤ Installable troubleshooting tools

WROX.COM CODE DOWNLOADS FOR THIS CHAPTER

The wrox.com code downloads for this chapter are found at www.wrox.com/remtitle .cgi?isbn=1118388044 on the Download Code tab.

At first glance, "Diagnostics and Troubleshooting" might not strike you as a very interesting chapter. Let's put you at ease from the beginning. Whether you are a casual IIS administrator or an IIS professional, you have probably run into many situations in which you wanted to find out why a page was taking a long time to load, why it hung, why it was consuming so much CPU, or why it failed. In this chapter, we will explore together many features and tools that will help you better manage your web platform.

IIS 8.0 brings with it a wealth of troubleshooting features that greatly enhance this latest version of Microsoft's web platform. It is easy to get excited about the ability that IIS gives us to get behind the scenes and gain access to a wealth of information.

This chapter starts off with many features that IIS 8.0 offers and then branches off into various other tools built into the operating system and some additional tools that can be downloaded, to make your troubleshooting skills the envy of your fellow administrators.

TYPES OF ISSUES

It is important to gain an understanding of the types of failures that can be encountered on your web server. IIS 8.0 has built-in support for the following types of errors:

➤ Specific errors

➤ Hang/time-out issues

➤ Resource-intensive issues

Specific Errors

The first type of error is a *specific error.* These are the errors that usually fail quickly and will show an HTTP Error page corresponding to the error (see Figure 23-1). Some errors (for example, those with a 500 HTTP status code) will have customized error pages with extensive information used for troubleshooting and debugging. Specific errors are often the easiest to troubleshoot because the error message will immediately narrow down the issue, and usually they are easy to reproduce and will fail the same way every time.

IIS 8.0 goes out of the way to give immediate and valid information that can be used to solve the specific issue. For example, consider a case in which you forget to put in a default document. The error page that IIS 8.0 serves up will tell you exactly what is happening, providing detailed error information, most likely causes, suggestions on what you can try, and links to further information.

Hang/Time-Out Issues

The second type of error is a *hang* or *time-out error.* In past versions of IIS, these were often very difficult to troubleshoot. The error would often simply say that there was a time-out, without giving any clues as to the cause. What makes these even more difficult to troubleshoot is that they can be hard to reproduce, and these types of errors will often take a long time before failing (90 seconds is a common script time-out value used by IIS and various web browsers); thus, each time you want to test or see the error again, you may need to wait a long time.

With IIS 8.0, troubleshooting hang and time-out issues get much easier with Failed Request Tracing and Runtime Status and Control (RSCA), which are covered in depth later in this chapter.

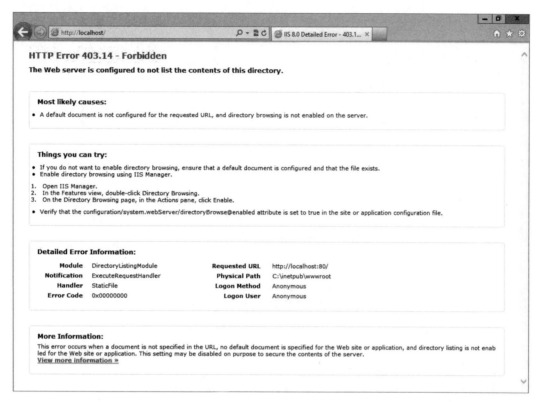

FIGURE 23-1

Resource-Intensive and Slowness Issues

The final category of errors is *resource-intensive* and *slowness issues*. They can cause the server's CPU to spike, cause excessive disk usage, high memory usage, or over utilize almost any resource. These are generally the most difficult issues to resolve. The negative effects of this issue are often not noticed immediately, and sometimes are not even caught during preproduction load testing if the issue occurs in a situation in which the testing team did not think to test. Instead, after a heavy load on the server or under certain unique circumstances, the site can start to bog down. When you start to troubleshoot the error, the only clue that you might have is that the site is running slower than normal. Now it is your responsibility to find out what is causing the slowness. It could be the server, the network, the database server, a third-party component — it could be nearly anything. Figure 23-2 shows the Windows Task Manager during an issue of intermittent but heavy CPU usage.

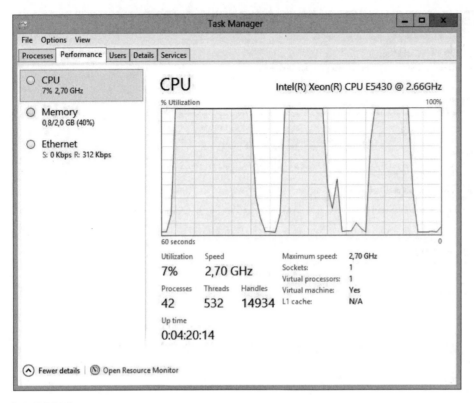

FIGURE 23-2

As with hang and time-out issues, Failed Request Tracing is at your service. IIS 8.0 enables you to determine which pages are taking a long time to run and what part of the page is currently being processed, usually leading to the cause of the issue.

It is also possible to have a combination of issues, either one error causing another error, or multiple independent issues that need to be solved at the same time. The rest of this chapter covers tools and troubleshooting steps to solve all three of these types of issues.

RUNTIME STATUS AND CONTROL API

IIS 8.0 allows you to look into the real-time state of the server, including all running page requests, application domains, and active sites — very useful for troubleshooting long-lasting page requests. This is done through the Runtime Status and Control API (RSCA). Don't let the term *API* in the name scare you. RSCA is used in many different ways, including with IIS Manager, PowerShell, and AppCmd.exe.

IIS Manager is one of the most straightforward means of viewing the RSCA data. Although the location in IIS Manager for RSCA makes sense when you think about it, it's not easy to find the first time. The next section shows how RSCA is used to view running worker processes.

Viewing Worker Processes

You can view the running requests at the server level in IIS Manager by double-clicking the Worker Processes icon (see Figure 23-3).

FIGURE 23-3

Double-click the Worker Processes icon at the server level to bring up a view of all running worker processes. Figure 23-4 shows the Worker Processes screen with one worker process running. Obviously, this can have many more than one worker process. There can be dozens or even hundreds of running worker processes, depending on how many sites and application pools you have on your server.

Because this is active data, only current worker processes will be shown here. This may change often. Chapter 8, "Web Application Pool Administration," discusses application pools in depth; however, as a general rule, if web gardens are not enabled, there should be one worker process for each application pool, and often not all application pools will have a running worker process. Application pools will not start until the first time they are used, and if the idle-time-out value is reached because a site has not been visited in a while, an application pool will shut down. In these cases, there will not be a worker process for that application pool.

In addition, since this is real-time data, if an application pool is recycled or killed, the process ID will change, and the worker process that you are watching may seem to disappear. This is the nature of real-time process information.

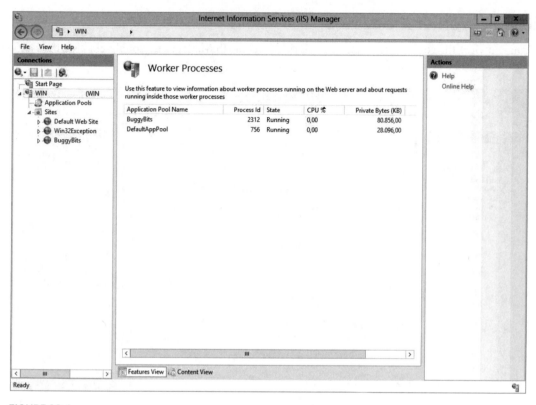

FIGURE 23-4

The Worker Processes View shows the Application Pool Name, Process ID, current State, CPU, Private Bytes, and Virtual Bytes.

Virtual Bytes and Private Bytes are interesting counters to understand. *Virtual Bytes* refers to the size in bytes of the virtual address space that the process is using. This doesn't necessarily correspond to physical memory or disk usage. *Private Bytes* refers to the size in bytes of memory that the process has allocated. This space cannot be shared by other processes. Because different tools in Windows Server 2012 display them differently, it is helpful to know the Private Bytes and Virtual Bytes values and what they correspond to within the different tools.

➤ **Task Manager** — In Task Manager, the Commit Size column corresponds to the Private Bytes value in RSCA. The Commit Size column is not shown by default, however. To display it, on the Details tab, right-click on the existing columns, click "Select columns," and add it. There is no matching column in Task Manager for Virtual Bytes.

➤ **Performance Monitor** — In Performance Monitor, both names match the RSCA names. The only difference between the two tools is that RSCA reports the value in kilobytes, whereas Performance Monitor reports it in bytes. To have the value match exactly, divide the Performance Monitor value by 1,024.

In Performance Monitor, you can view the memory usage for each worker process by selecting the Process counter and the `w3wp.exe` instance. On a busy server, there may be multiple `w3wp.exe` processes, which can make this more difficult. You will need to view the Process ID (PID) value to confirm which worker process it really is.

To see a list of started worker processes using PowerShell, run the following command (see Figure 23-5):

```
PS IIS:\appPools>dir
```

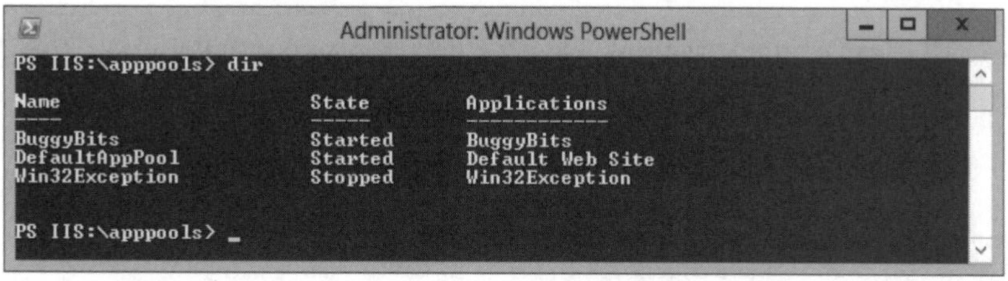

FIGURE 23-5

> **NOTE** *The WebAdministration module must be imported before navigating to the* `PS IIS:\appPools>` *directory. Refer to chapter 18 for more information about using PowerShell.*

To see a list of all running worker processes using `AppCmd.exe`, run the following command (see Figure 23-6):

```
appcmd.exe list wp
```

FIGURE 23-6

> **NOTE** `AppCmd.exe` *is in* `%windir%\system32\inetsrv`, *which isn't in the system path; thus, you must either add it to the system path, navigate to* `%windir%\`
> `system32\inetsrv`, *or enter the full page, as follows:*
>
> `%windir%\system32\inetsrv\appcmd.exe list wp.`
>
> *To add the* `inetsrv` *folder to the system path for the duration of the life of that command prompt session, run the following command:*
>
> `path=%path%;%windir%\system32\inetsrv.`
>
> *Lastly, to access the IIS cmdlets of PowerShell, you need to import the WebAdministration module first.*

This will do the equivalent of what `IISApp.vbs` did in IIS 6.0. If you were not familiar with `IISApp.vbs`, it was new to IIS 6.0 and had a single purpose, which was to list or recycle running worker processes on the server.

It is possible to filter based on the application pool name or worker process ID. For example, `appcmd.exe list wp /apppool.name:DefaultAppPool` or `appcmd.exe list wp /wp.name:2668` (`appcmd.exe list wp 2668` is a shorthand way to do the same thing), respectively.

Here is a simple VBScript example using WMI that will create output similar to `appcmd list wp`:

```
Set oService = GetObject("winmgmts:root\WebAdministration")

Set oWorkerProcesses = oService.InstancesOf("WorkerProcess")

For Each WP In oWorkerProcesses
    strPID = "WP """ & WP.ProcessId & """"
    strAppPool = "(applicationPool:" _
        & WP. AppPoolName & ")"
    WScript.echo(strPID & " " & strAppPool)
Next
```

This makes a call to the `WebAdministration` namespace, gets a list of all worker processes, and then loops through each worker process and outputs its Process ID and application pool name.

```
C:\Windows\System32\inetsrv>cscript list.vbs
Microsoft (R) Windows Script Host Version 5.8
Copyright (C) Microsoft Corporation. All rights reserved.
C:\Windows\System32\inetsrv\list.vbs(1, 1) (null): 0x8004100E
```

Viewing Page Requests

Now it's time to enter a hidden world that goes even deeper. At first glance, it's easy to miss that you can drill into the worker processes to see all running page requests. Double-click on the worker process that you want to drill into to see all the page requests for that worker process (see Figure 23-7).

Here you can find a list of all running page requests. These are active pages, so it will be difficult to catch any page that lives for less than a second. For testing, you can write a simple page that calls a `Sleep` command. Create a file (call it **sleep.aspx**) and place the following in it:

```
<% System.Threading.Thread.Sleep(10000) %>
Done
```

Since the time is in milliseconds, a value of `10000` will cause the page to sleep for 10 seconds.

> **NOTE** *The commands discussed in this section require that the Request Monitor and/or the IIS Management Scripts and Tools feature be installed. If you receive errors, make certain that these features are installed.*

After double-clicking on the worker process in the Worker Processes section, you will be taken to the Requests section, which shows the Web Site ID, Url, Verb, Client IP Address, State, Module Name, and Time Elapsed for each running page request. It is also interesting to note that if you hit a default page without putting the full path (for example, `http://localhost/`), it will show two requests: one for the default and one for the specific page.

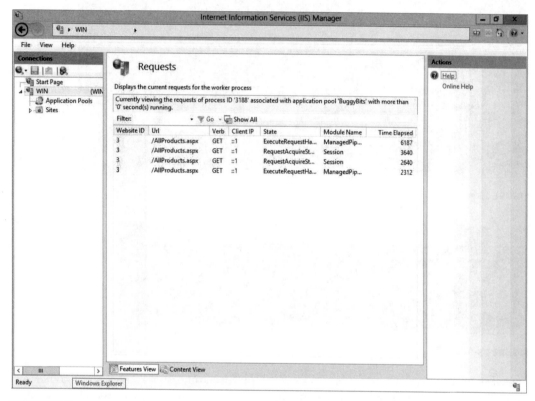

FIGURE 23-7

Requests can be filtered based on the time that they take to run, known as the *Time Elapsed*. Although it is not obvious, the Filter field in the Requests section is for the Time Elapsed. Enter a number of seconds between 0 and 2,147,482 into the Filter field and press Go. This will show all page requests that have been running for as long as or longer than the time you entered in the filter. To clear the filter, click the Show All button.

You can also use `AppCmd.exe` or the PowerShell WebAdministration module to obtain the same information. You can pass additional parameters to filter for the request ID, site name, worker process ID, application pool name, and time elapsed. To view all running requests on the server, run the following:

```
appcmd.exe list request
```

```
PS IIS:>Get-Item IIS:\AppPools\BuggyBits | Get-WebRequest
```

Figures 23-8 and 23-9, respectively, show PowerShell and `AppCmd.exe` run from the command line with long running requests.

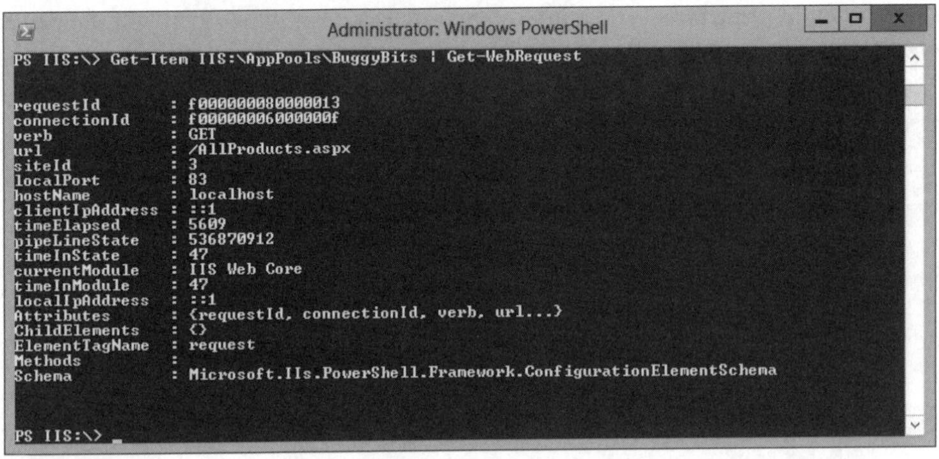

FIGURE 23-8

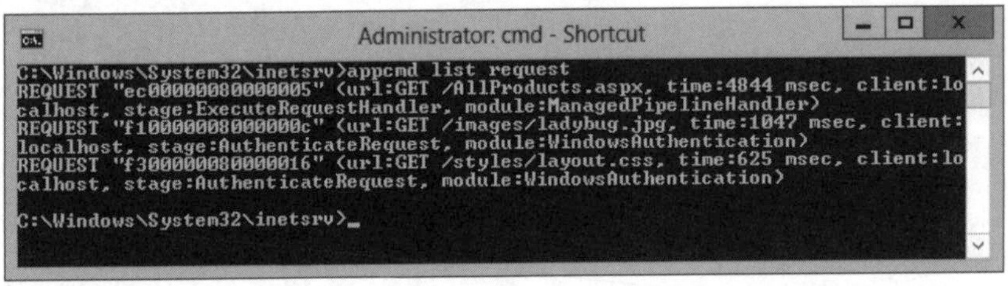

FIGURE 23-9

There can be many running requests on a server at any given time, so it is often useful to narrow them down further. The length of time that the pages have been running is a useful filter. Using AppCmd you can filter based on the identifier, worker process PID, application pool name, and website name. To get the syntax and examples for each, type **AppCmd.exe list request /?** from the `%windir%\system32\inetsrv` folder. Enter **Get-Help Get-WebRequest** in PowerShell to see the cmdlet's syntax. To see page requests that have been running for more than 5 seconds (5,000 milliseconds), run the following command (see Figure 23-10):

```
appcmd.exe list request /elapsed:5000
```

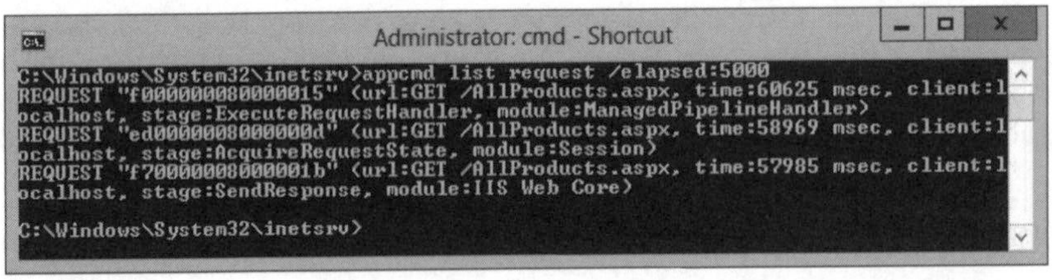

FIGURE 23-10

The same information can be retrieved using WMI or `Microsoft.Web.Administration` and is explained in more depth in Chapter 18, "Programmatic Configuration and Management."

Viewing Application Domains

Application domains (aka *AppDomains*) are a key part of ASP.NET, but historically they have been mostly hidden. An *application domain* is an isolated environment where applications exist. IIS creates separate AppDomains for each folder that is set as an application. Additionally, from code, developers can set their own AppDomains for code isolation.

The `WebAdministration` WMI namespace and `Microsoft.Web.Administration` each expose application domains and give the ability to unload them.

Here is a simple VBScript example using WMI that will allow you to view all the running application domains:

```
Set oService = GetObject("winmgmts:root\WebAdministration")

Set oAppDomains = oService.InstancesOf("AppDomain")

For Each AppDomain In oAppDomains
  WScript.echo("ID: " & AppDomain.Id)
  WScript.echo("  ApplicationPath: " & AppDomain.ApplicationPath)
  WScript.echo("  PhysicalPath:    " & AppDomain.PhysicalPath)
  WScript.echo("  Process Id:      " & AppDomain.ProcessId)
  WScript.echo("  SiteName:        " & AppDomain.SiteName)
  WScript.echo("  IsIdle:          " & AppDomain.IsIdle)
  WScript.echo("")
Next
```

This example uses the `WebAdministration` namespace, gets all AppDomains on the server, loops through them, and outputs key information on the AppDomain.

As you can see, RSCA offers a lot of information through a variety of methods. Using RSCA, the system administrator can view running processes, page requests, application domains, and much more. This can all be accessed in real time without installing a third-party product and without a system restart to install it.

IIS 8.0 ERROR PAGES

Like previous versions of IIS, IIS 8.0 can point to customized error pages. These can be created uniquely for your environment to allow you to customize what the end users see when they encounter an error — to hide the error details and display a friendly page that looks like the rest of the site. You can also create it to send detailed information to you when there is a failure. Custom error pages can be set for each HTTP status code and optionally substatus codes (status codes are covered in a later section).

IIS 8.0 can return two types of errors:

➤ **Custom errors** — Custom errors are errors that regular end users of the website will see. They contain a brief description of the error but should not contain any sensitive information that you do not want an end user to see. Because you can customize this, you can put as little or as much on this page as you want. Generally, however, it should hide the real error and display a friendly page to the end user.

> ➤ **Detailed errors** — Detailed errors contain a wealth of information meant for local administrators and developers. Because a detailed error can contain sensitive information about the error, it should not be shown to end users. Detailed errors are meant to provide valuable information to the administrators and developers to help troubleshoot failures and errors on the server.

IIS 8.0 has a convenient method of displaying a different error to end users than to administrators and developers. This method was modeled by ASP.NET, so if you know ASP.NET, you will already be familiar with this concept. By default, IIS 8.0 will display a detailed error when the page request comes from the local server, and display a custom error when the page request comes from anything but the local server. This allows the local administrator or developer to view the page while on the local server and receive a helpful and detailed error message, whereas the end users will receive a different error message that doesn't expose the sensitive information about the error.

> **NOTE** *Internet Explorer's default setting is to show a friendly error message. Microsoft implemented this feature because many web servers would return a plain HTTP status code and a one- or two-word description (such as "Internal Error"), which many novice users would struggle to understand. To disable this feature, select Tools ➪ Internet Options ➪ Advanced, and uncheck the checkbox titled "Show friendly HTTP error messages."*

The default behavior can be changed so that, rather than different error pages depending on where the page request originated from, you can have all requests be detailed errors or all requests be custom errors. This will be explained shortly.

Although IIS 8.0 has bona fide error-page handling, it hasn't taken over the error handling for ASP .NET pages by default. All pages that are handled by ASP.NET will still use the ASP.NET error handler and will still receive the custom and detailed error pages that ASP.NET provides. This can be confusing because some pages will have the IIS 8.0 custom error pages while others have the ASP .NET error pages. This is by design, but it can be changed. The `existingResponse` attribute on the `httpErrors` element can be set to the following:

> ➤ **Auto** — This allows the application (in this case, ASP.NET) to determine whether it should use its own error pages or allow IIS to use its error pages. This is the default, which means that ASP.NET pages will use the ASP.NET error pages, whereas most non-ASP.NET pages will use the IIS 8.0 custom error pages.

> ➤ **Replace** — This forces IIS to always use the IIS 8.0 error pages. The benefit is that the error pages will be consistent and will always be controlled in the same manner, but IIS 8.0 doesn't provide the same detailed information on ASP.NET requests as ASP.NET does.

> ➤ **PassThrough** — This allows the error pages of the application to pass through without IIS 8.0 intercepting them and displaying its own error pages. With this setting selected, not even static and other generic pages will display the IIS 8.0 custom error pages.

You can change between modes by using `AppCmd.exe` or PowerShell. Here is how you can set the mode to `Replace`:

```
appcmd.exe set config /section:httpErrors /existingResponse:Replace
```

```
Set-WebConfigurationProperty -pspath "MACHINE/WEBROOT/APPHOST"
                             -filter "system.webServer/httpErrors"
                             -name "existingResponse"
                             -value "Replace"
```

To change back to `Auto` or to change to `PassThrough`, just run the same command but change the `Replace` with `Auto` or `PassThrough`.

Customizing Custom Error Pages

IIS 8.0 error pages can be changed in IIS Manager at the server, site, or application level. The interface is essentially the same. Figure 23-11 shows the Error Pages icon at the site level.

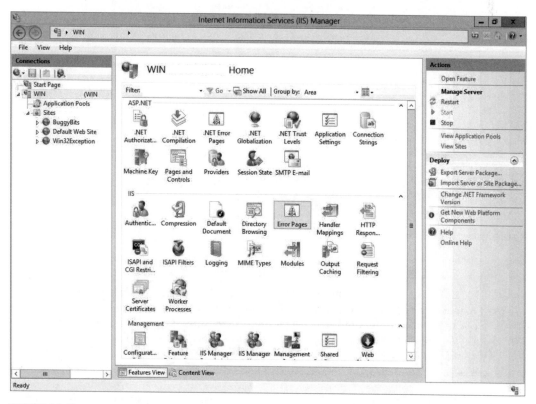

FIGURE 23-11

To manage error pages in IIS Manager, double-click the Error Pages icon. This will bring you to a list of status codes and their settings (see Figure 23-12). From here you can change any of the existing error pages or add new error pages. It's important to note that this allows you to change the custom error pages only, not the detailed error pages.

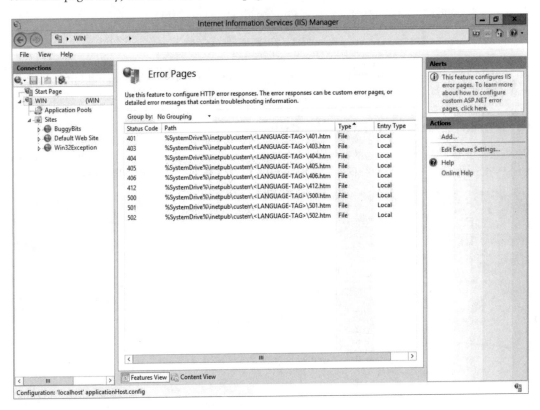

FIGURE 23-12

> **NOTE** *The detailed error pages cannot be changed unless you replace the CustomErrorModule (*custerr.dll*) Module in IIS 8.0, but you generally won't need to change the detailed error pages because they are meant to be seen by the system administrator or developer only and don't need to be customized to look like the rest of the site.*

From the IIS Manager Error Pages tool, you can edit the existing error pages or add a new error page. When adding new error pages, you can set the major status code and have the option to set the substatus code as well. This means, for example, that a 403.1 and 403.3 error page will return the same error page.

When creating or editing an error page, you can choose from one of three ways that IIS will display an error page:

➤ **Insert content from static file into the error response** — Displays a simple static page. This is the default, and it is fast because it is not preprocessed by the ASP.NET engine. You can select a file anywhere on the system. You can also serve up a different page for different languages, which will be covered in the next section.

➤ **Execute a URL on this site** — Displays the page that you specify, but it will process it with the ASP.NET engine to allow you to have dynamic content. It's important to note that this page must be a relative URL, and it must be in the same application pool as the page that caused the error.

➤ **Respond with a 302 redirect** — Redirects the page request to a new page, which can be on the same server or on a different server, so there is no requirement to be in the same application pool.

Within this same tool in IIS Manager, you can change between the three error response types:

➤ Custom error pages

➤ Detailed errors

➤ Detailed errors for local requests and custom error pages for remote requests

You can get to this setting window by clicking Edit Feature Settings from the right-hand Actions pane. Figure 23-13 shows the Edit Error Pages Settings window.

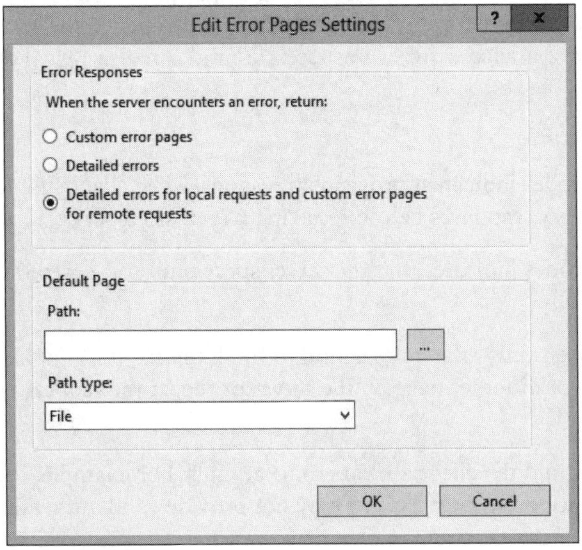

FIGURE 23-13

Multiple Language Support

IIS 8.0 supports multiple languages so that different error pages can be displayed for different browsers. Modern browsers send an HTTP header with the web request that specifies the language of the client. For example, a browser with a client language of English will send the following HTTP header: `Accept-Language: en-us`.

When setting custom error pages in IIS as described in the last section, if you select "Insert content from static file into the error response" for the Custom Error type, there is a checkbox that says "Try to return the error in the client language." If you check that, click on the "Set" button for a new box, which allows you to set the *Root directory path* and *Relative file path*. With this setting, when an error occurs, IIS will piece together the root directory + language + relative file path. The default Custom Error folder on an English version of Windows Server 2012 is `%SystemDrive%\inetpub\custerr\en-US\`.

Additional Language Packs can be obtained from `www.microsoft.com/downloads`.

The way that IIS handles substatus codes is by first checking if there is a specific error page set for the substatus code, and if there is not one set, it will check if there is a specific error page for the major status code. If there is no custom error page set for the major status code, it will check to see if a default error page has been set and use it.

HTTP Status Codes

When users try to access content on a server that is running IIS through HTTP or File Transfer Protocol (FTP), IIS returns a numeric code that indicates the status of the request. This status code is recorded in the IIS log, and it may also be displayed in the web browser or FTP client. The status code can indicate whether a particular request is successful or unsuccessful and can also reveal the exact reason that a request is unsuccessful.

Here is a list of the major status code categories:

➤ **1xx–Informational** — These status codes indicate a provisional response. The client should be prepared to receive one or more 1xx responses before receiving a regular response.

➤ **2xx–Success** — This class of status codes indicates that the server successfully accepted the client request.

➤ **3xx–Redirection** — The client browser must take more action to fulfill the request. For example, the browser may have to request a different page on the server or repeat the request by using a proxy server.

➤ **4xx–Client error** — An error occurs, and the client appears to be at fault. For example, the client may request a page that does not exist, or the client may not provide valid authentication information.

➤ **5xx–Server error** — The server cannot complete the request because it encounters an error.

FTP Status Codes

In addition to the HTTP status codes, there are several FTP status codes that can be used for troubleshooting FTP-related issues:

➤ **1xx–Positive preliminary reply** — These status codes indicate that an action has started successfully, but the client expects another reply before it continues with a new command.

➤ **2xx–Positive completion reply** — An action has successfully completed. The client can execute a new command.

➤ **3xx–Positive intermediate reply** — The command was successful, but the server requires additional information from the client to complete processing the request.

➤ **4xx–Transient negative completion reply** — The command was not successful, but the error is temporary. If the client retries the command, it may succeed.

➤ **5xx–Permanent negative completion reply** — The command was not successful, and the error is permanent. If the client retries the command, it receives the same error.

FAILED REQUEST TRACING

Failed Request Tracing is one of the most useful features in IIS 8.0. It enables you to gain detailed information about any page request and to be able to capture data based on the criteria that you define. This is not simply a tool for your development computer; this is a full-fledged, production-ready method of troubleshooting failures.

But what is even better is that as complex as it sounds, it really is not difficult at all. In the past, an IIS administrator would be required to rely on third-party tools to get inside the ASP.NET events to gain real-time insight into potential issues. These tools are usually expensive, have a steep learning curve, and often require a reset of IIS during installation. Tracing in some older versions of Windows Server brought the ability to see detailed debugging information free of charge and without installation downtime on the server, but the steps required to figure it out would scare the casual user.

With Failed Request Tracing in IIS 8.0, however, troubleshooting can be done at any time without downtime, with intangible performance overhead on the server, and with such ease of use that anyone can figure it out in a few minutes.

Failed Request Tracing was formally nicknamed *FREB*, or *Failed Request Event Buffering*, by the IIS development team. It is used to watch for all incoming requests that meet certain criteria and will save detailed information about the entire page request to disk in an easy-to-read XML format.

Three steps are required to start Failed Request Tracing logging to disk:

1. Ensure that Tracing is installed on the server.

a. Choose Server Manager ➪ IIS, and then scroll down to the Roles and Features section.

b. Expand the Tasks drop-down list and click Add Roles and Features.

   c. Expand the Web Server (IIS) Role ⇨ Web Server, and then check Tracing in the Health and Diagnostics section.

   d. Click Next twice to complete the installation.

2. Create a new tracing rule, as detailed in the following "Setting Up Failed Request Tracing Rules" section.

3. It is easy to miss this third step, which is to actually *turn it on*. Creating a rule does not automatically enable it, as you might assume. To enable Failed Request Tracing, go to the site level and double-click the Failed Request Tracing Rules icon. Then, in the Actions pane, click Edit Site Tracing. There is a checkbox labeled Enable that is off by default. Enable that and select OK.

Setting Up Failed Request Tracing Rules

It would not be practical to have all requests saved to disk, especially on a busy production server. You will want to narrow it down to capture the exact problem page. Failed Request Tracing provides filter options to narrow it down quite significantly. There are three steps to the wizard in IIS Manager:

1. Specify the content to trace.

2. Define the trace conditions.

3. Select the trace providers.

To begin creating a Failed Request Tracing rule from the server, site, or subfolder level, double-click the Failed Request Tracing Rules icon. This will open the Failed Request Tracing Rules tool, as shown in Figure 23-14.

To create a new Failed Request Tracing Rule, click the Add link in the Actions pane. The following three subsections will take you through the three pages of the wizard and cover the various options available to you.

Specifying Content to Trace

The first step of the wizard gives you the ability to choose all content or a specific type of content. You can choose All content, ASP.NET, Classic ASP, or Custom (see Figure 23-15).

This step is pretty straightforward. If you would like to narrow down to a single failed page, select Custom and enter the page name. For multiple pages, you must set up a new rule for each page. The Custom field does not allow you to enter multiple content types, although an asterisk (*) is allowed for wildcard characters. For example, **staff*.aspx** will catch `staff.aspx`, `staff_edit.aspx`, and any other pages that start with "staff" and have an extension of `.aspx`.

Click Next to go to the next step.

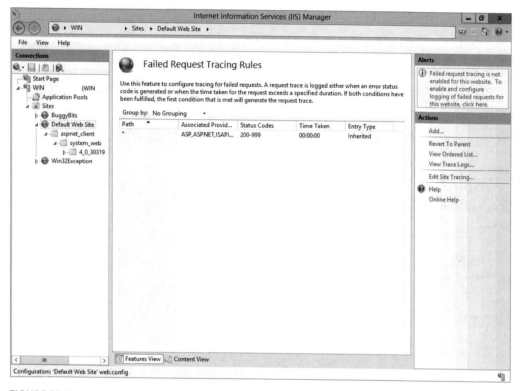

FIGURE 23-14

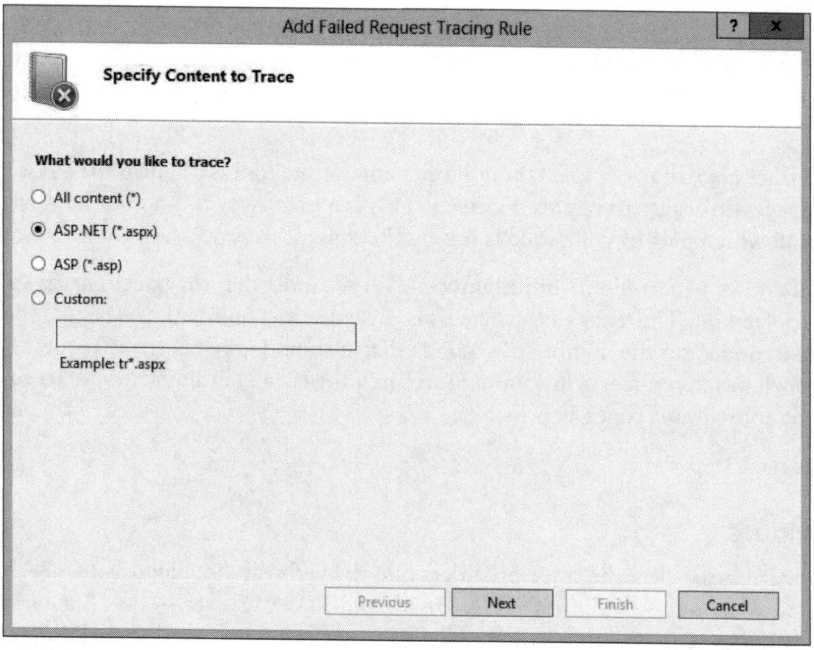

FIGURE 23-15

Defining Trace Conditions

The second filter step sets the *status code*, time taken, and event severity. The "Status code" field allows selecting multiple status code types, separated by a comma. For example, if you want to select all 500 errors, simply enter **500**. If you want to narrow it down to 500 and 401.5 errors ("Authorization failed by ISAPI/CGI application"), then you can enter **401.5,500** in the "Status code" box (see Figure 23-16).

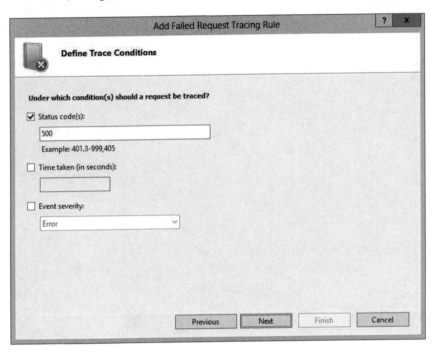

FIGURE 23-16

HTTP 200 status codes are also allowed. Even though the name of the tool is "Failed" Request Tracing, it will allow successful pages to be saved as well. This is a great way to find out how fast your code is running and which part of your code is taking the longest to process.

The "Time taken" field allows you to set the minimum time (in seconds) that the page must take to complete before it is reported on. This is as easy as it seems. Because it is optional, if desired, check the checkbox to enable it, and enter the number of seconds that it should take before a Request Page Trace is saved. Set it to whatever you feel is low enough to catch the issue, but high enough to capture the least amount of nonrelevant pages as possible.

Click Next to go to the next step.

Selecting Trace Providers

The final step of the wizard is to select the trace providers and the verbosity (see Figure 23-17). There are four providers by default — ASP, ASP.NET, ISAPI, and WWW Server — but, like virtually everything else in IIS, these can be extended or added to. Some providers overlap each other, and some are mutually exclusive. For example, the WWW Server provider gains information about every page request, whereas the ASP and ASP.NET providers will not both capture information for the same request.

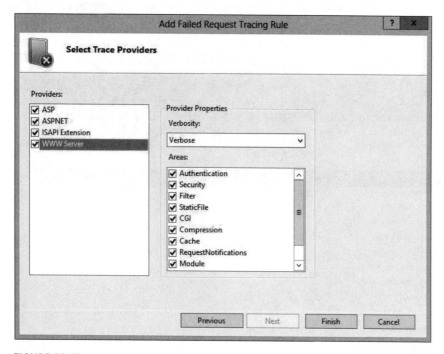

FIGURE 23-17

The default configuration has all providers selected with a Verbosity setting of Verbose. This will capture everything possible, but you can turn off anything that you do not require so that you can minimize the information that is captured.

After making your choices, select Finish. If tracing has not been enabled yet, finishing the wizard will not enable it for you. From the Failed Request Tracing Rules screen, click "Edit Site Tracing." The resulting screen allows you to enable tracing for that site. You can also set the path and the maximum number of trace files to store. Tracing is disabled by default. This is so that if you set certain tracing rules at the global level, tracing will not start writing to disk for all websites unless you purposefully turn them on.

Make sure to take note of the path where the trace files are placed. By default they are in `%SystemDrive%\inetpub\logs\FailedReqLogFiles\{subfolder}\`. When tracing writes to disk, it will place the trace files in a subfolder for that website (for example, `W3SVC1`).

Reading the XML Trace Logs

Once you have set up the files and captured some data, you can view the XML trace file by navigating to the logging folder. The files are numbered in successive order, with the file date stamp giving out the precise time that it was captured. Open the XML file that you want using your favorite

XML viewer (for example, Internet Explorer). The trace files include a wealth of information about the page request, ranging from the time that it takes to the failures that occur in each event. The `freb.xsl` file that comes with Windows Server 2012 has several tabs, including the Performance View tab, which shows details about each event of the page life cycle, sorted by the duration of time spent in each event (see Figure 23-18).

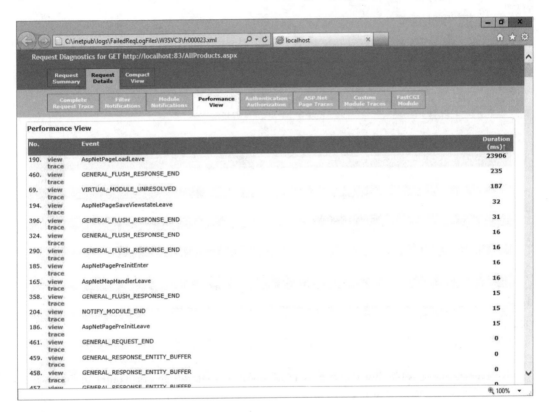

FIGURE 23-18

> **NOTE** *The first time that you attempt to view one of the Failed Request Tracing trace files in Internet Explorer, you may receive a warning that content is being blocked for "about:internet." Be sure to add "about:internet" to either the Local intranet or Trusted sites zone. If you don't, you will receive an error that says "Security settings do not allow the execution of script code within this stylesheet." You will get this message because the* `freb.xsl` *file has scripts in it that Internet Explorer will not run without specific authorization.*

> **NOTE** *If you have User Account Control (UAC) enabled, you may not see the Add button in the warning dialog box, so you will need to add the "about:internet" manually. Choose Tools (Alt+X) ⇨ Internet Options ⇨ Security Local intranet ⇨ Sites to add it.*

With this information in hand, you can tell which page caused the issue, if you didn't know that already; how long it took to run; and which event in the page life cycle took the most time.

> **NOTE** *The top line in the XML output file (see Figure 23-18) shows the URL that was used to make the request. It will not automatically include the default document name if the original request didn't include it. Therefore,* `http://localhost/` *is the request for whatever your default document is, which is commonly* `default.aspx`.

The other sections of the XML file contain valuable information about that particular page request. Failed Tracing may turn out to be a favorite for many system administrators trying to solve hang/time-out and resource-intensive and slowness issues.

LOGGING

No web server would be complete without detailed logging of every hit to the server. This includes not just page requests but images, files, HEAD requests, and virtually every request made to the web server. IIS has always had logging, and IIS 8.0 is no exception.

The default location for the log files is `%SystemDrive%\inetpub\logs\LogFiles`. By default, each website has its own set of logs, but this can be changed so that logging is per server.

> **NOTE** *The per-site logs are placed in their own folder, which is named by the site ID. Therefore, by default, a site with a site ID of 10 would have its log files saved to* `%SystemDrive%\inetpub\logs\LogFiles\w3svc10\`.

The log settings can be changed in IIS Manager at the server, site, application, or file level. However, not all settings are applicable at all levels. For example, the server level is the only place where you can set the encoding type and whether logging is per site or per server.

To change the log settings, double-click the Logging icon in IIS Manager. Most settings are set in the main Logging pane, but enabling and disabling logging is set in the Actions pane on the right.

> **NOTE** *Beside the Format dropdown list is a Select Fields button. This allows you to specify which fields are logged to disk. Three fields that aren't enabled by default that we recommend enabling are Bytes Sent, Bytes Received, and Cookie. (Time Taken is another good setting to watch; it is default in IIS 8.0.) These fields will be read by most statistics programs and provide valuable information that is worth recording. It is worth adding these fields with every new server built.*

Log files can be read in various ways and provide valuable information for troubleshooting. Logs can also be used by the website design team and marketing team, to know how many people have visited the site, where they spent time, how they got there, and what browser or tool they used to view the website.

The following are some common means of reading the log files:

➤ Using third-party programs such as Google Analytics, SmarterTools SmarterStats, Webtrends Analytics, or any of the multitude of choices out there.

➤ Viewing the files in their raw format using tools such as Notepad, NotePad++, and WordPad.

➤ Using a log reader tool like LogParser. (LogParser is explained in more detail later in this chapter.)

Log data files can be used for marketing and to know how visitors are using the site, but they can also be used to track hacking attempts, find out which pages are viewed when server resources spike, or to gather other valuable information.

ASP.NET TRACING

ASP.NET Tracing is a powerful tool to gain valuable information when troubleshooting dynamic code. Although there isn't anything new to IIS 8.0 in this tracing section, it is a key tool to understand.

ASP.NET Tracing provides detailed information about each page that is run. Unlike Failed Request Tracing, which records the information to an XML format saved to disk, page-level tracing can be displayed within the page itself, by using the ASP.NET Trace Viewer, or through code. This enables the developer or system administrator to easily view detailed information about the entire page request, including the precise timestamps of all of the page events, cookie and session state information, request and response and header information, and plenty of other information.

Figure 23-19 shows a small portion of a page-level trace. This trace is added to the bottom of the existing page, below your normal content. This is ideal during development but is obviously not meant for production because of the detailed information that is embedded into the page for everyone to see. Notice the custom trace information and the timestamps, which are approximately 1,000 milliseconds apart from each other.

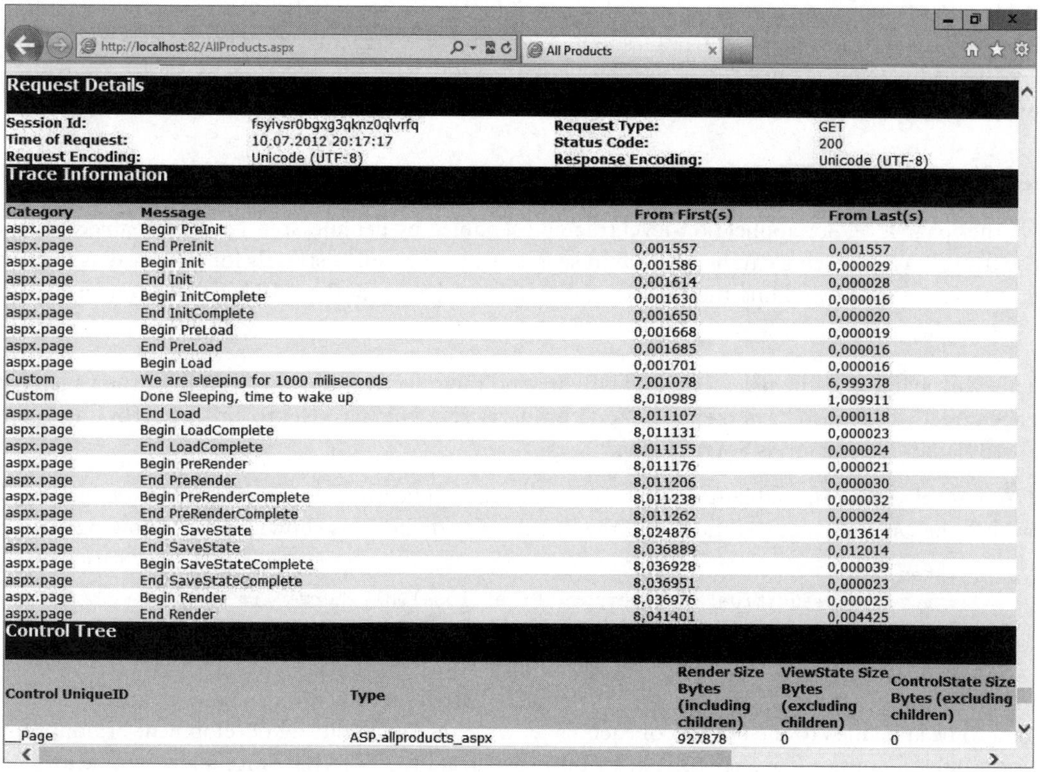

FIGURE 23-19

The following code was added to the page in Figure 23-19:

```
using System.Diagnostics;

public partial class _Default : System.Web.UI.Page
{
  Protected void Page_Load(object sender, EventArgs e)
  {
    ' Trace.Write information before the pause.
    Trace.Write("Custom", "We are Sleeping for 1000 milliseconds")

    ' Pause/Sleep for 1 second.
    System.Threading.Thread.Sleep(1000)

    ' Trace.Write to show when the pause has completed.
    Trace.Write("Custom", "Done sleeping, time to wake up.")
  }
}
```

As you can see, the custom information from the page is displayed in the trace report, including the time before and after the 1-second sleep. Notice that the "From First(s)" column increased by 1 second, which is what we instructed the page to do. As you can see, tracing allows you to troubleshoot the length of time that various parts of the page take to run, potentially uncovering performance issues on the websites that you troubleshoot. With ASP.NET Tracing, it makes it easier to tell if a slow-loading page is caused by a web service call, a database call, the time to render a custom image, or something else within the code.

Enabling ASP.NET Tracing

Neither page-level nor application-level tracing is enabled by default, so it must be enabled for you to use it. ASP.NET Tracing can be enabled in several ways. The most straightforward way is to enable it at the page level by adding the following directive to the top of the ASP.NET page code:

```
<%@ Page Trace="true" %>
```

This will enable it at the page level and will append the trace input to the bottom of the page. The page directive can also have the `traceMode` property set, which can set to either SortByCategory or SortByTime. The default is SortByTime.

Alternatively, you can enable ASP.NET Tracing at the application level within your `web.config` file. Within the `<system.web>` section, add the `<trace />` attribute, as shown in the following example:

```
<system.web>
  <trace enabled="true" pageOutput="true" localOnly="true" />
  . . . .
</system.web>
```

In this example, tracing is enabled with the `enabled` attribute. The `pageOutput` then sets the trace data to be appended to the bottom of each page, which is useful during development or nonproduction troubleshooting. The `localOnly` attribute instructs the ASP.NET Trace Viewer to be available only on the local server, and not for anyone trying to view it from another computer.

The following table shows the possible ASP.NET Tracing attributes and their values. These attributes can be set in your `web.config` file, from code, within your `global.asax` page, or from an HTTP module.

PROPERTY	DESCRIPTION
Enabled	Optional Boolean attribute. Read/Write value that specifies whether tracing is enabled for an application or a page. The default is `false`.
localOnly	Optional Boolean attribute. Specifies whether the ASP.NET Trace Viewer is available only on the host web server. If `false`, the ASP.NET Trace Viewer is available from any computer. The default is `true`.
mostRecent	Optional Boolean attribute. When `true`, the most recent page requests are displayed, while the oldest are rolled off the bottom end. When `false`, only the number of requests set in `requestLimit` is saved. New requests will be discarded if the `requestLimit` has been reached. The default is `false`.

pageOutput	Optional Boolean attribute. When `true`, the trace output is rendered at the end of each page. When `false`, it is only available from the ASP.NET Trace Viewer, and the page output is not affected. The default is `false`.
requestLimit	Optional `Int32` attribute. Specifies the number of trace requests to store on the server. See the `mostRecent` attribute description to see how to change the behavior when the `requestLimit` value is reached. The maximum value is 10,000. The default is 10.
traceMode	Optional `TraceDisplayMode` attribute. This attribute sets the "Sort by" value, to be used by the ASP.NET Trace Viewer. There are two possible values: SortByCategory and SortByTime. The default is SortByTime.
writeToDiagnosticsTrace	Optional Boolean attribute. This new .NET v2.0 attribute can be set to `true` to forward trace messages to the `System.Diagnostics` tracing infrastructure for further tracing abilities.

The ASP.NET Trace Viewer

When application-level ASP.NET Tracing is enabled, the ASP.NET Trace Viewer is available. Accessing the ASP.NET Trace Viewer is straightforward. By default, you can only view the ASP .NET Trace Viewer on the local host server, but using the attributes discussed in the previous section, you can override the default setting.

Accessing the ASP.NET Trace Viewer

Navigate to the application root, and append `trace.axd` to the end of the URL. For example, see `http://localhost/trace.axd`.

> **NOTE** *If you are unsure of your application root, simply add the following code to your website to find the path to the ASP.NET Trace Viewer:*
>
> ```
> <%= "Trace Viewer Path: " & Request("SERVER_NAME") _
>     & ":" & Request("SERVER_PORT") _
>     & Request.ApplicationPath _
>     & "/trace.axd" %>
> ```

The `trace.axd` file is a virtual file that is handled by an HTTP handler set in the root `web.config` file in the framework config folder. It is handled by the ASP.NET engine as if it were a real file, even though it does not physically exist.

The ASP.NET Trace Viewer provides the same information as the `pageOutput` tracing information, but it is not as intrusive because it is available from a separate tool and doesn't show in the web page itself (see Figure 23-20). From the List page in the ASP.NET Trace Viewer, click the page to view its trace report. The trace report provides the same information as the `pageOutput` tracing information, but the advantage is that it does not affect the look of the pages. Instead, it saves it to a report to be viewed by the system administrator.

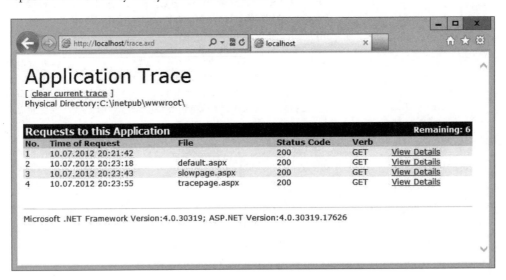

FIGURE 23-20

Password Protecting the ASP.NET Trace Viewer

If you set the localOnly attribute to false, allowing the ASP.NET Trace Viewer to be viewed from any computer, it is important to secure the ASP.NET Trace Viewer so that unauthorized people cannot gain access to privileged information. This can be done from web.config in the application root. Use the <location> element, which allows you to password-protect a specific file or folder:

```
<location path="trace.axd">
   <system.web>
      <authorization>
   <allow users="SteveBalmer" />
         <allow users="BillGates" />
         <deny users="*" />
      </authorization>
   </system.web>
</location>
```

You can add as many <allow> lines as you want. Attributes for <allow> are users and roles. For example, you can set <allow roles="admin" /> to allow everyone in the admin role to have access to trace.axd. Be sure to place this outside of the current <system.web> section, under the main <configuration> section.

When you are using Windows authentication in web.config, the user and password will be a Windows or Active Directory user. When using Forms authentication, you must use ASP.NET user-names and passwords.

With your password-protected ASP.NET Trace Viewer, you are now able to view full trace information for pages that your viewers view without them being able to view this sensitive information.

> **NOTE** *The ASP.NET Trace Viewer information is stored in the IIS worker process so that when the application pool is recycled or an application domain is restarted, the information will be lost. This also means that any change to* web .config *will cause previous ASP.NET Trace Viewer data to be lost.*

Extending Output Data

The ASP.NET Trace Viewer or the page-level `pageOutput` attribute can be extended to include information that you provide. This is similar to what developers often use with `Response.Write`, except that it has several advantages.

When debugging information is outputted to a trace report, it can be quickly and easily turned off or hidden from the casual user but still be available in the trace report. This allows you to leave your tracing output in place, even when your website is in production, without a performance penalty. When insight into your application is required, you can turn on the ASP.NET Trace Viewer and see the outputted information.

There are two methods for outputting the trace information — `Trace.Write` and `Trace.Warn`. The only difference is that `Trace.Write` is outputted with black text, and `Trace.Warn` is outputted in red.

```
public partial class _Default : System.Web.UI.Page
{
  Protected void Page_Load(object sender, EventArgs e)
  {
    ' Write key information to the trace output
    Trace.Write("The querystring information is: " + Request.QueryString;

    If (Request.QueryString.Count == 0)
    {
      Trace.Warn("No valid querystring is set.")
    }
  }
}
```

This will show in the trace report when it is run.

You are able to programmatically determine if tracing has been enabled by checking the `Tracecontext.Enabled` or `Context.Trace.IsEnabled` property. This will allow you to output non-trace information conditionally. For example, if you want to display a table only if tracing is enabled, you could do something like this:

```
public partial class _Default : System.Web.UI.Page
{
  Protected void Page_Load(object sender, EventArgs e)
  {
    If (Context.Trace.IsEnabled)
```

```
            {
              DataTable.Visible = true;
            }
            else
            {
              DataTable.Visible = false;
            }
        }
    }
```

Alternatively, the .NET `System.Diagnostics` namespace has even more debugging and tracing options, should you want to gain even further control over the ASP.NET tracing capabilities.

> **NOTE** *It is important to note that many types of errors will trigger an error before the* `pageOutput` *gets a chance to run. An unhandled programming error, for example, will throw a 500 status code, which will not show the trace data. In this case, you must use the ASP.NET Trace Viewer to view the trace report or handle the error in a* `Try...Catch` *block so that it fails gracefully enough for the trace information to be displayed.*

TROUBLESHOOTING TIPS

Where would a chapter on diagnostics be without some general-purpose troubleshooting tips? A great troubleshooter can often solve complex issues even if it is a new technology to them, simply from mastering troubleshooting skills. Excellent troubleshooting can take years to master, but here are some tips that can be used in almost any situation. This method of troubleshooting takes four steps, which you can memorize by using the acronym *RIFT* ("reproduce, isolate, fix, and test").

> **NOTE** *Before you start, it's important to back up your site and settings and to document all changes that you make. It's too easy, when something needs to be fixed "yesterday," to try random changes. But by the end, you're not sure what fixed the issue or how to get back to where you were before. These troubleshooting steps will help you make troubleshooting a deliberate and controlled methodology, but nothing replaces the importance of clear documentation. Be sure to take notes throughout the process and not depend on your memory alone to keep track of the changes that you made.*

Reproduce

Reproduce, reproduce, reproduce!

Before making any changes, be sure to *reproduce* the issue. Without properly seeing the issue for yourself, you will be "troubleshooting by mistake," which is a poor practice. When you see in advance exactly what the issue is, you are able to confirm that your fix did, indeed, resolve the issue.

Too often programmers and system administrators receive a report that something doesn't work, and instead of reproducing the issue to confirm that it is, indeed, broken, they make a quick change and ask the user to test again. The best troubleshooters always test before and after to confirm that they know exactly what their change fixed.

The ability to reproduce an issue is 50 percent of the battle. If you are able to quickly and easily reproduce the issue, you are well on your way to a complete solution.

Among the most difficult issues to resolve are those that do not happen often or on demand. In such cases, collect whatever information that you are able to, and use all the tools at your disposal until you are able to set up a test method of re-creating the issue.

Some examples of troubleshooting that you might perform include:

➤ Fixing a failed website that is throwing a 500 status code

➤ Resolving a password prompt on a page that should not have one

➤ Finding why an IIS worker process continues to fail prematurely

➤ Determining high CPU or memory usage

➤ Troubleshooting a failed connection from the web server to the database server

In preparation for the isolation stage, you should set up a test environment in which you can reproduce the issue quickly and make modifications without affecting a production site or application. The easier that you can reproduce the issue and make modifications, the quicker you will be able to perform the full RIFT process.

Isolate

Once you have reproduced the issue, it is time to find out the exact cause. Sometimes reproducing will not give any clues except at a very high level. The *isolation phase* will drill down to the exact cause. The goal with the isolation phase is to determine the single thing that is causing the failure. In some cases, there are compound issues, which makes it more difficult, but the principles are the same.

The following sections describe the five tricks that you should use to isolate the issue to its smallest factor.

Reproduce Trick

Reproduce, reproduce, reproduce! This may seem like a repeat of the first step, and it partially is, but reproducing the issue is something that you will do over and over again. Make sure that you can reproduce before you start, and then do it over and over again throughout the troubleshooting. This seems obvious, but it is amazing how often this is not done.

Fail Trick

This is a fun trick. Sometimes you may believe that you are addressing the correct issue, but you find out later that you were making a change to the wrong section, or even the wrong site. This can sometimes be called a "Double Fail trick," because your goal is to break the broken site to determine positively that you are changing what you intend to.

Consider an example of a website throwing a 500 error code on a web server with 100 websites that use host headers. You believe that you are modifying the correct content, but you aren't quite sure. Assuming that the rest of the site can spare a few seconds of downtime, a simple test is to stop the website and see if the error message changes. If it does, your change has confirmed that you are working with the correct website. If the error message does not change, you might be making changes to something unrelated.

The Fail trick can apply to almost anything — file permissions on disk, website, or application pools; IIS settings; code settings; or even network or database connectivity.

Only 1 Trick

The Only 1 trick is a way to get *something* working, even if it is very simple. Again, this trick determines that you are considering the correct factors. If you have a website that continues to fail and you are unsure if it is related to the code or the server configuration, it is helpful to run a simple test.

The goal is to get the site or issue working in its simplest form. It may be a static HTML page or a basic ASP.NET page, or you may create a new website on an unstable server so that you can see if that bare-bones website is also unstable. At first, you might completely ignore the issue itself and try to get a similar, but less complex, version of the site working.

Another way to consider this trick is as a "Hello World" test. The expression "Hello World" has been used for years to describe creating the first text output in a program. Many tutorials exist for creating a Hello World for COBOL, Java, JavaScript, Classic ASP, PHP, ASP.NET, or almost any programming language. Here, we share that term for any type of programming or administrative task where you get the most basic test working.

Once you have a basic test working, even if it is a long way from isolating the issue, you have the foundation in place for the Binary Halves Isolation trick, which can quickly take a complex failure and isolate it to its smallest factor.

Binary Halves Isolation Trick

Sometimes an issue is obvious; for example, you have an exact line number from which to work. But sometimes you do not have that luxury, for example, on a web page that fails without any error message. If you do not have any solid clue what is causing the issue, you may need to follow the Only 1 trick and then use the Binary Halves Isolation trick.

The Binary Halves Isolation trick involves breaking the issue into halves, and then halves again until you have determined the exact issue. To do this, you must be able to reproduce the failure and must have successfully carried out the Only 1 trick. Then pull out about half of the factors to see if it is still broken. From this, you can determine which half of the factors is causing the issue. Now repeat with about half of the remaining factors repeatedly until you have isolated the issue to the single item that is causing the failure.

As an IIS administrator, you will commonly be required to prove to a developer (even if that is also yourself) that the code is the problem. Even without extensive programming knowledge, it is possible to pull out parts of the code until you have proven the issue. A good troubleshooter can jump into almost any situation and isolate the issue, without being an expert in the technology or syntax of a programming language.

Another example would be to test a static HTML page on a server, or to temporarily remove or rename `web.config` and the ASP.NET application folders to determine if they are causing the failure.

A REAL-WORLD EXAMPLE OF BINARY HALVES ISOLATION

I recently found myself in a situation in which a web developer claimed that his website worked in his test environment but would not work on the server that I provisioned. I was confident in the server but had to help the developer solve his issue and to prove and build confidence in the web server.

My first step was to find out how to reproduce the issue. During the troubleshooting process, I set up a copy of the website on another server with a completely different configuration, and because the issue reoccurred there, I was quite confident that the issue wasn't caused by the server.

The website existed in a subfolder that was marked as an application, so on the test website I temporarily removed the `web.config` file at the site level to make sure that it was not the cause. The failure continued.

Then I temporarily removed the `web.config` file at the subfolder level to see if any HTTP modules or other references were causing the issue. The failure continued.

Next, I temporarily removed all the `app_*` folders, at which point the issue stopped. Obviously, the rest of the website didn't work as it should, but a simple "Hello World" proved that the cause of the issue existed in the `app_*` folders.

I added back half of the `app_*` folders and determined that the issue did not reoccur. I then added `App_Browsers`, one of the last two folders, and the issue reoccurred.

Now that I knew the exact folder, I carried out the Binary Halves Isolation trick on the files in the `App_Browsers` folder until I knew exactly which file was at fault.

Finally, I did the same thing with the sections of the file until I knew exactly what caused the issue.

It turned out that a login/membership module existed in the `App_Browsers` folder, but it required a matching DLL file to be placed in the `/bin` folder. The developer had placed it in the root `/bin` folder, but not in the `/application/bin` folder.

Without any awareness of the application, I was able to use these standard troubleshooting tricks to prove to the developer that he had improperly placed the module, causing his application to fail.

There are times when breaking the issue into parts is difficult — for example, if there are interwoven dependencies. This makes things more difficult, but the same principles still apply. Break the issue down to the smallest part, and then add back about half of the issue. It may mean creating some tests or making some modifications to the situation, but it can be done using the same methodology.

All but 1 Trick

Finally, when you believe that you have the exact issue determined, it is wise to do a final fail test with the single factor that you believe caused the issue. This determines with absolute confidence what the issue is. Remember, don't troubleshoot by mistake. Be certain of the issue.

To do this, pull out, or add in, the single factor that caused the issue, and watch the error reverse. There are many examples, but consider a file system permission issue. If you added three or four Windows users to the NTFS permissions and tweaked a few other settings during your troubleshooting and the issue was resolved, you may have opened up a security hole by not fully understanding the exact permission requirement. It would be wise to remove the NTFS permission that you believe was the cause so that it fails again, which proves the exact issue.

Again, it is possible that there are compounded issues — keep that possibility in mind during all your troubleshooting.

Fix

Once you have determined the exact cause, the obvious next step in the RIFT process is to *fix it*. This may be something that you have control over, or it may be something that you have to refer back to someone else to take over. Not much needs to be said about this step because the fix is dependent on isolating the issue. Often more work is done in the isolation step than in the fix step.

Test

Finally, it is important to *test* to ensure that everything is back to normal and working. There are three parts to the test step.

1. Reproduce, reproduce, reproduce! Don't walk away after fixing the issue without confirming that the change you made really works. It is amazing how often developers and system administrators will repair a bug or failure but not test it. It is also amazing how often it was not fixed even when the developer or administrator claimed that it was. Be sure to test that it is working afterward.

2. Ensure a clean environment when you are done. Be sure to clean up behind yourself. Remove any temporary users, files, folders, and notes that are floating around.

3. If there were specific lessons learned, be sure to document them in such a way that you and anyone else who requires it can benefit from them afterward. This can be done by updating company procedures or writing an article or blog or sending a memo to the applicable people.

Good troubleshooting skills transcend IIS 8.0 or even your areas of expertise. If you can master a few basic skills, troubleshooting can be a joy and sometimes a welcome challenge. Set yourself up for success in any type of issue that arises. Let the tools in this chapter enable you to walk through the RIFT steps to tackle the most challenging situations.

ADDITIONAL BUILT-IN TOOLS

Windows Server 2012 has several built-in tools that complement IIS troubleshooting. These tools are essential to isolating and solving the many types of issues that the system administrator is faced with. Many of these have been around since previous versions of Windows, some for many years, but their longevity just demonstrates their value all the more. This section includes tools that are either available out-of-the-box or as a separate install.

Task Manager

Task Manager is an old-time favorite that most administrators are familiar with. There is no quicker way to get a good handle on the current state of a server than to fire up Task Manager. Needless to say, it should be one of the first tools to look at during any troubleshooting, often before IIS Manager is started. You can access it quickly by right-clicking on the taskbar and selecting Task Manager.

Task Manager gives a quick overview of the system resources of the server. With Windows Server 2012, you can see not only the CPU and running applications, but also the disk usage, the network usage, and the resources used by Windows services.

The Processes and Performance tabs are often the most useful, but there is important information in each of the tabs. The Processes tab shows detailed information for the worker processes running on the server. The Performance tab shows two real-time graphs: one of the CPU and the other of the memory usage. You can also see a summary of the physical and kernel memory usage; some key system information, such as the number of handles, threads, and processes; and the uptime of this server.

In the Processes tab, two columns that are worth adding that are not there by default are:

➤ **PID** — The Process ID can help link the process in Task Manager with the one seen in IIS or other tools.

➤ **Commit Size** — Commit Size is the corresponding column that lines up with the Private Bytes in IIS. If you set the application pool Private Bytes limit, then the Commit Size in Task Manager is important to monitor to see how the w3wp.exe process runs compared with the application pool limit.

Another change worth making in the Processes tab is to check the checkbox at the bottom to "Show processes from all users." When troubleshooting IIS, the background processes running under different users are often most important, but they are not displayed unless this checkbox is selected.

These changes are required only once per server, per user. After the change is made, Task Manager will retain that setting even after logging out and in again.

Event Viewer

Event Viewer allows administrators quick access to application, security, and system details. Information ranging from errors to warnings to informational notices is recorded in this extensive log storage source.

Virtually all Microsoft Windows programs will write errors and warnings to Event Viewer, and many third-party programs do the same. This makes Event Viewer the "go-to place" to gain details on any type of failure.

IIS is no exception. In fact, many production servers have more IIS- and ASP.NET-related entries than any other type of entry. Whether it is an application pool shutting down because of inactivity or a worker process failing, Event Viewer offers a lot of clues to the issue at hand. In addition to failures and warnings, there are many informational messages such as the system update, reboot information, and new program installation data.

The information provided in Event Viewer is fairly detailed, but there are some errors that do not provide very useful information. An excellent website to bookmark and visit regularly is http://www.eventid.net. It allows you to enter the Event ID and Source of any event, and there are thousands of events, event sources, and user contributions about almost every Event ID. Many will offer the exact clue that you may require to solve a particularly difficult issue.

The data format of Event Viewer is now a standardized XML format that all programs must conform to. This makes it easier to tap into, extend, and to import and export.

To access Event Viewer, open Server Manager and choose Tools ⇨ Event Viewer. The GUI has the categories on the left, details in the middle, and Actions on the right, as shown in Figure 23-21. The following sections discuss some noteworthy points of interest.

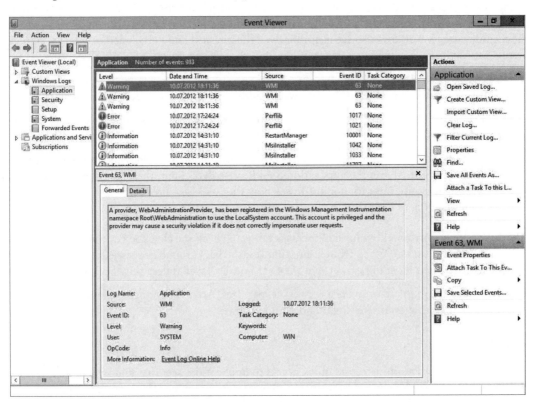

FIGURE 23-21

Attach Task to This Event

Among the best features of Event Viewer is the Attach Task to This Event option. By right-clicking on an event or a category and selecting this option, you can schedule a task that will be triggered if the event happens. This allows you to pop up a message, send an e-mail, or trigger an application when a particular event happens. Rather than Event Viewer being a reactive tool, it is now a proactive tool and can push critical information to you in whatever method that you specify.

Applications and Services Logs

Another feature in Event Viewer is the Applications and Services Logs section, which offers a wealth of information that was not previously available. These logs are for specific applications or services, rather than the system-wide logs in the Windows Logs section. A fresh install of Windows Server 2012 will already have dozens of categorized logs, and as more applications and services are installed, this list will grow. As you will quickly see, Windows Server 2012 provides some very useful tools for logging and monitoring.

By default, Analytic and Debug logs are hidden. You can enable them from the View menu at the top by selecting "Show Analytic and Debug Logs." This will add a few major categories and subcategories under the Applications and Services Logs category, which, in turn, will have one or more logs. The Analytic and Debug information is more detailed and not as easy to read casually, which is why it is disabled by default. When doing advanced troubleshooting, however, it is important to know of its existence and to enable it if desired.

Additionally, many of the logs are disabled by default; otherwise, it would quickly fill up your disk space. So, if there are any that you will need when troubleshooting a particular issue, be sure to confirm that they are enabled. You can enable a log by right-clicking on it and selecting Enable Log. If your only choice is Disable Log, then that category has been enabled already or was enabled by default. The default is different for each log; some are enabled already, but many are disabled out-of-the-box.

Subscriptions

The *Subscriptions section* allows you to centralize events from multiple servers. Once a subscription is active and events have been collected, you can view and manipulate these events as if they were locally stored events.

Forwarding uses the Windows Remote Management (WinRM) service and the Windows Event Collector (Wecsvc) service for this process.

Custom Views

In the past, filters were available to narrow a large set of event logs. Now there is a new category and tool called *Custom Views*. This allows you to set up a custom view that is always available to you for quick access.

You can create, import, view, or manage custom views from the Custom Views section on the left-hand pane. Another way to create a new custom view is to right-click on an existing folder (for example, Windows Logs ⇨ System) and select Create Custom View. This new custom view will be saved in the Custom Views section. Once you set up a custom view, it is always available to you unless you purposefully delete it.

Additionally, you can write your own XPath query in the XML tab of the Create Custom View dialog box. This allows you to use XML, if you so desire, to customize the filter even further, or to reuse a filter from one that you previously created.

Reliability and Performance Monitor

The *Reliability and Performance Monitor,* also known as *perfmon,* is one of the most valuable tools in the Windows arsenal. To open Performance Monitor from within Server Manager, select Tools ⇨ Performance Monitor (or press WIN+R and enter **perfmon**). Performance Monitor is not quite as quick and easy to use as Task Manager or Ping, but with a bit of practice, it is easy to master and very powerful.

There are hundreds and hundreds of counters, continuously exposing information on virtually every application and every part of the operating system. Perfmon makes all this information available in real time or by logging the data to be reviewed later.

In addition to counters, perfmon allows you to log and report on tracing information; system configuration information; and prepackaged statistics, lists, and summaries. One example is a top 10 list of the most disk-intensive applications.

For an IIS administrator, this information is valuable to get into the heart of IIS, system resources, ASP.NET databases, and many other important applications necessary to troubleshoot IIS. Many issues that an IIS administrator faces are related to the performance of the website. Issues can occur from hardware being underpowered, or a runaway script, to a particular resource bottleneck on the server. The trick is to find this information, understand it, and then deal with it accordingly.

Resource Overview

The Resource Overview screen, shown in Figure 23-22, provides a wealth of information on four main resources: CPU, Disk, Network, and Memory. This information is available in real time and includes both a live graph and detailed charts. You can see the Resource Overview section by clicking the Overview tab. You can also find more granular resource information by clicking on the specific CPU, Memory, Disk, or Network tab. All the categories can be expanded to show a breakdown of every active worker process on the system and how much of that particular resource it is using.

Performance Monitor

A tool that administrators of previous Windows operating systems are most used to is *Performance Monitor.* Performance Monitor has two purposes:

➤ To view the performance data on the system in real time

➤ To view historical data that was previously logged to disk

To view real-time counter data, select the Performance Monitor link from the left-hand pane, and follow these steps:

1. Click the green plus (+) button from the row of buttons at the top.

2. The Local computer will be selected by default, but you can point to a remote server if you desire.

3. In the middle left, you can select a counter. If there are multiple instances (for example, multiple disk volumes for PhysicalDisk), you can select _Total, <All instances>, or each individual instance.

4. When you have the counter(s) selected, click the Add > > button, which will move those counters to the right-hand pane.

5. Once you have all of the counters selected, press OK.

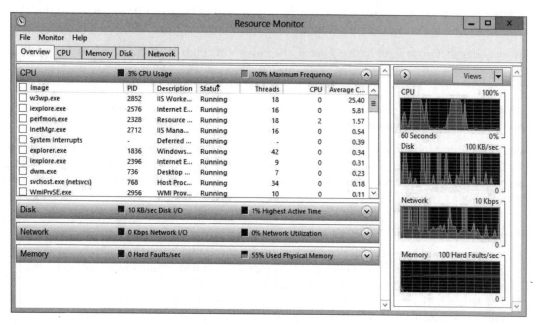

FIGURE 23-22

You will notice that the counters have been added to the list at the bottom, and more graph lines will start at the time that you add the counters.

> **NOTE** <All instances> *will add a counter for every instance, while* _Total *will add a single counter that is a sum of all the instances. When there is only one instance, they may appear to do the same thing, but they are really different.*

A convenient option is the Highlight feature. When you click on the icon that looks like a highlighter, the currently selected counter will be highlighted and stand out. This makes it much easier to find a particular line in the graph when there are many lines fighting to be viewed.

There are several features that you will appreciate about which we will not go into detail here — for example, the ability to pause, change graph types, copy data to the clipboard, graph properties, and many more. Take a few moments to familiarize yourself with these various features.

Reliability Monitor

Reliability Monitor is an impressive subtool within Performance Monitor. It has a daily timeline that shows five categories of events: Software (Un)Installs, Application Failures, Hardware Failures, Windows Failures, and Miscellaneous Failures. Using these categories of events, it graphs them in a visual chart and assigns your server an Index rating.

This information is extra valuable when seen in a timeline like this. For example, if you notice that your system is less stable starting on a particular date, you can check to see if there was a software installation that was performed just before the new pattern of failures. Or, you may find that there is a hardware failure that first occurred during that timeframe.

For each day that no failures have occurred, the Index will climb back up toward 10. Each type of error is weighted differently, and the length of time since the error and between errors also affects the Index.

Software installations do not affect the Index but are useful for comparing installations to system stability to see if there is any correlation.

With Reliability Monitor, it is possible to see at a glance the current stability of the system and to potentially forecast future issues and resolve them in advance. It is also easier than in the past to associate hardware failures or installations with other hardware or software failures, to find out the root cause of an issue.

Logging Historical Data to Disk

One of the powerful features of Reliability and Performance Monitor is the ability to log data to disk for retrieval at a later time. For example, you can record performance information to disk before an issue occurs, so that when it does occur, you can review the saved data to help isolate the cause of an issue. The logging feature has received some major improvements over time and has become a very valuable tool. Several logging and recording features are covered here.

User Defined Data Collector Sets

Data Collector Sets can be created to record and report on counters, events, and system configuration information. These Data Collector Sets can be customized to include specific information to provide an extensive report exactly to your specifications. They can also contain lists, summaries, tracing data, and customized wording and titles.

Figure 23-23 shows Performance Monitor with two User Defined Data Collector Sets.

To create a new Data Collector Set, perform the following steps:

1. Start Performance Monitor by going to Server Manager ➪ Tools ➪ Performance Monitor.
2. Expand Data Collector Sets.
3. Right-click the User Defined folder and select New ➪ Data Collector Set.

4. Give the Data Collector Set a name and select either "Create from a template" or "Create manually." Choosing "Create from a template" allows you to choose from one of three pre-existing Template Data Collector Sets or to browse for one that you may have obtained elsewhere. "Create manually" allows you to create your own Data Collector Set from scratch. You will be able to add your own Performance counters, Event trace data, and System configuration information counters, or, in the wizard, you can choose to set a Performance Counter Alert instead.

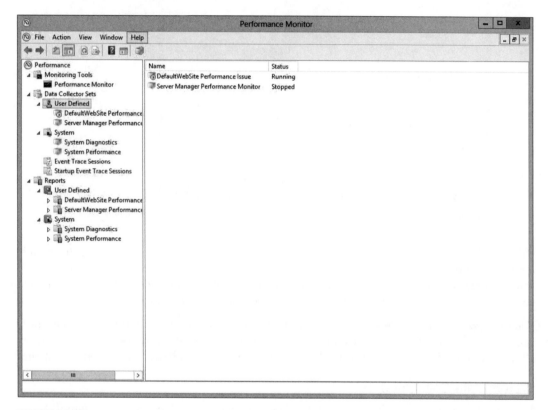

FIGURE 23-23

5. After choosing whether to create from a template or manually create a new set, complete the wizard with your preferred settings.

6. On the last step of the wizard, you have the options to "Open properties for this data collector set," "Start this data collector set now," or "Save and close" (see Figure 23-24). If you choose "Open properties for this data collector set" and click Finish, the properties window for the new Data Collector Set will appear, allowing you to customize it further. If you choose "Start this data collector set now" and click Finish, the wizard will complete and the new Data Collector Set will automatically start. The third option to "Save and close" will complete the wizard but will not start the Data Collector Set.

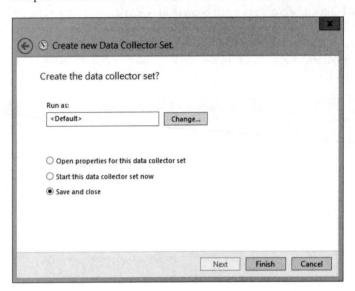

FIGURE 23-24

Once the data collector set is created, you can edit its properties and change various information, ranging from the folder where the data is saved to the schedule and stop conditions. You can also add new data collectors to an existing data collector set. A data collector can be performance counter data, event trace data, configuration data, or performance counter alerts.

You can save a Data Collector Set as an XML template by right-clicking on the Data Collector Set and clicking on Save Template. This offers a tremendous amount of control behind the scenes by allowing you to edit the XML file directly and create a new data collector set from this template.

System Data Collector Sets

Two data collector sets are already in place: *System Diagnostics* and *System Performance*. You can start these at any time, collect data for as long as you need, and then have a report generated for that data. These perform in the same way as the User Defined Data Collector Sets except that Microsoft has put together three recommended collectors to make your job easier.

Creating a Template from Real-Time Counters

If you have already added several real-time counters to Performance Monitor, you can save those as a template and log them to disk. This is convenient because you can visually tweak your list of counters before you begin logging, and then you can save it to a template when you are ready.

To save the real-time data as a template, perform the following steps:

1. Create the mix of counters that you are looking for in Performance Monitor.

2. In the right-hand pane, right-click Performance Monitor.

3. Select New ⇨ Data Collector Set.

4. Follow the wizard through the steps as you would to create a User Defined Data Collection Set (see above).

This will add a new user-defined data collector set. If you did not start it during the creation wizard, then start it when you are ready. Alternatively, you can have it started automatically based on an alert or a timed event. This will be covered shortly.

Reports

There is a *Reports section* that keeps a report for each time a data collector set instance is run. All reports are neatly organized for easy retrieval and are presented in a very intuitive and user-friendly manner. The report names are placed in a folder in the Reports section that matches the data collector set names. The filenames are named with the date when they were run.

Perfmon /Report

Possibly one of the most convenient means of getting a snapshot of the current state of a server is the perfmon /report option. From the desktop press WIN+R, and then type **perfmon /report**. This will start the System Diagnostics data collector for 60 seconds, after which it will display a detailed report of many of the server resources and settings. This is an invaluable tool to see the current state of the system resources.

Alerts and Threshold Starts

It is often desirable to have perfmon begin logging data as soon as a certain threshold is reached, rather than run it continuously. For example, let's say that once per week the CPU on the server runs wild, but you are unable to catch it before it recovers. You do not necessarily want detailed information logging around the clock until the issue occurs.

What you can do is set up an alert condition that starts the logging when the threshold is reached. This threshold can be set on any other performance counter, for example, when the CPU percentage is greater than a set value.

This can be set up with these steps:

1. Right-click Data Collector Sets/User Defined.

2. Select New ⇨ Data Collector Set.

3. Enter an applicable name for the collector set.

4. Select the "Create manually" radio button and click Next.

5. Select the Performance Counter Alert radio button and click Next.

6. Add one or more counters, set their threshold(s) and click Next.

7. Select the appropriate radio button — depending on if you desire to start the data collector set now or later.

8. Click Finish.

This does not specify an action for the alert yet. That takes another set of steps:

1. In the left-hand pane, select the new User Defined Data Collector Set that you just created.

2. In the main center pane, right-click the Data Collector that you want to set an alert action on and click Properties.

3. Select the Alert Action or Alert Task tab. The Alert Action tab allows you to specify that an entry will be added to the application event log in Event Viewer. In this tab, you can also specify a data collector set. It must be a user-defined set, but you can create a user-defined set based on a predefined set. The Alert Task tab allows you to run specific tasks when the alert condition is run.

4. Click OK when finished.

> **NOTE** *The one disadvantage of the Alert mechanism is that it checks the threshold at regular intervals, and, if after a single failure it hits the threshold, it will trip the alert. The problem is that many thresholds are frequently hit during normal healthy usage, and it is actually sustained usage that system administrators are most concerned about. For example, you may not be concerned about high CPU unless it remains high for several seconds. Opening Task Manager is an example of a task that can spike the CPU for a brief instant, potentially causing the CPU alert threshold to be reached, even though there was not a real concern. Therefore, be aware that there may be false positives, causing more logging than you may have planned.*

Viewing Logged Data

In addition to real-time data and reports, the Performance Monitor view is also used to view performance counter data that was previously saved to disk. To do so, press Ctrl+L or click the second icon from the left, which looks like an ice cube but actually represents a cube of data. Click the Log files radio button, and click Add. Locate the file from disk, and click Open and then OK.

This view is the same as the real-time view except that the data is static. In the properties of this view, you can narrow the time to a specific range.

Overlaying Multiple Servers

Have you ever wanted to view perfmon graphical data from multiple servers at the same time? In the past, it would require adding all the server counters together into one large Performance Monitor session.

With Windows Server 2012, you can overlay multiple windows to see them on top of each other. This is especially useful when you create a template with several counters and run them on multiple servers at the same time. It makes it convenient to compare several counters between servers.

The overlay option is available only in the standalone mode of Performance Monitor. You can open it by pressing WIN+R then typing **perfmon /sys /comp**.

In standalone mode, there is a menu called *Compare* that allows you to set the transparency of the current window and to snap to another window (see Figure 23-25).

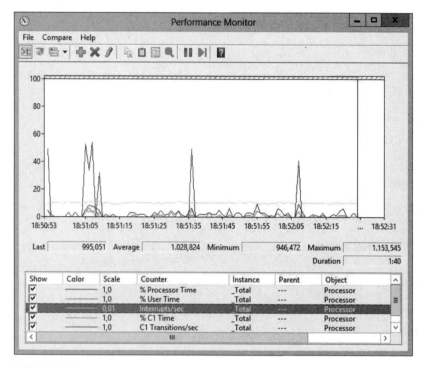

FIGURE 23-25

The Snap to Compare option will automatically resize and reposition the currently selected window so that it is the same size and is positioned exactly on top of the previously selected window.

> **NOTE** *If you have multiple Performance Monitor windows open, click the one that is already positioned and sized correctly, then select the one that you want to resize and reposition, and click Compare ⇨ Snap to Compare. The currently selected window will adjust to match the most recently "touched" window.*

Logging NTFS Failures to Disk

A little-known trick, available in Windows Server 2012 and previous operating systems, is to log all NTFS disk failures to Event Viewer. This can be very helpful when troubleshooting disk failures after they happen because it records them while you sleep, even if you were not anticipating a failure. It is helpful in finding incorrect permissions on files or folders.

This is accomplished by making two changes. First, the local group policy should be set to record failed objects, and then each disk volume should have Auditing enabled to record all failures.

Obviously, disk successes should not be recorded all the time because this would quickly fill your Event Viewer with useless information, but failures are not as common and are worth recording continuously.

You can make the group policy change by completing these steps:

1. Click WIN+R, and then enter **gpedit.msc**.

2. Under Computer Configuration, expand out to Windows Settings\Security Settings\Local Policies\Audit Policy.

3. Right-click the "Audit object access" item, and click Properties.

4. Check the Failure checkbox and click OK.

Additionally, you can set this at the domain level in a group policy. In fact, if there is a domain-based policy in play, it will override this setting.

Once the group policy is set to record all object failures, the disk volumes need also to be set for auditing:

1. Using Windows Explorer, navigate to the Computer section so that the disk volumes are visible.

2. Right-click on the first disk volume and select Properties.

3. Select the Security tab and click Advanced.

4. Select the Auditing tab.

5. Click the Add button, click the "Select a principle" link, enter **Everyone**, and then click OK.

6. In the Type dropdown, select Fail, and then click the Full Control checkbox, which will select all Failed options.

7. Click OK until everything has been acknowledged.

Now if there is a failure while attempting to access something on disk, the failed access will be logged to the Security section of Event Viewer. To view it, go to Event Viewer, Windows Logs and Security. Look for any Audit Failure errors, Event ID 4656, at the time of the failed attempt.

Figure 23-26 shows a partial view of the information available. By scrolling down, you can see the file that was denied access and the permission that it required.

The disk failure auditing described in this section is worth adding as part of the server build process because it does not fill up the logs too much under normal usage, and it is useful information to have after the fact.

ping, tracert, and pathping

ping and tracert have been around for many years and are probably common knowledge to most readers of this book, but it is still worth being reminded of their value in troubleshooting IIS and web applications. pathping is a somewhat newer tool for Windows and is available from the command line.

All three tools are available from the command prompt as command-line tools. Many third-party tools exist to enhance these or to provide similar functionality from a graphical user interface, but these basic tools still live on in all their simple glory. They are quick and easy to access on all Windows Server 2012 servers.

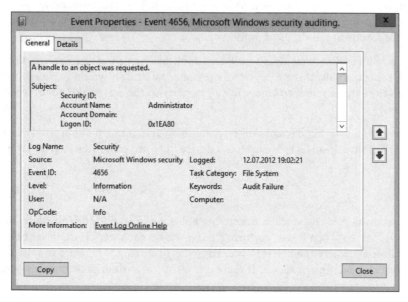

FIGURE 23-26

ping

`ping` sends a packet of data to measure the time, in milliseconds, that it takes to do a round trip to a destination server or device. It sends an ICMP "echo request" packet to the destination server and waits for a reply. If it doesn't receive a reply within the time-out period, it will report it as a time-out.

`ping` will also resolve a DNS name to an IP address before it begins the ICMP round trip, which doubles as another useful feature of this convenient tool (see Figure 23-27). There are about a dozen additional parameters to `ping`, but the one most worth keeping track of is `-t`, which will send a `ping` test continuously.

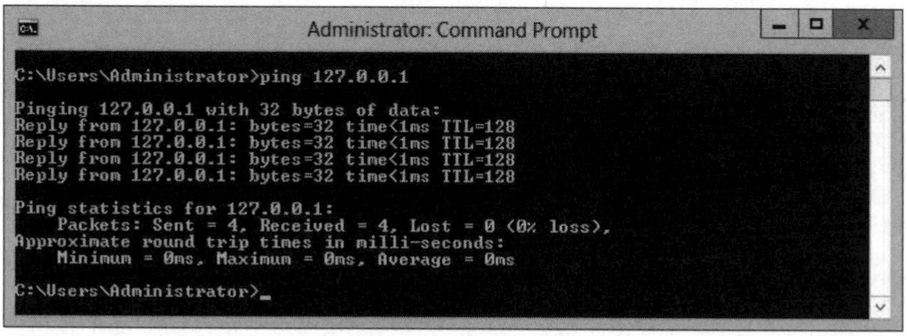

FIGURE 23-27

ping is useful to confirm that there is network connectivity between the client and server and that the connection is stable and fast. If the ping time is consistent and within a healthy range, it will confirm that the network is not the cause of an issue. A healthy ping time varies tremendously according to the location of the server relative to the client, and the network in between. Times can range from just a few milliseconds to hundreds of milliseconds.

If you receive a report of a failure while viewing a web-based application, a ping test can quickly confirm that the network is not at fault. If the ping times are not consistent, it would be worth running a few ping tests with the -t parameter to compare connectivity to the server and possibly some other key Internet locations.

It's important to note that not all Internet devices will respond to a ping. Some will purposely run in stealth mode to reduce their attack surface. So, even if a device does not respond to a ping, it may still be performing normally.

tracert

Like the ping tool, tracert tests basic network connectivity, but it will also find the full route, or path, between the client and server. Then it will perform a ping test on each step. If there are network issues, a tracert can show where the network breakdown is occurring. There are usually several hops across the Internet to a website or server. If there is an issue, it is often easy to spot where it occurred by performing a tracert test.

pathping

pathping is really a combination of the ping tool and the tracert tool, with some extra statistics included. It is particularly useful when looking at the network path between two computers to discover what is causing slowness or failures.

pathping is available out-of-the-box and installed by default. For detailed help, type **pathping /?** to list the nine possible parameters. A basic test of pathping bing.com will show the network connectivity between the client server and the www.bing.com data center that you are routed to.

telnet

telnet is a great tool for testing connectivity on a particular port and confirming access through a firewall. Just as Ping is used to check network connectivity, telnet can be used to check port availability.

telnet has several other uses, but the one that we describe here is specifically for port testing. Interestingly enough, the telnet Client is not installed by default with Windows Server 2012. To enable it the first time, open Server Manager and select Manage ➪ Add Roles or Features ➪ Features ➪ Telnet Client ➪ Next ➪ Install. Note that "Telnet *Server*" is a separate tool.

To test a particular port from the command line, type the following:

```
telnet {ServerName} {PortNumber}
```

For example:

```
telnet localhost 80
```

This will test that you have access to port 80 for the domain called `localhost`. You can test by IP as well. The result will be a blank `telnet` screen in this case, which is to be expected. If you know how to talk HTTP, you could talk to the `localhost` web server at this point. In this case, let's do a very simple test and type **GET http://localhost/**. Make sure that "GET" is in all capital letters. This will get the default homepage.

Some applications will give different information. Some start with a blank screen, whereas others will display some information right away. The key thing to note is that you don't get a time-out error. To compare this with a failed port, test by typing **telnet localhost 81**. It will show "Connecting To localhost..." for a while and eventually time out.

This underutilized trick makes a great port availability test using the built-in tools within Windows Server 2012.

INSTALLABLE TOOLS

In addition to built-in tools that enhance IIS 8.0 troubleshooting, there are some other Microsoft and third-party installable tools that should be a part of your toolkit. All these are production server-ready and can either be manually installed or have a well-tested installer. Some will require IIS to be reset so that they can listen to the active traffic. Just be sure that you understand each of the additional tools that you decide to install.

WFetch

WFetch is a simple but powerful tool to listen to all web traffic and see everything included in the communication between IIS and the web client, including the request, response, headers, body, content length, status codes, and more (see Figure 23-28). It is excellent for troubleshooting the actual web traffic between a web browser and the IIS server, because it allows you to see the entire conversation between the two sides.

Web Capacity Analysis Tool

Web Capacity Analysis Tool (WCAT) is a command-line tool that can be controlled using configuration files or from the command line directly. The output can be saved to a `.log` file or to an `.xml` file. There is a wealth of flexibility to create almost any type of test. This tool allows you to stress-test a website to know how it will perform under load, by simulating a large number of visitors to the website.

Multiple WCAT client servers can be running at the same time to generate even greater load. You can greatly increase the value of WCAT by using it in conjunction with other tools mentioned in this chapter. For example, Performance Monitor will allow you to watch how the web server performs during the simulated traffic. The output can be saved to a `.log` file or to an `.xml` file, depending on which you prefer.

Be careful about running this against a production server or running across a network where the cost of bandwidth is a concern. It can appear that a hacker is attacking the site and can bring a production site to its knees.

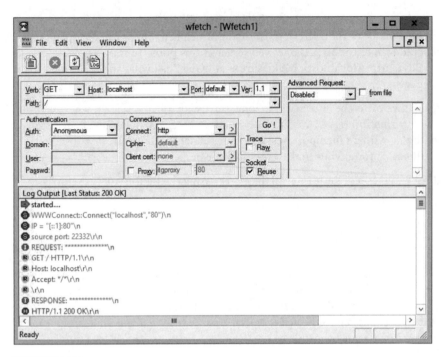

FIGURE 23-28

LogParser

LogParser is a dream come true for anyone wanting to dig into IIS logs, Event Viewer, registry, syslogs, XML data — you name it. Typically, it is used as a command-line tool, but there are several third-party GUIs that use LogParser. Many third-party tools have sprung up to add GUI wrappers for it, making it not only extremely powerful but quite easy. LogParser isn't necessarily for the faint of heart because of its power and flexibility in using SQL-like syntax, but it is easy enough for anyone to pick up after spending a bit of time with it. The time invested will pay back with great rewards.

To run LogParser, simply extract the zipped files in the download onto any computer, and either run across the network or copy `LogParser.exe` to the computer you want to work on. No install is necessary. This is production-server-ready, very stable, and extremely fast.

Because entire books and websites exist to support LogParser, this small space won't do justice to the options available. However, let's consider three examples:

Example 1 — To Search Event Viewer for All Error Entries in the System Log

The EventType value of 1 refers to Errors. You can specify the input format and output format, but LogParser will take an educated guess if you leave it off. In the following example, it will correctly guess the formats as `-i:EVT` for Event Viewer and `-o:NAT` for native format.

```
LogParser.exe "SELECT * FROM System WHERE EventType = 1 ORDER BY TimeWritten DESC"
```

Notice that the syntax is very much like what SQL used for database queries. That is intentional, and if you are familiar with SQL, writing LogParser queries won't take long to figure out. This example executes `LogParser.exe` and passes in a single parameter, which is the LogParser query. The query selects all (*) fields from the Event Viewer system log where the EventType is 1 (errors), and then sorts by the timestamp (`TimeWritten`) of the event entry, in descending order. The "`System`" keyword is a reserved word that tells LogParser to query the system log of Event Viewer. It also allows LogParser to know the input type without requiring you to specifically set it.

Example 2 — To Get the Registry Values of the Run Key for HKEY Local Machine and HKEY Current User

```
LogParser.exe "SELECT ValueName, Value FROM
\HKLM\Software\Microsoft\Windows\CurrentVersion\Run, \HKCU\Software\Microsoft\
               Windows\CurrentVersion\Run" -i:REG
```

This example is pretty straightforward, but notice that there are two Run keys, the HKEY Local Machine and HKEY Current User, separated by a comma. You can add as many Registry keys as you want, separated by commas. The `-i:REG` means that the input is from the Windows Registry. That is optional because LogParser is smart enough to figure that out based on the other information provided, but for the sake of the example, it's good to see that the input type can be set if necessary.

Example 3 — To Search the "Default Web Site" in IIS and Retrieve a Count of Hits for Each Web Page Extension

```
LogParser.exe
"SELECT TOP 20 EXTRACT_EXTENSION(cs-uri-stem), COUNT(*) AS Hits
FROM <Default Web Site>
GROUP BY EXTRACT_EXTENSION(cs-uri-stem)
ORDER BY Hits DESC"
```

In this example, `extract_extension` will pull out the page extension from the web filename (for example, aspx, gif, html), group by extension, and provide a count of how many visits were made to each of the top 20 visited extensions. Notice that `<Default Web Site>` causes LogParser to automatically query all of the log files for that website, simply by referencing the website's name. LogParser will go into IIS, find the path to the log file, and then query the log files for you. In this particular query example, the input type isn't set because LogParser is smart enough to figure that out.

Note that LogParser may take significant system resources to read through very large data stores, but other than that, it is safe to run on a production server.

DelegConfig

DelegConfig is a web application that helps to troubleshoot authentication issues on a server. It shows the Kerberos and delegating credentials, including Service Principal Names (SPNs), delegation settings, and the authentication method that is being used. This is particularly useful for Kerberos in a local domain environment because Kerberos is not used across the Internet.

To install DelegConfig, download it from the www.iis.net website, extract it, and copy it to a subfolder of a website. Then mark the Kerberos folder as an application.

> **NOTE** *If you are running in Integrated mode in IIS 8.0, the included* `web.config` *setting of* `Impersonate="true"` *is invalid. Edit the* `web.config` *file, and change to* `impersonate="false"`, *or delete the line completely for DelegConfig to work.*

To run DelegConfig, browse to the Kerberos folder on the website. The page has excellent explanations and gives a status beside each section with different icons, depending on whether it passes or fails the test.

Process Explorer

Process Explorer is like Task Manager on steroids (see Figure 23-29). Where Task Manager stops, Process Explorer takes over in an impressive way. Process Explorer allows you to dig into the processes and even into the threads of all running processes, in real time. You can see what is in memory for each thread, find out what is locking a file, find out how much CPU each process or thread is using, and see DLL dependencies.

Process	PID	CPU	Private Bytes	Working Set	Description	Company Name
System Idle Process	0		0 K	20 K		
System	4	0.32	112 K	260 K		
csrss.exe	348	< 0.01	1.204 K	3.384 K	Client Server Runtime Process	Microsoft Corporation
csrss.exe	416	0.13	1.916 K	26.084 K	Client Server Runtime Process	Microsoft Corporation
wininit.exe	424		820 K	3.372 K	Windows Start-Up Application	Microsoft Corporation
services.exe	512		3.316 K	7.236 K	Services and Controller app	Microsoft Corporation
svchost.exe	620		2.208 K	7.688 K	Host Process for Windows S...	Microsoft Corporation
svchost.exe	672		2.660 K	5.792 K	Host Process for Windows S...	Microsoft Corporation
svchost.exe	748	0.05	15.964 K	31.120 K	Host Process for Windows S...	Microsoft Corporation
svchost.exe	820		13.740 K	27.320 K	Host Process for Windows S...	Microsoft Corporation
svchost.exe	872		6.584 K	12.324 K	Host Process for Windows S...	Microsoft Corporation
svchost.exe	956	0.02	8.728 K	14.816 K	Host Process for Windows S...	Microsoft Corporation
svchost.exe	632		10.020 K	12.104 K	Host Process for Windows S...	Microsoft Corporation
spoolsv.exe	1068		2.784 K	8.204 K	Spooler SubSystem App	Microsoft Corporation
svchost.exe	1100		3.128 K	7.420 K	Host Process for Windows S...	Microsoft Corporation
inetinfo.exe	1120		4.532 K	11.292 K	Internet Information Services	Microsoft Corporation
sqlwriter.exe	1232		1.364 K	5.356 K	SQL Server VSS Writer - 64 Bit	Microsoft Corporation
Wex.Services.exe	1272		1.500 K	5.804 K	Wex.Services [v2.9.3k]	Microsoft Corporation
svchost.exe	1316		10.716 K	12.288 K	Host Process for Windows S...	Microsoft Corporation
svchost.exe	1336	0.01	4.208 K	8.644 K	Host Process for Windows S...	Microsoft Corporation
w3wp.exe	664	0.02	29.988 K	30.452 K	IIS Worker Process	Microsoft Corporation
w3wp.exe	2004	97.18	79.324 K	71.812 K	IIS Worker Process	Microsoft Corporation
svchost.exe	1624		2.804 K	7.472 K	Host Process for Windows S...	Microsoft Corporation
svchost.exe	1640		1.412 K	4.488 K	Host Process for Windows S...	Microsoft Corporation
svchost.exe	1656		1.780 K	6.092 K	Host Process for Windows S...	Microsoft Corporation
taskhost.exe	1048	< 0.01	4.328 K	8.324 K	Host Process for Windows T...	Microsoft Corporation
taskhost.exe	1936		1.920 K	6.688 K	Host Process for Windows T...	Microsoft Corporation
msdtc.exe	2628		2.892 K	7.012 K	Microsoft Distributed Transa...	Microsoft Corporation
lsass.exe	520		3.180 K	8.868 K	Local Security Authority Proc...	Microsoft Corporation
winlogon.exe	452		1.220 K	5.336 K	Windows Logon Application	Microsoft Corporation

CPU Usage: 100.00% | Commit Charge: 41.09% | Processes: 45 | Physical Usage: 39.46%

FIGURE 23-29

Process Explorer was written by Mark Russinovich and is available on `www.sysinternals.com`. Microsoft acquired Sysinternals, so this is now a Microsoft tool, but the `www.sysinternals.com` website is still valid.

Process Explorer is particularly useful to the IIS Administrator when isolating high CPU within a `w3wp.exe` worker process. It enables you to find out the CPU on each thread, and then see the contents of the thread itself. It also allows you, the system administrator, to see what is locking a file, and, if necessary, to release the lock. Figure 23-30 shows the System Information view of Process Explorer.

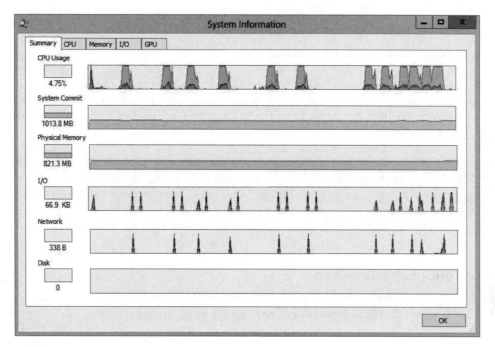

FIGURE 23-30

Simply running Process Explorer and reading the information can be done safely on a production server without any installation necessary and without any impact on the operation of the server. Download it from the website to any computer, and then copy `procexp.exe` to the server. Double-click on the file to start it.

> **WARNING** *Be careful with Process Explorer. It is powerful enough to kill critical system processes. If you kill the wrong process, you can take down the operating system. This gives all the power you need, so use it wisely.*

Process Monitor

One of the many useful tools in the Sysinternals Suite is Process Monitor. This tool observes, in real-time, file-system, process/thread, and registry activity. Process Monitor is especially useful for troubleshooting IIS access issues; however, it also has the capability to capture and view thread stacks for each operation, which can help find the root cause of the problem. The best way to become acquainted with Process Monitor's capabilities is to visit each of the menu items and options and to read the help file. In this section, the following topics are covered:

➤   Process Monitor column selection

➤   Adding filters, highlighting and counting occurrences

➤   Troubleshooting an IIS access denied issue

Many web applications running on IIS will write to a file, read from a file, or create a new file. By default, the account used to perform these read, write, or create activities is the application pools' identity of ApplicationPoolIdentity. At the same time, not all files or directories allow the default account the required privileges.

> **NOTE** *Prior to running this example, create a new website and install the contents found within the* CreateFile.zip *file. This file is downloadable from the* www.wrox.com.

Process Monitor Column Selection

To begin, download and extract the Process Monitor files, and then double-click the Procmon.exe file. Figure 23-31 shows the initial window. For now, simply select the default filters by clicking the OK button.

As described in the following table, the default columns are Time, Process Name, PID, Operation, Path, Result and Detail.

PROCESS MONITOR COLUMNS

COLUMN NAME	DESCRIPTION
Time	The time that the event happened.
Process Name	The name of the process that performed the event — for example, w3wp.exe, svchost.exe, lsass.exe, and so forth.
PID	The process id.

Operation	The operation performed during the event — for example, RegOpenKey, WriteFile, Thread Exit, Create File, and so forth.
Path	The registry, IP, directory, etc., path to the location of the entity upon which the operation was performed.
Result	The outcome of the operation — for example, SUCCESS, ACCESS DENIED, NAME NOT FOUND, and so forth.
Detail	Additional information about the event.
Duration	Not selected by default, this column displays the amount of time the process took to perform the specific task.

FIGURE 23-31

When you right-click a column header, a pop-up menu is rendered that allows you to add additional columns. Figure 23-32 displays the additional selectable columns.

A very valuable column to add is the Duration column. The Duration column logs the amount of time the process took to perform that specific event.

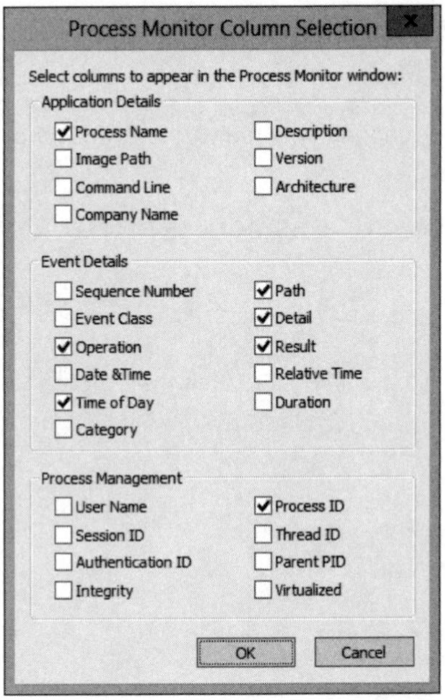

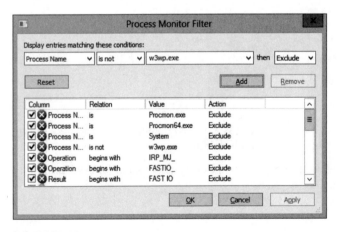

FIGURE 23-32

Adding Filters, Highlighting, and Counting Occurrences

When you open Process Monitor and begin monitoring the events on your system, you will immediately notice that a lot is happening and being logged. Without a filter, it is likely to take hours to find the specific event or group of events of interest. This is where the filter feature helps greatly.

After you have configured and accessed the example CreateFile website (or a website of your own), open Process Monitor and click the Filter menu on the toolbar and then the Filter... menu item. Add a filter so that only w3wp.exe processes are shown in the monitor. An example of this filter is shown in Figure 23-33.

FIGURE 23-33

Select the Add button and then OK to implement the filter. When you access the website again, only the events that are executed from a `w3wp.exe` process will be presented in the log (see Figure 23-34).

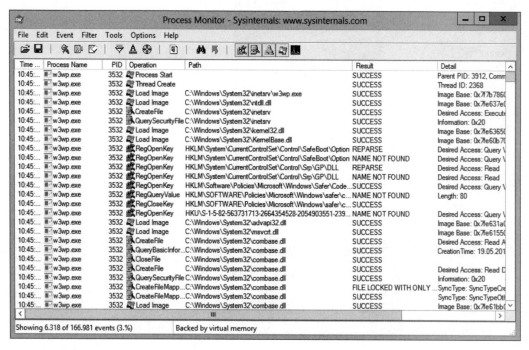

FIGURE 23-34

A large number of events still must be analyzed to determine why the website is not working as expected. Two very useful options help with the analysis:

➤ **Process Monitor Highlighting ➪ Filter ➪ Highlight** — This allows you to enter event criteria that you want highlighted. For example, you can highlight all the events that have a result of ACCESS DENIED. Then, when you are scrolling through the list of events, they are easy to pick out.

➤ **Tools ➪ Count Occurrences** — This provides the number of occurrences per selected column type. Figure 23-35 shows the number of times each Result has occurred when accessing the website. Double-clicking on the result automatically adds a filter to the log and only those events are shown. Therefore, double-clicking on the ACCESS DENIED results in seeing only the events, which have that result.

Troubleshooting an IIS Access Denied Issue

If you have used the `CreateFile.zip` example and filtered the log as previously discussed, you now have a very limited number of events to analyze. In this example, the CreateFile website is trying to create a directory and write a file to the `C:\Windows\System32\mySubDir` directory. Process Monitor, with a result of ACCESS DENIED, logs this event, as shown in Figure 23-36.

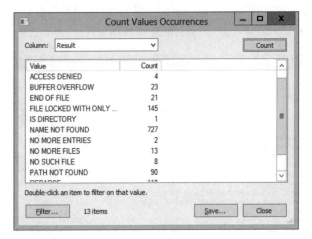

FIGURE 23-35

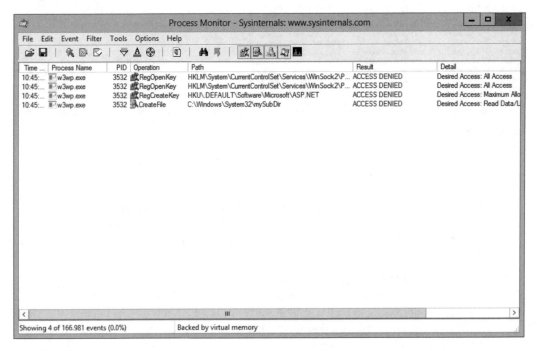

FIGURE 23-36

To resolve this ACCESS DENIED error, you should modify the identity of the application pool to use an identity that has permissions to perform the task. For more information on how to change the identity of an application pool, refer to Chapter 8.

The Debug Diagnostic Tool

Most of the features of the Debug Diagnostics Tool (DebugDiag) are now included within IIS 8.0 and are described above in this chapter, but it is worth taking note of this powerful tool because it is still supported on Windows Server 2012 and IIS 8.0.

DebugDiag is used for troubleshooting hangs, slow performance, memory leaks, and crashes. It is not just limited to IIS-related processes, although there are extra debugging scripts that target IIS and COM+ debugging.

DebugDiag was originally released as version 1.0 in the IIS Diagnostic Toolkit, but updated versions can be downloaded directly from `www.microsoft.com`.

DebugDiag runs as a GUI tool and allows the administrator to listen to a particular URL and watch for a Crash, IIS Hang, or Memory and Handle Leak. When those occur, a memory dump is generated, and then DebugDiag can be used to generate a report of the dump information. This information is valuable in finding out what is happening inside IIS and the IIS worker processes. It will report detailed information on the processes, threads, and memory.

Creating the Memory Dump

There are several ways to capture a memory dump using DebugDiag. The simplest method is to first select the Processes tab, as shown in Figure 23-37, which displays a list of all of the processes running on the machine. This is similar to what you see in Task Manager.

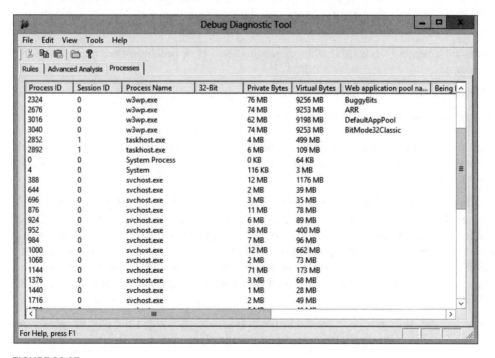

FIGURE 23-37

Focus on the entries with a Process Name equal to `w3wp.exe`. Notice that the process list provides the "Web application pool name." The "Web application pool name" is important if you have multiple worker processes running on the web server, because you need to take the memory dump of the worker process that is experiencing the problem.

After determining the application pool you need the memory dump of, right-click the row and you will be prompted via a pop-up menu to select the type of memory dump to take. The following options are available, as shown in Figure 23-38:

➤ **Monitor For Leaks** — When this menu item is selected, DebugDiag injects the Leak Track DLL (`LeakTrack.dll`) into the process. Attach the Leak Track to the process and leave it running for at least an hour before taking the memory dump. It helps track memory allocations and call stacks but is not useful for debugging managed code.

➤ **Create Full Userdump** — As the name implies, all consumed memory for this process will be dumped into a file. The size of the file will equal the amount of memory consumed by the process, so it can be large.

➤ **Create Mini Userdump** — This option creates a smaller memory dump that contains precise information about the call stacks that threw the first chance exception. This memory dump provides information for only limited analysis.

➤ **Create Userdump Series** — This option allows you to capture a certain number of memory dumps based on a configured timeframe. For example, you can create 10 memory dumps 3 seconds apart. This technique is useful to help solve memory consumption issues. Comparing the heaps between the memory dumps will show you which objects are increasing their consumption of the memory.

➤ **Attach Debugger** — Is helpful when debugging services or processes that are crashing at startup.

➤ **Terminate Process** — Ends the process.

➤ **Copy** — Copies the value into the cache.

Finally, select the item you require, and the tool will write the memory dump to disk. If successful, you will receive a message box containing the status and location of the memory dump, as shown in Figure 23-39.

The preceding example of creating a memory dump is considered a manual process. It is expected that the performance problem is happening at the time the memory dump is created. If the problem is not happening and you are not able to reproduce it easily, you can add a rule. This rule will create a memory dump based on a set of predetermined configurations that trigger the creation of the memory dump when those thresholds are breached. For example, you can add a rule that creates a memory dump when the CPU consumption exceeds 90 percent or memory exceeds 2 GB.

To do this, select the Rules tab, click the Add Rule button, and then select the type of rule to create (see Figure 23-40). The following table describes each rule type:

RULE TYPE	DESCRIPTION
Crash	Captures a memory dump when the process crashes. It is possible to configure the rule to create the memory dump based on a specific exception, at a specific breakpoint or when a specific event is fired.
Performance	Captures a memory dump when a specific performance trigger is breached — for example, CPU consumption, memory utilization, or request execution times. You can set the thresholds of most if not all of the monitors available in the Performance Monitor program.
Native (non-.NET) Memory and Handle Leak	Captures a memory dump of a non-managed-code process. You can use LeakTrack with native code to help you find a memory leak.

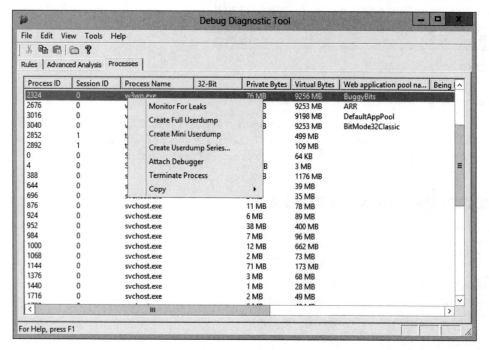

FIGURE 23-38

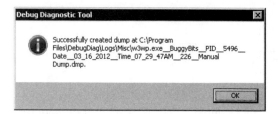

FIGURE 23-39

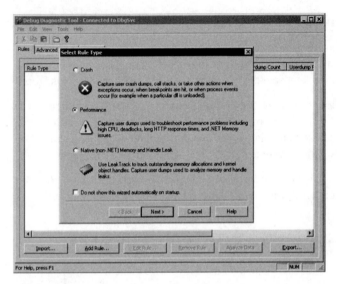

FIGURE 23-40

For this example, a Performance rule is created.

Select Next and then Performance Counters, as shown in Figure 23-41. Clicking the Next button opens a window allowing you to add performance triggers. For this example, a memory dump will be generated when the `'\Processor(_Total)\% Processor Time'` counter breaches 90 for 15 seconds.

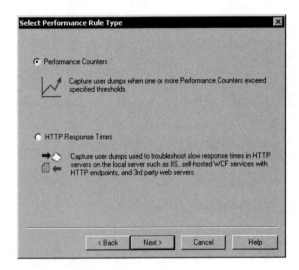

FIGURE 23-41

Select the Next button to select the target of the memory dump. Select Web application pool from the Target Type dropdown, and then the specific application pool you want the dump of.

> **NOTE** *The "HTTP Response Times" rule type allows you to specify a specific URL to monitor and associate it with a time-out trigger. It works in the same manner as Performance Monitor.*

The next window allows you to configure how many memory dumps you want to take when the rule is triggered. If you were having memory consumption issues, for example, you may want to take a series of memory dumps in order to compare what is happening between two or more dumps. Watching the memory consumption between the memory dump series may lead you to finding where the memory leak is coming from. However, for this example, the focus is CPU consumption, and therefore only a single memory dump is required. For this situation, make the changes as shown in Figure 23-42.

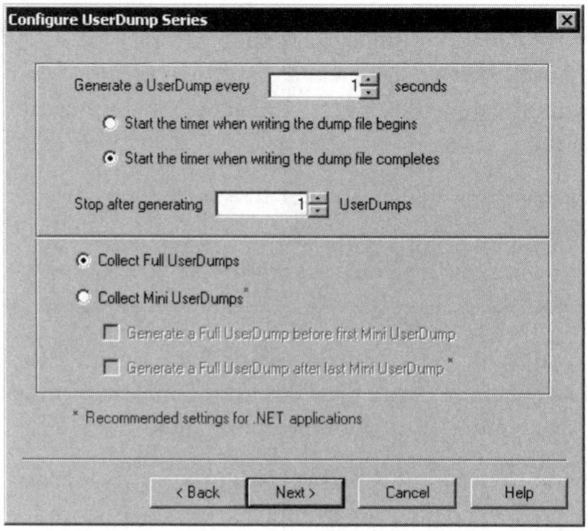

FIGURE 23-42

Lastly, enter the rule name and the location where the memory dump should be stored. Finish the creation of the rule by choosing to activate the rule "now" and wait for the counter to be breached. Once it is breached, select the rule and then the Analyze Data button, as shown in Figure 23-43.

Analyzing the Memory Dump

The analysis of a memory dump takes a lot of experience and in many cases is similar to detective work. You simply need to have a solid technical background and training. You need also to be able to gather bits and pieces together that enable you to create a big picture view. This big picture perspective can ultimately lead to the root cause of the problem. Because there are many books that cover in great detail how to analyze a memory dump, the analysis of the dump is not covered here. Nonetheless, the analysis performed by DebugDiag is very good and provides an Analysis Summary and Detail page that helps you identify or get you further along toward finding a solution.

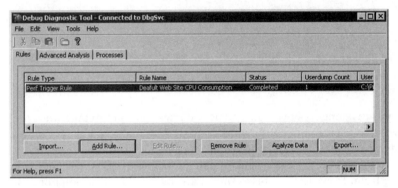

FIGURE 23-43

ProcDump

ProcDump is a command-line tool used to capture memory dumps that can later be analyzed with WinDbg or DebugDiag. ProcDump is especially useful when you need to capture a memory dump of a w3wp.exe process that is consuming large amounts of memory, experiencing CPU utilization spikes, or when the process becomes unresponsive.

> **NOTE** *By default, ProcDump takes a 32-bit memory dump. If you need to get a 64-bit dump, make sure you add the* -64 *parameter to the command line.*

There are several parameters supported by this program. I recommend you perform a search for "ProcDump" and review the official website. The official website provides all the information you need concerning the parameters. As well, there are a number of example commands.

The following command creates a full 64-bit memory dump of the w3wp.exe process with process id = 9999, when its memory consumption exceeds 1 GB. The memory dump, w3wp.dmp, is stored in the location from where the ProcDump command is executed:

```
C:\>procdump -64 -ma -m 1000 -o 9999 w3wp.dmp
```

A second example creates a full 64-bit memory dump when the CPU utilization exceeds 95 percent for more than 5 seconds:

```
C:\>procdump -64 -ma -c 95 -s 5 -o 9999 w3wp.dmp
```

If you are not able to configure ProcDump in a way that can create a memory dump via the command line, it is possible to temporarily configure ProcDump to execute directly in IIS 8.0. After downloading and installing ProcDump on your server, perform the following steps to capture a memory dump of the w3wp.exe process when it becomes unresponsive:

1. Open the Advanced Settings… for the application pool that you want to associate ProcDump with and take a memory dump of.

2. Scroll down until you find the Process Orphaning section and make the modifications shown in Figure 23-44.

3. Click OK.

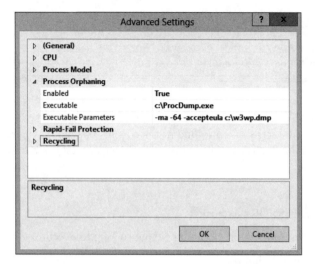

FIGURE 23-44

The next time the worker process for this application pool is orphaned, a memory dump is automatically created. You can then use this memory dump to find out what is causing or what caused the issue.

WinDbg

WinDbg is a tool used to analyze memory dumps. WinDbg provides commands and a user interface to examine memory dumps of processes running in kernel, user, or managed mode. The next two sections focus on finding a managed-code hang and crash within a w3wp.exe worker process. WinDbg is contained within the Debugging Tools for Windows kit and can be downloaded from http://msdn.microsoft.com/en-us/windows/hardware/gg463009.aspx. If the address is not valid, simply search for "Debugging Tools for Windows" and you'll find the most current address.

In previous sections of this chapter, you already learned that DebugDiag and ProcDump are tools to create a memory dump. Although DebugDiag provides some capabilities to analyze the memory dump, there are cases when a deeper look at the memory dump is required to find the root cause.

In the next section, you learn basic commands from the PSSCOR4 debugging extension and receive insight into finding the cause of the issue. Because this is not a Windows debugging book, only the initial steps to find the issue are discussed. Navigation all the way to the root cause and the construction of a solution exceeds the context of this book.

Troubleshooting a W3WP Hang

Many IIS administrators have experienced a situation in which a request is hanging — meaning that a user or customer has clicked a button on a browser, requesting a file or triggering an action on the IIS server, and the request simply hangs. Either it takes too long for IIS to answer the request or the page times out and nothing is returned.

> **NOTE** *Prior to executing this example, create a website using the code found in the* `WinDbgHang.zip` *file, downloadable from* `www.wrox.com`. *When you access the website, the* `w3wp.exe` *worker process will be visible.*

For this example, I have created an ASP.NET page that calls the `sleep` method in the `Page_Load` event. This is a very easy example; however, the steps taken to find it, the conclusions made, and lessons learned are very similar to a more complicated issue. The actions taken to troubleshoot a hang issue with WinDbg are as follows:

1. Create a series of memory dumps.
2. Open them in WinDbg and load the PSSCOR4 extension.
3. Execute some PSSCOR4 commands to find which method is taking so long to execute.
4. Perform the same on all captured memory dumps.
5. Refactor the code and see what the method looks like.

After installing the WinDbgHang website example in IIS, I ran it and due to the sleep call, the ASP.NET page waited and waited and waited until finally a response was rendered. From a user or customer perspective, all that is known is that the page is taking way too long to render and therefore the system is not usable. Action, therefore, must be taken to find the reason for this processing time.

A good approach for capturing this cause is to execute the following command while you are certain the hang is happening:

```
procdump -64 -ma -s 5 -n 3 PID w3wp-PID-hang.dmp
```

The previous command creates a 64-bit full memory dump, three times, 5 seconds apart. Once these dumps are created, compare them and see which method the thread is hung on. If you see that in all three dumps the thread is in the same method, then you have likely found the source of the problem.

Open the first W3WP memory dump in WinDbg and load the PSSCOR4 extension, as shown in Figure 23-45.

First, get a list of the ASPX request running at the time the memory dump was taken. This is achieved by entering the `!DumpHttpContext` command. The output is shown in Figure 23-46. Notice that the only request with an associated ThreadId is 37. This makes things very easy. However, if there were multiple requests running at the same time, you would need to look at the stack for each thread to get an understanding of what is happening during this hang.

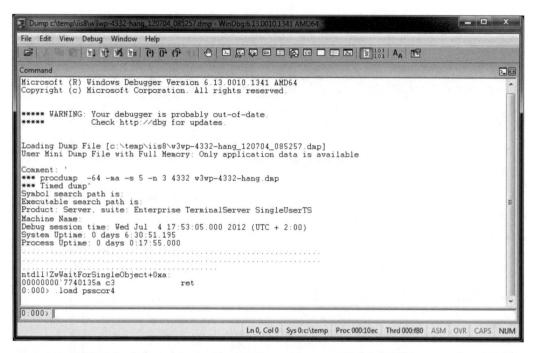

FIGURE 23-45

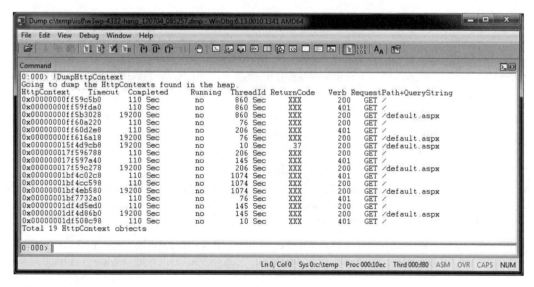

FIGURE 23-46

To look at the stack for ThreadId 37, enter **~37s** and focus will be placed onto this thread. Next, enter **!clrstack** to get the managed code stack of this thread. The result of !clrstack is shown in Figure 23-47.

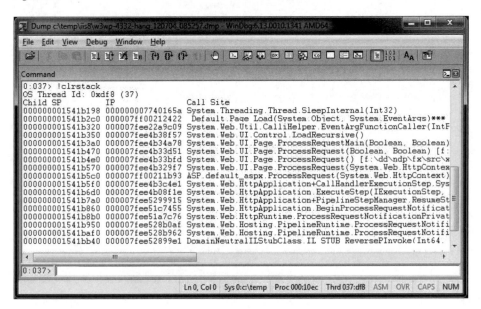

```
0:037> !clrstack
OS Thread Id: 0xdf8 (37)
Child SP               IP                Call Site
000000001541b198 000000007740165a System.Threading.Thread.SleepInternal(Int32)
000000001541b2c0 000007ff00212422  _Default.Page_Load(System.Object, System.EventArgs)***
000000001541b320 000007fee22a9c09 System.Web.Util.CalliHelper.EventArgFunctionCaller(IntP
000000001541b350 000007fee4b38f57 System.Web.UI.Control.LoadRecursive()
000000001541b3a0 000007fee4b34a78 System.Web.UI.Page.ProcessRequestMain(Boolean, Boolean)
000000001541b470 000007fee4b33d51 System.Web.UI.Page.ProcessRequest(Boolean, Boolean) [f:
000000001541b4e0 000007fee4b33bfd System.Web.UI.Page.ProcessRequest() [f:\dd\ndp\fx\src\x
000000001541b570 000007fee4b329f7 System.Web.UI.Page.ProcessRequest(System.Web.HttpContex
000000001541b5c0 000007ff00211b93 ASP.default_aspx.ProcessRequest(System.Web.HttpContext)
000000001541b5f0 000007fee4b3c4e1 System.Web.HttpApplication+CallHandlerExecutionStep.Sys
000000001541b6d0 000007fee4b08f1e System.Web.HttpApplication.ExecuteStep(IExecutionStep,
000000001541b7a0 000007fee5299915 System.Web.HttpApplication+PipelineStepManager.ResumeSt
000000001541b860 000007fee51c7455 System.Web.HttpApplication.BeginProcessRequestNotificat
000000001541b8b0 000007fee51a7c76 System.Web.HttpRuntime.ProcessRequestNotificationPrivat
000000001541b950 000007fee528b0af System.Web.Hosting.PipelineRuntime.ProcessRequestNotifi
000000001541baf0 000007fee528b962 System.Web.Hosting.PipelineRuntime.ProcessRequestNotifi
000000001541bb40 000007fee52899e1 DomainNeutralILStubClass.IL_STUB_ReversePInvoke(Int64.
```

FIGURE 23-47

Notice the reference to ASP.default_aspx in the stack. This matches what is shown in Figure 23-47. Moving up the stack you see the _Default.Page_Load() method and that it has called the System. Threading.Thread.SleepInternal() method. In this situation, the first question to ask is why this is happening. However silly this may seem, this is a rather common coding error made by junior developers.

In a real-world example, it is likely not so easy to find the method so fast. There may be a data access layer, a connection to the database, a concatenation of stings, a regular expression algorithm, and so on. Nonetheless, a good rule of thumb is that the method at the top of the managed stack is very likely the cause of the hang and as a result should be analyzed and optimized.

Open the other memory dumps and execute the same commands. Figure 23-48 shows the output of !DumpHttpContext. Notice how the Running column has increased from 10 Sec to 42 Sec and that it still has the same ThreadId. Compare Figures 23-38 and 23-40.

Run the !clrstack command and check if the stack is still waiting on the same method. In this example, it is, and if it is the same in your situation, then you have a good chance to solve this hang issue.

Lastly, if you have a background in development, then looking at the source can move the resolution even further along. Enter **!SaveAllModules C:\Temp\source (!sam)**, and WinDbg will refactor the managed code. There may be some components that are obfuscated or code that you do not have the symbols for and therefore will not refactor. Figure 23-49 shows the refactored code found within the Page_Load() method of the default page.

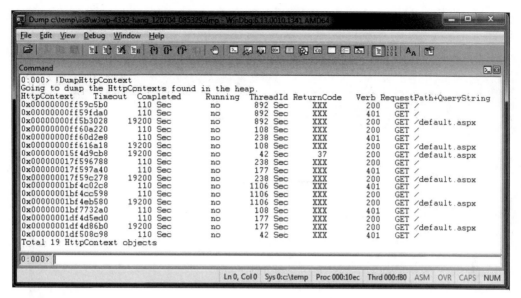

FIGURE 23-48

```
protected void Page_Load(object sender, EventArgs e)
{
    int millisecondsTimeout = 0x1388;
    Thread.Sleep(millisecondsTimeout);
    this.LabelSleep.Text = "Slept for " + millisecondsTimeout.ToString() + " miliseconds.";
}
```

FIGURE 23-49

Every performance issue needs a solution. Finding where it is happening is a challenge in itself. However, if you can find where it is happening and provide the solution at the same time, then that is really something!

Troubleshooting a W3WP Crash

A crash of the w3wp.exe worker process generally has significant impact on the system. In many cases, the worker process will terminate, not restart, and your users and customers will begin getting an HTTP status of 500 instead of the requested resource. In the sections covering ProcDump and DebugDiag, you learned how to capture a memory dump when the worker process terminates in general or when a specific exception is thrown.

> **NOTE** *Prior to executing this example, create a website using the code found in the* WinDbgCrash.zip *file, downloadable from* www.wrox.com. *When you access the website, the* w3wp.exe *worker process will be visible.*

Now you need to look at the memory dump and determine from where and, hopefully, why the exception is happening. Open the memory dump in WinDbg and you will notice that it navigates to the thread where the exception happened. Figure 23-50 shows the initial WinDbg window.

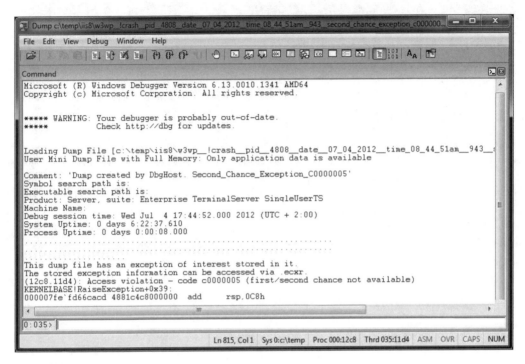

FIGURE 23-50

Load the PSSCOR4 extension by entering **.load psscor4**. Use the !clrstack command to view the stack. Figure 23-51 shows the result of this command. You may also look at the native call stack as well by entering **kb.** You will see the same method in the native call stack and likely have "KERNELBASE!RaiseException" at the top of the stack.

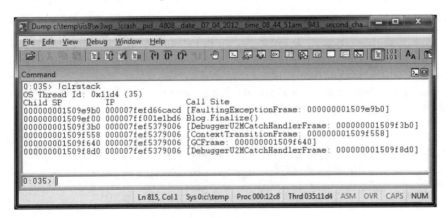

FIGURE 23-51

The crash is likely happening from within the finalizer of the Blog class. This is the first clue that can be sent to the developer team for further analysis. Or, as previously done, you can refactor the code, analyze it, and provide the solution to the developer team. The following code snippet shows the code that causes the exception.

```
~Blog()
{
  If (title.ToString() != string.Empty)
  {
    title = null;
  }
}
```

The exception is likely thrown because the `title.String()` is `null` and cannot be referenced, and therefore cannot be converted to a string.

> **NOTE** *Load the PSSCOR4 extension if the application pool where the exception occurred uses version 4.0 of the .NET Framework. If the application pool is using version 2.0, use PSSCOR2.*

Where to Go Next

The tools listed in this chapter are by no means an exhaustive list of the tools that are available for IIS 8.0 and Windows Server 2012 troubleshooting. It is important always to be on the lookout for new tools and to experiment with the various tools that are available. Microsoft's website `www.iis.net` has become the fully supported website that Microsoft and even the IIS Product group regularly use to get the latest tools and information. This is a site that should be at your fingertips to keep up-to-date on the latest tools.

INDEX

INDEX

A

ABOMapper, 635–636
access policies, IIS 8.0, 54–55
accounts, user accounts, 468–469
ACDS (Active Directory Certificate Services), CA generation, 485–487
ACEs (access control entries), 424
ACLs (access control lists), 424, 512
AcquireRequestState event, 345, 348, 364
actions (URL Rewrite), 683–686
Active Directory
    authentication, delegation, 458
    mapping, 450
    versus standalone, 45–46
Active Server Pages. *See* ASP
ADCS (Active Directory Certificate Services), 473
Administration Tool, extension, 388–391
    configuration control, 383–386
    module container, 386–388
    namespace references, 382–383
    new project, 382
administration.config, 28–29, 107–108, 600, 605
administrators, 222–223
ADSI (Active Directory Services Interfaces), 9
    programmatic configuration and, 635–636
ADUC (Active Directory Users and Computers), 232
Affinity traffic distribution, 547, 554
AHAdmin (Application Host Administration API), 639–641
AllocateRequestMemory function, 357
anonymous authentication, 424
    configuring, 428–430

Anonymous authentication (FTP server), 269
anonymous users, application pool security, 214–215
Apache, 19
API support, load balancing, 553
APIs (application programming interfaces), 7
    URL Rewrite and, 692
    WebSocket, 16
AppCmd.exe, 10, 97
    application pools, 655–656
        running processes, 209
    applications
        adding, 139–140
        deleting, 140
    attributes, 653–657
    backup and restore, 657–664
    collections, editing, 660–662
    commands, 647, 650–653
    compression configuration, 145
    configuration, 662–664
    help, 648–650
    host headers, 137
    IIS Manager delegation, 254
    listing configuration, 658–660
    MIME types, 147–149
    objects, 646–647, 653–655
    properties, 194, 660
    requests, currently executing, 656–657
    values, 653
    virtual directory creation, 142
    website creation, 124–126
    worker process state, 656
    XML piping, 664–665
application domains, RSCA and, 861
application folders, location tags, 246–247
Application Initialization, 30, 32, 176–177

application isolation, 151
application layer security, 420–421
Application Performance, 833–834
application pools, 6, 22–23
    Advanced Settings, 192–193
    AppCmd.exe, 199, 655–656
    applicationHost.config, 199–200
    applications, assigning, 196–200
    Basic Settings, 192
    bit settings, 215
    configuration, sandboxing, 466–468
    creating, 122–126 , 190–191
    hosting services and, 88–89
    integrated pipeline mode, 25
    .NET Framework version, 200–202
    optimization, 837–842
    recycling, 187–188, 210–212
    Recycling tool, 192
    running processes, 206–209
    security, 212–215
    setting, 91–94
    sites, assigning, 196–200
    starting/stopping, 210–212
    users, 216–220
    web application pool, 119
    web gardens, 188–190
Application Request Routing. *See* ARR
application root, 181
application server, 4
Application Settings module, 163–164
Application Warm-Up module, 16, 32
applicationHost.config, 27–28, 97, 107–108,
   199–200, 600, 605
application-level nodes (IIS Manager), 103–105
applications
    adding, 138–140
    assigning to application pools, 196–200
    capacity planning, 60–61
    definition, 180–183
    deleting, 140
    deployment, 56–57
        Web Deploy, 753–756
    integrated pipeline mode, 25
    isolation modes, 180
    overview, 119
    root application, 118, 119

    security, 50–51
    virtual directory comparison, 183–185
    Web Application Gallery, 746–750
    web application pool, 119
    web applications, 118
APTs (advanced persistent threats), 398
architecture
    application pools, 22–23
    ASP classic, 23
    ASP.NET, 23–24
    CGI, 22
    Http.sys, 21–22
    IIS 7.0 and later, 24–29
    IIS 8.0, 29–33
    IIS Admin services, 22
    inetinfo.exe, 20
    ISAP, 22
    Windows Server 2012, 35–36
ARR (Application Request Routing), 30, 545,
   558–559
    ARR Helper, 580–581
    ARR server farm, 561
    downloading, 560
    functionality, 559–560
    high availability, 589–590
    IIS site binding, 561
    installation, 560
    load balancing, 556
    optimizations, 588–589
    performance monitoring, 584
    SSL/TLS offloading, 579–580
    touchpoints, 561–562
    URL Rewrite rule, 561
    URL testing, 577–579
ASP (Active Server Pages), 4, 23
    configuration, 154–155
ASP Classic, 19, 23
ASP.NET
    CLR (Common Language Runtime), 23
    configuration, 155–156
    IIS pipeline and, 336–340
    integration, 7–8
    migration, 339
    web forms, 23
ASP.NET counter monitoring, 828–829
ASP.NET Development Server, 619

ASP.NET modules, 157–158
   .NET Authorization Rules, 158
   .NET Compilation, 158–159
ASP.NET Tracing, 874–876
   ASP.NET Trace Viewer, 877–880
   enabling, 876–877
AsyncCompletion event, 346, 348
attacks
   APTs (advanced persistent threats), 398
   DoS (denial-of-service), 396
   passive, 397–398
   poorly secured systems, 397
   privilege escalation, 396–397
   session replays, 420
   social engineering, 396
   SQL injection, 420
   vulnerability exploitation, 396
   XSS (cross-site scripting), 420
attributes
   AppCmd.exe, 653
      object associations, 654–657
   childConfig, 612
   delegation, 254
   inheritInChildApplications, 611
   lockAllAttributesExcept, 257–258
   lockAllElementsExcept, 257–258
   lockAttributes, 256
   lockElements, 256–257
   lockItem, 257
   overrideMode, 611–612
   path property, 608–609
   sourceConfig, 612
auditing, 49–50, 395
AuthenticateRequest event, 345, 348, 364
authentication, 9, 143, 395
   Active Directory, delegation, 458
   anonymous, 424, 428–430
   Anonymous (FTP server), 269
   basic, 424–425, 430–432
   client authentication, load balancing, 553
   Client Certificate, 425, 426–427
      configuring, 449–452
   digest, 425, 433–437
   forms-based, 425, 453-456
   IIS Manager, 229–231
   IWA (Integrated Windows authentication),
     425

   configuring, 437–439
   Kerberos, 443–447
   kernel mode, 447
   NTLM, configuring, 439–443
   overview, 423–424
   protocol transition configuration, 461
   SMTP server, 303
   UNC, 425, 448–449
   web farms, 447
   Windows, 231–232
authorization, 9, 143, 395
   configuration, 462–468
   overview, 424
   server-level, 232
   URL, 463–466
   web application-level, 232–233
   website-level, 232–233
AuthorizeRequest event, 345, 348, 364
automation, 98
   tools, 57–58
Azure, 545, 595–596

B

back-references (URL Rewrite), 683, 712–714
backups, 51–52, 555
Badmail folder (SMTP), 305–306
bandwidth throttling, 844
basic authentication, 424–425, 430–432
BeginRequest event, 345, 348, 364
Berners-Lee, Tim, 118
binary logging, 132–133
bindings, per server, 515
bit settings, application pools, 215
blind FTP, 263
BlockCrossLinks class, 357

C

CAB (change approval board), 786–787
caching
   ARR, enabling, 585
   duration, 586–587
   load balancing, 553
   managed content, 587
   modules, 323

output, 845–846

Output Caching, 719–721

pre-caching objects, 587

private browsing and, 691

security, 587–588

CALs (Client Access Licenses), 54, 229

capacity planning, 58–61

CAs (certificate authorities)

generating, 476–481

ADCS and, 485–487

importing, 483–484

installed, 473–474

private key, 476

public key, 476

website bindings, 484–485

CAS (Code Access Security), 542–543

CDN (content delivery network), 584–585

Central Certificate Store, 492

centralized binary logging, 829–831

centralized logging, 132–134

Certificate Enrollment Request, 479

certificates

Central Certificate Store, 492

CRLs (certificate revocation lists), 494

exporting/importing, 489–490

requests, submitting, 481–483

self-signed, 487

template management, 494

CGI (Common Gateway Interface), 4, 22, 316

configuration, 173

restrictions, 407–413

childConfig attribute, 612

childSource attribute, 516–517

Classic pipeline mode, 202

client affinity, load balancing, 554

client authentication, load balancing, 553

Client Certificate authentication, 425, 426–427

configuring, 449–452

client-side caching (CSC), 529–531

cloud architecture, Windows Server 2012, 35–36

cloud deployment, 53

CLR (Common Language Runtime), 23

clustering, 34

Hyper-V, 14

server farms and, 47–48

CN (Common Name), 473

code, writing, 623–625

collection items, direct configuration, 602–605

collections

AppCmd.exe, editing, 660–662

delegation, 254

locking, 257

COM+, 534–535

command line

LogParser and, 309–310

FTP client, 296–297

command-line management, 114–115

AppCmd.exe

attributes, 653

commands, 647

help, 648–650

list command, 650–653

objects, 646–647

values, 653

compression

configuration, 143–145

modules, 322

conditions (URL Rewrite), 682–683

configEncKey.key, 511

configSections, 112–113

configuration

administration consolidation, 108

application pools

isolation, 212–213

sandboxing, 466–468

ASP (Active Server Pages), 154–155

ASP.NET, 155–157

authentication, 428–432

authorization, 462–468

automated, 85–86

CGI (Common Gateway Interface), 173

Client Certificate authentication, 449–452

Compression, 143–145

custom modules, schema, 378

declarative schema, 111–113

delegation, 456–460

digest authentication, 433–437

direct configuration, 598–618

documents, default setting, 146

extending, 377–380

FastCGI, 174–176
FBA (forms-based authentication), 453–456
files
    bindings, 515
    childSource attribute, 516–517
    configSource attribute, 515–516
    copying, 510
    exporting, 504–506
    FTP administration, 294–296
    hierarchical naming structure, 110
    hierarchy, 107–108, 599–601
    IIS Manager, 244–246
    machine-neutral, 512–517
    moving, 506–508
    section groups, 110
    structure, 110–111
    system environment variables, 512–514
    XML, 28–29
file-specific, 109
FTP server, 264–265
    host name support, 290
    user security, 274–278
FTP sites, 271–274
FTPS (FTP over SSL), 286–288
host headers, 134–138
ISAPI, 172–173
IWA (Integrated Windows authentication), 437–439
Kerberos authentication, 443–447
location tags, 109–110
MIME (Multipurpose Internet Mail Extensions), 147–149
NTLM authentication, 439–443
optimization, 598–599
pipeline modes, 203–206
programmatic, 618
    ABO support, 635–636
    ADSI support, 635–636
    AHAdmin, 639–641
    API support, 635–636
    Microsoft.Web.Administration API, 626–634
    system requirements, 618–619
    Visual Web Developer, 619–626
protocol transition, 461

remote change notification, 108–109
sections, locking/unlocking, 113–114
security, 108
shared, 109
UNC authentication, 448–449
web.config files, distributed, 515
Configuration Editor, 33, 641–646
Connection strings module, 164
content configuration, 520–528
content filtering, load balancing, 553
content modules, 322
content replication, 524–527
Content View (IIS Manager), 105
cookie settings module, 169–170
CPU limits, 215–216
CPU throttling, 15–16
    active throttling, 31–32
CRLs (certificate revocation lists), 494
CSC (client-side caching), 529–531
CSR (Certificate Signing Request), 532
custom accounts, application pools, 219–220
custom modules, configuration extension, 377–381
CustomLoggingModule, 128
CustomRequestNotification event notification, 346, 348

D

Datacenter Edition, 41, 42, 43, 47, 48
DebugDiag (Debug Diagnostic Tool), 909–914
declarative schema, 111–113
decryption keys, 165
default installation, 65–66
    testing, 66–73
delegation, configuration, 456–460
DelegConfig, 901–902
deployment, 39–40
    applications, 56–57
    tools, 57–58
    WDS (Windows Deployment Services), 85–86
development environments, 55
DFS (Distributed File System), 119–120
    DFS Namespaces, 527

DFS-R (Distributed File System with Replication), 504, 526
  content replication and, 528
  IIS configuration files, 527–528
DHCP (Dynamic Host Configuration Protocol), 43
diagnostics, 10
  ASP.NET Tracing, 874–880
  error pages, 861–865
  errors, 852–853
  Failed Request Tracing, 867–873
  FTP status codes, 867
  HTTP status codes, 866
  languages, 866
  logging, 873–874
  resource-intensive issues, 853–854
  RSCA (Runtime Status and Control API), 854–861
  speed issues, 853–854
diagnostics modules, 323–324
dialog pages (IIS Manager), 103
digest authentication, 425
  configuring, 433–437
direct configuration, 598
  childConfig attribute, 612
  collection items, 602–605
  files, hierarchy, 599–601
  inheritance, 610–611
  location tag, 607–610
  locking, 611–612
  order of operation, 601–602
  paths, 612–613
  schema extensibility, 613–618
  schema files, 614
  sections
    administration.config, 605
    applicationHost.config, 605
    machine.config, 607
    redirection.config, 607
    web.config, 607
  sourceConfig attribute, 612
DirectAccess, 14
directories
  FTP server, 262–264
  permission setting, 89–91
  root virtual directory, 118
  virtual, 119–120
    application comparison, 183–185
    creating with AppCmd.exe, 142
    creating with IIS Manager, 140–141
    folders, 120
    PowerShell, 142
    root virtual directory, 118
directory structure, 87–88
disk I/O, monitoring, 826
DNS (domain name server), load balancing, 557–558
documents, 146
domain controller, 86
domain names, 572–573
domain restrictions, 399–405
DoS (denial-of-service) attacks, 396
Drop folder (SMTP), 306
DSR (Direct Server Return), load balancing, 549–551
DTLS (Datagram Transport Layer Security), 14–15
dynamic IP restrictions, 31, 404–405

E

elements, delegation, 254
e-mail, SMTP (Simple Mail Transport Protocol), 171
encryption
  BitLocker Drive Encryption, 36
  TLS, SMTP and, 304
Encryption Keys Password, 507
EndRequest event, 346, 348, 365
Enterprise Edition, 41, 42, 44
environment variables, 512–514
environments
  development, 55
  production, 55–56
  security, 398–399
error pages, 861–865
errors
  hang error, 852–853
  specific, 852
  time-out error, 852–853

Essentials Edition, 41, 42, 53
event logs, 49–50
event tracing from modules, 371–372
Event Viewer, troubleshooting and, 885–888, 895–896
events, 318
    global, 347
    nonsequential, 346
    notifications, 348
        managed code modules, 364–365
        methods, 348
        post-event notification, 348
        registering for native modules, 356
    pipeline request processing, 345–346
    trace events, managed code modules, 373–374
`ExecuteRequestHandler` event notification, 348
exporting configuration files, 504–506
extensibility, 8, 26, 98
    IIS Manager, 27
    overview, 344
    support modules, 324

F

Failed Request Tracing
    logs, 130
    rules setup, 868–871
    XML logs, 871–873
FailedRequestsTracingModule, 128
failover, 34
failure handling, load balancing and, 555
FastCGI, 30, 174–176
FBA (forms-based authentication), configuring, 453–456
Feature Delegation (IIS Manager), 105–106, 237–244
    Custom Web Site Delegation mode, 239–242
    Default Delegation mode, 239–242
filenames
    default, 181
    extensions, filtering by, 414–415
files
    configuration
        bindings, 515
        `childSource` attribute, 516–517

        `configSource` attribute, 515–516
        copying, 510
        exporting, 504–506
        FTP administration, 294–296
        hierarchical naming structure, 110
        hierarchy, 107–108, 599–601
        machine-neutral, 512–517
        moving, 506–508
        section groups, 110
        structure, 110–111
        system environment variables, 512–514
    schema, direct configuration, 614
file-specific configuration, 109
filtering, Request Filtering, 414–419
Firewall Friendly FTP, 260
firewalls, 49
    load balancing, 553
folders
    application, `location` tags, 246–247
    directories, virtual directories, 120
    SMTP, 305–306
forms-based authentication (FBA), 425
    configuring, 453–456
Foundation Edition, 41
FQDN (fully qualified domain name), 473
frameworks
    Azure, 595–596
    load balancing, 558
    WFF (Web Farm Framework), 594–595
FTP (File Transfer Protocol)
    blind FTP, 263
    command-line client, 296–297
    Firewall Friendly FTP, 260
    host name support, 290
    logon attempt restrictions, 293–294
    .NET accounts, membership, 278–286
    overview, 260–261
    Passive FTP, 260
    security, 261
    TLS and, 498–500
    user isolation, configuration, 288–289
FTP IP Address and Domain Restrictions, 292–293
FTP publishing, 759–763
FTP Request Filtering, 291–292

FTP server
    Advanced Settings, 272–273
    Anonymous authentication, 269
    configuration, 264–265
        user security, 274–278
    home directory, 272
    installation, 260–261, 264–265
        directory structure, 262–264
        planning, 261–264
        user isolation, 261–262
    Logging, 273–274
    messages, 274
    new site creation, 265–270
        PowerShell, 271
    site configuration, 271–274
    Telnet, 271
    user isolation, 263–234
FTP service, 6
    IIS 8 changes, 16–17
FTP status codes, 867
FTPS (FTP over SSL), 260, 261
    adding to sites, 294–295
    configuration, 286–288
Full Trust permissions, 160

G

GAC (Global Assembly Cache), 533–534
GetResponse function, 358
global events, 347
global variables, 379
GlobalApplicationResolveModules event, 347
GlobalApplicationStart event, 347
GlobalApplicationStop event, 347
GlobalCacheCleanup event, 347
GlobalCacheOperation event, 347
GlobalConfigurationChange event, 347
GlobalCustomNotification event, 347
GlobalFileChange event, 347
GlobalHealthCheck event, 347
GlobalPreBeginRequest event, 347
GlobalRSCAQuery event, 347
GlobalStopListening event, 347
GlobalThreadCleanup event, 347

GlobalTraceEvent event, 347
grid pages (IIS Manager), 102–103
GSLB (Global Server Load Balancing), 558
GUIs, Server with a GUI, 11

H

handshake, 473–476
hang errors, 852–853
HAProxy, 556
hardware
    content, 87
    load balancing, 555–556
    security modules, 494
    tamper-resistant, 493–494
health checking, load balancing, 553
Hidden Segments, filtering by, 416–417
hierarchy, configuration files, 107–108
    direct configuration, 599–601
High Trust permissions, 160
Home Server, 42
host headers, 30
    adding/removing, 136
    AppCmd.exe and, 137
    configuration, 134–138
    PowerShell and, 137–138
    SSL and, 138
host names
    FTP, 290
    support, 296
hosting services, 86–87
    application pools, 88–89
    directory structure, 87–88
    shared, managed code and, 89–94
    web server accounts, 88–89
hot-linking, URL Rewrite and, 729
HTTP (Hypertext Transfer Protocol), 118
    compression, 846–849
    host headers, 490–491
    modules
        Managed Code, 319, 325–326
        Native Code, 319, 320–324
    page headers, 842–843
    status codes, 866
HTTP Verbs, filtering by, 415

HttpLoggingModule, 127
  installation, 128–129
HttpModule class, 353–355
HTTP_PROTOCOL, URL Rewrite and, 731
HTTPS (HTTP Secure), 118
Http.sys, 21
  kernel mode, 21
  optimization, 835–836
  requests, 21
  TCP/IP connections, 21
  user mode, 21
HWC (hostable web core), 223
hwebcore.dll, 223–224
Hyper-V, 33–35
  clustering, 14
  replication, 14
  SR-IOV (Single-Root I/O Virtualization), 41
  version 3, 43
  virtual networking, 14

I

IANA (Internet Assigned Numbers Authority), 49
icacls.exe utility, 88
IHttpModule interface, 366–367
IIS (Internet Information Services)
  default option configuration, 149–150
  extensibility, 8
  introduction, 3
  management accounts, 54–55
  versions, 4–5
IIS 6.0 Metabase Compatibility, 636
IIS 6.0 WMI Compatibility, 636
IIS 7.0 and 7.5, 6
  upgrade to IIS 8.0, 80–81
IIS 8.0
  access policies, 54–55
  Application Warm-Up module, 16
  characteristics, 98
  CPU throttling, 15–16
  development environments, 55
  FTP, 16–17
  installation, decisions, 53
  production environments, 55–56
  replication, 56

Request Tracing, 59–60
requirements, 53
Server Core deployment, 56
Shared Configuration, 56
SMTP, 17
SSL (Secure Sockets Layer), changes, 15
upgrade from IIS 7.0, 80–81
WebSocket API, 16
IIS Admin service, 22
IIS Manager, 10
  appearance, 99
  application-level nodes, 103–105
  applications
    adding, 138–139
    deleting, 140
    folders, location tags, 246–247
  authentication, 229–231
  centralized certificates, 100
  CGI, restrictions, 99
  compression configuration, 143–145
  configuration files, 244–246
  Configuration Read Only, 250–251
  Configuration Read/Write, 250–251
  Content View, 105
  Copy Delegation, 252–254
  delegation
    AppCmd.exe and, 254
    Feature Delegation, 237–244
  dialog pages, 103
  directories, virtual, creating, 140–141
  extensibility, 27, 106
  FAST CGI settings, 99
  Feature Delegation, 105–106
  feature delegation, 100
  folders, right-clicking, 197–199
  ISAPI, restrictions, 99
  list pages, 101–102
  locking settings, 247–248
  Management Service, 100
    installation, 223–224
    WMSvc and, 224
  MIME types, 147–149
  .NET Profile, 101
  .NET Roles, 101
  .NET Users, 101

Not Delegated, 250
page requests, running, 209–210
property grid pages, 102–103
Read Only access, 249
Read/Write access, 249
remote connections, 106–107, 224–229
    remote installation, 234–235
Reset All Delegation, 251–252
Reset to Inherited, 251
`<section>` tags, 242–244
server certificates, 99
shared configuration, 100
SSL Settings, 101
users, 100
website-level nodes, 103–105
websites, creating, 121–122
worker processes, 99
workflow customization, 334–335
IIS native modules, 26
IIS service optimization, 835–842
`iistart.htm`, 72
independent worker processes, 317
`inetinfo.exe`, 20
inheritance, 610–611
`inheritInChildApplications` attribute, 611
InProc, 538
input variables, URL Rewrite, 701–704
installation
    automated, 85–86
    default, 65–73
    FTP server, 260–261, 264–265
        directory structure, 262–264
        new site creation, 265–270
        planning, 261–264
        user isolation, 261–262
    IIS 8.0
        decisions, 53
        features, 76–79
    LogParser, 309
    managed modules, 369–370
    minimal, security and, 8
    native modules, 361
    new, 43
    PHP, 174

PowerShell and, 79–80
remote, 234–235
security, 8–9
Server Manager and, 64–65
staggered, Shared Configuration, 517–520
upgrades, 43–44
Web PI (Web Platform Installer), 73–76
on Windows 7, 84–85
on Windows 8, 81–84
integrated pipeline mode, 25, 202, 203
interfaces
    IHttpModule, 366–367
    Minimal Server Interface, 11
    Server with a GUI, 11
    Windows Server 2012, 11–13
IP address-based bindings, 576
IP addresses, server farms, 573
IP restrictions, 31, 399–405
IPAM (IP Address Management), 36
IPS (intrusion prevention systems), 553
IPv6, 49
ISAPI (Internet Server Application Programming Interface), 4, 22
    configuration, 172–173
    legacy support, 340–341
    restrictions, 407–413
isolating applications, 151
    modes, 180
ITIL (IT Infrastructure Library), 780–781
ITSM (IT Service Management), 805
IWA (Integrated Windows authentication), 425
    configuring, 437–439

J–K

JScript, 4, 23
KDC (Key Distribution Center), 444
Kerberos, 425
    authentication
        delegation, 457
        enabling, 447
        overview, 444–445
        SPNs (Service Principal Names), 446
        web farms, 447

configuring, 443–447
    KDC (Key Distribution Center), 444
    TGT (Ticket Granting Ticket), 444
kernel mode
    authentication, 447
    `Http.sys`, 21

L

LAN (local area network), 46
languages, support, 866
layers of OSI model, 547
LDAP (Lightweight Directory Access Protocol), 49
least current request traffic distribution, 548
`list` command, `AppCmd.exe`, 650–653
list pages (IIS Manager), 101–102
listeners, trace listener, 375–376
load balancing, 47, 546
    client affinity, 554
    DSR (Direct Server Return), 549–551
    failure handling, 555
    frameworks, 558
    GSLB (Global Server Load Balancing), 558
    hardware, 555–556
    load balancers, 552–554
    NAT (Network Address Translation), 551–552
    NLB (network load balancing), 557
    NLBS (Network Load Balancing Services), 590–594
    OSI (Open Systems Interconnection) model, 546–547
    reverse proxy, 548–549
    round robin DNS, 557–558
    software, 556
    traffic distribution, 547–548
LoadLibrary, 223–224
local content, configuration, 520–521
Local Service accounts, 218
Local System accounts, 218
`location` tags, 607–610
    application folders, 246–247
    configuration and, 109–110
    Microsoft.Web.Administration API, 632–634

multiple, 609
nesting, 609
`lockAllAttributesExcept` attribute, 257–258
`lockAllElementsExcept` attribute, 257–258
`lockAttributes` attribute, 256
`lockElements` attribute, 256–257
locking, direct configuration and, 611–612
`lockItem` attribute, 257
logging, 49–50
    centralized
        binary logging, 132–133
        W3C, 133–134
    configuration, 127–134
    CustomLoggingModule, 128
    enabling, 128–134
    Failed Request Tracing, 130
    FailedRequestsTracingModule, 128
    HttpLoggingModule, 127
    RequestMonitorModule, 128
    TracingModule, 128
    troubleshooting, 873–874
    W3C (World Wide Consortium), 130–132
logging modules, 323–324
LogParser, 900–901
    bandwidth use, 311
    command line and, 309–310
    file leeching, 312
    files not found, 311
    installation, 309
    time taken, 311–312
`LogRequest` event, 346, 348, 365
Loopback Adapter, 551
Low Trust permissions, 160–161
LSASS (Local Security Authority Subsystem Service), 231–232
LUA (Least-Privileged User Account), 785

M

MAC (Message Authentication Code), 165
machine keys module, 165–166
`machine.config`, 108, 600, 607
`machineKey`, 535–536
managed code, shared hosting and, 89–94

managed code modules, 26, 363–364
    creating, 366–371
    design, 366
    event notifications, 364–365
    `IHttpModule` interface, 366–367
    installation, 369–370
    notifications
        implementation, 368–369
        registration, 367–368
    testing, 370–371
    trace events, 373–375
    trace results, 377
    `TraceSource` object, 372–373
    tracing support, namespace references, 372
Managed Code Modules (HTTP), 319, 325–326
managed engine, 26
ManagedEngine module, 363–364
management. *See* operations management
Management Service. *See also* WMSvc (Web
   Management Service)
    WMSvc and, 224
managing risk, 394–395
Many-to-One Client mapping, 450
`MapPath` event, 346, 348
mapping, 449
`MapRequestHandler` request event, 345,
   348, 365
Medium Trust permissions, 160
memory, monitoring, 824–852
metabase, 27–29
Microsoft.Web.Administration API, 626–634
    `ApplicationPool` object, 626
    attributes, editing, 630–632
    configuration classes, 627–629
    dynamic runtime classes, 629–630
    elements, editing, 630–632
    `location` tag, 632–634
    remote server access, 630
    `ServerManager` class, 627
    `Site` object, 626
    `VirtualDirectory` object, 626
    `WorkerProcess` object, 626–627
Microsoft.Web.Management API, 634–635
migration, Hyper-V, 35

MIME (Multipurpose Internet Mail Extensions),
   147–149
    server security and, 405–407
Minimal Server Interface, 11
Minimal Trust permissions, 161
minimum servers, 553, 570
MMC (Microsoft Management Console), 11
modules, 26
    Application Settings, 163–164
    configuration, schema, 378
    Connection strings, 164
    cookie settings, 169–170
    custom, configuration extension, 377–381
    event tracing, 371–372
    events, 345–347
    hardware security, 494
    IIS native, 26
    machine keys, 165–166
    managed, 26
    managed code, 363–364
        creating, 366–371
        design, 366
        event notifications, 364–365
        `IHttpModule` interface, 366–367
        installation, 369–370
        notification implementation, 368–369
        notification registration, 367–368
        testing, 370–371
        trace events, 373–374
        trace results, 377
        `TraceSource` object, 372–373
        tracing support, 372–377
    native
        building, 360–361
        creating, 352–362
        design, 351–352
        `HttpModule` class, 353–355
        installation, 361
        notification priority setting, 359–360
        `RegisterModule` function, 355–356
        SDK files, 352
        testing, 361–362
    .NET Error Pages, 159–160
    .NET Globalization, 160

.NET Trust Levels, 160–162
notifications, 347–351
Pages and Controls, 166–167
providers, 167–168
return codes, 348–349
session state, 168–170
SMTP e-mail, 171
utility, 26
MOF (Microsoft Operations Framework), 786–797
monitoring
    ASP.NET counters, 828–829
    centralized binary logging, 829–831
    disk I/O, 826
    memory usage, 824–852
    network bandwidth, 826
    processor utilization, 825
    web service counters, 827–828
    websites, 806–809
        Performance Monitor, 816–823
        Resource Monitor, 815–816
        Server Manager, 809–813
        Windows Task Manager, 813–815
MWA (Microsoft Web Administration), 98
MWM. *See* Microsoft.Web.Management API

N

namespaces
    custom module configuration, 379
    DFS Namespaces, 527
    references, managed code modules, 372
NAP (Network Access Protection), 37, 49
NAS (Network Attached Storage), 521
NAT (Network Address Translation), 14
    load balancing, 551–552
Native Code Modules (HTTP), 319
    caching modules, 323
    compression modules, 322
    content modules, 322
    diagnostics modules, 323–324
    extensibility support modules, 324
    HTTP modules, 320
    logging modules, 323–324

performance modules, 322
    security modules, 320–321
native modules
    building, 360–361
    creating, 352–362
    design, 351–352
    event notifications, registering for, 356
    HttpModule class, 353–355
    installation, 361
    new project creation, 353
    notifications, 356–360
    RegisterModule function, 355–356
    SDK files, 352
    testing, 361–362
NCSA (National Computer Security Association), 4
nesting, location tag, 609
.NET Authorization Rules module, 158
.NET Compilation module, 158–159
.NET Error Pages module, 159–160
.NET Framework, 23–24
    application pools and, 200–202
    configuration files, web farms and replication, 535–536
.NET Globalization module, 160
.NET membership, configuration, 278–286
.NET Trust Levels module, 160–162
network bandwidth monitoring, 826
Network Service accounts, 217
networks
    Active Directory, *versus* standalone, 45–46
    backups, 51–52
    NLB (network load balancing), 47
    planning, 45–48
    redundancy, 47
    security, 48–50
    server, location, 46
    server farms, 47–48
    Volume Shadow Copies, 52
New-Item cmdlet, 126
NLB (network load balancing), 47, 545, 552, 557
NLBS (Network Load Balancing Services), 590–594
nonsequential events, 347

notifications, 347–348
    event notifications, 348
        methods, 348
        registering for native modules, 356
    events, managed code modules, 364–365
    managed modules, 367–369
    native modules, priority setting, 359–360
    post-event notification methods, 348
    priority, 349–351
NT Option Pack, 4
NTFS, permissions, altering, 462–463
NTLM authentication, configuring, 439–443
NUMA (Non-Uniform Memory Access), 30

O

OCSP (Online Certificate Status Protocol), 494
offline folders, Shared Configuration, 529–531
OID (Object Identifier), 479
OnAcquireRequestState event notification method, 348
OnAsyncCompletion event notification method, 348
OnAuthenticateRequest event notification method, 348
OnAuthorizeRequest event notification method, 348
OnBeginRequest event notification method, 348, 357
OnCustomRequestNotification event notification method, 348
OnEndRequest event notification method, 348
One-to-One Client mapping, 449
OnExecuteRequestHandler event notification method, 348
OnLogRequest event notification method, 348
OnMapPath event notification method, 348
OnMapRequestHandler event notification method, 348
OnPostAcquireRequestState post-event notification method, 348
OnPostAuthenticationRequest post-event notification method, 348

OnPostAuthorizeRequest post-event notification method, 348
OnPostBeginRequest post-event notification method, 348
OnPostEndRequest post-event notification method, 348
OnPostExecuteRequestHandler post-event notification method, 348
OnPostLogRequest post-event notification method, 348
OnPostMapPath post-event notification method, 348
OnPostMapRequestHandler post-event notification method, 348
OnPostPreExecuteRequestHandler post-event notification method, 348
OnPostReadEntity post-event notification method, 348
OnPostReleaseRequestState post-event notification method, 348
OnPostSendResponse post-event notification method, 348
OnPostUpdateRequestCache post-event notification method, 348
OnPreExecuteRequestHandler event notification method, 348
OnReadEntity event notification method, 348
OnReleaseRequestState event notification method, 348
OnResolveRequestCache event notification method, 348
OnSendResponse event notification method, 348
OnUpdateRequestCache event notification method, 348
operating system optimization, 832–835
operation order, direct configuration, 601–602
operations management
    backup and restore, 797–804
    ITIL (IT Infrastructure Library), 780–781
    MOF (Microsoft Operations Framework), 781–784
        change management, 786–787
        emergency updates, 787–795
        hotfixes, 795–797

role-based administration, 785–786
optimization
    IIS service, 835–842
    operating system, 832–835
    website, 842–850
order of operation, direct configuration, 601–602
OSI (Open Systems Interconnection) model
    layers, 547
    load balancing, 546–547
Output Caching, 719–721
output caching, 845–846
overrideMode attribute, 611–612
OWASP (Open Web Application Security Project),
    397

P

page requests
    IIS Manager, 209–210
    RSCA and, 861
Pages and Controls module, 166–167
passive attacks, 397–398
Passive FTP, 260
passwords, authentication and, 430
path property, attributes, 608–609
pathping, 896–897, 898
paths, direct configuration, 612–613
performance modules, 322
Performance Monitor, 209, 816–823
performance tuning, 831–832
    IIS service optimization, 835–842
    operating system optimization, 832–835
    website optimization, 842–850
permissions, 89–91
    Full Trust, 160
    High Trust, 160
    Low Trust, 160–161
    Medium Trust, 160
    Minimal Trust, 161
    NTFS, altering, 462–463
PHP installation, 174
physical security, Windows server, 51
Pickup folder (SMTP), 306
ping, 896–897, 897–898

pipeline integration, 24–25
pipeline modes, 202–206
pipeline request-processing events, 347
PKI (Public Key Infrastructure), 492–495
poorly secured systems, 397
POP service, 6
port-based bindings, 576
PostAuthenticateRequest event, 345
PostAuthorizeRequest event, 345
PostLogRequest event, 346
PostMapRequestHandler event, 345
PostReleaseRequestState event, 346
PostRequestHandlerExecute event, 346
PostResolveRequestCache event, 345
PostUpdateRequestCache event, 346
PowerShell, 10
    backup and restore, 679–680
    cmdlets, 666–667
        activities, 671–673
    FTP site creation, 271
    help, 668–671
    host headers, 137–138
    improvements, 32–33
    installation and, 79–80
    management, 665–666
    MIME types, 148
    operational activities, 677–679
    virtual directories
        adding, 142
        removing, 142
    website attribute modification, 676–677
    website creation, 126, 673–676
PreExecuteRequestHandler event notification,
    348
PreRequestHandlerExecute event, 346, 365
priorities, notifications, 349–351
private key, 476
privilege escalation attacks, 396–397
ProcDump, 914–915
Process Explorer, 902–903
process isolation, 20
Process Monitor, 904–908
processor affinity, 22
    support, 216

processor utilization monitoring, 825
production environments, 55–56
programmatic configuration, 618
    ABO support, 635–636
    ADSI support, 635–636
    AHAdmin, 639–641
    API support, 635–636
    Microsoft.Web.Administration API
        Application object, 626
        ApplicationPool object, 626
        attributes, 630–632
        configuration classes, 627–629
        dynamic runtime classes, 629–630
        element, 630–632
        location tag, 632–634
        remote server access, 630
        ServerManager class, 627
        Site object, 626
        VirtualDirectory object, 626
        WorkerProcess object, 626–627
    Microsoft.Web.Management API,
      634–635
    system requirements, 618–619
    Visual Web Developer, 619–621
        code writing, 623–625
        running website, 625–626
        web form design, 621–623
properties, AppCmd.exe, editing, 660
property grid pages (IIS Manager), 102–103
protocol transition, configuring, 461
providers module, 167–168
proxies
    HAProxy, 556
    reverse proxy, 548–549
    transparent reverse proxy, 549
proxy servers, 49
public key, 476
publishing
    FTP publishing, 759–763
    Visual Studio, 768–776
    Web Deploy, 751–759
    Web PI, 744–750
    WebDAV, 763–768
PXE (Preboot eXecution Environment), 85

Q

QDig, 175
QoS prioritization, load balancing, 553
Queue folder (SMTP), 306

R

random traffic distribution, 547
RDC (Remote Differential Compression), 56
ReadEntity event, 346, 348
recovery, 51–52
recycling application pools, 187–188, 210–212
redirection.config, 28–29, 107–108, 600,
    607
    updating, 510–511
redundancy, 47
ReFS (Resilient File System), 36
regex (regular expressions), 705–712
registry replication, 533
ReleaseRequestState event, 346, 348, 365
remote access, 14
    delegation, 237–239
    enabling, WMSvc, 224–229
    Microsoft.Web.Administration API, 630
remote connections (IIS Manager), 106–107
    remote installation, 234–235
remote management, 9
replication, 34
    DFS-R (Distributed File System with
      Replication), 56
    Hyper-V, 14
    IIS 8.0, 56
    web farms
        COM+, 534–535
        GAC (Global Assembly Cache), 533–534
        machineKey, 535–536
        .NET configuration files, 535–536
        registry settings, 533
        session state, 536–542
        SSL certificates, 532–533
Request Filtering, 55, 413–419
Request Tracing, 59–60
RequestMonitorModule, 128

requests
   `AppCmd.exe`, currently executing, 656–657
   blocking, 729–730
   `Http.sys` and, 21
   pipeline, events, 347
   processing, 5–6
`ResolveRequestCache` event, 345, 348, 364
Resource Monitor, 815–816
response time traffic distribution, 548
return codes, 348–349
reverse proxy, 548–549
rewrite maps (URL Rewrite), 722–725
RIS (remote installation service), 57
risk management, 394–395
Robocopy, 528–529
root application, 118, 119
root objects, 119
root virtual directory, 118
round-robin traffic distribution, 547
   round robin DNS, 557–558
`RQ_NOTIFICATION_CONTINUE` return code, 348
`RQ_NOTIFICATION_FINISH_REQUEST` return code, 349
`RQ_NOTIFICATION_PENDING` return code, 348
RSA keys, syncing, 509–511
RSCA (Runtime Status and Control API), 503, 852–853, 854
   application domains, viewing, 861
   page requests, viewing, 858–860
   worker processes, viewing, 855–858
rules
   filtering by, 418
   priority, 403–404
   URL Rewrite, 682
     Canonical Domain Name template, 726
     hosting multiple domains, 732
     hot-link prevention, 729
     HTTP 503 code (down for maintenance), 726–728
     `HTTP_PROTOCOL`, 731
     `mod_rewrite` module and, 722
     outbound, 732–738
     preserving old URLs, 728–729
     query string logic, 732
     request blocking, 729–730
     subdomain redirect, 730–731
     templates, 695–700

S

SAM (Security Accounts Manager), 433
SAN (Storage Area Network), 523–524
SAN (Subject Alternate Name), 473
sandboxing application pools, 466–468
scalability, 60
schema
   Configuration Editor, modifying, 642–643
   custom modules, 378
   declarative, 111–113
   files, direct configuration, 614
`ScriptResource.axd`, 719
SDK, native modules, 352
`<section>` tags (IIS Manager), 242–244
secure systems, 394
security, 98. *See also* authentication; authorization
   application pools, 212–215
   attack types
     APTs (advanced persistent threats), 398
     DoS (denial-of-service), 396
     passive, 397–398
     privilege escalation, 396–397
     session replays, 420
     social engineering, 396
     SQL injection, 420
     vulnerability exploitation, 396
     XSS (cross-site scripting), 420
   auditing, 395
   authentication, 395
   authorization, 395
   caching, 587–588
   certificates
     exporting/importing, 489–490
     self-signed, 487
   default installation, 5
   detection tools, 397
   directory structure, 87–88
   documented baseline, 397
   environment, 398–399

FTP, 261
FTP server, users, 274–278
IIS-specific, 54–55
installation, minimal, 8
management, 9
  accounts, 54–55
  delegation, 54
network, 48–50
overview, 394
patches, 397
physical, 51
poorly secured systems, 397
risk management, 394–395
server, 399
  application layer, 420–421
  CGI restrictions, 407–413
  domain restrictions, 399–405
  dynamic IP restrictions, 404–405
  IP restrictions, 399–405
  ISAP extensions, 407–413
  logging, 421
  MIME-type extensions, 405–407
  Request Filtering, 413–419
  restrictions comparison, 405
  rules configuration, 401–403
  rules priority, 403–404
TLS (Transport Layer Security), 472
  CA import, 483–484
  Central Certificate Store, 492
  certificate export/import, 489–490
  certificate requests, 476–483
  FTP site, 498–500
  HTTP host headers, 490–491
  managed SSL/TLS-secure websites,
    487–491
  PKI (Public Key Infrastructure), 492–495
  SMTP virtual server, 496–497
  SNI (Server Name Indication), 491
  SSL/TLS handshake, 473–476
  website bindings, 484–485
web farms, CAS (Code Access Security),
  542–543
Windows server, 50–51
security modules, 320–321
self-signed certificates, generating, 487

SendResponse event, 346, 348
SEO (search engine optimization), URL Rewrite
  templates, 699–700
server
  location, 46
  migrating with Web Deploy, 756–759
  minimum servers, 570
  security, 399
    application layer security, 420–421
    CGI restrictions, 407–413
    domain restrictions, 399–405
    dynamic IP restrictions, 404–405
    IP restrictions, 399–405
    ISAPI extensions, 407–413
    logging, 421
    MIME-type extensions, 405–407
    Request Filtering, 413–419
    restrictions comparison, 405
    rules configuration, 401–403
    rules priority, 403–404
  security, Windows, 50–51
  synchronizing, 756–759
  variables, URL Rewrite, 715–716
  Volume Shadow Copies, 52
  web servers, 119
  workload, customization, 326–335
Server Core deployment, 56
Server Core option, 42
server farms, 47–48
  adding servers, 582
  caching, 584–588
  creating, 562–565
  disabling servers, 582–584
  editing server settings, 582
  enabling servers, 582–584
  explicit URL testing, 568–570
  health checks, 567–571
  live traffic testing, 567–568
  minimum servers, 570
  monitoring status, 584
  removing servers, 582
  rules, 565–567
  URL testing, 574–579
  web server bindings, 571–574
Server Manager, 11–13, 809–813

dashboard, 68
    installation and, 64–65
server virtualization, 42–43
Server with a GUI, 11
server-level authorization, 232–233
session replay attacks, 420
session state, web farms, 538–542
session state module, 168–170
SetPriorityForRequestNotification function, 349
SFTP (Secure FTP), 261
Shadow Copies, 52
share configuration, 109
Shared Configuration, 56, 502, 503–504
    bindings, 515
    `childSource` attribute, 516–517
    client-side caching, 529–531
    `configSource` attribute, 515–516
    DFS-R (Distributed File System Replication), 504
    files
        copying, 510
        exporting, 504–506
        moving, 506–508
    offline folders, 529–531
    reconnection, 511–512
    `redirection.config`, updating, 510–511
    RSA keys, syncing, 509–511
    staggered installations, 517–520
    system environment variables, 512–514
    UNC (Universal Naming Convention), 504
        polling, 508–509
    `web.config` files, distributed, 515
shared network content, configuration, 521–523
SIDs (security identifiers), application pools, 213–214
site administrators, 223
Small Business Server Edition, 41, 42
SMTP (Simple Mail Transport Protocol), 6, 171
    authentication, 303
    connection control, 304
    delivery configurations, 301–302
    domains, additional, 305
    e-mail module, 171
    folders, 305–306
    IIS 8.0, 17

log files, 307–309
    message limits, 300–301
    overview, 298
    relay restrictions, 304–305
    security, 302–303
    server, 298–302
    SMTPDiag tool, 306–307
    Telnet testing, 307
    TLS encryption, 304
    virtual server, 496–497
SNI (Server Name Indicator), 14–15, 30–31, 491
social engineering attacks, 396
software, load balancing, 556
sorry server, 553, 555
`sourceConfig` attribute, 612
specific errors, 852
SPNs (Service Principal Names), 446
SQL injection attacks, 420
SQL Server, session state, 539–542
SR-IOV (Single-Root I/O Virtualization), 41
SSL (Secure Sockets Layer), 14–15, 30–31, 471–472
    host headers and, 138
    HTTP host headers, 490–491
    IIS 8 changes, 15
    SSL offloading, 553
    SSL/TLS handshake, 473–476
SSL certificates, replication, web farms, 532–533
SSL/TLS offloading, 579–580
staggered installations, Shared Configuration, 517–520
standalone networks *versus* Active Directory, 45–46
Standard Edition, 41, 42, 43, 44, 47, 48
Sticky Sessions traffic distribution, 547
Storage Spaces, 523–524
`stronghost`, 551
system administrators, 222–223
system environment variables, 512–514
system requirements, programmatic configuration, 618–619
`System.Configuration`, 98
Systems Center Operations Manager, 49
`System.Web.Configuration`, 98

T

tamper-resistant hardware, 493–494

Task Manager, application pools, running processes, 207–208

TCP (Transmission Control Protocol), 260–261
  offloading and buffering, load balancing, 553
  stack tuning, 834–835

telnet, 898–899

Telnet, FTP Server testing, 271

templates
  certificates, 494
  URL Rewrite rules, 695–700

testing
  default installation, 66–73
  managed modules, 370–371
  native modules, 361–362

text editors, URL Rewrite and, 691

TFTP (Trivial File Transfer Protocol), 85

TGT (Ticket Granting Ticket), 444

time-out errors, 852–853

TLS (Transport Layer Security), 14–15, 118, 471–472
  CAs (certificate authorities), importing, 483–484
  Central Certificate Store, 492
  certificate export/import, 489–490
  certificate requests, submitting, 481–483
  encryption, SMTP and, 304
  FTP sites, 498–500
  HTTP host headers, 490–491
  PKI (Public Key Infrastructure), 492–495
  SMPT virtual server, 496–497
  SNI (Server Name Indication), 491
  website bindings, 484–485
  website security, 472
    certificate requests, 476–481
    SSL/TLS handshake, 473–476
    SSL/TLS-secure websites, 487–491

trace events, 373–376

trace listener, 375–376

TraceEvent() method, 374

tracert, 896–897, 898

TraceSource object, 372–373

Tracing, 376–377

TracingModule, 128

traffic, 58–59
  distribution, 547–548
  live traffic testing, 567–568

traffic treatment, load balancing, 553

troubleshooting. See also diagnostics
  DebugDiag, 909–914
  DelegConfig, 901–902
  Event Viewer and, 885–888
    NTFS disk failures, 895–896
  fixing, 884
  isolating, 881–884
  LogParser, 900–901
  pathping and, 896–897, 898
  ping and, 896–897, 897–898
  ProcDump, 914–915
  Process Explorer, 902–903
  Process Monitor, 904–908
  Reliability and Performance Monitor and, 888–895
  reproducing, 880–881
  Task Manager and, 885
  telnet and, 898–899
  testing, 884
  tracert and, 896–897, 898
  URL Rewrite, 738–741
  WCAT (Web Capacity Analysis Tool), 899–900
  WFetch, 899
  WinDbg, 915–921

U

UC (Unified Communications) certificates, 491

UNC (Universal Naming Convention), 504
  authentication, 425
    configuring, 448–449
  polling, 508–509

UpdateRequestCache event, 346, 348

upgrades
  IIS 7.0 to IIS 8.0, 80–81
  Windows Server 2012, 43–44

URL authorization, 463–466

URL information traffic distribution, 548

URL Rewrite
    actions, 682–686
    APIs, 692
    back-references, 683, 712–714
    conditions, 682–683
    IIS Manager and, 691
    input variables, 701–704
    installation, 686
    logging rewritten URLs, 722
    obtaining, 686
    Output Caching, 719–721
    redirecting to SSL, 716–718
    regex, 705–712
    request checking, 718–719
    rewrite maps, 722–725
    rules
        applying, 692–694
        Canonical Domain Name template, 726
        definition, 682
        hosting multiple domains, 732
        hot-link prevention, 729
        HTTP 503 code (down for maintenance),
          726–728
        HTTP_PROTOCOL, 731
        importing from mod_rewrite, 722
        outbound, 732–738
        preserving old URLs, 728–729
        query string logic, 732
        request blocking, 729–730
        subdomain redirect, 730–731
        templates, 695–700
    server variables, setting, 715–716
    text editors and, 691
    troubleshooting, 738–741
    walk-through, 687–691
    wildcards, 704–705
URL sequences, filtering by, 416
URL testing, server farms, 574–579
user accounts, 468–469
    security, 48–49
user information traffic distribution, 548
user mode, Http.sys, 21
usernames, authentication and, 430
users

application pools, 216–217
    custom accounts, 219–220
    Local Service accounts, 218
    Local System accounts, 218
    Network Service accounts, 217
    virtual accounts, 218–219
    isolating, 261–262
utility modules, 26

V

validation keys, 165
values, AppCmd.exe, 653
variables
    global, 379
    server, URL Rewrite, 715–716
    system environment variables, 512–514
VBScript, 4, 23
virtual accounts, 218–219
virtual directories, 119–120
    adding, PowerShell and, 142
    application comparison, 183–185
    creating, 140–142
    folders, 120
    removing, PowerShell, 142
    root virtual directory, 118
virtual networking, 34
    Hyper-V, 14
virtualization, 13, 33–35
    server virtualization, 42–43
    SR-IOV (Single-Root I/O Virtualization), 41
Visual Basic Scripting Language. *See* VBScript
Visual Studio, 769–776
Visual Web Developer, 619–626
volume automation, 58
Volume Shadow Copy service, 52
VPNs (virtual private networks), 14, 43
vulnerability exploitation, 396

W

W3C (World Wide Consortium) logging, 130–132
    centralized, 133–134
w3w.exe worker process, 185–190

WAN (wide area network), 46
WAS (Windows Process Activation Service), 29, 176
    application pool configuration isolation, 212–213
    virtual accounts, 218–219
WCAT (Web Capacity Analysis Tool), 59, 899–900
WDS (Windows Deployment Services), 85–86
Web Application Gallery, 746–750
web application pool, 119
web application-level authorization, 232–233
web applications, 118, 153
Web Deploy, 531–532
    application deployment, 753–756
    installation, 751–753
    server migration, 756–759
    server synchronization, 756–759
Web Edition, 41
web farms, 501–503
    authentication and, 447
    content configuration
        local content, 520–521
        SAN (Storage Area Network), 523–524
        shared network content, 521–523
        Storage Spaces, 523–524
    content replication, 524–528
    CSC (client-side caching), 529–531
    load balancing, 546–548
    offline folders, 529–531
    replication
        COM+, 534–535
        GAC (Global Assembly Cache), 533–534
        machineKey, 535–536
        .NET configuration files, 535–536
        registry settings, 533
        session state, 536–542
        SSL certificates, 532–533
    Robocopy, 528–529
    security, CAS (Code Access Security), 542–543
    Shared Configuration and, 502, 503–504
        file export, 504–506
        file relocation, 506–508
        machine-neutral files, 512–517

        reconnection, 511–512
        RSA key sync, 509–511
        staggered installations, 517–520
        UNC polling, 508–509
    Web Deploy, 531–532
web forms, 23
    design, 621–623
web gardens, 188–190
Web PI (Web Platform Installer), 73–76, 744–746
    Web Deploy, 751–753
        installation, 751–753
Web Platform Installer, 563
Web Server, role expansion, 76–77
web server accounts, hosting services and, 88–89
web servers, 87, 119
    bindings, 571–574
    CGI (Common Gateway Interface), 316
    independent worker processes, 317
    overview, 315–316
web services
    counters monitoring, 827–828
    starting/stopping, 150–151
web.config, 27–28, 97, 108, 600–601, 607
    application roots, 182
    distributed files, 515
    inheritance, 610–611
WebDAV, 743–744, 763–768
WebResources.axd, 719
website bindings, configuration, 484–485
website-level authorization, 232–233
website-level nodes (IIS Manager), 103–105
websites
    application pools, creating, 122–124
    creating, 121–126
    monitoring, 806–809
        Performance Monitor, 816–823
        Resource Monitor, 815–816
        Server Manager, 809–813
        Windows Task Manager, 813–815
    optimization, 842–850
    overview, 118–119
    as root objects, 119
    security, TLS, 472–481
    separation, 180
WebSocket API, 16

weight-based traffic distribution, 547
WFetch, 899
WFF (Web Farm Framework), 503, 545, 594–595
wildcards, URL Rewrite, 704–705
WinDbg, 915–921
Windows
    authentication, 231–232
    event logs, 49–50
    server, security, 50–51
Windows 7, installation on, 84–85
Windows 8, installation on, 81–84
Windows Certificate Services. *See* ADCS (Active
  Directory Certificate Services)
Windows Server 2012, 10
    Backup, 52
    BitLocker Drive Encryption, 36
    cloud architecture, 35–36
    cloud deployment, 53
    Datacenter, 11
    Deployment, 40–48
    DTLS (Datagram Transport Layer Security),
      14–15
    editions, 41. *See also specific editions*
    Enterprise, 11
    hardware, 44–45
    Home Server, 42
    Hyper-V, 13–14, 33–35
    IIS and, 19
    installation, new, 43
    IPAM (IP Address Management), 36
    MMC (Microsoft Management Console), 11
    NAP (Network Access Protection), 37
    ReFS (Resilient File System), 36
    remote access, 14

    Server Core option, 42
    Server Manager, 11–13
    SNI (Server Name Indicator), 14–15
    SSL (Secure Sockets Layer), 14–15
    Standard, 11
    TLS (Transport Layer Security), 14–15
    upgrades, 43–44
    user interface, 11–13
    virtualization, 13, 33–35
      server virtualization, 42–43
      SR-IOV (Single-Root I/O Virtualization),
        41
Windows Task Manager, 813–815
WMI (Windows Management Instrumentation),
  57, 598, 636–639
WMSvc (Web Management Service), 99
    authentication, Windows, 231–232
    HWC (hostable web core), 223
    installation, 223–224
    Management Service and, 224
    remote connections, enabling,
      224–229
worker process isolation mode, 20
worker processes
    RSCA and, 861
    `w3w.exe`, 185–190
writing code, 623–625
WSH (Windows Scripting Host), 636

X

XML (eXtensible Markup Language),
  configuration files, 28–29
XSS (cross-site scripting) attacks, 420